McGRAW-HILL'S

12 SAT PRACTICE TESTS AND PSAT

CHRISTOPHER BLACK

MARK ANESTIS

and the TUTORS of COLLEGE HILL COACHING™

D1399776

McGraw-Hill

NEW YORK / CHICAGO / SAN FRANCISCO / LISBON / LONDON / MADRID / MEXICO CITY
MILAN / NEW DELHI / SAN JUAN / SEOUL / SINGAPORE / SYDNEY / TORONTO

The McGraw·Hill Companies

1 2 3 4 5 6 7 8 9 0   QPD/QPD   0 1 2 1 0 9 8 7 6

ISBN-13: 978-0-07-147571-6
ISBN-10: 0-07-147571-0

Printed and bound by Quebecor/Dubuque.

McGraw-Hill books are available at special quantity discounts to use as pre-
miums and sales promotions, or for use in corporate training programs. For
more information, please write to the Director of Special Sales, McGraw-Hill
Professional, Two Penn Plaza, New York, NY 10121-2298. Or contact your
local bookstore.

SAT and PSAT are registered trademarks of the College Entrance
Examination Board, which was not involved in the production of, and does
not endorse, this product.

College Hill Coaching® is a registered trademark under the control of
Christopher F. Black.

CONTENTS

CHAPTER 1

WHAT YOU NEED TO KNOW ABOUT THE NEW SAT

Important Questions About a Tough Test

Why do colleges need to see my SAT scores? Aren't my grades and SAT Subject Test scores enough?

Good college admissions officers will use your SAT scores to help them assess your readiness to do tough college work. Although the SAT does not assess broad subject knowledge, it provides a universal benchmark that your high school transcript can't. It assess skills that are essential to success in a competitive liberal-arts college: written argumentation, critical reading, and mathematical analysis.

Competitive colleges need the SAT because course grades are, unfortunately, far from objective measures of your academic ability. Teachers rarely give out grades consistently and without bias. We all know that every school has easy graders and hard graders. Also, many teachers occasionally inflate or deflate grades for reasons unrelated to intellectual ability, like "effort" or personal preference. Even when objective standards are used, they vary widely from teacher to teacher and school to school. Achievement tests like AP exams and SAT Subject Tests are more objective, but they are designed to assess subject knowledge, which can be easily forgotten, rather than basic reasoning skills, which determine broader academic ability. Subject knowledge is effective only when it is incorporated into a meaningful and robust way of solving problems. The SAT, although not perfect, does a good job of measuring how well you reason under pressure, an important academic and life skill.

SAT-bashing has been a very popular pastime in the last 25 years or so, largely due to the "crack-the-test" SAT-prep franchises. Very few of their arguments against the SAT, however, hold any water. The fact is that more students take the SAT every year, and more colleges—not fewer—rely on the SAT every year.

Doesn't the SAT do a poor job of predicting first-year college grades?

SAT-bashers have long liked to claim that the SAT isn't valuable to colleges because it doesn't predict college grades very well. They miss two important points: first, smart college admissions officers don't *want* it to predict grades, and second, it correlates very well with something more important than grades—real success in academic fields like law, medicine, and the like.

As we just discussed, predicting grades is a wild-goose chase because grades are not objectively distributed: most any teacher can give out grades any way he or she wishes. Many students, as we all know, get good grades without having great intellectual ability. They just learn to "play the game" of school—seek the easy "A"s, suck up to teachers, and pad their transcripts.

Smart college admissions officers like the SAT because it often weeds the grade-grubbers out from the truly good thinkers. Rather than predicting your grades, your SAT scores indicate your ability to read critically, write cogently, solve math problems intelligently, and think under pressure. Thankfully, the SAT is not designed to predict how well you'll play the college grading game.

Doesn't the SAT just measure "test-taking skills"?

Unfortunately, most of the large SAT-prep franchises try to convince students that taking the SAT has nothing to do with real academic skills. They prefer you to believe that it's all about their test-taking "secrets." This is great marketing for them, but little help for you. Although there are a few basic test-taking skills that you should know about—process of elimination, intelligent guessing and checking, testing choices, and so on—these can be learned easily in a short afternoon, and don't earn you many points on the SAT. So what *does* get you big score improvements? SAT-taking practice (that's where this book comes in), focused concept review, and intelligent reasoning skills practice.

Many slick SAT-prep franchises portray the SAT as a scary and meaningless test concocted by a cabal of student-haters at the ETS. They claim the SAT can be "cracked" by simply memorizing their test-taking gimmicks. These scare tactics frighten a lot of students into expensive SAT-prep courses, but they are essentially lies. Of course, it's tempting to believe that the SAT is easy to crack, but do you really think that so many colleges would have been using the SAT for so long if it were a joke? (And don't you think that a lot more of their students would be acing the SAT?) Real success on the SAT takes hard work and the right attitude. Treating the SAT like a joke is definitely *not* the right attitude.

Despite what the SAT-prep franchises say, the SAT isn't written by a monopoly of sadists who hate students and want to make college admissions as arduous as possible. The Educational Testing Service (ETS) writes the SAT at the behest of the College Board, which is simply a nonprofit association of over 4,200 colleges whose goal is to promote high academic standards for students. More than likely, any college you apply to will be a member of the College Board.

The ETS changes the format and content of the SAT from time to time, not on its own whims, but through discussions with college and high school educators about their needs. For instance, in 2002, educators at the University of California, unhappy with the writing skills of their incoming freshmen, suggested that the SAT incorporate an essay and do away with some of the more "artificial" vocabulary-based questions so that it would better reflect actual college work. After much research, the ETS changed the SAT accordingly, and the most recent version of the SAT was implemented in 2005.

Why does so much ride on just one test?

It may seem unfair that a 4½ hour test is so important. Remember, though, that the SAT is not a one-shot, all-or-nothing affair. Your standardized test scores account for only about ⅕ to ⅓ of your college application, depending on where you apply. The other essential components include your grades, your curriculum, your essay, your recommendations, your special talents, and your extracurricular activities. Also, you can take the SAT many times, and colleges will consider only the top individual scores from all of your tests. In other words, if you take the SAT twice, and get scores of 460 Critical Reading, 530 Math and 500 Writing on the first test, and 540 Critical Reading, and 490 Math and 400 Writing on the second test, then your score is, for all practical purposes, 540 Critical Reading, 530 Math and 500 Writing. Colleges won't average the scores, or penalize you for being a bit inconsistent. They do this for their own benefit as well as yours: they fare better in the college rankings if they report higher scores!

The SAT is only "unfair" if you allow it to be by not taking it seriously. If, instead, you look at it as an opportunity to hone important academic reasoning skills, and prepare for it meaningfully, you'll find the process more rewarding and less nerve-racking.

Are SAT scores declining?

Every once in a while, you may hear someone claim that SAT scores are declining, and that this reflects the declining quality of our schools. Others claim that trends in average scores demonstrate that the SAT is getting easier or harder. Claims such as these are generally uninformed and demonstrate a basic lack of understanding about the SAT. Trends in average SAT scores mean nothing unless comparable populations of students take the test each year, and unless the difficulty of each SAT can be measured independently of the students who take it. Changes in the student populations who take the SAT and the evolution of the test itself make it hard to infer anything about trends in scores.

The first SAT was administered to a few thousand students, virtually all wealthy white males from new England prep schools. Today, the SAT is administered each year to more than one million students of both sexes representing all races and socioeconomic backgrounds in many countries. Furthermore, each year, the SAT is administered to a broader and more varied student population. In 2002, for instance, over one-third of all students taking the SAT were first-generation college applicants, and over one-third were minorities. These changes in demographics alone account for much of the year-to-year variations in test scores.

A fascinating recent study illustrates the dangers of drawing broad conclusions about trends in SAT scores. In 1997, the College Board conducted a study and discovered that, although overall verbal SAT scores had declined slightly over the previous decade, the verbal SAT scores of every significant racial group had actually *improved* over that time period—the scores of African-Americans had improved, the scores of Asian-Americans had improved, the scores of European-Americans had improved, and the scores of Hispanics had improved. So why, if the average score of nearly every group improved, did the overall score decline? The answer is a single word: distribution. The test-taking population was changing. A larger portion of students with historically lower scores were taking the SAT, thereby bringing the overall average down, even though the scores of each group were improving! In other words, 100% of the decline in scores was attributable to demographics, and had nothing to do with a decline in educational quality.

As a matter of fact, these data actually make the case that schools are actually doing a *better* job teaching students, since the scores of nearly every definable subgroup of students are improving!

Isn't the SAT unfair to minorities and biased toward rich white males?

This is one of the least substantial claims of the SAT-bashers. It *is* certainly true that the SAT is part of a long history of intelligence testing, and most of this history is quite dubious. (For an excellent review of this history, read *The Mismeasure of Man* by Stephen J. Gould.) Scientists who have studied "intelligence" in the past have almost certainly been susceptible to unconscious, if not overt, racial bias. But in recent decades, no one has been more at the forefront of eliminating cultural bias than psychometricians (psychologists who write and use tests).

In fact, the SAT was originally intended *not* to affirm the superiority of white males, but to open Ivy League admissions to racial minorities and the under privileged. It was intended to find the "best and brightest" students for the Ivy League, regardless of their backgrounds. The elite colleges of New England had become the exclusive domain of wealthy white males from elite New England prep schools, many of whom had dubious academic skills. The president of Harvard, James Bryant Conant, wanted to change that system to make American higher education more like a true meritocracy. The SAT was designed as a tool for achieving that goal. (You may question whether the SAT has really had its desired effects, or whether everyone who used the SAT used it in the same way, but these were clearly the goals of its chief proponents.)

Critics of the SAT like to say that the SAT is culturally biased toward rich white males, but they are notoriously unable to produce any evidence of this from recent decades. In fact, the ETS carefully reviews each test to minimize references to the American cultural elite and to ensure that historically under-represented populations are frequently mentioned. (Interestingly, the SAT-bashers frequently cite the SAT as being notoriously "politically correct;" I guess they want to have it both ways.)

Many complain that the SAT is unfair simply because certain minority groups have scored, on average, lower than whites. These discrepancies in scores, however, reveal less about bias in the test than about bias in educational opportunity and about the ill effects of certain environments on academic achievement. It is derelict of advocacy groups to blame the SAT rather than trying to solve the underlying educational problems it reveals.

Don't wealthy students who can afford expensive coaching have an unfair advantage?

Undoubtedly, the ability to afford the best coaching is an advantage. This should come as no surprise. Athletes and musicians certainly benefit from good personal coaching, and students are no different. This simply shows that the SAT is a test of ability, not race or any other innate quality. It is a test of reasoning skills, which can be learned. The right kind of training will pay off. If you follow the College Hill Method and take your preparation seriously, your efforts will be rewarded.

Is the SAT an intelligence test?

This isn't a simple question, so there's no simple answer. "Intelligence" can be used to refer to many different qualities, and certainly the SAT does not assess all of them. The common definition of intelligence as "an innate, general, and stable cognitive ability that determines one's ability to reason across a wide range of tasks" is outmoded and unhelpful. Most psychologists agree that humans possess many different "intelligences" that can improve or atrophy with use or disuse. These include musical intelligence, interpersonal intelligence, mechanical intelligence, verbal intelligence, mathematical intelligence, and analytical intelligence. The SAT measures only certain aspects of verbal, mathematical, and analytical intelligence.

When people ask whether the SAT is an "intelligence" test, usually they really mean: "Do my SAT scores put limits on how successful I can be?" The answer is: only if you misinterpret them. Rather than a measure of your innate "limits" for success, the SAT indicates your mastery of a few basic but essential academic skills. If you improve these skills, you will be more successful academically. Of course, academic success isn't the only kind of success. We can all find wonderful success stories about people who have become successful artists, politicians, and business leaders despite having low SAT scores. The SAT doesn't measure artistic, athletic, intrapersonal, or interpersonal skills, and these are often key elements to nonacademic success. You will find, however, that success in academic fields correlates quite highly (but not, of course, perfectly) with SAT scores.

Doesn't the College Board claim that you can't study for the SAT?

Despite claims to the contrary by SAT-bashers, the College Board openly states that you can and should study for the SAT, because it assesses very learnable skills. It strongly encourages preparation by focusing on *academic* skills. In fact, for decades the College Board has published materials to help students study for the SAT.

The College Board's research does shows quite clearly, however, that just learning test-taking tricks doesn't help much. Only solid practice in fundamental reasoning skills produces dramatic score improvements.

Do I have to take the SAT?

Probably, but not necessarily. Consult the web sites of the colleges you are interested in to see if they require the SAT or SAT Subject Tests. Most competitive schools will require the SAT or a test like it (such as the ACT), but some colleges do not. Even if your college does not require the SAT, you should consider taking it anyway. If you do well, your scores can make your application much more attractive. If you don't, just don't send them.

Do the colleges see all of my SAT Scores?

It's very important to remember that no college will see any of your SAT scores until you *tell* the College Board to release them. You will be given the opportunity to release your scores to specific schools when you register for the test, but be cautious about doing this. Don't—I repeat, *don't*—release your scores until either you're satisfied with your entire score report or you have no other choice (such as when a deadline is approaching).

When you release your score report to a college, the report will contain all of the scores of the SATs and SAT Subject Tests that you have taken up to that point. But remember: if you have taken any test more than once, the college will consider only the top score among all of the results.

Do I have to take SAT Subject Tests?

The SAT Subject Tests are one-hour subject area tests. They are offered in most academic subjects, like mathematics, physics, chemistry, biology, literature, history, languages, and so on. Some colleges do not require you to submit any SAT Subject Test scores, while others may require you to submit up to three SAT Subject Test scores. (But you may submit more than three if you wish.) If you are planning to apply to highly competitive colleges, you should plan to take three or more.

If you believe you have academic strengths that are not shown by your class grades, the SAT Subject Tests are an excellent way to show colleges those strengths.

When should I take the SAT and SAT Subject Tests?

It's usually best to take the SAT Subject Test in June for any course you've finished successfully, so that the subject material is fresh in your mind. For instance, if you do well in freshman biology, take the SAT Subject Test in biology in June of your freshman year. Likewise, consider taking the Math Level I after completing algebra II successfully, the Math Level II after precalculus, etc. You will want to take any SAT Subject Test in a subject when you feel you are "at your peak" in that subject.

Learn which SAT Subject Tests your colleges require, and try to complete them by June of your junior year. You can take up to three SAT Subject Tests on any one test date. After you take the PSAT in October of your junior year, you can take the SAT in late January, late March (or early April), or early May of your junior year and in early November, early December, and late January of your senior year.

Most of our students take the SAT in March and May of their junior year and, only if necessary, again in October of their senior year. Remember, if you submit more than one set of SAT scores, most colleges will use only your top scores.

How do I register for the SAT or SAT Subject Tests?

Since the cost and terms of registration change from time to time, check the College Board web site, *www.collegeboard.com* for all the necessary information about registration. The site also contains all the information you need to apply for special accommodations for students with disabilities.

Are my SAT and SAT Subject Test scores the most important part of my college application?

In most cases, no, but these scores are becoming more important as college admissions become more selective. Without exception, high SAT scores will provide you with an admission advantage regardless of what kind of school you are applying to. Most colleges are also very interested in your high school curriculum, your high school grades, your essay, your teacher recommendations, your special talents or experiences, and your extracurricular activities.

Generally, the more selective a college is, the more important the personal factors are, such as extracurricular activities and special talents. Some large or specialized schools will weigh the SAT or ACT scores more heavily than others, and even declare a cutoff score for applicants. If you have any questions about how heavily a certain college weighs your SAT or ACT scores, call the admissions office and ask.

Test Dates	Test	Registration Deadline	Late Deadline
November 4, 2006	SAT & Subject Tests	September 29, 2006	October 11, 2006
December 2, 2006	SAT & Subject Tests	November 1, 2006	November 9, 2006
January 27, 2007	SAT & Subject Tests	December 20, 2006	January 4, 2007
March 10, 2007	SAT only	February 2, 2007	February 14, 2007
May 5, 2007	SAT & Subject Tests	March 29, 2007	April 11, 2007
June 2, 2007	SAT & Subject Tests	April 27, 2007	May 9, 2007
October 6, 2007	SAT & Subject Tests		
November 3, 2007	SAT & Subject Tests		
December 1, 2007	SAT & Subject Tests		
January 26, 2008	SAT & Subject Tests		
March 1, 2008	SAT only		
May 3, 2008	SAT & Subject Tests		
June 7, 2008	SAT & Subject Tests		

How is the SAT scored?

Each of the three SAT sections (Critical Reading, Math and Writing) is scored on a scale from 200 to 800. The median (50th percentile) score for each section is usually between 490 and 530.

Each scaled score is based on a raw score for that section. This raw score increases by 1 point for every correct answer, and decreases by ¼ point for every wrong answer (except for the "grid-in" math questions, for which there is no penalty for wrong answers). If you skip a question, your raw score remains the same.

Should I guess if I don't know the answer to a question?

Because of the wrong answer penalty described above, blind guessing on multiple-choice questions will likely harm your score in the short run. If you are guessing on no more than five questions, be conservative and guess only when you can eliminate two or more choices.

If you are guessing on more than ten questions, though, you can be more aggressive. Answer all of the questions on which you can eliminate at least one choice before guessing.

On grid-in math questions, guessing can't harm your score, but it may help. So, if you have any kind of guess, fill it in.

Can I take the SAT with extended time?

Some students with special needs can take the SAT with accommodations such as extended time. These accommodations are available only to students with formal recommendations and are strictly proctored. If you have a learning disability that has been diagnosed by a psychologist and feel that special accommodations would benefit you, talk to your guidance counselor about how to qualify and register.

When will I receive my scores?

You can get your SAT or SAT Subject Test scores by phone or on the web about two weeks after you take the test. About ten days later, a written report will be mailed to you free of charge. Any schools to which you release your scores will receive them by mail at about the same time you do. If a college needs your scores sooner, you can "rush" them for a fee.

Can I get the actual test back when I receive my scores?

On some SAT administrations (usually those in October, January, and May), the College Board provides the Question and Answer Service (QAS) for a fee. This service provides you with a copy of the test booklet, a record of your answers, the answer key, scoring instructions, and information about the types and difficulty of each question. You may order this service when you register or up to five months after the date of the test. You may also order a copy of your answer sheet only for a smaller fee. You can find information about these services in your score report.

Are some SATs easier than others?

No. SATs are statistically "equated" so that one test should be, on average, just as difficult as any other. Many people think that, since the SAT is "graded on a curve," it is best to take the test when the "smart" kids are not taking the test, so the curve will be in your favor. They are wrong. The grading curves are determined ahead of time for each test. Don't let such misconceptions dictate when you take the test. Take it when you are best prepared for it.

CHAPTER 2

THE COLLEGE HILL METHOD

Smart Training for the SAT

What is the College Hill Method?

In the last few decades, the SAT-prep industry has been dominated by two general approaches: the "crack-the-test" approach and the "buckshot" approach. The "crack-the-test" approach assumes that acing the SAT (and tests like it) requires only memorizing a set of "proprietary" test-taking tricks. The "buckshot" approach assumes that acing the SAT requires memorizing scores and scores of "best strategies" for tackling every type of SAT question. (A shotgun sprays dozens of shotgun pellets over a wide area, hoping to hit something, in contrast to a rifle, which is far more accurate and efficient.)

Both approaches are occasionally somewhat helpful to students, but neither is close to an optimal approach. Just as sugar pills can give patients the feeling that they are getting better in the short run, yet cause serious harm in the long run by discouraging them from seeking real medical help, so do test-taking tricks give students a false sense of confidence. Worse, they often encourage poor thinking habits, which hurt students in college.

The "buckshot" approach also limits a student's potential on the SAT. Imagine any professional—a base ballplayer, for instance—training by simply memorizing standard procedures for every possible scenario that might arise. There are too many to count, so the effort is doomed from the start. Instead, real experts develop their expertise through active, structured and flexible knowledge, and robust general problem-solving skills that are particular to their field of expertise. A good baseball player learns to react to novel situations, to analyze situations on the fly, and to use his strengths flexibly. If a major-league hitter becomes too rigid and standardized in his approach, he will never be able to handle a new pitcher or a new hitting situation.

Since 2005, the SAT has raised its standards. It now includes a written essay, more reading passages, tougher math concepts, and questions about grammar and usage. It is, more than ever, an academic reasoning test, requiring creativity, analytical skill, insight, knowledge, logic, and genuine academic skills. Don't let the big SAT-prep franchises fool you: the test is less susceptible to their "tricks," and the colleges know it. Students who see very large score improvements on the SAT do it through smart practice and by systematically improving their creative problem-solving skills.

The College Hill Method, the focus of the successful McGraw-Hill SAT workbook series, is not focused on mere test-taking tricks or memorizing scores of procedures. Based on the work of Christopher Black, founder of College Hill Coaching in Greenwich, Connecticut, it focuses on two elements: structured core knowledge and robust, flexible problem-solving skills that apply to a wide array of problem situations.

Structured Core Knowledge

Structured core knowledge is the essential knowledge of the concepts, skills and relationships in a particular subject area. In mathematics, for instance, structured core knowledge includes the "basics" of such skills as adding, multiplying, dividing, and solving equations, but also includes a deep and fluent understanding of number relationships, operational equivalences (for instance, the fact that dividing by a number is the same as multiplying by its reciprocal, and that multiplication is commutative but raising to powers is not), and functional relationships(for instance, that squaring a positive number less than 1 makes it smaller). In reading and writing, structured core knowledge includes the "basics" of vocabulary and sentence-building skills, but also includes a deep and fluent understanding of the higher-order structure of words, sentences, paragraphs, long passages, and books, as well as an understanding of rhetorical strategies, etymology and literary devices.

In most game situations, chess masters instantly intuit the best move because of their vast structured core knowledge culled from actively analyzing hundreds of previous games. Similarly, good doctors can quickly diagnose their patients because of their vast structured core knowledge. With smart training, you will build your structured core knowledge of the SAT.

Robust problem-solving skills

Okay, so chess masters become masters by analyzing hundreds and hundreds of games. But how does this help you on the SAT? After all, you sure haven't taken hundreds of SATs before, and probably don't plan to in the near future.

But you *have* been reading, writing and doing math problems for many years, and if you have approached them mindfully, you have accumulated a great deal of structured core knowledge in those subject areas. The keys to success on the SAT are, first, *using* that structured core knowledge effectively on the SAT (rather than just applying standard test-taking tricks), and *building* your structured core knowledge through mindful problem-solving.

How do some people seem to learn so much more quickly than others? The key is in how they solve new problems. If you use mindful problem-solving skills, then every new problem reinforces old knowledge and builds new knowledge. Poor problem-solvers just apply a standardized procedure and move on to the next problem, hoping that they applied the procedure correctly. Good problem-solvers, on the other hand, mindfully employ the eight reasoning skills that we at College Hill Coaching summarize with the mnemonic MAPS CATCH: mapping, analyzing, finding patterns, simplifying, connecting to structured knowledge, considering alternatives, thinking logically, and checking work.

In this book, we don't have enough space to discuss the College Hill Method and MAPS CATCH in very much detail. It is discussed in more detail in books like *McGraw-Hill's SAT* and *Conquering the SAT Writing* and the upcoming *Brain Corps Training* series.

However, we can give you some important mindful questions to ask as you solve SAT problems that will help you to build your structured core knowledge:

- As you read critical reading passages, are you in control of how your eyes move through the page? Do you always know what to look for in a passage? Is your mind actively seeking to answer questions as you read and to "construct" a representation of what you read in your mind? Do you consolidate information as you read? Do you notice the structure of the passage as you read?
- As you write your essay, do you stay mindful of the central purpose of your essay? Do you think about different ways of phrasing and arranging your thoughts? Do you address the objections a reader might have to your points? Are you continually checking that your writing is clear and forceful to your reader?
- When solving a math problem, do you always represent the problem information in a way you can use, manipulate and check? Do you look for patterns or repetition in the problem so that you can simplify it? Do you consider the different approaches you could take to solving the problem? Do you have good strategies for checking your work?

Getting in the zone: mindful training for the SAT

SAT training is like marathon training. For one thing, those who finish happy are those who take their training seriously. Unfortunately, many students "train" to take the SAT merely by memorizing tricks and gimmicks for "cracking" the test. This is like training for a marathon merely by buying a pair of magic socks. The socks may give you a little bit of extra confidence, but they're not going to make a big difference. Second, the vast majority of marathon runners know that they don't have any chance of coming in first, but the good runners are happy just running their own race as best they can. They listen to their own bodies, rather than chasing the other runners around them. Similarly, good test takers don't pay attention to the students around them when they are taking a test. Instead, they know what they can do and what they can't do, and they don't stress out about not being able to answer every single question.

TRAIN YOUR BODY WITH YOUR MIND

There are two great reasons to combine a regimen of vigorous physical exercise with your preparation for the SAT. First, physical health yields mental benefits. Those who are in good physical shape can focus longer and think faster than those who don't exercise. Second, the task of getting your body in shape teaches you a lot about getting your mind in shape. When you are training to run a race like a marathon, for instance, you learn quickly that consistency pays off. Getting out there every day and logging miles is critical. Similarly, consistency pays off in SAT prep. If you set aside only one day a week to do your work, you won't see nearly as much benefit as if you had spread it out over the week. Also, physical training teaches you to listen to your body; you learn when it's okay to push yourself hard, and when you need to ease up. Similarly, good SAT training teaches you to listen to your mind; you learn which problems you can tackle easily, which are challenging but manageable, and which ones to skip. This will help you enormously on test day.

PRACTICE FOCUSING AND RELAXATION EXERCISES

Top athletes and performers often do focusing and relaxation exercises before they perform. These exercises help them to eliminate distractions and unnecessary tension so that they can do their best. You should practice these exercises, too. Here are some that work wonders.

I. FOCUSED BREATHING

Focused breathing is perhaps the oldest and most powerful technique for calming nerves and focusing the mind. It is also amazingly simple. Sit in an upright chair with your hands on your knees, or sit upright on the floor with your legs crossed. Close your eyes and focus your attention on your breathing. Do not alter your breathing at first, just notice it. After a few breaths, you will notice that it will become slower and deeper.

This deep breathing is the key to relaxation. When we are tense and anxious, our breathing becomes short and shallow, and the oxygen flow through the body is diminished.

Next, focus on gently controlling your breathing so that you extend both the in breath and the out breath. Your in breath should feel like you are filling your lungs completely with air. The out breath should be slow and controlled, and should produce a light, hollow, raspy sound at the back of your throat.

Do not hold your breath at any point. Your in breath should move smoothly into an out breath. After a few breaths like this, you will notice that your mind will begin to wander. You will think about other things, perhaps about responsibilities that you have, and your body will tense up briefly. Focus on "releasing" those thoughts from your mind in the same way that you are releasing the air from your lungs, and return your focus to the breath. This practice of noticing and releasing distractions is an essential part of focused breathing practice. It teaches you that these thoughts are normal, that you shouldn't get too anxious about them, and that you have control over them. You can "release" them from your mind.

After a few minutes of focused breathing, your body is relaxed and your mind is alert, so you are prepared to do your homework or take your test.

2. SYSTEMATIC RELAXATION

Another amazingly simple practice for releasing tension is systematic relaxation. Sit in an upright chair, or lie on the floor. Close your eyes. Bring your attention to the muscles in your head and face. These are usually the first muscles to become tense when we are anxious. As your attention moves around your face to the different muscles, "see" these muscles in your mind's eye at the same time that you consciously relax them. When your face and head feel relaxed, move to your neck and shoulders.

Don't rush. Often, the tension in your muscles goes so deep that you must focus on it for a minute or so before that tension will release. Then move systematically down to your arms, your torso and back, your hips, your legs, and your feet. With each stage of relaxation, you should feel the tension flowing out of you like sand from a bag. After several minutes of systematic relaxation, your body is relaxed, but your mind is focused, so you are ready to do your work.

3. YOGA AND MINDFUL EXERCISE

The problem with most exercise is that it is not mindful, and therefore can put more stress on your body than it should. If exercise to you means grunting out reps with a barbell, or running with music blasting from your earphones, then your exercise strategy may be more of an assault on your body and mind than a healthful practice.

Certain exercise disciplines have evolved over centuries to provide mindful, healthful practices. Yoga, for instance, is not just about bending and twisting your body into odd shapes. It is about pushing your body's strength, flexibility, and stamina to their limits in a mindful way, so that not only does your body become stronger and more flexible, but your mind develops a much deeper "body awareness" that is so essential to good health. T'ai Chi is also a great practice for developing body awareness, although it is generally not as physically demanding as yoga can be.

Learning these disciplines requires the help of an instructor. You can probably find such classes available at your local gym, or find some instruction tapes in the library or store. Incorporating these practices into your life can make you calmer and more prepared to handle life's problems.

Listen to your body

1. DON'T SLOUCH WHEN YOU WORK—SIT UP!

Your brain is constantly receiving signals from your body. When studying or taking a test, you don't want those signals to interfere with your thinking. When you slouch in your seat, or slump over your desk, your body tells your brain that it's time to rest, not to think. If you want to stay alert, sit upright and lean slightly forward over your work. You will find that this position helps you to process information much more efficiently than if you are in a more relaxed position.

2. LOOK AT YOUR TEST HEAD-ON, NOT AT AN ANGLE

You will find it much easier to read when your test book is facing you directly, rather than at an angle. As an exercise, try to read both ways. You will notice that your brain has to work harder to process the words when the book is at an angle. Don't make things harder than they need to be!

3. TAKE SHORT BREAKS WHEN YOU FEEL FATIGUED

Whenever you begin to feel fatigued from studying, take a five-minute break. But be strict—don't let your break get out of hand. Five minutes is enough time to get a snack or use the bathroom but not long enough to do much else. Don't take a break to watch your favorite show; you can do that after your homework is done. But a good short break can provide a great energy boost in the midst of your studying.

Eat smart and get your rest

Most high school students don't put nutrition and sleep near the top of their daily priorities. If you owned a $70,000 sports car, would you leave it out in hailstorms, neglect changing the oil or transmission fluid, and use only the cheapest gasoline? Obviously not. So don't think that your brain will work just fine even if you neglect its basic needs. Here are some simple tips to make sure that your mind and body are getting what they need.

1. DRINK FIVE GLASSES OF WATER A DAY

Even though water contains no calories or vitamins, it is the most important part of a nutritious diet. Water vitalizes your cells by helping transport essential nutrients to them. It also helps to flush out the toxic by-products that can build up in your system. Even though soda and juice are mostly water, they add lots of other unnecessary stuff that your cells don't need. All of your vital systems require an ample supply of pure water to function well.

2. TAKE A GOOD MULTIVITAMIN SUPPLEMENT DAILY

Even if you eat three square meals a day, you still may not be getting some of the nutrients your body and brain need to work at their best. Just one multivitamin supplement can ensure that you won't miss any nutrients even if you miss a meal. But remember: many essential nutrients, like Vitamin C, are not produced by your body, and so should be consumed regularly throughout the day. Vitamin supplements are helpful, but they can't substitute for good general eating habits.

3. EAT PROTEIN WITH EVERY MEAL

Protein, which is found in eggs, milk, fish, poultry, and meat, is essential to a good diet because it provides the "building blocks" for a healthy body. If you eat a lot of cereal and processed, packaged foods, you probably aren't getting enough protein. Egg whites, fish, chicken, lentils, tofu, and beans are the best sources of high-quality protein.

4. EAT WHOLE GRAINS AND LOTS OF VEGETABLES

There is some evidence that food additives can be harmful to the functioning of your organs, and this includes your brain. Try to eliminate processed foods from your diet: packaged crackers, cookies and cakes, processed cheeses, soda, and so on, because the additives in these foods generally offset any nutritional value they have. America is fat largely because of processed foods. Instead, eat more salads and green vegetables, fruits, and whole grains.

Instead of sugary processed cereal in the morning, try yogurt with fruit and oatmeal. Instead of a fast-food hamburger or pizza, try a grilled chicken sandwich with lettuce and tomato (keep the sauces to a minimum). Cutting out processed food is not too hard, and your energy will skyrocket and you'll feel (and think) much better.

5. TREAT SLEEP LIKE AN APPOINTMENT

Whenever a student a walks into my office with bleary eyes, I don't need an explanation. I usually get one anyway: she was up until 2 a.m. the previous night because she needed to finish an assignment that she had to postpone because of a softball game, or because her friend had an emotional crisis. Now, I'm not going to tell you to quit sports or abandon your friends, but you must understand something critical about sleep: if you don't get enough, your problems will snowball. If you have to stay up late to finish an assignment, then you'll be too tired to pay attention in class the next day, and you'll need to study harder to catch up, so you'll stay up even later the next night, and so on.

Think of it this way: if you plan your schedule so that you get eight hours of rest instead of six, you will probably find that you make up those two hours with better focus, energy, and productivity each day. So treat your bedtime like it's an important appointment, and you'll find you'll be much happier and get more done every day.

Smart test-taking tips

1. MAKE YOUR PRACTICE TESTS FEEL REAL

One essential part of SAT prep is taking realistic practice tests, like those in this book. When taking each practice SAT, try your best to replicate the experience of the actual test as much as possible:

- If you can't take the test in a proctored classroom, at least take it in some other "neutral" setting like a public library. If you absolutely must take it at home, take it at the dining room table and have a parent turn off the phones and time you on each section.
- Start your practice test in the morning since you'll probably start your official SAT between 8 and 9 am.
- If you are timing yourself, use a stopwatch that will beep when your time is up on each section.
- Take the test in one sitting, with only one or two 5-minute breaks.

It may help to build your test-taking stamina slowly. The SAT is a long test; the practice tests in this book are just under 4 hours in length, but the real SAT will take you over 4 hours. Just as marathoners don't start their training by running a full marathon, but instead work their way up to longer runs, you might want to take just a few sections at a time to start, building up gradually until, in the last few weeks before the SAT, you are taking full tests each week.

2. GET THE OXYGEN FLOWING—EXERCISE

To stay sharp, your brain needs a good supply of oxygen. So, a good aerobic exercise regimen can help your SAT preparation tremendously. If you don't already have a good exercise regime, get in the habit of doing at least 20 minutes of good aerobic exercise every day, preferably before you sit down to do your homework or take a practice test. This will get the oxygen flowing to your brain, relieve stress, and enhance your mental agility. But be careful—always check with your doctor before making dramatic changes in your physical activity level.

3. PREPARE YOUR STUDY AREA

When taking a practice test or just studying, preparing the area is important. Most students work inefficiently because they don't prepare their work space. Put yourself in a place where you can maintain mindful focus for an extended time. Do not study or take your tests on your bed. Your bed is a place for sleep, not study. When you recline, your brain becomes less alert. You can't study well if one part of your brain is sending sleep signals to the other parts! Instead, sit in a quiet area. Sit in an upright chair at a table or desk with good lighting. This makes it easier for your brain to absorb new information and solve new problems. Also, make sure that all the tools you will need are within easy reach: the test booklet, a calculator, and pencils with erasers.

4. TAKE CONTROL OF THE TEST

When you take the SAT, the test booklet is yours—mark it up freely. You get no points for neatness on the SAT. Jotting down notes, crossing off wrong answers, and marking up diagrams are essential to good test-takers.

Within any SAT section except the reading portion, the questions are in roughly ascending order of difficulty. But you can skip around as necessary—difficulty is a matter of opinion! Remember, your objective is to accumulate as many "raw points" as you possibly can, so don't get needlessly bogged down on any tough questions.

Be careful, though: if you skip around, make sure you keep extra careful track of your answers on the answer sheet!

> Write on the test when you need to. Mark up the diagrams on math problems, write in your own words in the Sentence Completion questions, and summarize each paragraph of the reading passages.
>
> *Alex Davidow (Syracuse '08, + 170 points CR)*

5. SET CLEAR GOALS

Head into each test with a well-formulated strategy for attacking the test. Have clear score goals in mind, and know what percentage of questions you will need to answer correctly to achieve those goals. The score conversion table below will tell you this. Remember that answering every question is a bad strategy unless you have a very realistic shot at breaking 700 per section. As a rule of thumb, remember that you need to get only about 50% (or ½) of the questions right in order to break 500, about 67% (or ⅔) of the questions right in order to break 600, and about 87.5% (or ⅞) of the questions right in order to break 700. It's best to focus the majority of your time on just that percentage of questions you will need to break your score goal. This strategy gives you more time to check your work on each question, and minimizes the chance of making careless errors. Use your PSAT scores or your Diagnostic Test scores as a starting point. Then decide what score will make you happy. You should know what the median SAT scores are for the schools you'd like to apply to. Set aggressive goals as you train (our students always expect to improve their scores by 100 points or so on each section) but pick a realistic goal as you get closer to the test date, based on your performance on the practice tests. If you've been getting 400s on all sections of your practice tests, don't expect to get 600s on the real thing!

6. REVIEW INTELLIGENTLY

After you take the practice tests in this book, you may need to review particular academic skills. Our review book, *McGraw-Hill's SAT*, provides a comprehensive review of all of the skills tested on the SAT. Are the geometry questions particularly tough for you? If so, focus on Chapter 13, "Essential Geometry Skills." Was pre-algebra so long ago that you forget what the commutative law and remainders are? If so, Chapter 10, "Essential Pre-Algebra Skills," is a good place to start. Look carefully at any troublesome critical reading questions on your tests. What part was toughest? If it was the vocabulary, focus on Chapter 6, "How to Build an Impressive Vocabulary with MAPS-CATCH." If you struggled in analyzing the passages, or finding their main points, focus on Chapter 7, "Critical Reading Skills." If you missed more sentence completion questions than you'd like, work on Chapter 8, "Sentence Completion Skills." Look carefully at any troublesome writing questions on your tests. Did you find yourself struggling with the essay? If so, Chapters 15 and 16 will teach you how to approach the essay more effectively, as will *Conquering the SAT Writing*. If the rules of grammar sometimes seem overwhelming, work on Chapter 18, "Essential Grammar Skills," and Chapter 17, "Attacking the Grammar Questions."

SAT Score Conversion Table

Use this table to help you set your strategy for reaching your score goals. Beneath each section heading, find your score goal. Then find the "raw score" that corresponds to it. This is the number of points you need in total for that section. For instance, if your score goal is 500 on the critical reading section, you need a raw score of 29 points. This means that you must get *at least* 29 correct answers in total on all of the critical reading section. Since there are 67 critical reading questions in total, this allows plenty of room to skip the harder questions.

Remember, however, that a wrong answer on any multiple-choice question deducts ¼ point from your raw score. Therefore, it is important to answer more questions than the minimum required for your goal, so that you give yourself room for error. If your goal is 500 on the critical reading section, for instance, you should plan to answer at least 35 questions to allow for a few wrong answers.

Raw Score	Critical Reading Scaled Score	Math Scaled Score	Writing Scaled Score	Raw Score	Critical Reading Scaled Score	Math Scaled Score	Writing Scaled Score
67	800			32	520	550	610
66	800			31	510	550	600
65	790			30	510	540	580
64	780			29	500	530	570
63	760			28	490	520	560
62	750			27	490	530	550
61	730			26	480	510	540
60	720			25	480	500	530
59	700			24	470	490	520
58	700			23	460	480	510
57	690			22	460	480	500
56	680			21	450	470	490
55	670			20	440	460	480
54	660	800		19	440	450	470
53	650	790		18	430	450	460
52	650	760		17	420	440	450
51	640	740		16	420	430	440
50	630	720		15	410	420	440
49	620	710	800	14	400	410	430
48	620	700	800	13	400	410	420
47	610	680	800	12	390	400	410
46	600	670	790	11	380	390	400
45	600	660	780	10	370	380	390
44	590	650	760	9	360	370	380
43	590	640	740	8	350	360	380
42	580	630	730	7	340	350	370
41	570	630	710	6	330	340	360
40	570	620	700	5	320	330	350
39	560	610	690	4	310	320	340
38	550	600	670	3	300	310	320
37	550	590	660	2	280	290	310
36	540	580	650	1	270	280	300
35	540	580	640	0	250	260	280
34	530	570	630	−1	230	240	270
33	520	560	620	−2 or less	210	220	250

> Take Practice Tests in the library, where there are no distractions, and go over each of your practice SATs for a second time soon after you take them to help you to understand where and why you are going wrong.
>
> *Joia Ramchandani (MIT '07, 700 CR 770 M)*

7. Practice, practice, practice!

Whatever strategies you want to use on the SAT, practice them on tests so that you don't spend energy re-thinking strategy during the real SAT. Don't get too focused on "point-counting" during the test. This will take your focus away from the real problems.

> Taking Practice Tests under real test conditions helps a lot!
>
> *Alex Davidow (Syracuse '08, +170 points CR)*

8. Familiarize yourself with the test format and instructions

One of the simplest ways to increase your chances of success on test day is to familiarize yourself with the format of the exam ahead of time. Know the format and instructions for each section of the SAT. This will save you time on the actual test. Why waste time reading the directions when you could memorize them beforehand? The rules won't change.

> Whenever you have the choice, turn off the TV and read a good book instead!
>
> *Elisha Barron (Yale '06, 800 CR 800 M)*

9. Know when to guess

The SAT is different from exams you take in the classroom because you get negative points for wrong answers. On a 100-question classroom math exam, if you answer 80 questions correctly and get 20 questions wrong, your score would be an 80. On the SAT, if you answer 80 questions correctly and get 20 questions wrong, your score would be a 75. Why? Because the

ETS includes a "wrong-answer penalty" to discourage random guessing. For 5-question multiple-choice questions, a correct answer is worth 1 "raw" point, a wrong answer costs you ¼ point, and an unanswered question costs you nothing. It's better to leave a question blank than it is to get it wrong. If you can eliminate two or more choices, however, you should probably make an educated guess. Work on your guessing strategy as you practice. When you take a Practice Test, write a "G" on the test booklet next to questions you guess on (not on the answer sheet). After the exam, check to see how many of those guesses you got right. If you consistently get more than 20% (or ⅕) of your guesses right, you are "beating the odds," and your guessing strategy is better than omitting those questions.

> Do some review almost every day rather than cramming it into just one or two days each week.
>
> *Joia Ramchandani (MIT '07, 700 CR 770 M)*

On SAT Day

1. The night before—relax!

The night before the SAT, your studying should all be behind you; cramming at this point will probably do more harm than good. Relax, go see a movie, grab dinner with your friends, do whatever you need to do to reward your brain for its efforts over the previous months. As long as you get a good night's rest, you're allowed to have some fun the evening before the exam. For a truly peaceful slumber, lay out everything you need for test day the night before.

> Prepare in advance, but don't study the night before, just get a good night's sleep. And don't forget a good breakfast the next morning! (Even if you're nervous!)
>
> *Julie MacPherson (+130 points CR)*

2. Get your stuff together

The night before the test, lay out everything you will need for the test on your night stand or kitchen table. Don't forget any of the following:

- Admission ticket
- Photo ID
- Several #2 pencils with erasers

- Calculator (with fresh batteries)
- Stopwatch
- A light snack, like a banana or granola bar
- Your brain
- Earplugs (if you need them to shut out distractions)
- Directions to the test site (if you haven't been there before)

Few things are as awful as having your calculator conk out ten minutes into your first math section, so put in fresh batteries the night before. Forgetting your ticket would be disastrous. And they rarely have a spare brain available if you happen to forget yours.

3. KNOW YOUR WAY

If you will be taking the SAT at an unfamiliar test site, make sure to get directions to the site well ahead of time. Drive (or take the bus or subway) to the test site at some point in the days before the test, so you can familiarize yourself with it. Even better, have someone else drive you to the test, but make sure that he or she knows the way, too. Leave yourself plenty of time to get to the test site by 8 am so that you don't stress out if you hit traffic or get a little lost.

4. BYOS—BRING YOUR OWN STOPWATCH

Your testing room will almost certainly have a clock, but it can be a big advantage to have your own stopwatch.(But make sure it doesn't make noise, or the proctor will confiscate it!) The best stopwatch is one that counts backwards from the time that you set.

Make sure you practice setting, starting, and stopping the watch before you get to the test site. This will help you to manage your time and avoid that annoying mental arithmetic you would have to do to tell how much time you have left. Practice using your stopwatch when taking your practice exams so that you feel comfortable using it.

> Bring a light snack for energy on SAT day to eat during one of the breaks.
>
> *Joia Ramchandani (MIT '07, 700 CR 770 M)*

5. DRESS WELL

Wear clothes that will keep you comfortable in any temperature. If it is late spring, bring an extra layer in case the room is too cold; if it is winter, wear layers so that you can remove clothing if you are too hot. Sometimes it seems as if NASA is using SAT testing rooms to test human endurance at extreme temperatures.

6. EAT A POWER BREAKFAST

Eat a good breakfast before the exam, with protein to give your brain the energy it will need. Oatmeal is a good option, or eggs and bacon. Try to stay away from sugary cereals and syrup. While eating, you may want to relax to some peaceful music, or you may want to "start your engine" by looking over an SAT critical reading passage or an interesting math problem to get your brain in the right mode.

7. GET THE EYE OF THE TIGER

Finally, head into the SAT with a positive attitude. If you go in with an "I don't want to be here" attitude, the SAT will eat you alive. Your attitude is critical to success on the SAT. Any negative energy will detract from your thinking power and cost you points. Positive energy serves as motivation and puts you into a sharper mindset, helping you to focus on the tough questions.

8. IT STARTS—FOCUS!

Good preparation will be wasted if you can't focus on test day. When you step into the classroom to take your SAT, you shouldn't be thinking about the things that could go wrong. Fight the urge to think about the sweet party you will go to that night, the argument that you had with your best friend the night before, or what you are going to have for lunch. Before the test begins, focus on relaxing and carrying out your game plan.

9. STAY ALERT DOWN THE STRETCH

The SAT is like a marathon, so pace yourself well. If you lose focus for the last section, it may cost you dearly. When you get near the end, don't think, "I'm almost out of here!" Focus by thinking, "Finish strong!" Keep yourself mentally sharp from beginning to end; don't allow yourself to let up until that final answer is filled in.

10. DON'T CHANGE YOUR ANSWER FOR DUMB REASONS

When should you change an answer and when should you leave it alone? The answer is simple: *only change your answer when you've reviewed the entire problem and discovered a mistake.* Don't change your answer for dumb reasons like, "This one can't be (A) because the last two answers were (A)!" or "It can't be that easy, it must be another answer!"

On your practice exams, whenever you change your answer, write a "Ch" next to the question in your test booklet. After you finish the exam, see how many of those changes were for the better. This will give you a better sense on test day of whether your checking strategy is an effective one.

11. WASTE NOT

Don't waste too much time on any one question. Some students lose 30–40 points on a section simply by being too stubborn to let a problem go. If a question is going to take too much time, circle the question number in the test booklet, skip it on your answer sheet, and come back to it later. If you return to the problem 10 or 15 minutes later, your refreshed brain may well see things more clearly and find a simple way to solve the problem!

12. Don't give the right answer to the wrong question

Don't go so fast that you answer the wrong question when doing a math problem. Always re-read the question to make sure you are giving the answer to the question it asks! For example, in the question

$3x + 6 = 12$, what is the value of $3x$?

even bright students often solve for x and give the answer of 2. However, the question asked for the value of $3x$, which is 6. This is an example of giving the right answer to the wrong question. If you occasionally make this kind of mistake, get into the habit of underlining what the question wants you to find. This will help you to focus on answering the right question.

13. Don't blow bubbles

Many SAT horror stories begin with a student putting answers in the wrong places on the answer sheet. To avoid this, practice using the answer sheets when taking your practice tests so that you get comfortable with them. Experiment with different methods of filling in your answer sheet. Some students like to slide the answer sheet from under the test booklet, revealing just one space at a time for each question. Others prefer to fill in the answer after every question, and some prefer to wait until they've answered all of the questions on a page (circling their answers on the test booklet before transferring them to the answer sheet). There is no one "best way" to do it; just find the approach that is best for you.

If you skip a problem, be extremely careful to skip that question on your answer sheet as well. A small erasable dash next to the question number on the answer sheet works well as a reminder.

14. Finish strong

If you budget your time wisely, you should have plenty of time to do everything you need to do on the SAT, and that probably includes leaving some hard questions unanswered. But what should you do if suddenly time is running out and you have several questions left that you need to answer? First, make sure that you really do need to answer them; answering too many questions is a common mistake. If you really do need to rush a bit, at least rush wisely. First answer the questions that can be done quickly. For example, a "word-in-context" critical reading question can usually be answered much more quickly than a "main idea" question. If your time is running out, attack the simplest questions!

CHAPTER 3

ATTACKING THE SAT ESSAY

Know What They're Looking For

Why an essay?

The first section of your SAT is a 25-minute writing assignment designed to assess how well you can express your ideas in writing—that is, make an argument using clear and specific examples, solid reasoning and fluent language. It is not simply an assessment of "what you know," and it isn't a spelling or grammar test. Many colleges regard this as one of the most important elements of the SAT, because essays are often an important part of college evaluation.

The assignment will be to answer a very broad question about human values or behavior, such as *Is an individual person responsible, through his or her example, for the behavior of others?* There is no "right" or "wrong" answer to the question; you may present any point of view you wish.

Writing an argumentative essay is not like writing a story or a letter to a friend. On the SAT essay, your job is not to entertain but to *persuade*. You may be funny and creative if you wish, but your primary task is to *explain and support an interesting point of view*, not to impress someone with flowery language or cute observations.

A good persuasive essay respects the reader's intelligence, yet explains an argument carefully. Although you *can* assume that your readers are smart and well-read, you *cannot* assume that they think exactly as you do, or that they will fill in logical gaps for you. You must show your reasoning.

How long should it be?

Quality is much more important than quantity. Nevertheless, you should try to fill both of the pages you're given for the essay. Plan to write four paragraphs, and add a fifth if you have enough time and substance.

Most essays that get perfect scores are four or five paragraphs long. Very few top-scoring essays have fewer than four paragraphs. The scorers will evaluate your essay's organization, and this includes how effectively you use paragraphs.

The five essential qualities of a good persuasive essay

Your SAT essay will be scored by two SAT English teachers who are trained by the ETS. They are looking for the five basic elements that all good humanities professors expect of good writing

1. INTERESTING, RELEVANT, AND CONSISTENT POINT OF VIEW

Do you take a thoughtful and interesting position on the issue? Do you answer the question as it is presented? Do you maintain a consistent point of view?

2. GOOD REASONING

Do you define any necessary terms to make your reasoning clear? Do you explain the reasons for and implications of your thesis? Do you acknowledge and address possible objections to your thesis without sacrificing its integrity?

3. SOLID SUPPORT

Do you give relevant and *specific* examples to support your thesis? Do you explain how these examples support your thesis?

4. LOGICAL ORGANIZATION

Does every paragraph relate clearly to your thesis? Do you provide logical transitions between paragraphs? Do you have a clear introduction and conclusion? Does the conclusion provide thoughtful commentary, rather than mere repetition of the thesis?

5. EFFECTIVE USE OF LANGUAGE.

Do you use effective and appropriate vocabulary? Do you vary sentence length and structure effectively? Do you avoid needless repetition? Do you use parallelism, metaphor, personification, or other rhetorical devices to good effect? Do you use strong verbs? Do you avoid needlessly abstract language? Do you avoid cliché?

PART 2

PRACTICE TESTS

PRACTICE TEST 1

ANSWER SHEET

Last Name: _____   First Name: _____

Date: _____   Testing Location: _____

Directions for Test

- Remove these answer sheets from the book and use them to record your answers to this test.
- This test will require 3 hours and 20 minutes to complete. Take this test in one sitting.
- The time allotment for each section is written clearly at the beginning of each section. This test contains six 25-minute sections, two 20-minute sections, and one 10-minute section.
- This test is 25 minutes shorter than the actual SAT, which will include a 25-minute "experimental" section that does not count toward your score. That section has been omitted from this test.
- You may take one short break during the test, of no more than 10 minutes in length.
- You may only work on one section at any given time.
- You must stop ALL work on a section when time is called.
- If you finish a section before the time has elapsed, check your work on that section. You may NOT work on any other section.
- Do not waste time on questions that seem too difficult for you.
- Use the test book for scratchwork, but you will receive credit only for answers that are marked on the answer sheets.
- You will receive one point for every correct answer.
- You will receive no points for an omitted question.
- For each wrong answer on any multiple-choice question, your score will be reduced by ¼ point.
- For each wrong answer on any numerical "grid-in" question, you will receive no deduction.

SECTION 2

1. Ⓐ Ⓑ Ⓒ Ⓓ Ⓔ   11. Ⓐ Ⓑ Ⓒ Ⓓ Ⓔ   21. Ⓐ Ⓑ Ⓒ Ⓓ Ⓔ   31. Ⓐ Ⓑ Ⓒ Ⓓ Ⓔ
2. Ⓐ Ⓑ Ⓒ Ⓓ Ⓔ   12. Ⓐ Ⓑ Ⓒ Ⓓ Ⓔ   22. Ⓐ Ⓑ Ⓒ Ⓓ Ⓔ   32. Ⓐ Ⓑ Ⓒ Ⓓ Ⓔ
3. Ⓐ Ⓑ Ⓒ Ⓓ Ⓔ   13. Ⓐ Ⓑ Ⓒ Ⓓ Ⓔ   23. Ⓐ Ⓑ Ⓒ Ⓓ Ⓔ   33. Ⓐ Ⓑ Ⓒ Ⓓ Ⓔ
4. Ⓐ Ⓑ Ⓒ Ⓓ Ⓔ   14. Ⓐ Ⓑ Ⓒ Ⓓ Ⓔ   24. Ⓐ Ⓑ Ⓒ Ⓓ Ⓔ   34. Ⓐ Ⓑ Ⓒ Ⓓ Ⓔ
5. Ⓐ Ⓑ Ⓒ Ⓓ Ⓔ   15. Ⓐ Ⓑ Ⓒ Ⓓ Ⓔ   25. Ⓐ Ⓑ Ⓒ Ⓓ Ⓔ   35. Ⓐ Ⓑ Ⓒ Ⓓ Ⓔ
6. Ⓐ Ⓑ Ⓒ Ⓓ Ⓔ   16. Ⓐ Ⓑ Ⓒ Ⓓ Ⓔ   26. Ⓐ Ⓑ Ⓒ Ⓓ Ⓔ   36. Ⓐ Ⓑ Ⓒ Ⓓ Ⓔ
7. Ⓐ Ⓑ Ⓒ Ⓓ Ⓔ   17. Ⓐ Ⓑ Ⓒ Ⓓ Ⓔ   27. Ⓐ Ⓑ Ⓒ Ⓓ Ⓔ   37. Ⓐ Ⓑ Ⓒ Ⓓ Ⓔ
8. Ⓐ Ⓑ Ⓒ Ⓓ Ⓔ   18. Ⓐ Ⓑ Ⓒ Ⓓ Ⓔ   28. Ⓐ Ⓑ Ⓒ Ⓓ Ⓔ   38. Ⓐ Ⓑ Ⓒ Ⓓ Ⓔ
9. Ⓐ Ⓑ Ⓒ Ⓓ Ⓔ   19. Ⓐ Ⓑ Ⓒ Ⓓ Ⓔ   29. Ⓐ Ⓑ Ⓒ Ⓓ Ⓔ   39. Ⓐ Ⓑ Ⓒ Ⓓ Ⓔ
10. Ⓐ Ⓑ Ⓒ Ⓓ Ⓔ   20. Ⓐ Ⓑ Ⓒ Ⓓ Ⓔ   30. Ⓐ Ⓑ Ⓒ Ⓓ Ⓔ   40. Ⓐ Ⓑ Ⓒ Ⓓ Ⓔ

SECTION 3

1. Ⓐ Ⓑ Ⓒ Ⓓ Ⓔ   11. Ⓐ Ⓑ Ⓒ Ⓓ Ⓔ   21. Ⓐ Ⓑ Ⓒ Ⓓ Ⓔ   31. Ⓐ Ⓑ Ⓒ Ⓓ Ⓔ
2. Ⓐ Ⓑ Ⓒ Ⓓ Ⓔ   12. Ⓐ Ⓑ Ⓒ Ⓓ Ⓔ   22. Ⓐ Ⓑ Ⓒ Ⓓ Ⓔ   32. Ⓐ Ⓑ Ⓒ Ⓓ Ⓔ
3. Ⓐ Ⓑ Ⓒ Ⓓ Ⓔ   13. Ⓐ Ⓑ Ⓒ Ⓓ Ⓔ   23. Ⓐ Ⓑ Ⓒ Ⓓ Ⓔ   33. Ⓐ Ⓑ Ⓒ Ⓓ Ⓔ
4. Ⓐ Ⓑ Ⓒ Ⓓ Ⓔ   14. Ⓐ Ⓑ Ⓒ Ⓓ Ⓔ   24. Ⓐ Ⓑ Ⓒ Ⓓ Ⓔ   34. Ⓐ Ⓑ Ⓒ Ⓓ Ⓔ
5. Ⓐ Ⓑ Ⓒ Ⓓ Ⓔ   15. Ⓐ Ⓑ Ⓒ Ⓓ Ⓔ   25. Ⓐ Ⓑ Ⓒ Ⓓ Ⓔ   35. Ⓐ Ⓑ Ⓒ Ⓓ Ⓔ
6. Ⓐ Ⓑ Ⓒ Ⓓ Ⓔ   16. Ⓐ Ⓑ Ⓒ Ⓓ Ⓔ   26. Ⓐ Ⓑ Ⓒ Ⓓ Ⓔ   36. Ⓐ Ⓑ Ⓒ Ⓓ Ⓔ
7. Ⓐ Ⓑ Ⓒ Ⓓ Ⓔ   17. Ⓐ Ⓑ Ⓒ Ⓓ Ⓔ   27. Ⓐ Ⓑ Ⓒ Ⓓ Ⓔ   37. Ⓐ Ⓑ Ⓒ Ⓓ Ⓔ
8. Ⓐ Ⓑ Ⓒ Ⓓ Ⓔ   18. Ⓐ Ⓑ Ⓒ Ⓓ Ⓔ   28. Ⓐ Ⓑ Ⓒ Ⓓ Ⓔ   38. Ⓐ Ⓑ Ⓒ Ⓓ Ⓔ
9. Ⓐ Ⓑ Ⓒ Ⓓ Ⓔ   19. Ⓐ Ⓑ Ⓒ Ⓓ Ⓔ   29. Ⓐ Ⓑ Ⓒ Ⓓ Ⓔ   39. Ⓐ Ⓑ Ⓒ Ⓓ Ⓔ
10. Ⓐ Ⓑ Ⓒ Ⓓ Ⓔ   20. Ⓐ Ⓑ Ⓒ Ⓓ Ⓔ   30. Ⓐ Ⓑ Ⓒ Ⓓ Ⓔ   40. Ⓐ Ⓑ Ⓒ Ⓓ Ⓔ

ANSWER SHEET

SECTION
4

1. Ⓐ Ⓑ Ⓒ Ⓓ Ⓔ   11. Ⓐ Ⓑ Ⓒ Ⓓ Ⓔ   21. Ⓐ Ⓑ Ⓒ Ⓓ Ⓔ   31. Ⓐ Ⓑ Ⓒ Ⓓ Ⓔ
2. Ⓐ Ⓑ Ⓒ Ⓓ Ⓔ   12. Ⓐ Ⓑ Ⓒ Ⓓ Ⓔ   22. Ⓐ Ⓑ Ⓒ Ⓓ Ⓔ   32. Ⓐ Ⓑ Ⓒ Ⓓ Ⓔ
3. Ⓐ Ⓑ Ⓒ Ⓓ Ⓔ   13. Ⓐ Ⓑ Ⓒ Ⓓ Ⓔ   23. Ⓐ Ⓑ Ⓒ Ⓓ Ⓔ   33. Ⓐ Ⓑ Ⓒ Ⓓ Ⓔ
4. Ⓐ Ⓑ Ⓒ Ⓓ Ⓔ   14. Ⓐ Ⓑ Ⓒ Ⓓ Ⓔ   24. Ⓐ Ⓑ Ⓒ Ⓓ Ⓔ   34. Ⓐ Ⓑ Ⓒ Ⓓ Ⓔ
5. Ⓐ Ⓑ Ⓒ Ⓓ Ⓔ   15. Ⓐ Ⓑ Ⓒ Ⓓ Ⓔ   25. Ⓐ Ⓑ Ⓒ Ⓓ Ⓔ   35. Ⓐ Ⓑ Ⓒ Ⓓ Ⓔ
6. Ⓐ Ⓑ Ⓒ Ⓓ Ⓔ   16. Ⓐ Ⓑ Ⓒ Ⓓ Ⓔ   26. Ⓐ Ⓑ Ⓒ Ⓓ Ⓔ   36. Ⓐ Ⓑ Ⓒ Ⓓ Ⓔ
7. Ⓐ Ⓑ Ⓒ Ⓓ Ⓔ   17. Ⓐ Ⓑ Ⓒ Ⓓ Ⓔ   27. Ⓐ Ⓑ Ⓒ Ⓓ Ⓔ   37. Ⓐ Ⓑ Ⓒ Ⓓ Ⓔ
8. Ⓐ Ⓑ Ⓒ Ⓓ Ⓔ   18. Ⓐ Ⓑ Ⓒ Ⓓ Ⓔ   28. Ⓐ Ⓑ Ⓒ Ⓓ Ⓔ   38. Ⓐ Ⓑ Ⓒ Ⓓ Ⓔ
9. Ⓐ Ⓑ Ⓒ Ⓓ Ⓔ   19. Ⓐ Ⓑ Ⓒ Ⓓ Ⓔ   29. Ⓐ Ⓑ Ⓒ Ⓓ Ⓔ   39. Ⓐ Ⓑ Ⓒ Ⓓ Ⓔ
10. Ⓐ Ⓑ Ⓒ Ⓓ Ⓔ   20. Ⓐ Ⓑ Ⓒ Ⓓ Ⓔ   30. Ⓐ Ⓑ Ⓒ Ⓓ Ⓔ   40. Ⓐ Ⓑ Ⓒ Ⓓ Ⓔ

SECTION
5

1. Ⓐ Ⓑ Ⓒ Ⓓ Ⓔ   5. Ⓐ Ⓑ Ⓒ Ⓓ Ⓔ
2. Ⓐ Ⓑ Ⓒ Ⓓ Ⓔ   6. Ⓐ Ⓑ Ⓒ Ⓓ Ⓔ
3. Ⓐ Ⓑ Ⓒ Ⓓ Ⓔ   7. Ⓐ Ⓑ Ⓒ Ⓓ Ⓔ
4. Ⓐ Ⓑ Ⓒ Ⓓ Ⓔ   8. Ⓐ Ⓑ Ⓒ Ⓓ Ⓔ

9. 10. 11. 12. 13.
14. 15. 16. 17. 18.

(Grid-in answer boxes 9–18)

ANSWER SHEET

SECTION 6

1. Ⓐ Ⓑ Ⓒ Ⓓ Ⓔ	11. Ⓐ Ⓑ Ⓒ Ⓓ Ⓔ	21. Ⓐ Ⓑ Ⓒ Ⓓ Ⓔ	31. Ⓐ Ⓑ Ⓒ Ⓓ Ⓔ
2. Ⓐ Ⓑ Ⓒ Ⓓ Ⓔ	12. Ⓐ Ⓑ Ⓒ Ⓓ Ⓔ	22. Ⓐ Ⓑ Ⓒ Ⓓ Ⓔ	32. Ⓐ Ⓑ Ⓒ Ⓓ Ⓔ
3. Ⓐ Ⓑ Ⓒ Ⓓ Ⓔ	13. Ⓐ Ⓑ Ⓒ Ⓓ Ⓔ	23. Ⓐ Ⓑ Ⓒ Ⓓ Ⓔ	33. Ⓐ Ⓑ Ⓒ Ⓓ Ⓔ
4. Ⓐ Ⓑ Ⓒ Ⓓ Ⓔ	14. Ⓐ Ⓑ Ⓒ Ⓓ Ⓔ	24. Ⓐ Ⓑ Ⓒ Ⓓ Ⓔ	34. Ⓐ Ⓑ Ⓒ Ⓓ Ⓔ
5. Ⓐ Ⓑ Ⓒ Ⓓ Ⓔ	15. Ⓐ Ⓑ Ⓒ Ⓓ Ⓔ	25. Ⓐ Ⓑ Ⓒ Ⓓ Ⓔ	35. Ⓐ Ⓑ Ⓒ Ⓓ Ⓔ
6. Ⓐ Ⓑ Ⓒ Ⓓ Ⓔ	16. Ⓐ Ⓑ Ⓒ Ⓓ Ⓔ	26. Ⓐ Ⓑ Ⓒ Ⓓ Ⓔ	36. Ⓐ Ⓑ Ⓒ Ⓓ Ⓔ
7. Ⓐ Ⓑ Ⓒ Ⓓ Ⓔ	17. Ⓐ Ⓑ Ⓒ Ⓓ Ⓔ	27. Ⓐ Ⓑ Ⓒ Ⓓ Ⓔ	37. Ⓐ Ⓑ Ⓒ Ⓓ Ⓔ
8. Ⓐ Ⓑ Ⓒ Ⓓ Ⓔ	18. Ⓐ Ⓑ Ⓒ Ⓓ Ⓔ	28. Ⓐ Ⓑ Ⓒ Ⓓ Ⓔ	38. Ⓐ Ⓑ Ⓒ Ⓓ Ⓔ
9. Ⓐ Ⓑ Ⓒ Ⓓ Ⓔ	19. Ⓐ Ⓑ Ⓒ Ⓓ Ⓔ	29. Ⓐ Ⓑ Ⓒ Ⓓ Ⓔ	39. Ⓐ Ⓑ Ⓒ Ⓓ Ⓔ
10. Ⓐ Ⓑ Ⓒ Ⓓ Ⓔ	20. Ⓐ Ⓑ Ⓒ Ⓓ Ⓔ	30. Ⓐ Ⓑ Ⓒ Ⓓ Ⓔ	40. Ⓐ Ⓑ Ⓒ Ⓓ Ⓔ

SECTION 7

1. Ⓐ Ⓑ Ⓒ Ⓓ Ⓔ	11. Ⓐ Ⓑ Ⓒ Ⓓ Ⓔ	21. Ⓐ Ⓑ Ⓒ Ⓓ Ⓔ	31. Ⓐ Ⓑ Ⓒ Ⓓ Ⓔ
2. Ⓐ Ⓑ Ⓒ Ⓓ Ⓔ	12. Ⓐ Ⓑ Ⓒ Ⓓ Ⓔ	22. Ⓐ Ⓑ Ⓒ Ⓓ Ⓔ	32. Ⓐ Ⓑ Ⓒ Ⓓ Ⓔ
3. Ⓐ Ⓑ Ⓒ Ⓓ Ⓔ	13. Ⓐ Ⓑ Ⓒ Ⓓ Ⓔ	23. Ⓐ Ⓑ Ⓒ Ⓓ Ⓔ	33. Ⓐ Ⓑ Ⓒ Ⓓ Ⓔ
4. Ⓐ Ⓑ Ⓒ Ⓓ Ⓔ	14. Ⓐ Ⓑ Ⓒ Ⓓ Ⓔ	24. Ⓐ Ⓑ Ⓒ Ⓓ Ⓔ	34. Ⓐ Ⓑ Ⓒ Ⓓ Ⓔ
5. Ⓐ Ⓑ Ⓒ Ⓓ Ⓔ	15. Ⓐ Ⓑ Ⓒ Ⓓ Ⓔ	25. Ⓐ Ⓑ Ⓒ Ⓓ Ⓔ	35. Ⓐ Ⓑ Ⓒ Ⓓ Ⓔ
6. Ⓐ Ⓑ Ⓒ Ⓓ Ⓔ	16. Ⓐ Ⓑ Ⓒ Ⓓ Ⓔ	26. Ⓐ Ⓑ Ⓒ Ⓓ Ⓔ	36. Ⓐ Ⓑ Ⓒ Ⓓ Ⓔ
7. Ⓐ Ⓑ Ⓒ Ⓓ Ⓔ	17. Ⓐ Ⓑ Ⓒ Ⓓ Ⓔ	27. Ⓐ Ⓑ Ⓒ Ⓓ Ⓔ	37. Ⓐ Ⓑ Ⓒ Ⓓ Ⓔ
8. Ⓐ Ⓑ Ⓒ Ⓓ Ⓔ	18. Ⓐ Ⓑ Ⓒ Ⓓ Ⓔ	28. Ⓐ Ⓑ Ⓒ Ⓓ Ⓔ	38. Ⓐ Ⓑ Ⓒ Ⓓ Ⓔ
9. Ⓐ Ⓑ Ⓒ Ⓓ Ⓔ	19. Ⓐ Ⓑ Ⓒ Ⓓ Ⓔ	29. Ⓐ Ⓑ Ⓒ Ⓓ Ⓔ	39. Ⓐ Ⓑ Ⓒ Ⓓ Ⓔ
10. Ⓐ Ⓑ Ⓒ Ⓓ Ⓔ	20. Ⓐ Ⓑ Ⓒ Ⓓ Ⓔ	30. Ⓐ Ⓑ Ⓒ Ⓓ Ⓔ	40. Ⓐ Ⓑ Ⓒ Ⓓ Ⓔ

SECTION 8

1. Ⓐ Ⓑ Ⓒ Ⓓ Ⓔ	11. Ⓐ Ⓑ Ⓒ Ⓓ Ⓔ	21. Ⓐ Ⓑ Ⓒ Ⓓ Ⓔ	31. Ⓐ Ⓑ Ⓒ Ⓓ Ⓔ
2. Ⓐ Ⓑ Ⓒ Ⓓ Ⓔ	12. Ⓐ Ⓑ Ⓒ Ⓓ Ⓔ	22. Ⓐ Ⓑ Ⓒ Ⓓ Ⓔ	32. Ⓐ Ⓑ Ⓒ Ⓓ Ⓔ
3. Ⓐ Ⓑ Ⓒ Ⓓ Ⓔ	13. Ⓐ Ⓑ Ⓒ Ⓓ Ⓔ	23. Ⓐ Ⓑ Ⓒ Ⓓ Ⓔ	33. Ⓐ Ⓑ Ⓒ Ⓓ Ⓔ
4. Ⓐ Ⓑ Ⓒ Ⓓ Ⓔ	14. Ⓐ Ⓑ Ⓒ Ⓓ Ⓔ	24. Ⓐ Ⓑ Ⓒ Ⓓ Ⓔ	34. Ⓐ Ⓑ Ⓒ Ⓓ Ⓔ
5. Ⓐ Ⓑ Ⓒ Ⓓ Ⓔ	15. Ⓐ Ⓑ Ⓒ Ⓓ Ⓔ	25. Ⓐ Ⓑ Ⓒ Ⓓ Ⓔ	35. Ⓐ Ⓑ Ⓒ Ⓓ Ⓔ
6. Ⓐ Ⓑ Ⓒ Ⓓ Ⓔ	16. Ⓐ Ⓑ Ⓒ Ⓓ Ⓔ	26. Ⓐ Ⓑ Ⓒ Ⓓ Ⓔ	36. Ⓐ Ⓑ Ⓒ Ⓓ Ⓔ
7. Ⓐ Ⓑ Ⓒ Ⓓ Ⓔ	17. Ⓐ Ⓑ Ⓒ Ⓓ Ⓔ	27. Ⓐ Ⓑ Ⓒ Ⓓ Ⓔ	37. Ⓐ Ⓑ Ⓒ Ⓓ Ⓔ
8. Ⓐ Ⓑ Ⓒ Ⓓ Ⓔ	18. Ⓐ Ⓑ Ⓒ Ⓓ Ⓔ	28. Ⓐ Ⓑ Ⓒ Ⓓ Ⓔ	38. Ⓐ Ⓑ Ⓒ Ⓓ Ⓔ
9. Ⓐ Ⓑ Ⓒ Ⓓ Ⓔ	19. Ⓐ Ⓑ Ⓒ Ⓓ Ⓔ	29. Ⓐ Ⓑ Ⓒ Ⓓ Ⓔ	39. Ⓐ Ⓑ Ⓒ Ⓓ Ⓔ
10. Ⓐ Ⓑ Ⓒ Ⓓ Ⓔ	20. Ⓐ Ⓑ Ⓒ Ⓓ Ⓔ	30. Ⓐ Ⓑ Ⓒ Ⓓ Ⓔ	40. Ⓐ Ⓑ Ⓒ Ⓓ Ⓔ

SECTION 9

1. Ⓐ Ⓑ Ⓒ Ⓓ Ⓔ	11. Ⓐ Ⓑ Ⓒ Ⓓ Ⓔ	21. Ⓐ Ⓑ Ⓒ Ⓓ Ⓔ	31. Ⓐ Ⓑ Ⓒ Ⓓ Ⓔ
2. Ⓐ Ⓑ Ⓒ Ⓓ Ⓔ	12. Ⓐ Ⓑ Ⓒ Ⓓ Ⓔ	22. Ⓐ Ⓑ Ⓒ Ⓓ Ⓔ	32. Ⓐ Ⓑ Ⓒ Ⓓ Ⓔ
3. Ⓐ Ⓑ Ⓒ Ⓓ Ⓔ	13. Ⓐ Ⓑ Ⓒ Ⓓ Ⓔ	23. Ⓐ Ⓑ Ⓒ Ⓓ Ⓔ	33. Ⓐ Ⓑ Ⓒ Ⓓ Ⓔ
4. Ⓐ Ⓑ Ⓒ Ⓓ Ⓔ	14. Ⓐ Ⓑ Ⓒ Ⓓ Ⓔ	24. Ⓐ Ⓑ Ⓒ Ⓓ Ⓔ	34. Ⓐ Ⓑ Ⓒ Ⓓ Ⓔ
5. Ⓐ Ⓑ Ⓒ Ⓓ Ⓔ	15. Ⓐ Ⓑ Ⓒ Ⓓ Ⓔ	25. Ⓐ Ⓑ Ⓒ Ⓓ Ⓔ	35. Ⓐ Ⓑ Ⓒ Ⓓ Ⓔ
6. Ⓐ Ⓑ Ⓒ Ⓓ Ⓔ	16. Ⓐ Ⓑ Ⓒ Ⓓ Ⓔ	26. Ⓐ Ⓑ Ⓒ Ⓓ Ⓔ	36. Ⓐ Ⓑ Ⓒ Ⓓ Ⓔ
7. Ⓐ Ⓑ Ⓒ Ⓓ Ⓔ	17. Ⓐ Ⓑ Ⓒ Ⓓ Ⓔ	27. Ⓐ Ⓑ Ⓒ Ⓓ Ⓔ	37. Ⓐ Ⓑ Ⓒ Ⓓ Ⓔ
8. Ⓐ Ⓑ Ⓒ Ⓓ Ⓔ	18. Ⓐ Ⓑ Ⓒ Ⓓ Ⓔ	28. Ⓐ Ⓑ Ⓒ Ⓓ Ⓔ	38. Ⓐ Ⓑ Ⓒ Ⓓ Ⓔ
9. Ⓐ Ⓑ Ⓒ Ⓓ Ⓔ	19. Ⓐ Ⓑ Ⓒ Ⓓ Ⓔ	29. Ⓐ Ⓑ Ⓒ Ⓓ Ⓔ	39. Ⓐ Ⓑ Ⓒ Ⓓ Ⓔ
10. Ⓐ Ⓑ Ⓒ Ⓓ Ⓔ	20. Ⓐ Ⓑ Ⓒ Ⓓ Ⓔ	30. Ⓐ Ⓑ Ⓒ Ⓓ Ⓔ	40. Ⓐ Ⓑ Ⓒ Ⓓ Ⓔ

Section 1

Time—25 minutes

Directions for Writing the Essay

Plan and write an essay that answers the question below. Do NOT write on another topic. An essay on another topic will receive a score of 0.

Two readers will grade your essay based on how well you develop your point of view, organize and explain your ideas, use specific and relevant examples to support your thesis, and use clear and effective language. How well you write is much more important than how much you write, but to cover the topic adequately you should plan to write several paragraphs.

Your essay must be written on separate lined sheets of paper. Keep your handwriting to a reasonable size. Your essay will be read by people who are not familiar with your handwriting, so write legibly.

You may use this sheet for notes and outlining, but these will not be graded as part of your essay.

Consider carefully the issue discussed in the following passage, then write an essay that answers the question posed in the assignment.

> The liberally educated person is one who is able to resist the easy and preferred answers, not because he is obstinate but because he knows others worthy of consideration.
> —Allan Bloom

Assignment: **What is one important "easy and preferred answer" that we should resist? That is, what dangerous misconception do people commonly hold?** Write an essay in which you answer this question and support your position logically with examples from literature, the arts, history, politics, science and technology, current events, or your experience or observation.

Write your essay on separate sheets of paper.

Section 2

Time—25 minutes
20 Questions

Directions for Multiple-Choice Questions

In this section, solve each problem, using any available space on the page for scratchwork. Then decide which is the best of the choices given and fill in the corresponding oval on the answer sheet.

- You may use a calculator on any problem. All numbers used are real numbers.
- Figures are drawn as accurately as possible EXCEPT when it is stated that the figure is not drawn to scale.
- All figures lie in a plane unless otherwise indicated.

Reference Information

$A = \pi r^2$ $A = \ell w$ $A = \frac{1}{2}bh$ $V = \ell wh$ $V = \pi r^2 h$ $c^2 = a^2 + b^2$ Special Right Triangles
$C = 2\pi r$

The arc of a circle measures 360°.
Every straight angle measures 180°.
The sum of the measures of the angles in a triangle is 180°.

---

1. If $3(m + n) + 3 = 15$, then $m + n =$

(A) 2
(B) 3
(C) 4
(D) 5
(E) 6

2. If Elena reads at a rate of r pages per minute for a total of m minutes, which of the following represents the total number of pages that Elena reads?

(A) rm

(B) $\dfrac{r}{m}$

(C) $\dfrac{m}{r}$

(D) $\dfrac{60r}{m}$

(E) $\dfrac{60m}{r}$

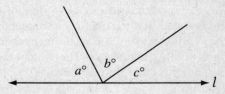

Note: Figure not drawn to scale.

3. In the figure above, if l is a line, $a + b = 120$ and $b + c = 100$, then what is the value of b?

(A) 10
(B) 20
(C) 30
(D) 40
(E) 50

GO ON TO THE NEXT PAGE ▶▶▶

4 If $6^n \times 6^4 = 6^{12}$, then $n =$

(A) 2
(B) 3
(C) 5
(D) 6
(E) 8

5 If $4x + b = x + 2$, what is b in terms of x?

(A) $5x + 2$
(B) $3x + 2$
(C) $2 - x$
(D) $2 - 3x$
(E) $2 - 5x$

RETAIL CAR PRICES			QUANTITY SOLD		
	Model A	Model B		Model A	Model B
1995	$15,000	$25,000	1995	200	100
2000	$20,000	$30,000	2000	220	150
2005	$25,000	$35,000	2005	200	200

6 The tables above show the retail prices of two car models and the quantities of those models sold at a particular car dealership in three different years. Based on these tables, how much greater was the total value of cars sold in 2005 than in 1995?

(A) $5,500,000
(B) $6,500,000
(C) $9,000,000
(D) $10,500,000
(E) $12,000,000

7 An isosceles triangle has one angle with a measure greater than 95° and another with a measure of $x°$. Which of the following must be true?

(A) $x > 85$
(B) $x = 85$
(C) $x = 42.5$
(D) $x < 42.5$
(E) $x > 42.5$

8 When m is divided by 7, the remainder is 2. What is the remainder when $4m$ is divided by 7?

(A) 1
(B) 2
(C) 3
(D) 4
(E) 5

9 If a is a multiple of 3 and b is an odd integer, then which of the following must be an odd integer?

(A) $\dfrac{a}{b}$
(B) ab
(C) $a + b$
(D) $2a + b$
(E) $a + 2b$

10 The point (a, b) is reflected over the x-axis, and then the reflected point is reflected over the y-axis. If a and b are both positive, which of the following represents the coordinates of the point after the second reflection?

(A) (a, b)
(B) (b, a)
(C) $(-a, -b)$
(D) $(-b, -a)$
(E) $(a, -b)$

11 A right circular cylinder with a radius of 1 and a height of 1 has a volume that is most nearly the same as the volume of a rectangular solid with dimensions

(A) 1 by 1 by 1
(B) 1 by 1 by 2
(C) 1 by 1 by 3
(D) 1 by 2 by 2
(E) 1 by 2 by 3

12 If the nth term of a sequence is $3n^2 - n$, then how much greater is the 10th term than the 3rd term?

(A) 242
(B) 266
(C) 281
(D) 286
(E) 290

13 What is the maximum number of points of intersection between a circle and a square that lie in the same plane?

(A) 4
(B) 6
(C) 7
(D) 8
(E) 9

14 If $x < x^3 < x^2$, then which of the following must be true?

(A) $x < -1$
(B) $-1 < x < 0$
(C) $0 < x < 1$
(D) $x > 1$
(E) x is not a real number

15 If $(m + n)^2 = 18$ and $mn = 4$, then what is the value of $m^2 + n^2$?

(A) 10
(B) 14
(C) 18
(D) 22
(E) 26

16 An isosceles triangle has two sides of length 5 and 12. Which of the following could be the perimeter of this triangle?

   I.   22
   II. 29
   III. 30
(A) II only
(B) I and II only
(C) I and III only
(D) II and III only
(E) I, II, and III

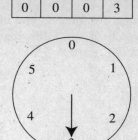

17 The figure above shows a digital counter above a dial counter showing the digits 0 through 5. Both counters are initially set to 0 and count upward together in increments of 1. For instance, when the digital counter reads 5 the dial counter also reads 5, but when the digital counter reads 6, the dial counter resets back to 0. What will the dial counter read when the digital counter reads 1000?

(A) 0
(B) 1
(C) 2
(D) 4
(E) 5

18 In a mixture of raisins and dates, the ratio by weight of raisins to dates is 7 to 3. How many pounds of raisins will there be in 7 pounds of this mixture?

(A) 2.1
(B) 2.3
(C) 2.8
(D) 3.0
(E) 4.9

GO ON TO THE NEXT PAGE ▶▶▶

19 If m and n are integers and $m = n{-}2/n{-}2/n^2$, then which of the following could be the value of m?

      I.   −5
     II.   −3
    III.   −1

(A) II only
(B) II and III only
(C) I and II only
(D) I and III only
(E) I, II, and III

3

20 Each of the k girls in a club agreed to raise an equal amount of money to give to a charity to which the club had pledged a total of x dollars. If p more girls later join the club and also agree to raise an equal share of the pledged amount, how much <u>less</u> would each of the original club members have to raise, in dollars, than she had originally agreed to raise?

(A) $\dfrac{x}{k}$

(B) $\dfrac{x}{k+p}$

(C) $\dfrac{px}{k+p}$

(D) $\dfrac{x(k+p)}{k}$

(E) $\dfrac{px}{k(k+p)}$

STOP

You may check your work, on this section only, until time is called.

Section 3

Time—25 Minutes
35 Questions

Directions for "Improving Sentences" Questions

Each of the sentences below contains one underlined portion. The portion may contain one or more errors in grammar, usage, construction, precision, diction (choice of words), or idiom. Some of the sentences are correct.

Consider the meaning of the original sentence, and choose the answer that best expresses that meaning. If the original sentence is best, choose (A), because it repeats the original phrasing. Choose the phrasing that creates the clearest, most precise and most effective sentence.

EXAMPLE:

The growth of the plant was so dramatic that the children <u>couldn't hardly believe their eyes</u>.

   (A)   couldn't hardly believe their eyes
   (B)   would not hardly believe their eyes
   (C)   could hardly believe their eyes
   (D)   couldn't nearly believe their eyes
   (E)   could hardly believe his or her eyes

Example answer: (C)

---

1 Andrews was one of the first employers to realize that employees are most productive when <u>he or she feels to be part of a family</u>.

   (A)   he or she feels to be part of a family
   (B)   they feel as if they are part of a family
   (C)   he or she feels part of a family
   (D)   it's more like a family for them
   (E)   feeling a part of a family is made possible

2 Several agents were dispatched to Europe <u>for the purpose of investigating</u> a lead that could potentially provide a break in the case.

   (A)   for the purpose of investigating
   (B)   to investigate on
   (C)   for the investigation of
   (D)   to investigate
   (E)   to investigate after

3 Although worried about the dangers of going into debt, <u>Helena's concern was more about the possibility of losing her business</u>.

   (A)   Helena's concern was more about the possibility of losing her business
   (B)   it was the possibility of losing her business that gave Helena more concern
   (C)   Helena was more concerned towards her business and the possibility of losing it
   (D)   the possibility of losing her business gave Helena more concern
   (E)   Helena was more concerned about the possibility of losing her business

4 Those who enjoy Marquez's <u>novels, being those who tend not to read</u> traditional fiction, preferring instead the intellectual challenge of magical realism.

   (A)   novels, being those who tend not to read
   (B)   novels, tending to be those who do not read
   (C)   novels tend not to read
   (D)   novels are the ones that tend not to be the ones reading
   (E)   novels being the ones tending not to read

5 The reason the event was cancelled was not so much the poor weather <u>as the lack of interest</u>.

   (A)   as the lack of interest
   (B)   than the lack of interest
   (C)   than because of the lack of interest
   (D)   but rather the lack of interest
   (E)   as it was lacking interest

GO ON TO THE NEXT PAGE ▶▶▶

6 The statute recently passed by the town gives the chief of police sole authority to determine <u>about which duties qualify for overtime pay</u>.

(A) about which duties qualify for over-time pay
(B) regarding the qualifications of duties for overtime pay
(C) whether overtime pay qualifies for certain duties or not
(D) for those duties that qualify for over-time pay
(E) which duties qualify for overtime pay

7 In baseball, the batter attempts to hit the ball within a ninety degree <u>quadrant, in cricket the batter can hit</u> the ball in any direction.

(A) quadrant, in cricket the batter can hit
(B) quadrant; but in cricket the batter can hit
(C) quadrant, but the batter can hit in cricket
(D) quadrant, but in cricket the batter can hit
(E) quadrant; the batter in cricket hitting

8 Skeptical of the abilities of prophets to tell the future, <u>Athens was where significant numbers of philosophers began to value reason over revealed truths</u>.

(A) Athens was where significant numbers of philosophers began to value reason over revealed truths
(B) it was a significant number of philosophers that began to value reason over revealed truths
(C) a significant number of philosophers in Athens began to value reason over revealed truths
(D) the valuing of reason over revealed truths was begun by a significant number of philosphers in Athens
(E) valuing of reason over revealed truths by philosophers in Athens was begun

9 As the investigation concludes, the debate over the origins of the scandal, the merits of the federal investigation, and <u>the legal authority of the prosecutor have</u> intensified greatly.

(A) the legal authority of the prosecutor have
(B) whether the prosecutor has legal authority has
(C) the legal authority of the prosecutor has
(D) what the legal authority of the prosecutor is has
(E) the prosecutor's legal authority have

10 Excited by the prospect of starting her own business, <u>Kyra's first decision needed to be where she could rent office space</u>.

(A) Kyra's first decision needed to be where she could rent office space
(B) Kyra first had to decide where it was to rent office space
(C) Kyra's first decision had to be regarding renting office space and where it would be
(D) Kyra first had to decide where to rent office space
(E) renting office space had to be what Kyra's first decision was about

---

Directions for Identifying Sentence Error Questions

The following sentences may contain errors in grammar, usage, diction (choice of words), or idiom. Some of the sentences are correct. No sentence contains more than 1 error.

If the sentence contains an error, it is underlined and lettered. The parts that are not underlined are correct.

If there is an error, select the part that must be changed to correct the sentence.

If there is no error, choose (E).

EXAMPLE:

By the time <u>they reached</u> the halfway point
           A
<u>in the race,</u> most <u>of the runners</u> <u>hadn't hardly</u>
  B   C   D
begun to hit their stride. <u>No error</u>
                 E

Example answer: (D)

---

11 <u>Elizabeth is a highly skilled teacher, in addition to being an outstanding pianist and composer, and these are talents she uses to get her students interested in music.</u>

(A) Elizabeth is a highly skilled teacher, in addition to being an outstanding pianist and composer, and these are talents she uses to get her students interested in music.

(B) A highly skilled teacher, Elizabeth uses her outstanding talents as a pianist and composer to get her students interested in music.

(C) Getting her students interested in music, Elizabeth uses her outstanding talents as a pianist and a composer, making her a highly skilled teacher.

(D) Elizabeth being an outstanding pianist and composer and a highly skilled teacher, she uses these talents to get her students interested in music.

(E) To get her students interested in music, Elizabeth uses her outstanding talents as a pianist and composer, her being a highly skilled teacher.

12 Yet to be discussed in the conference <u>is</u>
                              A
more than a dozen <u>proposals</u> for changes
                 B
<u>in</u> the procedural rules for <u>choosing</u>
C   D
new officers. <u>No error</u>
             E

13 Although the latest senatorial debate <u>focused</u>
                                  A
on the more <u>controversial</u> topics in the
          B
campaign, the candidates conducted

<u>themselves</u> much more <u>civil</u> than they
  C   D
had previously. <u>No error</u>
              E

14 <u>Having experienced</u> many realistic disaster
    A
drills in his months of training

<u>as a fire fighter,</u> Leon handled the disaster
        B
<u>calmly and effectively</u> and in fact is
       C
<u>credited</u> with saving several lives. <u>No error</u>
D   E

15 While the Athenians <u>were outraged</u> by the
                    A
oppressive and unenlightened Spartans,

<u>but the</u> Spartans were <u>indignant</u> about
  B   C
the Athenians' indifference <u>to the gods</u>
                        D
and religious matters. <u>No error</u>
                E

GO ON TO THE NEXT PAGE ▶▶▶

16 If some of the hikers <u>had not took</u> the
                           A
riskier but shorter route up the mountain,

<u>they</u> would probably not <u>have become</u> so
 B   C
<u>widely separated</u> by nightfall. <u>No error</u>
         D   E

3

17 Jason <u>was confused</u> by the theory, <u>about</u>
              A   B
which many of his classmates often

referred, <u>because</u> it seemed to <u>be based</u>
           C   D
on an obviously false premise. <u>No error</u>
                                     E

18 The pace at <u>which</u> industrial and
                    A
communications technologies

<u>are progressing</u> in developing countries
      B
<u>are</u> so rapid that many governments
 C
cannot anticipate the harm these

technologies <u>may do</u> to the
                 D
environment. <u>No error</u>
                 E

19 Every living creature on earth <u>owe their</u>
                                       A
existence <u>to</u> the chemical properties of atoms
          B
<u>that were forged</u> in stars billions of miles
       C
away and billions of <u>years ago</u>. <u>No error</u>
                          D   E

20 Having <u>such acute</u> senses of hearing, smell
              A
<u>and sight</u>, zebras often <u>provide</u> early
   B   C
warning to <u>other grazers</u> that predators are
              D
approaching. <u>No error</u>
                 E

21 Many students fail <u>to appreciate</u> <u>that</u> it is
                          A   B
much more difficult to teach someone

<u>how to write</u> good prose than <u>teaching</u>
    C   D
someone how to appreciate good prose

written by others. <u>No error</u>
                      E

22 Because the coach <u>was</u> so preoccupied <u>on</u>
                        A   B
developing and practicing trick plays, she

<u>did not spend</u> enough time <u>drilling</u> the
    C   D
fundamental skills. <u>No error</u>
                       E

23 <u>Without</u> our permission, our teacher
   A
assigned a new research topic to

<u>Jose and I</u> only two days before we
   B
<u>were</u> <u>to give</u> our presentation. <u>No error</u>
 C   D   E

24 Although statistical methods

<u>can rarely prove</u> causality, they can
        A
frequently <u>refute</u> theories by
              B
demonstrating that no correlation <u>exists</u>
                                      C
between <u>particular effects</u> and their
              D
presumed causes. <u>No error</u>
                     E

25 In the central courtyard <u>was</u> over a dozen
   A   B
different <u>varieties of lilies</u>, meticulously
              C
maintained <u>by</u> the gardener. <u>No error</u>
            D   E

26 Cara's <u>constant</u> improving race times
              A
proved that her new training <u>regimen</u> had
                                B
been <u>more effective</u> than even she
        C
<u>had hoped</u>. <u>No error</u>
    D   E

27 The devastation wrought by the hurricane

<u>was</u> so <u>widespread</u> that officials
 A   B
<u>had to suspend</u> many government services
     C
for an <u>indecisive</u> amount of time. <u>No error</u>
          D   E

28 High in isoflavones, protein, and <u>also in</u>
                                         A
fiber, soy beans <u>are</u> a flavorful food
                    B
<u>with</u> many <u>healthful</u> benefits. <u>No error</u>
   C   D   E

29 The project on nuclear energy

<u>that Jenna presented</u> to the science fair
        A
committee <u>was</u> considered superior to
              B
<u>the other students</u>, and <u>so</u> she was awarded
        C   D
the blue ribbon. <u>No error</u>
                     E

Directions for "Improving Paragraphs" Questions

The passage below is an early draft of an essay. It requires revision in many areas.

The questions that follow ask you to make improvements in sentence structure, diction, organization and development. Answering the questions may require you to understand the context of the passage as well as the rules of standard written English.

Questions 30–35 are based on the following passage.

(1) *Almost everyone knows about incentives and disincentives, even if they never actually heard the words.* (2) *People choose to do things because they perceive a benefit to doing them, or avoid things for which they perceive they will be punished.* (3) *That thing that makes them want to do it is called an incentive, and what makes them not want to do them would be a disincentive.* (4) *Business people are encouraged to make more money for the company through incentives like bonus pay and perks.* (5) *Students are constantly exposed to incentives like peer pressure, parental guilt and grades.* (6) *Peers use incentives to persuade others to become part of a group so that the group's influence can grow.* (7) *Parents use bribery or guilt to encourage you to behave in a way that makes them proud.* (8) *Teachers try to make their students do what they want by holding the gradebook that may determine their future.*

(9) *But what is surprising is that incentives don't always work in the way like they're supposed to.* (10) *For instance, in some schools they paid kids to read books one summer.* (11) *But people who studied such programs discovered that the kids ended up reading less in the long run, because paying them took the fun out of it.* (12) *Also, a day care center that imposed a 3 dollar an hour penalty on parents for picking up their kids late discovered that more parents, not fewer, started picking up their kids late.* (13) *This was because the parents no longer felt guilty because now they were paying the school for the extra service, but the penalty was cheap enough that they considered it a good deal.* (14) *The bottom line is that people who try to reward or punish things shouldn't assume that either rewards or punishments work the way they think they should.*

GO ON TO THE NEXT PAGE ▶▶▶

30 In context, which of the following is the best revision of sentence 3 (reproduced below)?

That thing that makes them want to do it is called an incentive, and what makes them not want to do them would be a disincentive.

(A) It is an incentive making someone want to do something, and a disincentive making them not want to do it.

(B) An incentive is what makes someone want to do something, and a disincentive is what makes someone want to avoid doing something.

(C) Incentives make someone want to do things, but disincentives are the things making them not want to do it.

(D) People are made to want to do something by incentives, and a disincentive is for not wanting to do it.

(E) It is incentives that make people want to do something, disincentives on the other hand being what makes people want to avoid doing something.

31 Which of the following changes to sentence 7 would best improve the coherence of the first paragraph?

(A) Change "you" to "their children."
(B) Change "use" to "also use."
(C) Begin the sentence with "Nevertheless."
(D) Begin the sentence with "For instance."
(E) Change "to behave" to "behaving."

32 Where is the best place to insert the following sentence?

Incentives are used to influence people in many walks of life.

(A) after sentence 2
(B) after sentence 3
(C) after sentence 4
(D) after sentence 5
(E) after sentence 6

33 Which of the following is the best version of sentence 9 (reproduced below)?

But what is surprising is that incentives don't always work in the way like they're supposed to.

(A) (as it is now)
(B) It is the surprising fact that incentives don't always work like they're supposed to.
(C) What is surprising, incentives don't always work like they should.
(D) Incentives don't always work as they should, it is surprising.
(E) Surprisingly, incentives don't always work as they should.

34 In context, what is the best version of the underlined portion of sentence 10 (reproduced below)?

For instance, <u>in some schools they</u> paid kids to read books one summer.

(A) in some schools where they
(B) some schools are where they
(C) some schools implemented programs that
(D) programs in some schools were where they
(E) in some school programs they

35 Which is the best sentence to insert between sentence 13 and sentence 14?

(A) Examples such as this demonstrate that incentives can be very effective.
(B) If the penalty had been greater, perhaps it would have had the desired effect.
(C) Clearly, rewards are more effective in most situations than punishments.
(D) Many schools have also implemented effective after-school reading programs.
(E) I'm not sure what the school decided to do with the program, since it wasn't working.

STOP

You may check your work, on this section only, until time is called.

Section 4

Time—25 Minutes
24 Questions

Each of the sentences below is missing one or two portions. Read each sentence, then select the word or words that most logically completes the sentence, taking into account the meaning of the sentence as a whole.

Example:

Rather than accepting the theory unquestioningly, Deborah regarded it with _____.

(A) mirth   (B) sadness
(C) responsibility (D) ignorance
(E) skepticism

Example answer: (E)

1 Geological evidence suggests that the earth's magnetic polarity has switched back and forth many times over the millennia; such ———— in the magnetic field may affect the ability of our planet to ward off cosmic radiation.

(A) intensifications (B) justifications
(C) records   (D) correlations
(E) fluctuations

2 Recent studies have demonstrated that even birds are capable of making and using tools, but scientists disagree as to whether such behavior is learned or ————.

(A) intelligent (B) impassive
(C) innate   (D) pragmatic
(E) suspect

3 Although doctors have been thus far successful at ———— the spread of tuberculosis in the United States, they are nonetheless concerned that ———— strains of the disease may yet arise.

(A) marginalizing . . innocuous
(B) controlling . . virulent
(C) obscuring . . indifferent
(D) imperilling . . responsive
(E) dismissing . . required

4 The lecturer admonished those who confused the carefully formulated ———— of the scientific method with the more wishful ———— of pseudoscience.

(A) theories . . divergences
(B) concessions . . estimates
(C) hypotheses . . conjectures
(D) paradigms . . restrictions
(E) hunches . . proofs

5 Unlike the first lecture, which was ———— and filled with irrelevant references, Ken's presentation was easy to understand and illustrated with ———— examples.

(A) obscure . . vague
(B) lucid . . pertinent
(C) convoluted . . petty
(D) concise . . esoteric
(E) abstruse . . germane

6 Although Ian's argument seemed plausible at first, his opponent in the debate dismissed it as mere ———— and refuted it thoroughly.

(A) sophistry (B) solicitousness
(C) acumen   (D) substantiation
(E) resolution

7 Glen is considered one of the most —— members of the group, having already read dozens of philosophical treatises and ——researched all new developments in his discipline.

(A) erudite . . assiduously
(B) contrite . . painstakingly
(C) cerebral . . hesitantly
(D) stoic . . lackadaisically
(E) argumentative . . generously

8 The establishment of international phone service in 1964 appeased those citizens of the tiny island who bemoaned the ———— of their community and longed for a greater connection to the world outside.

(A) obstinacy   (B) precociousness
(C) obsequiousness (D) insularity
(E) insinuation

GO ON TO THE NEXT PAGE ▶▶▶

The paired passages below are followed by questions based on their content and the relationship between the passages. Answer the questions on the basis of what is stated or implied in the passages and in any introductory material that may be provided.

Questions 9-12 are based on the following passages.

4

Passage 1

Line In polls, Kennedy is listed as one of the
greatest presidents ever to serve. How is it
that a man who barely served 1,000 days
and enacted few lasting policies, won no
5   wars and who was never much more popular
than his Republican rival, could be perceived
as greater than George Washington, James
Madison, Thomas Jefferson or Ronald Reagan?
The answer lies in the most consistent feature
10 of Baby Boomers, their narcissism. The
president of the "Me generation" trumps all
others, just as their war (Vietnam) is the
measuring stick by which all modern wars are
judged and their music (rock n' roll) continues
15 to dominate the air waves. History be damned;
if it didn't happen between 1960 and 1980, it's
irrelevant. If they didn't see it on television, it
might as well not have happened. JFK was
the first president to make effective use of
20 television.

Passage 2

Kennedy was the first President to be born in
the twentieth century and was very much a
man of his time. He was restless, seeking,
with a thirst of knowledge, and he had a
25 feeling of deep commitment, not only to
the people of the United States, but to the
peoples of the world. Many of the causes
he fought for exist today because of what he
did for the rights of minorities, the poor, the
30 very old and the very young. He never took
anything for granted and worked for everything
he owned. Perhaps Kennedy summed up his
life best in his own inaugural speech: "Ask not
what your country can do for you, but ask what
you can do for your country."

9 Unlike Passage 2, Passage 1 conveys a tone of

(A) cynicism
(B) hope
(C) objectivity
(D) fear
(E) humor

10 The question posed in lines 2–8 ("How is it … Ronald Reagan?") suggests that the author of Passage 1 believes that

(A) polls are unreliable gauges of real sentiments
(B) Kennedy's policies are what made him so popular
(C) Kennedy's high ranking is undeserved
(D) Kennedy was a savvy politician
(E) Kennedy himself was unconcerned with his own popularity

11 Passage 2 mentions "the very old and the very young" (lines 29–30) in order to make the point that Kennedy

(A) was elected by a very wide range of voters
(B) focused more on political issues than on moral ones
(C) was mourned by the entire nation
(D) was adept at manipulating the media
(E) supported policies that benefited divergent groups

12 With which of the following statements would BOTH authors most likely agree?

(A) American culture in the 60s and 70s was highly self-centered.
(B) Polls are powerful tools for assessing popular sentiments.
(C) Kennedy was one of the foremost advocates of minority rights.
(D) Kennedy was one of the hardest working American presidents
(E) Kennedy was in touch with the unique qualities of the era in which he governed.

GO ON TO THE NEXT PAGE ▶▶▶

First paragraph: http://www.renewamerica.us/columns/cox/031124
Second paragraph: http://www.studyworld.com/newsite/ReportEssay/Biography/
AmericanPresident%5CJFK_His_Life_and_Legacy-322663.htm

Questions 13–24 are based on the following passages.

The following passages discuss different perspectives on political dissent. The first passage, written in 1922 by H. L. Mencken, an American journalist and essayist, discusses real versus ideal government. The second, written in 1991 by Gordon S. Wood, a professor of history at Brown University, discusses the basis of the American Revolution.

Passage 1

Line All government, in its essence, is a conspiracy against the superior man: its one permanent object is to oppress him and cripple him. If it be aristocratic in organization, then it seeks
5 to protect the man who is superior only in law against the man who is superior in fact; if it be democratic, then it seeks to protect the man who is inferior in every way against both. One of its primary functions is to
10 regiment men by force, to make them as much alike as possible and as dependent upon one another as possible, to search out and combat originality among them. All it can see in an original idea is potential change,
15 and hence an invasion of its prerogatives. The most dangerous man, to any government, is the man who is able to think things out for himself, without regard to the prevailing superstitions and taboos. Almost inevitably
20 he comes to the conclusion that the government he lives in is dishonest, insane and intolerable, and so, if he is romantic, he tries to change it. And even if he is not romantic personally he is very apt to spread discontent
25 among those who are.

    There is seldom, if ever, any evidence that the new government proposed would be any better than the old one. On the contrary, all the historical testimony runs the other way.
30 Political revolutions do not often accomplish anything of genuine value; their one undoubted effect is simply to throw out one gang of thieves and put in another. After a revolution, of course, the successful revolutionists always
35 try to convince doubters that they have achieved great things, and usually they hang any man who denies it. But that surely doesn't

prove their case. In Russia, for many years, the plain people were taught that getting rid
40 of the Czar would make them all rich and happy, but now that they have got rid of him they are poorer and unhappier than ever before. Even the American colonies gained little by their revolt in 1776. For twenty-five
45 years after the Revolution they were in far worse condition as free states as they would have been as colonies. Their government was more expensive, more inefficient, more dishonest, and more tyrannical. It was only
50 the gradual material progress of the country that saved them from starvation and collapse, and that material progress was due, not to the virtues of their new government, but to the lavishness of nature. Under the British
55 hoof they would have got on just as well, and probably a great deal better.

    The ideal government of all reflective men, from Aristotle onward, is one which lets the individual alone—one which barely escapes
60 being no government at all. This ideal, I believe, will be realized in the world twenty or thirty centuries after I have passed from these scenes and take up my public duties in Hell.

Passage 2

    By the late 1760s and early 1770s a
65 potentially revolutionary situation existed in many of the colonies. There was little evidence of those social conditions we often associate with revolution (and some historians have desperately sought to find): no mass poverty,
70 no seething social discontent, no grinding oppression. For most white Americans there was greater prosperity than anywhere else in the world; in fact, the experience of that growing prosperity contributed to the
75 unprecedented eighteenth-century sense that people here and now were capable of ordering their own reality. Consequently, there was a great deal of jealousy and touchiness everywhere, for what could be
80 made could be unmade; the people were acutely nervous about their prosperity and the liberty that seemed to make it possible. With the erosion of much of what remained of traditional social relationships, more and

GO ON TO THE NEXT PAGE ▶▶▶

85 more individuals had broken away from their
families, communities, and patrons and were
experiencing the anxiety of freedom and
independence. Social changes, particularly
since the 1740s, multiplied rapidly, and many
90 Americans struggled to make sense of what
was happening. These social changes were
complicated, and they are easily misinterpreted.
Luxury and conspicuous consumption by
very ordinary people were increasing. So, too,
95 was religious dissent of all sorts. The rich
became richer, and aristocratic gentry
everywhere became more conspicuous and
self-conscious; and the numbers of poor in
some cities and the numbers of landless in
100 some areas increased. But social classes
based on occupation or wealth did not
set themselves against one another, for no
classes in this modern sense yet existed.
The society was becoming more unequal,
105 but its inequalities were not the source of
the instability and anxiety. Indeed, it was the
pervasive equality of American society that was
causing the problems—even in aristocratic
South Carolina.
110   Perhaps the society of no colony was more
unequal, more riven by discrepancies of rich
and poor, more dominated by an ostentatious
aristocracy than that of South Carolina.
"State and magnificence, the natural attendant
115 on great riches, are conspicuous among this
people," declared a wide-eyed New England
visitor in 1773. "In grandeur, splendour of
buildings, decorations, equipage, numbers,
commerce, shipping, and indeed in almost
120 everything, it far surpasses all I ever saw, or
ever expect to see in America." Yet, surprisingly,
in the opinion of Carolinian Christopher
Gadsden, society in his colony was most
remarkable, not for its inequality, but for its
125 equality, for the prevalence in it of substantial
hardworking farmers and artisans—that is, of
all those who "depend, almost, altogether
upon their own daily labour and industry, for
the maintenance of themselves and families."
130 These honest industrious white folk were
extraordinarily prosperous. Even "the poorest
of them (unless some very uncommon
instances indeed) but must find himself in a
very comfortable situation, especially when

135 he compares his condition with that of the
poor of other nations," or Gadsden might
have added, with that of the black slaves in
their own midst. The result, said Gadsden,
was that white society in South Carolina was
140 comparatively equal, "the distinctions ...
between the farmer and rich planter, the
mechanic and the rich merchant, being
abundantly more here, in imagination, than
reality."
145   Yet because such equality and prosperity
were so unusual in the Western world, they
could not be taken for granted. The idea of
labor, of hard work, leading to increased
productivity was so novel, so radical, in the
150 overall span of Western history that most
ordinary people, most of those who labored,
could scarcely believe what was happening to
them. Labor had been so long thought to be
the natural and inevitable consequence of
155 necessity and poverty that most people still
associated it with slavery and servitude.
Therefore any possibility of oppression, any
threat to the colonists' hard-earned prosperity,
any hint of reducing them to the poverty of
160 other nations, was especially frightening; for
it seemed likely to slide them back into the
traditional status of servants or slaves, into
the older world where labor was merely a
painful necessity and not a source of prosperity.
165 "The very apprehension thereof, cannot but
cause extreme uneasiness." "No wonder,"said
Gadsden, "that throughout *America*, we find
these men extremely anxious and attentive,to
the cause of liberty." These hardworking
170 farmers and mechanics were extraordinarily
free and well off and had much to lose, and
"this, therefore, naturally accounts for these
people, in particular, being so united and
steady, everywhere," in support of their
175 liberties against British oppression.

13   As it is used in line 3, "object" most nearly
means

(A)   disagreement
(B)   symbol
(C)   material thing
(D)   control
(E)   goal

14 Passage 1 suggests that an "aristocratic" (line 4) government is similar to a "democratic" (line 7) government primarily in its

(A) concern for commerce and private enterprise
(B) unpopularity among the common people
(C) oppression of its most creative citizens
(D) desire to implement fair and equitable laws
(E) promotion of new ideas

15 The "historical testimony" (line 29) most likely regards

(A) the social effects of political revolutions
(B) the causes of discontent that breeds rebellion
(C) the development of artistic movements
(D) the origins of superstitions and taboos
(E) the ascendancy of romantic sentiment

16 Passage 1 suggests that the post-revolutionary government of the American colonies eventually succeeded only because it

(A) was more responsive to the people
(B) enjoyed the benefit of natural resources
(C) established a more rigid framework of laws
(D) was more efficient than the previous government
(E) did not oppress its citizens

17 The author of Passage 1 believes that the "ideal government" (line 57) is characterized primarily by its

(A) commitment to putting educated citizens in power
(B) efficient systems of industry
(C) emphasis on law and order
(D) unintrusiveness
(E) support of broad social programs

18 According to Passage 2, the "revolutionary situation" (line 65) among the colonists included

(A) impoverishment
(B) political persecution
(C) envy
(D) hopelessness
(E) sharp class divisions

19 The author of Passage 2 suggests that "some historians" (line 68) believe that

(A) the situation in the American colonies prior to the revolution was not as dire as previously thought
(B) political upheaval is caused by social discontent
(C) American colonists had unprecedented power
(D) the American revolution was caused by jealousy
(E) colonial culture was highly traditional

20 As it is used in line 114, "state" most nearly means

(A) government
(B) pomp
(C) independence
(D) stage of physical development
(E) emotional condition

4

21 Christopher Gadsden refers to "the farmer and rich planter, the mechanic and the rich merchant" (lines 141–142) primarily as a means of highlighting

(A) the great range of occupations available in the colonies

(B) the fact that many kinds of citizens were willing to fight for their independence

(C) the profound discontent found throughout the colonies

(D) those who were most guilty of repressing their fellow colonists

(E) the relative lack of socioeconomic classes in South Carolina

22 With which of the following statements would the authors of BOTH passages most likely agree?

(A) The American Revolution is best characterized as a quest for religious freedom.

(B) Government is by its nature repressive.

(C) The transition to a democratic system of government dramatically benefited the American colonists.

(D) During and after the revolution, American colonists benefited from material prosperity.

(E) The post-revolutionary American government was unjust and tyrannical.

23 Passage 1 suggests that the American revolutionaries were inspired by

(A) impoverished conditions, while the author of Passage 2 suggests that they were inspired by class conflict

(B) lack of freedom, while the author of Passage 2 suggests that they were inspired by unjust taxation

(C) political idealism, while the author of Passage 2 suggests that they were inspired by fear of losing their wealth

(D) blind ideology, while the author of Passage 2 suggests that they were inspired by a lack of equality

(E) political repression, while the author of Passage 2 suggests that they were inspired by religious repression

24 Which of the following terms in Passage 2 is most similar in meaning to "hoof" in line 55 of Passage 1?

(A) "discontent" (line 70)

(B) "dissent" (line 95)

(C) "instability" (line 106)

(D) "magnificence" (line 114)

(E) "oppression" (line 157)

STOP

You may check your work, on this section only, until time is called.

Section 5

Time—25 Minutes
18 Questions

Directions for Multiple-Choice Questions

In this section, solve each problem, using any available space on the page for scratchwork. Then decide which is the best of the choices given and fill in the corresponding oval on the answer sheet.

- You may use a calculator on any problem. All numbers used are real numbers.
- Figures are drawn as accurately as possible EXCEPT when it is stated that the figure is not drawn to scale.
- All figures lie in a plane unless otherwise indicated.

Reference Information

$A = \pi r^2$ $A = \ell w$
$C = 2\pi r$ $A = \frac{1}{2}bh$ $V = \ell wh$ $V = \pi r^2 h$ $c^2 = a^2 + b^2$ Special Right Triangles

The arc of a circle measures 360°.
Every straight angle measures 180°.
The sum of the measures of the angles in a triangle is 180°.

---

1 If $4m - 2 = m + 7$, what is the value of m?

(A) 3.0
(B) 4.5
(C) 6.0
(D) 7.5
(E) 9.0

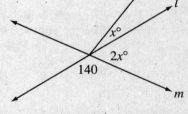

Note: Figure not drawn to scale.

2 In the figure above, l and m are lines. What is the value of x?

(A) 10
(B) 20
(C) 30
(D) 40
(E) 80

GO ON TO THE NEXT PAGE ▶▶▶

3   If $\frac{3}{8}$ of m is 48, what is $\frac{5}{8}$ of m?

(A) 80
(B) 64
(C) 60
(D) 40
(E) 30

5 ▶ **4**   Let a_n represent the nth term of a particular sequence. If $a_2 = 54$ and each term except the first is equal to the previous term divided by 3, then what is the first term that is NOT an integer?

(A) a_4
(B) a_5
(C) a_6
(D) a_7
(E) a_8

5   If $\sqrt{n} \times \sqrt{2}$ is an integer, which of the following could *not* be the value of n?

(A) 2
(B) 8
(C) 12
(D) 18
(E) 32

6   Four of the six faces of a cube are painted black, and the other two faces are painted white. What is the *least* number of vertices on this cube that could be shared by two or more black faces?

(A) eight
(B) seven
(C) six
(D) five
(E) four

7   If y varies directly as x, and if $y = 8$ when $x = a$ and $y = 12$ when $x = a + 10$, what is the value of a?

(A) 5
(B) 8
(C) 10
(D) 15
(E) 20

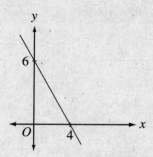

Note: Figure not drawn to scale.

8   The figure above shows the graph of the function $f(x) = ax + b$, where a and b are constants. What is the slope of the graph of the function $g(x) = -2f(x)$?

(A) -3

(B) $-\frac{4}{3}$

(C) $\frac{4}{3}$

(D) $\frac{3}{2}$

(E) 3

GO ON TO THE NEXT PAGE ▶▶▶

Directions for Student-Produced Response Questions

Each of the questions in this section requires you to solve the problem and enter your answer in a grid, as shown below.

- If your answer is ⅔ or .666..., you must enter **the most accurate value the grid can accommodate**, but you may do this in one of four ways.

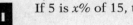

Start in first column — **2 / 3** — Grid result here

Start in second column — **2 / 3**

Grid as a truncated decimal — **. 6 6 6**

Grid as a rounded decimal — **. 6 6 7**

5

- In the example above, gridding a response of 0.67 or 0.66 is **incorrect** because it is less accurate than those above.
- The scoring machine cannot read what is written in the top row of boxes. You **MUST** fill in the numerical grid accurately to get credit for answering any question correctly. You should write your answer in the top row of boxes only to aid your gridding.
- Do **not** grid in a mixed fraction like $3\frac{1}{2}$ as ⎡3⎤⎡ ⎤⎡/⎤⎡2⎤ because it will be interpreted as $\frac{31}{2}$. Instead, convert it to an improper fraction like ½ or a decimal like 3.5 before gridding.
- None of the answers will be negative, because there is no negative sign in the grid.
- Some of the questions may have more than one correct answer. You must grid only one of the correct answers.
- You may use a calculator on any of these problems.
- All numbers in these problems are real numbers.
- Figures are drawn as accurately as possible EXCEPT when it is stated that the figure is not drawn to scale.
- All figures lie in a plane unless otherwise indicated.

---

9 If $x + 9$ is 50% greater than x, then what is the value of x?

11 If 5 is x% of 15, then what is x% of 60?

10 If a printer can print 5 pages in 20 seconds, then, at this rate, how many pages can it print in 5 minutes?

12 The measures of the four angles in a quadrilateral have a ratio of 2:3:6:7. What is the measure, in degrees, of the largest of these angles?

GO ON TO THE NEXT PAGE ▶▶▶

13 If a is $\frac{2}{5}$ of b, b is $\frac{1}{10}$ of c, and $c > 0$, then what is the value of $\frac{a}{c}$?

17 Each term in a sequence, except for the first, is equal to the previous term times a positive constant, k. If the 3rd term of this sequence is 12 and the 5th term is 27, what is the first term?

14 A rectangle and a triangle share the same base. If the area of the triangle is 6 times the area of the rectangle, and the height of the rectangle is 4, what is the height of the triangle?

5

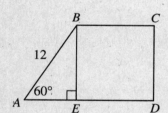

15 The median of a set of 5 integers is 10. If the greatest of these integers is 5 times the least integer, and if all the integers are different, what is the greatest possible sum of the numbers in this set?

Note: Figure not drawn to scale.

18 In the figure above, $2b = 3c$ and the area of the shaded triangle is $\frac{2}{5}$ the area of the rectangle. What is the slope of line l?

16 In the figure above, $BCDE$ is a square and $AB = 12$. What is the area of square $BCDE$?

STOP

You may check your work, on this section only, until time is called.

Section 6

Time—25 minutes
24 Questions

Each of the sentences below is missing one or two portions. Read each sentence, then select the word or words that most logically completes the sentence, taking into account the meaning of the sentence as a whole.

Example:

Rather than accepting the theory unquestioningly, Deborah regarded it with ———.

(A) mirth   (B) sadness
(C) responsibility (D) ignorance
(E) skepticism

Correct response: (E)

---

1 Although the party gained a clear majority in the election, its philosophy remained ———, never achieving a clear and consistent form.

(A) versatile   (B) indisputable
(C) homogenous   (D) nebulous
(E) appealing

2 The astronomer was ——— the evidence she was receiving from the radio telescope, because the data did not ——— her theory regarding the mass of the distant galaxy.

(A) concerned about . . refute
(B) disappointed by . . substantiate
(C) intimidated by . . ignore
(D) chastened . . conceal
(E) bolstered by . . exaggerate

3 Wildebeests are ——— creatures, often trekking over 1,000 miles in a typical year in search of food resources that shift according to the rainy season.

(A) itinerant   (B) indigenous
(C) subdued   (D) nocturnal
(E) arboreal

4 Carlos has always been ——— the motivations of politicians, often insisting that even their most seemingly ——— initiatives are in fact based on selfish impulses.

(A) skeptical of . . contemptible
(B) sanguine about . . magnanimous
(C) disparaging of . . callous
(D) enthusiastic about . . immaterial
(E) cynical about . . altruistic

5 Herbert was not ——— enough to be a good literary agent, often mistaking ——— prose for original and competent writing.

(A) discerning . . derivative
(B) gauche . . sublime
(C) obstinate . . proficient
(D) diligent . . innovative
(E) servile . . pedestrian

6

GO ON TO THE NEXT PAGE ▶▶▶

Each passage below is followed by questions based on its content. Answer each question based on what is stated or implied in the passage.

Questions 6–7 are based on the following passage.

Line Geologists use radiological methods to
      deduce the age of mineral samples. These
      methods rely on the fact that when a
      radioactive sample within a rock is first
   5 formed it is nearly pure, but gradually
      decays into a more stable element. Since
      this decay occurs at a predictable rate,
      measuring the proportion of each type of
      element within a rock can tell scientists
  10 how long it has been since that rock was
      formed. One problematic aspect of this
      dating method is that some of the stable
      element may have already been present when
      the mineral was formed, and therefore was
  15 not the result of radioactive decay.

6 The primary purpose of this passage is to

   (A)   introduce a scientific controversy
   (B)   refute a misconception
   (C)   explain a technique
   (D)   describe a historical fact
   (E)   examine a theory

7 According to the passage, radiological dating methods are most likely to yield inaccurate results when the radioactive mineral sample within a rock

   (A)   is exceptionally old
   (B)   comprises a large portion of the rock's mass
   (C)   decays into a stable element at a consistent rate
   (D)   originally contains samples of the element into which the radioactive element will decay
   (E)   decays into a stable element that remains in the rock, rather than being released into the atmosphere

Questions 8–9 are based on the following passage.

Line The tragic hero with Shakespeare need not
      be "good," though generally he is "good"
      and therefore at once wins sympathy in his
      error. But it is necessary that he should have
   5 so much of greatness that in his error and
      fall we may be vividly conscious of the
      possibilities of human nature. Hence, in the
      first place, a Shakespearean tragedy is never,
      like some miscalled tragedies, depressing.
  10 No one ever closes the book with the feeling
      that man is a poor mean creature. He may be
      wretched and he may be awful, but he is not
      small. His lot may be heart-rending and
      mysterious, but it is not contemptible. The
  15 most confirmed of cynics ceases to be a
      cynic while he reads these plays.

8 As it is used in line 13, "lot" most nearly means

   (A)   parcel of land   (B)   great quantity
   (C)   fate in life   (D)   motivation
   (E)   friend

9 The passage suggests that a "cynic" (line 16) is one who believes that

   (A)   Shakespeare's plays are self-serving
   (B)   human beings can be ignoble
   (C)   heroes should be imbued with greatness
   (D)   tragic heroes are worthy of sympathy
   (E)   Shakespeare's characters are unrealistic

GO ON TO THE NEXT PAGE ▶▶▶

Each passage below is followed by questions based on its content. Answer the questions based on what is stated or implied in each passage and in any introductory material that may be provided.

Questions 10–16 pertain to the following passage.

The following is an excerpt from a short story, written by an American author in 1909, regarding the crew of a sailing ship.

Line   She floated at the starting point of a long
        journey, very still in an immense stillness,
        the shadows of her spars flung far to the
        eastward by the setting sun. At that moment
5   I was alone on her decks. There was not a
        sound in her—and around us nothing moved,
        nothing lived, not a canoe on the water, not a
        bird in the air, not a cloud in the sky. In this
        breathless pause at the threshold of a long
10   passage we seemed to be measuring our
        fitness for a long and arduous enterprise, the
        appointed task of both our existences to be
        carried out, far from all human eyes, with
        only sky and sea for spectators and for
15   judges.
            There must have been some glare in the air
        to interfere with one's sight, because it was
        only just before the sun left us that my
        roaming eyes made out beyond the highest
20   ridges of the principal islet of the group
        something which did away with the
        solemnity of perfect solitude. The tide of
        darkness flowed on swiftly; and with tropical
        suddenness a swarm of stars came out above
25   the shadowy earth, while I lingered yet, my
        hand resting lightly on my ship's rail as if
        on the shoulder of a trusted friend. But,
        with all that multitude of celestial bodies
        staring down at one, the comfort of quiet
30   communion with her was gone for good. And
        there were also disturbing sounds by this
        time—voices, footsteps forward; the steward
        flitted along the main-deck, a busily
        ministering spirit; a hand bell tinkled
35   urgently under the poop deck.
            I found my two officers waiting for me
        near the supper table, in the lighted cuddy.

We sat down at once, and as I helped the chief mate, I said:
40   "Are you aware that there is a ship anchored inside the islands? I saw her mastheads above the ridge as the sun went down."
            He raised sharply his simple face, overcharged by a terrible growth of whisker,
45   and emitted his usual ejaculations:
            "Bless my soul, sir! You don't say so!"
            My second mate was a round-cheeked, silent young man, grave beyond his years, I thought; but as our eyes happened to meet I
50   detected a slight quiver on his lips. I looked down at once. It was not my part to encourage sneering on board my ship. It must be said, too, that I knew very little of my officers. In consequence of certain events
55   of no particular significance, except to myself, I had been appointed to the command only a fortnight before. Neither did I know much of the hands forward. All these people had been together for eighteen
60   months or so, and my position was that of the only stranger on board. I mention this because it has some bearing on what is to follow. But what I felt most was my being a stranger to the ship; and if all the truth must
65   be told, I was somewhat of a stranger to myself. The youngest man on board (barring the second mate), and untried as yet by a position of the fullest responsibility, I was willing to take the adequacy of the others for
70   granted. They had simply to be equal to their tasks; but I wondered how far I should turn out faithful to that ideal conception of one's own personality every man sets up for himself secretly.
75   Meantime the chief mate, with an almost visible effect of collaboration on the part of his round eyes and frightful whiskers, was trying to evolve a theory of the anchored ship. His dominant trait was to take all
80   things into earnest consideration. He was of a painstaking turn of mind. As he used to say, he "liked to account to himself" for practically everything that came in his way, down to a miserable scorpion he had found
85   in his cabin a week before. The why and the wherefore of that scorpion—how it got on board and came to select his room rather than the pantry (which was a dark place and more what a scorpion would be partial to),
90   and how on earth it managed to drown itself

6

in the inkwell of his writing desk—had exercised him infinitely. The ship within the islands was much more easily accounted for, and just as we were about to rise from table
95 he made his pronouncement. She was, he doubted not, a ship from home lately arrived. Probably she drew too much water to cross the bar except at the top of spring tides. Therefore she went into that natural harbor
100 to wait for a few days in preference to remaining in an open roadstead.

10 The tone of the first paragraph is primarily one of

(A) reflective anticipation
(B) anxious dread
(C) unrestrained excitement
(D) detached analysis
(E) incomprehension

11 The narrator mentions the "glare" (line 16) in order to make the point that

(A) the sea around him was filled with commotion
(B) his crew was not entirely reliable
(C) the ship was kept in very good condition
(D) the weather was about to change
(E) he did not see the distant masthead immediately

12 The "certain events" mentioned in line 54 pertain to the means by which

(A) the crew was chosen for the voyage
(B) the mysterious ship came to be docked nearby
(C) the second mate developed his grave disposition
(D) the narrator was chosen as captain
(E) the hands came to know each other

13 In lines 63–74 (But what I felt ... for himself secretly") the narrator conveys primarily his

(A) skepticism about the ability of his crewmen
(B) apprehensions about the mysterious ship
(C) excitement about the upcoming voyage
(D) lack of self-confidence
(E) pride in his accomplishments as such a young age

14 As it is used in line 78, the word "evolve" most nearly means

(A) destroy   (B) frighten
(C) generate   (D) dominate
(E) turn around

15 In the final paragraph, the chief mate is characterized primarily as being

(A) physically intimidating
(B) intelligent and erudite
(C) emotionally sensitive
(D) reserved and dull-witted
(E) meticulously thoughtful

16 As it is used in line 92, "exercised" most nearly means

(A) perplexed   (B) practiced
(C) strengthened   (D) eradicated
(E) weakened

Questions 17–24 pertain to the following passage.

The following passage discusses the study of language acquisition, the means by which humans learn to speak and understand language.

Line Language acquisition is one of the central topics in cognitive science. Every theory of cognition has tried to explain it; probably no other topic has aroused such controversy.
5 Possessing a language is the quintessentially human trait: all normal humans speak, no nonhuman animal does. Language is the main vehicle by which we know about other people's thoughts, and the two must be
10 intimately related. Every time we speak we are revealing something about language, so the facts of language structure are easy to come by; these data hint at a system of extraordinary complexity. Nonetheless,
15 learning a first language is something every child does successfully, in a matter of a few years and without the need for formal lessons. With language so close to the core of what it means to be human, it is not
20 surprising that children's acquisition of language has received so much attention. Anyone with strong views about the human mind would like to show that children's first few steps are steps in the right direction.
25   Is language simply grafted on top of cognition as a way of sticking communicable labels onto thoughts? Or does learning a language somehow mean learning to think in that language? A famous hypothesis, outlined
30 by Benjamin Whorf, asserts that the categories and relations that we use to understand the world come from our particular language, so that speakers of different languages conceptualize the world in different ways.
35 Language acquisition, then, would be learning to think, not just learning to talk.
This is an intriguing hypothesis, but virtually all modern cognitive scientists believe it is false. Babies can think before they can talk. Cognitive
40 psychology has shown that people think not just in words but in images and abstract logical propositions. And linguistics has shown that human languages are too ambiguous and schematic to use as a medium of internal

45 computation: when people think about "spring," surely they are not confused as to whether they are thinking about a season or something that goes "boing"—and if one word can correspond to two thoughts,
50 thoughts can't be words.
But language acquisition has a unique contribution to make to this issue. As we shall see, it is virtually impossible to show how children could learn a language unless you
55 assume they have a considerable amount of nonlinguistic cognitive machinery in place before they start.
All humans talk but no house pets or house plants do, no matter how pampered, so
60 heredity must be involved in language. But a child growing up in Japan speaks Japanese whereas the same child brought up in California would speak English, so the environment is also crucial. Thus there is no
65 question about whether heredity or environment is involved in language, or even whether one or the other is "more important." Instead, language acquisition might be our best hope of finding out how
70 heredity and environment interact. We know that adult language is intricately complex, and we know that children become adults. Therefore something in the child's mind must be capable of attaining that complexity. Any
75 theory that posits too little innate structure, so that its hypothetical child ends up speaking something less than a real language, must be false. The same is true for any theory that posits too much innate
80 structure, so that the hypothetical child can acquire English but not, say, Bantu or Vietnamese.
And not only do we know about the output of language acquisition, we know a
85 fair amount about the input to it, namely, parent's speech to their children. So even if language acquisition, like all cognitive processes, is essentially a "black box," we know enough about its input and output to
90 be able to make precise guesses about its contents.
The scientific study of language acquisition began around the same time as the birth of cognitive science, in the late

GO ON TO THE NEXT PAGE ▶▶▶

95 1950s. We can see now why that is not a
coincidence. The historical catalyst was
Noam Chomsky's review of Skinner's Verbal
Behavior. At that time, Anglo-American
natural science, social science, and philosophy
100 had come to a virtual consensus about the
answers to the questions listed above. The
mind consisted of sensorimotor abilities plus
a few simple laws of learning governing
gradual changes in an organism's behavioral
105 repertoire. Therefore language must be
learned; it cannot be a module; and thinking
must be a form of verbal behavior, since
verbal behavior is the prime manifestation of
"thought" that can be observed externally.
110 Chomsky argued that language acquisition
falsified these beliefs in a single stroke:
children learn languages that are governed by
highly subtle and abstract principles, and
they do so without explicit instruction or any
115 other environmental clues to the nature of
such principles. Hence language acquisition
depends on an innate, species-specific
module that is distinct from general
intelligence. Much of the debate in language
120 acquisition has attempted to test this once-
revolutionary, and still controversial,
collection of ideas. The implications extend
to the rest of human cognition.

17 This passage as a whole is best described as

(A)   a history of a new academic
discipline
(B)   a comparison of the traits of different
species
(C)   a discussion of a particular human
ability
(D)   biographical sketches of several
scientists
(E)   a refutation of an experimental
method

18 The "data" mentioned in line 13 most likely
include information regarding

(A)   the literacy levels of different
countries
(B)   the best methods for teaching infants
to speak
(C)   the ability of primates and other
mammals to communicate
(D)   the structure of the human brain
(E)   the intricacy of the expression of
human language

19 The sentence "Anyone ... direction" (lines
22–24) indicates that

(A)   Most parents are concerned about
their children's ability to read and
write correctly.
(B)   Language theorists tend to focus on
language acquisition more than later
language development.
(C)   Scientists are inclined to disregard
evidence that suggests that nonhuman
animals can use language.
(D)   More should be done to help children
who have difficulty learning
language.
(E)   Poor parenting usually leads to weak
oral language skills in children.

20 The statement "Babies can think before
they can talk" (line 39) is intended to show
that

(A)   learning to talk can sometimes be
difficult
(B)   verbal skill is not necessary to
cognition
(C)   psychologists should take into
account the desires of infants
(D)   speakers of different languages
conceptualize the world in
different ways
(E)   all cognitive skills develop according
to a rigid timeline

21 The statement "language acquisition might
be our best hope" (lines 68–69) means that

(A)   the ability to speak is a great asset to
the survival of the human species
(B)   studying how language is learned will
help answer deeper questions about
psychology
(C)   the study of linguistics is helping
to make cognitive science a more
popular subject
(D)   an individual who does not learn to
speak will not develop cognitive skills
(E)   cognitive science has been given little
notice until now

GO ON TO THE NEXT PAGE ▶▶▶

22 The "structure" mentioned in line 75 pertains to

(A) the grammatical rules of a language
(B) the derivations of particular words
(C) cognitive machinery
(D) a person's linguistic environment
(E) a means of investigating scientific claims

23 In line 99, "natural science, social science and philosophy" are mentioned as examples of disciplines that

(A) mutually accepted a single theory of how language is acquired
(B) questioned the need to study cognitive science as a separate discipline
(C) regarded an understanding of language acquisition to be beyond the scope of the scientific method
(D) did not put enough resources into the study of language acquisition
(E) disagreed about the manner in which human languages should be studied

24 Which of the following would most likely agree with the statement that "it cannot be a module" (line 106)?

(A) Noam Chomsky
(B) modern cognitive scientists
(C) philosophers from pre-1950
(D) modern comparative linguists
(E) adults who are learning a new language

6

STOP

You may check your work, on this section only, until time is called.

Section 7

Time—20 Minutes
16 Questions

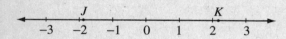

1 In the figure above, if the coordinates of points J and K are added together, this sum will be the coordinate of a point between

(A) −3 and −2
(B) −2 and −1
(C) 0 and 1
(D) 1 and 2
(E) 2 and 3

2 If $6x + 9y = 8$, then $2x + 3y =$

(A) $\frac{3}{8}$

(B) $\frac{4}{3}$

(C) 2

(D) $\frac{8}{3}$

(E) 3

3 Glenna had three boxes of pencils, each of which contained y pencils. She distributed these pencils by giving one to each student in her class, and had 9 pencils left over. If there are 21 students in Glenna's class, what is y?

(A) 3
(B) 4
(C) 6
(D) 8
(E) 10

4 If an integer n is divisible by both 12 and 20, then it must also be divisible by

(A) 15
(B) 24
(C) 32
(D) 80
(E) 240

GO ON TO THE NEXT PAGE ▶▶▶

5 A container in the shape of a right circular cylinder contains 12 liters of liquid when it is filled to $\frac{3}{4}$ of its height. How many liters does it contain when it is completely filled?

(A)   18
(B)   16
(C)   15
(D)   10
(E)   9

6 The profit that a company earns is equal to its revenue minus its expenses. If the revenue, in dollars, that a company makes for selling x items is given by the function $R(x) = 12x$ and the expenses it must pay for selling those x items is given by the function $E(x) = 3x + 12$, then which of the following expresses the profit, in dollars, that the company earns for selling those x items?

(A) $P(x) = 15x + 12$
(B) $P(x) = 15x - 12$
(C) $P(x) = 9x + 12$
(D) $P(x) = 9x - 12$
(E) $P(x) = 12 - 9x$

7 The average (arithmetic mean) of x and y is m, where $m \neq 0$. What is the average (arithmetic mean) of x, y, and $2m$?

(A) m

(B) $\frac{4}{3}m$

(C) $\frac{3}{2}m$

(D) $\frac{5}{3}m$

(E) $2m$

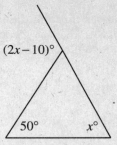

Note: Figure not drawn to scale.

8 In the figure above, what is the value of x?

(A)   30
(B)   40
(C)   50
(D)   60
(E)   70

9 For all real values of x and y, let $x \blacklozenge y$ be defined by the equation $x \blacklozenge y = 2 - xy$. If $-1 < a < 0$ and $0 < b < 1$, then which of the following must be true?

(A) $-2 < a \blacklozenge b < -1$
(B) $-1 < a \blacklozenge b < 0$
(C) $0 < a \blacklozenge b < 1$
(D) $1 < a \blacklozenge b < 2$
(E) $2 < a \blacklozenge b < 3$

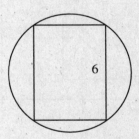

Note: Figure not drawn to scale.

10 The figure above shows a circle with an area of 25π square units. If each vertex of the rectangle is on the circle as shown, what is the area of the rectangle, in square units?

(A)   30
(B)   36
(C)   42
(D)   48
(E)   54

11 Line l passes through the origin and is perpendicular to the line given by the equation $2x + y = 8$. Which of the following points is NOT on line l?

(A) $(-4, -2)$
(B) $(-1, 1)$
(C) $(2, 1)$
(D) $(4, 2)$
(E) $(7, 3.5)$

12 If a and b are positive numbers, which of the following is equivalent to $a\%$ of $5b$?

(A) $\dfrac{ab}{20}$

(B) $\dfrac{ab}{5}$

(C) $\dfrac{a}{20b}$

(D) $\dfrac{a}{5b}$

(E) $\dfrac{b}{20a}$

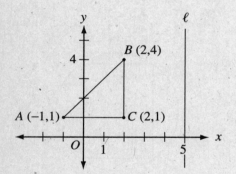

13 If the triangle in the figure above is reflected over line l, what will be the coordinates of the reflection of point A?

(A) $(4, 1)$
(B) $(6, 1)$
(C) $(10, 1)$
(D) $(11, 1)$
(E) $(12, 1)$

14 How many positive 3-digit integers contain only odd digits?

(A) 15
(B) 75
(C) 125
(D) 225
(E) 500

15 If k is a positive odd integer greater than 4, which of the following always represent the product of two even integers?

(A) $k^2 - 4$
(B) $k^2 + 4k - 5$
(C) $k^2 + 5k + 6$
(D) $k^2 + 3k - 10$
(E) $k^2 + k - 20$

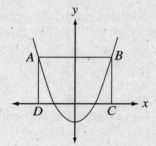

Note: Figure not drawn to scale.

16 The figure above shows the graph of the function $f(x) = x^2 - k$. Points A and B lie on the graph of the function and are the vertices of rectangle $ABCD$. If $AB = 6$ and the area of rectangle $ABCD$ is 20, what is the value of k?

(A) $\dfrac{17}{3}$

(B) $\dfrac{19}{3}$

(C) $\dfrac{34}{3}$

(D) $\dfrac{68}{3}$

(E) $\dfrac{98}{3}$

STOP

You may check your work, on this section only, until time is called.

Section 8

Time—20 minutes
19 Questions

Each of the sentences below is missing one or two portions. Read each sentence, then select the word or words that most logically completes the sentence, taking into account the meaning of the sentence as a whole.

Example:

Rather than accepting the theory unquestioningly, Deborah regarded it with ———.

(A) mirth   (B) sadness
(C) responsibility (D) ignorance
(E) skepticism

Correct response: (E)

1 As an advocate of ———, Gena has always believed that individuals who have been ——— deserve the opportunity to return to society as productive citizens.

(A) tolerance . . revered
(B) conservatism . . overlooked
(C) rehabilitation . . incarcerated
(D) perseverence . . championed
(E) independence . . criticized

2 Early researchers discovered that quinine produced ——— responses such as sweating and shivering when ingested by healthy individuals, but actually——— these effects in people who had malaria.

(A) beneficial . . assuaged
(B) physiological . . ameliorated
(C) circumstantial . . exacerbated
(D) premeditated . . rebuffed
(E) communicable . . concentrated

3 Even his friends believed that Yuri was too submissive to his superiors in the office, and told him that such ——— behavior might even harm his chances of promotion.

(A) headstrong   (B) tolerable
(C) complaisant   (D) truculent
(E) tactless

4 The efforts to ——— the local economy after the departure of the town's largest employer were ——— by the construction of a new arts center that would infuse the community with much-needed revenue.

(A) revive . . facilitated
(B) debilitate . . expedited
(C) reform . . postponed
(D) initiate . . tabled
(E) preempt . . subsidized

5 As ——— the value of free trade, Bennett was often called upon to give speeches around the world extolling the virtues of unencumbered commerce.

(A) an antagonist to
(B) a stalwart of
(C) a caviler about
(D) a diviner of
(E) a skeptic of

6 Federica expressed doubt about the existence of true altruism, claiming that no one makes a sacrifice without expecting it to be ——— in one form or another.

(A) requited   (B) repudiated
(C) portended   (D) rescinded
(E) expropriated

GO ON TO THE NEXT PAGE ▶▶▶

The passage below is followed by questions based on its content. Answer the questions based on what is stated or implied in each passage and in any introductory material that may be provided.

Questions 7–19 pertain to the following passage.

The following passage discusses Bohemianism, an unconventional and artistic lifestyle that had wide appeal in 19th century Europe and elsewhere.

Line   Bohemia is a land-locked country in central
        Europe, once a province of the Holy Roman
        Empire and until 1918 ruled from Vienna by
        the Austrian Hapsburgs. Today it constitutes
5   a part of modern Czechoslovakia and its
        major city, Prague, forms the nation's capital.
            Bohemia is also another, less clearly
        defined country, a country of the mind. This
        Bohemia in fact derives from misconceptions
10   about the true Bohemia and, in the English-
        speaking world, such misconceptions
        go back as far as Shakespeare. The
        designation of Bohemia as the spiritual
        habitation of artists stemmed from a
15   different misconception about the real
        country, because it was also once thought to
        be the homeland of the gypsies—a notion
        that quite ignored the "Egyptian" origin of
        "gypsy."
20   In 1843, when Michael William Balfe's once
        famous opera *The Bohemian Girl* premiered
        in London, this meaning was still widely
        current. A Bohemian had come to mean any
        wandering or vagabond soul, who need not
25   have been associated with the arts. It was the
        malnourished Parisian poet, Henry Murger,
        who was responsible for clinching the term's
        special association with the life of artists.
            In November 1849 a dramatized version
30   of the Latin Quarter tales Murger had written
        for the journal *Le Corsaire* was staged at the
        Theatre des Varietes with the title *La Vie de
        Boheme*. So extraordinarily successful did
        this prove that the stories themselves were
35   collected as *Scenes de la Vie de Boheme*. The
        public's appetite had been whetted and a
        popular cult of the gypsyartist was underway.
        Murger's volume of stories became the
        textbook for the artistic life throughout the

40   late nineteenth and early twentieth centuries.
            What were the basic elements of this
        Bohemia as it evolved under Murger? To start
        with, Bohemia belonged to the romantic
        movements which preached a doctrine of the
45   power of the individual imagination and
        came to adopt a secular religion of art.
            Like early Christianity it had its true
        believers and its heathens; the believers in
        this case being artists themselves, the elect of
50   the spirit, touched with the divine power of
        imagination, while the heathen were the
        commercial middle classes who had
        prospered and grown as a result of increased
        commodity production in the wake of the
55   Industrial Revolution.
            To the artists, these were people of no
        imagination who were only concerned with
        material things. As Philistines they virtually
        inhabited a different country from the
60   Bohemians, Murger's achievement was to
        define, quite persuasively, the boundaries of
        Bohemia in terms of a particular lifestyle. In
        his Bohemia, the production of art was in
        fact of less importance than the capacity
65   for art.
            Sensibility was what counted and *Scenes
        de la Vie de Boheme* does not celebrate artistic
        achievement so much as the gypsy life of
        being an artist and belonging to a creative
70   community.
            Murger was also responsible for the term
        "Bohemian" becoming inseparably linked
        with the supposedly unconventional,
        outlandish behaviour of artists, yet it is
75   evident that he did not invent Bohemianism.
        Most of its ingredients had been in existence
        in Paris for at least two decades before he
        started writing. Murger can thus be described
        as a Bohemian of the second generation,
80   which put him in a better position to
        reflect upon the experience and to idealize
        it than those who had been involved
        in the more chaotic process of its inception.
            Bohemia had been a haven for the political
85   rebel and, as the 19th century drew to a
        close, more than one French observer had
        seen it as the breeding-ground of cynicism,
        as the source of much potential danger.
        "It is quite clear," Jules Claretie wrote,
90   indignantly, in 1888, "that every country has
        its Bohemians. But they do not have the
        influence over the rest of the nation which
        they do in France—thanks to that poisonous

GO ON TO THE NEXT PAGE ▸▸▸

element in the French character which is
95   known as *la blague*—or cynicism." As
Augustin Challamel wrote in his *Souvenirs*:

Behind the "irregulars of the pen" came an
increasing number of Bohemians, affecting
the most profound disdain for what the
100   bourgeois called the "code of behaviour."
They posed as successors of Francois Villon[1],
playing the part of literary students,
habitues of the wine-bars, often of
places of ill-repute, breaking with the
105   customs of polite society, and believing, in
short, that everything is permissible to
men of intelligence...
Besides the false Romantic Byrons there
were some good men who fell into the
110   excesses of the literary revolution, and
practised debauchery and immorality.
Skeptical and materialistic, they elevated
poverty into a system. They were riddled
with debts, and they laughed at their
115   deliberate insolvency...
The Bohemian spirit spread wider still;
it did not only attach itself to literature
and art; gradually it spread to science and,
above all, to politics.

120   There were others who showed an active
sympathy for the Bohemians. Arsene
Houssaye, remembering his days in the
Impasse du Doyenne, had generously
befriended Bohemian poets. Yet Arsene
125   Houssaye was far from blind: he was well
aware that Bohemia included many
impostors. "I don't believe in the good faith
of the literary Bohemian," he had written as
early as 1856. "His disordered life is only a
130   journey in search of sensations, of the
documents and observations he needs to
produce his work. The real Bohemian is the
one who has no communication with the
public. He leads a vagabond existence for
135   himself alone, not for any readers or
spectators."

7   The overall purpose of this passage is to

(A)   analyze a historical period
(B)   define a broad cultural phenomenon
(C)   explain the merits of Henry Murger's
work
(D)   evaluate several literary works of a
particular genre
(E)   describe the culture of a particular
region

8   The "notion" (line 17) refers most directly to

(A)   a mistaken assumption
(B)   a bigoted point of view
(C)   a means of producing art
(D)   the celebration of a lifestyle
(E)   the inspiration for an opera

9   The author uses the word "Egyptian" (line 18)
in order to

(A)   refute the perception that Bohemians
are artists
(B)   compare African culture to European
culture
(C)   indicate the true source of a particular
term
(D)   refer to the origin of a style of art
(E)   acknowledge the culture that first
studied Bohemia

10   According to the passage, Henry Murger's
work is most notable for its ability to

(A)   reveal the historical inaccuracy of
certain accounts
(B)   justify the biases of a social class
(C)   inspire a fascination with a particular
lifestyle
(D)   revive the fortunes of a depressed
industry
(E)   establish a new field of study

11   In saying that Murger's stories became a
"textbook" (line 39) the author means that
these stories

(A)   were the first to apply historical
analysis to Bohemianism
(B)   predicted the political upheaval
that was to come in 19th and 20th
century Europe
(C)   provided a means of sustaining
interest in Bohemianism
(D)   warned against the social dangers of
Bohemianism
(E)   became a dry and lifeless depiction of
a once vibrant movement

GO ON TO THE NEXT PAGE ▶▶▶

[1] A medieval French poet who lived as a vagabond and a thief and wrote extensively about death and poverty

12 Murger was a "Bohemian of the second generation" (line 79) because he

(A) occasionally criticized the Bohemian lifestyle
(B) was an an observer of Bohemianism rather than a participant in it
(C) helped to transform Bohemianism from an artistic movement to a political one
(D) was not involved in the birth of Bohemianism
(E) could not maintain his romantic perspective on Bohemianism

13 In the sixth paragraph, lines 47–55, Bohemians are characterized primarily as being

(A) rebellious
(B) prosperous
(C) divinely selected
(D) traditionally pious
(E) insincere

14 The "people" (line 56) are

(A) early Christians
(B) the Bohemians
(C) artists of all types
(D) the ruling class
(E) the middle classes

15 Which of the following most accurately describes the difference between the Bohemians described by Jules Claretie and those described by Henry Murger?

(A) Claretie's Bohemians were optimistic, while Murger's Bohemians were cynical.
(B) Claretie's Bohemians are driven to acquire political power, while Murger's Bohemians have a need for secrecy.
(C) Claretie's Bohemians have no artistic talent, while Murger's Bohemians are artists with extraordinary skill.
(D) Claretie's Bohemians had very little social influence, while Murger's Bohemians shaped the culture of an entire nation.
(E) Claretie's Bohemians are a social blight, while Murger's Bohemians are uniquely creative and adventurous.

16 Augustin Challamel's quotation (lines 97–119) indicates that he regards Bohemianism as being characterized by all of the following EXCEPT

(A) affectation   (B) violence
(C) iconoclasm   (D) arrogance
(E) irresponsibility

17 The statement that Houssaye was "far from blind" (line 125) means that he

(A) understood the political benefits of Bohemianism
(B) did not hold the literary work of the Bohemians in high esteem
(C) did not have unquestioning sympathy for all Bohemians
(D) distrusted the social ambitions of Bohemians
(E) believed that Bohemians were too radical

18 Arsene Houssaye's attitude toward the Bohemians is best characterized as

(A) objectively analytical
(B) ambivalent
(C) morally outraged
(D) reverent
(E) mildly amused

19 Houssaye's quotation (lines 127–136) suggests that a "real Bohemian" is characterized primarily by his or her

(A) aloofness
(B) economic ambition
(C) respect for his or her literary audience
(D) comraderie with other Bohemians
(E) political idealism

STOP

You may check your work, on this section only, until time is called.

Section 9

Time—10 Minutes
14 Questions

Directions for "Improving Sentences" Questions

Each of the sentences below contains one underlined portion. The portion may contain one or more errors in grammar, usage, construction, precision, diction (choice of words), or idiom. Some of the sentences are correct.

Consider the meaning of the original sentence, and choose the answer that best expresses that meaning. If the original sentence is best, choose (A), because it repeats the original phrasing. Choose the phrasing that creates the clearest, most precise and most effective sentence.

EXAMPLE:

The growth of the plant was so dramatic that the children <u>couldn't hardly believe their eyes</u>.

- (A) couldn't hardly believe their eyes
- (B) would not hardly believe their eyes
- (C) could hardly believe their eyes
- (D) couldn't nearly believe their eyes
- (E) could hardly believe his or her eyes

Example answer: (C)

---

1 One way to improve student participation in the food drive <u>is by providing transportation for</u> those students who don't have cars.

- (A) is by providing transportation for
- (B) would be by providing transportation for
- (C) is to provide transportation for
- (D) is with transporting
- (E) is to be providing transportation to

2 Political reporters often must choose between currying favor with powerful officials to get inside information <u>or to gather</u> information as an objective outsider.

- (A) or to gather
- (B) as opposed to gathering
- (C) without gathering
- (D) and to gather
- (E) and gathering

3 Over 1,000 volunteers are available <u>to begin dispensing food and medicine after the order were given</u>.

- (A) to begin dispensing food and medicine after the order were given
- (B) if the order were given on the dispensing of food and medicine
- (C) for beginning to dispense food and medicine once the order is given
- (D) to begin dispensing food and medicine once the order is given
- (E) once the giving of the order about dispensing food and medicine

4 <u>With so many available</u>, an advisor should take time to help his or her students choose the courses that are best suited to them.

- (A) With so many available
- (B) Being that there are so many available
- (C) So many courses being available
- (D) With there being so many courses available
- (E) Because there are so many courses available

5 Very few high schools have such well-maintained athletic facilities <u>as our local school does</u>.

- (A) as our local school does
- (B) than our local school
- (C) compared to our local school
- (D) like our local school
- (E) like our local school does

9

GO ON TO THE NEXT PAGE ▸▸▸

6 Most scientists acknowledge <u>controlled studies to be most effective for</u> examining psychological hypotheses, but recognize that many such experiments are unethical to conduct on human subjects.

(A) controlled studies to be most effective for

(B) that controlled studies being most effective as

(C) controlled studies being most effective to

(D) that controlled studies are most effective for

(E) where controlled studies are most effective for

7 Although computer chips were once relatively large and expensive to manufacture, <u>they are now smaller and more affordable</u>.

(A) they are now smaller and more affordable

(B) it has become far smaller in recent years and they are more affordable

(C) their cost and size in recent years has decreased

(D) they have become less in terms of price and size in recent years

(E) it has become far smaller and more affordable in recent years

8 <u>To ignore</u> those who challenge your thesis is more insulting than attacking them outright.

(A) To ignore　　(B) In ignoring

(C) Ignoring　　(D) While ignoring

(E) When you ignore

9 The new wireless technology will allow doctors to diagnose patients, update files, and <u>let them access medical research without</u> leaving their homes.

(A) let them access medical research without

(B) to access medical research without the need for

(C) access medical research and not be

(D) to access medical research without

(E) access medical research without

10 The director of the agency was concerned that the latest advertisements <u>will not be regarded with the lightheartedness they were intended with</u>.

(A) will not be regarded with the lightheartedness they were intended with

(B) would not be regarded with the lightheartedness with which they had been intended

(C) would not be regarded with the lightheartedness that they were regarded to be intended with

(D) will not be regarded with the lightheartedness regarding with which they were intended

(E) would not be regarded with the lightheartedness with which they were intended to be regarded to have

11 The anthropologist was interested in studying the Maori people, <u>particularly their history, rituals, and social relationships</u>.

(A) particularly their history, rituals, and social relationships

(B) to study particularly their history, rituals, and social relationships

(C) particularly the study of their history, rituals, and social relationships

(D) particularly of their history and rituals in addition to their social relationships

(E) particularly studying their history, rituals, and social relationships

12 Although he was not elected as the captain, Omar <u>has become the team leader, him being</u> the most vocal and respected player on the team.

(A) has become the team leader, him being

(B) is being the team leader because of his being

(C) is the team leader for being

(D) has become the team leader because he is

(E) has become the team leader for having been

GO ON TO THE NEXT PAGE ▶▶▶

13 Most students thought that the new parking policy was <u>as restrictive, if not more, than</u> the previous policy.

    (A)   as restrictive, if not more, than
    (B)   as restrictive, if not more, as
    (C)   perhaps as restrictive, but perhaps more restrictive, as
    (D)   as restrictive as, if not more, than
    (E)   as restrictive as, if not more restrictive than,

14 The total revenue generated by the three drug therapies that the company unveiled this summer <u>are not likely to be as great as their newest drug</u>.

    (A)   are not likely to be as great as their newest drug
    (B)   are not likely to be as great as that generated by their newest drug
    (C)   is not likely to be as great as that generated by their newest drug
    (D)   is not likely to be as great as that generated by its newest drug
    (E)   is not likely to be as great as its newest drug

9

STOP

You may check your work, on this section only, until time is called.

ANSWER KEY

Section 2 Math	Section 5 Math	Section 7 Math	Section 4 Critical Reading	Section 6 Critical Reading	Section 8 Critical Reading	Section 3 Writing	Section 9 Writing
☐ 1. C	☐ 1. A	☐ 1. C	☐ 1. E	☐ 1. D	☐ 1. C	☐ 1. B	☐ 1. C
☐ 2. A	☐ 2. B	☐ 2. D	☐ 2. C	☐ 2. B	☐ 2. B	☐ 2. D	☐ 2. E
☐ 3. D	☐ 3. A	☐ 3. E	☐ 3. B	☐ 3. A	☐ 3. C	☐ 3. E	☐ 3. D
☐ 4. E	☐ 4. C	☐ 4. A	☐ 4. C	☐ 4. E	☐ 4. A	☐ 4. C	☐ 4. E
☐ 5. D	☐ 5. C	☐ 5. B	☐ 5. E	☐ 5. A	☐ 5. B	☐ 5. A	☐ 5. A
☐ 6. B	☐ 6. C	☐ 6. D	☐ 6. A	☐ 6. C	☐ 6. A	☐ 6. E	☐ 6. D
☐ 7. D	☐ 7. E	☐ 7. B	☐ 7. A	☐ 7. D	☐ 7. B	☐ 7. D	☐ 7. A
☐ 8. A	☐ 8. E	☐ 8. D	☐ 8. D	☐ 8. C	☐ 8. A	☐ 8. C	☐ 8. C
☐ 9. D	☐ 9. 18	☐ 9. E	☐ 9. A	☐ 9. B	☐ 9. C	☐ 9. C	☐ 9. E
☐ 10. C	☐ 10. 75	☐ 10. D	☐ 10. C	☐ 10. A	☐ 10. C	☐ 10. D	☐ 10. B
☐ 11. C	☐ 11. 20	☐ 11. B	☐ 11. E	☐ 11. E	☐ 11. C	☐ 11. B	☐ 11. A
☐ 12. B	☐ 12. 140	☐ 12. A	☐ 12. E	☐ 12. D	☐ 12. D	☐ 12. A	☐ 12. D
☐ 13. D	☐ 13. 1/25	☐ 13. D	☐ 13. E	☐ 13. D	☐ 13. C	☐ 13. D	☐ 13. E
☐ 14. B	or .04	☐ 14. C	☐ 14. C	☐ 14. C	☐ 14. E	☐ 14. E	☐ 14. D
☐ 15. A	☐ 14. 48	☐ 15. B	☐ 15. A	☐ 15. E	☐ 15. E	☐ 15. B	
☐ 16. A	☐ 15. 106	☐ 16. A	☐ 16. B	☐ 16. A	☐ 16. B	☐ 16. A	
☐ 17. D	☐ 16. 108		☐ 17. D	☐ 17. C	☐ 17. C	☐ 17. B	
☐ 18. E	☐ 17. 16/3		☐ 18. C	☐ 18. E	☐ 18. B	☐ 18. C	
☐ 19. B	or 5.33		☐ 19. B	☐ 19. B	☐ 19. A	☐ 19. A	
☐ 20. E	☐ 18. 5/6		☐ 20. B	☐ 20. B		☐ 20. E	
	or .833		☐ 21. E	☐ 21. B		☐ 21. D	
			☐ 22. D	☐ 22. C		☐ 22. B	
			☐ 23. C	☐ 23. A		☐ 23. B	
			☐ 24. E	☐ 24. C		☐ 24. E	
						☐ 25. B	
						☐ 26. A	
						☐ 27. D	
						☐ 28. A	
						☐ 29. C	
						☐ 30. B	
						☐ 31. A	
						☐ 32. B	
						☐ 33. E	
						☐ 34. C	
						☐ 35. B	

# Right (A):	Questions 1–8 # Right (A):	# Right (A):	# Right (A):	# Right (A):	# Right (A):	# Right (A)	# Right (A):
#Wrong (B):	_____ #Wrong (B):	#Wrong (B):	#Wrong (B):	#Wrong (B):	#Wrong (B):	#Wrong (B):	#Wrong (B):
# (A) – ¼ (B):	# (A) – ¼ (B):	# (A) – ¼ (B):	# (A) – ¼ (B):	# (A) – ¼ (B):	# (A) – ¼ (B):	# (A) – ¼ (B):	# (A) – ¼ (B):
	Questions 9–18 # Right (A):						

SCORE CONVERSION TABLE

How to score your test

Use the answer key on the previous page to determine your raw score on each section. Your raw score on each section except Section 4 is simply the number of correct answers minus ¼ of the number of wrong answers. On Section 4, your raw score is the sum of the number of correct answers for questions 1–8 minus ¼ of the number of wrong answers for questions 1–8 plus the total number of correct answers for questions 9–18. Next, add the raw scores from Sections 3, 4, and 7 to get your Math raw score, add the raw scores from Sections 2, 5, and 8 to get your Critical Reading raw score and add the raw scores from Sections 6 and 9 to get your Writing raw score. Write the three raw scores here:

Raw Critical Reading score: _____ Raw Math score: _____ Raw Writing score: _____

Use the table below to convert these to scaled scores.

Scaled scores: Critical Reading: _____ Math: _____ Writing: _____

Raw Score	Critical Reading Scaled Score	Math Scaled Score	Writing Scaled Score	Raw Score	Critical Reading Scaled Score	Math Scaled Score	Writing Scaled Score
67	800			32	520	550	610
66	800			31	510	550	600
65	790			30	510	540	580
64	780			29	500	530	570
63	760			28	490	520	560
62	750			27	490	530	550
61	730			26	480	510	540
60	720			25	480	500	530
59	700			24	470	490	520
58	700			23	460	480	510
57	690			22	460	480	500
56	680			21	450	470	490
55	670			20	440	460	480
54	660	800		19	440	450	470
53	650	790		18	430	450	460
52	650	760		17	420	440	450
51	640	740		16	420	430	440
50	630	720		15	410	420	440
49	620	710	800	14	400	410	430
48	620	700	800	13	400	410	420
47	610	680	800	12	390	400	410
46	600	670	790	11	380	390	400
45	600	660	780	10	370	380	390
44	590	650	760	9	360	370	380
43	590	640	740	8	350	360	380
42	580	630	730	7	340	350	370
41	570	630	710	6	330	340	360
40	570	620	700	5	320	330	350
39	560	610	690	4	310	320	340
38	550	600	670	3	300	310	320
37	550	590	660	2	280	290	310
36	540	580	650	1	270	280	300
35	540	580	640	0	250	260	280
34	530	570	630	−1	230	240	270
33	520	560	620	−2 or less	210	220	250

SCORE CONVERSION TABLE FOR WRITING COMPOSITE
[ESSAY + MULTIPLE CHOICE]

Calculate your writing raw score as you did on the previous page and grade your essay from a 1 to a 6 according to the standards that follow in the detailed answer key.

Essay score: _____ Raw Writing score: _____

Use the table below to convert these to scaled scores.

Scaled score: Writing: _____

Raw Score	Essay Score 0	Essay Score 1	Essay Score 2	Essay Score 3	Essay Score 4	Essay Score 5	Essay Score 6
−2 or less	200	230	250	280	310	340	370
−1	210	240	260	290	320	360	380
0	230	260	280	300	340	370	400
1	240	270	290	320	350	380	410
2	250	280	300	330	360	390	420
3	260	290	310	340	370	400	430
4	270	300	320	350	380	410	440
5	280	310	330	360	390	420	450
6	290	320	340	360	400	430	460
7	290	330	340	370	410	440	470
8	300	330	350	380	410	450	470
9	310	340	360	390	420	450	480
10	320	350	370	390	430	460	490
11	320	360	370	400	440	470	500
12	330	360	380	410	440	470	500
13	340	370	390	420	450	480	510
14	350	380	390	420	460	490	520
15	350	380	400	430	460	500	530
16	360	390	410	440	470	500	530
17	370	400	420	440	480	510	540
18	380	410	420	450	490	520	550
19	380	410	430	460	490	530	560
20	390	420	440	470	500	530	560
21	400	430	450	480	510	540	570
22	410	440	460	480	520	550	580
23	420	450	470	490	530	560	590
24	420	460	470	500	540	570	600
25	430	460	480	510	540	580	610
26	440	470	490	520	550	590	610
27	450	480	500	530	560	590	620
28	460	490	510	540	570	600	630
29	470	500	520	550	580	610	640
30	480	510	530	560	590	620	650
31	490	520	540	560	600	630	660
32	500	530	550	570	610	640	670
33	510	540	550	580	620	650	680
34	510	550	560	590	630	660	690
35	520	560	570	600	640	670	700
36	530	560	580	610	650	680	710
37	540	570	590	620	660	690	720
38	550	580	600	630	670	700	730
39	560	600	610	640	680	710	740
40	580	610	620	650	690	720	750
41	590	620	640	660	700	730	760
42	600	630	650	680	710	740	770
43	610	640	660	690	720	750	780
44	620	660	670	700	740	770	800
45	640	670	690	720	750	780	800
46	650	690	700	730	770	800	800
47	670	700	720	750	780	800	800
48	680	720	730	760	800	800	800
49	680	720	730	760	800	800	800

Detailed Answer Key

Section I

The following essay received 12 points out of a possible 12. It demonstrates *clear and consistent mastery* in that it

- develops an insightful point of view on the topic
- demonstrates exemplary critical thinking
- uses very effective examples, reasons, and other evidence to support its thesis
- is consistently focused, coherent, and well-organized
- demonstrates skillful and effective use of language and sentence structure
- is largely (but not necessarily completely) free of grammatical and usage errors

> The liberally educated person is one who is able to resist the easy and preferred answers, not because he is obstinate but because he knows others worthy of consideration.
>
> —Allan Bloom

Assignment: **What is one important "easy and preferred answer" that we should resist? That is, what dangerous misconception do people commonly hold**? Write an essay in which you answer this question and support your position logically with examples from literature, the arts, history, politics, science and technology, current events, or your experience or observation.

SAMPLE STUDENT ESSAY

One of the most dangerous misconceptions that people hold today is the idea that our enemies are fundamentally different from us. It is easy, to a certain extent, to understand how such a belief comes about. Most human societies must kill in order to survive, but must at the same time prohibit particular kinds of killing. Throughout our history, humans have been meat-eaters, and so must kill and eat animals in order to thrive (the minority of vegetarians notwithstanding). Also, societies must often defend themselves against violent enemies, necessitating the occasional use of deadly force. On the other hand, civilized societies must prohibit most killing within their own ranks, so that their populations do not die out or suffer needlessly.

So how do humans deal with this dichotomy: the need to kill, at least occasionally, to survive, and the need to prohibit killing within its ranks? Simply, humans have developed the concepts of "us" and "them." It is okay to kill and eat animals because they do not have the value of humans. Perhaps, too, a society may justify the killing of animals by adopting a belief system that says that animals are gifts to humans from a divine being or beings.

In much the same way, humans are inclined to put their enemies in the category of "other," that is, less than human, or to believe that a divine being has given them permission to kill those enemies. Paradoxically, those religious systems are also very likely to have severe restrictions against killing other human beings. In practice, most cultures regard these as restrictions merely against killing "their own kind." However, this type of thinking is counterproductive to the goal of building more just and functional societies. If one society can easily categorize another as an "enemy" and thereby reduce its foes to the status of animal, then the concept of universal human rights is abolished.

We see the dangers inherent in denying the humanity of our enemies in the United States today. Although the American Constitution champions the concept of inalienable rights that are due to all human beings, the United States Senate is actively engaged in undermining those rights. The right of habeas corpus, that is, the right of a person in custody to seek a hearing to determine whether or not he or she is being held justly, is a cornerstone of the United States Constitution. It is regarded as a fundamental element of a just society. Yet the Senate is seeking to eliminate that right for foreign detainees captured in the "war on terror." In other words, the mere suspicion of terrorism—not proof, but suspicion—is evidently reason enough to reduce a human being to the status of an animal. This heinous distinction of "us" versus "them" will surely have dire consequences for the United States, who will rightfully be seen as being grossly hypocritical on the matter of human rights.

Even beyond the trampling of human rights, the "us" versus "them" distinction is not even as useful in wartime as it may seem at first glance, because to defeat our enemy, we must understand our enemy. If we begin with the assumption that your enemy lacks human intelligence, desires and motivations, then we risk severely underestimating his ability. Therefore, if the United States continues down this

dangerous path, it runs the risk of losing not only the moral war but the actual war.

Reader's comments

This is an exceptionally well-reasoned and well-organized essay supporting the thesis that "it is a dangerous misconception to believe that our enemies are fundamentally different from us." The author demonstrates a strong understanding of the origins of a belief as well as its effects. The author consistently focuses on the dangers of reducing other human beings "to the status of animal," and uses the example of *habeas corpus* to excellent effect. The author also demonstrates strong facility and effective variety in diction and sentence structure. Its consistent critical reasoning and effective use of language merits a 12.

Detailed Answer Key

Section 2

1. C

$$3(m + n) + 3 = 15$$
Subtract 3: $\quad 3(m + n) = 12$
Divide by 3: $\quad m + n = 4$

2. A Recall the basic rate formula: *work = rate × time.* Since the rate is r pages per minute and the time is m minutes, the total amount of work is rm pages. It may also help you to give r and m simple numerical values, like 4 and 5, respectively, and calculate the numerical result, which is 20 pages, and confirm that choice (A) gives that result.

3. D Since there are 180° in a line, $a + b + c = 180$.

$$a + b = 120$$
$$\underline{b + c = 100}$$
Add equations: $\quad a + 2b + c = 220$
Subtract: $\quad \underline{-(a + b + c = 180)}$
$$b = 40$$

Alternately, you can solve for a and c separately:

$$a + b + c = 180$$
$$\underline{b + c = 100}$$
Subtract equations: $\quad a = 80$
$$a + b + c = 180$$
$$\underline{a + b = 120}$$
Subtract equations: $\quad c = 60$
Substitute into $\quad a + b + c = 180$:
$$80 + b + 60 = 180$$
Simplify: $\quad 140 + b = 180$
Subtract 140: $\quad b = 40$

4. E

$$6^n \times 6^4 = 6^{12}$$
Simplify: $\quad 6^{n+4} = 6^{12}$
Equate exponents: $\quad n + 4 = 12$
Subtract 4: $\quad n = 8$

5. D This question simply requires you to solve for b.

$$4x + b = x + 2$$
Subtract 4x: $\quad b = -3x + 2$
Commute: $\quad b = 2 + -3x = 2 - 3x$

6. B In 1995, 200 cars valued at \$15,000 and 100 cars valued at \$25,000 were sold, for a total value of $(200)(\$15,000) + (100)(\$25,000) = \$5,500,000$. In 2005, 200 cars valued at \$25,000 and 200 cars valued at \$35,000 were sold, for a total value of $(200)(\$25,000) + (200)(\$35,000) = \$12,000,000$. The difference is $\$12,000,000 - \$5,500,000 = \$6,500,000$.

7. D An isosceles triangle always contains two angles of equal measure. One of the angles has a measure greater than 95°, but neither of the other angles can measure more than 95°, because the sum of all three angles must be exactly 180°. The only way for this to be true is for the other two angles to be equal. If you choose a value of, say, 96° for the largest angle (of course, any value between 95° and 180° will do), and say that the others each measure x degrees, then $\quad x + x + 96 = 180$
Subtract 96: $\quad 2x = 84$
Divide by 2: $\quad x = 42$
Now notice that the only choice that is true is (D) $x < 42.5$.

8. A If m gives a remainder of 2 when divided by 7, then m must be 2 more than a multiple of 7. Choose any such value for m, like 2, 9, or 16. Then simply multiply this number by 4 and calculate the remainder when it is divided by 7. In each case, the result is the same: $4(2) = 8$, $4(9) = 36$, and $4(16) = 64$ all give a remainder of 1 when divided by 7.

9. D You might start by choosing simple values for a and b, like 6 and 5. (Always make sure that any numbers you choose satisfy the conditions in the problem—in this case, that a is a multiple of 3 and b is odd.) With these values, only choices (C) $6 + 5 = 11$ and (D) $2(6) + 5 = 17$ yield odd numbers, so the others can be eliminated. Trying new values like $a = 3$ and $b = 7$ shows that only choice (D) must always be odd. Alternately, you may notice that $2a$ must always be even, since it is a multiple of 2. When an even number is added to an odd number, b, the result must always be odd, so $2a + b$ will always be odd.

10. C When a point is reflected over the x-axis, it keeps its x-coordinate, but "negates" its y-coordinate. When it is reflected over the y-axis, it keeps its y-coordinate but negates its x-coordinate. The reflections look like this:

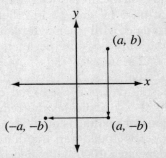

Therefore, the final position is $(-a, -b)$.

11. C The formula for the volume of a right cylinder is given in the Reference Information on the first page of every math section: $V = \pi r^2 h$. (Remember that a "right" cylinder is simply a cylinder in which the sides are perpendicular to the bases.) Therefore, a cylinder with radius 1 and height 1 has a volume of $\pi(1)^2(1) = \pi \approx 3.14$. The formula for the volume of a rectangular solid, which is also given in the Reference Information, is $V = lwh$. Therefore, the volumes of the boxes described in the choices are (A) 1, (B) 2, (C) 3, (D) 4 and (E) 6. The closest to π is (C) 3.

12. B Since the nth term is $3n^2 - n$, then the 3rd term is $3(3)^2 - 3 = 24$ and the 10th term is $3(10)^2 - 10 = 290$, and $290 - 24 = 266$.

13. D As this diagram shows, the maximum number of points of intersection is 8.

14. B Examining sample values from among the choices should make it clear that the inequality is only true when x takes a value between −1 and 0. For instance, if $x = -.5$, then $x^2 = (-.5)^2 = .25$ and $x^3 = (-.5)^3 = -.125$, and therefore $x < x^3 < x^2$.

15. A Simply "expand" and FOIL the expression to get $(m + n)^2 = (m + n)(m + n) = m^2 + 2mn + n^2$
Now simply substitute the values of the expressions that you are given. $(m + n)^2 = m^2 + 2mn + n^2$

Substitute:	$18 = m^2 + 2(4) + n^2$
Subtract 8:	$10 = m^2 + n^2$

16. A An isosceles triangle has two equal sides. If two of the sides have lengths of 5 and 12, then the only possible triangle is a 12–12–5 triangle. A 5–5–12 triangle is impossible, because the sum of any two sides of a triangle must be greater than the third side. (If you don't immediately see why, then just take three sticks and cut them to lengths of 5 in., 5 in. and 12 in., then try to construct a triangle with them. It can't be done!) Therefore the only possible perimeter of this triangle is $12 + 12 + 5 = 29$.

17. D Since the dial is cyclical and contains only the six digits 0–5, it indicates the remainder when the digital counter reading is divided by 6. If the digital counter reads 1000, then the dial will indicate the remainder when 1000 is divided by 6. You can

find this remainder through long division, or you can use your calculator. $1000 \div 6 = 166.66 \ldots$, and $6 \times .66 \ldots = 4$, so the dial reads 4.

18. E Since the ratio by weight of raisins to dates is 7 to 3, then 10 pounds of the mix would contain 7 pounds of raisins and 3 pounds of dates. In other words, 7/10 of the mix, by weight, is raisins. Therefore, in 7 pounds of the mix $(7/10)(7) = 4.9$ pounds is raisins.

19. B The key fact in this problem is that m and n must be integers. Start by considering simple integer values for n. Notice that if $n = 1$, then $m = 1 - 2/1 - 2/1 = -3$, which is an integer. Notice, also, that if n is greater than 1 or less than −1, then $2/n^2$ will not be an integer, and so m will not be an integer. The only other integer value of n that corresponds to an integer value of m is $n = -1$, which means $m = -1 - 2/(-1) - 2/(-1)^2 = -1 + 2 - 2 = -1$, which is an integer. Therefore, the only possible values of m are −3 and −1.

20. E You can approach this question numerically or algebraically. To take the numerical approach, consider simple values for k, x, and p. For instance, $k = 3$, $x = 12$, and $p = 1$. This means that 3 girls originally agreed to split $12, and so should have contributed $4 apiece, but then 1 more girl joined and so the $12 would have been split 4 ways, or $3 apiece, a savings of $1 per girl. Now plug the values in to each choice and see which gives a value of 1. The only choice that works is (E).
Alternately, you can take the algebraic approach. If k girls must raise a total of x dollars, then each must raise x/k dollars. If p more girls join, then $k + p$ girls must raise x dollars, or $x/(k + p)$ apiece. Now calculate the difference:
$$\frac{x}{k} - \frac{x}{k+p} = \frac{x(k+p)}{k(k+p)} - \frac{kx}{k(k+p)} = \frac{kx+px-kx}{k(k+p)} = \frac{px}{k(k+p)}$$

Section 3

1. B Since the pronoun here refers to *employees*, it should be the plural *they* rather than the singular *he* or *she*. Choice (D) uses the plural pronoun *them*, but it also uses the pronoun *it*, which lacks a clear antecedent.

2. D The phrase *for the purpose of investigating* is awkward and unidiomatic. The standard idiom is *to investigate*. The phrases *investigate on* and *investigate after* are also unidiomatic.

3. **E** The sentence begins with a modifying phrase based on the participle *worried*. The subject of this participle must be the subject of the main clause, but the subject of the main clause is *Helena's concern*. It is illogical to suggest that a *concern* is *worried*. The only logical subject of this participle is *Helena*, which is the subject in (C) and (E). Choice (C) is incorrect, however, because it is awkward and contains the unidiomatic phrase *concerned towards*.

4. **C** The original sentence lacks a verb. Both (C) and (D) correct this problem, but (C) is far more concise and effective.

5. **A** The original sentence is the most concise, idiomatic and effective.

6. **E** The phrase *determine about* is unidiomatic, as are *determine regarding* and *determine for*. The sentence is most effective if the needless preposition is simply eliminated. Choice (C) is grammatically sound, but it is logically nonsensical, since *pay* cannot *qualify for duties*.

7. **D** The original sentence contains a comma splice. Clearly, the two clauses contrast each other, so the conjunction *but* is clearly appropriate. Choice (B) is incorrect because the conjunction *but* cannot be used with a semicolon. Choice (C) is wrong because the phrase *in cricket* is misplaced.

8. **C** The modifying phrase that begins the sentence must modify the subject of the main clause. But the subject of the main clause is *Athens*, which cannot be *skeptical*. The only logical subject is *philosophers*, which is provided only by choice (C).

9. **C** The subject of the sentence is the singular noun *debate*, so the verb *have* is conjugated incorrectly, and should be changed to *has*. The sentence also contains a list which requires parallel phrasing: *the origins* and *the merits* should be combined with *the legal authority*. The only choice that corrects both problems is choice (C).

10. **D** The participle *excited* modifies the subject of the main clause of the sentence, but it is illogical to say that a *decision* is *excited*. The only logical subject is *Kyra*, but (B) is awkward and unidiomatic, so the best choice is clearly (D).

11. **B** The three ideas in the original sentence are coordinated awkwardly. An effective complex sentence must coordinate the ideas logically and concisely.

Choice (B) is concise, logical and effective. The participial phrases are very awkward in choice (C), the list in choice (D) is awkward and not parallel, and the gerund phrase at the end of choice (E) is awkward and illogical.

12. **A** The subject *proposals* is plural, therefore the verb should be changed to *are*.

13. **D** The modifier *civil* modifies the verb *conducted*, and therefore should be the adverb *civilly*.

14. **E** The original sentence is correct.

15. **B** The conjunction *but* is redundant, and should be eliminated, because the sentence already uses the contrasting conjunction *while*.

16. **A** The correct past participle of *to take* is *taken*, not *took*.

17. **B** The preposition *about* is unidiomatic. One refers *to* a theory, not *about* a theory.

18. **C** The main subject of the sentence is the singular noun *pace*, so the verb should be changed to *is*.

19. **A** The phrase *every living creature* is singular, so the phrase in (A) should be changed to *owes its*.

20. **E** The original sentence is correct.

21. **D** The comparison in the sentence is not parallel. How hard it is *to teach* one thing should be compared to how hard it is *to teach* another thing. Therefore choice (D) should be changed from *teaching* to *to teach*.

22. **B** The pronoun *on* is unidiomatic. The correct idiom is *preoccupied with*.

23. **B** Since the phrase *Jose and I* is the object of the preposition *to*, it must take the objective case *Jose and me*.

24. **E** The original sentence is correct.

25. **B** The subject of the sentence is *varieties*, so the verb should be changed to *were*.

26. **A** If Cara's race times are improving, they cannot be *constant*. This word should be changed to the adverb *constantly*, because it modifies the adjective *improving*.

27. **D** The word *indecisive* means *unable to make a decision*. Its use in this context is illogical. An amount of time cannot be *indecisive*, but it can be *indefinite*.

28. **A** The first two items in the list are simple nouns, so to maintain parallelism the phrase in choice (A) should be eliminated.

29. **C** The comparison between the *project* to *the other students* is illogical, so the phrase in (C) should be changed to *those of the other students*.

30. **B** The sentence is defining two terms, and choice (B) does so most effectively and concisely. Choice (A) uses the pronoun *it* without a clear antecedent, and uses two awkward participial phrases. Choice (C) is wordy and uses the pronoun *it* without a clear antecedent. Choices (D) and (E) are both unparallel and awkward.

31. **A** Since the paragraph is talking about general trends in behavior, the subjects and objects of discussion should all be in the third person. The pronoun *you* is therefore inappropriate and should be changed to *their children*.

32. **B** This sentence is best inserted after sentence 3 because it is a logical introduction to a discussion of specific uses of incentives, which is presented in sentences 4 through 8.

33. **E** The original sentence is wordy and uses the unidiomatic phrase *in the way like*. The most effective and idiomatic option is (E). Choice (B) is needlessly wordy, and choices (C) and (D) contain runons.

34. **C** The pronoun *they* has no clear antecedent in the original phrasing. The same error is repeated in choices (A), (B), (D), and (E). Choice (C), although not the most concise, is the most effective and grammatically correct.

35. **B** The inserted sentence follows a sentence discussing the reasons that a particular incentive program was ineffective, and precedes the concluding sentence of the passage. Therefore, the most effective sentence to insert here provides a concluding thought to the discussion of the incentive program, which choice (B) does. Since the paragraph discusses the reasons for the program's ineffectiveness, sentences (A) and (D) are illogical. Since the passage does not discuss the relative value of rewards and punishments, choice (C) is inappropriate. Sentence (E) does not convey any relevant information to the discussion at all.

Section 4

1. **E** Saying that *the earth's magnetic polarity has switched back and forth* is equivalent to saying that this polarity has *fluctuated* (varied irregularly). *correlations* = relationships between two variables

2. **C** The sentence indicates that scientists *disagree* about an issue. One position on the issue is that this particular bird behavior *is learned*. The opposing view must be that this behavior is *not* learned, and therefore was simply instinctive. Choice (C) *innate* means *present at birth*. *impassive* = lacking emotion; *pragmatic* = concerned with practical matters

3. **B** Since doctors try to cure diseases, it would be considered a success for them to *stop or slow* the spread of tuberculosis. They would be concerned, however, about *dangerous* strains arising. *marginalizing* = rendering irrelevant; *innocuous* = harmless; *virulent* = dangerous; *obscuring* = hiding from view; *indifferent* = uncaring; *imperilling* = putting in danger

4. **C** The first missing word represents something that is *carefully formulated* and is found in the scientific method, while the second missing word represents something that is *wishful* and found in *pseudoscience* (fake science). Since *concessions* (reluctant agreements) and *hunches* (intuitive guesses) are not part of the scientific method, choices (B) and (E) can be eliminated. Since *divergences* (departures from norms) and *restrictions* are not integral to pseudoscience and are not *wishful*, choices (A) and (D) can be eliminated. *conjectures* = guesses; *paradigms* = a set of assumptions and methods for solving problems or construing reality

5. **E** Since the two lectures are contrasted using parallel language, and since the first lecture is viewed negatively and the second positively, the first missing word must be the opposite of *easy to understand*, and the second missing word must be the opposite of *irrelevant*. *obscure* = little-known; *vague* = unclear; *lucid* = clear; *pertinent* = relevant; *convoluted* = confusing; *petty* = concerned with trivial matters; *concise* = brief and to the point; *esoteric* = intended to be understood only by a select group; *abstruse* = difficult to understand; *germane* = relevant

6. **A** Ian's argument was *thoroughly refuted*, although it *seemed plausible at first*. Therefore it was an example of *sophistry* (plausible but fallacious argumentation). *solicitousness* = anxious concern or eagerness; *acumen* = keen skill; *substantiation* = verifiable support for a claim; *resolution* = commitment

7. A One who has *read dozens of philosophical treatises* is clearly *well-read*, and such a person would likely have *thoroughly* researched new developments. *erudite* = well-educated; *assiduously* = with vigor and attention to detail; *contrite* = remorseful; *cerebral* = thoughtful and intelligent; *stoic* = deliberately unemotional; *lackadaisically* = inattentively and without energy

8. D Someone who seeks *a greater connection to the world outside* would likely *bemoan* (lament) the *insularity* (social isolation) of an island community. The *establishment of international phone service* would likely *appease* (ease the concerns of) those citizens. *obstinacy* = stubbornness; *precociousness* = characterized by early maturity; *obsequiousness* = servility; *insinuation* = subtle implication

9. A Passage 1 conveys a cynical tone in criticizing the *narcissism* (line 10) of the Baby Boomers and by mocking their self-centered point of view: *History be damned; if it didn't happen between 1960 and 1980, it's irrelevant* (lines 15–17). Passage 2 does not convey any such cynicism, and is in fact a uniformly positive depiction of Kennedy.

10. C This question is posed incredulously, implying that Kennedy should not *be perceived as greater than George Washington*. Therefore, the author believes that Kennedy's high ranking in polls is undeserved.

11. E This sentence discusses the good work that Kennedy did for *the rights of minorities, the poor, the very old and the very young*, thereby indicating that Kennedy supported policies that benefited divergent groups.

12. E Both passages agree that Kennedy was in touch with the unique qualities of the era in which he governed. Passage 1 states that he *was the first president to make effective use of television* (lines 18–20) and was held in high esteem by the Baby Boomers, and Passage 2 states that he was *very much a man of his time* (lines 22–23) and fought for the rights of many people who were suffering during that era.

13. E In saying that government's *one permanent object is to oppress* superior people, the author means that government's *goal* is to oppress them.

14. C The passage indicates that an *aristocratic* (line 4) government works *against the man who is superior in fact* (line 6), and that a *democratic* (line 7) government works against *both* those who are superior in law and those who are superior in fact. It then goes on to say that governments *combat originality* (line 13) among their citizens.

15. A In saying that *the historical testimony runs the other way* (line 29), the author is saying that this testimony contradicts the idea that *the new government would be any better than the old one* (lines 27–28). Therefore, such testimony must be about the effect of revolutions in trying to create better societies.

16. B Passage 1 states *that material progress was due, not to the virtues of their new government, but to the lavishness of nature* (lines 52–54). In other words, the government succeeded by the benefit of natural resources.

17. D The author of Passage 1 states that the ideal government *lets the individual alone* (lines 58–59) and is therefore characterized by its unintrusiveness.

18. C Passage 2 contends that the *revolutionary situation* did not include any *mass poverty ... seething social discontent* or *grinding oppression* (lines 69–71). It did, however, include *a great deal of jealousy* (line 78).

19. B These historians *desperately sought to find...mass poverty...seething social discontent...* and *grinding oppression* in order to explain the causes of the American Revolution. Therefore, they believed that political upheaval is caused by social discontent.

20. B In saying that *state and magnificence, the natural attendant on great riches, are conspicuous among this people*, the visitor is saying that the citizens of South Carolina conspicuously flaunt their wealth through ceremonious pomp. The word *state* most nearly means *pomp*.

21. E The quotation from Gadsden makes the point that *white society in South Carolina was comparatively equal* (lines 139–140). The distinctions among *the farmer and rich planter, the mechanic and the rich merchant ...* do not exist in reality.

22. D Both authors would agree that American colonists benefited from material prosperity. Passage 1 states that *material progress [in the colonies] was due, not to the virtues of their new government, but to the lavishness of nature* (lines 50–54), and Passage 2 states *that there was greater prosperity [in the colonies] than anywhere else in the world* (lines 72–73).

23. C Passage 1 states that *almost inevitably [the citizen] comes to the conclusion that the government he lives in is dishonest, insane and intolerable, and so, if he is romantic, he tries to change it* (lines 19–23). In other words, those who change the government, the revolutionaries, are motivated by romanticism or political idealism. Passage 2 states that the revolutionaries were motivated by *jealousy and touchiness everywhere* (lines 78–79). The revolutionaries *were acutely nervous about their prosperity and the liberty that seemed to make it possible* (lines 80–82). In other words, they were concerned about losing their wealth.

24. **E** In saying that American colonists lived *under the British hoof* (lines 54–55), the author of Passage 1 is saying that the British were guilty of *oppressing* the colonists. Therefore, *hoof* is being used as a metaphor for *oppression*.

Section 5

1. **A**

$$4m - 2 = m + 7$$

Subtract m: $3m - 2 = 7$
Add 2: $3m = 9$
Divide by 3: $m = 3$

2. **B** Since l is a line, and the measure of a straight angle is 180°,

$$140 + 2x = 180$$

Subtract 140: $2x = 40$
Divide by 2: $x = 20$

3. **A**

$\dfrac{3}{8}$ of m is 48

Translate: $\dfrac{3}{8}m = 48$

Multiply by 5/3: $\left(\dfrac{5}{3}\right)\dfrac{3}{8}m = \left(\dfrac{5}{3}\right)48$

Simplify: $\dfrac{5}{8}m = 80$

4. **C** Since each term is the previous term divided by 3, $a_2 = 54$, $a_3 = 18$, $a_4 = 6$, $a_5 = 2$, $a_6 = 2/3$. Therefore the first term that is not an integer is a_6.

5. **C** $\sqrt{n} \times \sqrt{2} = \sqrt{2n}$ is an integer only when $2n$ is a perfect square. The only choice that is not half of a perfect square is (C) 12. You should check to see that the other four choices are half of a perfect square, and so make $\sqrt{2n}$ an integer.

6. **C** The only way to prevent any of the vertices from touching at least two black faces is to paint the cube so that the two white faces are adjacent, as in the diagram below. (All unseen faces are black.)

Notice that here the two vertices that are circled touch only one black face. All of the others touch at least two black faces. Since there are 8 vertices in all, the minimum number of vertices that could be shared by two or more black faces is $8 - 2 = 6$.

7. **E** If y varies directly as x, then $y = kx$ for some constant k. Another way to express this relationship is to say $y/x = k$, that is, the ratio of y to x is always the same value. Therefore,

$$\frac{8}{a} = \frac{12}{a+10}$$

Cross-multiply: $8a + 80 = 12a$
Subtract $8a$: $80 = 4a$
Divide by 4: $20 = a$

8. **E** The original function is a line containing the points $(0, 6)$ and $(4, 0)$. Notice that the slope of the line (*rise/run*) or $(y_2 - y_1)/(x_2 - x_1)$.) is $(0 - 6)/(4 - 0) = -6/4 = -3/2$. If the function is multiplied by -2, the slope is also multiplied by -2, and $(-3/2)(-2) = 3$.

9. **18** The number that is 50% greater than x is $(x + .5x) = 1.5x$. If $x + 9$ is 50% greater than x,

$$x + 9 = 1.5x$$

Subtract x: $9 = .5x$
Multiply by 2: $18 = x$

10. **75** Since 60 seconds = 1 minute, there are $5(60) = 300$ seconds in 5 minutes. Recall the basic rate formula: *work = rate × time*.

$$\frac{5 \text{ pages}}{20 \text{ seconds}} \times 300 \text{ seconds} = \frac{1500}{20} \text{ pages} = 75 \text{ pages}$$

11. **20**

5 is $x\%$ of 15

Translate: $5 = x\%(15)$
Multiply by 4: $20 = x\%(60)$

12. **140** Since the measures of the four angles in a quadrilateral must have a sum of 360°, and the ratio of these angles is 2:3:6:7, then

$$2x + 3x + 6x + 7x = 360$$

Simplify: $18x = 360$
Divide by 18: $x = 20$

Therefore the four angles have measures of $2(20) = 40°$, $3(20) = 60°$, $6(20) = 120°$, and $7(20) = 140°$.

13. **1/25 or .04** You can approach this question numerically or algebraically. To approach it numerically, choose simple values for a, b, and c that satisfy the conditions. For instance, if you choose $c = 100$, then since b is 1/10 of c, $b = (1/10)(100) = 10$, and since a is 2/5 of b, $a = (2/5)(10) = 4$. Therefore, $a/c = 4/100 = 1/25$ or .04. To approach it algebraically, notice that you can express both a and c in terms of b.

Since a is 2/5 of b, $a = (2/5)b$, and since b is 1/10 of c, $c = 10b$. Therefore

$$\frac{a}{c} = \frac{\frac{2}{5}b}{10b} = \frac{\frac{2}{5}}{10} = \frac{2}{50} = \frac{1}{25} = .04$$

---

14. **48** Anytime a geometry question does not include a diagram, draw one. You are told that a triangle and a rectangle share the same base, and that the triangle has an area 6 times the area of the rectangle. Therefore, your diagram should look something like this:

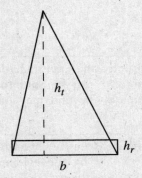

It should be pretty clear that the height of the triangle must be much greater than the height of the rectangle in order for the area of the triangle to be 6 times as great. To be more precise, set up an equation using the formulas for the area of a rectangle and the area of a triangle.

The triangle area is 6 times the rectangle area.

Translate:	$(bh_t)/2 = 6bh_r$
Multiply by 2:	$bh_t = 12bh_r$
Divide by b:	$h_t = 12h_r$
Substitute $h_r = 4$:	$h_t = 12(4) = 48$

---

15. **106** The median of a set of numbers is the value of the "middle" number. If the median of a set of 5 integers is 10, and if the greatest number is 5 times the least number, then the set of integers, listed in increasing order, can be expressed as

$$n, p, 10, r, 5n$$

Since n and p are different integers, and since they must be less than 10, the greatest values they can have are 8 and 9, respectively. This means that the greatest integer in the set is 5(8) = 40. So now the set is

$$8, 9, 10, r, 40$$

In order to maximize the sum, r must be chosen to be as large as possible, but since it must be an integer less than 40, its greatest possible value is 39. The greatest possible sum of these numbers, then, is $8 + 9 + 10 + 39 + 40 = 106$.

---

16. **108** Recall the relationships among the sides of a 30°–60°–90° triangle, which is always given in

the reference information at the beginning of each math section of the SAT. If you apply this relationship to the diagram, you can determine the length of each side. Write these values into the diagram as shown here:

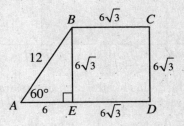

The area of the square is therefore $(6\sqrt{3})(6\sqrt{3}) = 36 \times 3 = 108$.

---

17. **16/3 or 5.33** Call the nth term of this sequence a_n. If each term after the first is equal to the previous term times k, then the first five terms can be expressed as

$$a_1, a_2 = ka_1, a_3 = k^2a_1, a_4 = k^3a_1, a_5 = k^4a_1$$

Since the 3rd term is 12 and the 5th term is 27, $k^2a_1 = 12$ and $k^4a_1 = 27$. You can divide these two equations to solve for k:

$$\frac{k^4 a_1}{k^2 a_1} = \frac{27}{12}$$

Simplify:

$$k^2 = \frac{9}{4}$$

Take the square root:

$$k = \frac{3}{2}$$

Substituting this value into the equation for the third term, you can solve for the first term:

$$k^2 a_1 = \left(\frac{3}{2}\right)^2 a_1 = 12$$

Simplify:

$$\frac{9}{4}a_1 = 12$$

Multiply by 4/9:

$$a_1 = 16/3 = 5.33$$

---

18. **5/6 or .833** Since the question provides information about the areas of the rectangle and the triangle, and since the formulas for these areas involve the base and height of each, it is best to start by examining these lengths. Notice that the rectangle has base b and height c, and the triangle

has base *b–a* and height *c*. Write these into the diagram:

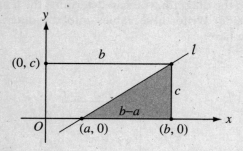

Recall the formulas for the area of a triangle and the area of a rectangle. Since the area of the shaded triangle is $\frac{2}{5}$ the area of the rectangle,

$$\frac{1}{2}(b-a)c = \frac{2}{5}bc$$

To simplify, multiply by 10:	$5(b-a)c = 4bc$
To simplify, divide by *c*:	$5(b-a) = 4b$
Distribute:	$5b - 5a = 4b$
Subtract 4*b*:	$b - 5a = 0$
Add 5*a*:	$b = 5a$
Recall that you are given the fact that	$2b = 3c$
Substitue *b* = 5*a*:	$2(5a) = 3c$
Simplify:	$10a = 3c$
Divide by 3:	$(10/3)a = c$

Now recall that you are trying to find the slope of the line, which is *rise/run = c/(b – a)*.

$$\frac{c}{b-a}$$

Substitute $c = (10/3)a$ and $b = 5a$:

$$\frac{\frac{10}{3}a}{(5a-a)} = \frac{\frac{10}{3}a}{4a} = \frac{10}{3} \times \frac{1}{4} = \frac{10}{12} = \frac{5}{6} = .833$$

Whew!
Obviously, a numerical approach would likely be easier here. Since you are told that $2b = 3c$, it is a good idea to start by choosing simple values for *b* and *c* that work in this equation, like *b* = 6 and *c* = 4. Of course, *a* is still an unknown, but one unknown is better than three! Write this information into the diagram:

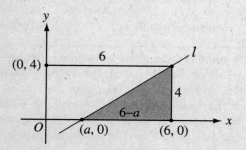

Since the area of the shaded triangle is $\frac{2}{5}$ the area of the rectangle,

$$\frac{1}{2}(6-a)4 = \frac{2}{5}(4)(6)$$

Simplify:	$12 - 2a = 9.6$
Subtract 9.6:	$2.4 - 2a = 0$
Add 2*a*:	$2.4 = 2a$
Divide by 2:	$1.2 = a$

Therefore the base of the triangle is 6 – 1.2 = 4.8, and the slope of the line is 4/4.8 = .833 = 5/6.

Section 6

1. **D** A philosophy that *never achiev[es] a clear and consistent form* can be said to be *nebulous* (vague). *indisputable* = beyond question; *homogenous* = uniform

2. **B** This sentence is somewhat ambiguous. Either she was *disappointed* by the evidence because it did not *support* her theory, or she *was pleased with* the evidence because it did not *contradict* her theory. The only choice that fits either of these interpretations is (B). *refute* = disprove; *substantiate* = provide substantial evidence for; *chasten* = correct by punishment; *bolstered* = supported

3. **A** An animal that travels so far in a given year is certainly *itinerant* (wandering from place to place). *indigenous* = native to a particular region; *subdued* = calm; *nocturnal* = night-active; *arboreal* = pertaining to trees

4. **E** Since Carlos believes that politicians are motivated by *selfish impulses*, he is *cynical about* their motives. He is so cynical that he doubts the motivation of even the politicians' most seemingly *altruistic* (selfless) initiatives. *skeptical* = inclined to doubting; *contemptible* = worthy of scorn; *sanguine* = cheerfully optimistic; *magnanimous* = generous; *disparaging* = criticizing; *callous* = emotionally hardened; *immaterial* = irrelevant; *cynical* = inclined to believe the worst about human motives

5. **A** The first word is clearly an adjective describing a *good literary agent*. Without the quality that this describes, the agent would think that some writing was *original and competent* when in fact it was not. This quality, then, must be *discernment* (the ability to distinguish good from bad), and writing that is not *original* is *derivative* (deriving from clichéd sources or formulas). *gauche* = socially

awkward; sublime = majestic; *obstinate* = stubborn; *proficient* = skilled; *diligent* = hard-working; *servile* = acting like a servant; *pedestrian* = ordinary

6. **C** This passage describes how *radiological methods* are used to *deduce the age of mineral samples* (lines 1–2). Therefore it is explaining a scientific technique.

7. **D** The passage states that *one problematic aspect of this dating method is that some of the stable element may have already been present when the mineral was formed, and therefore was not the result of radioactive decay* (lines 11–15). In other words, the technique is less reliable when the rock originally contained samples of the element into which the radioactive element will decay.

8. **C** In saying that *his lot may be heart-rending,* the author is saying that his *fate* may inspire pity.

9. **B** The paragraph is making the point that human beings, even tragic heroes, as depicted by Shakespeare, are *not contemptible* (line 14). The passage suggests that *cynics* are those who think otherwise about humanity, but who would be dissuaded from this belief by reading Shakespeare's tragedies.

10. **A** The paragraph conveys a clear tone of *reflective anticipation* by describing the *breathless pause at the threshold of a long passage* (lines 9–10) and the *appointed task of both our existences to be carried out* (lines 11–13).

11. **E** The narrator states *that there must have been some glare* (line 16) because it took him a while to notice *something which did away with the solemnity of perfect solitude* (lines 21–22), which turned out to be a ship in the distance. Therefore, the *glare* is mentioned to highlight the fact that the narrator did not see the ship's masthead immediately.

12. **D** The passage states that *in consequence of certain events ... I had been appointed to the command only a fortnight before* (lines 54–57). In other words, these events led to his being chosen as captain.

13. **D** The narrator says that *if all the truth must be told, I was somewhat of a stranger to myself ... I wondered how far I should turn out faithful to that ideal conception of one's own personality every man sets up for himself secretly* (lines 64–74). In other words, he was unsure if he was up to the task ahead of him, and wondered if he should *remain faithful* to his *ideal*

conception that he is a capable leader. He is not apprehensive about the ship, but rather about his own abilities.

14. **C** In saying that the chief mate *was trying to evolve a theory of the anchored ship*, the narrator means that he was trying to *generate* a theory to explain why the ship was there.

15. **E** The final paragraph characterizes the chief mate as being *meticulously thoughtful* by stating that *his dominant trait was to take all things into earnest consideration* (lines 79–80). The paragraph does not suggest at all that the chief mate was *intimidating, erudite* (well–read), *emotionally sensitive* or *dull-witted.*

16. **A** In saying that the *why and wherefore* (lines 85–86) of a scorpion *had exercised [the chief mate] infinitely* (lines 91–92), the narrator is continuing his discussion of the chief mate's need to *account to himself for practically everything that came in his* way (lines 82–83). Clearly, the chief mate had a difficult time explaining the scorpion because *the [mysterious] ship ... was more easily accounted for.* Therefore, the words *exercised* is being used to mean *perplexed.*

17. **C** The passage as a whole is concerned with discussing the ability of human beings to acquire language. Although it does state that *the scientific study of language acquisition began around the same time as the birth of cognitive science, in the late 1950s,* and is therefore a relatively new discipline, the passage as a whole is not concerned with the *history* of that discipline. The passage does not spend much time comparing species except to make the brief and obvious comments that *all normal humans speak, no nonhuman animal does* (lines 6–7) and that *all humans talk but no house pets or house plants do, no matter how pampered* (lines 58–59). The passage also clearly does not provide any *biographical sketches* or *refutations of an experimental method.*

18. **E** The phrase *these data* refers to *the facts of language structure* (line 12) which indicate *a system of extraordinary complexity.* This cannot refer to the structures inside the human brain, because these structures are not revealed *every time we speak* (line 10). These *data* therefore pertain to the intricacy of the expression of human language.

19. **B** The passage states that *it is not surprising that children's acquisition of language has received so much attention* (lines 19–21) because *anyone with strong views about the human mind would like to*

show that children's first few steps are steps in the right direction (lines 22–24). In other words, language theorists focus on language acquisition more than later language development.

20. **B** The passage states that *babies can think before they can talk* (line 39) as a way of refuting the assertion that *language acquisition [is equivalent to] learning to think* (lines 35–36). Therefore, the point of this statement is that verbal skill is not necessary to cognition (thinking).

21. **B** The passage states that *language acquisition might be our best hope of finding out how heredity and environment interact* (lines 68–70) in the development of human cognitive abilities.

22. **C** In the context of this discussion, *a theory that posits too much innate structure* (line 79) refers to a theory of language development that suggests that the human brain is born with so much "hard-wiring" that it can only learn a particular language. Therefore, the *structure* that this sentence refers to is the innate structure cognitive machinery of the human brain.

23. **A** The passage states that *natural science, social science, and philosophy had come to a virtual consensus* (lines 99–100) about whether language ability is learned or innate. In other words, they agreed on a single theory of language acquisition.

24. **C** The claim that *language must be learned; it cannot be a module; and thinking must be a form of verbal behavior* (lines 105–107) is attributed to those philosophers and other academics *in the late 1950s* (lines 94–95) who *had come to a virtual consensus* (line 100) about how language was acquired. Noam Chomsky, most modern cognitive scientists, and most modern linguists believe that the human brain is born with innate language-learning structures.

Section 7

1. **C** The simplest way to approach this question is to just approximate the value of the coordinates and add them, using your calculator if you need to. Point *J* seems to be around –1.8, and point *K* seems to be around 2.2. Their sum is –1.8 + 2.2 = .4, which is between 0 and 1.

2. **D** Notice that the expression that you are given and the expression you are asked to evaluate have a very simple relationship to one another: the first is 3 times the second.

	$6x + 9y = 8$
Divide by 3:	$2x + 3y = 8/3$

3. **E** If Glenna gave one pencil each to 21 students and had 9 left over, she must have had 30 pencils to start with. Since she had three boxes of pencils, each one must have contained $30 \div 3 = 10$ pencils.

4. **A** One efficient way to approach this question is just to find the least common multiple of 12 and 20. Since the greatest common factor of 12 and 20 is 4, the least common multiple is $12 \times 20 \div 4 = 60$. (Notice that 60 is 12×5 and also 20×3.) Notice that the only integer among the choices that is a factor of 60 is (A) 15.

5. **B** The container is only 3/4 filled when it contains 12 liters. Therefore 12 must be 3/4 of its total volume.

$$\frac{3}{4}x = 12$$

Multiply by 4/3:	$\left(\frac{4}{3}\right)\frac{3}{4}x = \left(\frac{4}{3}\right)12$
Simplify:	$x = 16$

6. **D** Profit, *P*, is equal to
$$R(x) - E(x) = (12x) - (3x + 12) = 12x - 3x - 12$$
$$= 9x - 12$$

7. **B** You can approach this question numerically or algebraically. To solve it numerically, simply pick simple values for *x*, *y*, and *m*. Since *m* must be the average of *x* and *y*, a good choice is $x = 3$, $y = 5$, and $m = 4$. Next find the average of *x*, *y*, and 2*m*: $(3 + 5 + 2(4))/3 = 16/3$. Now just plug these values into the choices and eliminate those that don't equal 16/3. Clearly, the only one that works is (B).
You can also take an algebraic approach. If the average of *x* and *y* is *m*, then

	$\dfrac{x+y}{2} = m$
Multiply by 2:	$x + y = 2m$
Express the average of *x*, *y* and *m*	$\dfrac{x+y+2m}{3}$
Substitute $x + y = 2m$:	$\dfrac{2m+2m}{3}$
Simplify:	$\dfrac{4m}{3}$

8. D The most efficient way to solve this is to use the external angle theorem, which states that the measure of an external angle in a triangle is equal to the sum of the two "remote interior" angles.

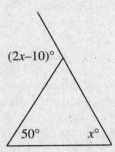

Therefore $2x - 10 = x + 50$
Subtract x: $x - 10 = 50$
Add 10: $x = 60$

9. E Simply choose values for a and b that satisfy the given conditions, and evaluate $a \blacklozenge b$ from the given equation. Notice that $a = -1/2$ and $b = 1/2$ satisfy the conditions.

$$a \blacklozenge b = 2 - ab$$
Substitute $a = -1/2$ and $b = 1/2$:
$$(-1/2) \blacklozenge (1/2) = 2 - (-1/2)(1/2)$$
Simplify: $= 2 + 1/4 = 2.25$
Since this value is between 2 and 3, the answer is (E).

10. D Begin by drawing a diagonal of the rectangle. It should be clear that this is also a diameter of the circle.

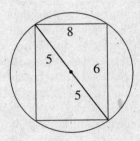

Since the area of the circle is 25π, $\pi r^2 = 25\pi$, and so $r = 5$. This means that the diameter $= 2r = 2(5) = 10$. The width of the rectangle now can be found with the Pythagorean Theorem, or simply by noticing that the rectangle consists of two 6–8–10 right triangles.

$$x^2 + 6^2 = 10^2$$
Simplify: $x^2 + 36 = 100$
Subtract 36: $x^2 = 64$
Take the square root: $x = 8$
Therefore the area of the rectangle is $(6)(8) = 48$.

11. B
$$2x + y = 8$$
Subtract $2x$: $y = -2x + 8$
Since this is in slope-intercept form, it should be clear that the slope of this line is –2. Recall that lines that are perpendicular in the x–y plane have slopes that are opposite reciprocals. The opposite reciprocal of –2 is 1/2. Therefore the line that goes through the origin and is perpendicular to the original line is $y = (1/2)x$. Notice that all of the coordinate pairs in the choices satisfy this equation with the exception of (B) (–1, 1),

12. A You can choose simple values for a and b and solve this problem numerically, or you can simply translate the expression $a\%$ of $5b$. Recall that % simply means *divided by 100* and *of* means *times*. Therefore $a\%$ of $5b$ is equivalent to $(a/100) = 5ab/100 = ab/20$.

13. D

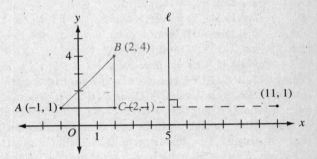

Since the question only asks about the reflection of point A, it is best to try to ignore the other points. A point and its reflection over a line are an equal distance from the line but on the opposite side of the line. Also, the line is the perpendicular bisector of the segment joining the point and its reflection. Since point A is $5 - (-1) = 6$ units away from the line, so its reflection must also be 6 units away from the line, and therefore has an x-coordinate of $5 + 6 = 11$. Since the reflected point must have the same y-coordinate as the original point, it has coordinates (11, 1).

14. C Trying to list all of these integers is too cumber-some a task. The key to simplifying the problem is to notice that each of the three digits can be chosen randomly from a set of five digits: 1, 3, 5, 7, and 9. Since the three digits can be chosen independently, the total number of such three-digit integers is $5 \times 5 \times 5 = 125$.

15. B Like so many problems, this can be attacked either numerically or algebraically, or some combination of the two. As usual, the algebraic approach is simpler but requires more abstract thinking. To take the logical-algebraic approach, you must know the "parity" (odd-even) rules and how to factor polynomials. First notice that each quadratic in the choices is factorable:

(A) $k^2 - 4 = (k - 2)(k + 2)$
(B) $k^2 + 4k - 5 = (k - 1)(k + 5)$
(C) $k^2 + 5k + 6 = (k + 2)(k + 3)$
(D) $k^2 + 3k - 10 = (k - 2)(k + 5)$
(E) $k^2 + k - 20 = (k - 4)(k + 5)$

Next, recall the basic parity rules:

odd × odd = odd
odd × even = even
even × even = even
odd + odd = even
odd + even = odd
even + even = even

Applying these rules to the factors shows that (B) is the only choice that *always* produces the product of two even integers. If k is odd, then

(A) $(k - 2)(k + 2)$ = odd × odd
(B) $(k - 1)(k + 5)$ = even × even
(C) $(k + 2)(k + 3)$ = odd × even
(D) $(k - 2)(k + 5)$ = odd × even
(E) $(k - 4)(k + 5)$ = odd × even

Clearly, choice (B) represents the product of 2 even integers. Since choices (C), (D) and (E) also produce even integers, it is *possible* that these numbers can be expressed as the product of two even integers, but not *always*. For instance, if $k = 5$, then choice (C) gives $(7)(8) = 56$, which *can* be expressed as the product of two even integers: $2 \times 28 = 56$. However, if $k = 7$, then (C) gives $(9)(10) = 90$, which *cannot* be expressed as the product of two even integers. On the other hand, choice (B) can *always* be expressed as the product of two even integers.

---

16. **A** The graph of the function $f(x) = x^2 - k$ is symmetric to the y-axis. Therefore, points A and B are the same distance from the y-axis. Since $AB = 6$, each point must be 3 units from the y-axis. Since the area of rectangle $ABCD$ is 20, you can calculate the height of the rectangle.

$$\text{Area} = 20 = base \times height = 6h$$
Divide by 6: $10/3 = h$
Be sure to write this information on the diagram.

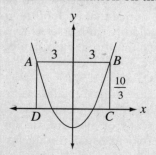

Point B, which has coordinates (3, 10/3), is on the parabola, so it must satisfy the equation $y = x^2 - k$

Substitute $y = 10/3$ and $x = 3$: $10/3 = 3^2 - k$
Subtract 9: $10/3 - 9 = -k$
Simplify: $-17/3 = -k$
Multiply by –1: $17/3 = k$

Section 8

---

1. **C** The sentence indicates that Gena believes that certain people *deserve the opportunity to return to society as productive citizens*. This suggests that these people were not part of society and are perhaps not always regarded as productive citizens. Such people were perhaps *incarcerated* (imprisoned) or *exiled*. One who believes that these people deserve the opportunity to return to society as productive citizens is an advocate of *rehabilitation* or *reform*. *revered* = held in high esteem; *perseverance* = steadfast in adhering to a course of action; *championed* = fought for.

---

2. **B** *Sweating and shivering* are examples of *physiological* (pertaining to the body) reactions. The contrasting conjunction *but* indicates a contrast between ideas; therefore, quinine must have had the opposite effect to *producing* those reactions; it must have *alleviated* them. *assuage* = to soothe; *ameliorate* = to make a bad situation better; *circumstantial* = incidental; *exacerbate* = make worse; *premeditated* = planned in advance; *rebuffed* = bluntly refused; *communicable* = contagious.

---

3. **C** His friends believe that Yuri was being too submissive; that is, they accused him of *complaisant* (cheerfully submissive) behavior. *headstrong* = adamant; *truculent* = disposed to fighting; *tactless* = lacking sensitivity.

---

4. **A** Efforts that *infuse the community with much–needed revenue* are clearly intended to *revive* (bring back to life) the economy, and the construction of the arts center would *facilitate* (help) such an effort. *debilitate* = to weaken; *expedite* = to help along, to make happen more quickly or easily; *reform* = improve; *initiate* = start; *table* = postpone consideration of; *preempt* = to take the place of; *subsidize* = to support financially.

---

5. **B** If Bennett *extoll[ed] the virtues of unencumbered* (free) *commerce*, then he is *a stalwart* (strong supporter) of free trade. *antagonist* = enemy; *caviler* = petty complainer; *diviner* = one who methodically foretells the future; *skeptic* = one inclined to doubting.

6. A *Altruism* is selflessness. If Federica *expressed doubt* about its existence, she must believe that people are basically selfish. Therefore she would believe that one would only make a sacrifice if he or she expects it to be *requited* (repaid). *repudiated* = rejected as invalid; *portended* = predicted; *rescinded* = made void; *expropriated* = stolen.

7. B Throughout the passage, the cultural phenomenon of Bohemianism is discussed. Although the first paragraph gives one definition of Bohemia as *a land-locked country in central Europe* (lines 1–2), the second paragraph makes it clear that Bohemia is more of a cultural phenomenon—a *country of the mind* (line 8). The passage then goes on to define the *basic elements* (line 41) of this phenomenon. Since one characterization of the phenomenon indicates that *every country has its Bohemians* (lines 90–91), it clearly is not discussing just one particular region.

8. A The *notion* referred to in line 17 is the idea that Bohemia was *the homeland of the gypsies* (line 17). The passage then states that this notion *ignored* (line 18) a critical fact, and is therefore mistaken. The passage does not suggest that this particular notion is bigoted, is a means of producing or inspiration for art, or is a celebration of a lifestyle.

9. C The author refers to *the "Egyptian" origin of "gypsy"* (lines 18–19) to make the point that since the word *gypsy* derives from the word *Egyptian*, gypsies likely originated in Egypt rather than Bohemia. Thus the word *Egyptian* is the source of the term *gypsy*.

10. C The passage states that, with the staging and publication of Murger's work, *the public's appetite had been whetted and a popular cult of the gypsy-artist was underway* (lines 35–37), that is, Murger's work inspired the popular fascination with the Bohemian lifestyle.

11. C Since this sentence concludes a paragraph discussing the origins of the public fascination with the Bohemian lifestyle, the statement that Murger's volume *became a textbook for the artistic life throughout the late nineteenth and early twentieth centuries* indicates that it sustained interest in that lifestyle for many decades.

12. D The passage states that Murger was a *Bohemian of the second generation* (line 79) because *he did not invent Bohemianism* (line 75) and indeed *most of [the] ingredients [of Bohemianism] had been in existence in Paris for at least two decades before he started writing* (lines 76–78). As a *malnourished Parisian poet* (line 26), Murger certainly participated

in the Bohemian lifestyle as it is described throughout the passage.

13. C In saying that the artists were *the elect of the spirit, touched with the divine power of imagination* (lines 49–51), the author characterizes Bohemians as being *divinely selected*.

14. E *The people of no imagination* (line 56) refers to the *commercial middle classes* (line 52).

15. E The Bohemians described by Jules Claretie *do not have the influence over the rest of the nation which they do in France—thanks to that poisonous element in the French character which is known as la blague—or cynicism* (lines 91–95). In other words, it is a *poisonous element* that allows the Bohemians to have influence in France, hence he believes that their influence is detrimental to French society. Henry Murger, on the other hand, characterizes Bohemians as *living the gypsy life of being an artist and belonging to a creative community* (lines 68–70).

16. B Challamel's quotation does characterize the Bohemians' affectation (*affecting the most profound disdain*, lines 98–99), iconoclasm (*breaking with the customs of polite society*, lines 104–105), arrogance (*believing, in short, that everything is permissible to men of intelligence*, lines 105–107), and irresponsibility (*debauchery and immorality*, line 111), but it does not mention violence.

17. C The passage states that Houssaye *had generously befriended Bohemian poets* (lines 123–124) but *was far from blind: he was well aware that Bohemia included many impostors* (lines 125–127). In other words, he did not have unquestioning trust in all Bohemians.

18. B Because he *generously befriended* many Bohemians, and yet said that he did not *believe in the good faith of the literary Bohemian* (lines 127–128), his attitude is best described as *ambivalent* (having conflicting feelings).

19. A Houssaye says that *the real Bohemian is the one who has no communication with the public* (lines 132–134), and is therefore *aloof*.

Section 9

1. C The subject of this sentence is *way* and the verb is the linking verb *is*. What follows the verb, then, must be a predicate adjective describing the *way*, or a predicate noun that is equivalent to the *way*.

The original sentence is grammatically incorrect because, rather than providing an adjective phrase or noun phrase, it provides a prepositional phrase that does not logically modify the subject. Choices (B) and (D) commit the same error. Choices (C) and (E) avoid this problem, because they both follow the verb with an infinitive, but only the infinitive in (C), *to provide*, is logically equivalent to *way*.

---

2. **E** The sentence describes a choice, and so should use parallelism in phrasing those choices. It must also use the standard idiomatic form *between A and B*. The first option is *currying favor*, a gerund phrase. To maintain parallel structure, the second option should also be a gerund phrase. The only option which uses parallel phrase and correct idiom is (E).

---

3. **D** In the original sentence, the subjunctive verb *were* is illogical, because the subjunctive mood suggests that the order is hypothetical or counter to fact. The rest of the sentence, particularly the indicative main verb *are*, suggests that the sentence is describing a real situation. Choice (D) corrects this error, and leaves the rest of the phrasing, which is correct, intact. Choice (B) is also incorrectly subjunctive; choice (C) uses the unidiomatic phrase *for beginning*; and (E) omits the verb in the second clause.

---

4. **E** The underlined phrase in the original sentence does not logically modify either the subject or verb of the main clause: notice that it makes no sense to say either that *the advisor* is *with so many available* or that *the taking* is *with so many available*. Clearly the sentence is trying to suggest that *there are so many courses available*. Choices (C) and (D) are likewise illogical modifiers. Choice (B) uses the non-standard idiom *being that*. Choice (E) corrects the problem most effectively, using the conjunction *because* to indicate a reason.

---

5. **A** The sentence is correct as written.

---

6. **D** The verb *acknowledge* is a transitive verb, which means that it requires a logical object. The object in the original sentence, *controlled studies to be*, is not logical. What is being acknowledged? The fact *that controlled studies are most effective*. Therefore the best answer is (D).

---

7. **A** The sentence is correct as written. Notice that the definite pronoun *they* refers to the plural noun *chips*, and that choices (B) and (E) incorrectly use a singular pronoun. The original phrasing is preferable to choices (C) and (D) because it provides the most parallel structure. Notice that

the adjectives *relatively large and expensive to manufacture* parallels the structure of *far smaller and more affordable*, and that the two clauses have the most similar structure overall in (A).

---

8. **C** The original sentence is not parallel. Since the sentence contrasts something to *attacking*, so it should be also phrased as a gerund: *ignoring*. Although choices (B) and (D) also use the gerund *ignoring*, they both insert extra words that violate the parallel structure.

---

9. **E** The sentence must be logical and use parallel form. The original sentence is redundancy because the underlined phrase includes *let them*, which needlessly repeats the idea expressed in *will allow*. Choices (B) and (D) are not parallel, and (C) is not idiomatic. The only choice that is both logical and parallel is (E).

---

10. **B** Since the sentence discusses a possible situation about which the director is concerned, the subjunctive mood is required for the verb in the underlined clause. Choices (B), (C) and (E) use the subjunctive auxiliary *would*, but (C) is illogical and (E) is awkward and wordy.

---

11. **A** The original phrasing is the best.

---

12. **D** In the original phrasing, *him being* is an awkward and non-standard phrase. Likewise, choices (B), (C) and (E) include non-standard or illogical phrases. Clearly, the sentence is providing a reason for a situation, and so the word *because* is logically appropriate.

---

13. **E** A sentence must remain grammatically and logically sound when any interrupting phrase is removed. The original sentence is not grammatically sound because the phrase *as restrictive than* is not idiomatic. Choices (C) and (D) are likewise not idiomatic when the interrupter is removed, and choice (B) is not idiomatic because the comparative adjective *more* requires the word *than*.

---

14. **D** The subject of the sentence is the singular *revenue*, and so the verb *are* does not agree in number with its subject. Second, the comparison in the sentence is illogical because it compares the *revenue* generated by three drug therapies to the *newest drug*, rather than the revenue it generates. Third, the pronoun *their* does not agree in number with the singular antecedent *company*. The only choice that fixes all three problems is (D).

PRACTICE TEST 2

ANSWER SHEET

Last Name: _____   First Name: _____

Date: _____   Testing Location: _____

Directions for Test

- Remove these answer sheets from the book and use them to record your answers to this test.
- This test will require 3 hours and 20 minutes to complete. Take this test in one sitting.
- The time allotment for each section is written clearly at the beginning of each section. This test contains six 25-minute sections, two 20-minute sections, and one 10-minute section.
- This test is 25 minutes shorter than the actual SAT, which will include a 25-minute "experimental" section that does not count toward your score. That section has been omitted from this test.
- You may take one short break during the test, of no more than 10 minutes in length.
- You may only work on one section at any given time.
- You must stop ALL work on a section when time is called.
- If you finish a section before the time has elapsed, check your work on that section. You may NOT work on any other section.
- Do not waste time on questions that seem too difficult for you.
- Use the test book for scratchwork, but you will receive credit only for answers that are marked on the answer sheets.
- You will receive one point for every correct answer.
- You will receive no points for an omitted question.
- For each wrong answer on any multiple-choice question, your score will be reduced by ¼ point.
- For each wrong answer on any numerical "grid-in" question, you will receive no deduction.

SECTION 2

1. Ⓐ Ⓑ Ⓒ Ⓓ Ⓔ
2. Ⓐ Ⓑ Ⓒ Ⓓ Ⓔ
3. Ⓐ Ⓑ Ⓒ Ⓓ Ⓔ
4. Ⓐ Ⓑ Ⓒ Ⓓ Ⓔ
5. Ⓐ Ⓑ Ⓒ Ⓓ Ⓔ
6. Ⓐ Ⓑ Ⓒ Ⓓ Ⓔ
7. Ⓐ Ⓑ Ⓒ Ⓓ Ⓔ
8. Ⓐ Ⓑ Ⓒ Ⓓ Ⓔ
9. Ⓐ Ⓑ Ⓒ Ⓓ Ⓔ
10. Ⓐ Ⓑ Ⓒ Ⓓ Ⓔ
11. Ⓐ Ⓑ Ⓒ Ⓓ Ⓔ
12. Ⓐ Ⓑ Ⓒ Ⓓ Ⓔ
13. Ⓐ Ⓑ Ⓒ Ⓓ Ⓔ
14. Ⓐ Ⓑ Ⓒ Ⓓ Ⓔ
15. Ⓐ Ⓑ Ⓒ Ⓓ Ⓔ
16. Ⓐ Ⓑ Ⓒ Ⓓ Ⓔ
17. Ⓐ Ⓑ Ⓒ Ⓓ Ⓔ
18. Ⓐ Ⓑ Ⓒ Ⓓ Ⓔ
19. Ⓐ Ⓑ Ⓒ Ⓓ Ⓔ
20. Ⓐ Ⓑ Ⓒ Ⓓ Ⓔ
21. Ⓐ Ⓑ Ⓒ Ⓓ Ⓔ
22. Ⓐ Ⓑ Ⓒ Ⓓ Ⓔ
23. Ⓐ Ⓑ Ⓒ Ⓓ Ⓔ
24. Ⓐ Ⓑ Ⓒ Ⓓ Ⓔ
25. Ⓐ Ⓑ Ⓒ Ⓓ Ⓔ
26. Ⓐ Ⓑ Ⓒ Ⓓ Ⓔ
27. Ⓐ Ⓑ Ⓒ Ⓓ Ⓔ
28. Ⓐ Ⓑ Ⓒ Ⓓ Ⓔ
29. Ⓐ Ⓑ Ⓒ Ⓓ Ⓔ
30. Ⓐ Ⓑ Ⓒ Ⓓ Ⓔ
31. Ⓐ Ⓑ Ⓒ Ⓓ Ⓔ
32. Ⓐ Ⓑ Ⓒ Ⓓ Ⓔ
33. Ⓐ Ⓑ Ⓒ Ⓓ Ⓔ
34. Ⓐ Ⓑ Ⓒ Ⓓ Ⓔ
35. Ⓐ Ⓑ Ⓒ Ⓓ Ⓔ
36. Ⓐ Ⓑ Ⓒ Ⓓ Ⓔ
37. Ⓐ Ⓑ Ⓒ Ⓓ Ⓔ
38. Ⓐ Ⓑ Ⓒ Ⓓ Ⓔ
39. Ⓐ Ⓑ Ⓒ Ⓓ Ⓔ
40. Ⓐ Ⓑ Ⓒ Ⓓ Ⓔ

SECTION 3

1. Ⓐ Ⓑ Ⓒ Ⓓ Ⓔ
2. Ⓐ Ⓑ Ⓒ Ⓓ Ⓔ
3. Ⓐ Ⓑ Ⓒ Ⓓ Ⓔ
4. Ⓐ Ⓑ Ⓒ Ⓓ Ⓔ
5. Ⓐ Ⓑ Ⓒ Ⓓ Ⓔ
6. Ⓐ Ⓑ Ⓒ Ⓓ Ⓔ
7. Ⓐ Ⓑ Ⓒ Ⓓ Ⓔ
8. Ⓐ Ⓑ Ⓒ Ⓓ Ⓔ
9. Ⓐ Ⓑ Ⓒ Ⓓ Ⓔ
10. Ⓐ Ⓑ Ⓒ Ⓓ Ⓔ
11. Ⓐ Ⓑ Ⓒ Ⓓ Ⓔ
12. Ⓐ Ⓑ Ⓒ Ⓓ Ⓔ
13. Ⓐ Ⓑ Ⓒ Ⓓ Ⓔ
14. Ⓐ Ⓑ Ⓒ Ⓓ Ⓔ
15. Ⓐ Ⓑ Ⓒ Ⓓ Ⓔ
16. Ⓐ Ⓑ Ⓒ Ⓓ Ⓔ
17. Ⓐ Ⓑ Ⓒ Ⓓ Ⓔ
18. Ⓐ Ⓑ Ⓒ Ⓓ Ⓔ
19. Ⓐ Ⓑ Ⓒ Ⓓ Ⓔ
20. Ⓐ Ⓑ Ⓒ Ⓓ Ⓔ
21. Ⓐ Ⓑ Ⓒ Ⓓ Ⓔ
22. Ⓐ Ⓑ Ⓒ Ⓓ Ⓔ
23. Ⓐ Ⓑ Ⓒ Ⓓ Ⓔ
24. Ⓐ Ⓑ Ⓒ Ⓓ Ⓔ
25. Ⓐ Ⓑ Ⓒ Ⓓ Ⓔ
26. Ⓐ Ⓑ Ⓒ Ⓓ Ⓔ
27. Ⓐ Ⓑ Ⓒ Ⓓ Ⓔ
28. Ⓐ Ⓑ Ⓒ Ⓓ Ⓔ
29. Ⓐ Ⓑ Ⓒ Ⓓ Ⓔ
30. Ⓐ Ⓑ Ⓒ Ⓓ Ⓔ
31. Ⓐ Ⓑ Ⓒ Ⓓ Ⓔ
32. Ⓐ Ⓑ Ⓒ Ⓓ Ⓔ
33. Ⓐ Ⓑ Ⓒ Ⓓ Ⓔ
34. Ⓐ Ⓑ Ⓒ Ⓓ Ⓔ
35. Ⓐ Ⓑ Ⓒ Ⓓ Ⓔ
36. Ⓐ Ⓑ Ⓒ Ⓓ Ⓔ
37. Ⓐ Ⓑ Ⓒ Ⓓ Ⓔ
38. Ⓐ Ⓑ Ⓒ Ⓓ Ⓔ
39. Ⓐ Ⓑ Ⓒ Ⓓ Ⓔ
40. Ⓐ Ⓑ Ⓒ Ⓓ Ⓔ

ANSWER SHEET

SECTION 4

1. Ⓐ Ⓑ Ⓒ Ⓓ Ⓔ
2. Ⓐ Ⓑ Ⓒ Ⓓ Ⓔ
3. Ⓐ Ⓑ Ⓒ Ⓓ Ⓔ
4. Ⓐ Ⓑ Ⓒ Ⓓ Ⓔ
5. Ⓐ Ⓑ Ⓒ Ⓓ Ⓔ
6. Ⓐ Ⓑ Ⓒ Ⓓ Ⓔ
7. Ⓐ Ⓑ Ⓒ Ⓓ Ⓔ
8. Ⓐ Ⓑ Ⓒ Ⓓ Ⓔ
9. Ⓐ Ⓑ Ⓒ Ⓓ Ⓔ
10. Ⓐ Ⓑ Ⓒ Ⓓ Ⓔ

11. Ⓐ Ⓑ Ⓒ Ⓓ Ⓔ
12. Ⓐ Ⓑ Ⓒ Ⓓ Ⓔ
13. Ⓐ Ⓑ Ⓒ Ⓓ Ⓔ
14. Ⓐ Ⓑ Ⓒ Ⓓ Ⓔ
15. Ⓐ Ⓑ Ⓒ Ⓓ Ⓔ
16. Ⓐ Ⓑ Ⓒ Ⓓ Ⓔ
17. Ⓐ Ⓑ Ⓒ Ⓓ Ⓔ
18. Ⓐ Ⓑ Ⓒ Ⓓ Ⓔ
19. Ⓐ Ⓑ Ⓒ Ⓓ Ⓔ
20. Ⓐ Ⓑ Ⓒ Ⓓ Ⓔ

21. Ⓐ Ⓑ Ⓒ Ⓓ Ⓔ
22. Ⓐ Ⓑ Ⓒ Ⓓ Ⓔ
23. Ⓐ Ⓑ Ⓒ Ⓓ Ⓔ
24. Ⓐ Ⓑ Ⓒ Ⓓ Ⓔ
25. Ⓐ Ⓑ Ⓒ Ⓓ Ⓔ
26. Ⓐ Ⓑ Ⓒ Ⓓ Ⓔ
27. Ⓐ Ⓑ Ⓒ Ⓓ Ⓔ
28. Ⓐ Ⓑ Ⓒ Ⓓ Ⓔ
29. Ⓐ Ⓑ Ⓒ Ⓓ Ⓔ
30. Ⓐ Ⓑ Ⓒ Ⓓ Ⓔ

31. Ⓐ Ⓑ Ⓒ Ⓓ Ⓔ
32. Ⓐ Ⓑ Ⓒ Ⓓ Ⓔ
33. Ⓐ Ⓑ Ⓒ Ⓓ Ⓔ
34. Ⓐ Ⓑ Ⓒ Ⓓ Ⓔ
35. Ⓐ Ⓑ Ⓒ Ⓓ Ⓔ
36. Ⓐ Ⓑ Ⓒ Ⓓ Ⓔ
37. Ⓐ Ⓑ Ⓒ Ⓓ Ⓔ
38. Ⓐ Ⓑ Ⓒ Ⓓ Ⓔ
39. Ⓐ Ⓑ Ⓒ Ⓓ Ⓔ
40. Ⓐ Ⓑ Ⓒ Ⓓ Ⓔ

SECTION 5

1. Ⓐ Ⓑ Ⓒ Ⓓ Ⓔ
2. Ⓐ Ⓑ Ⓒ Ⓓ Ⓔ
3. Ⓐ Ⓑ Ⓒ Ⓓ Ⓔ
4. Ⓐ Ⓑ Ⓒ Ⓓ Ⓔ

5. Ⓐ Ⓑ Ⓒ Ⓓ Ⓔ
6. Ⓐ Ⓑ Ⓒ Ⓓ Ⓔ
7. Ⓐ Ⓑ Ⓒ Ⓓ Ⓔ
8. Ⓐ Ⓑ Ⓒ Ⓓ Ⓔ

9. _grid-in answer box_
10. _grid-in answer box_
11. _grid-in answer box_
12. _grid-in answer box_
13. _grid-in answer box_

14. _grid-in answer box_
15. _grid-in answer box_
16. _grid-in answer box_
17. _grid-in answer box_
18. _grid-in answer box_

ANSWER SHEET

SECTION 6

1. Ⓐ Ⓑ Ⓒ Ⓓ Ⓔ
2. Ⓐ Ⓑ Ⓒ Ⓓ Ⓔ
3. Ⓐ Ⓑ Ⓒ Ⓓ Ⓔ
4. Ⓐ Ⓑ Ⓒ Ⓓ Ⓔ
5. Ⓐ Ⓑ Ⓒ Ⓓ Ⓔ
6. Ⓐ Ⓑ Ⓒ Ⓓ Ⓔ
7. Ⓐ Ⓑ Ⓒ Ⓓ Ⓔ
8. Ⓐ Ⓑ Ⓒ Ⓓ Ⓔ
9. Ⓐ Ⓑ Ⓒ Ⓓ Ⓔ
10. Ⓐ Ⓑ Ⓒ Ⓓ Ⓔ
11. Ⓐ Ⓑ Ⓒ Ⓓ Ⓔ
12. Ⓐ Ⓑ Ⓒ Ⓓ Ⓔ
13. Ⓐ Ⓑ Ⓒ Ⓓ Ⓔ
14. Ⓐ Ⓑ Ⓒ Ⓓ Ⓔ
15. Ⓐ Ⓑ Ⓒ Ⓓ Ⓔ
16. Ⓐ Ⓑ Ⓒ Ⓓ Ⓔ
17. Ⓐ Ⓑ Ⓒ Ⓓ Ⓔ
18. Ⓐ Ⓑ Ⓒ Ⓓ Ⓔ
19. Ⓐ Ⓑ Ⓒ Ⓓ Ⓔ
20. Ⓐ Ⓑ Ⓒ Ⓓ Ⓔ
21. Ⓐ Ⓑ Ⓒ Ⓓ Ⓔ
22. Ⓐ Ⓑ Ⓒ Ⓓ Ⓔ
23. Ⓐ Ⓑ Ⓒ Ⓓ Ⓔ
24. Ⓐ Ⓑ Ⓒ Ⓓ Ⓔ
25. Ⓐ Ⓑ Ⓒ Ⓓ Ⓔ
26. Ⓐ Ⓑ Ⓒ Ⓓ Ⓔ
27. Ⓐ Ⓑ Ⓒ Ⓓ Ⓔ
28. Ⓐ Ⓑ Ⓒ Ⓓ Ⓔ
29. Ⓐ Ⓑ Ⓒ Ⓓ Ⓔ
30. Ⓐ Ⓑ Ⓒ Ⓓ Ⓔ
31. Ⓐ Ⓑ Ⓒ Ⓓ Ⓔ
32. Ⓐ Ⓑ Ⓒ Ⓓ Ⓔ
33. Ⓐ Ⓑ Ⓒ Ⓓ Ⓔ
34. Ⓐ Ⓑ Ⓒ Ⓓ Ⓔ
35. Ⓐ Ⓑ Ⓒ Ⓓ Ⓔ
36. Ⓐ Ⓑ Ⓒ Ⓓ Ⓔ
37. Ⓐ Ⓑ Ⓒ Ⓓ Ⓔ
38. Ⓐ Ⓑ Ⓒ Ⓓ Ⓔ
39. Ⓐ Ⓑ Ⓒ Ⓓ Ⓔ
40. Ⓐ Ⓑ Ⓒ Ⓓ Ⓔ

SECTION 7

1. Ⓐ Ⓑ Ⓒ Ⓓ Ⓔ
2. Ⓐ Ⓑ Ⓒ Ⓓ Ⓔ
3. Ⓐ Ⓑ Ⓒ Ⓓ Ⓔ
4. Ⓐ Ⓑ Ⓒ Ⓓ Ⓔ
5. Ⓐ Ⓑ Ⓒ Ⓓ Ⓔ
6. Ⓐ Ⓑ Ⓒ Ⓓ Ⓔ
7. Ⓐ Ⓑ Ⓒ Ⓓ Ⓔ
8. Ⓐ Ⓑ Ⓒ Ⓓ Ⓔ
9. Ⓐ Ⓑ Ⓒ Ⓓ Ⓔ
10. Ⓐ Ⓑ Ⓒ Ⓓ Ⓔ
11. Ⓐ Ⓑ Ⓒ Ⓓ Ⓔ
12. Ⓐ Ⓑ Ⓒ Ⓓ Ⓔ
13. Ⓐ Ⓑ Ⓒ Ⓓ Ⓔ
14. Ⓐ Ⓑ Ⓒ Ⓓ Ⓔ
15. Ⓐ Ⓑ Ⓒ Ⓓ Ⓔ
16. Ⓐ Ⓑ Ⓒ Ⓓ Ⓔ
17. Ⓐ Ⓑ Ⓒ Ⓓ Ⓔ
18. Ⓐ Ⓑ Ⓒ Ⓓ Ⓔ
19. Ⓐ Ⓑ Ⓒ Ⓓ Ⓔ
20. Ⓐ Ⓑ Ⓒ Ⓓ Ⓔ
21. Ⓐ Ⓑ Ⓒ Ⓓ Ⓔ
22. Ⓐ Ⓑ Ⓒ Ⓓ Ⓔ
23. Ⓐ Ⓑ Ⓒ Ⓓ Ⓔ
24. Ⓐ Ⓑ Ⓒ Ⓓ Ⓔ
25. Ⓐ Ⓑ Ⓒ Ⓓ Ⓔ
26. Ⓐ Ⓑ Ⓒ Ⓓ Ⓔ
27. Ⓐ Ⓑ Ⓒ Ⓓ Ⓔ
28. Ⓐ Ⓑ Ⓒ Ⓓ Ⓔ
29. Ⓐ Ⓑ Ⓒ Ⓓ Ⓔ
30. Ⓐ Ⓑ Ⓒ Ⓓ Ⓔ
31. Ⓐ Ⓑ Ⓒ Ⓓ Ⓔ
32. Ⓐ Ⓑ Ⓒ Ⓓ Ⓔ
33. Ⓐ Ⓑ Ⓒ Ⓓ Ⓔ
34. Ⓐ Ⓑ Ⓒ Ⓓ Ⓔ
35. Ⓐ Ⓑ Ⓒ Ⓓ Ⓔ
36. Ⓐ Ⓑ Ⓒ Ⓓ Ⓔ
37. Ⓐ Ⓑ Ⓒ Ⓓ Ⓔ
38. Ⓐ Ⓑ Ⓒ Ⓓ Ⓔ
39. Ⓐ Ⓑ Ⓒ Ⓓ Ⓔ
40. Ⓐ Ⓑ Ⓒ Ⓓ Ⓔ

SECTION 8

1. Ⓐ Ⓑ Ⓒ Ⓓ Ⓔ
2. Ⓐ Ⓑ Ⓒ Ⓓ Ⓔ
3. Ⓐ Ⓑ Ⓒ Ⓓ Ⓔ
4. Ⓐ Ⓑ Ⓒ Ⓓ Ⓔ
5. Ⓐ Ⓑ Ⓒ Ⓓ Ⓔ
6. Ⓐ Ⓑ Ⓒ Ⓓ Ⓔ
7. Ⓐ Ⓑ Ⓒ Ⓓ Ⓔ
8. Ⓐ Ⓑ Ⓒ Ⓓ Ⓔ
9. Ⓐ Ⓑ Ⓒ Ⓓ Ⓔ
10. Ⓐ Ⓑ Ⓒ Ⓓ Ⓔ
11. Ⓐ Ⓑ Ⓒ Ⓓ Ⓔ
12. Ⓐ Ⓑ Ⓒ Ⓓ Ⓔ
13. Ⓐ Ⓑ Ⓒ Ⓓ Ⓔ
14. Ⓐ Ⓑ Ⓒ Ⓓ Ⓔ
15. Ⓐ Ⓑ Ⓒ Ⓓ Ⓔ
16. Ⓐ Ⓑ Ⓒ Ⓓ Ⓔ
17. Ⓐ Ⓑ Ⓒ Ⓓ Ⓔ
18. Ⓐ Ⓑ Ⓒ Ⓓ Ⓔ
19. Ⓐ Ⓑ Ⓒ Ⓓ Ⓔ
20. Ⓐ Ⓑ Ⓒ Ⓓ Ⓔ
21. Ⓐ Ⓑ Ⓒ Ⓓ Ⓔ
22. Ⓐ Ⓑ Ⓒ Ⓓ Ⓔ
23. Ⓐ Ⓑ Ⓒ Ⓓ Ⓔ
24. Ⓐ Ⓑ Ⓒ Ⓓ Ⓔ
25. Ⓐ Ⓑ Ⓒ Ⓓ Ⓔ
26. Ⓐ Ⓑ Ⓒ Ⓓ Ⓔ
27. Ⓐ Ⓑ Ⓒ Ⓓ Ⓔ
28. Ⓐ Ⓑ Ⓒ Ⓓ Ⓔ
29. Ⓐ Ⓑ Ⓒ Ⓓ Ⓔ
30. Ⓐ Ⓑ Ⓒ Ⓓ Ⓔ
31. Ⓐ Ⓑ Ⓒ Ⓓ Ⓔ
32. Ⓐ Ⓑ Ⓒ Ⓓ Ⓔ
33. Ⓐ Ⓑ Ⓒ Ⓓ Ⓔ
34. Ⓐ Ⓑ Ⓒ Ⓓ Ⓔ
35. Ⓐ Ⓑ Ⓒ Ⓓ Ⓔ
36. Ⓐ Ⓑ Ⓒ Ⓓ Ⓔ
37. Ⓐ Ⓑ Ⓒ Ⓓ Ⓔ
38. Ⓐ Ⓑ Ⓒ Ⓓ Ⓔ
39. Ⓐ Ⓑ Ⓒ Ⓓ Ⓔ
40. Ⓐ Ⓑ Ⓒ Ⓓ Ⓔ

SECTION 9

1. Ⓐ Ⓑ Ⓒ Ⓓ Ⓔ
2. Ⓐ Ⓑ Ⓒ Ⓓ Ⓔ
3. Ⓐ Ⓑ Ⓒ Ⓓ Ⓔ
4. Ⓐ Ⓑ Ⓒ Ⓓ Ⓔ
5. Ⓐ Ⓑ Ⓒ Ⓓ Ⓔ
6. Ⓐ Ⓑ Ⓒ Ⓓ Ⓔ
7. Ⓐ Ⓑ Ⓒ Ⓓ Ⓔ
8. Ⓐ Ⓑ Ⓒ Ⓓ Ⓔ
9. Ⓐ Ⓑ Ⓒ Ⓓ Ⓔ
10. Ⓐ Ⓑ Ⓒ Ⓓ Ⓔ
11. Ⓐ Ⓑ Ⓒ Ⓓ Ⓔ
12. Ⓐ Ⓑ Ⓒ Ⓓ Ⓔ
13. Ⓐ Ⓑ Ⓒ Ⓓ Ⓔ
14. Ⓐ Ⓑ Ⓒ Ⓓ Ⓔ
15. Ⓐ Ⓑ Ⓒ Ⓓ Ⓔ
16. Ⓐ Ⓑ Ⓒ Ⓓ Ⓔ
17. Ⓐ Ⓑ Ⓒ Ⓓ Ⓔ
18. Ⓐ Ⓑ Ⓒ Ⓓ Ⓔ
19. Ⓐ Ⓑ Ⓒ Ⓓ Ⓔ
20. Ⓐ Ⓑ Ⓒ Ⓓ Ⓔ
21. Ⓐ Ⓑ Ⓒ Ⓓ Ⓔ
22. Ⓐ Ⓑ Ⓒ Ⓓ Ⓔ
23. Ⓐ Ⓑ Ⓒ Ⓓ Ⓔ
24. Ⓐ Ⓑ Ⓒ Ⓓ Ⓔ
25. Ⓐ Ⓑ Ⓒ Ⓓ Ⓔ
26. Ⓐ Ⓑ Ⓒ Ⓓ Ⓔ
27. Ⓐ Ⓑ Ⓒ Ⓓ Ⓔ
28. Ⓐ Ⓑ Ⓒ Ⓓ Ⓔ
29. Ⓐ Ⓑ Ⓒ Ⓓ Ⓔ
30. Ⓐ Ⓑ Ⓒ Ⓓ Ⓔ
31. Ⓐ Ⓑ Ⓒ Ⓓ Ⓔ
32. Ⓐ Ⓑ Ⓒ Ⓓ Ⓔ
33. Ⓐ Ⓑ Ⓒ Ⓓ Ⓔ
34. Ⓐ Ⓑ Ⓒ Ⓓ Ⓔ
35. Ⓐ Ⓑ Ⓒ Ⓓ Ⓔ
36. Ⓐ Ⓑ Ⓒ Ⓓ Ⓔ
37. Ⓐ Ⓑ Ⓒ Ⓓ Ⓔ
38. Ⓐ Ⓑ Ⓒ Ⓓ Ⓔ
39. Ⓐ Ⓑ Ⓒ Ⓓ Ⓔ
40. Ⓐ Ⓑ Ⓒ Ⓓ Ⓔ

Section 1

Time—25 minutes

Directions for Writing the Essay

Plan and write an essay that answers the question below. Do NOT write on another topic. An essay on another topic will receive a score of 0.

Two readers will grade your essay based on how well you develop your point of view, organize and explain your ideas, use specific and relevant examples to support your thesis, and use clear and effective language. How well you write is much more important than how much you write, but to cover the topic adequately you should plan to write several paragraphs.

Your essay must be written on separate lined sheets of paper. Keep your handwriting to a reasonable size. Your essay will be read by people who are not familiar with your handwriting, so write legibly.

You may use this sheet for notes and outlining, but these will not be graded as part of your essay.

Consider carefully the issue discussed in the following passage, then write an essay that answers the question posed in the assignment.

> I have learned that success is to be measured not so much by the position that one has reached in life as by the obstacles which one has overcome while trying to succeed.
> —Booker T. Washington

Assignment: Is the struggle endured to achieve success more important than the accomplishment itself? Plan and write an essay in which you develop your point of view on this issue. Support your position with reasoning and examples taken from your reading, studies, experience, or observations.

Write your essay on separate sheets of paper.

Section 2

Time—25 Minutes
20 Questions

2 ▶ Directions for Multiple-Choice Questions

In this section, solve each problem, using any available space on the page for scratchwork. Then decide which is the best of the choices given and fill in the corresponding oval on the answer sheet.

- You may use a calculator on any problem. All numbers used are real numbers.
- Figures are drawn as accurately as possible EXCEPT when it is stated that the figure is not drawn to scale.
- All figures lie in a plane unless otherwise indicated.

Reference Information

   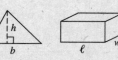

$A = \pi r^2$ $A = \ell w$
$C = 2\pi r$ $A = \frac{1}{2}bh$ $V = \ell wh$ $V = \pi r^2 h$ $c^2 = a^2 + b^2$ Special Right Triangles

The arc of a circle measures 360°.
Every straight angle measures 180°.
The sum of the measures of the angles in a triangle is 180°.

---

1. If $b = 4$ and $c = 7$, what is the value of $3b - 5c$?

(A) −27
(B) −23
(C) 3
(D) 6
(E) 20

2. If the average (arithmetic mean) of 4 and w is equal to the average of 2, 8, and w, what is the value of w?

(A) 2
(B) 4
(C) 6
(D) 8
(E) 10

(figure: coordinate plane with points M(−1, 5), N(4, 5), Q(−3, −2), R(x, −2))

3. In the figure above, the length of *MN* is equal to the length of *QR*. What is the value of *x*?

(A) −3
(B) −1
(C) 2
(D) 5
(E) 6

GO ON TO THE NEXT PAGE ▶▶▶

4 The cost of a highway toll was $0.75 in 2005. The following year the cost of the toll increased to $1.00. By what percent did the toll increase?

(A) 10%
(B) 20%
(C) 25%
(D) 33⅓%
(E) 50%

5 The cost of four oranges is d dollars. At this rate, what is the cost of 40 oranges?

(A) $\dfrac{d}{40}$

(B) $\dfrac{40}{d}$

(C) $10d$

(D) $20d$

(E) $40d$

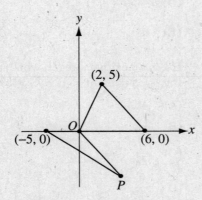

Note: Figure not drawn to scale.

6 If the areas of the two triangles in the figure above are equal, which of the following could be the coordinates of point P?

(A) $(3, -4)$
(B) $(4, -6)$
(C) $(2, -4)$
(D) $(2, -5)$
(E) $(1, -7)$

7 If $a - b = -4$, what is the value of $a^2 - 2ab + b^2$?

(A) −32
(B) −16
(C) 0
(D) 16
(E) 32

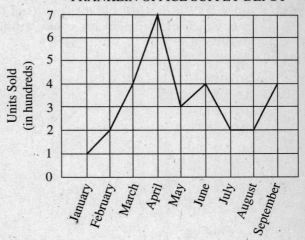

8 Between which two months did the Franklin Office Supply Depot experience the greatest change in the number of units sold?

(A) February to March
(B) March to April
(C) April to May
(D) June to July
(E) August to September

GO ON TO THE NEXT PAGE ▶▶▶

2

9 The ratio of r to s is 3 to 4. The ratio of s to t is 2 to 9. What is the ratio of r to t?

(A)　1 to 3
(B)　1 to 6
(C)　2 to 9
(D)　3 to 10
(E)　4 to 5

10 Points A, B, C, and D lie on a line, in that order. If $CD > BC > AB$ and the length of CD is 6, which of the following could be the length of AD?

(A)　17
(B)　18
(C)　19
(D)　20
(E)　21

x	4	5	6	7
$f(x)$	10	12	14	16

11 The table above gives values of the linear function f for selected values of x. Which of the following functions defines f?

(A)　$f(x) = \dfrac{3}{2}x + 4$

(B)　$f(x) = -\dfrac{2}{3}x - 3$

(C)　$f(x) = 2x + 2$

(D)　$f(x) = 3x - 3$

(E)　$f(x) = 4x - 6$

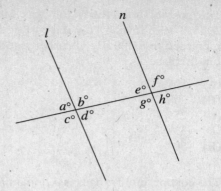

12 In the figure above, if $l \| n$, which of the following is NOT necessarily equal to e?

(A)　a

(B)　$\dfrac{(h+d)}{2}$

(C)　$\dfrac{(a+d)}{2}$

(D)　$\dfrac{(f+h)}{2}$

(E)　d

13 If k is a positive integer, which of the following is equivalent to $(2k^{1/2}k^{1/2})(2(k^{1/2})^{2/3})^{-2}$?

(A)　$4k$

(B)　$2k$

(C)　$\dfrac{1}{2k}$

(D)　$\dfrac{1}{4k}$

(E)　$\dfrac{1}{16k^2}$

14 If t is 40 percent greater than p, and p is 40 percent less than 600, what is the value of $t - p$?

(A)　144
(B)　240
(C)　360
(D)　504
(E)　1008

GO ON TO THE NEXT PAGE ▶▶▶

−2, 4, 8. . .

15 In the sequence above, each term after the second can be found by multiplying the two preceding terms together. For example, the third term is −2 × 4 = −8. How many of the first 139 terms of this sequence are negative?

(A) 46
(B) 70
(C) 74
(D) 92
(E) 93

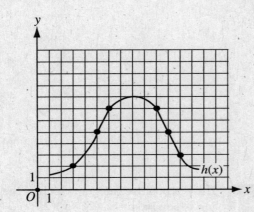

16 In the figure above, if the value of $h(5) = k$, then what is the value of $h(2k)$?

(A) 5
(B) 6
(C) 7
(D) 8
(E) 9

17 In a bag of marbles, $\frac{2}{5}$ of the marbles are red, $\frac{3}{10}$ of the marbles are white, and $\frac{1}{10}$ of the marbles are blue. If the remaining 10 marbles are green, how many marbles are in the bag?

(A) 15
(B) 20
(C) 35
(D) 45
(E) 50

18 If x and y are positive numbers greater than 1, and $\frac{wx}{y+w} = 1$ then $w =$

(A) $\dfrac{x-1}{y-1}$

(B) $\dfrac{y}{x-1}$

(C) $\dfrac{x+1}{y}$

(D) $\dfrac{x-y}{x+y}$

(E) $\dfrac{y}{x+1}$

GO ON TO THE NEXT PAGE ▶▶▶

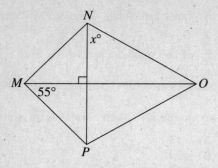

2 ➤

Note: Figure not drawn to scale.

19 In the quadrilateral above, $ON = OM = OP$. If $MN = MP$, then what is the value of x?

(A) 15
(B) 20
(C) 25
(D) 30
(E) 35

20 There are five roads from Wilton to Norwalk and four roads from Norwalk to Darien. If Kristina drives from Wilton to Darien and back, passes through Norwalk in both directions, and does not travel any road twice, how many different routes are possible for the round trip?

(A) 16
(B) 32
(C) 160
(D) 240
(E) 360

STOP

*You may check your work, on this
section only, until time is called.*

Section 3

Time—25 Minutes
35 Questions

Directions for "Improving Sentences" Questions

Each of the sentences below contains one underlined portion. The portion may contain one or more errors in grammar, usage, construction, precision, diction (choice of words), or idiom. Some of the sentences are correct.

Consider the meaning of the original sentence, and choose the answer that best expresses that meaning. If the original sentence is best, choose (A), because it repeats the original phrasing. Choose the phrasing that creates the clearest, most precise and most effective sentence.

EXAMPLE:

The growth of the plant was so dramatic that the children <u>couldn't hardly believe their eyes.</u>

(A) couldn't hardly believe their eyes
(B) would not hardly believe their eyes
(C) could hardly believe their eyes
(D) couldn't nearly believe their eyes
(E) could hardly believe his or her eyes

Example answer: (C)

1 The harmful effects of excessive alcohol intake on the hepatic system <u>is extensively documented by medical studies.</u>

(A) is extensively documented by medical studies
(B) is documented more extensively by medical studies
(C) are extensively documented by medical studies
(D) medical studies are extensively documenting
(E) has documented extensively by medical studies

2 Harper's Conservative Party <u>favors lower taxes, a more decentralized government, and the spending of less money</u> on imports.

(A) favors lower taxes, a more decentralized government, and the spending of less money
(B) has favored lower taxes, more decentralizing government, and spending less money
(C) favors lower taxes, a more decentralized government, and a lesser expenditure.
(D) favoring lower taxes, a more decentralized government, and less money spent
(E) favored lowering taxes, a more decentralized government, and spending less money

3 Exhausted by consecutive years of tropical-cyclone mayhem, <u>many people are asking about future trends, notes Kerry Emanuel, an atmospheric scientist at the Massachusetts Institute of Technology</u>, who focuses on weather and climate in the tropics.

(A) many people are asking about future trends, notes Kerry Emanuel, an atmospheric scientist at the Massachusetts Institute of Technology
(B) an atmospheric scientist at the Massachusetts Institute of Technology, notes Kerry Emanuel, many people are asking about future trends
(C) many people are asking about future trends, an atmospheric scientist notes Kerry Emanuel, at the Massachusetts Institute of Technology
(D) the Massachusetts Institute of Technology, notes Kerry Emanuel, finds that many people are asking about future trends
(E) future trends are a topic that many people are asking about, notes Kerry Emanuel, an atmospheric scientist at the Massachusetts Institute of Technology

4

If asked to name a famous explorer, <u>Christopher Columbus would probably be the person most of us would choose.</u>

(A) Christopher Columbus would probably be the person most of us would choose
(B) most of us would probably choose Christopher Columbus
(C) our choice for the most of us would probably be Christopher Columbus
(D) Christopher Columbus would probably get most of our choices
(E) most of our choices would probably be for Christopher Columbus

5

Located in Manhattan, <u>many sightseers like to visit the Empire State building, a massive skyscraper constructed during the Great Depression</u>.

(A) many sightseers like to visit the Empire State building, a massive skyscraper constructed during the Great Depression
(B) the Empire state building, a massive skyscraper constructed during the Great Depression many sightseers like to visit
(C) and constructed during the Great Depression, many tourists like to visit the Empire State Building
(D) the Empire State Building is a massive skyscraper constructed during the Great Depression, that many sightseers like to visit
(E) a massive skyscraper constructed during the Great Depression, the Empire State Building, is a place that sightseers like to visit

6

<u>The fact that the cancer, which was once thought to be untreatable, has gone into remission is still a mystery to the oncologists.</u>

(A) The fact that the cancer, which was once thought to be untreatable, has gone into remission is still a mystery to the oncologists
(B) Originally thought to be untreatable, the remission of the cancer is still a mystery to the oncologists
(C) The oncologists originally thought the cancer was untreatable and the remission still being a mystery
(D) The remission of the cancer is still a mystery to the oncologists, which originally thought it to be untreatable
(E) Still a mystery to the oncologists, originally thought to be untreatable was the remission of the cancer

7

<u>Being as he is a perfect gentleman</u>, Tommy is well known for his polite behavior even around strangers.

(A) Being as he is a perfect gentleman
(B) Although he is a perfect gentleman
(C) Being a gentleman perfectly
(D) A perfect gentleman
(E) In being a perfect gentleman

8

<u>Having poured down heavily throughout the night, Felisha observed that the rain had leaked into the cellar</u> through the cracked window.

(A) Having poured down heavily throughout the night, Felisha observed that the rain had leaked into the cellar
(B) Felisha observed that the rain, which had poured down heavily throughout the night, had leaked into the cellar
(C) Having poured down heavily throughout the night, the rain was observed by Felisha to have leaked into the cellar
(D) Felisha observed the rain, having poured down heavily throughout the night, had leaked into the cellar
(E) The rain, which poured down heavily throughout the night, leaked into the cellar as it was observed by Felisha

GO ON TO THE NEXT PAGE ▸▸▸

9 Sue Grafton, a mystery writer from Kentucky, is perhaps <u>best known for</u> the alphabet murder series she began writing in the 1980s.

(A) best known for
(B) best known by
(C) better known by
(D) better known for
(E) known better for

10 The validity of IQ tests as accurate measures of human intelligence <u>have been the subject of much debate.</u>

(A) have been the subject of much debate
(B) are often the subject of much debate
(C) has been the subject of much debate
(D) are a debate that is frequently held
(E) are something that many have been debating

11 <u>Bred in Portugal as a seafaring dog that carried messages between ships</u>, the Portuguese Water Dog is a strong and agile dog with enough stamina to do a full day's work.

(A) Bred in Portugal as a seafaring dog that carried messages between ships
(B) Breeding the seafaring dog that carried messages between ships in Portugal
(C) Although being bred in Portugal as a seafaring dog that carried messages between ships
(D) Since having been bred in Portugal as a seafaring dog that carried messages between ships
(E) Bred in Portugal carrying messages between ships as seafaring dogs

3

3

Directions for Identifying Sentences Error Questions

The following sentences may contain errors in grammar, usage, diction (choice of words), or idiom. Some of the sentences are correct. No sentence contains more than one error.

If the sentence contains an error, it is underlined and lettered. The parts that are not underlined are correct.

If there is an error, select the part that must be changed to correct the sentence.

If there is no error, choose (E).

EXAMPLE:

By the time <u>they reached</u> the halfway point
                    A

<u>in the race</u>, most <u>of the runners</u> <u>hadn't hardly</u>
     B   C   D

begun to hit their stride. <u>No error</u>
                                E

Example answer: (D)

12 Bob Hope, <u>long</u> <u>considered</u> a hero by many
                    A   B
members <u>of</u> the military, <u>were</u> very patriotic.
            C   D
<u>No error</u>
   E

13 <u>Between</u> the 32 NFL teams in 2005, the
        A
Indianapolis Colts <u>scored</u> the <u>most</u>
                        B   C
first half points and <u>allowed</u> the fewest
                          D
second half points. <u>No error</u>
                        E

14 <u>On April</u> 30, 1789, George Washington,
        A
<u>standing on</u> the balcony of Federal Hall on
     B
Wall Street in New York, <u>took</u> his oath
                              C
of office <u>as the first President</u> of the
               D
United States. <u>No error</u>
                  E

15 By virtue of <u>their</u> size and superior
                      A
technological advances, the Russian army

<u>was able</u> to quell the <u>aggressive</u> rebellion
     B   C
<u>with</u> unmatched efficiency. <u>No error</u>
   D   E

16 <u>Too much</u> sugar <u>causes</u> a cake to sag
        A   B
<u>in the center</u>, to brown excessively, and
     C
<u>having sticky</u>, thick crust. <u>No error</u>
     D   E

17 After <u>much</u> debate, Julia and Patricia
              A
<u>agreed</u> that they would go to the movies
   B
together on Friday, but at the last minute

<u>she</u> <u>changed</u> her mind. <u>No error</u>
   C   D   E

18 It has long been believed that our solar
        A
system came into existence when a
                B
huge cloud of gas and dust collapsed
                                    C
to form the sun and planets

approximately 4.5 billion years ago.
                    D
No error
    E

19 Some parents believe that a weekly
                    A
allowance help children to appreciate
            B   C
the importance of good money
                    D
management skills. No error
                        E

20 Quick to take advantage of his mother's
        A   B
preoccupation in proper nutrition,
        C
Jules convinced her to cook a large
            D
breakfast for him before he went to

the beach for the day. No error
                        E

21 After being led through the museum
        A
by a woman which they took to be the
                    B   C
curator, the patrons discovered that their
                    D
tour guide was actually the owner of the

museum. No error
            E

22 The surgical method of inserting the valve,
                        A
which includes making a small incision
    B
between the ribs, are intended to shorten
                    C
recovery time and reduce complications

associated with traditional open-heart
    D
surgery. No error
            E

3

23 Scientists are amassing evidence that
                A
the placebo affect is a physiological
                B
reaction, and that the expectation of a

benefit can trigger the same neurological
        C
pathways as real medication does. No error
                    D   E

24 In the aftermath of the Cuban Missile
        A
Crisis, the papers from all the national
                    B
security agencies involved were scattered
                        C   D
throughout the executive branch. No error
                                    E

25 After completing her examination of the
        A
patient, the medical intern informed the
                            B
chief resident that the patient was not only
                                C
feeling nauseous, but dizzy, and therefore
                    D
might have an infection. No error
                        E

3

26 That Erica dedicated so much of her
      A   B
time to charity work and she cared so little
                        C
about those less fortunate than she is
                D
surprising. No error
              E

27 When looking at satellite photographs
      A
of the area affected by Hurricane Katrina,
              B
the effects of the massive storm are
                                    C
clearly visible. No error
D   E

28 The play director has announced that
                                    A
if anyone wants to try out for the musical,
              B   C
they should do so immediately. No error
D   E

29 Neither Roger nor his sisters was able
                  A   B
to understand what the conductor was
                                    C
saying because they did not know how to
                    D
speak French. No error
              E

Directions for "Improving Paragraphs" Questions

The passage below is an early draft of an essay. It requires revision in many areas.

The questions that follow ask you to make improvements in sentence structure, diction, organization and development. Answering the questions may require you to understand the context of the passage as well as the rules of standard written English.

Questions 30–35 are based on the following passage.

(1) *Crocodiles descended from creatures that walked on their hind legs, and lived during the late Triassic period.* (2) *The crocodiles having survived the still unknown factors wiping out most of the reptile class at the end of the Mesozoic period.* (3) *The skull and hind legs of the crocodile still resemble in many ways those structures of its primitive relatives.* (4) *Walking on four legs, their two legged ancestry is revealed by their hind legs, which are longer than their front legs, making them slant forward when they stand.* (5) *The crocodile has a rather long, pointed skull, especially in the fish eating species of crocodiles.*

(6) *The palate is the flat bony part at the roof of the mouth.* (7) *In its relatives, the nostril holes in the palate were located under the outer nostrils, which were shifted to the far back of their snout.* (8) *However, in crocodiles, the nostrils are located at the front of the snout.* (9) *A problem came from this in keeping the breathing passages from filling with water.* (10) *Millions of years of evolution have solved this problem.* (11) *A second palate was formed, channeling the air above the mouth and into the throat passageway, where it can be opened and closed by a special flap or valve of skin.* (12) *Crocodiles are actually classified on the basis of how far back their secondary palate extends, ranging from those that have no secondary palate to those with a fully formed palate separating the air they breathe from the water in their mouths.*

30 In context, which is the best version of the underlined portion of sentence 2 (reproduced below)?

The crocodiles having survived the still unknown factors wiping out most of the reptile class at the end of the Mesozoic period.

(A) (As it is now)
(B) Crocodiles were somehow able to survive the unknown factors that wiped out most of the reptile class
(C) It is not clear how or why, but Crocodiles were able to survive the unknown factors wiping out most of the reptile class
(D) Having survived the unknown factors that wiped out most of the reptile class, it is not clear why crocodiles remained
(E) Most of the reptile class was wiped out by unknown factors but the crocodiles still have survived

31 In context, which is the best version of the underlined portion of sentence 4 (reproduced below)?

Walking on four legs, their two legged ancestry is revealed by their hind legs, which are longer than their front legs, making them slant forward when they stand.

(A) Though modern crocodiles walk on four legs,
(B) Four legged walkers,
(C) Modern Crocodiles, despite walking on four legs,
(D) As four legged walkers, modern crocodiles,
(E) Having four legs,

GO ON TO THE NEXT PAGE ▶▶▶

32 Which of the following should be done with sentence 5 (reproduced below)?

The crocodile has a rather long, pointed skull, especially in the fish eating species of crocodiles.

(A) Insert the phrase "In addition" at the beginning.

(B) Delete it; the sentence does not contain relevant information.

(C) Move it to the beginning of the essay as an introduction

(D) Move it to the middle of paragraph 2 after sentence 10.

(E) Insert the word "Interestingly" at the beginning.

33 Which of the following is the best sentence to insert at the beginning of the second paragraph?

(A) Crocodiles are able to run at incredible speeds despite their small stature.

(B) There are 23 living species of crocodile found mostly in the southern hemisphere, a living throwback to the age of the dinosaurs.

(C) The first crocodilians were called Protosuchians, living during the late Triassic to early Jurassic times.

(D) The biggest, most prominent change in the crocodile since its early days has been the change in its palate.

(E) Beginning in the Jurassic period, crocodiles became large and fully aquatic reptiles

34 In context, which of the following is the best way to revise and combine sentences 8 and 9 (reproduced below)?

However, in crocodiles, the nostrils are located at the front of the snout. A problem came from this in keeping the breathing passages from filling with water.

(A) No change is necessary

(B) However, because a crocodile's nostrils are located at the front of the snout, it was difficult to keep the breathing passages from filling with water.

(C) The nostrils of a crocodile are located at the front of the snout, however difficult it was to keep the breathing passages from filling with water.

(D) It was difficult keeping the breathing passages of the crocodile's nostrils from filling with water however, because they would be located at the front of the snout.

(E) Located at the front of the snout, water would get into the breathing passages of the crocodiles because of its nostrils.

35 In context, which is the best version of sentence 10 (reproduced below)?

Millions of years of evolution have solved this problem.

(A) (As it is now)

(B) This problem having been solved thanks to millions of years of evolution.

(C) It was after millions of years of evolution that the crocodile was able to solve this problem.

(D) This problem was no longer an issue after millions of years of evolution.

(E) The solver of this problem, after millions of years, was evolution.

STOP

You may check your work, on this section only, until time is called.

Section 4

Time—25 Minutes
24 Questions

Each of the sentences below is missing one or two portions. Read each sentence, then select the word or words that most logically completes the sentence, taking into account the meaning of the sentence as a whole.

Example:

Rather than accepting the theory unquestioningly, Deborah regarded it with ————.

(A) mirth   (B) sadness   (C) responsibility
(D) ignorance   (E) skepticism

Example answer: (E)

---

1 The earth minerals found within the thermal waters of the hot springs are known to —— and revitalize the skin.

(A) ingratiate   (B) invigorate
(C) exculpate   (D) enervate
(E) debilitate

2 Despite the ever-present curiosity about his life away from the presidency, Grover Cleveland enjoyed ———— that today's highly sought after public figures can only ————.

(A) a candor . . remember
(B) a popularity . . dissuade
(C) an animosity . . crave
(D) a privacy . . imagine
(E) a frivolity . . imitate

3 With unanimous approval, the Senate —— the new law that would prohibit companies from discriminating according to race in their hiring practices.

(A) ratified   (B) nullified
(C) refuted   (D) supplanted
(E) pilfered

4 Her closest friends saw her confinement to a wheelchair as an ————, but LaToya instead saw it as an ———— that pushed her to achieve things that many thought were impossible.

(A) atrocity . . irrelevance
(B) omen . . elocution
(C) invasion . . inspiration
(D) idiosyncracy . . extinction
(E) impediment . . impetus

5 During the struggle for Indian independence, Mahatma Gandhi was a ———— pacifist who may have steadfastly resisted authority but was never combative.

(A) fickle   (B) recalcitrant
(C) pugnacious   (D) lucrative
(E) spurious

6 Several months after the devastating ————, all that remained of Jamjang village was a circle of burned huts, wood-and-mud walls reduced to a sad ring of blackened ashes, and ———— smell of smoke that still hung in the air.

(A) wildfire . . a savory
(B) cacophony . . a pungent
(C) conflagration . . an acrid
(D) abomination . . a lethargic
(E) scourge . . an irascible

7 My editor's meticulousness is revealed in his ———— red scribbles, which show that he thought about each word, eliminated all unnecessary ones, and considered the flow of each sentence to the next.

(A) rapacious   (B) improvident
(C) convoluted   (D) copious
(E) ostentatious

8 In an effort to supplement his modest income, the ———— police officer would break the law for criminals who were willing to pay him adequately.

(A) clairvoyant   (B) impassive
(C) matriculated (D) scrupulous
(E) venal

GO ON TO THE NEXT PAGE ▶▶▶

The paired passages below are followed by questions based on their content and the relationship between the passages. Answer the questions on the basis of what is stated or implied in the passages and in any introductory material that may be provided.

Questions 9–12 are based on the following passages.

4

Passage 1

Line   Many medical researchers now believe that there is such a thing as being too clean. The "hygiene hypothesis" suggests that excessively sanitary conditions can lower a
5   person's resistance to disease. One recent study suggested that infection by the hepatitis A virus actually prevented certain individuals from developing allergies. But the protection was not exclusively environmental:
10   only those infected patients who had also inherited a particular gene saw the benefit.

Passage 2

The triumph of antibiotics over disease-causing bacteria is one of modern medicine's greatest success stories. Since these drugs
15   first became widely used in the World War II era, they have saved countless lives and blunted serious complications of many feared diseases and infections. After more than 50 years of widespread use, however, many
20   antibiotics don't pack the same punch they once did. Over time, some bacteria have developed ways to outwit the effects of antibiotics. Widespread use of antibiotics is thought to have spurred evolutionary changes
25   in bacteria that allow them to survive these powerful drugs. While antibiotic resistance benefits the microbes, it presents humans with two big problems: it makes it more difficult to purge infections from the body; and it
30   heightens the risk of acquiring infections in a hospital.

9   Both passages indicate that

(A)   recently developed medications are ineffectual
(B)   doctors should prescribe antibiotics more liberally
(C)   environment plays a far greater role than genetics in human health
(D)   unsanitary conditions are a risk to human health
(E)   certain factors are decreasing the human body's ability to ward off disease

10 The "benefit" mentioned in line 11 is

(A)   resistance to allergies
(B)   the ability to ward off hepatitis A
(C)   cleanliness
(D)   more disease-resistant genes
(E)   popular awareness

11 Passage 2 discusses antibiotics primarily with a tone of

(A)   strong optimism
(B)   dismissiveness
(C)   cynicism
(D)   qualified enthusiasm
(E)   jocularity

12 Unlike the "resistance" mentioned in line 5, the "resistance" in line 26 is a resistance to

(A)   bacteria rather than viruses
(B)   drugs rather than allergies
(C)   genetic diseases rather than infectious diseases
(D)   evolutionary changes rather than hepatitis A
(E)   infection rather than antibiotics

GO ON TO THE NEXT PAGE ▶▶▶

Questions 13-24 are based on the following passages.

The following passages discuss the American farm subsidy program, which makes direct payments to farmers in order to control the supply of agricultural goods available for domestic sale or for export.

Passage 1

Line   Something is rotten down on the farm. The U.S. Department of Agriculture has for decades managed the farm subsidy program, a multibillion-dollar system of direct payments
5   to American farmers. The General Accounting Office, the fact-finding agency of the United States Congress, recently studied the management of this program, and the findings should horrify lawmakers. But they
10   probably won't.

The GAO study revealed that government administrators of these subsidies are too ill-trained and that federal laws are too vague to properly monitor the hundreds of thousands
15   of farm subsidy payments granted each year. Many of the approved recipients were actually ineligible for the program. An analysis of a sample of subsidies that had already been reviewed and approved by the USDA revealed
20   that 30 percent of even these scrutinized subsidies were going to those who shouldn't be receiving them.

Such lack of USDA oversight is outrageous, given how much American taxpayers spend
25   each year to support farmers. From 1995 to 2002, Congress doled out more than $114 billion to farmers, and in 2002, just before the mid-term elections, President Bush increased subsidies to $190 billion over
30   the next 10 years. With so much money being freely handed out, the GAO report should inspire some tough questions for USDA officials on Capitol Hill. Yet, for all its detail, the 75-page report artfully avoids the bigger
35   question that no lawmaker wants to hear: why do we even have farm subsidies?

One popular misconception is that these subsidies produce lower food prices, and so are a boon to consumers. This analysis ignores

40   the fact that consumers are also paying for these subsidies through taxes. Because of the inefficiency of the program, the taxpayers—you and I—will probably pay more in excess taxes than we will ever get back in
45   lower corn or wheat prices.

In fact, farm subsidies are not intended to reduce food prices significantly. When prices are too low, farmers lose money. To prevent such a situation, Congress also pays farmers
50   to leave their land fallow, resulting in lower supply and thus higher prices. To obscure this intended effect, and because eschewing cultivation can improve the quality of soil, these payments are called "environmental
55   conservation" subsidies.

Another myth is that farm subsidies increase exports, and therefore benefit the American economy, by lowering the price of products and making them more attractive to
60   foreign consumers. This claim ignores at least two realities. First, just as farm subsidies transfer wealth from taxpayers to domestic consumers, so they transfer tax wealth to foreign consumers. Second, farm
65   subsidies are becoming a liability to American exporters. Last April, the World Trade Organization ruled that American cotton subsidies violated global trade rules, which could lead to billions of dollars in
70   retaliatory tariffs or fines. These realities are doing more harm than good to our country's economy.

Our most enduring and politically appealing illusion about subsidies is that we
75   must maintain them in order to save the small family farmer. Indeed, about 77 percent of Americans said that they support giving subsidies to small family farms, according to a 2004 poll. However, small family farmers
80   are not, by a long shot, the primary recipients of federal subsidies. According to the Environmental Working Group, a watchdog organization, 71 percent of farm subsidies go to the top 10 percent of beneficiaries, almost
85   all of which are large wealthy farms. In 2001, according to the USDA's own data, these wealthy farm households earned an average of over $135,000—more than 2½ times the income of non-farm households. In 2002,

GO ON TO THE NEXT PAGE ▸▸▸

Passage 1 © 2005 The Independent Institute. Adapted from an article by Nicolas Heidorn at *http://www.independent.org/newsroom/ article.asp?id=1340*

90 78 farms, none small or struggling, each
    received more than a million dollars in
    subsidies. The bottom 80 percent of farms—
    the struggling family farmers—each receive
    only $846 per year.
95   The result of subsidizing the rich, more
    landed farmers is that they can reduce the
    prices of their goods, making it much harder
    for small farmers to compete. Rather than
    saving family farmers, subsidies work
100 against them.
        Rich farmers are a powerful lobby in
    American politics. In 2003, crop producers
    gave $11.5 million in campaign contributions,
    according to the Center for Responsive
105 Politics, and they are likely to give much
    more in the future.
        So don't be surprised that the GAO's report
    won't be taken too seriously on Capitol Hill.
    Farm subsidies are more than just payoffs to
110 wealthy, large landowners. They are subsidies
    for elected officials, too.

Passage 2

    There has been much public outcry about the
    farm subsidy system, but its critics fail to
    recognize just how important these subsidies
115 really are. Farm subsidies protect farmers
    from damaging fluctuations in commodity
    prices that can result from wild fluctuations
    in the market or crop failure due to weather.
    At the same time, they protect consumers
120 from potential price spikes that can accompany
    steep drops in crop inventories. Before price
    supports became common in the 20th
    century, crop failure was a fact of life driven
    home with horrifying frequency.
125   Opponents of farm subsidies suggest that
    the system creates the problem of inventory
    oversupply. That is true, but this is only
    because regular shortfalls would be even
    more worrisome. The massive year-to-year
130 carryover of these inventories helps to
    safeguard against excessive price fluctuations
    that otherwise would follow natural or
    market-driven setbacks. Subsidies protect
    consumers from high prices and farmers
135 from low prices.

    One of the major misconceptions
    associated with farm subsidies, particularly
    among consumers, is that only the producers
    receive the benefits of this funding. This is
140 untrue. Subsidies virtually guarantee that
    products are produced in large amounts. This
    does indeed benefit the producers, but it also
    benefits others along the food processing,
    distribution and marketing chain. Farmers
145 receive direct benefits, but others along the
    way receive indirect benefits thanks to
    cheaper production inputs, which, in turn,
    contribute to lower production costs and
    thus lower prices for the consumers.
150   When assessing the costs and benefits of
    U.S. farm payments, it is important to compare
    these costs to those of other industrial nations.
    American farmers receive a much lower
    percentage of their incomes—about 20%—
155 from subsidies than do farmers from other
    countries. In some countries, more than
    70 percent of farm revenue is derived from
    government payments. The European Union
    spends more than twice as much annually
160 as the United States does on farm supports,
    despite having a smaller farm economy.
    When used efficiently, farm subsidies can
    be of great benefit. The farm subsidization
    system is not perfect, but its positive impacts
165 far outweigh its negative ones.

13 The "rotten" (line 1) thing is the fact that

(A) the government is not doing enough
     to help small farmers
(B) many American farmers are violating
     the law
(C) a governmental program is ineffective
     and unfair
(D) farmers are not taking advantage of
     important new technologies
(E) American farmers are unable to
     compete in international markets

GO ON TO THE NEXT PAGE ▶▶▶

14 The statement that "they probably won't" (line 10) is intended to indicate that

(A) the subsidy program is not as bad as it seems
(B) lawmakers are unlikely to see the report
(C) legislators are not likely to be persuaded by reports of mismanagement
(D) the GAO report is not entirely accurate
(E) legislators do not care enough about the concerns of farmers

15 The purpose of the fourth paragraph of Passage 1 (lines 37–45) is to

(A) describe a problem that farmers face
(B) show how increased agricultural production lowers taxes
(C) describe an authoritative study that supports the author's claim
(D) dispel a belief about the effectiveness of subsidies
(E) reveal a hidden benefit to agricultural subsidies

16 The author of Passage 1 uses quotation marks around the phrase "environmental conservation" (lines 54–55) in order to show that it is

(A) misleading
(B) being used only in the context of this passage
(C) intended to be taken humorously
(D) beyond the understanding of most readers
(E) derived from an obscure foreign phrase

17 The "2004 poll" (line 79) was intended to determine

(A) the political affiliation of farmers
(B) the rate of consumption of certain agricultural products
(C) opinions on environmental issues
(D) instances of the misuse of farm subsidies
(E) public sentiment for a governmental program

18 The statement that "They are subsidies for elected officials, too" (lines 110–111) means that legislators

(A) receive indirect political benefits from the subsidy program
(B) own the agricultural means of production
(C) are permitted to receive direct subsidies under USDA guidelines
(D) frequently compete with farmers for government funds
(E) are working to reduce inefficiencies in the farm subsidies program

19 Passage 2 indicates that the "problem of inventory over supply" (lines 126–127) is

(A) being alleviated by farm subsidy payments
(B) not as problematic as it may seem
(C) an unavoidable aspect of farming
(D) the result of excessive price fluctuations
(E) more dangerous to consumers than to farmers

20 The "chain" (line 144) is likely to include all of the following EXCEPT

(A) produce truck drivers
(B) fruit store owners
(C) legislators who support subsidies
(D) associations that promote agricultural products
(E) vegetable canning factories

21 Both passages agree that the American farm subsidies program

(A) is mismanaged
(B) benefits small farmers
(C) is not supported by most voters
(D) is employed more for political than economic ends
(E) can control the price of agricultural products

22 The author of Passage 1 would most likely respond to the claim that farm subsidies produce "lower prices for the consumers" (line 149) by claiming that

(A) this is untrue because crop failures that lead to higher prices are unavoidable

(B) the USDA pays too little in subsidies to provide such a benefit to consumers

(C) owners of large farms do not benefit from these lower prices

(D) higher prices can actually be beneficial to consumers

(E) these lower prices are not worth the tax increases to consumers that are needed to pay for it

23 The attitudes toward farm subsidies of Passage 1 and Passage 2, respectively, can best be described as

(A) cautiously optimistic and cynical

(B) disdainful and supportive

(C) critical and incredulous

(D) objectively analytical and sarcastic

(E) respectful and skeptical

24 Which of the following can be found in BOTH passages?

    I.   a verifiable statistic
    II. a refutation of a misconception
    III. a reference to political corruption

(A) I only

(B) I and II only

(C) I and III only

(D) II and III only

(E) I, II, and III

STOP

You may check your work, on this section only, until time is called.

Section 5

Time—25 Minutes
18 Questions

Directions for Multiple-Choice Questions

In this section, solve each problem, using any available space on the page for scratchwork. Then decide which is the best of the choices given and fill in the corresponding oval on the answer sheet.

- You may use a calculator on any problem. All numbers used are real numbers.
- Figures are drawn as accurately as possible EXCEPT when it is stated that the figure is not drawn to scale.
- All figures lie in a plane unless otherwise indicated.

Reference Information

$A = \pi r^2$ $A = \ell w$ $A = \frac{1}{2}bh$ $V = \ell wh$ $V = \pi r^2 h$ $c^2 = a^2 + b^2$ Special Right Triangles
$C = 2\pi r$

The arc of a circle measures 360°.
Every straight angle measures 180°.
The sum of the measures of the angles in a triangle is 180°.

---

1 If pens cost \$3 each and binders cost \$2 each, which of the following represents the cost, in dollars, of p pens and b binders?

(A) $5(b + p)$
(B) $3bp$
(C) $3p + 2b$
(D) $2(p + b)$
(E) $6bp$

2 Which of the following integers is divisible by 4 and 6, but is not divisible by 8?

(A) 12
(B) 24
(C) 48
(D) 64
(E) 72

3 If $8,755 = 85(x + 2)$, then $x =$

(A) 12
(B) 14
(C) 100
(D) 101
(E) 102

4 Let $x \Delta y \Delta z$ be defined by the equation

$$x \Delta y \Delta z = \left(\frac{x}{z}\right)y + xz$$

for all non-zero numbers x, y, and z. Which of the following is equal to an odd integer?

(A) $4\Delta8\Delta2$
(B) $3\Delta2\Delta1$
(C) $9\Delta3\Delta3$
(D) $8\Delta6\Delta4$
(E) $5\Delta7\Delta1$

GO ON TO THE NEXT PAGE ▶▶▶

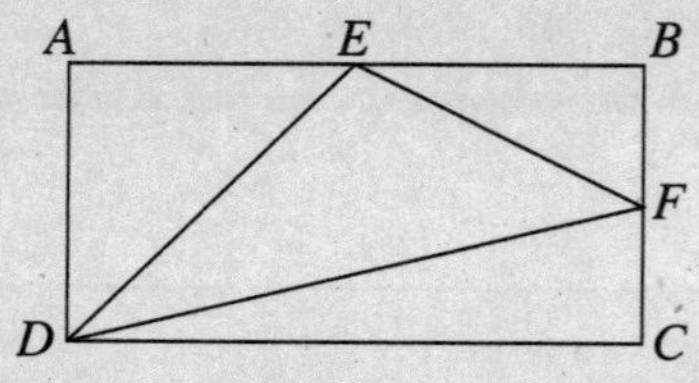

Note: Figure not drawn to scale.

5 In the figure above, *ABCD* is a rectangle. *DC* = 8, *AD* = 4, and *E* and *F* are midpoints of sides *AB* and *BC* respectively. What is the area of △*DEF*?

(A) 12
(B) 18
(C) 24
(D) 28
(E) 32

6 How many different four-digit integers can be formed using the digits 3, 4, 5, 6, 7, 8, 9 if the tens digit is 5 and no digit is repeated within an integer?

(A) 16
(B) 45
(C) 63
(D) 120
(E) 840

7 Zander drives to work at an average speed of 40 miles per hour and returns home along the same route at an average speed of 24 miles per hour. If his total travel time is 4 hours, what is the total number of miles in the roundtrip to and from work?

(A) 48
(B) 60
(C) 96
(D) 120
(E) 144

8 A swimming pool with a capacity of 20,000 gallons is one-quarter full. A pump can deliver *g* gallons of water every *m* minutes. If a company charges *d* dollars per minute for the use of the pump, then in terms of *g*, *m*, and *d*, how much will it cost, in dollars, to fill the pool?

(A) $\dfrac{15,000gd}{m}$

(B) $15,000gmd$

(C) $\dfrac{15,000md}{g}$

(D) $\dfrac{gd}{15,000m}$

(E) $\dfrac{gm}{15,000d}$

Directions for Student-Produced Response Questions

Each of the questions in this section requires you to solve the problem and enter your answer in a grid, as shown below.

- If your answer is ⅔ or .666 ..., you must enter **the most accurate value the grid can accommodate**, but you may do this in one of four ways:

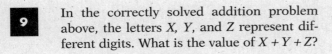

- In the example above, gridding a response of 0.67 or 0.66 is **incorrect** because it is less accurate than those above.
- The scoring machine cannot read what is written in the top row of boxes. You **MUST** fill in the numerical grid accurately to get credit for answering any question correctly. You should write your answer in the top row of boxes only to aid your gridding.
- Do **not** grid in a mixed fraction like $3\frac{1}{2}$ as 31/2 because it will be interpreted as $\frac{31}{2}$. Instead, convert it to an improper fraction like ⅞ or a decimal like 3.5 before gridding.
- None of the answers will be negative, because there is no negative sign in the grid.
- Some of the questions may have more than one correct answer. You must grid only one of the correct answers.
- You may use a calculator on any of these problems.
- All numbers in these problems are real numbers.
- Figures are drawn as accurately as possible EXCEPT when it is stated that the figure is not drawn to scale.
- All figures lie in a plane unless otherwise indicated.

$$\begin{array}{r} XYZ \\ +\ ZYX \\ \hline 848 \end{array}$$

9　In the correctly solved addition problem above, the letters X, Y, and Z represent different digits. What is the value of $X + Y + Z$?

10　A rectangular shaped field has a perimeter of 300 feet and a width of 60 feet. What is the area of the field in square feet?

GO ON TO THE NEXT PAGE ▸▸▸

$$f(x) = 8x - 4$$

$$g(x) = x^2 - 3$$

11 Given the functions above, what is the value of $f(g(3))$?

15 If $|-3x + 5| < 6$, what is one possible value of x if x must be a positive odd integer?

16 During a dance class, each of the twelve students is paired up with each of the other students twice. How many total pairings will there be during the class?

12 Points X and Y are on a circle with center O, and point Z is on the longer arc of the circle between X and Y. If the measure of angle XOY is 135°, the length of arc XZY is what fraction of the circumference of the circle?

17 The median of a set of 55 consecutive odd integers is 55. What is the greatest of these integers?

13 If $ab + \dfrac{1}{ab} = 4$, what is the value of $a^2b^2 + \dfrac{1}{a^2b^2}$?

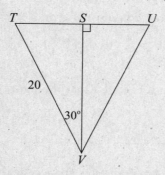

Note: Figure not drawn to scale.

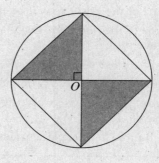

18 If the shaded region above has a perimeter of $24 + 12\sqrt{2}$ units, what is the area of the inscribed square?

14 In triangle TUV above, what is the length of TS?

STOP

You may check your work, on this section only, until time is called.

Section 6

Time—25 minutes
24 Questions

Each of the sentences below is missing one or two portions. Read each sentence, then select the word or words that most logically completes the sentence, taking into account the meaning of the sentence as a whole.

Example:

Rather than accepting the theory unquestioningly, Deborah regarded it with ———.

(A) mirth   (B) sadness
(C) responsibility   (D) ignorance
(E) skepticism

Example answer: (E)

1 The athlete committed such a ——— foul that the referee had no choice but to throw him out of the game and petition for a ———.

(A) blatant . . suspension
(B) miniscule . . fine
(C) egregious . . celebration
(D) obligatory . . decoration
(E) nautical . . ceremony

2 During her first two years at the firm, Tracy worked with a ——— that helped her to become the youngest partner in company history; no associate before her had ever accomplished so much with such a consistent standard of excellence.

(A) gratuity   (B) dormancy
(C) lethargy   (D) capriciousness
(E) diligence

3 Oprah Winfrey is one of her generation's most famous ———; she has a ——— for devoting her time and money to helping those who are less fortunate.

(A) altruists . . dislike
(B) charlatans . . prerequisite
(C) philanthropists . . penchant
(D) nihilists . . sympathy
(E) despots . . culpability

4 Although many actual criminal confessions take several hundred sentences elicited over several hours, in *Crime and Punishment*, Dostoevsky stages Raskolnikov's confession with relentlessly ——— plainness by using fewer than 20 words.

(A) laconic   (B) verbose
(C) lugubrious   (D) sonorous
(E) antiquated

5 Losing his championship title to a weaker opponent was such a humbling experience for the fighter that his swagger and ——— public demeanor were replaced by a more modest and self-effacing persona.

(A) lofty   (B) impecunious
(C) obligatory   (D) prescient
(E) pusillanimous

6

Each passage below is followed by questions based on its content. Answer each question based on what is stated or implied in the passage.

Questions 6–7 are based on the following passage.

Line The kareze system of irrigation was invented three thousand years ago during the height of the Persian Empire in what is now Iran. Persian engineers tapped water by first
5 sinking a well at the apex of an alluvial fan—the location where a mountain river deposits its sediment—until it reached the water table. These muqannis, as they were called, then calculated where a tunnel with a slight
10 downward slope would reach the surface near a village. From that point, a tunnel was built to the mother well, supplying the village with a steady supply of much-needed water. These systems were very time-consuming and
15 expensive to build. Typical tunnels were several kilometers in length, but some could run 50 kilometers and take many years to build. Once they were built, however, so dramatically did the kareze improve the conditions of life
20 for villagers that wholly new societal relations and systems were formed.

6 The primary purpose of the passage is to describe

(A) an architectural disaster
(B) a historical era
(C) a technological advance
(D) a geographical feature
(E) a social system

7 The "muqannis" (line 8) were

(A) common villagers
(B) Persian kings
(C) sedimentary deposits
(D) tunnels
(E) engineers

Questions 8–9 are based on the following passage.

Line The theory of evolution has been a boon not only to biologists, but also to anthropologists. Many customs can be explained as means of expressing or exaggerating genetic traits that
5 we have inherited from our forebears through the process of natural selection. For instance, sports can be seen as a means of expressing our genetic endowment as hunters, even though most societies no longer require
10 hunting. Likewise, face painting and body adornments can be seen as exaggerated expressions of those genetic traits that reflect health and virility. Expressing and exercising these inherited traits once had quite definite
15 survival value to individuals and societies. More mysterious to evolutionary anthropologists, however, is music. To what genetic trait can we attribute the universal love of music, and what survival benefit causes it to merit
20 selection by the evolutionary process?

8 The statement that "most societies no longer require hunting" (lines 9–10) is intended to emphasize the fact that

(A) technological progress has been very rapid in recent decades
(B) many political groups opposed the hunting of animals
(C) sports express vestigial genetic traits
(D) societies are becoming less violent over time
(E) hunting is not as competitive as most other sports

9 According to the passage, music is "mysterious" (line 16) because

(A) musical skill varies greatly from person to person within a population
(B) it is not as aggressive an activity as hunting is
(C) it is found in some cultures but not others
(D) it does not to appear to convey an obvious survival benefit
(E) musical skill cannot be inherited

GO ON TO THE NEXT PAGE ▶▶▶

Each passage below is followed by questions based on its content. Answer the questions based on what is stated or implied in each passage and in any introductory material that may be provided.

Questions 10-16 pertain to the following passage.

The following passage discusses the native Nepalese people, the Sherpa, who have long aided climbers of Mount Everest.

Line The cheerful smiles and legendary strength of
the Sherpas have been an integral part of
Everest climbing expeditions from the very
beginning. Indeed, very few significant
5   successes have been achieved without them.
    When Western mountaineers first set their
sights on the world's highest peak, they found
in the Sherpas a people ideally suited to the
rigors of high-altitude climbing, unfailingly
10   positive, stout at altitude, and seemingly
resistant to cold.
    Sherpas did not venture into the high
peaks until European mountaineers began
arriving to climb in the world's greatest
15   mountain range. Mount Everest, known as
Chomolungma or "Goddess Mother of the
Land" to Tibetan language speakers like
the Sherpas, was long revered as an abode of
the gods. Its slopes were considered off-limits
20   to humans.
    Although Everest now sees many a human
footprint, the Sherpas still regard the
mountain as a holy place. All modern
expeditions begin with a Puja ceremony in
25   which Sherpas and other team members
leave offerings and pay homage to the gods
of the mountain, hoping to remain in their
good graces throughout the climb.
    A Himalayan veteran in the early 1920s,
30   Alexander Kellas is generally regarded as the
first person to recognize the natural aptitude
of the Sherpa people for hard work and
climbing at high altitude. In his time, Kellas
was perhaps the world's leading expert on
35   mountain sickness and the effects of high
altitude. He recognized that Sherpas did not
feel these effects in the same way as others,
though it remains unclear what combination
of genetics and an upbringing at high altitude

40   allows the Sherpas to deal physiologically
with altitude better than others.
    Sherpas were first employed as porters,
tasked with carrying large amounts of
equipment to supply the military-style
45   expeditions of the day. The British climbers
were amazed at the strength of these people,
from the fittest of mature men to the young
and elderly. Arthur Wakefield described the
team of porters on one early expedition as "a
50   motley throng of old men, women, boys and
girls." Yet their accomplishments astonished
him. At 18,000 feet, how the Sherpas carried
their loads "completely puzzles me," he
wrote. "Some were 80 pounds!" In addition
55   to their loads, some of the women carried
along their babies. The whole troop slept
outside, using only rocks for shelter, as
temperatures dropped well below freezing.
    Stronger Sherpas soon graduated from
60   porter status and began to undertake
challenging climbing and work high on the
mountain. Those who distinguished themselves
high on the mountain were awarded the
Tiger Medal, and many aspired to this honor
65   and the higher pay rate it afforded.
    Unfortunately, Sherpas were also the first
to suffer the consequences that can come
from climbing high on Everest. A North Col
avalanche killed seven Sherpa porters on the
70   1922 expedition, the first recorded climbing
fatalities on the mountain. Even after the
disaster, however, the Sherpa people remained
enthusiastic about taking part in Everest
expeditions, which even then were becoming
75   an important source of revenue for a poor
mountain folk.

10   According to the passage, Sherpas supply which of the following to the climbers of Mount Everest?

  I.   ability to work in harsh
       environments
  II. expertise in treating altitude
       sickness
  III. physical strength and climbing
       ability

(A) I only
(B) I and II only
(C) I and III only
(D) II and III only
(E) I, II, and III

GO ON TO THE NEXT PAGE ▶▶▶

11 The passage indicates that, before Europeans arrived to climb Mount Everest, the Sherpas

(A) were unaware of the mountain
(B) regarded the mountain as evil
(C) had been climbing the mountain for centuries
(D) only climbed to the summit for religious purposes
(E) had not explored the highest part of the mountain

12 Wakefield's description of the Sherpas in lines 49–51 emphasizes their

(A) heterogeneity
(B) intelligence
(C) youth
(D) wisdom
(E) cheerfulness

13 Arthur Wakefield's attitude toward the Sherpas is best described as

(A) awed
(B) skeptical
(C) condescending
(D) antagonistic
(E) detached

14 The passage contains information to answer all of the following questions EXCEPT

(A) When were the first climbing fatalities on Mount Everest?
(B) Who was the first European to climb Mount Everest?
(C) What is the Tibetan name for Mount Everest?
(D) What is the name of the Sherpa religious ceremony that begins an expedition?
(E) Who was the first European to recognize the value of the Sherpas as climbing guides?

15 The reference to "rocks" in line 57 serves primarily to emphasize

(A) the challenges endured by the European climbers
(B) the barren landscape of Mount Everest
(C) the sacredness of the mountain to the Sherpas
(D) the ruggedness of the Sherpas
(E) the aloofness of the Sherpas

16 The passage indicates that the Sherpas continue to assist in Everest expeditions despite the dangers because

    I.   it has been a social custom for many centuries
    II. the climbing prowess of the Sherpas often reflects their social status
    III. it sustains their economy
    IV. it is a religious duty

(A) I and III only
(B) II and III only
(C) I, II, and III only
(D) I, II, and IV only
(E) II, III, and IV only

Questions 17–24 pertain to the following passage.

The following passage discusses recent research in the area of animal communication.

Line The fact that animals can communicate with
each other is obvious to anyone who has ever
watched a pack of dogs or a group of farm
cats interact, or listened to crows calling
5 to each other in the treetops. But just how
complex is animal communication? Clearly,
human language is far more complex than
anything we see elsewhere in the animal
kingdom. For instance, humans can
10 communicate about concepts, that is, things
that are not available to their immediate
senses, and about events in the past or in the
future. Can animal communication come
anywhere close to this level of complexity?
15 Information presented at an American
scientific conference in 2000 has shed a great
deal of light on this subject.
   The conference drew together animal
behaviorists studying species ranging from
20 parrots to whales. By bringing together
scientists who worked on many different
species and thus didn't often talk much
together, conference organizers hoped to gain
new insight into how animals communicate,
25 learn their own "culture," and maintain
social order.
   One of the more fascinating discoveries
reported was that sperm whales—the animals
with the largest brains on Earth—have a
30 female-dominated, egalitarian society similar
to that of the African elephant. Research has
also demonstrated another curious parallel
between these species. Elephants use
extremely low tones that can carry several
35 kilometers. These tones, called infrasound
because they are below the frequencies that
humans can hear, can be generated at an
energy of 90 decibels, about as loud as a
typical truck or tractor. Similarly, whales
40 generate clicks that can be as loud as a steel
gate clanging shut and carry enormous
distances—perhaps hundreds of miles—
through the water. Whales can hear nearly
all of the frequencies that humans can, as

45 well as many far higher than the human range.
Interestingly, it appears whales are talking
louder because of the increased noise in the
oceans from ships—just as humans talk
louder in a noisy bar than on a quiet beach.
50   Another species of animal with a highly
evolved brain is the dolphin. These graceful
creatures have long fascinated us. They have
a highly complex social life. For instance,
male dolphins will form alliances in pairs
55 and trios to herd females around for a month,
then form larger groupings to steal females
from other trios.
   To study dolphin communication, scientists
attach electronic tags to the animals so they
60 can quickly identify individuals, and tow
microphones behind boats to record the
dolphins' conversations. It appears that each
dolphin develops his or her own signature
signal, which researcher Vincent Janik
65 compares to an Internet screen name or
handle. Janik studied wild bottlenose dolphins
off Moray Firth, Scotland, recording 1,719
whistles in all. Each dolphin he studied made
a distinctive whistle that other dolphins would
70 imitate in response, presumably to keep in
touch. Janik employed human judges to
determine if calls were identical, because
computers are not yet up to the task.
   The dolphins also use a distinctive sound
75 when they find food, a low-pitched noise that
sounds very much like the braying of a donkey.
When one dolphin utters this call, other
dolphins rush in to feed.
   Janik doesn't like to call all this
80 communication "language," in deference to the
complexity of human interaction, preferring
to call it instead "a complex communication
system," and says it's very similar to what
scientists believe ancient humans' first steps
85 toward language would have resembled.
   Dolphins are studied in this field because
of their intelligence, as are apes and monkeys,
particularly chimpanzees, which some
scientists consider to be our closest relatives
90 among the animals. One study suggests that
"food barks" uttered by chimpanzees don't
only announce that they've found food, but
also provide some information as to the type
and quality of the food found. Similarly,

Excerpted from a column written by Edward Willett:
http://www.edwardwillett.com/Columns/animalcomm.htm

GO ON TO THE NEXT PAGE ▸▸▸

95 studies of monkeys have found that they
    utter cries that don't just warn of predators,
    but tell their fellow monkeys what kind of
    predator to look out for. A complementary
    study suggested that chimpanzee can
100 communicate silently. A researcher watched
    two chimpanzees cooperate with each other
    to catch, kill and eat a small monkey. They
    did so without a sound, possibly because
    they were within vocal range of other
105 members of their tribe and preferred not to
    share their lunch.

         Another study looked at chimpanzees'
    ability to read facial expressions. Chimpanzees
    were shown short videos depicting positive
110 and negative emotional events, and then
    were presented with images of two facial
    expressions, one of which conveyed an
    emotional meaning similar to that in the video.
    Without prompting, some of the chimps
115 associated negative facial expressions (such
    as screams and bared teeth) with scenes such
    as veterinary procedures and injection needles,
    and positive facial expressions with scenes of
    favorite foods and objects, indicating that they
120 can, indeed, inherently read facial expressions
    without being specifically trained to do so.

         Many chimpanzees have been taught
    American Sign Language, and others have
    been taught to work with numbers. That may
125 not seem too surprising in an animal so closely
    related to us, but other research presented at
    the conference indicated that even sea lions
    can reason via transitivity, that is, by logic
    analogous to "if A equals B, and B equals C,
130 then A equals C." For instance, in the wild,
    male sea lions will fight a male they have
    seen beaten by another that they in turn
    have beaten.

         Evolving research continues to show that
135 our animal cousins are more sophisticated
    communicators, and have more sophisticated
    societies, than we normally give them credit
    for. So keep an eye on your pet: he may be
    trying to tell you something.

---

17 Farm cats are mentioned in the first sentence primarily because they

(A) must often defend themselves against dogs
(B) hunt in groups
(C) are capable of exchanging information
(D) can communicate on a level that humans cannot
(E) are more intelligent than crows

18 According to the passage, the "conference organizers" (line 23) were primarily concerned with

(A) promoting the study of biology in public schools
(B) encouraging the preservation of endangered animals
(C) demonstrating the unique nature of human language
(D) teaching animals to communicate
(E) sharing information gained through recent research

19 The passage indicates that elephants are similar to sperm whales in terms of their

    I.   ability to hear frequencies below the range that the human ear can perceive
    II. social organization
    III. ability to communicate over long distances

(A) II only
(B) I and II only
(C) II and III only
(D) I and III only
(E) I, II, and III

20 In the analogy described in lines 48–49, ships are compared to

(A) crashing ocean waves
(B) loud bar patrons
(C) other whales
(D) humans on a beach
(E) steel gates

21 The phrase "It appears" (line 62) is intended to suggest that

(A) a conclusion can be drawn from scientific research
(B) most people agree about a certain issue
(C) a particular claim is obvious to all scientists
(D) certain data were sudden and unexpected
(E) a claim should be regarded with skepticism

22 The "task" in line 73 is the process of

(A) comparing underwater sounds
(B) counting the number of whistles
(C) determining why dolphins make certain noises
(D) recording sounds in the ocean
(E) communicating with dolphins

23 The author suggests that chimpanzees communicate "silently" (line 100) because they

(A) cannot cooperate as effectively with sound
(B) do not want to scare off their prey
(C) lack a broad vocal range
(D) do not want to alert other chimpanzees
(E) are too far apart to communicate vocally

24 Which of the following, if true, would most effectively refute the conclusion that the sea lions mentioned in lines 127–133 reasoned "via transitivity"?

(A) A male sea lion sometimes fights members of his own family.
(B) A male sea lion fights other sea lions only to assert social dominance.
(C) A male sea lion only fights other sea lions that he has seen defeated by others.
(D) A male sea lion fights other sea lions that he has seen defeat sea lions that have also defeated him.
(E) A male sea lion refuses to fight any other sea lions.

6

STOP

You may check your work, on this section only, until time is called.

Section 7

Time—20 Minutes
16 Questions

Directions for Multiple-Choice Questions

In this section, solve each problem, using any available space on the page for scratchwork. Then decide which is the best of the choices given and fill in the corresponding oval on your answer sheet.

- You may use a calculator on any problem. All numbers used are real numbers.
- Figures are drawn as accurately as possible EXCEPT when it is stated that the figure is not drawn to scale.
- All figures lie in a plane unless otherwise indicated.

Reference Information

$A = \pi r^2$ $A = \ell w$ $A = \frac{1}{2}bh$ $V = \ell wh$ $V = \pi r^2 h$ $c^2 = a^2 + b^2$ Special Right Triangles
$C = 2\pi r$

The number of degrees of arc in a circle is 360°.
The measure in degrees of a straight angle is 180°.
The sum of the measures in degrees of the angles of a triangle is 180°.

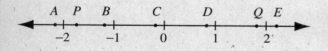

1 In the figure above, if the coordinates of points P and Q are multiplied together, the result will be closest to which of the following points?

(A) A
(B) B
(C) C
(D) D
(E) E

2 If $\frac{x}{8} = 5z$ and $\frac{1}{2z} = 5y$, then $xy =$

(A) 3
(B) 4
(C) 12
(D) 24
(E) 36

3 When a positive integer p is divided by 7, the remainder is 2. Which of the following expressions will yield a remainder of 4 when divided by 7?

(A) $p + 2$
(B) $p + 3$
(C) $p + 4$
(D) $p + 5$
(E) $p + 6$

GO ON TO THE NEXT PAGE ▸▸▸

SALARY GROWTH AT ACME PLUS CO.

YEARS WITH COMPANY	1	2	3	4	5
SALARY (in thousands)	32	33	36	42	51

4 Which of the following graphs best represents the information in the table above?

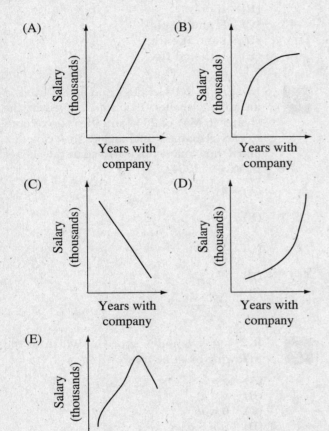

(A)

Salary (thousands) — Years with company

(B)

Salary (thousands) — Years with company

(C)

Salary (thousands) — Years with company

(D)

Salary (thousands) — Years with company

(E)

Salary (thousands) — Years with company

5 Four hundred dollars was invested at a yearly simple interest rate of x percent. If at the end of one year the investment had grown to 500 dollars, what is the value of x?

(A) 20
(B) 25
(C) 30
(D) 35
(E) 40

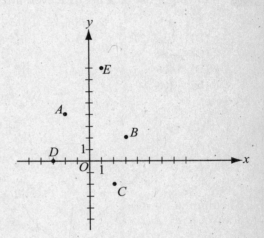

6 In the figure above, which of the following line segments (not shown) has a slope of -3?

(A) $\overline{AB}$

(B) $\overline{AC}$

(C) $\overline{AD}$

(D) $\overline{EB}$

(E) $\overline{DC}$

7 In a parking lot, ¾ of the vehicles are cars and ⅓ of the cars are more than 3 years old. If 20 cars in the lot are more than 3 years old, how many vehicles are there in total?

(A) 30
(B) 40
(C) 60
(D) 80
(E) 90

8 What is the average (arithmetic mean) of 8 consecutive *odd* integers if the smallest of those integers is n?

(A) $n + 5$
(B) $n + 6$
(C) $n + 7$
(D) $n + 8$
(E) $n + 9$

9 If w is an integer and $w \neq 0$, which of the following must be a positive even integer?

(A) w^4
(B) $(w - 2)^3$
(C) $4w^2$
(D) $4w$
(E) $3(w^2)$

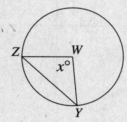

Note: Figure not drawn to scale.

10 In the circle above, W is the center of the circle and the length of ZY is 8. If the area of the circle is 64π, what is the value of x?

(A) 40
(B) 50
(C) 60
(D) 70
(E) 80

11 Which of the following expressions is equivalent to $16x^4$?

   I. $(64x^6)^{2/3}$

   II. $\left(\dfrac{1}{2x}\right)^{-4}$

   III. $\dfrac{x^2}{16x^{-1}}$

(A) I only
(B) II only
(C) II and III only
(D) I and II only
(E) I, II, and III

12 In April of 2004, d dogs and c cats lived in an animal shelter. If 4 cats arrived at the shelter in May of 2004 and the ratio of dogs to cats remained unchanged, in terms of c and d, how many dogs arrived at the shelter in May of 2004?

(A) 4

(B) $\dfrac{4d}{c}$

(C) $\dfrac{d}{c}$

(D) $d^2 - 4d$

(E) $\dfrac{2cd + 4d}{c}$

13 If $2 < |a| < 6$ and $3 < |b| < 6$, which of the following must be true?

(A) $a > b$
(B) $b > a$
(C) $0 < ab$
(D) $|ab| > 6$
(E) $36 < |a + b|$

14 When each side of a square is lengthened by 4 inches, the area of the square is increased by 112 square inches. What is the length, in inches, of one side of the original square?

(A) 10
(B) 11
(C) 12
(D) 13
(E) 14

15 $(-4x^4y^{-3})^{-3} =$

(A) $\dfrac{-4x}{y^6}$

(B) $\dfrac{-64y^9}{x^{12}}$

(C) $\dfrac{-64y^6}{x^7}$

(D) $-4x^{12}y^9$

(E) $\dfrac{y^9}{-64x^{12}}$

16 If the function h is defined by $h(x) = ax^2 + bx + c$, and both a and c are negative integers, which of the following could be the graph of the function h?

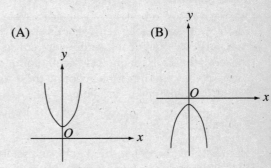

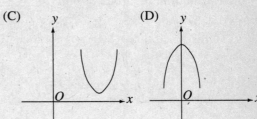

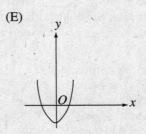

STOP

You may check your work, on this section only, until time is called.

Section 8

Time—20 minutes
19 Questions

Each of the sentences below is missing one or two portions. Read each sentence, then select the word or words that most logically completes the sentence, taking into account the meaning of the sentence as a whole.

Example:

Rather than accepting the theory unquestioningly, Deborah regarded it with _____.

(A) mirth   (B) sadness
(C) responsibility (D) ignorance
(E) skepticism

Example answer: (E)

8

1 As one of the most _____ writers of the 20th century, Jack Kerouac authored several books that _____ to a wide variety of readers.

(A) cryptic . . complained
(B) prolific . . appealed
(C) provocative . . attested
(D) arrogant . . spoke
(E) garish . . whispered

2 Since the downsizing, the company has shifted its focus from one that _____ many different points of view to one that _____ the voicing of different opinions.

(A) amplifies . . condemns
(B) eschews . . villifies
(C) embraces . . denounces
(D) seeks . . comprehends
(E) anticipates . . incorporates

3 The calculus problem was so difficult that even the most _____ mathematicians in the class struggled to derive the answer.

(A) agile   (B) adept
(C) abysmal   (D) insipid
(E) eloquent

4 The student's _____ was something the principal was not going to _____, and she punished the sophomore harshly for undermining the teacher's authority.

(A) insubordination . . condone
(B) dissemination . . assuage
(C) improvidence . . provoke
(D) subterfuge . . expedite
(E) impudence . . inundate

5 A good advertisement _____ potential customers to act, buy and consume; it persuades them that they must have the item on display.

(A) perpetuates   (B) thwarts
(C) consoles   (D) exhorts
(E) reproaches

6 Bartlett Jere Whiting's articles, though written long ago, demonstrate such a _____ and clarity of thinking that they still are included in bibliographies relating to this discipline.

(A) modicum   (B) respite
(C) dearth   (D) turpitude
(E) perspicacity

GO ON TO THE NEXT PAGE ▶▶▶

The passage below is followed by questions based on its content. Answer the questions based on what is stated or implied in each passage and in any introductory material that may be provided.

Questions 7-19 pertain to the following passage.

The following essay discusses the development of mathematics throughout history.

Line The trajectories of metaphysical and
mathematical thought have crossed myriad
times, and at many various angles and energies,
over the course of human civilization—often,
5 but not exclusively, to their mutual benefit.
Broadly speaking, the historical relationships
between religion and number fall into four
categories: the instrumental, the metaphorical,
the mystical, and the transformative. In
10 ancient civilizations, both arts were unified
by the fact that they were remote to the
multitude and by the fact that they were
occasionally practiced by the same priests,
but today their spheres are largely separated,
15 one dedicated to the manipulation of cultural
symbols to persuade believers, the other
dedicated to the manipulation of abstract
symbols to reveal the nature of truth.
    The Babylonians knew the instrumental
20 value of mathematics in the service of
engineering. They could calculate the number
of man-days[1] required to build a canal or dam,
or the quantity and arrangements of bricks
required to construct an edifice. They could
25 employ similar tools to predict the seasons
and other astronomical occurrences, and
because celestial bodies were regarded as
divine, mathematics came to be regarded as
an instrument of metaphysical exploration.
30 Likewise, geometric methods were used by
the Egyptians to construct the pyramids and
align them with the sacred heavens.
Reciprocally, the gods occasionally employed
mathematics to confound believers and set
35 their minds properly on the profundity of
logic, or so thought Plato when he interpreted
the oracle's demand that the Delians double

the volume of their altar, a task beyond Greek
mathematicians. (Each dimension cannot
40 merely be doubled, but rather multiplied by
the cube root of two, a number they had
approximated but not attained.)
    Proclus was likely inspired by this
instrumentality to infer that mathematics had
45 a deeper, metaphorical use in the service of
the divine, saying that mathematics "reminds
one of the invisible form of the soul ... [and]
awakens the mind and purifies the intellect."
Numbers could represent mystical beings,
50 even if they were not mystical themselves.
Such metaphors can be seen in Christianity's
Holy Trinity and the analogy between the
infinitude of the counting numbers and the
many presumed infinitudes of the divine.
55 Gregor Cantor, a Christian who contributed
greatly to the study of infinities, believed that
his theorems would offer Christianity for the
first time "the true theory of the infinite."
This metaphorical application reached a level
60 of absurdity when the number δ, the ratio of
the circumference of a circle to its diameter,
was taken to be precisely three by biblical
literalists in affirmation of the tripartite
nature of the Christian god. Ignorant of the
65 manner of mathematical reasoning, they took
their evidence directly from the book of
Kings, which proclaimed that a circular
cauldron in the temple of Solomon measured
ten cubits across and thirty cubits around.
70   Yet no power is so great as to be able to
construct a circle ten cubits across that could
be encircled with fewer than 31.4 cubits, and
this fact had been known for centuries before
the dawn of Christianity. The power of
75 mathematical deduction to establish irrefutable
truths beyond the arbitrary whims of spirits
and gods—and their priests on earth—has led
some to posit that numbers and their
relationships themselves hold mystical power
80 independent of their application to worldly
problems. This manner of thinking was taken
to its extreme by the cult of Pythagoras,
whose followers were called the mathematekoi,
or those who studied all things. Their creed
85 was "all is number;" and they pursued
religiously the purity of mathematical truth.
In the cult of Pythagoras, for the first time in

GO ON TO THE NEXT PAGE ▶▶▶

[1] One man-day is the amount of work an average man can complete in an average day.

human civilization, number acquired its own abstract plane beyond the physical world.

90   The mathematekoi believed that mathematics made itself known through nature, but was beyond nature, much in the same way that the spiritualists believed the gods were seen in nature yet supernatural. Mathematical

95   truths, unlike the revelations of the gods, could be known by a more reliable method available to all disciplined and pure devotees. The Pythagoreans eschewed meat, beans and animal skin clothing, and sought purity in all

100   things. Mathematics and reasoned philosophy was a means to spiritual purification, and the only way to achieve union with the divine.

Yet as with the elevation of any human endeavor to the plane of the metaphysical,

105   righteousness ascended. Ideological purity and political unity were celebrated with animal sacrifices upon every new proof and discovery, yet such seeming transgressions were punished with imperious and unreasoning

110   violence. When the mathematekos[2] Hipposus dared to prove that the length of the hypotenuse of a unitary isosceles right triangle is inexpressible as the ratio of whole numbers, the Pythagoreans threw him from a ship and

115   drowned him for denying their religious precept that all of reality can be described with whole numbers and the fundamental operations. Yet this hypotenuse (whose length is the square root of two) did not

120   cease to be irrational[3] by decree. Certainly either number or religious ideology would have to yield. The power of valid deduction, however, is absolute, unlike the more human philosophies. The realization of this fact has

125   led some to transform their sense of the origins of absolute truth. The Greeks were the first to rationalize nature—the word "rationalize" eventually shedding the arbitrary meaning of "expressing as ratio" and instead

130   encompassing all logical reasoning. They discovered that nature was not controlled by the capricious and obscure will of the gods, but rather by reliable and knowable mathematical laws. Although the explorers

135   occasionally stumbled in their quest for understanding, these missteps were inevitably found to be the fault of mistaken assumptions or inexact applications of logic. The inexorable march of reason toward the true understanding

140   of nature could not be denied.

[2] singular of mathematekoi
[3] inexpressible as a ratio of whole numbers

---

7 Which of the following is the best title for this passage?

(A)   Number and Religion in the Pythagorean Cult
(B)   The Religious Beliefs of Some Great Mathematicians
(C)   The Contribution of Geometry to Ancient Astronomy
(D)   The Historical Relationship between Mathematics and Metaphysics
(E)   The Legacy of the Babylonians

8 In line 3, the phrase "angles and energies" refers to

(A)   the motions of the planets
(B)   the rigidity of mathematical laws
(C)   the manner in which disciplines have intersected
(D)   the steadfast objectivity of historians
(E)   the mystical nature of some

9 The phrase "but not exclusively" (line 5) suggests that

(A)   some historians do not focus only on the development of mathematical and scientific thought
(B)   the relationship between mathematics and religion has not always been constructive
(C)   some people object to the application of mathematics to religious questions
(D)   many mathematical facts can easily coexist with religious precepts
(E)   some mathematical and religious ideas are beyond the understanding of the average person

10 The statement in lines 9–18 ("In ancient... truth") suggests that, over time, religion and mathematics have become more

(A) independent
(B) mystical
(C) interrelated
(D) difficult to understand
(E) popular

11 In line 14, the word "spheres" most nearly means

(A) social groups
(B) perfect forms
(C) domains of influence
(D) worldly objects
(E) mathematical laws

12 The word "Reciprocally" (line 33) is intended to convey the fact that

(A) mathematics was thought to be a tool for both humans and spiritual beings
(B) Plato was a mathematician as well as a moral philosopher
(C) the Egyptians contributed a great deal to Greek mathematics
(D) priests and mathematicians often posed problems to one another
(E) mathematicians were often employed in the building of

13 Plato is mentioned in line 36 because he

(A) solved a mathematical problem that had confused the oracle
(B) helped the Delians to construct an altar
(C) presented the Delians with knowledge that helped them to interpret a prophecy
(D) proclaimed that mathematical knowledge was independent of religious knowledge
(E) suggested that the oracle's demand was intended to mystify the Delians

14 The statement in lines 70–74 ("Yet no power ... dawn of Christianity") is intended to convey the fact that

(A) a proven mathematical fact cannot be contradicted
(B) religious laws are similar to mathematical laws
(C) ancient construction methods were inadequate
(D) many mathematical discoveries were made after the dawn of Christianity
(E) geometry was studied in great depth in the Christian era

15 The "manner of thinking" mentioned in line 81 includes the belief that

    I. the primary purpose of mathematics is to solve worldly problems
    II. mathematical laws are not arbitrary
    III. mathematics has mystical power

(A) III only
(B) I and II only
(C) I and III only
(D) II and III only
(E) I, II, and III

16 In line 89, "plane" most nearly means

(A) two-dimensional surface
(B) vehicle
(C) level
(D) struggle
(E) angle

17 In line 105, the statement "righteousness ascended" means that

(A) a mathematical theorem was proven
(B) historians acquired a biased point of view
(C) the Pythagoreans became ideologically intolerant
(D) many people rejected the cult of Pythagoras for religious reasons
(E) the cult of Pythagoras became politically divided

GO ON TO THE NEXT PAGE ▶▶▶

18 The final paragraph suggests that the "precept" mentioned in line 116 was

(A) factually incorrect
(B) only proven well after it was first declared
(C) later rejected by the Pythagoreans
(D) the foundation of many later discoveries
(E) obvious to many other Greek thinkers

19 The "explorers" (line 134) were those who

(A) sought mystical experiences
(B) investigated historical claims
(C) attempted to unify religion and mathematics
(D) endeavored to explain nature through reason
(E) adhered to the religious restrictions

8

STOP

You may check your work, on this section only, until time is called.

Section 9

Time—10 Minutes
14 Questions

Directions for "Improving Sentences" Questions

Each of the sentences below contains one underlined portion. The portion may contain one or more errors in grammar, usage, construction, precision, diction (choice of words), or idiom. Some of the sentences are correct.

Consider the meaning of the original sentence, and choose the answer that best expresses that meaning. If the original sentence is best, choose (A), because it repeats the original phrasing. Choose the phrasing that creates the clearest, most precise and most effective sentence.

EXAMPLE:

The growth of the plant was so dramatic that the children <u>couldn't hardly believe their eyes.</u>

(A)   couldn't hardly believe their eyes
(B)   would not hardly believe their eyes
(C)   could hardly believe their eyes
(D)   couldn't nearly believe their eyes
(E)   could hardly believe his or her eyes

Example answer: (C)

---

1   <u>Because the New York Yankees have spent the most money</u> of any franchise in baseball over the past five seasons, they have only managed to win one World Series in that time-span.

(A)   Because the New York Yankees have spent the most money
(B)   Although the New York Yankees have spent the most money
(C)   Having spent the most money, the New York Yankees
(D)   The New York Yankees, having spent the most money
(E)   The most money spent by the New York Yankees

2   Like most foreign visitors, <u>the canal system of Venice mesmerized the recently married couple</u>.

(A)   the canal system of Venice mesmerized the recently married couple
(B)   there was a canal system in Venice that mesmerized the recently married couple
(C)   the recently married couple, who was mesmerized by the canal system of Venice
(D)   the recently married couple was mesmerized by the canal system of Venice
(E)   the canal system of Venice having mesmerized the recently married couple

3   The new state <u>zoo, built on a four-hundred acre plot of land, and was paid for entirely by the state government</u>.

(A)   zoo, built on a four-hundred acre plot of land, and was paid for entirely by the state government
(B)   zoo was paid for by the state government, it was built on a four-hundred acre plot of land.
(C)   zoo is paid for by the state government while being built on a four-hundred acre plot of land
(D)   zoo, built on a four-hundred acre plot of land, was paid for entirely by the state government.
(E)   zoo, having been built on a four-hundred acre plot of land, and having been paid for entirely by the state government.

4   Many universities are developing new financial aid <u>programs that offer economic advantages to both the students and</u> their families.

(A) programs that offer economic advantages to both the students and

(B) programs, which offer economic advantage to not only students but

(C) programs, which offers economic advantages to both the students and

(D) programs; the economic advantages of which are offered to both students and

(E) programs: economic advantages are being offered to both the students in addition to

5   No sooner had Elizabeth accepted the job to teach AP biology at her daughter's private school <u>but her former boss persuaded her to return</u> to work at the laboratory.

(A) but her former boss persuaded her to return

(B) however she was persuaded by her former boss that she should

(C) but her former boss had her persuaded into returning

(D) when she was persuaded to return by her former boss

(E) than her former boss persuaded her to return

6   <u>His renown as a pioneer in the field of fuel-cell technology, Geoffrey Ballard almost equals</u> that of William Grove, the inventor of the world's first fuel cell, is the founder of Ballard Power Systems.

(A) His renown as a pioneer in the field of fuel-cell technology, Geoffrey Ballard almost equals

(B) Geoffrey Ballard's renown as a pioneer is in the field of fuel-cell technology almost equaling

(C) Geoffrey Ballard almost equals the renown as a pioneer in the field of fuel-cell technology

(D) As a pioneer, Geoffrey Ballard's renown as a pioneer in the field of fuel-cell technology almost equals

(E) Geoffrey Ballard, whose renown as a pioneer in the field of fuel-cell technology almost equals

7   <u>To clean the entire garage, Eric</u> decided to lie down and take a nap to restore his energy.

(A) To clean the entire garage, Eric

(B) Having cleaned the entire garage, Eric

(C) Eric cleaned the entire garage,

(D) In cleaning the entire garage, Eric

(E) Eric, cleaning the entire garage,

8   A brilliant songwriter who is able to adjust her style as she ages, <u>Madonna's songs always seem to fit with the music of the time</u>.

(A) Madonna's songs always seem to fit with the music of the time

(B) the songs of Madonna always seem to fit with the music of the time

(C) Madonna always writes songs that fit with the music of the time

(D) the music of the time is always fit by Madonna's songs

(E) Madonna always fits the music of the time when writing her songs

9   When you bake sugar cookies, <u>it is important that one remembers to chill the dough</u> before cutting the shapes.

(A) it is important that one remembers to chill the dough

(B) remembering to chill the dough is important

(C) it is important that you remember to chill the dough

(D) chilling the dough is important for you to have remembered

(E) to chill the dough is important for one to remember

10 When donating money to charity, <u>a non-profit organization that will use your dollars wisely should be your priority</u>.

- (A) a nonprofit organization that will use your dollars wisely should be your priority
- (B) you should make it your priority to choose a nonprofit organization that will use your dollars wisely
- (C) choose a nonprofit organization that will use your dollars wisely as your priority
- (D) a nonprofit organization should be your priority that will use your dollars wisely
- (E) using your dollars wisely should be your priority when choosing a nonprofit organization

11 In 2005, online shoppers in the United States charged more money to their credit cards <u>than</u> 2004.

- (A) than
- (B) than online shoppers for
- (C) than in
- (D) than would online shoppers in
- (E) than they did in

12 <u>Written in the late 18th century, modern audiences have enjoyed the musical theater's rendition of the opera *Don Giovanni* by Mozart</u>.

- (A) Written in the late 18th century, modern audiences have enjoyed the musical theater's rendition of the opera *Don Giovanni* by Mozart
- (B) Modern audiences have enjoyed the musical theater's rendition of the opera *Don Giovanni*, written in the late 18th century by Mozart.
- (C) Mozart's late 18th century opera *Don Giovanni* was enjoyed by modern audiences seeing the musical theater's rendition.
- (D) *Don Giovanni*, written by Mozart in the 18th century, was a musical theater's rendition of an opera that modern audiences had enjoyed.
- (E) Having been written in the late 18th century by Mozart, the musical theater's rendition of the opera *Don Giovanni* was enjoyed by modern audiences.

13 Surfing the Internet for hours at a time, <u>Claudia stares at her computer screen until her eyes begin to hurt</u>.

- (A) Claudia stares at her computer screen until her eyes begin to hurt
- (B) Claudia's eyes begin to hurt as she stares at her computer screen
- (C) staring at her screen until her eyes begin to hurt was Claudia
- (D) Claudia was staring at her computer screen until her eyes would begin to hurt
- (E) until her eyes began to hurt, Claudia staring at her computer screen

14 Dr. Sosa's delightful sense of humor and friendly smile <u>puts her patients</u> at ease.

- (A) puts her patients
- (B) having put her patients
- (C) her patients have been put
- (D) put her patients
- (E) putting her patients

STOP

You may check your work, on this section only, until time is called.

9

ANSWER KEY

Section 2 Math	Section 5 Math	Section 7 Math	Section 3 Critical Reading	Section 6 Critical Reading	Section 8 Critical Reading	Section 3 Writing	Section 9 Writing
☐ 1. B	☐ 1. C	☐ 1. A	☐ 1. B	☐ 1. A	☐ 1. B	☐ 1. C	☐ 1. B
☐ 2. D	☐ 2. A	☐ 2. B	☐ 2. D	☐ 2. E	☐ 2. C	☐ 2. C	☐ 2. D
☐ 3. C	☐ 3. D	☐ 3. A	☐ 3. A	☐ 3. C	☐ 3. B	☐ 3. A	☐ 3. D
☐ 4. D	☐ 4. B	☐ 4. D	☐ 4. E	☐ 4. A	☐ 4. A	☐ 4. B	☐ 4. A
☐ 5. C	☐ 5. A	☐ 5. B	☐ 5. B	☐ 5. A	☐ 5. D	☐ 5. D	☐ 5. E
☐ 6. B	☐ 6. D	☐ 6. D	☐ 6. C	☐ 6. C	☐ 6. E	☐ 6. A	☐ 6. E
☐ 7. D	☐ 7. D	☐ 7. D	☐ 7. D	☐ 7. E	☐ 7. D	☐ 7. D	☐ 7. B
☐ 8. C	☐ 8. C	☐ 8. C	☐ 8. E	☐ 8. C	☐ 8. C	☐ 8. B	☐ 8. C
☐ 9. B	☐ 9. 10	☐ 9. C	☐ 9. E	☐ 9. D	☐ 9. B	☐ 9. A	☐ 9. C
☐ 10. A	☐ 10. 5400	☐ 10. C	☐ 10. A	☐ 10. C	☐ 10. A	☐ 10. C	☐ 10. B
☐ 11. C	☐ 11. 44	☐ 11. D	☐ 11. D	☐ 11. E	☐ 11. C	☐ 11. A	☐ 11. E
☐ 12. D	☐ 12. ⅝ or .625	☐ 12. B	☐ 12. B	☐ 12. A	☐ 12. A	☐ 12. D	☐ 12. B
☐ 13. C		☐ 13. D	☐ 13. C	☐ 13. A	☐ 13. E	☐ 13. A	☐ 13. A
☐ 14. A	☐ 13. 14	☐ 14. C	☐ 14. C	☐ 14. B	☐ 14. A	☐ 14. E	☐ 14. D
☐ 15. E	☐ 14. 10	☐ 15. E	☐ 15. D	☐ 15. D	☐ 15. D	☐ 15. A	
☐ 16. C	☐ 15. 1 or 3	☐ 16. B	☐ 16. A	☐ 16. B	☐ 16. C	☐ 16. D	
☐ 17. E	☐ 16. 132		☐ 17. E	☐ 17. C	☐ 17. C	☐ 17. C	
☐ 18. B	☐ 17. 109		☐ 18. A	☐ 18. E	☐ 18. A	☐ 18. E	
☐ 19. B	☐ 18. 72		☐ 19. B	☐ 19. C	☐ 19. D	☐ 19. B	
☐ 20. D			☐ 20. C	☐ 20. B		☐ 20. C	
			☐ 21. E	☐ 21. A		☐ 21. B	
			☐ 22. E	☐ 22. A		☐ 22. C	
			☐ 23. B	☐ 23. D		☐ 23. B	
			☐ 24. B	☐ 24. D		☐ 24. E	
						☐ 25. D	
						☐ 26. C	
						☐ 27. A	
						☐ 28. D	
						☐ 29. B	
						☐ 30. B	
						☐ 31. A	
						☐ 32. B	
						☐ 33. D	
						☐ 34. B	
						☐ 35. A	

# Right (A):	Questions 1–8 # Right (A):	# Right (A):	# Right (A):	# Right (A):	# Right (A):	# Right (A)	# Right (A):
# Wrong (B):	_____ # Wrong (B):	# Wrong (B);	# Wrong (B):	# Wrong (B):	# Wrong (B):	# Wrong (B):	# Wrong (B):
# (A) – ¼ (B):	# (A) – ¼ (B):	# (A) – ¼ (B):	# (A) – ¼ (B):	# (A) – ¼ (B):	# (A) – ¼ (B):	# (A) – ¼ (B):	# (A) – ¼ (B):
	Questions 9–18 # Right (A):						

SCORE CONVERSION TABLE

How to score your test

Use the answer key on the previous page to determine your raw score on each section. Your raw score on each section except Section 4 is simply the number of correct answers minus ¼ of the number of wrong answers. On Section 4, your raw score is the sum of the number of correct answers for questions 1–8 minus ¼ of the number of wrong answers for questions 1–8 plus the total number of correct answers for questions 9–18. Next, add the raw scores from Sections 3, 4, and 7 to get your Math raw score, add the raw scores from Sections 2, 5, and 8 to get your Critical Reading raw score and add the raw scores from Sections 6 and 9 to get your Writing raw score.

Write the three raw scores here:

Raw Critical Reading score: _____ Raw Math score: _____ Raw Writing score: _____

Use the table below to convert these to scaled scores.

Scaled scores: Critical Reading: _____ Math: _____ Writing: _____

Raw Score	Critical Reading Scaled Score	Math Scaled Score	Writing Scaled Score	Raw Score	Critical Reading Scaled Score	Math Scaled Score	Writing Scaled Score
67				32		550	610
66	800			31	520	550	600
65	800			30	510	540	580
64	790			29	510	530	570
63	780			28	500	520	560
62	760			27	490	530	550
61	750			26	490	510	540
60	730			25	480	500	530
59	720			24	480	490	520
58	700			23	470	480	510
57	700			22	460	480	500
56	690			21	460	470	490
55	680			20	450	460	480
54	670	800		19	440	450	470
53	660	790		18	440	450	460
52	650	760		17	430	440	450
51	650	740		16	420	430	440
50	640	720		15	420	420	440
49	630	710	800	14	410	410	430
48	620	700	800	13	400	410	420
47	620	680	800	12	400	400	410
46	610	670	790	11	390	390	400
45	600	660	780	10	380	380	390
44	600	650	760	9	370	370	380
43	590	640	740	8	360	360	380
42	590	630	730	7	350	350	370
41	580	630	710	6	340	340	360
40	570	620	700	5	330	330	350
39	570	610	690	4	320	320	340
38	560	600	670	3	310	310	320
37	550	590	660	2	300	290	310
36	550	580	650	1	280	280	300
35	540	580	640	0	270	260	280
34	540	570	630	−1	250	240	270
33	530	560	620	−2 or less	230	220	250
	520				210		

SCORE CONVERSION TABLE FOR ESSAY + MULTIPLE CHOICE WRITING COMPOSITE

Calculate your writing raw score as you did on the previous page and grade your essay from a 1 to a 6 according to the standards that follow in the detailed answer key.

Essay score: _____ Raw Writing score: _____

Use the table below to convert these to scaled scores.

Scaled score: Writing _____

Raw Score	Essay Score 0	Essay Score 1	Essay Score 2	Essay Score 3	Essay Score 4	Essay Score 5	Essay Score 6
−2 or less	200	230	250	280	310	340	370
−1	210	240	260	290	320	360	380
0	230	260	280	300	340	370	400
1	240	270	290	320	350	380	410
2	250	280	300	330	360	390	420
3	260	290	310	340	370	400	430
4	270	300	320	350	380	410	440
5	280	310	330	360	390	420	450
6	290	320	340	360	400	430	460
7	290	330	340	370	410	440	470
8	300	330	350	380	410	450	470
9	310	340	360	390	420	450	480
10	320	350	370	390	430	460	490
11	320	360	370	400	440	470	500
12	330	360	380	410	440	470	500
13	340	370	390	420	450	480	510
14	350	380	390	420	460	490	520
15	350	380	400	430	460	500	530
16	360	390	410	440	470	500	530
17	370	400	420	440	480	510	540
18	380	410	420	450	490	520	550
19	380	410	430	460	490	530	560
20	390	420	440	470	500	530	560
21	400	430	450	480	510	540	570
22	410	440	460	480	520	550	580
23	420	450	470	490	530	560	590
24	420	460	470	500	540	570	600
25	430	460	480	510	540	580	610
26	440	470	490	520	550	590	610
27	450	480	500	530	560	590	620
28	460	490	510	540	570	600	630
29	470	500	520	550	580	610	640
30	480	510	530	560	590	620	650
31	490	520	540	560	600	630	660
32	500	530	550	570	610	640	670
33	510	540	550	580	620	650	680
34	510	550	560	590	630	660	690
35	520	560	570	600	640	670	700
36	530	560	580	610	650	680	710
37	540	570	590	620	660	690	720
38	550	580	600	630	670	700	730
39	560	600	610	640	680	710	740
40	580	610	620	650	690	720	750
41	590	620	640	660	700	730	760
42	600	630	650	680	710	740	770
43	610	640	660	690	720	750	780
44	620	660	670	700	740	770	800
45	640	670	690	720	750	780	800
46	650	690	700	730	770	800	800
47	670	700	720	750	780	800	800
48	680	720	730	760	800	800	800
49	680	720	730	760	800	800	800

Detailed Answer Key

Section 1

> The following essay received 12 points out of a possible 12. It demonstrates clear and consistent mastery in that it
>
> - develops an insightful point of view on the topic
> - demonstrates exemplary critical thinking
> - uses very effective examples, reasons, and other evidence to support its thesis
> - is consistently focused, coherent, and well-organized
> - demonstrates skillful and effective use of language and sentence structure
> - is largely (but not necessarily completely) free of grammatical and usage errors

SAMPLE STUDENT ESSAY

While there can certainly be value in the obstacles overcome in search of success, I disagree with the assertion that these struggles are more important than the accomplishment itself. Without question, individuals can learn valuable lessons from struggles, gaining insight into their own character or the nature of the struggles themselves and thus prepare for a future, less difficult path towards success. Far more often than not, however, struggle is defined by the pain it causes rather than by the lessons it teaches. This fact can be seen in a variety of sources throughout different walks of life.

Perhaps the most obvious example supporting my assertion that success without wounds leaves room for greater happiness, is war. Although countless films and novels have been written that describe the nobility of battle and the lessons learned in the midst of military struggle, ultimately, the price paid both by soldiers and innocent people caught up in the conflict significantly outweighs the positives described in such depictions. In international issues, success without conflict is ideal, even though it does not offer the compelling stories of soldiers' struggles and heroics. By avoiding conflict, peace is maintained and progress is made without interruptions. With war, nations are forced not only to overcome obstacles in the form of lost lives, but also to address the economic hardships involved in rebuilding infrastructure and paying off debt.

Another example that supports my assertion— one that is likely often used to support the opposite side of the argument—is the story of Lance Armstrong. In the past seven years, Armstrong has overcome a battle with cancer to win an unprecedented seven straight championships at the Tour de France. His story has inspired other cancer patients to dream of success and health and has led other cyclists to increase the intensity of their training in an attempt to end his streak. However, as wonderful as those side effects have been, the truth of the matter is that Armstrong was forced to face a nearly fatal illness, which was no doubt a horrific time for his friends and family. The question then becomes, is the value in Lance's accomplishments or in his struggles? Personally, I think his story would have been better if he had not been forced to overcome cancer. Winning seven straight titles without going through such personal difficulties would have made for a happier life, regardless of how such a shift would have affected the attractiveness of his story. A counter point to that argument would be that his health would have denied cancer patients one of their most powerfully inspired narratives; however, had Lance not battled cancer, another story would have filled that void, as the human spirit seeks ways to inspire itself in difficult times, and as such, it seems unfair to place value in the pain of any individual.

A final example supporting my assertion comes in the form of Alice Sebold. Now a famous writer, Ms. Sebold has been forced to overcome the effects of being raped while in college. The psychological effects of violent attacks are so severe that it would be quite difficult to overstate the magnitude of her struggles. However, she persevered and wrote two beautifully crafted works—one fiction (*The Lovely Bones*) and one non-fiction (*Lucky*)—based upon that tragic night. The battles faced by Ms.Sebold in the years leading up to her current success and state of mind helped to craft her work; this much is undeniable. However, those struggles are in no way a better measure of her success than the works themselves. A counter point might be that her stories might not have been so powerful had she not lived through these experiences herself and that her life made her the writer she is. I find this point to be off base, however, as I believe her status as a writer is unrelated to her status as a victim and that, without such pain in her life, she would have created different, but equally powerful stories.

Each of these examples points towards moments when people or groups of people were forced to take on a challenge and overcome loss before tasting success. Stories like these are well represented in books, films, and even daily news casts. They serve to inspire us, as they show us how much the human spirit can overcome on the path to success. The danger here, however, is in the potential for people to use the struggles of others as a crutch, depersonalizing their battles in an effort to feel less afraid of their own difficulties. There is absolutely nothing wrong with feeling inspired by a story of overcoming obstacles. In fact, when people say that such perseverance is an important measure of a person's character, they are correct. The mistake is in believing that the struggles somehow better represent success than do the accomplishments themselves, as though,

without the struggle, a person would somehow be less successful or less deserving of pride and admiration. Success without struggle can, at times, make for an anticlimactic story, but success without wounds leaves room for greater happiness, fewer losses, and better health. In my eyes, therefore, it seems unwise to see the struggles faced on the road to success as a better measure of accomplishment than are the actual successes themselves.

Reader's comments

This is an exceptionally well-reasoned and well-organized essay that disagrees with the thesis that "the struggle endured to achieve success is more important than the accomplishment itself." The author demonstrates a strong understanding of the origins of a belief as well as its effects. The author consistently focuses on the idea that while success can come from adversity, that success is not superceded by this struggle. The author also demonstrates strong facility and effective variety in diction and sentence structure. Its consistent critical reasoning and effective use of language merits a 12.

The following essay received 10 points out of a possible 12. It demonstrates reasonably consistent mastery in that it

- effectively develops a point of view on the topic
- demonstrates strong critical thinking
- uses good examples, reasons, and other evidence to support its thesis
- shows a good organization and consistent focus
- demonstrates consistent facility with language
- is mostly free of errors in grammar, usage, and mechanics

SAMPLE STUDENT ESSAY

When faced with adversity in some area of my life, I am often reminded of my mother's favorite saying that, "it is not about the ending—it is about the journey." Although it might seem like hackneyed advice to someone in the moment and frustrated by an obstacle that is difficult to overcome, the expression speaks the truth about success in life.

As I've gotten older, math class has become progressively more difficult for me. This year has been particularly difficult because I have worked my way into an advanced class. Each test seems like an obstacle or a hurdle that I have to get over and the tests seem to be getting progressively more difficult. So far this year, I have averaged a C+ in my math class, (which is not great) and my successes have been far and few between. When I have managed to succeed on a test, however, I know the good grade is the result of a lot of hard work and studying. In my opinion, the work I put into getting a good math grade is more a measure of my success as a person than the grade itself is. When I think back to the tests that I have done well on, what I remember clearly are the long nights of hard work and preparation that allowed me to achieve these rare successes and I feel very proud of the efforts.

Abraham Lincoln was a poor boy from a poor family, and the opportunity to become president was not handed to him as it might have been to someone with a higher social standing or with a greater disposable income. Lincoln made extraordinary efforts to gain knowledge while working on a farm, splitting rails for fences, and keeping store at New Salem, Illinois. He spent eight years in the Illinois legislature, and rode the circuit of courts for many years, as well. His colleagues said that his ambition was a little engine that knew no rest. In 1858 Lincoln ran against Stephen A. Douglas for Senator. He lost the election, but the famous Lincoln-Douglas debates helped him to gain a national reputation that won him the Republican nomination for President in 1860 and eventually the Presidency of the United States. When people think of Abraham Lincoln today, they think of "Honest Abe," one of the most influential and powerful Presidents in our history. The character he built by working hard to achieve his presidential position was more a measure of his success than it was an opportunity to call himself "President."

There are many examples of this belief that it is not about the ending—it is about the journey that can be found in other areas. The struggle to achieve a position teaches a person more about how to live than does the simple acquisition of the position. Using those valuable lessons throughout life will help make a person become more successful in the long run.

Reader's comments

This is a well-reasoned and well-organized essay supporting the thesis that "the struggle endured to achieve success is more important than the accomplishment itself." The author uses two well-organized examples to support her opinion. The essay does not get the highest possible score, however, because the author does not demonstrate strong enough facility with transition sentences. There is no flow from the second to the third paragraph—the author just jumps right into the Lincoln example without any sort of transition. In addition, her conclusion is not of the same quality and focus as the rest of the essay as it does not summarize the author's thoughts very clearly and strays a little from the main thesis. Nevertheless, the strong reasoning and effective examples in the essay merit a high score of 10.

The following essay received 4 points out of a possible 12, meaning that it demonstrates some incompetence in that it

- has a seriously limited point of view
- demonstrates weak critical thinking
- uses inappropriate or insufficient examples, reasons, and other evidence to support its thesis
- is poorly focused and organized, and has serious problems with coherence
- demonstrates frequent problems with language and sentence structure
- contains errors in grammar and usage that obscure the author's meaning seriously

SAMPLE STUDENT ESSAY

Success is not a measure of achievement but rather of heart. The novel *Huckleberry Finn* by Mark Twain shows how a black slave named Jim runs away from his masters' home in order to escape the threat of being sold to another slave owner. He joins Huck Finn, a ten year-old boy, and his ability to overcome obstacles and survive on the Mississippi River makes him successful. Similarly, as a tennis player, I always feel that I have succeeded if I have worked hard in practice and prepared the best that I could for tournaments. While winning means everything to me, I know that if I have come prepared to my tournament and executed my strategy, I have succeeded regardless of the result.

In *Huckleberry Finn*, Jim bravely runs away from his slave owner in order to be free. The fact that he and a ten year-old boy are able to survive as they travel down the river, both trying to escape the limitations of society, gives them ultimate success. Even though they had to disguise their identities and outsmart thieves, Huck and Jim were able to survive and continue their journey down the river until they were eventually found.

Similar to the experiences of Huck and Jim in *Huckleberry Finn*, I constantly struggle to achieve my goals. I have always been someone who has needed to work hard on my tennis game because I do not possess the natural talent that some of my adversaries

possess. Similarly, I have never been a fast kid so I have always had to work hard and improve my speed and agility in order to become faster and more nimble on the court. I have learned to realize that if I am training hard for my tournaments and spending a lot of attention on the aspects of my tennis game that I need to improve, I have already won. And often times, the result of my hard work is shown in my matches.

Reader's comments

The author attempts to answer the question posed in the prompt by discussing the struggle to achieve success. However, the author misses the mark and does not discuss the idea that the struggle is more important than the actual achievement. He instead defines success as a measure of an individual's "heart," an entirely different direction. The example in the second paragraph mentions a success achieved by Huck Finn that was not easy. This again strays from the question the prompt actually posed. Furthermore, the essay lacks a formal conclusion—it seems to end without warning. Lastly, the author demonstrates weak facility with language and structure, showing particular weakness in diction and transitions. This essay avoids a score of 0 (each reader giving it a 0) because it attempts to answer the question, and a score of 2 (each reader giving it a 1) because it attempts some reasoning and support for its claim.

Detailed Answer Key

Section 2

---

1. B

$$3b - 5c =$$

Substitute for b and c: $\quad 3(4) - 5(7) =$

Simplify: $\quad 12 - 35 = -23$

---

2. D First write the equation to find the average of 4 and w. Then, write the equation to find the average of 2, 8, and w. Set those two equations equal to each other and solve.

$$\frac{4+w}{2} = \frac{2+8+w}{3}$$

Cross-multiply: $\quad 3(4+w) = 2(10+w)$

Distribute: $\quad 12 + 3w = 20 + 2w$

Subtract $2w$: $\quad 12 + w = 20$

Subtract 12: $\quad w = 8$

---

3. C The length of MN can be determined by subtracting the x-coordinates of the two points M and N.

$$4 - (-1) = 5$$

The length of QR = the length of MN = 5.

The length of QR can be determined by subtracting the x-coordinates of the two points Q and R.

$$x - (-3) = 5$$
$$x + 3 = 5$$

Subtract 3: $\quad x = 2$

---

4. D To find the percent change use the formula:

$$\frac{final - original}{original} \times 100$$

The original (2005) was \$0.75
The final (2006) was \$1.00

$$\frac{\$1.00 - \$0.75}{\$0.75} \times 100 = \frac{\$0.25}{\$0.75} \times 100 = 33\frac{1}{3}\%$$

---

5. C Set up a proportion:

$$\frac{4\,oranges}{d\,dollars} = \frac{40\,oranges}{x\,dollars}$$

Cross multiply: $\quad 4x = 40d$

Divide by 4: $\quad x = 10d$

---

6. B

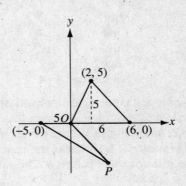

Area = ½(base)(height)

Start with the triangle on the right. The base rests along the x-axis and stretches from $x = 0$ to $x = 6$, so the base is 6 units. The height stretches from $y = 0$ to $y = 5$, so the height is 5 units. The area can now be calculated:

$$Area = \frac{1}{2}(6)(5) = 15$$

Because you are told the areas of the two triangles are equal, the area of the left triangle must also be 15. The base of this triangle stretches from $x = 0$ to $x = -5$ for a value of 5 units. We can use this to solve for its height:

$$Area = \frac{1}{2}(base)(height)$$

Substitute: $\quad 15 = \frac{1}{2}(5)(height)$

Simplify: $\quad 15 = 2.5(height)$

Divide by 2.5: $\quad 6 = height$

In order for the left triangle to have a height of 6 with a base on the x-axis, its height must equal 6 units, and answer choice (B) is the only point that is 6 units from the x-axis.

---

7. D Begin by factoring

$$a^2 - 2ab + b^2 = (a-b)(a-b)$$

Substitute for $(a - b)$: $\quad a^2 - 2ab + b^2 = (-4)(-4) = 16$

8. C Remember that the greatest change can be either positive or negative.

Month	#	Change
February	2	–
March	4	+2
April	7	+3
May	3	–4
June	4	+1
July	2	–2
August	2	0
September	4	+2

The biggest change occurs from April to May.

9. B You could plug in simple values to solve this question. Let's say $r = 3$. If that is the case, then $s = 4$ because the ratio of r to s is 3 to 4. The ratio of s to t is 2 to 9.

$$\frac{s}{t} = \frac{2}{9} = \frac{4}{t}$$

Cross multiply: $2t = 36$
Divide by 2: $t = 18$

So, if $s = 4$, then $t = 18$.

Therefore the ratio of r to t is 3 to 18 or 1 to 6.

10. A You may wonder why 15 is not an answer choice since $4 + 5 + 6 = 15$. But, remember that you cannot assume that numbers on the SAT are integers. It *could* be 15 if $AB = 4$, $BC = 5$ and $CD = 6$, but that's not one of the choices. If $BC = 5.6$ and $AB = 5.4$, then AD would be $5.4 + 5.6 + 6.0 = 17$.

It is impossible for AD to be 18 or greater if $CD = 6$ because CD is larger than the other two segments and the only way to get 18 would be for AB and/or BC to be larger than or equal to CD, which is not possible. Therefore the answer is (A).

11. C To solve this problem, plug in a value of x from the table above and cross out any function that does not give the proper value for f(x). Often times if you start with the first value in the table, three or more answers will work, so it can work to your advantage to start with a middle value. If you start with $x = 5$, a few choices can be eliminated:

(A) $f(5) = \frac{3}{2}(5) + 4 = 7.5 + 4 = 11.5$

(B) $f(5) = -\frac{2}{3}(5) - 3 = -\frac{10}{3} - 3 = -6\frac{1}{3}$

(C) $f(5) = 2(5) + 2 = 12$

(D) $f(5) = 3(5) - 3 = 12$

(E) $f(5) = 4(5) - 6 = 14$

This leaves you with two choices: C and D. Try the next value of x.   (C) $f(6) = 2(6) + 2 = 14$
                                                                             (D) $f(6) = 3(6) - 3 = 15$

Only (C) remains and so must be the correct answer.

12. D Because the lines are parallel you know that:

$a = e$ because they are corresponding angles.
$h = e$ because they are vertical angles.
$d = e$ because they are alternate interior angles.
f is supplementary to e but not necessarily equal to it.
    Look at each of the answer choices.
    (A) a is necessarily equal to e.
    (B) Because $h = e$ and $d = e$, you

can rewrite $\frac{(h+d)}{2}$ as $\frac{e+e}{2} = \frac{2e}{e} = e$

    (C) Because $a = e$ and $d = e$, you

can rewrite $\frac{(a+d)}{2}$ as $\frac{e+e}{2} = \frac{2e}{e} = e$

    (D) f is supplementary to e and therefore not necessarily equal to it. So $\frac{(f+h)}{2}$ is not necessarily equal to e.

    (E) d is necessarily equal to e.

13. C $(2k^{1/2}k^{1/2})(2(k^{3/2})^{2/3})^{-2} =$
Simplify $(2k^{1/2}k^{1/2})$: $(2k^{1/2}k^{1/2}) = (2k^{1/2 + 1/2}) = 2k$
Simplify $(2(k^{3/2})^{2/3})^{-2}$: $(2(k^{3/2})^{2/3})^{-2} = (2(k^{3/2 \times 2/3})^{-2} = (2k)^{-2}$

$(2k^{1/2}k^{1/2})(2(k^{3/2})^{2/3})^{-2} =$

Substitute: $(2k)(2k)^{-2} = \frac{2k}{(2k)^2} = \frac{1}{2k}$

14. A p is 40% less than 600: $p = 0.60(600) = 360$
t is 40% greater than p: $t = 1.40p$
Substitute: $t = 1.40(360) = 504$
                              $t - p = 504 - 360 = 144$

15. E Begin by writing out the first 6 to 8 terms of the sequence:

1st term = -2	–
2nd term = 4	+
3rd term = $-2(4) = -8$	–
4th term = $-8(4) = -32$	–
5th term = $-32(-8) = 256$	+
6th term = $256(-32) = -8,192$	–

It does not matter what the value of each term is. What matters is the sign of each term. The first 6 terms are $- + - - + -$. The pattern is $- + -$ and repeats every 3 terms with two negative terms in each repetition of the pattern. To find out how many of the first 139 terms are negative, divide 139 by 3 and find the remainder. $139 \div 3 = 46$ remainder 1.

This means that the pattern of three occurs 46 full times, which gives a total of 2 × 46 = 92 negative terms. The remainder of 1 means that the 139th term is the *first* term of the sequence, which is negative. This means there are a total of 92 + 1 = 93 negative terms.

---

16. **C** You are told that the value of $h(5) = k$. To find the value of k, go to $x = 5$ on the x-axis and find the y-value of the function at that point. $h(5) = 5$.

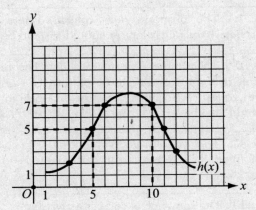

Therefore $k = 5$. The problem asks for the value of $h(2k)$ or $h(10)$. The value of $h(10)$ is 7.

---

17. **E** One challenging aspect of this problem is that some of the information is given as a fraction and some is given as an actual amount. Set up a table to help clarify the information:

	fraction	#
Red	$\frac{2}{5}$	?
White	$\frac{3}{10}$	?
Blue	$\frac{1}{10}$	?
Green	?	10
Total	1	?

The sum, of the fractional parts must be 1. This fact allows you to determine what fraction of the marbles are green. $\frac{2}{5} + \frac{3}{10} + \frac{1}{10} = \frac{8}{10}$ of the marbles are red, white or blue. Therefore $\frac{2}{10} = \frac{1}{5}$ = are green. Set up an equation and solve:

$$\frac{1}{5}x = 10$$

Multiply by 5: $x = 50$

---

18. **B**

$$\frac{wx}{y+w} = 1$$

Multiply by $(y + w)$: $\qquad wx = y + w$

Subtract w: $\qquad wx - w = y$

Factor out w: $\qquad w(x - 1) = y$

Divide by $(x - 1)$: $\qquad w = \dfrac{y}{x-1}$

---

19. **B** You are told that $ON = OM$.

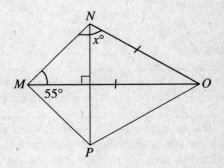

This means that $\angle ONM = \angle OMN$. You are also told that $ON = OP$.

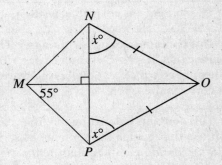

This means that $\angle ONP = \angle OPN = x$. Finally, you are told that $MN = MP$.

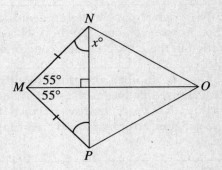

From this you can calculate the value of $\angle MNP$, which must be equal to 90°–55° = 35°. Because $\angle ONM = \angle OMN$, you know that $\angle ONM = 55°$. Therefore $x = 55°–35° = 20°$.

20. D To solve this problem, determine how many roads can be taken each step of the way. To go from Wilton to Norwalk, Kristina can choose from five roads. To go from Norwalk to Darien, she can choose from four roads. Heading back from Darien to Norwalk, she can now only choose from *three* roads because she can't travel the same road twice. Heading back from Norwalk to Wilton, she can now only choose from *four* roads for the same reason. This means there are a total of $5 \times 4 \times 3 \times 4 = 240$ possible routes.

Section 3

1. C The subject *harmful effects* (plural) disagrees with the verb *is* (singular). The verb should be *are*.

2. C The sentence is not parallel. The first two items in the list establish the pattern: *lower taxes* (concrete noun phrase), *a more decentralized government* (concrete noun phrase). So the last item in the list should also be a concrete noun phrase: *a lesser expenditure*.

3. A The sentence is correct as written.

4. B This contains a dangling modifier. The modifying phrase that begins the sentence describes *most of us* rather than *Christopher Columbus*. Answer choice (B) best corrects the error.

5. D This contains a dangling modifier. The modifying phrase that begins the sentence describes *the Empire State Building* rather than *many sightseers*. Answer choice (D) best corrects the error.

6. A The sentence is correct as written.

7. D The original phrasing is awkward and non-idiomatic. Answer choice (D) best corrects the construction in the most clear and concise manner.

8. B This is another dangling modifier. The modifying phrase that begins the sentence describes *Felisha* rather than *the rain*. Answer choice (B) eliminates the dangling error by properly rearranging the sentence.

9. A The sentence is correct as written.

10. C The subject *validity* (singular) disagrees with the verb *have* (plural). The verb should be *has* (singular).

11. A The sentence is correct as written.

12. D The subject *Bob Hope* (singular) disagrees with the verb *were* (plural). The verb should be *was* (singular).

13. A Since the Colts are one of 32 NFL teams *between* should instead be *among*.

14. E The sentence is correct as written.

15. A The pronoun *their* (plural) refers to *the Russian Army* (singular). It should instead be *its*.

16. D The sentence is not parallel. The first two items in the list establish the pattern: *to sag* (infinitive), *to brown* (infinitive). So the last item in the list should also be an infinitive *to have sticky thick crust.*

17. C The pronoun *she* is ambiguous. It is not clear whom *she* is referring to in this sentence—Julia or Patricia.

18. E The sentence is correct as written.

19. B The subject *allowance* (singular) disagrees with the verb *help* (plural). The verb should be *helps* (singular).

20. C This is an idiom error. The proper phrase is *preoccupation with*, not *in*.

21. B The pronoun *which* refers to the woman, and so should be replaced by the personal pronoun *whom*.

22. C The subject *technique* (singular) disagrees with the verb *are* (plural). The verb should be *is* (singular).

23. B This is a diction error. To *affect* means to influence. An *effect* is a result or consequence.

24. E The sentence is correct as written.

25. D The phrase *not only* A *but also* B indicates a parallel structure. To make the structure parallel, the phrase should instead be *but also feeling dizzy.*

26. C The word *and* connects the two thoughts as if they support each other. But they in fact contrast each other. The word *and* should be replaced with *even though, but* or *yet.*

27. A This contains a dangling modifier. Because *the effects*, the subject, is not underlined, it must be correct. *When looking* is a dangling participle because it suggests that the *effects* were *looking*, which is impossible. The sentence should begin with a phrase like *When one looks.*

28. **D** The pronoun *anyone* is singular. *They* should be replaced by *he* or *she.*

29. **B** When *neither .. nor ..* construction is used, the verb takes the same number as the noun that follows *nor*. In this case, *sisters* (plural) follows *nor*. So *was* should be changed to *were.*

30. **B** The original phrasing is not a complete sentence. Answer choice (B) provides the most logical, concise and clear phrasing.

31. **B** The original sentence contains a dangling modifier that needs to be corrected. The sentence suggests a bit of a contrast, so the *though* is an important addition to the correct selection.

32. **B** Sentence 5 does not contribute to the unity of the passage. The skull is not talked about in the rest of the passage.

33. **D** Answer choice (D) serves as a good introduction to the topic of the second paragraph since that paragraph focuses on the palate of the crocodile.

34. **B** Answer choice (B) provides the most logical and clear phrasing. Answer choice (C) creates an illogical contrast with its use of however. Answer choice (D) contains verb tense errors. Answer choice (E) creates a dangling modifier error.

35. **A** The sentence is best as written.

Section 4

1. **B** You are told that the minerals found in the waters do two things. They ___ and revitalize (bring new life to) the skin. The missing word should mean something similar to *revitalize. ingratiate* = to bring oneself into the good graces of another; *invigorate* = to impart vigor or strength; *exculpate* = to free of blame; *enervate* = to weaken; *debilitate* = to weaken.

2. **D** The word *despite* indicates a contrast. The sentence mentions an ever-present curiosity about Grover Cleveland, which suggests that his life was subject to much *scrutiny* (close examination). Despite this attention, though, he enjoyed *privacy*. This is something that other famous public figures would wish for or could only *imagine. candor* = honesty; *animosity* = bitter hostility; *frivolity* = inappropriate silliness.

3. **A** The senate unanimously *ratified* (formally approved) the law. *nullify* = to invalidate; *refute* = to argue against; *supplant* = to take the place of; *pilfer* = to steal.

4. **E** The *it* in the second half of the sentence refers to *her confinement to a wheelchair*. LaToya viewed it as something that *pushed* her to achieve. *Inspiration* and *impetus* are the two answer choices that would make sense in the second blank. The presence of the word *instead* indicates that LaToya's view was in opposition to the view of her friends, who must have seen it as a *problem. Impediment* (hurdle) is a good choice. *atrocity* = an appalling condition; *irrelevant* = unrelated to the subject; *omen* = a sign of something to come; *elocution* = a style of speaking; *idiosyncracy* = peculiar trait or habit; *impetus* = a driving force.

5. **B** Gandhi is described as *resistant to authority* without being *combative*. This takes *pugnacious* out of play and suggests that *recalcitrant* would be a good fit. *fickle* = known for unpredictable change; *recalcitrant* = hesitant to obey; *pugnacious* = combative; *lucrative* = profitable; *spurious* = fake.

6. **C** Whatever tragedy befell the Jamjang village resulted in *burned huts, blackened ashes*, and *a smell of smoke*. This suggests answer choices (A), *wildfire* and (C), *conflagration* (giant fire) are reasonable. The smell of smoke that hung in the air is probably not *savory* (appetizing) but instead *acrid* (unpleasantly sharp). *savory* = appetizing to the taste or smell; *cacophony* = harsh or discordant sounds; *pungent* = sharp taste or smell; *conflagration* = giant fire; *acrid* = unpleasantly sharp; *abomination* = disgust; *scourge* = a source of widespread suffering; *irascible* = easily angered.

7. **D** By looking at the editor's scribbles, the author could see how much thought he put into his work. The fact that he eliminates *all* unnecessary words suggests he makes a lot of marks on the page. *rapacious* = greedy; *improvident* = not providing for the future; *convoluted* = hard to follow; *copious* = abundant; *ostentatious* = showy.

8. **E** The officer is attempting to *supplement* (add to) his *modest income*. An individual who is willing to break the law for those who will pay enough money is one who *is able to be bribed (venal). clairvoyant* = having the ability to see things that cannot be perceived by the normal senses; *impassive* = lacking emotion; *matriculated* = having been admitted into a group; *scrupulous* = moral; *venal* = able to be bribed.

9. **E** Both passages indicate that "certain factors are decreasing the human body's ability to ward off disease." In Passage 1, this factor is "excessively sanitary conditions" (line 4) and in Passage 2 it is the "widespread use of antibiotics" (lines 19–20). Choice (A) is incorrect because neither passage suggests that "recently developed medications are ineffectual," even though Passage 2 suggests that antibiotics are becoming *less* ineffectual. Choice (B) is incorrect because Passage 1 does not discuss antibiotics, and Passage 2 suggests that their overuse may be a problem. Choice (C) is incorrect because Passage 1 indicates that *both* genetics and environment are essential to developing resistance to allergies. Choice (D) is incorrect because Passage 1 suggests that excessively *sanitary*, not unsanitary, conditions are problematic.

10. **A** The benefit referred to in line 11 is the ability of infection to prevent "certain individuals from developing allergies" (lines 7–8).

11. **D** Although the first two sentences of Passage 2 tout the benefits of antibiotics, this enthusiasm is muted by the discussion of the ways in which bacteria have come to "outwit" (line 22) those antibiotics. The overall tone is best described as one of "qualified [muted] enthusiasm."

12. **B** The "resistance" in line 5 is "a person's resistance to disease," specifically allergies. The "resistance" in line 26 is a bacteria's ability to "outwit the effects of antibiotics" (lines 22–23), which are a type of drug.

13. **C** Overall, the purpose of this passage is to criticize the USDA farm subsidy program for its mismanagement (lines 11–23), its inefficiency (lines 41–45), its unfairness (lines 79–94) and its ineffectiveness (lines 56–79). Therefore the "something rotten" mentioned in line 1 must refer to the farm subsidy program itself.

14. **C** Passage 1 explains its claim that the GAO report documenting mismanagement in the farm subsidies program "probably won't" (line 10) horrify lawmakers in the last two paragraphs (lines 101–111), where it suggests that lawmakers are unlikely to change a program that benefits a "powerful lobby in American politics" (lines 101–102).

15. **D** The fourth paragraph describes a "misconception" (line 37) and explains why it is wrong. The misconception is that subsidies lead to reduced costs to consumers, and the fourth paragraph suggests that it is not beneficial to consumers at all.

16. **A** This sentence suggests that the name given to these payments serves to "obscure [the] intended effect" (lines 51–52) of increasing food prices, and therefore is somewhat misleading.

17. **E** This poll revealed that "77 percent of Americans said that they support giving subsidies to small family farms" (lines 76–78), therefore it was intended to determine the feelings that the public had toward the federal farm subsidies program.

18. **A** The last two paragraphs (lines 101–111) suggest that subsidies are "for elected officials, too" (line 111) because these subsidies benefit "a powerful lobby" (line 101) that in turn contributes large sums to political campaigns. Therefore, politicians receive indirect benefits from the subsidy program. The passage does not suggest that legislators own farms, receive direct subsidies, compete with farmers for government funds, or work to reduce inefficiencies in the subsidies program.

19. **B** This paragraph indicates that "regular shortfalls would be even more worrisome" (lines 128–129) than inventory oversupply, thereby suggesting that oversupply is not as troublesome as it may seem. Since this oversupply is the result of subsidies, it certainly is not "being alleviated" by those payments. The passage does not suggest that oversupply is "unavoidable," and in fact suggests otherwise since the government is taking measures to ensure it. This oversupply "helps to safeguard against excessive price fluctuations" (lines 130–131) and therefore cannot be a result of those fluctuations. Also, the paragraph does not compare the harm these fluctuations do to farmers with the harm done to consumers.

20. **C** All of these choices represent parts of the "food processing [canning factories], distribution [truck drivers] and marketing [fruit store owners and promotional associations] chain" (lines 143–144) except for legislators.

21. **E** Both passages agree that subsidies "can control the price of agricultural products." Passage 1 indicates this in lines 49–51, where it says that "Congress also pays farmers to leave their land fallow, resulting in lower supply and thus higher prices." Passage 2 indicates this in lines 140–149, where it shows how "Subsidies ... contribute to ... lower prices for consumers."

22. **E** The author of Passage 1 discusses the fact that subsidies lower prices for consumers in lines 42–45, which conclude that "the taxpayers ... will probably pay

more in excess taxes than [they] will ever get back in lower corn or wheat prices." Therefore, the benefit of subsidies is not worth the higher taxes to consumers.

---

23. **B**   Passage 1 is disdainful of the farm subsidies program, saying that it "should horrify lawmakers" (line 9) because it is mismanaged, ineffective and unfair. Passage 2, however, generally supports the program by concluding that "its positive impacts far outweigh its negative ones" (lines 164–165).

---

24. **B**   Both passages contain a verifiable statistic: "30 percent of even these scrutinized subsidies were going to those who shouldn't be receiving them" (lines 20–22) and "more than 70 percent of farm revenue is derived from government payments" (lines 156–158); and a refutation of a misconception: "One popular misconception is that these subsidies... are a boon to consumers" (lines 37–39) and "One of the major misconceptions... is that only the producers receive the benefits of this funding" (lines 136–139). Passage 2 does not mention any instance of political corruption, however.

Section 5

---

1. **C**   Each pen costs $3, so if you buy p pens, it costs $3p$ dollars. Each binder costs $2, so b binders cost $2b$ dollars. Together they cost $3p + 2b$ dollars.

---

2. **A**   The first number that is divisible by both 4 and 6 is 12, which is not divisible by 8. Therefore the answer is (A). 24, 48, 64 and 72 are all divisible by 4, 6, *and* 8.

---

3. **D**

$$8,755 = 85(x + 2)$$

Divide by 85: $103 = x + 2$

Subtract 2: $x = 101$

---

4. **B**   To solve this problem, apply the definition to each of the answer choices and pick the one that gives you an odd number.

(A) $\frac{4}{2}(8) + 4(2) = 16 + 8 = 24$

(B) $\frac{3}{1}(2) + 3(1) = 6 + 3 = 9$

(C) $\frac{9}{3}(3) + 9(3) = 9 + 27 = 36$

(D) $\frac{8}{4}(6) + 8(4) = 12 + 32 = 44$

(E) $\frac{5}{1}(7) + 5(1) = 35 + 5 = 40$

Answer choice (B) is the only odd value.

---

5. **A**   Treat this like a shaded-area problem.

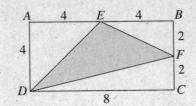

Because E and F are midpoints, you know that $AE = EB = 4$ and that $BF = FC = 2$. You can now find the area of the entire rectangle, and the area of the three unshaded triangles and subtract the area of the triangle from the area of the rectangle to get the area of triangle DEF.

Area of rectangle $ABCD = (8)(4) = 32$ units^2

Area of triangle $DCF = \frac{1}{2}(8)(2) = 8$ units^2

Area of triangle $EBF = \frac{1}{2}(4)(2) = 4$ units^2

Area of triangle $EAD = \frac{1}{2}(4)(4) = 8$ units^2

The area of triangle $DEF = 32 - 8 - 4 - 8 = 12$ units^2

---

6. **D**   Think about how many possible choices there are for each position and multiply those numbers together:

_____, _____ _____ _____
thousands hundreds tens   units

You are told that the tens digit is 5. Therefore there is only one possible choice for that position.

_____, _____ ___1___ _____
thousands hundreds tens   units

There are no other restrictions so when filling the units place, you can choose among *six* possible digits.

_____, _____ ___1___ ___6___
thousands hundreds tens   units

Now there are *five* digits left for the hundreds place.

_____, ___5___ ___1___ ___6___
thousands hundreds tens   units

Now there are *four* digits left for the thousands place.

___4___, ___5___ ___1___ ___6___
thousands hundreds tens   units

There are $4 \times 5 \times 1 \times 6 = 120$ possible integers.

---

7. **D**   This problem involves rates, so it helps to recall the rate equation: $d = rt$.

Because Zander returns home *along the same route*, you can use d for the distance both to and from work. Because he spends a total of 4 hours in the car, if he spends t hours on the way to work, he will spend $4 - t$ hours on the way home from work.

Set up rate equations for both legs of the trip:

To work:	$d = 40t$
From work:	$d = 24(4 - t)$
Set the expressions equal:	$40t = 24(4 - t)$
Distribute:	$40t = 96 - 24t$
Add 24t:	$64t = 96$
Divide by 64:	$t = 1.5$

Plug 1.5 in for t and solve for d: $d = 40(1.5) = 60$ miles to work. Therefore he travels $60 + 60 = 120$ miles to and from work that day.

---

8. C If a swimming pool that can hold 20,000 gallons is a quarter full, it holds ¼(20,000) = 5,000 gallons. It will take 20,000 − 5,000 = 15,000 more gallons to fill the pool. The pump is delivering water at a rate of g gallons per m minutes or $\frac{g}{m}$.

Use amount = rate × time to determine how long it will take to fill the pool:

$$15,000 = \frac{g}{m} \cdot (t)$$

Divide by $\frac{g}{m}$: $\frac{15,000m}{g} = t$

If it costs d dollars per minute, then the total cost is $\frac{15,000m}{g} \times d = \frac{15,000md}{g}$.

---

9. 10 The key to this problem is that the individual values of X and Z do not matter as much as their sum. Since the sum is a three digit number, there is no "carry" when X and Z are added. If you look at the far right column, you can see that $X + Z = 8$. The middle column tells you that $Y + Y = 4$, or $2Y = 4$. This means that $Y = 2$. The far left column confirms what you learned from the far right column: $Z + X = 8$. Therefore $Z + X + Y = 8 + 2 = 10$.

---

10. 5400

	Perimeter = $2L + 2W$
Substitute:	$300 = 2L + 2(60)$
Simplify:	$300 = 2L + 120$
Subtract 120:	$180 = 2L$
Divide by 2:	$90 = L$
Find the area:	Area = $LW = 90(60) = 5400$

---

11. 44

	$g(x) = x^2 - 3$
Find $g(3)$:	$g(3) = 3^2 - 3$
Simplify:	$g(3) = 6$
	$f(g(3)) = ?$
Substitute for $g(3)$:	$f(6) =$
	$f(x) = 8x - 4$
Find $f(6)$:	$f(6) = 8(6) - 4$
Simplify:	$f(6) = 44$

---

12. $\frac{5}{8}$ To solve this problem, it helps to draw a picture. Points X and Y are on the circle and Z can be found in between those two points on the longer arc of the circle as shown below:

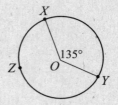

As shown, angle XOY is 135°. This means that the remainder of the circle makes up an angle of 360° − 135° = 225°. To find out what fraction of a circle this is, divide 225° by 360° $\frac{225}{360} = \frac{5}{8}$.

---

13. 14 Because you know that $ab + \frac{1}{ab} = 4$, it follows that if you square $ab + \frac{1}{ab}$, the result is $4^2 = 16$.

$$\left(ab + \frac{1}{ab}\right)\left(ab + \frac{1}{ab}\right) = a^2b^2 + \frac{ab}{ab} + \frac{ab}{ab} + \frac{1}{a^2b^2} = a^2b^2 + 2 + \frac{1}{a^2b^2}$$

$$16 = a^2b^2 + 2 + \frac{1}{a^2b^2}$$

Subtract 2: $14 = a^2b^2 + \frac{1}{a^2b^2}$

---

14. 10 This problem includes a 30°–60°–90° triangle.

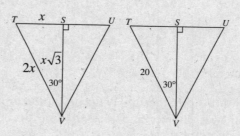

	$20 = 2x$
Divide by 2:	$10 = x$

---

15. 1or 3 $|-3x + 5| < 6$

Write as two separate inequalities:

$-3x + 5 < 6$ and $-3x + 5 + > -6$

Subtract 5: $-3x < 1$ and $3x > -11$

Divide by −3: $x > -\frac{1}{3}$ and $x < \frac{11}{3}$

The only odd integers between those two values are 1 and 3.

16. 132 Student A has 11 different partners: AB, AC, AD, AE, AF, AG, AH, AI, AJ, AK, AL
In fact, each student has 11 different partners, but you have to be careful to avoid counting the same pair more than once.

Student B has 11 different partners, but only 10 different partners that are not already counted: BC, BD, BE, BF, BG, BH, BI, BJ, BK, BL are new. BA was already counted.

Student C has 9 different partners not already counted: CD, CE, CF, CG, CH, CI, CJ, CK, and CL.

Student D has 8 different partners not already counted: DE, DF, DG, DH, DI, DJ, DK, and DL.

Student E has 7 different partners not already counted: EF, EG, EH, EI, EJ, EK, and EL

Student F has 6 different partners not already counted: FG, FH, FI, FJ, FK, and FL.

Student G has 5 different partners not already counted: GH, GI, GJ, GK, and GL.

Student H has 4 different partners not already counted: HI, HJ, HK, and HL

Student I has 3 different partners not already counted: IJ, IK, and IL

Student J has 2 different partners not already counted JK and JL

Student K has only 1 different partner not yet counted: KL

This yields a total of 11 + 10 + 9 + 8 + 7 + 6 + 5 + 4 + 3 + 2 + 1 = 66 total dance partnerships. Each student is paired up with each of the other students *twice*, so there are 66 × 2 = 132 different pairings.

17. 109 The median is the *middle* number. Aside from the median, there are 54 other numbers in the list. There are 27 numbers on each side of the median. The final term in the list can be found by adding 2 to the median twenty-seven times. 55 + 27(2) = 55 + 54 = 109

18. 72

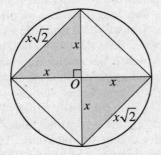

The shaded triangles are both 45°–45°–90° triangles as shown in the diagram above. To find the perimeter of the shaded region, add the 6 side lengths together:
$$x + x + x + x + x\sqrt{2} + x\sqrt{2} = 24 + 12\sqrt{2}$$

Combine terms: $4x + 2x\sqrt{2} = 24 + 12\sqrt{2}$

$4x = 24$, so x must be 6. If x is 6, then each side of the square is $x\sqrt{2}$ or $6\sqrt{2}$

The area of the square is $(6\sqrt{2})^2 = 72$.

Section 6

1. A The referee had no choice but to throw the athlete out of the game. This would indicate that the foul must have been pretty bad—*blatant* (obvious) and *egregious* (conspicuously bad or offensive) are two good choices. It is doubtful that the referee would petition for a *celebration* after the foul. A *suspension* would make sense for such an awful foul. *blatant* = obvious; *miniscule* = tiny; *egregious* = conspicuously bad or offensive; *nautical* = relating to shipping.

2. E Tracy became the youngest partner in firm history and no associate had ever performed with such a consistent *standard of excellence*. This would indicate she was a very *diligent* worker. *gratuity* = a gift given in return for service; *dormancy* = a period of inactivity; *lethargy* = fatigue; *capriciousness* = impulsiveness; *diligence* = hard work.

3. C Oprah is known for *helping those who are less fortunate*. This indicates that she is an *altruist* (selfless person) or a *philanthropist* (lover of mankind). Answer choice (A) does not make sense, however, because the second word, *dislike*, does not make sense in the context of the sentence. If she is an altruist, she won't have dislike for helping others. Answer choice (C) is a good fit because a *penchant* is an inclination to do something. *altruist* = selfless person; *charlatan* = a fraud; *prerequisite* = required as a prior condition; *philanthropist* = lover of mankind; *penchant* = inclination, a liking; *nihilist* = one who doubts the existence of knowable truths; *despot* = a tyrant; *culpability* = guilt.

4. A The word *although* establishes a contrast. Actual confessions take hours and several hundred sentences, whereas Dostoevsky's confession in his book takes a mere 20 words. You want to pick a word that suggests frugality with words. *laconic* = marked by the use of few words; *verbose* = wordy; *lugubrious* = exaggeratedly gloomy or mournful; *sonorous* = having a full deep sound; *antiquated* = outdated.

5. A The fighter was humbled by the experience of losing his title to a weaker opponent. His public demeanor changed to a *modest and self-effacing persona* from one that was previously not a modest one.

Lofty is a good fit for the missing word. *lofty* = exalted, arrogant; *impecunious* = penniless; *obligatory* = required; *prescient* = able to see the future; *pusillanimous* = cowardly.

6. **C** The passage as a whole describes the technological advance of *the kareze system of irrigation*, and describes some technical details of its construction and its effects on the Persian villagers.

7. **E** The phrase *these muqannis* (line 8) refers to the previous sentence, which describes how *Persian engineers* (line 4) constructed the kareze. Also, since these muqannis are said to have *calculated* the location of a tunnel, they must have been people, not inanimate things such as deposits or tunnels.

8. **C** The passage states that *sports can be seen [by evolutionary anthropologists] as a means of expressing our genetic endowment as hunters, even though most societies no longer require hunting* (lines 7–10). This implies that we have acquired genes for a trait that is no longer essential. In other words, these traits are *vestiges* (remain traces) we have inherited from our ancestors.

9. **D** In saying that music is *more mysterious to evolutionary anthropologists* (lines 15–16), the author means that the cultural need for musical expression is not as easily explained as sports is, that is, as an expression of *inherited traits* that once *had definite survival value to individuals and societies* (lines 14–15).

10. **C** The passages states that the Sherpas were *ideally suited to the rigors of high-altitude climbing ... stout at altitude, and seemingly resistant to cold* (lines 8–11). It also states that European climbers were *amazed at the strength of these people* (line 46). It does not, however, say that they had any *expertise in treating altitude sickness*.

11. **E** The passage states that *Sherpas did not venture into the high peaks until European mountaineers began arriving to climb in the world's greatest mountain range* (lines 12–15).

12. **A** In calling the team of porters a *motley (miscellaneous) throng of old men, women, boys and girls* (lines 50–51), Wakefield was clearly emphasizing their heterogeneity.

13. **A** The passage states of Wakefield that the accomplishments of the Sherpa *astonished him* (lines 51–52), and his expression of amazement in describing their ability to carry 80 pound loads reinforces this sentiment.

14. **B** The passage never answers the question *Who was the first European to climb Mount Everest*? It does, however, answer the questions regarding the first climbing fatalities on Everest (lines 68–71), the Tibetan name for Everest (line 16), the name of the Sherpa ceremony (line 24), and the first European to recognize the value of Sherpas (lines 31–33).

15. **D** This paragraph is primarily concerned with describing the ruggedness of the Sherpas, which was made clear in particular by their ability to sleep *using only rocks for shelter* (line 57). Although these rocks could perhaps indicate the *barren landscape of Mount Everest*, their mention in this sentence is clearly for another purpose.

16. **B** The passage states that *many [Sherpas] aspired to this honor [of the Tiger Medal] and the higher pay it afforded* (lines 64–65), and that assisting expeditions had become *an important source of revenue for a poor mountain folk* (lines 75–76). Since the Sherpa did not climb the mountain until the Europeans arrived, climbing could not have been a *social custom for many centuries*, and since the mountain was long considered *off-limits to humans* (lines 19–20) for religious reasons, climbing could not have been regarded as a *religious duty*.

17. **C** Farm cats are mentioned as examples of animals that *can communicate* (line 1), but the passage does not indicate that they can communicate on a level that humans cannot.

18. **E** The *conference organizers hoped to gain new insight into how animals communicate* (lines 23–24) by *bringing together scientists who worked on many different species* (lines 20–22). That is, they wanted to share information gained through recent research.

19. **C** Whales and elephants both have *a female-dominated, egalitarian society* (line 30) and can both communicate over long distances, elephants over *several kilometers* (lines 34–35) and whales over *perhaps hundreds of miles* (line 42). But while elephants use infrasound, which is below the frequencies that the human ear can detect, whales can hear *nearly all of the frequencies that humans can, as well as many higher than the human range* (lines 43–45), which suggests that elephants cannot hear frequencies lower than those that humans can. Therefore, the similarities are described by II and III but not I.

20. **B** The analogy in lines 48–49 suggests that whales speak more loudly in the presence of noisy ships just as humans talk louder in the presence of noisy bar patrons.

21. **A** This paragraph discusses how scientists study dolphins, and the phrase *it appears* introduces the conclusions based on data gathered in those studies. Therefore this phrase suggests that a conclusion can be drawn from scientific research.

22. **A** The passage states that human judges were employed to *determine if [dolphin] calls were identical*, that is, to compare underwater whistles.

23. **D** The passage says that the chimpanzees communicated *without a sound, possible because they were within vocal range of other members of their tribe and preferred not to share their lunch* (lines 103–106). In other words, they did not want to let the other chimpanzees know what they were doing.

24. **D** The passage suggests that sea lions can reason using the law of transitivity by inferring that "if sea lion A defeats sea lion B, and if I have defeated sea lion A, then I should be able to defeat sea lion B."

Section 7

1. **A** First, assign values to points P and Q. Point P is about -1.75 and point Q is about 1.75. Now multiply those two values in that vicinity together: $-1.75 \times 1.75 = -3.0625$. The only point in that vicinity is point A.

2. **B**

$$\frac{x}{8} = 5z$$

Multiply by 8: $\quad x = 40z$

$$\frac{1}{2z} = 5y$$

Divide by 5: $\quad \dfrac{1}{10z} = y$

$$xy =$$

Substitute: $\quad (40z)\dfrac{1}{10z} = 4$

3. **A** When p is divided by 7, it gives a remainder of 2. Think of a number for which this is a true statement and assign that number to be p. 9 divided by 7 is 1 with a remainder of 2. So, $p = 9$. Answer choice (A) becomes $9 + 2 = 11$. When 11 is divided by 7, the quotient is 1 with remainder 4.

4. **D** The best way to solve this problem is to plot the data points. As the x-values are increasing, the y values are increasing at a faster rate. So, the graph will be upward sloping with an increasing slope as it moves to the right. Answer choice D is a perfect fit.

5. **B** You can use the percent change formula to solve this problem. The original amount was \$400 and the final amount was \$500.

$$\frac{500 - 400}{400} \times 100 = \frac{100}{400} \times 100 = 25\%$$

6. **D** Begin by finding the coordinates of the 5 points:

A $(-2, 4)$
B $(3, 2)$
C $(2, -2)$
D $(-3, 0)$
E $(1, 8)$

The slope of AB is $\dfrac{4 - 2}{-2 - 3} = -\dfrac{2}{5}$

The slope of AC is $\dfrac{4 - (-2)}{-2 - 2} = -\dfrac{6}{4}$

The slope of AD is $\dfrac{4 - 0}{-2 - (-3)} = \dfrac{4}{1} = 4$

The slope of EB is $\dfrac{8 - 2}{1 - 3} = \dfrac{6}{-2} = -3$

The slope of DC is $\dfrac{0 - (-2)}{-3 - 2} = -\dfrac{2}{5}$

7. **D** ¾ of the vehicles are cars and ⅓ of the cars are older than 3 years. Therefore ¾ × ⅓ = ¼ of the vehicles are cars older than 3 years. You are told that there are 20 cars older than 3 years in the lot, which means that $20 = ¼$ (total)

Divide by ¼: $\quad$ total = 80 cars

8. **D** The smallest integer is n. Remember they are consecutive *odd* integers. The set of integers would be: $n, n + 2, n + 4, n + 6, n + 8, n + 10, n + 12, n + 14$ To average the integers, add them together and divide by 8:

$$\frac{n + (n + 2) + (n + 4) + (n + 6) + (n + 8) + (n + 10) + (n + 12) + (n + 14)}{8}$$

Combine terms: $\quad \dfrac{8n + 56}{8} = n + 7$

9. **C** You might solve this problem quickly with trial and error. Try $w = 1$.
   (A) $w^4 = 1^4 = 1$
   (B) $(w - 2)^3 = (1 - 2)^3 = -1^3 = -1$
   (C) $4w^2 = 4(1)^2 = 4(1) = 4$
   (D) $4w = 4(1) = 4$
   (E) $3(w^2) = 3(1^2) = 3(1) = 3$
Answer choices A, B, and E are out. Now try $w = -2$
   (C) $4w^2 = 4(-2)^2 = 4(4) = 16$
   (D) $4w = 4(-2) = -8$
Only answer choice (C) remains.

10. **C**

$$A = \pi r^2 = 64\pi$$

Divide by π: $r^2 = 64$

Take square root: $r = 8$

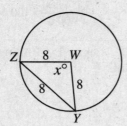

If the radius = 8 and $ZY = 8$, then triangle ZWY is an equilateral triangle and therefore $x = 60°$.

11. **D** This question tests your understanding of exponent rules. Simplify each of the three expressions:

$$\text{I. } (64x^6)^{\frac{2}{3}}$$

Take the cube root and then square that result:

cube root: $4x^2$

square: $16x^4$ equivalent

$$\text{II. } \left(\frac{1}{2x}\right)^{-4}$$

Rewrite without negative exponents: $(2x)^4$

raise to the fourth: $16x^4$

$$\text{III. } \frac{x^2}{16x^{-1}}$$

Rewrite without negative exponents: $\frac{x^3}{16}$

So only I and II are the same, and the answer is D.

12. **B** The original ratio of dogs to cats was $\frac{d}{c}$.

4 cats arrived, giving a total of $c + 4$ cats. You don't know how many dogs arrived, so call that number x, producing a total of $d + x$ dogs. The ratio remains unchanged, so set the new ratio of dogs to cats equal to the original ratio:

$$\frac{d + x}{c + 4} = \frac{d}{c}$$

Cross multiply: $c(d + x) = d(c + 4)$

Distribute: $cd + cx = cd + 4d$

Subtract cd: $cx = 4d$

Divide by c: $x = \frac{4d}{c}$

13. **D** To solve this problem, eliminate four of the five answer choices and you will be left with the one that *must* be true. Answer choice A says that $a > b$. If $b = 4$, and $a = 3$, this is not true.

Answer choice B says that $b > a$. If $b = 4$ and $a = 5$, this is not true.

Answer choice C says that $0 < ab$. If $a = -3$ and $b = 4$, then $ab = -12$ and this is not true.

Answer choice E says that $36 < |a + b|$. If $a = 3$ and $b = 4$, then $|a + b| = |3 + 4| = 7$. This leaves us with only answer choice D, which indeed must be true.

14. **C** The original side length of the square is x. This means that the original area is x^2. The new side length is $x + 4$. The new area would be $(x + 4)^2$ and is 112 square inches larger than the original area, x^2.

$$(x + 4)^2 = x^2 + 112$$

FOIL: $x^2 + 8x + 16 = x^2 + 112$

Subtract x^2: $8x + 16 = 112$

Subtract 16: $8x = 96$

Divide by 8: $x = 12$

15. **E** $(-4x^4y^{-3})^{-3} =$

Rewrite as a fraction: $\dfrac{1}{(-4x^4y^{-3})^{-3}}$

Raise everything in the denominator to the 3rd power:

$$\frac{1}{-64x^{12}y^{-9}}$$

Rewrite without negative exponents: $\dfrac{y^9}{-64x^{12}}$

16. **B** A negative a coefficient makes the quadratic open downward, which eliminates A, C and E. A negative c coefficient means that the vertex of the graph intersects the y-axis at a negative value. This leaves answer choice B as the correct answer.

Section 8

1. **B** If the first blank contains a positive word, then the second blank should contain a word such as *appeal*. If the first blank contains a negative word, the second blank should contain a word that means the opposite of *appeal*. The only word pairing of the bunch that makes sense is answer choice (B) *prolific* and *appealed*. *cryptic* = mysterious; *prolific* = producing abundant works; *provocative* = stimulating; *attest* = to affirm to be true; *garish* = excessively showy.

2. **C** The downsizing of the company has brought about change. It's not certain from the context whether the change has been good or bad. What's important is that the words you choose establish a change in practice. Answer choice (C) does so as

the company goes from one that embraces different points of view to one that *denounces* the voicing of different opinions.

3. **B**   The calculus problem was so extremely difficult that even the most *skilled* mathematicians struggled to derive the answer. *agile* = nimble; *adept* = skilled; *abysmal* = horrible; *insipid* = dull; *eloquent* = well-spoken.

4. **A**   The principal punished the student *harshly*, which suggests he or she must have misbehaved badly. The first word should be a word that relates to *misbehavior that undermines authority*. Two words fit that description well—*insubordination* (not submissive to authority) and *impudence* (rude boldness). The word *inundate* (to flood) does not make sense in the second blank, whereas *condone* (to excuse or overlook) does. Answer choice (A) is the best fit. *insubordination* = a failure to submit to authority; *condone* = to excuse or overlook; *disseminate* = to spread; *assuage* = to soothe; *improvident* = not providing for the future; *provoke* = to push into action; *subterfuge* = deceptiveness; *expedite* = to speed up; *impudence* = rude boldness; *inundate* = to flood.

5. **D**   A good advertisement is able to *persuade* consumers. *perpetuate* = to prolong the existence of; *thwart* = to prevent the occurrence of; *console* = to help ease the grief of another; *exhort* = to urge into action; *reproach* = criticism, disapproval.

6. **E**   Her articles are still used today, which suggests they must be of high quality. The missing word must be a positive word that relates to *clarity of thinking. modicum* = small amount; *respite* = a break; *dearth* = a lack; *turpitude* = depravity; *perspicacity* = acuteness of perception.

7. **D**   The first sentence of the passage indicates that the purpose of the passage is to discuss how *the trajectories of metaphysical and mathematical thought have crossed* (lines 1–2) throughout history, Although the passage does discuss the Babylonians and the Pythagoreans, they are not the focus of the passage as a whole.

8. **C**   These *angles and energies* describe the manner in *which the trajectories of metaphysical and mathematical thought have crossed* (lines 1–2) over the centuries, and therefore describe how two disciplines have intersected.

9. **B**   This qualifying phrase indicates that mathematics and religion have intersected *not exclusively* to their mutual benefit, suggesting that the relationship between these two disciplines has not always been constructive.

10. **A**   The sentence indicates that both disciplines *were unified in ancient times, but today their spheres are largely separated* (line 14), suggesting that the two disciplines have become more independent over time.

11. **C**   In saying that *their spheres are largely separated* (line 14), the author means that the two disciplines are largely independent in terms of what domains they influence.

12. **A**   This paragraph begins by describing the *instrumental* (line 19) relationship between religion in mathematics, particularly the use of mathematics by humans to describe the motions of the heavens and to construct temples. It then describes an incident in which the gods were thought to use mathematics to confound the believers. The word *reciprocally* shows that the "instrumentality" of mathematics went both ways between humans and the gods.

13. **E**   Plato is said to have suggested that the *gods occasionally employed mathematics to confound believers* (lines 33–34), particularly in the instance in which the oracle demanded that the worshippers double the size of their altar. Therefore, Plato suggested that the oracle's demand was intended to mystify the Delians.

14. **A**   This sentence states that it had *been known for centuries* that no circle ten cubits across can *be encircled with fewer than 31.4 cubits*, and that *no power is so great* as to violate this fact. Therefore, a particular geometric fact cannot be contradicted.

15. **D**   The *manner of thinking* being discussed in this paragraph was inspired by the *power of mathematical deduction to establish irrefutable truths beyond the arbitrary whims of spirits and gods* (lines 74–77) and includes the idea that *numbers and their relationships themselves hold mystical power* (lines 78–79). This *manner of thinking* did not include the belief that mathematics was primarily for solving worldly problems, and indeed it put mathematics on *its own abstract plane beyond the physical world* (lines 88–89). Therefore it includes beliefs II and III, but not I.

16. **C**   In saying that *number acquired its own abstract plane beyond the physical world*, the author means that mathematics was put on a *level* beyond the level of worldly concerns.

17. **C** This paragraph criticizes the Pythagoreans for *imperious and unreasoning violence* (lines 109–110) in drowning Hipposus for proving a mathematical facts that contradicted one of their religious precepts. The phrase *righteousness ascended* means that the Pythagoreans became ideologically intolerant.

18. **A** The *precept* in line 116 is the idea that *all of reality can be described with whole numbers and the fundamental operations* (lines 116–118). The first sentence of the final paragraph shows that this precept is incorrect: *this hypotenuse did not cease to be irrational by decree* (lines 118–120). In other words, there are indeed quantities that cannot be expressed in terms of whole numbers or their ratios.

19. **D** These *explorers* are said to be on a *quest for understanding* (lines 135–136) and that their errors were *inexact applications of logic* (line 138), but they were on an *inexorable march ... toward the true understanding of nature* (lines 138–140). In other words, they were trying to understand nature through logical reasoning.

Section 9

1. **B** The error in this sentence is the use of the word *because*. The sentence shows contrast rather than a cause and effect relationship. The Yankees have spent more money than any other franchise, and yet they have only won once. A contrasting conjunction like *although* better conveys the correct relationship.

2. **D** This sentence contains a dangling modifier. The modifying phrase that begins the sentence describes *the recently married couple rather than the canal system of Venice*. Answer choice (D) best corrects the error.

3. **D** The word *and* is extraneous and creates an awkward sentence. Remove the word *and* to fix the error.

4. **A** The sentence is correct as written.

5. **E** The expression *no sooner ... but* is not a correct idiom. The correct idiom is *no sooner ... than*.

6. **E** The sentence is awkwardly constructed. Answer choice (E) is clear, concise, and makes a logical comparison.

7. **B** Eric would not decide to lie down in order to clean the garage—he would probably lie down *after* he has cleaned the garage. Answer choice (B) best corrects the error.

8. **C** This contains a dangling modifier. The modifying phrase that begins the sentence describes *Madonna rather* than *Madonna's songs*. Answer choice (C) best corrects the error.

9. **C** This sentence is inconsistent with its use of pronouns. It is not proper to say *you* and then switch to *one*.

10. **B** This contains a dangling modifier. The original sentence implies that the nonprofit organization is donating money. It should instead be *you* that follows the comma because *you* are donating the money.

11. **E** This is a comparison error. You need to compare the *amount of money* online shoppers charged in 2005 to the *amount of money* online shoppers charged in 2004. As it is originally written, it is illogically comparing the amount of money charged in 2005 to the year 2004.

12. **B** Modern audiences were not written in the late 18th century. Answer choice (B) corrects the error in the most clear and concise manner.

13. **A** The sentence is correct as written.

14. **D** This is a subject-verb error. There are *two* things that put the patients at ease—her smile and her sense of humor. Therefore the subject is plural, which means that the verb should be *put*, the plural form.

PRACTICE TEST 3

ANSWER SHEET

Last Name: _____   First Name: _____

Date: _____   Testing Location: _____

Directions for Test

- Remove these answer sheets from the book and use them to record your answers to this test.
- This test will require 3 hours and 20 minutes to complete. Take this test in one sitting.
- The time allotment for each section is written clearly at the beginning of each section. This test contains six 25-minute sections, two 20-minute sections, and one 10-minute section.
- This test is 25 minutes shorter than the actual SAT, which will include a 25-minute "experimental" section that does not count toward your score. That section has been omitted from this test.
- You may take one short break during the test, of no more than 10 minutes in length.
- You may only work on one section at any given time.
- You must stop ALL work on a section when time is called.
- If you finish a section before the time has elapsed, check your work on that section. You may NOT work on any other section.
- Do not waste time on questions that seem too difficult for you.
- Use the test book for scratchwork, but you will receive credit only for answers that are marked on the answer sheets.
- You will receive one point for every correct answer.
- You will receive no points for an omitted question.
- For each wrong answer on any multiple-choice question, your score will be reduced by ¼ point.
- For each wrong answer on any numerical "grid-in" question, you will receive no deduction.

SECTION 2

1. Ⓐ Ⓑ Ⓒ Ⓓ Ⓔ
2. Ⓐ Ⓑ Ⓒ Ⓓ Ⓔ
3. Ⓐ Ⓑ Ⓒ Ⓓ Ⓔ
4. Ⓐ Ⓑ Ⓒ Ⓓ Ⓔ
5. Ⓐ Ⓑ Ⓒ Ⓓ Ⓔ
6. Ⓐ Ⓑ Ⓒ Ⓓ Ⓔ
7. Ⓐ Ⓑ Ⓒ Ⓓ Ⓔ
8. Ⓐ Ⓑ Ⓒ Ⓓ Ⓔ
9. Ⓐ Ⓑ Ⓒ Ⓓ Ⓔ
10. Ⓐ Ⓑ Ⓒ Ⓓ Ⓔ

11. Ⓐ Ⓑ Ⓒ Ⓓ Ⓔ
12. Ⓐ Ⓑ Ⓒ Ⓓ Ⓔ
13. Ⓐ Ⓑ Ⓒ Ⓓ Ⓔ
14. Ⓐ Ⓑ Ⓒ Ⓓ Ⓔ
15. Ⓐ Ⓑ Ⓒ Ⓓ Ⓔ
16. Ⓐ Ⓑ Ⓒ Ⓓ Ⓔ
17. Ⓐ Ⓑ Ⓒ Ⓓ Ⓔ
18. Ⓐ Ⓑ Ⓒ Ⓓ Ⓔ
19. Ⓐ Ⓑ Ⓒ Ⓓ Ⓔ
20. Ⓐ Ⓑ Ⓒ Ⓓ Ⓔ

21. Ⓐ Ⓑ Ⓒ Ⓓ Ⓔ
22. Ⓐ Ⓑ Ⓒ Ⓓ Ⓔ
23. Ⓐ Ⓑ Ⓒ Ⓓ Ⓔ
24. Ⓐ Ⓑ Ⓒ Ⓓ Ⓔ
25. Ⓐ Ⓑ Ⓒ Ⓓ Ⓔ
26. Ⓐ Ⓑ Ⓒ Ⓓ Ⓔ
27. Ⓐ Ⓑ Ⓒ Ⓓ Ⓔ
28. Ⓐ Ⓑ Ⓒ Ⓓ Ⓔ
29. Ⓐ Ⓑ Ⓒ Ⓓ Ⓔ
30. Ⓐ Ⓑ Ⓒ Ⓓ Ⓔ

31. Ⓐ Ⓑ Ⓒ Ⓓ Ⓔ
32. Ⓐ Ⓑ Ⓒ Ⓓ Ⓔ
33. Ⓐ Ⓑ Ⓒ Ⓓ Ⓔ
34. Ⓐ Ⓑ Ⓒ Ⓓ Ⓔ
35. Ⓐ Ⓑ Ⓒ Ⓓ Ⓔ
36. Ⓐ Ⓑ Ⓒ Ⓓ Ⓔ
37. Ⓐ Ⓑ Ⓒ Ⓓ Ⓔ
38. Ⓐ Ⓑ Ⓒ Ⓓ Ⓔ
39. Ⓐ Ⓑ Ⓒ Ⓓ Ⓔ
40. Ⓐ Ⓑ Ⓒ Ⓓ Ⓔ

SECTION 3

1. Ⓐ Ⓑ Ⓒ Ⓓ Ⓔ
2. Ⓐ Ⓑ Ⓒ Ⓓ Ⓔ
3. Ⓐ Ⓑ Ⓒ Ⓓ Ⓔ
4. Ⓐ Ⓑ Ⓒ Ⓓ Ⓔ
5. Ⓐ Ⓑ Ⓒ Ⓓ Ⓔ
6. Ⓐ Ⓑ Ⓒ Ⓓ Ⓔ
7. Ⓐ Ⓑ Ⓒ Ⓓ Ⓔ
8. Ⓐ Ⓑ Ⓒ Ⓓ Ⓔ
9. Ⓐ Ⓑ Ⓒ Ⓓ Ⓔ
10. Ⓐ Ⓑ Ⓒ Ⓓ Ⓔ

11. Ⓐ Ⓑ Ⓒ Ⓓ Ⓔ
12. Ⓐ Ⓑ Ⓒ Ⓓ Ⓔ
13. Ⓐ Ⓑ Ⓒ Ⓓ Ⓔ
14. Ⓐ Ⓑ Ⓒ Ⓓ Ⓔ
15. Ⓐ Ⓑ Ⓒ Ⓓ Ⓔ
16. Ⓐ Ⓑ Ⓒ Ⓓ Ⓔ
17. Ⓐ Ⓑ Ⓒ Ⓓ Ⓔ
18. Ⓐ Ⓑ Ⓒ Ⓓ Ⓔ
19. Ⓐ Ⓑ Ⓒ Ⓓ Ⓔ
20. Ⓐ Ⓑ Ⓒ Ⓓ Ⓔ

21. Ⓐ Ⓑ Ⓒ Ⓓ Ⓔ
22. Ⓐ Ⓑ Ⓒ Ⓓ Ⓔ
23. Ⓐ Ⓑ Ⓒ Ⓓ Ⓔ
24. Ⓐ Ⓑ Ⓒ Ⓓ Ⓔ
25. Ⓐ Ⓑ Ⓒ Ⓓ Ⓔ
26. Ⓐ Ⓑ Ⓒ Ⓓ Ⓔ
27. Ⓐ Ⓑ Ⓒ Ⓓ Ⓔ
28. Ⓐ Ⓑ Ⓒ Ⓓ Ⓔ
29. Ⓐ Ⓑ Ⓒ Ⓓ Ⓔ
30. Ⓐ Ⓑ Ⓒ Ⓓ Ⓔ

31. Ⓐ Ⓑ Ⓒ Ⓓ Ⓔ
32. Ⓐ Ⓑ Ⓒ Ⓓ Ⓔ
33. Ⓐ Ⓑ Ⓒ Ⓓ Ⓔ
34. Ⓐ Ⓑ Ⓒ Ⓓ Ⓔ
35. Ⓐ Ⓑ Ⓒ Ⓓ Ⓔ
36. Ⓐ Ⓑ Ⓒ Ⓓ Ⓔ
37. Ⓐ Ⓑ Ⓒ Ⓓ Ⓔ
38. Ⓐ Ⓑ Ⓒ Ⓓ Ⓔ
39. Ⓐ Ⓑ Ⓒ Ⓓ Ⓔ
40. Ⓐ Ⓑ Ⓒ Ⓓ Ⓔ

ANSWER SHEET

SECTION 4

1. Ⓐ Ⓑ Ⓒ Ⓓ Ⓔ	11. Ⓐ Ⓑ Ⓒ Ⓓ Ⓔ	21. Ⓐ Ⓑ Ⓒ Ⓓ Ⓔ	31. Ⓐ Ⓑ Ⓒ Ⓓ Ⓔ
2. Ⓐ Ⓑ Ⓒ Ⓓ Ⓔ	12. Ⓐ Ⓑ Ⓒ Ⓓ Ⓔ	22. Ⓐ Ⓑ Ⓒ Ⓓ Ⓔ	32. Ⓐ Ⓑ Ⓒ Ⓓ Ⓔ
3. Ⓐ Ⓑ Ⓒ Ⓓ Ⓔ	13. Ⓐ Ⓑ Ⓒ Ⓓ Ⓔ	23. Ⓐ Ⓑ Ⓒ Ⓓ Ⓔ	33. Ⓐ Ⓑ Ⓒ Ⓓ Ⓔ
4. Ⓐ Ⓑ Ⓒ Ⓓ Ⓔ	14. Ⓐ Ⓑ Ⓒ Ⓓ Ⓔ	24. Ⓐ Ⓑ Ⓒ Ⓓ Ⓔ	34. Ⓐ Ⓑ Ⓒ Ⓓ Ⓔ
5. Ⓐ Ⓑ Ⓒ Ⓓ Ⓔ	15. Ⓐ Ⓑ Ⓒ Ⓓ Ⓔ	25. Ⓐ Ⓑ Ⓒ Ⓓ Ⓔ	35. Ⓐ Ⓑ Ⓒ Ⓓ Ⓔ
6. Ⓐ Ⓑ Ⓒ Ⓓ Ⓔ	16. Ⓐ Ⓑ Ⓒ Ⓓ Ⓔ	26. Ⓐ Ⓑ Ⓒ Ⓓ Ⓔ	36. Ⓐ Ⓑ Ⓒ Ⓓ Ⓔ
7. Ⓐ Ⓑ Ⓒ Ⓓ Ⓔ	17. Ⓐ Ⓑ Ⓒ Ⓓ Ⓔ	27. Ⓐ Ⓑ Ⓒ Ⓓ Ⓔ	37. Ⓐ Ⓑ Ⓒ Ⓓ Ⓔ
8. Ⓐ Ⓑ Ⓒ Ⓓ Ⓔ	18. Ⓐ Ⓑ Ⓒ Ⓓ Ⓔ	28. Ⓐ Ⓑ Ⓒ Ⓓ Ⓔ	38. Ⓐ Ⓑ Ⓒ Ⓓ Ⓔ
9. Ⓐ Ⓑ Ⓒ Ⓓ Ⓔ	19. Ⓐ Ⓑ Ⓒ Ⓓ Ⓔ	29. Ⓐ Ⓑ Ⓒ Ⓓ Ⓔ	39. Ⓐ Ⓑ Ⓒ Ⓓ Ⓔ
10. Ⓐ Ⓑ Ⓒ Ⓓ Ⓔ	20. Ⓐ Ⓑ Ⓒ Ⓓ Ⓔ	30. Ⓐ Ⓑ Ⓒ Ⓓ Ⓔ	40. Ⓐ Ⓑ Ⓒ Ⓓ Ⓔ

SECTION 5

1. Ⓐ Ⓑ Ⓒ Ⓓ Ⓔ	5. Ⓐ Ⓑ Ⓒ Ⓓ Ⓔ
2. Ⓐ Ⓑ Ⓒ Ⓓ Ⓔ	6. Ⓐ Ⓑ Ⓒ Ⓓ Ⓔ
3. Ⓐ Ⓑ Ⓒ Ⓓ Ⓔ	7. Ⓐ Ⓑ Ⓒ Ⓓ Ⓔ
4. Ⓐ Ⓑ Ⓒ Ⓓ Ⓔ	8. Ⓐ Ⓑ Ⓒ Ⓓ Ⓔ

9. 10. 11. 12. 13.

14. 15. 16. 17. 18.

ANSWER SHEET

SECTION 6

1. Ⓐ Ⓑ Ⓒ Ⓓ Ⓔ
2. Ⓐ Ⓑ Ⓒ Ⓓ Ⓔ
3. Ⓐ Ⓑ Ⓒ Ⓓ Ⓔ
4. Ⓐ Ⓑ Ⓒ Ⓓ Ⓔ
5. Ⓐ Ⓑ Ⓒ Ⓓ Ⓔ
6. Ⓐ Ⓑ Ⓒ Ⓓ Ⓔ
7. Ⓐ Ⓑ Ⓒ Ⓓ Ⓔ
8. Ⓐ Ⓑ Ⓒ Ⓓ Ⓔ
9. Ⓐ Ⓑ Ⓒ Ⓓ Ⓔ
10. Ⓐ Ⓑ Ⓒ Ⓓ Ⓔ
11. Ⓐ Ⓑ Ⓒ Ⓓ Ⓔ
12. Ⓐ Ⓑ Ⓒ Ⓓ Ⓔ
13. Ⓐ Ⓑ Ⓒ Ⓓ Ⓔ
14. Ⓐ Ⓑ Ⓒ Ⓓ Ⓔ
15. Ⓐ Ⓑ Ⓒ Ⓓ Ⓔ
16. Ⓐ Ⓑ Ⓒ Ⓓ Ⓔ
17. Ⓐ Ⓑ Ⓒ Ⓓ Ⓔ
18. Ⓐ Ⓑ Ⓒ Ⓓ Ⓔ
19. Ⓐ Ⓑ Ⓒ Ⓓ Ⓔ
20. Ⓐ Ⓑ Ⓒ Ⓓ Ⓔ
21. Ⓐ Ⓑ Ⓒ Ⓓ Ⓔ
22. Ⓐ Ⓑ Ⓒ Ⓓ Ⓔ
23. Ⓐ Ⓑ Ⓒ Ⓓ Ⓔ
24. Ⓐ Ⓑ Ⓒ Ⓓ Ⓔ
25. Ⓐ Ⓑ Ⓒ Ⓓ Ⓔ
26. Ⓐ Ⓑ Ⓒ Ⓓ Ⓔ
27. Ⓐ Ⓑ Ⓒ Ⓓ Ⓔ
28. Ⓐ Ⓑ Ⓒ Ⓓ Ⓔ
29. Ⓐ Ⓑ Ⓒ Ⓓ Ⓔ
30. Ⓐ Ⓑ Ⓒ Ⓓ Ⓔ
31. Ⓐ Ⓑ Ⓒ Ⓓ Ⓔ
32. Ⓐ Ⓑ Ⓒ Ⓓ Ⓔ
33. Ⓐ Ⓑ Ⓒ Ⓓ Ⓔ
34. Ⓐ Ⓑ Ⓒ Ⓓ Ⓔ
35. Ⓐ Ⓑ Ⓒ Ⓓ Ⓔ
36. Ⓐ Ⓑ Ⓒ Ⓓ Ⓔ
37. Ⓐ Ⓑ Ⓒ Ⓓ Ⓔ
38. Ⓐ Ⓑ Ⓒ Ⓓ Ⓔ
39. Ⓐ Ⓑ Ⓒ Ⓓ Ⓔ
40. Ⓐ Ⓑ Ⓒ Ⓓ Ⓔ

SECTION 7

1. Ⓐ Ⓑ Ⓒ Ⓓ Ⓔ
2. Ⓐ Ⓑ Ⓒ Ⓓ Ⓔ
3. Ⓐ Ⓑ Ⓒ Ⓓ Ⓔ
4. Ⓐ Ⓑ Ⓒ Ⓓ Ⓔ
5. Ⓐ Ⓑ Ⓒ Ⓓ Ⓔ
6. Ⓐ Ⓑ Ⓒ Ⓓ Ⓔ
7. Ⓐ Ⓑ Ⓒ Ⓓ Ⓔ
8. Ⓐ Ⓑ Ⓒ Ⓓ Ⓔ
9. Ⓐ Ⓑ Ⓒ Ⓓ Ⓔ
10. Ⓐ Ⓑ Ⓒ Ⓓ Ⓔ
11. Ⓐ Ⓑ Ⓒ Ⓓ Ⓔ
12. Ⓐ Ⓑ Ⓒ Ⓓ Ⓔ
13. Ⓐ Ⓑ Ⓒ Ⓓ Ⓔ
14. Ⓐ Ⓑ Ⓒ Ⓓ Ⓔ
15. Ⓐ Ⓑ Ⓒ Ⓓ Ⓔ
16. Ⓐ Ⓑ Ⓒ Ⓓ Ⓔ
17. Ⓐ Ⓑ Ⓒ Ⓓ Ⓔ
18. Ⓐ Ⓑ Ⓒ Ⓓ Ⓔ
19. Ⓐ Ⓑ Ⓒ Ⓓ Ⓔ
20. Ⓐ Ⓑ Ⓒ Ⓓ Ⓔ
21. Ⓐ Ⓑ Ⓒ Ⓓ Ⓔ
22. Ⓐ Ⓑ Ⓒ Ⓓ Ⓔ
23. Ⓐ Ⓑ Ⓒ Ⓓ Ⓔ
24. Ⓐ Ⓑ Ⓒ Ⓓ Ⓔ
25. Ⓐ Ⓑ Ⓒ Ⓓ Ⓔ
26. Ⓐ Ⓑ Ⓒ Ⓓ Ⓔ
27. Ⓐ Ⓑ Ⓒ Ⓓ Ⓔ
28. Ⓐ Ⓑ Ⓒ Ⓓ Ⓔ
29. Ⓐ Ⓑ Ⓒ Ⓓ Ⓔ
30. Ⓐ Ⓑ Ⓒ Ⓓ Ⓔ
31. Ⓐ Ⓑ Ⓒ Ⓓ Ⓔ
32. Ⓐ Ⓑ Ⓒ Ⓓ Ⓔ
33. Ⓐ Ⓑ Ⓒ Ⓓ Ⓔ
34. Ⓐ Ⓑ Ⓒ Ⓓ Ⓔ
35. Ⓐ Ⓑ Ⓒ Ⓓ Ⓔ
36. Ⓐ Ⓑ Ⓒ Ⓓ Ⓔ
37. Ⓐ Ⓑ Ⓒ Ⓓ Ⓔ
38. Ⓐ Ⓑ Ⓒ Ⓓ Ⓔ
39. Ⓐ Ⓑ Ⓒ Ⓓ Ⓔ
40. Ⓐ Ⓑ Ⓒ Ⓓ Ⓔ

SECTION 8

1. Ⓐ Ⓑ Ⓒ Ⓓ Ⓔ
2. Ⓐ Ⓑ Ⓒ Ⓓ Ⓔ
3. Ⓐ Ⓑ Ⓒ Ⓓ Ⓔ
4. Ⓐ Ⓑ Ⓒ Ⓓ Ⓔ
5. Ⓐ Ⓑ Ⓒ Ⓓ Ⓔ
6. Ⓐ Ⓑ Ⓒ Ⓓ Ⓔ
7. Ⓐ Ⓑ Ⓒ Ⓓ Ⓔ
8. Ⓐ Ⓑ Ⓒ Ⓓ Ⓔ
9. Ⓐ Ⓑ Ⓒ Ⓓ Ⓔ
10. Ⓐ Ⓑ Ⓒ Ⓓ Ⓔ
11. Ⓐ Ⓑ Ⓒ Ⓓ Ⓔ
12. Ⓐ Ⓑ Ⓒ Ⓓ Ⓔ
13. Ⓐ Ⓑ Ⓒ Ⓓ Ⓔ
14. Ⓐ Ⓑ Ⓒ Ⓓ Ⓔ
15. Ⓐ Ⓑ Ⓒ Ⓓ Ⓔ
16. Ⓐ Ⓑ Ⓒ Ⓓ Ⓔ
17. Ⓐ Ⓑ Ⓒ Ⓓ Ⓔ
18. Ⓐ Ⓑ Ⓒ Ⓓ Ⓔ
19. Ⓐ Ⓑ Ⓒ Ⓓ Ⓔ
20. Ⓐ Ⓑ Ⓒ Ⓓ Ⓔ
21. Ⓐ Ⓑ Ⓒ Ⓓ Ⓔ
22. Ⓐ Ⓑ Ⓒ Ⓓ Ⓔ
23. Ⓐ Ⓑ Ⓒ Ⓓ Ⓔ
24. Ⓐ Ⓑ Ⓒ Ⓓ Ⓔ
25. Ⓐ Ⓑ Ⓒ Ⓓ Ⓔ
26. Ⓐ Ⓑ Ⓒ Ⓓ Ⓔ
27. Ⓐ Ⓑ Ⓒ Ⓓ Ⓔ
28. Ⓐ Ⓑ Ⓒ Ⓓ Ⓔ
29. Ⓐ Ⓑ Ⓒ Ⓓ Ⓔ
30. Ⓐ Ⓑ Ⓒ Ⓓ Ⓔ
31. Ⓐ Ⓑ Ⓒ Ⓓ Ⓔ
32. Ⓐ Ⓑ Ⓒ Ⓓ Ⓔ
33. Ⓐ Ⓑ Ⓒ Ⓓ Ⓔ
34. Ⓐ Ⓑ Ⓒ Ⓓ Ⓔ
35. Ⓐ Ⓑ Ⓒ Ⓓ Ⓔ
36. Ⓐ Ⓑ Ⓒ Ⓓ Ⓔ
37. Ⓐ Ⓑ Ⓒ Ⓓ Ⓔ
38. Ⓐ Ⓑ Ⓒ Ⓓ Ⓔ
39. Ⓐ Ⓑ Ⓒ Ⓓ Ⓔ
40. Ⓐ Ⓑ Ⓒ Ⓓ Ⓔ

SECTION 9

1. Ⓐ Ⓑ Ⓒ Ⓓ Ⓔ
2. Ⓐ Ⓑ Ⓒ Ⓓ Ⓔ
3. Ⓐ Ⓑ Ⓒ Ⓓ Ⓔ
4. Ⓐ Ⓑ Ⓒ Ⓓ Ⓔ
5. Ⓐ Ⓑ Ⓒ Ⓓ Ⓔ
6. Ⓐ Ⓑ Ⓒ Ⓓ Ⓔ
7. Ⓐ Ⓑ Ⓒ Ⓓ Ⓔ
8. Ⓐ Ⓑ Ⓒ Ⓓ Ⓔ
9. Ⓐ Ⓑ Ⓒ Ⓓ Ⓔ
10. Ⓐ Ⓑ Ⓒ Ⓓ Ⓔ
11. Ⓐ Ⓑ Ⓒ Ⓓ Ⓔ
12. Ⓐ Ⓑ Ⓒ Ⓓ Ⓔ
13. Ⓐ Ⓑ Ⓒ Ⓓ Ⓔ
14. Ⓐ Ⓑ Ⓒ Ⓓ Ⓔ
15. Ⓐ Ⓑ Ⓒ Ⓓ Ⓔ
16. Ⓐ Ⓑ Ⓒ Ⓓ Ⓔ
17. Ⓐ Ⓑ Ⓒ Ⓓ Ⓔ
18. Ⓐ Ⓑ Ⓒ Ⓓ Ⓔ
19. Ⓐ Ⓑ Ⓒ Ⓓ Ⓔ
20. Ⓐ Ⓑ Ⓒ Ⓓ Ⓔ
21. Ⓐ Ⓑ Ⓒ Ⓓ Ⓔ
22. Ⓐ Ⓑ Ⓒ Ⓓ Ⓔ
23. Ⓐ Ⓑ Ⓒ Ⓓ Ⓔ
24. Ⓐ Ⓑ Ⓒ Ⓓ Ⓔ
25. Ⓐ Ⓑ Ⓒ Ⓓ Ⓔ
26. Ⓐ Ⓑ Ⓒ Ⓓ Ⓔ
27. Ⓐ Ⓑ Ⓒ Ⓓ Ⓔ
28. Ⓐ Ⓑ Ⓒ Ⓓ Ⓔ
29. Ⓐ Ⓑ Ⓒ Ⓓ Ⓔ
30. Ⓐ Ⓑ Ⓒ Ⓓ Ⓔ
31. Ⓐ Ⓑ Ⓒ Ⓓ Ⓔ
32. Ⓐ Ⓑ Ⓒ Ⓓ Ⓔ
33. Ⓐ Ⓑ Ⓒ Ⓓ Ⓔ
34. Ⓐ Ⓑ Ⓒ Ⓓ Ⓔ
35. Ⓐ Ⓑ Ⓒ Ⓓ Ⓔ
36. Ⓐ Ⓑ Ⓒ Ⓓ Ⓔ
37. Ⓐ Ⓑ Ⓒ Ⓓ Ⓔ
38. Ⓐ Ⓑ Ⓒ Ⓓ Ⓔ
39. Ⓐ Ⓑ Ⓒ Ⓓ Ⓔ
40. Ⓐ Ⓑ Ⓒ Ⓓ Ⓔ

Section 1

Time—25 minutes
1 Question

Directions for Writing the Essay

Plan and write an essay that answers the question below. Do NOT write on another topic. An essay on another topic will receive a score of 0.

Two readers will grade your essay based on how well you develop your point of view, organize and explain your ideas, use specific and relevant examples to support your thesis, and use clear and effective language. How well you write is much more important than how much you write, but to cover the topic adequately you should plan to write several paragraphs.

Your essay must be written on separate lined sheets of paper. Keep your handwriting to a reasonable size. Your essay will be read by people who are not familiar with your handwriting, so write legibly.

You may use this sheet for notes and outlining, but these will not be graded as part of your essay.

Consider carefully the issue discussed in the following passage, then write an essay that answers the questions posed in the assignment.

> *If you believe you will succeed, you are probably right. If you think you will fail, you are also probably right.*

Assignment: **Which has a stronger effect on one's life: one's circumstances, or one's system of beliefs?** Write an essay in which you answer this question and support your position logically with examples from literature, the arts, history, politics, science and technology, current events, or your experience or observation.

Write your essay on separate sheets of paper.

Section 2

Time—25 minutes
24 Questions

Each sentence below has one or two blanks, each blank indicating that something has been omitted. Beneath the sentence are five words or sets of words labeled A through E. Choose the word or set of words that, when inserted in the sentence, *best* fits the meaning of the sentence as a whole.

Example:

Medieval kingdoms did not become constitutional republics overnight; on the contrary, the change was ———.

(A) unpopular   (B) unexpected
(C) advantageous (D) sufficient
(E) gradual

Correct response: (E)

1   From the 1930's until the 1960s, T.S. Eliot's reputation grew to mythic proportions, making him the most ——— English-speaking poet in the world.

(A) callous   (B) infamous
(C) aloof   (D) renowned
(E) obtuse

2   Because of the cold and rainy weather that has enveloped the resort areas this summer, the beaches have been ——— people.

(A) devoid of   (B) overpopulated by
(C) overrun with   (D) packed with
(E) manipulated by

3   Amid the controversy surrounding her reign, the queen decided to ——— her throne and retire to the countryside.

(A) commemorate   (B) abdicate
(C) rectify   (D) replicate
(E) disenfranchise

4   Although I expected ——— for raking my neighbor's lawn, I was surprised that she paid me so much because I had always been told that she was ———.

(A) remuneration . . frugal
(B) perquisite . . venal
(C) beneficiary . . penniless
(D) gratification . . arbitrary
(E) provisions . . thrifty

5   Despite having been ——— for several years, the vegetable garden had great potential, and Mrs. Nelson was excited about ——— it.

(A) fertile . . planting
(B) fallow . . cultivating
(C) aquatic . . fertilizing
(D) praiseworthy . . culminating
(E) painstaking . . sterilizing

6   Having never before been subjected to the rigors of a Presidential campaign, Senator Thomas found the ——— pace of the primaries overwhelming and as a result he took his name off the ballot.

(A) reticent   (B) mundane
(C) pastoral   (D) frenetic
(E) prosaic

7   The literature of Gabriel García Márquez has defined the "magical realism" genre of fiction; he writes of seemingly impossible and——— events that are woven flawlessly into the universal themes of love and war.

(A) plausible   (B) chimerical
(C) obsequious   (D) itinerant
(E) tenuous

8   The deliberation of the jury was ——— and even escalated to physical combat after two ——— jurors exchanged vicious invectives.

(A) dignified . . temperate
(B) decorous . . belligerent
(C) sedate . . amiable
(D) staid . . pugnacious
(E) contentious . . truculent

GO ON TO THE NEXT PAGE ▶▶▶

Each passage below is followed by one or two questions based on its content. Answer each question based on what is stated or implied in the passage that precedes it.

Questions 9–10 are based on the following passage.

Line   Johannes Kepler, whose audience was more
         friendly than Galileo's when it came to his
         theories concerning the universe, refined
         Galileo's telescope design. Kepler's refracting
5   telescope employed a convex-lens objective
         with a long focal length and a smaller
         convex-lens eyepiece with a short focal
         length. Unlike the galilean telescope, the
         keplerian refractor produces an inverted
10   image; it is upside-down and backwards. The
         distance between the objective and the
         eyepiece must be exactly equal to the sum of
         the focal lengths of the two lenses in order
         for the image to be clear. The magnification
15   factor depends on the ratio of the focal
         length of the objective to the focal length of
         the eyepiece.

9 The passage indicates that, unlike Kepler's theories, Galileo's theories were

(A)   not well researched
(B)   hindered by limited access to scientific instruments
(C)   not well received
(D)   rigorously tested
(E)   highly inventive

10 According to the passage, a Galilean telescope produces an image that is

(A)   precisely the distance from the objective to the eyepiece
(B)   clearer than that produced by the keplerian refractor
(C)   larger than that produced by the keplerian refractor
(D)   not inverted
(E)   larger than the distance from the objective to the eyepiece

Questions 11–12 are based on the following passage.

Line   As the nineteenth century progressed, the
         Romanticists ferreted out every possible
         subject of melodramatic or sentimental
         potentialities from history, literature, and the
5   strange portions of the globe. Whereupon the
         Impressionists turned the whole ingenious
         business on its ear as violently as possible in
         the name of progress, by insisting that the
         subject mattered not at all. Monet, high
10   priest of the Impressionist painters, said he
         would make great art the simplest thing he
         could think of, which was a couple of
         haystacks, and he did a whole series of
         canvases of them, at different times of the
15   day, under different atmospheric conditions,
         producing a wide variety of color effects
         according to the precise quality of changing
         light and shade.

11 The "ingenious business" mentioned in lines 6–7 is

(A)   the tendency of artists to choose emotional subjects
(B)   Monet's artwork as a whole
(C)   the use of natural forms in painting
(D)   the inventive use of light and shade
(E)   the inclination of artists to invent new modes of expression

12 The passage suggests that Monet most likely chose haystacks as his subject because they

(A)   evoked the peaceful feelings of a pastoral scene
(B)   had subtle and complex textures
(C)   were subjects that appealed to the Romanticists
(D)   were devoid of emotional content
(E)   could be depicted with a narrow range of hues

GO ON TO THE NEXT PAGE ▶▶▶

First paragraph: *Physics Demystified*, Stan Gibilisco, McGraw-Hill, 2002, p. 513
Second paragraph: *Sculpture Through the Ages*, Lincoln Rothschild, McGraw Hill, 1942, p. 238

The questions below are based on the content of the preceding passage. The questions are to be answered on the basis of what is stated or implied in the passage itself or the introductory material that precedes the passage.

2 ➤

Questions 13–18 are based on the following passage.

The following passage is an excerpt from a book written by a famous American composer, Aaron Copland, about what to listen for in music.

Line   It has often seemed to me that there is a
tendency to exaggerate the difficulty of
properly understanding music. We musicians
are constantly meeting some honest soul who
5   invariably says, in one form or another:
"I love music very much, but I don't
understand anything about it." My playwright
and novelist friends rarely hear any one say,
"I don't understand anything about the
10   theater or the novel." Yet I strongly suspect
that those very same people, so modest about
music, have just as much reason to be
modest about the other arts. Or, to put it
more graciously, have just as little reason to
15   be modest about their understanding of
music. If you have any feelings of inferiority
about your musical reactions, try to rid
yourself of them. They are often not justified.
     At any rate, you have no reason to be
20   downcast about your musical capacities until
you have some idea of what it means to be
musical. There are many strange popular
notions about what "being musical" consists
of. One is always being told, as the
25   unarguable proof of a musical person, that
he or she can "go to a show and then come
home and play all the tunes on the piano."
That fact alone bespeaks a certain musicality
in the person in question, but it does not
30   indicate the kind of sensitivity to music that
is under examination here. The entertainer
who mimics well is not yet an actor, and the
musical mimic is not necessarily a
profoundly musical individual. Another
35   attribute which is trotted forth whenever the
question of being musical arises is that of
having absolute pitch. To be able to recognize
the note A when you hear it may, at times, be
helpful, but it certainly does not prove, taken

40   by itself, that you are a musical person.
It should not be taken to indicate anything
more than a glib musicality which has only a
limited significance in relationship to the real
understanding of music which concerns us
45   here.
     There is, however, one minimum
requirement for the potentially intelligent
listener. He must be able to recognize a
melody when he hears it. If there is such a
50   thing as being tone-deaf, then it suggests the
inability to recognize a tune. Such a person
has my sympathy, but he cannot be helped;
just as the color-blind are a useless lot to the
painter. But if you feel confident that you can
55   recognize a given melody—not *sing* a melody,
but recognize it when played, even after an
interval of a few minutes and after other and
different melodies have been sounded—the
key to a deeper appreciation of music is in
60   your hands.
     It is insufficient merely to hear music in
terms of the separate moments at which it
exists. You must be able to relate what you
hear at any given moment to what just
65   happened before and what is about to come
afterward. In other words, music is an art
that exists in point of time. In that sense it is
like a novel, except that the events of a novel
are easier to keep in mind, partly because
70   real happenings are narrated and partly
because one can turn back and refresh one's
memory of them. Musical "events" are more
abstract by nature, so the act of pulling them
all together in the imagination is not so easy
75   as in reading a novel. That is why it is
necessary for you to be able to recognize a
tune. For the thing that takes the place of a
story in music is, as a rule, the melody. The
melody is generally what guides the listener.
80   If you can't recognize a melody on its first
appearance and can't follow its peregrinations
straight through to its final appearance, I fail
to see what you have to go on in listening.
You are just vaguely aware of the music. But
85   recognizing a tune means you know where
you are in the music and have a good chance
of knowing where you are going. It is the
only *sine qua non* of a more intelligent
approach to understanding music.

GO ON TO THE NEXT PAGE ▸▸▸

from *What to Listen for in Music*, Aaron Copland, McGraw-Hill 1957, pp. 4–6

13 Which of the following best describes the overall structure of the passage?

(A) A historical phenomenon is described and then evaluated.

(B) A problem is summarized and its effects on a wide range of situations are discussed.

(C) A story is told to illustrate a moral, and then this moral is discussed and generalized.

(D) The contributions of several artists are described and then evaluated.

(E) A common misconception is described and then followed by authoritative instruction.

14 Unlike the sentence that precedes it, the sentence beginning on line 13 ("Or, to put it ... understanding of music"), regards "those very same people" with

(A) condescension   (B) jocularity

(C) disdain   (D) respect

(E) indifference

15 According to the author, "being musical" (line 23) necessarily consists of which of the following?

     I. the ability to sing
     II. the ability to play an instrument
     III. the ability to detect a melody line

(A) I only

(B) III only

(C) I and III only

(D) II and III only

(E) I, II and III

16 In line 28, the word "bespeaks" most nearly means

(A) disproves   (B) discusses

(C) interrupts   (D) entertains

(E) indicates

17 In line 53, the word "lot" most nearly means

(A) group   (B) large amount

(C) empty region   (D) fate

(E) foundation

18 The passage indicates that appreciating music is more challenging than appreciating a novel because appreciating music necessarily involves

(A) the use of memory

(B) knowledge of the composer's life

(C) synthesis of abstract events

(D) the ability to recognize particular notes

(E) an understanding of musical theory

2

The questions below are based on the content of the preceding passage. The questions are to be answered on the basis of what is stated or implied in the passage itself or the introductory material that precedes the passage.

2

Questions 19–24 are based on the following passage.

The following is an excerpt from an essay on pragmatism by William James written in 1907.

Line　　The pragmatic method is primarily a method of settling metaphysical disputes that otherwise might be interminable. Is the world one or many?—fated or free?
5　—material or spiritual? Here are notions either of which may or may not hold good of the world, and disputes over such notions are unending. The pragmatic method in such cases is to try to interpret each notion by
10　tracing its respective practical consequences. What difference would it practically make to anyone if this notion rather than that notion were true? If no practical difference whatever can be traced, then the alternatives mean
15　practically the same thing, and all dispute is idle. Whenever a dispute is serious, we ought to be able to show some practical difference that must follow from one side or the other's being right.
20　　A glance at the history of the idea will show you still better what pragmatism means. The term is derived from the same Greek word *pragma*, meaning action, from which our words "practice" and "practical" come. It was
25　first introduced into philosophy by Mr. Charles Peirce in 1878. In an article entitled "How to Make Our Ideas Clear." Mr. Peirce, after pointing out that our beliefs are really rules for action, said that to develop a
30　thought's meaning, we need only determine what conduct it is fitted to produce: that conduct is for us its sole significance. And the tangible fact at the root of all our thought-distinctions, however subtle, is that
35　there is no one of them so fine as to consist in anything but a possible difference of practice. To attain perfect clearness in our thoughts of an object, then, we need only consider what conceivable effects of a

40　practical kind the object may involve—what sensations we are to expect from it, and what reactions we must prepare. Our conception of these effects, whether immediate or remote, is then for us the whole of our
45　conception of the object, so far as that conception has positive significance at all.
　　This is the principle of Peirce, the principle of pragmatism. It lay entirely unnoticed by anyone for twenty years, until I, in an
50　address before Professor Howison's philosophical union at the University of California, brought it forward again and made a special application of it to religion. By that date (1898) the times seemed ripe for
55　its reception. The word "pragmatism" spread, and at present it fairly spots the pages of the philosophic journals. On all hands we find the 'pragmatic movement' spoken of, sometimes with respect, sometimes with contumely,
60　seldom with clear understanding. It is evident that the term applies itself conveniently to a number of tendencies that hitherto have lacked a collective name, and that it has "come to stay."
65　　To take in the importance of Peirce's principle, one must get accustomed to applying it to concrete cases. I found a few years ago that Ostwald, the illustrious Leipzig chemist, had been making perfectly distinct
70　use of the principle of pragmatism in his lectures on the philosophy of science, though he had not called it by that name.
　　"All realities influence our practice," he wrote me; "and that influence is their
75　meaning for us. I am accustomed to putting questions to my classes in this way: In what respects would the world be different if this alternative or that were true? If I can find nothing that would become different, then
80　the alternative has no sense."
　　That is, the rival views mean practically the same thing, and meaning, other than practical, there is for us none. Ostwald in a published lecture gives this example of what
85　he means. Chemists have long wrangled over the inner constitution of certain bodies called "tautomerous." Their properties seemed equally consistent with the notion that an

GO ON TO THE NEXT PAGE ▶▶▶

90 unstable hydrogen atom oscillates inside of them, or that they are unstable mixtures of two bodies. Controversy raged; but never was decided. "It would never have begun," says Ostwald, "if the combatants had asked themselves what particular experimental fact 95 could have been made different by one or the other view being correct. For it would then have appeared that no difference of fact could possibly ensue; and the quarrel was as unreal as if, theorizing in primitive times 100 about the raising of dough by yeast, one party should have invoked a "brownie[1]," while another insisted on an "elf" as the true cause of the phenomenon."

19 According to the passage, the pragmatic method suggests that two claims are equivalent if they

(A) are based on the same premise
(B) have the same effect
(C) can be expressed mathematically
(D) do not contradict each other
(E) are made by people who have common sense

20 In line 35, the word "fine" most nearly means

(A) breakable (B) healthy
(C) meaningful (D) satisfactory
(E) subtle

21 In line 56, the phrase "fairly spots" most nearly means

(A) sees clearly
(B) considers superficially
(C) rejects completely
(D) tolerates
(E) abounds in

22 The passage indicates that Ostwald

(A) was present at the lecture the author gave at the University of California
(B) was well acquainted with Charles Peirce
(C) raised important objections to pragmatism
(D) applied the principles of pragmatism to science
(E) showed how to employ pragmatism in the analysis of religion

23 The passage suggests that the controversy surrounding "tautomerous" bodies would have been resolved in favor of one of the two competing theories if

(A) one of the theories had been proposed by a chemist as reputable as Ostwald
(B) the theories had predicted different outcomes to a feasible experiment
(C) the "tautomerous" bodies had been detected experimentally
(D) the theories had been examined by philosophical pragmatists
(E) the disputants had opened the debate to a wider audience

24 The final sentence refers to a "brownie" and an "elf" primarily to make the point that

(A) primitive people were superstitious
(B) modern scientists should avoid theories that involve mythical creatures
(C) scientists have now determined what causes yeast to rise
(D) a pragmatic perspective renders some arguments pointless
(E) knowledge about chemistry has accelerated in recent times

[1] A friendly sprite

STOP

You may check your work, on this section only, until time is called.

Section 3

Time—25 minutes
20 Questions

Directions for Multiple-Choice Questions

3 ▶

In this section, solve each problem, using any available space on the page for scratchwork. Then decide which is the best of the choices given and fill in the corresponding oval on the answer sheet.

- You may use a calculator on any problem. All numbers used are real numbers.
- Figures are drawn as accurately as possible EXCEPT when it is stated that the figure is not drawn to scale.
- All figures lie in a plane unless otherwise indicated.

Reference Information

$A = \pi r^2$
$C = 2\pi r$

$A = \ell w$

$A = \frac{1}{2}bh$

$V = \ell w h$

$V = \pi r^2 h$

$c^2 = a^2 + b^2$

Special Right Triangles

The arc of a circle measures 360°.
Every straight angle measures 180°.
The sum of the measures of the angles in a triangle is 180°.

---

1 If $2x + 7 = 4x + 5$, what is the value of x?

(A) 1
(B) 2
(C) 4
(D) 5
(E) 8

2 If n is any positive integer, which of the following must be even?

(A) $n + 2$
(B) $2n$
(C) $3n$
(D) n^2
(E) n^3

3 The length of a nail rounded to the nearest inch is 5 inches. Which of the following could be the actual length of the nail, in inches?

(A) 4.46
(B) 4.48
(C) 5.32
(D) 5.51
(E) 5.89

4 The walls of Jane's living room have an area of 340 square feet. If she can paint 60 square feet per hour, how many minutes after she starts painting will there be only 100 square feet left to paint?

(A) 120
(B) 150
(C) 180
(D) 240
(E) 270

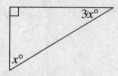

Note: Figure not drawn to scale.

5 In the right triangle above, what is the value of $3x$?

(A) 18.0
(B) 22.5
(C) 27.0
(D) 30.0
(E) 67.5

GO ON TO THE NEXT PAGE ▶▶▶

6 What is 50% of 60% of 180?

(A)　48
(B)　54
(C)　60
(D)　90
(E)　92

7 If $\dfrac{1}{c^2} = b^2 + 4b + 4$ then $c =$

(A)　$\dfrac{1}{(b-2)}$

(B)　$\dfrac{1}{\sqrt{(b-2)}}$

(C)　$\dfrac{1}{\sqrt{(4b+2)}}$

(D)　$\dfrac{1}{\sqrt{(b^2+2)}}$

(E)　$\dfrac{1}{(b+2)}$

8 If the average of $3y$, $4y$, and $(y-5)$ is 9, what is the value of y?

(A)　1.50
(B)　1.75
(C)　2.00
(D)　3.25
(E)　4.00

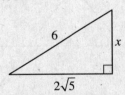

Note: Figure not drawn to scale.

9 In the figure above, right triangle ABC has side lengths as shown. What is the value of x?

(A)　2
(B)　3
(C)　4
(D)　5
(E)　6

10 Which of the following represents the domain of the function $f(x) = \dfrac{\sqrt{x+4}}{(x-6)}$?

(A)　$x \geq -4$
(B)　$x > -4$
(C)　$x \geq -4$ and $x \neq 6$
(D)　$x > -4$ and $x \neq 6$
(E)　$x \neq 6$

11 When the positive integer w is divided by 6, the remainder is 2. What is the remainder when $5w$ is divided by 6?

(A)　1
(B)　2
(C)　3
(D)　4
(E)　5

COLOUR OF VARIOUS PETS AT THE PET STORE

	white	black	brown	total
dogs	35	60	y	105
cats	x	37	16	w
pigs	15	5	8	28
total	75	m	34	z

12 Given the information in the table above, what is the value of $x + y + z$?

(A)　35
(B)　113
(C)　246
(D)　299
(E)　314

13 If a circle with center $(3, 4)$ is tangent to the x-axis, what is the circumference of the circle?

(A)　4π
(B)　6π
(C)　8π
(D)　12π
(E)　16π

14 If the length of line segment $\overline{DE}$ is 7, and the length of line segment $\overline{EF}$ is 9, which of the following could NOT be the length of line segment $\overline{DF}$?

(A)　6
(B)　8
(C)　12
(D)　16
(E)　18

GO ON TO THE NEXT PAGE ▶▶▶

3

3

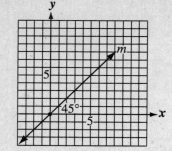

15 In the figure above, line *m* passes through the origin. Which of the following points lies on line *m*?

    I.   (−2, 1)
    II. (−2, −2)
    III. (1, 1)

(A) II only
(B) I and II only
(C) I and III only
(D) II and III only
(E) I, II, and III

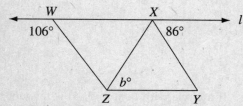

Note: Figure not drawn to scale.

16 In the figure above, $WX = XZ = ZY$. What is the value of *b*?

(A) 56
(B) 76
(C) 78
(D) 84
(E) 128

17 Mitchell spends 30% of his day sleeping, 35% of his day at work, 5% of his day at the gym, five additional hours at home and the rest of the day in the car. How many minutes does he spend in the car each day? (1 hour = 60 minutes)

(A) 2.2
(B) 60
(C) 120
(D) 132
(E) 432

18 What is the slope of the line containing the point (2, 5) and the midpoint of the line segment with endpoints (8, 8) and (6, −2)?

(A) $\dfrac{1}{2}$

(B) $-\dfrac{2}{5}$

(C) $-\dfrac{7}{4}$

(D) $-\dfrac{5}{2}$

(E) $-\dfrac{4}{7}$

19 A square has a diagonal of length *m*. Which of the following represents the area of the square in terms of *m*?

(A) $\dfrac{m^2}{2}$

(B) $2m$
(C) m^2
(D) m^3

(E) $\dfrac{2}{m^2}$

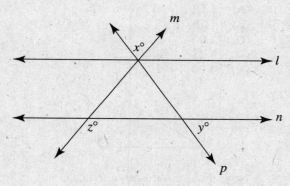

20 In the figure above, line *l* is parallel to line *n*. Which of the following represents the value of *x* in terms of *y* and *z*?

(A) $z - y$
(B) $z + y$
(C) $180 - z - y$
(D) $180 - z + y$
(E) $90 - y$

STOP

You may check your work, on this section only, until time is called.

Section 4

Time—25 Minutes
18 Questions

Directions for Multiple-Choice Questions

In this section, solve each problem, using any available space on the page for scratchwork. Then decide which is the best of the choices given and fill in the corresponding oval on the answer sheet.

- You may use a calculator on any problem. All numbers used are real numbers.
- Figures are drawn as accurately as possible EXCEPT when it is stated that the figure is not drawn to scale.
- All figures lie in a plane unless otherwise indicated.

Reference Information

$A = \pi r^2$
$C = 2\pi r$

$A = \ell w$

$A = \frac{1}{2}bh$

$V = \ell wh$

$V = \pi r^2 h$

$c^2 = a^2 + b^2$

Special Right Triangles

The arc of a circle measures 360°.
Every straight angle measures 180°.
The sum of the measures of the angles in a triangle is 180°.

---

1 Let $x \$ y$ be defined by the equation $x \$ y = x^y + 3$. What is the value of $4 \$ 2$?

(A) 9
(B) 11
(C) 19
(D) 20
(E) 25

2 If $m + n = 7$ and $2n - 3m = 6$, what is the value of $3n - 2m$?

(A) 7
(B) 13
(C) 14
(D) 17
(E) 18

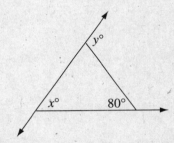

Note: Figure not drawn to scale.

3 In the triangle above, if x and y are integers and $x < 40$, what is the smallest possible value of y?

(A) 39°
(B) 61°
(C) 84°
(D) 119°
(E) 141°

GO ON TO THE NEXT PAGE ▶▶▶

4 Triangle *ABC* has side lengths that are all integers. If two of the sides are 7 and 11, how many possible values are there for the third side length?

(A)　11
(B)　12
(C)　13
(D)　14
(E)　15

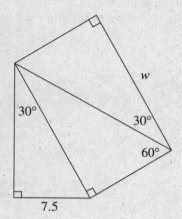

7.5

5 In the figure above, what is the value of *w*?

(A)　15
(B)　17
(C)　20
(D)　22
(E)　24

6 In 1995, the Jones family sold their home for $192,500. They spent $175,000 to buy the house in 1988. What percent profit did they make on the sale?

(A)　9%
(B)　10%
(C)　11%
(D)　12%
(E)　13%

7 How many different groups of four people can be assembled from a group of six people?

(A)　8
(B)　12
(C)　15
(D)　20
(E)　24

8　　　　　　　　　　−3, 6, −2 …

After the second term in the sequence above, each term is equivalent to the ratio of the preceding term to the term before that. For example, the third term, −2, is equal to the ratio of 6 to −3. How many of the first 100 terms of this sequence are negative?

(A)　33
(B)　34
(C)　50
(D)　66
(E)　67

Directions for Student-Produced Response Questions

Each of the questions in this section requires you to solve the problem and enter your answer in a grid, as shown below.

- If your answer is ⅔ or .666..., you must enter **the most accurate value the grid can accommodate**, but you may do this in one of four ways.

Start in first column — Grid result here: **2 / 3**

Start in second column: **2 / 3**

Grid as a truncated decimal: **. 6 6 6**

Grid as a rounded decimal: **. 6 6 7**

- In the example above, gridding a response of 0.67 or 0.66 is **incorrect** because it is less accurate than those above.
- The scoring machine cannot read what is written in the top row of boxes. You **MUST** fill in the numerical grid accurately to get credit for answering any question correctly. You should write your answer in the top row of boxes only to aid your gridding.
- Do **not** grid in a mixed fraction like $3\frac{1}{2}$ as $\boxed{3 \quad 1 \ / \ 2}$ because it will be interpreted as $\frac{31}{2}$. Instead, convert it to an improper fraction like $\frac{7}{2}$ or a decimal like 3.5 before gridding.
- None of the answers will be negative, because there is no negative sign in the grid.
- Some of the questions may have more than one correct answer. You must grid only one of the correct answers.
- You may use a calculator on any of these problems.
- All numbers in these problems are real numbers.
- Figures are drawn as accurately as possible EXCEPT when it is stated that the figure is not drawn to scale.
- All figures lie in a plane unless otherwise indicated.

---

9 If Liz's car can go 24 miles on one gallon of gasoline, then, at this rate, how many gallons will it take Liz to drive 96 miles?

10 If b is a positive number and $b^3 < b^2$, what is one possible value of b?

11 Eric is 40 pounds heavier than Bill. If together they weigh 320 pounds, how much does Eric weigh?

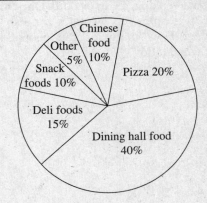

12 The circle graph above shows the results of a survey in which 3,000 college students indicated what they most often eat for dinner. How many fewer students eat snack food than dining hall food for dinner?

GO ON TO THE NEXT PAGE ▶▶▶

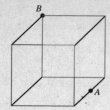

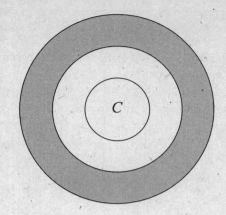

13 The cube shown above has edges of length 4. Point A is a midpoint on one of the edges. What is the length of AB (not shown)?

14 A cooler at a barbeque is filled with cans of soda and weighs 20 pounds. After two hours, three-quarters of the cans of soda have been consumed and the cooler holding the remaining sodas now weighs 14 pounds. If each can of soda weighs the same, how much does the empty cooler weigh?

15 Jim rides his bike to work each morning at an average speed of 15 miles per hour. He rides home along the same route at 10 miles per hour. If the total time of his commute to and from work is 60 minutes each day, how far, in miles, is Jim's trip to work?

16 Of 1,000 people surveyed, each person owned a dog, a cat, or both. One-third of the 630 people who owned a cat also owned a dog. How many of the people surveyed owned a dog?

17 The dart board above consists of three concentric circles with center C. The innermost circle has a radius of 1, the middle circle a radius of 2, and the outermost circle has a radius of 3. What is the probability that a dart thrown at random lands in the shaded area?

18 Every marble in a jar is either red or black, and either striped or unstriped. There are three times as many red marbles as black marbles. Among the red marbles, there are twice as many striped marbles as unstriped marbles. If you were to randomly select a marble from this jar, what is the probability that it would be an unstriped red marble?

You may check your work, on this section only, until time is called.

Section 5

**Time—25 minutes
24 Questions**

Each sentence below has one or two blanks, each blank indicating that something has been omitted. Beneath the sentence are five words or sets of words labeled A through E. Choose the word or set of words that, when inserted in the sentence, best fits the meaning of the sentence as a whole.

Example:

Medieval kingdoms did not become constitutional republics overnight; on the contrary, the change was ———.

(A) unpopular (B) unexpected
(C) advantageous (D) sufficient
(E) gradual

Correct response: (E)

1 The ——— odor was easily explained when Elmo found the bag of rotten garbage that he had forgotten to throw out three weeks earlier.

(A) putrid (B) delectable
(C) piquant (D) divine
(E) savory

2 Unable to ——— his mother's ——— handwriting, Doug had to call her for clarification when attempting to use the recipe.

(A) reconfigure . . illegible
(B) recapitulate . . lucid
(C) reiterate . . placid
(D) recognize . . cogent
(E) decipher . . unintelligible

3 The thousands of fragile artifacts that had been ——— by generations of archaeologists were stored without the requisite safeguards against ——— and so became utterly useless to students.

(A) collected . . preservation
(B) projected . . dissipation
(C) assembled . . retrieval
(D) amassed . . deterioration
(E) disseminated . . desiccation

4 The incontrovertible evidence presented by the prosecution proved conclusively the ——— of the defendant.

(A) apathy (B) culpability
(C) penitence (D) dexterity
(E) prescience

5 Throughout her life, Mother Teresa, the winner of the 1979 Nobel Peace Prize, was ——— with her time, devoting herself to providing medical care and nutrition to the dying poor of the world.

(A) rhetorical (B) munificent
(C) felicitous (D) austere
(E) mellifluous

GO ON TO THE NEXT PAGE ▸▸▸

Each passage below is followed by one or two questions based on its content. Answer each question based on what is stated or implied in the passage that precedes it.

Questions 6–7 are based on the following passage.

Line   As hominid history has unfolded, social and cultural means of adaptation have become increasingly important. In this process, humans have devised diverse ways
5   of coping with the range of environments and social systems they have occupied in time and space. The rate of cultural change has accelerated, particularly during the past 10,000 years. For millions of years, hunting
10   and gathering of nature's bounty—foraging— was the sole basis of hominid subsistence. However, it took only a few thousand years for food production (cultivation of plants and domestication of animals), which originated
15   in the Middle East 10,000 to 12,000 years ago, to replace foraging in most areas. People started producing their own food, planting crops and stockbreeding animals, rather than simply taking what nature had to offer.

6   The passage indicates that, unlike the practice of food gathering, the practice of food production among hominids

(A)   was not widely available
(B)   was introduced over one million years ago
(C)   developed rapidly
(D)   damaged the environment in which they lived
(E)   did not require great changes in behavior

7   According to the passage, which of the following is NOT an example of food production?

(A)   harvesting corn planted on a hillside
(B)   breeding fish in a protected lake
(C)   herding goats to gather their milk
(D)   organizing a group to hunt deer
(E)   transplanting wheat to a more hospitable location

Questions 8–9 are based on the following passage.

Line   In Egypt in 450 B.C., religion was the function of the priesthood, a mystic practice of elaborate ceremo nial performed in the depths of temple sanctuaries. In Greece
5   generally, and in the Panathenaea particularly, however, the temple served simply for the performance of the crucial rite of sacrifice. Various preliminaries were engaged in by all the citizens outside the
10   temple and in other parts of the city, which were of the very fabric of their lives. They witnessed or took part in games and activities that were familiar activities; the power of the Athenian state was expressed in the presence
15   of the tributaries, and her national prominence was implied in the six-day spectacle as a whole for it had consciously been elaborated to rival the time-honored Olympic games

8   The passage indicates that Egyptian religious rites differed from Greek religious rites primarily in terms of

(A)   the clothing worn by the priests
(B)   the degree to which the public participated
(C)   the length of the ceremonies
(D)   the willingness of the priests to participate
(E)   the elaborateness of the temples in which they were held

9   In line 9, the word "engaged" most nearly means

(A)   betrothed
(B)   entertained
(C)   loved
(D)   revealed
(E)   participated

GO ON TO THE NEXT PAGE ▶▶▶

First paragraph: *Anthropology: The Exploration of Human Diversity*, Conrad Phillip Kottak, McGraw-Hill, 1997, p. 3
Second paragraph: *Sculpture Through the Ages*, Lincoln Rothschild, McGraw-Hill, 1942, p. 62

Questions 10–16 are based on the following passage.

The following passage is an excerpt from a modern textbook on psychology.

Line   The cognitive strategies used to carry out the steps in problem-solving can be of three general types: trial and error, algorithmic, or heuristic. Let's look at each of these cognitive
5   strategies one at a time. We humans often approach problems without any cognitive strategy at all, simply trying one possible solution after another. This is usually referred to as the trial-and-error approach. Although
10 common, this approach to problem solving can be very time consuming and certainly does not guarantee that a solution will be discovered.

In contrast, algorithms are systematic
15 patterns of reasoning that (if followed) guarantee a correct solution. Computers generally use algorithms. Indeed computers are especially suited for them, since they can quickly consider the many alternatives
20 required by complex algorithms. Computers do not always use algorithms, however. For extremely complex problems, computers are sometimes programmed to use shortcuts known as heuristics. Heuristics are strategies
25 that increase the probabilities of finding a correct solution. But since they do not systematically evaluate every possible solution, heuristics do not guarantee finding the correct one. Indeed, they often lead to
30 poor solutions.

The concept of heuristic reasoning is derived partially from research that attempts to simulate human intelligence using computers. Efforts to program computers to
35 play the game of chess, for example, were originally frustrated by the enormous number of possible solutions that would have to be considered before making each move. To avoid such extensive algorithmic

40 programs, heuristic programs were written. For example, the program is written to maximize protection of the queen or to control the center of the board. Moves that meet these goals are executed, but the long-
45 range consequences of each move are not considered by the artificial intelligence program. That is why excellent chess players can generally beat computers at chess.

The concept of heuristic reasoning is an
50 important one because there is reason to believe that humans operate using heuristics more than algorithms. This is so either because algorithms require so much cognitive capacity and effort or because we
55 simply do not possess algorithms for most of the problems we face in life.

Suppose you are presented with the following problem: What occupation should Steve pursue in college? You are told that
60 Steve is shy, helpful, good with figures, and has a passion for detail. You are also told that you can ask for and receive additional information to use in solving the problem. How would you solve this problem?
65 Amos Tversky has identified two heuristics that are frequently used in human problem solving: representativeness and availability. The representativeness heuristic makes pre- dictions based on the similarity between the
70 information you have and the outcome you want to predict. For example, we might use this heuristic to predict Steve's best choice of an occupation on the basis of which occupation we believe his personality is most
75 representative of (accountant, pharmacist, etc.). This might be a good strategy, but it leads us not to seek and evaluate other information that might be helpful (such as Steve's preferences, his previous school
80 grades, or the employment opportunities in different occupations).

The availability heuristic bases decisions on the availability of relevant information in memory. Rather than seeking additional
85 information, we take another shortcut and use whatever information we can remember. In the case of predicting Steve's best occupation, we might recommend that he become an attorney based on our recollection

GO ON TO THE NEXT PAGE ▸▸▸

Psychology: An Introduction by Benjamin B. Lahey, McGraw-Hill, New York, 1998, p. 252

90 of an attorney to whom Steve bears a striking resemblance in ability and temperament. These cognitive shortcuts are obviously efficient in terms of effort but certainly do not always lead to effective problem solving.
95 However, humans frequently think heuristically.

10 This passage is primarily concerned with

(A) the origins of human error
(B) the computer as a model for human reasoning
(C) how human beings make decisions
(D) the development of algorithms
(E) comparing heuristics with trial-and-error methods

11 It can be inferred from the passage that the "research" mentioned in line 32 led to the conclusion that

(A) computers cannot be programmed to use heuristics
(B) computers are important aids to human reasoning
(C) computers can be programmed to defeat chess masters
(D) humans prefer using trial-and-error methods to using representativeness heuristics
(E) heuristics simulate human reasoning better than algorithms

12 The passage mentions the strategy of controlling the center of the board in a chess game as an example of

(A) a means of reducing the number of options to be evaluated before making a decision
(B) a thorough algorithmic approach that has been employed by most chess-playing programs
(C) a trial-and-error method that is easier for a computer to employ than a human
(D) an availability heuristic
(E) a representativeness heuristic

13 In line 44, the word "executed" most nearly means

(A) removed   (B) destroyed
(C) frustrated   (D) empowered
(E) carried out

14 The passage suggests that we humans tend to use heuristics more frequently than algorithms because heuristics

(A) are less mentally taxing than algorithms
(B) guarantee the correct answer
(C) evaluate more possible solutions than algorithms do
(D) are less systematic than trial-and-error approaches
(E) lead us to seek more information about a problem

15 The author suggests that the representativeness heuristic may be insufficient in helping Steve to choose an occupation because

(A) it does not take Steve's personality characteristics into account
(B) it does not take into account what Steve wants to do
(C) it requires an infinite amount of information
(D) it requires the use of an elaborate algorithm
(E) it is similar to a trial-and-error approach

16 According to the passage, the availability heuristic differs from the representativeness heuristic in that the availability heuristic relies more on the ability to

(A) compare current information about the problem to the desired outcome
(B) recall information
(C) follow a specified set of directions
(D) consider every possible solution to a problem
(E) test hypotheses

GO ON TO THE NEXT PAGE ▶▶▶

The questions below are based on the content of the preceding passage. The questions are to be answered on the basis of what is stated or implied in the passage itself or the introductory material that precedes the passage.

Questions 17–24 are based on the following passage.

The following passage is an excerpt from an essay about the relationship between politics and art in nineteenth century Europe.

Line   For two years after the fall of the Bastille, July 14, 1789, the vacillation of Louis XVI between liberal counselors like Mirabeau and Lafayette on the one hand, the blindly
5   reactionary queen Marie Antoinette and the conniving *émigré* nobles on the other, finally goaded the frantic forces of the Revolution to remove by violence the threat of a restoration of the *ancien régime*. However, it was many
10   years before France in the constitution of 1875 caught up politically with the grand trend toward parliamentary, constitutional rule, based upon wide popular suffrage with a stable and fairly high grade of civil
15   administration. Monarchists and clericals preached reaction and restoration on the Right; the new working class and socialist organizations, which arose with the mechanization of industry, called for
20   "completion" of the Revolution on the Left; and business sat solidly in the center trying to get a little order and stability without interference.
    Released politically and culturally as well
25   as economically from their anomalous subjection to an incapable and irresponsible nobility, the entrepreneurial groups in commerce and manufacture, the people who were working with astounding new methods of
30   making things, soon inaugurated an age of unparalleled growth. Technical advance of unbelievable speed and scope increased material production beyond measure and created services hitherto undreamed of.
35   Constructive as well as destructive influences of the development are reflected in the dynamic character and unprecedented activity of cultural expression.

    In the first place the individualistic
40   tendencies of the economy of opportunity reached their most extreme stage, producing an appearance of infinite variety in cultural expression. The various groups working for control represented forces with basically
45   distinct attitudes toward manners and art. But also, every factory owner, every large-scale merchant, after a brief period of stability and profit, felt himself a lord in his particular domain and proudly sought
50   appropriate distinction for his position. The number of people who might wish to own and could afford to buy some kinds of art became large in comparison with other periods. So that each might have the feeling
55   of making a personal choice expressive of his free, individual personality, "original" aspects of style achieved a special value. The artist exaggerated his every whim and impulse, which led inevitably to the development of
60   exotic and bizarre styles.
    It was an age of rapid and sometimes accidental accessions of wealth, tremendous profits in business often resulting from chance or from cutthroat competition as well
65   as from sagacity and service to the community, while great fortunes were rare or unattainable in the ranks of the professional and industrial employment. The wealthy, especially the parvenu,[1] wished to find means of indicating
70   that there was an intrinsic difference between themselves and others, partly because they believed it and partly because to justify the vast inequalities. This encouraged a debased intensification of artificiality in culture to a
75   point where it lost all direct contact with natural experience and might not readily be understood by those who had no special introduction. The more abstruse the forms of art, the more impenetrable to the uninitiated,
80   the greater their value as a distinction to the "connoisseur," which means precisely one who is "in the know." This is an important consideration in the extravagant forms of modern art, each of which starts out by being
85   notoriously "incomprehensible."

---

[1] One who has become suddenly wealthy and has risen to a higher social status

GO ON TO THE NEXT PAGE ▶▶▶

17 The first sentence portrays Louis XVI primarily as

(A) indecisive   (B) tyrannical
(C) reactionary   (D) liberal
(E) shrewd

18 It can be inferred from the passage that the French constitution of 1875 ensured which of the following?

    I. a powerful monarchy
    II. an expansion of the right to vote
    III. a well-organized system of government

(A) II only
(B) III only
(C) I and II only
(D) II and III only
(E) I, II, and III

19 In line 26, the word "subjection" most nearly means

(A) opinion
(B) theme
(C) state of submission
(D) course of study
(E) approval

20 The passage indicates that, in France in the late 18th century, entrepreneurs and business owners primarily sought

(A) favorable economic policies from the government
(B) freedom from political interference
(C) the right to vote
(D) a return to private ownership
(E) investment capital from the ruling elite

21 The passage indicates that the "economy of opportunity" (line 40) influenced the world of art primarily by

(A) allowing former merchants to become artists
(B) imposing universal standards for art
(C) eliminating distinctions between the wealthy and the poor
(D) providing more investment in public museums
(E) encouraging a wider range of individual expression

22 The description of the relationship between artists and merchants described in lines 46–60 assumes that many artists

(A) were working actively toward the restoration of the monarchy
(B) were largely able to ignore the political upheaval of the time
(C) were better trained than artists in previous centuries
(D) made aesthetic decisions based on the needs of patrons
(E) had much to lose in abandoning traditional forms

23 In line 62, the word "accessions" most nearly means

(A) wisdom   (B) accidents
(C) successions   (D) accumulation
(E) declines

24 The final paragraph suggests that, to the newly wealthy, the most valuable forms of art were those that were

(A) imitative of the works of the ancient masters
(B) produced with exotic materials
(C) created by artists with foreign backgrounds
(D) difficult to understand
(E) reflective of the political and social struggles of the time

From *Sculpture Through the Ages*, Lincoln Rothschild, © 1942, McGraw-Hill, pp. 208–209

STOP

You may check your work, on this section only, until time is called.

Section 6

Time—25 minutes
35 Questions

Directions for "Improving Sentences" Questions

Each of the sentences below contains one underlined portion. The portion may contain one or more errors in grammar, usage, construction, precision, diction (choice of words), or idiom. Some of the sentences are correct.

Consider the meaning of the original sentence, and choose the answer that best expresses that meaning. If the original sentence is best, choose (A), because it repeats the original phrasing. Choose the phrasing that creates the clearest, most precise and most effective sentence.

EXAMPLE:

The children couldn't hardly believe their eyes.

  (A) couldn't hardly believe their eyes
  (B) would not hardly believe their eyes
  (C) could hardly believe their eyes
  (D) couldn't nearly believe their eyes
  (E) could hardly believe his or her eyes

Example answer: (C)

---

1 She crouched <u>all quiet behind the couch, hoping that she would win</u> this round of hide and seek.

  (A) all quiet behind the couch, hoping that she would win
  (B) quietly behind the couch, and hoping that she would win
  (C) quiet behind the couch, hoping that she would win
  (D) quietly behind the couch, hoping to win
  (E) quietly behind the couch, in the hope to win

2 The most knowledgeable member of the group, <u>David's answers to all of the questions were correct</u>.

  (A) David's answers to all of the questions were correct
  (B) David answered all of the questions correctly
  (C) David's answers were all correct to the questions
  (D) David answered all the questions with complete correctness
  (E) David's answers to the questions were completely correct

3 Betsy founded the club, but <u>the meetings are not dominated by her</u>.

  (A) the meetings are not dominated by her
  (B) the meetings do not have her dominating them
  (C) she would not be dominating the meetings
  (D) she is not the one dominating over the meetings
  (E) she does not dominate the meetings

4 Jon was thrilled that his scores were so much better than <u>last time he took the test</u>.

  (A) last time he took the test
  (B) his previous test
  (C) his scores on his previous test
  (D) his scores on the previous test he took
  (E) those on the previous test that he had taken before

GO ON TO THE NEXT PAGE ▸▸▸

5 Frustrated by the lack of jobs in his home town, <u>Tyler sought opportunity in the city</u>, leaving behind a myriad of dreamless peers and wasted lives.

- (A) Tyler sought opportunity in the city
- (B) Tyler sought the city for the opportunities in it
- (C) Tyler's opportunity could be sought in the city
- (D) opportunity in the city was what Tyler sought
- (E) Tyler sought opportunity and he did it in the city

6 The tasks of <u>renting the van, packing the boxes, and the drive across town were much more time-consuming</u> than they had anticipated.

- (A) renting the van, packing the boxes, and the drive across town were much more time-consuming
- (B) renting the van, packing the boxes, and the drive across town were all things that took much more time
- (C) the renting of the van, packing of boxes, and the drive across town were all much more time-consuming
- (D) renting the van, packing the boxes, and driving across town were much more time-consuming
- (E) renting the van and packing the boxes together with driving across town was more time-consuming

7 Many scholars believe that a biography <u>of the sort that delves into J. D. Salinger's reclusive life</u> would be even more fascinating than another of his works of fiction.

- (A) of the sort that delves into J. D. Salinger's reclusive life
- (B) that had delved into the reclusive life of J. D. Salinger
- (C) of the type delving into J. D. Salinger's reclusive life
- (D) delving into J. D. Salinger's reclusive life
- (E) that would delve into the reclusive life of JD Salinger

8 Although Alison was neither the most <u>experienced nor the most well-educated candidate</u>, she was clearly the most enthusiastic of those who interviewed for the job.

- (A) experienced nor the most well-educated candidate
- (B) experienced or a well-educated candidate
- (C) experienced candidate and lacked the best education
- (D) experienced, nor was she well-educated as a candidate
- (E) experienced, nor a candidate who is best educated

9 Ralph Waldo <u>Emerson, who believed that the greatest obstacle in the way of</u> genius is the reliance on the ideas of previous generations.

- (A) Emerson, who believed that the greatest obstacle in the way of
- (B) Emerson believed that the greatest obstacle to
- (C) Emerson, believing that the greatest obstacle to
- (D) Emerson, in believing that the greatest obstacle to
- (E) Emerson, whose belief that the greatest obstacle in the way of

10 The coach of the women's softball team, a firm believer in equal opportunity, made sure that <u>every team member had their turn at bat</u>.

- (A) every team member had their turn at bat
- (B) every member of the team had their turn at bat
- (C) every team member had her turn at bat
- (D) every team member having their turn at bat
- (E) every member of the team having his turn at bat

11 <u>His French rusty after years of neglect</u>, Jeff stumbled through most of his conversations during his visit to Paris.

- (A) His French rusty after years of neglect
- (B) His French was rusty after years of neglect
- (C) His French, rusty after years of neglect
- (D) After years of neglect, his French was rusty
- (E) Rusty after years of neglecting his French

GO ON TO THE NEXT PAGE ▶▶▶

Directions for Identifying Sentence Error Questions

The following sentences may contain errors in grammar, usage, diction (choice of words), or idiom. Some of the sentences are correct. No sentence contains more than one error.

If the sentence contains an error, it is underlined and lettered. The parts that are not underlined are correct.

If there is an error, select the part that must be changed to correct the sentence. If there is no error, choose (E).

EXAMPLE:

By the time <u>they reached</u> the halfway
            A

point <u>in the race</u>, most <u>of the runners</u>
      B   C

<u>hadn't hardly</u> begun to hit their stride.
    D

<u>No error</u>
 E

Sample answer: (D)

---

12 Although she was <u>an expert climber</u>,
                    A
Marcie <u>struggled</u> <u>for ascending</u> the steep
        B   C
and <u>slippery precipice</u>. <u>No error</u>
     D   E

13 The logs that <u>had been piled</u> in the
             A
backyard throughout the long winter

<u>finally fell</u> over <u>when</u> the dog <u>had jumped</u>
  B   C   D
on them. <u>No error</u>
        E

14 Audrey <u>thought</u> that her ideas were better
        A
than <u>the rest of the class</u> and <u>was outraged</u>
      B   C
when her classmates <u>selected</u> another plan
              D
for the project. <u>No error</u>
         E

15 The <u>abstract and subjective</u> nature of
       A
modern art often <u>leaves observers</u> confused
           B
and unable to grasp the <u>subtle</u> messages
              C
<u>embedded</u> in its form. <u>No error</u>
  D   E

16 By the time election day arrived, he <u>shifted</u>
                  A
his position <u>on the bond issue</u> several
         B
times, <u>leaving even</u> his staunchest
     C
supporters <u>confused</u>. <u>No error</u>
      D   E

17 Exhausted and <u>being tired</u> of the noise
          A
from the back seat, Pedro <u>threatened</u> to
             B
turn the car around and <u>end the vacation</u>
            C
before it could <u>even begin</u>. <u>No error</u>
       D   E

18 Lithe in <u>both body and mind</u>, Horatio was
        A
<u>well-suited</u> to Greco-Roman <u>wrestling; he</u>
  B   C
was <u>often able</u> to out-smart as well as
    D
out-manouver his opponents. <u>No error</u>
                E

6

GO ON TO THE NEXT PAGE ▸▸▸

19 The design is <u>vastly superior</u> to those of
                          A
prior models, <u>but</u> a few inadequacies
                     B
<u>are expectant</u>, as perfection is not
        C
<u>an attainable goal</u>. <u>No error</u>
          D   E

20 <u>A vocal opponent</u> of the war, Veronica was
          A
<u>nevertheless</u> strongly in favor of giving the
        B
troops <u>his or her</u> proper compensation
              C
<u>upon returning</u> home. <u>No error</u>
          D   E

21 Noam Chomsky has long argued that the

media <u>plays</u> a large role in skewing
          A
<u>our perception</u> of reality, presenting images
        B
and <u>framing stories</u> in such a manner <u>as to</u>
          C   D
misrepresent the truth. <u>No error</u>
                                  E

22 The family of the victim <u>has reserved</u> its
                                        A
right to <u>sue</u> the defendant for civil
            B
damages, stating publicly that his prison

sentence <u>wasn't hardly</u> sufficient
              C
punishment <u>for the crime</u>. <u>No error</u>
                    D   E

23 Each of the stories <u>end</u> with a moral,
                                A
but some of these lessons are

<u>more obvious than others</u>, spelled out
              B
so as to <u>make</u> them impossible
              C
<u>to overlook</u>. <u>No error</u>
        D   E

24 The head of the used car dealership

<u>assured</u> the woman that <u>their</u> integrity
      A   B
was unshakable and that the

<u>odometer readings</u> were entirely
            C
<u>accurate</u>. <u>No error</u>
        D   E

25 The <u>rapid</u> growth in the <u>rate of construction</u>
              A   B
of private homes and apartment

buildings <u>have been</u> stimulated
                  C
<u>by low interest rates</u>. <u>No error</u>
            D   E

26 The work that Michael <u>did</u> at summer
                                  A
camp <u>to improve his soccer skills</u> <u>helped</u>
              B   C
him to become more <u>adapt</u> at passing and
                            D
shooting. <u>No error</u>
                E

27 The voters <u>in this state</u> should be concerned
                      A
about the outcome of this election, and

cast <u>his or her ballot</u> in November
            B
<u>to re-elect</u> the <u>incumbent</u>. <u>No error</u>
        C   D   E

28 Orlando did not want to <u>miss out on</u> the
                                    A

opportunity to try out <u>for the debate team</u>,
                                    B

so he <u>rescheduled</u> his music lesson <u>so that</u>
           C   D

he could stay after school. <u>No error</u>
                                    E

29 Justine practiced <u>her dance routine</u> for
                              A

several hours on Sunday, trying

<u>to make sure</u> that it would be
       B

<u>as graceful</u> as <u>the other dancers</u> when
       C   D

she performed it on Wednesday. <u>No error</u>
                                        E

GO ON TO THE NEXT PAGE ▸▸▸

Directions for Improving Paragraphs Questions

Below is an early draft of an essay. It requires revision in many areas.

The questions that follow ask you to make improvements in sentence structure, diction, organization, and development. Answering the questions may require you to understand the context of the passage as well as the rules of standard written English.

6

Questions 30–35 are based on the following passage.

(1) *One of the best-studied and most fascinating of the great apes is the chimpanzee.* (2) *This species, that is homo sapiens' closest living relative, is known for their intelligence and social complexity.* (3) *One of the ways in which chimpanzees are similar to humans is their degree of bonding with other members of the group.*

(4) *Chimpanzees live in complex and large groups of which include adults, adolescents, juveniles and infants and can include as many as 100 members.* (5) *Their social system is called 'fission-fusion' because they do not spend all of their time with their whole group, they often split into smaller parties to forage for food.* (6) *Female chimpanzees move to new groups when they mature and form new relationships there.*

(7) *An important aspect of chimpanzee society is the dominance hierarchy.* (8) *One individual will fight to become the alpha male, which means that he can have the best foods and the respect of the other individuals in the group.* (9) *However, being alpha male is not guaranteed for life, since other males also want the position of top dog, and the alpha has to defend his position against his rivals.* (10) *Dominance displays like chest-thumping are common in many other animal species.* (11) *This is where friendships and alliances become important.*

(12) *Female chimpanzees also compete with each other, but do not achieve alpha status because males are physically bigger and stronger.* (13) *Nevertheless, females can and do form complex relationships with each other and with their offspring, and also form bonds with adult males.* (14) *These are some of the reasons* why chimpanzees are so fascinating, and that make them so much like humans.

30 Which of the following is the best revision of the underlined section of sentence 2 (reproduced below)?

This species, that is homo sapiens' closest living relative, is known for their intelligence and social complexity.

(A) that is the closest relative to *homo sapiens*, is known for its intelligence and also its social complexity

(B) of which *homo sapiens'* is its closest relative, is known for their intelligence and social complexity

(C) the most closely related to *homo sapiens*, is known for how intelligent they are and for their social complexity

(D) the closest relative of *homo sapiens*, is known for its intelligence and social complexity

(E) of which it is *homo sapiens'* closest living relative, is known for its intelligence and its social complexity

31 Which of the following is the best revision of the underlined portion of sentence 4 (reproduced below)?

Chimpanzees live in complex and large groups of which include adults, adolescents, juveniles, and infants and can include as many as 100 members.

(A) large, complex groups of adults, adolescents, juveniles, and infants and can include as many as 100 members.

(B) complex and large groups which include adults, adolescents, juveniles, and infants and as many as 100 members.

(C) large, complex groups which would include adults, adolescents, juveniles, and infants and as many as 100 members.

(D) complex, large groups, which includes adults, adolescents, juveniles, and infants and can include as many as 100 members.

(E) large, complex groups containing as many as 100 members, including adults, adolescents, juveniles, and infants.

GO ON TO THE NEXT PAGE ▸▸▸

32 Which of the following is the best version of the underlined portion of sentence 5 (reproduced below)?

Their social system is called 'fission-fusion' because they do not spend all of their time with their whole group, they often split into smaller parties to forage for food.

(A) (as it is now)
(B) group; rather they often split
(C) group instead often split
(D) group and also often split
(E) group, but instead often splitting

33 Which is the best sentence to insert after sentence 6 to maintain the logic and unity of the second paragraph?

(A) Male chimpanzees are skilled hunters that prefer to prey on monkeys and small mammals.
(B) Female chimpanzees spend much of their time foraging for fruit.
(C) They are known for their use of tools, such as leaves as sponges.
(D) Male chimpanzees, on the other hand, stay in their natal group for life, and often form friendships with other males.
(E) Males, in contrast to females, are known for their loud dominance displays.

34 Which sentence contributes the least to the unity of the third paragraph?

(A) sentence 7
(B) sentence 8
(C) sentence 9
(D) sentence 10
(E) sentence 11

35 Where is the best place to insert the following sentence?

For instance, male chimpanzees often maintain strong bonds with allies who can support their challenge to the alpha male.

(A) after sentence 4
(B) after sentence 6
(C) after sentence 11
(D) after sentence 12
(E) There is no appropriate place for this sentence.

6

STOP *You may check your work, on this section only, until time is called.*

Section 7

Time—20 minutes
16 Questions

Directions for Multiple-Choice Questions

In this section, solve each problem, using any available space on the page for scratchwork. Then decide which is the best of the choices given and fill in the corresponding oval on your answer sheet.

- You may use a calculator on any problem. All numbers used are real numbers.
- Figures are drawn as accurately as possible EXCEPT when it is stated that the figure is not drawn to scale.
- All figures lie in a plane unless otherwise indicated.

Reference Information

$A = \pi r^2$ $A = \ell w$
$C = 2\pi r$ $A = \frac{1}{2}bh$ $V = \ell wh$ $V = \pi r^2 h$ $c^2 = a^2 + b^2$ Special Right Triangles

The number of degrees of arc in a circle is 360°.
The measure in degrees of a straight angle is 180°.
The sum of the measures in degrees of the angles of a triangle is 180°.

---

1 If $x^3 y = x^9$ and $x > 1$, then $y =$

- (A) 2
- (B) 3
- (C) 4
- (D) 5
- (E) 6

2 The ratio of 1 to 1.4 is equal to the ratio of

- (A) 1 to 4
- (B) 3 to 4
- (C) 5 to 7
- (D) 7 to 5
- (E) 4 to 3

$2x°$ \ $140°$

Note: Figure not drawn to scale.

3 A line and a ray intersect as shown above. What is the value of $2x + 5$?

- (A) 20
- (B) 25
- (C) 40
- (D) 45
- (E) 50

4 When three times a number is divided by two, the result is 39. What is that number?

- (A) 20
- (B) 21
- (C) 24
- (D) 26
- (E) 30

GO ON TO THE NEXT PAGE ▶▶▶

5 How much greater than $x - 5$ is $x + 5$?

(A) 2
(B) 5
(C) 7
(D) 10
(E) 12

6 Rectangle M has an area of A square feet. The length and width of another rectangle, N, are each triple the length and width of rectangle M. What is the area of rectangle N in terms of A?

(A) $2A$
(B) $3A$
(C) $6A$
(D) $9A$
(E) $12A$

7 If a circle has a circumference of 10, what is the ratio of the circumference of the circle to its diameter?

(A) $1 : 2\pi$
(B) $1 : \pi$
(C) $\pi : 1$
(D) $2\pi : 1$
(E) $\pi : 2$

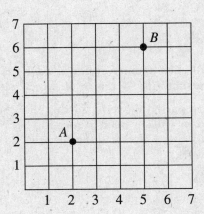

8 What is the distance from point A to point B in the figure above?

(A) 1
(B) 3
(C) 4
(D) 5
(E) 7

9 A theater purchases $500 worth of Sticky Bears and Chocolate Bombs. Each bag of Sticky Bears costs $1.50 and each bag of Chocolate Bombs costs $1.00. If a total of 400 bags of candy were purchased, how many bags of Chocolate Bombs did the theater buy?

(A) 100
(B) 150
(C) 200
(D) 250
(E) 300

10 The median of a set of seven consecutive even integers is 10. What is the average (arithmetic mean) of this set?

(A) 8
(B) 10
(C) 12
(D) 14
(E) 16

Questions 11 and 12 refer to the following tables.

NUMBER OF MOVIE TICKETS SOLD

	Adult	Child	Matinee (Adult or Child)
Village Theater	100	20	70
Bijou	120	30	20
Community Cinema	220	40	90
Triplex	x	30	0

PRICE OF MOVIE TICKETS AT ALL THEATERS

Adult	$9.00
Child	$6.00
Matinee (Adult or Child)	$6.00

GO ON TO THE NEXT PAGE ▶▶▶

11 The total revenue collected for movie tickets at the Bijou is what percent of the total revenue collected for movie tickets at the Community Cinema?

(A) 25%
(B) 50%
(C) 75%
(D) 100%
(E) 200%

12 If the Triplex has generated more ticket revenue than the Village Theater has, what is the least possible value of x?

(A) 145
(B) 146
(C) 147
(D) 148
(E) 149

7

13 If $\dfrac{1}{4y+6} = x^2$, which of the following represents the value of y in terms of x?

(A) $\dfrac{1}{4x^2} - \dfrac{3}{2}$

(B) $\dfrac{1}{4x^2} - \dfrac{3}{4}$

(C) $\dfrac{1}{x^2} - \dfrac{3}{2}$

(D) $\dfrac{1}{\sqrt{x}} + \dfrac{3}{2}$

(E) $\dfrac{1}{4x^2} - 24$

14 How many integers between 100 and 1000 contain only the digits 3, 4 or 5, if any digit may be repeated?

(A) 16
(B) 18
(C) 20
(D) 24
(E) 27

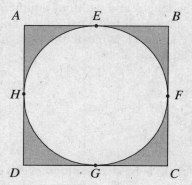

15 The inscribed circle touches square $ABCD$ at points E, F, G, and H, which are all midpoints of their respective sides. If the length of a side of the square is 6, what is the area of the shaded region?

(A) $36 - 9\pi$
(B) $36 - 36\pi$
(C) $24 - 9\pi$
(D) $36\pi - 36$
(E) $24 - 9\pi$

16 A chef spends c hours each day at her restaurant, $\dfrac{c}{3}$ hours of which she spends preparing desserts. At this rate, how many days will she need to spend at her restaurant to create desserts that require 24 hours of work?

(A) $\dfrac{c}{72}$

(B) $\dfrac{24}{c}$

(C) $\dfrac{c}{24}$

(D) $24c$
(E) $72c$

You may check your work, on this section only, until time is called.

Section 8

Time—20 minutes
19 Questions

Each of the sentences below is missing one or two portions. Read each sentence, then select the word or words that most logically completes the sentence, taking into account the meaning of the sentence as a whole.

Example: Rather than accepting the theory unquestioningly, Deborah regarded it with ———.

(A) mirth   (B) sadness
(C) responsibility (D) ignorance
(E) skepticism

Correct response: (E)

1 As the lunar cycle progresses in the coming days, the moon will continue to ——— in apparent size until it is not even visible next week

(A) progress   (B) wane
(C) debunk   (D) convoke
(E) coalesce

2 Because General Randolph's stratagem had been ——— by the opposing forces, his army was ——— by a well-coordinated and lethal counterattack.

(A) foreseen . . defoliated
(B) contradicted . . disavowed
(C) predicted . . decimated
(D) resolved . . destroyed
(E) established . . demarcated

3 During the presidential debate, the candidates practiced the art of ———; they used roundabout expressions and evasive tactics to avoid the questions they were asked.

(A) matriculation
(B) circumlocution
(C) contemplation
(D) homogeneity
(E) serendipity

4 It was George's propensity to ——— that caused his peers to view him as a ——— and grandiose individual.

(A) vacillate . . phlegmatic
(B) eulogize . . loquacious
(C) prophecy . . mercurial
(D) pilfer . . colloquial
(E) pontificate . . bombastic

5 Napoleon Bonaparte's ——— frame ——— his ability to dominate a room; in fact, people often remembered him as being much taller than he actually was.

(A) gargantuan . . disproved
(B) voluminous . . showed
(C) scanty . . exemplified
(D) diminutive . . belied
(E) meager . . propagated

6 The journalist's reputation for ——— has led many of his readers to doubt the ——— of his articles.

(A) candor . . legitimacy
(B) perfidiousness . . ingenuity
(C) fabrication . . veracity
(D) virtuosity . . aptitude
(E) perspicacity . . autonomy

8

GO ON TO THE NEXT PAGE ▶▶▶

The questions below are based on the content of the passage that precedes them. The questions are to be answered on the basis of what is stated or implied in the passage itself or the introductory material that precedes the passage.

Questions 7–19 are based on the following passage.

The following passages present two perspectives on the works and impact of twentieth century author Ernest Hemingway.

Passage 1

Line   For members of my generation, the young men born between 1918, roughly, and 1924, there was a special charm about Hemingway. By the time most of us were old enough to
5   read him he had become a legendary figure, a kind of twentieth-century Lord Byron; and like Byron, he had learned to play himself, his own best hero, with superb conviction. He was Hemingway of the rugged outdoor
10   grin and the hairy chest posing beside a marlin he had just landed or a lion he had just shot. He was Tarzan Hemingway, crouching in the African bush with elephant gun at ready, Bwana Hemingway
15   commanding his native bearers in terse Swahili; he was War Correspondent Hemingway writing a play in the Hotel Florida in Madrid while thirty fascist shells crashed through the roof; later on he was
20   Task Force Hemingway swathed in ammunition belts and defending his post singlehanded against fierce German attacks.
      But even without the legend he created around himself, the chest-beating,
25   wisecracking pose that was later to seem so incredibly absurd, his impact upon us was tremendous. The feeling he gave us was one of immense expansiveness and freedom and at the same time, of absolute stability and
30   control. We could put our whole faith in him and he would not fail us. We could follow him, ape his manner, his cold detachment, through all the doubts and fears of adolescence and come out pure and
35   untouched. The words he put down seemed to us to have been carved from the living stone of life. They were absolutely, nakedly true because the man behind them had reduced himself to the bare tissue of his soul
40   to write them and because he was a dedicated man. The words of Hemingway conveyed so exactly the taste, smell and feel of experience as it was, as it might possibly be, that we began unconsciously to translate
45   our own sensations into their terms and to impose on everything we did and felt the particular emotions they aroused in us.
      The Hemingway time was a good time to be young. It seems to me that we had much
50   then which the war later forced out of us and that in the end what many of us lost was something far greater than Hemingway and his strong formative influence. There are young writers today who, in losing or getting
55   rid of Hemingway, have been able to find nothing to put in his place, who have rejected his time as untrue for them only to fail at finding themselves in their own time. There are others, who, in their embarrassment at
60   the hold he once had over them, have not profited by the lessons he had to teach, and still others who were never touched by him at all. These last are perhaps the real unfortunates, for they have been denied
65   access to a powerful tradition, one that is as important and true as any my generation can ever have.

Passage 2

One wonders why *The Sun Also Rises* (1926) and *A Farewell to Arms* (1929) now seem
70   unable to evoke the same awesome sense of a tottering world, captured poignantly and precisely in language, which in the nineteen twenties established Ernest Hemingway's reputation. These novels should be speaking
75   to us. Our social structure is as shaken, our philosophical despair as great, our everyday experience as unsatisfying. We have had more war than Hemingway ever saw or dreamed of. Our violence—physical,
80   emotional and intellectual—is not inferior to that of the nineteen twenties. Yet, though Hemingway's books still offer great moments, they no longer seem to penetrate too deeply and steadily below the surface of existence;

GO ON TO THE NEXT PAGE ▶▶▶

First passage: John W. Aldridge, *After the Lost Generation*, McGraw Hill, 1951
Second passage: Brom Weber, *The American Novel and the 1920's*, McGraw Hill, 1971

85 one begins to doubt that they ever did so
significantly in the nineteen twenties,
It is not merely that our times are worse,
which they are. Life in the nineteen twenties,
after all, tended on the whole to be more
90 excruciating than life in the two previous
decades. In retrospect, however, Hemingway's
novels cajoled the dominant genteel tradition
in American culture while seeming to
repudiate it. They yielded to the functionalist,
95 technological aesthetic of the culture instead
of resisting in the manner of Frank Lloyd
Wright. Hemingway, in effect, became a dupe
of his culture rather than its moral-aesthetic
conscience. As a consequence, the import of
100 his work has diminished.
There is some evidence from his stylistic
evolution that Hemingway himself must have
felt as much, for Hemingway's famous
stylistic economy frequently seems to conceal
105 another kind of writer, with much richer
rhetorical resources to hand. So, *Death in the
Afternoon* (1932), Hemingway's bullfighting
opus and his first book after *A Farewell to
Arms* reveals great uneasiness over his earlier
110 accomplishment. One of the more important
of the aggressive defenses of his literary
method that appear in the work incorporates
a doctrine of ambiguity which justifies
confusion and encourages ambivalence:
115 *If a writer of prose knows enough about
what he is writing about he may omit
things that he knows and the reader, if the
writer is writing truly enough, will have a
feeling of those things as strongly as though
120 the writer had stated them.*
Hemingway made much the same
theoretical point in another way in *Death in
the Afternoon* apparently believing that a
formal reduction of aesthetic complexity was
125 the only kind of design that had value.
But in fact, Hemingway's famous economy
of prose was by no means as omnipresent as
he himself suggests; he had his own baroque
inclinations. His work is really a mixture of
130 stylistic forces. Thus a still greater irony of
Death in the Afternoon was its unmistakably
baroque prose, which he at one point
embarrassedly admitted was 'flowery'.
Reviewers, unable to challenge Hemingway's
135 expertise in the art of bullfighting and
confused by the eccentricities of the book,
noted that its style was 'awkward, tortuous,
[and] belligerently clumsy'.

Hemingway had written an extraordinarily
140 personal, self-indulgent, garrulous,
capricious, playful, bellicose and satiric book,
even more unruly and clownish than *The
Torrents of Spring*. There is no need here for
a schema of the book, beyond noting that it
145 contains scrambled chronology and thematic
arrangement, willful digressions, mock-
scholarly apparatus (for example, a
'bibliographical note' refers readers to a
Spanish bibliography—undated—for the
150 '2077 books and pamphlets in Spanish dealing
with or touching on tauromaquia[1]' which he
mock-modestly claimed to have read), fictional
interludes, scathing allusions and references
to contemporary writers and critics.

---

[1] bullfighting

7 Which of the following is the best title for
Passage 1?

(A) How Hemingway Influenced a
Generation
(B) Fiction and the Art of War
(C) Humor in Hemingway's Prose
(D) The Literary Giants of the 1920s
(E) Growing up in the 1920s

8 The sentence beginning on line 41 ("The
words of Hemingway ... they aroused in us")
indicates that Hemingway's readers were
inclined to

(A) emulate his style of writing
(B) look skeptically at his writing in light
of the horrors of war
(C) empathize deeply with his narratives
(D) view his writing more as poetry than
prose
(E) doubt the veracity of some of his
writing

GO ON TO THE NEXT PAGE ▶▶▶

9 Unlike the wars that Hemingway witnessed as described in the first paragraph of Passage 1, "the war" referred to in line 50 had the effect of

(A) discouraging young people from pursuing careers in writing
(B) encouraging the portrayal of soldiers as heroes
(C) inspiring many new authors to write about conflict
(D) disillusioning a generation
(E) elevating the status of Hemingway among literary critics

10 In line 57, "untrue" most nearly means

(A) not meaningful
(B) treacherous
(C) indecisive
(D) historically inaccurate
(E) intolerable

8 ▶

11 The author of Passage 1 indicates that writers of his generation differ from some young writers today in which of the following regards?

   I. their reverence for Hemingway
   II. their willingness to write about war
   III. their ability to find meaning in the period of history in which they live

(A) I only
(B) I and II only
(C) I and III only
(D) II and III only
(E) I, II and III

12 The last paragraph of Passage 1 suggests that the least fortunate of modern writers are those who

(A) have not experienced war first hand
(B) criticize Hemingway for his literary inadequacies
(C) have attempted to deviate from Hemingway's style
(D) have not been exposed to Hemingway's writing
(E) do not investigate the historical background of the 1920s before reading Hemingway

13 In saying that Hemingway's novels "should be speaking to us" (lines 74–75), the author of Passage 2 suggests that

(A) modern readers should be more educated
(B) literary critics are not doing their jobs properly
(C) educators should emphasize Hemingway's works
(D) readers prefer simplistic prose
(E) the modern world is similar to the world of Hemingway's time

14 The quotation from *Death in the Afternoon* in lines 115–120 suggests that Hemingway assumes that his readers

(A) prefer an ornate style of prose to an unadorned style
(B) can read beyond what is directly stated
(C) can empathize with the violence of his narratives
(D) are familiar with the European countryside he describes
(E) have read the works of writers who are contemporaries of Hemingway

15 Passage 2 indicates that Hemingway implied in his own prose that good writers must

(A) draw upon their own experiences
(B) imitate the great masters of the novel
(C) use a florid literary style
(D) continually endeavor to simplify their prose
(E) employ their knowledge of history in their writing

16 Passage 2 indicates that, over his entire literary career, Hemingway's literary style was in fact

(A) always sparse and simple
(B) persistently embellished
(C) inconsistent
(D) better suited to describing human relationships than the horrors of war
(E) consistently allegorical

GO ON TO THE NEXT PAGE ▶▶▶

17 The final paragraph of Passage 2 indicates that *Death in the Afternoon* contains which of the following?

    I.   descriptions of events that are ordered improperly
    II.   egocentric prose
    III.   recollections of Hemingway's wartime experiences

(A)   I only
(B)   II only
(C)   I and II only
(D)   I and III only
(E)   I, II, and III

18 Which of the following best describes how each passage characterizes Hemingway's relationship to the dominant culture of his time?

(A)   Passage 1 portrays him as a hero to his generation, while Passage 2 suggests that he was a conformist.
(B)   Passage 1 suggests that he felt out of place in his generation, while Passage 2 suggests that he was comfortable in the dominant culture.
(C)   Passage 1 suggests that he was persistently skeptical about the society in which he lived, while Passage 2 indicates that he always avoided social commentary.
(D)   Passage 1 suggests that he was only a marginal figure in his generation, while Passage 2 portrays him as the dominant writer of his time.
(E)   Both passages portray him as a rebel against the dominant culture.

19 Which of the following best describes the contrast in focus of the two passages?

(A)   Passage 1 focuses on Hemingway's wartime writing, while Passage 2 focuses on his writing about sports.
(B)   Passage 1 analyzes Hemingway's prose, while Passage 2 focuses on his cultural background.
(C)   Passage 1 examines the views of several literary critics, while Passage 2 objectively examines the inconsistencies in Hemingway's writings.
(D)   Passage 1 describes Hemingway's scholarly work, while Passage 2 describes the effect of his prose on a generation.
(E)   Passage 1 focuses on Hemingway as a man, while Passage 2 focuses on his literary style.

8

You may check your work, on this section only, until time is called.

Section 9

Time—10 Minutes
14 Questions

Directions for "Improving Sentences" Questions

Each of the sentences below contains one underlined portion. The portion may contain one or more errors in grammar, usage, construction, precision, diction (choice of words), or idiom. Some of the sentences are correct. Consider the meaning of the original sentence, and choose the answer that best expresses that meaning. If the original sentence is best, choose (A), because it repeats the original phrasing. Choose the phrasing that creates the clearest, most precise and most effective sentence.

EXAMPLE:

The children <u>couldn't hardly believe their eyes</u>.

  (A) couldn't hardly believe their eyes
  (B) would not hardly believe their eyes
  (C) could hardly believe their eyes
  (D) couldn't nearly believe their eyes
  (E) could hardly believe his or her eyes

Example answer: (C)

---

1 Having no more food in her backpack, <u>it was necessary for Maria</u> to begin foraging for edible berries.

  (A) it was necessary for Maria
  (B) made it necessary for Maria
  (C) Maria had
  (D) was why Maria had
  (E) required Maria

2 Anna Warren, an accomplished painter whose art has been shown in museums and galleries throughout America and Europe, <u>becoming as well known for her landscapes as for her still lifes</u>.

  (A) becoming as well known for her landscapes as for
  (B) in order to become as well known for her landscapes as
  (C) has become equally well known for her landscapes and still-lifes
  (D) has become as well known for her landscapes as
  (E) has become as well known for her landscapes as for

3 Some psychologists continue to believe that the mind is largely independent <u>of the body; most, however, believe</u> that human behavior can be explained solely in terms of the functions of the brain.

  (A) of the body; most, however, believe
  (B) from the body, but most however believe
  (C) of the body, most believe however
  (D) from the body; most though believe
  (E) from the body and most believe, however

4 The reason that television networks air such trashy programs is <u>because it is what the</u> viewers want to see.

  (A) because it is what the
  (B) that these are what
  (C) that this is what
  (D) because they are the things that
  (E) that is it these that

GO ON TO THE NEXT PAGE ▶▶▶

5 The greatest feature of this audio system is <u>it is able to play</u> music in almost any format.

(A) it is able to play
(B) it can play
(C) the fact of its being able to play
(D) its ability to play
(E) it being able to play

6 <u>If I wouldn't have been</u> in such a hurry to get to the reception, I would not have left my wallet at the hotel.

(A) If I wouldn't have been
(B) I had not been
(C) If I had not been
(D) Having been
(E) If not for being

7 The vacation cottage was tiny, dirty, and <u>it was lit with very dim lighting</u>.

(A) it was lit with very dim lighting
(B) it was dimly lit
(C) lit with very dim lighting
(D) the lighting was dim
(E) dimly lit

8 Although most people shudder when they recall analyzing sentences in school, <u>nevertheless a recent book about grammar has become a best seller</u>.

(A) nevertheless a recent book about grammar has become a best seller
(B) a recent book about grammar has become a best seller
(C) a recent book about grammar becoming a best seller
(D) a book has become a best seller recently about grammar
(E) yet a recent book about grammar became a best seller

9 As a writer, <u>it is surprising to me that so few</u> high school graduates can write a coherent sentence.

(A) it is surprising to me that so few
(B) it is surprising that hardly any
(C) I am surprised that so few
(D) it surprises me that so few
(E) I am surprised of the fact that so few

10 The coach gave Fernando a few words of encouragement before the <u>game, this was in order</u> to boost the pitcher's confidence.

(A) game, this was in order
(B) game
(C) game, this was
(D) game; in order
(E) game and this was

11 Although John Dewey profoundly influenced American philosophy of the 20th century, <u>modern philosophers do not find his ideas to be as resonant in the regard that they find his writings</u> almost incomprehensible.

(A) modern philosophers do not find his ideas to be as resonant in the regard that they find his writings.
(B) modern philsophers are not so much influenced by the resonance of his ideas in that they find that his writings are
(C) his ideas are not as resonant with modern philosophers being that to them his writings are
(D) his ideas do not resonate as well with modern philosophers in the sense that they find his writings to be
(E) his ideas do not resonate as well with modern philosophers, who find his writings

12 A hierarchical power structure is not <u>a necessity of modern society, and actually that is antithetical to</u> true democracy.

(A) a necessity of modern society, and actually that is antithetical to
(B) necessarily needed by modern society, and is antithetical of
(C) necessary to modern society; in fact, it is antithetical to
(D) needed for modern society and so is antithetical to
(E) necessary to modern society; in fact is antithetical of

9

13 When one of my seizures <u>strikes, I feel as if I were</u> paralyzed, if only for a moment.

(A)   strikes, I feel as if I were
(B)   strikes, I feel as if I was
(C)   strike, I feel like I was
(D)   strikes, it is a feeling like being
(E)   strikes, I feel like being

14 Completely devoid of artistic merit, the film used shock tactics in an effort to gain publicity <u>and increasing their ticket sales.</u>

(A)   increasing their ticket sales
(B)   increase ticket sales
(C)   increasing the sales of their tickets
(D)   and tickets
(E)   and, as such, their increasing ticket sales

ANSWER KEY

Section 3 Math	Section 4 Math	Section 7 Math	Section 2 Critical Reading	Section 5 Critical Reading	Section 8 Critical Reading	Section 6 Writing	Section 9 Writing
☐ 1. A	☐ 1. C	☐ 1. B	☐ 1. D	☐ 1. A	☐ 1. B	☐ 1. D	☐ 1. C
☐ 2. B	☐ 2. B	☐ 2. C	☐ 2. A	☐ 2. E	☐ 2. B	☐ 2. B	☐ 2. E
☐ 3. C	☐ 3. D	☐ 3. D	☐ 3. B	☐ 3. D	☐ 3. C	☐ 3. E	☐ 3. A
☐ 4. D	☐ 4. C	☐ 4. D	☐ 4. A	☐ 4. B	☐ 4. E	☐ 4. C	☐ 4. B
☐ 5. E	☐ 5. A	☐ 5. D	☐ 5. B	☐ 5. B	☐ 5. D	☐ 5. A	☐ 5. D
☐ 6. B	☐ 6. B	☐ 6. D	☐ 6. D	☐ 6. C	☐ 6. C	☐ 6. D	☐ 6. C
☐ 7. E	☐ 7. C	☐ 7. C	☐ 7. B	☐ 7. D	☐ 7. A	☐ 7. D	☐ 7. E
☐ 8. E	☐ 8. E	☐ 8. D	☐ 8. E	☐ 8. B	☐ 8. C	☐ 8. A	☐ 8. B
☐ 9. C	☐ 9. 4	☐ 9.	☐ 9. C	☐ 9. E	☐ 9. D	☐ 9. B	☐ 9. C
☐ 10. C	☐ 10. $0 < b < 1$	☐ 10. B	☐ 10. D	☐ 10. C	☐ 10. A	☐ 10. C	☐ 10. B
☐ 11. D	☐ 11. 180	☐ 11. B	☐ 11. A	☐ 11. E	☐ 11. C	☐ 11. A	☐ 11. E
☐ 12. C	☐ 12. 900	☐ 12. E	☐ 12. D	☐ 12. A	☐ 12. D	☐ 12. C	☐ 12. C
☐ 13. B	☐ 13. 6	☐ 13. E	☐ 13. A	☐ 13. E	☐ 13. E	☐ 13. D	☐ 13. A
☐ 14. E	☐ 14. 12	☐ 14. A	☐ 14. D	☐ 14. A	☐ 14. B	☐ 14. B	☐ 14. C
☐ 15. D	☐ 15. 6	☐ 15. A	☐ 15. B	☐ 15. B	☐ 15. D	☐ 15. E	
☐ 16. A	☐ 16. 580	☐ 16. E	☐ 16. E	☐ 16. B	☐ 16. C	☐ 16. A	
☐ 17. D	☐ 17. $\frac{5}{9}$ or		☐ 17. A	☐ 17. A	☐ 17. C	☐ 17. A	
☐ 18. B	.555 or		☐ 18. C	☐ 18. D	☐ 18. A	☐ 18. E	
☐ 19. A	.556		☐ 19. B	☐ 19. C	☐ 19. E	☐ 19. C	
☐ 20. A	☐ 18. $\frac{1}{4}$		☐ 20. E	☐ 20. B		☐ 20. C	
			☐ 21. E	☐ 21. E		☐ 21. E	
			☐ 22. D	☐ 22. D		☐ 22. C	
			☐ 23. D	☐ 23. D		☐ 23. A	
			☐ 24. D	☐ 14. D		☐ 24. B	
						☐ 25. C	
						☐ 26. C	
						☐ 27. D	
						☐ 28. A	
						☐ 29. D	
						☐ 30. D	
						☐ 31. E	
						☐ 32. B	
						☐ 33. D	
						☐ 34. D	
						☐ 35. C	

# Right (A): ___	Questions 1–8 # Right (A): ___	# Right (A): ___	# Right (A): ___	# Right (A): ___	# Right (A): ___	# Right (A) ___	# Right (A): ___
#Wrong (B): ___	#Wrong (B): ___	#Wrong (B): ___	#Wrong (B): ___	#Wrong (B): ___	#Wrong (B): ___	#Wrong (B): ___	#Wrong (B): ___
# (A) – ¼ (B): ___	# (A) – ¼ (B): ___	# (A) – ¼ (B): ___	# (A) – ¼ (B): ___	# (A) – ¼ (B): ___	# (A) – ¼ (B): ___	# (A) – ¼ (B): ___	# (A) – ¼ (B): ___
	Questions 9–18 # Right (A): ___						

SCORE CONVERSION TABLE

How to score your test

Use the answer key on the previous page to determine your raw score on each section. **Your raw score on each section except Section 4 is simply the number of correct answers minus ¼ of the number of wrong answers. On Section 4, your raw score is the sum of the number of correct answers for questions 1–8 minus ¼ of the number of wrong answers for questions 1–8 plus the total number of correct answers for questions 9–18.** Next, add the raw scores from Sections 3, 4, and 7 to get your Math raw score, add the raw scores from Sections 2, 5, and 8 to get your Critical Reading raw score and add the raw scores from Sections 6 and 9 to get your Writing raw score. Write the three raw scores here:

Raw Critical Reading score: _____   Raw Math score: _____   Raw Writing score: _____

Use the table below to convert these to scaled scores.

Scaled scores: Critical Reading: _____   Math: _____   Writing: _____

Raw Score	Critical Reading Scaled Score	Math Scaled Score	Writing Scaled Score	Raw Score	Critical Reading Scaled Score	Math Scaled Score	Writing Scaled Score
67	800			32	520	550	610
66	800			31	510	550	600
65	790			30	510	540	580
64	780			29	500	530	570
63	760			28	490	520	560
62	750			27	490	530	550
61	730			26	480	510	540
60	720			25	480	500	530
59	700			24	470	490	520
58	700			23	460	480	510
57	690			22	460	480	500
56	680			21	450	470	490
55	670			20	440	460	480
54	660	800		19	440	450	470
53	650	790		18	430	450	460
52	650	760		17	420	440	450
51	640	740		16	420	430	440
50	630	720		15	410	420	440
49	620	710	800	14	400	410	430
48	620	700	800	13	400	410	420
47	610	680	800	12	390	400	410
46	600	670	790	11	380	390	400
45	600	660	780	10	370	380	390
44	590	650	760	9	360	370	380
43	590	640	740	8	350	360	380
42	580	630	730	7	340	350	370
41	570	630	710	6	330	340	360
40	570	620	700	5	320	330	350
39	560	610	690	4	310	320	340
38	550	600	670	3	300	310	320
37	550	590	660	2	280	290	310
36	540	580	650	1	270	280	300
35	540	580	640	0	250	260	280
34	530	570	630	−1	230	240	270
33	520	560	620	−2 or less	210	220	250

SCORE CONVERSION TABLE FOR WRITING COMPOSITE
[ESSAY + MULTIPLE CHOICE]

Calculate your writing raw score as you did on the previous page and grade your essay from a 1 to a 6 according to the standards that follow in the detailed answer key.

Essay score: _____Raw Writing score: _____

Use the table below to convert these to scaled scores.

Scaled score: Writing: _____

Raw Score	Essay Score 0	Essay Score 1	Essay Score 2	Essay Score 3	Essay Score 4	Essay Score 5	Essay Score 6
−2 or less	200	230	250	280	310	340	370
−1	210	240	260	290	320	360	380
0	230	260	280	300	340	370	400
1	240	270	290	320	350	380	410
2	250	280	300	330	360	390	420
3	260	290	310	340	370	400	430
4	270	300	320	350	380	410	440
5	280	310	330	360	390	420	450
6	290	320	340	360	400	430	460
7	290	330	340	370	410	440	470
8	300	330	350	380	410	450	470
9	310	340	360	390	420	450	480
10	320	350	370	390	430	460	490
11	320	360	370	400	440	470	500
12	330	360	380	410	440	470	500
13	340	370	390	420	450	480	510
14	350	380	390	420	460	490	520
15	350	380	400	430	460	500	530
16	360	390	410	440	470	500	530
17	370	400	420	440	480	510	540
18	380	410	420	450	490	520	550
19	380	410	430	460	490	530	560
20	390	420	440	470	500	530	560
21	400	430	450	480	510	540	570
22	410	440	460	480	520	550	580
23	420	450	470	490	530	560	590
24	420	460	470	500	540	570	600
25	430	460	480	510	540	580	610
26	440	470	490	520	550	590	610
27	450	480	500	530	560	590	620
28	460	490	510	540	570	600	630
29	470	500	520	550	580	610	640
30	480	510	530	560	590	620	650
31	490	520	540	560	600	630	660
32	500	530	550	570	610	640	670
33	510	540	550	580	620	650	680
34	510	550	560	590	630	660	690
35	520	560	570	600	640	670	700
36	530	560	580	610	650	680	710
37	540	570	590	620	660	690	720
38	550	580	600	630	670	700	730
39	560	600	610	640	680	710	740
40	580	610	620	650	690	720	750
41	590	620	640	660	700	730	760
42	600	630	650	680	710	740	770
43	610	640	660	690	720	750	780
44	620	660	670	700	740	770	800
45	640	670	690	720	750	780	800
46	650	690	700	730	770	800	800
47	670	700	720	750	780	800	800
48	680	720	730	760	800	800	800
49	680	720	730	760	800	800	800

Detailed Answer Key

Section 1

The following essay received 12 points out of a possible 12, meaning that it demonstrates *clear and consistent competence* in that it

- develops an insightful point of view on the topic
- demonstrates exemplary critical thinking
- uses effective examples, reasons, and other evidence to support its thesis
- is consistently focused, coherent and well-organized
- demonstrates skilful and effective use of language and sentence structure
- is largely (but not necessarily completely) free of grammatical and usage errors

Consider carefully the issue discussed in the following passage, then write an essay that answers the question posed in the assignment.

> *If you believe you will succeed, you are probably right. If you think you will fail, you are also probably right.*

Assignment: **Which has a stronger effect on one's life: one's circumstances, or one's system of beliefs?** Write an essay in which you answer this question and support your position logically with examples from literature, the arts, history, politics, science and technology, current events, or your experience or observation.

SAMPLE STUDENT ESSAY

Our success is based, to a large degree, on our self confidence. Very self confident people generally succeed because they are comfortable with themselves, and they are assertive, aggressive, and enthusiastic. Since they believe that they will succeed, confident people make more opportunities for themselves. Yet, many confident and idealistic people struggle nevertheless, because success so often requires luck and the help of others.

During the early twentieth century, masses of immigrants from eastern and southern Europe and China flooded into the United States. They all came in search of opportunity and success, confident that America's "streets paved with gold" would deliver them to riches and power. These immigrants, though, no matter how deeply they believed that they would succeed, struggled. Americans who had lived in the Unites States for generations saw these immigrants as impostors who would accept lower wages and dilapidated working conditions, thereby thrusting the American union workers out of jobs. These indigent immigrants were stuck in tenement apartments that were so small they could not fit entire families at one time. "Nativist" American families regarded each immigrant group as having

unique and appalling traits. In Jacob Riis's "How the Other Half Lives," a progressive documentation of immigrant communities, black, Italian, and Chinese neighborhoods are all described as filled with dirty, ignorant, unwelcoming and lazy people. The dreams of success in America that were illustrated by exceptional men like Andrew Carnegie, who emigrated to America from Scotland and worked his way to world renown and economic success, pervaded immigrant communities, even though it was often futile for most immigrants to try to gain decent lives in America.

There are, as well, many people who believe that they will not succeed at their endeavors, and yet attain them because they are lucky, or because the belief that one might fail pushes that person to work harder to attain success. In the novel "Into Thin Air," a team of hikers and climbers, all from different walks of life and of different ages, attempts to climb Mount Everest. The voyage up the Greta mountain goes smoothly until, when the team has almost reached the summit, a huge storm blows in and overtakes the team, killing a majority of the climbers. A few men, however, survived the storm and the fury of Everest. These people did not believe that they would survive but, miraculously, and through the aid of rescue teams that combed the mountain after the storm, were saved, hospitalized, and nursed back to health.

Success, as it is experienced in the real world, is made in part of ambition, in part confidence and belief, and in large part opportunity, without which belief and ambition are irrelevant. It has been said that "luck is when preparation meets opportunity," and so, if furnished with the opportunity, ambitious and confident people are predisposed to succeed in their endeavors. There are situations, though, that occur randomly and unexpectedly, that no one can prepare for or avoid. It is, therefore, important and healthy to believe in one's self, with the knowledge that belief and confidence are but two of the many factors that contribute to attaining success.

The following essay received 8 points out of a possible 12, meaning that it demonstrates *adequate competence* in that it

- develops a point of view on the topic
- demonstrates some critical thinking, but perhaps not consistently
- uses some examples, reasons, and other evidence to support its thesis, but perhaps not adequately
- shows a general organization and focus, but shows occasional lapses in this regard
- demonstrates adequate but occasionally inconsistent facility with language
- contains occasional errors in grammar, usage, and mechanics

---

SAMPLE STUDENT ESSAY

Failure and success are often dependent on your attitude. If one thinks that one is going to fail, that means that you are not setting goals for yourself. If you don't have high goals, then it is impossible to achieve incredible things.

For instance last year, I tried out for the golf team. I thought I wasn't good enough to get on the team, and I ended up playing way over my handicap. I wasn't confident and it effected how I played. I was instead worrying about what excuse I would give for why I missed a shot so badly. I was missing some putts by 10 feet or more. I was cut after the first tryout. Over the summer I played a lot of golf by myself and that gives a person a lot of time to ponder. I reflected on my experiences about how badly I played at the tryouts, and how well I was playing during the summer. Then I was playing like a completely different person. I realized that this was because I was not worried about what others thought. I knew what I was capable of and did not feel the need to prove it to other people. I knew right then that I needed to play with others the way I played by myself—with mental toughness and confidence.

I was able to try and correct this problem when I was partnered up with someone I had never played with before but who was the defending club champion which made me nervous. This guy shoots barely over par every round. He's a formidable opponent. The "old" me would have crumpled under the pressure and thought before each shot how nervous I was that he'd say my swing was horrible looking or that he had never seen someone slice a golf ball so horribly before. But, instead the new me visualized the perfect shot before each swing and I played one of the best rounds of my life. He even said I should join the club championship later that month, which was an enormous compliment coming from him. (I actually was not able to play in that tournament because I was out of town.) The only difference between my round that day and my rounds during the tryouts the previous year was my attitude.

I think if you try hard you can do anything. When I tried out for the team again I knew I had improved over the summer. I decided to focus on the game and not worry or think about what would happen if I failed. I am happy to say that as I write this essay, I am the third ranked player on our high school golf team.

> The following essay received 4 points out of a possible 12, meaning that it demonstrates *some incompetence* in that it
>
> - has a seriously limited point of view
> - demonstrates weak critical thinking
> - uses inappropriate or insufficient examples, reasons, and other evidence to support its thesis
> - is poorly focused and organized, and has serious problems with coherence
> - demonstrates frequent problems with language and sentence structure
> - contains errors in grammar and usage that obscure the author's meaning

SAMPLE STUDENT ESSAY

It's hard to say really whether just because you believe something it will happen. I think that's sometimes true, but not always. Like I think most basketball teams think they can win the championship, or they believe it, but they don't because only one team can and there are twenty in the league. But the winner of the bicycle race the Tour de France shows that you can do great things if you believe in yourself and you give it 110%. He had cancer and people accused him of taking steroids when he was racing in a foreign country, but he won anyways three times in a row.

More people should be like Lance Armstrong because he didn't let anything get in his way. Sometimes when you feel that things are too much or things are getting in your way or you feel depressed you should think about a guy who rode his bike up steep mountains with competitors trying to kick his bike and people yelling things at him but winning never the less. All this in addition to overcoming the disease of cancer and the chemotherapy that goes along with it and saps your energy. My uncle had to go through chemotherapy and, thank god it worked and he's better now, but it really took a lot of his energy out. So its even more remarkable that he could overcome that.

Also, many characters in books and movies prove that when you think positively you can accomplish great things. Macbeth for instance became the king of Scotland because it was his dream and he did everything he could to do it. He was tenacious in his endeavors, therfore proving that great things come to those who work hard and believe in himself or herself.

Detailed Answer Key

Section 2

1. **D** If his reputation grew to *mythic proportions*, he has achieved great fame. *callous* = hardened, insensitive; *infamous* = famous for bad things; *aloof* = distant physically or emotionally; *renowned* = famous; *obtuse* = unintelligent, dense.

2. **A** When the weather is *cold and rainy* people do not tend to go to the beach, so it would be empty. *devoid of* = lacking; *overpopulated by* = overcrowded; *overrun with* = overflowing.

3. **B** A *controversy* would encourage the queen to *step down from* her throne and *retire to the country-side*. *commemorate* = to honor; *abdicate* = to give up power; *rectify* = to set right; *replicate* = to copy; *disenfranchise* = to deprive the rights of.

4. **A** *Although* indicates contrast. Someone would expect to receive *payment* for raking the neighbor's lawn. The *surprise* suggests that the woman is not very generous with her money. *remuneration* = payment; *frugal* = economical; *perquisite* = a tip, gratuity; *venal* = able to be bribed; *beneficiary* = one that receives benefit; *gratification* = pleasure; *arbitrary* = whimsical; *provisions* = supplies; *thrifty* = economical.

5. **B** *Although* suggests that this garden with *great potential* must have been less than great in the past. Given the potential for greatness, it would make sense for Mrs. Nelson to be excited to *plant or grow* things. *fertile* = capable of growth; *fallow* = left unseeded; inactive; *cultivate* = to prepare to grow on; *culminate* = to climax, to come to a conclusion; *painstaking* = diligent.

6. **D** If the senator was not used to the *rigors* (demands) of the campaign, he would be overwhelmed by a *frantic* pace *reticent* = reluctant to share feelings; *mundane* = common; *pastoral* = relating to country life; *frenetic* = frantic; *prosaic* = dull.

7. **B** If his writing defines *magical realism*, he must write about *fantastical* events. *plausible* = conceivable; *chimerical* = fantastical; *obsequious* = overly submissive; *itinerant* = traveling from place to place; *tenuous* = flimsy.

8. **E** The deliberation escalated to physical violence which would indicate it was definitely a heated discussion. Jurors exchanging vicious *invectives* (abusive language) would be understandably agitated. *dignified* = full of dignity; *temperate* = self-restrained; *decorous* = proper; *belligerent* = war-like; *sedate* = calm; *amiable* = friendly; *staid* = calm and dignified; *pugnacious* = ready to fight; *contentious* = quarrelsome; *truculent* = ready to fight.

9. **C** The passage says that Kepler's *audience was more friendly than Galileo's* (lines 1–2) regarding their theories.

10. **D** The keplerian refractor produces an *inverted image* (lines 9–10), *unlike the Galilean telescope*.

11. **A** The Impressionists *turned the whole ingenious business on its ear* (lines 6–7), meaning they rebelled against the Romanticist tendency to use *every possible subject of melodramatic or sentimental potentialities* (lines 2–4)

12. **D** Because Monet was the *high priest* (lines 9–10) of the Impressionists, who believed that *subject mattered not at all* (line 9), and rebelled against the sentimentality of the Romanticists, must have chosen haystacks because they are not sentimental.

13. **A** This passage does not discuss any *historical phenomenon or the contributions of artists*. The first two paragraphs discuss the misconception that it is difficult to properly understand music. The last two paragraphs describe what is required to properly understand music, according to the author who is a famous composer, and so this portion of the passage can be considered *authoritative instruction*.

14. **D** The previous sentence suggests that those people know as little about the theater and novel as they say they know about music, but the sentence that follows is more respectful of their *understanding*.

15. **E** Saying that *the fact bespeaks a certain musicality* is like saying that *the fact indicates* (*that they have*) *a certain musicality*.

16. **B** The passage clearly states that the *minimum skill required to appreciate music is the ability to recognize a melody* (lines 48–49).

17. **A**   Saying that *the color-blind are a useless lot to the painter* is like saying *the color-blind are a useless group of people to the painter.*

18. **C**   The passage says that *musical "events" are more abstract by nature, so the act of pulling them all together (that is, synthesizing them) is not so easy as in reading a novel* (lines 72–75). 18. **E** In saying that *experience ... is a traffic between the object and the subject,* the author means that there is interaction or communication between them.

19. **B**   The passage states that *if no practical difference whatever can be traced (in their effects), then the alternatives mean practically the same thing, and all dispute is idle* (lines 13–16).

20. **E**   Saying that *the root of all our thought-distinctions, however subtle, is that there is no one of them so fine as to consist in anything but a possible difference of practice* is equivalent to saying that *no distinction is so subtle that it is anything but a difference in practical outcome.*

21. **E**   Saying that *at present it fairly spots the pages of the philosophic journals* is the same as saying that *it now abounds in the pages of philosophic journals.*

22. **D**   The passage states that Ostwald *had been making perfectly distinct use of the principle of pragmatism in his lectures on the philosophy of science* (lines 69–71).

23. **B**   The thesis of the passage is that scientific theories are only distinguishable if they imply different outcomes that can be detected, so that observation could determine which theory is true.

24. **D**   The discussion of the competing theories about what causes dough to rise emphasizes the point that, to a pragmatist, competing theories that do not imply different results are equivalent, and arguing about them is pointless.

Section 3

1. **A**

	$2x + 7 = 4x + 5$
Subtract 5:	$2x + 2 = 4x$
Subtract $2x$:	$2 = 2x$
Divide by 2	$1 = x$

2. **B**   Pick any positive integer for n and plug it into the equation and eliminate anything that is odd. Try $n = 3$. (A) $= n + 2 = 3 + 2 = 5$. (B) $= 2(n) = 2(3) = 6$. (C) $= 3n = 3(3) = 9$. (D) $= n^2 = 3^2 = 9$. (E) $= n^3 = 3^3 = 27$. Only answer choice B is even.

3. **C**   When rounding to the nearest inch, answer choices A and B become 4. ($4.00 < x < 4.50$ is rounded down to 4). Answer choices D and E become 6. ($5.50 < x < 6.00$ is rounded up to 6.00)

4. **D**   When there are 100 ft² left to paint, Jane has already painted $340 - 100 = 240$ ft². You can construct a rate pyramid for this problem:

If a problem gives you two of the quantities, just put them in their places in the pyramid and do the operation between them to find the missing quantity:

$240 \div 60 = 4$ hrs.

There are 60 minutes in an hour. $4 \times 60 = 240$ minutes.

5. **E**   There are 180° in a triangle:

	$90° + 3x + x = 180°$
Subtract 90:	$4x = 90°$
Divide by 4:	$x = 22.5°$
Multiply by 3:	$3x = 67.5°$

(Chapter 13, Lesson 2: Triangles)

6. **B**   50% of 60% of $180 = (.5)(.6)(180) = 54$

7. **E**

	$\dfrac{1}{c^2} = b^2 + 4b + 4$
Factor:	$\dfrac{1}{c^2} = (b+2)^2$
Take reciprocals:	$c^2 = \dfrac{1}{(b+2)^2}$
Take the square root:	$c = \dfrac{1}{\sqrt{(b+2)^2}} = \dfrac{1}{b+2}$

8. **E**   Set up an equation to find the average.

	$\dfrac{3y + 4y + (y-5)}{3} = 9$
Multiply by 3:	$3y + 4y + (y - 5) = 27$
Combine like terms:	$8y - 5 = 27$
Add 5:	$8y = 32$
Divide by 8:	$y = 4$

9. C   Use the Pythagorean Theorem to solve for x.

$$(x)^2 + (2\sqrt{5})^2 = (6)^2$$

Square each part:	$x^2 + 20 = 36$
Subtract 20:	$x^2 = 16$
Take the square root:	$x = 4$

10. C   Both "domain rules" discussed in Chapter 14 apply:

$(x - 6) \neq 0$	$(x + 4) \geq 0$
Add 6:	$x \neq 6$
Subtract 4:	$x \geq -4$

11. D   Pick a value for w that satisfies the condition. It must be 2 more than a multiple of 6, like $6 + 2 = 8$. If $w = 8$, then $5w = 40$. When 40 is divided by 6, the remainder is 4.

12. C

In the "dogs" row:	$35 + 60 + y = 105$
Combine:	$95 + y = 105$
Subtract 95:	
In the "white" column:	$35 + x + 15 = 75$
Combine:	$50 + x = 75$
Subtract 50:	$x = 25$
In the "cats" row:	$x + 37 + 16 = w$
Substitute 25 for x:	$25 + 37 + 16 = w$
Solve for w:	$78 = w$
In the "total" column:	$105 + w + 28 = z$
Substitute 78 for w:	$105 + 78 + 28 = z$
Solve for z:	$246 = z$

13. B   If the circle is tangent to the x-axis, it only touches the axis at one point. The x-intercept will share the same x-value as the center point. The center of the circle is $(3, 4)$ and the circle must touch the x-axis at the point $(3, 0)$ and thus the radius = $4 - 0 = 4$.

$$\text{Circumference} = 2\pi r = 2(\pi)(4) = 8\pi$$

14. E   The triangle inequality theorem states that $EF - DE < DF < EF + DE$
Substitute 9 for EF and 7 for DE: $9 - 7 < DF < 9 + 7$
$2 < DF < 16$

15. D

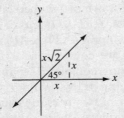

If the line creates an angle of 45° with the x-axis, then its equation is $y = x$ and therefore any point where the x and y coordinate are the same is on the line.

$$y = 10$$

16. A   Mark the information on the diagram, and use the facts that (1) "linear" angles have a sum of 180°, (2) angles in a triangle have a sum of 180°, and (3) in a triangle, angles across from equal sides are equal. Your diagram should look like this:

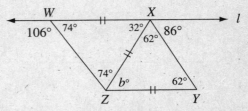

Therefore $62 + 62 + b = 180$ and so $b = 56$

17. D   A chart may help you organize the information.

	%	Hours	
sleep	30	7.2	$(.30)(24) = 7.2$
work	35	8.4	$(.35)(24) = 8.4$
gym	5	1.2	$(.05)(24) = 1.2$
home		5.0	
car		x	
total	100	24.0	

$(\%)(24)$ = hours

Hours in car $= 24 - 7.2 - 8.4 - 1.2 - 5.0 = 2.2$ hours
2.2 hours × 60 minutes/hour = 132 minutes.

18. B   First find the midpoint of $(8, 8)$ and $(6, -2)$.

$$\text{midpoint} = \left(\frac{X_1 + X_2}{2}, \frac{Y_1 + Y_2}{2}\right)$$

$$\text{midpoint} = \left(\frac{8 + 6}{2}, \frac{8 + -2}{2}\right)$$

$$\text{midpoint} = (7, 3)$$

Next find the slope of the line connecting the two points $(7, 3)$ and $(2, 5)$.

$$\text{slope} = \frac{(Y_2 - Y_1)}{(X_2 - X_1)} = \frac{(3 - 5)}{(7 - 2)} = -\frac{2}{5}$$

19. A   The diagonal of a square splits it into two 45°–45°–90° triangles. The sides of a 45°–45°–90° triangle are x, x, and $x\sqrt{2}$. So if the sides of the square have length x, the diagonal has length $x\sqrt{2}$.

Therefore	$x\sqrt{2} = m$
Divide by $\sqrt{2}$:	$x = m/\sqrt{2}$

The area of a square is x^2 or $\dfrac{m^2}{2}$

20. **A**   Since vertical angles are equal, label the two interior angles x and y. The quickest method is to notice that z is the measure of an "exterior angle" to the triangle, and so it equals the sum of the two "remote interior" angles. Therefore $z = x + y$ and so $x = z - y$.

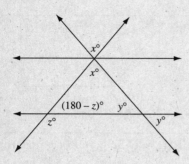

Or you can "plug in:"

Let's say $x = 40°$ and $y = 70°$

There are 180° in a triangle:
$$40° + 70° + (180 - z) = 180°$$
Subtract 290: $-z = -110°$
Divide by –1: $z = 110°$

Next, plug the values for z and y into the answer choices and pick the one that equals 40°: $z - y = 110° - 70° = 40°$.

Section 4

1. **C** $x \$ y = x^y + 3$
   Plug in for x and y: $4 \$ 2 = 4^2 + 3 = 19$

2. **B**   When given a system of equations and asked to evaluate another expression, begin by writing the two expressions on top of each other and see if adding or subtracting yields the answer.
$$n + m = 7$$
$$2n - 3m = 6$$
Add the two together: $3n - 2m = 13$ Done!

3. **D**   In order to find the smallest value of y, you must make x as large as possible. Since you know that $x < 40$, and x and y are both positive integers, it follows that the largest possible value of x is 39. Since y is the measure of an exterior angle to the triangle, $y = 39 + 80 = 119$

4. **C**   The triangle inequality theorem states that:
$$11 - 7 < x < 11 + 7$$
$$4 < x < 18$$
Therefore x can be any integer from 5 to 17, which includes $17 - 5 + 1 = 13$ possible integers.

5. **A**

All three of the triangles in the figure are $30 - 60 - 90$.

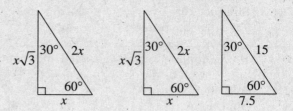

The side across from the 30° in the triangle on the far left is 7.5. The hypotenuse is double that or $2(7.5) = 15$.

That hypotenuse is the $x\sqrt{3}$ side of the middle triangle.

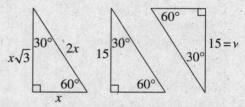

Both are $30 - 60 - 90$ triangles and they share the same hypotenuse. This means that they are exactly the same and since w is also across from the 60°, it too is equal to 15.

6. **B**   Use the percent change formula:

$$\text{percent change} = \frac{\text{final} - \text{original}}{\text{original}} \times 100\%$$

$$= \frac{192{,}500 - 175{,}000}{175{,}000} \times 100\%$$

$$= \frac{17{,}500}{175{,}000} \times 100\% = 10\%$$

7. **C**   To simplify the problem, notice that for every group of four people chosen, another group of two people is "left out," so the number of two-person groups is equal to the number of four-person groups. To count the number of two-person groups, Think of the people as A, B, C, D, E and F. How many two-person groups contain A? Five: AB, AC, AD, AE and AF. Once these are counted, ask: how many more two-person groups contain B? Four: BC, BD, BE, and BF. Continuing in this manner, you can see that the total number of two-person groups is $5 + 4 + 3 + 2 + 1 = 15$. Therefore, the number of four-person groups is also 15.

8. **E** Just focus on the sign of each term. The signs of the first three terms are −, +, − respectively. The sign of the fourth term is (−) ÷ (−) = +. The sign of the fifth term is (−) ÷ (+) = −. The sign of the sixth term is (+) ÷ (−) = −. The signs of first 6 terms of the sequence are: −, +, −, −, +, −.

The pattern of three terms. −,+,−, repeats indefinitely. This pattern repeats 100 ÷ 3 = 33 1/3⅓ times. Each repetition contains 2 negative numbers. The 33 full repetitions (which account for the first 99 terms) contain 33 × 2 = 66 negative numbers. The 100th term is also negative, giving a total of 66 + 1 = 67 negative terms.

---

9. **4** Set up a ratio and solve:

$$\frac{24}{1}\frac{miles}{gallon} = \frac{96}{x}\frac{miles}{gallons}$$

Cross Multiply: $24x = 96$
Divide by 24: $x = 4$ gallons

---

10. **0** $< b < 1$ In order for b^3 to be less than b^2, b must be a fraction between 0 and 1. When a fraction between zero and one is multiplied by itself, its value decreases.

---

11. **180** Begin by writing equations that represent what you are told in the problem: E = Eric, B = Bill.

$$E = 40 + B$$
$$E + B = 320$$

Plug $(40 + B)$ in for E: $(40 + B) + B = 320$
Subtract 40: $2B = 280$
Divide by 2: $B = 140$
Solve for E: $E = 40 + 140 = 180$

---

12. **900** Using the pie chart, first calculate how many students eat dining hall food and how many students eat snack food.

Snack: 10% of 3,000 = (.10)(3,000) = 300 Students
Dining Hall: 40% of 3,000 = (.40)
                  (3,000) = 1,200 students

1,200 − 300 = 900 students

---

13. **6**

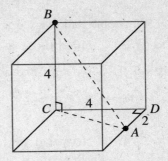

Each side of the cube is 4 units long. $AD = 2$ because point A is the midpoint of that side. To find the distance from A to B set up a right triangle ($\triangle ABC$) where the length you're trying to find is a side. You know that the value of BC is 4 because it is an edge of the cube. To find AB, you need to first find the value of AC, which can be found by solving right triangle ADC using the Pythagorean Theorem:

$$2^2 + 4^2 = AC^2$$

Combine: $20 = AC^2$
Take the square root: $\sqrt{20} = AC$

Next, solve right triangle ABC to find the value of AB.

$$AC^2 + BC^2 = AB^2$$

Substitute: $(\sqrt{20})^2 + 4^2 = AB^2$
Combine: $36 = AB^2$
Take the square root: $6 = AB$

---

14. **12** Begin by writing a system of equations: S = weight of soda cans; C = weight of cooler

$$C + S = 20$$
$$C + ¼ S = 14$$

Subtract two equations: $¾S = 6$
Divide by ¾: $S = 8$
Plug in 8 for S and solve: $C + 8 = 20$
Subtract 8: $C = 12$

---

15. **6** First set up a distance = (rate)(time) equation for the trips to and from work.

to work: $d = 15(t)$
from work: $d = 10(1 − t)$
Set 2 equations equal: $15t = 10(1 − t)$
Distribute: $15t = 10 − 10t$
Add 10t: $25t = 10$

Divide by 25: $t = \dfrac{2}{5}$

Plug in for t: $d = 15(t) = 15\left(\dfrac{2}{5}\right) = 6$ miles

16. **580**   Set up a Venn diagram to solve this problem:

1,000 − 630 = 370 people had just a dog. 630 people had a cat, and $\frac{1}{3}$ (630) = 210 of those also had a dog.

Therefore 210 + 370 − 580 people had dogs.

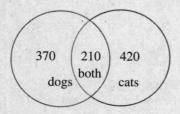

17. **5/9 or .555 or .556**

Find area of middle circle: $\pi r^2 = \pi\,(2)^2 = 4\pi$
Find area of outermost circle: $\pi r^2 = \pi\,(3)^2 = 9\pi$
The area of the shaded region = $9\pi - 4\pi = 5\pi$
The probability that the dart will land in the shaded area is $5\pi/9\pi = 5/9$.

20. **0.25 or ¼**

If there are three times as many red marbles as black marbles, then if there are x black marbles, there are $3x$ red marbles. This means there are a total of $x + 3x = 4x$ marbles, $3x$ of which are black. Therefore the probability of choosing a red marble is $3x/4x = ¾$. Of these red marbles, twice as many are striped as unstriped, so if there are y unstriped red marbles, there are $2y$ striped red marbles, for a total of $3y$ red marbles, y of which are unstriped. Therefore $y/3y = ⅓$ of the red marbles are unstriped. $¼ × ⅓ = ¼$, so the probability of choosing an unstriped red marble at random is ¼.

Section 5

1. **A**   A bag of rotten garbage that had been sitting there for three weeks would probably be disgusting. *putrid* = rotten; *delectable* = delightful; *piquant* = pleasant tasting; *savory* = tasty

2. **E**   Doug had to call his mother for *clarification*, which would indicate that he was confused when attempting to use the handwritten recipe. *reconfigure*= to rearrange; *illegible* = unable to be read; *recapitulate* = to summarize; *lucid* = clear; *reiterate* = to recap; *placid* = calm; *cogent* = convincing; *decipher* = to figure out; *unintelligible* = incapable of being understood.

3. **D**   Fragile artifacts that archaeologists *collect* require safeguards against *deterioration*. *projected* = extended forward into space or time; *dissipation*= wasteful expenditure; *amassed* = collected; *disseminated* = scattered as seed; *desiccation* = drying out.

4. **B**   *Incontrovertible* (indisputable) evidence presented by a prosecutor would be bad news for a defendant and would probably prove his or her guilt. *apathy* = lack of feeling; *culpable* = guilty; *penitence* = regret; *dexterity* = grace and skill; *prescience* = foresight.

5. **B**   Mother Teresa was *selfless or generous* with her time. *rhetorical* = used to persuade; *munificent* = generous; *felicitous* = apt, well suited; *austere* = severe; *mellifluous* = smooth flowing.

6. **C**   The passage says that the *rate of cultural change has accelerated* (lines 7–8) in recent history, and uses the development of food production as an example.

7. **D**   Food production, according to the passage, involves any kind of *cultivation of plants* or *domestication of animals* (line 13–14).

8. **B**   The first sentence describes Egyptian rites as *mystic* practices *performed in the depths of temple sanctuaries* exclusively by priests. The Greek rituals, however, were *engaged in by all citizens* (line 9).

9. **E**   Saying that *preliminaries were engaged in by citizens* is the same as saying that *preliminaries were participated in by citizens*.

10. **C**   The passage as a whole discusses the different ways that humans make decisions: trial and error, algorithms and heuristics.

11. **E**   The *research* is described as what led to the derivation of *the concept of heuristic reasoning* (line 31). Furthermore, this research was designed to *simulate human intelligence using computers* (lines 33–34). Therefore, the attempt to simulate human intelligence must have led researchers to believe that heuristics simulate human thinking.

12. **A**   This strategy is described as a response to frustration over the *enormous number of possible solutions* (line 37) involved in making a chess move.

13. **E**   In saying that *moves that meet these goals are executed*, the author means that helpful moves are carried out. Since moves are not people, they *cannot* be *empowered* or *frustrated*.

14. A The passage suggests that one reason why we use heuristics is *because algorithms require so much cognitive capacity and effort* (lines 53–54).

15. B The author states that the representativeness heuristic *leads us not to seek and evaluate other information that might be helpful ... such as Steve's preferences* (lines 77–79). Such a heuristic does take personality characteristics into account. Also, it does not require an infinite amount of information or an elaborate algorithm and it is quite distinct from the trial-and-error approach described earlier in the passage.

16. B Unlike the representativeness heuristic, the availability heuristic *bases decisions on the availability of relevant information in memory* (lines 82–84).

17. A Louis is said to *vacillate* (waver) between liberal and reactionary counselors. Thus he was indecisive.

18. D The constitution ended the monarchy and safeguarded *wide popular suffrage* (voting rights) ... *and fairly high grade of civil administration* (lines 13–15).

19. C In saying that the entrepreneurial groups were *released politically and culturally as well as economically from their anomalous subjection to an incapable and irresponsibly nobility* (lines 24–27), the author is saying that entrepreneurs became free of the nobility, to whom they previously had to submit politically and economically. Therefore, the word *subjection* most nearly means *state of submission*.

20. B The passage says that *business sat solidly in the center trying to get a little order and stability without interference* (lines 21–23).

21. E The economy of opportunity is said to produce *an appearance of infinite variety in cultural expression* (lines 42–43) and encouraged art that was *expressive of ... free, individual personality* (lines 55–56).

22. D The paragraph says that merchants sought *distinction for (their) position* (line 50) and used art to that end. The merchant bought art *expressive of his free, individual personality* and as a result the *artist exaggerated his every whim and impulse* (lines 55–58). Therefore the needs of the patrons influenced the aesthetic decisions of the artists.

23. D In saying that *it was an age of rapid and sometimes accidental accessions of wealth*, the author is saying that many merchants of this time acquired sudden wealth. Therefore *accessions* most nearly means *accumulation*.

24. D The passage says *the more abstruse the forms of art, the more impenetrable to the uninitiated, the greater their value as a distinction to the "connoisseur"* (lines 78–81).

Section 6

1. D *All quiet* is slang and *hoping that she would win* is non-standard form. Choice D is clear, concise and standard.

2. B The non-underlined phrase is an **appositive**, and should be followed by its equivalent *David*.

3. E The first clause is in the active voice, so the second clause should maintain the active voice.

4. C This is a comparison error. Jon's *scores* can only be compared to other *scores*.

5. A The original phrasing is best.

6. D This is a violation of parallelism. The items in the list should have similar grammatical forms. Choice D creates a concise phrasing in which all of the items are **gerunds**.

7. D The phrase *of the sort that delves* is wordy and non-standard.

8. A The original phrasing is best.

9. B The original phrasing produces a sentence fragment. Choice B creates a complete thought concisely.

10. C The phrase *every member* is singular, but the pronoun *their* is plural. Choice C provides pronoun-antecedent agreement.

11. A The original phrasing is best.

12. C The phrase *for ascending* contains an idiom error. The idiom is *struggle to*, so the phrase in C should be *to ascend*.

13. D The past perfect tense is incorrect because the *jumping* occurred at the same time as the *falling*. This should be the simple past tense *jumped*.

14. B This is a comparison error. Audrey's *ideas* should not be compared to a *class*. The correction is *those of the rest of the class*.

15. **E**   The sentence is correct.

16. **A**   This is a tense error. Since the shifting had occurred many times before election day *arrived* (simple past tense), it should take the past perfect tense, *had shifted*.

17. **A**   This is a violation of parallelism. Omit the word *being*.

18. **E**   This sentence is correct.

19. **C**   This is a diction error. *Expectant* means *eagerly awaiting*, and inadequacies can't await things. The proper word is *expected*.

20. **C**   This is a pronoun-antecedent disagreement. The antecedent is *troops* which is plural, so the proper pronoun is *their*.

21. **A**   The word *media* is plural. (The singular form is *medium*.) Therefore the proper verb conjugation is *play*.

22. **C**   The phrase *wasn't hardly* is a double negative, and should be changed to *wasn't* or *was hardly*.

23. **A**   The subject of the verb is *each*, which is singular. The correct conjugation, then, is *ends*.

24. **B**   Ambiguous pronoun antecedent. The pronoun *their* indicates a plural antecedent, but none is available in the sentence. Since the salesman is most logically talking about his own integrity, the pronoun should be *his* or *her*.

25. **C**   The subject of the verb *have been stimulated* is the singular subject *growth*, and so it does not agree. It should be changed to *has been*.

26. **C**   The word *adapt* is a verb meaning *change for a specific purpose*, and so is used improperly here. The correct word is the adjective *adept*.

27. **D**   The pronouns *his* or *her* have a plural antecedent, *the voters*. Therefore, this phrase should be changed to *their ballots*.

28. **A**   The phrase *miss out on* is a non-standard idiom because it is needlessly wordy. It should be re-phrased to simply *miss*.

29. **D**   This is an illogical comparison. Since the comparison is being made to *her dance routine*, this should be rephrased as *the routines of the other dancers*.

30. **D**   The phrase *closest living relative* pertains to a specific living person rather than a species. Also, *species* is a singular noun.

31. **E**   The original phrasing is very awkward and unclear. The several ideas in the sentence do not coordinate logically.

32. **B**   The original phrasing contains a comma splice. Choice B separates the independent clauses with a semicolon and coordinates the ideas logically.

33. **D**   This sentence logically follows the sentence about female social habits.

34. **D**   Sentence 10 contributes the least to the unity because it is the only sentence that deviates from the topic of the chimpanzee society.

35. **C**   This sentence expands upon sentence 11 and provides a solid conclusion to the paragraph.

Section 7

1. **B**   Since the exponentials have the same base, you can disregard the base and set the exponents equal to each other: $3y = 9$
Divide by 3: $y = 3$

2. **C** $\dfrac{1}{1.4} = .7143$

"Divide out" the fractions and look for the same quotient.
Answer choice C: $5 \div 7 = .7143$

3. **D**   Angles that form a line have a sum of 180°.
Write an equation: $2x + 140° = 180°$
Subtract 140°: $2x = 40°$
Add 5 to both sides: $2x + 5 = 40° + 5°$
Combine like terms: $2x + 5 = 45°$

4. **D**   Write an equation: $\dfrac{3x}{2} = 39$

Multiply by 2: $3x = 78$
Divide by 3: $x = 26$

5. **D**
To find out how much greater $x + 5$ is than $x - 5$, subtract them from each other:
$$(x + 5) - (x - 5)$$
Distribute: $x + 5 - x + 5$
Combine like terms: 10

6. D

Find Area of Rectangle M: $(L)(W) = LW = A$
Find Area of Rectangle P: $(3L)(3W) = 9LW$
Substitute A for LW: $9LW = 9A$.

7. C There is no need to actually calculate the length of the diameter. You should know that, by definition, the number π is the ratio of the circumference to the diameter of *any* circle. (Just remember the formula $c = \pi d$ so $\pi = c/d$.) The actual length of the circumference doesn't matter. Therefore, the ratio is π:1.

8. D Draw $\overline{AB}$ and construct a right triangle:

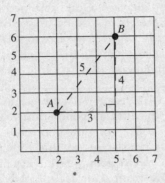

You should notice that this forms a "special" 3–4–5 right triangle, so calculating the distance algebraically is unnecessary. If you don't notice this, however, you can use the Pythagorean Theorem:
$$3^2 + 4^2 = (AB)^2$$
Simplify: $\qquad\qquad 25 = (AB)^2$
Take the square root: $\qquad 5 = AB$

9. C Begin by writing a system of equations:
s = # of bags of sticky bears
c = # of bags of chocolate bombs
Total cost is $500: $\quad 1.50s + 1.00c = 500$
400 bags were bought: $s + c = 400$
Solve for s: $\qquad\qquad s = 400 - c$
Subst. into first eq.: $\quad 1.50(400 - c) + c = 500$
Distribute: $\qquad\qquad 600 - 1.50c + c = 500$
Subtract 600: $\qquad\qquad -0.50c = -100$
Divide by -0.50: $\qquad c = 200$

10. B The simplest way to solve this is to remember from Chapter 12, Lesson 4, that, in a set of "evenly spaced" numbers, the median and the mean are always equal. Since consecutive even integers are certainly "evenly spaced," the average (arithmetic mean) must also be 10.
Alternately, you can construct a set of 7 consecutive even integers that has 10 as its middle number:
4, 6, 8, 10, 12, 14, 16
$$\text{mean} = \frac{(4+6+8+10+12+14+16+)}{7} = 10$$

11. B First calculate the revenue for each theater.
Bijou = 120(9) + 30(6) + 20(6) = $1380
Community = 220(9) + 40(6) + 90(6) = $2760
1380 is what percent of $2760?

$$1380 = \frac{x}{100}(2760)$$

Simplify: $\qquad\qquad 1380 = 27.6x$
Divide by 27.6: $\qquad 50 = x$
So the total revenue the Bijou receives is 50% of the revenue the Community Cinema receives.

12. E The total revenue at the Triplex is
$$9.50x + 28(6.50) = 9.5x + 162$$
The total revenue at the Village Theater is
110(9.50) + 20(6.50) + 70(6.00) = 1600
Set up inequality: 182 + 9.5x > 1600
Subtract 182: $\qquad 9.5x = 1418$
Divide by 9.5: $\qquad x = 149.3$
Therefore the Triplex sold at least 149 adult tickets.

13. E Remember that any digit may be repeated. Because the number has three digits, you can regard this as a "counting" problem with three choices. There are three choices for each digit, so the total number of distinct integers is $3 \times 3 \times 3 = 27$.

14. A Take reciprocal of both sides: $\dfrac{1}{x^2} = 4y + 6$

Subtract 6: $\qquad \dfrac{1}{x^2} - 6 = 4y$

Divide by 4: $\qquad \dfrac{1}{4x^2} - \dfrac{6}{4} = \dfrac{1}{4x^2} - \dfrac{3}{2} = y$

15. A To find the area of the shaded region, subtract the area of the circle from the area of the square.
Area of the square = $(\text{side})^2 = 6^2 = 36$
Area of the circle = $\pi(r)^2 = \pi(3)^2 = 9\pi$
Shaded area = $36 - 9\pi$

16. E Try plugging in values. If $c = 12$, for instance, then she spends $12 \div 3 = 4$ hours each day preparing desserts. Desserts that require 24 hours of preparation would take $24 \div 4 = 6$ days to make. Plug $c = 12$ into the answer choices and eliminate those that do NOT equal 6.

(A) $\quad \dfrac{c}{72} = \dfrac{12}{72} = \dfrac{1}{6}$ $\qquad$ (B) $\quad \dfrac{24}{c} = \dfrac{24}{12} = 2$

(C) $\quad \dfrac{c}{24} = \dfrac{12}{24} = \dfrac{1}{2}$ $\qquad$ (D) $\quad 24c = 24(12) = 288$

(E) $\dfrac{72}{c} = \dfrac{72}{12} = 6$

Alternatively, you can solve this problem using your algebra skills. This is a "rate" problem, so use the formula

$$Amount\ of\ work = rate \times time$$

The amount of work is 24 "dessert hours." The rate at which she prepares desserts is c/3 "dessert hours per day,"

so $\qquad\qquad 24 = \dfrac{c}{3} \times time$ (in days)

Multiply by 3: $\qquad 72 = c \times time$ (in days)

Divide by c: $\qquad\qquad \dfrac{72}{c} = time$ (in days)

Section 8

1. B The size of the moon is changing such that it will soon no longer be visible. It must be getting smaller. *desiccate* = to dry out; *wane* = to shrink in size; *debunk* = to expose something as false; *convoke* = to call together; *coalesce* = to fuse together.

2. C The *opposing forces* saw the attack coming, so they could prepare themselves for the attacking army and defeat them badly. *foreseen* = predicted; *defoliate* = to lose leaves; *disavowed* = sworn off; *decimate* = to destroy; *resolved* = brought to a resolution; *demarcate* = to set boundaries.

3. B The candidates used *roundabout expressions* and *evasive tactics* to *avoid* the questions. They were speaking *around the subject*. This makes *circumlocution* a perfect fit. *matriculation* = the admission to a group, usually a university; *circumlocution* = evasive speech; *contemplation* = thoughtfulness; *homogeneity* = the state of being similar; *serendipity* = good luck in making a fortunate discovery.

4. E A *propensity* is a tendency to do something. George does something that causes his peers to look at him as a *grandiose*, or pompous person. *vacillate* = to go back and forth; *phlegmatic* = sluggish; *eulogize* = to praise; *loquacious* = very talkative; *prophesy* = to tell the future; *mercurial* = changing, volatile; *pilfer* = to steal; *colloquial* = using everyday language, conversational; *pontificate* = to speak in an arrogant way; *bombastic* = grandiloquent, pompous.

5. D If he was remembered as being *taller than she actually was*, he is actually small. Despite being small, he is able to *dominate a room*. *gargantuan* = gigantic; *voluminous* = of large capacity; *scanty* = insufficient; *exemplify* = to serve as an example; *diminutive* = tiny; *belied* = misrepresented; *meager* = lacking in quantity; *propagate* = to grow or multiply.

6. C The journalist has an *infamous* (notorious) history, which indicates he has not behaved properly in the past. A reputation for *fabrication* (making things up) would lead his readers to doubt the authenticity or truth of his articles. *candor* = honesty; *perfidiousness* = unfaithfulness; *ingenuity* = cleverness; *fabrication* = something invented, a lie; *veracity* = truth; *virtuosity* = great skill; *aptitude* = talent; *perspicacity* = ability to discern or understand; *autonomy* = independence.

7. A Passage 1 discusses the impact of Hemingway on writers of the author's generation, *the young men born between 1918, roughly, and 1924* (lines 1–2). The author is consistent on this topic, discussing Hemingway's *impact upon us* (line 26) in the second paragraph, and comparing Hemingway's impact on his generation to his impact on today's generation in the final paragraph.

8. C The author states that the impact of Hemingway's words on his generation was so great that *we began unconsciously to translate our own sensations into their term*. This kind of translation is *empathy*.

9. D The *war* mentioned in line 50 is said to have *forced (much) out of us* ... and the author says that this loss *was something far greater than Hemingway and his formative influence* ... In other words, this war disillusioned them on the images of war presented in Hemingway's writing.

10. A In saying that *many young writers ... have rejected (Hemingway's) time as untrue*, the author is saying that those writers have decided that Hemingway's depiction of his times have little meaning for them.

11. C Statement I is supported in line 5, *he had become a legendary figure (to my generation)* and in the final paragraph, in which the author states that today's writers *have not profited (from Hemingway) or were never touched by him at all*. Statement III is supported by lines 57–58, in which the author says that modern writers have failed *at finding themselves in their own time*, while his own generation, as he says in lines 48–49, felt that the *Hemingway time was a good time to be young*.

12. D The author states that *perhaps the real unfortunates* are those who *have been denied access to a powerful tradition* (in Hemingway's writings) (lines 63–65).

13. E In this first paragraph of Passage 2, the author describes the similarities between Hemingway's world and the modern world, to suggest that Hemingway's writing should have meaning for us because of those similarities.

14. B This excerpt in lines 115–120 says that a reader *will have a feeling of those things* which are not directly mentioned by the author. This would require the ability to read beyond what an author has explicitly stated.

15. D The author of Passage 2 says that *Hemingway's famous economy of prose was by no means as omnipresent as he himself suggests* in *Death of the Afternoon* which discusses his literary method. In other words, he claimed that writers should write *economically* but did not always do so himself.

16. C Passage 2 mentions that Hemingway's writing seems to be influenced by *a mixture of stylistic forces* (lines 129–130).

17. C Choice I is supported in line 145, which says that Hemingway's writing *contains scrambled chronology*. Choice II is supported by line 140, which says that the book is *self-indulgent*. There is no mention that the book contains recollections of his wartime experiences.

18. A Passage 1 clearly states that Hemingway *had become a legendary figure* (line 5) to his generation. Passage states that Hemingway *became a dupe of his culture* (lines 97–98) who *yielded to the functionalist, technological aesthetic of the culture instead of resisting* (lines 94–96).

19. E The first passage is concerned with the influence of Hemingway as a hero to his generation, but does not delve into his literary style. The second passage, however, is concerned almost exclusively with Hemingway's writing style.

Section 9

1. C Since the sentence begins with a participial phrase modifying *Maria*, the clause that follows should begin with *Maria*.

2. E As it is originally phrased, the sentence has no verb, and so isn't even a sentence! Choices (C), (D), and (E) correct that problem, but only (E) contains a clear and idiomatic phrasing of the comparison.

3. A The original phrasing is best. It is parallel and idiomatic and uses the semicolon correctly.

4. B The clause *the reason is because* is illogical, because the word *because* is neither a noun nor a pronoun and so cannot be equated with a noun. Since *programs* is plural, (B) is the best choice.

5. D The word *feature* can only be equated with a noun phrase that represents a feature. Choice (D) does this in the most concise way.

6. C Choice (C) is the only one that contains a standard phrasing in the subjunctive mood.

7. E Choice (E) is the most concise and parallel.

8. B The use of *nevertheless* in the original phrasing is redundant, since the sentence starts with *although*.

9. C The opening participial phrase *as a writer*, should be followed by the noun or pronoun that it modifies, which is *I*. Choice (C) does this most clearly.

10. B The original sentence contains a comma splice and a pronoun, *this*, with an unclear antecedent. Choice (B) corrects both of these problems.

11. E The original phrasing is wordy and nonstandard. Choice (E) is the most concise and clear.

12. **C** The phrase *a necessity of* uses wordy and non-standard diction. Also, the two ideas are not strongly coordinated in the original phrasing. Choice (C) uses parallel phrasing to strengthen the coordination between the ideas, provides a more logical coordinator, *in fact*, and uses more concise and standard diction.

---

13. **A** The original phrasing is best. Since the *feeling* in the second clause is in the subjunctive mood, because it is counter to fact, the correct verb form is *were*.

14. **C** The *phrase every member* is singular, but the pronoun *their* is plural. Choice C provides pronoun-antecedent agreement.

PRACTICE TEST 4

ANSWER SHEET

Last Name: _____   First Name: _____

Date: _____   Testing Location: _____

Directions for Test

- Remove these answer sheets from the book and use them to record your answers to this test.
- This test will require 3 hours and 20 minutes to complete. Take this test in one sitting.
- The time allotment for each section is written clearly at the beginning of each section. This test contains six 25-minute sections, two 20-minute sections, and one 10-minute section.
- This test is 25 minutes shorter than the actual SAT, which will include a 25-minute "experimental" section that does not count toward your score. That section has been omitted from this test.
- You may take one short break during the test, of no more than 10 minutes in length.
- You may only work on one section at any given time.
- You must stop ALL work on a section when time is called.
- If you finish a section before the time has elapsed, check your work on that section. You may NOT work on any other section.
- Do not waste time on questions that seem too difficult for you.
- Use the test book for scratchwork, but you will receive credit only for answers that are marked on the answer sheets.
- You will receive one point for every correct answer.
- You will receive no points for an omitted question.
- For each wrong answer on any multiple-choice question, your score will be reduced by ¼ point.
- For each wrong answer on any numerical "grid-in" question, you will receive no deduction.

SECTION 2

1. Ⓐ Ⓑ Ⓒ Ⓓ Ⓔ 11. Ⓐ Ⓑ Ⓒ Ⓓ Ⓔ 21. Ⓐ Ⓑ Ⓒ Ⓓ Ⓔ 31. Ⓐ Ⓑ Ⓒ Ⓓ Ⓔ
2. Ⓐ Ⓑ Ⓒ Ⓓ Ⓔ 12. Ⓐ Ⓑ Ⓒ Ⓓ Ⓔ 22. Ⓐ Ⓑ Ⓒ Ⓓ Ⓔ 32. Ⓐ Ⓑ Ⓒ Ⓓ Ⓔ
3. Ⓐ Ⓑ Ⓒ Ⓓ Ⓔ 13. Ⓐ Ⓑ Ⓒ Ⓓ Ⓔ 23. Ⓐ Ⓑ Ⓒ Ⓓ Ⓔ 33. Ⓐ Ⓑ Ⓒ Ⓓ Ⓔ
4. Ⓐ Ⓑ Ⓒ Ⓓ Ⓔ 14. Ⓐ Ⓑ Ⓒ Ⓓ Ⓔ 24. Ⓐ Ⓑ Ⓒ Ⓓ Ⓔ 34. Ⓐ Ⓑ Ⓒ Ⓓ Ⓔ
5. Ⓐ Ⓑ Ⓒ Ⓓ Ⓔ 15. Ⓐ Ⓑ Ⓒ Ⓓ Ⓔ 25. Ⓐ Ⓑ Ⓒ Ⓓ Ⓔ 35. Ⓐ Ⓑ Ⓒ Ⓓ Ⓔ
6. Ⓐ Ⓑ Ⓒ Ⓓ Ⓔ 16. Ⓐ Ⓑ Ⓒ Ⓓ Ⓔ 26. Ⓐ Ⓑ Ⓒ Ⓓ Ⓔ 36. Ⓐ Ⓑ Ⓒ Ⓓ Ⓔ
7. Ⓐ Ⓑ Ⓒ Ⓓ Ⓔ 17. Ⓐ Ⓑ Ⓒ Ⓓ Ⓔ 27. Ⓐ Ⓑ Ⓒ Ⓓ Ⓔ 37. Ⓐ Ⓑ Ⓒ Ⓓ Ⓔ
8. Ⓐ Ⓑ Ⓒ Ⓓ Ⓔ 18. Ⓐ Ⓑ Ⓒ Ⓓ Ⓔ 28. Ⓐ Ⓑ Ⓒ Ⓓ Ⓔ 38. Ⓐ Ⓑ Ⓒ Ⓓ Ⓔ
9. Ⓐ Ⓑ Ⓒ Ⓓ Ⓔ 19. Ⓐ Ⓑ Ⓒ Ⓓ Ⓔ 29. Ⓐ Ⓑ Ⓒ Ⓓ Ⓔ 39. Ⓐ Ⓑ Ⓒ Ⓓ Ⓔ
10. Ⓐ Ⓑ Ⓒ Ⓓ Ⓔ 20. Ⓐ Ⓑ Ⓒ Ⓓ Ⓔ 30. Ⓐ Ⓑ Ⓒ Ⓓ Ⓔ 40. Ⓐ Ⓑ Ⓒ Ⓓ Ⓔ

SECTION 3

1. Ⓐ Ⓑ Ⓒ Ⓓ Ⓔ 11. Ⓐ Ⓑ Ⓒ Ⓓ Ⓔ 21. Ⓐ Ⓑ Ⓒ Ⓓ Ⓔ 31. Ⓐ Ⓑ Ⓒ Ⓓ Ⓔ
2. Ⓐ Ⓑ Ⓒ Ⓓ Ⓔ 12. Ⓐ Ⓑ Ⓒ Ⓓ Ⓔ 22. Ⓐ Ⓑ Ⓒ Ⓓ Ⓔ 32. Ⓐ Ⓑ Ⓒ Ⓓ Ⓔ
3. Ⓐ Ⓑ Ⓒ Ⓓ Ⓔ 13. Ⓐ Ⓑ Ⓒ Ⓓ Ⓔ 23. Ⓐ Ⓑ Ⓒ Ⓓ Ⓔ 33. Ⓐ Ⓑ Ⓒ Ⓓ Ⓔ
4. Ⓐ Ⓑ Ⓒ Ⓓ Ⓔ 14. Ⓐ Ⓑ Ⓒ Ⓓ Ⓔ 24. Ⓐ Ⓑ Ⓒ Ⓓ Ⓔ 34. Ⓐ Ⓑ Ⓒ Ⓓ Ⓔ
5. Ⓐ Ⓑ Ⓒ Ⓓ Ⓔ 15. Ⓐ Ⓑ Ⓒ Ⓓ Ⓔ 25. Ⓐ Ⓑ Ⓒ Ⓓ Ⓔ 35. Ⓐ Ⓑ Ⓒ Ⓓ Ⓔ
6. Ⓐ Ⓑ Ⓒ Ⓓ Ⓔ 16. Ⓐ Ⓑ Ⓒ Ⓓ Ⓔ 26. Ⓐ Ⓑ Ⓒ Ⓓ Ⓔ 36. Ⓐ Ⓑ Ⓒ Ⓓ Ⓔ
7. Ⓐ Ⓑ Ⓒ Ⓓ Ⓔ 17. Ⓐ Ⓑ Ⓒ Ⓓ Ⓔ 27. Ⓐ Ⓑ Ⓒ Ⓓ Ⓔ 37. Ⓐ Ⓑ Ⓒ Ⓓ Ⓔ
8. Ⓐ Ⓑ Ⓒ Ⓓ Ⓔ 18. Ⓐ Ⓑ Ⓒ Ⓓ Ⓔ 28. Ⓐ Ⓑ Ⓒ Ⓓ Ⓔ 38. Ⓐ Ⓑ Ⓒ Ⓓ Ⓔ
9. Ⓐ Ⓑ Ⓒ Ⓓ Ⓔ 19. Ⓐ Ⓑ Ⓒ Ⓓ Ⓔ 29. Ⓐ Ⓑ Ⓒ Ⓓ Ⓔ 39. Ⓐ Ⓑ Ⓒ Ⓓ Ⓔ
10. Ⓐ Ⓑ Ⓒ Ⓓ Ⓔ 20. Ⓐ Ⓑ Ⓒ Ⓓ Ⓔ 30. Ⓐ Ⓑ Ⓒ Ⓓ Ⓔ 40. Ⓐ Ⓑ Ⓒ Ⓓ Ⓔ

ANSWER SHEET

SECTION 4

1. Ⓐ Ⓑ Ⓒ Ⓓ Ⓔ   11. Ⓐ Ⓑ Ⓒ Ⓓ Ⓔ   21. Ⓐ Ⓑ Ⓒ Ⓓ Ⓔ   31. Ⓐ Ⓑ Ⓒ Ⓓ Ⓔ
2. Ⓐ Ⓑ Ⓒ Ⓓ Ⓔ   12. Ⓐ Ⓑ Ⓒ Ⓓ Ⓔ   22. Ⓐ Ⓑ Ⓒ Ⓓ Ⓔ   32. Ⓐ Ⓑ Ⓒ Ⓓ Ⓔ
3. Ⓐ Ⓑ Ⓒ Ⓓ Ⓔ   13. Ⓐ Ⓑ Ⓒ Ⓓ Ⓔ   23. Ⓐ Ⓑ Ⓒ Ⓓ Ⓔ   33. Ⓐ Ⓑ Ⓒ Ⓓ Ⓔ
4. Ⓐ Ⓑ Ⓒ Ⓓ Ⓔ   14. Ⓐ Ⓑ Ⓒ Ⓓ Ⓔ   24. Ⓐ Ⓑ Ⓒ Ⓓ Ⓔ   34. Ⓐ Ⓑ Ⓒ Ⓓ Ⓔ
5. Ⓐ Ⓑ Ⓒ Ⓓ Ⓔ   15. Ⓐ Ⓑ Ⓒ Ⓓ Ⓔ   25. Ⓐ Ⓑ Ⓒ Ⓓ Ⓔ   35. Ⓐ Ⓑ Ⓒ Ⓓ Ⓔ
6. Ⓐ Ⓑ Ⓒ Ⓓ Ⓔ   16. Ⓐ Ⓑ Ⓒ Ⓓ Ⓔ   26. Ⓐ Ⓑ Ⓒ Ⓓ Ⓔ   36. Ⓐ Ⓑ Ⓒ Ⓓ Ⓔ
7. Ⓐ Ⓑ Ⓒ Ⓓ Ⓔ   17. Ⓐ Ⓑ Ⓒ Ⓓ Ⓔ   27. Ⓐ Ⓑ Ⓒ Ⓓ Ⓔ   37. Ⓐ Ⓑ Ⓒ Ⓓ Ⓔ
8. Ⓐ Ⓑ Ⓒ Ⓓ Ⓔ   18. Ⓐ Ⓑ Ⓒ Ⓓ Ⓔ   28. Ⓐ Ⓑ Ⓒ Ⓓ Ⓔ   38. Ⓐ Ⓑ Ⓒ Ⓓ Ⓔ
9. Ⓐ Ⓑ Ⓒ Ⓓ Ⓔ   19. Ⓐ Ⓑ Ⓒ Ⓓ Ⓔ   29. Ⓐ Ⓑ Ⓒ Ⓓ Ⓔ   39. Ⓐ Ⓑ Ⓒ Ⓓ Ⓔ
10. Ⓐ Ⓑ Ⓒ Ⓓ Ⓔ   20. Ⓐ Ⓑ Ⓒ Ⓓ Ⓔ   30. Ⓐ Ⓑ Ⓒ Ⓓ Ⓔ   40. Ⓐ Ⓑ Ⓒ Ⓓ Ⓔ

SECTION 5

1. Ⓐ Ⓑ Ⓒ Ⓓ Ⓔ   5. Ⓐ Ⓑ Ⓒ Ⓓ Ⓔ
2. Ⓐ Ⓑ Ⓒ Ⓓ Ⓔ   6. Ⓐ Ⓑ Ⓒ Ⓓ Ⓔ
3. Ⓐ Ⓑ Ⓒ Ⓓ Ⓔ   7. Ⓐ Ⓑ Ⓒ Ⓓ Ⓔ
4. Ⓐ Ⓑ Ⓒ Ⓓ Ⓔ   8. Ⓐ Ⓑ Ⓒ Ⓓ Ⓔ

9.   10.   11.   12.   13.

14.   15.   16.   17.   18.

(Grid-in bubble answer fields numbered 0–9)

ANSWER SHEET

SECTION 6

1. Ⓐ Ⓑ Ⓒ Ⓓ Ⓔ   11. Ⓐ Ⓑ Ⓒ Ⓓ Ⓔ   21. Ⓐ Ⓑ Ⓒ Ⓓ Ⓔ   31. Ⓐ Ⓑ Ⓒ Ⓓ Ⓔ
2. Ⓐ Ⓑ Ⓒ Ⓓ Ⓔ   12. Ⓐ Ⓑ Ⓒ Ⓓ Ⓔ   22. Ⓐ Ⓑ Ⓒ Ⓓ Ⓔ   32. Ⓐ Ⓑ Ⓒ Ⓓ Ⓔ
3. Ⓐ Ⓑ Ⓒ Ⓓ Ⓔ   13. Ⓐ Ⓑ Ⓒ Ⓓ Ⓔ   23. Ⓐ Ⓑ Ⓒ Ⓓ Ⓔ   33. Ⓐ Ⓑ Ⓒ Ⓓ Ⓔ
4. Ⓐ Ⓑ Ⓒ Ⓓ Ⓔ   14. Ⓐ Ⓑ Ⓒ Ⓓ Ⓔ   24. Ⓐ Ⓑ Ⓒ Ⓓ Ⓔ   34. Ⓐ Ⓑ Ⓒ Ⓓ Ⓔ
5. Ⓐ Ⓑ Ⓒ Ⓓ Ⓔ   15. Ⓐ Ⓑ Ⓒ Ⓓ Ⓔ   25. Ⓐ Ⓑ Ⓒ Ⓓ Ⓔ   35. Ⓐ Ⓑ Ⓒ Ⓓ Ⓔ
6. Ⓐ Ⓑ Ⓒ Ⓓ Ⓔ   16. Ⓐ Ⓑ Ⓒ Ⓓ Ⓔ   26. Ⓐ Ⓑ Ⓒ Ⓓ Ⓔ   36. Ⓐ Ⓑ Ⓒ Ⓓ Ⓔ
7. Ⓐ Ⓑ Ⓒ Ⓓ Ⓔ   17. Ⓐ Ⓑ Ⓒ Ⓓ Ⓔ   27. Ⓐ Ⓑ Ⓒ Ⓓ Ⓔ   37. Ⓐ Ⓑ Ⓒ Ⓓ Ⓔ
8. Ⓐ Ⓑ Ⓒ Ⓓ Ⓔ   18. Ⓐ Ⓑ Ⓒ Ⓓ Ⓔ   28. Ⓐ Ⓑ Ⓒ Ⓓ Ⓔ   38. Ⓐ Ⓑ Ⓒ Ⓓ Ⓔ
9. Ⓐ Ⓑ Ⓒ Ⓓ Ⓔ   19. Ⓐ Ⓑ Ⓒ Ⓓ Ⓔ   29. Ⓐ Ⓑ Ⓒ Ⓓ Ⓔ   39. Ⓐ Ⓑ Ⓒ Ⓓ Ⓔ
10. Ⓐ Ⓑ Ⓒ Ⓓ Ⓔ   20. Ⓐ Ⓑ Ⓒ Ⓓ Ⓔ   30. Ⓐ Ⓑ Ⓒ Ⓓ Ⓔ   40. Ⓐ Ⓑ Ⓒ Ⓓ Ⓔ

SECTION 7

1. Ⓐ Ⓑ Ⓒ Ⓓ Ⓔ   11. Ⓐ Ⓑ Ⓒ Ⓓ Ⓔ   21. Ⓐ Ⓑ Ⓒ Ⓓ Ⓔ   31. Ⓐ Ⓑ Ⓒ Ⓓ Ⓔ
2. Ⓐ Ⓑ Ⓒ Ⓓ Ⓔ   12. Ⓐ Ⓑ Ⓒ Ⓓ Ⓔ   22. Ⓐ Ⓑ Ⓒ Ⓓ Ⓔ   32. Ⓐ Ⓑ Ⓒ Ⓓ Ⓔ
3. Ⓐ Ⓑ Ⓒ Ⓓ Ⓔ   13. Ⓐ Ⓑ Ⓒ Ⓓ Ⓔ   23. Ⓐ Ⓑ Ⓒ Ⓓ Ⓔ   33. Ⓐ Ⓑ Ⓒ Ⓓ Ⓔ
4. Ⓐ Ⓑ Ⓒ Ⓓ Ⓔ   14. Ⓐ Ⓑ Ⓒ Ⓓ Ⓔ   24. Ⓐ Ⓑ Ⓒ Ⓓ Ⓔ   34. Ⓐ Ⓑ Ⓒ Ⓓ Ⓔ
5. Ⓐ Ⓑ Ⓒ Ⓓ Ⓔ   15. Ⓐ Ⓑ Ⓒ Ⓓ Ⓔ   25. Ⓐ Ⓑ Ⓒ Ⓓ Ⓔ   35. Ⓐ Ⓑ Ⓒ Ⓓ Ⓔ
6. Ⓐ Ⓑ Ⓒ Ⓓ Ⓔ   16. Ⓐ Ⓑ Ⓒ Ⓓ Ⓔ   26. Ⓐ Ⓑ Ⓒ Ⓓ Ⓔ   36. Ⓐ Ⓑ Ⓒ Ⓓ Ⓔ
7. Ⓐ Ⓑ Ⓒ Ⓓ Ⓔ   17. Ⓐ Ⓑ Ⓒ Ⓓ Ⓔ   27. Ⓐ Ⓑ Ⓒ Ⓓ Ⓔ   37. Ⓐ Ⓑ Ⓒ Ⓓ Ⓔ
8. Ⓐ Ⓑ Ⓒ Ⓓ Ⓔ   18. Ⓐ Ⓑ Ⓒ Ⓓ Ⓔ   28. Ⓐ Ⓑ Ⓒ Ⓓ Ⓔ   38. Ⓐ Ⓑ Ⓒ Ⓓ Ⓔ
9. Ⓐ Ⓑ Ⓒ Ⓓ Ⓔ   19. Ⓐ Ⓑ Ⓒ Ⓓ Ⓔ   29. Ⓐ Ⓑ Ⓒ Ⓓ Ⓔ   39. Ⓐ Ⓑ Ⓒ Ⓓ Ⓔ
10. Ⓐ Ⓑ Ⓒ Ⓓ Ⓔ   20. Ⓐ Ⓑ Ⓒ Ⓓ Ⓔ   30. Ⓐ Ⓑ Ⓒ Ⓓ Ⓔ   40. Ⓐ Ⓑ Ⓒ Ⓓ Ⓔ

SECTION 8

1. Ⓐ Ⓑ Ⓒ Ⓓ Ⓔ   11. Ⓐ Ⓑ Ⓒ Ⓓ Ⓔ   21. Ⓐ Ⓑ Ⓒ Ⓓ Ⓔ   31. Ⓐ Ⓑ Ⓒ Ⓓ Ⓔ
2. Ⓐ Ⓑ Ⓒ Ⓓ Ⓔ   12. Ⓐ Ⓑ Ⓒ Ⓓ Ⓔ   22. Ⓐ Ⓑ Ⓒ Ⓓ Ⓔ   32. Ⓐ Ⓑ Ⓒ Ⓓ Ⓔ
3. Ⓐ Ⓑ Ⓒ Ⓓ Ⓔ   13. Ⓐ Ⓑ Ⓒ Ⓓ Ⓔ   23. Ⓐ Ⓑ Ⓒ Ⓓ Ⓔ   33. Ⓐ Ⓑ Ⓒ Ⓓ Ⓔ
4. Ⓐ Ⓑ Ⓒ Ⓓ Ⓔ   14. Ⓐ Ⓑ Ⓒ Ⓓ Ⓔ   24. Ⓐ Ⓑ Ⓒ Ⓓ Ⓔ   34. Ⓐ Ⓑ Ⓒ Ⓓ Ⓔ
5. Ⓐ Ⓑ Ⓒ Ⓓ Ⓔ   15. Ⓐ Ⓑ Ⓒ Ⓓ Ⓔ   25. Ⓐ Ⓑ Ⓒ Ⓓ Ⓔ   35. Ⓐ Ⓑ Ⓒ Ⓓ Ⓔ
6. Ⓐ Ⓑ Ⓒ Ⓓ Ⓔ   16. Ⓐ Ⓑ Ⓒ Ⓓ Ⓔ   26. Ⓐ Ⓑ Ⓒ Ⓓ Ⓔ   36. Ⓐ Ⓑ Ⓒ Ⓓ Ⓔ
7. Ⓐ Ⓑ Ⓒ Ⓓ Ⓔ   17. Ⓐ Ⓑ Ⓒ Ⓓ Ⓔ   27. Ⓐ Ⓑ Ⓒ Ⓓ Ⓔ   37. Ⓐ Ⓑ Ⓒ Ⓓ Ⓔ
8. Ⓐ Ⓑ Ⓒ Ⓓ Ⓔ   18. Ⓐ Ⓑ Ⓒ Ⓓ Ⓔ   28. Ⓐ Ⓑ Ⓒ Ⓓ Ⓔ   38. Ⓐ Ⓑ Ⓒ Ⓓ Ⓔ
9. Ⓐ Ⓑ Ⓒ Ⓓ Ⓔ   19. Ⓐ Ⓑ Ⓒ Ⓓ Ⓔ   29. Ⓐ Ⓑ Ⓒ Ⓓ Ⓔ   39. Ⓐ Ⓑ Ⓒ Ⓓ Ⓔ
10. Ⓐ Ⓑ Ⓒ Ⓓ Ⓔ   20. Ⓐ Ⓑ Ⓒ Ⓓ Ⓔ   30. Ⓐ Ⓑ Ⓒ Ⓓ Ⓔ   40. Ⓐ Ⓑ Ⓒ Ⓓ Ⓔ

SECTION 9

1. Ⓐ Ⓑ Ⓒ Ⓓ Ⓔ   11. Ⓐ Ⓑ Ⓒ Ⓓ Ⓔ   21. Ⓐ Ⓑ Ⓒ Ⓓ Ⓔ   31. Ⓐ Ⓑ Ⓒ Ⓓ Ⓔ
2. Ⓐ Ⓑ Ⓒ Ⓓ Ⓔ   12. Ⓐ Ⓑ Ⓒ Ⓓ Ⓔ   22. Ⓐ Ⓑ Ⓒ Ⓓ Ⓔ   32. Ⓐ Ⓑ Ⓒ Ⓓ Ⓔ
3. Ⓐ Ⓑ Ⓒ Ⓓ Ⓔ   13. Ⓐ Ⓑ Ⓒ Ⓓ Ⓔ   23. Ⓐ Ⓑ Ⓒ Ⓓ Ⓔ   33. Ⓐ Ⓑ Ⓒ Ⓓ Ⓔ
4. Ⓐ Ⓑ Ⓒ Ⓓ Ⓔ   14. Ⓐ Ⓑ Ⓒ Ⓓ Ⓔ   24. Ⓐ Ⓑ Ⓒ Ⓓ Ⓔ   34. Ⓐ Ⓑ Ⓒ Ⓓ Ⓔ
5. Ⓐ Ⓑ Ⓒ Ⓓ Ⓔ   15. Ⓐ Ⓑ Ⓒ Ⓓ Ⓔ   25. Ⓐ Ⓑ Ⓒ Ⓓ Ⓔ   35. Ⓐ Ⓑ Ⓒ Ⓓ Ⓔ
6. Ⓐ Ⓑ Ⓒ Ⓓ Ⓔ   16. Ⓐ Ⓑ Ⓒ Ⓓ Ⓔ   26. Ⓐ Ⓑ Ⓒ Ⓓ Ⓔ   36. Ⓐ Ⓑ Ⓒ Ⓓ Ⓔ
7. Ⓐ Ⓑ Ⓒ Ⓓ Ⓔ   17. Ⓐ Ⓑ Ⓒ Ⓓ Ⓔ   27. Ⓐ Ⓑ Ⓒ Ⓓ Ⓔ   37. Ⓐ Ⓑ Ⓒ Ⓓ Ⓔ
8. Ⓐ Ⓑ Ⓒ Ⓓ Ⓔ   18. Ⓐ Ⓑ Ⓒ Ⓓ Ⓔ   28. Ⓐ Ⓑ Ⓒ Ⓓ Ⓔ   38. Ⓐ Ⓑ Ⓒ Ⓓ Ⓔ
9. Ⓐ Ⓑ Ⓒ Ⓓ Ⓔ   19. Ⓐ Ⓑ Ⓒ Ⓓ Ⓔ   29. Ⓐ Ⓑ Ⓒ Ⓓ Ⓔ   39. Ⓐ Ⓑ Ⓒ Ⓓ Ⓔ
10. Ⓐ Ⓑ Ⓒ Ⓓ Ⓔ   20. Ⓐ Ⓑ Ⓒ Ⓓ Ⓔ   30. Ⓐ Ⓑ Ⓒ Ⓓ Ⓔ   40. Ⓐ Ⓑ Ⓒ Ⓓ Ⓔ

Section 1

Time—25 minutes
1 Question

Directions for Writing the Essay

Plan and write an essay that answers the question below. Do NOT write on another topic. An essay on another topic will receive a score of 0.

Two readers will grade your essay based on how well you develop your point of view, organize and explain your ideas, use specific and relevant examples to support your thesis, and use clear and effective language. How well you write is much more important than how much you write, but to cover the topic adequately you should plan to write several paragraphs.

Your essay must be written on separate lined sheets of paper. Keep your handwriting to a reasonable size. Your essay will be read by people who are not familiar with your handwriting, so write legibly.

You may use this sheet for notes and outlining, but these will not be graded as part of your essay.

Consider carefully the issue discussed in the following passage, then write an essay that answers the question posed in the assignment.

> *None know the unfortunate and the fortunate do not know themselves.*
> —Benjamin Franklin

Assignment: **Are people today generally too unaware of their good fortune?** Write an essay in which you answer this question and support your position logically with examples from literature, the arts, history, politics, science and technology, current events, or your experience or observation.

Write your essay on separate sheets of paper.

Section 2

Time—25 minutes
24 Questions

2 ➤

> Each sentence below has one or two blanks, each blank indicating that something has been omitted. Beneath the sentence are five words or sets of words labeled A through E. Choose the word or set of words that, when inserted in the sentence, best fits the meaning of the sentence as a whole.
>
> Example:
>
> Medieval kingdoms did not become constitutional republics overnight; on the contrary, the change was ——.
>
> (A) unpopular   (B) unexpected
> (C) advantageous   (D) sufficient
> (E) gradual
>
> **Correct response: (E)**

1 After the doctor administered the ——, Ingrid could no longer feel the left side of her face, allowing the doctor to stitch the wound without causing any further pain.

(A) emollient   (B) antibody
(C) antidote   (D) cathartic
(E) anesthetic

2 This particular strain of the flu is extremely —— and leaves its victims ——, often unable even to get out of bed.

(A) benign . . exhausted
(B) mild . . incapacitated
(C) harmless . . energized
(D) debilitating . . lethargic
(E) popular . . revitalized

3 The earthquake —— the entire village; not a single building survived the disaster and thousands were injured.

(A) preserved   (B) reiterated
(C) debunked   (D) razed
(E) salvaged

4 The newly released version of Shakespeare's *Othello* was condemned by critics for being just another —— remake that fails to bring anything new to the movie screen.

(A) innovative   (B) hackneyed
(C) novel   (D) quixotic
(E) profound

5 After the sharp economic downturn, the airline industry was on the verge of collapse, and many companies survived only because of a large government —— that provided a vital —— of cash that helped pay off the accumulated debt.

(A) subsidy . . infusion
(B) censure . . influx
(C) endowment . . emission
(D) endorsement . . alimony
(E) allowance . . emanation

6 Having been —— himself in college, Mr. Davis found it difficult to —— his daughter for her inability to stay away from parties while at school.

(A) an ascetic . . castigate
(B) an altruist . . extol
(C) a sybarite . . censure
(D) a philanthropist . . accommodate
(E) a hedonist . . rebuke

7 While writing *Walden*, Henry David Thoreau lived alone in a one room shack, but did not live the life of ——; he made many trips to the nearby village and entertained frequently at his house.

(A) a miscreant   (B) an exhibitionist
(C) a recluse   (D) a curator
(E) a polemicist

8 The saleswoman has a —— that helps her sell more cars than anyone else at the dealership; she is —— in her efforts to close a deal.

(A) doggedness . . inexorable
(B) pertinacity . . lackadaisical
(C) diffidence . . submissive
(D) temerity . . munificent
(E) tenacity . . indolent

GO ON TO THE NEXT PAGE ▶▶▶

Each passage below is followed by one or two questions based on its content. Answer each question based on what is stated or implied in the passage that precedes it.

Questions 9–10 are based on the following passage.

Line   Strategy is the employment of the battle to gain the end of the war; it must therefore give an aim to the whole military action, which must be in accordance with the object
5   of the war; in other words, strategy forms the plan of the war; and to this end it links together the series of acts which are to lead to the final decision; that is to say it makes the plans for the separate campaigns and
10   regulates the combats to be fought in each. As these are all things which to a great extent can only be determined on conjectures some of which turn out incorrect, while a number of other arrangements pertaining to details
15   cannot be made at all beforehand, it follows, as a matter of course, that strategy must go with the army to the field in order to arrange the particulars on the spot, and to make the modifications to the general plan which
20   incessantly become necessary in war.

9 In line 4, "object" most nearly means

(A)   weapon   (B)   opposition
(C)   observation   (D)   goal
(E)   link

10 The reference to "modifications" in line 19 serves primarily to emphasize the observation that war is

(A)   dangerous   (B)   inspirational
(C)   unpredictable   (D)   easily controlled
(E)   an ancient art

Questions 11–12 are based on the following passage.

Line   It was a strange figure—like a child: yet not so like a child as like an old man, viewed through some supernatural medium, which gave him the appearance of having receded
5   from the view, and being diminished to a child's proportions. Its hair, which hung about its neck and down its back, was white as if with age; and yet the face had not a wrinkle in it, and the tenderest bloom was on
10   the skin. The arms were very long and muscular; the hands the same, as if its hold were of uncommon strength. Its legs and feet, most delicately formed, were, like those upper members, bare. It wore a tunic of the
15   purest white and round its waist was bound a lustrous belt, the sheen of which was beautiful. It held a branch of fresh green holly in its hand; and, in singular contradiction of that wintry emblem, had its dress trimmed with
20   summer flowers.

11 In line 3, the word "medium" most nearly means

(A)   average   (B)   clairvoyant
(C)   substance   (D)   artistic work
(E)   impossibility

12 The reference to the "bloom" (line 9) serves primarily to emphasize the figure's

(A)   old age   (B)   long hair
(C)   eeriness   (D)   strength
(E)   youthful appearance

First passage: *On War*, Clausewitz; Bibliomania.com
Second passage: *A Christmas Carol*, Charles Dickens, 1893

GO ON TO THE NEXT PAGE ▸▸▸

The questions below are based on the content of the preceding passage. The questions are to be answered on the basis of what is stated or implied in the passage itself or the introductory material that precedes the passage.

Questions 13–17 are based on the following passage.

The following passage is excerpted from a recent book written by Dr. Patricia McConnell, an applied animal behaviorist and dog trainer, that discusses the relationship between dogs and humans.

Line   All dogs are brilliant at perceiving the
        slightest movement that we make, and they
        assume that each tiny motion has meaning.
        So do we humans, if you think about it.
5   Remember that minuscule turn of the head
        that caught your attention when you were
        dating? Think about how little someone's lips
        have to move to change a sweet smile into a
        smirk. How far does an eyebrow have to rise
10   to change the message we read from the face
        it's on–a tenth of an inch? You'd think that
        we would automatically generalize this
        common knowledge to our interactions with
        our dogs. But we don't. We are often
15   oblivious to how we're moving around our
        dogs. It seems to be very human not to know
        what we're doing with our body, unconscious
        of where our hands are or that we just tilted
        our head. We radiate random signals like
20   some crazed semaphore flag, while our dogs
        watch in confusion, their eyes rolling around
        in circles like cartoon dogs.
            These visual signals, like all the rest of our
        actions, have a profound influence on what
25   our dogs do. Who dogs are and how they
        behave are partly defined by who we humans
        are and how we ourselves behave. Domestic
        dogs, by definition, share their lives with
        another species: us.
30   Our species shares so much with dogs. If
        you look across the vast range of all animal
        life, from beetles to bears, humans and dogs
        are more alike than we are different. Like
        dogs, we make milk for our young and raise

35   them in a pack. Our babies have lots to learn
        while growing up; we hunt cooperatively; we
        play silly games even as adults; we snore; we
        scratch and blink and yawn on sunny
        afternoons. Look at what Pam Brown, a New
40   Zealand poet, had to say about people and
        dogs in the book *Bond for Life*:
            "Humankind is drawn to dogs because they
            are so like ourselves—bumbling,
            affectionate, confused, easily disappointed,
45   eager to be amused, grateful for kindness
            and the least attention."
            These similarities allow the members of
        two different species to live together
        intimately, sharing food, recreation, and even
50   bearing young together. Lots of animals live
        closely linked to others, but our level of
        connection with our dogs is profound.
            Most of us exercise with our dogs, play
        with our dogs, eat at the same time as our dogs
55   (and sometimes the same food), and sleep
        with our dogs. Some of us still depend on our
        dogs for our work. Sheep ranchers in
        Wyoming and dairy farmers in Wisconsin
        need their dogs as much as or more than
60   they do machinery or high-tech feeding
        systems. We know that dogs enrich the lives
        of many of us, providing comfort and joy to
        millions around the world. Studies even show
        that they decrease the probability of a second
65   heart attack. We don't put up with shedding
        and barking and carrying pooper scoopers on
        walks for nothing.

13   Which of the following is the best title for
        this passage?

(A)   Visual Acuity in Dogs
(B)   The Ties That Bind Dogs and Humans
(C)   The Utility of Animals in the
      Workplace
(D)   Close Relationships in the Animal
      Kingdom
(E)   How to Communicate with
      your Dog

GO ON TO THE NEXT PAGE ▸▸▸

14 The passage mentions the "minuscule turn of the head" (line 5) primarily as an example of

(A) a common gesture that dogs perform
(B) a small action that has meaning to humans
(C) something that dogs often detect but humans don't
(D) something that is difficult to measure
(E) an action that binds dogs and humans

15 The reference to the "semaphore flag" in line 20 serves primarily to emphasize the author's observation that dogs

(A) are more confused than they seem
(B) are in constant motion
(C) cannot detect many of the signals that are intended for them
(D) are capable of conveying sophisticated information
(E) can detect unintended signals

16 The passage indicates that humans and dogs are alike in all the following aspects EXCEPT

(A) eating habits
(B) the ability to detect small movements
(C) child rearing practices
(D) the need for attention
(E) acute hearing

17 The author mentions "high-tech feeding systems" (lines 60–61) as examples of

(A) technologies that can benefit dogs
(B) resources for all pet owners
(C) advances that have yet to be developed
(D) equipment that some farmers find necessary
(E) systems that require further study

The questions below are based on the content of the preceding passage. The questions are to be answered on the basis of what is stated or implied in the passage itself or the introductory material that precedes the passage.

2

Questions 18–24 are based on the following passage.

The following is an excerpt from an essay written by Ralph Waldo Emerson in 1841.

Line What right have I to write on Prudence, whereof I have little, and that of the negative sort? My prudence consists in avoiding and going without, not in the inventing of means
5 and methods, not in adroit steering, not in gentle repairing. I have no skill to make money spend well, no genius in my economy, and whoever sees my garden discovers that I must have some other garden. Yet I love
10 facts, and hate lubricity[1] and people without perception. Then I have the same title to write on prudence that I have to write on poetry or holiness. We write from aspiration and antagonism, as well as from experience.
15 We paint those qualities which we do not possess. The poet admires the man of energy and tactics; the merchant breeds his son for the church or the bar; and where a man is not vain and egotistic you shall find what he
20 has not by his praise. Moreover it would be hardly honest in me not to balance these fine lyric words of Love and Friendship with words of coarser sound, and whilst my debt to my senses is real and constant, not to own
25 it in passing.

Prudence is the virtue of the senses. It is the science of appearances. It is the outmost action of the inward life. It is God taking thought for oxen. It moves matter after the
30 laws of matter. It is content to seek health of body by complying with physical conditions, and health of mind by the laws of the intellect.

The world of the senses is a world of shows; it does not exist for itself, but has a
35 symbolic character; and a true prudence or law of shows recognizes the co-presence of other laws and knows that its own office is

[1]lewdness or shiftiness

GO ON TO THE NEXT PAGE ▸▸▸

2 ➤

subaltern;[2] knows that it is surface and not centre where it works. Prudence is false when
40 detached. It is legitimate when it is the Natural History of the soul incarnate, when it unfolds the beauty of laws within the narrow scope of the senses.

There are all degrees of proficiency in
45 knowledge of the world. It is sufficient to our present purpose to indicate three. One class live to the utility of the symbol, esteeming health and wealth a final good. Another class live above this mark to the beauty of the
50 symbol, as the poet and artist and the naturalist and man of science. A third class live above the beauty of the symbol to the beauty of the thing signified; these are wise men. The first class have common sense; the
55 second, taste; and the third, spiritual perception. Once in a long time, a man traverses the whole scale, and sees and enjoys the symbol solidly, then also has a clear eye for its beauty, and lastly, whilst he pitches his
60 tent on this sacred volcanic isle of nature, does not offer to build houses and barns thereon, reverencing the splendor of the God which he sees bursting through each chink and cranny.
65   The world is filled with the proverbs and acts of a base prudence, which is a devotion to matter, as if we possessed no other faculties than the palate, the nose, the touch, the eye and ear; a prudence which never subscribes,
70 which never gives, which seldom lends, and asks but one question of any project: will it bake bread? This is a disease like a thickening of the skin until the vital organs are destroyed. But culture, revealing the high
75 origin of the apparent world and aiming at the perfection of the man as the end, degrades every thing else, as health and bodily life, into means. It sees prudence not to be a several[3] faculty, but a name for
80 wisdom and virtue conversing with the body and its wants. Cultivated men always feel and speak so, as if a great fortune, the achievement of a civil or social measure, great personal influence, a graceful and commanding
85 address, had their value as proofs of the energy of the spirit. If a man lose his balance and immerse himself in any trades or pleasures for their own sake, he may be a good wheel or pin, but he is not a cultivated man.

[2]secondary
[3]distinct

---

18 In saying that others discover that the author "must have some other garden" (line 9), he suggests that he

(A) owns a great deal of land
(B) is not adept at growing things
(C) enjoys gardening a great deal
(D) is frequently disoriented
(E) wants to acquire more land

19 In line 11, the word "title" most nearly means

(A) ownership
(B) name
(C) literary work
(D) right
(E) opposition

20 In the first paragraph, the author argues that he is justified in writing about prudence because he

(A) exercises prudence in many different areas
(B) has written many stories with prudent characters
(C) understands the topic from studying classic philosophy
(D) admires prudence more than he possesses it
(E) is an expert gardener

21 According to the passage, members of the "third class" (line 51) are superior to the members of the other classes primarily in their ability to

(A) create art
(B) solve practical problems
(C) perceive supernatural qualities
(D) establish facts scientifically
(E) reason logically

GO ON TO THE NEXT PAGE ▶▶▶

22 The reference to "houses and barns" (line 61) serves primarily to emphasize the fact that one who "traverses the whole scale" (line 57) appreciates

(A) the transience of life
(B) the importance of sturdy construction
(C) the necessity of capturing the beauty of nature through art
(D) the nobility of farm life
(E) the dangers of religious fervor

23 The sentence "The world is filled with... will it bake bread?" (lines 65–72) suggests that the "base prudence" of proverbs is

(A) too preachy
(B) not taught with enough care
(C) too concerned with practical things
(D) insufficiently sensual
(E) difficult to understand

24 In the final paragraph, the author's attitude toward culture is best characterized as

(A) reverential
(B) jocular
(C) objective
(D) indifferent
(E) critical

2

STOP

You may check your work, on this section only, until time is called.

Section 3

Time—25 minutes
20 Questions

Directions for Multiple-Choice Questions

In this section, solve each problem, using any available space on the page for scratchwork. Then decide which is the best of the choices given and fill in the corresponding oval on the answer sheet.

- You may use a calculator on any problem. All numbers used are real numbers.
- Figures are drawn as accurately as possible EXCEPT when it is stated that the figure is not drawn to scale.
- All figures lie in a plane unless otherwise indicated.

Reference Information

$A = \pi r^2$ $A = \ell w$ $A = \frac{1}{2}bh$ $V = \ell wh$ $V = \pi r^2 h$ $c^2 = a^2 + b^2$ Special Right Triangles
$C = 2\pi r$

The arc of a circle measures 360°.
Every straight angle measures 180°.
The sum of the measures of the angles in a triangle is 180°.

---

1 How many CD cases, each holding 120 CDs, are needed to hold 20 dozen CDs? (1 dozen = 12 CDs)

(A) 1
(B) 2
(C) 3
(D) 4
(E) 5

2 Which of the following has the digit 4 in both the units place and the thousandths place?

(A) 4,004.040
(B) 4,000.400
(C) 3,004.004
(D) 3,040.444
(E) 4,040.004

3 If $f(x) = 2x^2 + 8$, what is the value of $f(8)$?

(A) 116
(B) 133
(C) 136
(D) 256
(E) 264

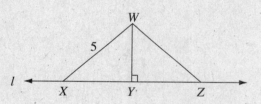

4 In the figure above, points X, Y, and Z lie on line l, and $\overline{WY}$ bisects $\overline{XZ}$. If $XZ = 8$, what is the length of $\overline{WY}$?

(A) 2
(B) 3
(C) 4
(D) $4\sqrt{3}$ (approximately 6.93)
(E) $5\sqrt{3}$ (approximately 8.66)

GO ON TO THE NEXT PAGE ▶▶▶

5 At a science fair, the prize money of $3,000 is to be split in the ratio 3:2:1 by the first, second, and third place finishers, respectively. What is the amount of the third prize?

(A) $500
(B) $1,000
(C) $1,500
(D) $2,000
(E) $2,500

6 If $(x - y) = -2$, then $(x - y)^2 =$

(A) −4
(B) −2
(C) 0
(D) 2
(E) 4

11	B	7	3
A	1	10	9
4	12	2	16
5	8	C	D

7 In the table above, all of the columns and rows have the same sum. What is the value of $A + B + C + D$?

(A) 48
(B) 56
(C) 62
(D) 74
(E) 90

8 If $a < b < -1$, which of the following has the greatest value?

(A) $-3a + b$
(B) $-(a-b)$
(C) $-(3a + b)$
(D) $3a$
(E) $a-b$

9 A piece of paper is folded in half about side AB. Cuts are then made along the dotted lines. Which of the following best represents the result when unfolded?

(A)

(B)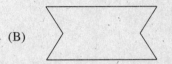

(C)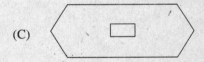

(D)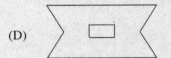

(E)

10 How many integers from the set of all integers from 1 to 100 inclusive are NOT the cube of an integer?

(A) 93
(B) 94
(C) 95
(D) 96
(E) 97

GO ON TO THE NEXT PAGE ▸▸▸

11 In a pet store, there are three times as many goldfish as there are tropical fish. There are twice as many orange goldfish as there are black goldfish. What is the probability that a randomly selected fish from the store is a black goldfish?

(A) $\dfrac{1}{12}$

(B) $\dfrac{1}{6}$

(C) $\dfrac{1}{4}$

(D) $\dfrac{1}{2}$

(E) $\dfrac{3}{4}$

12 The ideal gas law states that pressure, P, varies inversely as volume, V, and directly as the temperature, T. If $P = 700$ and $V = 10$, then $T = 350$. What is the value of T when $P = 500$ and $V = 20$?

(A) 20
(B) 120
(C) 200
(D) 350
(E) 500

$$x - 2y > 13$$
$$y + x < 13$$

13 Which of the following ordered pairs (x, y) is a solution of both of the inequalities above?

(A) (3, −1)
(B) (12, 3)
(C) (8, 3)
(D) (10, 2)
(E) (1, 5)

14 After Andrea gives Chris $10 and Liz $3, Chris gives $4 to Liz. At this point, Andrea has $10 more than Chris and $16 more than Liz. How much more money did Andrea have than Chris originally?

(A) $10
(B) $20
(C) $24
(D) $29
(E) $36

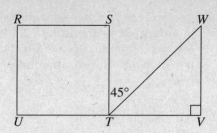

Note: Figure not drawn to scale.

15 In the figure above, points U, T, and V lie on the same line and point T is the midpoint of $\overline{UV}$. What is the ratio of the perimeter of square $RSTU$ to the perimeter of triangle TVW?

(A) $2 + \sqrt{2} : 4$

(B) $4 : 2 + \sqrt{2}$

(C) $2 : 1$

(D) $4 : 2 + \sqrt{3}$

(E) $2 + \sqrt{3} : 6$

16 A parking lot has 5 spots remaining and 5 different cars in line waiting to be parked. If one of the cars is too big to fit in the two outermost spots, in how many different ways can the five cars be arranged?

(A) 15
(B) 54
(C) 72
(D) 96
(E) 120

17 Seven students took a quiz and their average (arithmetic mean) score was 83. If the average score for three of the students was 79, what was the average score for the other four students?

(A) 85
(B) 86
(C) 87
(D) 88
(E) 89

Federal Hourly Minimum Wage History	
1974	$2.00
1976	$2.30
1978	$2.65
1980	$3.10
1982	$3.35

18 According to the data listed in the table above, the minimum wage in 1980 was what percent larger than the minimum wage in 1974?

(A)   30%
(B)   55%
(C)   64.5%
(D)   110%
(E)   155%

8, 13, 21...

19 After the first two terms in the sequence above, each subsequent term is the sum of the two immediately preceding numbers. For example, 21 = 13 + 8. How many of the first 60 terms of this sequence are odd?

(A)   20
(B)   30
(C)   33
(D)   40
(E)   44

20 A snow-removal company charges a business d dollars for removing any amount of snow from their parking lot up to 6 inches, and f dollars for each additional inch of snow. Which of the following represents the cost of hiring the company to shovel p inches of snow from the parking lot, if $p > 6$?

(A) $pd + pf$
(B) $fd + p$
(C) $f + d - p$
(D) $fp - 6f + 6d$
(E) $f(p - 6) + d$

STOP

You may check your work, on this section only, until time is called.

Section 4

Time—25 minutes
24 Questions

4

Each sentence below has one or two blanks, each blank indicating that something has been omitted. Beneath the sentence are five words or sets of words labeled A through E. Choose the word or set of words that, when inserted in the sentence, best fits the meaning of the sentence as a whole.

Example:

Medieval kingdoms did not become constitutional republics overnight; on the contrary, the change was ———.

(A) unpopular   (B) unexpected
(C) advantageous   (D) sufficient
(E) gradual

Correct response: (E)

1. Rita was understandably consumed by ____ when she was forced to put her beloved seventeen year-old cat to sleep.

(A) inversion (B) anguish
(C) frivolity (D) hilarity
(E) sluggishness

2. The doctors were astonished by the incredible rate at which the virus was ____; few had ever seen anything replicate at such a remarkable speed.

(A) pontificating (B) diverging
(C) saturating (D) proliferating
(E) dissipating

3. Despite being from the wealthiest family in Australia, Leah was ____ and sometimes even ____ with her money, refusing to waste even a few dollars.

(A) prudent . . munificent
(B) thrifty . . stingy
(C) frugal . . outspoken
(D) extravagant . . improvident
(E) reckless . . miserly

4. After two consecutive weeks of grueling midterms Tony got a much needed ____ from his studies with the arrival of spring break.

(A) continuance
(B) encore
(C) respite
(D) commencement
(E) conviction

5. Throughout his time in medical school, Emil has always been a ____; his ____ antics may have won favor with some of the doctors, but most could see through his superficial flattery.

(A) toady . . irreverent
(B) sycophant . . fawning
(C) lackey . . insubordinate
(D) mercenary . . intractable
(E) clairvoyant . . altruistic

Each passage below is followed by one or two questions based on its content. Answer each question based on what is stated or implied in the passage that precedes it.

Questions 6–7 are based on the following passage.

Line   Suppose that a mass attached to the end of a string is set in motion. The mass comes to rest at the top of its swing, then falls back in the other direction, gains speed, reaches
5   maximum speed at the bottom of its swing, rises on the other side, and again comes to rest at the top of its swing. Then the process repeats. If there were no friction and no outside disturbance, the pendulum would
10   keep swinging forever.
    If we make the string very light, the pendulum bob is essentially the only mass in the system. Since the bob changes height during its swing, its gravitational energy
15   changes. The pendulum has zero speed and therefore zero kinetic energy at the top of its swing, at maximum height, when its gravitational energy is largest; it has maximum speed and therefore maximum
20   kinetic energy at the bottom of its swing, when its gravitational energy is smallest. Total energy will be conserved if the gain of kinetic energy exactly equals the loss of gravitational energy.

6   The passage suggests that the gravitational energy of the bob depends on

(A)   its distance from the ground
(B)   the length of its string
(C)   the force applied to it
(D)   its speed
(E)   the time it takes for one full swing

7   Which of the following best describes the relationship between gravitational energy and kinetic energy of the bob as it is explained in the passage?

(A)   As kinetic energy increases, gravitational energy increases.
(B)   As kinetic energy increases, gravitational energy decreases.
(C)   Gravitational energy remains constant, even as kinetic energy changes.
(D)   Kinetic energy remains constant, even as gravitational energy changes.
(E)   Kinetic energy and gravitational energy are exactly equal when the bob is at the bottom of its swing.

Questions 8–9 are based on the following passage.

Line   The old woman was a gnarled and leathery person-age who could don, at will, an expression of great virtue. She possessed a small music-box capable of one tune, and a
5   collection of "God bless yehs" pitched in assorted keys of fervency. Each day she took a position upon the stones of Fifth Avenue, where she crooked her legs under her and crouched immovable and hideous, like an
10   idol. She received daily a small sum in pennies. It was contributed, for the most part, by persons who did not make their homes in that vicinity.

8   It can be inferred from the passage that the old woman is most likely a

(A)   shop owner   (B)   beggar
(C)   recluse   (D)   musician
(E)   mother

9   In line 6, the word "keys" most nearly means

(A)   tones of voice   (B)   principles
(C)   necessities   (D)   tools
(E)   sponsors

First passage: *Great Ideas in Physics*, Alan Lightman; McGraw Hill, July 2000
Second passage: *Maggie, A Girl of the Streets*, Stephen Crane. Public Domain

GO ON TO THE NEXT PAGE ▶▶▶

Questions 10–16 are based on the following passage.

The following passage is an excerpt taken from a discussion about the pros and cons of government surveillance and the phenomenon known as "Big Brother."

Line   The first video surveillance systems were installed in the early 1970s to assist in road traffic management and deter bank robbers. During the 1980s their use spread rapidly to
5   public transport, shops, the workplace, leisure venues and the approaches to public buildings. A further step in this direction was taken at the beginning of the 1990s, when cameras were installed on public highways,
10   in sports stadiums and on the streets of certain cities.

     This new form of surveillance aroused misgivings from the onset. In France, the CNIL (National Committee on Computer
15   Data and Individual Freedom) proposed the first legal safeguards at the end of the 1980s. But the general public accepted the new technology, as a means of crime prevention. However, a survey carried out in 1996
20   showed that social acceptability varied according to the type of application. Only 9% of respondents considered the presence of cameras in car parks and shops as an invasion of privacy. On the other hand, 51%
25   thought that showing pictures of a person taken in a public place without that person's consent was a serious violation.

     The cameras involved are more and more powerful. Some have a full 360° range of
30   vision. Others are fitted with zoom lenses that can read the figures on cash registers or car number plates at a distance of 300 meters. There are even "smart" cameras equipped with sensors that trigger alarm
35   systems when incidents occur. The transmission of images over public telephone networks means that people can be kept under surveillance worldwide without regard to national frontiers.
40   Once installed, video surveillance systems can be used for purposes other than those for which they were originally intended. The use of the cameras of Beijing's Tiananmen Square to identify and arrest demonstrators in June
45   1989 is a notorious example.

     It is becoming apparent that the closed circuit systems installed in large department stores in order to counter shoplifting are now being used for staff surveillance. They have
50   become an instrument for monitoring work and productivity. This is confirmed by the large number of instances in which video evidence is offered in court in alleged cases of wrongful dismissal. Video systems can also
55   be used to monitor specific aspects of consumer behavior. Detailed analysis of tiny movements and gestures enables stores to optimize the positioning of goods and devise the most effective shopping itineraries.
60   Video recordings of shoplifters can be used to build photo archives of suspects and persistent offenders. Currently, research is being conducted into software that can automatically identify wanted persons among
65   the faces filmed in group scenes.

     Video surveillance is a new form of control. An abstract, remote, impersonal, automatic, bureaucratic, largely invisible and inherently mysterious device enables a
70   machine to create information and, if need be, initiate action. Here, the essence of control is manipulation rather than coercion, as if a distant hand were pulling invisible strings. The person under surveillance is
75   reduced to an object of information. His records are contained in countless files, and everywhere he goes he leaves electronic traces of his passage. As if this were not enough, his activities are rendered even more
80   transparent by video cameras that track his image. The subject himself remains ignorant of the processes and manipulation of data going on behind his back.

     In democracies, where freedoms are
85   guaranteed by law, the loss of privacy entailed in the taking of pictures must not be disproportionate to the end in view. It may be justified in certain places where security is at risk, but it is not justified in all cases. In a
90   Belgian secondary school, smokers were

GO ON TO THE NEXT PAGE ▶▶▶

Excerpted from: http://mondediplo.com/1998/03/11video, Big Brother is Watching you on Video; March, 1998

Available on subscription,
email: lmdsubs@granta.com
or visit our website: www.mondediplo.com>

pursued right into the toilets, where cameras were installed to catch them in the act. Department store fitting rooms are kept under surveillance by hidden cameras to

95 reduce the theft of clothing. It has also been established that cameras installed on the public highway, or set up outside department stores to keep watch on the entrances, can see into adjacent houses and apartment

100 blocks. Safeguarding the rights of persons subjected to video surveillance is absolutely essential if a proper balance is to be struck between security and freedom.

10 The purpose of the first paragraph is to

(A) state a thesis
(B) provide a brief history of a phenomenon
(C) describe the nature of a culture
(D) summarize a misconception
(E) describe one individual's unique point of view

11 It can be inferred from the passage that, at the end of the 1980s, the CNIL was concerned with

(A) making video surveillance less expensive
(B) road traffic management
(C) potential misuses of electronic surveillance
(D) encouraging wider use of electronic surveillance
(E) deterring bank theft

12 The statistics cited in the second paragraph suggest that people's concerns about electronic surveillance of their activities depend on

(A) whether the surveillance is indoors or outdoors
(B) what kinds of crimes are prevented with its use
(C) how expensive the equipment is to install and maintain
(D) how accurate the equipment is
(E) what control they have over how the information is distributed after it is gathered

13 The "aspects of consumer behavior" mentioned in lines 55–56 can be inferred to include

(A) shoplifting
(B) purchasing habits
(C) sensitivity to surveillance
(D) concerns about safety
(E) eating habits

14 In line 78, the word "passage" most nearly means

(A) death   (B) writing
(C) entryway   (D) activity
(E) objection

15 The list of adjectives in lines 67–69 serve primarily to characterize electronic surveillance as

(A) effective   (B) expensive
(C) detached   (D) useless
(E) coercive

16 The author objects to the use of cameras "installed on the public highway" (lines 96–97) chiefly because

(A) they can be used to invade the privacy of non-drivers
(B) the use of cameras in a public place is never justified
(C) they can be easily damaged
(D) they have not been proven to prevent traffic accidents
(E) they are insufficiently accurate

GO ON TO THE NEXT PAGE ▶▶▶

Questions 17–24 are based on the following passage.

The following passage is an excerpt from an essay written in 1896 on women in the northeastern United States.

Line   The exodus of women, for one reason or
another, to the cities in the last ten years
parallels that of men. They have come from
the West in regiments, and from the South in
5   brigades. Each year they come younger and
younger. They have ameliorated the customs
and diversified the streets.

New York and perhaps city women in
general, when they are suddenly called upon
10   to earn their livings, are much more
independent about it, and more original in
their methods than women in smaller places,
where womanly pursuits, as they are called,
follow more closely prescribed lines. The
15   New York woman has more knowledge of
the world, and she knows that one can do
pretty much what one pleases, if it is done
with a certain dash, *élan*, carrying-all-before-
it air. When she comes to work for her living
20   she profits by this knowledge. Instead of
becoming a governess or a teacher of music,
she tries to get hold of something original
that will excite interest. When she has found
it she holds it up, as it were, on a blazoned
25   banner, inscribed with this legend, "I have
not a penny to my name, and I'm going to
work." She accepts the situation with the
greatest good-humor and makes herself more
acceptable to the old set by relating her
30   discouragements, trials, and mistakes so
comically that she is better company than
before. If her story is not bad enough she
embroiders it to the proper point of
attractiveness.

35   In the measure that women are
determining their own lives, they want their
own homes. The desire is entirely reasonable.
The woman who is occupied with daily work
needs greater freedom of movement, more
40   isolation, more personal comforts, and the
exemption, moreover, from being agree-able
at all times and places. She wants to be able
to shut her doors against all the world, and
not to be confined within four walls herself;

45   and she wants to open her doors when it
pleases her, and to exercise the rites
of hospitality unquestioned. In fact, she
wants many things that cannot be had except
in her own home. It is an interesting fact in
50   natural history that women in their first
breathing-spell should revert to constructing
homes as their natural background, to which
is added the male realization that the home is
the proper stimulus to achievement.

55   To be the mistress of a home, to extend
hospitalities, briefly to be within the
circumference of a social circle, instead of
gliding with uneasy foot on the periphery, is
the reasonable desire of every woman. When
60   this is achieved many temptations, so freely
recognized that nobody disputes them, are
eliminated. It is a noticeable fact that in all
women-bachelor households, no matter how
humble, that the rugs are scarcely down and
65   the curtains up, until the kettle is lighted and
the reign of hospitality has begun. It is
interesting to observe how soon the shyest
novice over the tea-cup loses her timidity,
and assumes that air of confidence that once
70   was the enviable property of only married
women.

17   The passage suggests that, compared to city
women, women who live in "smaller places"
(line 12) are

(A)   better educated
(B)   more aggressive
(C)   less attractive
(D)   more traditional
(E)   wealthier

GO ON TO THE NEXT PAGE ▶▶▶

from "Women Bachelors" by Mary Gay Humphreys, 1896, in *Early American Women* © 1992 by Nancy Woloch, Wadsworth Publishing Company, pp. 550–552

18 In line 18, the word "dash" most nearly means

(A) carelessness   (B) properness
(C) quickness   (D) danger
(E) flair

19 The "knowledge" referred to in line 20 is knowledge of

(A) music
(B) how to make one's self interesting to others
(C) the superiority of women over men
(D) how to sustain a traditional profession
(E) how to maintain a home

20 The "attractiveness" referred to in line 34 refers to

(A) a woman's outward appearance
(B) the pitifulness of a woman's situation
(C) a woman's wealth
(D) the formal education a woman has achieved
(E) a woman's desire to help others become beautiful

21 The third paragraph (lines 35–54) indicates that women who work outside of the home need which of the following?

    I. the ability to entertain when they wish
   II. the freedom to abstain from propriety
  III. free access to higher education

(A) I only
(B) II only
(C) I and II only
(D) II and III only
(E) I, II, and III

22 The phrase "uneasy foot on the periphery" (line 58) refers to some women's

(A) exclusion from certain social groups
(B) inability to maintain a home
(C) lack of success in acquiring employment
(D) superior skills at public speaking
(E) warm hospitality

23 In line 68, the phrase "over the tea-cup" most nearly means

(A) when purchasing dinner
(B) when cleaning dishes
(C) when hosting guests
(D) when looking for a job
(E) when moving to the city

24 The last paragraph suggests most directly that owning and maintaining her own home makes a woman more

(A) confident
(B) affluent
(C) emotionally stable
(D) adept at making household repairs
(E) attractive to men

STOP

You may check your work, on this section only, until time is called.

Section 5

Time—25 Minutes
18 Questions

Directions for Multiple-Choice Questions

In this section, solve each problem, using any available space on the page for scratchwork. Then decide which is the best of the choices given and fill in the corresponding oval on the answer sheet.

- You may use a calculator on any problem. All numbers used are real numbers.
- Figures are drawn as accurately as possible EXCEPT when it is stated that the figure is not drawn to scale.
- All figures lie in a plane unless otherwise indicated.

Reference Information

$A = \pi r^2$
$C = 2\pi r$

$A = \ell w$

$A = \frac{1}{2}bh$

$V = \ell wh$

$V = \pi r^2 h$

$c^2 = a^2 + b^2$

Special Right Triangles

The arc of a circle measures 360°.
Every straight angle measures 180°.
The sum of the measures of the angles in a triangle is 180°.

---

1 If $3 - x = 2x - 6$, what is the value of x?

(A) 1
(B) 2
(C) 3
(D) 6
(E) 9

$$\begin{array}{r} RP \\ + \ 7T \\ \hline 15P \end{array}$$

2 In the correctly worked addition problem above, R, P, and T, represent different digits. What is the value of R?

(A) 0
(B) 2
(C) 5
(D) 8
(E) 9

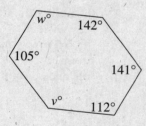

3 In the figure above, what is the value of $w + v$?

(A)   40°
(B)   125°
(C)   140°
(D)   220°
(E)   300°

GO ON TO THE NEXT PAGE ▶▶▶

4 One number is twice as large as another positive number, and their difference is 4. What is the greater of the two numbers?

(A) 4
(B) 6
(C) 8
(D) 10
(E) 12

5 In a movie theater, $\frac{1}{3}$ of the seats were filled when the previews started. After 50 more people came in, $\frac{3}{4}$ of the seats were filled. How many seats are in the movie theater?

(A) 90
(B) 120
(C) 150
(D) 170
(E) 190

6 How many of the first fifty positive integers contain the digit 4?

(A) 12
(B) 13
(C) 14
(D) 15
(E) 16

7 If $3x = y + z$, $y = 6 - z$, and $z + x = 8$, what is the value of $\frac{y}{z}$?

(A) 0
(B) 2
(C) 4
(D) 5
(E) 7

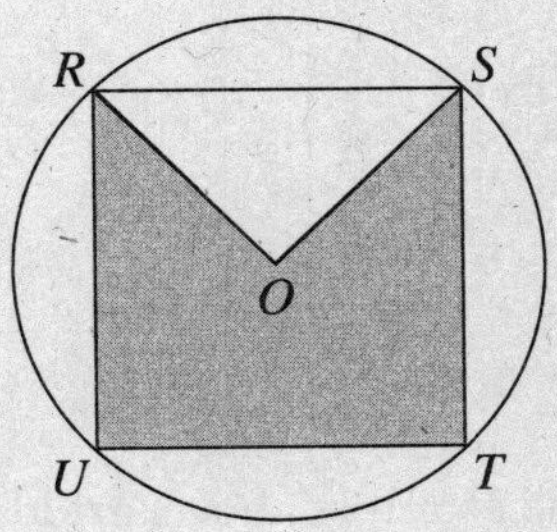

8 In the figure above, the four vertices of square RSTU lie on circle O, which has a radius of 8. What is the area of the shaded region?

(A) 32
(B) 96
(C) 128
(D) 150
(E) 166

Directions for Student-Produced Response Questions

Each of the questions in this section requires you to solve the problem and enter your answer in a grid, as shown below.

- If your answer is ⅔ or .666..., you must enter **the most accurate value the grid can accommodate**, but you may do this in one of four ways:

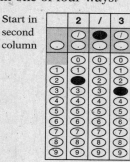

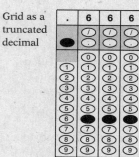

- In the example above, gridding a response of 0.67 or 0.66 is **incorrect** because it is less accurate than those above.
- The scoring machine cannot read what is written in the top row of boxes. You **MUST** fill in the numerical grid accurately to get credit for answering any question correctly. You should write your answer in the top row of boxes only to aid your gridding.
- Do **not** grid in a mixed fraction like $3\frac{1}{2}$ as $\boxed{3}\ \boxed{1}\ \boxed{/}\ \boxed{2}$ because it will be interpreted as $\frac{31}{2}$. Instead, convert it to an improper fraction like $\frac{7}{2}$ or a decimal like 3.5 before gridding.
- None of the answers will be negative, because there is no negative sign in the grid.
- Some of the questions may have more than one correct answer. You must grid only one of the correct answers.
- You may use a calculator on any of these problems.
- All numbers in these problems are real numbers.
- Figures are drawn as accurately as possible EXCEPT when it is stated that the figure is not drawn to scale.
- All figures lie in a plane unless otherwise indicated.

9 If $f(x) = 3x + 7$ and $g(x) = x^2 - 1$, what is the value of $g(f(2))$?

10 At Streams Elementary School, the four homeroom classes have 14, 18, 21, and 23 students. What is the fewest number of students that would have to change homerooms for each class to contain the same number of students?

Time Allocation for Activities
in an Average Day for an
Average College Student

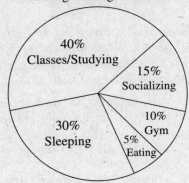

11 According to the data in the circle graph above, how many combined hours does an average college student spend at the gym and socializing during an average seven day week?

12 Two sides of a triangle have lengths of 6 and 8. The length of the third side is unknown. What is the largest possible area of this triangle?

13 If x is a positive integer and $| 2x + 6 | > 10$, what is the least possible value of x?

14 A pile of five coins consists of one penny (1 cent), one nickel (5 cents), one dime (10 cents), one quarter (25 cents) and one 50-cent piece. If two different coins are selected at random, what is the probability that the sum of these coins will be less than 35 cents?

15 If one can of paint costs $15.00 and contains enough paint to cover an area of 300 square feet, what is the cost, in dollars, of the paint needed to cover a large rectangular ballroom that measures 150 feet by 100 feet? (Disregard the dollar sign when gridding your answer.)

16 If a rectangular solid has side lengths of 6, 4, and 3. If its surface area is m square units, and its volume is n cubic units, what is the value of m/n?

Set X is the set of positive integers between 1 and 50 (inclusive)
Set Y is the set of positive integers between 1 and 100 (inclusive)

17 If x is a member of set X and y is a member of set Y, what is the greatest value of $x + y$ such that both $x + y$ and xy are members of set Y?

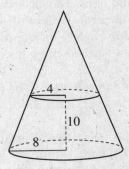

18 The radius of the base of a right circular cone is 8. A parallel cross section is made through the cone and has a radius of 4. If the distance between the cross section and the base of the cone is 10, what is the height of the cone?

STOP

You may check your work, on this section only, until time is called.

Section 6

Time—25 Minutes
35 Questions

Directions for Improving Sentences Questions

Each of the sentences below contains one underlined portion. The portion may contain one or more errors in grammar, usage, construction, precision, diction (choice of words), or idiom. Some of the sentences are correct.

Consider the meaning of the original sentence, and choose the answer that best expresses that meaning. If the original sentence is best, choose (A), because it repeats the original phrasing. Choose the phrasing that creates the clearest, most precise and most effective sentence.

EXAMPLE:

The children <u>couldn't hardly believe their eyes.</u>

(A) couldn't hardly believe their eyes
(B) would not hardly believe their eyes
(C) could hardly believe their eyes
(D) couldn't nearly believe their eyes
(E) could hardly believe his or her eyes

Example answer: (C)

1 Although it is often dismissed as a vulgar popular phenomenon, hip hop culture has actually <u>introduced many innovations of the musical sort, inspiring</u> artists in many divergent genres.

(A) introduced many innovations of the musical sort, inspiring
(B) introduced the musical innovations and inspirations for
(C) introduced many musical innovations, inspiring
(D) introducing many musical innovations and inspiring
(E) introduced many musical innovations, inspired

2 Jeremy had not realized that such a career path even existed until he spoke with his uncle <u>who had also, at another point in time in the past, followed such a route.</u>

(A) who had also, at another point in time in the past, followed such a route.
(B) who had also, therefore, followed such a route.
(C) who once had followed that very route.
(D) who, at one point, had followed that very exact same route.
(E) who had also, henceforth, followed such a route.

3 Charles denied any wrongdoing, claiming <u>there was no way he could of known</u> that his friend had lied.

(A) there was no way he could of known
(B) there wasn't any way he could of known
(C) there was no way he could have known
(D) there wasn't no way he could have known
(E) the way he could have known was not

4 Although many children dream of owning a pet, <u>the responsibility of taking care of them is something few of them consider.</u>

(A) the responsibility of taking care of them is something few of them consider.
(B) it is the responsibility of taking care of them that so many children do not consider.
(C) taking care of one is the responsibility that so few consider.
(D) it is rarely considered, the responsibility of taking care of one.
(E) few consider the responsibility that comes with taking care of one.

5 Ronald's daily workout regimen is intense: <u>he runs, swims, and he likes to lift weights.</u>

(A) he runs, swims, and he likes to lift weights.
(B) he runs, swims, and lifts weights.
(C) he is a runner, a swimmer, and lifts weights.
(D) he runs, swims and lifts weights.
(E) running, swimming, and lifting weights.

6 <u>It is the debate of historians whether</u> the New Deal of World War II actually provided the economic stimulus that ended the Great Depression.

(A) It is the debate of historians whether
(B) Historians have their debate of whether
(C) Whether or not historians debate over
(D) Historians debate whether
(E) Of the debate, historians think

7 <u>The tragic sadness of unrequited love</u> often serves as inspiration to artists and musicians.

(A) The tragic sadness of unrequited love
(B) Unrequited love is tragically sad,
(C) It is a tragically sad phenomenon, unrequited love, which
(D) Unrequited love being tragically sad
(E) For the tragic sadness of unrequited love

8 James Joyce's novel *Finnegans Wake* is not easily accessible, <u>being that it often is requiring of hours of research to interpret a single sentence.</u>

(A) being that it often is requiring of hours of research to interpret a single sentence.
(B) and often requiring hours of research to interpret a single sentence.
(C) often requiring hours of research to interpret a single sentence.
(D) with its requirement of hours of research for a single sentence to be interpreted.
(E) the interpretation of which often requires hours of research to interpret a single sentence.

9 Many critics believe that film can never do justice to literature, <u>a failure to consider the depth added by visual representation.</u>

(A) a failure to consider the depth added by visual representation.
(B) a failing in consideration of the depth added by visual representation.
(C) failing, considering the depth added by visual representation.
(D) failing to consider the depth added by visual representation.
(E) a failure, considering the depth added by visual representation.

10 Harry <u>Truman, facing the onerous decision of</u> whether or not to use the atomic bomb and usher in the age of nuclear warfare.

(A) Truman, facing the onerous decision of
(B) Truman faced the onerous decision of
(C) Truman had faced the onerous decision, debating
(D) Truman, as he faced the onerous decision of
(E) Truman faced the onerous decision which was debating

11 In a symbol of unity, the students gathered in the court yard, <u>their lighting candles to express hope</u> that the labor dispute would be resolved.

(A) their lighting candles to express hope
(B) in the hope of lighting candles for
(C) expressing hope and lighting candles so
(D) which lit candles to express hope
(E) lighting candles to express hope

GO ON TO THE NEXT PAGE ▶▶▶

12 After Tara was <u>aroused</u> from sleep by a sharp
                 A
noise, she <u>raced</u> for the front <u>door; fearing</u>
        B   C
the <u>presence</u> of an intruder. <u>No error</u>
     D   E

13 <u>Asked what he wanted</u> for his birthday,
           A
Virgil <u>turned around</u> and quickly <u>replied</u>
        B   C
that he would like a bike, a new computer,

and <u>staying up</u> past nine o'clock. <u>No error</u>
   D   E

14 Every day, John sits in his garage <u>admiring</u>
                          A
his vintage cars, each of which <u>runs</u> as
                       B
though <u>it was</u> brand new, <u>never driven</u> out
       C   D
of the show room. <u>No error</u>
                E

15 <u>When placed</u> in new surroundings, even the
     A
<u>most lively</u> cats <u>sink</u> to the floor,
   B   C
<u>seeming to be suspicious</u> of all they see.
          D
<u>No error</u>
  E

16 The new governor, <u>who was more radical</u> than
                  A
his <u>predecessor, came</u> to power <u>on a platform</u>
      B   C
of reform, equality, and <u>being honest</u>. <u>No error</u>
              D   E

17 <u>Unable to find</u> her <u>driver's license</u>, Mary
    A   B
asked the agent if a credit card would be

<u>sufficient enough</u> evidence <u>to prove</u> her
     C   D
identity. <u>No error</u>
       E

18 The new movie was <u>disliked</u> by critics who
               A
<u>expected</u> it to be <u>as well-written</u> and as
  B   C
tightly acted as <u>those of the director's</u>
              D
previous films, which included several

award winners. <u>No error</u>
         E

19 Each of the boys wanted to hear <u>their</u> name
                                                      A
<u>called</u> as the coach <u>announced</u> the final
   B   C
roster for the <u>upcoming season.</u> <u>No error</u>
                        D   E

20 Although he has matured <u>in many ways</u>,
                                                 A
Gordon still occasionally <u>resorted</u> to childish
                                        B
habits <u>when he feels sad</u>, using memories
            C
from youth to <u>help him through</u> tough times.
                        D
<u>No error</u>
   E

21 <u>Overwhelmed by</u> the speed of the city,
         A
Catherine <u>often hid</u> in her hotel room, only
                  B
<u>occasionally braving</u> the streets and the
         C
<u>swarming crowds</u> of holiday shoppers.
         D
<u>No error</u>
   E

22 Peter, <u>the store manager</u>, assured the
                     A
customers that <u>their prices</u> were comparable
                         B
to <u>those of their competitors</u> on all items,
         C
<u>even the most</u> expensive ones. <u>No error</u>
   D   E

23 <u>Admired by</u> his peers, adored by his family,
         A
and <u>a man respected</u> even by his enemies,
         B
Chadwick <u>was confident</u> that he had lived a
                  C
good life, <u>completely devoid</u> of selfish
                     D
motives. <u>No error</u>
               E

24 Erica was <u>irritated by</u> her husband's
                     A
<u>impulsive</u> shopping <u>because she knew that</u>
   B   C
the price of video equipment at Joe's
Applicances was higher <u>than Acme Video.</u>
                                    D
<u>No error</u>
   E

25 Only after David <u>had wrote</u> the first two
                              A
paragraphs <u>of his essay</u> did he <u>realize that</u>
                  B   C
he was not entirely <u>convinced</u> of the
                              D
validity of his own argument. <u>No error</u>
                                          E

26 Renee's <u>responsibilities at</u> the aquarium
                     A
were not only <u>to train</u> and perform with
                     B
the seals, but also <u>in feeding</u> them
                              C
<u>according to</u> a very strict dietary regimen.
         D
<u>No error</u>
   E

27 The festival was more a celebration of jazz
culture than simply <u>like a series of concerts;</u>
                              A
it <u>included</u> many exhibits and lectures
      B
<u>on the various</u> movements and eras
      C
<u>that influenced</u> the art form. <u>No error</u>
      D   E

GO ON TO THE NEXT PAGE ▸▸▸

28 The four hurricanes <u>that struck</u> Florida
                              A
<u>in the summer of 2004</u> were unparalleled
            B
in their effects; <u>it was something</u> that the
                          C
citizens <u>had never experienced</u> before.
                      D
<u>No error</u>
      E

29 The concerns that consumers

<u>have recently voiced</u> about the safety
            A
of sport utility vehicles

<u>have been addressed</u> <u>by manufacturers</u>,
            B   C
although many critics still claim that the

designs of these trucks can

be <u>dramatically improved</u>. <u>No error</u>
            D   E

Directions for Improving Paragraphs Questions

Below is an early draft of an essay. It requires revision in many areas.

The questions that follow ask you to make improvements in sentence structure, diction, organization, and development. Answering the questions may require you to understand the context of the passage as well as the rules of standard written English.

Questions 30–35 are based on the following passage.

(1) *The structure of television news has undergone massive changes and many of those changes have occurred during the past fifty years.* (2) *In the industry's early years, networks were required by law to provide "public service" programming.* (3) *News shows fell under the category of public service.* (4) *As such, news was originally viewed not as a profit-making venture, but rather as a way to fulfill a requirement.* (5) *Due to a lack of financial pressure, producers were able to create expansive intellectual documentaries, and in them, they put long excerpts from political speeches and worldwide visually stunning imagery.* (6) *However, the airwaves were devoid of much in the way of investigative journalism.*

(7) *In 1969, 60 Minutes debuted on CBS.* (8) *The first television "news magazine," the show provided short sound bites, a dramatic narrative structure, and a promise to uncover hidden truths.* (9) *Suddenly, a new perspective was born: journalists became the public watchdog, perpetually seeking the unjust and corrupt lurking behind the closed doors of government and corporate offices.*

(10) *Amid all these changes, many ethical issues were raised.* (11) *Does sensationalizing the news make the information less valuable?* (12) *Is public opinion being skewed to fit a particular network's political leanings or are people still able to sift through balanced information on their own?*

(13) *Without question, the new television news shows have attracted wide audiences and are profitable to the networks.* (14) *Their ratings often compete with those of the most popular sitcoms.* (15) *Television journalists regularly achieve celebrity status unknown to journalists in the 1950s.* (16) *60 Minutes remains at the top of the ratings, continuing to generate enormous revenues for CBS.* (17) *The world as we see it today is born in a studio and crafted by intelligent professionals with the talent of Hollywood producers.*

30 Which of the following is the best version of the under lined portion of sentence 1 (reproduced below)?

The structure of television news has undergone massive changes and all of those changes have occurred over the past fifty years.

(A) (as it is now)
(B) and those changes have all occurred over the past fifty years.
(C) all of which have occurred over the past fifty years.
(D) over the past fifty years.
(E) and it has happened over fifty years.

31 In context, which of the following is the best way to combine sentences 2 and 3?

(A) In the industry's early years, networks were required by law to provide "public service" programming, and news being under that category.
(B) In the industry's early years, networks were required by law to provide "public service" programming, which included news.
(C) News had been under a category of "public service" programming, which would have been required of the industry in its early years by law.
(D) The category of "public service" programming included news and was a requirement of the industry in the early years by law.
(E) In the industry's early years, networks were required by law to provide "public service" programming, as such, the news fell under that category.

32 Which of the following is the best version of the underlined portion of sentence 5 (reproduced below)?

Because there was little financial pressure, producers could create expansive intellectual documentaries, <u>and in them, they put long excerpts from political speeches and worldwide visually stunning imagery.</u>

(A)   (as it is now)
(B)   often including long excerpts from political speeches and visually stunning imagery from around the world.
(C)   often including excerpts from political speeches that were long and imagery from around the world that were stunning.
(D)   and in them, they included long excerpts from political speeches and visually stunning imagery from around the world.
(E)   often including long excerpts and visually stunning imagery from political speeches and around the world.

33 Which of the following revisions of sentence 7 provides the most effective transition from the first paragraph to the second paragraph?

(A)   All this changed in 1969, when *60 Minutes* debuted on CBS.
(B)   And so it was not surprising when *60 Minutes* debuted on CBS in 1969.
(C)   Another example of this phenomenon was *60 Minutes,* which debuted on CBS in 1969.
(D)   Therefore it was in 1969 that *60 Minutes* debuted on CBS,
(E)   The debut of *60 Minutes* on CBS in 1969 signaled the end of an era.

34 Where is the best place to insert the following sentence?

Such questions still concern media observers, but the harshness of their critiques is mitigated by the great popularity of such news magazines.

(A)   after sentence 6, to end the first paragraph
(B)   after sentence 9, to end the second paragraph
(C)   after sentence 10
(D)   after sentence 12, to end the third paragraph
(E)   after sentence 13

35 In context, which of the following is the most effective version of sentence 14 (reproduced below)?

Their ratings often compete with those of the most popular sitcoms.

(A)   (as it is now)
(B)   Ratings of theirs compete with the most popular sitcoms.
(C)   Ratings of sitcoms compete with the ones of news programs.
(D)   Ratings compete with those of sitcoms, even the most popular ones.
(E)   Ratings are competitive with sitcoms.

STOP

You may check your work, on this section only, until time is called.

Section 7

Time—20 minutes
16 Questions

Directions for Multiple-Choice Questions

In this section, solve each problem, using any available space on the page for scratchwork. Then decide which is the best of the choices given and fill in the corresponding oval on your answer sheet.

- You may use a calculator on any problem. All numbers used are real numbers.
- Figures are drawn as accurately as possible EXCEPT when it is stated that the figure is not drawn to scale.
- All figures lie in a plane unless otherwise indicated.

Reference Information

$A = \pi r^2$ $A = \ell w$
$C = 2\pi r$ $A = \frac{1}{2}bh$ $V = \ell wh$ $V = \pi r^2 h$ $c^2 = a^2 + b^2$ Special Right Triangles

The arc of a circle measures 360°.
Every straight angle measures 180°.
The sum of the measures of the angles in a triangle is 180°.

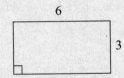 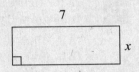

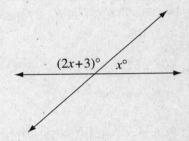

1 If the rectangles shown above have the same perimeter, what is the value of x?

(A) 2
(B) 3
(C) 4
(D) 5
(E) 6

2 If b represents a positive integer, which of the following expressions necessarily represents an even integer?

(A) $2b$
(B) $b + 2$
(C) $2b + 1$
(D) $3b$
(E) $2b - 1$

Note: Figure not drawn to scale.

3 Two lines intersect as shown in the figure above, what is the value of x?

(A) 54
(B) 56
(C) 57
(D) 59
(E) 62

GO ON TO THE NEXT PAGE ▶▶▶

4 If x and y are both positive, which of the following is equivalent to $(x^6 y^4)^{-\frac{1}{2}}$?

(A) $x^3 y^2$

(B) $x^{12} y^8$

(C) $\dfrac{1}{x^3 y^2}$

(D) $\dfrac{1}{x^6 y^4}$

(E) $\dfrac{1}{x^{12} y^8}$

Final Exam Grades
Mr. Price's Class

Grade	Number of students
95	4
90	3
85	4
80	3
75	1
60	2

5 Based on the information in the table above, what is the median final exam grade for Mr. Price's class?

(A) 75
(B) 80
(C) 85
(D) 90
(E) 95

6 If $a = b^3$, and b is positive, then by what factor does a increase if b is tripled?

(A) 3
(B) 8
(C) 9
(D) 27
(E) 81

7 If $f(x) = (x - 2)^2 + 4$, what is the least value in the range of $f(x)$?

(A) 0
(B) 1
(C) 2
(D) 3
(E) 4

8 If $20^w = 5^3 \times 4^3$, what is the value of w?

(A) 1
(B) 3
(C) 6
(D) 8
(E) 10

Step 1: Subtract 5 from x
Step 2: Multiply this difference by 2
Step 3: Add 6 to this product

9 Which of the following represents the result if the three operations above are performed in sequence?

(A) $x - 4$
(B) $2x + 1$
(C) $2x - 4$
(D) $2x - 6$
(E) $2x + 2$

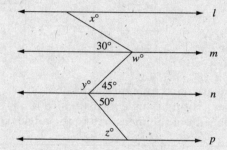

10 In the figure above, $l \parallel m \parallel n \parallel p$. What is the value of $w + x + y + z$?

(A) 100°
(B) 160°
(C) 280°
(D) 310°
(E) 350°

11 Two towns located x miles apart are p centimeters apart on a roadmap that is drawn to scale. How many miles apart are two towns that are $p + 5$ centimeters apart on this map?

(A) $\dfrac{p + 5x}{p}$

(B) $\dfrac{px + 5x}{p}$

(C) $\dfrac{p - 5x}{x}$

(D) $\dfrac{p}{px + 5}$

(E) $\dfrac{x}{p + 5x}$

GO ON TO THE NEXT PAGE ▶▶▶

12 For any positive integer, n, let $\int n$ be defined as the integer obtained when each digit in n has been replaced with the corresponding digit in the table below, ignoring any leading zeroes.

For example, $\int 326 = 548$ and $\int 86 = 08 = 8$.

Digit in n	Digit in $\int n$
0	2
1	3
2	4
3	5
4	6
5	7
6	8
7	9
8	0
9	1

Which of the following is equivalent to $\int 820 + \int 104$?

(A) $\int 146$ (B) $\int 368$ (C) $\int 580$
(D) $\int 621$ (E) $\int 746$

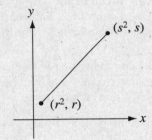

13 In the figure above, if $r \neq s$, what is the slope of the line segment?

(A) $r + s$
(B) $r - s$

(C) $\dfrac{s^2 - s}{r^2 - r}$

(D) $\dfrac{1}{(s+r)}$

(E) $\dfrac{1}{(s-r)}$

14 If the point $(3, 4)$ is on a circle with center at $(0, 0)$, which of the following points is outside of the circle?

(A) $(2, 4)$
(B) $(5, 0)$
(C) $(-3, -4)$
(D) $(-2, -5)$
(E) $(-4, -3)$

15 Both m and x are positive integers and $m + x = 8$. If $16m^2 + 56m + 49 = (mx + 7)^2$, what is the value of $m - x$?

(A) -8
(B) -4
(C) 0
(D) 4
(E) 8

$$\frac{b+a}{a} = x$$

$$\frac{b-a}{a} = y$$

16 In the equations above, if $a \neq 0$, which of the following is equal to $(x - y)(x + y)$?

(A) $-4a$
(B) $-4b$

(C) $\dfrac{-4b}{a}$

(D) $\dfrac{(b^2 - a^2)}{a}$

(E) $\dfrac{(b^2 - a^2)}{a^2}$

 **STOP**

You may check your work, on this section only, until time is called.

Section 8

Time—20 minutes
19 Questions

Each of the sentences below is missing one or two portions. Read each sentence, then select the word or words that most logically completes the sentence, taking into account the meaning of the sentence as a whole.

Example:

Rather than accepting the theory unquestioningly, Deborah regarded it with ———.

(A) mirth   (B) sadness
(C) responsibility   (D) ignorance
(E) skepticism

Correct response: (E)

8

1 The decade following the Great Depression in was one of ———: the United States began the slow return to economic stability.

(A) inflammation   (B) acrimony
(C) mirth   (D) aggregation
(E) rehabilitation

2 As a gourmet, Jorge bemoaned the ——— of good restaurants in his new home city.

(A) paucity   (B) quality
(C) surfeit   (D) conglomeration
(E) consumption

3 Before Tamaya Shutkin's well-publicized experiments proved that the new fuel source was clean and effective, environmentalists argued that the innovation was too ——— to put into use nationally.

(A) speculative   (B) lucid
(C) dynamic   (D) fastidious
(E) monotonous

4 Although the ——— despot had spent much of the previous thirty years persecuting his citizens, his recent near-death experience has turned him into a much less ——— ruler.

(A) repugnant . . beneficent
(B) cantankerous . . abominable
(C) nefarious . . odious
(D) patriarchal . . vile
(E) malevolent . . mellifluous

5 Several of Jane Austen's characters are so ——— that their very natures prevent them from ——— to the social standards of their times.

(A) heretical . . denouncing
(B) obsequious . . assimilating
(C) recalcitrant . . migrating
(D) itinerant . . habituating
(E) iconoclastic . . conforming

6 Despite being one of the least ——— dancers in the troupe, she moves with ——— that belies her lack of grace.

(A) agile . . an ineptitude
(B) nimble . . a deftness
(C) graceful . . a treachery
(D) cunning . . an aptitude
(E) dexterous . . an idiosyncrasy

GO ON TO THE NEXT PAGE ▶▶▶

The questions below are based on the content of the passage that precedes them. The questions are to be answered on the basis of what is stated or implied in the passage itself or the introductory material that precedes the passage.

Questions 7–19 are based on the following passages.

The following passages debate the ethics of the use of animals for the advancement of scientific knowledge.

Passage 1

Line   To deny science the use of animals in research is, it might be said, to bring scientific and allied medical progress to a halt, and that is reason enough to oppose it. The claim that
5   progress would be "brought to a halt" is an exaggeration certainly. It is not an exaggeration to claim that, given its present dominant tendency, the rights view requires massive redirection of scientific research. The
10   dominant tendency involves routinely harming animals. It should come as no surprise that the rights view has principled objections to its continuation.
        If we are seriously to challenge the use of
15   animals in research, we must challenge the *practice* itself, not only individual instances of it or merely the liabilities in its present methodology. The rights view issues such a challenge. Routine use of animals in research
20   assumes that their value is reducible to their possible utility relative to the interests of others. The rights view rejects this view of animals and their value, as it rejects the justice of institutions that treat them as
25   renewable resources. They, like us, have a value of their own, logically independent of their utility for others and of their being the object of anyone else's interests. To treat them in ways that respect their value,
30   therefore, requires that we *not* sanction practices that institutionalize treating them as if their value was reducible to their possible utility relative to our interests. Scientific research, when it involves routinely harming
35   animals in the name of possible "human and

humane benefits," violates this requirement of respectful treatment. Animals are not to be treated as mere receptacles or as renewable resources. Thus does the practice of scientific
40   research on animals violate their rights. Thus ought it to cease, according to the rights view. It is not enough first conscientiously to look for nominal alternatives and then, having failed to find any, to resort to using animals.
45   Though that approach is laudable as far as it goes, and though taking it would mark significant progress, it does not go far enough. It assumes that it is all right to allow practices that use animals as if their
50   value were reducible to their possible utility relative to the interests of others, provided that we have done our best not to do so. The rights view's position would have us go further in terms of "doing our
55   best." *The best we can do in terms of not using animals is not to use them.* Their inherent value does not disappear—just because we have failed to find a way to avoid harming them in pursuit of our chosen goals.
60   Their value is independent of these goals and their possible utility in achieving them.
        The rights view does not oppose using what is learned from conscientious efforts to treat a
65   sick animal (or human) to facilitate and improve the treatment tendered other animals (or humans). In *this* respect, the rights view raises no objection to the "many human and humane benefits" that flow from medical
70   science and the research with which it is allied. What the rights view opposes are practices that cause intentional harm to laboratory animals preparatory to "looking for something that just might yield some human or humane
75   benefit." Whatever benefits happen to accrue from such a practice are irrelevant to assessing its tragic injustice. Lab animals are not our tasters; we are not their kings.

Passage 2

        Whether animals have rights is a question of
80   great importance because if they do, those rights must be respected, even at the cost of

GO ON TO THE NEXT PAGE ▶▶▶

First passage: Tom Regan, *"The Case Against Animal Research"*, Contemporary Issues in Bioethics, Wadsworth Publishing Company, 1999
Second passage: Carl Cohen, *"Do Animals Have Rights?"*, Contemporary Is-sues in Bioethics, Wadsworth Publishing Company, 1999

great burdens for human beings. A right
(unlike an interest) is a valid claim, or potential
claim, made by a moral agent, under
85   principles that govern both the claimant and
the target of the claim. Rights are precious;
they are dispositive; they count.

       You have the right to the return of money
you lent me; we both understand that. It may
90   be very convenient for me to keep the money,
and you may have no need of it whatever; but
my convenience and your needs are not to
the point. You have a *right* to it, and we have
95   courts of law partly to ensure that such rights
will be respected.

       If you make me a promise, I have a moral
right to its fulfillment–even though there may
be no law to enforce my right. It may be very
much in your interest to break that promise,
100   but your great interests and the silence of the
law cut no mustard when your solemn promise
has been given.

       Some persons believe that animals have
rights and they therefore look on the uses of
105   animals in medical investigations with moral
loathing. If animals have rights they certainly
have the right not to be killed, even to
advance our important interests.

       Some may say, "Well, they have rights, but
110   we have rights too, and our rights override
theirs." That may be true in some cases, but it
will not solve the problem because, although
we may have a weighty *interest* in learning,
say, how to vaccinate against polio or other
115   diseases, we do not have a *right* to learn such
things. Nor could we honestly claim that we
kill research animals in self-defense; they did
not attack us. If animals have rights, they
certainly have the right not to be killed to
120   advance the interests of others, whatever rights
those others may have.

       In 1952 there were about 58,000 cases of
polio reported in the United States and 3,000
polio deaths; my parents, parents everywhere,
125   trembled in fear for their children at camp or
away from home. Polio vaccination became
routine in 1955, and cases dropped to about
a dozen a year; today polio has been
eradicated completely from the Western
130   Hemisphere. The vaccine that achieved this
could have been developed *only* with the
substantial use of animals.

       Many obligations are owed by humans to
animals; few will deny that. But it certainly

135   does not follow from this that animals have
rights because it is certainly not true that
every obligation of ours arises from the rights
of another. Not at all. We need to be clear
and careful here. Rights entail obligations. If
140   you have a right to the return of the money
I borrowed, I have an obligation to repay it.
No issue. But the proposition *all rights entail
obligations* does not convert simply, as the
logicians say. From the true proposition that
145   all trees are plants, it does not follow that all
plants are trees. Similarly, not all obligations
are entailed by rights. Some obligations, like
mine to repay the money I borrowed from you,
do arise out of rights. But many obligations
150   are owed to persons or other beings who
have no rights whatever in the matter.

       I emphasize this because, although
animals have no rights, it surely does not
follow from this that one is free to treat them
155   with callous disregard. Animals are not stones;
they feel. A rat may suffer; surely we have the
obligation not to torture it gratuitously, even
though it be true that the concept of a right
could not possibly apply to it.

160   Animals cannot be the bearers of rights
because the concept of rights is essentially
human; it is rooted in, and has force within,
a human moral world. Humans must deal
with rats and must be moral in their dealing
165   with them; but a rat can no more be said to
have rights than a table can be said to have
ambition. To say of a rat that it has rights is
to confuse categories, to apply to its world a
moral category that has content only in the
170   human moral world.

7   The author of Passage 1 indicates that those
who subscribe to the "rights view" referred to
in Passage 1 necessarily

   (A)   deny that animals can feel pain
   (B)   value medical progress over animal
          rights
   (C)   oppose medical research that harms
          animals
   (D)   believe that the rights of the sick
          supersede the rights of the healthy
   (E)   believe that only human beings have
          rights

8 The passage indicates that the "institutions" mentioned in line 24 often assume that animals used for medical research

(A) should be set free
(B) do not suffer during testing
(C) have a biochemical makeup that is similar to that of humans
(D) will remain in abundance
(E) are capable of distinguishing between right and wrong

9 In line 30, the word "sanction" most nearly means

(A) penalize
(B) approve
(C) destroy
(D) formally decree
(E) control

10 According to the passage, the "approach" mentioned in line 45 is one that

(A) acknowledges the impracticality of animal research
(B) tries to eliminate animal research on moral grounds
(C) utilizes animal research only as a last resort
(D) attempts to minimize the expense of medical research
(E) represents the mainstream of established medical practice

11 In line 66, the word "tendered" most nearly means

(A) administered to
(B) denied to
(C) relinquished to
(D) inspired by
(E) reduced to

12 In line 81, the statement that the rights of animals "must be respected" is made because this claim

(A) is the author's main thesis
(B) represents the dominant view of medical researchers
(C) is part of a proposition that the author refutes
(D) is a quotation from a respected authority
(E) represents a principle that the author believes should be upheld by the courts

13 Passage 2 indicates that, unlike an interest, a right is necessarily

(A) representative of an individual need
(B) a factor in social decisions
(C) something that animals can have
(D) beyond ethical analysis
(E) binding to more than one party

14 The statistics cited in the discussion of polio in the sixth paragraph of Passage 2 are intended primarily to support the author's claim that animals

(A) can contract diseases as easily as humans can
(B) often carry dangerous diseases
(C) are invaluable in the campaign to eradicate disease
(D) do not have the same rights as humans have
(E) share our concern for the well-being of children

15 The function of the seventh paragraph of Passage 2 (lines 133–151) is primarily to

(A) discuss a logical fallacy
(B) cite an authority on an issue
(C) provide historical background to a debate
(D) illustrate the suffering of animals under certain conditions
(E) present a moral objection to medical research performed on animals

16 In saying that a certain statement "does not convert simply" (line 143), the author of Passage 2 means that such a statement

(A) cannot be easily translated into another language
(B) is not based on factual evidence
(C) is logically impossible
(D) does not logically imply another statement
(E) does not easily change the minds of skeptics

17 The author of Passage 2 would likely characterize the use of the word "rights" in line 40 as

(A) a misnomer
(B) an anachronism
(C) a moral necessity
(D) a clever application
(E) inconsistent with the "rights view" discussed in Passage 1

8

18 Which of the following statements follows logically from the arguments presented by both authors?

(A) Animals do not have rights that bind human beings.
(B) Medical research cannot proceed if the use of animals in such research is prohibited.
(C) Animals are renewable resources.
(D) Gratuitous violence to animals is never morally justified.
(E) Humans have a right to learn how to prevent disease.

19 The two passages differ in their perspectives on animal experimentation in medical research in that Passage 1

(A) considers it a moral obligation, while Passage 2 does not
(B) devalues it, while Passage 2 values it highly
(C) claims that it harms animals, while Passage 2 claims that it does not
(D) claims that it requires harming the animals, while Passage 2 states that it does not
(E) states that the researchers who engage in it are moral agents, while Passage 2 states that they are not

STOP

You may check your work, on this section only, until time is called.

Section 9

Time—10 Minutes
14 Questions

Directions for Improving Sentences Questions

Each of the sentences below contains one underlined portion. The portion may contain one or more errors in grammar, usage, construction, precision, diction (choice of words), or idiom. Some of the sentences are correct.

Consider the meaning of the original sentence, and choose the answer that best expresses that meaning. If the original sentence is best, choose (A), because it repeats the original phrasing. Choose the phrasing that creates the clearest, most precise and most effective sentence.

EXAMPLE:

The children <u>couldn't hardly believe their eyes.</u>

   (A)   couldn't hardly believe their eyes
   (B)   would not hardly believe their eyes
   (C)   could hardly believe their eyes
   (D)   couldn't nearly believe their eyes
   (E)   could hardly believe his or her eyes

Example answer: (C)

---

1 Richard Avedon has created photographic portraits <u>and these capture unique</u> and often bizarre aspects of their subjects' personalities.

   (A)   and these capture unique
   (B)   which are capturing unique
   (C)   that uniquely capture
   (D)   that capture unique
   (E)   in capturing unique

2 Generally, <u>election years especially</u>, viewers should be careful not to obtain political information from only one source.

   (A)   election years especially
   (B)   and especially in election years
   (C)   election year's especially
   (D)   especially election year's
   (E)   and election years

3 The change in seasons, while beautiful, <u>often cause</u> people to fall ill.

   (A)   often cause
   (B)   often causing
   (C)   often causes
   (D)   therefore causes
   (E)   however, causes

4 Suddenly faced with an opportunity to earn lavish <u>incomes, recent</u> college graduates often forsake personal happiness for the pursuit of material wealth.

   (A)   incomes, recent
   (B)   incomes; recent
   (C)   incomes recent
   (D)   incomes, recently
   (E)   incomes of recent

5 The patient, unable to tolerate the seemingly interminable wait, <u>angrily leaving the doctor's office.</u>

   (A)   angrily leaving the doctor's office
   (B)   left the doctor's office room with anger
   (C)   left the doctor's office in a state of anger
   (D)   angrily left the doctor's office
   (E)   left angrily the doctor's office

9

GO ON TO THE NEXT PAGE ▶▶▶

6 Bill was ecstatic about the new accounting software, which allowed <u>organization of his current finances and to construct a detailed financial plan.</u>

(A) organization of his current finances and to construct a detailed financial plan
(B) organization of his current finances and let him construct a detailed financial plan
(C) him to organize his current finances and for a detailed financial plan to be constructed
(D) him to organize his current finances and construct a detailed financial plan
(E) him to organize his current finances and for the construction of a detailed financial plan

7 During the meeting, the board <u>created a plan where teachers would receive</u> pay raises according to their students' performance on standardized examinations.

(A) created a plan where teachers would receive
(B) creates a plan in which teachers are receiving
(C) created a plan where teachers receive
(D) creates a plan for teachers receiving
(E) created a plan in which teachers would receive

8 <u>The beleaguered fans left the game silently,</u> unable to envision a time when their team would once again stand tall in victory.

(A) The beleaguered fans left the game silently
(B) The beleaguered fans, in silence, had left the game
(C) They left the game silently, the beleaguered fans
(D) The beleaguered fans leaving the game silently
(E) Leaving the game silently, the beleaguered fans

9 When he lost his internet connection, Rufus punched his computer <u>monitor and this clearly demonstrates</u> his dire need for anger management therapy.

(A) monitor and this clearly demonstrates
(B) monitor, clearly demonstrating
(C) monitor, clearly to demonstrate
(D) monitor; clearly demonstrating
(E) monitor, clearly by demonstrating

10 The mentor program requires that its members <u>provide guidance, act respectfully, and act patiently</u> even when things are not going well.

(A) provide guidance, act respectfully, and act patience
(B) provide guidance, respectful action, and to show patience
(C) provide guidance, respectful action, and to show patience
(D) provide guidance, act respectfully, and show patience
(E) guidance, respectful action, and patience

11 The <u>country, once on the brink of financial collapse, now</u> boasts a thriving economy.

(A) country, once on the brink of financial collapse, now
(B) country that was once on the brink of financial collapse, now
(C) country, being once on the brink of financial collapse and now
(D) country being on the brink of financial collapse now
(E) country, that was once on the brink of financial collapse but now

12 The claim that a nation's strength depends on its military capabilities is belied by the fact that many of the world's economic <u>powers, like Japan, has almost no</u> soldiers beyond their own borders.

(A) powers, like Japan, has almost no
(B) powers, Japan being one, have just about no
(C) powers, like Japan, have almost no
(D) powers like Japan, has almost no
(E) powers have almost, like Japan, no

13 Being an affluent metropolitan area with a large fan base, the baseball commissioner decided that Washington, DC would be a fine city to host a new franchise.

(A) Being an affluent metropolitan area with a large fan base, the baseball commissioner decided that Washington, DC

(B) The fact that it is an affluent metropolitan area with a large fan base was why the baseball commissioner decided that Washington, DC

(C) The baseball commissioner decided that Washington, DC, an affluent metropolitan area with a large fan base,

(D) Because of it being an affluent metropolitan area with a large fan base, the baseball commissioner decided that Washington, DC

(E) An affluent metropolitan area with a large fan base, the baseball commissioner decided that Washington, DC

14 Completely devoid of artistic merit, the film used shock tactics in an effort to gain publicity and increasing their ticket sales.

(A) increasing their ticket sales
(B) increase ticket sales
(C) increasing the sales of their tickets
(D) and tickets
(E) and, as such, their increasing ticket sales

9

STOP   *You may check your work, on this section only, until time is called.*

ANSWER KEY

Section 3 Math	Section 5 Math	Section 7 Math	Section 2 Critical Reading	Section 4 Critical Reading	Section 8 Critical Reading	Section 6 Writing	Section 9 Writing
☐ 1. B	☐ 1. C	☐ 1. A	☐ 1. E	☐ 1. B	☐ 1. E	☐ 1. C	☐ 1. D
☐ 2. C	☐ 2. D	☐ 2. A	☐ 2. D	☐ 2. D	☐ 2. A	☐ 2. C	☐ 2. B
☐ 3. C	☐ 3. D	☐ 3. D	☐ 3. D	☐ 3. B	☐ 3. A	☐ 3. C	☐ 3. C
☐ 4. B	☐ 4. C	☐ 4. C	☐ 4. B	☐ 4. C	☐ 4. C	☐ 4. E	☐ 4. A
☐ 5. A	☐ 5. B	☐ 5. C	☐ 5. A	☐ 5. B	☐ 5. E	☐ 5. B	☐ 5. D
☐ 6. E	☐ 6. C	☐ 6. D	☐ 6. E	☐ 6. A	☐ 6. B	☐ 6. D	☐ 6. D
☐ 7. A	☐ 7. A	☐ 7. E	☐ 7. C	☐ 7. B	☐ 7. C	☐ 7. A	☐ 7. E
☐ 8. C	☐ 8. B	☐ 8. B	☐ 8. A	☐ 8. B	☐ 8. D	☐ 8. C	☐ 8. A
☐ 9. D	☐ 9. 168	☐ 9. C	☐ 9. D	☐ 9. A	☐ 9. B	☐ 9. D	☐ 9. B
☐ 10. D	☐ 10. 6	☐ 10. E	☐ 10. C	☐ 10. B	☐ 10. C	☐ 10. B	☐ 10. D
☐ 11. C	☐ 11. 42	☐ 11. B	☐ 11. C	☐ 11. C	☐ 11. A	☐ 11. E	☐ 11. A
☐ 12. E	☐ 12. 24	☐ 12. A	☐ 12. E	☐ 12. E	☐ 12. C	☐ 12. C	☐ 12. C
☐ 13. D	☐ 13. 3	☐ 13. D	☐ 13. B	☐ 13. B	☐ 13. E	☐ 13. D	☐ 13. C
☐ 14. D	☐ 14. $\frac{1}{2}$ or	☐ 14. D	☐ 14. B	☐ 14. D	☐ 14. C	☐ 14. C	☐ 14. D
☐ 15. B	0.5	☐ 15. C	☐ 15. E	☐ 15. C	☐ 15. A	☐ 15. E	
☐ 16. C	☐ 15. 750	☐ 16. C	☐ 16. E	☐ 16. A	☐ 16. D	☐ 16. D	
☐ 17. B	☐ 16. 1.5		☐ 17. D	☐ 17. D	☐ 17. A	☐ 17. C	
☐ 18. B	or $\frac{3}{2}$		☐ 18. B	☐ 18. E	☐ 18. D	☐ 18. D	
☐ 19. D	☐ 17. 100		☐ 19. D	☐ 19. B	☐ 19. B	☐ 19. A	
☐ 20. E	☐ 18. 20		☐ 20. D	☐ 20. B		☐ 20. B	
			☐ 21. C	☐ 21. C		☐ 21. E	
			☐ 22. A	☐ 22. A		☐ 22. B	
			☐ 23. C	☐ 23. C		☐ 23. B	
			☐ 24. E	☐ 24. A		☐ 24. D	
						☐ 25. A	
						☐ 26. C	
						☐ 27. A	
						☐ 28. C	
						☐ 29. E	
						☐ 30. D	
						☐ 31. B	
						☐ 32. B	
						☐ 33. A	
						☐ 34. D	
						☐ 35. A	

# Right (A): _____	Questions 1–8 # Right (A): _____	# Right (A): _____	# Right (A): _____	# Right (A): _____	# Right (A): _____	# Right (A): _____	# Right (A): _____
# Wrong (B): _____	# Wrong (B): _____	# Wrong (B): _____	# Wrong (B): _____	# Wrong (B): _____	# Wrong (B): _____	# Wrong (B): _____	# Wrong (B): _____
# (A) – $\frac{1}{4}$(B): _____	# (A) – $\frac{1}{4}$(B): _____	# (A) – $\frac{1}{4}$(B): _____	# (A) – $\frac{1}{4}$(B): _____	# (A) – $\frac{1}{4}$(B): _____	# (A) – $\frac{1}{4}$(B): _____	# (A) – $\frac{1}{4}$(B): _____	# (A) – $\frac{1}{4}$(B): _____
	Questions 9–18 # Right (A): _____						

SCORE CONVERSION TABLE

How to score your test

Use the answer key on the previous page to determine your raw score on each section. **Your raw score on each section except Section 4 is simply the number of correct answers minus ¼ of the number of wrong answers. On Section 4, your raw score is the sum of the number of correct answers for questions 1–8 minus ¼ of the number of wrong answers for questions 1–8 plus the total number of correct answers for questions 9–18.** Next, add the raw scores from Sections 3, 4, and 7 to get your Math raw score, add the raw scores from Sections 2, 5, and 8 to get your Critical Reading raw score and add the raw scores from sections 6 and 9 to get your Writing raw score. Write the three raw scores here:

Raw Critical Reading score: _____   Raw Math score: _____   Raw Writing score: _____

Use the table below to convert these to scaled scores.

Scaled scores: Critical Reading: _____ Math: _____ Writing: _____

Raw Score	Critical Reading Scaled Score	Math Scaled Score	Writing Scaled Score	Raw Score	Critical Reading Scaled Score	Math Scaled Score	Writing Scaled Score
67	800			32	520	550	610
66	800			31	510	550	600
65	790			30	510	540	580
64	780			29	500	530	570
63	760			28	490	520	560
62	750			27	490	530	550
61	730			26	480	510	540
60	720			25	480	500	530
59	700			24	470	490	520
58	700			23	460	480	510
57	690			22	460	480	500
56	680			21	450	470	490
55	670			20	440	460	480
54	660	800		19	440	450	470
53	650	790		18	430	450	460
52	650	760		17	420	440	450
51	640	740		16	420	430	440
50	630	720		15	410	420	440
49	620	710	800	14	400	410	430
48	620	700	800	13	400	410	420
47	610	680	800	12	390	400	410
46	600	670	790	11	380	390	400
45	600	660	780	10	370	380	390
44	590	650	760	9	360	370	380
43	590	640	740	8	350	360	380
42	580	630	730	7	340	350	370
41	570	630	710	6	330	340	360
40	570	620	700	5	320	330	350
39	560	610	690	4	310	320	340
38	550	600	670	3	300	310	320
37	550	590	660	2	280	290	310
36	540	580	650	1	270	280	300
35	540	580	640	0	250	260	280
34	530	570	630	−1	230	240	270
33	520	560	620	−2 or less	210	220	250

SCORE CONVERSION TABLE FOR WRITING COMPOSITE [ESSAY + MULTIPLE CHOICE]

Calculate your writing raw score as you did on the previous page and grade your essay from a 1 to a 6 according to the standards that follow in the detailed answer key.

Essay score: _____ Raw Writing score: _____

Use the table below to convert these to scaled scores.

Scaled score: Writing: _____

Raw Score	Essay Score 0	Essay Score 1	Essay Score 2	Essay Score 3	Essay Score 4	Essay Score 5	Essay Score 6
−2 or less	200	230	250	280	310	340	370
−1	210	240	260	290	320	360	380
0	230	260	280	300	340	370	400
1	240	270	290	320	350	380	410
2	250	280	300	330	360	390	420
3	260	290	310	340	370	400	430
4	270	300	320	350	380	410	440
5	280	310	330	360	390	420	450
6	290	320	340	360	400	430	460
7	290	330	340	370	410	440	470
8	300	330	350	380	410	450	470
9	310	340	360	390	420	450	480
10	320	350	370	390	430	460	490
11	320	360	370	400	440	470	500
12	330	360	380	410	440	470	500
13	340	370	390	420	450	480	510
14	350	380	390	420	460	490	520
15	350	380	400	430	460	500	530
16	360	390	410	440	470	500	530
17	370	400	420	440	480	510	540
18	380	410	420	450	490	520	550
19	380	410	430	460	490	530	560
20	390	420	440	470	500	530	560
21	400	430	450	480	510	540	570
22	410	440	460	480	520	550	580
23	420	450	470	490	530	560	590
24	420	460	470	500	540	570	600
25	430	460	480	510	540	580	610
26	440	470	490	520	550	590	610
27	450	480	500	530	560	590	620
28	460	490	510	540	570	600	630
29	470	500	520	550	580	610	640
30	480	510	530	560	590	620	650
31	490	520	540	560	600	630	660
32	500	530	550	570	610	640	670
33	510	540	550	580	620	650	680
34	510	550	560	590	630	660	690
35	520	560	570	600	640	670	700
36	530	560	580	610	650	680	710
37	540	570	590	620	660	690	720
38	550	580	600	630	670	700	730
39	560	600	610	640	680	710	740
40	580	610	620	650	690	720	750
41	590	620	640	660	700	730	760
42	600	630	650	680	710	740	770
43	610	640	660	690	720	750	780
44	620	660	670	700	740	770	800
45	640	670	690	720	750	780	800
46	650	690	700	730	770	800	800
47	670	700	720	750	780	800	800
48	680	720	730	760	800	800	800
49	680	720	730	760	800	800	800

Detailed Answer Key

Section I

The following essay received 12 points out of a possible 12, meaning that it demonstrates *clear and consistent competence* in that it

- develops an insightful point of view on the topic
- demonstrates exemplary critical thinking
- uses effective examples, reasons, and other evidence to support its thesis
- is consistently focused, coherent, and well-organized
- demonstrates skilful and effective use of language and sentence structure
- is largely (but not necessarily completely) free of grammatical and usage errors

Consider carefully the issue discussed in the following passage, then write an essay that answers the question posed in the assignment.

> *None know the unfortunate and the fortunate do not know themselves.*
>
> —Benjamin Franklin

Assignment: **Are people today generally too unaware of their good fortune?** Write an essay in which you answer this question and support your position logically with examples from literature, the arts, history, politics, science and technology, current events, or your experience or observation.

SAMPLE STUDENT ESSAY

When running against George Bush for governor of Texas, Ann Richards said that the future president "was born on third base but thinks he hit a triple," and was born "with a silver foot in his mouth." Not only do these turns of phrase belong in the political humor hall of fame, but they also reveal an important truth. Governor Richard's comments could as easily apply to millions of us Americans as it did to George Bush, which is, in part, why we elected him as president in 2000. We have no real sense of our privilege as nation, and mistakenly think that it is simply the product of our hard work and worthiness.

In fact, the origin of our privilege as a nation is not hard to determine, and it has very little to do with our moral or intellectual superiority as a people. This is not to say that America is not filled with good, smart, honest and hard-working people, but that it is a profoundly dangerous mistake to imagine, as so many of us do, that our status of superpower is simply a natural product of our superiority as a people.

So often, modern neo-conservatives claim that we are so productive and powerful as a nation because our "American values" of hard work and freedom are superior to those of other cultures. What they rarely acknowledge, however, yet what is painfully obvious, is that the history of "American values" has included such beliefs as that Africans are not human, that women should not have the right to

vote, that money and possessions are virtues, and that violence solves every problem. Furthermore, we have succeeded economically not because of these "American values" but despite them. Our country is uniquely endowed with rich natural resources, free access to water on two oceans, friendly neighbors, and geographical barriers from our enemies. These were not achieved through hard work or a dedication to high moral standards, but a willingness to conquer the native people and appropriate their lands.

What is perhaps even more dangerous than assuming that we have earned our prosperity by hard work and virtue alone is assuming that poorer countries fail to prosper merely because they aren't "democratic" or "free" enough. Our country has been run long enough by those with this privileged mindset, who believe that they have not only the right but the duty to impose their values on others.

This kind of thinking is precisely what the rest of the world hates about America. So many of our citizens seem genuinely befuddled by the fact that the world consumes our music, our films and our technology, yet so many people in the world hate us. It is not so hard to understand when one realizes that the vast majority of the world's people are not born into countries so isolated from their enemies and so abundant in natural resources. Most are born in the third world, not on third base.

> The following essay received 8 points out of a possible 12, meaning that it demonstrates *adequate competence* in that it
> - develops a point of view on the topic
> - demonstrates some critical thinking, but perhaps not consistently
> - uses some examples, reasons, and other evidence to support its thesis, but perhaps not adequately
> - shows a general organization and focus, but shows occasional lapses in this regard
> - demonstrates adequate but occasionally inconsistent facility with language
> - contains occasional errors in grammar, usage, and mechanics

SAMPLE STUDENT ESSAY

While Franklin's quotation serves as a valid consideration for much of the world's population, it is not a totally universal fact. Most people in the world are quite lucky to be where they are. Most people in this fortunate position are unaware of the scope of their luck. Even worse, a large percentage of these people are ignorant to the difficulties faced by those who do not share in their blessings. But to accept this situation as a truth without exception, would be an error in judgment, for many people are quite aware how lucky they are and many of those people are more than willing to face and fight for the pain of those less fortunate.

Perhaps no moment in history was more indicative of the flaws in Ben Franklin's quote than the summer of 1964, Freedom Summer. With a presidential election on the horizon, America was in the midst of unprecedented social upheaval. Racial tension had reached a boiling point and conservatives unwilling to accept social change in the South were excluding African-Americans from voting, threatening them with violence in order to maintain the status quo. To battle this situation, northern white college students, many of them privileged upper class Ivy Leaguers, drove down to Mississippi in an effort to help African-Americans register to vote. Facing the threat of violent repercussions, these intrepid youths took it upon themselves to bridge a racial and economic gap and push for a cause far removed from their own sheltered lives.

History is littered with such instances of selflessness. Whether demonstrated through a course of action as difficult and substantial as Freedom Summer or through a simple charitable contribution, the virtue remains the same. Their good deeds, however, often remain unseen simply because they are not newsworthy. Most of what we hear about today has to deal with crime and hate. What we miss are the optimistic stories where people step outside of their own lives to make a difference. Altruism, it seems, does not sell newspapers. While there are many people ignorant of their own good luck and blind to the pain of others, there are also many who understand their position in life and do what they can to improve the fortunes of others.

The following essay received 4 points out of a possible 12, meaning that it demonstrates *some incompetence* in that it
- has a seriously limited point of view
- demonstrates weak critical thinking
- uses inappropriate or insufficient examples, reasons, and other evidence to support its thesis
- is poorly focused and organized, and has serious problems with coherence
- demonstrates frequent problems with language and sentence structure
- contains errors in grammar and usage that obscure the author's meaning

SAMPLE STUDENT ESSAY

This quote by Ben Franklin says that people who are lucky do not realize they are fortunate. But this is not always true. There are many examples in life of people being very thankful for the things that they have. The most obvious example of this is the very existence of the annual holiday called Thanksgiving, where families come together and name the things they are most thankful for. This is one of the only holidays that the entire country celebrates, regardless of religion or background, and it shows how important people believe it is to be aware of one's good fortune.

People also often talk about having a streak of good luck, for example saying that good things come in threes, or that their good luck charm must be working. When I have a streak of good luck, I always notice it, and hope that it will last, and am thankful for it. I know that I am fortunate when this happens.

Also, there are many examples of people being aware of poor and starving people. People give to charities and give money to beggars on the street. They know that misfortune exists and wish that it were not the case and they do every little thing that they can to help out those in need. I have spent three years volunteering for the Key Club at my school, which is an organization that helps out with community projects, often helping those less fortunate. This has been a great experience for me, because it has opened my eyes to those who need help.

Sometimes you are lucky and you don't even know why. To you, it may be just your everyday life but when you compare it with what some other people go through, you can realize that you are actually very fortunate. This is a very important quality in life, one that we should all strive to achieve.

Detailed Answer Key

Section 2

1. **E**   Doctors often *administer* medication, and this medication left Ingrid without feeling on the left side of her face and removed the pain. *emollient* = something that softens; *antibody* = body substance that fights infection; *antidote* = a remedy to a poison; *cathartic* = something that assists in removing substances from the body; *anesthetic* = something that causes a loss of sensation.

2. **D**   This strain of the flu leaves its victims ____. Because she is unable to get out of bed, this strain must be particularly *harsh* or *harmful*. *benign* = harmless; *incapacitated* = disabled; *debilitating* = removing the strength from someone; *lethargic* = sluggish, lacking energy; *revitalized* = restored with life and energy.

3. **D**   A *gigantic earthquake* would cause serious damage. The fact that not a single building survived and so many were injured supports the idea. Look for a word that means *destroyed*. *preserve* = to maintain; *reiterate* = to state again; *debunk* = to disprove; *raze* = to destroy completely, to demolish; *salvage* = to save from destruction.

4. **B**   The newly released version of *Othello* was *condemned* (criticized) because it was just like the other remakes and did not bring anything new to the screen. *innovative* = new, fresh; *hackneyed* = overused, trite; *novel* = new; *quixotic* = idealistic, lacking realism; *profound* = deep, insightful.

5. **A**   The *airline industry was on the verge of collapse* and some businesses somehow survived because of government intervention. The intervention must have given the airlines money and such an intervention is known as a *subsidy*. *subsidy* = financial assistance; *infusion* = a flowing inward; *censure* = harsh criticism; *influx* = a flowing in; *endowment* = donated funds; *emission* = a substance that is discharged; *endorsement* = support; *alimony* = an allowance; *emanation* = something that comes off a source.

6. **E**   The father behaved in a manner similar to his daughter. Therefore, he would find it hard to *punish* his daughter for her excessive partying. He must also be a *hedonist* or pleasure-seeker. *ascetic* = one who leads a life of self denial; *castigate* = to criticize

harshly; *altruist* = a selfless individual; *extol* = to praise; *sybarite* = one who seeks luxury; *censure* = to publicly criticize; *philanthropist* = one who loves mankind; *hedonist* = pleasure seeker; *rebuke* = to scold harshly.

7. **C**   While writing his famous book, the author lived alone in a shack, much as a *hermit* would. But, the sentence explains that he did not lead the life of a hermit and that he instead actually did many social things such as go to the village and entertain at his house. *miscreant* = villain; *recluse* = a hermit; *curator* = a manager; *arborist* = a tree specialist.

8. **A**   The saleswoman *sells more cars than anyone else*, so she must be good at what she does. She would most likely be *unrelenting* in her efforts to close a deal. *inexorable* = relentless; *doggedness* = unwillingness to surrender; *lackadaisical* = uninterested; *pertinacity* = stubborn persistence; *submissive* = willing to yield; *diffident* = lacking confidence; *munificent* = generous; *temerity* = recklessness; *indolent* = lazy; *tenacity* = persistent.

9. **D**   The statement *the whole military action...must be in accordance with the object of the war* is saying that the strategy should fit with the *goal*.

10. **C**   The passage states that *modifications to the general plan...incessantly become necessary in war*, thereby suggesting that war is unpredictable.

11. **C**   The figure is viewed *through some supernatural medium*, which is perhaps a substance like a fog.

12. **E**   The face, which *had not a wrinkle in it*, must have therefore looked youthful. The phrase *tenderest bloom* reinforces this image.

13. **B**   Each paragraph, and hence the passage as a whole, explains how *our species shares so much with dogs* (line 30).

14. **B**   This action, in the context of a date between two human beings, is meant to describe a small but meaningful gesture.

15. **E**   The term *crazed semaphore flag* is a simile to describe what humans seem like to dogs, that is, we constantly send unintended signals that dogs pick up.

16. **E** The passage specifically indicates that dogs and humans are alike in all these ways except in sharpness of hearing.

17. **D** The passage says that farmers *need their dogs as much as or more than they do machinery or high-tech feeding systems*, thereby implying that these feeding systems are necessary to some farmers.

18. **B** The author is describing some of his inadequacies: *My prudence consists … not in the inventing of mans and methods … I have no skill to make money well …* he therefore is suggesting in line 9 that he is no good at gardening, either.

19 **D** By saying *I have the same title to write on prudence as I have to write on poetry or holiness …* the author is saying that he has the right, and indeed he is exercising that right throughout the passage.

20. **D** The author states in the first line that he has little prudence and that what he has is *of the negative sort* (lines 2–3). He later states that *we write from aspiration and antagonism* (lines 13–14) and that *we paint those qualities which we do not possess* (lines 15–16). Therefore, he is claiming the right to write about prudence because he admires it more than he possesses it.

21. **C** The *third class* is described as those who *live above* those of the second class, who are the artists and scientists. This third class is the *wise men* who have *spiritual perception*.

22. **A** By saying that the wise person *does not offer to build houses and barns* on the *sacred volcanic isle of nature*, the author is saying metaphorically that a wise person can see beyond nature to the *Splendor of the God* and does not see earthly life as his or her permanent status.

23. **C** This *base prudence* was described as a *devotion to matter* which concerns the five senses, rather than what lies beyond. This is a clear reference to the *first class* described in the previous paragraph, which lives *to the utility of the symbol*, or is concerned primarily with practical matters.

24. **E** In this paragraph, the author says that *culture … degrades every thing else, as health and bodily life, into means*, and then goes on to say that *cultivated men* in this sense of *culture* are not truly cultivated. Therefore, he is criticizing culture for the way it defines human activity.

Section 3

1. **B**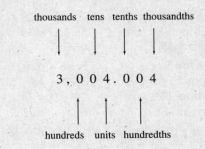

$$20 \text{ dozen CDs} \times \frac{12\,\text{CDs}}{1\,\text{dozen}} = 240 \text{ CDs}.$$

$$240 \text{ CDs} \times \frac{1\,\text{case}}{120\,\text{CDs}} = 2 \text{ cases}.$$

2. **C**

thousands tens tenths thousandths
↓   ↓   ↓   ↓

3 , 0 0 4 . 0 0 4

↑   ↑   ↑

hundreds units hundredths

3. **C** This question can be read as: "What is the value of y when $x = 8$?"
Plug 8 in for x and solve for y: $f(x) = 2x^2 + 8$
$$y = 2(8)^2 + 8$$
$$y = 2(64) + 8 = 136$$

4. **B**

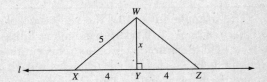

Line segment $\overline{WY}$ bisects $\overline{XZ}$. Therefore if $XZ = 8$, $XY = YZ = 4$.
Solve for x using the Pythagorean Theorem:
$$4^2 + x^2 = 5^2$$
$$16 + x^2 = 25$$
Subtract 16: $x^2 = 9$
Take square root: $x = 3$

5. **A**
They split the money in the ratio $3x:2x:1x$.
Write an equation: $3x + 2x + x = \$3,000$
Combine like terms: $6x = \$3,000$
Divide by 6: $x = \$500$

6. **E** Don't do more work than you have to here. The question asks for the value of $(x - y)^2$ and it tells you that $(x - y) = -2$.

                  $(x - y)^2$
Plug in -2 for $(x - y)$: $(-2)^2$
Simplify: 4

7. A Use the third row to find the common sum:
$$4 + 12 + 2 + 16 = 34$$

Solve for B: $11 + B + 7 + 3 = 34$
Combine like terms: $21 + B = 34$
Subtract 21: $B = 13$

Solve for A: $A + 1 + 10 + 9 = 34$
Combine like terms: $20 + A = 34$
Subtract 20: $A = 14$

Solve for C: $7 + 10 + 2 + C = 34$
Combine like terms: $19 + C = 34$
Subtract 19: $C = 15$

Solve for D: $5 + 8 + C + D = 34$
Plug in 15 for C: $5 + 8 + 15 + D = 34$
Combine like terms: $28 + D = 34$
Subtract 28: $B = 6$

$$A + B + C + D = 14 + 13 + 15 + 6 = 48$$

8. C Pick values for a and b and see which is greatest. Plug in -3 for a and -2 for b:
(A) $-3a + b = -3(-3) + (-2) = 9 + -2 = 7$
(B) $-(a + b) = -((-3) + (-2)) = -(-5) = 5$
(C) $-(3a + b) = -(3(-3) + (-2)) = -(-9 + -2) = 11$
(D) $3a = 3(-3) = -9$
(E) $a - b = (-3) - (-2) = -3 + 2 = -1$

9. D The triangle cut out of the right side of the folded piece of paper will take a triangular chunk out of both sides of the unfolded product. This eliminates answer choice E. The loss of the triangle on each end will make the paper smaller. This eliminates answer choices A and C. The rectangular piece cut off of side AB will leave a hole in the middle, which eliminates choice B.

10. D One simple way is to find out how many integers between 1 and 100 **are** the cube of an integer.

$1^3 = 1$; $2^3 = 8$; $3^3 = 27$; $4^3 = 64$
Four integers **are**, therefore $100 - 4 = 96$ are not.

11. C If there are three times as many goldfish as there are tropical fish, then 3 out of every 4 fish are goldfish.

The probability of selecting a goldfish at random is $\dfrac{3}{4}$.

There are twice as many orange as black goldfish, so 1/3 of the goldfish are black, and the probability

of selecting a black goldfish is $\dfrac{1}{3} \times \dfrac{3}{4} = \dfrac{3}{12} = \dfrac{1}{4}$.

12. E

Set up an equation: $P = \dfrac{kT}{V}$

Plug in given values: $700 = \dfrac{k(350)}{(10)} = 35k$

Divide by 35: $k = 20$

Write new equation: $P = \dfrac{20T}{V}$

Plug in new values: $500 = \dfrac{20T}{20}$; $500 = T$

13. D Plug in the ordered pairs listed and see which one works: $x - 2y > 5$
$y + x < 13$

(A)	$3 - 2(-1) > 5$; $5 > 5$	NO
	$3 + -1 < 13$, $2 < 13$	works
(B)	$12 - 2(3) > 5$; $6 > 5$	works
	$3 + 12 < 13$; $15 < 13$	NO
(C)	$8 - 2(3) > 5$; $2 > 5$	NO
	$8 + 3 < 13$; $11 < 13$	works
(D)	$10 - 2(2) > 5$; $6 > 5$	works
	$2 + 10 < 13$; $12 < 13$	works
(E)	$1 - 2(5) > 5$; $-9 > 5$	NO
	$1 + 5 < 13$	works

14. D Let a be the number of dollars Andrea had to start, let c be the number of dollars Chris had to start, and let l be the number of dollars Liz had to start. The question asks for the value of c. After Andrea gives \$10 to Chris she has $a - 10$ dollars and Chris has $c + 10$ dollars. Andrea then gives \$3 to Liz leaving her with $a - 13$ dollars and Liz with $l + 3$ dollars. Chris then gives \$4 to Liz leaving him with $c + 6$ dollars and Liz now has $l + 7$ dollars. If Andrea still has \$10 more than Chris, then:

$$(a - 13) = (c + 6) + 10$$
Simplify: $a - 13 = c + 16$
Add 13: $a = c + 29$

Therefore, Andrea has \$29 more than Chris.
Alternatively, you could plug in numbers to solve this problem: Let's say Andrea finished with \$30. She had \$10 more than Chris and \$16 more than Liz.
Final Totals: Andrea = \$30; Chris = \$20; Liz = \$14
Before Andrea gave \$10 to Chris, she had \$30 + \$10 = \$40 and Chris had \$20 − \$10 = \$10.
Before Andrea gave \$3 to Liz, she had \$40 + \$3 = \$43
Before Chris gave \$4 to Liz, he had \$10 + \$4 = \$14, and \$43 − \$14 = \$29.

15. B

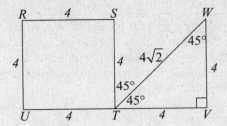

Because we know that T is a midpoint of line segment $\overline{UV}$ we know that $UT = TV$. Let's say that the length of a side of the square is 4. That would make the perimeter of the square $4 + 4 + 4 + 4 = 16$.

The two legs of right triangle TVW would also be 4 and the hypotenuse can be found using the Pythagorean theorem: $4^2 + 4^2 = \left(TW\right)^2$

Simplify: $\quad\quad\quad\quad\quad\quad 32 = \left(TW\right)^2$

Take square root: $\quad\quad\quad \sqrt{32} = TW = 4\sqrt{2}$

The perimeter of the triangle is $4 + 4 + 4\sqrt{2} = 8 + 4\sqrt{2}$

Set up ratio: $\quad\dfrac{\text{perimeter of square}}{\text{perimeter of triangle}} = \dfrac{16}{8 + 4\sqrt{2}}$

Divide numerator and denominator by 4: $\dfrac{4}{2 + \sqrt{2}}$

16. C "Park" the cars to solve this problem. You have 5 parking spaces to fill. Deal with the restrictions first. One of the cars is too big to fit in the two spots closest to the street so you only have 4 choices for the spot closest to the street. Once you have parked one of those four cars in that spot, you have 3 choices for the spot that is the second closest to the street. Now the restrictions are lifted and you have 3 choices for the third spot, then 2 choices for the fourth spot, and 1 choice for the last spot. $4 \times 3 \times 3 \times 2 \times 1 = 72$

17. B Remember your average pyramid from Chapter 12, Lesson 2. A total of 7 students took the quiz and had an average score of 83, so the sum of their scores is $(83)(7) = 581$ points. Three of the students had an average score of 79, so the sum of their scores is $(79)(3) = 237$ points. Therefore the four remaining students scored $581 - 237 = 344$ points. Find the average: $\quad 344 \div 4 = 86$ points

18. B First look at the table to find the minimum wage in each of those two years:

1980: $3.10
1974: $2.00

Percent change $= \dfrac{\text{final} - \text{original}}{\text{original}} \times 100\%$

Plug in values: $\dfrac{3.10 - 2.00}{2.00}(100\%) = \dfrac{1.10}{2.00}(100\%) = 55\%$

19. D Write out the first nine terms: $t_3 = 13 + 8 = 21$; $t_4 = 21 + 13 = 34$; $t_5 = 34 + 21 = 55$; $t_6 = 55 + 34 = 89$; $t_7 = 89 + 55 = 144$; $t_8 = 144 + 89 = 233$; $t_9 = 233 + 144 = 377$. So the sequence is:

8, 13, 21, 34, 55, 89, 144, 233, 377...
E, O, O, E, O, O, E, O, O

The repeating pattern is {even, odd, odd} which repeats every three terms. In 60 terms, the pattern repeats $60 \div 3 = 20$ times. In each repetition there are 2 odd numbers, so in 20 full repetitions there are $20 \cdot 2 = 40$ odd numbers.

20. E Break this problem into two parts: the cost of the first 6 inches, and the cost of the additional inches. They charge d dollars total for the first 6 inches and f dollars for *each* additional inch. Be careful to remember to remove the first 6 inches from the calculation of the "additional" inches to be shoveled.

Cost of first 6 inches: $\quad\quad d$
Cost of additional: $\quad\quad\quad (p - 6)f$
Total cost: $\quad\quad\quad\quad\quad \text{Cost} = d + (p - 6)f$

Section 4

1. B Rita's cat was *beloved*, so putting it to sleep would be a sad experience. You would expect her to be consumed by grief. *inversion* = the act of turning upside-down; *anguish* = agonizing emotional pain; *frivolity* = silliness; *hilarity* = extreme humor.

2. D If the virus was replicating *at a remarkable speed*, then it was *proliferating*. *pontificate* = to speak pompously; *diverge* = to move apart; *saturate* = to fill completely; *proliferate* = to grow; *dissipate* = to disperse.

3. B Leah came from a wealthy family. The word *Despite* indicates that we should expect an irony, so she must be behaving differently from how you would expect a rich woman to behave. If she won't waste *even a few dollars* she must be relatively *stingy*. The phrase *sometimes even* indicates a greater degree. *prudent* = wise; *munificent* = generous; *thrifty* = conservative with money; *stingy* = unwilling to part with money; *frugal* = good with your money; *outspoken* = inclined to speak one's mind; *improvident* = wasteful; *miserly* = stingy.

4. C If his midterms were *grueling*, they tired him out. He must be in need of a rest. *encore* = an additional performance; *respite* = a break, a rest; *commencement* = a beginning; *conviction* = strong belief.

5. B Emil has *always been* a particular way throughout medical school. He is prone to *superficial flattery*, so he is a flatterer. *toady* = one who flatters; *irreverent* = disrespectful; *sycophant* = one who flatters; *fawning* = giving excessive praise; *lackey* = a servant; *insubordinate* = resistant to authority; *mercenary* = one who is paid to fight; *intractable* = stubborn; *clairvoyant* = able to see the future; *altruistic* = selfless.

6. A The passage says that *since the bob changes height ... its gravitational energy changes*, thereby suggesting that gravitational energy depends on height.

7. B Lines 15–21 indicate the inverse relationship between gravitational and kinetic energy.

8. B The fact that she *took a position on the stones* in the street and *received daily a small sum in pennies* which were *contributed* by others implies that she is a beggar.

9. A The *keys* describe the way she says "God bless yeh," so it indicates her tones of voice.

10. B This paragraph is simply stating a brief history of video surveillance. This paragraph contains no central thesis. It is preventing objective facts, and so it is also not describing a *misconception* or presenting an *individual's point of view*.

11. C Since CNIL *proposed safeguards* against electronic surveillance, they must be concerned with potential misuses.

12. E The statistics suggest that people do not disapprove widely of the use of video surveillance, but are widely disapproving of *showing pictures of a person taken in a public place without that person's consent*.

13. B The stores *monitor specific aspects of consumer behavior* like *movements and gestures* in order to *optimize the position of goods*.

14. D In saying that *everywhere he goes he leaves electronic traces of his passage*, the author means that the person's activities are being surveilled by electronic detectors everywhere he goes.

15. C Adjectives like *remote, impersonal* and *largely invisible* indicate that electronic surveillance is *detached*.

16. A The central topic of the passage is the invasion of privacy. The author states that the *loss of privacy entailed in the taking of pictures ... may be justified in certain places where security is at risk, but it is not justified in all cases* (lines 85–89). The examples that are then cited represent examples where the taking of pictures has stepped over the line of prudent security. The author's objection to the cameras on the highway is that they *can see into adjacent houses and apartment blocks* (lines 98–100), thereby invading the privacy of non-drivers.

17. D The passage says that *city women* are *more original ... than women in smaller places* (lines 8–12). Therefore, women in smaller places are more traditional.

18. E This *dash* is *something original that will excite interest* (lines 22–23).

19. B This *knowledge* is the *knowledge of the world* that allows one to *excite interest*.

20. B The *attractiveness* of her story is enhanced by *relating her discouragements, trials and mistakes* (line 30) to make her *better company.*

21. C The paragraph says that such women need to *exercise the rites of hospitality unquestioned* (lines 46–47), which supports statement I. It also says that they need *the exemption ... from being agreeable at all times and places* (lines 39–42), which supports statement II. The paragraph says nothing about education.

22. A The sentence conveys the idea that women want to *be within the circumference of a social circle* rather than *on the periphery.*

23. C This paragraph discusses the value of a woman bachelor extending *hospitalities* (line 56), and in saying that *the shyest novice over the tea cup loses her timidity*, the author is saying that women become more bold when they are hosting guests.

24. A The passage states that a woman with her own home *loses her timidity* (line 68).

Section 5

1. C $3 - x = 2x - 6$

Add x: $3 = 3x - 6$

Add 6: $9 = 3x$

Divide by 3: $3 = x$

2. D The rightmost (units) column seems to indicate that $P + T = P$ and so $T = 0$. There can be no "carry" as long as T is less than 10, which it must be. According to the tens column, $R + 7 = 15$, so $R = 8$.

3. D The sum of the angles in an n-sided polygon is $(n - 2) 180° =$ degrees because any n-sided polygon can be divided into $n-2$ triangles. The sum of the angles in a 6-sided polygon, then, is $(6 - 2)180°$ $= 4(180°) = 720°$

So, $142° + 141° + 112° + 105° + w° + v° = 720°$

Simplify: $500° + w° + v° = 720°$

Subtract 500° : $w° + v° = 220°$

4. C Write equations to represent the information:

$$x = 2y$$
$$x - y = 4$$

Substitute $2y$ for x: $2y - y = 4$

Combine like terms: $y = 4$

Solve for x: $x = 2y = 2(4) = 8$

The greater of these two numbers is 8.

5. B Let $n =$ the number of seats in the theater

$$\frac{1}{3}n + 50 = \frac{3}{4}n$$

Subtract $\frac{1}{3}n$: $50 = \frac{5}{12}n$

Divide by $\frac{5}{12}$: $n = 120$

6. C Just write them out, keeping in mind that the 4 can be in the ones or tens place:

4, 14, 24, 34, 40, 41, 42, 43, 44, 45, 46, 47, 48, 49

(A common mistake here is to count 44 twice because it contains two 4s)

7. A You must combine the equations to solve:

$$
\begin{array}{ll}
\text{(a)} & 3x = y + z \\
\text{(b)} & y = 6 - z \\
\text{(c)} & z + x = 8
\end{array}
$$

Substitute $(6 - z)$ for y: $3x = (6 - z) + z$

Combine like terms: $3x = 6$

Divide by 3: $x = 2$

Plug in 2 for x: $z + 2 = 8$

Subtract 2: $z = 6$

Plug in 6 for z: $y = 6 - 6 = 0$

Divide y by z: $\dfrac{y}{z} = \dfrac{0}{6} = 0$

---

8. B The diagonal of the square is the diameter of the circle.

$$d = 2r = 2(8) = 16$$

The diagonal of a square divides it into two 45°– 45° –90° triangles as shown here:

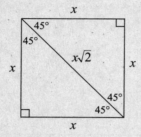

The diagonal $= 16 = x\sqrt{2}$

Divide by $\sqrt{2}$:

$$\frac{16}{\sqrt{2}} = \frac{16\sqrt{2}}{2} = 8\sqrt{2} = x$$

$$\text{Area}_{\text{square}} = \text{side}^2 = \left(8\sqrt{2}\right)^2 = 128$$

Now you might notice that the shaded region is ¾ of the whole square, so its area is ¾(128) = 96. Or, you might notice that the shaded region is the square minus the area of triangles *ROS:*

$$\text{Area}_{\triangle ROS} = \frac{1}{2}(\text{base})(\text{height}) = \frac{1}{2}(8)(8) = 32$$

Shaded Area $= \text{Area}_{\text{square}} - \text{Area}_{\text{triangle}} = 128 - 32 = 96$

---

9. 168 If two things are equal, you can substitute either one for the other. $f(x) = 3x + 7$

Substitute: $g(f(x)) = g(3x + 7)$

Use the definition of $g(x)$: $g(3x + 7) = (3x + 7)^2 - 1$

Plug in 2 for x: $y = (3(2) + 7)^2 - 1$

Simplify: $y = 13^2 - 1 = 168$

---

10. 6 First find out how many students would be in each homeroom if they were all the same size. You can do this by finding the average size of the classes:

$$\text{Average} = \frac{14 + 18 + 21 + 23}{4} = 19$$

This means each class must have 19 students when you are done moving children around. Start with the largest class, 23 students, and move 4 of those students into the class with 14. This leaves us with classes with

$$18 \quad 18 \quad 21 \quad 19$$

Next move one from the class with 21 students into each of the 18-student classes to move those three classes to 19 students as well. This means a total of 6 must be moved.

---

11. 42 The pie chart shows that 15 + 10 = 25% of an average day is spent either socializing or at the gym: (0.25)(24 hours) = 6 hours per day. So in a seven-day week, the student would spend 6 × 7 = 42 hours.

---

12. 24 You are given only two sides of a triangle, with the third as an unknown. To find the maximum area, first set it up as if it were a *right* triangle:

$$\text{Area} = \frac{1}{2}(\text{base})(\text{height})$$

$$\text{Area} = \frac{1}{2}(6)(8) = 24$$

It doesn't have to be a right triangle though, it could look like these:

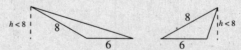

But these have smaller heights, and therefore smaller areas. Therefore the right triangle has maximum area.

---

13. 3 $|2x + 6| > 10$

Translate without the absolute value:

$$2x + 6 > 10 \text{ or } 2x + 6 < -10$$

Subtract 6: $2x > 4$ $2x < -16$

Divide by 2: $x > 2$ $x < -8$

Since x is a positive integer, it must be greater than 2. The least integer greater than 2 is 3.

14. $\frac{1}{2}$ or .5

There are ten possible combinations of two coins: $1 + 5 = 6$; $1 + 10 = 11$; $1 + 25 = 26$; $1 + 50 = 51$; $5 + 10 = 15$; $5 + 25 = 30$; $5 + 50 = 55$; $10 + 25 = 35$; $10 + 50 = 60$; $25 + 50 = 75$

Five of these have a sum that is less than 35 cents, so the probability is $\frac{1}{2}$ or 0.5.

15. **750**

Area of ballroom = $150 \times 100 = 15,000$ ft^2

Set up ratio: $\dfrac{1 \text{ can}}{300 \text{ ft}^2} = \dfrac{x \text{ cans}}{15,000 \text{ ft}^2}$

Cross multiply: $300x = 15,000$
Divide by 300: $x = 50$ cans of paint

Set up ratio: $\dfrac{1 \text{ can}}{\$15.00} = \dfrac{50 \text{ cans}}{y}$

Cross multiply: $y = \$750.00$

16. **1.5** or $\dfrac{3}{2}$

Volume = $n = lwh$
Plug in values: $n = (6)(4)(3) = 72$
Surface Area = $m = 2lw + 2hw + 2lh$
Plug in: $m = 2(6)(4) + 2(3)(4) + 2(6)(3)$
Simplify: $m = 48 + 24 + 36 = 108$
$m/n = 108/72 = 1.5$

17. **100** First remember that "inclusive" means including the smallest and largest numbers listed. In order for xy to be a member of set Y, it must be a positive integer between 1 and 100. To maximize the sum, find the largest numbers possible. 99 from set Y and 1 from set X will give you a sum of 100 and a product of 99, both of which are in set Y.

18. **20** This problem can be solved using similar triangles. Draw two right triangles, one with a base of 4, and the other with a base of 8. The first triangle has a height of x, and the other has a height of $x + 10$.

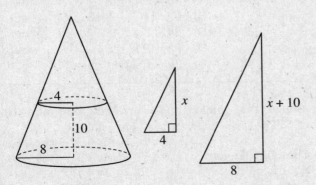

Set up a ratio and solve for x: $\dfrac{x}{4} = \dfrac{x+10}{8}$

Cross multiply: $8x = 4(x + 10)$
Distribute: $8x = 4x + 40$
Subtract $4x$: $4x = 40$
Divide by 4: $x = 10$
Therefore the height of the cone is $10 + 10 = 20$
(Chapter 13, Lesson 6: Similar Figures)

Section 6

1. **C** Choice C is the most concise and grammatically appropriate choice.

2. **C** The phrase *at another point in time in the past* is unnecessarily wordy and redundant, because the tense conveys the time.

3. **C** The phrase *could of* is a common diction error that stems from mispronunciation of the contraction *could've*. *Could have* is the correct phrase.

4. **E** Choice E is most parallel with the preceding clause.

5. **B** This choice follows the rules of parallel structure, keeping the entire list in the same format.

6. **D** The original phrase is unclear because it uses a weak verb and the "dummy" subject *It*. Choice D is most clear and concise.

7. **A** The sentence is best as written.

8. **C** The phrase *being that* is a non-standard form of *because*. The use of the participial phrase *often requiring ...* to describe the novel is most concise and clear.

9. **D** The original phrase is an **appositive,** which should only be used next to a noun that describes the same thing as the appositive. Since this phrase does not describe *literature*, it is inappropriate. The participial phrase in D is most appropriate and effective.

10. **B** The original choice produces a sentence fragment: it contains no verb. Choice B conveys the idea most directly and completely.

11. **E** The phrase *their lighting candles to express hope* is a noun phrase in the place where a participial phrase belongs.

12. C A comma is better suited for joining the two phrases. The second phrase is not an independent clause, so the semi-colon is inappropriate.

13. D Answer choice D is incorrect because it does not follow the rules of parallel structure. One alternative would be *permission to stay up*.

14. C The cars are not brand new, so the statement *it was brand new* is counter to fact, and is therefore in the subjunctive mood. The proper form is *it were*.

15. E The sentence is correct.

16. D Choice D does not follow the rules of parallel structure. The correct word is *honesty*.

17. C The phrase *sufficient enough* is redundant.

18. D The comparison is illogical. The sentence is comparing one *movie* to other *movies*, so the phrase *those of* should be eliminated.

19. A The pronoun does not agree in number with its antecedent, *each*, which is singular. The correct pronoun is *his*.

20. B The use of the present perfect *has matured* and the present tense *feels* implies the present tense for the verb in choice B. Therefore, the correct word is *resorts*.

21. E The sentence is correct.

22. B The pronoun *their* has no clear antecedent. It logically refers to the store, so it should be replaced with *the store's prices* or *the prices the store offered*.

23. B Answer choice B violates the rules of parallel structure. The correction is *respected*.

24. D This is a comparison error. It is not logical to suggest that the *price of video equipment at Joe's Appliances* is more than *Acme Video*. A better phrasing would be *those at Acme Video*.

25. A The past perfect tense requires the use of the past participle. The past participle of *to write* is *written*, not *wrote*.

26. C The parallel construction of the list requires that the phrase in (C) be changed to *to feed*.

27. A The parallel construction *more A than B* requires that the phrases A and B be parallel. Therefore, the word *like* should be omitted.

28. C The antecedent of the pronoun *it* is the plural noun *storms*; the two do not agree in number, so the phrase should be changed to *they were something*.

29. E The sentence is correct

30. D This choice conveys the right idea in the fewest words.

31. B Choice B is most concise and clear.

32. B This option is more concise than the others and maintains a logical structure.

33. A Choice A most effectively conveys the idea that *60 Minutes* changed the nature of television journalism.

34. D This sentence serves as a transition from the ideas of paragraph 3 into those of paragraph 4.

35. A The sentence is most effective as it is.

Section 7

1. A
Perimeter = length + length + width + width
The perimeter of the 1st rectangle is $6 + 6 + 3 + 3 = 18$
The perimeter of the 2nd rectangle is $7 + 7 + x + x = 18$

Combine like terms:	$14 + 2x = 18$
Subtract 14:	$2x = 4$
Divide by 2:	$x = 2$

2. A
To solve this problem, pick an odd number for b:
Let's say $b = 1$.

(A)	$2b = 2(1) = 2$	ok
(B)	$b + 2 = 1 + 2 = 3$	out
(C)	$2b + 1 = 2(1) + 1 = 3$	out
(D)	$3b = 3(1) = 3$	out
(E)	$2b - 1 = 2(1) - 1 = 1$	out

3. D
Angles that make up a straight line add up to 180°.

$$2x + 3° + x = 180°$$

Combine like terms:	$3x + 3° = 180°$
Subtract 3°:	$3x = 177°$
Divide by 3:	$x = 59°$

4. C

$$\left(x^6 y^4\right)^{-\frac{1}{2}} = \left(x^{-3} y^{-2}\right) = \frac{1}{\left(x^3 y^2\right)}$$

5. C

The median is the middle value. Write out the final exam grades from smallest to largest, then cross off the "outer" terms two at a time:
~~60, 60, 75, 80, 80, 80, 85, 85,~~ 85, ~~85, 90, 90, 90, 95, 95, 95, 95~~
This leaves 85 as the median.

6. D

$$a = b^3$$
Choose a simple value like 1 for b: $a = 1^3 = 1$
Now triple b and find a: $a = 3^3 = 27$
Therefore, the value of a is multiplied by 27.

7. E

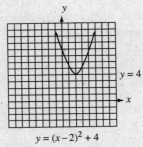

$$y = (x-2)^2 + 4$$

A quick way to solve this problem is to graph it on your calculator:
As you can see on the graph, $y = 4$ at its minimum value. Alternately, you may simply notice that the smallest the square of a real number can be is 0. This means that the smallest $(x - 2)^2$ can be is 0, so the smallest that y can be is 4. Be careful not to pick 2 as your answer. This is the value of x that *yields* the minimum value of the function, but is not actually the minimum value. Sometimes they will ask which value of x gives the minimum value of y, so you will sometimes look for that as an answer.

8. B $(5^3)(4^3) = (5 \times 4)^3 = 20^3 = 20^w$ so $w = 3$

9. C
Subtract 5 from x: $x - 5$
Multiply by 2: $2(x - 5)$
Add 6: $2(x - 5) + 6$
Distribute: $2x - 10 + 6$
Combine like terms: $2x - 4$

10. E

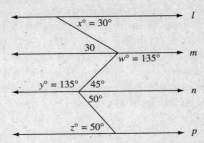

Remember, with parallel lines, angles that make a "Z" are equal. Mark up the diagram as shown.
$w + x + y + z = 135 + 30 + 135 + 50 = 350$

11. B   Set up a ratio: $\dfrac{x \text{ miles}}{p \text{ cms}} = \dfrac{y \text{ miles}}{p + 5 \text{ cms}}$

Cross multiply: $x(p + 5) = yp$
Distribute: $xp + 5x = yp$

Divide by p: $\dfrac{xp + 5x}{p} = y$

12. A   The question asks the value of $\sqrt{820} + \sqrt{104}$.
$$\sqrt{820} = 042$$
$$\sqrt{104} = 326$$
$$\sqrt{820} + \sqrt{104} = 042 + 326 = 368$$
Careful! Don't pick answer B, $\sqrt{368}$, which equals 580. Answer choice A, $\sqrt{146} = 368$

13. D $\text{Slope} = m = \dfrac{y_2 - y_1}{x_2 - x_1} = \dfrac{s - r}{s^2 - r^2}$

Factor: $\dfrac{s - r}{(s - r)(s + r)} = \dfrac{1}{(s + r)}$

14. D

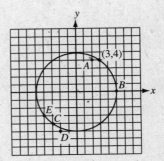

Using the distance formula to find the distance from $(0, 0)$ to $(3, 4)$ you can find that the radius = 5. Sketch a circle centered at the origin with a radius of 5, and plot the 5 answer choices. Answer choice D would be outside the circle. The others are either inside the circle or on it.

15. C $16m^2 + 56m + 49 = (mx + 7)^2$

Since $m + x = 8$, substitute $8 - m$ for x:

$16m^2 + 56m + 49 = (m(8 - m) + 7)^2$

Simplify: $16m^2 + 56m + 49 = (-m^2 + 8m + 7)^2$

Factor: $(4m + 7)^2 = (-m^2 + 8m + 7)^2$

Take the square root: $|4m + 7| = |-m^2 + 8m + 7|$

Since m is positive but less than 8, both $4m + 7$ and $-m^2 + 8m + 7$ are positive, so $4m + 7 = -m^2 + 8m + 7$

Add $m^2 - 8m - 7$: $m^2 - 4m = 0$

Divide by m: $m - 4 = 0$

Add 4: $m = 4$

Substitute into $m + x = 8$: $4 + x = 8$

Subtract 4: $x = 4$

So $m - x = 4 - 4 = 0$

---

16. C

$(x - y)(x + y) = x^2 - y^2$. Plug in and simplify:

$$x^2 - y^2 = \left(\frac{b-a}{a}\right)^2 - \left(\frac{b+a}{a}\right)^2$$

Square both expressions:

$$\left(\frac{b^2 - 2ab + a^2}{a^2}\right) - \left(\frac{b^2 + 2ab + a^2}{a^2}\right)$$

Combine the fractions:

$$\frac{\left(b^2 - 2ab + a^2\right) - \left(b^2 + 2ab + a^2\right)}{a^2}$$

Combine like terms:

$$\left(\frac{-4ab}{a^2}\right) = \frac{-4b}{a}$$

Alternatively, if you wish to avoid the algebra, pick a value for b and a and see which answer choice works.

Let's say $a = 2$ and $b = 4$:

$$\left(\frac{b-a}{a}\right)^2 - \left(\frac{b+a}{a}\right)^2 = \left(\frac{4-2}{2}\right)^2 - \left(\frac{4+2}{2}\right)^2 = 1 - 9 = -8$$

Answer choice C: $\dfrac{-4b}{a} = \dfrac{-4(4)}{2} = -8$

Section 8

1. E The colon indicates an explanation. The decade witnessed a *slow return to economic stability*, which is a rehabilitation. *acrimony* = harsh words; *mirth* = laughter; *aggregation* = making up a whole of something; *rehabilitate* = to return to health.

---

2. A If Jorge is a *gourmet*, he enjoys fine food. A gourmet would logically *bemoan* (complain about) a *lack* of good restaurants. *paucity* = a lack; *multitude* = a large number; *surfeit* = an excess; *conglomeration* = a combination.

---

3. A Before evidence came out that suggested that the *new* fuel source was effective and clean, environmentalists argued that the *innovation* (new idea) was too _____. If the evidence proved that it was clean and effective, they must have worried it would not be effective because they did not know enough about the fuel. *speculative* = based on inconclusive evidence; *lucid* = clear; *dynamic* = full of energy; *fastidious* = difficult to please, meticulously attentive to detail; *monotonous* = boring.

---

4. C A *despot* is a tyrannical leader. The fact that he has spent much of the past thirty years *persecuting his citizens* confirms this. The word *Although* indicates a contrast, so his experience must have made him less mean. *repugnant* = causes feelings of disgust; *beneficent* = kind, generous; *cantankerous* = cranky; *abominable* = abhorrent; *nefarious* = wicked; *odious* = worthy of hatred; *patriarchal* = ruled by males; *vile* = disgusting; *malevolent* = evil-wishing; *mellifluous* = smooth flowing.

---

5. E This sentence can be completed in two different logical ways. Clearly the *very natures* of these characters prevent them from *conforming* to the social standards of their times, in which case they are *rebels*, or their natures prevent them from *straying from* the social standards of their times, in which case they are *conformists. heretic* = an individual with controversial opinions; *denounce* = to condemn; *obsequious* = overly submissive; *assimilate* = to make similar; *recalcitrant* = hesitant to obey; *itinerant* = wandering; *iconoclast* = one who attacks tradition; *conform* = to do what is expected.

---

6. B The dancer moves with —— that *belies* (misrepresents) *her lack of grace*. The *despite* indicates a contrast in the sentence and the second half of the sentence discusses her lack of grace. It would follow that she would move with *grace* or *skill* and that she is one of the *least* graceful dancers in the troupe.

agile = quick, nimble; *inept* = incompetent, clumsy; *nimble* = deft, highly skilled; *deft* = skillful; *treachery* = betrayal; *cunning* = deceptiveness, cleverness; *aptitude* = skill, ability; *dexterous* = good with one's hands; *idiosyncrasy* = an unusual mannerism or characteristic

7. **C** Passage 1 states that *the rights view has principled objections* (line 12) to the continuation of animal research because it harms animals.

8. **D** The passage states that these institutions *treat (animals) as renewable resources* (line 25).

9. **B** The passage states that treating animals well requires *that we not sanction practices* that deny them their rights. This means that we should not *approve* such practices.

10. **C** This approach is one that looks *for nominal alternatives (to research on animals) and then, having failed to find any, (resorts) to using animals* (lines 43–44).

11. **A** The phrase *treatment tendered other animals* the author means *treatment administered to other animals.*

12. **C** The assumption made in this statement—*if they do (have rights), those rights must be respected*—is the claim that the passage attempts to refute.

13. **E** The passage explains that *a right (unlike an interest) is a valid claim, or potential claim, made by a moral agent, under principles that govern both the claimant and the target of the claim* (lines 82–86). This suggests that they bind more than one party.

14. **C** These statistics illustrate the fact that important medical breakthroughs, like the elimination of polio, depended on the use of animal experimentation.

15. **A** This paragraph discusses the logical-fallacy which is "Since rights entail obligations, obligations imply rights."

16. **D** The point of this paragraph is that the converse of the statement "All rights entail obligations" is not true, so this statement does not logically imply another.

17. **A** Since the author of Passage 2 argues that animals cannot have rights because the concepts of rights is *essentially human*, then the author would regard this use of the term as incorrect.

18. **D** Both passages suggest that the statement in choice D is true. Passage 1 argues that harming animals is wrong even if such harms brings benefits to humans. Passage 2 states that *surely we have the obligation not to torture it (a rat) gratuitously* (lines 156–157).

19. **B** Passage 1 devalues animal experimentation by saying that stopping it would not bring medical research *to a halt* (line 5) and that only research performed in treating animals that are sick is morally justified. Passage 2 states that polio could not have been cured without such animal experimentation.

Section 9

1. **D** The phrasing in (D) is most concise and clear.

2. **B** The underlined phrase must be parallel with the opening modifier, *generally*, which is an adverb. Choice (B) is the only one that provides the correct adverbial form.

3. **C** Since the subject of the sentence is *change*, which is singular, the correct verb form is *causes*. Choices (D) and (E) include illogical coordinators.

4. **A** The modifying phrase that opens the sentence should be set apart from the main clause by a comma.

5. **D** The original phrasing is not a complete sentence. The phrases *with anger* and *in a state of anger* are not idiomatic. Choice (D) is preferable to choice (E) because the object *the doctor's office* should not be separated from its verb *left*.

6. **D** The original phrasing is not parallel. Choice (D) provides the most concise and parallel phrasing.

7. **E** Since a plan is not a place, the use of *where* in the original phrasing is incorrect. Choice (B) is incorrect because the verb *are receiving* is in the wrong tense. Choice (D) is incorrect because the verb *causes* is in the wrong tense. Choice (E) uses the correct tense and pronouns.

8. **A** The original phrasing is the most logical and concise. The verb in choice (B) is in the wrong tense. Choice (C) contains a misplaced appositive. Choices (D) and (E) produce sentence fragments.

9. **B**   Choice (B) is the only phrasing that logically coordinates the two clauses in the sentence.

10. **D**   Choice (D) is the only phrasing that includes logical and parallel phrasing

11. **A**   The original phrasing is clear, concise and logical.

12. **C**   In the original phrasing, the verb *has* does not agree with its subject *powers*. Choice (C) corrects this problem and uses thie modifying phrase correctly.

13. **C**   The original phrasing contains a dangling participle, *being*. Choice (B) is awkward and contains a pronoun, *it*, with an unclear antecedent. Choice (D) begins with a non-standard phrasing, *because of it being*. Choice (E) contains a misplaced appositive.

14. **D**   This choice best follows the law of parallelism.

PRACTICE TEST 5

ANSWER SHEET

Last Name: _____   First Name: _____

Date: _____   Testing Location: _____

Directions for Test

- Remove these answer sheets from the book and use them to record your answers to this test.
- This test will require 3 hours and 20 minutes to complete. Take this test in one sitting.
- The time allotment for each section is written clearly at the beginning of each section. This test contains six 25-minute sections, two 20-minute sections, and one 10-minute section.
- This test is 25 minutes shorter than the actual SAT, which will include a 25-minute "experimental" section that does not count toward your score. That section has been omitted from this test.
- You may take one short break during the test, of no more than 10 minutes in length.
- You may only work on one section at any given time.
- You must stop ALL work on a section when time is called.
- If you finish a section before the time has elapsed, check your work on that section. You may NOT work on any other section.
- Do not waste time on questions that seem too difficult for you.
- Use the test book for scratchwork, but you will receive credit only for answers that are marked on the answer sheets.
- You will receive one point for every correct answer.
- You will receive no points for an omitted question.
- For each wrong answer on any multiple-choice question, your score will be reduced by ¼ point.
- For each wrong answer on any numerical "grid-in" question, you will receive no deduction.

SECTION 2

1. Ⓐ Ⓑ Ⓒ Ⓓ Ⓔ
2. Ⓐ Ⓑ Ⓒ Ⓓ Ⓔ
3. Ⓐ Ⓑ Ⓒ Ⓓ Ⓔ
4. Ⓐ Ⓑ Ⓒ Ⓓ Ⓔ
5. Ⓐ Ⓑ Ⓒ Ⓓ Ⓔ
6. Ⓐ Ⓑ Ⓒ Ⓓ Ⓔ
7. Ⓐ Ⓑ Ⓒ Ⓓ Ⓔ
8. Ⓐ Ⓑ Ⓒ Ⓓ Ⓔ
9. Ⓐ Ⓑ Ⓒ Ⓓ Ⓔ
10. Ⓐ Ⓑ Ⓒ Ⓓ Ⓔ
11. Ⓐ Ⓑ Ⓒ Ⓓ Ⓔ
12. Ⓐ Ⓑ Ⓒ Ⓓ Ⓔ
13. Ⓐ Ⓑ Ⓒ Ⓓ Ⓔ
14. Ⓐ Ⓑ Ⓒ Ⓓ Ⓔ
15. Ⓐ Ⓑ Ⓒ Ⓓ Ⓔ
16. Ⓐ Ⓑ Ⓒ Ⓓ Ⓔ
17. Ⓐ Ⓑ Ⓒ Ⓓ Ⓔ
18. Ⓐ Ⓑ Ⓒ Ⓓ Ⓔ
19. Ⓐ Ⓑ Ⓒ Ⓓ Ⓔ
20. Ⓐ Ⓑ Ⓒ Ⓓ Ⓔ
21. Ⓐ Ⓑ Ⓒ Ⓓ Ⓔ
22. Ⓐ Ⓑ Ⓒ Ⓓ Ⓔ
23. Ⓐ Ⓑ Ⓒ Ⓓ Ⓔ
24. Ⓐ Ⓑ Ⓒ Ⓓ Ⓔ
25. Ⓐ Ⓑ Ⓒ Ⓓ Ⓔ
26. Ⓐ Ⓑ Ⓒ Ⓓ Ⓔ
27. Ⓐ Ⓑ Ⓒ Ⓓ Ⓔ
28. Ⓐ Ⓑ Ⓒ Ⓓ Ⓔ
29. Ⓐ Ⓑ Ⓒ Ⓓ Ⓔ
30. Ⓐ Ⓑ Ⓒ Ⓓ Ⓔ
31. Ⓐ Ⓑ Ⓒ Ⓓ Ⓔ
32. Ⓐ Ⓑ Ⓒ Ⓓ Ⓔ
33. Ⓐ Ⓑ Ⓒ Ⓓ Ⓔ
34. Ⓐ Ⓑ Ⓒ Ⓓ Ⓔ
35. Ⓐ Ⓑ Ⓒ Ⓓ Ⓔ
36. Ⓐ Ⓑ Ⓒ Ⓓ Ⓔ
37. Ⓐ Ⓑ Ⓒ Ⓓ Ⓔ
38. Ⓐ Ⓑ Ⓒ Ⓓ Ⓔ
39. Ⓐ Ⓑ Ⓒ Ⓓ Ⓔ
40. Ⓐ Ⓑ Ⓒ Ⓓ Ⓔ

SECTION 3

1. Ⓐ Ⓑ Ⓒ Ⓓ Ⓔ
2. Ⓐ Ⓑ Ⓒ Ⓓ Ⓔ
3. Ⓐ Ⓑ Ⓒ Ⓓ Ⓔ
4. Ⓐ Ⓑ Ⓒ Ⓓ Ⓔ
5. Ⓐ Ⓑ Ⓒ Ⓓ Ⓔ
6. Ⓐ Ⓑ Ⓒ Ⓓ Ⓔ
7. Ⓐ Ⓑ Ⓒ Ⓓ Ⓔ
8. Ⓐ Ⓑ Ⓒ Ⓓ Ⓔ
9. Ⓐ Ⓑ Ⓒ Ⓓ Ⓔ
10. Ⓐ Ⓑ Ⓒ Ⓓ Ⓔ
11. Ⓐ Ⓑ Ⓒ Ⓓ Ⓔ
12. Ⓐ Ⓑ Ⓒ Ⓓ Ⓔ
13. Ⓐ Ⓑ Ⓒ Ⓓ Ⓔ
14. Ⓐ Ⓑ Ⓒ Ⓓ Ⓔ
15. Ⓐ Ⓑ Ⓒ Ⓓ Ⓔ
16. Ⓐ Ⓑ Ⓒ Ⓓ Ⓔ
17. Ⓐ Ⓑ Ⓒ Ⓓ Ⓔ
18. Ⓐ Ⓑ Ⓒ Ⓓ Ⓔ
19. Ⓐ Ⓑ Ⓒ Ⓓ Ⓔ
20. Ⓐ Ⓑ Ⓒ Ⓓ Ⓔ
21. Ⓐ Ⓑ Ⓒ Ⓓ Ⓔ
22. Ⓐ Ⓑ Ⓒ Ⓓ Ⓔ
23. Ⓐ Ⓑ Ⓒ Ⓓ Ⓔ
24. Ⓐ Ⓑ Ⓒ Ⓓ Ⓔ
25. Ⓐ Ⓑ Ⓒ Ⓓ Ⓔ
26. Ⓐ Ⓑ Ⓒ Ⓓ Ⓔ
27. Ⓐ Ⓑ Ⓒ Ⓓ Ⓔ
28. Ⓐ Ⓑ Ⓒ Ⓓ Ⓔ
29. Ⓐ Ⓑ Ⓒ Ⓓ Ⓔ
30. Ⓐ Ⓑ Ⓒ Ⓓ Ⓔ
31. Ⓐ Ⓑ Ⓒ Ⓓ Ⓔ
32. Ⓐ Ⓑ Ⓒ Ⓓ Ⓔ
33. Ⓐ Ⓑ Ⓒ Ⓓ Ⓔ
34. Ⓐ Ⓑ Ⓒ Ⓓ Ⓔ
35. Ⓐ Ⓑ Ⓒ Ⓓ Ⓔ
36. Ⓐ Ⓑ Ⓒ Ⓓ Ⓔ
37. Ⓐ Ⓑ Ⓒ Ⓓ Ⓔ
38. Ⓐ Ⓑ Ⓒ Ⓓ Ⓔ
39. Ⓐ Ⓑ Ⓒ Ⓓ Ⓔ
40. Ⓐ Ⓑ Ⓒ Ⓓ Ⓔ

ANSWER SHEET

SECTION 4

1. Ⓐ Ⓑ Ⓒ Ⓓ Ⓔ
2. Ⓐ Ⓑ Ⓒ Ⓓ Ⓔ
3. Ⓐ Ⓑ Ⓒ Ⓓ Ⓔ
4. Ⓐ Ⓑ Ⓒ Ⓓ Ⓔ
5. Ⓐ Ⓑ Ⓒ Ⓓ Ⓔ
6. Ⓐ Ⓑ Ⓒ Ⓓ Ⓔ
7. Ⓐ Ⓑ Ⓒ Ⓓ Ⓔ
8. Ⓐ Ⓑ Ⓒ Ⓓ Ⓔ
9. Ⓐ Ⓑ Ⓒ Ⓓ Ⓔ
10. Ⓐ Ⓑ Ⓒ Ⓓ Ⓔ

11. Ⓐ Ⓑ Ⓒ Ⓓ Ⓔ
12. Ⓐ Ⓑ Ⓒ Ⓓ Ⓔ
13. Ⓐ Ⓑ Ⓒ Ⓓ Ⓔ
14. Ⓐ Ⓑ Ⓒ Ⓓ Ⓔ
15. Ⓐ Ⓑ Ⓒ Ⓓ Ⓔ
16. Ⓐ Ⓑ Ⓒ Ⓓ Ⓔ
17. Ⓐ Ⓑ Ⓒ Ⓓ Ⓔ
18. Ⓐ Ⓑ Ⓒ Ⓓ Ⓔ
19. Ⓐ Ⓑ Ⓒ Ⓓ Ⓔ
20. Ⓐ Ⓑ Ⓒ Ⓓ Ⓔ

21. Ⓐ Ⓑ Ⓒ Ⓓ Ⓔ
22. Ⓐ Ⓑ Ⓒ Ⓓ Ⓔ
23. Ⓐ Ⓑ Ⓒ Ⓓ Ⓔ
24. Ⓐ Ⓑ Ⓒ Ⓓ Ⓔ
25. Ⓐ Ⓑ Ⓒ Ⓓ Ⓔ
26. Ⓐ Ⓑ Ⓒ Ⓓ Ⓔ
27. Ⓐ Ⓑ Ⓒ Ⓓ Ⓔ
28. Ⓐ Ⓑ Ⓒ Ⓓ Ⓔ
29. Ⓐ Ⓑ Ⓒ Ⓓ Ⓔ
30. Ⓐ Ⓑ Ⓒ Ⓓ Ⓔ

31. Ⓐ Ⓑ Ⓒ Ⓓ Ⓔ
32. Ⓐ Ⓑ Ⓒ Ⓓ Ⓔ
33. Ⓐ Ⓑ Ⓒ Ⓓ Ⓔ
34. Ⓐ Ⓑ Ⓒ Ⓓ Ⓔ
35. Ⓐ Ⓑ Ⓒ Ⓓ Ⓔ
36. Ⓐ Ⓑ Ⓒ Ⓓ Ⓔ
37. Ⓐ Ⓑ Ⓒ Ⓓ Ⓔ
38. Ⓐ Ⓑ Ⓒ Ⓓ Ⓔ
39. Ⓐ Ⓑ Ⓒ Ⓓ Ⓔ
40. Ⓐ Ⓑ Ⓒ Ⓓ Ⓔ

SECTION 5

1. Ⓐ Ⓑ Ⓒ Ⓓ Ⓔ
2. Ⓐ Ⓑ Ⓒ Ⓓ Ⓔ
3. Ⓐ Ⓑ Ⓒ Ⓓ Ⓔ
4. Ⓐ Ⓑ Ⓒ Ⓓ Ⓔ

5. Ⓐ Ⓑ Ⓒ Ⓓ Ⓔ
6. Ⓐ Ⓑ Ⓒ Ⓓ Ⓔ
7. Ⓐ Ⓑ Ⓒ Ⓓ Ⓔ
8. Ⓐ Ⓑ Ⓒ Ⓓ Ⓔ

9. 10. 11. 12. 13.

14. 15. 16. 17. 18.

[Grid-in answer bubbles numbered 9–18, each containing columns with decimal points, fraction slashes, and digits 0–9]

ANSWER SHEET

SECTION 6

1. Ⓐ Ⓑ Ⓒ Ⓓ Ⓔ
2. Ⓐ Ⓑ Ⓒ Ⓓ Ⓔ
3. Ⓐ Ⓑ Ⓒ Ⓓ Ⓔ
4. Ⓐ Ⓑ Ⓒ Ⓓ Ⓔ
5. Ⓐ Ⓑ Ⓒ Ⓓ Ⓔ
6. Ⓐ Ⓑ Ⓒ Ⓓ Ⓔ
7. Ⓐ Ⓑ Ⓒ Ⓓ Ⓔ
8. Ⓐ Ⓑ Ⓒ Ⓓ Ⓔ
9. Ⓐ Ⓑ Ⓒ Ⓓ Ⓔ
10. Ⓐ Ⓑ Ⓒ Ⓓ Ⓔ
11. Ⓐ Ⓑ Ⓒ Ⓓ Ⓔ
12. Ⓐ Ⓑ Ⓒ Ⓓ Ⓔ
13. Ⓐ Ⓑ Ⓒ Ⓓ Ⓔ
14. Ⓐ Ⓑ Ⓒ Ⓓ Ⓔ
15. Ⓐ Ⓑ Ⓒ Ⓓ Ⓔ
16. Ⓐ Ⓑ Ⓒ Ⓓ Ⓔ
17. Ⓐ Ⓑ Ⓒ Ⓓ Ⓔ
18. Ⓐ Ⓑ Ⓒ Ⓓ Ⓔ
19. Ⓐ Ⓑ Ⓒ Ⓓ Ⓔ
20. Ⓐ Ⓑ Ⓒ Ⓓ Ⓔ
21. Ⓐ Ⓑ Ⓒ Ⓓ Ⓔ
22. Ⓐ Ⓑ Ⓒ Ⓓ Ⓔ
23. Ⓐ Ⓑ Ⓒ Ⓓ Ⓔ
24. Ⓐ Ⓑ Ⓒ Ⓓ Ⓔ
25. Ⓐ Ⓑ Ⓒ Ⓓ Ⓔ
26. Ⓐ Ⓑ Ⓒ Ⓓ Ⓔ
27. Ⓐ Ⓑ Ⓒ Ⓓ Ⓔ
28. Ⓐ Ⓑ Ⓒ Ⓓ Ⓔ
29. Ⓐ Ⓑ Ⓒ Ⓓ Ⓔ
30. Ⓐ Ⓑ Ⓒ Ⓓ Ⓔ
31. Ⓐ Ⓑ Ⓒ Ⓓ Ⓔ
32. Ⓐ Ⓑ Ⓒ Ⓓ Ⓔ
33. Ⓐ Ⓑ Ⓒ Ⓓ Ⓔ
34. Ⓐ Ⓑ Ⓒ Ⓓ Ⓔ
35. Ⓐ Ⓑ Ⓒ Ⓓ Ⓔ
36. Ⓐ Ⓑ Ⓒ Ⓓ Ⓔ
37. Ⓐ Ⓑ Ⓒ Ⓓ Ⓔ
38. Ⓐ Ⓑ Ⓒ Ⓓ Ⓔ
39. Ⓐ Ⓑ Ⓒ Ⓓ Ⓔ
40. Ⓐ Ⓑ Ⓒ Ⓓ Ⓔ

SECTION 7

(1–40, Ⓐ Ⓑ Ⓒ Ⓓ Ⓔ)

SECTION 8

(1–40, Ⓐ Ⓑ Ⓒ Ⓓ Ⓔ)

SECTION 9

(1–40, Ⓐ Ⓑ Ⓒ Ⓓ Ⓔ)

Section 1

Time—25 minutes

I

Directions for Writing the Essay

Plan and write an essay that answers the question below. Do NOT write on another topic. An essay on another topic will receive a score of 0.

Two readers will grade your essay based on how well you develop your point of view, organize and explain your ideas, use specific and relevant examples to support your thesis, and use clear and effective language. How well you write is much more important than how much you write, but to cover the topic adequately you should plan to write several paragraphs.

Your essay must be written on separate lined sheets of paper. Keep your handwriting to a reasonable size. Your essay will be read by people who are not familiar with your handwriting, so write legibly.

You may use this sheet for notes and outlining, but these will not be graded as part of your essay.

Consider carefully the issue discussed in the following passage, then write an essay that answers the question posed in the assignment.

> In any contest between power and patience, bet on patience.
>
> —W.B. Prescott

Assignment: **Which is a more powerful force of social change: power or patience?** Write an essay in which you answer this question and support your position logically with examples from literature, the arts, history, politics, science and technology, current events, or your experience or observation.

Write your essay on separate sheets of paper.

GO ON TO THE NEXT PAGE ▸▸▸

Section 2

Time—25 minutes
20 Questions

2 ▶

Directions for Multiple-Choice Questions

In this section, solve each problem, using any available space on the page for scratchwork. Then decide which is the best of the choices given and fill in the corresponding oval on the answer sheet.

- You may use a calculator on any problem. All numbers used are real numbers.
- Figures are drawn as accurately as possible EXCEPT when it is stated that the figure is not drawn to scale.
- All figures lie in a plane unless otherwise indicated.

Reference Information

$A = \pi r^2$ $A = \ell w$ $A = \frac{1}{2}bh$ $V = \ell wh$ $V = \pi r^2 h$ $c^2 = a^2 + b^2$ Special Right Triangles
$C = 2\pi r$

The arc of a circle measures 360°.
Every straight angle measures 180°.
The sum of the measures of the angles in a triangle is 180°.

---

1 If $a = 3 + b$ and $a = 2b$, then $b =$

(A) 1.5
(B) 2
(C) 3
(D) 4
(E) 6

2 If 1 pound of cheese costs $1.50 and 2 pounds of beef costs $4.00, then how much more expensive is 6 pounds of beef than 6 pounds of cheese?

(A) $1.50
(B) $2.00
(C) $3.00
(D) $4.00
(E) $6.00

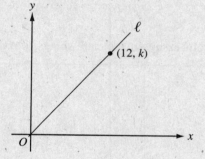

3 In the figure above, line l passes through the origin and has a slope of 2. What is the value of k?

(A) 2
(B) 4
(C) 6
(D) 12
(E) 24

4 If x is 5 less than y, then what is the value of $5(x - y)$?

(A) −25
(B) −5
(C) 0
(D) 5
(E) 25

5 On a certain map that is drawn to scale, a distance of 50 miles is represented by 1 inch. How many inches on the map would represent a distance of 240 miles?

(A) 2.4
(B) 4.8
(C) 6.4
(D) 8.0
(E) 12.0

6 Three students have a total of 30 CDs among them. If one student has 40% of the CDs, and another has 33 ⅓% of the CDs, how many CDs does the third student have?

(A) 6
(B) 8
(C) 9
(D) 10
(E) 12

7 The average (arithmetic mean) of Marianne's scores on 3 tests is 85. If she scored 90 on both of the first two tests, what was her score on the third test?

(A) 70
(B) 75
(C) 80
(D) 85
(E) 90

$$-1, 0, 1, -1, 0, 1, ...$$

8 The numbers −1, 0 and 1 repeat in a sequence, as shown above. If this pattern continues, what will be the sum of the first 100 terms of this sequence?

(A) −1
(B) 1
(C) 33
(D) 34
(E) 100

9 Fifty plastic balls numbered 1 to 50, inclusive, are placed in a bowl and one ball is to be selected at random. What is the probability that the ball selected will have a number that is a multiple of 3?

(A) $\dfrac{3}{50}$

(B) $\dfrac{3}{25}$

(C) $\dfrac{8}{25}$

(D) $\dfrac{1}{3}$

(E) $\dfrac{9}{25}$

10 If $a + b = 5$, $a - c = 15$, and $a = 10$, then $c - b =$

(A) −10
(B) −5
(C) 0
(D) 5
(E) 10

$$\begin{array}{r} 3A \\ B7 \\ 4B \\ +\ 27 \\ \hline 178 \end{array}$$

11 In the correctly worked addition problem above, A and B represent digits. What is digit A?

(A) 5
(B) 6
(C) 7
(D) 8
(E) 9

GO ON TO THE NEXT PAGE ▶▶▶

Note: Figure not drawn to scale.

12 In the figure above, point D (not shown) is drawn so that point C is the midpoint of $\overline{AD}$. If $CD = 4x$, then what is the length of AB in terms of x?

(A) $3x$
(B) $\sqrt{15}x$
(C) $4x$
(D) $\sqrt{17}x$
(E) $\sqrt{63}x$

13 The line that passes through $(-2, 4)$ and $(1, 6)$ also passes through which of the following points?

(A) $(4, 8)$
(B) $(4, 10)$
(C) $(5, 7)$
(D) $(5, 8)$
(E) $(5, 9)$

14 For which of the following sets of numbers is the first number equal to the sum of the second number and the square of the third number?

(A) 6, 4, 2
(B) 9, 6, 9
(C) 10, 9, 4
(D) 16, 7, 3
(E) 19, 16, 15

15 $3^x + 3^x + 3^x + 3^x + 3^x + 3^x + 3^x + 3^x + 3^x =$

(A) 3^{x+8}
(B) 3^{9x}
(C) 3^{x+2}
(D) 27^x
(E) $9(3^{9x})$

16 Which of the following graphs represents the set of all solutions of the statement $2 - |x + 1| < 0$?

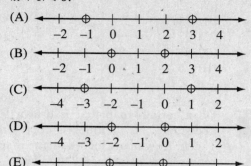

17 A publishing company wants to increase the price of one of its books by 10%. Research shows that this increase in price would decrease sales of the book by only 5%. By what percent would this change increase the money received through sales of this book?

(A) 4.0%
(B) 4.5%
(C) 5.0%
(D) 5.5%
(E) 6.0%

18 A total of 32 teams play in a single-elimination tournament. In the first round, every team plays one game against another team, and the losing teams are eliminated from the tournament. No game ends in a tie. Every winning team procedes to the next round, in which they play another winning team. This single-elimination procedure continues until only one team remains. If each game takes precisely 2 hours to play, what is the total length of games played in the tournament, in hours?

(A) 30
(B) 32
(C) 48
(D) 62
(E) 64

GO ON TO THE NEXT PAGE ▸▸▸

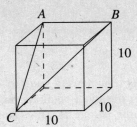

19 In the figure above, points A, B, and C are vertices of the cube shown. What is the area of triangle ABC?

(A) 50

(B) $50\sqrt{2}$

(C) $50\sqrt{3}$

(D) $100\sqrt{2}$

(E) $100\sqrt{3}$

20 A jar contains only red and black marbles. Originally, the ratio of black marbles to red marbles was 4:5. After 18 black marbles were added, the ratio of black marbles to red marbles became 5:4. How many marbles were in the jar originally?

(A) 45

(B) 54

(C) 63

(D) 72

(E) 81

2

You may check your work, on this section only, until time is called.

Section 3

Time—25 minutes
24 Questions

3

Each of the sentences below is missing one or two portions. Read each sentence, then select the word or words that most logically completes the sentence, taking into account the meaning of the sentence as a whole.

Example:

Rather than accepting the theory unquestioningly, Deborah regarded it with ———.

(A) mirth   (B) sadness   (C) responsibility
(D) ignorance   (E) skepticism

Correct response: (E)

1 Journalists often have strong personal opinions about the political events they analyze, and so have great difficulty in remaining ——————— in their writing.

(A) eloquent
(B) converted
(C) neutral
(D) biased
(E) emotional

2 Although the topic of the lecture fascinated me, the speaker's presentation style was so ——————— that I found it difficult to stay awake.

(A) monotonous
(B) rude
(C) provocative
(D) authoritative
(E) trustworthy

3 Because space travel is becoming increasingly ———————, within a few decades it is possible that excursions to the moon will be as ——— as international flights are today.

(A) dangerous . . pedestrian
(B) responsive . . formal
(C) inescapable . . challenging
(D) mundane . . exciting
(E) inexpensive . . commonplace

4 The fact that viewers seem to ——— the stars of even the most vacuous popular television programs suggests that Americans value sheer ——— over talent or achievement.

(A) exalt . . intelligence
(B) lionize . . fame
(C) criticize . . popularity
(D) envy . . obscurity
(E) tolerate . . aesthetics

5 Anthropologists have discovered that many cultures employ only ——— strategies for resolving conflicts, in contradiction to those who suggest that warfare is ———.

(A) ineffective . . dangerous
(B) violent . . common
(C) peaceful . . universal
(D) restricted . . deleterious
(E) idiosyncratic . . novel

6 Francisco Goya's cheerful ——— of social conditions in 18th century Spain was later ——— by a harshly critical view of its politics and society.

(A) celebration . . supported
(B) espousal . . returned
(C) repression . . succeeded
(D) acceptance . . supplanted
(E) denunciation . . replaced

7 The pace with which the country's infrastructure was rebuilt after the war can best be described as ———; the government leaders reasoned that a hasty approach would likely create more problems later on.

(A) accelerated
(B) dexterous
(C) indifferent
(D) deliberate
(E) dilapidated

8 Although racquetball was invented in 1949 in Greenwich, Connecticut, in fact many of its rules were ——— from older, well-established sports like handball and squash.

(A) appropriated
(B) discarded
(C) advocated
(D) elucidated
(E) compensated

GO ON TO THE NEXT PAGE ▶▶▶

Each passage below is followed by one or two questions based on its content. Answer each question based on what is stated or implied in the preceding passage.

Questions 9–10 are based on the following passage.

The following passage is from an essay on American education and political values written in 2004.

Line American public schools teach capitalism not so much by directly instructing students in the function and benefits of free markets as by embodying capitalistic qualities in their
5   very structure. For instance, they encourage students to compete for capital resources called grades, which teachers often keep arbitrarily scarce, thereby espousing the values of individual achievement and
10   competition. In socialist and communist countries, in contrast, we find schools in which cooperation is stressed far more than competition. Students in socialist systems regularly engage in practices that American
15   students would characterize as "cheating;" in such systems, knowledge is regarded as something that everyone should be willing to share. The American emphasis on knowledge as a source of competition contrasts starkly
20   with the American democratic ideal of universal education.

9 The passage indicates that the means by which capitalistic values are conveyed to American students is

(A) socialistic
(B) implicit
(C) illegal
(D) direct
(E) challenging

10 In line 12, the word "stressed" most nearly means

(A) anxious
(B) under pressure
(C) fragile
(D) evaluated
(E) emphasized

Questions 11–12 are based on the following passage.

The following passage discusses the life of F. Scott Fitzgerald, a famous American novelist of the early 20th century.

Line The life of F. Scott Fitzgerald was sharply divided in every sense. The years of youth, of his first maturity and his early success in the 1910s and 1920s, contrast markedly with the
5   years full of personal and public happenings that led to his premature death in 1940. These later years, full of disillusionment and suffering, though identified with human and artistic growth, were cut off at the very
10   moment when Fitzgerald's career seemed about to bear its best fruits. But Fitzgerald's life was divided above all in a personal and human sense. It was divided between the pursuit of the artistic ideal and the continual,
15   too frequent concessions to the taste of the moment or to the lure of easy success; it was divided between a rigorous application to the craft of fiction and the waste of precious energy in purely commercial literary activity.
20   Fitzgerald was a victim, in so many ways, of the myth of success and money, the false gods, as Hemingway was to call them in *Green Hills of Africa*, on whose altars so many promising young writers were sacrificed.

11 According to the author, Fitzgerald's pursuit of the "artistic ideal" (line 14) is best described as

(A) compromised
(B) premature
(C) effortless
(D) secretive
(E) uninterrupted

12 It can be inferred from the passage that, in *Green Hills of Africa*, Hemingway directly criticizes

(A) Fitzgerald's early writing
(B) those who depart from a stark literary style
(C) the pursuit of money
(D) Fitzgerald's public life
(E) those who adhere to strict artistic ideals

GO ON TO THE NEXT PAGE ▶▶▶

The questions below are based on the content of the passage that precedes them. The questions are to be answered on the basis of what is stated or implied in the passage itself or the introductory material that precedes the passage.

Questions 13–24 are based on the following passage.

The following is an excerpt from a biography of Ayn Rand, a 20th century American philosopher and novelist.

Line   The life of Ayn Rand was the material of fiction. But if one attempted to write it as a novel, the result would be preposterously unbelievable. Everything about her life and
5   her person was of an epic scale. Her seventy-seven years encompassed the outer limits of triumph and defeat, of exaltation and tragedy, of passionate love and intransigent hatred, of dedicated effort and despairing
10   passivity. Her person encompassed the grandeur of the heroes of her novels, their iron determination, their vast powers of intellect and imagination, their impassioned pursuit of their goals, their worship of
15   achievement, their courage, their pride, and their love of life—as well as the terrors, the self-doubts, the lack of emotional balance, the private agonies that are so alien to an Ayn Rand hero. Her virtues were larger than
20   life—and so were her shortcomings.

    Few figures in this century have been so admired and so savagely attacked. She is viewed as goddess and malefactor, as a seminal genius and an ominously dangerous
25   corrupter of the young, as the mightiest of voices for reason and the destroyer of traditional values, as the espouser of joy and the exponent of mindless greed, as the great defender of freedom and the introducer of
30   malevolent values into the mainstream of American thought. It is all but impossible to find a neutral voice among the millions who have read her works; each reader takes an unequivocal stand for or against what she
35   represents. When her name is mentioned in any gathering, it is met with explosions of grateful, loving admiration or enraged disapproval.

    Yet despite the furor her ideas have
40   generated, little is known about the human being who was Ayn Rand. Her public and professional activities took place on a lighted stage; her private life was lived backstage, curtained from view.

45   I first met Ayn Rand in 1950. At the age of forty-five, she had already achieved a singular renown as the author of *The Fountainhead*, and was writing her magnum opus, *Atlas Shrugged*—the work that was to
50   skyrocket her to international fame and place her in the center of a hurricane of controversy.

    I shall not forget my first sight of Ayn Rand. When the door to her home opened
55   that spring evening in 1950, I found myself facing the most astonishing human being I had ever encountered. It was the eyes. The eyes were dark, too large for the face, fringed with dark lashes, alive with an intensity of
60   intelligence I had never imagined human eyes could hold. They seemed the eyes of a human being who was composed of the power of sight.

    As the years passed, I was to observe all
65   the many changes of expression of those incredible eyes. I saw them ferocious with concentration on a new idea or question that had not occurred to her before. I saw them cold, so icily, inhumanly cold that they froze
70   one's heart and mind. I saw them radiant with the uninhibited delight of a child. I saw them menacing with anger at any hint of what she considered the irrational in human action. I saw them kind, touchingly kind,
75   tender with the desire to help and to protect. I saw the merciless, accusing eyes of the moralist, judging, condemning, unforgiving, the power of her reason becoming a whip to scourge the heretic. But I never saw those
80   eyes without the light of a vast, consuming intelligence, the light of a ruthless intellect that was at once cold and passionate; this was the core of her life, the motor of her soul.

    There was something I never saw in Ayn
85   Rand's eyes. They never held an inward look—a look of turning inside to learn one's own spirit and consciousness. They gazed only and always outward. It was many years before I was to understand the absence of
90   that inward look, and what it revealed. It was

GO ON TO THE NEXT PAGE ▶▶▶

to require all the knowledge of all the years to understand it.

95 Those who worship Ayn Rand and those who damn her do her the same disservice; they make her unreal and they deny her humanity. She was infinitely more fascinating and infinitely more valuable than either goddess or sinner. She was a human being. She lived, she loved, she fought her battles, and she knew

100 triumph and defeat. The scale was epic; the principle is inherent in human existence.

13 The main purpose of this passage is to

(A) refute some of Ayn Rand's theories
(B) critique Ayn Rand's novels
(C) bemoan Ayn Rand's obscurity
(D) reveal how fame damaged Ayn Rand's life
(E) humanize Ayn Rand

14 The first paragraph (lines 1–20) characterizes Ayn Rand's life primarily as

(A) impoverished
(B) introspective
(C) majestic
(D) charitable
(E) humble

15 The sentence beginning on line 10, "Her person encompassed ... an Ayn Rand hero," suggests that Rand

(A) had difficulty depicting some of the characters in her novels
(B) identified intellectually with the characters in her novels
(C) imbued the heroes of her novels with many emotional imperfections
(D) was indifferent to the controversy her ideas generated
(E) shared the fears that the heroes of her novels exhibited

16 The first paragraph suggests that Rand shared which of the following with the heroes of her novels?

  I.   a passion for achievement
  II. self-doubt
  III. equanimity

(A) I only
(B) I and II only
(C) I and III only
(D) II and III only
(E) I, II, and III

17 The second paragraph suggests that, as a group, those who have read Ayn Rand's works are

(A) united in their admiration of her ideals
(B) polarized
(C) critical of her literary style
(D) respectful of her life experiences
(E) unaware of the breadth of her work

18 The sixth paragraph (lines 64–84) contains all of the following EXCEPT

(A) metaphor
(B) stark contrast
(C) parallel sentence structure
(D) a definition of a term
(E) characterization

19 The author suggests that Ayn Rand lacked

(A) childlike delight
(B) logical rigor
(C) introspection
(D) tenderness
(E) ruthlessness

20 The sentence beginning on line 90, "It was to require...to understand it" suggests that the author of this passage

(A) disagreed with an important tenet of Rand's philosophy
(B) needed a great deal of time to appreciate an aspect of Rand's demeanor
(C) lacked Rand's moral courage
(D) shared Rand's judgmentalism
(E) was unable to appreciate the literary inventiveness of Rand's writing style

21 The passage describes the contrast between which of the following?

  I.   Rand's private life and her public life
  II. Rand's philosophy and her literary style
  III. The author's philosophy and Rand's philosophy

(A) I only
(B) I and II only
(C) I and III only
(D) II and III only
(E) I, II, and III

GO ON TO THE NEXT PAGE ▸▸▸

22 The author of this passage would most likely agree with which of the following statements?

(A)   Rand's works have long been unappreciated

(B)   Very few who read Rand's works closely have a negative opinion of her.

(C)   Rand's greatest works were published after her death

(D)   Rand's novels served to unify American thinkers

(E)   Although Rand lived an epic life, she is better appreciated as a flawed human being.

23 It can be inferred from the passage that the author

(A)   met Ayn Rand only once

(B)   met Ayn Rand before she became famous

(C)   knew Ayn Rand intimately over a long period of time

(D)   only saw Ayn Rand on social occasions

(E)   was Ayn Rand's literary editor

24 This passage contains enough information to answer all of the following questions EXCEPT

(A)   How were Rand's ideas received by the American public?

(B)   In what decade was Ayn Rand born?

(C)   What was considered to be Rand's greatest work?

(D)   In what country was Ayn Rand born?

(E)   How old was Rand when she died?

STOP

You may check your work, on this section only, until time is called.

Section 4

Time—25 Minutes
35 Questions

Directions for "Improving Sentences" Questions

Each of the sentences below contains one underlined portion. The portion may contain one or more errors in grammar, usage, construction, precision, diction (choice of words), or idiom. Some of the sentences are correct.

Consider the meaning of the original sentence, and choose the answer that best expresses that meaning. If the original sentence is best, choose (A), because it repeats the original phrasing. Choose the phrasing that creates the clearest, most precise and most effective sentence.

EXAMPLE:

The children <u>couldn't hardly believe their eyes</u>.

   (A) couldn't hardly believe their eyes
   (B) would not hardly believe their eyes
   (C) could hardly believe their eyes
   (D) couldn't nearly believe their eyes
   (E) could hardly believe his or her eyes

Example answer: (C)

---

1 Geothermal heat is not only an abundant and renewable energy source but also <u>clean as a fuel which emits</u> virtually no harmful gases.

   (A) clean as a fuel which emits
   (B) a clean fuel that emits
   (C) clean as a fuel which is emitting
   (D) the clean fuel emitting
   (E) a clean fuel for emitting

2 In the most recent election, voters were neither energized <u>about the importance of the campaign and they lacked awareness of the issues</u> that directed it.

   (A) about the importance of the campaign and they lacked awareness of the issues
   (B) to how important the campaign was nor to their lack of awareness of the issues
   (C) about how important the campaign was nor about their awareness of the issues
   (D) on the importance of the campaign nor the awareness of the issues
   (E) about the importance of the campaign nor aware of the issues

3 Many existentialistic works, such as Samuel Becket's *Malone Dies*, <u>which subordinates</u> the role of plot to the role of introspection.

   (A) which subordinates
   (B) which subordinate
   (C) subordinate
   (D) subordinates
   (E) that subordinate

4 Although Allen popularized the use of angst-ridden monologue in film, <u>the device was not invented by him</u>.

   (A) the device was not invented by him
   (B) the device had not been invented by him
   (C) he was not the inventor of the particular device
   (D) he would not have invented the device
   (E) he did not invent the device

5 Western culture has thrived because it values the open inquiry of science <u>more than the closed dogma</u> of state religion.

   (A) more than the closed dogma
   (B) to the closed dogma
   (C) over the closed nature of the dogma of
   (D) more than that of the closed dogma
   (E) more than it values things like the closed dogma

GO ON TO THE NEXT PAGE ▶▶▶

6 Enormously creative yet focused on his own commercial success, <u>the film depicts Warhol as</u> a complex and enigmatic figure.

(A) the film depicts Warhol as
(B) the film is a depiction of Warhol as
(C) Warhol in the film has been the depiction of
(D) Warhol is depicted in the film as
(E) Warhol is depicted by the film for

7 The first African American to lead an Ivy League institution, Ruth Simmons, <u>who has not shrunk from controversial issues regarding</u> the role of the university in American society.

(A) who has not shrunk from controversial issues regarding
(B) has not shrunk from controversial issues regarding
(C) has not shrunken from controversial issues for
(D) who has not shrunk from controversial issues in
(E) has not shrank from controversial issues regarding

8 Most animals are able to produce vitamin C internally, but <u>there is no production by humans</u> and therefore they must incorporate it into their diets.

(A) there is no production by humans
(B) humans cannot be the producers of it
(C) there is no human production A
(D) humans cannot
(E) there is not by humans

9 The invention of the plow over 12,000 years ago enabled large populations to sustain themselves without <u>needing of migration in search of food</u>.

(A) needing of migration in search of food
(B) the need of migration for the search of food
(C) needing to be migratory for search of food
(D) the need to migrate in search of food
(E) the need for migration in the search for food

10 The interconnectivity of the thousands of electrical generators and relay stations <u>is able to magnify a small failure into</u> one of catastrophic proportions.

(A) is able to magnify a small failure into
(B) are able to magnify a small failure into
(C) is able to magnify a small failure for
(D) are able to magnify that of a small failure into
(E) is able to magnify that of a small failure into

11 The film not only employs fine actors, <u>nevertheless it also gives them outstanding roles to play as well</u>.

(A) nevertheless it also gives them outstanding roles to play as well
(B) for it gives them also outstanding roles to play
(C) but outstanding roles as well
(D) but also the actors' roles are outstanding
(E) but also gives them outstanding roles to play

Directions for "Improving Sentences" Questions

The following sentences may contain errors in grammar, usage, diction (choice of words), or idiom. Some of the sentences are correct. No sentence contains more than one error.

If the sentence contains an error, it is underlined and lettered. The parts that are not underlined are correct.

If there is an error, select the part that must be changed to correct the sentence.

If there is no error, choose (E).

EXAMPLE:

By the time <u>they reached</u> the halfway point
                    A
<u>in the race,</u> most <u>of the runners</u> <u>hadn't hardly</u>
    B   C   D
begun to hit their stride. <u>No error</u>
                                    E

Sample answer: (D)

12 The devastating failure <u>of the experiment</u>
                                        A
<u>surprised</u> the scientists, who were expecting
    B
a <u>successive</u> outcome to <u>confirm</u> their
        C   D
theory. <u>No error</u>
            E

13 Once I finish <u>reading</u> this book, <u>I have read</u>
                        A   B
every novel and essay that John Steinbeck

ever published, <u>including those</u> that were
                            C
released <u>posthumously</u>. <u>No error</u>
                D   E

14 Most linguists <u>are convinced</u> that the
                            A
ability to speak, while uniquely human,

<u>is simply</u> a combination of <u>cognitive skills</u>
    B   C
that have been passed on <u>to our species</u>
                                    D
through evolution. <u>No error</u>
                        E

15 Our friends seemed <u>to think that</u> the movie
                                A
was one of the best adventure films

<u>of recent years</u>, but it <u>did not seem</u> that
        B   C
way to <u>David and I</u>. <u>No error</u>
            D   E

16 The dispute <u>between the teachers' union</u>
                            A
and the board of education <u>became</u> less
                                    B
heated once <u>it agreed</u> to follow
                    C
<u>the rules of arbitration</u>. <u>No error</u>
            D   E

17 Recent articles <u>have indicated</u> that
                            A
individuals who <u>work on</u> professions that
                    B
require a great deal of desk work have

<u>a higher rate</u> of obesity <u>than those who</u>
        C   D
work outdoors. <u>No error</u>
                    E

18 Although <u>there is</u> a lot more than twenty
                    A
copies of the book left <u>in the storeroom</u>,
                                B
they will sell out quickly, so I <u>recommend</u>
                                        C
that <u>we order more</u> now. <u>No error</u>
            D   E

19 The work involved <u>in doing research</u> on
                                A
one's ancestors <u>has become</u> much less
                        B
arduous because <u>you can now find</u> a great
                        C
deal of genealogical information

<u>on the internet</u>. <u>No error</u>
        D   E

GO ON TO THE NEXT PAGE ▶▶▶

20 Many literary historians <u>regard</u> the novels
                           A

of Zora Neale Hurston, with their

<u>rich characterizations</u>, as being among the
              B

<u>most significant</u> works
        C

<u>of the late Harlem Renaissance</u>. <u>No error</u>
             D   E

4 ➤

21 Health researchers <u>have accumulated</u>
                        A

evidence <u>suggesting</u> that daily vitamin C
          B

supplements <u>can reduce</u> the risk of both
            C

heart disease <u>in addition to stroke</u>.
                  D

<u>No error</u>
  E

22 The multitude of similarities <u>between</u> the
                       A

dozens <u>of Europeans languages</u>
          B

<u>can be attributed</u> in large measure
    C

<u>to the early development</u> of international
         D

commerce. <u>No error</u>
        E

23 There was <u>very little debate</u> among the
            A

conference participants <u>about the issue</u> of
              B

whether the salaries of professional women

<u>should be</u> comparable <u>to men</u>. <u>No error</u>.
  C   D   E

24 Being a <u>popular and well-respected</u>
          A

member of the community, <u>Andrea is</u>
            B

clearly favored <u>to win</u> the nomination
        C

<u>for representative</u> to the city council.
       D

<u>No error</u>
  E

25 The <u>entertaining and informative</u> lecture
           A

by the <u>eminent</u> cosmologist inspired Andre
       B

<u>for reading</u> more about astronomy
  C

<u>and to take</u> more science courses. <u>No error</u>
  D   E

26 Although they <u>would have preferred</u> to
             A

have several candidates

<u>from which to choose,</u> the voters
        B

nevertheless <u>excepted</u> the unopposed
        C

<u>candidacy of Senator Frumm</u>. <u>No error</u>
        D   E

27 We walked for many hours through the

thick forests and <u>over the rocky hills</u> until
             A

we <u>had reached</u> the clearing <u>in which</u> we
    B   C

would pitch our tent <u>for the night</u>. <u>No error</u>
              D   E

28 Over nearly four hundred acres in the

valley <u>sprawl</u> the <u>majestic</u> Rancho Coronado,
      A   B

<u>which</u> <u>has been owned</u> by the same family
  C   D

for over two hundred years. <u>No error</u>
                  E

29 Several writers who are <u>critics toward</u> the
                  A

president's environmental policy

<u>have published</u> an anthology of essays and
  B

research documents describing how

<u>to improve</u> the country's
  C

<u>commitment to ecology</u> without impeding
      D

economic progress. <u>No error</u>
          E

GO ON TO THE NEXT PAGE ▶▶▶

Directions for "Improving Paragraphs" Questions

Below is an early draft of an essay. It requires revision in many areas.

The questions that follow ask you to make improvements in sentence structure, diction, organization and development. Answering the questions may require you to understand the context of the passage as well as the rules of standard written English.

Questions 30–35 pertain to the following passage.

(1) *For most young people in America who are approaching voting age, choosing a president is very much like the process by which you choose a homecoming queen.* (2) *They simply select the candidate whose personality they like the most.* (3) *They don't realize that choosing a leader is a much more serious task than that.* (4) *The more informed the voters are, the more likely it is that they will pick a good and capable leader.*

(6) *The first step to making a reasonable choice for president is to read a good international newspaper every day.* (7) *This will give you a better perspective on both domestic and international issues.* (8) *The next step is to decide what issues are most important to you?* (9) *What are your interests that the president has some control over?* (10) *For instance, one candidate might want to eliminate environmental regulations so his industrial supporters can get richer.* (11) *But you have asthma that is affected by the pollution or you'd rather not swim in a lake that has become polluted because of it.* (12) *Or, you might be just the right age for a draft and one of the candidates wants to fight a new war that you don't approve of.* (13) *So many political commercials seem to focus on cutting the opponent down rather than discussing the important issues.* (14) *The fact is that the president can do a lot of things that influence your life and you may not be aware of it.*

(15) *Also, very few young adults really think about what kinds of qualifications and what skills the candidates might or might not have, they just pick the one whom their parents or their friends like.* (16) *They should be asking whether this person is going to solve the problems that are important to me because he or she is qualified to solve them?* (17) *For instance, is someone who has been in Congress his whole adult life really prepared to*

represent people who run small businesses, or work in manual labor, or teach school? (18) *Even if you may like someone's personality from an ad, they still might not be making very good decisions for you and your family.* (19) *It's important to look into a candidate's past for yourself rather than relying on political ads to tell you what the candidates are like.* (20) *Then, become an active participant in the politcal process rather than a passive observer.*

30 Which of the following is the best revision of the underlined portion of sentence 1 (reproduced below)?

For most young people in America who are approaching voting age, choosing a president is very much like the process by which you choose a homecoming queen.

(A) (as it is now)
(B) the process of choosing a homecoming queen
(C) that of choosing a homecoming queen
(D) the way you choose a homecoming queen
(E) choosing a homecoming queen

31 Which of the following is the best way to combine sentences 2 and 3 (reproduced below)?

They simply select the candidate by picking the one whose personality they like the most. They don't realize that choosing a leader is a much more serious task than that.

(A) They don't realize that choosing a leader is more serious than that, selecting the one whose personality they like the most.

(B) Selecting the one that has the personality they like most, they don't realize that it's more serious than that.

(C) Not realizing how serious a task it is to choose a leader, they simply select the candidate whose personality they like most.

(D) Because of not realizing how serious it is choosing a leader, they simply select the candidate whose personality they like most.

(E) Because they simply select the candidate with the personality they like the most, they don't realize that choosing a leader is more serious than that.

GO ON TO THE NEXT PAGE ▶▶▶

32 Which of the following is the best version of the underlined portions of sentences 10 and 11 (reproduced below)?

For instance, one candidate might want to eliminate environmental regulations <u>so his industrial supporters can get richer. But you have asthma that is affected by the pollution or you'd rather not swim in a lake that has become polluted because of it</u>.

(A) (as it is now)
(B) for the financial benefit of his industrial supporters, but to the detriment of your asthma and your favorite swimming lake, which are harmed by pollution.
(C) for his industrial supporters' wealth, but you have asthma and your favorite swimming lake is getting worse because of pollution.
(D) for his industrial supporters' wealth, but not for your asthma and your favorite swimming lake is harmed by pollution.
(E) for the financial benefit of his industrial supporters, but to the detriment of your asthma and your favorite swimming lake are harmed by pollution.

33 Which of the following sentences contributes least to the unity of the second paragraph?

(A) Sentence 10
(B) Sentence 11
(C) Sentence 12
(D) Sentence 13
(E) Sentence 14

34 Which of the following is the best version of the underlined portion of sentence 15 (reproduced below)?

Also, very few young adults really think about <u>what kinds of qualifications and skills the candidates might or might not have, they</u> just pick the one whom their parents or their friends like.

(A) (as it is now)
(B) the qualifications and skills of the candidates, but instead
(C) what kinds of qualifications and skills the candidates might have, they instead
(D) the qualifications and skills of the candidates, they
(E) what are the qualifications and skills of the candidates, they instead

35 Which of the following is the best revision of the underlined portion of sentence 16 (reproduced below)?

They should be asking whether <u>this candidate is able to solve the problems that are important to me because he or she is qualified to solve them</u>?

(A) the candidate is qualified to solve the problems that are important to them.
(B) the candidate is qualified to solve the problems that are important to me?
(C) is this candidate able to be qualified to solve the problems that are important to me?
(D) the candidate is qualified to solve the problems that are important to him or her.
(E) the candidate is or is not qualified to solve the problems that are important to him or her.

STOP

You may check your work, on this section only, until time is called.

Section 5

Time—25 minutes
18 Questions

1 If $\frac{p}{9}$ and $\frac{p}{27}$ are both integers, then what is the least possible positive value of p?

(A) 3
(B) 6
(C) 9
(D) 18
(E) 27

2 If $4(x + 3) = 15$, then what is the value of $4x + 3$?

(A) 0.75
(B) 1.50
(C) 6.00
(D) 10.00
(E) 15.00

3 In a road race, a $4,000 prize is split among the first three finishers in the ratio of 5:2:1. What is the greatest amount, in dollars, that any of the three prize winners receives?

(A) 500
(B) 1000
(C) 1500
(D) 2000
(E) 2500

4 Point O is the center of the circle above, arc MNP has a length of 6π and MOP has a measure of 120°. What is the length of PO?

(A) 6
(B) 9
(C) 12
(D) 15
(E) 18

GO ON TO THE NEXT PAGE ▶▶▶

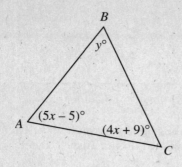

Note: Figure not drawn to scale.

5 In the figure above, $AB = BC$. What is the value of y?

(A)   40
(B)   50
(C)   65
(D)   70
(E)   75

6 The average (arithmetic mean) of f, g and h is one greater than their median, and $f < g < h$. If $f = 6$ and $h = 20$, then what is the value of g?

(A)   0.75
(B)   1.33
(C)   2.00
(D)   3.50
(E)   4.75

7 A jar contains marbles that are either red, white or blue. If the ratio of white marbles to red marbles is 3 to 5 and the ratio of red marbles to blue marbles is 6 to 5, then what is the least possible number of marbles in the jar?

(A)   18
(B)   25
(C)   63
(D)   73
(E)   80

8 The volume of a certain quantity of gas varies inversely as the pressure (in atmospheres) and directly as the temperature (in degrees Kelvin). If this quantity of gas occupies 10 liters at a pressure of 2 atmospheres and a temperature of 300 degrees Kelvin, what volume, in liters, will it occupy at 1 atmosphere and 450 degrees Kelvin?

(A)   15
(B)   30
(C)   90
(D)   300
(E)   450

Directions for Student-Produced Response Questions

Each of the questions in this section requires you to solve the problem and enter your answer in a grid, as shown below.

- If your answer is ⅔ or .666 ..., you must enter **the most accurate value the grid can accommodate**, but you may do this in one of four ways:

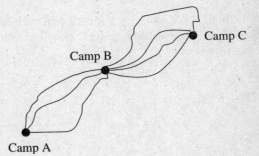

- In the example above, gridding a response of 0.67 or 0.66 is **incorrect** because it is less accurate than those above.
- The scoring machine cannot read what is written in the top row of boxes. You **MUST** fill in the numerical grid accurately to get credit for answering any question correctly. You should write your answer in the top row of boxes only to aid your gridding.
- Do **not** grid in a mixed fraction like $3\frac{1}{2}$ as $\boxed{3\,|\,1\,|\,/\,|\,2}$ because it will be interpreted as $\frac{31}{2}$. Instead, convert it to an improper fraction like $\frac{7}{2}$ or a decimal like 3.5 before gridding.
- None of the answers will be negative, because there is no negative sign in the grid.
- Some of the questions may have more than one correct answer. You must grid only one of the correct answers.
- You may use a calculator on any of these problems.
- All numbers in these problems are real numbers.
- Figures are drawn as accurately as possible EXCEPT when it is stated that the figure is not drawn to scale.
- All figures lie in a plane unless otherwise indicated.

9 If 25% of 16 is x, then what is x% of 200?

10 The figure above represents all of the paths between Camp A and Camp B, and all of the possible paths from Camp B to Camp C. If you wish to travel from Camp A to Camp C using only these available paths and passing through Camp B only once, how many different routes can you chose from?

GO ON TO THE NEXT PAGE ▶▶▶

11 If $\dfrac{2}{x} = w$, then $(wx)^{-3} =$

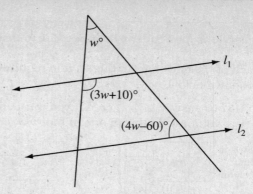

12 Adding 2 to a number, x, then dividing this result by 4 is equivalent to multiplying x by $\dfrac{1}{4}$ and then adding what number?

5 ➤

15 In the figure above, if $l_1 \| l_2$, then what is the value of w?

16 If $x^2 - y^2 = 24$ and $x + y = 72$, then what is the value of $x - y$?

13 If n and p are positive integers and $n^{-2p} = \dfrac{1}{16^p}$, what is the value of n?

17 If $f(x) = x - k$ where k is a constant, and the points $(6, 1)$ and $(8, 1)$ lie on the graph of $y = f(x)$, what is the value of $f(0)$?

14 If $f(x) = -(x - 1)^2 + 2$ for all real values of x, then what is the greatest possible value of $f(x) + 3$?

Note: Figure not drawn to scale.

18 In the figure above, A, B and C are points on the number line with coordinates as shown. If $AC = 5AB$, then what is the value of x?

You may check your work, on this section only, until time is called.

Section 6

Time—25 minutes
24 Qestions

Each of the sentences below is missing one or two portions. Read each sentence, then select the word or words that most logically completes the sentence, taking into account the meaning of the sentence as a whole.

Example:

Rather than accepting the theory unquestioningly, Deborah regarded it with ————.

(A) mirth (B) sadness (C) responsibility
(D) ignorance (E) skepticism

Correct response: (E)

1 The fossil record suggests that new species do not arise ————, but instead develop gradually from other, existing species.

(A) quietly   (B) scientifically
(C) instantaneously
(D) permanently (E) falsely

2 Howard has a reputation for ————; although his self-serving claims always seem plausible, they are rarely true.

(A) genius   (B) prevarication
(C) fervency   (D) contemplation
(E) forthrightness

3 Many psychoanalysts have claimed that great artists and composers constantly battle with derangement, theorizing that ———— and genius cannot ————.

(A) equanimity .. conflict
(B) sanity .. coexist
(C) psychosis .. coincide
(D) productivity .. differ
(E) aesthetics .. interface

4 American oceanographers of the 1950s were relegated to using ———— maps of the ocean floor, because the highly detailed charts produced by the navy were ———— so that they did not fall into the hands of the Soviets.

(A) counterfeit .. distributed
(B) lucid .. apprehended
(C) deficient .. classified
(D) temporary .. disseminated
(E) sketchy .. improved

5 Although he was a sincere Catholic, Galileo was considered by the Church to be ———— because his astronomic theories conflicted with its teachings.

(A) an apostate
(B) a conformist
(C) a relic
(D) an ascetic
(E) a despot

GO ON TO THE NEXT PAGE ▶▶▶

Each passage below is followed by one or two questions based on its content. Answer each question based on what is stated or implied in the passage.

Questions 6–7 are based on the following passage.

The following is an excerpt from a book on the planet Mars by astronomer Percival Lowell.

Line Once in about every fifteen years a startling
visitant makes his appearance upon our
midnight skies—a great red star that rises at
sunset through the haze about the
5 eastern horizon, and then, mounting higher
with the deepening night, blazes forth against
the dark background of space with a
splendor that outshines Sirius and rivals the
giant Jupiter himself. Startling for its size,
10 the stranger looks the more fateful for being
a fiery red. Small wonder that by many folk it
is taken for a portent. Certainly, no one who
had not followed in their courses what the
Greeks so picturesquely called "the wanderers"
15 (hoi planetai) would recognize in the
apparition an orderly member of our own
solar family. Nevertheless, one of the
wanderers it is, for that star is the planet
Mars, large because for the moment near,
20 having in due course again been overtaken by
the Earth, in her swifter circling about the
Sun, at that point in space where his orbit
and hers make their closest approach.

6 The passage suggests that, to many people, the redness of Mars indicates its

(A)   ominousness
(B)   ability to support life
(C)   proximity to the sun
(D)   enormous size
(E)   swiftness

7 In line 16, the word "apparition" most nearly means

(A)   evil spirit
(B)   figment of the imagination
(C)   spectacle
(D)   foreshadowing
(E)   calculation

Questions 8–9 are based on the following passage.

Line Man is the only creature that consumes
without producing. He does not give milk, he
does not lay eggs, he is too weak to pull the
plough, he cannot run fast enough to catch
5 rabbits. Yet he is lord of all the animals. He
sets them to work, he gives back to them the
bare minimum that will prevent them from
starving, and the rest he keeps for himself.
Our labor tills the soil, our dung fertilizes it,
10 and yet there is not one of us who owns more
than his bare skin. You cows that I see before
me, how many thousands of gallons of milk
have you given during this last year? And
what has happened to that milk which should
15 have been breeding up sturdy calves? And
you hens, how many eggs have you laid in
this last year, and how many of those eggs
ever hatched into chickens? The rest have all
gone to market to bring in money for Jones
20 and his men. And you, Clover, where are
those four foals you bore, who should have
been the support and pleasure of your old
age? Each was sold at a year old; you will
never see one of them again. In return
25 for your confinements and all your labour in
the fields, what have you ever had except
your bare rations and a stall?

8 This passage is written from the point of view of

(A)   a man running for public office
(B)   an underpaid farm worker
(C)   a member of the clergy
(D)   an owner of a large farm
(E)   a farm animal

9 The questions posed in lines 11–23 indicate the speaker's dissatisfaction with

(A)   the low level of overall production of the farm animals
(B)   inefficient farming practices
(C)   the unfairness of the relationship between humans and animals
(D)   the excessive cost of maintaining a farm
(E)   the fact that some animals work harder than others

GO ON TO THE NEXT PAGE ▶▶▶

First paragraph: "Mars," Percival Lowell, www.bibliomania.com, Public Domain, Chapter 1, "As a Star," p. 1
Second paragraph: George Orwell, *Animal Farm*, Public Domain

The questions below are based on the content of the preceding passage. The questions are to be answered on the basis of what is stated or implied in the passage itself or the introductory material that precedes the passage.

Questions 10–17 pertain to the following passage.

The following passage discusses medical advances in the fight against viruses.

Line   Vaccination is one of medicine's cleverest tricks: making the body believe it is sick and thus causing it to marshal just the right forces to ward off that particular sickness
5   The development of this practice stands as a twentieth-century accomplishment, but its roots reach far back into the past. Centuries ago, the Chinese and the Turks knew enough to produce a medicine against smallpox by
10   grinding up the scabs of people with mild cases of the disease. In 1796, Dr. Edward Jenner found he could induce resistance to smallpox by using the vaccinia virus (vacca is Latin for cow) to infect people with the
15   relatively mild cowpox. But it was Louis Pasteur, working a century later, who did the research that finally gave the field of immunology the creative boost that would propel it to the forefront of modern medicine.
20   In 1895, Pasteur produced a rabies vaccine without actually realizing that he was enhancing the body's own immune system; he knew only that the vaccine worked.
       But what was the infectious agent that
25   vaccines fought? Could it have been a bacterium? In Germany, in 1882, Robert Koch had shown that just such a germ caused tuberculosis. Microscopic parasites with similarities both to plants and animals,
30   bacteria were certainly the cause of much human misery. But they were not to play the starring role in the vaccine story.
       The first tantalizing awareness of a virus— a microorganism even stranger than the
35   invisible bacteria and like nothing else ever known before—came in 1898 when Martinus Willem Beijerinick discovered a minuscule

living thing he described with a name, "virus," derived from the Latin for poisonous
40   slime. A virus is really no more than a protein bag carrying its own set of genetic instructions. A virus cannot reproduce on its own. It must attach itself to a cell, impregnate the cell with the viral genes, and then,
45   parasite that it is, turn that cell into a reproductive machine for the virus's benefit. The body, for the most part, is able to recognize these viruses as foreign invaders by the signature proteins on their surface.
50   It then attacks them with antibodies and sends killer cells to destroy the cells that have already been infected. If the immune system is overwhelmed by the invasion, the body becomes sick and may die. If the body wins,
55   then its immune system keeps a record of this particular enemy and is better prepared to resist the next time. Sometimes the immunity is lifelong.
       Thanks to advances in modern vaccines,
60   measles are nearly gone, and chicken pox, whooping cough, typhoid, and cholera are under control. From a purely psychological point of view, perhaps the biggest vaccine success of the century was the almost total
65   victory over polio, an effort that called upon everything scientists had learned in the new fields of immunology and virology. Polio was thought to be a true childhood plague, a crippler and a destroyer of young lives. It
70   seemed to come from nowhere in 1916 and was virtually eradicated fifty years later.
       The advances against viruses continue. There is now a vaccine for the vicious hepatitis B virus, and vaccines for the
75   potentially deadly influenza viruses. But herpes, another viral affliction, still flourishes, and the most ubiquitous of all the viral maladies—the common cold, caused by well over a hundred different viruses—may
80   never be thwarted by a vaccine because the viruses are too numerous. Scientists have come a long way in the fight against viruses, but further advances are necessary as it seems new viruses appear as old viral foes
85   are eradicated. The fight will probably never be completely won.

6

GO ON TO THE NEXT PAGE ▸▸▸

Excerpted from "Medicine's Great Journey", Schering Laboratories, Calloway Editions, Inc, © 1992, p 27-31.

10 Which of the following is the best title for this passage?

(A)   Medical Breakthroughs of the 19th Century
(B)   The Fight Against Bacterial Infections
(C)   The Power and Promise of Vaccines
(D)   How the Human Immune System Works
(E)   The Work of Edward Jenner

11 The passage mentions the "Chinese and the Turks" (line 8) as examples of cultures that

(A)   identified viruses by name
(B)   employed early forms of vaccination
(C)   were nearly eradicated by viral diseases
(D)   mistook bacteria for viruses
(E)   used treatments that exacerbated rather than eliminated diseases

12 The passage indicates that viruses cause all of the following EXCEPT

(A)   tuberculosis
(B)   cowpox
(C)   polio
(D)   herpes
(E)   hepatitis

13 Which of the following relationships is most similar to the relationship between the virus and the cell as it is described in the third paragraph (lines 33–58)?

(A)   the relationship between two birds of different species, in which one bird lays its eggs in the nest of the other, which raises the young as its own
(B)   the relationship between a bear and a salmon, in which the bear captures and eats the salmon before it spawns
(C)   the relationship between a tickbird and a rhinoceros, in which the tickbird cleans parasites off the rhinoceros
(D)   the relationship between a bumblebee and a flower, in which the bumblebee carries pollen from the flower with which to fertilize other flowers
(E)   the relationship between two scavengers that fight over the same carcass

14 According to the passage, bacteria are like viruses in that they

(A)   cannot reproduce on their own
(B)   have been virtually eradicated
(C)   played a major role in the discovery of vaccines
(D)   are parasitic
(E)   are largely beneficial

15 In line 49, the word "signature" most nearly means

(A)   dangerous
(B)   official
(C)   identifying
(D)   invisible
(E)   beneficial

16 Which of the following best describes the relationship between the last two paragraphs?

(A)   The final paragraph makes a generalization based on the specific examples mentioned in the previous paragraph.
(B)   The final paragraph answers a question raised in the previous paragraph.
(C)   The final paragraph explains the time sequence of the events described in the previous paragraph.
(D)   The final paragraph gives an example of a concept defined in the previous paragraph.
(E)   The final paragraph qualifies the triumphant tone of the previous paragraph.

17 The passage cites which of the following as major impediments to eradicating viruses?

   I.   the abundance of viruses
   II. the inability of viruses to replicate on their own
   III. the ability of new viruses to replace old ones

(A)   I only
(B)   III only
(C)   I and II only
(D)   I and III only
(E)   I, II, and III

GO ON TO THE NEXT PAGE ▸▸▸

The questions below are based on the content of the preceding passage. The questions are to be answered on the basis of what is stated or implied in the passage itself or the introductory material that precedes the passage.

Questions 18–24 are based on the following passage.

The following is an excerpt taken from the memoirs of a Chinese woman born and raised in China during times of war.

Line My older brother, Ching-chung, six years older than I, was protective and vigilant; he was in my eyes a man. He supervised my schooling and checked my home-work nightly; but most
5 of all I loved the stories he told me.

The Chinese language is a poetic one, and conversation—even among peasants—is often indirect and metaphorical, reflecting a philosophical turn of mind intrinsic to the
10 Chinese. Thus the teachings of Confucius or Buddha, codes of behavior, morality, and the like are often taught through the retelling, generation after generation, of the exploits of legendary heroes and heroines and stories
15 exemplifying the Chinese ideals.

Since both of my parents were so preoccupied—father with his business, and mother again pregnant—Ching-chung took it upon himself to be my teacher. Each day I
20 would wait impatiently for another story to begin. They always involved supreme sacrifice: the loyal servant ever ready to die for his master, the peasant equally willing to sacrifice himself for his emperor and country, the
25 good son eager to bring honor to his family.

As I was a girl, my brother would tell me of many heroines who sacrificed themselves for their fathers, brothers, or husbands, always practicing the virtues of humility,
30 modesty, and servitude. My favorite heroine was one Mu-lan, or "Wild Orchid." She was an only child when war broke out (the story took place centuries earlier) and her father was obliged to fight. Being fifty years old, a
35 sanctified age at that time, he was far too old for battle. Because she loved her father and was imbued with the Chinese spirit of sacrifice, she dressed herself as a man and took her father's place in battle. Throughout

40 the fierce fighting no one realized she was female, and when the Emperor, in recognition of her achievements, offered her a distinguished wife, Mu-lan was forced to reveal her true sex.

45 These daily stories, exemplifying basic Chinese obligations and principles, made an enormous impression on me, and would affect my attitude and personal philosophy throughout my life.

50 But my brother had his tyrannical side as well. He went through a period during which he forced me to memorize the Four Chinese Classics—*The Analects of Confucius, The Great Learning, The Doctrine of the Mean*, and *The*
55 *Works of Mencius*—none of which I understood. He also made me memorize and copy out in careful calligraphy such maxims as: Render filial piety to parents, show respect to seniors by the generation age order, remain in
60 harmony with clan members and the community, teach and discipline sons and grandsons, attend to one's vocation properly, do not commit what the law forbids.

From Ching-chung, I learned that sons
65 were to be filial to their fathers, wives dutiful to their husbands, and brothers affectionate to each other; and that laziness, extravagance, violence, and gambling were the most offensive conduct. He insisted that I copy out
70 each and every maxim. After holding the brush for hours on end, my fingers became cramped and useless. One day I simply burst into tears and, thoroughly exhausted, sat down on the floor and refused to get up.
75 Fortunately my father intervened, and my brother's tyranny came to an abrupt and permanent end.

My reading was not confined exclusively to Chinese literature, however. Although my
80 father continued to make us all read and recite the tenets of certain Mandarin sages, by this time my adolescent, pre-teen tastes tended toward romantic European novels, many of them translated into Chinese. I
85 preferred to read the English translations of books like *The Three Musketeers* and *The Count of Monte Cristo*. It was this latter title that made the deepest impression on me. I knew whole passages by heart, and even took
90 the trouble to reread the book in Chinese, the title of which translates as *The Vengeance and the Gratitude of the Count of Monte Cristo*,

Excepted from *Journey in Tears*, Chow Ching-Li, McGraw-Hill.©1978 p25-27

GO ON TO THE NEXT PAGE ▶▶▶

reflecting a more Chinese concept in its translation.

95   In either version, I loved this strong and willful character who was so undeserving of all the misfortune that befell him. I suffered far more from his unhappiness than I delighted in his revenge; and like him, I felt I

100 should always be grateful to those people who had been kind to me.

18 The main purpose of this passage is to

(A)   compare Asian literature to English literature
(B)   explore one child's relationship with literature
(C)   critique certain Chinese childrearing practices
(D)   show the contrast between Chinese traditions and Western traditions
(E)   reveal a painful episode between siblings

19 The passage mentions "peasants" in line 8 in order to make the point that

(A)   some Chinese people tell stories because they are unable to read
(B)   legends are retold mainly by people in the lower classes
(C)   figurative and moralistic language is used by a wide range of Chinese people
(D)   in China, the types of stories that are told differ widely from class to class
(E)   most people in China are taught to write poetry

20 The passage suggests that, at first, the author's attitude towards her brother's stories was one of

(A)   fear
(B)   indignation
(C)   ambivalence
(D)   eagerness
(E)   reluctant acceptance

21 The passage suggests that the author's brother expressed his "tyrannical side" (line 50) primarily through

(A)   physical beatings
(B)   stealing valued possessions
(C)   cruel demands
(D)   failing to acknowledge the author
(E)   public humiliation

22 It can be inferred from the passage that the "more Chinese concept" mentioned in line 93 likely incudes an emphasis on

(A)   brevity
(B)   wealth
(C)   Asian history
(D)   thankfulness
(E)   tyranny

23 According to the author, one significant difference between the story of *The Count of Monte Cristo* and *The Great Learning* was that

(A)   one was about Chinese nobility and the other was about Chinese peasants
(B)   she studied one book willingly and the other unwillingly
(C)   one espoused violence as a virtue and the other condemned it
(D)   one was widely popular, while the other was relatively obscure
(E)   one was a comedy and the other a tragedy

24 As it is used in line 90, the word "trouble" most nearly means

(A)   mental effort
(B)   precarious situation
(C)   emotional turmoil
(D)   ethical difficulty
(E)   reluctance.

STOP   *You may check your work, on this section only, until time is called.*

Section 7

Time—20 minutes
16 Questions

Directions for Multiple-Choice Questions

In this section, solve each problem, using any available space on the page for scratchwork. Then decide which is the best of the choices given and fill in the corresponding oval on the answer sheet.

- You may use a calculator on any problem. All numbers used are real numbers.
- Figures are drawn as accurately as possible EXCEPT when it is stated that the figure is not drawn to scale.
- All figures lie in a plane unless otherwise indicated.

Reference Information

$A = \pi r^2$ $A = \ell w$ $A = \frac{1}{2}bh$ $V = \ell wh$ $V = \pi r^2 h$ $c^2 = a^2 + b^2$ Special Right Triangles
$C = 2\pi r$

The number of degrees of arc in a circle is 360°.
The measure in degrees of a straight angle is 180°.
The sum of the measures in degrees of the angles in a triangle is 180°.

---

1 If one of the angles in a triangle is 100°, what is the average (arithmetic mean) of the measures, in degrees, of the other two angles?

(A) 20°
(B) 30°
(C) 40°
(D) 60°
(E) 80°

2 If k is an integer that is one less than a multiple of 6, which of the following could be $k + 1$?

(A) 16
(B) 17
(C) 18
(D) 19
(E) 20

3 Which of the following expresses the number that is 15 more than the product of 3 and $m - 2$?

(A) $3m - 21$
(B) $3m - 13$
(C) $3m - 6$
(D) $3m + 9$
(E) $3m + 13$

GO ON TO THE NEXT PAGE ▶▶▶

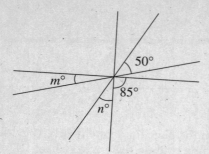

Note: Figure not drawn to scale

4 In the figure above, four line segments intersect at a single point. What is the value of $m + n$?

(A)   45
(B)   50
(C)   60
(D)   65
(E)   85

5 If $x\%$ of 30 is 12, what is $4x\%$ of 15?

(A)   6
(B)   12
(C)   18
(D)   24
(E)   48

6 If $0 < x < 1$ then which of the following must be true?

  I. $\frac{1}{x} < x$
  II. $x^2 > x$
  III. $-x < -1$

(A)   none
(B)   I only
(C)   II only
(D)   III only
(E)   I and III only

7 If every gadget costs p dollars to make, and each one sells for m dollars, then which of the following expressions represents the profit made if 10 gadgets are made but only 9 are sold?

(A) $10m - 9p$
(B) $9m - 10p$
(C) $10(m - p) - 9m$
(D) $9p + 10m$
(E) $10(m - p) + 9m$

8 If $y = f(x)$ such that y varies inversely as x, and the points (4, 6) and (2, m) lie on the graph of $y = f(x)$, what is the value of m?

(A)   4
(B)   6
(C)   8
(D)   10
(E)   12

9 A machine can fill 200 boxes of cereal in 5 minutes. At this rate, how many <u>hours</u> will it take this machine to fill 24,000 boxes of cereal? (60 minutes = 1 hour)

(A)   10
(B)   24
(C)   100
(D)   210
(E)   600

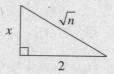

10 In the figure above, what is the value of x in terms of n?

(A) $\sqrt{n-4}$
(B) $\sqrt{n-2}$
(C) $\sqrt{n+4}$
(D) $\sqrt{n+2}$
(D) $\sqrt{n+4}$

$$(r - 5)^2 = (r + 2)^2$$

11 Which of the following represents all possible solutions to the equation above?

(A)   −5 and 2 only
(B)   5 and −2 only
(C)   3.5 only
(D)   1.5 only
(E)   0 only

GO ON TO THE NEXT PAGE ▸▸▸

12 A certain class has 8 boys and 10 girls. How many different sets of four class officers—president, vicepresident, treasurer and secretary—can be formed from students in this class if the president and treasurer must be girls and the vice president and secretary must be boys?

(A) 25,600
(B) 6,400
(C) 5,040
(D) 3,200
(E) 2,520

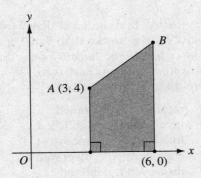

Note: Figure not drawn to scale.

13 In the figure above, if the shaded region has an area of 15, what is the slope of *AB*?

(A) $\dfrac{3}{5}$

(B) $\dfrac{2}{3}$

(C) $\dfrac{3}{4}$

(D) 1

(E) $\dfrac{3}{2}$

14 If $m > 1$, then $\dfrac{m - \dfrac{1}{m}}{1 - \dfrac{1}{m}} =$

(A) $m + 1$
(B) m
(C) $m - 1$
(D) -1

(E) $\dfrac{m}{m - 1}$

15 If a circle on the coordinate plane has a center at (6, −6), which of the following could NOT be the number of points on the circle that also lie on a coordinate axis?

    I. 1
    II. 2
    III. 3

(A) I only
(B) II only
(C) I and II only
(D) I and III only
(E) II and III only

16 A certain car race consists of three legs of equal distance. On the first two legs of the race, a car travels an average of 50 miles per hour. On the last leg of the race, the car travels at an average of 75 miles per hour. What is the average speed, in miles per hour, for this car over the entire race?

(A) 52.00
(B) 56.25
(C) 58.33
(D) 62.50
(E) 66.67

STOP

You may check your work, on this section only, until time is called.

Section 8

Time—20 minutes
19 Questions

Each of the sentences below is missing one or two portions. Read each sentence, then select the word or words that most logically completes the sentence, taking into account the meaning of the sentence as a whole.

Example:

Rather than accepting the theory unquestioningly, Deborah regarded it with ———.

(A) mirth   (B) sadness
(C) responsibility   (D) ignorance
(E) skepticism

Correct response: (E)

8

1 A clear model of the atom ——— physicists for decades; although they reasoned that the atom must exist, its ——— remained a mystery.

(A) eluded .. structure
(B) persuaded .. forces
(C) inspired .. interest
(D) mystified .. reality
(E) investigated .. configuration

2 In contrast to the other interns who were exhausted by the drudgery of the 60-hour work week, Alynna seemed ———.

(A) petrified   (B) extensive
(C) agitated   (D) indefatigable
(E) corrupted

3 Airborne germs are ———, yet surprisingly few are ———; despite the fact we inhale them with nearly every breath, the vast majority of them are innocuous and are neutralized easily by our immune systems.

(A) omnipresent .. harmless
(B) ubiquitous .. virulent
(C) scarce .. malevolent
(D) intolerable .. inconsequential
(E) plentiful .. benign

4 Unlike *Vanity Fair*, which is occasionally didactic, *Middlemarch* is morally ———, challenging the reader to make his or her own ethical evaluations of the characters' actions.

(A) resolute   (B) corrupt
(C) enervating (D) pedantic
(E) ambiguous

5 The theory that humans have inhabited Australia for no more than 8,000 years was ——— when *Homo sapiens* bones that were discovered in the outback were ——— to be more than 50,000 years old.

(A) refuted .. accustomed
(B) invalidated .. established
(C) introduced .. demonstrated
(D) corroborated .. displayed
(E) disproven .. deplored

6 Judge Webster gave her instructions to the jury in such a ——— way that there was no doubt that they were to be obeyed strictly.

(A) loquacious
(B) desultory
(C) phlegmatic
(D) peremptory
(E) torpid

GO ON TO THE NEXT PAGE ▸▸▸

The questions below are based on the content of the passage that precedes them. The questions are to be answered on the basis of what is stated or implied in the passage itself or the introductory material that precedes the passage.

Questions 7–19 are based on the following passages.

The following are two recent essays on the economics of environmentalism.

Passage 1

Line   Many proponents of recycling regard it as a
       universal good. They assume that re-using
       the remnants of any industrial or commercial
       process is better than putting them in a
5   landfill. Many opponents of recycling, on the
       other hand, scrutinize the economic costs of
       recycling. They suggest that recycling is often
       a bad idea because municipal recycling
       programs often waste more money than they
10   save, and companies can often produce new
       products more cheaply than they can recycle
       old ones. The debate rarely gets anywhere
       because it is too often politicized as a battle
       between a healthy economy and a healthy
15   environment. Of course, most of us want
       both. We must first stop the demonization;
       recycling proponents are not all economic
       ignoramuses, and recycling opponents are
       not all greedy troglodytes. We also must
20   learn to appreciate the real costs of recycling
       (or not recycling) to industry as well as the
       environment.
           When discussing recycling, both
       environmentalists and industrialists must
25   examine the full life cycle of the commercial
       materials in question, and the effect that they
       have on the broader environment and
       economy throughout these life cycles. When
       debating the cost of a new road, for instance,
30   it is not enough to simply consider how
       much the contractors will charge or whether
       the materials are recycled. We must ask
       broader environmental questions like: what
       are the effects of things like the reduction of
35   natural water filtration, the leaching of
       dangerous elements from the road materials
       into the soil, the extra warming produced by
       the dark heat-absorbing materials, and the
       removal of flora and animal habitats in the

40   construction? Where will the road materials
       be in a thousand years? Will they be innocuous
       soil material, or environmental toxins? How
       will the extra traffic affect air quality?
           We must also must consider broader
45   economic questions like: is the road made of
       local or imported materials? If they are
       imported, are they imported from countries
       with whom we have positive political and
       economic relations? Can the taxpayers afford
50   it? Is the money better spent elsewhere? Is the
       construction performed efficiently and by
       companies that were chosen through a fair
       and open bidding process? Will the road
       enhance commerce? How might the road
55   surface affect the life span or efficiency of the
       cars driving on it? How much will annual
       maintenance cost?
           These are all responsible questions that
       the stewards of both our environment and
60   our economy should ask. They may lead us to
       interesting answers. Perhaps nature can do a
       more efficient and safer job of reusing waste
       matter in a landfill than a recycling plant
       can. Perhaps an economic system that
65   accounts for environmental costs and
       benefits will lead to a much better standard
       of living for the average citizen. Perhaps
       inserting some natural resources into a
       responsible "industrial cycle" is better for
70   the environment than "conserving" those
       resources. Perhaps some recycling practices
       only delay environmental damage rather than
       preventing it. Asking such questions openly,
       respectfully and rigorously will help the
75   debaters to appreciate the attitudes of their
       opponents, lead to a less rancorous debate
       and a healthier economy and environment.

Passage 2

           The costs and benefits of preserving our
       natural environment seem almost impossible
80   to quantify. One difficulty lies in the
       diffuseness of the costs and benefits of
       nature. Economists have a relatively easy
       time with commerce, because money and
       goods can be tracked through a series of
85   point-to-point exchanges. For instance, when
       I give a store clerk a dollar, she gives me a
       pack of gum. Part of the dollar I give her
       goes to the gum company, some goes toward
       the costs of running the store, some goes to

GO ON TO THE NEXT PAGE ▶▶▶

90   the government as tax, and some goes to her
as profit. It is all easily accounted for.
        The benefits that ecosystems provide, like
biodiversity, the filtration of groundwater, the
maintenance of the oxygen and nitrogen
95   cycles, and climate stability, however, are not
simply bought-and-sold commodities.
They clearly benefit us, because without them
our lives would deteriorate dramatically, but
they are not part of a clear exchange, so they
100   fall into the class of benefits and costs that
economists call "externalities."
        When you choose something, even if money
is not involved, the exchange is often clear.
When you pick an apple from a tree, the tree
105   loses an apple, and you gain one. If money is
involved—for instance, when an apple is
purchased—the exchange can be compared
with the billions of other monetary
transactions that occur in the economic
110   world every day. The diffuse, unchosen costs
and benefits that affect all of us daily—
annoying commercials or a beautiful sunset,
for instance—are much harder to valuate.
        The "good feeling" that many people have
115   about recycling and maintaining
environmental quality is just such an
externality. Anti-environmentalists tend to
ridicule such feelings as unquantifiable and
hence irrelevant to economic decisions. But
120   its value is real: many investors will only
purchase the stock of companies with good
environmental records, and protests and
litigation against polluters can have steep
costs in terms of money and goodwill.
125   Some scientists have attempted to quantify
"external" ecological benefits rigorously.
Robert Costanza, formerly of the Center for
Environmental Science at the University of
Maryland, has estimated the value of nature
130   by tallying the cost to replace its services.
Imagine, for instance, that we paved over the
Florida Everglades and atop it somehow built
systems that maintained all of the functions
of the ecosystem we destroyed: gas
135   conversion and sequestering, food production,
water filtration, weather regulation, et cetera.
How much would it cost to keep these systems
running? Even though these systems almost
certainly would not account for some of the
140   most important externalities, like natural
beauty, the cost would be extraordinarily high.
Costanza places the cost "conservatively" at
$33 trillion dollars annually, far more than the
combined annual gross national products of

145   all of the countries in the world.
        Some in the fields of both economics and
environmental science object to Costanza's
attempt to valuate nature. Environmentalists
argue that it simply cannot be done—how do
150   you put a price on the smell of heather and a
cool breeze? Industrialists argue that it
depends largely on speculation and renders
economic decision-making more cumbersome.
Nevertheless, Costanza's work is among the
155   most cited in the fields of environmental
science and economics. For any flaws it might
have, his work is giving a common
vocabulary to industrialists and
environmentalists alike, which we must do
160   if we are to coordinate intelligent
environmental policy with responsible
economic policy.

7   The primary purpose of the first four
sentences of Passage 1 is to

(A)   introduce a discussion with a story
(B)   establish the author's main thesis
(C)   define several key concepts
(D)   provide the historical background
        to a debate
(E)   characterize two positions on an issue

8   The sentence beginning on line 16, "We
must first stop ... greedy troglodytes" suggests that those who debate the issue of
recycling tend to

(A)   mischaracterize their opponents
(B)   ignore statistics
(C)   use weak logical arguments
(D)   employ misleading ad campaigns
(E)   avoid personal confrontations

9   As they pertain to the "new road" mentioned
in line 29, the "life cycles" mentioned in line
28 are those of

(A)   the plants that are destroyed by road
        construction
(B)   the animals that may be displaced by
        a new road
(C)   economic and industrial trends
(D)   the substances that constitute the road
(E)   the companies involved in construct-
        ing the road

10 The questions listed in the second paragraph (lines 33–40) directly address all of the following possibilities EXCEPT

(A) the destruction of animals' natural homes
(B) the leakage of poisons into the soil
(C) the creation of landslides from soil displacement
(D) the emission of harmful car fumes
(E) the reduction of natural water purification

11 In line 69, the word "responsible" most nearly means

(A) guilty
(B) reactionary
(C) well-governed
(D) pleasant
(E) mature

12 The exchange with the "store clerk" (line 86) is used to represent

(A) an example of recycling
(B) an illustration of the value of human emotions
(C) a poorly understood and uncommon phenomenon
(D) a particular difficulty in economic analysis
(E) a transaction that is easily accounted for

13 Which of the following examples serves the same rhetorical purpose as that served by the "pack of gum" in line 87?

(A) the "apple" in line 104
(B) the "groundwater" in line 93
(C) the "climate stability" in line 95
(D) the "good feeling" in line 114
(E) the "beautiful sunset" in lines 113

14 In saying that the benefits of ecosystems are not "commodities" (line 96) Passage 2 suggests that they

(A) are less expensive to maintain than factories
(B) are difficult to track and evaluate
(C) are not as beneficial to consumers as purchased goods
(D) do not represent a financial burden if they are destroyed
(E) are found everywhere in abundance

15 Which of the following would be an example of an "externality" as it is defined in Passage 2?

(A) the extra revenue produced by increasing the price of a service
(B) the annual cost of maintaining a municipal recycling program
(C) the value of a beaver pelt in the wholesale market
(D) the irritating noise caused by a neighbor's motor-cycle
(E) the salaries paid to environmental workers

16 Passage 2 indicates that Costanza himself considers the true value of the world's ecosystems to be

(A) a subject more for psychologists than economists
(B) impossible to determine
(C) likely greater than his estimate
(D) independent of the value of human emotions
(E) roughly equal to the value of the gross national product of the United States

17 Which of the following is mentioned in Passage 2 as one of the potential "flaws" (line 156) in Costanza's work?

(A) contradictions with well-known theories of economics
(B) excessively technical language
(C) a failure to consider any externalities
(D) excessive reliance on guesswork
(E) incomplete mathematical models

8

18 The two passages differ in their perspectives on the debate between industrialists and environmentalists mainly in that Passage 1 emphasizes

(A) mathematics, while Passage 2 emphasizes psychology

(B) deficiencies in the debate, while Passage 2 emphasizes progress in the debate

(C) the irrelevance of externalities, while Passage 2 emphasizes their importance

(D) the impact on taxpayers, while Passage 2 emphasizes the views of politicians

(E) pollution, while Passage 2 emphasizes recycling

8

19 Both passages include which of the following elements?

    I.   a discussion of the importance of human feelings in a debate

   II.   a citation of an authoritative scientific study

   III.   a reference to global warming

(A) I only

(B) II only

(C) I and II only

(D) II and III only

(E) I, II, and III

STOP

You may check your work, on this section only, until time is called.

Section 9

Time—10 Minutes
14 Questions

Directions for "Improving Sentence" Questions

Each of the sentences below contains one underlined portion. The portion may contain one or more errors in grammar, usage, construction, precision, diction (choice of words), or idiom. Some of the sentences are correct.

Consider the meaning of the original sentence, and choose the answer that best expresses that meaning. If the original sentence is best, choose (A), because it repeats the original phrasing. Choose the phrasing that creates the clearest, most precise and most effective sentence.

EXAMPLE:
The children couldn't hardly believe their eyes.

    (A) couldn't hardly believe their eyes
    (B) would not hardly believe their eyes
    (C) could hardly believe their eyes
    (D) couldn't nearly believe their eyes
    (E) could hardly believe his or her eyes

Example answer: (C)

1 Brian wanted to prepare well for the <u>exam; staying up</u> all night studying his textbook.

    (A) exam; staying up
    (B) exam; and staying up
    (C) exam in staying up
    (D) exam, so he stayed up
    (E) exam and staying up

2 Many athletes use yoga to enhance their flexibility <u>and so that they might improve their mind-body awareness</u>.

    (A) and so that they might improve their mind-body awareness
    (B) and to improve their mind-body awareness
    (C) as well as improving their mind-body awareness
    (D) and for improving their mind-body awareness
    (E) and improve their mind-body awareness also

3 Without speaking so much as a syllable, <u>Chaplin's emotions and intentions were clearly portrayed on the screen</u>.

    (A) Chaplin's emotions and intentions were clearly portrayed on the screen
    (B) Chaplin clearly on the screen portrayed his emotional intentions
    (C) Chaplin's emotions and intentions on the screen were clearly portrayed by him
    (D) Chaplin emotionally portrayed his intentions on the screen clearly
    (E) Chaplin clearly portrayed his emotions and intentions on the screen

4   The conversation between <u>Anna and me about her future plans was</u> frank and productive.

(A)   Anna and me about her future plans was

(B)   Anna and I about her future plans were

(C)   Anna and me about her future plans were

(D)   me and Anna about her future plans were

(E)   Anna and I about her future plans was

5   <u>The fact of the island's strong natural defenses made it a natural choice by the naval commander to station his ships there</u>.

(A)   The fact of the island's strong natural defenses made it a natural choice by the naval commander to station his ships there.

(B)   The naval commander chose to station his ships on the island because it had strong natural defenses.

(C)   The island's strong natural defenses made the naval commander choose to station his ships on it.

(D)   Due to its strong natural defenses, the naval commander stationed his ships on the island by choice.

(E)   The island was the choice for the naval commander's stationing his ships because of its strong natural defenses.

6   Much of the night sky has never been examined carefully because <u>of the cumbersome nature of telescopes and the fact that they can only peer</u> into a tiny patch of the sky at one time.

(A)   of the cumbersome nature of telescopes and the fact that they can only peer

(B)   telescopes are cumbersome and can only peer

(C)   of the cumbersomeness of telescopes and the fact of their peering only

(D)   telescopes are cumbersome enough without peering

(E)   telescopes are too cumbersome yet unable to peer

7   Only recently have neural scientists come to realize that new nerve cells can, in certain situations, <u>be generated to assume</u> the function of dead or damaged ones.

(A)   be generated to assume

(B)   be generated for the assuming of

(C)   have been generated to assume

(D)   assume, being generated,

(E)   generate the assuming of

8   Prospective students should consider not only a school's curriculum and prestige, but also <u>what kind of student support programs it provides</u>.

(A)   what kind of student support programs it provides

(B)   how good are its student support programs

(C)   what its student support programs are

(D)   what student support programs they provide

(E)   its student support programs

9   William F. Buckley, <u>wrote his first book when he was 23</u>, also founded the *National Review*.

(A)   wrote his first book when he was 23

(B)   who wrote his first book when he was 23

(C)   who when he would have published his first book was 23

(D)   wrote, at 23, his first book

(E)   would write his first book at 23

10   <u>If they would not have been led astray by the faulty map</u>, the troop would have found camp by nightfall.

(A)   If they would not have been led astray by the faulty map

(B)   If the faulty map would not have led it astray

(C)   Had they not have been led astray by the faulty map

(D)   Had it not been led astray by the faulty map

(E)   Would they not have been led astray by the faulty map

11 Barely able to speak because of the cold, <u>the communication among the two explorers had to be done through gestures</u>.

(A) the communication among the two explorers had to be done through gestures

(B) the communication between the two explorers had to be done through gestures

(C) the two explorers had to communicate through gestures

(D) the two explorers had to communicate between themselves from gestures

(E) gestures were used to communicate between the two explorers

12 The cost of crude oil is influenced dramatically not only by supply but also <u>by what the current geopolitical events are like</u>.

(A) by what the current geopolitical events are like

(B) because of current geopolitical events

(C) by current geopolitical events

(D) by what current geopolitical events are

(E) because current geopolitical events influence it

13 The Ivy League was founded as a sports conference <u>and many think it was founded as an academic conference</u>.

(A) and many think it was founded as an academic conference

(B) and not, as many think, as an academic conference

(C) but many people think instead that it was founded as an academic conference

(D) yet many think mistakenly that it was founded as an academic conference instead

(E) but not as an academic conference as many think

14 <u>They expended so much effort and money to be able to witness</u> the transit of Venus, the surveyors could not return to Europe without the valuable data they sought.

(A) They expended so much effort and money to be able to witness

(B) They had expended so much effort and money for witnessing

(C) Having expended so much effort and money to be able to witness

(D) The money and effort having been expended already to witness

(E) To be able to witness, having expended so much effort and money

9

STOP

You may check your work, on this section only, until time is called.

ANSWER KEY

Section 2 Math	Section 5 Math	Section 7 Math	Section 3 Critical Reading	Section 6 Critical Reading	Section 8 Critical Reading	Section 4 Writing	Section 9 Writing
☐ 1. C	☐ 1. E	☐ 1. C	☐ 1. C	☐ 1. C	☐ 1. A	☐ 1. B	☐ 1. D
☐ 2. C	☐ 2. C	☐ 2. C	☐ 2. A	☐ 2. B	☐ 2. D	☐ 2. E	☐ 2. B
☐ 3. E	☐ 3. E	☐ 3. D	☐ 3. E	☐ 3. B	☐ 3. B	☐ 3. C	☐ 3. E
☐ 4. A	☐ 4. B	☐ 4. A	☐ 4. B	☐ 4. C	☐ 4. E	☐ 4. E	☐ 4. A
☐ 5. B	☐ 5. B	☐ 5. D	☐ 5. C	☐ 5. A	☐ 5. B	☐ 5. A	☐ 5. B
☐ 6. B	☐ 6. C	☐ 6. A	☐ 6. D	☐ 6. A	☐ 6. D	☐ 6. D	☐ 6. B
☐ 7. B	☐ 7. D	☐ 7. B	☐ 7. D	☐ 7. C	☐ 7. E	☐ 7. B	☐ 7. A
☐ 8. A	☐ 8. B	☐ 8. E	☐ 8. A	☐ 8. E	☐ 8. A	☐ 8. D	☐ 8. E
☐ 9. C	☐ 9. 8	☐ 9. A	☐ 9. B	☐ 9. C	☐ 9. D	☐ 9. D	☐ 9. B
☐ 10. C	☐ 10. 12	☐ 10. B	☐ 10. E	☐ 10. C	☐ 10. C	☐ 10. A	☐ 10. D
☐ 11. D	☐ 11. 1/8	☐ 11. D	☐ 11. A	☐ 11. B	☐ 11. C	☐ 11. E	☐ 11. C
☐ 12. B	☐ 12. 0.5 or	☐ 12. E	☐ 12. C	☐ 12. A	☐ 12. E	☐ 12. C	☐ 12. C
☐ 13. A	½	☐ 13. B	☐ 13. C	☐ 13. A	☐ 13. A	☐ 13. B	☐ 13. B
☐ 14. D	☐ 13. 4	☐ 14. A	☐ 14. C	☐ 14. D	☐ 14. B	☐ 14. E	☐ 14. C
☐ 15. C	☐ 14. 5	☐ 15. A	☐ 15. B	☐ 15. C	☐ 15. D	☐ 15. D	
☐ 16. C	☐ 15. 35	☐ 16. B	☐ 16. A	☐ 16. E	☐ 16. C	☐ 16. C	
☐ 17. B	☐ 16. 333 or		☐ 17. B	☐ 17. D	☐ 17. D	☐ 17. B	
☐ 18. D	⅓		☐ 18. D	☐ 18. B	☐ 18. B	☐ 18. A	
☐ 19. B	☐ 17. 7		☐ 19. C	☐ 19. A	☐ 19. A	☐ 19. C	
☐ 20. D	☐ 18. 7/6 or		☐ 20. B	☐ 20. D		☐ 20. E	
	1.16 or		☐ 21. A	☐ 21. C		☐ 21. D	
	1.17		☐ 22. E	☐ 22. D		☐ 22. A	
			☐ 23. C	☐ 23. B		☐ 23. D	
			☐ 24. D	☐ 24. A		☐ 24. E	
						☐ 25. C	
						☐ 26. C	
						☐ 27. B	
						☐ 28. A	
						☐ 29. A	
						☐ 30. E	
						☐ 31. C	
						☐ 32. B	
						☐ 33. D	
						☐ 34. B	
						☐ 35. A	

Right (A): _____

Questions 1–8
Right (A): _____

Right (A): _____

Right (A): _____

Right (A): _____

Right (A): _____

Right (A): _____

Right (A): _____

#Wrong (B): _____

#Wrong (B): _____

#Wrong (B): _____

#Wrong (B): _____

#Wrong (B): _____

#Wrong (B): _____

#Wrong (B): _____

#Wrong (B): _____

(A) − ¼B: _____

(A) − ¼B: _____

(A) − ¼B: _____

(A) − ¼B: _____

(A) − ¼B: _____

(A) − ¼B: _____

(A) − ¼B: _____

(A) − ¼B: _____

Questions 9–18
Right (A): _____

SCORE CONVERSION TABLE

How to score your text

Use the answer key on the previous page to determine your raw score on each section. Your raw score on each section except Section 4 is simply the number of correct answers minus ¼ of the number of wrong answers. On Section 4, your raw score is the sum of the number of correct answers for questions 1–8 minus ¼ of the number of wrong answers for questions 1–8 plus the total number of correct answers for questions 9–18. Next, add the raw scores from Sections 3, 4, and 7 to get your Math raw score, add the raw scores from Sections 2, 5, and 8 to get your Critical Reading raw score and add the raw scores from Sections 6 and 9 to get your Writing raw score. Write the three raw scores here:

Raw Critical Reading score: _____ Raw Math score: _____ Raw Writing score: _____

Use the table below to convert these to scaled scores.

Scaled scores: Critical Reading: _____ Math: _____ Writing: _____

Raw Score	Critical Reading Scaled Score	Math Scaled Score	Writing Scaled Score	Raw Score	Critical Reading Scaled Score	Math Scaled Score	Writing Scaled Score
67	800			32	520	550	610
66	800			31	510	550	600
65	790			30	510	540	580
64	780			29	500	530	570
63	760			28	490	520	560
62	750			27	490	530	550
61	730			26	480	510	540
60	720			25	480	500	530
59	700			24	470	490	520
58	700			23	460	480	510
57	690			22	460	480	500
56	680			21	450	470	490
55	670			20	440	460	480
54	660	800		19	440	450	470
53	650	790		18	430	450	460
52	650	760		17	420	440	450
51	640	740		16	420	430	440
50	630	720		15	410	420	440
49	620	710	800	14	400	410	430
48	620	700	800	13	400	410	420
47	610	680	800	12	390	400	410
46	600	670	790	11	380	390	400
45	600	660	780	10	370	380	390
44	590	650	760	9	360	370	380
43	590	640	740	8	350	360	380
42	580	630	730	7	340	350	370
41	570	630	710	6	330	340	360
40	570	620	700	5	320	330	350
39	560	610	690	4	310	320	340
38	550	600	670	3	300	310	320
37	550	590	660	2	280	290	310
36	540	580	650	1	270	280	300
35	540	580	640	0	250	260	280
34	530	570	630	−1	230	240	270
33	520	560	620	−2 or less	210	220	250

SCORE CONVERSION TABLE FOR WRITING COMPOSITE
[ESSAY + MULTIPLE CHOICE]

Calculate your writing raw score as you did on the previous page and grade your essay from a 1 to a 6 according to the standards that follow in the detailed answer key.

Essay score: _____ Raw Writing score: _____

Use the table below to convert these to scaled scores.

Scaled score: Writing: _____

Raw Score	Essay Score 0	Essay Score 1	Essay Score 2	Essay Score 3	Essay Score 4	Essay Score 5	Essay Score 6
−2 or less	200	230	250	280	310	340	370
−1	210	240	260	290	320	360	380
0	230	260	280	300	340	370	400
1	240	270	290	320	350	380	410
2	250	280	300	330	360	390	420
3	260	290	310	340	370	400	430
4	270	300	320	350	380	410	440
5	280	310	330	360	390	420	450
6	290	320	340	360	400	430	460
7	290	330	340	370	410	440	470
8	300	330	350	380	410	450	470
9	310	340	360	390	420	450	480
10	320	350	370	390	430	460	490
11	320	360	370	400	440	470	500
12	330	360	380	410	440	470	500
13	340	370	390	420	450	480	510
14	350	380	390	420	460	490	520
15	350	380	400	430	460	500	530
16	360	390	410	440	470	500	530
17	370	400	420	440	480	510	540
18	380	410	420	450	490	520	550
19	380	410	430	460	490	530	560
20	390	420	440	470	500	530	560
21	400	430	450	480	510	540	570
22	410	440	460	480	520	550	580
23	420	450	470	490	530	560	590
24	420	460	470	500	540	570	600
25	430	460	480	510	540	580	610
26	440	470	490	520	550	590	610
27	450	480	500	530	560	590	620
28	460	490	510	540	570	600	630
29	470	500	520	550	580	610	640
30	480	510	530	560	590	620	650
31	490	520	540	560	600	630	660
32	500	530	550	570	610	640	670
33	510	540	550	580	620	650	680
34	510	550	560	590	630	660	690
35	520	560	570	600	640	670	700
36	530	560	580	610	650	680	710
37	540	570	590	620	660	690	720
38	550	580	600	630	670	700	730
39	560	600	610	640	680	710	740
40	580	610	620	650	690	720	750
41	590	620	640	660	700	730	760
42	600	630	650	680	710	740	770
43	610	640	660	690	720	750	780
44	620	660	670	700	740	770	800
45	640	670	690	720	750	780	800
46	650	690	700	730	770	800	800
47	670	700	720	750	780	800	800
48	680	720	730	760	800	800	800
49	680	720	730	760	800	800	800

Detailed Answer Key

Section 1

The following essay received 12 points out of a possible 12, meaning that it demonstrates *clear and consistent mastery* in that it

- develops an insightful point of view on the topic
- demonstrates exemplary critical thinking
- uses effective examples, reasons, and other evidence to support its thesis
- is consistently focused, coherent, and well-organized
- demonstrates skilful and effective use of language and sentence structure
- is largely (but not necessarily completely) free of grammatical and usage errors

Consider carefully the issue discussed in the following passage, then write an essay that answers the question posed in the assignment.

> In any contest between power and patience, bet on patience.
>
> —W.B. Prescott

Assignment: **Which is a more powerful force of social change: power or patience?** Write an essay in which you answer this question and support your position logically with examples from literature, the arts, history, politics, science and technology, or your experience or observation.

Write your essay on separate sheets of paper.

SAMPLE STUDENT ESSAY

Although the first two centuries of the American experiment have been characterized by the systematic disenfrachisement of African Americans, women, the destitute, and those from the "wrong" political party, democracy has slowly and patiently evolved and strengthened, not through military victories, but by patient commitment to an idea. Indeed, democracy is the antithesis of concentrated power. Yet, tragically, recent American leaders act as if it can be forced upon a people, in ignorance of the true history of their own democracy, and of the nature of democracy itself. They have come to believe that America, by dint of its relative success with democracy at home, has earned the right to exert its unbridled will throughout the world. They will fail because they do not understand the value of patience over power, of ideas over arms, of compassion over strategy. The patient commitment to true democracy will, in the long run, be more powerful than the strongest army on earth.

The current war in Iraq was first proclaimed as a "preemptive" strike against terrorists in order to protect our homeland. When it was revealed beyond doubt that Iraq in fact posed no threat to us, our leaders re-cast the war as one to "free Iraq" and "bring democracy to an oppressed people." But this could not possibly be so. Such proclamations express only the wishes of politicians, not human reality. Democracy is the patient triumph of ideas over might. It is a waging of words rather than a waging of war; it is a faith in humanity to choose what is right and good, not to force-feed a single-minded view down the throats of the masses.

But, the neoconservatives say, our own freedom, our own democracy, was earned only through wars like the Revolutionary War, the Civil War and the World Wars. We must exert our power and perhaps spill the blood of our brave soldiers so that freedom will reign! But this is true only for one's own freedom, not the freedom of others. Each people must earn its own freedom. No country on this earth will ever accept that it has been "given" democracy by an invading force. It's story must belong to its people, just as the story of our freedom is our own.

We have a long way to go before we understand democracy well enough to preach it to others, let alone force it down their throats. True leaders lead by example, not by force. When our leaders learn the true meaning of democracy well enough to live it, then they will have earned the right to speak it, and the world will follow their example. To reach that point, we need patient faith in an idea, not the powers of arms.

The following essay received 10 points out of a possible 12, meaning that it demonstrates *reasonably consistent* mastery in that it

- effectively develops a point of view on the topic
- demonstrates strong critical thinking
- uses good examples, reasons, and other evidence to support its thesis
- shows a good organization and consistent focus
- demonstrates consistent facility with language
- is mostly free of errors in grammar, usage, and mechanics

SAMPLE STUDENT ESSAY

Patience does bring about greater change than does power. We tend to see the world in terms of power. Our televisions are filled with scenes of powerful politicians and tycoons, of powerful bombs and natural disasters, but if our televisions could show us the world as it really is, we would see a lot more patient waiting than powerful expressions of force. Even though the universe may have been created in one huge big bang, life has only evolved to its current level patiently over millions and millions of years.

Our economy is supported more by the millions of workers who do their jobs faithfully and patiently day by day than by the mega-powerful CEOs with billion dollar salaries. In fact, the most successful CEOs become successful only by learning the patience of the common people. McDonald's is successful because it consistently gives the people the food they want, day in and day out. Dell has become a successful company because it patiently listens to its consumers and helps them with difficulties they may have with their computers.

Another good example of the strength of patience is a colony of ants. No one ant has any extraordinary ability, but when they patiently do their jobs as a group, they create and maintain an enormous ecosystem almost as complex as a city. There are no tycoons in an ant colony.

It is wise to remember that patience is more important than power. For instance, great athletes become great by patiently and consistently working on their skills, their strength and their agility. If they tried to do all of their training in one powerful burst, they would quickly burn themselves out or get injured. Even one who is merely trying to stay in shape, or to learn a subject, should remember that steady patient work is more important than natural power.

The following essay received 4 points out of a possible 12, meaning that it demonstrates *some incompetence* in that it

- has a seriously limited point of view
- demonstrates weak critical thinking
- uses inappropriate or insufficient examples, reasons, and other evidence to support its thesis
- is poorly focused and organized, and has serious problems with coherence
- demonstrates frequent problems with language and sentence structure
- contains errors in grammar and usage that obscure the author's meaning seriously

SAMPLE STUDENT ESSAY

If to bet on patience means that you should just wait for things to happen, I don't think you should do that. Sometimes the most important thing is to take some action and show that you have some power. If somebody is trying to attack you, then patience isn't going to help you much, but having a gun probably will. That's just the way things are.

A lot of times people will tell me that it's better if you just wait and good things will happen. But when you see people who have made their mark in the world you see people have just took charge and did things on their own terms. Power works. Everybody can tell when somebody walks into the room who has confidence in themselves. It's very appealing and people like that tend to have a lot of infuence over people and things.

I don't want to just sit around and wait for things to happen that's why I try to make things happen. That's a lot better for all different areas like sports, business and politics.

Detailed Answer Key

Section 2

---

1. C First substitute $2b$ for a:

$$a = 3 + b$$

Substitute: $\quad\quad\quad\quad\quad\quad 2b = 3 + b$

Subtract b: $\quad\quad\quad\quad\quad\quad b = 3$

---

2. C 6 pounds of cheese cost $6 \times \$1.50 = \$9.00$.
6 pounds of beef cost $3 \times \$4.00 = \$12.00$.
$\$12.00 - \$9.00 = \$3.00$

---

3. E The slope of a line is the "rise divided by the run" between any two points. Use the origin as one point and $(12, k)$ as the other. The "rise" between these points is $k - 0 = k$. The "run" is $12 - 0 = 12$. If the slope is 2, then $k/12 = 2$, and therefore $k = 24$.

---

4. A The statement "x is 5 less than y" translates into

$$x = y - 5$$

Subtract y: $\quad\quad x - y = -5$

therefore: $\quad\quad 5(x - y) = 5(-5) = -25$

You may also choose simple values for x and y, where x is 5 less than y, like $x = 2$ and $y = 7$.

---

5. B On a map that is drawn to scale, all distances are proportional to their corresponding lengths in the real world. Therefore, we can set up a proportion:

$$\frac{50 \text{ miles}}{1 \text{ inch}} = \frac{240 \text{ miles}}{x \text{ inches}}$$

Cross-multiply: $\quad\quad 50x = 240$

Divide by 50: $\quad\quad\quad x = 4.8$

---

6. B One student has 40% of the CDs, and 40% of $30 = .40(30) = 12$ CDs. The other student has $33\frac{1}{3}\%$, or $\frac{1}{3}$ of the CDs. $\frac{1}{3}$ of $30 = 10$. Therefore the third student has $30 - 12 - 10 = 8$ CDs.

---

7. B If the average score of Marianne's 3 tests is 85, then the sum of the three scores is $85 \times 3 = 255$. If she scored 90 on the first two tests, then she must have received $255 - 90 - 90 = 75$ on the third test.

---

8. A The sequence consists of the repetition of three numbers, -1, 0 and 1 which have a sum of 0. In the first 100 terms, this pattern is repeated $33\frac{1}{3}$ times. The first 33 repetitions yield a sum of $33(0) = 0$, but this leaves one more term, which is -1. Therefore the overall sum is $0 + -1 = -1$.

---

9. C Since $50 \div 3 = 16\frac{2}{3}$, there are 16 multiples of 3 between 1 and 50, the last one being $16 \times 3 = 48$. Therefore the probability of choosing a multiple of 3 is $16/50 = 8/25$.

---

10. C Substitute $a = 10$ into both of the other equations and solve for b and c: $10 + b = 5$

Subtract 10: $\quad\quad\quad\quad b = -5$

$$10 - c = 15$$

Subtract 10: $\quad\quad\quad -c = 5$

Divide by -1: $\quad\quad\quad c = -5$

So $c - b = -5 - (-5) = 0$

---

11. D Examine the "ones" column first. $A + 7 + B + 7$ must equal either 18 or 28 in order to produce an 8 in the ones column as a result. (Think about why it can't equal 8 or 38 or greater.) Therefore $A + B = 4$ or 14. If $A + B = 4$, then there is a "carry" of 1 into the tens column, and so $1 + 3 + B + 4 + 2 = 17$ and $B = 7$. But this is impossible, because we had assumed that $A + B$ is only 4. Therefore, $A + B$ must equal 14, and the "carry" is 2. This means that $2 + 3 + B + 4 + 2 = 17$, and so $B = 6$. therefore $A = 8$.

---

12. B Draw point D so that C is the midpoint of AD. If $CD = 4x$, then $AC = 4x$ also. Then you can find AB by the Pythagorean Theorem:

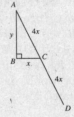

$$y^2 + x^2 = (4x)^2$$

Simplify: $\quad\quad\quad y^2 + x^2 = 16x^2$

Subtract x^2: $\quad\quad\quad\quad y^2 = 15x^2$

Take the square root: $\quad\quad\quad y = \sqrt{15}x$

13. A   A quick sketch of the two points may be helpful:

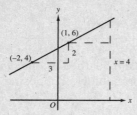

One approach is to determine the equation of the line joining the two points, but this is time consuming, then seeing which point "works" in the equation. (The equation is $y = (2/3)x + 16/3$.) A simpler method is to notice that, to get from the first point to the second, you need only move to the right 3 units and up 2 units. Repeating this again from the second point puts you at (4, 8).

14. D   This is just a matter of checking each choice. Don't forget that *squaring* something is **not** the same as taking the *square root*. (If you made this mistake, you probably chose (B) as your answer.) The only choice that "works" is (D) because $16 = 7 + 3^2$.

15. C $3^y + 3^y + 3^y + 3^y + 3^y + 3^y + 3^y + 3^y + 3^y = 9(3^y)$
Notice that 9 is a power of 3: $9(3^y) = 3^1(3^y)$
Add exponents when multiplying exponentials with a common base: $3^2(3^y) = 3^{y+2}$

16. C   One approach is to "test" points and work by process of elimination. For instance, you might notice that 0 doesn't work (because $2 - |0 + 1|$ is not < 0), but 2 does work (because $2 - |2 + 1| < 0$. Therefore the solution set contains 2 but not 0. This eliminates choices (A) and (B). You can proceed like this until only one choice remains.

Another approach is to simplify the inequality and "translate" it. $2 - |x + 1| < 0$
Subtract 2: $-|x + 1| < -2$
Divide by -1 and "flip": $|x + 1| > 2$
Represent sum as a
difference: $|x - (-1)| > 2$
This means that the distance from x to -1 is greater than 2. The graph that shows all values more than 2 units away from -1 is choice (C).

17. B   Assume that the original price of the book is p and the total number of books sold at that price is n. At this price, the book would produce a revenue of np. The new price is 10% greater, or $1.1p$, and the new sales number is 5% less, or $.95n$. This would produce a revenue of $(1.1p)(.95n) = 1.045np$, which represents an increase in revenue of 4.5%.

18. D   In the first round, 16 games are played and 16 teams are eliminated. In the next round, 8 games are played and 8 are eliminated, and so on. Each round contains half as many games as the previous round. The total number of games played is $16 + 8 + 4 + 2 + 1 = 31$. (A simpler method of counting the games is simply to notice that 31 teams of the 32 must be eliminated in order to decide the one remaining champion!) Since each game takes 2 hours, the total number of hours is $31(2) = 62$ hours.

19. B   Sides AB and AC are perpendicular, so their lengths can be used as the base and height of the triangle. $AB = 10$, and since AC is the hypotenuse of an isosceles right triangle with legs of length 10, its length is $10\sqrt{2}$.

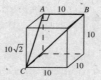

Therefore the area of the triangle is $(1/2)(10)(10\sqrt{2}) = 50\sqrt{2}$.

20. D   Let x represent the total of number of marbles in the jar to start. Since the ratio of black marbles to red marbles is 4:5, 4/9 of the marbles are black and 5/9 of the marbles are red. So there are $(4/9)x$ black marbles and $(5/9)x$ red marbles to start. After 18 black marbles are added, there are $(4/9)x + 18$ black marbles. Since the new ratio is 5:4,

$$\frac{\frac{4}{9}x + 18}{\frac{5}{9}x} = \frac{5}{4}$$

Cross-multiply: $\dfrac{16}{9}x + 72 = \dfrac{25}{9}x$

Multiply by 9: $16x + 648 = 25x$
Subtract $16x$: $648 = 9x$
Divide by 9: $72 = x$

Section 3

1. C If journalists have *strong personal opinion*, they must have a difficult time remaining *unbiased*. *eloquent* = well spoken; *converted* = changed into something else; *neutral* = unbiased; *biased* = partial.

2. A If the speaker found it *difficult to stay awake*, the lecture must have been very *dull*. *monotonous* = dull; *provocative* = inspiring a strong reaction; *authoritative* = characterized by authority.

3. E International flights today are very common, but few people can travel into space because of the enormous *expense*. If it is possible that space excursions will soon be like international flights, they must be getting *less expensive*. *pedestrian* = commonplace; *responsive* = reacting quickly to stimuli; *mundane* = ordinary.

4. B If audiences *value* stars of *vacuous* (empty-headed) programs, they must value *fame* over talent. *exalt* = praise highly; *lionize* = treat as a celebrity; *obscurity* = the quality of being hard to recognize; *aesthetics* = the philosophy of beauty.

5. C The two logical ways of completing this idea are to say that cultures use a variety of *war-like* strategies to resolve conflicts, contradicting those who think warfare is *rare*, or to say that cultures use a wide variety of *peaceful* strategies to resolve conflicts, contradicting those who think warfare is *dominant*. *universal* = found everywhere; *deleterious* = harmful; *idiosyncratic* = unique and odd.

6. D The terms *cheerful* and *harshly* suggest a change in attitude. Goya must have *tolerated* the social conditions early in life, but then *changed* this attitude. *espousal* = public embrace of an idea; *repression* = hiding of one's feelings; *succeeded* = followed; *supplanted* = replaced; *denunciation* = public criticism.

7. D If they believed that a *hasty* approach would cause problems, they must have preferred a *slow and careful* approach. *accelerated* = sped up; *dexterous* = nimble; *indifferent* = uncaring; *deliberate* = slow and careful; *delapidated* = run-down.

8. A The sentence suggests that although the game is relatively new, many aspects of it are old. The rules were *adapted from* or *taken from* older games. *appropriated* = taken and made one's own; *discarded* = thrown out; *advocated* = supported vocally; *elucidated* = explained in detail; *compensated* = made amends.

9. B The passage states that schools teach capitalism *not so much by directly instructing students* (lines 1–2) but by simply *embodying capitalistic qualities*. This suggests that capitalism is taught *implicitly*.

10. E By saying that *cooperation is stressed far more than competition*, the author means that *cooperation is emphasized over competition*.

11. A The passage states that Fitzgerald was guilty of *too frequent concessions to the taste of the moment* (lines 15–16) rather than steadfast pursuit of the *artistic ideal*. This means that he *compromised* that ideal.

12. C The passage states that Hemingway referred to *success and money as false gods* (line 21) in his work.

13. A The constant focus on the human qualities of Ayn Rand—*her life and her person* (lines 4–5), *astonsihing human being* (line 56), *eyes of a human being* (line 62), *she was a human being* (line 98)—in relation to the *epic* (lines 5 and 100) scale of her life indicate the author's purpose to *humanize* Ayn Rand.

14. C The author states that Rand's life was *preposterously unbelievable* (line 3), that *she herself encompassed ... grandeur* (line 11) and that her *virtues were larger than life* (lines 19–20). These clearly characterize Rand's life as majestic.

15. B This sentence indicates that Ayn Rand shared a *vast powers of intellect* (lines 13–14) with her heroes.

16. A The first paragraph indicates that Rand shared an *impassioned pursuit of...goals* (line 14) with her heroes, but that she possessed *self-doubt* (line 17) which they lacked, and they possessed *emotional balance* (line 17) which she lacked.

17. B This paragraph suggests that Rand's readers take one of two extreme positions on her philosophy: *grateful, loving admiration or enraged disapproval* (lines 37–38)

18. D This paragraph contains metaphor (*her reason becoming a whip* (line 78), stark contrast (*menacing with anger ... touchingly kind* (lines 72–74), parallel sentence structure (*I saw them...*), and characterization of Rand herself, but no definitions.

19. C Although the author mentions that Rand possessed the *delight of a child* (line 71) and *the power of ... reason* (line 78), and was *tender* (line 75) and *merciless* (line 76), it suggests that she lacked an *inward look* (lines 85–86).

20. **B**   This sentence indicates that it would take *all the years* for the author to understand *the absence of* (Rand's) *inward look* (lines 89–90).

21. **A**   The only one of these contrasts that is described in the passage is that between Rand's public life and private life: *Her public ... activities took place on a lighted stage; her private life was lived backstage* (lines 41–43).

22. **E**   The author clearly conveys the idea that Rand had both *epic virtues and epic shortcoming* (lines 19–20). The final sentence reinforces and summarizes this theme by emphasizing both the epic and the human qualities of her life.

23. **C**   The author states that *as the years passsed,* (she) *was to observe all the many changes* of Rand's eyes, thereby suggesting that she knew Rand intimately over a long period of time.

24. **D**   The passage contains information about how her ideas were received: *each reader takes an unequivocal stand for or against what she represents ... and her name is met with explosions of grateful, loving admiration or enraged disapproval* (lines 36–38). It also indicates that she was born in the first decade of the 20th century, since she was *45 years old in 1950* (line 45), and that Rand was 77 years old when she died (line 5). It does not, however, indicate where Ayn Rand was born (but, if you're interested, it was St. Petersburg, Russia).

Section 4

1. **B**   The phrase *not only...but also* indicates **parallel structure**. Choice B provides the most parallel structure.

2. **E**   The sentence should have a *neither...nor* parallel structure. Choice E is most **parallel**.

3. **C**   The sentence must be an **independent clause**, and the **verb must agree** with the plural subject *works*.

4. **E**   The two clauses should be parallel, since they have the same subject. **The active** voice keeps the second clause parallel with the first.

5. **A**   The original phrasing is best.

6. **D**   The **modifying phrase** should be followed by the noun it modifies, which is *Warhol*. Choice D is also the most idiomatic.

7. **B**   The original phrasing is a sentence **fragment**. Choice B is most idiomatic.

8. **D**   The original phrasing is **wordy and awkward**. Choice D is most concise.

9. **D**   the original phrasing is **wordy and awkward**. Choice D is most concise.

10. **A**   The original phrasing is best.

11. **E**   The phrase *not only* suggests a **parallel** phrasing in the form *not only A but also B*.

12. **C**   This is a **diction error**. The correct word is *successful*. *Successive* means *following one after another*.

13. **B**   This verb is the **wrong tense**. Since the book has not been finished yet, this verb should be in the **future** perfect tense: *will have read*.

14. **E**   This sentence is correct.

15. **D**   This pronoun is in the **wrong case**. Since it is the object of a preposition, it should have the **objective case**: *to David and me*.

16. **C**   This pronoun has a **vague antecedent**. It could refer to the *union* or the *board*, so it should be made more specific.

17. **B**   This is an **improper idiom**. The correct idiom is *work in*.

18. **A**   This is a **subject-verb disagreement**. Since the subject of the verb is *copies*, the phrase should read *there are*.

19. **C**   This is a **pronoun shift**. Since the pronoun *one's* has already been used, it should be maintained: *one can now find*.

20. **E**   The sentence is correct.

21. **D**   This phrase is **redundant** and non-idiomatic. It should read *and stroke*.

22. **A**   The word *between* should only be used to refer to two things, not dozens. the correct word is *among*.

23. **D** This is an **illogical comparison**. The *salaries of professional women* should be compared to *the salaries of professional men.*

24. **E** The sentence is correct.

25. **C** This uses **incorrect idiom**. The correct phrase is to *read.*

26. **C** This is a **diction error**. The correct word is *accepted. Excepted* means left out.

27. **B** This is an improper use of the **perfect tense**. Since the *reaching* was not completed before the *walking*, it should take the simple past tense: *reached.*

28. **A** This is a **subject-verb disagreement**. Since the subject of the verb is the singular *Rancho Coronado*, it should be *sprawls.*

29. **A** This uses **incorrect idiom**. The correct idiom is *critics of.*

30. **E** The **comparison** requires parallel form: *choosing … is like choosing.*

31. **C** Choice C coordinates the ideas most **logically**, without the use of any **unclear pronoun antecedents.**

32. **B** The ideas are **coordinated most logically** in choice B.

33. **D** Sentence 13 is out of place because the main idea of the sentence is about how voters should inform themselves about political candidates and issues, not about the negativity of political ads.

34. **B** The original phrasing is needlessly **wordy and awkward**. Choice B is preferable to D because D creates a run-on sentence.

35. **A** Choice A is best because it is concise and avoids the **pronoun shift** of the others.

Section 5

1. **E** 27 is the least common multiple of 9 and 27.

2. **C**

$$4(x + 3) = 15$$
Distribute: $\quad 4x + 12 = 15$
Subtract 9: $\quad 4x + 3 = 6$

3. **E** If the winnings are split in the ratio of 5:2:1, then each portion is 5/8, 2/8 and 1/8 of the total, respectively. The largest portion, then is (5/8)($4,000) = $2500.

4. **B** Since 120° is 1/3 of 360°, arc *MNP* is 1/3 of the circumference. So the circumference is $3(6\pi) = 18\pi$. Since circumference $= 2\pi r = 18\pi$, $r = 9$.

5. **B** If $AB = BC$, then the angles opposite those sides are equal, too: $\quad 5x - 5 = 4x + 9$
Subtract $4x$ $\qquad x - 5 = 9$
Add 5: $\qquad\qquad x = 14$
Substituting for x, this tells you that the base angles are both 65°. Since $65 + 65 + y = 180$, $y = 50$.

6. **C** The median is the "middle number" in the set, which is g because $f < g < h$. If $f = 6$ and $h = 20$, then the average of the three numbers is

$$\frac{6 + g + 20}{3} = \frac{g + 26}{3}$$

If the average is 1 greater than the median, then

$$\frac{g + 26}{3} = g + 1$$

Multiply by 3: $\qquad g + 26 = 3g + 3$
Subtract g: $\qquad\quad 26 = 2g + 3$
Subtract 3: $\qquad\quad 23 = 2g$
Divide by 2: $\qquad 11.5 = g$

7. **D** If the ratio of white marbles to red marbles is 3 to 5, then the total number of red marbles must be a multiple of 5. If the ratio of red marbles to blue marbles is 6 to 5, then the number of red marbles must also be a multiple of 6. The least multiple of both 5 and 6 is 30, so the least number of red marbles is 30. Use the two ratios to find the number of white and blue marbles:
3/5 = (# white marbles)/30, so # white marbles = 18
6/5 = 30/(# blue marbles), so # blue marbles = 25
Therefore the total number of marbles is 30 + 18 + 25 = 73

8. **B** If the volume varies inversely as the pressure and directly as the temperature, then $V = kT/P$ where k is a constant. You are given that $10 = k(300)/2$, therefore $k = 1/15$. So to find the volume at 1 atmosphere and 450 degrees, use the formula $V = (1/15)(450)/1 = 30$

9. 8   Translate into an equation:

$$25\% \text{ of } 16 \text{ is } x$$
$$0.25(16) = x$$

Simplify: $4 = x$
Substitute: 4% of 200
$$.04(200) = 8$$

---

10. 12   Since, in choosing a route, you must first choose from 3 paths from A to B, then from 4 paths from B to C, the total number of routes is $3 \times 4 = 12$.

---

11. 1/8 or .125 $2/x = w$
Multiply by x: $2 = xw$
Raise to the –3 power: $1/8 = (wx)^{-3}$

---

12. 1/2 or 0.5 If we add 2 to x and then divide by 4, the result is $\dfrac{x+2}{4}$. Distributing, we can see that this is equivalent to $x/4 + 2/4 = x/4 + 1/2$.

---

13. 4 $n^{-2p} = \dfrac{1}{16^p}$

simplify: $\dfrac{1}{n^{2p}} = \dfrac{1}{16^p}$

Take the reciprocal: $n^{2p} = 16^p$
Take the pth root: $n^2 = 16$
Take the square root: $n = 4$

---

14. 5 The graph of the function $f(x) = -(x - 1)^2 + 2$ is a parabola with a vertex at $(1, 2)$, as shown here.

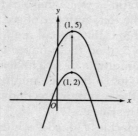

The graph of $y = f(x) + 3$ is simply the same graph shifted up 3 units. Its highest point is at $(1,5)$, so the greatest value of the function is 5. If you'd rather not graph, just notice that $f(x) = -(x - 1)^2 + 2$ can get no greater than 2 because the greatest $-(x - 1)^2$ can be is 0 (since "squares" cannot be negative). Therefore the greatest that $-(x - 1)^2 + 2 + 3$ can be is 5.

---

15. 35

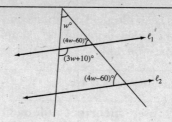

Focus on the "upper" triangle. Notice that one of its interior angles is equal to $(4w - 60)°$, because of the parallel lines theorem. By the exterior angle theorem

$$3w + 10 = (4w - 60) + w$$

Simplify: $3w + 10 = 5w - 60$
Subtract $3w$ $10 = 2w - 60$
Add 60: $70 = 2w$
Divide by 2: $35 = w$

---

16. 1/3 or .333   Recall the factoring formula
$$x^2 - y^2 = (x - y)(x + y)$$
Substitute: $24 = (x - y)(72)$
Divide by 72: $1/3 = (x - y)$
Don't worry about solving for x and y!

---

17. 7 $f(x) = y = |x - k|$
Substitute (6, 1): $1 = |6 - k|$
Translate: $6 - k = 1$ or -1
Subtract 6: $-k = -5$ or -7
Multiply by -1: $k = 5$ or 7
Substitute (8, 1): $1 = |8 - k|$
Translate: $8 - k = 1$ or -1
Subtract 8: $-k = -7$ or -9
Multiply by -1: $k = 7$ or 9
Therefore $k = 7$ and $f(x) = |x - 7|$ and $f(0) = |0 - 7| = 7$

---

18. 7/6 or 1.16 or 1.67

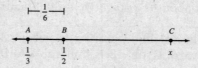

The distance from A to B is $1/2 - 1/3 = 1/6$. If $AC = 5AB$, then $AC = 5(1/6) = 5/6$. Therefore the coordinate of point C is $1/3 + 5/6 = 2/6 + 5/6 = 7/6$.

Section 6

1. C If the species arise *gradually*, they must not arise *quickly*. *instantaneously* = in an instant.

2. B If his claims are *rarely true*, then he must have a reputation for *lying*. *prevarication* = stretching or avoiding the truth; *fervency* = passion; *contemplation* = deep thought; *forthrightness* = honesty, candor.

3. B A *tortured* life is one filled with severe emotional difficulties that can produce *insanity*. *equanimity* = level-headedness; *coexist* = live together; *psychosis* = severe mental disease; *coincide* = occur at the same time or place; *aesthetics* = the study of beauty; *interface* = a place where two things meet.

4. C To keep the maps from falling into the hands of the Soviets, the maps would have to have been *kept secret*. Without these *detailed charts*, the oceanographers must have been relegated to using *incomplete* ones. *counterfeit* = fake; *lucid* = clear; *apprehended* = captured; *deficient* = lacking in important ways; *classified* = categorized as secret; *disseminated* = scattered or spread, as seed; *sketchy* = incomplete.

5. A The word *although* indicates a contrast. One whose ideas conflict with those of his declared religion is a *heretic* or *apostate*. *apostate* = one who challenges a core tenet of his or her religion; *conformist* = one who does what is expected; *relic* = an object left over from ancient times; *ascetic* = one who lives a life of self-denial; *despot* = absolute ruler.

6. A The passage states that *the stranger looks more fateful (ominous) for being a fiery red* (line 11).

7. C The *apparition* refers to the spectacular appearance of Mars in the night sky.

8. E The fact that the speaker speaks of *man* in the third person indicates that he or she is not a man. In saying that *our labor tills the soil, our dung fertilizes it* and so on, the speaker is indicating that he or she is a farm animal.

9. C These questions reflect the perspective that animals do a great deal of work in a farm, but receive very little in return.

10. C The passage does describe a medical breakthrough—vaccination—but does not focus exclusively on the 19th century or on the entire range of medical breakthroughs of the 19th century; therefore, (A) is a poor choice for a title. The passage focuses on viral infections, not bacterial ones, so (B) is also a poor choice. The passage does not focus on how the immune system works as a whole, but only on those aspects of the immune system that are affected by vaccines, so (D) is a weak choice for a title. Finally, Edward Jenner's work is described only briefly in the first paragraphs, so (E) is a poor choice. The best title is (C).

11. B This reference is given as an example of the *roots* (line 7) of the practice of vaccination.

12. A Lines 26–27 indicate that tuberculosis is caused by a bacterium.

13. A The passage states that the virus attaches itself to the cell and inserts its genes so that the cell can become a reproductive machine (line 46) for the virus. This is analogous to a bird's laying its eggs in the nest of another bird who then becomes a reproductive machine for a line of genes that is not its own.

14. D Line 28 refers to bacteria as *parasites* and line 45 uses the same term to describe a virus.

15. C The *signature* proteins are those by which *the body…is able to recognize* viruses (line 45), so they are able to *identify* the viruses.

16. E The final paragraph states that *the common cold…may never be thwarted* (lines 78–80) and that the general fight against viruses *will probably never be completely won* (lines 85–86). This contrasts with the triumphant tones of the previous paragraph which describes the victory of vaccinations over polio, measles and many other diseases.

17. D The final paragraph states that the common cold may never be thwarted because *the viruses are too numerous* and because *new viruses appear as old viral foes are eradicated*. The fact that viruses cannot reproduce on their own is not cited as an impediment to their eradication.

18. B The idea that unifies all of the paragraphs is that of a child developing a relationship with literature. She does not compare English and Chinese literature in depth, and the painful episode between the author and her brother is only mentioned in two of the paragraphs.

19. **A**   This paragraph states that Chinese...conversation...is often indirect and metaphorical, reflecting a philosphical turn of mind, and that this conversation involves retelling codes of behavior and morality. It adds that this is true even among peasants, thereby suggesting that such language is not restricted to the upper classes.

20. **D**   The author states that she would *wait impatiently for another story to begin* (line 20), indicating that she was eager to hear more.

21. **C**   The author states that her brother *forced me to memorize* Chinese classics and *insisted that I copy* the maxims until *my fingers became cramped and useless*.

22. **D**   The author states that the Chinese translation of the title of *The Count of Monte Cristo* is *The Vengeance and Gratitude of the Count of Monte Cristo*. Since the author states that this *reflects a more Chinese concept*, it can be inferred that this includes an emphasis either on honor and vengeance or gratitude and thankfulness.

23. **B**   The author states that she was forced to memorize *The Great Learning*, which she did not understand, but that she *tended* (line 98) toward books like *The Count of Monte Cristo*, which *made the deepest impression* (line 103) on the author.

24. **A**   In saying that she *took the trouble to reread the book in Chinese*, she meant that it was an extra mental effort that she was willing to endure.

Section 7

1. **C**   The sum of the angles in a triangle is 180°. If one has a measure of 100°, the other two must have a sum of 80°, so their average measure is 80°/2 = 40°.

2. **C**   If k is one less than a multiple of 6, then $k + 1$ must be a multiple of 6. The only multiple of 6 among the choices is (C) 18.

3. **D**   15 more than the product of 3 and $m - 2$ means $15 + 3(m - 2)$
Distribute: $15 + 3m - 6$
Combine like terms: $3m + 9$

4. **A**

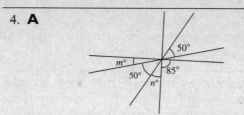

Draw in the measure of the angle that is "vertical" to the 50° angle and therefore equal. Notice that the four "bottom" angles have a sum of 180°.
$$m + 50 + n + 85 = 180$$
Simplify: $m + n + 135 = 180$
Subtract 135: $m + n = 45$

5. **D** $x\%$ of 30 is 12
Translate: $x\% \times 30 = 12$
Multiply by 4: $4x\% \times 30 = 48$
Divide by 2: $4x\% \times 15 = 24$

6. **A**   Choosing $x = 0.5$ shows that none of the three statements is necessarily true. Plugging this in to statement I gives $1/0.5 < 0.5$, which simplifies to $2 < 0.5$ which is not true. (Notice that this eliminates choices (B) and (E).) Plugging in to statement II gives $(0.5)^2 > 0.5$ which simplifies to $0.25 > 0.5$ which is also not true. (Notice that this eliminates choice (C).) Finally, plugging in to statement III gives $-0.5 < -1$, which is also false, leaving only choice (A).

7. **B**   If each gadget sells for m dollars, then selling 9 of them will generate $9m$ dollars in revenue. If it costs p dollars to make each one, then making 10 of them costs $10p$ dollars. So the profit would be $9m - 10p$

8. **E**   If y varies inversely as x, then the product of x and y is always the same. Since $(4, 6)$ is a point on the graph, then the product of x and y is always $4 \times 6 = 24$. Since $(2, m)$ is also on the graph, $2m = 24$ also, so $m = 12$.

9. **A**   The phrase "at this rate" suggests a proportion:
$$\frac{200 \text{ boxes}}{5 \text{ minutes}} = \frac{24{,}000 \text{ boxes}}{x \text{ minutes}}$$
Cross-multiply: $200x = 120{,}000$
Divide by 200: $x = 600$ minutes
Convert to hours:
600 minutes ÷ 60 minutes/hour = 10 hours

10. B   Since the triangle is a right triangle, you can use the Pythagorean Theorem: $x^2 + 2^2 = \left(\sqrt{n}\right)^2$

Simplify:	$x^2 + 4 = n$
Subtract 4:	$x^2 = n - 4$
Take the square root:	$x = \sqrt{n-4}$

11. D

	$(r-5)^2 = (r+2)^2$
Distribute:	$r^2 - 10r + 25 = r^2 + 4r + 4$
Subtract r^2:	$-10r + 25 = 4r + 4$
Add $10r - 4$:	$21 = 14r$
Divide by 14:	$1.5 = r$

12. E   Since the president must be a girl, there are 10 choices for president. Since the treasurer must also be a girl, there are 9 choices left for treasurer. Since the vice president must be a boy, there are 8 choices for vice president, and once he is chosen there are 7 choices left for secretary. This gives the total number of possibilities as $10 \times 9 \times 8 \times 7 = 5,040$.

13. B

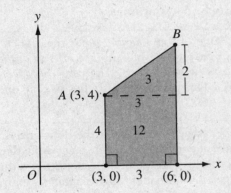

Mark up the diagram as shown. Notice that the shaded region consists of a right triangle and a rectangle. The area of the rectangle is $3 \times 4 = 12$, and since the total area is 15, the triangle must have an area of 3. Since the area of a triangle is one-half the base times the height, $(1/2)(3)(h) = 3$ and therefore $h = 2$. This means that the slope of AB is 2/3 (the "rise" over the "run").

14. A   One simple approach to this problem is simply to pick a value for m like 2. (Remember the condition that $m > 1$!) Plug this in to the expression and evaluate:

$$\frac{2 - \frac{1}{2}}{1 - \frac{1}{2}} = \frac{1.5}{0.5} = 3$$

Plugging in to the choices gives (A) 2+1 (B) 2 (C) 2–1 (D) –1 (E) 2/(2–1). The only choice that is equal to 3 is (A).

Alternately, you can simplify the expression by first multiplying by m/m, factoring, and canceling:

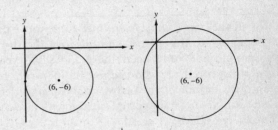

15. A   Careful here: notice that the question asks which could NOT be the number of points on the circle that lie on a coordinate axis. These figures show how it is possible to have 2 or 3 such points, but it is impossible to have just 1.

16. B   Imagine, for convenience, that each leg of the race is 150 miles. If the car averages 50 miles per hour for the first 2 legs, then the time for each leg is 150/50 = 3 hours. The time for the last leg is 150/75 = 2 hours. This means that the total distance of 150 + 150 + 150 = 450 miles is covered in 3 + 3 + 2 = 8 hours, so the car's average speed is 450 miles ÷ 8 hours = 56.25 miles per hour.

Section 8

1. A   Some aspect of the atom *remained a mystery*, so a clear model of the atom, which reveals its *structure*, must have *eluded* them. *eluded* = avoided capture; *configuration* = arrangement of parts.

2. D   If Alynna contrasted with the exhausted interns, she must have seemed *untiring*. *petrified* = turned to stone; *agitated* = riled up; *indefatigable* = untiring; *corrupted* = morally tainted.

3. **B**   If we *inhale them* (germs) *with nearly every breath* they must be quite common. The vast majority of them are *innocuous* (harmless) and our immune system is able to defeat them quite easily. This would suggest that few are *dangerous*. *omnipresent* = present at all times; *ubiquitous* = omnipresent; *virulent* = capable of causing disease; *scarce* = in short supply; *malevolent* = wishing harm on others; *benign* = harmless.

4. **E**   If it is not *didactic* (preachy), and leaves the reader *to make his or her own ethical evaluations*, it must be morally *ambiguous*. *resolute* = determined and steadfast; *corrupt* = morally tainted; *enervating* = weakening; *pedantic* = acting like a know-it-all; *ambiguous* = unclear.

5. **B**   If the bones were *determined* to be more than 50,000 years old, this fact would *disprove* the theory that humans had only been there for 8,000 years. *refuted* = disproved; *accustomed* = used to; *invalidated* = disproven or made unworthy; *established* = determined; *corroborated* = supported a claim with evidence; *deplored* = regretted.

6. **D**   The missing word must mean so *forceful as to leave no room for interpretation*. *loquacious* = talkative; *desultory* = aimless; *phlegmatic* = sluggish; *peremptory* = serving to end debate, expecting to be obeyed; *torpid* = lacking physical or mental energy.

7. **E**   The first four sentences characterize the positions of the proponents and opponents of recycling.

8. **A**   This sentence suggests that the debaters have "demonized" each other incorrectly.

9. **D**   The passage states that *we must examine the full life cycle of the commercial materials in question*. The *commercial materials* of the new road are the *substances that constitute the road*.

10. **C**   The questions do not address the problem of mudslides, but they do address (A) *the removal of…animal habitats* (line 39), (B) *the leaching of dangerous elements into the soil* (lines 35–37), (D) the *air quality* as it is effected by *extra traffic* (line 43), and (E) *the reduction of natural water filtration* (line 35).

11. **C**   The *responsible "industrial cycle"* refers to a means of processing resources that could be *better for the environment* than even *"conserving"* those *resources*. This suggests that the industrial cycle manages the resources well.

12. **E**   This exchange is described as something where all of the value is *easily accounted for* (line 92).

13. **A**   The *pack of gum* represents an item that is involved in a clear economic exchange. The *apple* in line 105 is part of a similar exchange.

14. **B**   The passage suggests that *bought-and-sold commodities* are like the pack of gum in the first paragraph, which is *easily accounted for*. By saying that the benefits of ecosystems are not commodities, the passage suggests that they are more difficult to track and evaluate.

15. **D**   The passage states that externalities are a *class of costs and benefits* that *are not part of a clear exchange*. The only choice that is not part of a clear economic exchange is the noise caused by a motorcycle.

16. **C**   The passage states that *Costanza places the cost "conservatively" at $33 trillion dollars* (lines 142–143). This suggests that Costanza considers this to be a low estimate.

17. **D**   One of the *potential flaws* mentioned in the last paragraph is that *industrialists argue that (Costanza's work) depends largely on speculation* (line 152). This means that it relies heavily on guesswork.

18. **B**   Passage 1 focuses on the deficiencies in the debate about environmentalism, suggesting that there is little progress and too much *demonization* (line 16), and suggesting a broader range of analysis than is currently being used. Passage 2, however, suggests that Costanza's work *is giving a common vocabulary to industrialists and environmentalists alike* (lines 157–158), and so facilitating progress in the debate.

19. **A**   Neither passage mentions global warming (even though Passage 1 mentions localized warming produced by road materials in line 37), and Passage 1 does not cite any scientific study. Both passages, however, discuss the importance of human feelings: Passage 1 mentions the harm done by *demonization* (line 16) of the debators, and their need to *appreciate the attitudes of their opponents* (lines 75–76), and Passage 2 emphasizes that the *"good feeling"* some people get from recycling has a real value.

Section 9

1. **D**   Choice (D) is most logical, standard and clear.

2. **B**   Choice B provides the most **parallel** phrasing.

3. **E**   The **participial phrase dangles** in the original sentence. Choice E corrects this without **awkwardness**.

4. **A**   The original phrasing is best. The pronoun *me* is properly in the **objective** case, and the subject of the verb *was* is the singular *conversation*.

5. **B**   The original sentence is vague and awkward. Choice B is clearest and most concise.

6. **B**   The original phrasing is awkward and wordy. Also, the phrasing *because of (noun phrase)* is almost always less clear than the phrasing *because (independent clause)*.

7. **A**   The original phrasing is best.

8. **E**   Choice E is the most concise and clear, and the phrasing is **parallel**.

9. **B**   The underlined clause should be phrased as a dependent clause.

10. **D**   The original phrase uses **incorrect subjunctive form**. Also, the antecedent *troop* is singular.

11. **C**   The original phrasing produces a **misplaced modifying phrase**, which is corrected in choice C.

12. **C**   The original phrasing is **awkward** and wordy.

13. **B**   The original phrasing is **awkward** and wordy. Choice B is preferable to E because E contains a double negative *but not*.

14. **C**   The original phrasing is a **run-on** or a **comma splice**. Choice C correctly subordinates the clause as a **participial phrase**.

PRACTICE TEST 6

ANSWER SHEET

Last Name: _____   First Name: _____

Date: _____   Testing Location: _____

Directions for Test

- Remove these answer sheets from the book and use them to record your answers to this test.
- This test will require 3 hours and 20 minutes to complete. Take this test in one sitting.
- The time allotment for each section is written clearly at the beginning of each section. This test contains six 25-minute sections, two 20-minute sections, and one 10-minute section.
- This test is 25 minutes shorter than the actual SAT, which will include a 25-minute "experimental" section that does not count toward your score. That section has been omitted from this test.
- You may take one short break during the test, of no more than 10 minutes in length.
- You may only work on one section at any given time.
- You must stop ALL work on a section when time is called.
- If you finish a section before the time has elapsed, check your work on that section. You may NOT work on any other section.
- Do not waste time on questions that seem too difficult for you.
- Use the test book for scratchwork, but you will receive credit only for answers that are marked on the answer sheets.
- You will receive one point for every correct answer.
- You will receive no points for an omitted question.
- For each wrong answer on any multiple-choice question, your score will be reduced by ¼ point.
- For each wrong answer on any numerical "grid-in" question, you will receive no deduction.

SECTION 2

1. Ⓐ Ⓑ Ⓒ Ⓓ Ⓔ   11. Ⓐ Ⓑ Ⓒ Ⓓ Ⓔ   21. Ⓐ Ⓑ Ⓒ Ⓓ Ⓔ   31. Ⓐ Ⓑ Ⓒ Ⓓ Ⓔ
2. Ⓐ Ⓑ Ⓒ Ⓓ Ⓔ   12. Ⓐ Ⓑ Ⓒ Ⓓ Ⓔ   22. Ⓐ Ⓑ Ⓒ Ⓓ Ⓔ   32. Ⓐ Ⓑ Ⓒ Ⓓ Ⓔ
3. Ⓐ Ⓑ Ⓒ Ⓓ Ⓔ   13. Ⓐ Ⓑ Ⓒ Ⓓ Ⓔ   23. Ⓐ Ⓑ Ⓒ Ⓓ Ⓔ   33. Ⓐ Ⓑ Ⓒ Ⓓ Ⓔ
4. Ⓐ Ⓑ Ⓒ Ⓓ Ⓔ   14. Ⓐ Ⓑ Ⓒ Ⓓ Ⓔ   24. Ⓐ Ⓑ Ⓒ Ⓓ Ⓔ   34. Ⓐ Ⓑ Ⓒ Ⓓ Ⓔ
5. Ⓐ Ⓑ Ⓒ Ⓓ Ⓔ   15. Ⓐ Ⓑ Ⓒ Ⓓ Ⓔ   25. Ⓐ Ⓑ Ⓒ Ⓓ Ⓔ   35. Ⓐ Ⓑ Ⓒ Ⓓ Ⓔ
6. Ⓐ Ⓑ Ⓒ Ⓓ Ⓔ   16. Ⓐ Ⓑ Ⓒ Ⓓ Ⓔ   26. Ⓐ Ⓑ Ⓒ Ⓓ Ⓔ   36. Ⓐ Ⓑ Ⓒ Ⓓ Ⓔ
7. Ⓐ Ⓑ Ⓒ Ⓓ Ⓔ   17. Ⓐ Ⓑ Ⓒ Ⓓ Ⓔ   27. Ⓐ Ⓑ Ⓒ Ⓓ Ⓔ   37. Ⓐ Ⓑ Ⓒ Ⓓ Ⓔ
8. Ⓐ Ⓑ Ⓒ Ⓓ Ⓔ   18. Ⓐ Ⓑ Ⓒ Ⓓ Ⓔ   28. Ⓐ Ⓑ Ⓒ Ⓓ Ⓔ   38. Ⓐ Ⓑ Ⓒ Ⓓ Ⓔ
9. Ⓐ Ⓑ Ⓒ Ⓓ Ⓔ   19. Ⓐ Ⓑ Ⓒ Ⓓ Ⓔ   29. Ⓐ Ⓑ Ⓒ Ⓓ Ⓔ   39. Ⓐ Ⓑ Ⓒ Ⓓ Ⓔ
10. Ⓐ Ⓑ Ⓒ Ⓓ Ⓔ   20. Ⓐ Ⓑ Ⓒ Ⓓ Ⓔ   30. Ⓐ Ⓑ Ⓒ Ⓓ Ⓔ   40. Ⓐ Ⓑ Ⓒ Ⓓ Ⓔ

SECTION 3

1. Ⓐ Ⓑ Ⓒ Ⓓ Ⓔ   11. Ⓐ Ⓑ Ⓒ Ⓓ Ⓔ   21. Ⓐ Ⓑ Ⓒ Ⓓ Ⓔ   31. Ⓐ Ⓑ Ⓒ Ⓓ Ⓔ
2. Ⓐ Ⓑ Ⓒ Ⓓ Ⓔ   12. Ⓐ Ⓑ Ⓒ Ⓓ Ⓔ   22. Ⓐ Ⓑ Ⓒ Ⓓ Ⓔ   32. Ⓐ Ⓑ Ⓒ Ⓓ Ⓔ
3. Ⓐ Ⓑ Ⓒ Ⓓ Ⓔ   13. Ⓐ Ⓑ Ⓒ Ⓓ Ⓔ   23. Ⓐ Ⓑ Ⓒ Ⓓ Ⓔ   33. Ⓐ Ⓑ Ⓒ Ⓓ Ⓔ
4. Ⓐ Ⓑ Ⓒ Ⓓ Ⓔ   14. Ⓐ Ⓑ Ⓒ Ⓓ Ⓔ   24. Ⓐ Ⓑ Ⓒ Ⓓ Ⓔ   34. Ⓐ Ⓑ Ⓒ Ⓓ Ⓔ
5. Ⓐ Ⓑ Ⓒ Ⓓ Ⓔ   15. Ⓐ Ⓑ Ⓒ Ⓓ Ⓔ   25. Ⓐ Ⓑ Ⓒ Ⓓ Ⓔ   35. Ⓐ Ⓑ Ⓒ Ⓓ Ⓔ
6. Ⓐ Ⓑ Ⓒ Ⓓ Ⓔ   16. Ⓐ Ⓑ Ⓒ Ⓓ Ⓔ   26. Ⓐ Ⓑ Ⓒ Ⓓ Ⓔ   36. Ⓐ Ⓑ Ⓒ Ⓓ Ⓔ
7. Ⓐ Ⓑ Ⓒ Ⓓ Ⓔ   17. Ⓐ Ⓑ Ⓒ Ⓓ Ⓔ   27. Ⓐ Ⓑ Ⓒ Ⓓ Ⓔ   37. Ⓐ Ⓑ Ⓒ Ⓓ Ⓔ
8. Ⓐ Ⓑ Ⓒ Ⓓ Ⓔ   18. Ⓐ Ⓑ Ⓒ Ⓓ Ⓔ   28. Ⓐ Ⓑ Ⓒ Ⓓ Ⓔ   38. Ⓐ Ⓑ Ⓒ Ⓓ Ⓔ
9. Ⓐ Ⓑ Ⓒ Ⓓ Ⓔ   19. Ⓐ Ⓑ Ⓒ Ⓓ Ⓔ   29. Ⓐ Ⓑ Ⓒ Ⓓ Ⓔ   39. Ⓐ Ⓑ Ⓒ Ⓓ Ⓔ
10. Ⓐ Ⓑ Ⓒ Ⓓ Ⓔ   20. Ⓐ Ⓑ Ⓒ Ⓓ Ⓔ   30. Ⓐ Ⓑ Ⓒ Ⓓ Ⓔ   40. Ⓐ Ⓑ Ⓒ Ⓓ Ⓔ

ANSWER SHEET

SECTION 4

1. Ⓐ Ⓑ Ⓒ Ⓓ Ⓔ
2. Ⓐ Ⓑ Ⓒ Ⓓ Ⓔ
3. Ⓐ Ⓑ Ⓒ Ⓓ Ⓔ
4. Ⓐ Ⓑ Ⓒ Ⓓ Ⓔ
5. Ⓐ Ⓑ Ⓒ Ⓓ Ⓔ
6. Ⓐ Ⓑ Ⓒ Ⓓ Ⓔ
7. Ⓐ Ⓑ Ⓒ Ⓓ Ⓔ
8. Ⓐ Ⓑ Ⓒ Ⓓ Ⓔ
9. Ⓐ Ⓑ Ⓒ Ⓓ Ⓔ
10. Ⓐ Ⓑ Ⓒ Ⓓ Ⓔ

11. Ⓐ Ⓑ Ⓒ Ⓓ Ⓔ
12. Ⓐ Ⓑ Ⓒ Ⓓ Ⓔ
13. Ⓐ Ⓑ Ⓒ Ⓓ Ⓔ
14. Ⓐ Ⓑ Ⓒ Ⓓ Ⓔ
15. Ⓐ Ⓑ Ⓒ Ⓓ Ⓔ
16. Ⓐ Ⓑ Ⓒ Ⓓ Ⓔ
17. Ⓐ Ⓑ Ⓒ Ⓓ Ⓔ
18. Ⓐ Ⓑ Ⓒ Ⓓ Ⓔ
19. Ⓐ Ⓑ Ⓒ Ⓓ Ⓔ
20. Ⓐ Ⓑ Ⓒ Ⓓ Ⓔ

21. Ⓐ Ⓑ Ⓒ Ⓓ Ⓔ
22. Ⓐ Ⓑ Ⓒ Ⓓ Ⓔ
23. Ⓐ Ⓑ Ⓒ Ⓓ Ⓔ
24. Ⓐ Ⓑ Ⓒ Ⓓ Ⓔ
25. Ⓐ Ⓑ Ⓒ Ⓓ Ⓔ
26. Ⓐ Ⓑ Ⓒ Ⓓ Ⓔ
27. Ⓐ Ⓑ Ⓒ Ⓓ Ⓔ
28. Ⓐ Ⓑ Ⓒ Ⓓ Ⓔ
29. Ⓐ Ⓑ Ⓒ Ⓓ Ⓔ
30. Ⓐ Ⓑ Ⓒ Ⓓ Ⓔ

31. Ⓐ Ⓑ Ⓒ Ⓓ Ⓔ
32. Ⓐ Ⓑ Ⓒ Ⓓ Ⓔ
33. Ⓐ Ⓑ Ⓒ Ⓓ Ⓔ
34. Ⓐ Ⓑ Ⓒ Ⓓ Ⓔ
35. Ⓐ Ⓑ Ⓒ Ⓓ Ⓔ
36. Ⓐ Ⓑ Ⓒ Ⓓ Ⓔ
37. Ⓐ Ⓑ Ⓒ Ⓓ Ⓔ
38. Ⓐ Ⓑ Ⓒ Ⓓ Ⓔ
39. Ⓐ Ⓑ Ⓒ Ⓓ Ⓔ
40. Ⓐ Ⓑ Ⓒ Ⓓ Ⓔ

SECTION 5

1. Ⓐ Ⓑ Ⓒ Ⓓ Ⓔ
2. Ⓐ Ⓑ Ⓒ Ⓓ Ⓔ
3. Ⓐ Ⓑ Ⓒ Ⓓ Ⓔ
4. Ⓐ Ⓑ Ⓒ Ⓓ Ⓔ

5. Ⓐ Ⓑ Ⓒ Ⓓ Ⓔ
6. Ⓐ Ⓑ Ⓒ Ⓓ Ⓔ
7. Ⓐ Ⓑ Ⓒ Ⓓ Ⓔ
8. Ⓐ Ⓑ Ⓒ Ⓓ Ⓔ

9.   10.   11.   12.   13.

14.   15.   16.   17.   18.

ANSWER SHEET

SECTION 6

1. Ⓐ Ⓑ Ⓒ Ⓓ Ⓔ	11. Ⓐ Ⓑ Ⓒ Ⓓ Ⓔ	21. Ⓐ Ⓑ Ⓒ Ⓓ Ⓔ	31. Ⓐ Ⓑ Ⓒ Ⓓ Ⓔ
2. Ⓐ Ⓑ Ⓒ Ⓓ Ⓔ	12. Ⓐ Ⓑ Ⓒ Ⓓ Ⓔ	22. Ⓐ Ⓑ Ⓒ Ⓓ Ⓔ	32. Ⓐ Ⓑ Ⓒ Ⓓ Ⓔ
3. Ⓐ Ⓑ Ⓒ Ⓓ Ⓔ	13. Ⓐ Ⓑ Ⓒ Ⓓ Ⓔ	23. Ⓐ Ⓑ Ⓒ Ⓓ Ⓔ	33. Ⓐ Ⓑ Ⓒ Ⓓ Ⓔ
4. Ⓐ Ⓑ Ⓒ Ⓓ Ⓔ	14. Ⓐ Ⓑ Ⓒ Ⓓ Ⓔ	24. Ⓐ Ⓑ Ⓒ Ⓓ Ⓔ	34. Ⓐ Ⓑ Ⓒ Ⓓ Ⓔ
5. Ⓐ Ⓑ Ⓒ Ⓓ Ⓔ	15. Ⓐ Ⓑ Ⓒ Ⓓ Ⓔ	25. Ⓐ Ⓑ Ⓒ Ⓓ Ⓔ	35. Ⓐ Ⓑ Ⓒ Ⓓ Ⓔ
6. Ⓐ Ⓑ Ⓒ Ⓓ Ⓔ	16. Ⓐ Ⓑ Ⓒ Ⓓ Ⓔ	26. Ⓐ Ⓑ Ⓒ Ⓓ Ⓔ	36. Ⓐ Ⓑ Ⓒ Ⓓ Ⓔ
7. Ⓐ Ⓑ Ⓒ Ⓓ Ⓔ	17. Ⓐ Ⓑ Ⓒ Ⓓ Ⓔ	27. Ⓐ Ⓑ Ⓒ Ⓓ Ⓔ	37. Ⓐ Ⓑ Ⓒ Ⓓ Ⓔ
8. Ⓐ Ⓑ Ⓒ Ⓓ Ⓔ	18. Ⓐ Ⓑ Ⓒ Ⓓ Ⓔ	28. Ⓐ Ⓑ Ⓒ Ⓓ Ⓔ	38. Ⓐ Ⓑ Ⓒ Ⓓ Ⓔ
9. Ⓐ Ⓑ Ⓒ Ⓓ Ⓔ	19. Ⓐ Ⓑ Ⓒ Ⓓ Ⓔ	29. Ⓐ Ⓑ Ⓒ Ⓓ Ⓔ	39. Ⓐ Ⓑ Ⓒ Ⓓ Ⓔ
10. Ⓐ Ⓑ Ⓒ Ⓓ Ⓔ	20. Ⓐ Ⓑ Ⓒ Ⓓ Ⓔ	30. Ⓐ Ⓑ Ⓒ Ⓓ Ⓔ	40. Ⓐ Ⓑ Ⓒ Ⓓ Ⓔ

SECTION 7

1. Ⓐ Ⓑ Ⓒ Ⓓ Ⓔ	11. Ⓐ Ⓑ Ⓒ Ⓓ Ⓔ	21. Ⓐ Ⓑ Ⓒ Ⓓ Ⓔ	31. Ⓐ Ⓑ Ⓒ Ⓓ Ⓔ
2. Ⓐ Ⓑ Ⓒ Ⓓ Ⓔ	12. Ⓐ Ⓑ Ⓒ Ⓓ Ⓔ	22. Ⓐ Ⓑ Ⓒ Ⓓ Ⓔ	32. Ⓐ Ⓑ Ⓒ Ⓓ Ⓔ
3. Ⓐ Ⓑ Ⓒ Ⓓ Ⓔ	13. Ⓐ Ⓑ Ⓒ Ⓓ Ⓔ	23. Ⓐ Ⓑ Ⓒ Ⓓ Ⓔ	33. Ⓐ Ⓑ Ⓒ Ⓓ Ⓔ
4. Ⓐ Ⓑ Ⓒ Ⓓ Ⓔ	14. Ⓐ Ⓑ Ⓒ Ⓓ Ⓔ	24. Ⓐ Ⓑ Ⓒ Ⓓ Ⓔ	34. Ⓐ Ⓑ Ⓒ Ⓓ Ⓔ
5. Ⓐ Ⓑ Ⓒ Ⓓ Ⓔ	15. Ⓐ Ⓑ Ⓒ Ⓓ Ⓔ	25. Ⓐ Ⓑ Ⓒ Ⓓ Ⓔ	35. Ⓐ Ⓑ Ⓒ Ⓓ Ⓔ
6. Ⓐ Ⓑ Ⓒ Ⓓ Ⓔ	16. Ⓐ Ⓑ Ⓒ Ⓓ Ⓔ	26. Ⓐ Ⓑ Ⓒ Ⓓ Ⓔ	36. Ⓐ Ⓑ Ⓒ Ⓓ Ⓔ
7. Ⓐ Ⓑ Ⓒ Ⓓ Ⓔ	17. Ⓐ Ⓑ Ⓒ Ⓓ Ⓔ	27. Ⓐ Ⓑ Ⓒ Ⓓ Ⓔ	37. Ⓐ Ⓑ Ⓒ Ⓓ Ⓔ
8. Ⓐ Ⓑ Ⓒ Ⓓ Ⓔ	18. Ⓐ Ⓑ Ⓒ Ⓓ Ⓔ	28. Ⓐ Ⓑ Ⓒ Ⓓ Ⓔ	38. Ⓐ Ⓑ Ⓒ Ⓓ Ⓔ
9. Ⓐ Ⓑ Ⓒ Ⓓ Ⓔ	19. Ⓐ Ⓑ Ⓒ Ⓓ Ⓔ	29. Ⓐ Ⓑ Ⓒ Ⓓ Ⓔ	39. Ⓐ Ⓑ Ⓒ Ⓓ Ⓔ
10. Ⓐ Ⓑ Ⓒ Ⓓ Ⓔ	20. Ⓐ Ⓑ Ⓒ Ⓓ Ⓔ	30. Ⓐ Ⓑ Ⓒ Ⓓ Ⓔ	40. Ⓐ Ⓑ Ⓒ Ⓓ Ⓔ

SECTION 8

1. Ⓐ Ⓑ Ⓒ Ⓓ Ⓔ	11. Ⓐ Ⓑ Ⓒ Ⓓ Ⓔ	21. Ⓐ Ⓑ Ⓒ Ⓓ Ⓔ	31. Ⓐ Ⓑ Ⓒ Ⓓ Ⓔ
2. Ⓐ Ⓑ Ⓒ Ⓓ Ⓔ	12. Ⓐ Ⓑ Ⓒ Ⓓ Ⓔ	22. Ⓐ Ⓑ Ⓒ Ⓓ Ⓔ	32. Ⓐ Ⓑ Ⓒ Ⓓ Ⓔ
3. Ⓐ Ⓑ Ⓒ Ⓓ Ⓔ	13. Ⓐ Ⓑ Ⓒ Ⓓ Ⓔ	23. Ⓐ Ⓑ Ⓒ Ⓓ Ⓔ	33. Ⓐ Ⓑ Ⓒ Ⓓ Ⓔ
4. Ⓐ Ⓑ Ⓒ Ⓓ Ⓔ	14. Ⓐ Ⓑ Ⓒ Ⓓ Ⓔ	24. Ⓐ Ⓑ Ⓒ Ⓓ Ⓔ	34. Ⓐ Ⓑ Ⓒ Ⓓ Ⓔ
5. Ⓐ Ⓑ Ⓒ Ⓓ Ⓔ	15. Ⓐ Ⓑ Ⓒ Ⓓ Ⓔ	25. Ⓐ Ⓑ Ⓒ Ⓓ Ⓔ	35. Ⓐ Ⓑ Ⓒ Ⓓ Ⓔ
6. Ⓐ Ⓑ Ⓒ Ⓓ Ⓔ	16. Ⓐ Ⓑ Ⓒ Ⓓ Ⓔ	26. Ⓐ Ⓑ Ⓒ Ⓓ Ⓔ	36. Ⓐ Ⓑ Ⓒ Ⓓ Ⓔ
7. Ⓐ Ⓑ Ⓒ Ⓓ Ⓔ	17. Ⓐ Ⓑ Ⓒ Ⓓ Ⓔ	27. Ⓐ Ⓑ Ⓒ Ⓓ Ⓔ	37. Ⓐ Ⓑ Ⓒ Ⓓ Ⓔ
8. Ⓐ Ⓑ Ⓒ Ⓓ Ⓔ	18. Ⓐ Ⓑ Ⓒ Ⓓ Ⓔ	28. Ⓐ Ⓑ Ⓒ Ⓓ Ⓔ	38. Ⓐ Ⓑ Ⓒ Ⓓ Ⓔ
9. Ⓐ Ⓑ Ⓒ Ⓓ Ⓔ	19. Ⓐ Ⓑ Ⓒ Ⓓ Ⓔ	29. Ⓐ Ⓑ Ⓒ Ⓓ Ⓔ	39. Ⓐ Ⓑ Ⓒ Ⓓ Ⓔ
10. Ⓐ Ⓑ Ⓒ Ⓓ Ⓔ	20. Ⓐ Ⓑ Ⓒ Ⓓ Ⓔ	30. Ⓐ Ⓑ Ⓒ Ⓓ Ⓔ	40. Ⓐ Ⓑ Ⓒ Ⓓ Ⓔ

SECTION 9

1. Ⓐ Ⓑ Ⓒ Ⓓ Ⓔ	11. Ⓐ Ⓑ Ⓒ Ⓓ Ⓔ	21. Ⓐ Ⓑ Ⓒ Ⓓ Ⓔ	31. Ⓐ Ⓑ Ⓒ Ⓓ Ⓔ
2. Ⓐ Ⓑ Ⓒ Ⓓ Ⓔ	12. Ⓐ Ⓑ Ⓒ Ⓓ Ⓔ	22. Ⓐ Ⓑ Ⓒ Ⓓ Ⓔ	32. Ⓐ Ⓑ Ⓒ Ⓓ Ⓔ
3. Ⓐ Ⓑ Ⓒ Ⓓ Ⓔ	13. Ⓐ Ⓑ Ⓒ Ⓓ Ⓔ	23. Ⓐ Ⓑ Ⓒ Ⓓ Ⓔ	33. Ⓐ Ⓑ Ⓒ Ⓓ Ⓔ
4. Ⓐ Ⓑ Ⓒ Ⓓ Ⓔ	14. Ⓐ Ⓑ Ⓒ Ⓓ Ⓔ	24. Ⓐ Ⓑ Ⓒ Ⓓ Ⓔ	34. Ⓐ Ⓑ Ⓒ Ⓓ Ⓔ
5. Ⓐ Ⓑ Ⓒ Ⓓ Ⓔ	15. Ⓐ Ⓑ Ⓒ Ⓓ Ⓔ	25. Ⓐ Ⓑ Ⓒ Ⓓ Ⓔ	35. Ⓐ Ⓑ Ⓒ Ⓓ Ⓔ
6. Ⓐ Ⓑ Ⓒ Ⓓ Ⓔ	16. Ⓐ Ⓑ Ⓒ Ⓓ Ⓔ	26. Ⓐ Ⓑ Ⓒ Ⓓ Ⓔ	36. Ⓐ Ⓑ Ⓒ Ⓓ Ⓔ
7. Ⓐ Ⓑ Ⓒ Ⓓ Ⓔ	17. Ⓐ Ⓑ Ⓒ Ⓓ Ⓔ	27. Ⓐ Ⓑ Ⓒ Ⓓ Ⓔ	37. Ⓐ Ⓑ Ⓒ Ⓓ Ⓔ
8. Ⓐ Ⓑ Ⓒ Ⓓ Ⓔ	18. Ⓐ Ⓑ Ⓒ Ⓓ Ⓔ	28. Ⓐ Ⓑ Ⓒ Ⓓ Ⓔ	38. Ⓐ Ⓑ Ⓒ Ⓓ Ⓔ
9. Ⓐ Ⓑ Ⓒ Ⓓ Ⓔ	19. Ⓐ Ⓑ Ⓒ Ⓓ Ⓔ	29. Ⓐ Ⓑ Ⓒ Ⓓ Ⓔ	39. Ⓐ Ⓑ Ⓒ Ⓓ Ⓔ
10. Ⓐ Ⓑ Ⓒ Ⓓ Ⓔ	20. Ⓐ Ⓑ Ⓒ Ⓓ Ⓔ	30. Ⓐ Ⓑ Ⓒ Ⓓ Ⓔ	40. Ⓐ Ⓑ Ⓒ Ⓓ Ⓔ

Section 1

Time—25 minutes

Directions for Writing the Essay

Plan and write an essay that answers the question below. Do NOT write on another topic. An essay on another topic will receive a score of 0.

Two readers will grade your essay based on how well you develop your point of view, organize and explain your ideas, use specific and relevant examples to support your thesis, and use clear and effective language. How well you write is much more important than how much you write, but to cover the topic adequately you should plan to write several paragraphs.

Your essay must be written on separate lined sheets of paper. Keep your handwriting to a reasonable size. Your essay will be read by people who are not familiar with your handwriting, so write legibly.

You may use this sheet for notes and outlining, but these will not be graded as part of your essay.

Consider carefully the issue discussed in the following passage, then write an essay that answers the question posed in the assignment.

> All art is a lie, and all art is the truth. The beholder determines which.

Assignment: **Do artistic endeavors such as music, painting and drama enhance our understanding of reality or provide escape from reality?** Write an essay in which you agree or disagree with the statement above, using an example or examples from history, politics, literature, the arts, current events, or your experience or observation.

Write your essay on separate sheets of paper.

Section 2

Time—25 Minutes
20 Questions

Directions for Multiple-Choice Questions

In this section, solve each problem, using any available space on the page for scratchwork. Then decide which is the best of the choices given and fill in the corresponding oval on the answer sheet.

- You may use a calculator on any problem. All numbers used are real numbers.
- Figures are drawn as accurately as possible EXCEPT when it is stated that the figure is not drawn to scale.
- All figures lie in a plane unless otherwise indicated.

Reference Information

$A = \pi r^2$ $A = \ell w$ $A = \frac{1}{2}bh$ $V = \ell w h$ $V = \pi r^2 h$ $c^2 = a^2 + b^2$ Special Right Triangles
$C = 2\pi r$

The arc of a circle measures 360°.
Every straight angle measures 180°.
The sum of the measures of the angles in a triangle is 180°.

---

1 If $(x - y) = -2$, then $3(x - y)(x - y)(x - y) =$

(A) −24
(B) −12
(C) 0
(D) 12
(E) 24

2 If $w \neq 0$, then 40 percent of $20w$ is equal to

(A) $2w$
(B) $4w$
(C) $8w$
(D) $20w$
(E) $80w$

x	3	4	5	6
y	10	14	18	22

3 The table above shows a relationship between two variables, x and y. Which of the following equations could describe this relationship?

(A) $y = x + 7$
(B) $y = 4x - 2$
(C) $y = 3x + 1$
(D) $y = 5x - 5$
(E) $y = 2x + 4$

4 The points W, X, Y, and Z lie on a line in that order. If $XY = 50$, WY is 30 more than XY, and $WX = YZ$, what is XZ?

(A) 30
(B) 50
(C) 70
(D) 80
(E) 100

GO ON TO THE NEXT PAGE ▶▶▶

2

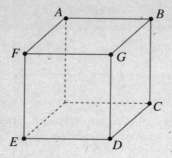

5 In the cube in the figure above, all of the following line segments is the same length EXCEPT

(A) AG
(B) BE
(C) BD
(D) EG
(E) AE

6 If $3^{y+4} = 81$, what is the value of y?

(A) −2
(B) −1
(C) 0
(D) 1
(E) 2

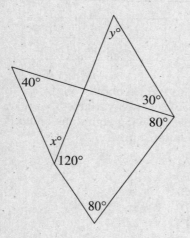

7 In the figure above, what is the value of $x + y$?

(A) 120
(B) 110
(C) 100
(D) 90
(E) 80

8 If a and b are non-zero integers and $a > b$, which of the following must be true?

I. $ab \neq 0$
II. $a - b > 0$
III. $a \div b > 1$

(A) I only
(B) II only
(C) I and II only
(D) I and III only
(E) I, II, and III

9 The distance from Appletown to Brickton is 6 miles and the distance from Brickton to Caper City is 9 miles. Which of the following could be the distance, in miles, from Appletown to Caper City?

(A) 14
(B) 16
(C) 17
(D) 18
(E) 19

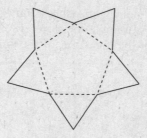

10 The figure above shows five triangles arranged around a regular pentagon. All of the solid line segments are equal in length. If the perimeter of the figure indicated by the solid segments is 100 and the perimeter of the pentagon indicated by the dotted lines is 60, what is the area of one of the triangles?

(A) 24
(B) 32
(C) 36
(D) 48
(E) 64

11 The sum of two numbers is 71. If one number is 2 greater than one-half of the other number, what is the value of the greater number?

(A)   23
(B)   25
(C)   42
(D)   43
(E)   46

12 Points A, B, C, and D lie on line l and points D, E, F, and G lie on line m. If lines l and m are distinct, how many lines can be drawn such that each line passes through exactly 2 of these 7 points?

(A)   4
(B)   5
(C)   6
(D)   9
(E)   12

13 What fraction of the even integers between 2 and 16, inclusive, satisfy the statement $3w - 2 > 28$?

(A) $\dfrac{1}{8}$

(B) $\dfrac{1}{4}$

(C) $\dfrac{3}{8}$

(D) $\dfrac{1}{2}$

(E) $\dfrac{5}{8}$

14 If a is 20 percent less than b, and b is 20 percent greater than 400, then what is the value of $b - a$?

(A)   80
(B)   96
(C)   100
(D)   104
(E)   108

15 If $m = n(n - 3)$, what is the value of $-3m$ in terms of n?

(A) $3n + 3n^2$
(B) $9n + 3n^2$
(C) $3n + 9n^2$
(D) $3n - 3n^2$
(E) $9n - 3n^2$

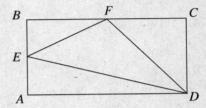

16 In the figure above, $ABCD$ is a rectangle and points E and F are midpoints of their respective sides. If $BC = 2AB = 8$, what is the area of $\triangle EFD$?

(A)   8
(B)   12
(C)   16
(D)   20
(E)   24

17 What is the average (arithmetic mean) of 8 consecutive odd integers if the least of these integers is x?

(A) $x + 5$
(B) $x + 6$
(C) $x + 7$
(D) $x + 8$
(E) $x + 9$

GO ON TO THE NEXT PAGE ▶▶▶

Note: Figure not drawn to scale.

18 In the figure above, $20 < b < 30$ and $a > c > b$. If a, b and c are integers, what is the largest possible value of a?

(A)   119
(B)   121
(C)   140
(D)   137
(E)   139

19 If $\dfrac{4}{v} + w = 6$ and $v \neq 0$, which of the following expresses v in terms of w ?

(A) $\dfrac{4}{6 - w}$

(B) $\dfrac{w}{6 - w}$

(C) $\dfrac{w}{4 - w}$

(D) $\dfrac{w - 6}{w}$

(E) $\dfrac{w - 2}{4}$

20 The distance from the center of a clock to the tip of the minute hand is 4 inches. What is the length of the arc, in <u>feet,</u> that this tip traces between 2:45 pm and 7:15 pm? (1 foot = 12 inches)

(A) 3π
(B) 12π
(C) 16π
(D) 24π
(E) 36π

You may check your work, on this section only, until time is called.

Section 3

Time—25 Minutes
24 Questions

Each of the sentences below is missing one or two portions. Read each sentence, then select the word or words that most logically completes the sentence, taking into account the meaning of the sentence as a whole.

Example:

Rather than accepting the theory unquestioningly, Deborah regarded it with ———.

(A) mirth   (B) sadness   (C) responsibility
(D) ignorance   (E) skepticism

Correct response: (E)

1 Ptolemy's theory that the universe revolved around the sun was ——— by his contemporaries, but is ——— today for its naive assumptions.

(A) believed .. supported
(B) counteracted .. satirized
(C) accepted .. ridiculed
(D) mesmerized .. corroborated
(E) affiliated .. mocked

2 Although the rebels attacked with great ferocity, the ——— and undisciplined manner in which they assaulted the fort left no doubt that they would be defeated.

(A) haphazard   (B) spartan
(C) apathetic   (D) civilized
(E) strict

3 Only after the massive rains and winds produced by Hurricane Alysha had ——— were the volunteer crews able to come to the aid of those ——— by the storm.

(A) commenced .. enthralled
(B) ebbed .. encouraged
(C) compounded .. masticated
(D) intensified .. harmed
(E) abated .. afflicted

4 Madonna's musical work over the past 20 years is more ——— than that of many popular singers; she has incorporated a wide variety of styles into her songs.

(A) repugnant   (B) negligent
(C) banal   (D) eclectic
(E) incompetent

5 Early in his medical school career, Blake realized that his ——— personality was not ideally suited to a career in therapy; he could not provide a stabilizing influence on his patients if he himself was so easily ———.

(A) cantankerous .. placated
(B) irascible .. riled
(C) equanimous .. infuriated
(D) euphoric .. provoked
(E) choleric .. assuaged

6 The talk show host was taken aback by the ——— demeanor of his guest, having never been so harshly accosted before.

(A) jocular   (B) congenial
(C) impudent   (D) urbane
(E) erudite

7 Bicycle champion Lance Armstrong showed incredible ——— in overcoming cancer to become the first person to win six consecutive Tour de France victories.

(A) perspicacity   (B) magnanimity
(C) delirium   (D) vanity
(E) pertinacity

8 The senator ——— the claims of the opposing party that he had lied about his health care policies, arguing that he had actually kept all of his campaign promises.

(A) championed   (B) impugned
(C) emulated   (D) lauded
(E) concurred with

GO ON TO THE NEXT PAGE ▶▶▶

Each passage below is followed by one or two questions based on its content. Answer each question based on what is stated or implied in the preceding passage.

Questions 9–10 are based on the following passage.

The following passage is an excerpt from a novel set in modern-day Africa.

Line   Na-ne's absence now is a vertiginous[1] hollow
in my being, a dark hole that is my constant
companion. I did not know the gravity of
such holes, of the extra weight on
5   every organ, of the soul becoming an old
man. My son Semu runs about oblivious, like
a goat; he is not even two full years, and his
happiness is inaccessible to me. He calls
"Papa, papa, look," but I cannot look. He bats
10   at my hand and he climbs on my leg. He is
Na-ne as I remember him, and so he is a
shadow. My brother was this age when I was
nearly ten. I may tell Semu "Na-ne, mother
wants us to get more thatch," and he looks
15   at me and smiles, and I do not know if he is
happy to be Na-ne, but he is happy.

[1]causing dizziness

9   It can be inferred from the passage that Na-ne is Semu's

(A)   father
(B)   son
(C)   uncle
(D)   nephew
(E)   grandfather

10   Unlike the quotation in line 9, the quotation in lines 13–14

(A)   uses figurative language
(B)   conveys a request
(C)   addresses an absent person
(D)   describes a happy scene
(E)   is spoken with great urgency

Questions 11–12 are based on the following passage.

The following is from a book about American public policy written in 1982.

Line   For most of human history the plight of the
poor has been easily excluded from the
consciousness of those with the power to act.
Inaction was justified by elaborate theories
5   that the poor were by nature inferior or
happy in their condition or both. But human
society confronts a new reality: pressures of
population and technology on the fragile
balance of our planet's ecosystem are
10   compelling the rich not only to re-examine
their own lifestyles, but also to take a greater
interest in the lifestyles of the poor whose
conditions leave them dependent for
short-term survival on large families and the
15   destructive use of crop lands, forests, and
watersheds—thus posing a threat to the
affluent more certain in its occurrence and
consequences than the threat of armed
revolution. Poverty has become salient to
20   the powerful and the implications are far
reaching.

11   According to the passage, before the "new reality"(line 7), some powerful people

(A)   depended on large families for their survival
(B)   destroyed crop land
(C)   took a great interest in the poor
(D)   were self-conscious about their lifestyles
(E)   believed that the poor enjoyed their status

12   The passage suggests that the poor affect the lives of the affluent chiefly by

(A)   draining money from the government
(B)   damaging the natural environment
(C)   making the wealthy feel guilty for their relative affluence
(D)   making unrealistic political demands
(E)   threatening armed revolution

GO ON TO THE NEXT PAGE ▶▶▶

The questions below are based on the content of the passage that precedes them. The questions are to be answered on the basis of what is stated or implied in the passage itself or the introductory material that precedes the passage.

Questions 13–17 are based on the following passage.

The following is a story taken from a collection of short stories written by Heinrich Böll.

Line They have patched up my legs and given me
a job I can do sitting down: I count the
people crossing the new bridge. They get
such a kick out of it, documenting their
5 efficiency with figures; that senseless nothing
made up of a few numbers goes to their
heads, and all day long, all day long, my
soundless mouth ticks away like clockwork,
piling number on number, just so I can
10 present them each evening with the triumph
of a figure.

They beam delightedly when I hand over
the result of my day's labors, the higher the
figure the broader their smiles, and they have
15 every reason to hug themselves when
they climb into bed, for many thousands
of pedestrians cross their new bridge
every day...

But their statistics are wrong. I am sorry,
20 but they are wrong. I am an untrustworthy
soul, although I have no trouble giving an
impression of sterling integrity.

Secretly it gives me pleasure to do them
out of one pedestrian every so often, and
25 then again, when I feel sorry for them, to
throw in a few extra. I hold their happiness
in the palm of my hand. When I am mad at
the world, when I have smoked all my
cigarettes, I just give them the average,
30 sometimes less than the average; and when
my spirits soar, when I am in a good mood,
I pour out my generosity in a five-digit
number. It makes them so happy! They
positively snatch the sheet from my hand,
35 their eyes light up, and they pat me on
the back. How blissfully ignorant they are!

And then they start multiplying, dividing,
working out percentages, God knows what
all. They figure out how many people crossed
40 the bridge per minute today, and how many
will have crossed the bridge in ten years.
They are in love with the future-present
tense, the future-perfect is their specialty—
and yet I can't help being sorry that the
45 whole thing is a fallacy.

When my little sweetheart crosses the
bridge—which she does twice a day—my heart
simply stops beating. The tireless ticking of
my heart just comes to a halt until she has
50 turned into the avenue and disappeared.
And all the people who pass by during that
time don't get counted. Those two minutes
are mine, all mine, and nobody is going to
take them away from me. And when she
55 returns every evening from her ice-cream
parlor, when she walks along on the far side,
past my soundless mouth which must count,
count, then my heart stops beating again,
and I don't resume counting until she is out
60 of sight. And all those who are lucky enough
to file past my unseeing eyes during those
minutes will not be immortalized in
statistics: shadow-men and shadow-women,
creatures of no account, they are barred from
65 the parade of future-perfect statistics.

Needless to say, I love her. But she hasn't
the slightest idea, and I would rather she
didn't find out. I don't want her to suspect
what havoc she wreaks in all those
70 calculations, I want her to walk serenely off
to her ice-cream parlor, unsuspecting and
innocent with her long brown hair and
slender feet, and go get lots of tips. I love her.
It must surely be obvious that I love her.

75 Not long ago they checked up on me.
My partner, who sits across the street and has
to count the cars, gave me plenty of warning,
and that day, I was a lynx-eyed devil. I
counted like crazy, no speedometer could do
80 better. The chief statistician, no less, posted
himself across the street for an hour, and
then compared his tally with me. I was only
one short. My little sweetheart had walked
past, and as long as I live I won't allow that
85 adorable child to be whisked off into the
future-perfect tense; they're not going to take

GO ON TO THE NEXT PAGE ▶▶▶

Excerpted from *The Stories of Heinrich Böll: At the Bridge*, Heinrich Böll, Alfred A Knopfl. '1986' p156–157.

my little sweetheart and multiply her and divide her and turn her into a meaningless percentage. It made my heart bleed to have
90 to go on counting without turning round to watch her, and I am certainly grateful to my partner across the street who has to count the cars. It might have cost me my job, my very existence.
95 The chief statistician clapped me on the shoulder and said I was a good fellow, trustworthy and loyal. "To be out one in one hour," he said, "really makes no odds. We allow for a certain margin of error
100 anyway. I'm going to apply for your transfer to horse-drawn vehicles."
 Horse-drawn vehicles are, of course, a piece of cake. There's nothing to it. There are never more than a couple of dozen
105 horse-drawn vehicles a day, and to tick over the next number in your brain once every half hour—what a cinch!
 Horse-drawn vehicles would be terrific. Between four and eight they are not allowed
110 across the bridge at all, and I could walk to the ice-cream parlor, feast my eyes on her or maybe walk her partway home, my little uncounted sweetheart.

13 The first paragraph suggests that the narrator regards his task with

(A) disdain
(B) unreserved excitement
(C) subdued respect
(D) extreme fear
(E) mild trepidation

14 The second paragraph suggests that the narrator's superiors are primarily concerned with

(A) allowing the narrator to work in comfort
(B) ensuring the quality of the narrator's work
(C) determining the number of people who cross the bridge
(D) giving the narrator tedious tasks
(E) avoiding demanding work

15 In line 43, the reference to the "future perfect" suggests

(A) the narrator's anticipation of seeing his sweetheart
(B) the narrator's need to deceive his supervisors
(C) the narrator's hope to be finished with his task
(D) the supervisors' inhumane treatment of the narrator
(E) the supervisors' obsession with extrapolation

16 The passage suggests that a "lynx-eyed devil"(line 78) is one who

(A) can deceive without being caught
(B) can tally quickly and accurately
(C) walks across the bridge without being detected
(D) keeps a sharp eye on workers he is supervising
(E) is concerned with speed rather than accuracy

17 In line 98, the word "odds" most nearly means

(A) difference   (B) advantage
(C) probability   (D) ignorance
(E) idiosyncracy

Questions 18–24 are based on the following passage.

The following is an excerpt taken from a textbook on the interpretation of art.

Line Look around you. Do you see art in your
immediate surroundings? What qualities
determine that certain things are art?
Definitions of art vary widely, but most tend
5   to fall within general notions developed over
the centuries. The technical ability of an
ancient Egyptian potter to produce a
well-made clay vessel defined his "art."
By extension, the ceramic pot itself, the
10   product of such skillful execution, also
qualified as art. In Europe 600 years ago,
all the trade and professional associations,
from shoemaking to banking, still held to this
broad definition of art as skill or craft in a
15   particular field. The currently popular notion
of the artist as the creator and definer of
art—put simply, "Art is what artists create"—
is a relatively recent concept. The social and
professional role of the artist, and the
20   identification of his or her works as art,
began to develop about six centuries ago in
the ancient artisan tradition.

According to the ancient, encompassing
definition of art as products and activities
25   skillfully done, the finely made clothes you
are wearing, the well-crafted chair you are
sitting on, and the masterful athletic
performance you watched the other day are
considered art. So are mass-media forms
30   such as compact disc covers, posters,
magazine advertisements, music videos and
Internet Web sites, because all of these show
human skill and technical ability.

Some items and activities in our
35   environment, however, stand out from the
rest. They are somehow more artistic, more
"art" than other buildings, chairs, album
covers, and athletic performances. Their
appearance or form, that is, the way their
40   line, color, shape, texture, and other visual
elements combine to please the senses, is so
satisfying or perfect that we call them
beautiful. We apply this notion when we call
a graceful bridge or majestic skyscraper
45   "a beauty," a stellar basketball play
"beautiful," and the stunning photograph of
the player "a work of art".

Prior to the twentieth century, most
aestheticians, or philosophers of art, believed
50   that beauty was the central defining feature
of art. Aesthetics, the philosophy of art,
centered on the study of the nature of art and
beauty. By the turn of the twentieth century,
however, some aestheticians had begun to
55   find this identification of beauty with art
insufficient. Some called the expression of
emotion art's defining characteristic; others
argued that the effective communication of
feelings and ideas to the viewer defined art.
60   One group of influential aesthetic theorists,
the formalists, emphasized the unique effect
of artistic form on the viewer. They
hypothesized that an object or activity
qualifies as art if its visual form is sufficiently
65   compelling or inspiring or beautiful to
provoke an intensely felt, sensory-based
response or aesthetic experience. This
concept echoed the ancient Greek definition
of aesthetic, meaning "of or pertaining to the
70   senses" or "sensuous perception." You might
think that aesthetic experiences are extremely
rare. They are not. If you have ever felt
yourself swept away in the sensuous
experience of a sports event, a musical
75   performance, a film, a sunset, or a painting
of a sunset, you have had an aesthetic
experience.

Look around again. How much of your
surroundings do you consider visually
80   captivating or beautiful, expressive or
communicative? Do any objects in your field
of vision provoke an aesthetic experience? Do
you consider these things art? Is it skill,
beauty, expression, communication,
85   compelling form, aesthetic experience, or all
of the above that make these art for you?
Or is it some quality not mentioned here,
such as originality or creativity, that makes
these objects or activities stand out as art?
90   Might a change in setting or context more
fully establish you selections as art? If it were
moved into the impressive surroundings of
an art museum, would a sports photo or CD
cover become more fully art in you eyes?
95   According to aesthetician George Dickie's
"institutional theory of art," major art
institutions such as museums determine
what is and is not art in a given culture.

GO ON TO THE NEXT PAGE ▶▶▶

Excerpted from *Responding to Art*, Robert Bersson, McGraw-Hill. © 2004, p2–4.

As you can see, art has been defined in a
100 variety of ways. Given this diversity
of definitions, many contemporary
aestheticians conclude that there can be no
single, fixed definition of art. Instead, they
subscribe to the notion of art as a concept
105 that evolves as we and the artwork of our
period change. Your own concept of art
might build upon the definitions of the past,
but it will also be influenced by those of the
present and changed by the art and ideas
110 of the future. From this array of possibilities
you yourself will ultimately determine,
like an aesthetician, your definition or
concept of art.

18 The primary purpose of this passage is to

(A) explain the connection between art
and craftsmanship
(B) trace the origins of the institutional
theory of art
(C) explain the role of aestheticians in
the broader field of philosophy
(D) refute an ancient theory of art
(E) discuss the variety of definitions of
art through the ages

19 In line 9, the "extension" refers to a connection between

(A) Egyptian art and European art
(B) a skill and a physical object
(C) crafts and fine arts
(D) ancient philosophy and modern
philosophy
(E) a potter's skill and a critic's
evaluation of it

20 The first paragraph suggests that, over the
centuries, conceptions of art have become
focused more on

(A) the skills of businessmen than on the
skills of painters and sculptors
(B) the monetary value of art than on the
aesthetic value of art
(C) the activities of individual artists
than on the skills of artisans
(D) the ideas of consumers than on the
theories of philosophers
(E) industrial values than on agricultural
values

21 The author uses the word "somehow" in line
36 to make the point that

(A) very few people who paint are true
artists
(B) most people do not regard
commercial art as beautiful
(C) our senses often deceive us
(D) the criteria for beauty are often
difficult to explain
(E) we tend to believe that only works in
museums are true art

22 Unlike the "ancient, encompassing definition of art" (line 23–24) the "ancient
Greek definition of aesthetic" (lines 68–69)
emphasized

(A) the experiences of the viewer
(B) the intent of the artist
(C) popular opinion
(D) skillful execution
(E) historical value

23 According to the the "institutional theory
of art"(line 96), a photograph can only be
considered art if it

(A) elicits a strong sensory response in
viewers
(B) is produced by a skillful and
renowned photographer
(C) attempts to convey a deep emotion
of the photographer
(D) is sanctioned by an official body
(E) is purchased by an art connoisseur

24 In line 103, the word "fixed" most nearly
means

(A) repaired
(B) subtle
(C) undetermined
(D) unchanging
(E) focused

STOP

*You may check your work, on this
section only, until time is called.*

Section 4

Time—25 Minutes
35 Questions

Directions for Improving Sentences Questions

Each of the sentences below contains one underlined portion. The portion may contain one or more errors in grammar, usage, construction, precision, diction (choice of words), or idiom. Some of the sentences are correct.

Consider the meaning of the original sentence, and choose the answer that best expresses that meaning. If the original sentence is best, choose (A), because it repeats the original phrasing. Choose the phrasing that creates the clearest, most precise and most effective sentence.

EXAMPLE:

The growth of the plant was so dramatic that the children <u>couldn't hardly believe their eyes.</u>

  (A) couldn't hardly believe their eyes
  (B) would not hardly believe their eyes
  (C) could hardly believe their eyes
  (D) couldn't nearly believe their eyes
  (E) could hardly believe his or her eyes

Example answer: (C)

---

1 My favorite activity at this camp is <u>you get to swim.</u>

  (A) you get to swim
  (B) getting to go swimming
  (C) the swimming
  (D) to swim so much
  (E) the swimming you get to do

2 The newer video games for children are very engaging, <u>but ones that don't have anything in the way of real</u> educational value.

  (A) but ones that don't have anything in the way of real
  (B) but lack any real
  (C) and do not have any real
  (D) but no real
  (E) but not any real

3 We could not reach the clearing <u>having a large tree that had fallen blocking</u> our path.

  (A) having a large tree that had fallen blocking
  (B) because a large tree had fallen and blocked
  (C) for a large tree that fell blocking
  (D) due to a large tree that fell and had been blocking
  (E) because a large tree which fell blocking

4 Having run with little effort for over an hour, <u>Jane was disheartened to feel a sudden pain in her knee.</u>

  (A) Jane was disheartened to feel a sudden pain in her knee
  (B) it was disheartening for Jane to feel a sudden pain in her knee
  (C) the sudden pain in her knee disheartened Jane
  (D) Jane's sudden pain in her knee was disheartening to her
  (E) Jane's sudden pain in her knee disheartened her

5 Americans like to hear stories of those who have amassed fortunes through their own hard work, <u>and so seem also happy to see</u> those same tycoons fall in disgrace.

  (A) and so seem also happy to see
  (B) but so seem also happy seeing
  (C) but seem also happy in seeing
  (D) yet also seem happy to see
  (E) seeming also happy to see

6 Curators of modern museums understand that they must create exhibits that are not only informative <u>but also attract visitors.</u>

  (A) but also attract visitors
  (B) and also attractive to visitors
  (C) as well as attractive to visitors
  (D) but also attracting visitors
  (E) but also attractive to visitors

GO ON TO THE NEXT PAGE ▸▸▸

7 Many absurdist writers, notably Eugene Ionesco, believed that novels and plays <u>need not</u> rely on plot.

(A) need not
(B) don't have to need to
(C) would not need to
(D) should not have to need to
(E) need not have to

8 Several of the protestors began to question their methods when they realized that, <u>perhaps because they were promoting confrontation rather than dialogue</u>, they were not changing the minds of their opponents.

(A) perhaps because they were promoting confrontation rather than dialogue
(B) perhaps because their promotion was of confrontation rather than of dialogue
(C) because they have been promoting confrontation rather than dialogue, perhaps
(D) maybe for promoting confrontation instead of dialogue
(E) because they would promote confrontation rather than dialogue

9 Einstein formulated nearly all of his most influential theories in the course of a single year, <u>1905, which have had</u> a profound effect on the whole world of physics, from consumer electronics to quantum theory and space travel.

(A) 1905, which have had
(B) 1905; having
(C) 1905, and these theories have had
(D) 1905; but these theories have had
(E) 1905, however, these have had

10 Sandra's coaching style <u>had been uncompromising and she was</u> more sensitive after many of her players broke down in tears.

(A) had been uncompromising and she was
(B) was uncompromising when she became
(C) had been uncompromising, but she became
(D) was uncompromising, but she had become
(E) was uncompromising, nevertheless she was

11 Although many universities embrace the responsibility of training students to get jobs, <u>there is more of a focus on learning for elevating the mind among other universities.</u>

(A) there is more of a focus on learning for elevating the mind among other universities
(B) there is more of a focus among other universities on learning as a way to elevate the mind
(C) others have a focus on learning as a way of elevating the mind
(D) other universities focus on having learning be a way of elevating the mind
(E) others focus on learning as a way to elevate the mind

Directions for Identifying Sentence Error Questions

The following sentences may contain errors in grammar, usage, diction (choice of words), or idiom. Some of the sentences are correct. No sentence contains more than one error.

If the sentence contains an error, it is underlined and lettered. The parts that are not underlined are correct.

If there is an error, select the part that must be changed to correct the sentence.

If there is no error, choose (E).

EXAMPLE:

By the time <u>they reached</u> the halfway point
                    A

in the race, most <u>of the runners</u> <u>hadn't hardly</u>
        B   C   D

begun to hit their stride. <u>No error</u>
                                    E

Example answer: (D)

12 Although our football team <u>does not win</u>
                                          A

all of its games, Coach Palmer

<u>usually never</u> fails to put every one
        B

<u>of his players into the game,</u> because he
                    C

feels that they <u>have earned</u> the right
                            D

to play. <u>No error</u>
                E

13 The bombs <u>destroyed</u> much of the
                        A

infrastructure of the city,

<u>but it did not disrupt</u> commerce
            B

<u>in the busy markets</u> for <u>more than</u>
            C   D

a few days. <u>No error</u>
                    E

14 By the time <u>the first light of morning</u>
                            A

showed <u>above the trees</u>, the circus workers
                B

<u>had took</u> all of the equipment out of the
    C

trucks and had <u>begun</u> to erect the tents.
                        D

<u>No error</u>
    E

15 We <u>could not have hoped</u> for better
                A

conditions <u>in which to play</u> the game;
                        B

not only was the weather perfect, <u>but also</u>
                                            C

the field <u>had never been</u> in better shape.
                    D

<u>No error</u>
    E

16 As soon as the gun sounded, the racers

<u>had begun</u> to jostle one another for
    A

position <u>at the front</u> of the pack,
                B

<u>safely away from</u> the <u>peril</u> of flying knees
            C   D

and elbows. <u>No error</u>
                    E

17 The effort <u>required</u> to study
                        A

<u>for seven final exams</u> within the span of
                B

four days <u>are far more</u> than the typical
                    C

student <u>can manage</u>. <u>No error</u>
                D   E

18 After <u>having eaten</u> nothing <u>but nuts</u> and
                A   B

berries for forty days <u>in the wilderness</u>,
                                C

Jon had no desire <u>of eating</u> more fruit.
                            D

<u>No error</u>
    E

GO ON TO THE NEXT PAGE ▸▸▸

19 Appearing <u>like an apparition</u> in the distance
                        A
<u>was</u> the beautiful Blue Ridge Mountains,
   B
<u>where</u> we <u>were going to spend</u> the last
   C   D
week of our vacation. <u>No error</u>
                              E

20 Neither the president, <u>who was</u> on
                              A
vacation, <u>or even</u> the vice-president,
            B
who was ill, <u>was</u> available <u>to give</u> the
              C   D
keynote address. <u>No error</u>
                        E

21 Many <u>of the voters</u> who came to the
             A
meeting <u>voiced</u> their <u>concerns for</u> the
          B   C
mayor's new plan to create a new

municipal parking lot <u>next to</u> the
                        D
elementary school. <u>No error</u>
                          E

22 The ability of insects <u>to detect</u> members
                              A
of their own species from

<u>hundreds of meters</u> away <u>is</u> actually quite
       B   C
different from <u>whales</u>. <u>No error</u>
                  D   E

23 The damage to the building

<u>would not have been</u> so great <u>if</u> the roof
        A   B
<u>had been constructed</u> according
        C
<u>to the recently adopted</u> specifications.
        D
<u>No error</u>
   E

24 Without the expertise <u>of Alan and I</u> at their
                              A
disposal, the researchers <u>struggled</u> to
                              B
interpret the documents <u>they</u> had found
                              C
<u>in the archives</u>. <u>No error</u>
       D   E

25 The investment required <u>to develop</u>
                              A
new technologies <u>are</u> often so enormous
                  B
that very few energy companies <u>are able</u> to
                                  C
undertake <u>innovative</u> ventures. <u>No error</u>
            D   E

26 The petition <u>requesting that</u> the president
                        A
reconsider his <u>stance on</u> stem-cell research
                  B
<u>included</u> the signatures of dozens of
   C
<u>imminent</u> scientists. <u>No error</u>
   D   E

27 For many students, the realization that

<u>his or her</u> academic success can be <u>affected</u>
   A   B
<u>by dietary habits</u> <u>comes</u> as a great surprise.
       C   D
<u>No error</u>
   E

28 The fingerprints that <u>were found</u> at the
                              A
scene of the crime <u>clearly did not</u> match
                        B
<u>the defendant</u>, so the prosecuting team
   C
<u>was forced</u> to alter its original theory.
   D
<u>No error</u>
   E

29 The athletes standing <u>on the podium</u> were
                              A
clearly affected <u>about</u> the warm <u>reception</u>
                  B   C
that they received <u>from the audience.</u>
                        D
<u>No error</u>
   E

GO ON TO THE NEXT PAGE ▶▶▶

Questions 30–35 pertain to the following passage.

(1) *Do we idolize sports heroes too much?* (2) *Since the beginning of recorded history, every major culture has had sports and sports heroes.* (3) *In the United States, the Hollywood movie industry is the only thing that outdoes professional sports in regards to attracting viewers and the money it makes in entertainment.* (4) *Some people think that sports are just a distraction from important things like how some guys spend more time thinking about who is the best quarterback than about who should be president.* (5) *Others say that it's worse than a waste of time, that it promotes violence and immaturity.* (6) *They cite all of the crime and drug abuse committed by athletes, some of whom can even get away with murder if they're famous enough.* (7) *Nevertheless, we will always look up to most good athletes, because sports perform important services for a society.* (8) *The Taleban tried to get rid of sports completely as being against their religion.*

(9) *Sports provide a civilization with a way for its warriors to hone the skills they need for fighting.* (10) *So in worshipping sports heroes we are kind of paying respect to our soldiers.* (11) *But many anthropologists claim that the instinct to play sports comes from an activity that is not war but something similar but much older which is hunting.* (12) *You can easily see that the skills used in sports are precisely the skills required for being a successful hunter: throwing things accurately, running quickly, tackling things, hitting things with sticks and acting deceptively.* (13) *This instinct is not something we*

can just get rid of; we may not need to hunt any more, so we need to play sports. (14) *Our need to play sports is like a kitten playing with string: it is our brain's way of helping us learn the skills needed for hunting.*

(15) *It is true that we idolize sports figures far too much.* (16) *Since they are only doing what, essentially, their most basic instincts tell them to do, they are not nearly as worthy of admiration as those who actually use their minds and creativity to improve humanity.*

30 Which of the following is the best revision of sentence 4 (reproduced below)?

Some people think that sports are just a distraction from important things like how some guys spend more time thinking about who is the best quarterback than about who should be president.

(A) Some people think that sports distract us from important things like thinking about who is the best quarterback rather than who should be president.

(B) Some people complain that sports distract us from important things, focusing us on questions like who is the best quarterback rather than who is the best presidential candidate.

(C) Who is the best quarterback, for instance, is one distraction from questions like who should be president that is caused by sports.

(D) Some people think that who should be president is much more important than who is the best quarterback, but also that sports distract us from that.

(E) Some people complain about the distraction of sports, focusing on questions like who is the best quarterback instead of who is the best presidential candidate.

31 Which of the following is the best version of the underlined portion of sentence 5 (reproduced below)?

In the United States, the Hollywood movie industry is the only <u>thing that outdoes professional sports in regards to attracting viewers and the money it makes in entertainment.</u>

(A)   (as it is now)
(B)   things that are more attractive and money-making than professional sports
(C)   form of entertainment more attractive of viewers and making more money than professional sports
(D)   thing attracting more viewers and making more money in the entertainment field than professional sports makes
(E)   form of entertainment that attracts more viewers and makes more money than professional sports

32 Which sentence in the first paragraph contributes the least to the logical coherence of the paragraph?

(A)   sentence 4   (B)   sentence 5
(C)   sentence 6   (D)   sentence 7
(E)   sentence 8

33 Which of the following is the best version of the underlined portion of sentence 11 (reproduced below)?

But many anthropologists claim that the instinct to play sports comes <u>from an activity that is not war but something similar but much older which is hunting.</u>

(A)   (as it is now)
(B)   from hunting, which is not war but similar but much older
(C)   not from war but from hunting, a similar but much older activity
(D)   from hunting, which is similar to war and which is older
(E)   not from war but instead it comes from hunting, which is an older activity than war but still similar

34 In context, which of the following revisions of the underlined portion of sentence 13 (reproduced below) provides the clearest logical transition?

<u>This instinct</u> is not something we can just get rid of; we may not need to hunt any more, so we need to play sports.

(A)   Nevertheless, this instinct
(B)   The instinct to use these skills
(C)   Instead, this instinct
(D)   All the while this instinct
(E)   For example, this instinct

35 Which of the following is the best version of the underlined portion of sentence 14 (reproduced below)?

Our need to play sports is like a <u>kitten playing with string:</u> it is our brain's way of helping us learn the skills needed for hunting.

(A)   a kitten when it is playing with a string
(B)   the way that a kitten plays with a string
(C)   the string that a kitten plays with
(D)   a kitten when it needs to play with string
(E)   a kitten's need to play with string

STOP

You may check your work, on this section only, until time is called.

Section 5

Time—25 Minutes
18 Questions

Directions for Multiple-Choice Questions

In this section, solve each problem, using any available space on the page for scratchwork. Then decide which is the best of the choices given and fill in the corresponding oval on the answer sheet.

- You may use a calculator on any problem. All numbers used are real numbers.
- Figures are drawn as accurately as possible EXCEPT when it is stated that the figure is not drawn to scale.
- All figures lie in a plane unless otherwise indicated.

Reference Information

$A = \pi r^2$ $A = \ell w$ $A = \frac{1}{2}bh$ $V = \ell wh$ $V = \pi r^2 h$ $c^2 = a^2 + b^2$ Special Right Triangles

$C = 2\pi r$

The arc of a circle measures 360°.
Every straight angle measures 180°.
The sum of the measures of the angles in a triangle is 180°.

---

1 If $\dfrac{a}{2} = \dfrac{b}{2}$ and $a = 36$, then $b =$

(A) 12
(B) 24
(C) 28
(D) 32
(E) 54

2 If $2c + d = 9.25$, then $6c + 3d + 3 =$

(A) 22.75
(B) 24.75
(C) 27.75
(D) 30.75
(E) 32.75

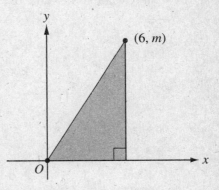

Note: Figure not drawn to scale.

3 If the shaded triangle in the figure above has an area of 12, what is the value of m ?

(A) 2
(B) 4
(C) 6
(D) 8
(E) 10

GO ON TO THE NEXT PAGE ▶▶▶

4

A pizzeria offers one or more of the following toppings on its pizzas: pepperoni, mushrooms, meatballs. How many different combinations of one or more toppings are possible? (Assume that the order of the toppings does not matter.)

(A) 5
(B) 6
(C) 7
(D) 8
(E) 9

5

If the perimeter of a rectangle is 5 times the width of the rectangle, then the length of the rectangle is how many times longer than the width?

(A) $\dfrac{2}{3}$

(B) $\dfrac{3}{2}$

(C) 2

(D) $\dfrac{5}{2}$

(E) 3

6

If $16^{w+2} = 2^{11}$, what is the value of w?

(A) 0.75
(B) 1.33
(C) 2.00
(D) 3.50
(E) 4.75

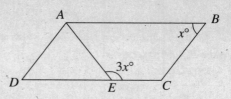

Note: Figure not drawn to scale.

7

In the figure above, $ABCD$ is a parallelogram and AE bisects $\angle DAB$. What is the value of x ?

(A) 24
(B) 28
(C) 32
(D) 36
(E) 40

8

The width of a rectangle is 75% the length of the rectangle. The perimeter of the rectangle is 84 centimeters. A circle is drawn that contains all four vertices of this rectangle. If the area of this circle is $k\pi$ square centimeters, what is the value of k?

(A) 160
(B) 175
(C) 185
(D) 210
(E) 225

Directions for Student-Produced Response Questions

Each of the questions in this section requires you to solve the problem and enter your answer in a grid, as shown below.

- If your answer is ⅔ or .666 ..., you must enter **the most accurate value the grid can accommodate**, but you may do this in one of four ways:

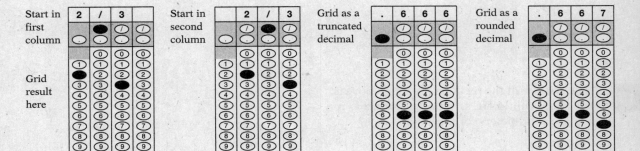

Start in first column   Start in second column   Grid as a truncated decimal   Grid as a rounded decimal

Grid result here

- In the example above, gridding a response of 0.67 or 0.66 is **incorrect** because it is less accurate than those above.
- The scoring machine cannot read what is written in the top row of boxes. You **MUST** fill in the numerical grid accurately to get credit for answering any question correctly. You should write your answer in the top row of boxes only to aid your gridding.
- Do **not** grid in a mixed fraction like $3\frac{1}{2}$ as $\boxed{3\,|\,1\,|\,/\,|\,2}$ because it will be interpreted as $\frac{31}{2}$. Instead, convert it to an improper fraction like ⁷⁄₂ or a decimal like 3.5 before gridding.
- None of the answers will be negative, because there is no negative sign in the grid.
- Some of the questions may have more than one correct answer. You must grid only one of the correct answers.
- You may use a calculator on any of these problems.
- All numbers in these problems are real numbers.
- Figures are drawn as accurately as possible EXCEPT when it is stated that the figure is not drawn to scale.
- All figures lie in a plane unless otherwise indicated.

9 If a car travels at a constant rate of 75 miles per hour, how many <u>minutes</u> will it take to travel 100 miles? (60 minutes = 1 hour)

11 The average (arithmetic mean) of five different integers is 30. If the least of these integers is 7, what is the greatest possible value of any of the numbers?

10 What is the only integer that satisfies the statement |3x − 5| < 1.2?

12 The ratio of girls to boys at a certain school is 8:5. If there are 520 students at the school altogether, how many boys are at the school?

GO ON TO THE NEXT PAGE ▶▶▶

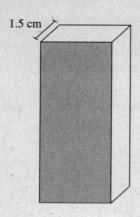

1.5 cm

5 ➤ **13**

The volume of the rectangular solid above is 27 cubic centimeters. What is the area, in square centimeters, of the shaded face?

14

At the beginning of the year, the price of stock A was 35% greater than the price of stock B. Over the course of the year, the price of stock A doubled while the price of stock B decreased by 10%. At the end of the year, how many times greater was the price of stock A than the price of stock B?

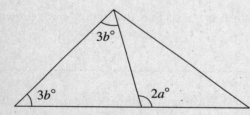

$3b°$

$3b°$ $2a°$

Note: Figure not drawn to scale.

15

In the triangle above, a and b are odd integers. If $50 > a > 60$, then what is one possible value of b?

16

If L represents the sum of the first three terms of a geometric sequence in which the second and third terms are 1 and 3, respectively, and M represents the sum of the first three terms of a geometric sequence in which the second and third terms are 3 and 1, respectively, then what is $M - L$?

17

If the range of the function $y = f(x)$ is all real numbers between -1 and 12, inclusive, then what is the maximum value of $g(x)$ if $g(x) = 2f(x-1) + 3$?

18

Let #x represent the greatest even number less than x. If $20 < x < 30$, then what is the maximum possible value of #$5x - $#$4x$?

STOP

You may check your work, on this section only, until time is called.

Section 6

Time—25 minutes
24 Questions

Each of the sentences below is missing one or two portions. Read each sentence, then select the word or words that most logically completes the sentence, taking into account the meaning of the sentence as a whole.

Example:

Rather than accepting the theory unquestioningly, Deborah regarded it with ———.

(A) mirth   (B) sadness
(C) responsibility   (D) ignorance
(E) skepticism

Correct response: (E)

1 Veteran coaches can often reflect on past experiences to draw lessons for the present; young players, however, rarely have the advantage of such ———.

(A) vagueness   (B) misconceptions
(C) hindsight   (D) antagonism
(E) premonitions

2 The males of many bird species rely on ——— displays like elaborate plumage and energetic dances to attract females, yet such exhibitions are ——— for the many males who are not chosen as mates.

(A) eternal . . tolerable
(B) misleading . . successful
(C) carnivorous . . irrelevant
(D) ostentatious . . futile
(E) passive . . inexplicable

3 The memoir was filled with entertaining ——— about the author's experiences as an army nurse, but many readers thought that the disjointed nature of these stories detracted from the ——— of the book.

(A) pluralities . . consistency
(B) themes . . implausibility
(C) missives . . frivolity
(D) treatises . . authenticity
(E) vignettes . . cohesiveness

4 Fast horses often tend to be hard to control, so riders who are concerned about safety should look for steeds that are slower and more ———.

(A) nimble
(B) irascible
(C) tractable
(D) recalcitrant
(E) erroneous

5 One critical flaw of the new trade regulations is that they require much greater oversight of commerce, but do not ——— the necessary funds for such an increase in ———.

(A) appropriate . . vigilance
(B) provide . . taxation
(C) determine . . empathy
(D) embezzle . . organization
(E) sequester . . industry

Each passage below is followed by one or two questions based on its content. Answer each question based on what is stated or implied in the passage.

Questions 6–7 are based on the following passage.

The following is an excerpt from a biography of Albert Einstein that discusses his relationship with the American silent film star Charlie Chaplin.

Line   The essence of Einstein's profundity lay in his simplicity, and the essence of his science lay in his artistry—his phenomenal sense of beauty. He is, of course, best known for his theory of
5   relativity, which brought him world fame. But with fame came a form of near idolatry that Einstein found incomprehensible. To his amazement, he became a living legend, a veritable folk hero, looked upon as an oracle,
10   entertained by royalty, statesmen, and other celebrities, and treated by public and press as if he were a movie star rather than a scientist. When, in Hollywood's glittering heyday, Chaplin took Einstein to the gala opening of
15   his film *City Lights*, the crowds surged around the limousine as much to gape at Einstein as at Chaplin. Turning in bewilderment to his host, Einstein asked, "What does it mean?" to which the worldly-
20   wise Chaplain bitterly replied, "Nothing."

6   The passage suggests that, unlike Einstein, Chaplin

(A)   was widely adored by the public
(B)   understood the nature of celebrity
(C)   did not consider himself an artist
(D)   knew people in powerful positions
(E)   was annoyed by the press

7   Einstein's question in line 19 is inquiring about

(A)   a piece of art
(B)   a scientific puzzle
(C)   a social phenomenon
(D)   a polite gesture
(E)   an invitation

Questions 8–9 are based on the following passage.

The following is an excerpt from a book about bio-medical ethics.

Line   Traditional codes of medical ethics, as well as other traditional expositions, emphasize the moral obligations of health-care professionals rather than the moral rights of patients.
5   Physicians are expected to perform those actions which will benefit their patients and to refrain from performing those that will harm them. Thus traditional medical ethics stresses two fundamental principles as governing the
10   physician-patient relationship—the principles of *beneficence* and *nonmaleficence*. Both of these are expressed in the dictum, "Benefit and do no harm to the patient." In contrast, recent discussions of medical ethics speak
15   more and more about the moral rights of patients, especially about the right to make their own medical decisions. These discussions emphasize the right of patients to act as autonomous decision makers, determining for
20   themselves what will be done to their bodies. This change of emphasis reflects a growing change in lay attitudes toward health-care professionals, especially physicians.

8   The sentence beginning on line 5 ("Physicians are expected to … harm them") represents the perspective of

(A)   theorists with whom the author adamantly disagrees
(B)   modern physicians
(C)   patients with life-threatening illnesses
(D)   long-established tenets
(E)   recent treatises on medical ethics

9   The passage indicates that "lay attitudes" (line 22) are becoming increasingly focused on

(A)   traditional codes
(B)   the behavior of professionals
(C)   emotional health
(D)   the rights of physicians
(E)   the rights of those receiving treatment

GO ON TO THE NEXT PAGE ▶▶▶

First paragraph: *Albert Einstein, Creator & Rebel*, Banesh Hoffman, © 1992, Penguin Books, p 3.
Second paragraph: *Biomedical Ethics*, Thomas Mappes, Jane Zempaty, McGraw Hill. © 1981, pp 44–45

Questions 10–16 pertain to the following passage.

The following excerpt is taken from a book devoted to the argumentation, particularly with regard to its merits, purposes and techniques.

Line Why do we argue? Why do we make trouble? Why are we obnoxious and disagreeable? Why not just go along and not make waves? Because we are constantly faced with decisions.
5 In order to make good decisions we have to consider the issues and the relevant arguments and positions. It is necessary to decide what issues are the most important, what topics the most vital.
10 Arguing provides the opportunity to explore and probe the claims and positions offered. In arguing we have a chance to examine exactly what the position rests upon. The territorial limit should be extended to two hundred miles
15 off-shore: Why? What rights are involved? Who will suffer and who will gain? Are there alternatives to the move? What problem forced this solution? What will happen if it is not extended? In arguing we need not disagree
20 with a position in order to attack it. We need only want to test or explore it. One major reason for arguing, then, is to learn: to explore, probe, and test in order to examine a belief.
Very often when we engage in arguments
25 we already have a conviction but argue to persuade others. Sometimes we are being persuaded, at other times we are doing the persuading. This aspect of argument is around us at all times. When the daily newspaper
30 editorial supports compulsory seat-belt legislation and offers arguments, the aim is to convince us, the readers. The same holds for all arguments and positions presented on television and radio. In these situations we
35 do not have the opportunity to reply. The argument is stated and there it is, we can take it or leave it. We are presented with very polished and convincing arguments but cannot ourselves object.
40 Other forms of argument designed to persuade us are the advertising messages that reach us by way of commercials, posters, jingles, and so on. The reasons presented for trying a product can be good, such as
45 efficiency or low cost, or poor, such as prestige or an irrelevant endorsement. The errors in reasoning one finds in advertising are the same as elsewhere. When Polly Politician says, "Unemployment may be reduced as
50 much as 22 percent in the next six months," she relies on the same "hedge-words" as an advertisement saying, "Shine toothpaste may reduce cavities by as much as 36 percent." Both use the expression "as much as,"
55 indicating only an outside possibility, and both use the word "may" instead of "will." We often aim to convince someone of our view. When we suggest to a colleague that opening a new branch might not be a
60 good idea, we are arguing. He might, at the same time, be aiming to convince us that it is a good idea. In these situations we must be very quick. Someone presenting us with a position expects either assent or disagreement. If we
65 dissent, then there is a responsibility to explain why we disagree. If we cannot come up with a reason, then we are expected to agree.
Arguments can also be fun, especially when they are not about something too vital. Arguing
70 is like playing, and to appreciate it on its own, without any desire to achieve some other end, is not only possible, but desirable. Arguing when nothing is at stake can be a valuable experience, like playing a friendly game of
75 tennis to prepare for a tournament. We are more at ease, and so can pay more attention to what we are saying and how we are saying it. We can take more risks on outrageous maneuvers, maybe try out a new shot.
80 A common old saying is that one should never argue about religion or politics. This is nonsense. One of our aims is to have true beliefs. In this sense we all seek the truth. Yet the adage warns us not to examine or test the
85 most important and basic of beliefs. Should these be left alone? No. These are just the beliefs that should be most carefully examined. By spotting weaknesses, mistakes, and falsehoods we stand a much better
90 chance of holding and acting on true beliefs. The advantage of this is success: making decisions on false beliefs can only lead to error and trouble.

GO ON TO THE NEXT PAGE ▸▸▸

Excerpted from *How to Win an Argument*, Michael A. Gilbert, McGraw-Hill. © 1979, p 5–7.

10 In the first paragraph, the author assumes that the reader

(A) understands the basic value of argumentation
(B) lives in a democratic society
(C) wants to act judiciously
(D) reads newspapers
(E) has had experience in dealing with obnoxious people

11 Unlike the questions in the first paragraph, the questions in the second paragraph

(A) pertain to argumentation
(B) are not questions that the author believes are appropriate
(C) have answers that are already well-known
(D) are not answered in this passage
(E) are not related to any particular policy

12 The main purpose of the second and third paragraphs is to

(A) describe different purposes of argumentation
(B) illustrate different methods of arguing
(C) present opposite perspectives on a political issue
(D) describe some common misconceptions about argumentation
(E) summarize the findings of researchers

13 The passage suggests that "Polly Politician" (line 48) is guilty of

(A) corruption
(B) inefficiency
(C) ignorance
(D) egotism
(E) equivocation

14 The "arguments" mentioned in line 31 differ significantly from the argument described in the fifth paragraph (lines 57–66) chiefly in that they are

(A) about petty topics
(B) poorly reasoned
(C) one-sided
(D) for entertainment purposes
(E) irrefutable

15 According to the analogy used in the sixth paragraph, the "outrageous maneuvers" (line 78) are like

(A) novel ways of making a point in casual conversation
(B) tricks used by politicians in debates
(C) the deceptive practices of journalists
(D) unethical practices in business
(E) unorthodox coaching practices

16 The purpose of the last paragraph (lines 80–93) is to

(A) continue an analogy from the previous paragraph
(B) refute a misconception
(C) provide a specific example that supports a political theory
(D) support the author's thesis by citing an authoritative opinion
(E) present a personal reflection

Questions 17–24 are based on the following passage

The following passage is from a memoir written in 1970 by Lady Mary Dolling Sanders O'Malley, who wrote under the pseudonym Ann Bridge.

Line   In 1924 George Mallory set out with the third
        expedition to attempt to reach the summit of
        Mount Everest. My brother Jack and I had
        first met George at Zermatt in 1909, and both
5   made friends with him. Till my marriage in
        1913, George and I climbed a great deal
        together in Wales; we met in the Alps; he
        often stayed with us in London.
            Naturally, I took great interest in his
10   Everest expeditions. With George I pored
        over the routes and studied the photographs;
        when he was first asked to lecture about it I
        went and stayed with them, and George tried
        out his original lecture on Ruth (his wife) and
15   me, in his roomy study at The Holt—he was
        rather nervous, but in fact the lectures were a
        great success, delivered in his beautiful voice,
        with an engaging hint of shyness. Both Ruth
        and I noticed, though, before he left for the
20   third time, that some of the happy enthusiasm
        that had been so evident before the two earlier
        expeditions was lacking—he was what he
        himself called "heavy," a frame of mind he
        detested if it took him before or during a climb.
25   We read of course in the papers every
        scrap of news that came from the expedition—
        always with a time-lag of about a fortnight
        while despatches were being brought down
        through Tibet by runners to the nearest
30   telegraph office.
            One night at the end of the first week in
        that June, at Bridge End, our house in Surrey,
        I had a peculiarly vivid dream. In it Ruth and
        I decided to go out and visit the Everest
35   expedition. With the absurd inconsequence
        so frequent in dreams we took the train to
        Chur, in eastern Switzerland, and then drove
        in an open two-horse carriage through streets
        of high gray stone-built houses, till we reached
40   the headquarters of the expedition. We went
        in; the men were all out, and we decided to
        get tea ready for them; there was no milk, so
        we took a large jug to the *Meierei*, the dairy
        along the street, and filled it—I clearly
45   remember explaining the word *Meierei* to
        Ruth, who knew no German. Then the men
        came in, hungry and cheerful, with snowy
        boots, and we all had tea. And afterwards
        George took me into what he called the

50   maproom, where there was a huge
        enlargement of a photograph of the ridge of
        Everest, running down to the North Col, on
        the wall; he took a thing like a billiard-cue and
        showed me the new camps, and explained
55   how certain it was that they would reach the
        summit tomorrow. Then he put down the
        cue, and we sat on the big table in the middle
        of the room, swinging our legs, and talked—
        George spoke, more fully and openly than he
60   had ever done before to me of what mountains
        and his relationship to mountains meant to
        him—he spoke with a strange mixture of
        reverence and what I can only call rapture.
            This dream frightened me terribly. He had
65   been so alive, so near, in it—just as when a
        beloved friend whom one has not seen for some
        time comes to stay, and for days after they have
        left the whole house is glowing and warm from
        their recent presence—so Bridge End, next
70   morning, as I went about my daily tasks, was
        full of the presence of George. I did not want
        to worry Ruth, but I wrote to Marjorie Turner,
        her sister, at Westbrook, saying I had been
        worried by a dream, and asking what the
75   latest news was of George? In reply I got a
        laconic post-card: "Last heard from R. three
        days ago; he was all right then. M."
            I don't think I even tried to comfort myself
        with the absurd setting of the dream, like the
80   Everest Expedition's headquarters being in a
        stone-built house in a Swiss town—I was too
        accustomed to the inconsequent dottiness of
        dreams. And on a Saturday morning nearly a
        fortnight later Owen came out to me where I
85   was sorting linen in the big workroom behind
        the kitchen with the newspaper in his hand.
        "I've got some bad news for you," he said.
        "George and Irvine have been killed on
        Everest."
90   Odell reported having his last sight of the
        pair after noon on 8 June, above the last step,
        on the open arête, "going strongly for the
        top." Having climbed a lot with George, I
        cannot believe, with only a perfectly straight-
95   forward snow ridge between him and the
        summit, the last obstacle surmounted, that
        he did not reach it. And when in 1933 a later
        expedition found an ice-axe *below* the first
        rock step, it confirmed my belief, and that of

GO ON TO THE NEXT PAGE ▶▶▶

Excerpted from *Moment of Knowing*, Ann Bridge, Mcgraw-Hill. © 1970, p 24–27.

100 many others, that Mallory and Irvine had
reached the top, and that disaster had
overtaken them on the way down. Descent is
always more difficult than ascent; and who
would leave an ice-axe behind, with that
105 snow arête still in front of him? Certainly not
George.
   In 1953 Everest was successfully climbed
by Hunt's party. I was in Ireland, but our
daughter Jane, George's godchild, who was in
110 London, telephoned me the news first thing.
I was especially glad to hear it from her.

5 ▶

17 In line 24, the word "took" most nearly means

(A) acquired
(B) derived from
(C) overcame
(D) required
(E) endured

18 The narrator uses the phrase "every scrap"
in lines 25–26 in order to convey

(A) the unreliable nature of the news
(B) the slow speed of the news
(C) her lack of interest in the
    technicalities of climbing
(D) the awkward relationship between
    the narrator and Ruth
(E) her eagerness to hear news of the
    expedition

19 The "absurd inconsequence" in the narrator's dream is the

(A) absence of milk in the expedition
    headquarters
(B) cheerfulness of the men
(C) location of the expedition headquarters
(D) speed of the train ride
(E) photograph of Mount Everest

20 In the author's dream, Mallory's attitude
toward the mountains can best be described
as

(A) awed
(B) fearful
(C) cavalier
(D) objectively analytical
(E) ambivalent

21 In saying that she was "too accustomed to
the inconsequent dottiness of dreams"
(line 83) the author suggests that she was
unable to

(A) warn Mallory of the dangers of his
    climb
(B) appease the anxiety caused by her
    dream
(C) allow herself to be affected by her
    dream
(D) understand the symbolism of her
    dream
(E) determine the location of the expedi-
    tion's headquarters

22 The references to "a fortnight" in both lines
27 and line 84 are significant because, when
considered together, they suggest that

(A) communications technology had
    improved significantly
(B) the ascent took far longer than
    Mallory had anticipated
(C) the information that the author
    received about Mallory's expedition
    was unreliable
(D) Mallory had insufficient time to pre-
    pare for his ascent
(E) the author's dream roughly coincided
    with Mallory's death

23 In the sentence beginning on line 93,
"Having climbed ... did not reach it" the
author expresses her opinion that Mallory

(A) lacked some important mountain
    climbing skills
(B) was hindered by weather
(C) was an exceptionally able climber
(D) was not killed
(E) was misled by his fellow climbers

24 It can be inferred from the passage that the
narrator was "especially glad" (line 111)
that the news of a successful climb came
from her daughter because her daughter

(A) had been away for a long time
(B) was an adept climber
(C) rarely communicated with other
    members of the family
(D) had had a special relationship with
    George Mallory
(E) was not accustomed to good news

STOP

*You may check your work, on this
section only, until time is called.*

Section 7

Time—20 Minutes
16 Questions

Directions for Multiple-Choice Questions

In this section, solve each problem, using any available space on the page for scratchwork. Then decide which is the best of the choices given and fill in the corresponding oval on your answer sheet.

- You may use a calculator on any problem. All numbers used are real numbers.
- Figures are drawn as accurately as possible EXCEPT when it is stated that the figure is not drawn to scale.
- All figures lie in a plane unless otherwise indicated.

Reference Information

$A = \pi r^2$ $\quad$ $A = \ell w$ $\quad$ $A = \frac{1}{2}bh$ $\quad$ $V = \ell wh$ $\quad$ $V = \pi r^2 h$ $\quad$ $c^2 = a^2 + b^2$ $\quad$ Special Right Triangles
$C = 2\pi r$

The number of degrees of arc in a circle is 360°.
The measure in degrees of a straight angle is 180°.
The sum of the measures in degrees of the angles of a triangle is 180°.

$$\underset{A}{\bullet} \overset{x+4}{\rule{2cm}{0.4pt}} \underset{B}{\bullet} \overset{2x-3}{\rule{2cm}{0.4pt}} \underset{C}{\bullet} \overset{6}{\rule{1.5cm}{0.4pt}} \underset{D}{\bullet} \overset{3x+4}{\rule{2cm}{0.4pt}} \underset{E}{\bullet}$$

1 In the figure above, what is the length of line segment AE in terms of x?

(A) $3x + 11$
(B) $5x + 14$
(C) $7x + 8$
(D) $6x + 11$
(E) $6x + 17$

2 A video store charges an annual account fee of \$3.00 per customer and has a total of 5,400 members. If everyone pays the fee, what is the total amount collected from the members?

(A) \$16.20
(B) \$162.00
(C) \$1,620.00
(D) \$16,200.00
(E) \$162,000.00

3 A plastic container contains 2 pints of water. If 8 tablespoons of water are poured out, what fraction of the original amount remains?

(A) $\dfrac{1}{8}$

(B) $\dfrac{1}{4}$

(C) $\dfrac{1}{2}$

(D) $\dfrac{3}{4}$

(E) $\dfrac{7}{8}$

1 pint = 2 cups
1 cup = 16 tablespoons

GO ON TO THE NEXT PAGE ▶▶▶

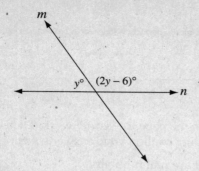

Note: Figure not drawn to scale.

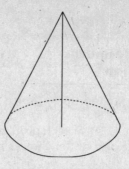

Note: Figure not drawn to scale.

4 Lines m and n intersect, as shown, in the figure above. What is the value of y?

(A) 52
(B) 58
(C) 62
(D) 68
(E) 72

7 The radius of the base of the right circular cone above is 4 inches and the height of the cone is 14 inches. A cut is made parallel to the circular base such that it produces a smaller cone with a radius of 3 inches. What is the height, in inches, of the smaller cone?

(A) 3.5
(B) 6.0
(C) 7.0
(D) 10.5
(E) 11.0

5 Elysha uses air-conditioning year round and spends, on average, $125 per month to cool her apartment. A new energy-efficient air conditioning system would cost her $3,000 to install and only $25 per month thereafter to cool the apartment. If she installs the new system, how many months will it take for her total savings in cooling costs to equal the cost of the system?

(A) 30
(B) 35
(C) 40
(D) 45
(E) 50

8 A right triangle has side lengths of $x - 1$, $x + 1$, and $x + 3$. What is its perimeter?

(A) 7
(B) 24
(C) 28
(D) 32
(E) 36

$$0.2\overline{4516} = 0.245162451624516 \ldots$$

9 In the repeating decimal above, what is the 3,000th digit to the right of the decimal?

(A) 2
(B) 4
(C) 5
(D) 1
(E) 6

$$\begin{array}{r} BA \\ +6B \\ \hline CAB \end{array}$$

6 In the correctly worked addition problem above, A, B, and C represent different digits. What is the value of B?

(A) 0
(B) 1
(C) 4
(D) 5
(E) 8

GO ON TO THE NEXT PAGE ▶▶▶

Housing Situation of Glenville Families

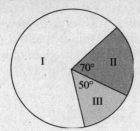

Region I: Families who own their own homes
Region II: Families who own condominiums
Region III: Families who rent apartments

10 The pie graph above shows the housing situation of families in Glenville. If there are 12,000 families in Glenville, then how many families own their own homes?

(A)   3,000
(B)   4,000
(C)   6,000
(D)   8,000
(E)   9,000

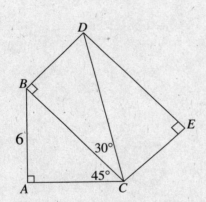

Note: Figure not drawn to scale.

11 In the figure above, $BD \parallel CE$. What is the length of DE?

(A) $6\sqrt{3}$

(B) $6\sqrt{2}$

(C) $2\sqrt{6}$

(D) $4\sqrt{6}$

(E) $3\sqrt{5}$

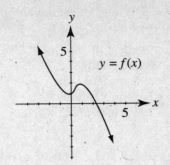

12 Given the graph of $y = f(x)$ above, which of the following represents the graph of $y = f(x + 3) + 3$?

(A) 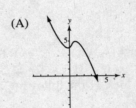   (B)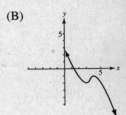

(C) 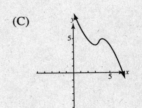   (D)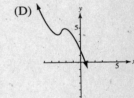

(E)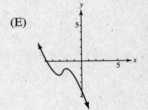

13 If $n = 5^{2000} + 5^{2002}$, then what are the prime factors of n?

(A) 5 only
(B) 2 and 5 only
(C) 2, 5, and 10 only
(D) 2, 5, and 13 only
(E) 2, 5, 1000, and 1001 only

14 If $r = s^6 = t^4$ and r is positive, then $st =$

(A) $r^{1/24}$
(B) $r^{1/10}$
(C) $r^{5/12}$
(D) r^{10}
(E) r^{24}

15 Let $x \, \Omega \, y$ be defined by $x \, \Omega \, y = (x - y)^2$ for all values of x and y. If $x \, \Omega \, y = 2y \, \Omega \, 3$ and $x = y - 3$, then which of the following could be the value of y?

(A) -1
(B) 1
(C) 3
(D) 4
(E) 6

16 In the Connecticut State Championships, Rodrigo runs the 1-mile race four different times. He finishes with times of a minutes, b minutes, c minutes and d minutes. What was his average speed, in <u>miles per hour</u>, for all four races combined?

(A) $\dfrac{a + b + c + d}{4}$

(B) $\dfrac{a + b + c + d}{240}$

(C) $\dfrac{a + b + c + d}{15}$

(D) $\dfrac{4}{a + b + c + d}$

(E) $\dfrac{240}{a + b + c + d}$

STOP

You may check your work, on this section only, until time is called.

Section 8

Time—20 minutes
19 Questions

Each of the sentences below is missing one or two portions. Read each sentence, then select the word or words that most logically completes the sentence, taking into account the meaning of the sentence as a whole.

Example:

Rather than accepting the theory unquestioningly, Deborah regarded it with ———.

(A) mirth   (B) sadness
(C) responsibility   (D) ignorance
(E) skepticism

Correct response: (E)

1 Donna's aggressive style was a ——— when she was a young student, but it turned into an asset when she became a trial lawyer.

(A) liability   (B) novelty
(C) compliment   (D) symbol
(E) protection

2 Although the report is ———, it would be ——— of the committee to accept it without revision; it discusses the topic thoroughly, but contains several significant errors that need to be corrected.

(A) flawed . . foreign
(B) inarticulate . . negligent
(C) comprehensive . . remiss
(D) complete . . acceptable
(E) subtle . . irresponsible

3 Davis was confident in her ability to win the race, but not so ——— as to believe that she could do so without her greatest effort.

(A) thorough
(B) doubtful
(C) complacent
(D) coherent
(E) latent

4 The diet and exercise regimen did not work to invigorate Dina as the doctors had hoped; indeed she felt ——— by the effort and more ——— than ever.

(A) defeated . . sanguine
(B) weakened . . lithe
(C) energized . . torpid
(D) conciliated . . despondent
(E) enervated . . phlegmatic

5 The film contains a ——— of sophisticated symbols, far more than even a perspicacious critic can interpret in several viewings.

(A) modicum
(B) rectitude
(C) surfeit
(D) dearth
(E) deficit

6 Planning to divert their pursuers with a ——— lead, the conspirators knew they would escape if no one unraveled their ——— plan.

(A) veritable . . venerable
(B) contrived . . decrepit
(C) specious . . forthright
(D) credible . . scheming
(E) spurious . . duplicitous

GO ON TO THE NEXT PAGE ▶▶▶

The questions below are based on the content of the passage that precedes them. The questions are to be answered on the basis of what is stated or implied in the passage itself or the introductory material that precedes the passage.

Questions 7-19 are based on the following passages.

The following passages present two perspectives on author Nathaniel Hawthorne and his works. The first passage was written by an American author and critic in 1872, and the second passage was written as a response 8 years later.

Passage 1

Line   Mr. Hawthorne is having a posthumous productivity almost as active as that of his lifetime. Six volumes have been compounded from his private journals, an unfinished
5   romance is doing duty as a "serial[1]," and a number of his letters, with other personal memorials, have been given to the world. These liberal excisions from the privacy of so reserved and shade-seeking a genius suggest
10   forcibly the general question of the proper limits of curiosity as to that passive personality of an artist of which the elements are scattered in portfolios and table-drawers. The question is really brought to an open
15   dispute between the instinct of self-conservatism and the general fondness for squeezing an orange dry. Artists, of course, as time goes on, will be likely to take the alarm, empty their table-drawers, and level the
20   approaches to their privacy. The critics, psychologists, and gossip-mongers may then glean amid the stubble.
        Our remarks are not provoked by any visible detriment conferred on Mr. Hawthorne's
25   fame by these recent publications. He has very fairly withstood the ordeal; which, indeed, is as little as possible an ordeal in his case, owing to the superficial character of the documents. His journals throw little light on
30   his personal feelings, and even less on his genius *per se*. Their general effect is difficult to express. They deepen our sense of that genius, while they singularly diminish our impression of his general intellectual power.

[1]A novel published in installments in a periodical
First passage: "*Nathaniel Hawthorne*", The Nation, March 14, 1872. Henry James,
Second passage: "*Review of Hawthorne, by Henry James*" William Dean Howells, 1880.

35   They represent him, judged with any real critical rigor, as superficial, uninformed, incurious, inappreciative; but from beginning to end they cast no faintest shadow upon the purity of his peculiar gift. The truth is that
40   Mr. Hawthorne belonged to the race of magicians, and that his genius took its nutriment as insensibly—to our vision—as the flowers take the dew. He was the last man to have attempted to explain himself, and these
45   pages offer no adequate explanation of him. They show us one of the gentlest, lightest, and most leisurely of observers, strolling at his ease among foreign sights in blessed intellectual irresponsibility, and weaving his
50   chance impressions into a tissue as smooth as fireside gossip. Mr. Hawthorne had what belongs to genius—a style individual and delightful; he seems to have written as well for himself as he did for others—to have
55   written from the impulse to keep up a sort of literary tradition in a career singularly devoid of the air of professional authorship; but as regards substance, his narrative flows along in a current as fitfully diffuse and shallow as
60   a regular correspondence with a distant friend—a friend familiar but not intimate—sensitive but not exacting. With all allowance for suppressions, his entries are never confidential; the author seems to have been
65   reserved even with himself. They are a record of things slight and usual. Some of the facts noted are incredibly minute; they imply a peculiar *leisure* of attention. How little his journal was the receptacle of Mr. Hawthorne's
70   deeper feelings is indicated by the fact that during a long and dangerous illness of his daughter in Rome, which he speaks of later as "a trouble that pierced into his very vitals," he never touched his pen.

Passage 2

75   Mr. James's book on Hawthorne, in Morley's *English Men of Letters* series, merits far closer examination and carefuller notice than we can give it here, alike for the interest of its subject, the peculiarity of its point of view,
80   and the charm and distinction of its literature. An American author writing of an American author for an English public incurs risks with his fellow-countrymen which Mr. James must have faced, and is much more
85   likely to possess the foreigner whom he addresses with a clear idea of our conditions than to please the civilization whose portrait

GO ON TO THE NEXT PAGE ▶▶▶

is taken. Forty-six, fifty, sixty-four, are not
dates so remote, nor are Salem and Concord
90 societies so extinct, that the people of those
periods and places can be safely described as
"provincial[2]," not once, but a dozen times;
and we foresee, without any very powerful
prophetic lens, that Mr. James will be in
95 some quarters attainted of high treason. For
ourselves, we will be content with saying that
the provinciality strikes us as somewhat over-
insisted upon, and that, speaking from the
point of not being at all provincial ourselves,
100 we think the epithet is sometimes mistaken.
If it is not provincial for an Englishman to be
English, or a Frenchman French, then it is
not so for an American to be American; and if
Hawthorne was "exquisitely provincial," one
105 had better take one's chance of universality
with him than with almost any Londoner or
Parisian of his time. Provinciality, we
understand it, is a thing of the mind or the
soul; but if it is a thing of the experiences,
110 then that is another matter, and there is no
quarrel. Hawthorne undoubtedly saw less of
the world in New England than one sees in
Europe, but he was no cockney[3], as
Europeans are apt to be.
115   We think, too, that, in his conscience against
bragging and chauvinism, Mr. James puts too
slight a value upon some of Hawthorne's work.
It is not enough to say of a
book so wholly unrivaled as *The Scarlet Letter*
120 that it was "the finest piece of imaginative
writing put forth in America," as if it had its
parallel in any literature. No one better than
Mr. James knows the radical difference
between a romance and a novel, but he speaks
125 now of Hawthorne's novels, and now of his
romances, throughout, as if the terms were
convertible; whereas the romance and the
novel are as distinct as the poem and the
novel. Hawthorne's fictions being always and
130 essentially, in conception and performance,
romances, and not novels, something of all
Mr. James's special criticism is invalidated by
the confusion which, for some reason not
made clear, he permits himself.
135   What gives us entire satisfaction, however,
is Mr. James's characterization, or illustrations
of Hawthorne's own nature. He finds him an
innocent, affectionate heart, extremely
domestic, a life of definite, high purposes

140 singularly un-baffled, and an "unperplexed
intellect." This strikes us as beautifully
reasonable and true, and we will not cloud it
with comment of ours. But satisfactorily as
Mr. James declares Hawthorne's personality
145 in large, we do not find him sufficient as to
minor details and facts. His defect, or his
error, appears most often in his discussion of
the notebooks, where he makes plain to
himself the simple, domestic, democratic
150 qualities in Hawthorne, and yet maintains
that he sets down slight and little aspects of
nature because his world is small and vacant.
Hawthorne noted these because he loved
them, and as a great painter, however full
155 and vast his world is, continues to jot down
whatever strikes him as picturesque and
characteristic. As a romance, the twelve years
of boyhood which he spent in the wild
solitudes of Maine were probably of greater
160 advantage to him than if they had been passed
at Eton and Oxford. At least, until some other
civilization has produced a romantic genius at
all comparable to his, we must believe this.

7   In the second sentence, the author of
Passage 1 lists several works of Hawthorne
that

(A)   were roundly criticized by other
authors
(B)   were published without his consent
(C)   were not as popular as his other works
(D)   were superior to most of his other
works
(E)   demonstrated Hawthorne's need for
adulation

8   The "orange" in line 17 is intended to
represent

(A)   the greed of certain publishers
(B)   the creative work of an author or artist
(C)   the conservative nature of writers
(D)   the published musings of gossip-
mongers
(E)   the respect for the privacy of artists

[2]Unsophisticated and narrow-minded

[3]A resident of London's East End who is looked down upon by
some Londoners as being unsophisticated.

GO ON TO THE NEXT PAGE ▶▶▶

9   The first sentence of the second paragraph makes the concession that

(A) Hawthorne became famous only after his death

(B) few of Hawthorne's manuscripts acquired after his death have actually been published

(C) Hawthorne approved of most of the publications under discussion

(D) Hawthorne's works are inferior to those of his contemporaries

(E) Hawthorne's reputation has not been damaged by the posthumous publication of his works

10   The reference to Hawthorne as the "last man" (line 43) serves to emphasize

(A) the lack of self-consciousness in his writing

(B) the difficulty he had in articulating his observations

(C) his lack of moral responsibility

(D) his inability to notice details

(E) the deep symbolism in his writing

11   In the last paragraph of Passage 1, the author indicates that Hawthorne's journals are characterized by

I. repressed feelings
II. intellectual casualness
III. an engaging style

(A) I only   (B) I and II only
(C) I and III only   (D) II and III only
(E) I, II and III

12   As it is used in line 95, the word "quarters" most nearly means

(A) segments of society

(B) housing units

(C) postures

(D) criticisms

(E) mercies

13   The author of Passage 2 foresees that James will be accused of "high treason" (line 95) because he has

(A) suggested that Hawthorne is an inferior author

(B) failed to acknowledge basic historical facts

(C) criticized the American government

(D) mischaracterized certain Americans

(E) violated a federal law

14   The author of Passage 2 mentions the "Parisian" in line 107 primarily as an example of one who

(A) lacks sophistication

(B) would not understand Hawthorne's work

(C) has not visited New England

(D) is widely regarded as being cosmopolitan

(E) is unfamiliar with Hawthorne's work

15   In the first two sentences of the second paragraph (lines 115–122), the author of Passage 2 criticizes James for

(A) showing bias toward American writers and against British writers

(B) maligning Hawthorne's writing style

(C) being insufficiently enthusiastic in his praise for Hawthorne

(D) focusing on Hawthorne's personal life rather than Hawthorne's work

(E) being too romantic

16   Which of the following best describes that attitude of the author of Passage 2 toward Nathaniel Hawthorne and his works?

(A) affectionate

(B) harshly critical

(C) mildly disapproving

(D) ambivalent

(E) incredulous

17 With which of the following statements about romance literature would the author of Passage 2 most likely agree?

(A) an international perspective enhances the quality of romances

(B) all romances are novels, but not all novels are romances

(C) the best romances reflect simple lifestyles, but not simple minds

(D) romance literature is inferior to poetry

(E) romance literature is intellectually challenging

18 The two authors differ in their evaluations of Hawthorne's journals primarily in that the author of Passage 1

(A) feels that they deserved to be published, while the author of Passage 2 does not

(B) feels that they have been unjustly criticized, while the author of Passage 2 feels that the criticisms are valid

(C) criticizes them for being too sophisticated, while the author of Passage 2 criticizes them for being too provincial

(D) praises them for their candidness, while the author of Passage 2 criticizes them for it

(E) suggests that they do not reflect Hawthorne's true genius, while the author of Passage 2 suggests that they do

19 How would the author of Passage 2 most likely respond to the statement in Passage 1 that Hawthorne's journals "show us one of the gentlest, lightest, and most leisurely of observers" (lines 46–47)?

(A) He would agree, and use this fact to criticize Hawthorne's style.

(B) He would disagree, and suggest that Hawthorne is in fact a very analytical observer.

(C) He would agree, and add that these are aspects of his genius.

(D) He would suggest that this fact is irrelevant to Hawthorne's work.

(E) He would suggest that this observation would apply to almost all American writing.

8

STOP

You may check your work, on this section only, until time is called.

Section 9

Time—10 Minutes
14 Questions

Directions for "Improving Sentences" Questions

Each of the sentences below contains one underlined portion. The portion may contain one or more errors in grammar, usage, construction, precision, diction (choice of words), or idiom. Some of the sentences are correct.

Consider the meaning of the original sentence, and choose the answer that best expresses that meaning. If the original sentence is best, choose (A), because it repeats the original phrasing. Choose the phrasing that creates the clearest, most precise and most effective sentence.

EXAMPLE:

The children <u>couldn't hardly believe their eyes.</u>

- (A) couldn't hardly believe their eyes
- (B) would not hardly believe their eyes
- (C) could hardly believe their eyes
- (D) couldn't nearly believe their eyes
- (E) could hardly believe his or her eyes

Example answer: (C)

---

1 Voters seem as interested in this <u>election, if not more so, than the last one.</u>

- (A) election, if not more so, than the last one
- (B) election as the last one, if not more so
- (C) election, if not more than, as the last one
- (D) election as it was for the last one, if not more so
- (E) election, if not more, than the last one

2 An indefatigable researcher as well as an engaging writer, <u>Tony Horwitz's book *Blue Latitudes* explores the journeys of James Cook.</u>

- (A) Tony Horwitz's book *Blue Latitudes* explores the journeys of James Cook
- (B) the book *Blue Latitudes* is where Tony Horwitz explores the journeys of James Cook
- (C) Tony Horwitz explores the journeys of James Cook in the book *Blue Latitudes*
- (D) Tony Horwitz explores the journeys, in the book *Blue Latitudes*, of James Cook
- (E) *Blue Latitudes*, a book by Tony Horwitz, explores the journeys of James Cook

3 His grade on the test <u>came as a surprise to Isaac, being since he had</u> studied so hard the previous night.

- (A) came as a surprise to Isaac, being since he had
- (B) came as a surprising fact for Isaac, being that he had
- (C) was surprising to Isaac for the fact that he had
- (D) surprised Isaac, especially because he had
- (E) surprised Isaac being that he had

4 <u>As opposed to women during the industrial revolution</u>, the treatment of women in today's work force is close to being equitable, although there is still much progress to be made.

- (A) As opposed to women during the industrial revolution
- (B) Unlike the treatment of women during the industrial revolution
- (C) Unlike women in the industrial revolution
- (D) As compared to women and their treatment of the industrial revolution
- (E) Unlike women's treatment of the industrial revolution

GO ON TO THE NEXT PAGE ▶▶▶

5 Finding a fulfilling second career is particularly important for former professional athletes, <u>most of them retire</u> from their first careers before they reach the age of forty.

(A) most of them retire
(B) although most of them retire
(C) most of whom retire
(D) while most of them retire
(E) but most of them retiring

6 Because the rules governing the behavior of electrons are so unlike any rules we commonly <u>experience is the reason why understanding</u> quantum physics is difficult.

(A) experience is the reason why understanding
(B) experience, understanding
(C) experience is why anyone's understanding
(D) experience, is why understanding
(E) experience, is the reason why to understand

7 Mark Twain's *Huckleberry Finn* is regarded not only as a classic of literature, <u>it is a scathing attack on</u> nineteenth century American society.

(A) it is a scathing attack on
(B) it attacks scathingly
(C) but it attacks scathingly
(D) but also as a scathing attack on
(E) but also it scathingly attacks

8 <u>Reading magazine advertisements carefully</u>, the writers seem more interested in impact than in correct grammatical form.

(A) Reading magazine advertisements carefully
(B) While we read magazine advertisements carefully
(C) Reading carefully the contents of magazine advertisements
(D) When you read magazine advertisements carefully
(E) As a careful reading of magazine advertisements demonstrates

9 The committee charged with finding a new chief executive wanted to find someone with a strong track record, a good reputation, and <u>someone with an ability to inspire the workers</u>.

(A) someone with an ability to inspire the workers
(B) they wanted someone to inspire the workers
(C) someone to inspire the workers
(D) an ability to be able to inspire the workers
(E) an ability to inspire the workers

10 <u>Nearly every summer afternoon, the park fills with the sounds of children who come to swim and play with their friends</u>.

(A) Nearly every summer afternoon, the park fills with the sounds of children who come to swim and play with their friends.
(B) Coming to swim and play with their friends nearly every summer afternoon, the park fills with the sounds of children.
(C) The sounds of children fill the park nearly every summer afternoon, them coming to swim and play with their friends.
(D) Coming to swim and play with their friends, the park fills with the sounds of children nearly every summer afternoon.
(E) The park fills with the sounds of children nearly every summer afternoon, who come to swim and play with their friends.

11 The campaign was not as much fun as Eleanor <u>had hoped, being</u> pursued by the press and attacked by her opponent at almost every turn.

(A) had hoped, being
(B) hoped in the sense that she was
(C) had hoped: she was
(D) had hoped because of being
(E) hoped; she has been

GO ON TO THE NEXT PAGE ▶▶▶

12 The artificial reef, constructed to protect coral and other anemones, occupies a large portion of the <u>inlet; but, therefore, obstructs</u> the migration of larger fish and sea mammals.

(A) inlet; but, therefore, obstructs
(B) inlet and therefore obstructs
(C) inlet; thereby obstructing
(D) inlet but because of this obstructs
(E) inlet but therefore obstructing

13 Being accelerated by a rocket in space provides the same experience to an observer as <u>if by gravity</u>.

(A) if by gravity
(B) gravity
(C) by gravity
(D) being accelerated by gravity
(E) acceleration by gravity

14 When applying to graduate school, one should visit the schools in person, <u>as the campus environment at one may differ vastly from another university</u>.

(A) as the campus environment at one may differ vastly from another university.
(B) since the campus environment may differ vastly from another university to this one.
(C) because the campus environment may differ greatly from university to university
(D) because the campus environment is greatly different from one another.
(E) as the campus environment at one may be vastly different from another university.

9

STOP

You may check your work, on this section only, until time is called.

ANSWER KEY

Section 2 Math	Section 5 Math	Section 7 Math	Section 3 Critical Reading	Section 6 Critical Reading	Section 8 Critical Reading	Section 4 Writing	Section 9 Writing
☐ 1. A	☐ 1. B	☐ 1. D	☐ 1. C	☐ 1. C	☐ 1. A	☐ 1. C	☐ 1. B
☐ 2. C	☐ 2. D	☐ 2. D	☐ 2. A	☐ 2. D	☐ 2. C	☐ 2. B	☐ 2. C
☐ 3. B	☐ 3. B	☐ 3. E	☐ 3. E	☐ 3. E	☐ 3. C	☐ 3. B	☐ 3. D
☐ 4. D	☐ 4. C	☐ 4. C	☐ 4. D	☐ 4. C	☐ 4. E	☐ 4. A	☐ 4. B
☐ 5. B	☐ 5. A	☐ 5. A	☐ 5. B	☐ 5. A	☐ 5. C	☐ 5. D	☐ 5. C
☐ 6. C	☐ 6. A	☐ 6. C	☐ 6. C	☐ 6. B	☐ 6. E	☐ 6. E	☐ 6. B
☐ 7. D	☐ 7. D	☐ 7. D	☐ 7. E	☐ 7. C	☐ 7. B	☐ 7. A	☐ 7. D
☐ 8. C	☐ 8. E	☐ 8. B	☐ 8. D	☐ 8. D	☐ 8. B	☐ 8. A	☐ 8. E
☐ 9. A	☐ 9. 80	☐ 9. E	☐ 9. E	☐ 9. E	☐ 9. E	☐ 9. C	☐ 9. E
☐ 10. D	☐ 10. 18	☐ 10. D	☐ 10. C	☐ 10. C	☐ 10. A	☐ 10. C	☐ 10. A
☐ 11. E	☐ 11. 116	☐ 11. B	☐ 11. E	☐ 11. D	☐ 11. E	☐ 11. E	☐ 11. C
☐ 12. D	☐ 12. 200	☐ 12. D	☐ 12. B	☐ 12. A	☐ 12. A	☐ 12. B	☐ 12. B
☐ 13. C	☐ 13. 18	☐ 13. D	☐ 13. A	☐ 13. E	☐ 13. D	☐ 13. B	☐ 13. D
☐ 14. B	☐ 14. 3	☐ 14. C	☐ 14. C	☐ 14. C	☐ 14. D	☐ 14. C	☐ 14. C
☐ 15. E	☐ 15. 17	☐ 15. C	☐ 15. E	☐ 15. A	☐ 15. C	☐ 15. E	
☐ 16. B	or 19	☐ 16. E	☐ 16. B	☐ 16. B	☐ 16. A	☐ 16. A	
☐ 17. C	☐ 16. 26/3		☐ 17. A	☐ 17. C	☐ 17. C	☐ 17. C	
☐ 18. D	or 8.66		☐ 18. E	☐ 18. E	☐ 18. E	☐ 18. D	
☐ 19. A	or 8.67		☐ 19. B	☐ 19. C	☐ 19. C	☐ 19. B	
☐ 20. A	☐ 17. 27		☐ 20. C	☐ 20. A		☐ 20. B	
	☐ 18. 30		☐ 21. D	☐ 21. B		☐ 21. C	
			☐ 22. A	☐ 22. E		☐ 22. D	
			☐ 23. D	☐ 23. C		☐ 23. E	
			☐ 24. D	☐ 24. D		☐ 24. A	
						☐ 25. B	
						☐ 26. D	
						☐ 27. A	
						☐ 28. C	
						☐ 29. B	
						☐ 30. B	
						☐ 31. E	
						☐ 32. E	
						☐ 33. C	
						☐ 34. B	
						☐ 35. E	

Right (A): _____

Questions 1–8
Right (A): _____

Right (A): _____

Right (A): _____

Right (A): _____

Right (A): _____

Right (A) _____

Right (A): _____

Wrong (B): _____

Wrong (B): _____

Wrong (B): _____

Wrong (B): _____

Wrong (B): _____

Wrong (B): _____

Wrong (B): _____

(A) – ¼ (B): _____

(A) – ¼ (B): _____

(A) – ¼ (B): _____

(A) – ¼ (B): _____

(A) – ¼ (B): _____

(A) – ¼ (B): _____

(A) – ¼ (B): _____

Questions 9–18
Right (A): _____

SCORE CONVERSION TABLE

How to score your test

Use the answer key on the previous page to determine your raw score on each section. **Your raw score on each section except Section 4 is simply the number of correct answers minus ¼ of the number of wrong answers. On Section 4, your raw score is the sum of the number of correct answers for questions 1–8 minus ¼ of the number of wrong answers for questions 1–8 plus the total number of correct answers for questions 9–18.** Next, add the raw scores from Sections 3, 4, and 7 to get your Math raw score, add the raw scores from Sections 2, 5, and 8 to get your Critical Reading raw score and add the raw scores from Sections 6 and 9 to get your Writing raw score. Write the three raw scores here:

Raw Critical Reading score: _____ Raw Math score: _____ Raw Writing score: _____

Use the table below to convert these to scaled scores.

Scaled scores: Critical Reading: _____ Math: _____ Writing: _____

Raw Score	Critical Reading Scaled Score	Math Scaled Score	Writing Scaled Score	Raw Score	Critical Reading Scaled Score	Math Scaled Score	Writing Scaled Score
67	800			32	520	550	610
66	800			31	510	550	600
65	790			30	510	540	580
64	780			29	500	530	570
63	760			28	490	520	560
62	750			27	490	530	550
61	730			26	480	510	540
60	720			25	480	500	530
59	700			24	470	490	520
58	700			23	460	480	510
57	690			22	460	480	500
56	680			21	450	470	490
55	670			20	440	460	480
54	660	800		19	440	450	470
53	650	790		18	430	450	460
52	650	760		17	420	440	450
51	640	740		16	420	430	440
50	630	720		15	410	420	440
49	620	710	800	14	400	410	430
48	620	700	800	13	400	410	420
47	610	680	800	12	390	400	410
46	600	670	790	11	380	390	400
45	600	660	780	10	370	380	390
44	590	650	760	9	360	370	380
43	590	640	740	8	350	360	380
42	580	630	730	7	340	350	370
41	570	630	710	6	330	340	360
40	570	620	700	5	320	330	350
39	560	610	690	4	310	320	340
38	550	600	670	3	300	310	320
37	550	590	660	2	280	290	310
36	540	580	650	1	270	280	300
35	540	580	640	0	250	260	280
34	530	570	630	−1	230	240	270
33	520	560	620	−2 or less	210	220	250

CONVERSION TABLE FOR WRITING COMPOSITE
[ESSAY + MULTIPLE CHOICE]

Calculate your writing raw score as you did on the previous page and grade your essay from a 1 to a 6 according to the standards that follow in the detailed answer key. Essay score: _____ Raw Writing score: _____

Use the table below to convert these to scaled scores.

Scaled scores: Writing _____

Raw Score	Essay Score 0	Essay Score 1	Essay Score 2	Essay Score 3	Essay Score 4	Essay Score 5	Essay Score 6
−2 or less	200	230	250	280	310	340	370
−1	210	240	260	290	320	360	380
0	230	260	280	300	340	370	400
1	240	270	290	320	350	380	410
2	250	280	300	330	360	390	420
3	260	290	310	340	370	400	430
4	270	300	320	350	380	410	440
5	280	310	330	360	390	420	450
6	290	320	340	360	400	430	460
7	290	330	340	370	410	440	470
8	300	330	350	380	410	450	470
9	310	340	360	390	420	450	480
10	320	350	370	390	430	460	490
11	320	360	370	400	440	470	500
12	330	360	380	410	440	470	500
13	340	370	390	420	450	480	510
14	350	380	390	420	460	490	520
15	350	380	400	430	460	500	530
16	360	390	410	440	470	500	530
17	370	400	420	440	480	510	540
18	380	410	420	450	490	520	550
19	380	410	430	460	490	530	560
20	390	420	440	470	500	530	560
21	400	430	450	480	510	540	570
22	410	440	460	480	520	550	580
23	420	450	470	490	530	560	590
24	420	460	470	500	540	570	600
25	430	460	480	510	540	580	610
26	440	470	490	520	550	590	610
27	450	480	500	530	560	590	620
28	460	490	510	540	570	600	630
29	470	500	520	550	580	610	640
30	480	510	530	560	590	620	650
31	490	520	540	560	600	630	660
32	500	530	550	570	610	640	670
33	510	540	550	580	620	650	680
34	510	550	560	590	630	660	690
35	520	560	570	600	640	670	700
36	530	560	580	610	650	680	710
37	540	570	590	620	660	690	720
38	550	580	600	630	670	700	730
39	560	600	610	640	680	710	740
40	580	610	620	650	690	720	750
41	590	620	640	660	700	730	760
42	600	630	650	680	710	740	770
43	610	640	660	690	720	750	780
44	620	660	670	700	740	770	800
45	640	670	690	720	750	780	800
46	650	690	700	730	770	800	800
47	670	700	720	750	780	800	800
48	680	720	730	760	800	800	800
49	680	720	730	760	800	800	800

Detailed Answer Key

Section I

The following essay received 12 points out of a possible 12, meaning that it demonstrates *clear and consistent competence* in that it

- develops an insightful point of view on the topic
- demonstrates exemplary critical thinking
- uses effective examples, reasons, and other evidence to support its thesis
- is consistently focused, coherent, and well-organized
- demonstrates skillful and effective use of language and sentence structure
- is largely (but not necessarily completely) free of grammatical and usage errors

Consider the following statement:

> *All art is a lie, and all art is the truth.* The beholder determines which.

Assignment: **Do artistic endeavours such as music, painting and drama enhance our understanding of reality or provide escape from reality?** Write an essay in which you agree or disagree with the statement above, using an example or examples from history, politics, literature, the arts, current events, or your experience or observation.

SAMPLE STUDENT ESSAY

For centuries, aestheticians and common people alike have wondered about the nature of art. Most of us haven't formulated a philosophical definition of art, but we "know it when we see it." Although this does not constitute a formal definition of art, it indicates an important aspect of art: it must have a significant impact on the viewer (or reader or listener). Of course, any particular painting, or book, or piece of music, no matter how well-crafted, is not likely to have the same impact on all who experience it. Thus, it may be art for some but not for others; it has meaning or "truth" for some, but not for others. In this regard, all art is a lie, and all art is the truth.

Art that is "a lie" is art that does not "ring true," that is, it does not resonate with our beings. I remember taking a trip into Manhattan to visit the Metropolitan Museum of Art with my parents when I was ten years old. My father wanted us to see the ancient artifacts of the Greek and Mesopotamian civilizations. We had to pass huge colorful paintings of gallant men on horses and vibrant depictions of battle to get to the musty motionless stone statues of heads. None of the heads, it seemed, smiled. They didn't welcome us, they didn't want us to be there. These may have been "true" depictions of ancient heads, but to me they were a lie; they did not resonate in my soul.

The oil paintings in the upstairs galleries were a different story, though. Although my sophisticated 10 year-old brain told me that knights almost certainly did not carry their armor so lightly, that the clouds did not gleam so brightly above them, and that their horses could not have been so spotless and majestic, somehow they were nevertheless "true." They communicated to me. They told me that the people of 18th century Europe valued gallantry and adventure and romance, even if they may not have experienced it as vividly as these paintings suggested. They put me in touch with a people, if only in terms of their ideals and not their reality. The motionless, lifeless heads and torsos in the basements communicated nothing to me.

As we were eating ten-dollar sandwiches in the museum cafeteria, my dad said "It gives me chills to see those ancient statues and think about the artisans who carved them three or four thousand years ago. I feel like I'm touching one of those ancient Mesopotamians himself when I touch those statues." I knew he wasn't just saying that for my sake or my brother's sake. He really felt that way. The statues were "the truth" to him. A few years later, when I studied Greek civilization with a great teacher, I began to appreciate my father's words. But when I was ten, those statues were a lie.

The following essay received 10 points out of a possible 12, meaning that it demonstrates *adequate competence* in that it

- develops a point of view on the topic
- demonstrates some critical thinking, but perhaps not consistently
- uses some examples, reasons, and other evidence to support its thesis, but perhaps not adequately
- shows a general organization and focus, but shows occasional lapses in this regard
- demonstrates adequate but occasionally inconsistent facility with language
- contains occasional errors in grammar, usage, and mechanics

SAMPLE STUDENT ESSAY

Every work of art reveals some degree of truth about the artist. The choice of subject matter, the arrangement of the parts, the use of color, and so on, tell us perhaps more about who created the art than what the art is about. On the other hand, it is true that no piece of art can capture the whole truth.

A good example of a great work of art is the Mona Lisa. It is considered great perhaps not only because it conveys a great truth about beauty, but because it also leaves so much unsaid for the viewer to interpret. Who is this woman? What is her relationship with the artist? What does her elusive smile mean?

Leonardo Da Vinci perhaps left such questions unanswered because he wanted to "hide" something, so perhaps in that sense the work is a "lie." But is that such a bad thing? The challenge of interpretation and discovering some answers to questions that may not be perfectly answerable is one of the great challenges of appreciating art. Also, perhaps that is one of its greatest pleasures.

What makes any piece of art—a painting, a sculpture, a building, a piece of music—truly great is not it's ability to "reveal" a great truth but to merely hint at a greater beauty beyond the surface. Great music, like Beethoven's Ninth Symphony, take the listener to new places. It almost doesn't matter whether these new places are "true" or not, but just that they take us there

The following essay received 2 points out of a possible 12, meaning that it demonstrates *some incompetence* in that it

- has a seriously limited point of view
- demonstrates weak critical thinking
- uses inappropriate or insufficient examples, reasons, and other evidence to support its thesis
- is poorly focused and organized, and has serious problems with coherence
- demonstrates frequent problems with language and sentence structure
- contains errors in grammar and usage that obscure the author's meaning

SAMPLE STUDENT ESSAY

I don't know how you could say that all art is the truth and all art is a lie at the same time. It's saying two completely different things! What I think is that all art is fake basically. It doesn't really show the world like it is it only shows the way one guy sees it. People who are just artists don't always get out and see what is going on in the world, instead they spend a lot of time by themselves doing there art.

So maybe it isn't a lie but it isn't the truth because its just what one person thinks. A painting of someone sitting on a chair doesn't look exactly like her. Also, the amount of money people pay for some paintings is ridiculous. A lot of the paintings that sell for millions of dollars look like things that I could do easy. It makes me angry to think that some people can throw paint on a canvas in a couple of minutes and then have somebody pay them millions of dollars for it.

Detailed Answer Key

Section 2

1. A

$(x - y) = -2.$

$3(x - y)(x - y)(x - y) =$

Plug in: $3(-2)(-2)(-2) = -24$

---

2. C

What is 40% of 20ω?

Write equation: $x = 0.40(20\omega)$

Simplify: $x = 8\omega$

---

3. B   Notice that whenever an x-value increases by 1, the corresponding y-value increases by 4. This means that the "slope" of the linear equation is 4. This suggests that choice (B) is best, but you should plug in to check:

(A) $y = x + 7$

Plug in 3 for x: $y = 3 + 7 = 10$ OK

Plug in 4 for x: $y = 4 + 7 = 11$ NO

(B) $y = 4x - 2$

Plug in 3 for x: $y = 12 - 2 = 10$ OK

Plug in 4 for x: $y = 16 - 2 = 14$ OK

Plug in 5 for x: $y = 20 - 2 = 18$ OK

Plug in 6 for x: $y = 24 - 2 = 22$ OK

So (B) is clearly best!

---

4. D

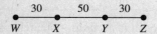

You are told that $XY = 50$ and that WY is 30 more than that. Therefore $WY = 80$, which means that $WX = 30 = YZ$. Therefore $XZ = 50 + 30 = 80$.

---

5. B   Segments AG, BD, EG, and AE are each diagonals of a face of the cube, but BE goes through the center of the cube and is longer than the others.

---

6. C

$3^{y + 4} = 81$

$3^4 = 81$

$3^4 = 3^{y + 4}$

Remove bases: $4 = y + 4$

Subtract 4: $y = 0$

---

7. D   Starting with quadrilateral at the bottom of the figure, solve for one the unmarked angle using the fact that there are 360° in a quadrilateral:

$80° + 80° + 120° + \omega = 360°$

Combine like terms: $280° + \omega = 360°$

Subtract 280°: $\omega = 80°$

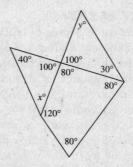

Since linear pairs have a sum of 180°, the two triangles contain angles of 100°.

There are 180° in a triangle: $x + 40 + 100 = 180$

Combine like terms: $x + 140 = 180$

Subtract 140°: $x = 40$

There are 180° in a triangle: $y + 30 + 100 = 180$

Combine like terms: $y + 130 = 180$

Subtract 130°: $y = 50$

$x + y = 40 + 50 = 90$

---

8. C   If neither a not b is 0, then ab cannot possibly equal 0, hence statement I is true. This eliminates choice (B). Since $a > b$, then $a - b$ must be positive. (Try a few examples with positive and negative numbers to convince yourself that this is true.) Therefore, statement II is true. This eliminates choices (A) and (D). Notice that a could equal 3 and b could equal -1, and so $a \div b$ could equal -3. So, statement III is false, leaving choice (C).

---

9. A   The closest the two towns can be to each other is $9 - 6 = 3$ miles. The farthest apart the two towns can be from each other is $9 + 6 = 15$ miles.

10. D If the perimeter of the solid-line figure is 100, then each side is $100 \div 10 = 10$ units long. If the pentagon has a perimeter of 60, then each of its sides is $60 \div 5 = 12$ units long. The altitude of one of the triangles, shown below, is one leg of a right triangle with a leg of 6 and hypotenuse of 10. You can find h, then, with the Pythagorean Theorem: $h^2 + 6^2 = 10^2$. This gives $h = 8$. So each triangle has a base of 12 and height of 8, so it has an area of $(1/2)(12)(8)=48$.

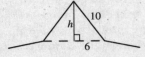

11. E The sum is 71:
The sum is 71:	$x + y = 71$
One is 2 + half the other:	$x = 2 + 0.5y$
Substitute for x:	$2 + 0.5y + y = 71$
Combine like terms:	$2 + 1.5y = 71$
Subtract 2:	$1.5y = 69$
Divide by 1.5:	$y = 46$

Since the sum is 71, the other number must be $71 - 46 = 25$, and the larger number is 46.

12. D A good diagram makes it clear:

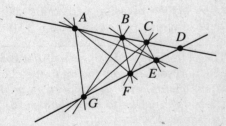

There are nine possible paths.

13. C There are 8 even integers between 2 and 16, inclusive: 2, 4, 6, 8, 10, 12, 14 and 16.
Solve:	$3\omega - 2 > 28$
Add 2:	$3\omega > 30$
Divide by 3:	$\omega > 10$

There are only three integers in the set greater than 10, so the fraction is 3/8.

14. B First solve for b: b is 20% greater than 400:
$$b = 1.20(400) = 480$$
Next solve for a: a is 20 percent less than b
$$a = 0.80(b) = 0.80(480) = 384$$
$$b - a = 480 - 384 = 96$$

15. E
	$m = n(n - 3)$
Multiply by -3:	$-3m = -3n(n - 3)$
Distribute:	$-3m = -3n^2 + 9n$
Rearrange:	$-3m = 9n - 3n^2$

16. B Don't try to find the area of the triangle directly(with $A = (1/2)bh$), because finding the base and height is too much work. Instead, find it *indirectly:* find the area of the rectangle and subtract the areas of the three "surrounding" triangles. The area of the rectangle = $(8)(4) = 32$. The area of $\triangle BEF = \frac{1}{2}(4)(2) = 4$. The area of $\triangle FCD = \frac{1}{2}(4)(4) = 8$. The area of $EAD = \frac{1}{2}(8)(2) = 8$. Therefore the area of $\triangle EFD = 32 - 4 - 8 - 8 = 12$.

17. C Eight consecutive odd integers can be represented as: $x, x + 2, x + 4, x + 6, x + 8, x + 10, x + 12$ and $x + 14$.
You can find their average with the formula:

$$\frac{x + (x + 2) + (x + 4) + (x + 6) + (x + 8) + (x + 10) + (x + 12) + (x + 14)}{8}$$

Combine like terms: $\dfrac{8x + 56}{8}$

Simplify: $x + 7$

18. D To get the largest possible value of a, you must make the other angles as *small* as possible. The smallest possible value of b is $21°$, and, because $c > b$, the smallest possible value of c is $22°$. There are $180°$ in a triangle, so set up an equation to find the largest possible value of a:
	$a + b + c = 180°$
Plug in for b and c:	$a + 21° + 22° = 180°$
Combine like terms:	$a + 43° = 180°$
Subtract $43°$:	$a = 137°$

19. **A**   Set up and solve: $\dfrac{4}{v} + w = 6$

Subtract $:\omega$ $\dfrac{4}{v} = 6 - w$

Divide by 4: $\dfrac{1}{v} = \dfrac{6-w}{4}$

Take reciprocal of both sides: $v = \dfrac{4}{6-w}$

20. **A**   The radius, *r*, of the arc that the tip traces is 4 inches. So in one full hour the minute hand traces an arc equal to the full circumference of the circle.

$$C = 2\pi r$$

Plug in for *r*: $C = 2\pi(4) = 8\pi$

Each hour, the tip of the minute hand moves 8π inches. From 2:40 to 7:10 is $5^{1}/_{2}$ hours, so in that time the tip traces an arc of $(5.5)8\pi = 36\pi$ inches. Since there are 12 inches in a foot, this distance is $36\pi \div 12 = 3\pi$ feet.

Section 3

1. **C**   The word *but* indicates a contrast. *Contemporaries* are individuals that live in the same time period. *Naive assumptions* are ignorant, and so may be *mocked*. The *acceptance* of his contempraries would contrast the *lack of acceptance* today. *ridicule* = to make fun of; *corroborate* = to support; *affiliate* = to associate with; *mock* = to make fun of.

2. **A**   The word *although* indicates contrast. The rebels' *ferocity* will help their cause, but they are also *undisciplined*, a fact which will lead to their defeat. the missing word must go with *undisciplined*. *haphazard* = random, without form; *spartan* = disciplined; *apathetic* = lacking concern

3. **E**   The crews would be better able to help others after the massive rains and winds had *stopped*. The storm's *wrath* (fury) would "hurt" those in its path. *subside* = to settle down; *enthrall* = to thrill, *ebb* = to weaken; *compound* = to make worse; *masticate* = to chew; *abate* = to reduce in amount; *afflicted* = harmed.

4. **D**   The *wide variety of styles* suggests that her collection is *diverse*. *repugnant* = disgusting; *negligent* = lacking care; *banal* = boring, common; *eclectic* = of a wide variety; *incompetent* = lacking skill.

5. **B**   Blake's personality is not an ideal fit for a therapist because he cannot *provide a stabilizing influence* on his patients. This suggests that he is *irritable* and easily *riled* up. *cantankerous* = cranky; *placate* = to calm; *irascible* = easily angered; *riled* = upset; *equanimous* = even tempered; *infuriated* = angered; *euphoric* = full of joy; *provoked* = riled up, bothered; *choleric* = easily angered; *assuaged* = soothed.

6. **C**   The host was *taken aback* (surprised) by the demeanor of his guest. It was unusual for him to be so *harshly accosted* (attacked). The missing word should mean something like *confrontational*. *jocular* = joking; *congenial* = polite, friendly; *impudent* = bold, rude; *urbane* = polite; *erudite* = learned.

7. **E**   *Overcoming cancer* to win championships requires a large amount of determination. *perspicacity* = the ability to sense what others are feeling. *magnanimity* = generosity; *delirium* = a state of mental confusion; *vanity* = obsession with one's self; *pertinacity* = determination.

8. **B**   The opposing party suggested that the senator had lied, and so he is *responding to* the claims by his attackers. *champion* = to support; *impugn* = to attack as false; *emulate* = to copy; *laud* = to praise; *concur* = to agree

9. **C**   The narrator refers to *my son Semu* (line 6) and the quote in lines 13–14 makes it clear that Na-ne is the narrator's dead brother. Therefore Na-ne is Semu's uncle.

10. **C**   The first line makes it clear that Na-ne is absent, and perhaps has died. Therefore the quote in lines 13-14 addresses an absent person.

11. **E**   The passage states that before the *new reality*, some with the *power to act* had *elaborate theories that the poor were ... happy in their condition* (lines 4–5).

12. **B**   The passage states that *pressures ... on the fragile balance of our planet's ecosystem are compelling the rich. To take greater interest* in the poor and their *destructive use of crop lands, forests and watersheds* (lines 8–17).

13. A The narrator describes his task as *senseless nothing* (line 5), indicating that he regards his task with scorn or disdain.

14. C The paragraph indicates that his superiors are interested only in the *number* that the narrator presents to them, and this number represents the number of people who have crossed the bridge.

15. E The narrator says of his superiors that *the future perfect is their specialty* (line 42) *after having stated that they figure out ... how many people will have crossed the bridge in ten years* (line 40). This last statement, which uses the future-perfect tense, refers to his superior's need to use the current Numbers to predict future numbers. This task is called *extrapolation*.

16. B In saying that he *was a lynx-eyed devil*, the narrator says that *no speedometer could do better*, meaning that he counted accurately and quickly.

17. A In saying that the difference between their two counts really makes no odds, the chief statistician is saying that it does not matter. That is it makes no real difference because they allow for a *certain margin of error* (line 83).

18. E The purpose of the passage is to discuss various definitions of art, like *technical ability* (line 6) of artisans, the *product of such skillful execution* (line 10), *what artists create* (line 17), the *expression of emotion* (lines 56–57), and so on.

19. B The *extension* refers to the fact that a ceramic pot (an object) can be considered art because it is the result of *skillful execution* (line 10). therefore this refers to a connection between a skill and an object.

20. C The first paragraph suggests that, while earlier definitions of art focused on *technical ability* (line 6), the *currently popular* notion of art is that art is *what artists create* (line 7).

21. D In saying that *some items and activities in our environment... are somehow more artistic than others*, the author is saying that it is often hard to explain why some things seem beautiful to our senses.

22. A The *ancient, encompassing definition of art* (lines 23–24) defines art *as products and activities skillfully done*. The *ancient Greek definition of aesthetic* (lines 68–70), however, focuses on *sensuous perception*, emphasizing the experiences of the viewer.

23. D According to this theory, *major art institutions ...determine what is and what is not art* (lines 97–98).

24. D In referring to a *fixed definition of art* (line 104), the author is contrasting a theory *that evolves* (line 105). Therefore, *fixed* means *not evolving*.

Section 4

1. C The phrase that follows *is* should be logically and grammatically equivalent to *activity*, like *the swimming*.

2. B Choice B provides the most concise, yet logically parallel, alternative.

3. B The original sentence does not show the logical relationship between the ideas. Choice B shows the most logical relationship and contains a logical sequence of tenses.

4. A The sentence is correct. The sentence begins with a **participial phrase**, which must be followed by the subject of the participle, which is *Jane*.

5. D The two ideas contrast each other, and so require a contrasting conjunction. Also, the correct **idiom** is *happy to see*, not *happy in seeing*.

6. E The original sentence is not **parallel**. The phrase *not only A but also B* requires that *A* and *B* be in the same grammatical form.

7. A The sentence is correct.

8. A The sentence is correct. It contains the clearest verb and the least awkward phrasing.

9. C The pronoun *which* in the original sentence has an unclear antecedent. Choices (B) and (D) misuse the semicolon, and choice (E) contains a **comma splice**.

10. C The ideas must be joined with a contrasting conjunction, and the tense sequence must be logical. Choice (C) shows correct temporal and logical sequencing.

11. E   The original phrasing is wordy, awkward, and vague. Choice (E) is the most concise and clear.

12. B   The phrase *usually never* is **illogical**, because *usually* and *never* are logically exclusive terms. The word *usually* should be eliminated.

13. B   The pronoun *it* is singular, but its **antecedent**, *bombs*, is plural. The pronoun should be *they*.

14. C   This verb tense, the past perfect, requires a **past participle**. The past participle of the verb *to take* is *taken*.

15. E   The sentence is correct.

16. A   This verb is in the **past perfect** tense, but it should not be, because it refers to an action that occurred at the same time as the *gun sounded*, and so should be in the **simple past** tense: *began*. (Chapter 18, Lesson 9)

17. C   The verb *are* is conjugated for a plural subject, but its subject is *effort*, which is singular. The verb should be changed to *is*.

18. D   This is an incorrect **idiom**. The correct idiom is *desire to eat*.

19. B   This is an **inverted sentence**, in which the subject comes after the verb. The subject of the verb *was* is *Blue Ridge Mountains*, which is a plural subject. Therefore the verb should be *were*.

20. B   This is an incorrect **parallel form**. The correct form is *neither A nor B*.

21. C   This is an incorrect **idiom**. The correct idiom is *voiced concerns **about***.

22. D   This is an **illogical comparison**. The *ability of insects* is not the same kinds of things as *whales*. this should be changed to *the ability of whales*.

23. E   The sentence is correct.

24. A   The word *I* is a pronoun in the **improper case**. Since it is the object of a preposition, *of*, it should be in the **objective case**, *me*.

25. B   The subject of this verb is *investment*, which is singular. Therefore, the verb should be *is*.

26. D   This is a **diction error**. *Imminent* means *likely to happen soon*, but *eminent* means *well-known and well-respected*.

27. A   The **antecedent** of these pronouns is *students*. The pronoun should therefore be plural: *them*.

28. C   This is an **illogical comparison**. The *fingerprints* cannot logically match the *defendant*, but rather the *defendant's fingerprints*.

29. B   This is an **improper idiom**. One is *affected by* things rather than *affected about* them.

30. B   Choice (B) provides the most logical, concise and clear phrasing.

31. E   Choice (E) provides the most logical, concise and clear phrasing.

32. E   Sentence 8 is not logically related to the topic of the paragraph, which is the meaning of sports and the idolization of sports figures in the United States.

33. C   Choice (C) provides the most logical, concise and clear phrasing.

34. B   Choice (B) provides the most logical transition from the previous sentence, which discusses particular *skills* related to both sports and hunting.

35. E   Choice (E) provides the most parallel and logical comparison with *our need to play sports*.

Section 5

1. B

	$a/3 = b/2$
Substitute $a = 36$:	$36/3 = b/2$
Simplify:	$12 = b/2$
Multiply by 2:	$24 = b$

2. D

	$2c + d = 9.25$
Multiply by 3:	$6c + 3d = 27.75$
Add 3:	$6c + 3d + 3 = 30.75$

3. B   The fact that the vertex of the triangle has coordinates $(6, m)$ means that the triangle has a base of 6 and a height of m. Use the formula *area* $= (1/2)bh$

Substitute:	$12 = (1/2)m(6)$
Simplify:	$12 = 3m$
Divide by 3	$4 = m$

4. **C** The seven possible combinations: 1) just pepperoni, 2) just mushrooms, 3) just meatballs, 4) pepperoni and mushroom, 5) pepperoni and meatballs, 6) meatballs and mushroom, 7) all 3.

5. **B** If the length of a rectangle is l and its width is w, then its perimeter is $2l + 2w$. If the perimeter is 5 times the width, then

$$2l + 2w = 5w$$
Subtract $2w$: $\qquad 2l = 3w$
Divide by 2: $\qquad l = 1.5w$

6. **A**
$$16^{w+2} = 2^{11}$$
Notice that 16 is equal to 2^4: $\qquad (2^4)^{w+2} = 2^{11}$
Simplify: $\qquad (2)^{4w+8} = 2^{11}$
Equate exponents: $\qquad 4w + 8 = 11$
Subtract 8: $\qquad 4w = 3$
Divide by 4: $\qquad w = 3/4$ or 0.75

7. **D** In a parallelogram, consecutive angle must be supplementary. Therefore, if the angle at B is $x°$, the angles at A and C are each $180-x°$. Since the angle at A is bisected, it is divided into two angles each with measure $90 - \frac{1}{2}x°$.

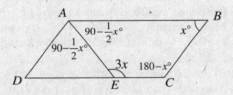

Now you can use the fact that the sum of the angles in a quadrilateral is $360°$. In quadrilateral $ABCE$,

$$x + (180 - x) + 3x + (90 - \tfrac{1}{2}x) = 360$$
Simplify: $\qquad 2.5x + 270 = 360$
Subtract 270: $\qquad 2.5x = 90$
Divide by 2.5: $\qquad x = 36$

8. **E** Since the width of the rectangle is 75% as long as the length, $w = .75l$. The perimeter, then, is $l + l + .75l + .75l = 3.5l$.

$\qquad 3.5l = 84$
Divide by 3.5: $\qquad l = 24$
Find the width: $\qquad w = (.75)(24) = 18$

Now you can find the diagonal of the rectangle with the Pythagorean Theorem: $\qquad d^2 = 18^2 + 24^2$
Simplify: $\qquad d^2 = 900$
Take the square root: $\qquad d = 30$
Therefore the diagonal of the circle is 30, and its radius is $30/2 = 15$. The area of the circle, then, is $\pi(15)^2 = 225\pi$.

9. **80** Recall the *formula distance = rate × time*.
Substitute: $\qquad 100$ miles $= 75$ mph $\times$ *time*
Divide by 75 mph: $\qquad 4/3$ hours $=$ *time*
Convert: $4/3$ hours $\times 60$ min/hr $= 80$ minutes

10. **18**
$\qquad |3x - 53| < 1.2$
Translate: $\qquad -1.2 < 3x - 53 < 1.2$
Add 53: $\qquad 51.8 < 3x < 54.2$
Divide by 3: $\qquad 17.3 < x < 18.1$
The only integer in that range is 18.

11. **116** If the average of five numbers is 30, then their sum must be $5 \times 30 = 150$. To maximize one of these numbers, you must minimize the sum of the other four. If they are all *different integers*, and the least of them is 7, then the least possible sum of four of these numbers is $7 + 8 + 9 + 10$. To find the greatest value,

$\qquad 7 + 8 + 9 + 10 + x = 150$
Simplify: $\qquad 34 + x = 150$
Subtract 34: $\qquad x = 116$

12. **200** If the ratio of girls to boys is 8:5, then (since the "whole" is $8 + 5 = 13$) girls are 8/13 of the class and boys are 5/13 of the class. The total number of boys, then is 5/13 of $520 = 200$.

13. **18** The volume of a rectangular solid is given by the formula *volume = l × w × h*. Since the width of this box is 1.5 and its volume is 27, then $\qquad 27 = (1.5)(l \times h)$
Divide by 1.5: $\qquad 18 = l \times h$
This formula, $l \times h$, gives the area of the shaded face.

14. **3** Perhaps the simplest approach is to assume that the price of stock B is $100. If the price of stock B is 35% greater than the price of stock B to start, then stock A starts at $135. If the price of stock A doubles, then it ends up at $2 \times \$135 = \$270$. If the price of stock B decreases by 10%, it ends up at $(0.9)(\$100) = \$90$. $270/90 = 3$, so stock A ends up at 3 times the price of stock B.

15. **17 or 19**   Here, the key is noticing that the $2a°$ angle is an "exterior" angle to the triangle on the left, and so is equal to the sum of the two "remote interior" angles.

Therefore	$2a = 3b + 3b$
Simplify:	$2a = 6b$
Divide by 2:	$a = 3b$

Since the problem states that a and b are integers, this means that a is a multiple of 3. Since the problem also states that a is odd and between 50 and 60, the only possibilities for a are 51 and 57.

16. **26/3 or 8.66 or 8.67**   A geometric sequence is one in which each term is calculated by multiplying the previous term by some constant. The problem states that $L = a + 1 + 3$, and $M = b + 3 + 1$. If these are both geometric sequences, then in the first sequence, we are multiplying by 3, and in the second sequence, we are multiplying by 1/3. Therefore, you can calculate to find the missing terms: $L = 1/3 + 1 + 3$ and $M = 9 + 3 + 1$. So $M - L = 13 - 4\ 1/3 = 8\ 2/3$ which is 26/3 or 8.666 . . .

17. **27**   If the range of $y = f(x)$ is all real numbers between -1 and 12, inclusive, then its greatest possible value is 12. The graph of the function $y = f(x-1)$ is simply the graph of $y = f(x)$ "shifted right" 1 unit. This means that the range of y values remains the same, and the maximum value is still 12. Finding the maximum value of $g(x) = 2f(x-1) + 3$ is a tiny bit trickier, but just involves substituting 12 as the maximum value for $f(x-1)$. This gives $2(12) + 3 = 27$.

18. **30** $20 < x < 30$
Choose x to be a number very close to 30, like 29.9. This means $5x = 149.5$ and $4x = 119.6$. Therefore #$5x = 148$ and #$4x = 118$, and $148-118 = 30$.

Section 6

1. **C**   The ability to *reflect on past experiences* is called *hindsight* or *retrospection*. *vagueness* = lack of clarity; *misconceptions* = erroneous ideas; *hindsight* = ability to reflect on past experiences; *antagonism* = personal dislike; *premonitions* = predictions

2. **D**   *Elaborate plumage and energetic dances* are examples of *showy* displays; but if they are used by males who are not chosen as mates, they are *pointless*. *carnivorous* = meat-eating; *ostentatious* = showy; *futile* = having no effect; *passive* = not active

3. **E**   the passage states that these are *entertaining stories*, but the fact that they are *disjointed* would detract from the *cohesiveness* of the story. *pluralities* = multitudes; *implausibility* = incredibleness; *missives* = written letters; *frivolity* = lack of seriousness; *treatises* = formal written analyses; *vignettes* = humorous or telling stories; *cohesiveness* = focus, lack of digression

4. **C**   If *fast* horses are *hard to control*, then *slower* horses would be relatively *easy to control*. *nimble* = quick and flexible; *irascible* = easily angered; *tractable* = easy to control; *recalcitrant* = stubborn

5. **A**   A *greater oversight* is an *increase in vigilance*. If this requires funds, then not providing them would be a *critical flaw*. *appropriate* = to set aside for a specific purpose; *vigilance* = watchfulness; *empathy* = deep sympathy; *embezzle* = steal from one's employer; *sequester* = to place in isolation; *industry* = diligent, productive work

6. **B**   The passage says that Einstein found fame *incomprehensible*, but that Chaplin was *worldly-wise*, and Chaplin's response to Einstein demonstrates that he understands the nature of celebrity.

7. **C**   Einstein's question is asking why people are treating him like a celebrity.

8. **D**   This sentence summarizes something that *traditional codes of medical ethics ... emphasize* (lines 1–2). therefore it comes from a long-established tenet.

9. **E**   The passage states that these attitudes are reflected in discussions that *speak more and more about the moral rights of patients* (lines 14–15).

10. **C**   The first paragraph states that we do such a disagreeable thing as arguing because we want to *make good decisions* (line 5), or act judiciously.

11. **D**   The purpose of the passage as a whole is to answer the questions in the first paragraph, which pertain to the purpose of argumentation. The questions in the second paragraph, however, are examples of questions that might help someone to explore a particular issue, but which are not answered in this passage.

12. **A**   The purpose of the passage as a whole is to discuss the different purposes of argumentation. The second paragraph describes arguing as *an opportunity to explore and probe ... claims*. The third paragraph describes the ability of an argument to *persuade others*.

13. **E**   *Polly Politician* is described as using *"hedge Words"* which render her claims very vague. This is also called *equivocation*, which is a failure to make definitive statements.

14. **C**   The *arguments* mentioned in the third paragraph are *situations (in which) we do not have the opportunity to reply*, unlike those in the fifth paragraph, in which *someone presenting us with a position expects either assent or disagreement*, and also expects us to *explain* our position. The latter Arguments are dialogues, while the former are one-sided.

15. **A**   The analogy is used to liken an informal argument with *a friendly game of tennis*, and the *outrageous maneuvers* are intended to parallel novel methods of making a persuasive point.

16. **B**   This paragraph refutes the misconception that one should never argue about religion or politics (lines 80–81) by explaining why doing so helps us to avoid problems.

17. **C**   In saying that a frame of mind *took him before or during a climb* (line 24), the author means that it *overcame* him.

18. **E**   The statement *we read ... every scrap* conveys the idea that they eagerly awaited every bit of news that came to them about Mallory's expedition.

19. **C**   The narrator mentions in the previous paragraph (line 29) that the expedition was in Tibet, which is where Mount Everest is located. In the dream, however, the expedition headquarters was in Switzerland. the narrator restates the absurdity of this aspect of her dream in line 79, where she refers to the absurd setting of the dream, and particularly that the headquarters was in a Swiss town. (An inconsequence is something that does not follow logically.)

20. **A**   Mallory's attitude is said to be characterized by *a strange mixture of reverence and what I can only call rapture* (line 63). These clearly express a feeling of awe.

21. **B**   When the author says that she is *too accustomed to the inconsequent dottiness of dreams* (lines 83–84), she is saying that she knows too well that dreams can have very silly elements in them, but this quality is *inconsequent* because she *could not comfort (herself)* (line 78) with the thought that it was a dream, and was still *frightened ... terribly* (line 64).

22. **E**   The first reference to a *fortnight (two weeks)* mentions that it took about that long for information about the expedition to reach the author. The second reference mentions that she received notice of George's death one fortnight after her dream, suggesting that her dream and his death may have occurred at about the same time.

23. **C**   This sentence states that the author *cannot believe* that George did not reach the summit, because she had climbed with him before and was confident of his skill.

24. **D**   The passage as a whole focuses on the narrator's relationship with George Mallory, who was killed on Mount Everest. The narrator mentions that her daughter was George's godchild (line 109) and therefore had a special connection to Mallory.

Section 7

1. **D**   Just combine like terms:
   $(x + 4) + (2x - 3) + 6 + (3x + 4) = 6x + 11$

2. **D**   To find the total amount, find the product of those two numbers: $\$3.00 \times 5,400 = \$16,200$

3. **E**   The container contains 2 pints of water. Since there are 2 cups in 1 pint, it contains $2 \times 2 = 4$ cups. Since there are 16 tablespoons in 1 cup, it contains $4 \times 16 = 64$ tablespoons. If 8 tablespoons are poured out, there are $64 - 8 - 56$ remaining of the original 64. $56/64 = 7/8$.

4. C There are 180° on one side of a line.

$$y° + (2y - 6)° = 180°$$

Combine like terms: $3y - 6° = 180°$

Add 6°: $3y = 186°$

Divide by 3: $y = 62°$

---

5. A The question asks, essentially, how long it will take her to make up the $3,000 she spends on her air-conditioning system. She saves $125 – $25 = $100 per month. It would therefore take her $3,000 ÷ $100 = 30 months to make up the cost.

---

6. C Start in the "units" column at the far right: if there is no "carry," then $A + B = B$, and $A = 0$. Then look at the hundreds column and notice that C must equal 1 because the sum of two two-digit numbers cannot exceed 198. Now you can rewrite the problem as:

$$\begin{array}{r} B\,0 \\ +\,6B \\ \hline 10\,B \end{array}$$

From the tens column, $B + 6 = 10$, so $B = 4$.

---

7. D

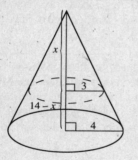

Dividing the cone with a parallel cross section forms similar triangles as shown in the diagram above. To solve for the height of the smaller cone set up a ratio:

$$\frac{14}{4} = \frac{x}{3}$$

Cross multiply: $42 = 4x$

Divide by 4: $10.5 = x$

---

8. B The longest side of the triangle is the hypotenuse, which is $x + 3$. The legs are $x + 1$ and $x - 1$.

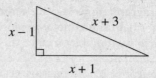

Now, solve for x using the Pythagorean Theorem:

$$(x + 1)^2 + (x - 1)^2 = (x + 3)^2$$

FOIL: $(x^2 + 2x + 1) + (x^2 - 2x + 1) = (x^2 + 6x + 9)$

Combine like terms: $2x^2 + 2 = x^2 + 6x + 9$

Subtract x^2: $x^2 + 2 = 6x + 9$

Subtract $6x$: $x^2 - 6x + 2 = 9$

Subtract 9: $x^2 - 6x - 7 = 0$

Factor: $(x - 7)(x + 1) = 0$

Find zeroes: $x = 7$ or $x = -1$

Of course, x cannot be –1 because the sides cannot have a negative length, so $x = 7$ and the sides are 6, 8, and 10. The perimeter therefore = 6 + 8 + 10 = 24

---

9. E The pattern repeats every 5 terms, to find which digit is in the 3,000th place divide 3,000 by 5 and find the remainder: 3,000 ÷ 5 = 600.00. Since there is no remainder, the term must be the last one in the pattern.

---

10. D The portions of the pie graph dedicated to regions II and III constitute 70° + 50° = 120°, which is 1/3 of the whole circle (1/3 of 360° = 240°). Therefore, region I represents 2/3 of the whole, and 2/3 of 12,000 is 8000.

---

11. B

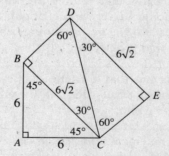

The figure consists of a 45–45–90 triangle and two identical 30–60–90 triangles. You know that they are identical because you are told that side BD and CE are parallel and thus hypotenuse CD creates alternate interior angles that are equal to each other. Because triangle *BAC* is a 45–45–90 triangle, the sides are $x - x - x\sqrt{2}$. Therefore the hypotenuse of the triangle is $6\sqrt{2}$. Because the two 30–60–90 triangles are identical, you do not need to do any further math as side *DE* will be the same as side *BC*.

12. D The graph of the function $y = f(x + 3) + 3$ is equivalent to the function $y = f(x)$ shifted to the LEFT 3 and UP 3, as shown in answer choice D.

---

13. D Don't calculate; the number is too big, so you will need to use your factoring skills and knowledge of exponents. $5^{2000} + 5^{2002} = 5^{2000}(1 + 5^2) = 5^{2000}(26) = 5^{2000}(13)(2)$. This is a complete prime factorization, so the prime factors are 2, 5, and 13.

---

14. C   If $r = s^6$, then it follows that $s = r^{1/6}$.
If $r = t^4$, then it follows that $t = r^{1/4}$.
$st = (r^{1/6})(r^{1/4})$

Add exponents: $st = r^{((1/6)+(1/4))}$
Simplify: $st = r^{5/12}$

---

15. C
$x\,\Omega\,y = (x - y)^2$
$x\,\Omega\,y = 2x\,\Omega\,3$
$(x - y)^2 = (2x - 3)^2$

Substitute $(y - 3)$ for x: $((y - 3) - y)^2 = (2x - 3)^2$
Combine like terms: $(-3)^2 = (2x - 3)^2$
FOIL: $9 = 4x^2 - 6x - 6x + 9$
Combine like terms: $0 = 4x^2 - 12x$
Factor: $0 = 4x(x - 3)$
Divide by x: $4x = 0$ or $x - 3 = 0$
Use the zero-product property: $x = 0$ or $x = 3$

---

16. E To find his average speed in miles per hour for the four races combined, divide the total distance traveled (in miles) by the total time of the races (in hours). Each race was 1 mile, so he ran a total distance of 4 miles. He finished the four races in a combined $(a + b + c + d)$ minutes, which is equivalent to $(a + b + c + d)/60$ <u>hours</u>.

$$\frac{4 \text{ miles}}{\dfrac{a + b + c + d}{60} \text{ hours}} = \frac{240}{a + b + c + d} \text{ mph}$$

Section 8

1. A The word *but* indicates a contrast; the opposite of an asset is a *liability*. *liability* = handicap; *novelty* = new experience; *compliment* = kind words.

---

2. C The *although* indicates an impending contrast. The fact that they would consider *accepting it without revision* suggests that it must be a quality report. After the semi-colon the sentence states that the report was *thorough* (complete), but contained errors. So, it would be inappropriate (*remiss*) to accept it without first correcting those errors. *inarticulate* = incomprehensible at speech; *negligent* = characterized by careless informality; *comprehensive* = complete; *remiss* = exhibiting carelessness.

---

3. C Davis was confident, but not *excessively confident*. *complacent* = overconfident; *coherent* = clear-headed; *latent* = present, but hidden.

---

4. E The doctors hoped the regimen would *energize* Dina, but it did not. The word *indeed* indicates that it in fact had the opposite effect, so she must have felt *weakened* and more *sluggish* than ever. *sanguine* = cheerfully optimistic; *lithe* = graceful and flexible; *torpid* = lethargic, lacking energy; *conciliated* = placated; *despondent* = depressed; *enervated* = weakened; *phlegmatic* = sluggish.

---

5. C If there are *far more (symbols) than even a perspicacious (keenly perceptive) critic can interpret*, it must have *tons* of them! *modicum* = small amount; *rectitude* = properness; *surfeit* = excessive amount; *dearth* = lack; *sequester* = to place in isolation.

---

6. E The criminals are planning to *divert* (distract) their pursuers; a *false* lead would do that. Such a plan is very *sneaky*. *venerable* = worthy of respect; *veritable* = genuine, real; *decrepit* = old, worn down; *contrived* = planned, calculated; *forthright* = honest; *specious* = false but plausible; *scheming* = sneaky; *credible* = legitimate; *duplicitous* = sneaky; *spurious* = false.

---

7. B These works are described as *liberal excisions from the privacy* (line 6) of Hawthorne. This means that they were taken from a man who wanted them kept private, so they were published without his permission.

---

8. B The *orange* being squeezed dry, in this case, is Hawthorne's genius, which is being exploited by those who wish to publish his posthumous (after-death) works.

9. E The sentence says that there is no *visible detriment conferred on Mr. Hawthorne's fame*, that is, that his reputation is not harmed, by the publication of these works.

10. A By saying that Hawthorne was *the last man to have attempted to explain himself*, the author is saying that Hawthorne was not concerned with his own emotions or motivations in his writings.

11. E The last paragraph states that Hawthorne's journals were characterized by repressed feelings (*the author seems to have been reserved even with himself*, lines 64–65), intellectual casualness (*strolling ... in blessed intellectual irresponsibility*, lines 48–49), and an engaging style (*a style individual and delightful*, lines 53–54).

12. A In saying that James will *in some quarters be attainted of high treason*, the author means that some people in American society will be very upset with James' characterizations of them.

13. D The *treason* is the description of the people of Salem and Concord as *"provincial,"* when, according to the author, they are not.

14. D The *Parisian of his time* is intended to provide an ironic contrast to the "provincial" Hawthorne, whom, the author of Passage 2 claims, is actually more *universal* than most city-dwellers.

15. C The author complains that James *puts too slight a value upon Hawthorne's work*, or does not praise it highly enough.

16. A The author of Passage 2 expresses great affection for Hawthorne by calling him *a romantic genius* (line 163) and for his works by saying that they have no parallel in any literature (lines 123–124).

17. C The two central points in this passage are that Hawthorne is not a *provincial*, that is, simple-minded man, and that he is a singularly masterful writer of romances, which are characterized by *simple, domestic, democratic* qualities. Therefore, romances are the products of simple lifestyles, but not simple minds.

18. E The author of passage 1 states that Hawthorne's journals *singularly diminish our impression of his general intellectual power* (lines 33–34), while the author of Passage 2 says that they reflect his thoughts as a *great painter* (line 155).

19. C In the first three sentences of the final paragraph of Passage 2, the author summarizes these same qualities of Hawthorne in making the point that Hawthorne is a *romantic genius* (line 163).

Section 9

1. B The phrase *if not more so* is an interrupter. When an interrupter is removed, the remaining sentence should be logically and grammatically correct. Choice (B) provides a clear re-phrasing.

2. C The sentence begins with an **appositive**, which is a noun phrase that is adjacent to another noun or noun phrase and which explains it. This appositive clearly refers to *Tony Horwitz* and not his book. Choice (C) corrects the dangling appositive, and places the other modifiers correctly.

3. D The phrase *being since* is not standard. Choice (D) is most logical, standard and clear.

4. B The original comparison is **illogical**. The *treatment of women* cannot logically oppose *women*. Choice (C) provides the most logical comparison.

5. C As it is phrased, the original sentence is a **run-on** or a **comma splice**. The clause that follows the commas must be a **dependent clause**, like the one in (C).

6. B The word *because* allows for a very concise phrasing to relate the two clauses. Choice (B) is the most concise.

7. D The phrase *not only A but also B* requires that *A* and *B* be parallel. Choice (D) is most parallel.

8. E The original sentence starts with a **dangling participial phrase**, that is a participial phrase without a noun to modify. Choice (E) provides a logical and complete phrasing.

9. E The original phrasing is **not parallel**. The three items in the list are most parallel with choice (E).

10. A The original sentence is best.

11. **C** In the original phrasing, the participle *being* is misplaced. The second clause explains the first, so the semicolon in (C) provides a logical conjunction.

12. **B** Phrases joined by a semicolon must be **independent clauses**, and so the original phrasing is incorrect. Choice (B) joins independent clauses with a conjunction, and the logical coordinator *therefore*.

13. **D** The comparison in the original sentence is **illogical**. Choice (D) provides a logical and parallel comparison.

14. **C** The comparison in the original sentence is **illogical**. Choice (C) provides a logical and parallel comparison.

PRACTICE TEST 7

ANSWER SHEET

Last Name: _____   First Name: _____

Date: _____   Testing Location: _____

Directions for Test

- Remove these answer sheets from the book and use them to record your answers to this test.
- This test will require 3 hours and 20 minutes to complete. Take this test in one sitting.
- The time allotment for each section is written clearly at the beginning of each section. This test contains six 25-minute sections, two 20-minute sections, and one 10-minute section.
- This test is 25 minutes shorter than the actual SAT, which will include a 25-minute "experimental" section that does not count toward your score. That section has been omitted from this test.
- You may take one short break during the test, of no more than 10 minutes in length.
- You may only work on one section at any given time.
- You must stop ALL work on a section when time is called.
- If you finish a section before the time has elapsed, check your work on that section. You may NOT work on any other section.
- Do not waste time on questions that seem too difficult for you.
- Use the test book for scratchwork, but you will receive credit only for answers that are marked on the answer sheets.
- You will receive one point for every correct answer.
- You will receive no points for an omitted question.
- For each wrong answer on any multiple-choice question, your score will be reduced by ¼ point.
- For each wrong answer on any numerical "grid-in" question, you will receive no deduction.

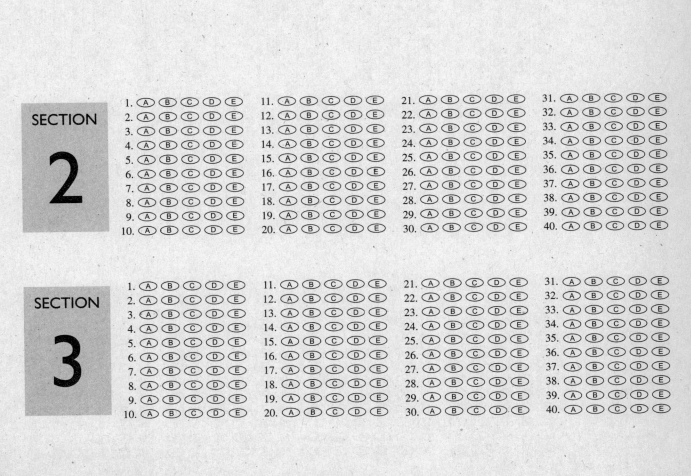

ANSWER SHEET

SECTION 4

1. Ⓐ Ⓑ Ⓒ Ⓓ Ⓔ   5. Ⓐ Ⓑ Ⓒ Ⓓ Ⓔ
2. Ⓐ Ⓑ Ⓒ Ⓓ Ⓔ   6. Ⓐ Ⓑ Ⓒ Ⓓ Ⓔ
3. Ⓐ Ⓑ Ⓒ Ⓓ Ⓔ   7. Ⓐ Ⓑ Ⓒ Ⓓ Ⓔ
4. Ⓐ Ⓑ Ⓒ Ⓓ Ⓔ   8. Ⓐ Ⓑ Ⓒ Ⓓ Ⓔ

9. 10. 11. 12. 13.

14. 15. 16. 17. 18.

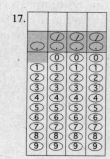

SECTION 5

1. Ⓐ Ⓑ Ⓒ Ⓓ Ⓔ   11. Ⓐ Ⓑ Ⓒ Ⓓ Ⓔ   21. Ⓐ Ⓑ Ⓒ Ⓓ Ⓔ   31. Ⓐ Ⓑ Ⓒ Ⓓ Ⓔ
2. Ⓐ Ⓑ Ⓒ Ⓓ Ⓔ   12. Ⓐ Ⓑ Ⓒ Ⓓ Ⓔ   22. Ⓐ Ⓑ Ⓒ Ⓓ Ⓔ   32. Ⓐ Ⓑ Ⓒ Ⓓ Ⓔ
3. Ⓐ Ⓑ Ⓒ Ⓓ Ⓔ   13. Ⓐ Ⓑ Ⓒ Ⓓ Ⓔ   23. Ⓐ Ⓑ Ⓒ Ⓓ Ⓔ   33. Ⓐ Ⓑ Ⓒ Ⓓ Ⓔ
4. Ⓐ Ⓑ Ⓒ Ⓓ Ⓔ   14. Ⓐ Ⓑ Ⓒ Ⓓ Ⓔ   24. Ⓐ Ⓑ Ⓒ Ⓓ Ⓔ   34. Ⓐ Ⓑ Ⓒ Ⓓ Ⓔ
5. Ⓐ Ⓑ Ⓒ Ⓓ Ⓔ   15. Ⓐ Ⓑ Ⓒ Ⓓ Ⓔ   25. Ⓐ Ⓑ Ⓒ Ⓓ Ⓔ   35. Ⓐ Ⓑ Ⓒ Ⓓ Ⓔ
6. Ⓐ Ⓑ Ⓒ Ⓓ Ⓔ   16. Ⓐ Ⓑ Ⓒ Ⓓ Ⓔ   26. Ⓐ Ⓑ Ⓒ Ⓓ Ⓔ   36. Ⓐ Ⓑ Ⓒ Ⓓ Ⓔ
7. Ⓐ Ⓑ Ⓒ Ⓓ Ⓔ   17. Ⓐ Ⓑ Ⓒ Ⓓ Ⓔ   27. Ⓐ Ⓑ Ⓒ Ⓓ Ⓔ   37. Ⓐ Ⓑ Ⓒ Ⓓ Ⓔ
8. Ⓐ Ⓑ Ⓒ Ⓓ Ⓔ   18. Ⓐ Ⓑ Ⓒ Ⓓ Ⓔ   28. Ⓐ Ⓑ Ⓒ Ⓓ Ⓔ   38. Ⓐ Ⓑ Ⓒ Ⓓ Ⓔ
9. Ⓐ Ⓑ Ⓒ Ⓓ Ⓔ   19. Ⓐ Ⓑ Ⓒ Ⓓ Ⓔ   29. Ⓐ Ⓑ Ⓒ Ⓓ Ⓔ   39. Ⓐ Ⓑ Ⓒ Ⓓ Ⓔ
10. Ⓐ Ⓑ Ⓒ Ⓓ Ⓔ   20. Ⓐ Ⓑ Ⓒ Ⓓ Ⓔ   30. Ⓐ Ⓑ Ⓒ Ⓓ Ⓔ   40. Ⓐ Ⓑ Ⓒ Ⓓ Ⓔ

ANSWER SHEET

SECTION 6

1. (A) (B) (C) (D) (E)
2. (A) (B) (C) (D) (E)
3. (A) (B) (C) (D) (E)
4. (A) (B) (C) (D) (E)
5. (A) (B) (C) (D) (E)
6. (A) (B) (C) (D) (E)
7. (A) (B) (C) (D) (E)
8. (A) (B) (C) (D) (E)
9. (A) (B) (C) (D) (E)
10. (A) (B) (C) (D) (E)

11. (A) (B) (C) (D) (E)
12. (A) (B) (C) (D) (E)
13. (A) (B) (C) (D) (E)
14. (A) (B) (C) (D) (E)
15. (A) (B) (C) (D) (E)
16. (A) (B) (C) (D) (E)
17. (A) (B) (C) (D) (E)
18. (A) (B) (C) (D) (E)
19. (A) (B) (C) (D) (E)
20. (A) (B) (C) (D) (E)

21. (A) (B) (C) (D) (E)
22. (A) (B) (C) (D) (E)
23. (A) (B) (C) (D) (E)
24. (A) (B) (C) (D) (E)
25. (A) (B) (C) (D) (E)
26. (A) (B) (C) (D) (E)
27. (A) (B) (C) (D) (E)
28. (A) (B) (C) (D) (E)
29. (A) (B) (C) (D) (E)
30. (A) (B) (C) (D) (E)

31. (A) (B) (C) (D) (E)
32. (A) (B) (C) (D) (E)
33. (A) (B) (C) (D) (E)
34. (A) (B) (C) (D) (E)
35. (A) (B) (C) (D) (E)
36. (A) (B) (C) (D) (E)
37. (A) (B) (C) (D) (E)
38. (A) (B) (C) (D) (E)
39. (A) (B) (C) (D) (E)
40. (A) (B) (C) (D) (E)

SECTION 7

1. (A) (B) (C) (D) (E)
2. (A) (B) (C) (D) (E)
3. (A) (B) (C) (D) (E)
4. (A) (B) (C) (D) (E)
5. (A) (B) (C) (D) (E)
6. (A) (B) (C) (D) (E)
7. (A) (B) (C) (D) (E)
8. (A) (B) (C) (D) (E)
9. (A) (B) (C) (D) (E)
10. (A) (B) (C) (D) (E)

11. (A) (B) (C) (D) (E)
12. (A) (B) (C) (D) (E)
13. (A) (B) (C) (D) (E)
14. (A) (B) (C) (D) (E)
15. (A) (B) (C) (D) (E)
16. (A) (B) (C) (D) (E)
17. (A) (B) (C) (D) (E)
18. (A) (B) (C) (D) (E)
19. (A) (B) (C) (D) (E)
20. (A) (B) (C) (D) (E)

21. (A) (B) (C) (D) (E)
22. (A) (B) (C) (D) (E)
23. (A) (B) (C) (D) (E)
24. (A) (B) (C) (D) (E)
25. (A) (B) (C) (D) (E)
26. (A) (B) (C) (D) (E)
27. (A) (B) (C) (D) (E)
28. (A) (B) (C) (D) (E)
29. (A) (B) (C) (D) (E)
30. (A) (B) (C) (D) (E)

31. (A) (B) (C) (D) (E)
32. (A) (B) (C) (D) (E)
33. (A) (B) (C) (D) (E)
34. (A) (B) (C) (D) (E)
35. (A) (B) (C) (D) (E)
36. (A) (B) (C) (D) (E)
37. (A) (B) (C) (D) (E)
38. (A) (B) (C) (D) (E)
39. (A) (B) (C) (D) (E)
40. (A) (B) (C) (D) (E)

SECTION 8

1. (A) (B) (C) (D) (E)
2. (A) (B) (C) (D) (E)
3. (A) (B) (C) (D) (E)
4. (A) (B) (C) (D) (E)
5. (A) (B) (C) (D) (E)
6. (A) (B) (C) (D) (E)
7. (A) (B) (C) (D) (E)
8. (A) (B) (C) (D) (E)
9. (A) (B) (C) (D) (E)
10. (A) (B) (C) (D) (E)

11. (A) (B) (C) (D) (E)
12. (A) (B) (C) (D) (E)
13. (A) (B) (C) (D) (E)
14. (A) (B) (C) (D) (E)
15. (A) (B) (C) (D) (E)
16. (A) (B) (C) (D) (E)
17. (A) (B) (C) (D) (E)
18. (A) (B) (C) (D) (E)
19. (A) (B) (C) (D) (E)
20. (A) (B) (C) (D) (E)

21. (A) (B) (C) (D) (E)
22. (A) (B) (C) (D) (E)
23. (A) (B) (C) (D) (E)
24. (A) (B) (C) (D) (E)
25. (A) (B) (C) (D) (E)
26. (A) (B) (C) (D) (E)
27. (A) (B) (C) (D) (E)
28. (A) (B) (C) (D) (E)
29. (A) (B) (C) (D) (E)
30. (A) (B) (C) (D) (E)

31. (A) (B) (C) (D) (E)
32. (A) (B) (C) (D) (E)
33. (A) (B) (C) (D) (E)
34. (A) (B) (C) (D) (E)
35. (A) (B) (C) (D) (E)
36. (A) (B) (C) (D) (E)
37. (A) (B) (C) (D) (E)
38. (A) (B) (C) (D) (E)
39. (A) (B) (C) (D) (E)
40. (A) (B) (C) (D) (E)

SECTION 9

1. (A) (B) (C) (D) (E)
2. (A) (B) (C) (D) (E)
3. (A) (B) (C) (D) (E)
4. (A) (B) (C) (D) (E)
5. (A) (B) (C) (D) (E)
6. (A) (B) (C) (D) (E)
7. (A) (B) (C) (D) (E)
8. (A) (B) (C) (D) (E)
9. (A) (B) (C) (D) (E)
10. (A) (B) (C) (D) (E)

11. (A) (B) (C) (D) (E)
12. (A) (B) (C) (D) (E)
13. (A) (B) (C) (D) (E)
14. (A) (B) (C) (D) (E)
15. (A) (B) (C) (D) (E)
16. (A) (B) (C) (D) (E)
17. (A) (B) (C) (D) (E)
18. (A) (B) (C) (D) (E)
19. (A) (B) (C) (D) (E)
20. (A) (B) (C) (D) (E)

21. (A) (B) (C) (D) (E)
22. (A) (B) (C) (D) (E)
23. (A) (B) (C) (D) (E)
24. (A) (B) (C) (D) (E)
25. (A) (B) (C) (D) (E)
26. (A) (B) (C) (D) (E)
27. (A) (B) (C) (D) (E)
28. (A) (B) (C) (D) (E)
29. (A) (B) (C) (D) (E)
30. (A) (B) (C) (D) (E)

31. (A) (B) (C) (D) (E)
32. (A) (B) (C) (D) (E)
33. (A) (B) (C) (D) (E)
34. (A) (B) (C) (D) (E)
35. (A) (B) (C) (D) (E)
36. (A) (B) (C) (D) (E)
37. (A) (B) (C) (D) (E)
38. (A) (B) (C) (D) (E)
39. (A) (B) (C) (D) (E)
40. (A) (B) (C) (D) (E)

Section 1

Time—25 minutes
1 Question

Directions for Writing Essays

Plan and write an essay that answers the question below. Do NOT write on another topic. An essay on another topic will receive a score of 0.

Two readers will grade your essay based on how well you develop your point of view, organize and explain your ideas, use specific and relevant examples to support your thesis, and use clear and effective language. How well you write is much more important than how much you write, but to cover the topic adequately you should plan to write several paragraphs.

Your essay must be written on separate lined sheets of paper. Keep your handwriting to a reasonable size. Your essay will be read by people who are not familiar with your handwriting, so write legibly.

You may use this sheet for notes and outlining, but these will not be graded as part of your essay.

Consider carefully the issue discussed in the following passage, then write an essay that answers the question posed in the assignment.

> A year is a long time—365 individual days. In that span, the earth has made a full revolution around the sun, entire species have evolved while others have become extinct, and governments have formed and dissolved. If we cannot reflect on the last 12 months and say how we have changed for the better, we must change the way we are living."

Assignment: **What is the most important thing that you have learned in the past year?** Write an essay in which your answer this question and support your position logically with examples from literature, the arts, history, politics, science and technology, current events, or your experience or observation.

Write your essay on separate sheets of paper.

Section 2

Time — 25 minutes
24 Questions

Each sentence below has one or two blanks, each blank indicating that something has been omitted. Beneath the sentence are five words or sets of words labeled A through E. Choose the word or set of words that, when inserted in the sentence, <u>best</u> fits the meaning of the sentence as a whole.

Example:

Medieval kingdoms did not become constitutional republics overnight; on the contrary, the change was ———.

(A) unpopular   (B) unexpected
(C) advantageous   (D) sufficient
(E) gradual

Correct response: (E)

1 The ——— of good Sunday afternoon television shows became apparent when David watched yet another mindless infomercial.

(A) influx   (B) scarcity
(C) glut   (D) abundance
(E) authenticity

2 *Morningside*, the winner of the Triple Crown, was easy to handle all morning, but then turned suddenly ——— and refused to take a rider.

(A) energetic   (B) obstinate
(C) monotonous   (D) cooperative
(E) tractable

3 The already ——— Middle East peace talks were ——— when a destructive car bombing broke the cease-fire agreement between the two countries.

(A) placid . . aborted
(B) harmonious . . terminated
(C) tenuous . . abandoned
(D) volatile . . enhanced
(E) fragile . . complemented

4 The prosecutor's _____ evidence was impossible to _____ and as such, the defendant knew that he would go to prison.

(A) ironclad . . refute
(B) dubious . . disprove
(C) indisputable . . authenticate
(D) irrefutable . . corroborate
(E) surreptitious . . invalidate

5 On January 24th, 1975, McDonald's opened the world's first drive through window in Sierra Vista, Arizona, an ——— concept that revolutionized the fast food industry.

(A) inane   (B) insipid
(C) innocuous   (D) innovative
(E) intrepid

6 President Nixon's ——— actions during the Watergate scandal brought him much deserved public censure and led to his resignation.

(A) commendable   (B) inconceivable
(C) laudable   (D) exemplary
(E) reprehensible

7 As has been the case with many scientists throughout history, Gregor Mendel's success in unraveling the mechanisms of inheritance was ———; he stumbled upon the precise species of pea that produced the outcome he was looking for.

(A) serendipitous   (B) deliberate
(C) outlandish   (D) premeditated
(E) intangible

8 The critics ——— the most recent publication as derivative and ———; it offered nothing new or insightful to the materials already available to the scientific community.

(A) decried . . mundane
(B) hailed . . hackneyed
(C) condemned . . ingenious
(D) lauded . . vapid
(E) maligned . . avant-garde

GO ON TO THE NEXT PAGE ▶▶▶

2

Each passage below is followed by one or two questions based on its content. Answer each question based on what is stated or implied in the passage that precedes it.

Questions 9–10 are based on the following passage.

Line To trace and analyze a continuity of theme or obsession in a film director's work can be an intriguing exercise, but it does not prove that director to be an artist, or his films to be worth
5 writing about. To abstract films from the notion of value, whether artistic or moral, and to write about them not in relation to life, but in relation to concepts and themes, to abstracted philosophical, psychoanalytical
10 or sociological theory, or to each other ("Movies are about movies"), can certainly make the critics task a great deal easier. Taking refuge in intellectualism, he does not have to expose himself (or herself) to judgment
15 by the quality of his own experience or life, or by his capacity to evaluate and interpret it. "Value judgments" are not irrelevent to criticism, they are the very heart of it; but they do expose the critic to the same risks as
20 are run by the artist every time he ventures on the creative act.

9   As a whole, the passage cautions film critics against

(A)   becoming obsessed with the work of particular directors
(B)   taking risks
(C)   confusing art with reality
(D)   focusing exclusively on abstract analysis
(E)   failing to employ accepted philosophical standards

10   It can be inferred from the passage that the "risks" (line 19) include

(A)   being excessively analytical
(B)   creating an unattractive work of art
(C)   making a movie that is not lucrative
(D)   alienating one's peers
(E)   having one's work judged by others

Questions 11–12 are based on the following passage.

Line Structure is often a cause of friction in the relationship between the architect and his structural engineer. A good architect today must be a generalist, well versed in space
5 distribution, construction techniques, and electrical and mechanical systems, but also knowledgable in financing, real estate, human behavior and social conduct. In addition, he is an artist, entitled to the expression of his
10 aesthetic tenets. He must know about so many specialties that he is sometimes said to know nothing about everything. The engineer, on the other hand, is by training and mental make-up a pragmatist. He is an expert in
15 certain specific aspects of engineering and in those aspects only. There are today not only structural engineers, but structural engineers who specialize only in concrete design or only in the design of concrete domes or even
20 in the design of concrete domes of one particular shape. No wonder the engineer is said to be a man who knows everything about nothing! The personalities of these two are bound to clash. Lucky is the client whose
25 architect understands structure and whose structural engineer appreciates the aesthetics of architecture.

11   In saying that architects are sometimes said "to know nothing about everything," (line 12) the author means that they

(A)   value function over beauty
(B)   do not understand how to fund construction projects
(C)   require more education in human behavior
(D)   are too pragmatic
(E)   have a knowledge that is broad but shallow

GO ON TO THE NEXT PAGE ▸▸▸

First paragraph: *About John Ford*, Lindsay Anderson, McGraw Hill, ©1981, p 202
Second paragraph: *Why Buildings Stand Up*, Mario Salvadori, McGraw Hill, ©1980, p 24

12 In lines 20–21, the author mentions "concrete domes of one particular shape" to make the point that

(A) concrete is a particularly easy construction material to work with

(B) architects often prefer simple geometric shapes

(C) some engineers are highly specialized

(D) architects and engineers can collaborate successfully

(E) engineers are sometimes insufficiently trained

The questions below are based on the content of the preceding passage. The questions are to be answered on the basis of what is stated or implied in the passage itself or the introductory material that precedes the passage.

2

Questions 13–24 are based on the following passage.

The following passage is from a book about the appreciation of literature.

Line Reading literature is a common experience; it is by no means a simple experience. Literature may seem a simple matter of fact when one thinks of it as being black marks

5 on white pages; but as soon as the reader recognizes the marks as words—and as phrases, and sentences, and paragraphs—he has begun to leave the realm of the simple experience of the "real" object, the printed

10 page, and has begun to move in the world of abstractions. The black marks are soon seen to be symbols of other things, to "stand for" objects, processes, and situations.

In spite of the abstract quality of language,
15 there is a comforting familiarity about the printed page, for the words can be appreciated as common sounds and meanings remembered from conversation. Even when the words are unfamiliar, the dictionary will tell the reader

20 the correct sound and meaning. It all seems real enough and simple enough, for language is second nature with the adult and he does not think much about it. Indeed, it is probably true that for most readers books are palliatives,

25 something to fill the awkward pauses between periods of significant activity. Books pour from the presses and are read without being remembered—but "when literature is not memorable it is nothing."

30 Readers who believe that literature provides a memorable experience, who take the printed page seriously as an opportunity to enjoy a significant experience, are sometimes regarded with suspicion, as if they had lost

35 their touch with reality and become escapists victimized by the unrealities of the imagined world of fiction. Such suspicions are groundless, for the very world of reality in which we all live our daily lives is filled

GO ON TO THE NEXT PAGE ▶▶▶

2

40 with imagined experience. We look out the
    window at the street and we say, "It is wet
    out." This is an imagined experience, for
    wetness is a tactile sensation, not visual.
    We can judge weight of a stone without
45 lifting it because our visual response to the
    stone stimulates through our imagination
    (recollections of past experiences with stones)
    kinaesthetic sensations of muscular tensions.
    Much of thought proceeds by hypothesis—
50 that is, by trial and error. Imagination, the
    representation of things not present, is
    essential to our lives.

        Those who feel strongly the separation
    between literature and life, who are reluctant
55 to suspend their disbelief, have in a great
    measure missed out on one of the most
    profoundly civilizing of processes—the
    education of the senses and the pleasurable
    acquisition of that knowledge which is
60 necessary for our understanding of human
    experience.

        Yet life is not literature, nor is literature
    life; the two are distinct, but so much has
    been made of the distinction that they are
65 often seen as alien to one another. It is the
    alienation that does so much damage, that
    allows the writer to grow careless in his art
    and the reader to become casual and
    uncritical. It is when the reality of life and
70 the imagination of literature are brought
    together that the writer is honored for his
    skill and the reader is alerted to the
    importance of the art of reading. A reader's
    experience with a book is no different in
75 its nature than his experience with other
    objects in life. All experience is interactive; it
    is a traffic between the object and the
    subject. Actuality, the sense of living through
    an event with its emotional quality
80 of enjoyment or suffering, characterizes the
    experience of reading as it does the
    experience of living.

        In life, objects appear to us and we have
    sensations and impressions of them as they
85 impinge on our sensory organs; we adjust to
    the objects with every confidence that they
    are real. How often we are mistaken in our
    impression of the sensation, our judgment of
    the impression! Theseus, in *A Midsummer*
90 *Night's Dream*, speaks of the errors we make
    in judging: "in the night, imagining some
    fear, how easy is a bush supposed a bear!"
    The corrected impression may come in time
    or too late or it may never come at all.

95   In literature as in life the magic of the
    imagination creates vivid images that may
    develop in the reader a disposition to accept
    the images as physical reality, and what was
    at first imagined becomes at last directly
100 sensed. John Keats went so far as to express
    a *preference* for the imagined when he said,
    "Heard melodies are sweet, but those
    unheard are sweeter ..."

        Perhaps Keats was an uncommon reader,
105 for most of us still cling to the notion that we
    enjoy direct, lively sensations in life, but only
    the pale, reflected image of those sensations
    in literature. Generally, however, we
    underestimate the power of literature to affect
110 us directly. Indeed, we may not want it to
    move us deeply; in that case, when the
    images threaten to transcend their mirrorlike
    flatness and to become solidly real, we seek
    refuge in further abstractness: we become
115 more "educated," and a consciousness of
    words as words replaces the images evoked
    by the words, and consequently we are at a
    further and safer remove from life.

13 The statement that literature "is by no means
        a simple experience" (line 2) means that

    (A) it is very difficult to write good prose
    (B) literary analysis requires a great deal
         of technical knowledge
    (C) good literature elicits very powerful
         emotions
    (D) the process of interpreting words is
         complex
    (E) many of the best books are not
         widely available

14 The word "move" in line 10 refers to the
        progress of

    (A) a literary movement
    (B) a social phenomenon
    (C) a particular writer's work
    (D) a reader's thought process
    (E) literary criticism

GO ON TO THE NEXT PAGE ▶▶▶

15 The quotation in lines 28–29 is intended to contrast directly with the belief that

(A) books serve primarily to comfort readers
(B) a good story should be intellectually stimulating
(C) literature provides readers with vivid sensory experiences
(D) those who read a great deal are often poor conversationalists
(E) few people read great literature

16 The "suspicions" mentioned in line 37 are held by those who believe that literature

(A) can be too difficult for many readers to interpret
(B) is a highly rewarding experience
(C) can alienate readers from reality
(D) is not taught well in schools
(E) contains too little moral instruction

17 The "damage" mentioned in line 66 is caused by

(A) bringing life experiences together with literary ones
(B) the failure to acknowledge the work history of an author
(C) writing that is dull and unimaginative
(D) writing that focuses on escapist fantasies
(E) the emphasis on distinguishing between literary experiences and life experiences

18 In line 77, the word "traffic" most nearly means

(A) congestion
(B) merchandise
(C) detour
(D) crowd
(E) communication

19 The passage mentions "confidence" in line 86 to make the point that

(A) we often cannot detect objects in our immediate environment
(B) writers must rely on their creative instincts
(C) we usually trust that our sensory perceptions are correct
(D) we should not allow the fantasy world of novels to influence our everyday decisions
(E) critics are often biased in their judgments of literature

20 In line 88, the word "impression" most nearly means

(A) interpretation
(B) imitation
(C) stamp
(D) questioning
(E) approval

21 According to the passage, the "stone" in line 44 is similar to the "bush" in line 92 in that both

(A) represent literary metaphors
(B) are easily confused with other objects
(C) convey a particular mood
(D) are incapable of emotion
(E) are apprehended through the imagination

22 In the final two paragraphs, John Keats is mentioned primarily as an example of

(A) a writer who used imagery in his work
(B) one who had a vivid imagination
(C) a poet who departed from tradition
(D) one who warned against overeducation
(E) one who preferred real experience to imagination

GO ON TO THE NEXT PAGE ▶▶▶

2

23 According to the author, those who "become more 'educated'" (line 115) do so chiefly in order to

(A) learn the backgrounds of authors
(B) appreciate the nuances of a story they are reading
(C) become better writers
(D) avoid becoming too affected by literature
(E) change careers

24 Which of the following best summarizes the main idea of the passage?

(A) Schools should expose students to a wider range of literature.
(B) The power of literature is grasped through imagined experience.
(C) Escapist fiction is not true literature.
(D) Reading teachers should help students to translate words rather than to develop their imaginations.
(E) Good literature is comforting and familiar.

STOP

You may check your work, on this section only, until time is called.

Section 3

Time — 25 minutes
20 Questions

Directions for Multiple-Choice Questions

In this section, solve each problem, using any available space on the page for scratchwork. Then decide which is the best of the choices given and fill in the corresponding oval on the answer sheet.

- You may use a calculator on any problem. All numbers used are real numbers.
- Figures are drawn as accurately as possible EXCEPT when it is stated that the figure is not drawn to scale.
- All figures lie in a plane unless otherwise indicated.

3

Reference Information

$A = \pi r^2$ $A = \ell w$ $A = \frac{1}{2}bh$ $V = \ell wh$ $V = \pi r^2 h$ $c^2 = a^2 + b^2$ Special Right Triangles

$C = 2\pi r$

The arc of a circle measures 360°.
Every straight angle measures 180°.
The sum of the measures of the angles in a triangle is 180°.

---

1 If $6x + 4 = 7x - 3$, what is the value of x?

(A) 3
(B) 4
(C) 5
(D) 6
(E) 7

2 A batch of 3 dozen cookies requires 2 cups of sugar. How many cups of sugar are needed to bake 108 cookies? (1 dozen = 12 cookies)

(A) 4
(B) 5
(C) 6
(D) 7
(E) 8

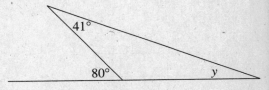

Note: Figure not drawn to scale.

3 In the figure above, what is the value of y?

(A) 39°
(B) 41°
(C) 43°
(D) 45°
(E) 47°

4 If 20 is 40% of w, what is 20% of w?

(A) 5
(B) 10
(C) 15
(D) 20
(E) 25

GO ON TO THE NEXT PAGE ▶▶▶

3

5 If each of the following lengths of rope is cut into the maximum possible number of 4-inch lengths, which will produce the greatest amount of excess rope?

(A) 15.0 inches
(B) 15.5 inches
(C) 16.0 inches
(D) 16.5 inches
(E) 17.0 inches

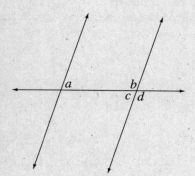

Note: Figure not drawn to scale.

6 In the figure above $l > m$ and $a = 80°$. What is the value of $b + c + d$?

(A) 200°
(B) 220°
(C) 260°
(D) 280°
(E) 320°

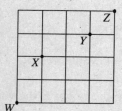

7 In the figure above, a continuous path is to be drawn from W to Z moving only up or to the right on the segments shown. How many such paths can be drawn that do not contain either X or Y?

(A) 10
(B) 12
(C) 14
(D) 16
(E) 18

8 Which of the following sets of numbers has the property that the sum of any two numbers in the set is also a number in the set?

    I.   The set of all odd integers
    II. The set of all even integers
    III. The set of all positive integers

(A) II only
(B) III only
(C) I and II only
(D) II and III only
(E) I, II, and III

9 Let the function f be defined by the equation $f(x) = 4x - 3$. Let g be defined by the equation $g(x) = x^2 + 3$. Which of the following represents $g(f(x))$?

(A) $16x^2 - 24x + 9$
(B) $16x^2 - 24x + 12$
(C) $16x^2 + 6$
(D) $16x^2 + 9$
(E) $16x^2 - 12x + 12$

10 If an integer, a, is divided by 6, the remainder is 5. What is the remainder when $4a$ is divided by 6?

(A) 1
(B) 2
(C) 3
(D) 4
(E) 5

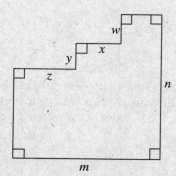

11 Which of the following is equal to the perimeter of the figure above?

(A) $2m + 2n$
(B) $m + n - (w + x + y + z)$
(C) $2(m + n) + (w + x + y + z)$
(D) $2(m + n) - (w + x + y + z)$
(E) $m + n + w + x + y + z$

GO ON TO THE NEXT PAGE ▶▶▶

12 Let $\begin{vmatrix} a & b \\ d & c \end{vmatrix}$ be defined for all real numbers

a, b, c, and d by the equation $\begin{vmatrix} a & b \\ d & c \end{vmatrix} = ab + cd$.

If $f = \begin{vmatrix} 2 & 3 \\ 5 & 4 \end{vmatrix}$, what is the value of $\begin{vmatrix} 2 & 7 \\ 3 & f \end{vmatrix}$?

(A) 26
(B) 34
(C) 70
(D) 92
(E) 108

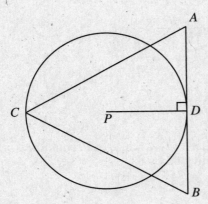

13 In the figure above, $\triangle ABC$ is equilateral. If the area of circle P is 75π, what is the perimeter of the triangle?

(A) $40 + 20\sqrt{3}$

(B) $40 + 10\sqrt{3}$

(C) 60

(D) $20 + 10\sqrt{3}$

(E) $20 + 20\sqrt{3}$

14 If the degree measures of the angles of a triangle are in the ratio of 3 : 4 : 5, what is the sum of the two smaller angles?

(A) 45°
(B) 60°
(C) 75°
(D) 105°
(E) 150°

15 A right circular cylinder has a height of 8. If the volume of the cylinder is 200π, what is the circumference of the base?

(A) 8π
(B) 10π
(C) 12π
(D) 24π
(E) 30π

16 The sum of two numbers is w and their difference is 4. In terms of w, what is the value of the lesser of the two numbers?

(A) $w - 4$

(B) $\dfrac{w - 4}{2}$

(C) $\dfrac{2w - 4}{3}$

(D) $\dfrac{w + 4}{2}$

(E) $w + 4$

17 A teacher picks three boys and four girls to participate in a game. She begins by arranging them in a line at the front of the room. If the students are arranged girl/boy/girl/boy/girl/boy/girl, how many different arrangements are possible?

(A) 24
(B) 48
(C) 72
(D) 96
(E) 144

$1, 2, -1, 3, -4 \ldots$

18 The first five terms in a sequence are shown above. After the second term, each term can be obtained by subtracting the previous term from the term before that. For example, the third term can be found by subtracting the second term from the first term: $-1 = 1 - 2$. How many of the first 42 terms of this sequence are negative?

(A) 18
(B) 19
(C) 20
(D) 21
(E) 22

GO ON TO THE NEXT PAGE ▶▶▶

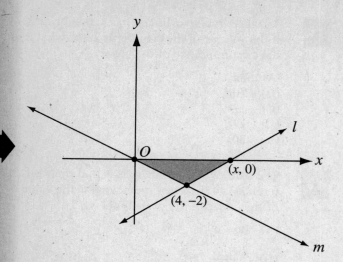

Note: Figure not drawn to scale.

19 In the figure above, if line l is perpendicular to line m, what is the area of the shaded triangle?

(A) 5
(B) 10
(C) 15
(D) 20
(E) 25

20 A group of s college students agreed to split equally the costs of a trip that costs a total of d dollars. If g students back out at the last minute, which of the following represents the extra amount that each student must pay as a result?

(A) $\dfrac{dg}{s^2 - sg}$

(B) $\dfrac{ds - dg}{s^2 - sg}$

(C) $\dfrac{ds}{g^2 - s}$

(D) $\dfrac{d}{s^2 - g}$

(E) $\dfrac{sg}{d^2 - sg}$

STOP

You may check your work, on this section only, until time is called.

Section 4

Time—25 Minutes
18 Questions

Directions for Multiple-Choice Questions

In this section, solve each problem, using any available space on the page for scratchwork. Then decide which is the best of the choices given and fill in the corresponding oval on the answer sheet.

- You may use a calculator on any problem. All numbers used are real numbers.
- Figures are drawn as accurately as possible EXCEPT when it is stated that the figure is not drawn to scale.
- All figures lie in a plane unless otherwise indicated.

Reference Information

$A = \pi r^2$
$C = 2\pi r$

$A = \ell w$

$A = \frac{1}{2}bh$

$V = \ell wh$

$V = \pi r^2 h$

$c^2 = a^2 + b^2$

Special Right Triangles

The arc of a circle measures 360°.
Every straight angle measures 180°.
The sum of the measures of the angles in a triangle is 180°.

---

1 When 4 times a number, n, is decreased by 6, the result is 26. What is the square of n?

(A) 8
(B) 16
(C) 32
(D) 36
(E) 64

2 A chef pours ¼ cup of oil into a measuring cup. How many cups of water must the chef add for the mixture to be 10% oil and 90% water?

(A) 1.75
(B) 2.00
(C) 2.25
(D) 2.50
(E) 2.75

```
  6        7
  8        4
  a        b
  b        c
  7        9
+ 5      + 6
 42       51
```

3 In the correctly worked addition problem above, what is the value of $c - a$?

(A) 6
(B) 9
(C) 16
(D) 25
(E) 41

4 If y is a positive integer and $2|y| + 4 < 14$, then what is the largest possible value of y?

(A) 2
(B) 4
(C) 5
(D) 8
(E) 9

GO ON TO THE NEXT PAGE ▶▶▶

5 If $4n^2 = 20$ and $3m^2 = 12$, what is the value of $(n - m)(n + m)$?

(A)   1
(B)   2
(C)   4
(D)   8
(E)   12

4 ➤ **6** The average (arithmetic mean) of five different positive integers is 30. What is the greatest possible value of any of these integers?

(A)   130
(B)   134
(C)   138
(D)   140
(E)   146

7 Every freshman at Alston Academy is required to participate in at least one spring after-school sports program among softball, soccer, and tennis. No student is allowed to participate in more than 2 sports. If 80 students play softball, 60 students play soccer, 90 students play tennis and 40 play 2 of the 3 sports, how many freshmen are there at Alston Academy?

(A)   150
(B)   190
(C)   230
(D)   260
(E)   270

8 Miguel drove to his office in the morning at an average speed of 30 miles per hour. He returned home, along the same route, at 20 miles per hour. If Miguel spent a total of two hours commuting to and from work, what is the distance from his office to his home?

(A)   12.0
(B)   18.0
(C)   20.0
(D)   24.0
(E)   37.5

Directions for Student-Produced Response Questions

Each of the questions in this section requires you to solve the problem and enter your answer in a grid, as shown below.

- If your answer is ⅔ or .666 ..., you must enter **the most accurate value the grid can accommodate**, but you may do this in one of four ways:

Start in first column

Grid result here

Start in second column

Grid as a truncated decimal

Grid as a rounded decimal

- In the example above, gridding a response of 0.67 or 0.66 is **incorrect** because it is less accurate than those above.
- The scoring machine cannot read what is written in the top row of boxes. You **MUST** fill in the numerical grid accurately to get credit for answering any question correctly. You should write your answer in the top row of boxes only to aid your gridding.
- Do **not** grid in a mixed fraction like $3\frac{1}{2}$ as $\boxed{3\,|\,1\,|\,/\,|\,2}$ because it will be interpreted as $\frac{31}{2}$. Instead, convert it to an improper fraction like ⅞ or a decimal like 3.5 before gridding.
- None of the answers will be negative, because there is no negative sign in the grid.
- Some of the questions may have more than one correct answer. You must grid only one of the correct answers.
- You may use a calculator on any of these problems.
- All numbers in these problems are real numbers.
- Figures are drawn as accurately as possible EXCEPT when it is stated that the figure is not drawn to scale.
- All figures lie in a plane unless otherwise indicated.

9   If $4x = 10$ and $5y = 9$, then $8x - 10y =$

10   When a positive odd integer, p, is increased by 20 percent of itself, the result is an integer between 40 and 55. What is one possible value of p?

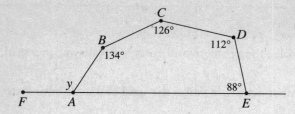

Note: Figure not drawn to scale.

11 In the figure above, F, A, and E lie on the same line. What is the value of y?

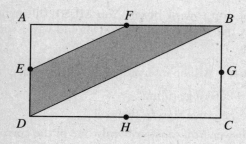

12 In rectangle $ABCD$ above, $AF = BF = AD$. If $EA = ED$, and $DC = 8$, what is the area of the shaded region?

13 If $4^{p+r} = 1,024$ and $2^p = 16$, then what is the value of 2^r?

14 If y divided by one-fourth is 32, what is the value of $y^{\frac{1}{3}}$?

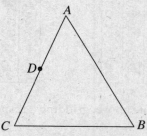

Note: Figure not drawn to scale.

15 In the figure above, $AD = DC = 10$. If the area of the triangle in the figure above is 240 square inches, and $\angle BAC = \angle BCA$, what is its perimeter?

GO ON TO THE NEXT PAGE ▶▶▶

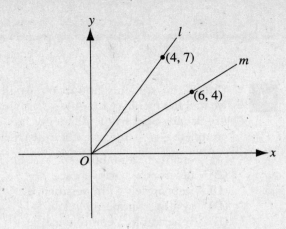

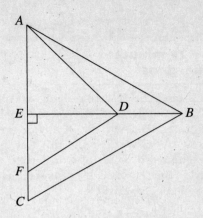

Note: Figure not drawn to scale.

16 Line n (not shown) passes through the origin and it passes in between lines l and m. What is one possible value of the slope of line n?

17 In $\triangle ABC$ above, $\dfrac{EB}{ED} = \dfrac{4}{3}$ and $\dfrac{AC}{AF} = \dfrac{5}{4}$. What is the quotient formed when the area of $\triangle ABC$ is divided by the area of $\triangle ADF$?

18 A jar contains 32 black, red, and yellow marbles. There are 4 times as many yellow marbles as red marbles, and 3 times as many black marbles as red marbles. What is the probability that, if 3 marbles are selected at random from the jar, without replacement, all of them are yellow?

You may check your work, on this section only, until time is called.

Section 5

Time—25 minutes
24 Questions

Each sentence below has one or two blanks, each blank indicating that something has been omitted. Beneath the sentence are five words or sets of words labeled A through E. Choose the word or set of words that, when inserted in the sentence, <u>best</u> fits the meaning of the sentence as a whole.

Example:

Medieval kingdoms did not become constitutional republics overnight; on the contrary, the change was ———.

(A) unpopular   (B) unexpected
(C) advantageous   (D) sufficient
(E) gradual

Correct response: (E)

1 A fight broke out in the high school cafeteria when one student made ——— remark about another student's mother.

(A) a gracious   (B) an impromptu
(C) a barren   (D) a derogatory
(E) a complimentary

2 Portuguese water dogs are _____ breed known for the extreme drive and determination with which they perform their assigned tasks.

(A) a corpulent   (B) a languid
(C) a diligent   (D) a dilatory
(E) a vacuous

3 The politician's excessively ——— demeanor, while perhaps justified because he had never lost an election, was costing him votes because the American public did not appreciate ———.

(A) haughty . . an egotist
(B) conceited . . a prevaricator
(C) diffident . . an extrovert
(D) cavalier . . an augur
(E) meticulous . . an autocrat

4 Unlike the students at Lincoln High who treated the faculty with ———, the students at Broad Spectrum Academy act with complete ——— towards their instructors.

(A) civility . . amiability
(B) deference . . irreverence
(C) impropriety . . impertinence
(D) apathy . . impunity
(E) veneration . . compliance

5 During the seventeenth and eighteenth centuries, the written works of African American authors were often ——— by others and as a result the contributions of the original authors have been ———.

(A) filched . . exonerated
(B) expurgated . . undisclosed
(C) appropriated . . misattributed
(D) commiserated . . miscalculated
(E) pilfered . . celebrated

GO ON TO THE NEXT PAGE ▶▶▶

Each passage below is followed by one or two questions based on its content. Answer each question based on what is stated or implied in the passage that precedes it.

Questions 6–7 are based on the following passage.

Line There are two ways in which paper-and-pencil tests fail to represent the whole domain of intelligent behavior. One has to do with the nature of the tests themselves. Most
5 real-life problems cannot be posed in the form of conventional test items without seriously distorting the problem; even a "what would you do?" question about how to deal with, say, disruptive behavior in a classroom cannot
10 possibly capture the complexity and immediacy of the real-life situation. Furthermore, the use of the multiple-choice format tends to limit the kinds of items that are written and in some instances the nature of the cognitive
15 processes involved in taking a test. The other major limitation of conventional testing is that there is very little variation in the situations in which data are collected. Tests are typically administered in academic settings
20 where the expectation is that one should strive for as many "right" answers as possible, following specified time limits and procedures. In real life, one might decide to settle for an approximation or a probability that satisfies
25 his or her own needs rather than strive for an optimal solution; or one might postpone the problem until he or she can talk to someone or get a book off the shelf.

6 This passage is concerned primarily with

(A) defining intelligent behavior
(B) demonstrating how to improve multiple-choice tests
(C) showing deficiencies in a method of assessment
(D) explaining different methods of solving problems
(E) analyzing a domain of scientific research

7 According to the passage, unlike solutions to test questions, "real-life" solutions are often

(A) excessively emotional
(B) based on logic
(C) the result of erroneous information
(D) provisional
(E) multiple-choice

5

GO ON TO THE NEXT PAGE ▸▸▸

A Question of Intelligence, Daniel Seligman, ©1992, Birch Lane Press p 21.

Questions 8–9 are based on the following passage.

Line   Both the heart and the blood, which oversee
the maintenance of the body's internal
environment, rely totally on the breath to
supply them with oxygen and remove gaseous
5   waste. Unlike other nutrients that feed the
body such as vitamins, minerals and proteins,
oxygen cannot be stored within the body and
must continually be replenished. Every minute
that we are alive we require steady and
10   constant provisions of fresh oxygen. On the
average we breathe about fifteen times a
minute. What makes the respiration process
unique in our body is that it functions both
automatically and voluntarily. Unlike the flow
15   of our blood or the beat of our heart, we are
able to change the rate and pattern of our
breath whenever we wish. The breathing
process is also designed to operate completely
on its own, without interference from the rest
20   of our lives.

8   Which of the following statements, if true,
would directly contradict a claim made in
this passage?

(A)   Vitamin C cannot be stored in the
human body.
(B)   The blood is used to carry nutrients
to the cells in the human body.
(C)   Humans can change their breathing
rate at will.
(D)   Humans can sometimes breathe at a
rate of over 50 times per minute.
(E)   The heart is controlled by impulses
from the brain.

9   According to the passage, human respiration is unlike other biological systems primarily in that it

(A)   requires our constant attention
(B)   operates at varying rates throughout
the day
(C)   depends on other systems in the body
(D)   must function constantly to keep us
alive
(E)   works with or without our conscious
control

Question 10 is based on the following passage.

Line   Long before the New World was discovered,
men apprenticed themselves to masters to
learn a trade and receive support. Englishmen
did not consider it strange, therefore, when
5   Jamestown's original settlers agreed to work
for the Virginia Company—which owned the
land—for seven years in exchange for their
passage to America and food, clothing and
shelter. When the men had finished their
10   term of service they were free to return to
England or stay on in the settlement. Those
who remained struck out on their own instead
of offering themselves as salaried laborers.
They asked the Virginia company to send
15   indentured servants whom they would hire.

10   The passage suggests that Jamestown's original settlers, before they finished their terms
of service, were most like

(A)   salaried laborers
(B)   master craftsmen
(C)   land owners
(D)   apprentices
(E)   entrepreneurs

GO ON TO THE NEXT PAGE ▶▶▶

First paragraph: *Total Breathing*, Philip Smith, ©1980, McGraw Hill, p 2
Second paragraph: *America Fever, The Story of American Immigration*, Barbara Greenleaf, Four Winds Press, ©1970 p 10
Excerpted from *Private Lives, Public Lives: Tangled Together Like Badly Cast Fishing Line*, Ann L. Putnam, University of North Texas
    Press, ©1995, p 7–9

Questions 11–16 are based on the following passage.

The following is from a recent essay by an American author about the challenges of being a mother and a writer.

Line   Then at last I was alone. Truth to tell, I was lonely. Absolutely dazed by the silence. I have become so connected to the rhythms of my children, I have lost my edge. Unaccustomed
5   as I am to the quiet and the solitude, I fear my affections will take some weaning, for such habits of mind and heart are not easily broken. I must learn all over again how to be *alone but not solitary*. I know instantly
10   that I will need days to recover, to discover the rhythms of my psyche, the edges of my soul, days I will not have, not in time.
    I finally settle down and the ideas begin to roll. I'd earned this day, I'd done my homework,
15   gathered ideas, taken notes, made outlines, done all the reading, all the things you can do in bits and snatches, and now I was going to bring it all to the "boiling point." What I needed was the opening line, a first line
20   with the rhetorical distances just right, one which would tangle the reader in my own entanglings.
    I had decided ahead of time that I was *not* going to answer the phone. "Do you have any
25   reusable clothing to donate, carpets to clean, furniture to shampoo, chimneys to sweep, cemetery plots, life insurance, home insurance, auto insurance, will you buy a ticket to send a child to the circus, march in the cancer
30   crusade, the heart campaign, keep kids off drugs, out of gangs, off the streets?" So when the phone rings an hour later, of course I answer it.
    It's my little girl. She's lost her field trip
35   permission slip to spend the day with her class on a marine biology ship. She'll have to spend the whole day in the library, could I please bring it over? If I went to the school it would cost me the morning and I was getting
40   panicky about the way this paper wasn't getting written. But could I really work, trying not to think of her sitting there in the library all day? For once I would say *no*! If she lost the note, well, it would be a learning
45   experience. I would try to claim, for once, the boundaries of my own autonomy. I would *not* get caught in those tangled, entangling lines, phone or otherwise. I did not have to answer to their every pull and tug.
50   But it wasn't as easy as that. If my day felt long, wouldn't hers feel longer? How would I switch off that inevitable and automatic response to her, such that I too would sit in the hot September library eating my sack
55   lunch all alone? Other than death, I do believe that having a child is probably the most life-altering experience a person can have. Certain ways of feeling, thinking, reacting, reading, writing, my very epistemology, the
60   way I know things, are changed forever. I would go to school.
    But then it's after lunch and I'm comfortably settled back at the computer with what's left of the day. At least I'd have the
65   afternoon. By now the computer was downright warm to the touch, but only because it had been sitting there humming to itself all morning.
    The dog, with whom I can be "alone but
70   not solitary," has settled down beneath the computer table, by my feet. She follows me everywhere, makes no demands I cannot meet, my eighty-five pound, black and white shadow friend. She's lying under the
75   computer table chewing on an old sock. Time flies. Or maybe it stops. Anyway, the screen begins to fill with green letters that turn into words, into sentences, into actual *paragraphs*. I'd written the introduction, laid claim to my
80   thesis, had just written about the tug I had always felt in trying to be a wife, mother, and daughter on the one hand, and to do what I have always considered to be my work in the world on the other. But then I'm interrupted
85   by a funny sound coming from under the table. The dog is making a funny noise, sort of like choking or gagging.
    "Alex, what are you *doing*?" I say. But she's watching the rug in front of her, waiting for

GO ON TO THE NEXT PAGE ▸▸▸

Excerpted from *Private Lives, Public Lives* Tangled Together Like Badly Cast Fishing Line, by Ann L. Putnam. University of North Texas Press, © 1995, p 7–9.

90 something to happen. I start to rush her
    outside, but whatever was going to come up
    must have gone back down, because now
    she's sitting there, looking up at me, wagging
    her tail. Then I notice that the sock is gone.
95   The trip to the vet, even when taking into
    account my accelerated speed, the half-hour
    wait in the office, the examination, x-rays
    and diagnosis, pretty well took care of the
    rest of the afternoon.
100   "It certainly was lucky you were home
    today," the vet said. "It could have been life
    threatening." Ah, there it is, I'm thinking,
    proving once again the shifty presence of that
    old pale rider and the necessity of my constant
105 vigilance. But I get weary, keeping track of
    everything. I know where the room I need is,
    and it's the one inside my head, in the
    country of my imagination. But always I am
    drawn back by those lines whose tugs and
110 pulls are the center of my heart.
        Now where was my unassailable center,
    my still, quiet center of concentration? I'd
    never begun to reach the "boiling point."

11 It can be inferred that by "my edge" (line 4)
        the author means

    (A)   her skills as a mother
    (B)   those things that distract her from
          her writing
    (C)   her writing ability
    (D)   her loneliness
    (E)   her dog

12 As it is used in this passage, the term "boil-
        ing point" refers to the point at which the
        author feels

    (A)   unbearably frustrated with writing
    (B)   anxious about abandoning her child
    (C)   that her writing can begin to flow
    (D)   annoyed with her dog
    (E)   profoundly lonely

13 The questions listed in lines 24–31 represent

    (A)   the author's doubts about her ability
          to write
    (B)   the author's thoughts about writing
          topics
    (C)   alternatives to writing that the author
          is considering
    (D)   potential distractions to the author
    (E)   things that the author's children say

14 The author mentions the "hot September
        library" (line 54) to emphasize her

    (A)   need to get away so that she can
          write
    (B)   empathy for her daughter
    (C)   dissatisfaction with the results of her
          current project
    (D)   unpleasant memories of her child-
          hood
    (E)   process of generating creative ideas

15 According to the author, she "would go to
        school" (line 61) in order to

    (A)   learn more about writing
    (B)   bring her daughter something
    (C)   set the boundaries of her autonomy
    (D)   study child development
    (E)   discover something about herself

16 The sentence beginning on line 76
        ("Anyway...actual *paragraphs*") is intended
        to convey the author's

    (A)   amazement
    (B)   disgust
    (C)   frustration
    (D)   maternal instinct
    (E)   moral integrity

The questions below are based on the content of the preceding passage. The questions are to be answered on the basis of what is stated or implied in the passage itself or the introductory material that precedes the passage.

Questions 17–24 are based on the following passage.

The following is an excerpt from a book about cinematic criticism and in particular the works of film director John Ford.

Line The best way to approach the films of Ford is the way he himself approached the business of making them, empirically, practicing his trade. He was a creator, a poet in the original
5 Greek sense of the word—"one who makes, a maker ... the creator of a poem." From the start, and all his life, he was a teller of tales. And like Homer with his "blooming lyre," his tales were traditional, told for an audience
10 who wanted only to be entertained, were not looking for originality or enlightenment, were happy to hear old tales well told.

He entertained, of course, in a very distinctive, entirely individual way. His
15 personality was strong; his accent was always his own. The better one knows Ford, the more powerful seems the influence of his Irish background, his Irish consciousness. Not just for the pull of rebelliousness,
20 consanguinity and strong drink—forceful though that was. But also for the complementary lyricism of the Celtic temperament, the sweetness of it and its underlying melancholy, the consciousness of
25 time and transience, of partings that must sever the closest bonds of family and friendship, of men who march away, loved ones who disappear into distance, the eternal longing of the dispossessed. It is this
30 apprehension of impermanence, this sense of man's ultimate isolation that makes so dear and so joyous the bulwarks we erect against the assault of mortality. Bulwarks of comradeship, family, love.
35 He was capable of sentimentalism, but he was not soft; he was a disciplinarian, and he could be shockingly undisciplined; he demanded more loyalty than he was prepared to give. With all his vices and ambiguities,

40 though, he carried an ideal, "hidden within him," and it was this ideal that inspired his poetry. He told tales. He did not make films "about" things, about conceptions of history, or revaluations of Western Myth. Experience,
45 not abstract ideas, is the stuff of the work.

And yet the hidden ideal is there. An ideal implies a morality: Ford's poetic gift was essentially a moral one, not abstracted from the business of living or standing aside from
50 it, but wholly involved in it. In this way (and in this way only) he was a "committed" artist. His films give the lie to the commonly received notion that evil is so much more "interesting" or attractive than goodness.
55 Ford's villains are bad, unpleasant, and not in the least seductive; his heroes are charming, humorous, warm-blooded. Generosity, fidelity, truthfulness: these are not just respectable, they are lovable, life-enhancing.

60 Ford's tales at their best always mean more than they seem to: they transcend narrative. They have a soul, and this is why we call them "poetic." He was born, it seems, with this gift of telling stories clearly,
65 understandably, so that they could appeal to the simplest, least thinking in his audience; and simultaneously he could transform them into poems, for those who have eyes to see and ears to hear. The magic is in his style,
70 which with its undeviating simplicity and directness expresses the real content, as opposed to the mere circumstances of the story. It is a powerful style, not an assertive one. For all the strength of personality
75 behind it, it never proclaims itself. Ford's aim—though he would have never used the term—was always *empathetic*. Nothing should come between the audience and the experience; and what is to be experienced is
80 not "the movie" but a story, a situation, a character, a sharing of feeling.

To say that an artist sticks to his guns may mean a number of different things. It may mean insistence on a personal, original style,
85 incomprehensible to his contemporaries. It may mean commitment to views repugnant to his fellow man. It may mean rejection of authority at a time of conformism, or loyalty to tradition in a time of revolution. For John

GO ON TO THE NEXT PAGE ▶▶▶

From *About John Ford,* by Lindsey Anderson. Used by permission of Plexus Publishing.

90 Ford, it meant above all the preservation of
an unyielding integrity of personality, both as
an artist and as a man. His ideas and
emotions matured; and changing circumstance
provoked him to changing reactions. But his
95 essential character did not change; nor did
his feelings, his values or his conviction.
     Poet of faith in an age of unbelief, he saw
the world going in a way he could neither
approve nor wholly understand, and this
100 made him sad. But John Ford was not a man
or an artist who ever surrendered himself to
bitterness or disillusion. He had a great
heart, and so was able and still is able to
"make us feel," to "loose our hearts with
105 tears." Such smiles, such tears, such
restorative energy—"the freshness of the
early world"—are the gifts that John Ford has
left us in his films.

17 The first paragraph suggests that Homer's
tales were

(A) innovative
(B) told in many languages
(C) violent
(D) politically charged
(E) not enlightening

18 The passage suggests that Ford acquired his
"sense of man's ultimate isolation" (line 31)
from his

(A) early education
(B) ethnic heritage
(C) experiences with other directors
(D) knowledge of classic Greek
        storytellers
(E) sentimental relationship with his
        family

19 In line 30, the word "apprehension" most
nearly means

(A) fear
(B) physical possession
(C) perception
(D) desire
(E) will

20 In saying that Ford "did not make films 'about'
things" (lines 42–43) the author means that

(A) Ford's characters were not realistic
(B) Ford's films focused on the concrete
        and sensory rather than the abstract
(C) Ford was not a disciplined filmmaker
(D) the narratives in Ford's films were
        not cohesive
(E) Ford was always conscious of repre-
        senting his idealism on screen

21 In saying that Ford's villains are "not in the
least seductive" (line 56) the author means
that they

(A) do not appeal to audiences
(B) are respectable
(C) commit illegal acts but not
        immoral acts
(D) are not well-developed as characters
(E) are incomprehensible

22 As it is used in line 73, the word "assertive"
most nearly means

(A) obtrusive
(B) powerful
(C) intentional
(D) personal
(E) sympathetic

23 In the seventh paragraph (lines 82–96),
Ford's artistic style is characterized primarily as

(A) conformist
(B) dynamic
(C) innovative
(D) steadfast
(E) repugnant

24 The final paragraph suggests that Ford found
the modern world outside of his movies to be

(A) generous
(B) joyous
(C) restorative
(D) foreboding
(E) bewildering

 **STOP**

*You may check your work, on this
section only, until time is called.*

Section 6

Time—25 Minutes
35 Questions

Directions for "Improving Sentences" Questions

Each of the sentences below contains one underlined portion. The portion may contain one or more errors in grammar, usage, construction, precision, diction (choice of words), or idiom. Some of the sentences are correct.

Consider the meaning of the original sentence, and choose the answer that best expresses that meaning. If the original sentence is best, choose (A), because it repeats the original phrasing. Choose the phrasing that creates the clearest, most precise and most effective sentence.

EXAMPLE:

The children <u>couldn't hardly believe their eyes</u>.

  (A) couldn't hardly believe their eyes
  (B) would not hardly believe their eyes
  (C) could hardly believe their eyes
  (D) couldn't nearly believe their eyes
  (E) could hardly believe his or her eyes

Example answer: (C)

---

1   Alina always volunteers to help at school charity fundraisers, believing that <u>to be in aide to ones</u> fellow humans beings is a noble pursuit.

  (A) to be in aide to ones
  (B) to aide one's
  (C) to aid ones
  (D) to aid one's
  (E) aiding for one's

2   The jury deliberated for several hours, <u>in the uncertainty as to whether the defendant could of</u> prevented the accident.

  (A) in the uncertainty as to whether the defendant could of
  (B) uncertain as to whether the defendant could have
  (C) uncertain as to whether the defendant could of
  (D) uncertain regarding that whether the defendant could have
  (E) being uncertain as to the fact of whether the defendant could have

3   Giraffes are forced to eat <u>less plants and drink less water during the dry season when their food supply is diminished</u>.

  (A) less plants and drink less water during the dry season when their food supply is diminished.
  (B) less plants and water during the dry season when their food supply is diminished.
  (C) fewer plants and drink less water during the dry season, when their food supply is diminished
  (D) fewer plants and drink less water during the dry season, when their food supply would have been diminished
  (E) less plants and drink less water during the dry season when their food supply was diminished.

4   We were disappointed that the birthday present for my mother <u>had took so many days to get</u> to her house.

  (A) had took so many days to get
  (B) had took so many days getting
  (C) had taken so many days to get
  (D) had taken so many days in getting
  (E) had already been so long in getting

GO ON TO THE NEXT PAGE ▸▸▸

5 The council session focused <u>on deciding who would</u> organize the general election

(A) on deciding who would
(B) on the one who would be chosen to
(C) around the decision of who would
(D) on who would be the one chosen to
(E) around to whom the choice
     would go to

6 If you would like to know more about lactose intolerance, come talk to Jon <u>and I: we both cannot</u> tolerate any dairy products.

(A) and I: we both cannot
(B) and me: since we both cannot
(C) and me: because neither can
(D) and me: neither of us can
(E) and I: neither of us can

7 David's laptop computer would not start this morning <u>because he left it</u> in the rain all yesterday afternoon.

(A) because he left it
(B) being that he had left it out
(C) for his leaving it out
(D) because of his having left it
(E) because he had left it

8 We wanted to find a waiter who was able to work long hours, handle a busy dining room, and, above all, <u>he or she must keep the diners happy</u>.

(A) he or she must keep the diners happy
(B) they should keep the diners happy
(C) keep the diners happy
(D) keeping the diners happy
(E) be able to keep the diners happy

9 <u>If I had to choose between</u> eggplant, zucchini, and green beans, I would always choose zucchini.

(A) If I had to choose between
(B) If I had to choose among
(C) If I were to be choosing between
(D) If I was to choose among
(E) If I chose between

10 <u>Although the prospective student was</u> interested in studying human evolution, she eventually wanted to write a dissertation on chimpanzees.

(A) Although the prospective student was
(B) Although the perspective student was
(C) Although the prospective student is
(D) Although the perspective student is
(E) Despite the fact that the perspective student was

11 Jogging together in the park, <u>it surprised us to see an enormous festival on the green</u>.

(A) it surprised is to see an enormous festival on the green
(B) an enormous festival on the green surprised us
(C) we were surprised to see an enormous festival on the green
(D) we were suprised in seeing an enormous festival on the green
(E) we were surprised to see a festival on the green, and it was enormous

---

Directions for Identifying Sentence Error Questions

The following sentences may contain errors in grammar, usage, diction (choice of words), or idiom. Some of the sentences are correct. No sentence contains more than one error.

If the sentence contains an error, it is underlined and lettered. The parts that are not underlined are correct.

If there is an error, select the part that must be changed to correct the sentence.

If there is no error, choose (E).

EXAMPLE:

By the time <u>they reached</u> the halfway
           A
point <u>in the race</u>, most <u>of the runners</u>
     B   C
<u>hadn't hardly</u> begun to hit their stride.
    D
<u>No error</u>
  E

Sample answer: (D)

---

12 <u>After</u> the month of July, <u>there are</u> usually a
    A   B
large rush of visitors <u>to the beaches</u> of
                  C
Southern Florida because hotel room

<u>rates drop</u> dramatically. <u>No error</u>
  D   E

13 <u>Regardless</u> of where they come from
    A
or <u>what period they arrive in</u>, immigrants
     B
always seem <u>to appreciate</u> the economic
         C
opportunities <u>in the United States</u>.
           D
<u>No error</u>
  E

14 After Christopher saw an <u>extraordinary</u>
                A
pitching performance <u>at a baseball game</u>,
             B
he knew immediately <u>that he wanted</u>
            C
to be <u>one</u> when he grew up. <u>No error</u>
     D   E

15 Any comprehensive study of Greek

literature <u>would show</u> that the ancient
        A
influence <u>of</u> Hellenic authors
       B
<u>is still reflected</u> in <u>modern Greek prose</u>.
  C   D
<u>No error</u>
  E

16 The graphics of this video game <u>is not much</u>
                     A
better than <u>those of the previous version</u>
            B
of the same game, <u>which many critics</u>
             C
<u>heralded</u> as the <u>best</u> of all time. <u>No error</u>
  D   E

17 The new carpet <u>was damaged</u> not only by
           A
flooding, <u>but</u> also <u>because of</u> the splatter
      B   C
from the irresponsible painters

<u>who finished</u> the room. <u>No error</u>
  D   E

18 Although <u>most of</u> the short stories in the
       A
anthology were <u>attributed to</u> their authors
          B
by name, <u>a few of</u> the submissions were
       C
written <u>unanimously</u>. <u>No error</u>
     D   E

6

GO ON TO THE NEXT PAGE ▶▶▶

19 Now that Jessica <u>had finished</u> reading a
                        A
book about Roman mythology, she

<u>feels more confident</u> about <u>taking the test</u>
          B   C
on <u>ancient religions</u>. <u>No error</u>
      D   E

20 The <u>display of fireworks</u> thrilled the
              A
spectators, <u>they provided</u> a fitting end
                    B
<u>to the week-long</u> celebration of the town's
        C
<u>centennial</u>. <u>No error</u>
    D   E

21 <u>After being</u> traumatized by a boy in her class
        A
<u>that</u> taunted her until she cried, <u>Eliza ran</u>
  B   C
from the room, <u>sobbing uncontrollably</u>.
                        D

<u>No error</u>
  E

22 A recent survey <u>suggests that</u> shock
                        A
tactics in health care advertisements

<u>are more effective</u> because Americans
        B
react more intensely <u>to this</u> than to the
                        C
more objective <u>distribution of</u> information.
                    D

<u>No error</u>
  E

23 Her obsession with cleanliness <u>compelled her</u>
                                        A
to wash the walls of her apartment

<u>twice a week</u> and <u>scrubbing</u> the floor of
        B   C
her kitchen <u>each night</u>. <u>No error</u>
                  D   E

24 <u>Although</u> routine monitoring
        A
<u>of the fetal heart</u> for regular rhythms is
        B
<u>suggested by</u> obstetricians, midwives often
        C
forgo such invasive procedures unless the

fetus <u>shows</u> signs of distress. <u>No error</u>
          D   E

25 The Actors' Guild, which <u>has funded</u>
                                  A
numerous scholarships for city children

over the past twenty years, <u>was lauded</u>
                                  B
<u>by the media</u> for <u>their</u> undying generosity.
      C   D
<u>No error</u>
  E

26 The Chief of Police explained that the

decrease in funding <u>would have</u>
                        A
detrimental effects on public safety

because <u>less</u> police officers <u>on duty</u>
          B   C
would lead <u>to more crime</u>. <u>No error</u>
                D   E

GO ON TO THE NEXT PAGE ▶▶▶

27 To many critics, the rate <u>at which</u> many
A
baseball players <u>are hitting</u> home runs
B
today <u>are indicative of the fact</u> that many
C
athletes <u>are using</u> performance-enhancing
D
drugs. <u>No error</u>
E

28 <u>Although</u> we had been told to expect a
A
terrible meal, <u>we were</u> actually quite
B
<u>satisfied at</u> the quality of food <u>we received</u>
C   D
in the hospital cafeteria. <u>No error</u>
E

29 Even though our summer home

<u>had attracted</u> numerous bids <u>from</u>
A   B
potential buyers, <u>my parents decided</u>
C
not to sell it because they wanted it to

remain available for <u>my brothers and I</u>.
D

<u>No error</u>
E

Directions for "Improving Paragraph" Questions

Below is an early draft of an essay. It requires revision in many areas.

The questions that follow ask you to make improvements in sentence structure, diction, organization and development. Answering the questions may require you to understand the context of the passage as well as the rules of standard written English.

Questions 30–35 are based on the following passage.

(1) *Although Greece is home to one of the most ancient civilizations in the world, it is actually a rather small country population-wise. (2) There are actually only about ten million people who live there. (3) Nevertheless, it also has a small geographic area compared to most countries, covering only about 50,000 square miles.*

(4) *Much of this land is in the form of islands. (5) Popular tourist destinations, the islands are perhaps the most well-known geographic feature of Greece. (6) However, the country actually has a very diverse landscape and habitat, with areas that get a lot of rainfall and a lot of the country is mountainous. (7) As the seasons change, so do the preferred tourist destinations in Greece. (8) Many people believe that Greece is always hot, but in reality the winters are somewhat wet and cold, and as a result the islands aren't as popular during those months, but that is when the ski regions are more popular.*

(9) *Greece borders on Albania and has an uncomfortable political and economic relationship with Turkey. (10) In recent years, the country has seen a wave of immigration from Albania, which has changed the dynamics of the local economy. (11) Most people who live in Greece are part of the Greek Orthodox Church, which is an important part of life for them. (12) The economy depends largely on summer tourist season, and this is what sustains many people especially who live near the islands for the rest of the year. (13) Many Greeks have a job on one of the islands during the summer catering to tourist's needs, but then move back to the mainland for fall, winter and spring. (14) Overall, Greece is a*

fascinating country, and worthy of your study as well as your coming to visit.

30 Which of the following revisions of the underlined portion best combines sentences 1 and 2?

Although Greece is home to one of the most ancient civilizations in the world, <u>it is actually a rather small country population-wise. There are actually only about ten million people who live there.</u>

(A) it has a relatively small population of only about ten million people.

(B) it is actually a rather small country in terms of population, with only about ten million people who live there

(C) it has a relatively small population, and there are actually only about ten million people living there

(D) it is actually a small population: only about ten million people

(E) it is small population-wise: only about ten million people

31 Which of the following is the best revision of the underlined portion of sentence 3 (reproduced below)?

<u>Nevertheless, it also has a small geographic area</u> compared to most countries, covering only about 50,000 square miles

(A) For example, it also has a small geographic area

(B) It also has a small geographic area

(C) Nevertheless, its geographic area is small

(D) Truth be told, it even has a small geographic area

(E) Nevertheless, it also has a small geographic area

32 Which of the following is the best revision of the underlined portion of sentence 6 (reproduced below)?

However, the country actually has a very diverse landscape and habitat, <u>with areas that get a lot of rainfall and a lot of the country is mountainous</u>.

(A) with a great deal of rainfall in areas and much of the country is mountainous

(B) with rainfall plentiful in some places and mountainous regions

(C) with rainy areas and including many mountainous regions

(D) including regions that are very rainy and others that are very mountainous

(E) including a lot of rainfall and a large proportion of mountainous terrain

33 In context, which of the following is the best revision of sentence 8 (reproduced below)?

Many people believe that Greece is always hot, but in reality the winters are somewhat wet and cold, and as a result the islands aren't as popular during those months, but that is when the ski regions are more popular.

(A) In the hot summer months, the islands draw more tourists, but in the cold and wet winter months the northern ski regions are more popular.

(B) Although Greece is hot in the summer, during the winter tourism on the islands drops off because the weather is wet and cold, but then the northern ski regions are better.

(C) Although many people believe that Greece is always hot, that isn't the case and in winter tourists prefer the northern ski regions instead of the islands.

(D) The islands are hot during the summer months, but in the winter the tourists go to the northern ski regions because they like it more.

(E) Since the winters are wet and cold, tourists go to the northern ski regions instead of the islands in the hot summer months.

34 Which of the following sentences contributes the least to the overall unity of paragraph 3?

(A) sentence 9
(B) sentence 10
(C) sentence 11
(D) sentence 12
(E) sentence 13

35 Which of the following is the best revision of the underlined portion of sentence 12 (reproduced below)?

The economy depends largely on the summer tourist season, <u>and this is what sustains many people especially who live near the islands for the rest of the year</u>.

(A) the profits of which happen to sustain especially many who live near the islands through the rest of the year

(B) where especially many people who live near the islands make enough money to support themselves for the rest of the year

(C) although this results in the fact that some people, especially those who live near the islands, are supported for the rest of the year

(D) which sustains many people, especially those who live near the islands, for the remainder of the year

(E) and specially financially sustains many people who live near the islands

6

STOP

You may check your work, on this section only, until time is called.

Section 7

Time—20 minutes
16 Questions

Directions for Multiple-Choice Questions

In this section, solve each problem, using any available space on the page for scratchwork. Then decide which is the best of the choices given and fill in the corresponding oval on your answer sheet.

- You may use a calculator on any problem. All numbers used are real numbers.
- Figures are drawn as accurately as possible EXCEPT when it is stated that the figure is not drawn to scale.
- All figures lie in a plane unless otherwise indicated.

Reference Information

$A = \pi r^2$ $A = \ell w$ $A = \frac{1}{2}bh$ $V = \ell wh$ $V = \pi r^2 h$ $c^2 = a^2 + b^2$ Special Right Triangles
$C = 2\pi r$

The number of degrees of arc in a circle is 360°.
The measure in degrees of a straight angle is 180°.
The sum of the measures in degrees of the angles of a triangle is 180°.

---

1 If $4x = 9$, what is the value of $4x - 7$?

(A) 29
(B) 16
(C) 13
(D) 7
(E) 2

2 At the local market, 6 apples cost \$1.20 and 5 oranges cost \$1.20. If Monique buys twelve apples and ten oranges at this rate, how much change will she get back if she pays with a \$5 bill?

(A) \$0.20
(B) \$0.60
(C) \$1.00
(D) \$1.20
(E) \$2.60

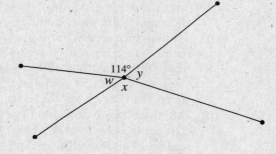

3 In the figure above, what is the value of $w + x + y$?

(A) 66
(B) 106
(C) 186
(D) 246
(E) 256

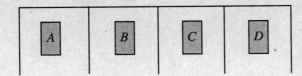

4 The figure above shows four cars in a parking lot. Each car belongs to only one person, and each person owns only one car. Tom's car is parked next to Eric's car and Felisha's car is parked next to Eric's and Latoya's car. Which car could belong to Tom?

(A) A only
(B) C only
(C) D only
(D) A or D
(E) C or D

5 If $3x + 4y = 7$ and $5x - 6y = 12$, what is the value of $8x - 2y$?

(A) 9
(B) 13
(C) 19
(D) 21
(E) 24

A D E G J

6 Three letters are to be picked from the letters listed above. If the second letter must be a vowel and the first or third letter must be G, how many different arrangements can be formed if no letters can be repeated?

(A) 12
(B) 14
(C) 16
(D) 18
(E) 20

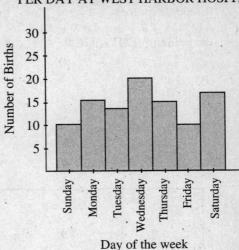

AVERAGE NUMBER OF BIRTHS
PER DAY AT WEST HARBOR HOSPITAL

7 According to the graph above, which of the following is the closest approximation of the percent of births that occur on Friday, Saturday, and Sunday combined?

(A) 27%
(B) 37%
(C) 40%
(D) 42%
(E) 45%

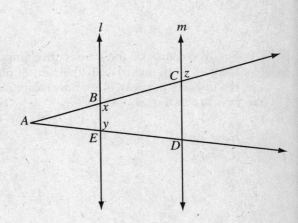

8 In the figure above, if $l = m$ and $AC = AD$, what is the value of $x + y + z$?

(A) 113°
(B) 180°
(C) 226°
(D) 293°
(E) 339°

GO ON TO THE NEXT PAGE ▸▸▸

9 For all integers n greater than 1, let $f(n)$ = p, where p is the sum of all positive integer factors of n. For instance, $f(12) = 1 + 2 + 3 + 4 + 6 + 12 = 28$. What is the value of $f(24) - f(16)$?

(A) 16
(B) 24
(C) 29
(D) 31
(E) 60

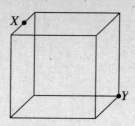

12 The cube shown above has a volume of 64 and X is the midpoint of one edge. What is the length of the line segment XY (not shown)?

(A) $2\sqrt{5}$

(B) $\sqrt{30}$

(C) 6

(D) $2\sqrt{10}$

(E) $\sqrt{42}$

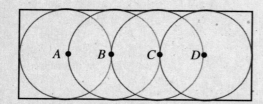

10 In the figure above, A, B, C, and D are the centers of the four circles. If each circle has a circumference of 6π, what is the perimeter of the rectangle?

(A) 42
(B) 48
(C) 60
(D) 66
(E) 84

13 If x and y are different positive integers and $5x + 2y = 41$, what is the product of all of the possible values of x?

(A) 1
(B) 3
(C) 15
(D) 105
(E) 945

11 Set W consists of the consecutive integers from -8 to w inclusive. If the sum of all of the integers in set W is 30, how many numbers are in the set?

(A) 16
(B) 18
(C) 19
(D) 20
(E) 22

GO ON TO THE NEXT PAGE ▶▶▶

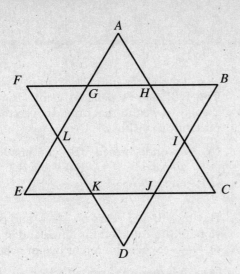

7

14 The figure above consists of a regular hexagon surrounded by six equilateral triangles. If the perimeter of triangle AGH is 30, what is the area of the hexagon?

(A) $120\sqrt{3}$

(B) $150\sqrt{3}$

(C) 175

(D) $120\sqrt{2}$

(E) $150\sqrt{2}$

15 If $4^a = b$, which of the following expresses $64b$ in terms of a?

(A) 4^{3+a}

(B) 4^{a^2}

(C) 4^{3a}

(D) $4^{3/a}$

(E) $4^a + 4^3$

16 Bill runs at a constant rate of b miles per hour, Ty runs at a constant rate of t miles per hour, and $0 < t < b$. If they run a race that is m miles long, how many more hours, in terms of b, t, and m, will it take Ty to finish the race than Bill?

(A) $tm - bm$

(B) $\dfrac{t}{m} - \dfrac{b}{m}$

(C) $t - m$

(D) $\dfrac{t+m}{2b}$

(E) $\dfrac{m}{t} - \dfrac{m}{b}$

You may check your work, on this section only, until time is called.

Section 8

Time—20 minutes
19 Questions

Each of the sentences below is missing one or two portions. Read each sentence, then select the word or words that most logically completes the sentence, taking into account the meaning of the sentence as a whole.

Example:

Rather than accepting the theory unquestioningly, Deborah regarded it with ———.

(A) mirth   (B) sadness
(C) responsibility   (D) ignorance
(E) skepticism

Correct response: (E)

8

1 The women's rights movement in the 1960s and 1970s was ——— campaign during which many individuals from ——— backgrounds came together as one to further a cause.

(A) a cooperative . . indistinguishable
(B) an acrimonious . . disparate
(C) a belligerent . . contrasting
(D) a harmonious . . outlandish
(E) a united . . diverse

2 After four straight days of filming, the crew and cast took a two day ——— to rest up for the final few scenes.

(A) enervation   (B) mastication
(C) fluctuation   (D) dividend
(E) hiatus

3 The billionaire's palacial estate is ——— display of wealth that offends even the most pretentious visitors.

(A) an undecorated   (B) an unadorned
(C) a spartan   (D) a garish
(E) an austere

4 Having suffered years of ——— and oppression, the defector left his homeland in search of ———, where he might live in peace.

(A) inhumanity . . an affliction
(B) forbearance . . an asylum
(C) magnanimity . . a refuge
(D) truculence . . a travesty
(E) persecution . . a haven

5 Although comprehensiveness is often helpful, this textbook presents ——— of information on the subject that overwhelms the readers and often leaves them confused.

(A) a surfeit   (B) a paucity
(C) a promulgation   (D) a bastion
(E) a vestige

6 The 1996 California government ——— created for crop farmers provided a vast ——— of money that was not equitably divided; nearly two-thirds of the funds went to fewer than five percent of all the farms in the state.

(A) installment. . confiscation
(B) endowment . . abatement
(C) referendum . . diminution
(D) subsidy . . appropriation
(E) indemnity . . efflux

GO ON TO THE NEXT PAGE ▶▶▶

Both passages excerpted form: "Genetic Engineering", Pro & Con, Frederic Golden © 1983. Stonesong Press. p 147 -150

Questions 7–19 are based on the following passages.

The following passages present two perspectives on the issue of the dangers and benefits of genetic engineering. They were written in 1983, when the technology was in its infancy.

Passage 1

Line   The cries of alarm over genetic engineering are a mix of naiveté and demagoguery. After the first experiments in gene splicing became widely known, a public outcry was heard.
5   Fortunately, however, the voices of scientific Cassan dras were not heeded. Work on splicing genes and recombinant DNA, the basic building block of life and heredity, has been allowed to continue under strict federal
10   guidelines. The results have been nothing short of dazzling. "Genetic Engineering means design and development for the benefit of mankind," says pioneering gene-splicer Herbert Boyer, founder of Genentech, Inc.
15   Not a single mishap has been reported since the first gene-transplanting experiment. Not a single lethal bug has escaped the lab to cause biological havoc. Popular fears of an Andromeda Strain have proven completely
20   unfounded.
        Medicine is only one discipline affected by the marvels of genetic engineering. Scientists are also revolutionizing agriculture with new breeds of plants that are hardier, more
25   resistant to disease, and easier to grow. Geneticists hope to endow such food crops as wheat, rice, and corn with the capability of drawing their nitrogen directly from the air, rather than from the soil, thus reducing the
30   need for expensive fertilizers. Also in the offing are a variety of specially designed small bugs—ones that will help make fuels, plastics and other chemicals. Other specially created bacteria, thriving on materials that
35   only they can digest, might be utilized in mining and refining processes, dissolving scarce minerals from the earth.
        Even as a research tool, gene splicing has proven invaluable. By inserting a single gene
40   of unknown purpose into an active cluster of known genes, scientists are able to determine the purpose of an unspecified bit of DNA. Eventually, by examining one gene after another, they hope to learn the identity of the
45   entire complement of human genes, totaling perhaps a hundred thousand or more different packets of genetic instructions. According to molecular biologist Charles Weissmann of the University of Zurich, a pioneering gene-splicer:
50   "Biology has become as unthinkable without gene-splicing techniques as sending an explorer into the jungle without a compass."
        The charge that such tampering with genetic structures amounts to gross
55   interference with the natural order of things is pure nonsense. Gene-splicer Stanley Cohen of Stanford notes, for instance, that humans were interfering with heredity by crossbreeding animals and creating hybrid plants long
60   before they even knew of the existence of genes. Indeed, it was through such mingling of genes, even when done unwittingly, that humans made the transition from primitive hunter-gatherers to civilized farmers.
65   Besides, nature's own genetic engineering can hardly be held up as an example of benevolence. Cohen points out that it was, after all, "evolutionary wisdom" that gave us the gene combinations for bubonic plague,
70   smallpox, yellow fever, typhoid, polio, and cancer.
        During all of this success, no genetic monster has been created to slither out of the lab. Nor is that possibility likely. "Those who
75   claim we are letting loose an Andromeda Strain [of virulent pathogens] are either hysterics or are trying to wreck a whole new field of research," says microbiologist Bernard David of Harvard Medical School.
80   Also, scientists would find it infinitely harder to redesign the complex machinery of humans—a fear often cited by critics of

8

GO ON TO THE NEXT PAGE ▶▶▶

Both passages excerpted from: *Genetic Engineering, Pro & Con*, Frederic Golden ©1983. Stonesong Press. p 147–150

genetic engineering–than to splice a gene or two into a simple single-celled organism.
85 In view of their splendid record to date, the genetic engineers should not be halted—nor should we try to restrain the inevitable advance of human knowledge—when they are on the verge of what may be even more
90 promising achievements.

Passage 2

Some say it is an attempt by scientists to play God. That may sound like an exaggeration, but the description is not far from the truth. Genetic engineering is a
95 calculated effort to restructure things in a fundamental way. It is as if the scientists have presumed to play the Lord's role as described in Genesis—"Let us make man in our image"—rather than obey His laws
100 revealed in Leviticus—"Thou shall not let thy cattle gender with a diverse kind; thou shall not sow thy field with mingled seed."

The altering of life by genetic engineers is already under way. Animal growers regularly
105 use frozen sperm, artificial insemination, and even surrogate mothers to produce improved breeds. Some have suggested, and even tried, using all of these techniques on humans. Although cloning animals (that is, creating a
110 genetic-copy offspring from a single parent) was once dismissed as the far-out speculation of a few science-fiction writer, biologist are now routinely cloning frogs, mice, and other lowly species. As scientists continue to improve
115 their skills, the possibility of cloning humans will no longer be a wild nightmarish fantasy. Indeed, molecular biologists have already ushered in their own Brave New World. With frightening ease, they are shuffling
120 genes within species and from one species to another. Genes of bacteria are spliced onto those of mice, and possibly onto those of humans. When they make such transfers of DNA (the master molecule that is the coding
125 of genes) researchers create entirely new life-forms with their own characteristics—organisms that may never have existed before on the face of the earth.

The justification for such work is

130 invariably high-minded. The proponents of gene-splicing, or recombinant DNA as it is known in the jargon, say that it will help improve food supplies by creating hardier and more productive plants and animals.
135 They also say it will help in the fight against disease, perhaps even wiping out such scourges as sickle cell anemia or hemophilia. But such goals can be achieved by other means and would involve far fewer risks. Who can say
140 for certain that a re-engineered microbe, containing unexpectedly lethal gene combinations, will not escape from the laboratory into the environment, unleashing a mysterious and uncontrollable ailment?

145 Still another fear is that the new Fausts of molecular biology will not only attempt to repair genetic defects but also try to "improve" the species. They have the potential to manipulate genes and characteristics in
150 humans; with a moral blindness men may adopt Adolf Hitler's immoral vision that "we will create the perfect race."

Most worrisome of all are genetic engineering's unforeseen consequences.
155 Myriads of life forms inhabit our world, each having its own special niche and purpose, and each the end product of nature's own processes of trial and error. No one can say what the side effects may be when science
160 interferes with evolution. Says biologist Robert Sinsheimer, chancellor of the University of California at Santa Cruz: "Biologists have become, without wanting it, the custodians of great and terrible power. It is idle to pretend
165 otherwise. Do we really wish to replace the fateful but impartial workings of chance with the purposeful self-interested workings of human will?"

Biochemist Erwin Chargaff, whose own
170 explorations into the structure of DNA helped bring about today's biological revolution, puts the question even more bluntly: "Have we the right to counteract, irreversibly, the evolutionary wisdom of millions of years in
175 order to satisfy the ambition and curiosity of a few scientists?" Chargaff, like many, feels the answer is no. "If you can modify a cell," he says, "it's only a short step to modifying a mouse, and if you can modify a mouse, it's

180 only a short step to modifying a higher animal, even man." Although scientists may blindly consider this a great triumph, it is a disturbing Pandora's box that society should not open.

7 The quotation at the end of the first paragraph (lines 11–13) can be considered a weakness in the argument of Passage 1 because

(A) it presents a claim which is later disproved
(B) the speaker has no experience in the technology he is speaking about
(C) it is self-contradictory
(D) it is a business owner's evaluation of his own business
(E) it is based on an outmoded definition

8 Which of the following is most like the "Andromeda Strain" mentioned in Passage 1?

(A) the "expensive fertilizers" of line 30
(B) the "small bugs" of line 32
(C) the "complement of human genes" in line 45
(D) the "pure nonsense" in line 56
(E) the "genetic monster" of line 72–73

9 The purpose of the third paragraph (lines 21–37) is to

(A) reveal a flaw in the thinking of those who oppose genetic engineering
(B) define several important biological terms
(C) present the opinion of an authority
(D) provide a brief historical background of genetic engineering
(E) discuss potential benefits of genetic engineering

10 The quotation in lines 50–52 ("Biology has become ... a compass") expresses the opinion that genetic engineering

(A) requires more funding
(B) has become complex and dangerous
(C) is indispensable to progress in biology
(D) has lost its focus
(E) requires very precise instruments

11 In line 68, the phrase "evolutionary wisdom" is placed in quotation marks in order to convey a sense of

(A) awe
(B) irony
(C) objective detachment
(D) light-hearted humor
(E) benevolence

12 The final paragraph of Passage 1 contains which of the following?

I. an authoritative perspective
II. a personal reflection
III. an attempt to allay a fear
IV. an expression of hope

(A) III and IV only
(B) I, II, and III only
(C) II, III, and IV only
(D) I, III, and IV only
(E) I, II, III, and IV

13 The author of Passage 2 regards the possibility of scientists continuing "to improve their skills" (line 114) as

(A) highly remote
(B) potentially hopeful
(C) dangerous
(D) unequivocally triumphant
(E) irrelevant

14 Which of the following statements, if true, would most directly contradict a claim made in the fourth paragraph of Passage 2 (lines 129–144)?

(A) Some diseases cannot be cured safely without the use of genetic engineering
(B) Most genetic engineers have high ethical standards.
(C) Gene splicing can produce hardier plants.
(D) Many companies that perform genetic engineering are highly profitable.
(E) Genetic engineering is relatively inexpensive.

GO ON TO THE NEXT PAGE ▶▶▶

15 In line 164, the word "idle" most nearly means

(A) dormant
(B) irresponsible
(C) unemployed
(D) slow
(E) admirable

16 According to the author of Passage 2, the most troublesome aspect of the new science of genetic engineering is

(A) the uncertainty of its application
(B) the lack of skill of its practitioners
(C) its financial costs
(D) its ineffectiveness
(E) the bureaucratic hurdles it must face

17 How would the author of Passage I most likely regard the question posed in lines 139–144 of Passage 2 ("Who can say ... uncontrolled ailment")?

(A) It represents a central and legitimate concern which has not been adequately addressed.
(B) It represents a legitimate concern that is beginning to be addressed by a small number of scientists.
(C) It is not a question that concerns most opponents of genetic engineering.
(D) It is naive and hysterical.
(E) It does not go far enough in addressing the potential dangers of genetic engineering.

18 Unlike the author of Passage 1, the author of Passage 2 regards the genetic engineering of hardier plants as

(A) desirable
(B) impossible
(C) perilous
(D) safe
(E) inevitable

19 Which of the following claims made in Passage 2 is directly addressed in the last paragraph of Passage 1?

(A) "Genetic engineering is a calculated effort to restructure things in a fundamental way." (lines 93–96)
(B) "...they are shuffling genes within species and from one species to another." (lines 119–121)
(C) "They also say it will help in the fight against disease..." (lines 135–136)
(D) "Myriads of life forms inhabit our world." (line 155)
(E) "...it's only a short step to modifying a higher animal, even man." (lines 179–181)

STOP

You may check your work, on this section only, until time is called.

Section 9

Time—10 Minutes
14 Questions

Directions for "Improving Sentences" Questions

Each of the sentences below contains one underlined portion. The portion may contain one or more errors in grammar, usage, construction, precision, diction (choice of words), or idiom. Some of the sentences are correct.

Consider the meaning of the original sentence, and choose the answer that best expresses that meaning. If the original sentence is best, choose (A), because it repeats the original phrasing. Choose the phrasing that creates the clearest, most precise and most effective sentence.

EXAMPLE:

The children couldn't hardly believe their eyes.

- (A) couldn't hardly believe their eyes
- (B) would not hardly believe their eyes
- (C) could hardly believe their eyes
- (D) couldn't nearly believe their eyes
- (E) could hardly believe his or her eyes

Example answer: (C)

---

1 Larry Peters is almost as skilled an actor as he is a singer.

- (A) almost as skilled an actor as he is a singer
- (B) equally skilled as an actor than a singer
- (C) of the same skill as a writer and as an actor
- (D) a skillful actor, with equal skill as a singer
- (E) skillful as an actor, also the same as a singer

2 Underestimating the amount of time taking to get to school, many students are late to class each morning.

- (A) Underestimating the amount of time taking to get to school, many students are late to class each morning.
- (B) Many students are late to class each morning because they underestimate the time of getting to school.
- (C) Many students are late to class each morning because they underestimate how long it takes to get to school.
- (D) Late to class each morning, students underestimate the amount of time it takes to get to school.
- (E) Underestimating the time it takes students to get to the school makes them late to class each morning.

3 Its being in the context of the discussion, the phrase "at all costs" is used to indicate the importance of the mission.

- (A) Its being in the context of the discussion
- (B) In the context of the discussion
- (C) The context of the discussion states that
- (D) Considering the discussion's context
- (E) In understanding the context of the discussion,

4 Hungry from having missed her last three meals, Stephanie's search for a restaurant was urgent.

- (A) Stephanie's search for a restaurant was urgent
- (B) Stephanie searched urgently for a restaurant
- (C) a restaurant was what Stephanie urgently searched for
- (D) a restaurant Stephanie urgently searched for
- (E) Stephanie urgently searching for a restaurant.

5 After midnight, the snack bar in the train station is closed, inconveniencing <u>what people, if any, that are</u> left in the building.

(A) what people, if any, that are
(B) which people, if any, that are
(C) whatever people that are
(D) any people
(E) any of the people that are

6 Now working as a substitute mathematics teacher at Greenfield Prep Academy, <u>Martha will next teach</u> a two-week biology seminar at Westville High.

(A) Martha will next teach
(B) Martha will then teach
(C) but Martha will then do
(D) her Martha's teaching job will be
(E) Martha's next assignment is

7 <u>Unlike 30 years ago, students today</u> have instantaneous access to their friends through technology.

(A) Unlike 30 years ago, students today
(B) Unlike 30 years ago, today's students
(C) Different from their counterparts, 30 years ago students
(D) Unlike their counterparts 30 years ago, students in this day and age
(E) Students today, unlike those 30 years ago,

8 Guillermo loved to read <u>books, by which he found biographies to be the most entertaining</u>.

(A) books, by which he found biographies to be the most entertaining
(B) books, and biographies were the ones of these that he found to be most entertaining
(C) books, and found biographies to be the most entertaining
(D) books: and biographies were the most entertaining for him
(E) books, having found biographies to be the most entertaining of all

9 The graduate students were honored to study with Dr. Flounders, <u>an imminent</u> historian, and author of many texts.

(A) an imminent
(B) who was an imminent
(C) the imminent
(D) an eminent
(E) being an eminent

10 By far the most challenging aspect of the descent is <u>we have to coordinate it perfectly</u> so that we do not suffer from altitude sickness.

(A) we have to coordinate it perfectly
(B) we must coordinate it perfectly
(C) our coordination of it perfectly
(D) coordinating it perfectly
(E) perfectly to coordinate it

11 <u>If we had not stopped at the bank</u>, we probably would not have had enough money to pay for dinner.

(A) If we had not stopped at the bank
(B) If we would not have stopped at the bank
(C) If we didn't have stopped at the bank
(D) Because we had stopped at the bank
(E) If not for having stopped at the bank

12 The hurricane <u>had the effect of damaging the hotel and the obliteration of the bridge</u> connecting it to the mainland.

(A) had the effect of damaging the hotel and the obliteration of the bridge
(B) had the effect of damaging the hotel and obliterating the bridge as well
(C) damaged the hotel and obliterated the bridge
(D) damaged both the hotel and obliterated the bridge
(E) damaged the hotel and the obliteration of the bridge

13 <u>Jerry Seinfeld's hallmark is to turn mundane situations into comedy</u>, is widely considered to be one of the funniest comics of all time.

(A) Jerry Seinfeld's hallmark is to turn mundane situations into comedy, is

(B) Jerry Seinfeld and his hallmark of turning mundane situations into comedy is

(C) Jerry Seinfeld's hallmark is to turn mundane situations into comedy, and is

(D) Jerry Seinfeld turns mundane situations into comedy and his hallmark is

(E) Jerry Seinfeld, whose hallmark is to turn mundane situations into comedy, is

14 While training for a marathon, <u>it is important to hydrate, stretch, and sleeping enough</u>.

(A) it is important to hydrate, stretch, and sleeping enough.

(B) it is important, hydrating, stretching, and sleeping enough.

(C) hydrating, stretching, and to sleep enough are important.

(D) it is important to hydrate, stretch, and get enough sleep.

(E) it is important, to hydrate, stretch, and getting enough sleep.

9

 **STOP**

You may check your work, on this section only, until time is called.

ANSWER KEY

Section 2 Math	Section 5 Math	Section 7 Math	Section 2 Critical Reading	Section 5 Critical Reading	Section 8 Critical Reading	Section 3 Writing	Section 9 Writing
1. E	1. E	1. E	1. B	1. D	1. E	1. D	1. A
2. C	2. C	2. A	2. B	2. C	2. E	2. B	2. C
3. A	3. B	3. D	3. C	3. A	3. D	3. C	3. B
4. B	4. B	4. D	4. A	4. B	4. E	4. C	4. B
5. B	5. A	5. C	5. D	5. C	5. A	5. A	5. D
6. D	6. D	6. A	6. E	6. C	6. D	6. D	6. A
7. E	7. B	7. B	7. A	7. D	7. D	7. E	7. E
8. D	8. D	8. D	8. A	8. A	8. E	8. C	8. C
9. B	9. 2	9. C	9. D	9. E	9. E	9. B	9. D
10. B	10. 35 or 45	10. A	10. E	10. D	10. C	10. A	10. D
11. A	11. 100	11. D	11. E	11. C	11. B	11. C	11. A
12. D	12. 12	12. C	12. C	12. C	12. B	12. B	12. C
13. C	13. 2	13. D	13. D	13. D	13. C	13. B	13. E
14. D	14. 2	14. C	14. D	14. B	14. A	14. D	14. D
15. B	15. 72	15. A	15. A	15. B	15. B	15. E	
16. B	16. $\frac{2}{3} < x < \frac{7}{4}$	16. E	16. C	16. A	16. A	16. A	
17. E	17. 1.66 or 1.67 or $\frac{5}{3}$		17. E	17. E	17. D	17. C	
18. C	18. .113 or $\frac{7}{62}$		18. E	18. B	18. C	18. D	
19. A			19. C	19. C	19. E	19. A	
20. A			20. A	20. B		20. B	
			21. E	21. A		21. B	
			22. B	22. A		22. C	
			23. D	23. D		23. C	
			24. B	24. E		24. E	
						25. D	
						26. B	
						27. C	
						28. C	
						29. D	
						30. A	
						31. B	
						32. D	
						33. A	
						34. C	
						35. D	

Right (A): ___ | Questions 1–8 # Right (A): ___ | # Right (A): ___ | # Right (A): ___ | # Right (A): ___ | # Right (A): ___ | # Right (A) ___ | # Right (A): ___

Wrong (B): ___ | # Wrong (B): ___ | # Wrong (B): ___ | # Wrong (B): ___ | # Wrong (B): ___ | # Wrong (B): ___ | # Wrong (B): ___ | # Wrong (B): ___

(A) − ¼ (B): ___ | # (A) − ¼ (B): ___ | # (A) − ¼ (B): ___ | # (A) − ¼ (B): ___ | # (A) − ¼ (B): ___ | # (A) − ¼ (B): ___ | # (A) − ¼ (B): ___ | # (A) − ¼ (B): ___

Questions 9–18 # Right (A): ___

SCORE CONVERSION TABLE

How to score your test

Use the answer key on the previous page to determine your raw score on each section. **Your raw score on each section except Section 4 is simply the number of correct answers minus ¼ of the number of wrong answers. On Section 4, your raw score is the sum of the number of correct answers for questions 1–8 minus ¼ of the number of wrong answers for questions 1–8 plus the total number of correct answers for questions 9–18.** Next, add the raw scores from Sections 3, 4, and 7 to get your Math raw score, add the raw scores from Sections 2, 5, and 8 to get your Critical Reading raw score and add the raw scores from Sections 6 and 9 to get your Writing raw score. Write the three raw scores here:

Raw Critical Reading score: _____　Raw Math score: _____　Raw Writing score: _____

Use the table below to convert these to scaled scores.

Scaled scores:　Critical Reading: _____　Math: _____　Writing: _____

Raw Score	Critical Reading Scaled Score	Math Scaled Score	Writing Scaled Score	Raw Score	Critical Reading Scaled Score	Math Scaled Score	Writing Scaled Score
67	800			32	520	550	610
66	800			31	510	550	600
65	790			30	510	540	580
64	780			29	500	530	570
63	760			28	490	520	560
62	750			27	490	530	550
61	730			26	480	510	540
60	720			25	480	500	530
59	700			24	470	490	520
58	700			23	460	480	510
57	690			22	460	480	500
56	680			21	450	470	490
55	670			20	440	460	480
54	660	800		19	440	450	470
53	650	790		18	430	450	460
52	650	760		17	420	440	450
51	640	740		16	420	430	440
50	630	720		15	410	420	440
49	620	710	800	14	400	410	430
48	620	700	800	13	400	410	420
47	610	680	800	12	390	400	410
46	600	670	790	11	380	390	400
45	600	660	780	10	370	380	390
44	590	650	760	9	360	370	380
43	590	640	740	8	350	360	380
42	580	630	730	7	340	350	370
41	570	630	710	6	330	340	360
40	570	620	700	5	320	330	350
39	560	610	690	4	310	320	340
38	550	600	670	3	300	310	320
37	550	590	660	2	280	290	310
36	540	580	650	1	270	280	300
35	540	580	640	0	250	260	280
34	530	570	630	−1	230	240	270
33	520	560	620	−2 or less	210	220	250

SCORE CONVERSION TABLE FOR WRITING COMPOSITE
[ESSAY + MULTIPLE]

Calculate your writing raw score as you did on the previous page and grade your essay from a 1 to a 6 according to the standards that follow in the detailed answer key.

Essay score: _____ Raw Writing score: _____

Use the table below to convert these to scaled scores.

Scaled score: Writing: _____

Raw Score	Essay Score 0	Essay Score 1	Essay Score 2	Essay Score 3	Essay Score 4	Essay Score 5	Essay Score 6
−2 or less	200	130	250	280	310	340	370
−1	210	240	260	290	320	360	380
0	230	260	280	300	340	370	400
1	240	270	290	320	350	380	410
2	250	280	300	330	360	390	420
3	260	290	310	340	370	400	430
4	270	300	320	350	380	410	440
5	280	310	330	360	390	420	450
6	290	320	340	360	400	430	460
7	290	330	340	370	410	440	470
8	300	330	350	380	410	450	470
9	310	340	360	390	420	450	480
10	320	350	370	390	430	460	490
11	320	360	370	400	440	470	500
12	330	360	380	410	440	470	500
13	340	370	390	420	450	480	510
14	350	380	390	420	460	490	520
15	350	380	400	430	460	500	530
16	360	390	410	440	470	500	530
17	370	400	420	440	480	510	540
18	380	410	420	450	490	520	550
19	380	410	430	460	490	530	560
20	390	420	440	470	500	530	560
21	400	430	450	480	510	540	570
22	410	440	460	480	520	550	580
23	420	450	470	490	530	560	590
24	420	460	470	500	540	570	600
25	430	460	480	510	540	580	610
26	440	470	490	520	550	590	610
27	450	480	500	530	560	590	620
28	460	490	510	540	570	600	630
29	470	500	520	550	580	610	640
30	480	510	530	560	590	620	650
31	490	520	540	560	600	630	660
32	500	530	550	570	610	640	670
33	510	540	550	580	620	650	680
34	510	550	560	590	630	660	690
35	520	560	570	600	640	670	700
36	530	560	580	610	650	680	710
37	540	570	590	620	660	690	720
38	550	580	600	630	670	700	730
39	560	600	610	640	680	710	740
40	580	610	620	650	690	720	750
41	590	620	640	660	700	730	760
42	600	630	650	680	710	740	770
43	610	640	660	690	720	750	780
44	620	660	670	700	740	770	800
45	640	670	690	720	750	780	800
46	650	690	700	730	770	800	800
47	670	700	720	750	780	800	800
48	680	720	730	760	800	800	800
49	680	720	730	760	800	800	800

Detailed Answer Key

Section 1

> The following essay received 12 points out of a possible 12, meaning that it demonstrates *clear and consistent competence* in that it
>
> - develops an insightful point of view on the topic
> - demonstrates exemplary critical thinking
> - uses effective examples, reasons, and other evidence to support its thesis
> - is consistently focused, coherent, and well-organized
> - demonstrates skillful and effective use of language and sentence structure
> - is largely (but not necessarily completely) free of grammatical and usage errors
>
> Consider carefully the following statement. Then plan and write your essay as directed.
>
> > "A year is a long time—365 individual days. In that span, the earth has made a full revolution around the sun, entire species have evolved while others have become extinct, and governments have formed and dissolved. If we cannot reflect on the last 12 months and say how we have changed for the better, we must change the way we are living."
>
> **Assignment:** **"What is the most important thing that you have learned in the past year?"** Write an essay in which you answer this question and support your position logically with examples from literature, the arts, history, politics, science and technology, current events, or your experience or observation.

SAMPLE STUDENT ESSAY

The most important lesson I learned this year was that you don't have to officially win something to feel like you've won. In some situations, winning has more to do with a personal feeling of achievement than receiving an actual prize.

My best friend Steven and I have often trained together each fall for cross-country and we got to a point where we could run eight miles in under 50 minutes. The furthest we ever ran in one race was twelve miles, a rather grueling journey with a much slower time per mile than we were used to. Although we both had considered training to run a full 26-plus mile marathon, the 12-mile race instilled some doubt. Last year, at the end of our sophomore year, we were crazy enough to take on that formidable challenge: we decided to run in a marathon together in the coming fall.

We took out books from the library that suggested training regimens for running a marathon and followed them to the letter. We even changed our diets, reading up on what foods one should and should not eat in the months leading up to a race. We ran six days per week, easing our way into the process in terms of distance; first four mile runs with an occasional six, several weeks later six mile runs with an occasional eight. Within another month we topped our personal bests, running twelve miles more quickly, and, importantly, more easily than we had before. Twelve weeks into our training, we ran an eighteen mile loop. It was easily the hardest physical challenge of my life and I was exhausted at its completion. It left me wondering if I could possibly squeeze out another eight miles to complete the marathon one month later.

The day of the race came, and we were both giddy and nervous in anticipation of the monstrous task in front of us. We were carbohydrate-loaded (as the books all suggested) and thus well-fueled. Steven and I had agreed that we would not feel compelled to run the race together, freeing one of us to press ahead of the other depending on how we were feeling. For the first eighteen miles we ran at the exact same pace, proceeding at a rate that to be honest I didn't think I was capable of achieving. The adrenaline was helping! As I finished out that eighteenth mile I began to doubt whether I had enough left in me to complete the race. Steven started pulling away from me and I told him to leave me behind because I was running out of steam. He ran about one-hundred yards in front of me but never pulled much further away than that. He was sacrificing his time so that he could help pace me through the rest of the race and get me to the finish line (which still seemed like an impossible dream).

The following essay received 8 points out of a possible 12, meaning that it demonstrates *adequate competence* in that it
- develops a point of view on the topic
- demonstrates some critical thinking, but perhaps not consistently
- uses some examples, reasons, and other evidence to support its thesis, but perhaps not adequately
- shows a general organization and focus, but shows occasional lapses in this regard
- demonstrates adequate but occasionally inconsistent facility with language
- contains occasional errors in grammar, usage, and mechanics

SAMPLE STUDENT ESSAY

But I just kept going. Just over an hour later, we were coming down the home stretch ... 26.2 miles about to be completed. Steven slowed up so I could catch up to him, and we crossed the finish line together.

We finished behind 855 other runners that day, but I have never felt like more of a winner than I did that afternoon. My friend and I accomplished something together that we did not think possible just twelve months earlier. We set our minds to achieving this goal and overcame the challenge together. I don't know if I will ever run a marathon again in my life, but I know that if I am faced with a challenge that seems impossible, I will think about that marathon to help me get through it.

The most important lesson I learned this year was that there is truly no place like home. This past year has easily been the most complex and overwhelming year of my life. About 6 months ago, I wanted nothing to do with my family, was annoyed at every single member of my family, and could not wait until I went away to college. All it took was two months abroad and I have come to realize just how wrong these desires were.

The year began with what was supposed to be one of the most amazing experiences of my life. I was finally busting free from my "prison" at home! I was spending the first semester abroad in Madrid, Spain as part of an emersion program offered by my school's language department. All five students in our school who took part in the program were assigned to live with a family that spoke little to no English. I will admit that this had me feeling a little nervous since my Spanish was good but by no means fluent. But this concern was far lower on the list than the desire to get away from the craziness at home.

As it turned out, my concern about being able to communicate effectively was legitimate as I did indeed struggle to express many of my every day needs in Spanish. Who would have guessed how hard it would be to get someone to understand that you wanted your eggs without cheese?!?! But, as it turns out, this inability to communicate was the least of my concerns.

The family I was matched with did not want to participate in the exchange program and was forced to take me because only four families signed up to host a student and five of us came to Spain. I was matched with a family of six that lived in a house that should really only hold four. The house was tiny! The four children lived in two rooms that were each not much larger than the bunk beds they slept on. The only other rooms in the house were a tiny master bedroom for the parents, a small galley kitchen and a 10 foot by 10 foot "living room". Upon my arrival, the two youngest children came up to me and said to me in Spanish, "Oh, you're the one forcing us to move our bunk beds for 2 months. You stink." That's about as friendly as my interaction got with them all semester.

It didn't get much better from there. The two oldest sons, with whom I was supposed to go to school each day, were apparently going through a mischief phase and wanted nothing to do with going to classes. The first day I was there they were supposed to walk to school with me. Just two minutes after we left the house, they took off their backpacks, hid them in the woods, and headed in the opposite direction of the school. I missed the entire first half of the day because it took me 3 hours to even find the school on my own.

I tried to force myself to spend as much time as possible at the school learning and communicating in Spanish (and English!) with the teachers because I just didn't want to head back to that awful house. But, I could only spend so much time at the school each afternoon and I had to go home eventually. When I would arrive at the house from school, it was honestly like I was invisible. No one in the family would speak to me, the two youngest sons would walk into me as if they didn't know I was there and even the parents acted like I was a nuisance and that I was interrupting their every day life. I got to a point where I felt like I was Harry Potter living with the Dursley's under their stairwell, except I didn't know any magic tricks to make things better when the times were rough.

The following essay received 4 points out of a possible 12, meaning that it demonstrates *some incompetence* in that it

- has a seriously limited point of view
- demonstrates weak critical thinking
- uses inappropriate or insufficient examples, reasons, and other evidence to support its thesis
- is poorly focused and organized, and has serious problems with coherence
- demonstrates frequent problems with language and sentence structure
- contains errors in grammar and usage that obscure the author's meaning

SAMPLE STUDENT ESSAY

What was supposed to be the greatest and most exciting experience of my life was one of the disappointing and loneliest times I've ever had. To spend two months in a foreign country living with a family that really didn't want you around in the first place was quite a tiresome ordeal. Just weeks before I left for Spain I was trying to find ways to convince my parents to make my younger brother move out of our house so I could turn his room into a video game palace. After 2 weeks in Spain, I couldn't wait to come back home so I could hang out with him and listen to his endless whining. I realized on that journey that I actually had it amazingly good at home. I have a family that loves me, wants me around, and actually interacts with me on a daily basis.

The most important lesson I learned in the last year was to think before I spoke. I had a great job working at the country club near my house waiting tables. A lot of the people who eat there are pretty rich and get pretty rude towards the workers.

One afternoon this past summer, I was having a particularly bad day and was in a horrible mood. My parents had just told me that we were going to be moving in a year and I was furious—I didn't really even want to go to work.

When I got to work I realized it was the day of the club championship at the golf course so I knew that I was in for a long and busy day. Two of the waiters that were supposed to show up that day did not make it so my already hectic day immediately got a lot worse.

I normally worked four tables at one time, that day I had eight! The kitchen was way behind schedule, people were starting to get cranky and they were taking it out on me. I got to one of my tables and the customer asked (politely actually now that I think about it) when her food would be coming. I lost it and started yelling at her, taking out all my frustrations on an innocent bystander. I called her a snob, I called her stupidly rich, I told her she should just go buy her own restaurant and cook her own meal if she didn't want to wait any longer. I think I even called her fat! (She was thin)

She looked at me, horrified, shocked that I would yell at her in this manner. She asked me for my name and badge number. I mocked her by asking for her name and she handed me her card—"Director of Admissions—Dartmouth" . . . my top choice school. Upon reading that I muttered a quick apology, walked away quietly and vowed never again to let myself speak without thinking.

Section 2

1. B David was watching a *mindless* infomercial, which implies that it is not of high quality. The fact that he is watching a low quality show would suggest that there is a *lack* of good Sunday afternoon television. *influx* = a flowing in; *scarcity* = a lack; *glut* = an oversupply; *abundance* = a large amount.

2. B The horse was easy to handle all morning and then turned suddenly ————. If the horse refused to take a rider it would indicate he was being *difficult* or *stubborn*. *obstinate* = stubborn; *monotonous* = boring, tediously repeating; *cooperative* = willing to work with others; *tractable* = easy to handle.

3. C A destructive car bombing broke the cease fire and would have a negative impact on the peace talks. The word in the second blank should be negative, which eliminates D and E. The sentence suggests that this violence is not unusual because the talks were already —— when the bombing occurred. The first blank should mean something like *shaky*. *placid* = calm; *aborted* = terminated; *harmonious* = melodious, peaceful; *tenuous* = flimsy, easily shaken; *volatile* = explosive; *fragile* = easily broken; *complemented* = completed, made whole.

4. A The fact that the defendent knew he was going to go to prison indicates that the prosecutor had a very solid case against him. The evidence would be *strong* and difficult to argue against. *ironclad* = without flaw; *refute* = to prove false; *dubious* = doubtful; *indisputable* = undeniable; *authenticate* = to prove genuine; *corroborate* = to support; *surreptitious* = sneaky; *invalidate* = to nullify.

5. D The drive through was a first, something *new* and it revolutionized the fast food industry. *inane* = pointless; *insipid* = dull; *innocuous* = harmless; *innovative* = new and interesting. *intrepid* = fearless.

6. E His ———— actions brought him *censure* (public criticism) and led to his resignation. His actions must have been *inappropriate* and *worthy of criticism*. *commendable* = worthy of praise; *inconcievable* = difficult to grasp or understand; *laudable* = worthy of praise; *exemplary* = worthy of imitation; *reprehensible* = worthy of criticism.

7. A This sentence suggests there is a similarity between Mendel's success and that of many scientists before him and that he was *lucky* to "stumble upon" a species that worked for him. You want a word that suggests *luck*. *serendipitous* = the act of making a discovery by good fortune; *deliberate* = with intent;

outlandish = unconventional, bizarre; *premeditate* = to plan or plot ahead of time; *intangible* = unable to be felt.

8. A The critics described the publication as derivative (*adapted from other works*) and ————. The information after the semi-colon explains what the word in the second blank should mean. The critics said the book *offered nothing new or insightful*, so the second word should mean *common*. Since the critics are criticizing the work, the first blank should contain a word that is negative and means "criticized". *decry* = to openly criticize; *mundane* = boring, common, everyday; *hailed* = praised; *hackneyed* = overused, trite; *condemned* = strongly disapproved of; *lauded* = praised; *vapid* = tasteless, dull; *maligned* = wronged, treated with malice; *avant-garde* = innovative.

9. D The main idea of the passage is that *"Value judgments" are not irrelevant to criticism* and that critics should not merely *take refuge in intellectualism*.

10. E The *risks* include having *to expose himself (or herself) to judgment by the quality of his own experience or life, or by his capacity to evaluate and interpret it*.

11. E The passage states that architects must be knowledgeable in *space distribution, construction techniques...mechanical systems . . . financing* and so on, suggesting that their knowledge is broad. But to say they *know nothing* suggests that this knowledge is also shallow.

12. C The *concrete domes of one particular shape* are the objects of specialization for particular structural engineers.

13. D The first paragraph explains how reading is a complex task in that the *simple experience of the ... printed page* moves into the *world of abstractions* (lines 10–11).

14. D The word *move* here refers to the process in a reader's mind of translating words on a page into abstract thoughts.

15. A This quote presents a perspective that contrasts the idea in the previous sentence that *books are palliatives (objects of comfort)* (line 24).

16. C The *suspicions* are those of people who think that close readers have *lost their touch with reality* (line 35).

17. E The passage states that it is the alienation that does so much damage (lines 64–65), and this alienation is described in the previous sentence as the distinction between life and literature.

18. E In saying that *experience...is a traffic between the object and the subject*, the author means that there is interaction or communication between them.

19. C This sentence states that we adjust to the objects with every confidence that they are real when we have sensations and impressions of objects (lines 83–85). In other words, we act under the belief that our perceptions are of real objects, and not illusions.

20. A The phrase *impression of the sensation* here means *interpretation of the experience*.

21. E The stone is said to *stimulate...our imagination* (line 46) and the bush, likewise, is said to be an *impression of the sensation* (line 88) which can be mistaken when *imagining some fear* (line 93).

22. B Keats is described as one who expressed *a preference for the imagined* (line 101), and as an *uncommon reader* (line 104). The passage does not discuss Keats' writing at all.

23. D The author suggests that *becoming more educated* is how some people *seek refuge in ... abstractness* (line 114) in order to avoid the *lively sensations* (line 106) of literature.

24. B Each paragraph maintains a consistent focus on the importance of imagination in the interpretation and appreciation of literature.

Section 3

1. E $6x + 4 = 7x - 3$
Add 3: $6x + 7 = 7x$
Subtract $6x$: $7 = x$

2. C First figure out how many dozen cookies there are in 108 cookies:

$$108 \text{ cookies} \times \frac{1 \text{ dozen}}{12 \text{ cookies}} = 9 \text{ dozen}$$

Next, solve:

$$9 \text{ dozen} \times \frac{2 \text{ cups}}{3 \text{ dozen}} = 6 \text{ cups}$$

3. A

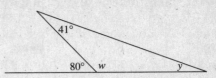

There are 180° on one side of a line:
$$w + 80° = 180°$$
Subtract 80: $w = 100°$
There are 180° in a triangle:
$$41° + 100° + y = 180°$$
Combine like terms: $141° + y = 180°$
Subtract 141: $y = 39°$

4. B First, solve for w.
                          20 is 40% of w
                          $20 = .40(w)$
Divide by 0.40: $w = 50$
Next, find 20% of 50
                          x is 20% of 50
                          $x = 0.20(50)$
Simplify: $x = 10$

5. B Find the amount of excess rope each answer choice would produce by dividing by 4:
Answer choice A: $15 \div 4 = 3$ remainder 3
Answer choice B: $15.5 \div 4 = 3$ remainder 3.5
Answer choice C: $16 \div 4 = 4$ remainder 0
Answer choice D: $16.5 \div 4 = 4$ remainder 0.5
Answer choice E: $17 \div 4 = 4$ remainder 1
Answer choice B has the largest amount left over.

6. D

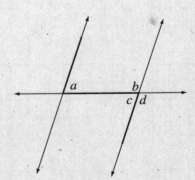

A "Z" can be drawn that shows us that angle a is equal to angle c. Therefore $a = c = 80°$.

Remember that there are 180° on one side of a line, so $c + b = 180°$. Substitute in 80° for c and we see that $b = 100°$.

Because angle b and angle d are vertical angles, $b = d = 100°$.

Therefore $b + c + d = 100° + 80° + 100° = 280°$

---

7. **E** This one is just a matter of drawing out all the possibilities:

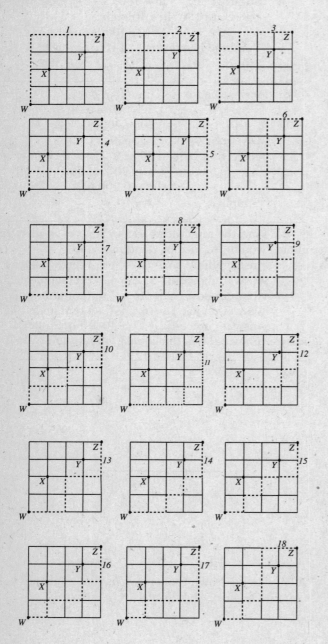

8. **D** Just try a few numbers from each of the sets and see which always work.

I. *The set of odd integers:* Try 5 and 7. $5 + 7 = 12$. Since 12 is even, Roman numeral I is already eliminated.

II. *The set of even integers:* Try 4 and 8. $4 + 8 = 12$. How about 6 and 18? $6 + 18 = 24$. This one works!

III. *The set of positive integers:* any positive integer added to another positive integer is positive. So this one works.

---

9. **B** $g(f(x)) =$
Substitute for $f(x)$: $g(4x - 3) =$
Plug $(4x - 3)$ into $g(x)$: $g(4x - 3) = (4x - 3)^2 + 3$
F.O.I.L.: $g(4x - 3) = 16x^2 - 12x - 12x + 9 + 3$
Combine like terms: $g(f(x)) = 16x^2 - 24x + 12$

---

10. **B** Choose a value of a that is 5 more than some multiple of 6, like $a = 11$. Then, find the value of $4a$: $4(11) = 44$. Next, find the remainder when 44 is divided by 6:

$$6\overline{)44} \quad \begin{array}{r} 7 \\ \hline \end{array}$$

The answer is 7 Remainder 2: $\dfrac{-42}{2}$

---

11. **A**

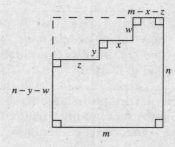

If you wish, label all of the sides and add them up. Starting from the top right and moving down:

$n + m + (n - y - w) + z + y + x + w + (m - x - z)$
$n + n + m + m - y + y - w + w + z - z + x - x$

Combine like terms: $2m + 2n$

Or, much more simply, you can notice that the perimeter of this figure must be the same as the surrounding rectangle, which clearly has perimeter $2m + 2n$.

12. D

First find the value of f: $\begin{vmatrix} a & b \\ d & c \end{vmatrix} = ab + cd$.

$f = \begin{vmatrix} 2 & 3 \\ 5 & 4 \end{vmatrix}$ $f = 2(3) + 4(5) = 6 + 20 = 26$

Plug in 26 for f and solve:

$\begin{vmatrix} 2 & 7 \\ 3 & 26 \end{vmatrix} = 2(7) + 3(26) = 92$

13. C

Area of a circle:	$\pi r^2 = 75\pi$
Divide by π:	$r^2 = 75$
Take square root:	$r = \sqrt{75} = 5\sqrt{3}$

Because this is an equilateral triangle, it can be split into two 30-60-90 triangles.

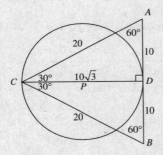

The perimeter is equal to $10 + 10 + 20 + 20 = 60$.

14. D

Rewrite ratio:	$3x : 4x : 5x$
180° in a Δ:	$3x + 4x + 5x = 180°$
Combine like terms:	$12x = 180°$
Divide by 12:	$x = 15$
Plug in for x:	$45° : 60° : 75°$
Add 2 smallest together:	$45° + 60° = 105°$

15. B

Volume of cylinder:	$V = \pi r^2 h$
Plug in given values:	$200\pi = \pi(r)^2(8)$
Divide by π:	$200 = (r)^2(8)$
Divide by 8:	$25 = r^2$
Take square root:	$5 = r$
Circumference of circle:	$C = 2\pi r$
Plug in for r:	$C = 2\pi(5) = 10\pi$

16. B

Let the *smaller* number be x, and the *larger* number be $x + 4$, since they differ by 4.

Find the sum of the two:	$x + (x + 4) = w$
Combine like terms:	$2x + 4 = w$
Add 4:	$2x = w - 4$
Divide by 2:	$x = \dfrac{w - 4}{2}$

17. E

Try to "construct" the order in the front of the room. You have seven spots to fill, and thus seven decisions to make and seven numbers to multiply. The first spot must be filled by a girl, so you have four choices for the first spot. The second spot a boy, so three choices, The third spot a girl, you've already placed one girl so now you have three choices. The fourth spot a boy, you now have two choices. The fifth spot a girl, you now have two choices, the sixth spot a boy, you only have one choice and the seventh spot a girl, you only have one choice.

There are $4 \times 3 \times 3 \times 2 \times 2 \times 1 \times 1 = 144$ possibilities.

18. C

Find a couple more terms to see if you can find the pattern. The sixth term = $3 - (-4) = 7$. The seventh term = $-4 - 7 = -11$. The eighth term = $7 - (-11) = 18$. A pattern has formed (just focus on + and − since that is what they are asking about):

$$+, +, -, +, -, +, -, +, -, \ldots$$

Starting with the second term, the sequence alternates between + and -. The pattern repeats every 2 terms. You know the first term of the sequence is +, and you want to see how many of the next 41 are negative. Divide 41 by 2 and see how many times the pattern repeats: $41 \div 2 = 20$ remainder 1. There is one negative term in each repetition of the pattern, so there are $20 \times 1 = 20$ negative terms. The 42ns term is positive since the first term of each repetition is +. There are 20 negative terms.

19. A

If line l is perpendicular to line m, then the slope of line l is the opposite reciprocal of the slope of line m. Begin by finding the slope of line m:

$$\frac{y_2 - y_1}{x_2 - x_1} = \frac{-2 - 0}{4 - 0} = -\frac{2}{4} = -\frac{1}{2}$$

This means that the slope of line l must be 2. Use the slope formula to find the value of x:

$$\frac{y_2 - y_1}{x_2 - x_1} = \frac{0 - (-2)}{x - 4} = \frac{2}{x - 4} = 2$$

Cross Multiply:	$2(x - 4) = 2$
Distribute:	$2x - 8 = 2$
Add 8:	$2x = 10$
Divide by 2:	$x = 5$

Now we need to find the area of the triangle by finding the base and the height. The height is 2 and the base is 5. Area = $\frac{1}{2}$(base)(height) = $\frac{1}{2}(5)(2) = 5$.

20. A

Perhaps the easiest way to solve this problem is to plug in numbers. Imagine a group of $s = 20$ students agreed to split a trip that cost $d = \$1000$ equally. [They would each pay $\$1,000/20 = \$50$.] But, $g = 5$ students backed out meaning that now each student would pay $\$1,000/15 = \$66.67$—a difference of $\$16.67$. Plug in the values of g, s, and d into the answer choices and pick the one that gives you $\$16.67$.

$$\frac{dg}{s^2 - sg} = \frac{(1000)(5)}{(20)^2 - (20)(5)} = \frac{5000}{400 - 100} = 16.67$$

Section 4

1. E

Begin by writing an equation:	$4n - 6 = 26$
Add 6:	$4n = 32$
Divide by 4:	$n = 8$

Careful: the question asks for the SQUARE of 8:

Square both sides:	$n^2 = 64$

2. C

You can actually solve this problem most easily by realizing that the ¼ cup of oil already added is equal to 10% of the total. Solve the following:

$$\frac{1}{4} \text{ is 10% of what?}$$
$$\frac{1}{4} = 0.10x$$

Divide by 0.10: $2.5 = x$

There will be 2.5 cups total, so you must add $2.5 - 0.25 = 2.25$ cups.

3. B

Begin by combining the like terms in both equations to get the following equations:

$$26 + b + c = 51$$
$$\underline{26 + a + b = 42}$$

Subtract straight down: $c - a = 9$

4. B

	$2|y| + 4 < 14$
Subtract 4:	$2|y| < 10$
Divide by 2:	$|y| < 5$

The largest possible value of y is 4 since it must be < 5.

5. A

It pays to recognize that $(n - m)(n + m)$ is the same thing as $n^2 - m^2$.

	$4n^2 = 20$
Divide by 4:	$n^2 = 5$
	$3m^2 = 12$
Divide by 3:	$m^2 = 4$
	$n^2 - m^2$
Substitute:	$5 - 4 = 1$

6. D

Set up an equation to find the average:

$$\frac{a + b + c + d + e}{5} = 30$$

Multiply by 5: $a + b + c + d + e = 150$

To find the greatest possible value, you want to make all the other as **small** as possible. They must all be different so you cannot repeat any numbers. Make $a = 1$, $b = 2$, $c = 3$, and $d = 4$ and solve for e:

	$1 + 2 + 3 + 4 + e = 150$
Combine like terms:	$10 + e = 150$
Subtract 10:	$e = 140$

7. B This problem can be solved by drawing a Venn diagram.

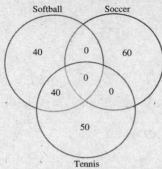

Let's say all 40 of the students that play two sports play both tennis and softball. This means that 0 students play both tennis and soccer, 0 students play both soccer and softball, and 0 students play all three sports. If 80 students in total play softball and 40 are playing softball *and* tennis, then 80 − 40 = 40 students play *just* softball. If 90 students in total play tennis and 40 are playing softball *and* tennis, then 90 − 40 = 50 students play *just* tennis. There are 60 students that play just soccer. The total number of students can now be found by adding together all the values in the diagram: 40 + 40 + 60 + 50 = 190.

8. D This problem involves rates, so it helps to recall the rate equation: $d = rt$.

Because he travels home *along the same route*, you can use d for the distance both to and from work. Because he spends a total of 2 hours in the car, if he spends t hours going to work, he will spend $2 - t$ hours on the way home from work.

Set up the rate equations for both legs of the trip:

To work:	$d = 30t$
From work:	$d = 20(2 - t)$
Set the expressions equal:	$30t = 20(2 - t)$
Distribute:	$30t = 40 - 20t$
Add 20t:	$50t = 40$
Divide by 50:	$t = 0.80$

Plug 0.80 in for t and solve for d: $d = 30(0.80) = 24$
Check by confirming that plugging $t = 0.80$ into the other rate equation gives the same distance from home to work.

9. 2
The question asks for the value of $8x - 10y$. They tell you that $4x = 10$ and $5y = 9$. Don't solve for x and y individually, recognize that $8x$ is twice $4x$, so $8x = 2(10) = 20$ and that $10y$ is twice $5y$, so $10y = 2(9) = 18$. Plug those into $8x - 10y = 20 - 18 = 2$.

10. 35 or 45
First, take note that it must be an **odd** positive integer.

Let's write an equation for it:	$40 < p + 0.20p < 55$
Combine like terms:	$40 < 1.20p < 55$
Divide by 1.20:	$33.33 < p < 45.83$

There are 6 odd integers in that range: 35, 37, 39, 41, 43, 45. In order for it to form an integer when increased by 20% of itself, it must be divisible by 5. 35 or 45 work.

11. 100
There are 540° in a pentagon:

	$134° + 126° + 112° + 88° + x = 540°$
Combine like terms:	$460° + x = 540°$
Subtract 460°:	$x = 80°$

There are 180° on one side of a line:

	$80° + y = 180°$
Subtract 80°:	$y = 100°$

12. 12

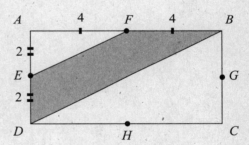

Find the area of the entire rectangle = length × width
$$\text{Area} = (8)(4) = 32$$
Area of $\triangle ABD = \frac{1}{2}(\text{Area rectangle } ABCD) = \frac{1}{2}(32) = 16$.
To find the shaded area, subtract the area of $\triangle AFE$ from the area of $\triangle ABD$.
$$\text{Area of } \triangle AFE = \frac{1}{2}(2)(4) = 4$$
Shaded Area = Area of $\triangle ABD$ − Area of $\triangle AFE$
Shaded Area = $16 - 4 = 12$

13. 2

$$4p^{+r} = 1,024$$

Since $4^5 = 1,024$, it follows that $p + r = 5$

$$2^p = 16$$

Since $2^4 = 16$, it follows that $p = 4$.

$$p + r = 5$$

Substitute: $4 + r = 5$

Subtract 4: $r = 1$

$$2^r = 2^1 = 2$$

---

14. 2

Set up an equation: $y \div \frac{1}{4} = 32$

Multiply by $\frac{1}{4}$: $y = 8$

Raise 8 to the $\frac{1}{3}$: $8^{1/3} = 2$

---

15. 72

Don't be afraid to rotate a triangle on the page to make it easier to work with when trying to find the area. If the base of the triangle is 20 and the area is 240, solve to find the height:

$$A = \frac{1}{2}(base)(height)$$
$$240 = \frac{1}{2}(20)(h)$$

Divide by 10: $24 = height$

The larger triangle is composed of two 5-12-13 triangles, except that they are 10-24-26. The perimeter of the larger triangle is found by adding 26 + 26 + 10 + 10 = 72.

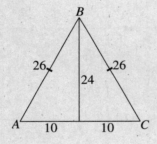

16. 2/3 <x × 7/4 or .666 < 1.75

Find the slope of each of the lines; line n will have a slope between those two.

line l: $\dfrac{y_2 - y_1}{x_2 - x_1} = \dfrac{(7-0)}{(4-0)} = \dfrac{7}{4}$

line m: $\dfrac{y_2 - y_1}{x_2 - x_1} = \dfrac{(4-0)}{(6-0)} = \dfrac{2}{3}$

Therefore, the slope of line n is between $\frac{2}{3}$ and $\frac{7}{4}$.

---

17. 1.66 or 1.67 or 5/3

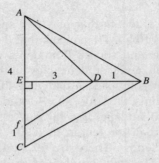

Using the ratios that they give in the problem you can fill in the information shown above. Now just calculate the areas of the two triangles mentioned:

Area $\triangle ABC = \frac{1}{2}(5)(4) = 10$

Area $\triangle ADF = \frac{1}{2}(4)(3) = 6$

Now find the quotient: $\dfrac{\text{Area } \triangle ABC}{\text{Area } \triangle ADF} = \dfrac{10}{6} = \dfrac{5}{3}$

---

18. 0.113 or 7/62

Set up ratios for the various relationships:

$$\frac{yellow}{red} = \frac{4}{1} \qquad \frac{black}{red} = \frac{3}{1}$$

Pretend there was only 1 red marble. There would be 3 black marbles and 4 yellow marbles – 1 + 3 + 4 = 8 total. They tell us that there are 32 total marbles, so there are 4 red, 12 black and 16 yellow. The probability that 3 marbles selected at random, without replacement, can be found by multiplying the probability that each of the first three draws would be yellow.

The probability that the first draw is yellow: $\frac{16}{32}$

The probability that the second draw is yellow: $\frac{15}{31}$

The probability that the third draw is yellow: $\frac{14}{30}$

Multiply the probabilities: $\frac{16}{32} \times \frac{15}{31} \times \frac{14}{30} = .113$

Section 5

1. D If a fight broke out as a result of the remark, the remark must have been *insulting*. *impromptu* = done without preparation; *barren* = lacking production, infertile; *derogatory* = belittling, insulting.

2. C The waterdogs are a breed known for showing extreme drive and determination, which is *diligence*. *corpulent* = fat; *languid* = weak; *diligent* = hard working; *dilatory* = delaying; *vacuous* = lacking substance.

3. A The politician had never lost so he was probably pretty confident, and perhaps overly so. His behavior related to this fact was *costing him votes*. The two words should be negative. *haughty* = overly proud; *conceited* = cocky; *prevaricator* = a liar; *diffident* = timid, shy; *cavalier* = overly proud; *augur* = a prophet, one who can tell the future; *meticulous* = attentive to detail; *autocrat* = a ruler with unlimited power.

4. B The *unlike* at the beginning of the sentence introduces an impending contrast. Therefore you are looking for words in the two blanks that oppose each other. Ultimately the students at Lincoln High must behave in an opposite manner to the students at Broad Spectrum. Answer choice B is a perfect fit because *deference* and *irreverence* are virtual antonyms. *civility* = politeness; *amiability* = friendliness; *deference* = respect; *irreverence* = disrespect; *impropriety* = improper behavior; *impertinence* = rudeness; *apathy* = lack of caring; *impunity* = exemption from penalty; *veneration* = respect, worship; *compliance* = willingness to follow the rules.

5. C That time period was not a time of equality for African Americans, and one can infer that their works were *stolen* by others. This would make it difficult for their contributions to be *noted* or *appropriately recognized*. *filch* = to steal; *exonerate* = to free of blame; *expurgate* = to edit to remove profanity; *undisclosed* = not made known; *appropriate* = to take possesion of; *misattribute* = to assign to the wrong person; *commiserate* = to sympathize with; *pilfer* = to steal.

6. C The passage explains some reasons why pencil-and- paper tests may not reflect real ability. It does not suggest any ways to improve them, or to solve problems in general.

7. D The passage states that *in real life, one might settle* for a solution *that satisfies his or her own needs* (lines 23–24), which means that such a solution is provisional.

8. A The passage states the *unlike nutrients... such as vitamins...oxygen cannot be stored within the body* (lines 5–8), thereby suggesting that vitamins can be stored in the body. Statement (A) would contradict this.

9. E The passage states that *what makes the respiration process unique in our body is that it functions both automatically and voluntarily* (lines 13–15), that is, it works with and without our conscious control.

10. D The passage states that it was not *strange* for the original settlers to become indentured servants because it followed the tradition of those who *apprenticed themselves*.

11. C In saying I have lost my edge (line 4) the author means that she has lost her ability to write because she is *so connected to the rhythms of my children*. (lines 3–4)

12. C The author uses the term *"boiling point"* twice, in line 18 and line 118) to describe a point after which she had done her research in preparation for writing, but had not yet begun to write productively.

13. D These questions represent the distracting questions that people might ask her on the telephone.

14. B This paragraph describes the author's feelings as she imagines her daughter's experience if she had to stay home from her field trip. She says that *I too would sit in the hot September library* to indicate that she empathizes strongly with her daughter.

15. B This statement represents the author's acquiescence to go to her daughter's school to bring her the misplaced permission slip discussed in the previous paragraph.

16. A In this sentence, the author is expressing amazement that she is finally beginning to write despite all of the *tugs and pulls* in her life that distract her.

17. E The passage states that John Ford's tales were like Homer's in that they were *told for an audience who. . . were not looking for . . . enlightenment* (line 11). Therefore, it suggests that Homer's tales were not enlightening.

18. B The passage attributes this sense to *the influence of his Irish background* (line 18).

19. C The *apprehension of impermanence* in this sentence refers to the *sense or perception of mortality*.

20. B The sentence that follows this statement explains it: *Experience, not abstract ideas, is the stuff of the work* (lines 44–45). In other words, Ford did not make films about the abstract, but rather about concrete experiences.

21. A The author states that Ford's villains are *not in the least seductive* to contrast the *commonly received notion that evil is so much more "interesting or attractive than goodness* (line 54), thereby suggesting that his villains are not attractive to audiences.

22. A The author says that Ford's style is *powerful...not assertive*, and goes on to explain that, while it has a strong effect, it *never proclaims itself* (line 75). Therefore the author is suggesting that Ford's style is not *obtrusive*.

23. D The author uses phrases like *sticks to his guns* (line 82), *unyielding integrity* (line 91) and *his essential character did not change* (line 95) to convey Ford's steadfast artistic style.

24. E The final paragraph states that Ford *saw the world going in a way he could...(not) wholly understand.* Therefore, he found it difficult to comprehend.

Section 6

1. D Because *fellow man* is being treated as a possessed object, *one's* must have an apostrophe.

2. B Choice (B) is the most concise and clear. Recognize that *could of* is a diction error: the correct for is *could have*.

3. C The phrase *less plants* is incorrect because plants are countable, so there are *fewer* of them.

4. C The past participle of *to take* is *taken*, not *took*, and the phrase *to get* is more idiomatic than *in getting*.

5. A The original phrasing is best. The correct idiom is *focused on*.

6. D The pronoun is part of a prepositional phrase, and so should be in the objective case: *me*. Also, remember that a colon separates two **independent clauses** in which the second explains the first.

7. E Because the *leaving* is a completed action, it should be in the past **perfect tense**: *had left*.

8. C The phrasing in answer C is both clear and parallel.

9. B Use *between* when comparing exactly 2 things, and *among* when comparing more than 2 things.

10. A The original phrasing is best.

11. C The sentence begins with a participial phrase that modifies *we*, so the original phrasing creates a dangling participle. Choice (C) corrects this problem, and coordinates the ideas clearly.

12. B The subject of verb is *rush*, which is singular, so the verb should be *is*.

13. B The phrase *what period they arrived in* is awkward; *when they arrived* is simpler and more parallel.

14. D The pronoun *one* is ambiguous. It should be replaced by *a pitcher*.

15. E The sentence is correct.

16. A The subject of the verb is *graphics*, which is plural, so the verb should be *are*.

17. **C**   The phrase *because of* is not parallel. In the construction *not only* A *but also* B, the phrases that replace A and B must be parallel: *because of* should be replaced with *by*.

18. **D**   The word *unanimously* means that everyone is in agreement. The proper word is *anonymously*.

19. **A**   The verb is in the wrong tense. Since the sentence refers to *now*, the correct tense is present perfect: *has finished*.

20. **B**   As it is, the sentence is a **run on** since two sentences are joined with only a comma. Two acceptable corrections are *and they provided* or *providing*.

21. **B**   The pronoun *that* is not appropriate in reference to a boy. The correct pronoun is *who*.

22. **C**   The pronoun *this* does not agree in number with its antecedent *tactics*, and should be replaced by *them*.

23. **C**   This is an error in parallelism. The phrase *to wash the walls* uses an infinitive, so *scrubbing* should also be in the infinitive form: *to scrub*.

24. **E**   The sentence is correct.

25. **D**   Because *the Actor's Guild* is singular, *their* is the wrong number and should be replaced by *its*.

26. **B**   Because *police* are countable, *fewer* should be used instead of *less*.

27. **C**   The subject of the verb is *rate*, which is singular, so the verb does not agree with its subject and its diction is awkward. A good correction is *indicates*.

28. **C**   This is an **idiom error**. People are satisfied *with* things not *at* them.

29. **D**   The underlined phrase is the object of a prepositional phrase, and so should take the objective case: *my brothers and me*.

30. **A**   Choice A is the most conscise and logical.

31. **B**   The coordinators *nevertheless* and *for example* are illogical in this context.

32. **D**   This option is most concise and parallel, while conveying all the necessary information.

33. **A**   Choice (A) provides the most logical follow-up to sentence 7.

34. **C**   Sentence 11 mentions the Greek Orthodox Church for the only time in the passage. This sentence could easily be removed without changing any central idea of the passage.

35. **D**   This option is the most concise, while conveying the same overall meaning.

Section 7

1. E

$$4x - 7 =$$
Plug in 9 for $4x$: $9 - 7 = 2$
(Chapter 11, Lesson 1: Solving Equations)

2. A

If she buys a dozen apples and apples cost $1.20 for 6 apples, she will spend 2(1.20) = $2.40 on the apples. If she buys 10 oranges and oranges cost $1.20 for 5 oranges, she will spend 2(1.20) = $2.40 on the oranges. She will spend a total of $2.40 + $2.40 = $4.80.

If she pays with a $5.00 bill she will get $5.00 – $4.80 = $0.20 back in change.

3. D

All four angles together must add up to 360°
$$114° + w + x + y = 360°$$
Subtract 114°: $w + x + y = 246°$

4. D

This is purely a logic problem. Felisha's car must be parked next to Eric's and Latoya's car. This means that Felisha's car is in the middle of the two, either in spot B:

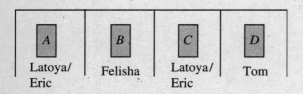

Or in spot C:

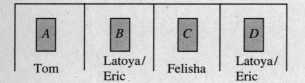

Because Latoya and Eric's cars must always be on either side of Felisha's car, it leaves Tom's car in either spot A or spot D, depending on if Felisha's car is in spot B or spot C.

5. C

Stack them and add straight down:

$$
\begin{array}{r}
3x + 4y = 7 \\
+\ \underline{5x - 6y = 12} \\
8x - 2y = 19
\end{array}
$$

6. A

You have three decisions to make in this problem. You must choose where to put the G, then choose which vowel to put in the second spot, then choose the final letter. Since the G may be placed in either the first or third spot, there are 2 options. Since a second letter must be a vowel, there are 2 options. The final spot there are three options because there are 3 letters left. This means there are 2 × 2 × 3 = 12 possibilities.

7. B

Begin by estimating how many births there were, on average, per day of the week: Sunday: 10, Monday: 15, Tuesday: 13, Wednesday: 20, Thursday: 15, Friday: 10, Saturday: 17.

Add them up: 10 + 15 + 13 + 20 + 15 + 10 + 17 = 100
The total of 100 makes it easy to calculate a percentage.

On Fri, Sat and Sun there were 10 + 10 + 17 = 37 births.

37 is what percent of 100? 37%

8. D

The fact that $AC = AD$ tells us that $\triangle ACD$ is isosceles and thus we know that angles ACD and ADC are equal.

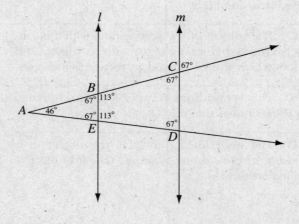

The fact that the lines l and m are parallel lets us know that angles ABE and AEB are equal as well. The fact that we're given angle BAE allows us to fill out that small triangle because

$$46° + w + w = 180°$$

Subtract 46°: $\quad\quad\quad 2w = 134°$

Divide by 2: $\quad\quad\quad\quad w = 67°$

There are 180° on one side of a line:

$$180° - 67° = x = 113°$$

Because of complimentary angles:

$$\angle ACD = \angle ADC = 67°$$

Because of vertical angles: $\quad\quad z = 67°.$

$$x + y + z =$$

Plug in: $\quad 113° + 113° + 67° = 293°$

---

9. C

p represents the sum of all the factors of n.

$f(24) = 1 + 2 + 3 + 4 + 6 + 8 + 12 + 24 = 60$

$f(16) = 1 + 2 + 4 + 8 + 16 = 31$

$f(24) - f(16) = 60 - 31 = 29$

---

10. A

Start by finding the radius of each circle: $\quad C = 2\pi r$

Plug in 6π for C: $\quad\quad\quad\quad\quad 6\pi = 2\pi r$

Divide by 2π: $\quad\quad\quad\quad\quad\quad\quad 3 = r$

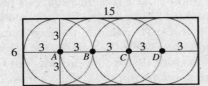

Fill in the radii and the perimeter is

$$15 + 15 + 6 + 6 = 42$$

---

11. D

At first, this problem can seem quite daunting because you think you have to start adding up all of the integers starting at negative eight and continue until you get to a sum of 30. But, use a little logic here:

$-8 + -7 + -6 + -5 + -4 + -3 + -2 + -1 + 0 + 1 + 2 + 3 + 4 + 5 + 6 + 7 + 8$

Notice, that all of those numbers above will cancel out when added together: $-8 + 8 = 0$; $-7 + 7 = 0$, etc. . . . So the sum of all the numbers from -8 to $+8$ is zero! Now, starting at 9, add numbers until you get to 30. $9 + 10 = 19 + 11 = 30$. This means that $w = 11$. From -8 to 11 there are 20 numbers.

---

12. C

The cube's volume is 64 which means that each side of the cube is 4. To solve this problem you need to construct right triangles and use the Pythagorean Theorem.

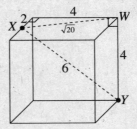

Find the value of XW: $\quad\quad 2^2 + 4^2 = (XW)^2$

Combine like terms: $\quad\quad\quad\quad 20 = (XW)^2$

Take the square root: $\quad\quad\quad \sqrt{20} = XW$

Find the value of XY: $\quad (\sqrt{20})^2 + 4^2 = (XY)^2$

Combine like terms: $\quad\quad\quad\quad\quad 36 = (XY)^2$

Take the square root: $\quad\quad\quad\quad\quad 6 = XY$

---

13. D

You might first come up with all the possible values of x.

$\quad\quad 5x + 2y = 41$

If $x = 1$: $\quad\quad\quad\quad 5(1) + 2y = 41$

Subtract 5: $\quad\quad\quad\quad 2y = 36$

Divide by 2: $\quad\quad\quad\quad y = 18$ OK

If $x = 2$: $\quad\quad\quad\quad 5(2) + 2y = 41$

Subtract 10: $\quad\quad\quad 2y = 31$

Divide by 2: $\quad\quad\quad\quad y = 15.5$ [not integer]

If $x = 3$: $\quad\quad\quad\quad 5(3) + 2y = 41$

Subtract 15: $\quad\quad\quad 2y = 26$

Divide by 2: $\quad\quad\quad\quad y = 13$ OK

If $x = 4$: $\quad\quad\quad\quad 5(4) + 2y = 41$

Subtract 20: $\quad\quad\quad 2y = 21$

Divide by 2: $\quad\quad\quad\quad y = 10.5$ [not integer]

If $x = 5$: $\quad\quad\quad\quad 5(5) + 2y = 41$

Subtract 25: $\quad\quad\quad 2y = 16$

Divide by 2: $\quad\quad\quad\quad y = 8$ OK

If $x = 6$: $\quad\quad\quad\quad 5(6) + 2y = 41$

Subtract 30: $\quad\quad\quad 2y = 11$

Divide by 2: $\quad\quad\quad\quad y = 5.5$ [not integer]

If $x = 7$: $\quad\quad\quad\quad 5(7) + 2y = 41$

Subtract 35: $\quad\quad\quad 2y = 6$

Divide by 2: $\quad\quad\quad\quad y = 3$ OK

If $x = 8$: $\quad\quad\quad\quad 5(8) + 2y = 41$

Subtract 40: $\quad\quad\quad 2y = 1$

Divide by 2: $\quad\quad\quad\quad y = 0.5$ [not integer]

x can be 1, 3, 5, or 7. The product is

$$1 \times 3 \times 5 \times 7 = 105$$

14. A

Since it is a regular hexagon, it can be divided into 6 equilateral triangles. Because each side of the hexagon is part of one of the 6 identical equilateral triangles that surrounds the polygon, the area of the polygon can be found by finding the area of one of the surrounding equilateral triangles and multiplying that result by 6.

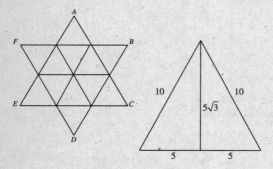

Area = ½ (10)(5√3) = 25√3

Since the hexagon is composed of 6 of these triangles, the area of the hexagon can be found by multiplying

25√3 × 6 = 150√3

15. A

If $4^a = b$, substitute that in: $64b = 64(4^a)$
$64 = 4^3$, substitute that in: $64b = 4^3(4^a)$
Using the rules of exponentials: $64b = 4^{3+a}$

16. E

If Bill's rate is b miles per hour and he goes a distance of m miles in m/b hours. Similarly, Ty covers the m miles at t miles per hour in m/t hours. Since Bill is going faster than Ty, he is running for less time. To find how much longer it took Ty to finish

the race subtract the two times: $\dfrac{m}{t} - \dfrac{m}{h}$

Section 8

1. E   The individuals from ——— came together as one to further the women's rights movement. A word like *diverse* is a perfect fit for the second blank. Because all these individuals *came together*, it would make sense for *united* to be the word in the first blank. *acrimonious* = bitter, harsh; *disparate* = different, dissimilar; *belligerent* = warlike; *outlandish* = unconventional.

2. E   After four straight days of filming, the crew was probably in need of a *break*. The crew took two days off to rest up for the final days of filming. *enervate* = to weaken; *mastication* = the act of chewing; *fluctuate* = to go back and forth; *dividend* = a payment; *hiatus* = a break.

3. D   The estate is a display of wealth that offends even *pretentious* (showy) visitors. This indicates that the palace must be a *showy* display of wealth. *unadorned* = undecorated; *spartan* = simple; *garish* = excessively showy; *austere* = severe, unadorned.

4. E   A *defector* is someone who abandons one cause for another. The sentence suggests that he has *suffered* and that he wants to find a place where he can live in *peace*. The word in the first blank should suggest *suffering*, while the word in the second blank should be a word that would provide him the peace he is seeking. *inhumanity* = lack of compassion; *affliction* = a condition of pain; *forbearance* = patience; *asylum* = a place of safety; *magnanimity* = generosity; *refuge* = a place of safety; *truculence* = cruel actions or behavior; *travesty* = something that imitates another in a comedic fashion; *persecution* = suffering; *haven* = a safe place.

5. A   The *although* indicates a contrast. The sentence indicates that *comprehensiveness* (completeness in detail) is good, but that the textbook *overwhelms* the reader which suggests it has too much information. *surfeit* = a huge excess; *paucity* = a lack; *promulgation* = a formal announcement; *bastion* = a stronghold, a fortress; *vestige* = a remaining trace.

6. D   The fact that it provided a vast ——— of money that was not evenly divided indicates that it was some sort of *donation* or inflow of *money*. Choice D, *appropriation* is a good choice. *installment* = scheduled partial payment; *confiscation* = the act of taking into custody; *endowment* = funds or property donated; *abatement* = a reduction; *referendum* = a legislative act; *diminution* = a reduction; *subsidy* = monetary assistance; *appropriation* = funds set apart to be given for a particular use; *indemnity* = legal exemption from damages; *efflux* = an outward flow.

---

7. **D** It is not surprising to hear the founder of a company speak positively of his business; therefore, the quotation is not particularly compelling.

---

8. **E** The *"Andromeda Strain"* refers to *virulent pathogens* (line 75), and so the *genetic monster* described in line 71 is most similar to this.

---

9. **E** This paragraph discusses some of the *marvels of genetic engineering* that go beyond medicine.

---

10. **C** Because a compass is indispensable to an explorer, the sentence is making the point that gene-splicing is indispensable to biology.

---

11. **B** The term here is being used ironically, because the point is that evolution does not always produce things that benefit mankind, for instance *bubonic plague, smallpox*, et cetera.

---

12. **D** The authoritative perspective is given by the quote from *microbiologist Bernard David* (lines 74–78); the attempt to allay a fear is given in lines 73–74 in which the author states that a *genetic monster* is unlikely; and the expression of hope is given in the last sentence in which the author states that scientists *are on the verge of ... even more promising achievements*. The paragraph contains no personal reflection, however.

---

13. **C** The author states that *as scientists continue to improve their skills, the possibility of cloning humans will no longer be a wild nightmarish fantasy*. In other words, from the author's point of view, the nightmare will become a reality, so these skills are dangerous.

---

14. **A** This paragraph makes the claim that *such goals (as safely wiping out diseases) can be achieved by... means* other than genetic engineering. If the statement in (A) were true, it would directly contradict this.

---

15. **B** In saying that *it is idle to pretend otherwise*, the author is saying that it is irresponsible to claim that biologists do *not* hold a *great and terrible power* (line 164). Therefore *idle* means *irresponsible*.

---

16. **A** The author of Passage 2 states that *most worrisome of all are genetic engineering's unforeseen consequences* (lines 153–154).

---

17. **D** The author of Passage 1 states that *the cries of alarm over genetic engineering are a mix of naiveté and demagoguery* (lines 1–2), in other words, they are based on either ignorance or intentional deceit. He later states that *popular fears of an Andromeda strain have proven completely unfounded* (lines 19–20), and quotes a scientist who refers to those who proclaim such fears as *hysterics (those who let their emotions get the better of their reasoning)* (line 77). Therefore, he would most likely regard such a question as being naive and hysterical.

---

18. **C** The author of Passage 1 describes the genetic engineering of hardier plants as *revolutionizing agriculture* (line 23) for the better, while the author of Passage 2 suggests that *creating hardier and more productive plants* involves potential risks like *unleashing a mysterious and uncontrollable ailment* (lines 143–144). Remember that *perilous* means *risky*.

---

19. **E** The last paragraph of Passage 1 states that *scientists would find it infinitely harder to redesign the complex machinery of humans* (lines 80–83), thereby refuting the claim in Passage 2 that *it is only a short step to modifying a higher animal, even man* (lines 180–181).

Section 9

1. **A**   The original phrasing is best.

2. **C**   This phrasing is most logical and concise.

3. **B**   The phrase *Its being in the context* is non-standard. Choice (C) is illogical, and (D) and (E) produce dangling participles.

4. **B**   The original sentence suggests that Stephanie's *search* was hungry , when of course it is Stephanie who is hungry. Answer choice (B) most concisely expresses the true meaning of the sentence.

5. **D**   This phrasing is most logical and concise.

6. **A**   The original phrasing is best.

7. **E**   The original sentence contains an illogical comparison. The students today must be compared with the *students* of 30 years ago. The original sentence illogically compares the students of today with the time *30 years ago*.

8. **C**   This phrasing is most logical, idiomatic and concise.

9. **D**   Something that is *imminent* is about to occur, whereas someone who is *eminent* is prominently distinguished.

10. **D**   The phrase that follows the linking verb *is* must be a phrase that represents the aspect that is the *most challenging*. It should not be an independent clause. Answer choice (D) provides the best phrasing.

11. **A**   The original phrasing is best.

12. **C**   Choice (C) provides the most concise and parallel phrasing.

13. **E**   This phrasing is most logical and concise.

14. **D**   Choice (D) provides the most concise and parallel phrasing.

PRACTICE TEST 8

ANSWER SHEET

Last Name: _____   First Name: _____

Date: _____   Testing Location: _____

Directions for Test

- Remove these answer sheets from the book and use them to record your answers to this test.
- This test will require 3 hours and 20 minutes to complete. Take this test in one sitting.
- The time allotment for each section is written clearly at the beginning of each section. This test contains six 25-minute sections, two 20-minute sections, and one 10-minute section.
- This test is 25 minutes shorter than the actual SAT, which will include a 25-minute "experimental" section that does not count toward your score. That section has been omitted from this test.
- You may take one short break during the test, of no more than 10 minutes in length.
- You may only work on one section at any given time.
- You must stop ALL work on a section when time is called.
- If you finish a section before the time has elapsed, check your work on that section. You may NOT work on any other section.
- Do not waste time on questions that seem too difficult for you.
- Use the test book for scratchwork, but you will receive credit only for answers that are marked on the answer sheets.
- You will receive one point for every correct answer.
- You will receive no points for an omitted question.
- For each wrong answer on any multiple-choice question, your score will be reduced by ¼ point.
- For each wrong answer on any numerical "grid-in" question, you will receive no deduction.

SECTION 2

1. Ⓐ Ⓑ Ⓒ Ⓓ Ⓔ   11. Ⓐ Ⓑ Ⓒ Ⓓ Ⓔ   21. Ⓐ Ⓑ Ⓒ Ⓓ Ⓔ   31. Ⓐ Ⓑ Ⓒ Ⓓ Ⓔ
2. Ⓐ Ⓑ Ⓒ Ⓓ Ⓔ   12. Ⓐ Ⓑ Ⓒ Ⓓ Ⓔ   22. Ⓐ Ⓑ Ⓒ Ⓓ Ⓔ   32. Ⓐ Ⓑ Ⓒ Ⓓ Ⓔ
3. Ⓐ Ⓑ Ⓒ Ⓓ Ⓔ   13. Ⓐ Ⓑ Ⓒ Ⓓ Ⓔ   23. Ⓐ Ⓑ Ⓒ Ⓓ Ⓔ   33. Ⓐ Ⓑ Ⓒ Ⓓ Ⓔ
4. Ⓐ Ⓑ Ⓒ Ⓓ Ⓔ   14. Ⓐ Ⓑ Ⓒ Ⓓ Ⓔ   24. Ⓐ Ⓑ Ⓒ Ⓓ Ⓔ   34. Ⓐ Ⓑ Ⓒ Ⓓ Ⓔ
5. Ⓐ Ⓑ Ⓒ Ⓓ Ⓔ   15. Ⓐ Ⓑ Ⓒ Ⓓ Ⓔ   25. Ⓐ Ⓑ Ⓒ Ⓓ Ⓔ   35. Ⓐ Ⓑ Ⓒ Ⓓ Ⓔ
6. Ⓐ Ⓑ Ⓒ Ⓓ Ⓔ   16. Ⓐ Ⓑ Ⓒ Ⓓ Ⓔ   26. Ⓐ Ⓑ Ⓒ Ⓓ Ⓔ   36. Ⓐ Ⓑ Ⓒ Ⓓ Ⓔ
7. Ⓐ Ⓑ Ⓒ Ⓓ Ⓔ   17. Ⓐ Ⓑ Ⓒ Ⓓ Ⓔ   27. Ⓐ Ⓑ Ⓒ Ⓓ Ⓔ   37. Ⓐ Ⓑ Ⓒ Ⓓ Ⓔ
8. Ⓐ Ⓑ Ⓒ Ⓓ Ⓔ   18. Ⓐ Ⓑ Ⓒ Ⓓ Ⓔ   28. Ⓐ Ⓑ Ⓒ Ⓓ Ⓔ   38. Ⓐ Ⓑ Ⓒ Ⓓ Ⓔ
9. Ⓐ Ⓑ Ⓒ Ⓓ Ⓔ   19. Ⓐ Ⓑ Ⓒ Ⓓ Ⓔ   29. Ⓐ Ⓑ Ⓒ Ⓓ Ⓔ   39. Ⓐ Ⓑ Ⓒ Ⓓ Ⓔ
10. Ⓐ Ⓑ Ⓒ Ⓓ Ⓔ   20. Ⓐ Ⓑ Ⓒ Ⓓ Ⓔ   30. Ⓐ Ⓑ Ⓒ Ⓓ Ⓔ   40. Ⓐ Ⓑ Ⓒ Ⓓ Ⓔ

SECTION 3

1. Ⓐ Ⓑ Ⓒ Ⓓ Ⓔ   11. Ⓐ Ⓑ Ⓒ Ⓓ Ⓔ   21. Ⓐ Ⓑ Ⓒ Ⓓ Ⓔ   31. Ⓐ Ⓑ Ⓒ Ⓓ Ⓔ
2. Ⓐ Ⓑ Ⓒ Ⓓ Ⓔ   12. Ⓐ Ⓑ Ⓒ Ⓓ Ⓔ   22. Ⓐ Ⓑ Ⓒ Ⓓ Ⓔ   32. Ⓐ Ⓑ Ⓒ Ⓓ Ⓔ
3. Ⓐ Ⓑ Ⓒ Ⓓ Ⓔ   13. Ⓐ Ⓑ Ⓒ Ⓓ Ⓔ   23. Ⓐ Ⓑ Ⓒ Ⓓ Ⓔ   33. Ⓐ Ⓑ Ⓒ Ⓓ Ⓔ
4. Ⓐ Ⓑ Ⓒ Ⓓ Ⓔ   14. Ⓐ Ⓑ Ⓒ Ⓓ Ⓔ   24. Ⓐ Ⓑ Ⓒ Ⓓ Ⓔ   34. Ⓐ Ⓑ Ⓒ Ⓓ Ⓔ
5. Ⓐ Ⓑ Ⓒ Ⓓ Ⓔ   15. Ⓐ Ⓑ Ⓒ Ⓓ Ⓔ   25. Ⓐ Ⓑ Ⓒ Ⓓ Ⓔ   35. Ⓐ Ⓑ Ⓒ Ⓓ Ⓔ
6. Ⓐ Ⓑ Ⓒ Ⓓ Ⓔ   16. Ⓐ Ⓑ Ⓒ Ⓓ Ⓔ   26. Ⓐ Ⓑ Ⓒ Ⓓ Ⓔ   36. Ⓐ Ⓑ Ⓒ Ⓓ Ⓔ
7. Ⓐ Ⓑ Ⓒ Ⓓ Ⓔ   17. Ⓐ Ⓑ Ⓒ Ⓓ Ⓔ   27. Ⓐ Ⓑ Ⓒ Ⓓ Ⓔ   37. Ⓐ Ⓑ Ⓒ Ⓓ Ⓔ
8. Ⓐ Ⓑ Ⓒ Ⓓ Ⓔ   18. Ⓐ Ⓑ Ⓒ Ⓓ Ⓔ   28. Ⓐ Ⓑ Ⓒ Ⓓ Ⓔ   38. Ⓐ Ⓑ Ⓒ Ⓓ Ⓔ
9. Ⓐ Ⓑ Ⓒ Ⓓ Ⓔ   19. Ⓐ Ⓑ Ⓒ Ⓓ Ⓔ   29. Ⓐ Ⓑ Ⓒ Ⓓ Ⓔ   39. Ⓐ Ⓑ Ⓒ Ⓓ Ⓔ
10. Ⓐ Ⓑ Ⓒ Ⓓ Ⓔ   20. Ⓐ Ⓑ Ⓒ Ⓓ Ⓔ   30. Ⓐ Ⓑ Ⓒ Ⓓ Ⓔ   40. Ⓐ Ⓑ Ⓒ Ⓓ Ⓔ

ANSWER SHEET

SECTION 4

1. Ⓐ Ⓑ Ⓒ Ⓓ Ⓔ
2. Ⓐ Ⓑ Ⓒ Ⓓ Ⓔ
3. Ⓐ Ⓑ Ⓒ Ⓓ Ⓔ
4. Ⓐ Ⓑ Ⓒ Ⓓ Ⓔ
5. Ⓐ Ⓑ Ⓒ Ⓓ Ⓔ
6. Ⓐ Ⓑ Ⓒ Ⓓ Ⓔ
7. Ⓐ Ⓑ Ⓒ Ⓓ Ⓔ
8. Ⓐ Ⓑ Ⓒ Ⓓ Ⓔ
9. Ⓐ Ⓑ Ⓒ Ⓓ Ⓔ
10. Ⓐ Ⓑ Ⓒ Ⓓ Ⓔ

11. Ⓐ Ⓑ Ⓒ Ⓓ Ⓔ
12. Ⓐ Ⓑ Ⓒ Ⓓ Ⓔ
13. Ⓐ Ⓑ Ⓒ Ⓓ Ⓔ
14. Ⓐ Ⓑ Ⓒ Ⓓ Ⓔ
15. Ⓐ Ⓑ Ⓒ Ⓓ Ⓔ
16. Ⓐ Ⓑ Ⓒ Ⓓ Ⓔ
17. Ⓐ Ⓑ Ⓒ Ⓓ Ⓔ
18. Ⓐ Ⓑ Ⓒ Ⓓ Ⓔ
19. Ⓐ Ⓑ Ⓒ Ⓓ Ⓔ
20. Ⓐ Ⓑ Ⓒ Ⓓ Ⓔ

21. Ⓐ Ⓑ Ⓒ Ⓓ Ⓔ
22. Ⓐ Ⓑ Ⓒ Ⓓ Ⓔ
23. Ⓐ Ⓑ Ⓒ Ⓓ Ⓔ
24. Ⓐ Ⓑ Ⓒ Ⓓ Ⓔ
25. Ⓐ Ⓑ Ⓒ Ⓓ Ⓔ
26. Ⓐ Ⓑ Ⓒ Ⓓ Ⓔ
27. Ⓐ Ⓑ Ⓒ Ⓓ Ⓔ
28. Ⓐ Ⓑ Ⓒ Ⓓ Ⓔ
29. Ⓐ Ⓑ Ⓒ Ⓓ Ⓔ
30. Ⓐ Ⓑ Ⓒ Ⓓ Ⓔ

31. Ⓐ Ⓑ Ⓒ Ⓓ Ⓔ
32. Ⓐ Ⓑ Ⓒ Ⓓ Ⓔ
33. Ⓐ Ⓑ Ⓒ Ⓓ Ⓔ
34. Ⓐ Ⓑ Ⓒ Ⓓ Ⓔ
35. Ⓐ Ⓑ Ⓒ Ⓓ Ⓔ
36. Ⓐ Ⓑ Ⓒ Ⓓ Ⓔ
37. Ⓐ Ⓑ Ⓒ Ⓓ Ⓔ
38. Ⓐ Ⓑ Ⓒ Ⓓ Ⓔ
39. Ⓐ Ⓑ Ⓒ Ⓓ Ⓔ
40. Ⓐ Ⓑ Ⓒ Ⓓ Ⓔ

SECTION 5

1. Ⓐ Ⓑ Ⓒ Ⓓ Ⓔ
2. Ⓐ Ⓑ Ⓒ Ⓓ Ⓔ
3. Ⓐ Ⓑ Ⓒ Ⓓ Ⓔ
4. Ⓐ Ⓑ Ⓒ Ⓓ Ⓔ

5. Ⓐ Ⓑ Ⓒ Ⓓ Ⓔ
6. Ⓐ Ⓑ Ⓒ Ⓓ Ⓔ
7. Ⓐ Ⓑ Ⓒ Ⓓ Ⓔ
8. Ⓐ Ⓑ Ⓒ Ⓓ Ⓔ

9. 10. 11. 12. 13.

14. 15. 16. 17. 18.

(Grid-in answer boxes numbered 9 through 18, each with columns for digits 0–9, decimal points, and fraction bars.)

ANSWER SHEET

SECTION 6

1. Ⓐ Ⓑ Ⓒ Ⓓ Ⓔ	11. Ⓐ Ⓑ Ⓒ Ⓓ Ⓔ	21. Ⓐ Ⓑ Ⓒ Ⓓ Ⓔ	31. Ⓐ Ⓑ Ⓒ Ⓓ Ⓔ
2. Ⓐ Ⓑ Ⓒ Ⓓ Ⓔ	12. Ⓐ Ⓑ Ⓒ Ⓓ Ⓔ	22. Ⓐ Ⓑ Ⓒ Ⓓ Ⓔ	32. Ⓐ Ⓑ Ⓒ Ⓓ Ⓔ
3. Ⓐ Ⓑ Ⓒ Ⓓ Ⓔ	13. Ⓐ Ⓑ Ⓒ Ⓓ Ⓔ	23. Ⓐ Ⓑ Ⓒ Ⓓ Ⓔ	33. Ⓐ Ⓑ Ⓒ Ⓓ Ⓔ
4. Ⓐ Ⓑ Ⓒ Ⓓ Ⓔ	14. Ⓐ Ⓑ Ⓒ Ⓓ Ⓔ	24. Ⓐ Ⓑ Ⓒ Ⓓ Ⓔ	34. Ⓐ Ⓑ Ⓒ Ⓓ Ⓔ
5. Ⓐ Ⓑ Ⓒ Ⓓ Ⓔ	15. Ⓐ Ⓑ Ⓒ Ⓓ Ⓔ	25. Ⓐ Ⓑ Ⓒ Ⓓ Ⓔ	35. Ⓐ Ⓑ Ⓒ Ⓓ Ⓔ
6. Ⓐ Ⓑ Ⓒ Ⓓ Ⓔ	16. Ⓐ Ⓑ Ⓒ Ⓓ Ⓔ	26. Ⓐ Ⓑ Ⓒ Ⓓ Ⓔ	36. Ⓐ Ⓑ Ⓒ Ⓓ Ⓔ
7. Ⓐ Ⓑ Ⓒ Ⓓ Ⓔ	17. Ⓐ Ⓑ Ⓒ Ⓓ Ⓔ	27. Ⓐ Ⓑ Ⓒ Ⓓ Ⓔ	37. Ⓐ Ⓑ Ⓒ Ⓓ Ⓔ
8. Ⓐ Ⓑ Ⓒ Ⓓ Ⓔ	18. Ⓐ Ⓑ Ⓒ Ⓓ Ⓔ	28. Ⓐ Ⓑ Ⓒ Ⓓ Ⓔ	38. Ⓐ Ⓑ Ⓒ Ⓓ Ⓔ
9. Ⓐ Ⓑ Ⓒ Ⓓ Ⓔ	19. Ⓐ Ⓑ Ⓒ Ⓓ Ⓔ	29. Ⓐ Ⓑ Ⓒ Ⓓ Ⓔ	39. Ⓐ Ⓑ Ⓒ Ⓓ Ⓔ
10. Ⓐ Ⓑ Ⓒ Ⓓ Ⓔ	20. Ⓐ Ⓑ Ⓒ Ⓓ Ⓔ	30. Ⓐ Ⓑ Ⓒ Ⓓ Ⓔ	40. Ⓐ Ⓑ Ⓒ Ⓓ Ⓔ

SECTION 7

1. Ⓐ Ⓑ Ⓒ Ⓓ Ⓔ	11. Ⓐ Ⓑ Ⓒ Ⓓ Ⓔ	21. Ⓐ Ⓑ Ⓒ Ⓓ Ⓔ	31. Ⓐ Ⓑ Ⓒ Ⓓ Ⓔ
2. Ⓐ Ⓑ Ⓒ Ⓓ Ⓔ	12. Ⓐ Ⓑ Ⓒ Ⓓ Ⓔ	22. Ⓐ Ⓑ Ⓒ Ⓓ Ⓔ	32. Ⓐ Ⓑ Ⓒ Ⓓ Ⓔ
3. Ⓐ Ⓑ Ⓒ Ⓓ Ⓔ	13. Ⓐ Ⓑ Ⓒ Ⓓ Ⓔ	23. Ⓐ Ⓑ Ⓒ Ⓓ Ⓔ	33. Ⓐ Ⓑ Ⓒ Ⓓ Ⓔ
4. Ⓐ Ⓑ Ⓒ Ⓓ Ⓔ	14. Ⓐ Ⓑ Ⓒ Ⓓ Ⓔ	24. Ⓐ Ⓑ Ⓒ Ⓓ Ⓔ	34. Ⓐ Ⓑ Ⓒ Ⓓ Ⓔ
5. Ⓐ Ⓑ Ⓒ Ⓓ Ⓔ	15. Ⓐ Ⓑ Ⓒ Ⓓ Ⓔ	25. Ⓐ Ⓑ Ⓒ Ⓓ Ⓔ	35. Ⓐ Ⓑ Ⓒ Ⓓ Ⓔ
6. Ⓐ Ⓑ Ⓒ Ⓓ Ⓔ	16. Ⓐ Ⓑ Ⓒ Ⓓ Ⓔ	26. Ⓐ Ⓑ Ⓒ Ⓓ Ⓔ	36. Ⓐ Ⓑ Ⓒ Ⓓ Ⓔ
7. Ⓐ Ⓑ Ⓒ Ⓓ Ⓔ	17. Ⓐ Ⓑ Ⓒ Ⓓ Ⓔ	27. Ⓐ Ⓑ Ⓒ Ⓓ Ⓔ	37. Ⓐ Ⓑ Ⓒ Ⓓ Ⓔ
8. Ⓐ Ⓑ Ⓒ Ⓓ Ⓔ	18. Ⓐ Ⓑ Ⓒ Ⓓ Ⓔ	28. Ⓐ Ⓑ Ⓒ Ⓓ Ⓔ	38. Ⓐ Ⓑ Ⓒ Ⓓ Ⓔ
9. Ⓐ Ⓑ Ⓒ Ⓓ Ⓔ	19. Ⓐ Ⓑ Ⓒ Ⓓ Ⓔ	29. Ⓐ Ⓑ Ⓒ Ⓓ Ⓔ	39. Ⓐ Ⓑ Ⓒ Ⓓ Ⓔ
10. Ⓐ Ⓑ Ⓒ Ⓓ Ⓔ	20. Ⓐ Ⓑ Ⓒ Ⓓ Ⓔ	30. Ⓐ Ⓑ Ⓒ Ⓓ Ⓔ	40. Ⓐ Ⓑ Ⓒ Ⓓ Ⓔ

SECTION 8

1. Ⓐ Ⓑ Ⓒ Ⓓ Ⓔ	11. Ⓐ Ⓑ Ⓒ Ⓓ Ⓔ	21. Ⓐ Ⓑ Ⓒ Ⓓ Ⓔ	31. Ⓐ Ⓑ Ⓒ Ⓓ Ⓔ
2. Ⓐ Ⓑ Ⓒ Ⓓ Ⓔ	12. Ⓐ Ⓑ Ⓒ Ⓓ Ⓔ	22. Ⓐ Ⓑ Ⓒ Ⓓ Ⓔ	32. Ⓐ Ⓑ Ⓒ Ⓓ Ⓔ
3. Ⓐ Ⓑ Ⓒ Ⓓ Ⓔ	13. Ⓐ Ⓑ Ⓒ Ⓓ Ⓔ	23. Ⓐ Ⓑ Ⓒ Ⓓ Ⓔ	33. Ⓐ Ⓑ Ⓒ Ⓓ Ⓔ
4. Ⓐ Ⓑ Ⓒ Ⓓ Ⓔ	14. Ⓐ Ⓑ Ⓒ Ⓓ Ⓔ	24. Ⓐ Ⓑ Ⓒ Ⓓ Ⓔ	34. Ⓐ Ⓑ Ⓒ Ⓓ Ⓔ
5. Ⓐ Ⓑ Ⓒ Ⓓ Ⓔ	15. Ⓐ Ⓑ Ⓒ Ⓓ Ⓔ	25. Ⓐ Ⓑ Ⓒ Ⓓ Ⓔ	35. Ⓐ Ⓑ Ⓒ Ⓓ Ⓔ
6. Ⓐ Ⓑ Ⓒ Ⓓ Ⓔ	16. Ⓐ Ⓑ Ⓒ Ⓓ Ⓔ	26. Ⓐ Ⓑ Ⓒ Ⓓ Ⓔ	36. Ⓐ Ⓑ Ⓒ Ⓓ Ⓔ
7. Ⓐ Ⓑ Ⓒ Ⓓ Ⓔ	17. Ⓐ Ⓑ Ⓒ Ⓓ Ⓔ	27. Ⓐ Ⓑ Ⓒ Ⓓ Ⓔ	37. Ⓐ Ⓑ Ⓒ Ⓓ Ⓔ
8. Ⓐ Ⓑ Ⓒ Ⓓ Ⓔ	18. Ⓐ Ⓑ Ⓒ Ⓓ Ⓔ	28. Ⓐ Ⓑ Ⓒ Ⓓ Ⓔ	38. Ⓐ Ⓑ Ⓒ Ⓓ Ⓔ
9. Ⓐ Ⓑ Ⓒ Ⓓ Ⓔ	19. Ⓐ Ⓑ Ⓒ Ⓓ Ⓔ	29. Ⓐ Ⓑ Ⓒ Ⓓ Ⓔ	39. Ⓐ Ⓑ Ⓒ Ⓓ Ⓔ
10. Ⓐ Ⓑ Ⓒ Ⓓ Ⓔ	20. Ⓐ Ⓑ Ⓒ Ⓓ Ⓔ	30. Ⓐ Ⓑ Ⓒ Ⓓ Ⓔ	40. Ⓐ Ⓑ Ⓒ Ⓓ Ⓔ

SECTION 9

1. Ⓐ Ⓑ Ⓒ Ⓓ Ⓔ	11. Ⓐ Ⓑ Ⓒ Ⓓ Ⓔ	21. Ⓐ Ⓑ Ⓒ Ⓓ Ⓔ	31. Ⓐ Ⓑ Ⓒ Ⓓ Ⓔ
2. Ⓐ Ⓑ Ⓒ Ⓓ Ⓔ	12. Ⓐ Ⓑ Ⓒ Ⓓ Ⓔ	22. Ⓐ Ⓑ Ⓒ Ⓓ Ⓔ	32. Ⓐ Ⓑ Ⓒ Ⓓ Ⓔ
3. Ⓐ Ⓑ Ⓒ Ⓓ Ⓔ	13. Ⓐ Ⓑ Ⓒ Ⓓ Ⓔ	23. Ⓐ Ⓑ Ⓒ Ⓓ Ⓔ	33. Ⓐ Ⓑ Ⓒ Ⓓ Ⓔ
4. Ⓐ Ⓑ Ⓒ Ⓓ Ⓔ	14. Ⓐ Ⓑ Ⓒ Ⓓ Ⓔ	24. Ⓐ Ⓑ Ⓒ Ⓓ Ⓔ	34. Ⓐ Ⓑ Ⓒ Ⓓ Ⓔ
5. Ⓐ Ⓑ Ⓒ Ⓓ Ⓔ	15. Ⓐ Ⓑ Ⓒ Ⓓ Ⓔ	25. Ⓐ Ⓑ Ⓒ Ⓓ Ⓔ	35. Ⓐ Ⓑ Ⓒ Ⓓ Ⓔ
6. Ⓐ Ⓑ Ⓒ Ⓓ Ⓔ	16. Ⓐ Ⓑ Ⓒ Ⓓ Ⓔ	26. Ⓐ Ⓑ Ⓒ Ⓓ Ⓔ	36. Ⓐ Ⓑ Ⓒ Ⓓ Ⓔ
7. Ⓐ Ⓑ Ⓒ Ⓓ Ⓔ	17. Ⓐ Ⓑ Ⓒ Ⓓ Ⓔ	27. Ⓐ Ⓑ Ⓒ Ⓓ Ⓔ	37. Ⓐ Ⓑ Ⓒ Ⓓ Ⓔ
8. Ⓐ Ⓑ Ⓒ Ⓓ Ⓔ	18. Ⓐ Ⓑ Ⓒ Ⓓ Ⓔ	28. Ⓐ Ⓑ Ⓒ Ⓓ Ⓔ	38. Ⓐ Ⓑ Ⓒ Ⓓ Ⓔ
9. Ⓐ Ⓑ Ⓒ Ⓓ Ⓔ	19. Ⓐ Ⓑ Ⓒ Ⓓ Ⓔ	29. Ⓐ Ⓑ Ⓒ Ⓓ Ⓔ	39. Ⓐ Ⓑ Ⓒ Ⓓ Ⓔ
10. Ⓐ Ⓑ Ⓒ Ⓓ Ⓔ	20. Ⓐ Ⓑ Ⓒ Ⓓ Ⓔ	30. Ⓐ Ⓑ Ⓒ Ⓓ Ⓔ	40. Ⓐ Ⓑ Ⓒ Ⓓ Ⓔ

Section 1

Time—25 minutes
1 Question

Directions for Writing the Essay

Plan and write an essay that answers the question below. Do NOT write on another topic. An essay on another topic will receive a score of 0.

Two readers will grade your essay based on how well you develop your point of view, organize and explain your ideas, use specific and relevant examples to support your thesis, and use clear and effective language. How well you write is much more important than how much you write, but to cover the topic adequately you should plan to write several paragraphs.

Your essay must be written on separate lined sheets of paper. Keep your handwriting to a reasonable size. Your essay will be read by people who are not familiar with your handwriting, so write legibly.

You may use this sheet for notes and outlining, but these will not be graded as part of your essay.

Consider carefully the issue discussed in the following passage, then write an essay that answers the question posed in the assignment.

> In a culture obsessed with superficial appearances, our leaders should be those who can see beyond the surface. Judging a book by its cover is the job of the consumer, but reading the book—pondering its contents and perhaps seeking to write new chapter—is the job of a leader.

Assignment: **How important is it to look beyond superficial appearances?** Write an essay in which you answer this question and discusss your point of view on this issue. Support your position logically with examples from literature, the arts, history, politics, science and technology, current events, or your experience or observation.

Write your essay on separate sheets of paper.

GO ON TO THE NEXT PAGE ▶▶▶

Section 2

Time —25 minutes
20 questions

2

1 If $2m + k = 12$ and $k = 10$, what is the value of m?

(A) 0
(B) 3/4
(C) 1
(D) 2
(E) 4

2 The average (arithmetic mean) of three numbers is 50. If two of the numbers are 35 and 50, what is the third number?

(A) 45
(B) 50
(C) 55
(D) 60
(E) 65

3
$$
\begin{array}{r}
A5 \\
A3 \\
A5 \\
+\,2A \\
\hline
157
\end{array}
$$

In the correctly worked addition problem above, each A represents the same digit. What is the value of A?

(A) 1
(B) 2
(C) 3
(D) 4
(E) 6

4 What number is the same percent of 225 as 9 is of 25?

(A) 27
(B) 45
(C) 54
(D) 64
(E) 81

GO ON TO THE NEXT PAGE ▶▶▶

5 If $2^{x-1} = 32$, what is the value of x?

(A) 4
(B) 6
(C) 9
(D) 16
(E) 17

VOTING RESULTS FOR REFERENDUM

	Yes	No	Total
Men	26		
Women			76
Total	59		137

6 The table above, representing the results of a vote taken by the Zoning Commission on a recent referendum, is only partially completed. Based on the table, how many women on the Commission voted no?

(A) 43
(B) 48
(C) 57
(D) 61
(E) 78

7 Kenny and Mike each begin with the same number of baseball cards. After Mike gives Kenny 12 cards, Kenny has twice as many as Mike. How many cards do they have all together?

(A) 36
(B) 48
(C) 60
(D) 72
(E) 84

8 A bag of Texas Tillie's Trail Mix contains x ounces of walnuts, 15 ounces of peanuts, and 20 ounces of pecans. Which of the following expressions gives the fraction of the mix that is walnuts?

(A) $\dfrac{x}{35}$

(B) $\dfrac{35}{x}$

(C) $\dfrac{x}{35 + x}$

(D) $\dfrac{35 + x}{x}$

(E) $\dfrac{35 - x}{35 + x}$

9

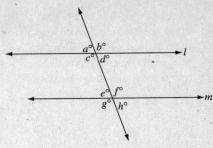

In the diagram above, if $l \| m$, which of the following is equivalent to $a + d + f + g$?

(A) $2c + 2f$
(B) $b + c + e + h$
(C) $2d + 2e$
(D) $a + d + e + h$
(E) $2b + 2g$

10 For which of the following ordered pairs (x, y) is $2x + 3y > 6$ and $x - y > 6$?

(A) $(7, -1)$
(B) $(7, 1)$
(C) $(4, -3)$
(D) $(3, 3)$
(E) $(-3, 4)$

11 When n is divided by 12, the remainder is 6. What is the remainder when n is divided by 6?

(A) 0
(B) 1
(C) 2
(D) 3
(E) 4

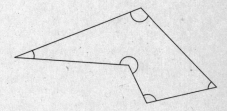

12 The figure above shows a polygon with five sides. What is the average (arithmetic mean) of the measures, in degrees, of the five angles shown?

(A) 85°
(B) 108°
(C) 120°
(D) 324°
(E) 540°

GO ON TO THE NEXT PAGE ▶▶▶

13 At a pet store, if d represents the number of dogs and c represents the number of cats, then which of the following is equivalent to the statement "There are 3 fewer than 4 times as many dogs as cats?"

(A) $4d + 3 = c$
(B) $4d - 3 = c$
(C) $d = 4c + 3$
(D) $d = 4c - 3$
(E) $4d - 3c = 0$

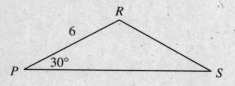

14 In the figure above, if $PR = RS$, what is the area of triangle PRS?

(A) $9\sqrt{2}$

(B) $9\sqrt{3}$

(C) $18\sqrt{2}$

(D) $18\sqrt{3}$

(E) $36\sqrt{3}$

15 A \$50,000 prize is divided among four winners in a ratio of 4:3:2:1. What is the greatest amount of money that any winner receives?

(A) \$5,000
(B) \$10,000
(C) \$12,500
(D) \$20,000
(E) \$40,000

16 For all non-zero integers a and b, let

$$a\{b\} = \frac{a^2}{b^2}$$

If $m\{n\} = 9$, which of the following must be true?

    I. $m > n$
    II. $m^2 - n^2 = 8n^2$
    III. $|n|$ is a factor of $|m|$.

(A) II only
(B) I and II only
(C) II and III only
(D) I and III only
(E) I, II, and III

17 A jar contains only red, white, and blue marbles. It contains twice as many red marbles as white marbles, and three times as many white marbles as blue marbles. If a marble is drawn at random, what is the probability that it is white?

(A) $\dfrac{1}{10}$

(B) $\dfrac{1}{6}$

(C) $\dfrac{3}{10}$

(D) $\dfrac{1}{3}$

(E) $\dfrac{3}{5}$

18 A certain class has 6 girls and 5 boys. Four of these students are to line up in the front of the room, with two girls on either end and two boys in between. How many such arrangements are possible?

(A) 20
(B) 200
(C) 462
(D) 600
(E) 900

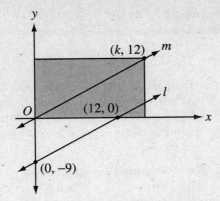

Note: Figure not drawn to scale.

19 In the figure above, if $m \parallel l$, what is the area of the shaded rectangle?

(A)   96
(B)   108
(C)   144
(D)   192
(E)   204

20 A rectangular solid has a volume of p cubic centimeters, where p is an odd integer. The length, width, and height of the solid, in centimeters, are r, s, and t. If r, s, and t are all positive integers, which of the following must be true?

    I. $p + s + t$ is odd.

    II. $r = \dfrac{p}{st}$

    III. The total surface area of the solid, in square centimeters, has an even value.

(A)   I only
(B)   I and II only
(C)   I and III only
(D)   II and III only
(E)   I, II, and III

2

You may check your work, on this section only, until time is called.

Section 3

Time—25 minutes
24 questions

3

Each of the sentences below is missing one or two portions. Read each sentence, then select the word or words that most logically completes the sentence, taking into account the meaning of the sentence as a whole.

Example:

Rather than accepting the theory unquestioningly, Deborah regarded it with ———

(A) mirth   (B) sadness
(C) responsibility (D) ignorance
(E) skepticism

Correct response: (E)

1 They enjoyed each other's company enormously, but they rarely agreed on any issue; in fact, one could be sure that on any important topic their opinions would ———.

(A) diverge   (B) coincide
(C) retreat   (D) assemble
(E) truncate

2 Once accepted as an incontrovertible truth, the theory that nine planets revolve around our sun is now regarded by astronomers as ———.

(A) enacted   (B) irrefutable
(C) universal   (D) dubious
(E) conclusive

3 Having lost his wife and three children to untimely deaths, Rembrandt entered his dark period in 1642, when his immersion in painting often seemed his only ——— from abject ———.

(A) salvation ... prudence
(B) remorse ... adulation
(C) solace ... melancholy
(D) elation ... poverty
(E) departure ... cheerfulness

4 Many proponents of the new curriculum considered its omission of Romance literature to be ———, while the more conservative educators considered such a removal ———.

(A) repugnant ... premature
(B) innocuous ... deplorable
(C) reprehensible ... benevolent
(D) malicious ... disgraceful
(E) auspicious ... encouraging

5 As the expedition leader quickly realized, the recently accelerated program to acclimate the climbers to high altitudes was ———; as a result, several team members were soon ——— by the lack of oxygen.

(A) illusory ... initiated
(B) excessive ... mitigated
(C) appropriate ... confused
(D) ineffective ... enervated
(E) venerable ... absolved

6 Although the mainstream of most societies reviles the ———, nearly every culture reserves at least some small place for those who question its treasured norms and mores.

(A) charlatan   (B) surrogate
(C) philanthropist (D) pragmatist
(E) iconoclast

GO ON TO THE NEXT PAGE ▶▶▶

7 Steven Pinker is far from ——— about the heated controversy of whether the human mind is a *tabula rasa*; he stands ——— in the negative camp.

(A) ambivalent ... unequivocally
(B) apathetic ... furtively
(C) impartial ... reluctantly
(D) adamant ... vehemently
(E) subjective ... stubbornly

8 Although Ivan Illich was dismissed as a ——— by many of his contemporaries, many modern thinkers now regard his revolutionary insights on the dehumanization of society as ———.

(A) pedant . . . derivative
(B) neophyte ... vociferous
(C) radical ... visionary
(D) partisan ... conciliatory
(E) hermit ... simplistic

Each passage below is followed by one or two questions based on its content. Answer each question based on what is stated or implied in the passage.

Questions 9–12 are based on the following passages.

Passage 1

Line   In many instances, the study of life on Earth ultimately involves the study of the molecules of which living organisms are composed. How does photosynthesis convert the energy
5   of sunlight into the energy of sugar molecules? What is the structure of the cell membrane, and how does it function in controlling the movement of materials into and out of the cell? How do muscles contract? How do the
10   nerve cells in your brain communicate with one another? What causes cancer? To understand the answers to these questions, you must first learn about energy and matter, the properties of atoms, and how atoms interact
15   with one another to form molecules.

Passage 2

For centuries the idea that photosynthesis supports the earth's biosystem had been fundamental to our understanding of life on Earth. If the sun went out, we assumed, life
20   would soon follow. Yet in the 1970s, scientists discovered organisms thriving in deep-sea hydrothermal vents far from any light energy required for photosynthesis. These organisms relied on bacteria that harvest energy not
25   from light but from the chemical bonds in sulfides and other molecules that poured from the heat vents. This process is called chemosynthesis. Other organisms eat these bacteria or house the living bacteria in their
30   tissues. Such relationships mirror the myriad complex relationships we see in the photosynthetic food chain, in which bacteria are either consumed or co-opted by organisms to aid in breaking down or synthesizing
35   chemicals that the organisms' own tissues cannot.

GO ON TO THE NEXT PAGE ▸▸▸

9　Both passages focus primarily on

- (A) how groups of cells form tissues
- (B) the origin of life on Earth
- (C) biochemical processes
- (D) the importance of the sun to life on Earth
- (E) unusual life forms

3

10　The questions listed in lines 5–11 of Passage 1 are presented as those that

- (A) biologists have yet to explore in great depth
- (B) inspire controversy within the scientific community
- (C) necessarily concern those who are interested in a deep understanding of biology
- (D) are difficult to investigate with current methods and technology
- (E) researchers have not considered to be as important as those that concern ecology

11　Which of the five questions posed in Passage 1 is most relevant to the discussion in Passage 2?

- (A) How does photosynthesis convert the energy of sunlight into the energy of sugar molecules?
- (B) What is the structure of the cell membrane, and how does it function in controlling the movement of materials into and out of the cell?
- (C) How do muscles contract?
- (D) How do the nerve cells in your brain communicate with one another?
- (E) What causes cancer?

12　Which of the following concepts is mentioned in Passage 2 but NOT in Passage 1?

- (A) the structure of cells
- (B) the conversion of light energy to food energy
- (C) disease
- (D) relationships among separate organisms
- (E) bonds within molecules

The passages below are followed by questions based on their content. Answer the questions on the basis of what is stated or implied in the passage itself or the introductory material that precedes the passage.

Questions 13–18 are based on the following passage.

The following is an excerpt from a popular book on "innumeracy," the common inability of people to deal rationally with numbers.

Line　Without some appreciation of common large numbers, it's impossible to react with the proper scepticism to terrifying reports that more than a million American kids are
5　kidnapped each year, or with the proper sobriety to a warhead carrying a megaton of explosive power—the equivalent of a million tons (or two billion pounds) of TNT.
　　And if you don't have some feeling for
10　probabilities, automobile accidents might seem a relatively minor problem of local travel, whereas being killed by terrorists might seem to be a major risk when going overseas. As often observed, however, the 45,000 people
15　killed annually on American roads are approximately equal in number to all American dead in the Vietnam War. On the other hand, the seventeen Americans killed by terrorists in 1985 were among the 28 million
20　of us who traveled abroad that year—that's one chance in 1.6 million of becoming a victim. Compare that with these annual rates in the United States: one chance in 68,000 of choking to death; one chance in 75,000 of dying
25　in a bicycle crash; one chance in 20,000 of drowning; and one chance in only 5,300 of dying in a car crash.
　　Confronted with these large numbers and with the correspondingly small probabilities
30　associated with them, the innumerate will inevitably respond with the non sequitur,[1] "Yes, but what if you're that one," and then nod knowingly, as if they've demolished your argument with penetrating insight. This

GO ON TO THE NEXT PAGE ▶▶▶

Excerpted from *Innumeracy* by John Allen Paulos, Hill and Wang, New York, 1988, pp.7–8.
[1] A non sequitur is a statement that does not follow logically from previous statements

35 tendency to personalize is a characteristic of many who suffer from innumeracy. Equally typical is a tendency to equate the risk from some obscure and exotic malady with the chances of suffering from heart and
40 circulatory disease, from which about 12,000 Americans die each week.

There's a joke I like that's marginally relevant. An old married couple in their nineties contact a divorce lawyer, who pleads
45 with them to stay together. "Why get divorced now after seventy years of marriage?" The little old lady finally pipes up in a creaky voice: "We wanted to wait until the children were dead."
50 A feeling for what quantities or time spans are appropriate in various contexts is essential to getting the joke. Slipping between millions and billions or between billions and trillions should in this sense be equally funny, but it
55 isn't, because we too often lack an intuitive grasp for these numbers.

A recent study by Drs. Kronlund and Phillips of the University of Washington showed that most doctors' assessments of the
60 risks of various operations, procedures, and medications (even in their own specialties) were way off the mark, often by several orders of magnitude. I once had a conversation with a doctor who, within approximately
65 20 minutes, stated that a certain procedure he was contemplating (a) had a one-chance-in-a million risk associated with it; (b) was 99 percent safe; and (c) usually went quite well. Given the fact that so many doctors seem to
70 believe that there must be at least eleven people in the waiting room if they're to avoid being idle, I'm not surprised at this new evidence of their innumeracy.

13 Which of the following can be inferred to be the author's view of the "reports that more than a million American kids are kidnapped each year" (lines 3–5)?

(A) They are typical examples of American journalism.
(B) They are evidence of a terrible problem that must be addressed.
(C) They are probably untrue.
(D) They properly use a number to convey a simple fact.
(E) They demonstrate an American obsession with statistics.

14 What fact is the list of probabilities cited in lines 22–27 intended to illustrate?

(A) that probability can be used in many different ways in everyday life
(B) that terrorism is far less a threat to Americans than many other common dangers
(C) that the world is filled with many dangers
(D) that a knowledge of probability can help Americans decide where to travel most safely abroad
(E) that bicycles are nearly as dangerous as cars

15 Which of the following is *not* an element of the discussion in this passage?

(A) a personal recollection
(B) a verifiable statistic
(C) a reference to an authoritative study
(D) a discussion of a common misconception
(E) a refutation of a scientific theory

16 What is the author's view of the "penetrating insight" mentioned in line 34?

(A) It is the result of careful analysis.
(B) It does not exist.
(C) It demolishes a statistical argument.
(D) It does not sufficiently personalize the situation being discussed.
(E) It is not found enough in everyday discussions.

17 In what way does the author suggest that the joke described in lines 42–49 is like "slipping between millions and billions" (lines 52–53)?

(A) They both involve a lack of appreciation for particular quantities.
(B) They both describe mistakes the elderly are likely to make.
(C) They both illustrate a common scenario.
(D) They both reveal the value of understanding probabilities.
(E) They both illustrate humor in mathematics.

GO ON TO THE NEXT PAGE ▶▶▶

18 The author mentions the time span of "approximately 20 minutes" (line 65) in order to emphasize

(A) the doctor's inability to appreciate relevant time spans
(B) the comparison with the elderly couple in the preceding joke
(C) the frequency with which the doctor contradicted himself
(D) the common need to approximate rather than use precise numbers
(E) how quickly he was able to get an appointment

Questions 19–24 are based on the following passage:

The following is an excerpt from a memoir of Richard Feynman, a Nobel-Prize-winning physicist, in which he describes the experience of having an artist friend named Jerry teach him to draw.

Line   I promised to work, but still bet that he couldn't teach me to draw. I wanted very much to learn to draw, for a reason that I kept to myself: I wanted to convey an emotion I
5   have about the beauty of the world. It's difficult to describe because it's an emotion. It's analogous to the feeling one has in religion that has to do with a god that controls everything in the universe: there's a generality
10   aspect that you feel when you think about how things that appear so different and behave so differently are all run "behind the scenes" by the same organization, the same physical laws. It's an appreciation of the
15   mathematical beauty of nature, of how she works inside; a realization that the phenomena we see result from the complexity of the inner workings between atoms; a feeling of how dramatic and wonderful it is. It's a
20   feeling of awe—of scientific awe—which I felt could be communicated through a drawing to someone who had also had this emotion. It could remind him, for a moment, of this feeling about the glories of the universe.
25   Jerry turned out to be a very good teacher. He told me first to go home and draw anything. So I tried to draw a shoe; then I tried to draw a flower in a pot. It was a mess!
       The next time we met I showed him my
30   attempts: "Oh, look!" he said. "You see, around in back here, the line of the flower pot doesn't touch the leaf." (I had meant the line to come up to the leaf.) "That's very good. It's a way of showing depth. That's very
35   clever of you."
       "And the fact that you don't make all the lines the same thickness (which I *didn't* mean to do) is good. A drawing with all the lines the same thickness is dull." It continued like

GO ON TO THE NEXT PAGE ▶▶▶

40 that: everything that I thought was a mistake,
    he used to teach me something in a positive
    way. He never said it was wrong; he never put
    me down. So I kept on trying, and I gradually
    got a little bit better, but I was never satisfied.

19 In line 13, the word "organization" most
     nearly means

(A) corporation
(B) rules of physics
(C) social group
(D) arrangement of objects
(E) system of emotional expression

20 Which of the following experiences is closest
     to what the author describes as "dramatic
     and wonderful" (line 19)?

(A) proving a physical law
(B) creating a beautiful sculpture
(C) appreciating the power of physical
    laws in nature
(D) teaching another person how to play
    an instrument
(E) seeing a masterful painting for the
    first time

21 What assumption does the author make
     about the appreciation of art?

(A) It comes only through the experience
    of creating art.
(B) It is enhanced by having experiences
    similar to those that inspired the artist.
(C) It is not as important as the apprecia-
    tion of science.
(D) It is difficult for a scientist.
(E) It requires an understanding of the
    historical period in which the piece
    was created.

22 If Jerry is really a "very good teacher"
     (line 25) in the way that the author suggests,
     what would he most likely have done if the
     author had drawn the flower pot with lines
     of all the same thickness?

(A) Jerry would have shown the author
    how to vary the thickness of his lines.
(B) Jerry would have shown the author
    examples of how line thickness
    affects the quality of a drawing.
(C) Jerry would have mentioned that the
    drawing was dull, but could be made
    more lively with color.
(D) Jerry would have found something
    positive elsewhere in the drawing.
(E) Jerry would have made the author
    re-do the drawing.

23 The author suggests that the "way of showing
     depth" (line 34) is actually

(A) unintentional
(B) unattractive
(C) difficult to accomplish
(D) not characteristic of true art
(E) a reflection of the author's theory of
    nature

24 In what way was the author "never satisfied"
     (line 44)?

(A) He was never able to fully appreciate
    great art.
(B) He was never able to draw a realistic
    flower pot.
(C) He was not able to replicate his
    teacher's talent for emphasizing the
    positive in his students.
(D) He never fully appreciated the talent
    of his teacher.
(E) He was never able to convey ade-
    quately his feelings about the beauty
    of the world.

3

STOP

*You may check your work, on this
section only, until time is called.*

Section 4

Time—25 minutes
35 questions

Directions for "Improving Sentences" Questions

Each of the sentences below contains one underlined portion. The portion may contain one or more errors in grammar, usage, construction, precision, diction (choice of words), or idiom. Some of the sentences are correct.

Consider the meaning of the original sentence, and choose the answer that best expresses that meaning. If the original sentence is best, choose (A), because it repeats the original phrasing. Choose the phrasing that creates the clearest, most precise, and most effective sentence.

EXAMPLE:

The children <u>couldn't hardly believe their eyes</u>.

- (A) couldn't hardly believe their eyes
- (B) would not hardly believe their eyes
- (C) could hardly believe their eyes
- (D) couldn't nearly believe their eyes
- (E) could hardly believe his or her eyes

Example answer: (C)

---

1 The anthology contains mostly the work of modern poets, but <u>which includes a few significant older works as well.</u>

- (A) which includes a few significant older works as well
- (B) it includes a few significant older works as well
- (C) also it contains a few significant older works as well
- (D) as well, it also includes a few significant older works
- (E) which also include a few significant older works

2 The coach worked long and hard into the night <u>for preparing the team's strategy</u> for the next game.

- (A) for preparing the team's strategy
- (B) in preparing the team's strategy
- (C) for the preparation of the team's strategy
- (D) in order for proper preparation of the team's strategy
- (E) to prepare the team's strategy

3 Although usually unflappable even in front of a crowd, <u>Carla's anxiety overwhelmed her</u> during the recital.

- (A) Carla's anxiety overwhelmed her
- (B) her anxiety overwhelmed Carla completely
- (C) Carla being overwhelmed by anxiety
- (D) Carla was overwhelmed by anxiety
- (E) nevertheless Carla's anxiety was overwhelming

4 Those students who sit through her lectures <u>day after day, having been numbed into thinking</u> that history could never be even remotely interesting.

- (A) day after day, having been numbed into thinking
- (B) day after day being numbed into thinking
- (C) day after day have been numbed into thinking
- (D) day after day of being numbed into thinking
- (E) day after day of having been numbed into thinking

GO ON TO THE NEXT PAGE ▶▶▶

5 Swimming in the deepest part of the lake, <u>the current pushed Justine farther from shore.</u>

(A) the current pushed Justine farther from shore
(B) Justine had been pushed farther from shore by the current
(C) Justine was pushed farther from shore by the current
(D) the current's push made sure that Justine moved farther from shore
(E) the push of the current moved Justine farther from shore

6 Writing a good twenty-page research paper is more difficult than <u>when you have to write</u> two good ten-page papers.

(A) when you have to write
(B) when one must write
(C) the writing of
(D) writing
(E) one's writing of

7 <u>If we had not stopped for gas,</u> we probably would have arrived in time for the movie.

(A) If we had not stopped for gas
(B) If we would not have stopped for gas
(C) If we didn't have stopped for gas
(D) Because we had stopped for gas
(E) If not for having been stopped for gas

8 The spectators watched <u>agape, they could not believe</u> what they were seeing on the playing field.

(A) agape, they could not believe
(B) agape having not believed
(C) agape, for the reason that they could not believe
(D) agape: they could not believe
(E) agape, therefore they could not believe

9 The evidence for clairvoyance has never been <u>persuasive, and many people continue to believe</u> that it is a widespread phenomenon.

(A) persuasive, and many people continue to believe
(B) persuasive; nevertheless, many people continue to believe
(C) persuasive, so many people continue to believe
(D) persuasive: and people continue to believe anyway
(E) persuasive, which is why people continue to believe

10 The strange theories that explain the atom <u>reveals how deeply the common and the bizarre are entwined</u> in the physical world.

(A) reveals how deeply the common and the bizarre are entwined
(B) reveal how common the entwining of the bizarre is
(C) reveals the deep bizarre common entwining
(D) reveal how the common and the bizarre are so entwined deeply
(E) reveal how deeply the common and the bizarre are entwined

11 The transportation board announced <u>their anonymous approval</u> of the new contract at the press conference that afternoon.

(A) their anonymous approval
(B) its anonymous approval
(C) their unanimous approval
(D) its unanimous approval
(E) about its unanimous approval

4 ▶

Directions for Identifying Sentence Error Questions

The following sentences may contain errors in grammar, usage, diction (choice of words), or idiom. Some of the sentences are correct. No sentence contains more than one error.

If the sentence contains an error, it is underlined and lettered. The parts that are not underlined are correct.

If there is an error, select the part that must be changed to correct the sentence.

If there is no error, choose (E).

EXAMPLE:

By the time <u>they reached</u> the halfway point
           A
<u>in the race,</u> <u>most of the runners</u> <u>hadn't hardly</u>
   B   C   D
begun to hit their stride. <u>No error</u>
                 E

Sample answer: (D)

12 The reporters failed to notice the

discrepancies in the report that the
<u>A</u>

Congressman presented, because

<u>his staff and him</u> had <u>successfully</u> diverted
   B   C

the media's attention <u>to other issues.</u>
                      D

<u>No error</u>
  E

13 The Warren family, whose ancestors

<u>founded</u> the town over <u>three hundred</u> years
 A   B
ago, <u>have ran</u> the general store <u>for</u> seven
    C   D
generations. <u>No error</u>
           E

14 <u>Surprisingly</u> absent from the game <u>were</u> the
   A   B
crowd's <u>customary</u> <u>taunting</u> of the opposing
        C   D
players. <u>No error</u>
       E

15 <u>Much</u> of the class time <u>was dedicated</u> to
 A   B

discussing those theories that <u>seemed to be</u>
                    C

most commonly misconstrued

<u>by the students.</u> <u>No error</u>
    D   E

16 The refraction of light as it <u>passes from</u> air
                      A

into a denser <u>medium</u> like water or glass
        B

often <u>produce</u> interesting kaleidoscopic
     C

<u>effects.</u> <u>No error</u>
 D   E

17 Of the two films <u>that made</u> money
              A
<u>for the studio</u> this year, the <u>least</u> expensive
   B   C
garnered the more <u>favorable</u> reviews.
             D
<u>No error</u>
  E

18 Having invested so much effort in getting

her team <u>so far</u> <u>in the tournament,</u>
     A   B
Coach Moran could hardly be blamed for

reacting so <u>emotional</u> <u>to the foul</u> called on
         C   D
her player in the waning seconds of the

game. <u>No error</u>
      E

19 To its most eminent proponents, anarchism

implies not a desire for lawlessness or chaos,
A

but rather it is a respect for the ability of
B   C

individuals to manage their own affairs
D

justly without the intervention of a

government. No error
E

20 The senate adopted new rules to prevent

representatives from serving on a committee
A

while at the same time maintaining an
B

interest in any company that conducts
C

business that is affected by that committee's
D

decisions. No error
E

21 The labor coalition, which consists of
A

representatives from all of the skilled labor

unions, have expressed concern about the
B   C

new hiring policies enacted by the board.
D

No error
E

22 Most cognitive scientists now believe that
A

the way the human brain stores information
B

is different in many significant ways from
C

a computer hard drive. No error
D   E

23 The museum, which has sponsored free
A

programs in the arts for city children since

the late 1960s, was cited by the mayor for
B   C

their many civic contributions. No error
D   E

24 When given the choice, Harlow's monkeys
A

clearly preferred the warmer, cloth-covered

surrogate mother more than the wire
B

surrogate, even when the latter was able
C

to provide them with nourishment. No error
D   E

25 Although both films accurately depict the
A

horrors of fighting on the front lines, *Saving*
B

Private Ryan is by far the most graphic.
C   D

No error
E

26 The debate team, which included
A

Emma and I, was stuck on the bus for
B   C

more than two hours. No error
D   E

27 By the time he reached the island, David
A

had already swam further than anyone
B   C

else ever had. No error
D   E

28 Far from being a liberal fanatic, Davis
     A
actually espouses very conservative
         B
views on social and economic issues.
  C   D
No error
  E

29 For building vocabulary skills, students
    A
should try to speak and write new words in
      B
appropriate contexts, rather than merely
  C   D
memorizing definitions. No error
             E

4

GO ON TO THE NEXT PAGE ▶▶▶

Questions 30–35 are based on the following passage.

(1) *Maria Montessori, who was born in 1870, was a remarkable woman for her time.* (2) *She surprised her parents by telling them that she wanted to study engineering when she was young, a position that they thought was unladylike.* (3) *She later decided to switch to medicine and became the first female physician in Italy.* (4) *As a doctor, the treatment of children who they said were "deficient" bothered her.* (5) *She realized that isolating them and depriving them of stimulation was doing them a lot of harm.*

(6) *In 1907 Maria opened her Casa dei Bambini, or "Children's House," a daycare center where impoverished children could receive a stimulating learning environment.* (7) *She believed that there are specific time schedules where children's minds are ready to learn particular things at their own pace, and these periods are different for every child.* (8) *She decided it was important to help each child through his or her own curriculum rather than a standardized one for everybody.* (9) *What was most amazing, the children who used to be aggressive and unmanageable became very proud of their accomplishments and eager to learn more when they were taught skills that gave them control and independence.* (10) *There were fifty students in her first class.*

(11) *One of the things that Dr. Montessori did that might be the most important is not just treat children as small adults, but as people with their own special needs.* (12) *She designed special furniture, toys, and learning aids that were appropriate for their size and abilities.*

(13) *Her philosophy has had a profound effect on education throughout the world.* (14) *Today, even the most traditional and regimented schools acknowledge many contributions of Maria Montessori.*

30 Which of the following is the best revision of sentence 2 (reproduced below)?

She surprised her parents by telling them that she wanted to study engineering when she was young, a position that they thought was unladylike.

(A) When she was young, she surprised her parents by telling them that she wanted to study the unladylike position of engineering, they thought.

(B) When she was young, she surprised her parents by telling them that she wanted to study engineering, a subject they thought was unladylike.

(C) She surprised her parents by telling them that she wanted to study engineering, a subject that they thought was unladylike when she was young.

(D) She surprised her parents by telling them that she wanted to study the unladylike, so her parents thought, subject of engineering when she was young.

(E) She surprised her parents when she was young by telling them, who thought it was unladylike, that she wanted to study engineering.

GO ON TO THE NEXT PAGE ▶▶▶

31   Which of the following is the best way to revise the underlined portion of sentence 4 (reproduced below)?

As a doctor, <u>the treatment of children who they said were "deficient" bothered her</u>.

(A) she was bothered by the treatment of children who were said to be "deficient."

(B) the way children were treated who they said were "deficient" bothered her.

(C) the treatment bothered her of children who they said were "deficient."

(D) she was bothered by those children they said were "deficient" and the way they were treated.

(E) she was bothered by the children treated who were said to be "deficient."

32   The unity of the second paragraph can best be improved by deleting which of the following sentences?

(A) sentence 6   (B) sentence 7
(C) sentence 8   (D) sentence 9
(E) sentence 10

33   Where is the best place to insert the following sentence?

It was developed according to her theories about learning.

(A) after sentence 6
(B) after sentence 7
(C) after sentence 8
(D) after sentence 9
(E) after sentence 10

34   Which of the following is the best revision of sentence 7 (reproduced below)?

She believed that there are specific time schedules where children's minds are ready to learn particular things at their own pace, and these periods are different for every child.

(A) She believed that there are specific time schedules, and these schedules are different for every child, where children's minds are ready at their own pace to learn particular things.

(B) She believed that there are different time periods for every child where their minds are ready to learn particular things at their own pace.

(C) She believed different children at their own pace each have their own time schedules where they are ready to learn particular things.

(D) She believed that each child's mind has its own unique pace and schedule for learning.

(E) She believed that there are specific schedules that are different for every child's mind that make them able to learn at their own pace.

35   Which is the best sentence to insert between sentence 8 and sentence 9?

(A) Her need to blaze trails persisted well into her old age.

(B) It wasn't long until Dr. Montessori was recognized for her efforts.

(C) This focus on the individual child produced amazing results.

(D) She soon opened many of these schools throughout Italy.

(E) Even though she was a physician by training, she earned eminence as a teacher.

STOP   *You may check your work, on this section only, until time is called.*

Section 5

Time—25 minutes
18 questions

Directions for Multiple-Choice Questions

In this section, solve each problem, using any available space on the page for scratchwork. Then decide which is the best of the choices given and fill in the corresponding oval on the answer sheet.

- You may use a calculator on any problem. All numbers used are real numbers.
- Figures are drawn as accurately as possible EXCEPT when it is stated that the figure is not drawn to scale.
- All figures lie in a plane unless otherwise indicated.

Reference Information

$A = \pi r^2$ $A = \ell w$
$C = 2\pi r$ $A = \frac{1}{2}bh$ $V = \ell wh$ $V = \pi r^2 h$ $c^2 = a^2 + b^2$ Special Right Triangles

The arc of a circle measures 360°.
Every straight angle measures 180°.
The sum of the measures of the angles in a triangle is 180°.

---

1 If $5y - 2 = 3y + 7$, what is the value of y?

(A) 3.0
(B) 4.5
(C) 6.0
(D) 7.5
(E) 9.0

2

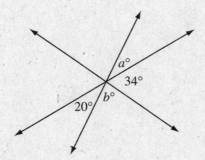

In the figure above, three lines intersect in a single point. What is the value of $a + b$?

(A)   20
(B)   54
(C)   126
(D)   146
(E)   252

3 If $(2x)(3x) = \left(\dfrac{2}{8}\right)\left(\dfrac{3}{2}\right)$, and $x > 0$, what is the value of x?

(A) $\frac{1}{16}$
(B) $\frac{1}{8}$
(C) $\frac{1}{4}$
(D) $\frac{1}{3}$
(E) $\frac{1}{2}$

4 Two positive integers are "compatible" if their greatest common factor is a prime number. For instance, 15 and 25 are compatible because their greatest common factor is 5, which is prime. If m and 98 are compatible, and m is an odd number, then what is the greatest common factor of m and 98?

(A)   2
(B)   5
(C)   7
(D)   14
(E)   49

GO ON TO THE NEXT PAGE ▶▶▶

5 For how many integer values of k is $|k - 0.5| < 10$?

(A)   17
(B)   18
(C)   19
(D)   20
(E)   21

7 If m and n are integers and $1 < m^3 = n^2 < 100$, what is the value of $m + n$?

(A)   4
(B)   8
(C)   12
(D)   16
(E)   32

6 What is the greatest possible value of $f(x)$ over the interval $-1 \le x \le 2$ if $f(x)$ is defined by the equation $f(x) = \dfrac{10 - x^2}{2}$?

(A)   3.0
(B)   3.5
(C)   4.0
(D)   4.5
(E)   5.0

8 Amanda travels to work from home in 60 minutes. If, on her way home, she increases her average speed by 20% and she travels by the exact same route, how many minutes will it take her to get home?

(A)   48
(B)   50
(C)   54
(D)   60
(E)   64

GO ON TO THE NEXT PAGE ▶▶▶

Directions for Student-Produced Response Questions

Each of the questions in this section requires you to solve the problem and enter your answer in a grid, as shown below.

- If your answer is ⅔ or .666..., you must enter **the most accurate value the grid can accommodate**, but you may do this in one of four ways.

Start in first column

Grid result here

Start in second column

Grid as a truncated decimal

Grid as a rounded decimal

- In the example above, gridding a response of 0.67 or 0.66 is **incorrect** because it is less accurate than those above.
- The scoring machine cannot read what is written in the top row of boxes. You **MUST** fill in the numerical grid accurately to get credit for answering any question correctly. You should write your answer in the top row of boxes only to aid your gridding.
- Do **not** grid in a mixed fraction like $3\frac{1}{2}$ as ⟨ 3 1 / 2 ⟩ because it will be interpreted as $\frac{31}{2}$. Instead, convert it to an improper fraction like ½ or a decimal like 3.5 before gridding.
- None of the answers will be negative, because there is no negative sign in the grid.
- Some of the questions may have more than one correct answer. You must grid only one of the correct answers.
- You may use a calculator on any of these problems.
- All numbers in these problems are real numbers.
- Figures are drawn as accurately as possible EXCEPT when it is stated that the figure is not drawn to scale.
- All figures lie in a plane unless otherwise indicated.

9 What is 0.5 percent of 80?

10 If d is the middle number of three consecutive odd integers whose sum is s, what is the value of d divided by s?

11 If $\frac{4}{9}$ of c^2 is 24, what is $\frac{5}{9}$ of c^2?

12 The measures of the four angles in a quadrilateral have a ratio of 3:4:5:6. What is the measure, in degrees, of the smallest of these angles?

GO ON TO THE NEXT PAGE ▶▶▶

13 If $5a + 6b = 13$ and $4a + 5b = 9$, then what is the value of $7a + 7b$?

14 If $m = \dfrac{1}{3}$, what is the value

of $\dfrac{\dfrac{1}{m+1} + \dfrac{1}{m-1}}{\dfrac{1}{m^2 - 1}}$?

5

15 If x and y are positive integers such that $x^2 + y^2 = 41$, then what is the value of $(x + y)^2$?

16 A jar contains fifteen marbles, five of which are white and the rest black. What is the *least* number of white marbles that must be added to the jar so that at least three-fifths of the marbles will be white?

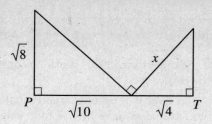

17 In the figure above, $\overline{PT}$ is a straight line segment. What is the value of x?

18 In one basketball game, Tamara made 50% of her shots, and in the next game, she made 60% of her shots. In the two games, she made 52% of her shots altogether. If she took a shots in the first game and b shots in the second game, what is the value of $\dfrac{a}{b}$?

STOP

You may check your work, on this section only, until time is called.

Section 6

Time —25 minutes
24 questions

Each of the sentences below is missing one or two portions. Read each sentence, then select the word or words that most logically complete the sentence, taking into account the meaning of the sentence as a whole.

Example:

Rather than accepting the theory unquestioningly, Deborah regarded it with ———.

(A) mirth   (B) sadness
(C) responsibility   (D) ignorance
(E) skepticism

Correct response: (E)

1 Rather than giving Sandra thoughtful and useful advice, her father admonished her with hollow clichés and ——— platitudes.

(A) irate   (B) inane
(C) homogeneous   (D) flamboyant
(E) altruistic

2 Maintaining a courageous ——— even while in prison, Nelson Mandela spent years trying to convince others that the fight against apartheid was not ———.

(A) optimism ... worthwhile
(B) will ... treacherous
(C) hope ... futile
(D) fortitude ... premeditated
(E) instability ... porous

3 The ——— of the construction near the building rendered the school far less ——— to learning; the teachers could hardly hear themselves talk.

(A) din ... conducive
(B) efficiency ... accustomed
(C) noise ... averse
(D) precision ... discernible
(E) racket ... irascible

4 Although no real problem in physics can be solved ———, an approximate solution by a simplified method is sufficient so long as the complicating factors are ———.

(A) precisely ... large
(B) completely ... difficult
(C) exactly ... negligible
(D) plausibly ... minimal
(E) ethically ... nonexistent

5 The ——— of a civil war depends on the factions' access to martial resources; the conflict may drag on for years or even decades so long as each side has sufficient ——— to continue fighting.

(A) violence ... mediation
(B) popularity ... opposition
(C) length ... reluctance
(D) duration ... means
(E) value ... skill

GO ON TO THE NEXT PAGE ▶▶▶

Each passage below is followed by questions based on its content. Answer each question based on what is stated or implied in the passage or the introductory material that precedes it.

Questions 6–7 are based on the following passage.

Line   Jung was never dogmatic as to a single "cause" of schizophrenia,[1] although he inclined to the belief that a psychological, rather than a physical, origin was probable. He was also
5   modest in his therapeutic claims, recognizing that only a limited number of cases responded to analysis, and that partial alleviation was more common than cure. Jung considered that there were many schizophrenics who
10   never came near a mental hospital. If such people consulted him, he was cautious and sometimes dismissed them without attempting psychoanalysis. Jung was one of the first to recognize that a psychotic episode could be
15   precipitated by psychoanalysis.

6   Based on the information in the passage, with which of the following statements would Jung most likely agree?

(A)   Schizophrenia is much more common than most psychologists acknowledge.
(B)   Schizophrenia has a single common cause.
(C)   Psychoanalysis is not helpful to all mentally ill patients.
(D)   Schizophrenia might be caused by physical trauma.
(E)   Psychoanalysis, in the right measure, can cure all schizophrenic patients.

7   In context, "precipitated by" (line 15) most nearly means

(A)   hastened by
(B)   cured by
(C)   responsive to
(D)   made more efficient by
(E)   composed of

Questions 8–9 are based on the following passage.

Line   The tragic (and the dramatic)—it is said—are *universal.* At a distance of centuries we still grieve at the tribulations of Oedipus and Orestes, and even without sharing the ideology
5   of Homais we are distressed by the tragedy of Emma Bovary. The comic, on the other hand, seems bound to its time, society, cultural anthropology. We understand the drama of the protagonist of *Rashomon,* but we don't
10   understand when and why the Japanese laugh. It is an effort to find Aristophanes comic, and it takes more culture to laugh at Rabelais than it does to weep at the death of the paladin Orlando.

8   Which of the following would the author consider most difficult for a modern American to find humorous?

(A)   a farcical musical about animals who talk
(B)   a comic film about gangsters set in Chicago
(C)   a satirical poem written in 16th-century China
(D)   a situation comedy based on the life of a plumber
(E)   a funny movie with a tragic ending

9   The "effort" (line 11) to which the author refers is a task that requires which of the following?

(A)   great planning
(B)   the work of more than one person
(C)   overcoming cultural obstacles
(D)   a great many natural resources
(E)   emotional fortitude

GO ON TO THE NEXT PAGE ▶▶▶

First paragraph: Anthony Storr, *The Essential Jung.* © 1983 by Princeton University Press. Reprinted by permission of Princeton University Press.
Second paragraph: *The Comic and the Rule* in *Travels in Hyperreality,* by Umberto Eco, Harcourt, Brace, Jovanovich, 1983, p. 269.

[1]Schizophrenia is a type of mental illness characterized by a withdrawal from reality and, occasionally, delusions and mood disorders.

The questions below are based on the content of the preceding passage. The questions are to be answered on the basis of what is stated or implied in the passage itself or the introductory material that precedes the passage.

Questions 10–16 are based on the following passage:

The following is an excerpt from a book on the writing process in which the author describes an interview he gave by telephone to a radio show to promote a writer's conference.

Line The appointed evening arrived, and my
      phone rang, and the host came on and
      greeted me with the strenuous joviality of his
      trade. He said he had three lovely ladies in
 5   the studio with him and he was eager to find
      out what we all thought of the present state
      of literature and what advice we had for all
      his listeners who were members of the literati
      and had literary ambitions themselves. This
 10   hearty introduction dropped like a stone in
      our midst, and none of the three lovely ladies
      said anything in response, which I thought
      was the proper response.
          The silence lengthened, and finally I said,
 15   "I think we should banish all further mention
      of the words 'literature' and 'literary' and
      'literati.'" I knew that the host had been
      briefed about what kind of writers we were
      and what we wanted to discuss. But he had
 20   no other frame of reference. "Tell me," he
      said, "what insights do you have about the
      literary experience in America today?" Silence
      also greeted this question. Finally I said,
      "We're here to talk about the craft of writing."
 25   He didn't know what to make of that, and
      he began to involve the names of authors like
      Ernest Hemingway and Saul Bellow and
      William Styron, whom we surely regarded as
      literary giants. We said those writers didn't
 30   happen to be our models, and we mentioned
      people like Lewis Thomas and Joan Didion
      and Garry Wills. He had never heard of them.
      One of them mentioned Tom Wolfe's *The
      Right Stuff*, and he hadn't heard of that. We
 35   explained that these were writers we admired
      for their ability to harness the issues and
      concerns of the day.
          "But don't you want to write anything
      literary?" our host said. The three women

 40   said they felt they were already doing satisfying
      work. That brought the program to another
      halt, and the host began to accept phone calls
      from his listeners, all of whom were
      interested in the craft of writing and
 45   wanted to know how we went about it. "And
      yet, in the stillness of the night," the host said
      to several callers, "don't you ever dream of
      writing the great American novel?" They
      didn't. They had no such dreams—in the
 50   stillness of the night or any other time. It was
      one of the all-time lousy radio talk shows.
          The story sums up a situation that any
      particular practitioner of nonfiction will
      recognize. Those of us who are trying to
 55   write well about the world we live in, or to
      teach students to write well about the world
      they live in, are caught in a time warp, where
      literature by definition still consists of forms
      that were certified as "literary" in the 19th
 60   century: novels and short stories and poems.
      But in fact the great preponderance of what
      writers now write and sell, what book and
      magazine publishers publish and what
      readers demand is nonfiction.

10 In the first paragraph, the author suggests that he regards the host's introduction to be

(A) insincere   (B) inappropriate
(C) erudite   (D) flattering
(E) incoherent

11 Throughout the passage, the author uses the term "literary" to mean

(A) well-written
(B) with regard to love stories
(C) pertaining to the writing of fiction and poetry
(D) concerning contemporary issues
(E) persuasive

GO ON TO THE NEXT PAGE ▶▶▶

Excerpted from *On Writing Well* by William Zinsser, Harper Perennial, New York, 6th edition, 1998, pp. 95–97.

12 What is the main substance of the misunderstanding between the interviewer and the interviewees?

(A) The interviewer believed that the writers had written books that they actually had not.
(B) The interviewer lacked a frame of reference on writing beyond literary fiction.
(C) The interviewees wanted to be more critical of classic authors, while the interviewer wanted to praise them.
(D) The interviewer wanted to discuss current issues, while the writers wanted to discuss 19th-century literary forms.
(E) The interviewer disagreed with the writers on the merits of *The Right Stuff*.

13 The authors in lines 31–32 are mentioned as examples of

(A) the most popular authors of the time
(B) authors who had set the trend for the "literary" style of that era
(C) authors who had influenced the work of the writers being interviewed
(D) authors whose works followed in the manner of Hemingway, Bellow, and Styron
(E) authors who wrote experimental fiction

14 In context, the word "harness" (line 36) most nearly means

(A) dominate
(B) make easier to understand
(C) influence the direction of
(D) witness
(E) reinforce

15 If the callers shared the sensibilities of the interviewees, then by saying that they had "no such dreams" (line 49), the callers were most likely suggesting that they

(A) did not wish to pursue literary fame in such a competitive environment
(B) had disdain for those who wrote fiction for profit
(C) knew that the public did not care for writers like Thomas, Didion, and Wills
(D) had been discouraged by their negative experiences with publishers in the literary world
(E) were happy doing what they were doing

16 In context, the word "preponderance" (line 61) most nearly means

(A) evidence
(B) domination
(C) majority
(D) heaviness
(E) quality

as Democritus and Archimedes. Two sets of
phenomena seemed important: the movements
of animals, and the movements of the heavenly
bodies. To the modern man of science, the
45 body of an animal is a very elaborate machine,
with an enormously complex physico-
chemical structure; every new discovery
consists in diminishing the apparent gulf
between animals and machines. To the Greek,
50 it seemed more natural to assimilate apparently
lifeless motions to those of animals. A child
still distinguishes live animals from other
things by the fact that they can move them;
to many Greeks, and especially to Aristotle,
55 this peculiarity suggested itself as the basis of
a general theory of physics.

But how about the heavenly bodies? They
differ from animals by the regularity of their
60 movements, but this may be only due to their
superior perfection. Every Greek philosopher,
whatever he may have come to think in adult
life, had been taught in childhood to regard
the sun and moon as gods; Anaxagoras was
65 prosecuted for impiety because he thought
that they were not alive. It was natural that a
philosopher who could no longer regard the
heavenly bodies themselves as divine should
think of them as moved by the will of a Divine
70 Being who had a Hellenic love of order and
geometric simplicity. Thus the ultimate
source of all movement is Will: on earth the
capricious Will of human beings, but in heaven
the unchanging Will of the Supreme Artificer.

Questions 17–24 are based on the following passage.

*The following is from a book on the history of
Western philosophy by Bertrand Russell, in which
he discusses ancient Greek philosophy.*

Line To understand the views of Aristotle, as of
most Greeks, on physics, it is necessary to
apprehend his imaginative background.
Every philosopher, in addition to the formal
5 system which he offers to the world, has
another much simpler system of which he
may be quite unaware. If he is aware of it, he
probably realizes that it won't quite do; he
therefore conceals it, and sets forth something
10 more sophisticated, which he believes
because it is like his crude system, but which
he asks others to accept because he thinks he
has made it such as cannot be disproved. The
sophistication comes in by way of refutation
15 of refutations, but this alone will never give a
positive result: it shows, at best, that a theory
may be true, not that it *must* be. The positive
result, however little the philosopher may
realize it, is due to his imaginative
20 preconceptions, or to what Santayana calls
"animal faith."

In relation to physics, Aristotle's
imaginative background was very different
from that of a modern student. Nowadays,
25 students begin with mechanics, which, by its
very name, suggests machines. They are
accustomed to automobiles and airplanes;
they do not, even in the dimmest recesses of
their subconscious imagination, think that an
30 automobile contains some sort of horse inside,
or that an airplane flies because its wings are
those of a bird possessing magical powers.
Animals have lost their importance in our
imaginative pictures of the world, in which
35 humans stand comparatively alone as masters
of a mainly lifeless and largely subservient
material environment.

To the ancient Greek, attempting to give
a scientific account of motion, the purely
40 mechanical view hardly suggested itself,
except in the case of a few men of genius such

17 Which of the following best summarizes the
overall purpose of this passage?

(A) to compare Aristotle's philosophy
with those of Democritus and
Archimedes
(B) to describe the preconceptions
behind Aristotle's physical theories
(C) to uncover the flaws in ancient Greek
astronomy
(D) to show how Aristotle's theories facilitated the development of modern
technology
(E) to contrast the modern conception of
the animal with that of the ancient
Greeks

GO ON TO THE NEXT PAGE ▶▶▶

Excerpted from *A History of Western Philosophy* by Bertrand
Russell, Touchstone, Simon & Schuster, New York, 1945, 1972,
pp. 203–204.

18 According to the passage, in what way have animals "lost their importance". (line 33)?

(A) Humans no longer treat animals as respectfully as they once did.

(B) Humans no longer need animals to do hard labor.

(C) Few religions today require animal sacrifices.

(D) Modern writers rarely write stories or fables with animals as main characters.

(E) Animals no longer inspire modern physical theories.

19 Which of the following is most similar to the "imaginative preconceptions" (line 19) of Aristotle?

(A) the belief that animals are inferior to humans

(B) the belief that all scientific problems can be solved through rigorous philosophical analysis

(C) the belief that computers have minds and souls like humans or animals

(D) the belief that the body of an animal is a complicated machine

(E) the belief that the sun and moon are not alive

20 What does the author imply about the "men of genius" (line 41)?

(A) They believed that physics is essentially the study of the mechanics of motion rather than spirits or wills.

(B) They were able to precisely determine the orbits of the planets.

(C) They regarded the sun and moon as gods.

(D) They alone saw the similarity between the motion of animals and the motion of heavenly bodies.

(E) They regarded all movement as being produced by a Divine Being.

21 According to the passage, modern scientists diminish "the apparent gulf between animals and machines" (lines 49–50) by

(A) using machines to train animals

(B) studying the motivations of animals

(C) working to make machines function more like animals

(D) using technology to improve the lives of animals

(E) uncovering the mechanical laws behind biology

22 In line 51, the word "assimilate" most nearly means

(A) compare   (B) repeat

(C) attach   (D) refer

(E) elevate

23 In the final paragraph, which of the following does the author imply about Greek philosophers?

(A) Some of them were not rigorous in demonstrating their theories through experiment.

(B) They were more concerned with popularizing their theories than proving them.

(C) Some of them departed dramatically from their childhood teachings.

(D) They all regarded the planetary bodies as divine.

(E) Most of them disagreed strongly with Aristotle.

24 The "Hellenic love of order and geometric simplicity" (line 70) attributed to the "Divine Being" (line 69) can be inferred to involve which of the following?

I. a need to simplify mathematical equations

II. desire to make astronomical objects move in elegant paths

III. a need to unify the laws of motion with a single theory

(A) I only

(B) II only

(C) I and II only

(D) II and III only

(E) I, II, and III

STOP

You may check your work, on this section only, until time is called.

Section 7

Time—20 minutes
16 questions

Directions for Multiple-Choice Questions

In this section, solve each problem, using any available space on the page for scratchwork. Then decide which is the best of the choices given and fill in the corresponding oval on your answer sheet.

- You may use a calculator on any problem. All numbers used are real numbers.
- Figures are drawn as accurately as possible EXCEPT when it is stated that the figure is not drawn to scale.
- All figures lie in a plane unless otherwise indicated.

Reference Information

$A = \pi r^2$ $A = \ell w$ $A = \frac{1}{2}bh$ $V = \ell wh$ $V = \pi r^2 h$ $c^2 = a^2 + b^2$ Special Right Triangles
$C = 2\pi r$

The number of degrees of arc in a circle measures 360°.
Every straight angle measures 180°.
The sum of the measures of the angles in a triangle is 180°.

---

1 The number that is $\frac{2}{3}$ of 60 is what fraction of 80?

(A) $\frac{1}{6}$

(B) $\frac{1}{3}$

(C) $\frac{1}{2}$

(D) $\frac{3}{4}$

(E) $\frac{8}{9}$

2 If $4x + 2y = 8$, then $x + \frac{1}{2}y =$

(A) 0.25
(B) 0.5
(C) 1
(D) 2
(E) 4

3 29 apples, 21 pears, and 64 oranges are to be distributed among three baskets, with each basket getting an equal number of apples, each basket getting an equal number of pears, and each basket getting an equal number of oranges. If as much of the fruit as possible is distributed in this way, what fruit will remain undistributed?

(A) 2 apples, 2 pears, and 1 orange
(B) 2 apples, 1 pear, and 1 orange
(C) 2 apples and 1 orange
(D) 1 pear and 1 orange
(E) 1 apple only

GO ON TO THE NEXT PAGE ▶▶▶

4 For all values of x and y, let "x & y" be defined by the equation x & $y = x(x - 1) + y(y - 1)$. What is the value of 1 & 2?

(A) 1
(B) 2
(C) 3
(D) 4
(E) 5

5 In $\triangle ABC$, $AB = 15$ and $BC = 9$. Which of the following could *not* be the length of AC?

(A)   5
(B)   7
(C)   9
(D) 16
(E) 22

6 What is the surface area of a cube that has a volume of 64 cubic centimeters?

(A)   64 square centimetres
(B)   96 square centimetres
(C) 256 square centimetres
(D) 288 square centimetres
(E) 384 square centimeters

7 The average (arithmetic mean) of x, 2, 6, and 10 is 8. What is the *median* of x, 2, 6, and 10?

(A) 4
(B) 6
(C) 7
(D) 8
(E) 9

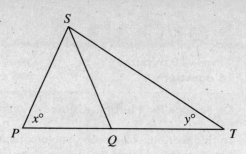

Note: Figure not drawn to scale.

8 In the figure above, $PS = SQ$ and $SQ = QT$. Which of the following expresses y in terms of x?

(A) $\dfrac{x}{2}$

(B) $90 - x$

(C) $90 - \dfrac{x}{2}$

(D) $180 - 2x$
(E) $180 - x$

9

$$-4 \;\; -3 \;\; -2 \;\; -1 \;\; 0 \;\; 1 \;\; 2 \;\; 3 \;\; 4$$

The graph above represents the set of all possible solutions to which of the following statements?

(A) $|x-1| > 1$
(B) $|x+1| < 1$
(C) $|x-1| < 1$
(D) $|x+1| > 1$
(E) $|x+1| > -1$

10
$a > b$
$b < c$
$a = 2c$

If a, b, and c represent different integers in the statements above, which of the following statements must be true?

    I. $a > c$
    II. $2c > b$
    III. $ac > b2$

(A) I only
(B) II only
(C) I and II only
(D) II and III only
(E) I, II, and III

GO ON TO THE NEXT PAGE ▶▶▶

11 How many different positive three-digit integers begin with an odd digit and end with an even digit?

(A) 125
(B) 180
(C) 200
(D) 225
(E) 250

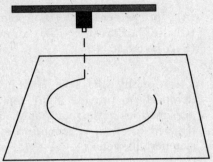

12 A machine uses a laser beam to cut circles from a sheet of plastic, as shown in the figure above. The beam cuts at the rate of 3 cm per second. If circle A has an area of 64π square centimeters and circle B has an area of 16π square centimeters, how many more seconds will it take the machine to cut circle A than circle B?

(A) 2π seconds

(B) $\dfrac{8\pi}{3}$ seconds

(C) $\dfrac{16\pi}{3}$ seconds

(D) 8π seconds

(E) $\dfrac{48\pi}{3}$ seconds

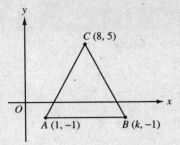

Note: Figure not drawn to scale

13 In the figure above, the slope of AC is the opposite of the slope of CB. What is the value of k?

(A) 9
(B) 10
(C) 12
(D) 14
(E) 15

14 If m is the product of all of the integers from 1 to 10, inclusive, and 2^n is a factor of m, then what is the greatest possible value of n?

(A) 2
(B) 4
(C) 8
(D) 16
(E) 32

15 An equilateral triangle with area $36\sqrt{3}$ square centimeters is divided into two triangles by the bisector of one of its angles. What is the sum of the perimeters of these two triangles?

(A) $18 + 6\sqrt{3}$

(B) $18 + 9\sqrt{3}$

(C) $36 + 6\sqrt{3}$

(D) $36 + 12\sqrt{3}$

(E) $36 + 18\sqrt{3}$

16 A culture of bacteria doubles in population every 2 hours. A sample of 100 bacteria grows to 1,000 bacteria by 4:00 pm. At what time were there 250 bacteria in this sample?

(A) 11:30 am
(B) 12 noon
(C) 12:30 pm
(D) 1:00 pm
(E) 2:00 pm

You may check your work, on this section only, until time is called.

Section 8

Time—20 minutes
19 questions

Each of the sentences below is missing one or two portions. Read each sentence, then select the word or words that most logically complete the sentence, taking into account the meaning of the sentence as a whole.

Example:

Rather than accepting the theory unquestioningly, Deborah regarded it with ————.

(A) mirth   (B) sadness
(C) responsibility   (D) ignorance
(E) skepticism

Correct response: (E)

8

1 To Clara's relief, the biopsy revealed that the tumor on her skin was ————.

(A) malignant   (B) irreverent
(C) serene   (D) benign
(E) mortal

2 The speaker's message was ———— by jargon that rendered it decipherable only to those few audience members familiar with her particular area of expertise.

(A) elated   (B) revealed
(C) obscured   (D) enlightened
(E) consoled

3 To those consumers who are more influenced by style than by performance, the ——— value of the sports car outweighs its functional flaws.

(A) utilitarian   (B) pragmatic
(C) approximate   (D) aesthetic
(E) inexplicable

4 A student becomes a thinker only when he or she realizes that most so-called facts are merely ———— claims, each serving its purpose only temporarily.

(A) provisional   (B) polemical
(C) authoritative   (D) dramatic
(E) pedantic

5 Traditionally, the role had been played demurely to provide a foil for the bolder personalities in the play, but Ms. Linney has decided to ———— convention and emphasize her character's ————.

(A) respect ... bluster
(B) abandon ... solitude
(C) forgo ... coyness
(D) uphold . . . bombast
(E) eschew ... impudence

6 Despite the attempts of popular analysts to depict the stock market as driven by predictable financial principles, an increasing number of investors believe that the price of any security is ————.

(A) invaluable   (B) complacent
(C) capricious   (D) responsive
(E) obscure

GO ON TO THE NEXT PAGE ▶▶▶

The questions below are based on the content of the two passages that precede them and the relationship between the passages. The questions are to be answered on the basis of what is stated or implied in the passage itself or the introductory material that precedes the passage.

Questions 7–19 are based on the following passages.

Since 1996, when scientists at the Roslin Institute in England cloned a sheep from the cells of another adult sheep, many inside and outside the scientific community have debated the ethics of cloning the cells of human beings. The following passages are excerpts of arguments on this issue.

Passage 1

Line   With the specter of human cloning looming on the horizon, the dominant ethical question is: what is a human being? Until now, our respect for human life has rested
5   fundamentally on the deep understanding that human life is perhaps the ultimate gift of nature or God. This gift is made even more profound by the fact that we ourselves are not only its recipients but also its conduits:
10   we receive life and we help create it. But our participation in the creation of life must never be misconstrued as control. Rather, we must be humbled by the power of the life force at the moment of conception.
15   The idea of "outsourcing" the creation of human life, of relegating it to a laboratory, of reducing the anticipation of childbirth to a trip to the mall or a selection from a catalog, leaves us with a profoundly hollow feeling.
20   The mystery is replaced by design; the surrender to nature is replaced by arrogant control. Should we turn our noses up at one who would offer us the most precious gift in the universe, only to say: "Sorry, but I think
25   I can do better?"
       Cloning is the engineering of human life. We have for the first time the ability to determine the exact genetic makeup of a human being, to thwart the essential random
30   (or seemingly random) processes that form the basis of natural selection, to employ unnatural selection. A child can be created that is no longer a unique creation but the end product of an assembly line, with carefully

35   designed and tested features. Are the astonishing products of natural selection that we find around us somehow deficient? Are we so full of hubris[1] as to think we have a better way than nature or God?
40   If human cloning becomes acceptable, we will have created a new society in which the essence of human life is marginalized. Industries will arise that turn human procreation into a profitable free-market
45   enterprise. The executive boards of these companies, rather than nature or God, will decide the course of human evolution, with more concern for quarterly profit reports than for the fate of humanity.
50   These are not idle concerns. Even as we ponder the ethical implications of human cloning, companies are forging ahead with the cloning of human stem cells for seemingly beneficial purposes, marching steadily toward
55   a Brave New World[2] in which humanity will be forever different from what it is today.

Passage 2

       The irrational fears about human cloning that abound from all parts of the political spectrum should not surprise anyone who
60   knows a little bit about the history of technology. Hardly anything significant has been invented that no segment of the population has denounced as evil: factories, trains, automobiles, telephones, televisions,
65   computers. Not even medicine has been spared this vituperation, despite its obvious benefits to humanity. Before the merits of surgery became obvious, it was unimaginable that slicing the flesh of a human being could
70   do more harm than good.
       At first glance, it might seem that cloning is a whole new ballgame. After all, cloning is "the engineering of human life," isn't it? It is the mass production of designer babies. It is
75   the end of evolution, or at least the beginning of its corporate management. It is certainly a slap in the face of God. Or is it?
       One of scariest things to the opponents of cloning is the prospect of human beings having

GO ON TO THE NEXT PAGE ▶▶▶

[1] Excessive pride or arrogance
[2] A futuristic novel by Aldous Huxley that describes the mass production of genetically identical human babies.

80 identical genetic codes. As cloning foe Jeremy
   Rifkin has said: "It's a horrendous crime to
   make a Xerox of someone. You're putting a
   human into a genetic straitjacket." Logically,
   then, Mr. Rifkin must be repulsed by natural-
85 born identical multiples: there is no scientific
   way to distinguish the DNA of one's genetically
   identical twin from that of one's clone.
   Perhaps the whole system of natural human
   procreation is suspect, if it is capable
90 of occasionally churning out such
   monstrosities.
       We need nothing more than the most
   rudimentary common sense to see how
   vacuous such an argument is. We all know
95 identical twins who have their own unique
   thoughts, talents, experiences, and beliefs.
   They are not horrendous monsters. Human
   beings are more than merely their DNA;
   they are the products of the continual and
100 inscrutably complex interactions of
   environment and biology. Human clones
   would be no different.
       The most common objection we hear
   from the anti-cloning lobby is that those who
105 would clone human beings are "playing
   God," and trespassing into territory that can
   only bring the wrath of nature or its creator.
   Most of these arguments are basically
   theological, and rest on the most effective
110 tool of human control ever invented: fear
   of God. We can easily get people to hate
   something by calling it "unnatural." But this
   argument is even more easily demolished than
   the previous one, because it falls so easily in
115 line with so many obviously silly claims. This
   argument rests on the assumption that human
   ingenuity has essentially no value, that
   improving on nature is the height of hubris.
   This is the reasoning of the Dark Ages.
120 Nature presents vegetables and meats only in
   raw form, so isn't the cooking of food a
   human transgression against nature? Nature
   gives us feet, not wheels, so aren't bicycles
   evil? If we were to abandon all of the
125 "unnatural" practices and products from our
   lives, we would be shivering in caves eating
   uncooked leaves and bugs.
       Maybe human procreation is a different
   arena, however, more sacred than all of the
130 others. But then, why have the technologies
   of fertility enhancement, in vitro fertilization,
   embryo transfer, and birth control become so
   widely accepted? They are telling examples:
   each of these procreational technologies had

135 legions of vocal opponents—*at first*—but over
   time the protests mellowed as people realized
   that the sky wouldn't fall after all. Familiarity
   dissipates fear.
       What most opponents of genetic technology
140 don't realize is that their supposedly "moral"
   objections are impeding true moral progress.
   With genetic engineering and stem cell
   research, scientists finally have within their
   grasp technologies that can produce ample
145 food for a starving world and cure devastating
   illnesses. Only ignorant superstition stands in
   their way.

7 The "control" mentioned in line 12 is
      control over

      (A)   the effects of cloning
      (B)   the development of genetic
            technologies
      (C)   the process of conception
      (D)   the moral debate about cloning
      (E)   activities in a laboratory

8 Which of the following best describes the
      attitude of the author of Passage 1 toward
      "outsourcing" (line 15)?

      (A)   reluctant approval
      (B)   disdain
      (C)   strong support
      (D)   ironic detachment
      (E)   ambivalence

9 The statement "sorry, but I think I can do
      better" (lines 24–25) is intended to represent
      a comment from

      (A)   a religious person to a nonreligious
            person
      (B)   an opponent of cloning to a scientist
      (C)   a voter to a politician
      (D)   the author to the reader
      (E)   an advocate of cloning to nature
            or God

10 The parenthetical comment in line 30 is intended to account for the possibility that

(A) life might be designed by a power beyond humanity
(B) cloning technologies might become uncontrollable
(C) two human beings might have the same genetic makeup by chance alone
(D) some scientific theories might not be reliable
(E) cloning technology might not succeed

11 Passage 1 mentions which of the following as elements of "unnatural selection" (line 32)?

　　I.　mechanical procedures
　　II.　random processes
　　III.　selection of characteristics

(A) I only
(B) III only
(C) I and II only
(D) I and III only
(E) I, II, and III

12 In the first paragraph of Passage 2, the author suggests that the opponents of human cloning, as a group, are all of the following EXCEPT

(A) very religious
(B) unreasonable about the implications of cloning
(C) from widely varied political orientations
(D) ignorant of scientific history
(E) fearful of new ideas

13 Surgery is mentioned in lines 68–70 as an example of

(A) a practice that requires a great deal of education
(B) something that most people still fear
(C) a medical technology that was once denounced
(D) a viable alternative to genetic technologies
(E) a skill in need of more practitioners

14 The author of Passage 2 quotes Jeremy Rifkin (lines 81–83) in order to

(A) illustrate the dangers of cloning
(B) show a well-reasoned perspective
(C) indicate an illogical claim
(D) represent the views of medical professionals
(E) show how others support the author's thesis

15 The author of Passage 2 mentions that identical human twins "have their own unique thoughts" (lines 95–96) in order to suggest that those twins

(A) would likely oppose human cloning
(B) are not simply the product of their DNA
(C) are among the most vocal advocates of cloning
(D) are able to provide alternatives to procreational technologies
(E) are less likely to be swayed by illogical theories

16 Passage 2 suggests that those individuals who had previously denounced "procreational technologies" (line 134) have since come to accept them because those individuals

(A) became more familiar with the technologies
(B) realized that the technologies were indeed "natural"
(C) understood the theories behind the technologies
(D) realized that the technologies were inexpensive
(E) themselves needed to use those technologies

17 The tone of the last paragraph of Passage 2 is best described as

(A) indignant
(B) analytical
(C) resigned
(D) humorous
(E) whimsical

GO ON TO THE NEXT PAGE ▸▸▸

18 Which of the following best describes the relationship between the pair of questions presented in Passage 1 ("Are the astonishing products . . . nature or God?" [lines 35–39]) and the pair of questions presented in Passage 2 ("Nature presents . . . evil?" [lines 120–124])?

(A) The first two are not intended to be answered, while the second two are.

(B) The first two are scientific questions, while the second two are moral questions.

(C) Both pairs of questions indicate points of view criticized by their respective authors.

(D) The first two are intended as questions from cloning opponents, while the second two are intended as questions from cloning advocates.

(E) The first two are common questions, the second two are asked only by experts.

19 The last paragraphs of both passages indicate that both authors share what assumption?

(A) Cloning needs more scientific study.

(B) Genetic engineering will have profound global effects.

(C) Cloning will marginalize human life.

(D) Procreational technology can benefit the poor.

(E) Scientists are ill-suited to make moral decisions.

STOP

You may check your work, on this section only, until time is called.

Section 9

Time—10 minutes
14 questions

Directions for "Improving Sentences" Questions

Each of the sentences below contains one underlined portion. The portion may contain one or more errors in grammar, usage, construction, precision, diction (choice of words), or idiom. Some of the sentences are correct.

Consider the meaning of the original sentence, and choose the answer that best expresses that meaning. If the original sentence is best, choose (A), because it repeats the original phrasing. Choose the phrasing that creates the clearest, most precise, and most effective sentence.

EXAMPLE:

The children couldn't hardly believe their eyes.

   (A) couldn't hardly believe their eyes
   (B) would not hardly believe their eyes
   (C) could hardly believe their eyes
   (D) couldn't nearly believe their eyes
   (E) could hardly believe his or her eyes

Example answer: **(C)**

---

1 One way to improve the effectiveness of the treatment is by moving the source of radiation more closely to the patient.

   (A) by moving the source of radiation more closely
   (B) to move the source of radiation more closely
   (C) to move the source of radiation closer
   (D) in moving the source of radiation closer
   (E) to move more closely the source of radiation

2 Until becoming more affordable by standardizing its technology, cell phones were quite rare.

   (A) until becoming more affordable by standardizing its technology
   (B) having become more affordable through standardizing their technology
   (C) becoming more affordable through standardized technology
   (D) until they became more affordable in standardized technology
   (E) until standardized technology made them more affordable

3 The airline industry has adopted new pricing procedures; seeming to benefit both the consumers as well as the companies.

   (A) procedures; seeming to benefit both the consumers as well as
   (B) procedures; seemingly benefiting both the consumers and
   (C) procedures seemingly in benefit of both the consumers as well as
   (D) procedures that seem benefiting of both the consumers and
   (E) procedures that seem to benefit both the consumers and

4 The thirty-foot-high stone wall, built over the course of eighty years, once protecting the city from invaders.

   (A) wall, built over the course of eighty years, once protecting
   (B) wall, built over the course of eighty years, once protected
   (C) wall was built over the course of eighty years, which protected
   (D) wall was built over the course of eighty years in protecting
   (E) wall, built over the course of eighty years; it once protected

9

GO ON TO THE NEXT PAGE ▶▶▶

5 A concise and informative guide for writers, <u>William Zinsser's *On Writing Well* has sold nearly one million copies.</u>

(A) William Zinsser's *On Writing Well* has sold nearly one million copies

(B) nearly one million copies of William Zinsser's *On Writing Well* have been sold

(C) William Zinsser wrote *On Writing Well*, which has sold nearly one million copies

(D) William Zinsser's *On Writing Well* having sold nearly one million copies

(E) *On Writing Well* has sold nearly one million copies by William Zinsser

6 When you submit personal information to a website, <u>one should make sure</u> that it won't be used for unauthorized purposes.

(A) one should make sure
(B) and make sure
(C) then make sure
(D) be sure of
(E) make sure

7 Although passenger pigeons once filled the skies over Michigan, <u>relentless hunting eliminated their entire population by 1901.</u>

(A) relentless hunting eliminated their entire population by 1901

(B) it was relentless hunting eliminating their entire population by 1901

(C) its entire population was eliminated by relentless hunting by 1901

(D) by 1901 it was relentless hunting eliminating their entire population

(E) relentless hunting having eliminated their entire population by 1901

8 The failure of the relief effort was more a result of <u>poor coordination than because of blatant corruption.</u>

(A) poor coordination than because of blatant corruption

(B) coordination being poor than by blatant corruption

(C) poor coordination than by blatant corruption

(D) poor coordination than of blatant corruption

(E) coordination being poor than corruption being blatant

9 <u>Until revealing that she had been working</u> at a design firm, few of her friends realized that Amanda was interested in art.

(A) Until revealing that she had been working

(B) Having revealed that she had been working

(C) Until she revealed that she had been working

(D) Being that she revealed she had worked

(E) Until she revealed about her working

10 Inspired by reading about the great explorers, <u>it was Gerald's decision to sail around the world.</u>

(A) it was Gerald's decision to sail around the world

(B) Gerald decided to sail around the world

(C) the decision was made by Gerald to sail around the world

(D) sailing around the world was what Gerald decided to do

(E) Gerald having decided to sail around the world

11 The results of the election were so close that the club <u>had it decided that they would have co-presidents.</u>

(A) had it decided that they would have co-presidents

(B) decided to have co-presidents

(C) would have decided to have co-presidents

(D) decided they would have co-presidents

(E) had decided that they would have co-presidents

GO ON TO THE NEXT PAGE ▶▶▶

12 Writing skills are waning because the widespread use of e-mail and instant <u>messaging discourages students from developing their ideas and supporting</u> those ideas logically.

(A) messaging discourages students from developing their ideas and supporting
(B) messaging discourage students to develop their ideas and support
(C) messaging, which discourages students from developing their ideas and supporting
(D) messaging discouraging students from developing their ideas and supporting
(E) messaging discouraging students to develop their ideas and support

13 <u>To acknowledge</u> opposing viewpoints does not mean subverting your own thesis, and in fact usually creates a more cogent essay.

(A) to acknowledge
(B) in acknowledging
(C) acknowledging
(D) while acknowledging
(E) for the acknowledgment of

14 To get the full benefit of any medication, avoid problems, and <u>for the reduction of possible side effects,</u> discuss your prescription with your doctor.

(A) for the reduction of possible side effects
(B) for reducing possible side effects
(C) reducing possible side effects
(D) also to reduce possible side effects
(E) reduce possible side effects

9

STOP

You may check your work, on this section only, until time is called.

ANSWER KEY

Section 2 Math	Section 5 Math	Section 7 Math	Section 3 Critical Reading	Section 6 Critical Reading	Section 8 Critical Reading	Section 4 Writing	Section 9 Writing
1. C	1. B	1. C	1. A	1. B	1. D	1. B	1. C
2. E	2. D	2. D	2. D	2. C	2. C	2. E	2. E
3. D	3. C	3. C	3. C	3. A	3. D	3. D	3. E
4. E	4. C	4. B	4. B	4. C	4. A	4. C	4. B
5. B	5. D	5. A	5. D	5. D	5. E	5. C	5. A
6. A	6. E	6. B	6. E	6. C	6. C	6. D	6. E
7. D	7. C	7. D	7. A	7. A	7. C	7. A	7. A
8. C	8. B	8. A	8. C	8. C	8. B	8. D	8. D
9. B	9. 0.4	9. D	9. C	9. C	9. E	9. B	9. C
10. A	10. 333 or 1/3	10. B	10. C	10. B	10. A	10. E	10. B
11. A	11. 30	11. E	11. A	11. C	11. D	11. D	11. B
12. B	12. 60	12. B	12. D	12. B	12. A	12. B	12. A
13. D	13. 28	13. E	13. C	13. C	13. C	13. C	13. C
14. B	14. 666 or 667 or 2/3	14. C	14. B	14. B	14. C	14. B	14. E
15. D	15. 81	15. D	15. E	15. E	15. B	15. E	
16. C	16. 10	16. B	16. B	16. C	16. A	16. C	
17. C	17. 3		17. A	17. B	17. A	17. C	
18. D	18. 4		18. C	18. E	18. C	18. C	
19. D			19. B	19. C	19. B	19. B	
20. E			20. C	20. A		20. B	
			21. B	21. E		21. B	
			22. D	22. A		22. D	
			23. A	23. C		23. D	
			24. E	24. B		24. B	
						25. D	
						26. B	
						27. B	
						28. E	
						29. A	
						30. B	
						31. A	
						32. E	
						33. A	
						34. D	
						35. C	

Right (A): _____
Wrong (B): _____
(A)–¼(B): _____

Questions 1–8
Right (A): _____
Wrong (B): _____
(A)–¼(B): _____

Questions 9–18
Right (A): _____

Right (A): _____
Wrong (B): _____
(A)–¼(B): _____

Right (A): _____
Wrong (B): _____
(A)–¼(B): _____

Right (A): _____
Wrong (B): _____
(A)–¼(B): _____

Right (A): _____
Wrong (B): _____
(A)–¼(B): _____

Right (A): _____
Wrong (B): _____
(A)–¼(B): _____

Right (A): _____
Wrong (B): _____
(A)–¼(B): _____

SCORE CONVERSION TABLE

How to score your test

Use the answer key on the previous page to determine your raw score on each section. **Your raw score on each section except Section 5 is simply the number of correct answers minus ¼ of the number of wrong answers. On Section 5, your raw score is the sum of the number of correct answers for questions 1–8 minus ¼ of the number of wrong answers for questions 1–8 plus the total number of correct answers for questions 9–18.** Next, add the raw scores from Sections 3, 4, and 7 to get your Math raw score, and add the raw scores from Sections 6 and 9 to get your Writing raw score. Write the three raw scores here:

Raw Critical Reading score: _____   Raw Math score: _____   Raw Writing score: _____

Use the table below to convert these to scaled scores.

Scaled scores: Critical Reading: _____   Math: _____   Writing: _____

Raw Score	Critical Reading Scaled Score	Math Scaled Score	Writing Scaled Score	Raw Score	Critical Reading Scaled Score	Math Scaled Score	Writing Scaled Score
67	800			32	520	550	610
66	800			31	510	550	600
65	790			30	510	540	580
64	780			29	500	540	570
63	760			28	490	530	560
62	750			27	490	520	550
61	730			26	480	510	540
60	720			25	480	500	530
59	700			24	470	490	520
58	700			23	460	480	510
57	690			22	460	480	500
56	680			21	450	470	490
55	670			20	440	460	480
54	660	800		19	440	450	470
53	650	790		18	430	450	460
52	650	760		17	420	440	450
51	640	740		16	420	430	440
50	630	720		15	410	420	440
49	620	710	800	14	400	410	430
48	620	700	800	13	400	410	420
47	610	680	800	12	390	400	410
46	600	670	790	11	380	390	400
45	600	660	780	10	370	380	390
44	590	650	760	9	360	370	380
43	590	640	740	8	350	360	380
42	580	630	730	7	340	350	370
41	570	630	710	6	330	340	360
40	570	620	700	5	320	330	350
39	560	610	690	4	310	320	340
38	550	600	670	3	300	310	320
37	550	590	660	2	280	290	310
36	540	580	650	1	270	280	300
35	540	580	640	0	250	260	280
34	530	570	630	−1	230	240	270
33	520	560	620	−2 or less	210	220	250

SCORE CONVERSION TABLE FOR WRITING COMPOSITE
[ESSAY + MULTIPLE CHOICE]

Calculate your writing raw score as you did on the previous page and grade your essay from a 1 to a 6 according to the standards that follow in the detailed answer key.

Essay score: _____ Raw Writing score: _____

Use the table below to convert these to scaled scores.

Scaled score: Writing: _____

Raw Score	Essay Score 0	Essay Score 1	Essay Score 2	Essay Score 3	Essay Score 4	Essay Score 5	Essay Score 6
-2 or less	200	230	250	280	310	340	370
-1	210	240	260	290	320	360	380
0	230	260	280	300	340	370	400
1	240	270	290	320	350	380	410
2	250	280	300	330	360	390	420
3	260	290	310	340	370	400	430
4	270	300	320	350	380	410	440
5	280	310	330	360	390	420	450
6	290	320	340	360	400	430	460
7	290	330	340	370	410	440	470
8	300	330	350	380	410	450	470
9	310	340	360	390	420	450	480
10	320	350	370	390	430	460	490
11	320	360	370	400	440	470	500
12	330	360	380	410	440	470	500
13	340	370	390	420	450	480	510
14	350	380	390	420	460	490	520
15	350	380	400	430	460	500	530
16	360	390	410	440	470	500	530
17	370	400	420	440	480	510	540
18	380	410	420	450	490	520	550
19	380	410	430	460	490	530	560
20	390	420	440	470	500	530	560
21	400	430	450	480	510	540	570
22	410	440	460	480	520	550	580
23	420	450	470	490	530	560	590
24	420	460	570	500	540	570	600
25	430	460	480	510	540	580	610
26	440	470	490	520	550	590	610
27	450	480	504	530	560	590	620
28	460	490	510	540	570	600	630
29	470	500	520	550	580	610	640
30	480	510	530	560	590	620	650
31	490	520	540	560	600	630	660
32	500	530	570	570	610	640	670
33	510	540	580	580	620	650	680
34	510	550	560	590	630	660	690
35	520	560	570	600	640	670	700
36	530	560	580	610	650	680	710
37	540	570	590	620	660	690	720
38	550	580	600	630	670	700	730
39	560	606	610	640	680	710	740
40	580	610	620	650	690	720	750
41	590	620	640	660	700	730	760
42	600	630	650	680	710	740	770
43	610	640	690	690	720	750	780
44	620	660	670	707	740	770	800
45	640	670	690	720	750	780	800
46	650	690	700	730	770	800	800
47	670	700	720	750	780	800	800
48	680	720	730	760	800	800	800
49	680	720	730	760	800	800	800

Detailed Answer Key

Section I

The following essay received 12 points out of a possible 12, meaning that it demonstrates *clear and consistent competence* in that it

- develops an insightful point of view on the topic
- demonstrates exemplary critical thinking
- uses effective examples, reasons, and other evidence to support its thesis
- is consistently focused, coherent, and well-organized
- demonstrates skillful and effective use of language and sentence structure
- is largely (but not necessarily completely) free of grammatical and usage errors

Consider carefully the issue discussed in the following passage, then write an essay that answers the question posed in the assignment.

> In a culture obsessed with superficial appearances, our leaders should be those who can see beyond the surface. Judging a book by its cover is the job of the plebeian or the consumer, but reading the book—pondering its contents and perhaps seeking to write new chapters—is the job of a leader.

Assignment: How important is it to look beyond superficial appearances? Write an essay in which you answer this question and discuss your point of view on this issue. Support your position logically with examples from literature, the arts, history, politics, science and technology, current events, or your experience or observation.

SAMPLE STUDENT ESSAY

The creature that Victor Frankenstein created was horrible to all who saw it, including Victor himself. Huge, misshapen and awkward, the creature was not even considered human. Indeed, the creature began to fulfill the only role that humans allowed him to occupy: the role of a bloodthirsty monster. Yet what Mary Shelley's *Frankenstein* shows us is not so much how rare and horrible it is to alter the natural order, but how tragically simple it is to create a monster. Victor Frankenstein created a monster not by contravening nature, as many would believe, but by judging the creature by his outward appearance and treating him like an unworthy freak.

How simple it is to hate others, to consider them less than human, based on superficial analysis. Hatred is the desperate accomplice of fear. In recent years, too many of us Americans—denizens of the land of the free and home of the brave—have become imprisoned by our hatred and cowed by our fear for the unknown. Our leaders are too often

complicit in rousing this fear and fueling this hate, and in mistaking a quick trigger finger for bravery in the face of threat. They become quick to imprison or kill people who scare us at first, rather than acknowledge that they are humans with rights. They see the populace cringing at foreigners because foreigners attacked us in 2001. They can't see past their irrational fear to the enormous need to reach out to disenfranchised and subjugated cultures and listen to their concerns. If only Victor Frankenstein had tried to learn what his creature would need once it was given life.

Our leaders are often the blindest of all because, to survive, they must not edify but pander. They see the populace cringing in fear at the prospect of human cloning because they imagine Frankenstein's monster. They can't see past their irrational fear to the huge potential medical benefits of stem cell research. They refuse to see that clones are indistinguishable from twins, and that twins are not horrible monstrosities. We can't really expect politicians or the media—who pander to popularity polls and big corporate donations—to see the world for what it truly is. They judge the world book by its cover, as did the angry villagers of Ingolstadt.

Our current situation will get better only once a critical mass of the American population begins to see that we are creating monsters everywhere by our irrational fear of the new and the foreign. We value instant polls of superficial and uninformed opinions more than careful thought and deep analysis. Perhaps it's time to open the book and read it carefully rather than just glancing at the cover.

The following essay received 8 points out of a possible 12, meaning that it demonstrates *adequate competence* in that it

- develops a point of view on the topic
- demonstrates some critical thinking, but perhaps not consistently
- uses some examples, reasons, and other evidence to support its thesis, but perhaps not adequately
- shows a general organization and focus, but shows occasional lapses in this regard
- demonstrates adequate but occasionally inconsistent facility with language
- contains occasional errors in grammar, usage, and mechanics

---

SAMPLE STUDENT ESSAY

Whoever said you can't judge a book by its cover probably never had to drive on the highway behind a Hummer. Americans are obsessed with making a first impression, usually an impression of aggression and wealth. Certainly, first impressions about human beings are usually wrong, but American culture is, unfortunately, being increasingly defined by consumer items that give an aggressive first impression and last impression. These items, unlike human beings, are designed carefully, and their first impressions are intended to convey the entire product.

A good example of this is the Super Bowl. It has become a flashy, decadent display of consumption rather than what it should be, a display of athletic prowess. Our obsession with consumer goods that make us seem more attractive or stronger and more powerful have made it clear that we're not concerned with substance as much as appearances. Every commercial shouts at you that first appearances are everything. Our schools are filled with people who think that the most important things in their lives are what shoes they wear or what cell phone they use.

Popular psychologists like Dr. Phil appear on television and tell us how important it is for us to be ourselves and not let other people tell us who we are, and then a string of commercials comes on telling you how a beer or car or deodorant makes you look more attractive. Which message do we really hear?

The following essay received 4 points out of a possible 12, meaning that it demonstrates *some incompetence* in that it

- has a seriously limited point of view
- demonstrates weak critical thinking
- uses inappropriate or insufficient examples, reasons, and other evidence to support its thesis
- is poorly focused and organized, and has serious problems with coherence
- demonstrates frequent problems with language and sentence structure
- contains errors in grammar and usage that obscure the author's meaning seriously

SAMPLE STUDENT ESSAY

I think that definitely you can't judge a book by its cover. Like my friend Cal is a really good wrestler and he even got into the state finals for his weight class. Everybody thinks he's a total jock but not a lot of people know also that he works really hard every day after practice at his uncle's garage and a lot of people think he's as good as a lot of other mechanics. He's a lot smarter than people give him credit for and he get's really good grades in math.

As a matter of fact he's in the honors level of math and will probably take calculus next year, so he's not just a jock or even just a great mechanic. When you look at him, especially when he's got his game face on just before a match, you would hardly believe that he could be a good student.

The next time you see an athlete, don't assume that he is just a dumb jock. Professional athletes have sometimes become senators and business leaders, so sometimes they have minds as well as muscles.

Detailed Answer Key

Section 2

1. **C** Substitute $k = 10$ into $2m + k = 12$ to get
$$2m + 10 = 12$$
Subtract 10: $2m = 2$
Divide by 2: $m = 1$

2. **E** If the average of three numbers is 50, then their sum must be $3(50) = 150$. If two of the numbers are 35 and 50, then the third is $150 - 35 - 50 = 65$

3. **D** Since the ones column has only one A, it is easy to figure out its value from there. The only value for A that yields a 7 in the ones column is 4.

4. **E** The problem is best solved with a proportion:
$\frac{9}{25} = \frac{x}{225}$. Cross-multiply: $25x = 2025$

Divide by 25: $x = 81$

5. **B** Since $32 = 2^5$, we can substitute: $2^{x-1} = 32$
$$2^{x-1} = 2^5$$
$$x - 1 = 5$$
Add 1: $x = 6$

6. **A** Since there were 59 yes votes, 26 of which were from men, $59 - 26 = 33$ of them were from women. Since there were 76 women in total, 33 of whom voted yes, $76 - 33 = 43$ of them must have voted no.

7. **D** They both start with x cards. After Mike gives Kenny 12 cards, Mike has $x - 12$ and Kenny has $x + 12$ cards. If Kenny has twice as many as Mike, then
$$x + 12 = 2(x - 12)$$
Distribute: $+ 12 = 2x - 24$
Add 24: $+ 36 = 2x$
Subtract x: $36 = x$
Since they each had 36 cards to start, they had a total of $36 + 36 = 72$.

8. **C** The fraction that is walnuts equals the amount of walnuts divided by the total amount:

$$\frac{x}{(x + 15 + 20)}$$

Simplify: $\frac{x}{(x + 35)}$

9. **B** You might simplify this problem by plugging in possible values for the angle measures, remembering the parallel lines theorem. Your diagram might look like this:

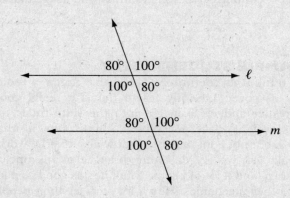

This example shows that $a + d + f + g = 360°$, and the only other sum among the choices that equals 360° is (B).

10. **A** Either plug in the ordered pairs to check, or draw a graph, as long as you can do it quickly. Notice that the point $(7, -1)$ satisfies both inequalities:
$2(7) + 3(-1) > 6$ and $7 - (-1) > 6$

11. **A** If n has a remainder of 6 when it is divided by 12, it must be 6 more than a multiple of 12. Pick any one you like: 18, for example. When 18 is divided by 6, the remainder is 0.

12. **B** Any five-sided polygon can be divided into three triangles like so:

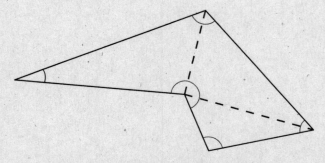

Since the sum of the angles in a triangle is 180°, the sum of the angles in this figure is $3(180) = 540°$. The average measure of the five angles, then, is $540/5 = 108°$.

13. D It is perhaps simplest to rephrase the statement in terms of the number of dogs and the number of cats, so that it is easy to turn into an equation: "There are 3 fewer than 4 times as many dogs as cats" is the same as saying "The number of dogs is 3 fewer than 4 times the number of cats." This can be translated into $d = 4c - 3$.

---

14. B Mark up the diagram with the information given:

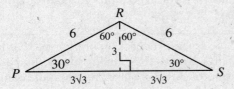

To find the area of the triangle, you need to use the formula *area = base × height*/2. Since the height divides the triangle into two 30° – 60° – 90° triangles, the other sides have lengths shown. The base of the triangle is $6(\sqrt{3})$ and the height is 3, so the area is

$$\frac{6\left(\sqrt{3}\right)(3)}{2} = 9\sqrt{3}.$$

---

15. D The sum of the parts is $4 + 3 + 2 + 1 = 10$. Therefore, the parts are $\dfrac{4}{10}$, $\dfrac{3}{10}$, $\dfrac{2}{10}$, and $\dfrac{1}{10}$ of the whole. The largest share, then, is ($50,000) $(4/10) = \$20,000$

---

16. C Use the definition to translate the equation:
$$m[n] = 9$$
Translate: $m^2/n^2 = 9$

Now think about what values of m and n will work. Notice that 3 and 1 will work, but so will –3 and –1. Now plug these into the statements, and see if any are false. Since –3 is not greater than –1, statement I can be eliminated, and so can answers (B), (D), and (E). Notice that this means you don't have to check statement II, because it's in both remaining answers. You can show that statement III is true by taking the square root of both sides of the equation: $\dfrac{|m|}{|n|} = 3$. This means that |n| goes into |m| 3 times, so it is a factor.

---

17. C Let's say there are x blue marbles in the jar. This means there are $3x$ white marbles, and $2(3x) = 6x$ red marbles, for a total of $10x$ marbles. Since $3x$ are white the probability of picking a white is $3x/10x = 3/10$.

18. D Think about how many options you have to fill each place, from left to right. Since the first person must be a girl, you have 6 options. Since the next must be a boy, you have 5 options. Since the next must be a boy, you have 4 options (one is already up there). Since the next must be a girl, you have 5 options left. This means that the total number of possible arrangements is $(6)(5)(4)(5) = 600$. (Chapter 12, Lesson 5: Counting Problems)

---

19. D If the two lines are parallel, then they have the same slope. The slope of l is $\dfrac{9}{12} = \dfrac{3}{4}$, so the slope of m must be $\dfrac{3}{4}$ as well. Therefore $\dfrac{12}{k} = \dfrac{3}{4}$

Cross-multiply: $3k = 48$
Divide by 3: $k = 16$
Therefore, the rectangle has a width of 16 and a height of 12, so its area is $(16)(12) = 192$.

---

20. E If p is the volume of the solid, then $r \times s \times t = p$. Solving this for r gives $r = \dfrac{p}{(st)}$, so statement II is true. This lets you eliminate choices (A) and (C). If r, s, and t are integers and p is odd, then r, s, and t must be odd, because if any of them were even, then p would be even. Therefore $p + s + t$ is odd, and statement I is true. This eliminates choice (D). To check statement III, you need to find an expression for the surface area of the solid, which is $2(rs) + 2(rt) + 2(st) = 2(rs + rt + st)$. Since this is a multiple of 2, it must be even, and statement III is true. So the answer is (E).

Section 3

1. A The fact that they *rarely agreed* implies that their opinions would often *differ*. diverge = differ or move apart; *coincide* = fit together or occur simultaneously; *retreat* = move away; *assemble* = put together; *truncate* = cut short.

---

2. D The sentence implies a contrast between what *once was* and what *is now*. If it is no longer an *incontrovertible* (irrefutable) *truth*, it must now be *in doubt*. enacted = put into effect officially; *irrefutable* = impossible to disprove; *universal* = true at all places and times; *dubious* = doubtful; *conclusive* = acting as final proof.

3. **C** One who has encountered such tragedy would be expected to look to his painting as a *departure* from such *abject* (wretched) *sorrow*. *prudence* = conservative wisdom; *remorse* = regret; *adulation* = admiration; *solace* = peaceful respite; *melancholy* = sadness; *elation* = extreme happiness.

4. **B** *Proponents of a new curriculum* are people who support the change, while *conservative educators* are those who want to keep things the same. *repugnant* = disgusting; *innocuous* = harmless; *deplorable* = regrettable; *reprehensible* = worthy of scorn; *benevolent* = kind; *malicious* = evil; *auspicious* = favorable.

5. **D** What effect should a *lack of oxygen* have on climbers? It should be expected to *weaken* them. But this implies that the expedition leader's plan to acclimate them (get them used to the environment) was a *failure*. *illusory* = like an illusion; *initiated* = started; *mitigated* = soothed or made better; *enervated* = weakened; *venerable* = worthy of honor; *absolved* = forgiven.

6. **E** One who *questions norms* (conventions) *and mores* (moral standards) is a *rebel* of sorts. *charlatan* = a fake; *surrogate* = one who stands in place of another; *philanthropist* = one who gives to charity; *pragmatist* = one concerned with practical matters; *iconoclast* = one who destroys sacred objects or traditions.

7. **A** If he *stands in the negative camp*, then he must have a firm opinion about the issue. *ambivalent* = having conflicting opinions on an issue; *unequivocally* = without doubt; *apathetic* = lacking concern; *furtively* = secretively; *impartial* = fair and unbiased; *adamant* = stubborn; *vehemently* = passionately; *subjective* = being a matter of opinion.

8. **C** If he was *dismissed* by his contemporaries, they must have thought negatively of him. The *although* implies a contrast, so modern thinkers must now think positively of him. *pedant* = a know-it-all; *derivative* = deriving from the work of others; *neophyte* = beginner; *vociferous* = loudly opinionated; *radical* = one with an extreme opinion; *visionary* = able to envision the future; *partisan* = marked by party loyalty; *conciliatory* = bringing people together; *hermit* = one who prefers to live alone.

9. **C** Passage 1 focuses on *the study of molecules of which living organisms are composed*. Passage 2 discusses the ways in which organisms harvest energy through chemical processes like photosynthesis and chemosynthesis, which are biochemical processes.

10. **C** The main point of the paragraph is in the first sentence: the *study of life on Earth ultimately involves the study of molecules*. The questions that follow are therefore questions about molecules that concern those who study life on Earth, that is, biologists.

11. **A** Passage 2 focuses on organisms that harvest energy in a way that is analogous to, but different from, photosynthesis. The process of converting energy into food for the organism, then, is a relevant topic for Passage 2.

12. **D** Passage 2 discusses how *other organisms* utilize the bacteria that harvest energy from sulfides, either by consuming them or incorporating them into their tissues. This concept is not discussed in Passage 1. Both passages discuss the *conversion of light energy to food energy, and bonds within molecules*. Only Passage 1 discusses the *structure of cells and disease*, specifically cancer.

13. **C** The author indicates that one should react with *proper skepticism* to those reports, thereby implying that they are *probably untrue*.

14. **B** The author asks (in line 22) the reader to *compare* the probability of being a victim of terrorism to the list of probabilities that follow, which are much greater, thereby implying that terrorism is not much of a threat.

15. **E** The personal recollection begins on line 63: *I once had a conversation ...* The verifiable statistics abound in paragraphs 1, 2, and 3. The authoritative study is mentioned in lines 56–63. Common misconceptions are mentioned multiple times, as in lines 12–13: *being killed by terrorists might seem to be a major risk.*

16. **B** The author says that this *penetrating insight* is really a *non sequitur*, that is, something that doesn't follow logically. Therefore it is not a penetrating insight at all.

17. A The author says that a *feeling for what quantities or time spans are appropriate in various contexts is essential to getting the joke* (lines 50–53), thereby implying that the couple, like those who slip *between millions and billions*, lack an appreciation for particular quantities.

18. C In the span of *approximately 20 minutes* the doctor said three different things about the procedure, so he contradicted himself frequently.

19. B The passage refines the usage of the word by saying *the same organization, the same physical laws*, thereby suggesting that the author meant *rules of physics* when he said *organization*.

20. C In lines 16–19, the author describes the *realization that the phenomena we see result from the complexity of the inner workings between atoms* as being dramatic and wonderful.

21. B In lines 20–22, the author says that his feeling of awe *could be communicated through a drawing to someone who had also had this emotion*, thereby suggesting that appreciating such art depends on having a similar experience as the artist.

22. D The author says that Jerry is a *very good teacher in that everything that I thought was a mistake, he used to teach me something in a positive way. He never said it was wrong; he never put me down*. We can infer, then, that Jerry would have done something positive and affirming.

23. A The parenthetical comment that precedes this sentence indicates that the fact that the line did not touch the flower pot was unintentional.

24. E The main point of the passage is that the author wanted to learn to draw to convey the awe he felt about the workings of nature and the physical world. So when he finishes by saying *I was never satisfied*, we know that he was *never able to convey adequately his feelings about the beauty of the world*.

Section 4

1. B The pronoun *which* is out of place because it is assumed to refer to the preceding noun *poets*. If the pronoun is eliminated, the meaning is clearer and the two clauses are **parallel.**

2. E This is an awkward usage of the gerund *preparing*. To convey purpose, the infinitive *to prepare* is much more effective.

3. D This contains a **dangling modifier.** The modifying phrase that begins the sentence describes *Carla* rather than *Carla's anxiety*.

4. C This is a sentence fragment without a verb. Choice (C) completes the thought and makes a complete sentence.

5. C The participle *swimming* **dangles** in this sentence. *Justine* should follow the **participial phrase** because she is the one swimming, not *the current*.

6. D The comparison is not **parallel.** The sentence should say that *writing* one thing is *more difficult than* **writing** something else.

7. A This sentence is correct.

8. D This is a **run-on sentence, or a comma splice.** Two sentences cannot be "spliced" together with only a comma; you must use a conjunction, a semicolon, or a colon. Since the second clause explains the idea in the first clause, a colon is most appropriate.

9. B The two clauses are not properly coordinated. Since the second clearly contradicts the first, a contrasting conjunction like *but* or a contrasting coordinating adverb like *nevertheless* should be used.

10. E The verb *reveals* does not agree with the subject *theories* and should be *reveal* instead.

11. D The pronoun *their* does not agree in number with its antecedent *board* and should be changed to *its*.

12. B The phrase *his staff and him* serves as the subject of the verb *had diverted*, and so it must be in the subjective case: *his staff and he*.

13. C This is incorrect **past participle** form; the **present perfect** form of *to run* is *have run*.

14. **B**   The subject of the verb *were* is *taunting*. (This is an **inverted sentence** because the subject comes after the verb.) Since *taunting* is singular, the verb should be *was*.

15. **E**   The sentence is correct.

16. **C**   The verb *produce* does not agree with its subject *refraction*. It should be changed to *produces*.

17. **C**   Since the sentence compares only **two** films, one of them is the *less* expensive.

18. **C**   This word answers the question *how did she react?* Therefore it modifies a verb and should be in the form of an **adverb:** *emotionally*.

19. **B**   This phrase is part of a **parallel construction:** "*not A but B.*" The construction is parallel only if this phrase is eliminated.

20. **B**   This phrase is **redundant.** The word *while* means *at the same time*, so the second phrase should be eliminated.

21. **B** The verb *have expressed* does not agree with its subject *coalition*, and should be changed to *has expressed*.

22. **D**   This is an **illogical comparison.** A *way* cannot be compared to a *hard drive*. The phrase should be *the way a computer hard drive stores information*.

23. **D**   The pronoun *their* does not agree with its **antecedent** *museum*, and should be changed to *its*.

24. **B**   This is an **idiom error.** The correct form of this comparison is "*prefer A to B*" not "*prefer A more than B.*"

25. **D**   Since only two films are being compared, the comparative adjective *more* is required.

26. **B**   The phrase *Emma and I* is the object of the verb *included*, and therefore should take the objective case *Emma and me*.

27. **B**   The past perfect tense requires the past participle *swum*.

28. **E**   The sentence is correct as written.

29. **A**   The participle *building* dangles in the original sentence. It should be changed to the infinitive *to build* so that it properly modifies the verb *try*.

30. **B**   The modifying phrases are awkwardly placed. Modifiers should obey the **law of proximity** and be as close as possible to the words they modify.

31. **A**   The modifying phrase at the beginning is **dangling.** Since *she* is *a doctor*, *she* should follow the opening phrase. (D) and (E) do not work because they improperly imply that she was bothered by the *children* rather than their *treatment*. You might notice that the correct choice contains verbs in the passive voice. Although you should minimize the use of the passive voice, it is not always incorrect.

32. **E**   This paragraph discusses Montessori's methods and results in the *Casa dei Bambini*, and so the trivial and unrelated fact that *there were fifty students in her first class* is out of place.

33. **A**   The pronoun *it* refers to Montessori's day care center, and so this sentence should follow the one that mentions the day care center, but precede the sentence that discusses her *theories* in detail.

34. **D**   Revision (D) is the most concise and effective of the choices.

35. **C**   Sentences 8 and 9 discuss Montessori's philosophy and its effectiveness. Sentence 8 indicates that Montessori *decided it was important to help each child through his or her own curriculum*, which is clearly a *focus on the individual child*.

Section 5

1. B

$$5y - 2 = 3y + 7$$
Subtract $3y$: $\quad\quad\quad 2y - 2 = 7$
Add 2: $\quad\quad\quad\quad\quad 2y = 9$
Divide by 2: $\quad\quad\quad\quad y = 4.5$

2. D   Since vertical angles are equal, $a = 20$. Since angles that form a straight line have a sum of $180°$, $20 + b + 34 = 180$. Therefore $b = 126$. So $a + b = 20 + 126 = 146$.
(Chapter 13, Lesson 1: Lines and Angles)

3. C

$$(2x)(3x) = (2/8)(3/2)$$
Simplify: $\quad\quad\quad\quad 6x^2 = 6/16$
Divide by 6: $\quad\quad\quad x^2 = 1/16$
Take the square root: $\quad x = 1/4$

4. C   Since the prime factorization of 98 is $2 \times 7 \times 7$, and since the greatest common factor of m and 98 is a prime number, that greatest common factor must be 2 or 7. Since it is not even, it must be 7.

5. D

$$|k - 0.5| < 10$$
Translate: $\quad\quad -10 < k - 0.5 < 10$
Add 0.5: $\quad\quad\quad -9.5 < k < 10.5$
The smallest possible integer value for k is -9 and the greatest is 10. The total number of integers between -9 and 10, inclusive, is $10 - (-9) + 1 = 20$.

6. E   To maximize the value of $(10 - x^2)/2$, you must minimize the value of x^2. The smallest value that x^2 can have is 0, if $x = 0$. Since 0 is within the domain given, the maximum value of $f(x)$ is $(10 - 0)/2 = 5$.

7. C   It helps to know the perfect squares and the perfect cubes. The first seven perfect squares greater than 1 are 4, 9, 16, 25, 36, 49, and 64. The first three perfect cubes are 8, 27, and 64. Clearly, the only integer between 1 and 100 that is both a perfect cube and a perfect square is $64 = 4^3 = 8^2$. Therefore $m = 4$ and $n = 8$, so $m + n = 4 + 8 = 12$.

8. B   This is a rate problem, so remember the basic rate formula: *distance = rate × time*. Start by picking a value for the distance from Amanda's home to work. No matter what distance you choose, the final answer will be the same, so choose a distance that's easy to calculate with, like 50 miles. If it takes her 60 minutes (1 hour) to get to work, she must be going 50 miles/hour. If she increases her speed by 20% for the trip home, then her speed coming home is (1.20) $(50 \text{ miles/hour}) = 60 \text{ miles/hour}$. To travel 50 miles at 60 miles/hour will take her $(50 \text{ miles})/(60 \text{ mph}) = 5/6$ hour, which is $5/6(60 \text{ minutes}) = 50 \text{ minutes}$.
(Chapter 12, Lesson 4: Rate Problems)

9. 0.4   Remember that "percent" means "divided by 100," so 0.5 percent of 80 means $0.5 \div 100 \times 80 = 0.4$.

10. 0.333 or 1/3   Just pick three consecutive odd integers, like 1, 3, and 5. Since d is the middle of these, $d = 3$. Since s is the sum of these, $s = 1 + 3 + 5 = 9$. So d divided by s is 3/9 or 1/3.

11. 30   4/9 of c^2 is 24
Translate: $\quad\quad\quad\quad\quad\quad (4/9)(c^2) = 24$
Multiply by 5/4: $\quad (5/4)(4/9)(c^2) = (5/4)(24)$
Simplify: $\quad\quad\quad\quad\quad\quad (5/9)(c^2) = 30$

12. 60   The sum of the four angles in a quadrilateral is $360°$. The sum of the parts in the ratio is $3 + 4 + 5 + 6 = 18$. Therefore the angles are 3/18, 4/18, 5/18 and 6/18 of the whole, which is $360°$. So the smallest angle measures $(3/18)(360°) = 60°$.

13. 28   Subtract the equations:
$$\begin{aligned} 5a + 6b &= 13 \\ -(4a + 5b) &= 9) \\ \hline a + b &= 4 \end{aligned}$$
Multiply by 7: $\quad\quad 7a + 7b = 28$

14. 0.666 or 0.667 or 2/3   A good way to simplify the messy fraction is to multiply the numerator and denominator by the least common multiple of all the denominators in the "smaller" fractions. Since $m^2 - 1 = (m + 1)(m - 1)$, $m^2 - 1$ is the least common multiple. Multiplying by $(m^2 - 1)/(m^2 - 1)$ simplifies the expression:

$$\frac{m^2 - 1}{m^2 - 1} \times \frac{\dfrac{1}{m + 1} \times \dfrac{1}{m - 1}}{\dfrac{1}{m^2 - 1}} = \frac{(m - 1) + (m + 1)}{1} = 2m$$

Since $m = \dfrac{1}{3}$, $2m = \dfrac{2}{3}$

15. 81   By guessing and checking positive integers, you should be able to see that the only positive integers that satisfy the equation are 5 and 4. Therefore $(x + y)^2 = (5 + 4)^2 = 81$.

16. 10 Five out of the 15 marbles are white. If x more white marbles are added, the probability of choosing a white marble is $\dfrac{(5+x)}{(15+x)}$. This fraction must be at least $\dfrac{3}{5}$, so $\dfrac{(5+x)}{(15+x)} \geq 3/5$

Cross-multiply:	$25 + 5x \geq 45 + 3x$
Subtract $3x$:	$25 + 2x \geq 45$
Subtract 25:	$2x \geq 20$
Divide by 2:	$x \geq 10$.

17. 3 By inspecting the angles of the two triangles, you can see that they must be similar, as the diagram shows.

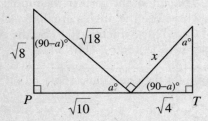

This implies that the corresponding sides are proportional. Using the Pythagorean Theorem, you can find the hypotenuse of the larger triangle:

$$\sqrt{8}^2 + \sqrt{10}^2 = 8 + 10 = h^2, \text{ so } h = \sqrt{18}$$

Then you can set up a proportion of the corresponding sides:

$$\frac{\sqrt{8}}{\sqrt{4}} = \frac{\sqrt{18}}{x}$$

Cross multiply:	$x\sqrt{8} = \sqrt{72}$
Divide by $\sqrt{8}$:	$x\sqrt{9} = 3$

18. 4 If she took a shots in her first game, and made 50% of them, then she made $.5a$ shots in the first game. Similarly, she made $.6b$ shots in the second game. If she made 52% of her shots altogether, then

$$\frac{.5a + .6b}{a + b} = .52$$

Cross-multiply:	$.5a + .6b = .52a + .52b$
Subtract $.5a$ and $.52b$:	$.08b = .02a$
Divide by $0.2b$:	$4 = \dfrac{a}{b}$

Section 6

1. B Sandra's father's words were not *thoughtful* or *useful*, but rather they were *hollow clichés*. They were *overused* and *thoughtless. irate* = angry; *inane* = pointless; *homogeneous* = the same throughout; *flamboyant* = lively; *altruistic* = selfless

2. C If he was *courageous* in prison, he must not have given up his fight. *treacherous* = deceitful; *futile* = having no hope of success; *fortitude* = strength; *premeditated* = planned in advance; *porous* = full of holes.

3. A Since the teachers couldn't hear themselves talk, the construction must have been noisy, and therefore was not very *constructive* to learning (no pun intended). *din* = noise; *conducive* = helpful, constructive; *averse* = opposed to; *discernible* = detectable; *irascible* = easily angered

4. C The sentence implies that solutions to physics problems are *approximate*, so they cannot be *exact*. The approximate solution would be sufficient as long as the complicating factors are *small. negligible* = not significant; *plausibly* = with a good likelihood of success; *ethically* = with regard to moral standards.

5. D *Martial resources* are those resources that sustain an army's ability to fight; they are the *means* to continue fighting. If the factions both have *access* to these resources, the fight is likely to drag on. *mediation* = attempt to resolve a conflict

6. C Since Jung was *modest in his therapeutic claims* (line 5) and *cautious* (line 11) when consulted by schizophrenics, we can conclude that he did not yet believe that his therapy worked for all mentally ill patients.

7. A The sentence indicates that psychoanalysis could *bring about* a psychotic episode.

8. C The passage says that the *comic ... seems bound to its time, society, cultural anthropology* (lines 7–8). This implies that it's harder to find something humorous if it is from another culture or time. Choice (C) is the most foreign to modern Americans.

9. C Because the passage says that it is harder to understand the comedy of other societies and eras because of cultural obstacles, the *effort* is in overcoming these obstacles.

10. B   The author states that the host's introduction *dropped like a stone in our midst* (line 10), and that no response at all to this introduction was *the proper response* (line 13). The rest of the essay makes clear that the author considers the host's comments, particularly with its focus on *literature,* to be inappropriate.

11. C   The author defines the term somewhat in line 60 by listing the forms to which the term *literary* is applied: *novels and short stories and poems.* Throughout the passage, also the author distinguishes *literary* works from works of nonfiction, which can be very well-written.

12. B   The interviewer asked the writers about the *"literary experience"* (line 22) of the day, and then whether they *"write anything literary"* (lines 38–39), when in fact they did not write literature at all, but rather nonfiction.

13. C   Those writers are mentioned as *our models* by the author, suggesting that the author and the other writers have been influenced by them.

14. B   In saying that writers were admired for *their ability to harness the issues,* the author is saying that they make them easy to understand for their readers.

15. E   The writers being interviewed had said that *they felt they were already doing satisfactory work* (lines 40–41). The callers implied that they felt the same way.

16. C   The phrase *the great preponderance of what writers now write and sell* refers to the *majority* of what they write and sell.

17. B   The first sentence indicates the purpose of this passage: *To understand . . . Aristotle . . . it is necessary to apprehend his imaginative background* (lines 1–3), in other words, to understand the preconceptions behind his theories.

18. E   This paragraph discusses the ancient Greek idea that mechanical devices are somehow imbued with the spirit of animals with similar abilities, for instance, an airplane having the spirit of a bird. The comment that *animals have lost their importance in our imaginative pictures of the world* indicates that modern thinkers no longer suppose any link between the life-spirit of animals and the behavior of machines.

19. C   The *imaginative preconceptions* of Aristotle are explained in the second and third paragraphs, where it says that *to the Greek, it seemed more natural to assimilate apparently lifeless motions to those of animals* (lines 50–53).

20. A   The passage says that *the . . . mechanical view hardly suggested itself, except in the case of a few men of genius* (lines 40–41). So these men of genius had the *mechanical view.*

21. E   The passage says that *to the modern man of science, the body of an animal is a very elaborate machine* (line 46). The difference between animals and machines is diminished with discoveries about the *physico-chemical structure* (lines 47–48) of animals, or the mechanical and chemical nature of biology.

22. A   In saying that, to the ancient Greek, *it seemed more natural to assimilate apparently lifeless motions to those of animals* (lines 50–52), the author is saying that Greeks were inclined to compare the motions of lifeless things to the motions of living things, and that these comparisons were *the basis of a general theory of physics* (lines 56–57).

23. C   The passage says that *Every Greek philosopher ... had been taught in childhood to regard the sun and moon as gods* (lines 61–64), and then that *Anaxagoras was prosecuted for impiety because he thought that they were not alive* (lines 64–66). This implies that he *departed dramatically from his childhood teachings.*

24. B   The *Hellenic love of order and geometric simplicity* (line 70) is attributed to the Divine Being who moves the heavenly bodies. These heavenly bodies were said to move with *regularity* (line 59) and *superior perfection* (line 61). Therefore, it can be inferred that this *love of order and geometric simplicity* pertains to the movement of the heavenly bodies.

Section 7

1. C $\frac{2}{3}$ of 60 is 40, and $\frac{40}{80} = 50\%$

2. D
$$4x + 2y = 8$$

Divide by 4: $x + \left(\frac{1}{2}\right)y = 2$

3. C This question is asking what the remainder is when 29, 21, and 64 are each divided by 3. When 29 is divided by 3 the remainder is 2; when 21 is divided by 3 the remainder is 0; and when 64 is divided by 3 the remainder is 1.

---

4. B   1 & 2

Substitute using definition: $1(1 - 1) + 2(2 - 1)$

Simplify: $0 + 2 = 2$

---

5. A In a triangle, any side must have a length that is less than the sum of the two other lengths but greater than the difference of the two other lengths.

Therefore, the third side must have a length between $15 - 9 = 6$ and $15 + 9 = 24$, so a length of 5 is impossible.

---

6. B The volume of a cube is equal to s^3, where s is the length of one edge. If $s^3 = 64$, then $s = 4$, and so each square face has an area of $s^2 = 4^2 = 16$. Since a cube has six faces, the total surface area is $6(16) = 96$.

---

7. D $\dfrac{(x + 2 + 6 + 10)}{3} = 8$, so $x + 2 + 6 + 10 = 32$

Simplify: $x + 18 = 32$
Subtract 18: $x = 14$

So the numbers are 2, 6, 10, and 14. The median is the average of the two middle numbers: $\dfrac{(6 + 10)}{2} = 8$.

---

8. A Indicate the congruent sides with tick marks: in a triangle, the angles across from equal sides are equal; indicate this in the diagram. Your angles should be marked as shown. Since the angles in a triangle have a sum of 180°, $y + y + 180 - x = 180$

Subtract 180: $2y - x = 0$
Add x: $2y = x$

Divide by 2: $y = \dfrac{x}{2}$

---

9. D Notice that the graph is of all the points that are more than 1 unit away from −1. The distance from a point to −1 is $|x - (-1)|$; or $|x + 1|$; if this distance is greater than one, then $|x + 1| > 1$.

---

10. B "Must be true" kinds of questions are often best answered by process of elimination with examples. Begin with a simple set of values, for instance $a = 0$, $b = -1$, and $c = 0$. Notice that these values satisfy all of the given information. This example clearly shows that statement I need not be true, because 0 is not greater than 0, and that statement III need not be true, because $(0)(0)$ is not greater than $(-1)^2$. This leaves only statement II as a possibility, so the answer must be (B).

---

11. E You have five choices for the first digit: 1, 3, 5, 7, and 9; ten choices for the middle digit (any digit will do), and five choices for the last digit: 0, 2, 4, 6, and 8. So the total number of possibilities is $5 \times 10 \times 5 = 250$.

---

12. B To find how many more seconds it will take the machine to cut circle A than circle B, you can find the length of time it takes to cut each circle and subtract them. The laser cuts the circumference of each circle, so you must find that first. Circle A has an area of 64π. Since the area of a circle is πr^2, the radius of the circle is 8. Since the area of circle B is 16π, its radius is 4. The circumference of a circle is $2\pi r$, so the circumference of A is $2\pi(8) = 16\pi$ and the circumference of B is $2\pi (4) = 8\pi$. The difference of their radii is $16\pi - 8\pi = 8\pi$. The time it takes to cut that length is given by the formula *time = distance/rate*.

$$\frac{(8\pi \text{ cm})}{(3 \text{ cm/second})} = \frac{8\pi}{3 \text{ sec}}$$

---

13. E The slope of AC is $rise/run = \dfrac{(5 - (-1))}{(8 - 1)} = 6/7$.

Therefore the slope of CB is −6/7. Using the slope formula: $\dfrac{(5 - (-1))}{(8 - k)} = -6/7$

Simplify: $\dfrac{6}{(8 - k)} = -6/7$

Cross-multiply: $-6(8 - k) = 42$
Divide by 6: $-8 + k = 7$
Add 8: $k = 15$

14. C $m = 1 \times 2 \times 3 \times 4 \times 5 \times 6 \times 7 \times 8 \times 9 \times 10$. You can factor even further in terms of primes: $m = 1 \times 2 \times 3 \times (2 \times 2) \times 5 \times (2 \times 3) \times 7 \times (2 \times 2 \times 2) \times (3 \times 3) \times (2 \times 5)$. This shows that there are a maximum of eight factors of 2, so the greatest power of 2 that is a factor of m is 2^8.

15. D First draw a diagram to see how the area of an equilateral triangle is related to the lengths of the sides:

Notice that the height (which is also the bisector of the "top" angle) divides the triangle into two 30°–60°–90° triangles, with sides as shown. The area of a triangle is $base \times height/2$, which in this case is

$\dfrac{(2x)(x\sqrt{3})}{2} = x^2\sqrt{3}$. Since the area is given as $36\sqrt{3}$,

x must equal 6. Substituting this into the diagram, each smaller triangle has sides of length 6, $6\sqrt{3}$, and 12. Therefore the sum of the perimeters of the two triangles is $36 + 12\sqrt{3}$.

16. B At 4:00 pm, there are 1,000 bacteria. Since the population doubles every two hours, there must have been half as many two hours ago. So at 2:00 pm there were 500 bacteria, and at 12:00 noon there were 250 bacteria. (Notice that the fact that there were 100 bacteria to start is irrelevant.)
(Chapter 12, Lesson 4: Rate Problems)

Section 8

1. D If she was relieved, the tumor must not have been dangerous. *malignant* = dangerous; *irreverent* = disrespectful; *serene* = calm; *benign* = harmless; *mortal* = capable of dying.

2. C If the jargon rendered the speech *decipherable only to* a few audience members, then it rendered the speech *undecipherable* to the rest of the audience. Therefore the message was *obscured*.

3. D If one prefers *style* to *performance*, then the *cosmetic* appeal of the car would be most important. *utilitarian* = concerned with practical uses; *pragmatic* = concerned with function; *aesthetic* = pertaining to beauty.

4. A If something *serves its purpose only temporarily,* then it is by definition *provisional. provisional* = serving a temporary purpose; *polemical* = relating to a controversial intellectual position; *pedantic* = acting like a know-it-all.

5. E A *foil* is a character that provides a dramatic contrast to the personality of another character. The *but* in the sentence indicates that Ms. Linney is *going against the tradition,* and does not portray her character *demurely* (modestly). *bluster* = brashness; *forgo* = abandon an inclination or plan; *coyness* = shyness; *bombast* = pompous speech; *eschew* = abandon; *impudence* = impertinence, rudeness.

6. C *Despite* implies an ironic situation. If analysts have tried to depict the stock market as *driven by predictable principles,* it would be ironic if people believed that it was not predictable at all. *invaluable* = very valuable; *complacent* = self-satisfied; *capricious* = arbitrary, whimsical; *responsive* = tending to respond quickly; *obscure* = not widely known.

7. C The *control* is mentioned in the context of *the creation of life* (line 11). This is the *process of conception.*

8. B The author says that this *"outsourcing" ... leaves us with a profoundly hollow feeling* (lines 15–19). This indicates a *disdain.*

9. E This statement is from those who *turn [their] noses up at one who would offer us the most precious gift in the universe,* that is, the advocates of cloning are turning up their noses at nature or God.

10. A The parenthetical comment suggests that the *essential random . . . processes that form the basis of natural selection* may be only *seemingly* random. This suggests that these processes may be planned rather than random.

11. D The *"unnatural selection"* is described as involving *an assembly line* (line 34), which is a type of *mechanical procedure,* and *carefully designed and tested features* (line 35), which implies a *selection of characteristics.* The *random processes* (line 30) are attributed to *natural* selection.

12. A The passage implies that those who know *a little bit about the history of technology* (lines 60–61) would not have such *irrational fears about human cloning* (line 57). Therefore you can eliminate choice (D). The fact that these *fears* are called *irrational* eliminates choices (B) and (E). Since these fears are said to *abound from all parts of the political spectrum* (line 58), you can eliminate choice (C). The passage never mentions that the opponents are *very religious,* so the answer is (A).

13. C Surgery is mentioned in line 68 as something *significant* (line 61) that was once *denounced* (line 63).

14. C After quoting Mr. Rifkin, the author then goes on to describe the illogic behind the quote.

15. B The passage mentions that human twins *"have their own unique thoughts"* in order to refute the claim that identical genes put *a human into a genetic straitjacket* (line 83).

16. A The passage says that *familiarity* [with procreational technologies] *dissipates fear* (line 138), implying that these technologies become more acceptable as they become more familiar.

17. A This paragraph says that *ignorant superstition* (line 146) stands in the way of *technologies that can produce ample food for a starving world and cure devastating illnesses* (lines 145–146). This indicates anger at an unjust situation.

18. C In each case, the questions represent the perspective that the author argues against.

19. B The first passage says that cloning technologies will make the world *forever different from what it is today* (line 56), and the second says that these technologies *can produce ample food for a starving world and cure devastating illnesses* (lines 145–146).

Section 9

1. C The infinitive *to move* more effectively conveys purpose than does the phrase *by moving*. Also, the modifier *more closely* has the incorrect form. It should be in adjectival form *closer,* because it modifies the noun *source.*

2. E The original sentence illogically suggests that cell phones standardized their own technology. The only choice that logically coordinates the ideas is choice E.

3. E The colon is misused in the original sentence, since it does not introduce a list of examples or an independent explanatory clause. Choice B has the same problem. Choices C and D use improper idioms. Only choice E conveys the idea clearly and idiomatically.

4. B The original phrasing is a sentence fragment; it contains no verb. Choices B, C, and D correct this mistake, but C and D do not clearly convey what protected the city. Only choice B conveys the idea logically.

5. A The original sentence is correct. The phrase preceding the comma is an appositive modifying *On Writing Well.* Therefore, B and C cause this modifier to be misplaced. Choice D is a fragment and E misplaces the modifier *by William Zinsser.*

6. E The original phrase shifts the pronoun from *you* to *one.* Choices B and C are illogical and D is unidiomatic. Choice E is concise and avoids these problems.

7. A The original sentence conveys the idea clearly and effectively. Choices B and C misuse the singular pronoun *it* to refer to the plural noun *pigeons.* Choice D is awkward and E produces a fragment.

8. D Choice D is the only choice that makes the comparison idiomatic, logical, and parallel.

9. C In the original sentence, the participle *revealing* is misplaced, since it does not modify the closest noun *friends.* Choice B repeats this error, and choices D and E are unidiomatic. The only choice that fixes this problem and conveys the logical sequence of ideas is choice C.

10. B The participle *inspired* is left dangling in the original sentence. Its subject, *Gerald,* must follow the comma. Since choice E produces a sentence fragment, the best choice is B.

11. **B** The original phrasing does not clearly convey who *decided*. Also, the noun *club* is singular, so the plural pronoun *they* is inappropriate. Choice B concisely and clearly fixes these problems.

12. **A** The original phrasing is clear, logical, and effective.

13. **C** Since this sentence is giving general advice about a general practice, the gerund *acknowledging* is more effective than the infinitive *to acknowledge*. Further, the gerund is parallel with the gerund *subverting* with which it is compared.

14. **E** The sentence is not parallel. The first two items in the list establish the pattern: *get ... avoid ...* So the last item should be *reduce...*

PRACTICE TEST 9

ANSWER SHEET

Last Name: _____   First Name: _____

Date: _____   Testing Location: _____

Directions for Test

- Remove these answer sheets from the book and use them to record your answers to this test.
- This test will require 3 hours and 20 minutes to complete. Take this test in one sitting.
- The time allotment for each section is written clearly at the beginning of each section. This test contains six 25-minute sections, two 20-minute sections, and one 10-minute section.
- This test is 25 minutes shorter than the actual SAT, which will include a 25-minute "experimental" section that does not count toward your score. That section has been omitted from this test.
- You may take one short break during the test, of no more than 10 minutes in length.
- You may only work on one section at any given time.
- You must stop ALL work on a section when time is called.
- If you finish a section before the time has elapsed, check your work on that section. You may NOT work on any other section.
- Do not waste time on questions that seem too difficult for you.
- Use the test book for scratchwork, but you will receive credit only for answers that are marked on the answer sheets.
- You will receive one point for every correct answer.
- You will receive no points for an omitted question.
- For each wrong answer on any multiple-choice question, your score will be reduced by ¼ point.
- For each wrong answer on any numerical "grid-in" question, you will receive no deduction.

SECTION 2

1. Ⓐ Ⓑ Ⓒ Ⓓ Ⓔ 11. Ⓐ Ⓑ Ⓒ Ⓓ Ⓔ 21. Ⓐ Ⓑ Ⓒ Ⓓ Ⓔ 31. Ⓐ Ⓑ Ⓒ Ⓓ Ⓔ
2. Ⓐ Ⓑ Ⓒ Ⓓ Ⓔ 12. Ⓐ Ⓑ Ⓒ Ⓓ Ⓔ 22. Ⓐ Ⓑ Ⓒ Ⓓ Ⓔ 32. Ⓐ Ⓑ Ⓒ Ⓓ Ⓔ
3. Ⓐ Ⓑ Ⓒ Ⓓ Ⓔ 13. Ⓐ Ⓑ Ⓒ Ⓓ Ⓔ 23. Ⓐ Ⓑ Ⓒ Ⓓ Ⓔ 33. Ⓐ Ⓑ Ⓒ Ⓓ Ⓔ
4. Ⓐ Ⓑ Ⓒ Ⓓ Ⓔ 14. Ⓐ Ⓑ Ⓒ Ⓓ Ⓔ 24. Ⓐ Ⓑ Ⓒ Ⓓ Ⓔ 34. Ⓐ Ⓑ Ⓒ Ⓓ Ⓔ
5. Ⓐ Ⓑ Ⓒ Ⓓ Ⓔ 15. Ⓐ Ⓑ Ⓒ Ⓓ Ⓔ 25. Ⓐ Ⓑ Ⓒ Ⓓ Ⓔ 35. Ⓐ Ⓑ Ⓒ Ⓓ Ⓔ
6. Ⓐ Ⓑ Ⓒ Ⓓ Ⓔ 16. Ⓐ Ⓑ Ⓒ Ⓓ Ⓔ 26. Ⓐ Ⓑ Ⓒ Ⓓ Ⓔ 36. Ⓐ Ⓑ Ⓒ Ⓓ Ⓔ
7. Ⓐ Ⓑ Ⓒ Ⓓ Ⓔ 17. Ⓐ Ⓑ Ⓒ Ⓓ Ⓔ 27. Ⓐ Ⓑ Ⓒ Ⓓ Ⓔ 37. Ⓐ Ⓑ Ⓒ Ⓓ Ⓔ
8. Ⓐ Ⓑ Ⓒ Ⓓ Ⓔ 18. Ⓐ Ⓑ Ⓒ Ⓓ Ⓔ 28. Ⓐ Ⓑ Ⓒ Ⓓ Ⓔ 38. Ⓐ Ⓑ Ⓒ Ⓓ Ⓔ
9. Ⓐ Ⓑ Ⓒ Ⓓ Ⓔ 19. Ⓐ Ⓑ Ⓒ Ⓓ Ⓔ 29. Ⓐ Ⓑ Ⓒ Ⓓ Ⓔ 39. Ⓐ Ⓑ Ⓒ Ⓓ Ⓔ
10. Ⓐ Ⓑ Ⓒ Ⓓ Ⓔ 20. Ⓐ Ⓑ Ⓒ Ⓓ Ⓔ 30. Ⓐ Ⓑ Ⓒ Ⓓ Ⓔ 40. Ⓐ Ⓑ Ⓒ Ⓓ Ⓔ

SECTION 3

1. Ⓐ Ⓑ Ⓒ Ⓓ Ⓔ 11. Ⓐ Ⓑ Ⓒ Ⓓ Ⓔ 21. Ⓐ Ⓑ Ⓒ Ⓓ Ⓔ 31. Ⓐ Ⓑ Ⓒ Ⓓ Ⓔ
2. Ⓐ Ⓑ Ⓒ Ⓓ Ⓔ 12. Ⓐ Ⓑ Ⓒ Ⓓ Ⓔ 22. Ⓐ Ⓑ Ⓒ Ⓓ Ⓔ 32. Ⓐ Ⓑ Ⓒ Ⓓ Ⓔ
3. Ⓐ Ⓑ Ⓒ Ⓓ Ⓔ 13. Ⓐ Ⓑ Ⓒ Ⓓ Ⓔ 23. Ⓐ Ⓑ Ⓒ Ⓓ Ⓔ 33. Ⓐ Ⓑ Ⓒ Ⓓ Ⓔ
4. Ⓐ Ⓑ Ⓒ Ⓓ Ⓔ 14. Ⓐ Ⓑ Ⓒ Ⓓ Ⓔ 24. Ⓐ Ⓑ Ⓒ Ⓓ Ⓔ 34. Ⓐ Ⓑ Ⓒ Ⓓ Ⓔ
5. Ⓐ Ⓑ Ⓒ Ⓓ Ⓔ 15. Ⓐ Ⓑ Ⓒ Ⓓ Ⓔ 25. Ⓐ Ⓑ Ⓒ Ⓓ Ⓔ 35. Ⓐ Ⓑ Ⓒ Ⓓ Ⓔ
6. Ⓐ Ⓑ Ⓒ Ⓓ Ⓔ 16. Ⓐ Ⓑ Ⓒ Ⓓ Ⓔ 26. Ⓐ Ⓑ Ⓒ Ⓓ Ⓔ 36. Ⓐ Ⓑ Ⓒ Ⓓ Ⓔ
7. Ⓐ Ⓑ Ⓒ Ⓓ Ⓔ 17. Ⓐ Ⓑ Ⓒ Ⓓ Ⓔ 27. Ⓐ Ⓑ Ⓒ Ⓓ Ⓔ 37. Ⓐ Ⓑ Ⓒ Ⓓ Ⓔ
8. Ⓐ Ⓑ Ⓒ Ⓓ Ⓔ 18. Ⓐ Ⓑ Ⓒ Ⓓ Ⓔ 28. Ⓐ Ⓑ Ⓒ Ⓓ Ⓔ 38. Ⓐ Ⓑ Ⓒ Ⓓ Ⓔ
9. Ⓐ Ⓑ Ⓒ Ⓓ Ⓔ 19. Ⓐ Ⓑ Ⓒ Ⓓ Ⓔ 29. Ⓐ Ⓑ Ⓒ Ⓓ Ⓔ 39. Ⓐ Ⓑ Ⓒ Ⓓ Ⓔ
10. Ⓐ Ⓑ Ⓒ Ⓓ Ⓔ 20. Ⓐ Ⓑ Ⓒ Ⓓ Ⓔ 30. Ⓐ Ⓑ Ⓒ Ⓓ Ⓔ 40. Ⓐ Ⓑ Ⓒ Ⓓ Ⓔ

ANSWER SHEET

SECTION 4

1. (A) (B) (C) (D) (E)	11. (A) (B) (C) (D) (E)	21. (A) (B) (C) (D) (E)	31. (A) (B) (C) (D) (E)
2. (A) (B) (C) (D) (E)	12. (A) (B) (C) (D) (E)	22. (A) (B) (C) (D) (E)	32. (A) (B) (C) (D) (E)
3. (A) (B) (C) (D) (E)	13. (A) (B) (C) (D) (E)	23. (A) (B) (C) (D) (E)	33. (A) (B) (C) (D) (E)
4. (A) (B) (C) (D) (E)	14. (A) (B) (C) (D) (E)	24. (A) (B) (C) (D) (E)	34. (A) (B) (C) (D) (E)
5. (A) (B) (C) (D) (E)	15. (A) (B) (C) (D) (E)	25. (A) (B) (C) (D) (E)	35. (A) (B) (C) (D) (E)
6. (A) (B) (C) (D) (E)	16. (A) (B) (C) (D) (E)	26. (A) (B) (C) (D) (E)	36. (A) (B) (C) (D) (E)
7. (A) (B) (C) (D) (E)	17. (A) (B) (C) (D) (E)	27. (A) (B) (C) (D) (E)	37. (A) (B) (C) (D) (E)
8. (A) (B) (C) (D) (E)	18. (A) (B) (C) (D) (E)	28. (A) (B) (C) (D) (E)	38. (A) (B) (C) (D) (E)
9. (A) (B) (C) (D) (E)	19. (A) (B) (C) (D) (E)	29. (A) (B) (C) (D) (E)	39. (A) (B) (C) (D) (E)
10. (A) (B) (C) (D) (E)	20. (A) (B) (C) (D) (E)	30. (A) (B) (C) (D) (E)	40. (A) (B) (C) (D) (E)

SECTION 5

1. (A) (B) (C) (D) (E)	5. (A) (B) (C) (D) (E)
2. (A) (B) (C) (D) (E)	6. (A) (B) (C) (D) (E)
3. (A) (B) (C) (D) (E)	7. (A) (B) (C) (D) (E)
4. (A) (B) (C) (D) (E)	8. (A) (B) (C) (D) (E)

9.   10.   11.   12.   13.

14.   15.   16.   17.   18.

ANSWER SHEET

SECTION 6

1. (A) (B) (C) (D) (E)	11. (A) (B) (C) (D) (E)	21. (A) (B) (C) (D) (E)	31. (A) (B) (C) (D) (E)
2. (A) (B) (C) (D) (E)	12. (A) (B) (C) (D) (E)	22. (A) (B) (C) (D) (E)	32. (A) (B) (C) (D) (E)
3. (A) (B) (C) (D) (E)	13. (A) (B) (C) (D) (E)	23. (A) (B) (C) (D) (E)	33. (A) (B) (C) (D) (E)
4. (A) (B) (C) (D) (E)	14. (A) (B) (C) (D) (E)	24. (A) (B) (C) (D) (E)	34. (A) (B) (C) (D) (E)
5. (A) (B) (C) (D) (E)	15. (A) (B) (C) (D) (E)	25. (A) (B) (C) (D) (E)	35. (A) (B) (C) (D) (E)
6. (A) (B) (C) (D) (E)	16. (A) (B) (C) (D) (E)	26. (A) (B) (C) (D) (E)	36. (A) (B) (C) (D) (E)
7. (A) (B) (C) (D) (E)	17. (A) (B) (C) (D) (E)	27. (A) (B) (C) (D) (E)	37. (A) (B) (C) (D) (E)
8. (A) (B) (C) (D) (E)	18. (A) (B) (C) (D) (E)	28. (A) (B) (C) (D) (E)	38. (A) (B) (C) (D) (E)
9. (A) (B) (C) (D) (E)	19. (A) (B) (C) (D) (E)	29. (A) (B) (C) (D) (E)	39. (A) (B) (C) (D) (E)
10. (A) (B) (C) (D) (E)	20. (A) (B) (C) (D) (E)	30. (A) (B) (C) (D) (E)	40. (A) (B) (C) (D) (E)

SECTION 7

1. (A) (B) (C) (D) (E)	11. (A) (B) (C) (D) (E)	21. (A) (B) (C) (D) (E)	31. (A) (B) (C) (D) (E)
2. (A) (B) (C) (D) (E)	12. (A) (B) (C) (D) (E)	22. (A) (B) (C) (D) (E)	32. (A) (B) (C) (D) (E)
3. (A) (B) (C) (D) (E)	13. (A) (B) (C) (D) (E)	23. (A) (B) (C) (D) (E)	33. (A) (B) (C) (D) (E)
4. (A) (B) (C) (D) (E)	14. (A) (B) (C) (D) (E)	24. (A) (B) (C) (D) (E)	34. (A) (B) (C) (D) (E)
5. (A) (B) (C) (D) (E)	15. (A) (B) (C) (D) (E)	25. (A) (B) (C) (D) (E)	35. (A) (B) (C) (D) (E)
6. (A) (B) (C) (D) (E)	16. (A) (B) (C) (D) (E)	26. (A) (B) (C) (D) (E)	36. (A) (B) (C) (D) (E)
7. (A) (B) (C) (D) (E)	17. (A) (B) (C) (D) (E)	27. (A) (B) (C) (D) (E)	37. (A) (B) (C) (D) (E)
8. (A) (B) (C) (D) (E)	18. (A) (B) (C) (D) (E)	28. (A) (B) (C) (D) (E)	38. (A) (B) (C) (D) (E)
9. (A) (B) (C) (D) (E)	19. (A) (B) (C) (D) (E)	29. (A) (B) (C) (D) (E)	39. (A) (B) (C) (D) (E)
10. (A) (B) (C) (D) (E)	20. (A) (B) (C) (D) (E)	30. (A) (B) (C) (D) (E)	40. (A) (B) (C) (D) (E)

SECTION 8

1. (A) (B) (C) (D) (E)	11. (A) (B) (C) (D) (E)	21. (A) (B) (C) (D) (E)	31. (A) (B) (C) (D) (E)
2. (A) (B) (C) (D) (E)	12. (A) (B) (C) (D) (E)	22. (A) (B) (C) (D) (E)	32. (A) (B) (C) (D) (E)
3. (A) (B) (C) (D) (E)	13. (A) (B) (C) (D) (E)	23. (A) (B) (C) (D) (E)	33. (A) (B) (C) (D) (E)
4. (A) (B) (C) (D) (E)	14. (A) (B) (C) (D) (E)	24. (A) (B) (C) (D) (E)	34. (A) (B) (C) (D) (E)
5. (A) (B) (C) (D) (E)	15. (A) (B) (C) (D) (E)	25. (A) (B) (C) (D) (E)	35. (A) (B) (C) (D) (E)
6. (A) (B) (C) (D) (E)	16. (A) (B) (C) (D) (E)	26. (A) (B) (C) (D) (E)	36. (A) (B) (C) (D) (E)
7. (A) (B) (C) (D) (E)	17. (A) (B) (C) (D) (E)	27. (A) (B) (C) (D) (E)	37. (A) (B) (C) (D) (E)
8. (A) (B) (C) (D) (E)	18. (A) (B) (C) (D) (E)	28. (A) (B) (C) (D) (E)	38. (A) (B) (C) (D) (E)
9. (A) (B) (C) (D) (E)	19. (A) (B) (C) (D) (E)	29. (A) (B) (C) (D) (E)	39. (A) (B) (C) (D) (E)
10. (A) (B) (C) (D) (E)	20. (A) (B) (C) (D) (E)	30. (A) (B) (C) (D) (E)	40. (A) (B) (C) (D) (E)

SECTION 9

1. (A) (B) (C) (D) (E)	11. (A) (B) (C) (D) (E)	21. (A) (B) (C) (D) (E)	31. (A) (B) (C) (D) (E)
2. (A) (B) (C) (D) (E)	12. (A) (B) (C) (D) (E)	22. (A) (B) (C) (D) (E)	32. (A) (B) (C) (D) (E)
3. (A) (B) (C) (D) (E)	13. (A) (B) (C) (D) (E)	23. (A) (B) (C) (D) (E)	33. (A) (B) (C) (D) (E)
4. (A) (B) (C) (D) (E)	14. (A) (B) (C) (D) (E)	24. (A) (B) (C) (D) (E)	34. (A) (B) (C) (D) (E)
5. (A) (B) (C) (D) (E)	15. (A) (B) (C) (D) (E)	25. (A) (B) (C) (D) (E)	35. (A) (B) (C) (D) (E)
6. (A) (B) (C) (D) (E)	16. (A) (B) (C) (D) (E)	26. (A) (B) (C) (D) (E)	36. (A) (B) (C) (D) (E)
7. (A) (B) (C) (D) (E)	17. (A) (B) (C) (D) (E)	27. (A) (B) (C) (D) (E)	37. (A) (B) (C) (D) (E)
8. (A) (B) (C) (D) (E)	18. (A) (B) (C) (D) (E)	28. (A) (B) (C) (D) (E)	38. (A) (B) (C) (D) (E)
9. (A) (B) (C) (D) (E)	19. (A) (B) (C) (D) (E)	29. (A) (B) (C) (D) (E)	39. (A) (B) (C) (D) (E)
10. (A) (B) (C) (D) (E)	20. (A) (B) (C) (D) (E)	30. (A) (B) (C) (D) (E)	40. (A) (B) (C) (D) (E)

Section 1

Time—25 minutes

Directions for Writing the Essay

Plan and write an essay that answers the question below. Do NOT write on another topic. An essay on another topic will receive a score of 0.

Two readers will grade your essay based on how well you develop your point of view, organize and explain your ideas, use specific and relevant examples to support your thesis, and use clear and effective language. How well you write is much more important than how much you write, but to cover the topic adequately you should plan to write several paragraphs.

Your essay must be written on separate lined sheets of paper. Keep your handwriting to a reasonable size. Your essay will be read by people who are not familiar with your handwriting, so write legibly.

You may use this sheet for notes and outlining, but these will not be graded as part of your essay.

Consider carefully the issue discussed in the following passage, then write an essay that answers the question posed in the assignment.

> An entertainment-driven culture runs the risk of encouraging passivity among its citizens. If they can experience something vicariously through a movie, television show, or video game why should they get involved with the activity itself? It's safer, after all, to watch someone scale a mountain than to do it youreself. The effect of this passivity, of course, is an apathetic frame of mind. We cease to care deeply about so many things because they are experienced, at best, second-hand.

Assignment: **Is apathy a problem in today's society?** Write an essay in which you answer this question and discuss your point of view on this issue. Support your position logically with examples from literature, the arts, history, politics, science and technology, current events, or your experience or observation.

Write your essay on separate sheets of paper.

Section 2

Time—25 minutes
20 Questions

1 If $x = 3$ and $5x = 3x + y$, then $y =$

(A) 1.5
(B) 2
(C) 3
(D) 4
(E) 6

2 A store sells a package of 6 batteries for $4 and a package of 24 of the same batteries for $12. If you need to buy 48 of these batteries, how much money will you save by buying them in packages of 24 rather than packages of 6?

(A) $4
(B) $8
(C) $12
(D) $16
(E) $20

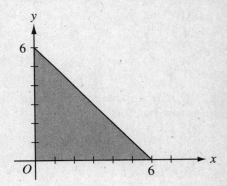

3 Which of the following points does NOT lie in the shaded region above?

(A) (1, 1)
(B) (1, 4)
(C) (3, 3)
(D) (4, 1)
(E) (5, 5)

GO ON TO THE NEXT PAGE ▶▶▶

2

4 If $\frac{1}{3}$ of $2x$ is 5, what is $\frac{2}{3}$ of $4x$?

(A) 5
(B) 10
(C) 15
(D) 20
(E) 25

5 If n is a positive integer that is divisible by 12 and 16, then n must also be divisible by

(A) 28
(B) 32
(C) 48
(D) 96
(E) 192

6

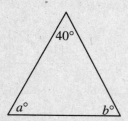

Note: Figure not drawn to scale

In the figure above, if $a - b = 10$, then $a =$

(A) 60
(B) 65
(C) 70
(D) 75
(E) 80

7 If n is an integer, which of the following must be even?

(A) $\frac{n}{2}$
(B) $n + 2$
(C) $2n + 1$
(D) n^2
(E) $n^2 + n$

8 Mike sold a total of 48 sodas at a snack stand. The stand sells only cola and root beer. If he sold twice as many colas as root beers, how many root beers did he sell?

(A) 32
(B) 24
(C) 18
(D) 16
(E) 8

9 If m and n are both squares of integers, which of the following is NOT necessarily the square of an integer?

(A) $9m$
(B) mn
(C) m^2
(D) $9mn$
(E) $9m - 9n$

10 If $a + b = 9$, $a - c = 14$, and $a = 10$, then $c - b =$

(A) −5
(B) −3
(C) 3
(D) 5
(E) 23

11 If set $M = \left\{ \frac{1}{6}, \frac{1}{4}, \frac{2}{3}, \frac{5}{6} \right\}$ and if x and y are both elements of set M, then what is the maximum possible value of $5x - 5y$?

(A) $\frac{10}{3}$
(B) 4
(C) $\frac{25}{6}$
(D) $\frac{14}{3}$
(E) 5

0	1	2	3	4	5
1	2	4			
2					
3			x		
4					
5					

12 With the exception of the shaded squares, every square in the figure above contains the sum of the number in the square directly above it and the number in the square directly to its left. For example, the number 4 in the unshaded square above is the sum of the 2 in the square above it and the 2 in the square directly to its left. What is the value of x?

(A) 6
(B) 7
(C) 8
(D) 15
(E) 30

GO ON TO THE NEXT PAGE ▶▶▶

13 If a, b, and c are positive even integers such that $a < b < c$ and $a + b + c = 60$, then the greatest possible value of c is

(A) 36
(B) 40
(C) 42
(D) 54
(E) 57

14 The population of Bumpton increased by 10% from 1980 to 1990 and decreased by 10% from 1990 to 2000. What is the net percent change in the population of Bumpton from 1980 to 2000?

(A) −9%
(B) −1%
(C) +0%
(D) +1%
(E) +9%

15 Each female of a certain species of fish lays 100 eggs each fall and then dies. If only 30% of these eggs mature to become egg-producing females the next year, then how many egg-producing females will descend from a single egg-producing female 2 years after she first lays eggs?

(A) 900
(B) 9,000
(C) 18,000
(D) 27,000
(E) 810,000

16 If $x > 0$ and $x = 5y$, then $\sqrt{x^2 - 2xy + y^2} =$

(A) $2y$
(B) $y\sqrt{6}$
(C) $4y$
(D) $16y$
(E) $24y$

17 If $x > x^2$, which of the following must be true?

   I. $x < 1$
  II. $x > 0$
 III. $x^2 > 1$
(A) I only
(B) II only
(C) I and II only

(D) I and III only
(E) I, II, and III

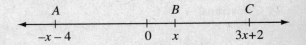

18 Which of the following represents the distance from the midpoint of $\overline{AB}$ to the midpoint of $\overline{BC}$ on the number line above?

(A) $\dfrac{3x + 2}{2}$

(B) $2x - 1$
(C) $2x + 3$
(D) $3x + 1$
(E) $4x$

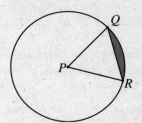

19 P is the center of the circle above and $PQ = QR$. If $\triangle PQR$ has an area of $9\sqrt{3}$, what is the area of the shaded region?

(A) $36\pi - 9\sqrt{3}$

(B) $24\pi - 9\sqrt{3}$

(C) $18\pi - 9\sqrt{3}$

(D) $9\pi - 9\sqrt{3}$

(E) $6\pi - 9\sqrt{3}$

20 In a class of 160 seniors, the ratio of boys to girls is 3 to 5. In the junior class, the ratio of boys to girls is 3 to 2. When the two classes are combined, the ratio of boys to girls is 1 to 1. How many students are in the junior class?

(A) 400
(B) 360
(C) 200
(D) 180
(E) 160

STOP

You may check your work, on this section only, until time is called.

Section 3

Time—25 minutes
24 Questions

Each of the sentences below is missing 1 or 2 portions. Read each sentence, then select the word or words that most logically complete the sentence, taking into account the meaning of the sentence as a whole.

Example:

Rather than accepting the theory unquestioningly, Deborah regarded it with ———.

(A)　mirth　　　　　(B)　sadness
(C)　responsibility　(D)　ignorance
(E)　skepticism

Correct response: (E)

1 Julia feared that her 6-month hiatus from playing the piano would cause her musical skills to ———.

(A)　atrophy　　(B)　align
(C)　develop　　(D)　reconcile
(E)　disseminate

2 Senator Harris is widely viewed as a ——— orator; his speeches are full of ——— commentary and domineering opinions.

(A)　vindictive ... pedantic
(B)　conciliatory ... treacherous
(C)　didactic ... moralizing
(D)　dogmatic ... meek
(E)　simplistic ... prosaic

3 Walter's ——— was beginning to annoy his coworkers; although they appreciated the thought he gave to his decisions, his inability to make up his mind was growing tiresome.

(A)　vacillation
(B)　solicitation
(C)　rejuvenation
(D)　admonishment
(E)　professionalism

4 To succeed as a writer, one needs a great deal of ———; successful writers are ——— even in the face of countless rejections.

(A)　affluence ... haughty
(B)　pertinacity ... apologetic
(C)　intimidation ... resilient
(D)　tenacity ... relentless
(E)　stoutness ... craven

5 Although direct, forceful stances usually appeal to voters on the campaign trail, candidates usually resort to ——— during debates to avoid alienating any potential supporters.

(A)　pontification
(B)　circumlocution
(C)　logic
(D)　exaggeration
(E)　brevity

6 Counselors in the prison rehabilitation program must have faith in the ——— of those who have committed felonies, yet be wary of ———; they must believe that criminals can change, but know that they can often return to their old habits.

(A)　mutability ... astuteness
(B)　variability ... consistency
(C)　coarseness ... responsibility
(D)　persuasion ... transcendence
(E)　malleability ... relapse

7 Marullus' reference to "chimney-tops" during his monologue in *Julius Caesar* is considered by some historians ———, since such things are unlikely to have existed in Rome in the 1st century B.C.

(A)　a miscalculation
(B)　an anachronism
(C)　an idiom
(D)　an interlocutor
(E)　a mirage

GO ON TO THE NEXT PAGE ▶▶▶

8 The letter "h" at the end of Pittsburgh is ——— of American sentiments soon after World War I; it was added as part of a movement during that time to make the names of American cities sound less German.

(A) an inference   (B) an analogy
(C) a vestige   (D) an anomaly
(E) a quandary

Each passage below is followed by one or two questions based on its content. Answer each question based on what is stated or implied in the preceding passage.

Questions 9–10 are based on the following passage.

3

Line Although countries can construct redoubtable stone barriers to separate "us" from "others," no barrier is stronger than language. We infer volumes from the language of another,
5 whether he is erudite or philistine, whether she is noble or mean. Our labels, too, can be impenetrable walls: we are "freedom fighters," they are "terrorists"; we are the "faithful," they are the "infidels." Those people who use
10 such wall-language are the Manichaeans,[1] those who refuse to see, or cannot see, shades of gray, the subtle truths of humanity. Their "truths" are the most dangerous weapons, wielded by the blind and the
15 ignorant.

9 In this paragraph, language is characterized primarily as

(A) biased
(B) enlightening
(C) difficult to understand
(D) unifying
(E) changeable

10 In line 4, the word "volumes" most nearly means

(A) spaces   (B) editions
(C) measurements   (D) an abundance
(E) capacities

GO ON TO THE NEXT PAGE ▶▶▶

[1] Those who believe in absolute good and evil
Second paragraph: *Educational Psychology: A Developmental Approach*, Norman A. Sprinthall *et al.*, McGraw-Hill 1994, p. 149

Questions 11–12 are based on the following passage.

Line   It may be difficult for adults to learn not to
interfere but rather to support the child's
desire for freedom and autonomy. For
example, if you watch a boy of three trying
5   to tie his shoes, you may see him work with
extraordinary motivation even though the
loops aren't matched, and well over half the
time as he tries for the final knot, he ends up
with two separate laces, one in each hand.
10   Then watch his parents as they watch their
children attempt a task like this. Too often
the parent will step in and take over, tie the
shoes the "right way" and defeat the child's
growing attempt at self-mastery. The same
15   goes for putting on boots, coats, and even
playing with toys. It is exceedingly easy to fall
into the trap of almost always responding
negatively to a child at this age. Commonly, a
parent might say no up to 200 times a day at
20   this stage. Such nagging not only is aversive
in the extreme, but also a constant reminder
to the child of his or her lack of self-control.

11   The passage suggests that helping a boy to
tie his shoes the "right way" (line 13) can be

(A)   necessary to his self-esteem
(B)   important to his personal hygiene
(C)   appropriate only if the boy has the
necessary fine motor skills
(D)   essential to teaching him patience
(E)   harmful to his autonomous
development

12   The passage indicates that negative
responses to a child can lead to the child's

(A)   rebellion
(B)   feeling of helplessness
(C)   persistence in the task
(D)   mimicking of the negative behavior
(E)   anger

The questions below are based on the content
of the preceding passage. The questions are to
be answered on the basis of what is stated or
implied in the passage itself or the introductory material that precedes the passage.

Questions 13–18 are based on the following passage.

The following is an essay about T. S. Eliot, an American poet of the early 20th century, and the Modernist movement, of which he was a part.

Line   Modernism is the most peculiar of all artistic
movements of the twentieth century and the
most difficult to pin down since people started
coming up with "movements" in the first
5   place. Modernism is the only thing that
strikes more fear into the heart of an English
undergraduate than the idea of going to a
lecture. Critics and academics, not unwisely,
prefer their artistic movements to be readily
10   comprehensible and clearly enough defined
to make some logical sense. Modernism,
however, will not be tamed. It is straggly,
begins nowhere and with no one in particular,
and ends only when its writers have started
15   to baffle even themselves. One treads
carefully through its key texts: James Joyce's
Ulysses, T. S. Eliot's *The Waste Land* (both
1922), and Virginia Woolf's *Mrs. Dalloway*
(1925). The authors of these aberrations,
20   these posturing, egotistical, lunatic,
kaleidoscopic works of blatant and self-
conscious genius, have laid literary
landmines throughout their works. Joyce said
of *Ulysses* that "I've put in so many enigmas
25   and puzzles that it will keep the professors
busy for centuries arguing over what I meant,
and that's the only way of insuring one's
immortality." This statement sums up the
enigma of modernism (if one can be said to
30   sum up an enigma) in that it contains
arrogance mingling with modesty, cleverness
tied up in self-effacing humour, and above all
absurdity with a purpose. Plots, such as they
exist at all in modernist writing, are

GO ON TO THE NEXT PAGE ▶▶▶

35 submerged beneath wave upon wave of
classical allusions, archaisms, neologisms,
foreign languages, quotations, swear words
and other hyper-literary and meta-literary
indulgences. If I haven't made it clear
40 already, it is hard not to love modernism.
It is hard to work out what exactly it is.
   Recently, while browsing in an Oxford
bookshop, a friend of mine picked up a copy
of *Finnegans Wake*—James Joyce's final
45 book—and read the first page. Between tears
of laughter, he managed to indicate to me
that he couldn't understand a word of it. It is
hard not to sympathise with the outsider's
attitude so amply demonstrated by my friend's
50 outburst of shock and wonder. To find one of
our most famous authors writing gibberish is
rather heartening. Yet we remain outsiders to
the work. *Finnegans Wake,* you see, is
emblematic of all that is right and wrong
55 with modernism. It took a spectacularly long
time to write and was finally published in
1939, seventeen years after its predecessor,
Ulysses. That probably had something to do
with the fact that over 40 different languages
60 crept into its catalogue of portmanteau words
(ersatz words consisting of two or more real
words or word elements, like those of Lewis
Carroll in his poem "Jabberwocky"). The
resulting book is uniquely inventive and at
75 the same time uniquely confusing. In that
sense, it is the perfect example of a
modernist text. It alienates its readers just as
it tries to mimic how they think. The English
modernist novel is a sociopath and a cad:
70 dangerous and reprehensible but somehow
roguishly likeable.

13 In the first paragraph, the author characterizes Modernism as which of the following?

   I.   self-centered
   II. ill-defined
   III. politically oriented

(A) I only   (B) II only
(C) I and II only   (D) II and III only
(E) I, II, and III

14 The passage suggests that critics and academics dislike artistic movements that are

(A) enigmatic
(B) comprehensible
(C) wide-ranging
(D) inventive
(E) socially conscious

15 The "landmines" in line 23 are

(A) episodes in novels that refer to
    violence
(B) criticisms of the works of other
    novelists
(C) new methods of analyzing literature
(D) literary devices intended to baffle
    academics
(E) limitations that publishers place on
    an author's work

16 The reference to "wave upon wave" (line 35)
suggests that, in Modernist fiction, plot is

(A) a powerfully moving element
(B) secondary to other considerations
(C) dominant over diction
(D) characterized by redundancy
(E) dangerous

17 The author's overall attitude toward
Modernism can best be described as

(A) ambivalent   (B) reverential
(C) cynical   (D) indignant
(E) jocular

18 The final sentence of the passage employs
each of the following EXCEPT

(A) simile   (B) juxtaposition
(C) personification (D) contrast
(E) metaphor

Transducing the Genome, Gary Zweiger, McGraw-Hill, pp. xi–xii

GO ON TO THE NEXT PAGE ▶▶▶

3

Questions 19–24 are based on the following passage.

The following is an excerpt from a book on genomics, the new science of gathering and using the information encoded in the genes of an organism.

Line Biology is being reborn as an information
      science, a progeny of the Information Age.
      As information scientists, biologists concern
      themselves with the messages that sustain
  5   life, such as the intricate series of signals
      that tell a fertilized egg to develop into a
      full-grown organism, or the orchestrated
      response the immune system makes to an
      invading pathogen. Molecules convey
 10   information, and it is their messages that are
      of paramount importance. Each molecule
      interacts with a set of other molecules and
      each set communicates with another set,
      such that all are interconnected. Networks of
 15   molecules give rise to cells; networks of cells
      produce multicellular organisms; networks of
      people bring about cultures and societies;
      and networks of species encompass
      ecosystems. Life is a web and the web is life.
 20   Ironically, it was the euphoria for molecules
      that touched off this scientific revolution. In
      the 1980s only a tiny percentage of the
      millions of different molecular components
      of living beings was known. In order to gain
 25   access to these molecules, a new science and
      even a new industry had to be created.
      Genomics is the development and application
      of research tools that uncover and analyze
      thousands of different molecules at a time.
 30   This new approach to biology has been so
      successful that universities have created
      entire departments devoted to it, and all
      major pharmaceutical companies now have
      large genomics divisions. Genomics has
 35   granted biologists unprecedented access to
      the molecules of life, but this is more than
      just a technological revolution. Through

genomics massive amounts of biological
information can be converted into an
 40 electronic format. This directly links the life
sciences to the information sciences, thereby
facilitating a dramatically new framework for
understanding life.
      Information is a message, a bit of news.
 45 It may be encoded or decoded. It may be
conveyed by smoke signals, pictures, sound
waves, electromagnetic waves, or innumerous
other media, but the information itself is not
made of anything. It has no mass.
 50 Furthermore, information always has a sender
and an intended receiver. This implies an
underlying intent, meaning, or purpose.
Information theory thus may seem unfit for
the cold objectivism of science. The focus of
 55 the information sciences, however, is not so
much on information content, but rather on
how messages are conveyed, processed, and
stored.
      Advances in this area have been great and
 60 have helped to propel the remarkable
development of the computer and
telecommunication industries. Could these
forces be harnessed to better understand the
human body and to improve human health?

19 The primary purpose of this passage is to

(A) refute a theory
(B) describe the origins of a misconception
(C) analyze different perspectives on a phenomenon
(D) describe a new trend in a field of study
(E) suggest a new method of teaching

20 The passage mentions each of the following as an example of elements interrelating to form a larger whole EXCEPT

(A) molecules forming a cell
(B) organisms forming an ecosystem
(C) pathogens forming the immune system
(D) individuals forming a society
(E) cells forming an organism

21 The passage mentions the "orchestrated response" (line 7) primarily as an example of

(A) the coordinated efforts of scientists
(B) molecules conveying information
(C) the work being done to promote genomics
(D) the similarity between cells and computers
(E) an unrealized potential

22 According to the passage, the "dramatically new framework" (line 40) is one in which

(A) new university buildings are being built
(B) the immune system attacks a pathogen
(C) networks of molecules give rise to cells
(D) genomics research receives more federal funding
(E) biological data is translated into a new form

23 According to the passage, information theory "may seem unfit for the cold objectivism of science" (lines 53–54) because

(A) it is better suited to commercial industry than to academic study
(B) it can be conveyed by sound waves
(C) it suggests that messages may have meaning or purpose
(D) it is not rigorously studied
(E) it analyzes biological information

24 Which of the following best describes the function of the final paragraph in relation to the rest of the passage?

(A) It modifies a theory presented earlier.
(B) It provides a solution to a problem mentioned earlier.
(C) It raises doubts about the value of genomics.
(D) It indicates actual and potential consequences of genomics.
(E) It mentions a viable alternative to genomics.

3

STOP

You may check your work, on this section only, until time is called.

Section 4

Time—25 minutes
35 Questions

---

4 →

Directions for "Improving Sentences" Questions

Each of the sentences below contains one underlined portion. The portion may contain one or more errors in grammar, usage, construction, precision, diction (choice of words), or idiom. Some of the sentences are correct.

Consider the meaning of the original sentence, and choose the answer that best expresses that meaning. If the original sentence is best, choose (A), because it repeats the original phrasing. Choose the phrasing that creates the clearest, most precise, and most effective sentence.

EXAMPLE:

The children <u>couldn't hardly believe their eyes</u>.

- (A) couldn't hardly believe their eyes
- (B) would not hardly believe their eyes
- (C) could hardly believe their eyes
- (D) couldn't nearly believe their eyes
- (E) could hardly believe his or her eyes

Example answer: (C)

---

1 The controversial themes, which resonate with recent political events, <u>explain why the book is selling at such a feverish pace</u>.

- (A) explain why the book is selling at such a feverish pace
- (B) explains the feverish pace of the book
- (C) explain the reason for the pace of the book's feverish sales
- (D) explains why the book's selling pace is so feverish
- (E) is why the book is selling well.

2 One of the best features of the journalist's lifestyle is <u>you never know what's next</u>.

- (A) you never know what's next
- (B) it's so unpredictable
- (C) that you never know what's next
- (D) one can never predict what's next
- (E) its unpredictability

3 Despite having an engaging personality and an outstanding education, <u>Greg's search for a satisfying job was fruitless</u>.

- (A) Greg's search for a satisfying job was fruitless
- (B) Greg searched fruitlessly for a satisfying job
- (C) Greg's job search was fruitless because he insisted on a satisfying job
- (D) the satisfying job that Greg sought was nowhere to be found
- (E) Greg searched for a satisfying job, but it was fruitless

4 The plot of the movie was neither plausible <u>and it was not even faithful to the novel</u>.

- (A) and it was not even faithful to the novel
- (B) nor was it faithful to the novel
- (C) nor faithful to the novel
- (D) and certainly not faithful to the novel
- (E) yet hardly faithful to the novel

5 We were astonished that the package had <u>took so long to get to its destination</u>.

- (A) had took so long to get
- (B) had took so long getting
- (C) had taken so long in its getting
- (D) had taken so long to get
- (E) had been so long getting

6 The committee agreed that the new principal should be able to inspire teachers, uphold tradition, and, above all, <u>he or she must maintain a scholarly atmosphere</u>.

- (A) he or she must maintain a scholarly atmosphere
- (B) they should maintain a scholarly atmosphere
- (C) maintain a scholarly atmosphere
- (D) keep things scholarly
- (E) he or she should keep things scholarly

GO ON TO THE NEXT PAGE ▶▶▶

7 Although critics say that many have portrayed Othello with more passion than <u>he, they can't help but admire his acting</u>.

    (A) he, they can't help but admire his acting

    (B) him, they can't help but admire his acting

    (C) he, they can't help but admire him acting

    (D) him, they can't help but admire him acting

    (E) him, they must only admire his acting

8 <u>Neither of the battling rams seemed to feel the pain of their wounds</u>.

    (A) Neither of the battling rams seemed to feel the pain of their wounds.

    (B) Neither of the battling rams seemed to feel the pain of his wounds.

    (C) Neither ram, that was battling, seemed to feel the pain of their wounds.

    (D) Neither ram, who were battling, seemed to feel the pain of his wounds.

    (E) Neither of the battling rams seemed to feel the pain of his wounds.

9 Walking into her house after a hard day's work, <u>Liz's family surprised her with a warm, delicious meal and a clean house</u>.

    (A) Liz's family surprised her with a warm, delicious meal and a clean house

    (B) Liz was surprised to find a warm, delicious meal and a clean house, courtesy of her family

    (C) Liz's family made her a warm, delicious meal and cleaned the house, surprising her

    (D) Liz found a warm, delicious meal and a clean house surprising her from her family

    (E) a warm, delicious meal and a clean house surprised Liz, courtesy of her family

10 An increasing number of students are coming to realize that an education at a public university can be <u>as good, if not better, than an elite private college</u>.

    (A) as good, if not better, than an elite private college

    (B) as good, if not better, as one at an elite private college

    (C) as good as, if not better, than an elite private college education

    (D) as good an education as, if not better, than one at an elite private college

    (E) as good as, if not better than, one at an elite private college

11 <u>S. J. Perelman, whose hallmark of a grandiloquent writing style is</u> widely regarded as one of the finest American wits of all time.

    (A) S. J. Perelman, whose hallmark of a grandiloquent writing style is

    (B) Being that his hallmark is a grandiloquent writing style, S. J. Perelman is

    (C) S. J. Perelman's grandiloquent writing style is his hallmark and is

    (D) S. J. Perelman and his hallmark of a grandiloquent writing style are

    (E) S. J. Perelman, whose hallmark is a grandiloquent writing style, is

GO ON TO THE NEXT PAGE ▸▸▸

Directions for Identifying Sentence Error Questions

The following sentences may contain errors in grammar, usage, diction (choice of words), or idiom. Some of the sentences are correct. No sentence contains more than 1 error.

If the sentence contains an error, it is underlined and lettered. The parts that are not underlined are correct.

If there is an error, select the part that must be changed to correct the sentence.

If there is no error, choose (E).

EXAMPLE:

By the time <u>they reached</u> the halfway point
             A
<u>in the race</u>, most <u>of the runners</u> <u>hadn't hardly</u>
  B   C   D
begun to hit their stride. <u>No error</u>
                    E

Sample answer: **(D)**

12 The lack of progress

<u>in international relations</u> <u>reveals</u> that
      A   B
governments <u>must study</u> the art of
           C
diplomacy <u>much closer</u>. <u>No error</u>
          D   E

13 Because Deborah <u>has been</u> a representative
               A
for over 20 years and <u>also her popularity</u>
                  B
among <u>her constituents</u>, few are willing
      C
<u>to challenge</u> her in an election. <u>No error</u>
  D   E

14 Caravaggio <u>demonstrated</u> the great range
           A
<u>of his artistic talent</u> <u>in such paintings as</u>
      B   C
"Bacchus" and "Basket of Fruit," painted in

1593 and 1596, <u>respectfully</u>. <u>No error</u>
           D   E

15 Grizzly bears <u>rarely show aggression</u>
             A
toward <u>humans, but</u> they will protect their
        B
territory <u>from anyone</u> whom they
        C
<u>would have considered</u> to be a threat.
       D
<u>No error</u>
 E

16 The choir's rendition of "America the

Beautiful" <u>was stirring</u>, particularly after
        A
the children <u>had finished</u> <u>their</u> presentation
         B   C
on <u>the meaning of</u> freedom. <u>No error</u>
    D   E

17 Andre suggested <u>to the board</u> that both the
           A
fund deficit and the <u>disillusionment</u> of the
            B
investors were <u>a problem</u> that
        C
<u>had to be addressed</u> immediately. <u>No error</u>
     D   E

18 Because Phillips reasoned that either

<u>accepting</u> or rejecting the proposal <u>were</u>
 A   B
going to upset some <u>political faction</u>,
           C
he decided to delay the vote until

<u>after his reelection</u>. <u>No error</u>
  D   E

19 The Attorney General <u>spoke at length</u>
                                          A
about the detrimental <u>effects</u> of having <u>less</u>
                            B   C
defense attorneys <u>to serve</u> indigent
                          D
defendants. <u>No error</u>
                    E

20 The service <u>at Centro</u> is much better than
                          A
<u>the other restaurants</u> we frequent, so
         B
<u>we prefer</u> to go there when
      C
<u>we are entertaining</u> guests. <u>No error</u>
             D   E

21 Before the curtain <u>rose</u>, Anthony wished
                                   A
that <u>he were</u> back in bed, only <u>dreaming</u>
         B   C
about performing in front of

<u>hundreds of strangers</u> rather than actually
                D
doing it. <u>No error</u>
                  E

22 James, like many parents, <u>believes</u> that if a
                                              A
child can read <u>at a very young age</u>, <u>they</u>
                        B   C
will grow to have <u>exceptional</u> literary
                              D
talent. <u>No error</u>
                 E

23 The <u>decline</u> of the Enlightenment
              A
<u>was hastened</u> not only by tyrants but also
         B
<u>because</u> of intellectual <u>opposition</u>. <u>No error</u>
      C   D   E

24 Although he pitched <u>professionally</u> for 3
                                   A
decades, Nolan Ryan <u>never lost</u> any
                              B
velocity on his fastball, and few <u>maintained</u>
                                              C
such <u>control over</u> so many pitches as he.
              D
<u>No error</u>
      E

25 The Senator and his <u>opponent</u>, Thomas
                                   A
Cowher, were running a very tight

race until <u>he</u> made a <u>racially insensitive</u>
                  B   C
comment that <u>offended</u> many voters.
                      D
<u>No error</u>
      E

26 Just when <u>those who</u> were observing
                          A
the heart transplant procedure assumed

<u>the worst</u>, the surgeons themselves <u>are</u>
      B   C
<u>most</u> confident. <u>No error</u>
      D   E

27 <u>Although</u> testing <u>for unsafe</u> levels of
         A   B
asbestos particles is widely <u>advocated for</u>
                                              C
houses <u>built before</u> 1950, many home
              D
owners ignore this suggestion. <u>No error</u>
                                                E

28 Between my brother <u>and I</u> <u>existed</u> a strong
                           A   B

bond that did not weaken even <u>when</u> he
                                       C

chose to live <u>thousands of miles</u> away on a
                     D

different continent. <u>No error</u>
                          E

29 <u>Writing about</u> the folk duo, *The Indigo*
        A

Girls, one critic <u>has suggested</u> that <u>their</u>
                     B   C

longevity is <u>due</u> to its ability to remain
               D

faithful to an honest musical style while

stretching the boundaries of convention.

<u>No error</u>
  D

Questions 30–35 pertain to the following passage.

(1) *For thousands of years, philosophers have debated whether humans discover mathematics or it is something that has been invented. (2) Plato believed that perceived mathematical objects like lines were only vague shadows of abstract "ideals" that exist outside of human experience.*

(3) *Circular objects or circles drawn on paper aren't "really" circles. (4) Rather, they are just a flawed approximation of the perfect circular form. (5) So, in this sense, Plato believed that mathematics was something revealed imperfectly to humans, not invented by them. (6) Many students surely wish that mathematics had not been invented at all. (7) A position that opposes Plato's idealism is called mathematical intuitionism, which is the belief that all mathematics is the product of human minds.*

(8) *There is one good way to understand the difference between idealism and intuitionism. (9) Look at big numbers. (10) An idealist would say that all numbers, no matter how large, truly exist, even if no one has ever actually calculated them. (11) An intuitionist, on the other hand, might say that some numbers may be so big that they are physically impossible to calculate or express in a meaningful way, and so do not truly "exist."*

(12) *Another point of view that is different from these ones is one that says that it is a pointless thing to ask the question as to whether mathematical objects "really exist" or not. (13) This view simply regards mathematics as a tool for interpreting information from the world around us. (14) This view is essentially a*

compromise between idealism and intuitionism. (15) *Although it acknowledges that mathematics reaches beyond the mind of a mathematician, it also denies that it has any meaning outside of the mind. (16) The concept of a circle is not a reflection of an abstract "ideal," and also it is not completely a human invention. (17) Instead it is a concept that we form in our minds after perceiving and thinking about many circular objects in the world around us.*

30 Which of the following is the best revision of the underlined portion of sentence 1 (reproduced below)?

For thousands of years, philosophers have debated whether <u>humans discover mathematics or it is something that has been invented</u>.

(A) humans discover mathematics or invent it
(B) humans so much discover mathematics as they do invent it
(C) the discovery of mathematics is what humans do or the invention
(D) humans discover mathematics or if it is invented
(E) mathematics is something discovered or if humans invent it

31 In context, which of the following is the most logical revision of the underlined portion of sentence 3 (reproduced below)?

<u>*Circular objects*</u> *or circles drawn on paper aren't "really" circles.*

(A) nevertheless, circular objects
(B) according to his reasoning, circular objects
(C) furthermore, circular objects
(D) secondly, circular objects
(E) all the while, circular objects

GO ON TO THE NEXT PAGE ▶▶▶

32 Which of the following is the best revision of sentence 4 (reproduced below)?

Rather, they are just a flawed approximation of the perfect circular form.

(A) But instead they are only a flawed approximation of the perfect circular form.

(B) Rather, they are only flawed approximations of the perfect circular form.

(C) Rather, their forms are merely an approximation of circular perfection alone.

(D) Instead, their approximation of the perfect circular form mentioned above is imperfect.

(E) Rather, their perfection as circular forms is only an approximation of it.

33 Which of the following sentences contributes least to the unity of the first paragraph?

(A) sentence 3   (B) sentence 4
(C) sentence 5   (D) sentence 6
(E) sentence 7

34 Which of the following is the best way to combine sentences 8 and 9 (reproduced below)?

There is one good way to understand the difference between idealism and intuitionism. Look at big numbers.

(A) One good way to understand the difference between idealism and intuitionism is the following: look at large numbers.

(B) It is a good way to understand the difference between idealism and intuitionism in considering large numbers.

(C) The consideration of large numbers provides one good way toward the understanding of the difference between idealism and intuitionism.

(D) To consider large numbers is to have one good way of understanding the difference between idealism and intuitionism.

(E) One good way to understand the difference between idealism and intuitionism is to consider large numbers.

35 In context, which of the following is the best revision of sentence 12 (reproduced below)?

Another point of view that is different from these ones is one that says that it is a pointless thing to ask the question as to whether mathematical objects "really exist" or not.

(A) A third point of view regards it as pointless to ask whether mathematical objects "really exist."

(B) Another, completely different, point of view is the one that regards asking whether or not mathematical objects "really exist" as pointless.

(C) Asking whether mathematical objects "really exist" is pointless, according to another, third, different point of view.

(D) The asking of whether mathematical objects "really exist" is a pointless thing, says a third point of view.

(E) Another different point of view says it is pointless to ask about whether mathematical objects "really exist" or not.

STOP

You may check your work, on this section only, until time is called.

Section 5

Time—25 miinutes
20 Questions

Directions for Multiple-Choice Questions

In this section, solve each problem, using any available space on the page for scratchwork. Then decide which is the best of the choices given and fill in the corresponding oval on your answer sheet.

- You may use a calculator on any problem. All numbers used are real numbers.
- Figures are drawn as accurately as possible EXCEPT when it is stated that the figure is not drawn to scale.
- All figures lie in a plane unless otherwise indicated.

Reference Information

$A = \pi r^2$ $A = \ell w$

$C = 2\pi r$ $A = \frac{1}{2}bh$ $V = \ell wh$ $V = \pi r^2 h$ $c^2 = a^2 + b^2$ Special Right Triangles

The arc of a circle measures 360°.
Every straight angle measures 180°.
The sum of the measures of the angles in a triangle is 180°.

---

1 If $2x = 10$ and $3y = 12$, then $4x + 6y =$

(A) 10
(B) 12
(C) 22
(D) 32
(E) 44

2 The average (arithmetic mean) of three numbers is 5. If one of the numbers is 4, what is the sum of the other two numbers?

(A) 8
(B) 9
(C) 10
(D) 11
(E) 12

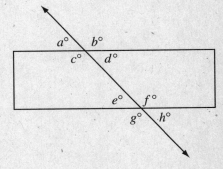

3 The figure above shows a rectangle intersected by a line. If $b = 2a$, then $d + e + g + h =$

(A) 120
(B) 240
(C) 300
(D) 320
(E) 360

4 For all real numbers x where $x \geq 1$, let $f(x) = \sqrt{\sqrt{x} - 1}$. What is the value of $f(100)$?

(A) 3
(B) 9
(C) 10
(D) 27
(E) 100

5 If $3^{k+m} = 243$ and $2^m = 8$, then what is the value of 2^k?

(A) 2
(B) 4
(C) 6
(D) 8
(E) 10

6 The average (arithmetic mean) of four different even integers is 50. If none of the numbers is greater than 60, what is the least possible value of any one of the numbers?

(A) 26
(B) 27
(C) 28
(D) 29
(E) 30

7 In a certain soccer league, each of the five teams plays every other team in the league exactly three times each season. How many games are played in total in one season?

(A) 15
(B) 24
(C) 30
(D) 60
(E) 120

8 Pump A, working alone, can fill a tank in 3 hours, and pump B can fill the same tank in 2 hours. If the tank is empty to start and pump A is switched on for one hour, after which pump B is also switched on and the two work together, how many *minutes* will pump B have been working by the time the pool is filled?

(A) 48
(B) 50
(C) 54
(D) 60
(E) 64

Directions for Student-Produced Response Questions

Each of the questions in this section requires you to solve the problem and enter your answer in a grid, as shown below.

- If your answer is ⅔ or .666 ..., you must enter **the most accurate value the grid can accommodate**, but you may do this in one of four ways.

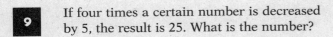

Start in first column   Grid result here

Start in second column

Grid as a truncated decimal

Grid as a rounded decimal

- In the example above, gridding a response of 0.67 or 0.66 is **incorrect** because it is less accurate than those above.
- The scoring machine cannot read what is written in the top row of boxes. You **MUST** fill in the numerical grid accurately to get credit for answering any question correctly. You should write your answer in the top row of boxes only to aid your gridding.
- Do **not** grid in a mixed fraction like $3\frac{1}{2}$ as $\boxed{3}\ \boxed{1}\ \boxed{/}\ \boxed{2}$ because it will be interpreted as $\frac{31}{2}$. Instead, convert it to an improper fraction like ⅞ or a decimal like 3.5 before gridding.
- None of the answers will be negative, because there is no negative sign in the grid.
- Some of the questions may have more than one correct answer. You must grid only one of the correct answers.
- You may use a calculator on any of these problems.
- All numbers in these problems are real numbers.
- Figures are drawn as accurately as possible EXCEPT when it is stated that the figure is not drawn to scale.
- All figures lie in a plane unless otherwise indicated.

---

9   If four times a certain number is decreased by 5, the result is 25. What is the number?

10   For every integer m greater than 1, let $<<m>>$ be defined as the sum of the integers from 1 to m, inclusive. For instance, $<<4>> = 1 + 2 + 3 + 4 = 10$. What is the value of $<<7>> - <<5>>$?

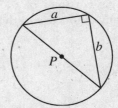

11   If the circumference of the circle above is 10π, then what is the value of $a^2 + b^2$?

GO ON TO THE NEXT PAGE ▶▶▶

12

A, B, C, D

How many different three-letter arrangements of the letters above are possible if no letter may be repeated? (An arrangement like *ABC* is distinct from an arrangement like *BCA*.)

13 If $96,878 \times x^2 = 10,200$, then $\dfrac{10,200}{5x^2 \times 96,878} =$

5

17 The perimeter of the isosceles triangle above is 24. If the ratio of *a* to *b* is 2 to 3, what is the value of *b*?

14 Every term in a certain sequence is one less than three times the previous term. If the fourth term of this sequence is 95, what is the 1st term of the sequence?

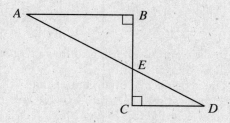

Note: Figure not drawn to scale.

15 If $4 + \sqrt{b} = 7.2$, what is the value of $4 - \sqrt{b}$?

18 In the figure above, $AB = 6$, $BC = 6$, and $CD = 2$. What is AD?

16 Admission to a museum is $10 for each adult and $5 for each child. If a group of 30 people pays a total of $175 in admission, how many adults are in the group?

You may check your work, on this section only, until time is called.

Section 6

Time—25 minutes
24 Questions

Each of the sentences below is missing one or two portions. Read each sentence, then select the word or words that most logically complete the sentence, taking into account the meaning of the sentence as a whole.

Example:

Rather than accepting the theory unquestioningly, Deborah regarded it with ———.

(A) mirth   (B) sadness
(C) responsibility   (D) ignorance
(E) skepticism

Correct response: (E)

1 The strange signal detected by the radio telescope, rather than being taken as evidence of a new cosmological phenomenon, was instead treated as merely ——— of the equipment itself.

(A) a malfunction
(B) a bulwark
(C) an anthology
(D) a mutation
(E) a transfer

2 The long-standing divisions among the indigenous ethnic groups in the region have created an ——— problem that may never be solved without international intervention.

(A) impotent   (B) intractable
(C) evanescent   (D) irate
(E) insipid

3 The ease with which the army's defenses were breached surprised the opposing general, who expected resistance to be far more ——— than it was.

(A) ephemeral
(B) compatible
(C) egregious
(D) tolerable
(E) imposing

4 Although dependence on electronic devices has ——— in recent years, the increased efficiency of common appliances has ——— the demand on the power grid.

(A) abated ... decreased
(B) surged ... attenuated
(C) increased ... compromised
(D) diminished ... reduced
(E) flourished ... elevated

5 Although persecution at the hands of ——— landowners vanquished the will of many, it ——— the dreams of revolution among the hardier insurgents.

(A) despotic ... squandered
(B) cruel ... destroyed
(C) amenable ... bore
(D) celebrated ... initiated
(E) ruthless ... forged

6

Each passage below is followed by questions based on its content. Answer each question based on what is stated or implied in the passage or the introductory material that precedes it.

Questions 6–9 are based on the following passages.

Passage 1

The following is from a recent commentary on Jean-Jacques Rousseau (1712–1778), a French philosopher during the Enlightenment.

Line Taken as a whole, Rousseau's writings
attacked the Age of Reason, gave impetus
to the Romantic movement by emphasizing
feeling (leading Goethe to say that "feeling
5   is all"), revived religion even though he had
doubts about some traditional teachings,
provided a new direction for education (his
book *Émile* was considered by some the best
work on education since Plato's *Republic*),
10   inspired the French Revolution, made a
unique impact on political philosophy,
and, more than the writing of any of his
contemporaries, influenced several
subsequent philosophers, especially
15   Immanuel Kant. On one occasion, Kant was
so absorbed in reading Rousseau's *Émile* that
he forgot to take his celebrated daily walk.
While Kant admitted that it was David Hume
who awakened him from his dogmatic
20   slumbers regarding the theory of knowledge,
it was Rousseau who showed him the way to
a new theory of morality. So impressed was
Kant by the insights of Rousseau that he
hung a picture of him on the wall of his
25   study, convinced that Rousseau was the
Newton of the moral world.

Passage 2

The roses we lay at Rousseau's feet for this
theory of Natural Rights tend to overwhelm
the less fragrant of his ideas. He persisted in
30   believing in the nobility of the primitive state
of nature, and that women's nature was to
serve men. His assertions about Natural
Rights of Man laid the philosophical
foundation of American independence, but
35   his worship of emotion over reason and of
"negative education" gave generations of
parents permission to ignore the need to
discipline and teach their children.

6 Passage 1 suggests that Goethe

(A) was at the forefront of the Age of Reason
(B) was a traditionalist
(C) was influenced by Rousseau
(D) opposed the Romantic movement
(E) inspired much of Rousseau's work

7 Passage 1 mentions Kant's "daily walk" (line 17) in order to emphasize

(A) Kant's forgetfulness
(B) Kant's commitment to healthful practices
(C) the dogmatic nature of Rousseau's writings
(D) the effect of Rousseau's philosophy on Kant
(E) Kant's close friendship with Rousseau

8 Unlike Passage 1, Passage 2 characterizes Rousseau's emphasis on emotion as

(A) insincere   (B) innovative
(C) harmful   (D) temporary
(E) necessary

9 Both passages credit Rousseau with

(A) attacking the Age of Reason
(B) inspiring revolutionary thought
(C) encouraging discipline
(D) praising the primitive state of nature
(E) establishing the Romantic movement

GO ON TO THE NEXT PAGE ▶▶▶

The questions below are based on the content of the preceding passage. The questions are to be answered on the basis of what is stated or implied in the passage itself or the introductory material that precedes the passage.

Questions 10–16 pertain to the following passage.

The following passage was written by an American essayist in 2003 about the status of capitalism.

Line   In response to a journalist's question, "What do you think about Western civilization?" Mahatma Gandhi is said to have replied, "It would be a good idea." Any honest person
5 who values the concept of the free market, who believes in the promise of open economic competition, would say the same thing about capitalism. We hear our politicians, and of course the corporate news and entertainment
10 media, speaking as if the United States were a model of free-market capitalism, as if anyone could start a business to create and sell a product or service without the obstruction of the government. The truth is
15 quite different. Those we hear saying such things are quite often voices that are bankrolled by large corporations, which themselves are often protected from competition by mutual agreement with the
20 federal government.

    The concept of free trade is simple: if Company A can produce and distribute a product more efficiently and at a higher quality than Company B, it should be allowed
25 to do so, and to charge any price for it that free consumers are willing to pay. Although Company B would likely suffer as a result, humanity would benefit from freer and cheaper access to high-quality goods.
30 Sometimes free trade works nicely, as when Company A is in the United States and Company B is in India. Then, agreements are signed to "open up" India to the cheaper goods made by Company A, even if doing so
35 crushes Company B because, we say, consumers have a right to cheap, high-quality goods. But if Company A were in India and Company B were in the United States, the story would likely be very different.

40   This isn't an idle example. India developed a pharmaceutical industry many years ago that could produce drugs very cheaply that would save tens of thousands of lives each year. In a free-market economy, the Indian
45 pharmaceutical industry would have been allowed to make drugs and get them to the people who needed them. But that would mean that western pharmaceutical companies would make less profit. Of course,
50 it's not that the American pharmaceutical companies don't care about Indian children dying because they can't get drugs; it's just that their responsibility is to their stockholders. They must maximize profits.
55 But the "free market" was getting in the way. So they simply changed the rules.

    Thus, in 1994 India "agreed" (that is, gave in to Western pressure) to "liberalize" its pharmaceutical industry by allowing its
60 largest drug companies to be sold to Western interests, thereby reducing competition. Drug prices predictably shot up, putting them out of reach of people who needed them, but the Western corporations made more money. It
65 was a big triumph for the "liberalization" of markets, but a great blow to free markets.

    In a free economy, businesses are also expected to wager their own capital on success in the marketplace. The adventurous
70 entrepreneur is a moral icon in the United States. The American pharmaceutical industry, however, receives over half a billion dollars annually in federal tax dollars in the form of research grants to develop medications
75 and vaccines that they can then patent and sell back to consumers at monopolistic prices. The legislators who sponsor these grants know that their campaigns will likely receive reciprocal monetary benefit as a
80 result. What is worse, most American voters accept this system happily because they believe that they are simply helping to find cures for diseases. The reality, however, is very different: by discouraging the
85 competition that leads to real progress, this system of protectionism is actually a huge impediment to the elimination of disease.

GO ON TO THE NEXT PAGE ▶▶▶

10 The quotation from Mahatma Gandhi (lines 3–4) suggests that Gandhi believed that Western civilization was

(A) on the decline
(B) the beneficiary of unfair economic practices
(C) antithetical to progress in Asia
(D) a great triumph
(E) an unrealized concept

11 The "voices" mentioned in line 17 can be inferred to include all of the following EXCEPT

(A) American politicians
(B) leaders like Mahatma Gandhi
(C) television journalists
(D) some leaders of large corporations
(E) those who believe that the United States is faithful to the capitalist ideal

12 The primary function of the second paragraph (lines 21–39) is to

(A) illustrate a debate
(B) provide a statistical analysis
(C) explain a concept
(D) give historical background
(E) describe a popular viewpoint

13 By saying that "the story would likely be very different" (lines 38–39), the passage suggests that

(A) the rules of a free market are selectively applied
(B) trade laws favor smaller countries
(C) American companies produce the best products
(D) Asian countries are moving away from the free market
(E) American companies share the same interests as Indian companies

14 The quotation marks around particular words in the fourth paragraph (lines 57–66) serve primarily to indicate that those words are

(A) being used ironically
(B) technical economic terms
(C) adaptations of foreign words
(D) recently coined
(E) direct quotations from a document described earlier

15 The "triumph" described in line 65 is characterized as

(A) a rare success for free markets
(B) a legislative victory
(C) a breakthrough in the development of inexpensive drugs
(D) a tragic violation of the principle of free trade
(E) a success that was based on luck

16 The passage suggests that the "entrepreneur" (line 70) differs from executives in the pharmaceutical industry in that the entrepreneur

(A) does not abide by free-market ideals
(B) risks his or her own money
(C) does not hire employees from overseas
(D) works more closely with representatives in Washington
(E) needs less money to start a typical business

GO ON TO THE NEXT PAGE ▶▶▶

Questions 17–24 pertain to the following passage.

The following passage is an excerpt from Mary Shelley's Frankenstein, *written in 1831.*

Line Natural philosophy, and particularly
chemistry, became nearly my sole occupation.
I read with ardor those works, so full of
genius and discrimination, that modern
5   inquirers have written on these subjects.
I attended the lectures and cultivated the
acquaintance of the men of science of the
university. In M. Waldman I found a true
friend. His gentleness was never tinged by
10   dogmatism, and his instructions were given
with an air of frankness and good nature that
banished every idea of pedantry. In a
thousand ways he smoothed for me the path
of knowledge and made the most abstruse
15   inquiries clear and facile to my
apprehension.
    As I applied so closely, it may be easily
conceived that my progress was rapid. My
ardor was indeed the astonishment of the
20   students, and my proficiency that of the
masters. None but those who have
experienced them can conceive of the
enticements of science. A mind of moderate
capacity which closely pursues one study
25   must infallibly arrive at great proficiency in
that study; and I, who continually sought the
attainment of one object of pursuit and was
solely wrapped up in this, improved so
rapidly that at the end of two years I made
30   some discoveries in the improvement of some
chemical instruments, which procured me
great esteem and admiration at the
university. When I had arrived at this point
and had become as well acquainted with the
35   theory and practice of natural philosophy as
depended on the lessons of any of the
professors at Ingolstadt, my residence there
being no longer conducive to my
improvements, I thought of returning to my

40   friends and my native town, when an
incident happened that protracted my stay.
    Whence, I often asked myself, did the
principle of life proceed? It was a bold
question, and one which has ever been
45   considered as a mystery; yet with how many
things are we upon the brink of becoming
acquainted, if cowardice or carelessness did
not restrain our inquiries. I revolved these
circumstances in my mind and determined
50   thenceforth to apply myself more particularly
to those branches of natural philosophy
which relate to physiology. Unless I had been
animated by an almost supernatural
enthusiasm, my application to this study
55   would have been irksome and almost
intolerable. To examine the causes of life, we
must first have recourse to death. I became
acquainted with the science of anatomy, but
this was not sufficient; I must also observe
60   the natural decay and corruption of the
human body. In my education my father had
taken the greatest precautions that my mind
should be impressed with no supernatural
horrors. I do not ever remember to have
65   trembled at a tale of superstition or to have
feared the apparition of a spirit. Darkness
had no effect upon my fancy, and a
churchyard was to me merely the receptacle
of bodies deprived of life, which, from being
70   the seat of beauty and strength, had become
food for the worm. I saw how the fine form
of man was degraded and wasted; I beheld
the corruption of death succeed to the
blooming cheek of life; I saw how the worm
75   inherited the wonders of the eye and brain.
I paused, examining and analyzing all the
minutiae of causation, as exemplified in the
change from life to death, and death to life,
until from the midst of this darkness a
80   sudden light broke in upon me—a light so
brilliant and wondrous, yet so simple, that
while I became dizzy with the immensity of
the prospect which it illustrated, I was
surprised that among so many men of genius
85   who had directed their inquiries towards the
same science, that I alone should be reserved
to discover so astonishing a secret.

GO ON TO THE NEXT PAGE ▸▸▸

17 In the first paragraph, the narrator indicates that the instruction given to him by M. Waldman was

(A) haughty
(B) challenging
(C) easily understood
(D) obscure
(E) expensive

18 In line 16, the word "apprehension" most nearly means

(A) fear
(B) reservation
(C) imprisonment
(D) understanding
(E) arrest

19 The narrator indicates that proficiency in an academic study requires which of the following?

     I. genius
     II. diligence
     III. financial resources

(A) I only
(B) II only
(C) I and II only
(D) II and III only
(E) I, II, and III

20 The narrator indicates that he considered leaving Ingolstadt because he

(A) had learned all he could from its instructors
(B) was acutely homesick
(C) was offered another job
(D) had a negative experience with a professor there
(E) had become ill

21 In saying that he was "animated by an almost supernatural enthusiasm" (lines 53–54) the narrator suggests that he

(A) was easily influenced by superstition
(B) loved lecturing at Ingolstadt
(C) was passionate about studying the physiology of life and death
(D) was excited about the prospect of returning home
(E) wanted to learn more about the origin of certain superstitions

22 The "seat of beauty and strength" (line 70) is a reference to

(A) the churchyard
(B) the human body
(C) the worm
(D) the university at Ingolstadt
(E) the narrator's studies

23 In line 73, the phrase "succeed to" most nearly means

(A) inspire   (B) thrive
(C) replace   (D) proceed to
(E) promote

24 The final sentence of the passage suggests that the narrator feels

(A) intimidated by the enormous task before him
(B) grateful to those who instructed him
(C) anxious about the moral dilemma posed by his work
(D) baffled by particular scientific principles
(E) privileged to be on the verge of a momentous discovery

STOP

You may check your work, on this section only, until time is called.

Section 7

Time—20 miinutes
16 Questions

1 Which of the following integers is 2 greater than a multiple of 7?

(A) 14
(B) 15
(C) 16
(D) 17
(E) 18

2 A store sells oranges for 20 cents each, but for every 4 oranges you buy, you may buy a fifth for only 5 cents. How many oranges can you buy from this store for $3.40?

(A) 14
(B) 17
(C) 18
(D) 19
(E) 20

3 If r is a positive number and s is a negative number, all of the following must represent positive numbers EXCEPT:

(A) $-r + s$
(B) $r - s$
(C) $\dfrac{r}{s^2}$
(D) rs^2
(E) $(rs)^2$

4 Which of the following expresses the number that is 12 less than the product of 3 and $x + 1$?

(A) $x - 8$
(B) $x + 37$
(C) $3x - 11$
(D) $3x - 9$
(E) $3x + 15$

GO ON TO THE NEXT PAGE ▶▶▶

5 One bag of grass seed covers 5,000 square feet. If each bag costs $25, how much will it cost to buy enough grass seed to cover a square area that is 200 feet by 200 feet?

(A) $25
(B) $100
(C) $200
(D) $1,000
(E) $2,000

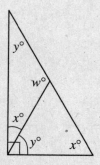

Note: Figure not drawn to scale.

6 In the right triangle above, what is the value of w?

(A) 30
(B) 60
(C) 90
(D) 120
(E) 150

7 Three integers have a sum of 7 and a product of 0. If the difference of the greatest number and the least numbers is 11, then the least of these numbers is

(A) −18
(B) −11
(C) −9
(D) −2
(E) 0

8 Four points lie on a circle. How many different triangles can be drawn with 3 of these points as vertices?

(A) 4
(B) 5
(C) 6
(D) 7
(E) 8

9 If a, b, and c are consecutive positive integers such that $a < b < c$ and abc is NOT a multiple of 4, then which of the following must be true?

(A) a is even
(B) b is even
(C) c is even
(D) $a + b + c$ is odd
(E) abc is odd

Questions 10–12 refer to the following graph.

PARTICIPATION IN FUND RAISER
FOR 5 CLASSES

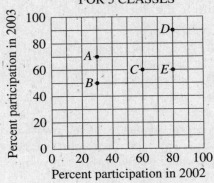

10 For which class was the change in percent participation the greatest from 2002 to 2003?

(A) A
(B) B
(C) C
(D) D
(E) E

11 If class *B* and class *E* each had 100 students in 2002 and 2003, then, in total, how many more students participated in the fund raiser from class *E* than from class *B* over the 2 years?

(A) 10
(B) 20
(C) 30
(D) 40
(E) 60

12 In 2002, the same number of students participated in the fund raiser from class *C* as from class *D*. If class *D* contained 120 students in 2002, how many students were there in class *C* in 2002?

(A) 90
(B) 100
(C) 120
(D) 140
(E) 160

13 If $x = -1$ is a solution of the equation $x^2 = 4x + c$ where c is a constant, what is another value of x that satisfies the equation?

(A) −5
(B) −2
(C) 1
(D) 2
(E) 5

14 1, 2, 6, 7, 9 A three-digit integer is to be formed from the digits listed above. If the first digit must be odd, either the second or the third digit must be 2, and no digit may be repeated, how many such integers are possible?

(A) 6
(B) 9
(C) 18
(D) 24
(E) 30

15 If 1 pound of grain can feed 5 chickens or 2 pigs, then 10 pounds of grain can feed 20 chickens and how many pigs?

(A) 8
(B) 10
(C) 12
(D) 24
(E) 40

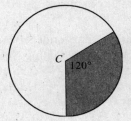

16 Point *C* is the center of the circle on the figure above. The shaded region has an area of 3π square centimeters. What is the *perimeter* of the shaded region in centimeters?

(A) $2\pi + 6$
(B) $2\pi + 9$
(C) $2\pi + 12$
(D) $3\pi + 6$
(E) $3\pi + 12$

You may check your work, on this section only, until time is called.

Section 8

Time—20 minutes
19 Questions

> Each of the sentences below is missing one or two portions. Read each sentence, then select the word or words that most logically complete the sentence, taking into account the meaning of the sentence as a whole.
>
> Example:
>
> Rather than accepting the theory unquestioningly, Deborah regarded it with ———.
>
> (A) mirth   (B) sadness
> (C) responsibility (D) ignorance
> (E) skepticism
>
> **Correct response: (E)**

8 ➤

1 The studio's most recent movies reflect a ——— of many different artistic visions rather than the ——— of a single director.

(A) conglomeration ... insubordination
(B) prudence ... unity
(C) bastion ... despair
(D) synthesis ... dominance
(E) conspiracy ... retreat

2 Rather than endeavoring to write timeless fiction with lasting value, many novelists cater to the ——— tastes of those modern readers who read a book once and then discard it.

(A) immoral   (B) fleeting
(C) valuable   (D) solid
(E) intellectual

3 Although many investors may tolerate short-term declines in the value of their securities, few will accept a ——— downturn in the stock market.

(A) protracted
(B) contemporaneous
(C) transient
(D) surreptitious
(E) fickle

4 In most societies, athletes are ——— in the same way that successful warriors were celebrated by civilizations in years past.

(A) invoked   (B) repudiated
(C) lionized   (D) vilified
(E) beguiled

5 Dobson's overconfident and arrogant manner during press conferences was beginning to irritate his associates; there was no need to be ——— about the success of an endeavor that had yet to be launched.

(A) superficial   (B) capricious
(C) pious   (D) deferential
(E) supercilious

6 Although few literary critics approved of her criticism of the ——— society in which she lived, Virginia Woolf remained a ——— opponent of the male hegemony that hindered women's pursuit of professional and artistic success.

(A) matriarchal ... pugnacious
(B) patriarchal ... vociferous
(C) avuncular ... belligerent
(D) prejudiced ... rudimentary
(E) liberal ... negligent

GO ON TO THE NEXT PAGE ▸▸▸

The passages below are followed by questions based on their content and the relationship between the passages. The questions are to be answered on the basis of what is stated or implied in the passages themselves or the introductory material that precedes them.

Questions 7–19 pertain to the following passages.

The following are 2 essays on the American English spelling reform movement. Passage 1 was written in 1906 by the humorist Ellis Parker Butler. Passage 2 was written by a modern American writer in 2003.

Passage I

Line My own opinion of the spelling profession is
that it has nothing to do with genius, except
to kill it. I know that Shakespeare was a
promiscuous sort of speller, even as to his
5 own name, and no one can deny that he was
a greater genius than Noah Webster. The
reason America so long lagged behind
Europe in the production of genius is that
America, for many decades, was the slave of
10 the spelling-book. No man who devotes the
fiery days of his youth to learning to spell has
time to be a genius.

Serena says, and I agree with her, that it is
the jealousy of a few college professors who
15 are trying to undermine the younger writers.
They know that it is excusable to spell
incorrectly now, but they want this new
phonetic spelling brought into use so that
there shall be no excuse for bad spelling, and
20 that then, Serena says, self-made authors like
me, who never can spell but who simply
blaze with genius, will be hooted out of the
magazines to make room for a stupid sort of
literature that is spelled correctly. Serena
25 looks upon the whole thing as a direct,
personal stab at me. I look at it more
philosophically.

To me it seems that the spelling reformers
are entirely on the wrong track. Their
30 proposed changes are almost a revolution,
and we Americans do not like sudden
changes. We like our revolutions to come
about gradually. Think how gradually
automobiles have come to pass. If, in our
35 horse age, the streets had suddenly been
covered with sixty horsepower snorters going

thirty miles an hour and smelling like an
eighteenth-century literary debate, and killing
people right and left, we Americans would
40 have arisen and destroyed every vestige
of the automobile. But the automobile came
gradually—first the bicycle, then the
motorcycle, and so, by stages, to the present
monsters. So slowly and progressively did the
45 automobile increase in size and number that
it seemed a matter of course. We take to
being killed by the automobile quite naturally
now.

Of course, the silent letters in our words
50 are objectionable. They are lazy letters. We
want no idle class in America, whether
tramp, aristocrat, or silent letter, but we do
not kill the tramp and the aristocrat. We set
them to work, or we would like to. My theory
55 of spelling reform is to set the idle letters to
work.

Take that prime offender, *although*. *Altho*
does all the work, and *ugh* sits on the fence
and whittles. I would put *ugh* to work. *Ugh* is
60 a syllable in itself. I would have the *ugh*
follow the pronounced *altho* as a third
syllable. Doubtless the asthmatic islanders
who concocted our English language actually
pronounced it so.

65 I propose to have some millionaire endow
my plan, and Serena and I will then form
a society for the reforming of English
pronunciation. I will not punch out the *i*
of any chief, nor shall any one drag *me* from
70 any programme, however dull. I will
pronounce *programme* as it should be
pronounced— *programmy*—and, as for *chief*,
he shall be pronounced *chy-ef*.

The advantage of this plan is manifest. It is
75 so manifest that I am afraid it will never be
It is so adopted.

Serena's plan is, perhaps, less intellectual,
but more American. Serena's plan is to ignore
all words that contain superfluous letters.
80 She would simply boycott them. Serena
would have people get along with such words
as are already phonetically spelled. Why
should people write *although*, when they can
write *notwithstanding that*, and not have a
85 silent letter in it? I have myself often written
a phrase twelve words long to stand instead
of a single word I did not know how to spell.
In fact, I abandoned my Platonic friendship
for Serena, and replaced it with ardent love,

GO ON TO THE NEXT PAGE ▸▸▸

90   because I did know how to spell *sweetheart,*
but could not remember whether she was my
friend or *freind.*

Passage 2

For centuries, thinkers as notable as
Benjamin Franklin have registered the
95   same complaint about English spelling: it is
needlessly complicated and inconsistent in
pronunciation. Silent letters abound, and
ough is pronounced six different ways in the
words *tough, bough, through, bought, although,*
100   and *cough.* Franklin wanted to change the
alphabet and institute new spelling rules to
make English more sensible, more usable,
and easier to learn. Such good ideas have
been around a long time, and we should put
105   them to rest for three good reasons.

First, English, like most languages, has
dialects. In Boston, *Korea* and *career* are
homophones. In San Francisco, they are not.
To spell them the same way would be to
110   impose a "preferred" dialect on all
Americans, forcing us all to talk like South
Enders and violating our precious value of
democracy over elitism. Failure to do so
would result in chaos. Would a novelist from
115   Alabama who was educated at Brown write
in her native drawl, her adopted New
England dialect, or the homogenized English
of the educated elite? In a democratic society,
isn't one of the great benefits of a language-
120   wide spelling system that it obscures those
spoken dialects that are so often used to
stratify and separate us?

Second, languages evolve, adopting words
from other languages, coining new ones, and
125   changing pronunciations over time. The
silent letters in the word *eight,* a bane of the
"rational" speller, are the echoes of the
German *acht,* the Latin *octo,* the Greek *okto*
and even (faintly) the Sanskrit *asta.* The
130   spelling may be vexing to some, but it is a
historical treasure trove to others. Furthermore,
this example shows the folly of trying to
standardize spelling by linking it with
pronunciation. The words won't stand still.
135   Third, languages are not influenced very
much by plan or reason; they develop by
evolving conventions of usage. They are
cultural artifacts, not legislated standards.
Spelling is like football: there may be lots of
140   silly and illogical things in it, but that doesn't
mean you have a snowball's chance in hell of
replacing the rules.

7   In the first paragraph of Passage 1, Noah
Webster is mentioned as an example of

(A)   a genius who was a poor speller
(B)   one of the first spelling reformers
(C)   a man devoted to proper spelling
(D)   a famous playwright
(E)   one who shares the author's opinion

8   Serena regards phonetic spelling as a
"personal stab" (line 26) at the author of
Passage 1 because its proponents

(A)   have a history of vindictiveness
(B)   do not like hard work
(C)   are well educated
(D)   are wealthy
(E)   want to eliminate the author's excuse
     for poor spelling

9   The success of "Serena's plan" (line 77)
depends on the ability of people to

(A)   change their habits of pronunciation
(B)   spell correctly
(C)   perfect their handwriting skills
(D)   learn an entirely new alphabet
(E)   change their writing habits

10   By saying that Serena's plan is "more
American" (line 78), the author of Passage 1
implies that Americans

(A)   are good spellers
(B)   regard writers with disdain
(C)   are inclined to protest
(D)   do not read enough
(E)   can't take a joke

11   In Passage 1, the author's theory of spelling
reform differs from that of Serena in that
the author

(A)   wants to alter the pronunciation of
     words that Serena wants to ignore
(B)   regards Shakespeare as a genius but
     Serena does not
(C)   wants to change the alphabet but
     Serena does not
(D)   seeks to simplify spelling, while
     Serena does not
(E)   understands how to alter American
     habits but Serena does not

12 The author of Passage 1 claims to have fallen in love with Serena because

(A) his spelling skills were weak
(B) they agreed on a plan for phonetic spelling
(C) she helped him to understand philosophy
(D) they shared a distaste for automobiles
(E) they were both writers

13 The "chaos" mentioned in line 114 refers to

(A) the difficulty of spelling words with silent letters
(B) the challenge of getting scholars to agree
(C) the many ways of pronouncing *ough*
(D) the possibility of many sets of spelling rules for different dialects
(E) the disagreement among linguists regarding spelling reform

14 According to Passage 2, "one of the great benefits of a language-wide spelling system" (lines 119–120) is that it

(A) simplifies commonly misspelled words
(B) discourages social distinctions implied by pronunciation
(C) eliminates silent letters
(D) makes it easier to translate words from English to other languages
(E) imposes a preferred dialect

15 Passage 2 mentions the word "eight" as an example of

(A) a word with a spelling that is edifying to some
(B) a commonly mispronounced word
(C) a word with a spelling that the author believes should be simplified
(D) a recently coined term
(E) a word that has remained unchanged for centuries

16 The tone of the two passages differs in that Passage 1 is

(A) jocular, whereas Passage 2 is logical
(B) cynical, whereas Passage 2 is whimsical
(C) analytical, whereas Passage 2 is lighthearted
(D) scientific, whereas Passage 2 is satirical
(E) strident, whereas Passage 2 is reflective

17 With which of the following statements would the authors of both passages most likely agree?

(A) The rules of English spelling need to be changed.
(B) Modern conventions of grammar are illogical.
(C) Americans are lazy.
(D) Conventions of language are not easily changed.
(E) Writers should read widely to perfect their craft.

8

18 If the author of Passage 1 were serious about his plan for reforming English pronunciation, the author of Passage 2 would likely regard that plan as

(A) a necessary addition to phonetic spelling
(B) a logical alternative to the current system
(C) inferior to the plan for phonetic spelling
(D) unworkable because it disregards the way that conventions of language develop
(E) a more plausible plan than Serena's

19 In both passages, the word "although" is regarded as

(A) a word that is commonly mispronounced
(B) a word that is difficult to spell
(C) an example of an idiosyncracy of English that some consider problematic
(D) a word that reveals much about the development of the English language
(E) a word that can easily be eliminated from the English language

STOP

You may check your work, on this section only, until time is called.

Section 9

Time—10 minutes
14 Questions

Directions for "Improving Sentences" Questions

Each of the sentences below contains one underlined portion. The portion may contain one or more errors in grammar, usage, construction, precision, diction (choice of words), or idiom. Some of the sentences are correct.

Consider the meaning of the original sentence, and choose the answer that best expresses that meaning. If the original sentence is best, choose (A), because it repeats the original phrasing. Choose the phrasing that creates the clearest, most precise, and most effective sentence.

EXAMPLE:

The children <u>couldn't hardly believe their eyes</u>.

  (A)   couldn't hardly believe their eyes
  (B)   would not hardly believe their eyes
  (C)   could hardly believe their eyes
  (D)   couldn't nearly believe their eyes
  (E)   could hardly believe his or her eyes

Example answer: (C)

---

1   <u>The chef's assistant cut the vegetables and laid them on the table, he</u> then started to prepare the meat.

  (A)   The chef's assistant cut the vegetables and laid them on the table, he
  (B)   The vegetables were cut and laid on the table by the chef's assistant when he
  (C)   After cutting the vegetables and laying them on the table, the chef's assistant
  (D)   The chef's assistant, having cut the vegetables and laying them on the table,
  (E)   Laying on the table, the chef's assistant who cut the vegetables

2   Practicing their rebuttals ahead of time <u>helps the forensics team members to become a better debater</u>.

  (A)   helps the forensics team member to become a better debater
  (B)   helps forensic team members to become better debaters
  (C)   helping the forensics team members to become better debaters
  (D)   is helpful to the forensics team members who become better debaters
  (E)   the forensics team member becomes a better debater

3   *Billy the Bobcat,* <u>like other children's stories, have</u> elements that can only be fully appreciated by adults.

  (A)   like other children's stories have
  (B)   like other children's stories, has
  (C)   a children's story, like others, has
  (D)   is like other stories for children in that they have
  (E)   like that of other children's stories, has also

4   Ernest Rutherford, <u>a New Zealand scientist when measuring the charge and mass of alpha particles</u>, discovered that they are virtually identical to the nuclei of helium atoms.

  (A)   a New Zealand scientist when measuring the charge and mass of alpha particles,
  (B)   a New Zealand scientist who measured the charge and mass of alpha particles
  (C)   a New Zealand scientist which measured the charge and mass of alpha particles,
  (D)   measuring the charge and mass of alpha particles, was a scientist when he
  (E)   being the one who measured the mass and charge of alpha particles as a scientist

GO ON TO THE NEXT PAGE ▶▶▶

5 Oxytocin is the hormone that triggers uterine contractions during <u>labor, as well as</u> the preliminary contractions known as Braxton Hicks.

(A)   labor, as well as
(B)   labor, as well as being the hormone that triggers
(C)   labor, causing as well
(D)   labor; and also causes
(E)   labor; also causing

6 During the Clinton presidency, <u>the U.S. enjoyed more than any time in its history peace and economic well being</u>.

(A)   the U.S. enjoyed more than any time in its history peace and economic well being
(B)   the U.S. enjoying more than any other time in its history peace and economic well being
(C)   more peace and economic well being was enjoyed by the U.S. than any other time
(D)   economic peace and well being was enjoyed by the U.S. more so than any other time in the country's history
(E)   the U.S. enjoyed more peace and economic well being than at any other time in its history

7 The final three months of the year tend to be profitable for technology companies <u>because of increased consumer demand being around the holidays</u>.

(A)   because of increased consumer demand being around the holidays
(B)   because of increasing consumer demand occurs around the holidays
(C)   an increased consumer demand around the holidays makes it so
(D)   because consumer demand increases around the holidays
(E)   because the increased consumer demand is what occurs around the holidays

8 As his moviemaking career began to wane, Jerry Lewis remained in the public eye by hosting a variety show and <u>on an annual telethon with benefits for the Muscular Dystrophy Association</u>.

(A)   on an annual telethon with benefits for the Muscular Dystrophy Association
(B)   an annual telethon with benefits to the Muscular Dystrophy Association
(C)   benefiting the Muscular Dystrophy Association with his annual telethon
(D)   an annual telethon benefiting the Muscular Dystrophy Association
(E)   the Muscular Dystrophy Association with an annual telethon

9 The development of bebop is attributed in large part to Dizzy Gillespie and also saxophonist Charlie Parker; <u>and their unique styles helped to contribute to and typified the bebop sound</u>.

(A)   and their unique styles helped to contribute to and typified the bebop sound
(B)   their unique styles contributed to and typified the bebop sound
(C)   it was their unique styles that contributed to and were typifying the bebop sound
(D)   but their unique styles helped contribute to the typical bebop sound
(E)   the bebop sound was helped by the contributions of their unique styles and typified it

10 Many critics believe that video games <u>are harmful to children that contain violent imagery</u>.

(A)   are harmful to children that contain violent imagery
(B)   containing violent imagery are harmful to children
(C)   that contain violent imagery that harms children
(D)   containing violent imagery that are harmful to children
(E)   harmful to children containing violent imagery

GO ON TO THE NEXT PAGE ▶▶▶

11 Walking hand-in-hand along the boardwalk, <u>a vendor stopped the couple to try to sell them lemonade</u>.

(A) a vendor stopped the couple to try to sell them lemonade

(B) the couple was stopped by a vendor who tried to sell them lemonade

(C) trying to sell them lemonade, a vendor stopped the couple

(D) a vendor stopped the couple to try and sell them lemonade

(E) the couple having been stopped by the vendor who tried to sell them lemonade

12 Professor Peterson had just stepped into the classroom <u>and that was when he discovered</u> that several lab manuals were missing.

(A) and that was when he found out

(B) and then he discovered

(C) when he discovered

(D) after which he discovered

(E) discovering soon thereafter

9 ➤

13 Parents today spend more time working <u>than</u> 30 years ago.

(A) than

(B) than have

(C) than of the parents of

(D) than did parents

(E) than of the parents

14 The anthropologists would have considered their research a success <u>if they would have found a language that shares lexical elements with the Borneans they were studying</u>.

(A) if they would have found a language that shares lexical elements with the Borneans they were studying

(B) had they found a language that shares lexical elements with that of the Borneans they were studying

(C) if they found a language that shares lexical elements with the Borneans they were studying

(D) if they had found a language that shares lexical elements with the Borneans they were studying

(E) if they would have found a language that shares lexical elements with that of the Borneans they were studying

STOP

You may check your work, on this section only, until time is called.

ANSWER KEY

Section 2 Math	Section 5 Math	Section 7 Math	Section 3 Critical Reading	Section 6 Critical Reading	Section 8 Critical Reading	Section 4 Writing	Section 9 Writing
☐ 1. E	☐ 1. E	☐ 1. C	☐ 1. A	☐ 1. A	☐ 1. D	☐ 1. A	☐ 1. C
☐ 2. B	☐ 2. D	☐ 2. E	☐ 2. C	☐ 2. B	☐ 2. B	☐ 2. E	☐ 2. B
☐ 3. E	☐ 3. C	☐ 3. A	☐ 3. A	☐ 3. E	☐ 3. A	☐ 3. B	☐ 3. B
☐ 4. D	☐ 4. A	☐ 4. D	☐ 4. D	☐ 4. B	☐ 4. C	☐ 4. C	☐ 4. B
☐ 5. C	☐ 5. B	☐ 5. C	☐ 5. B	☐ 5. E	☐ 5. E	☐ 5. D	☐ 5. A
☐ 6. D	☐ 6. A	☐ 6. C	☐ 6. E	☐ 6. C	☐ 6. B	☐ 6. C	☐ 6. E
☐ 7. E	☐ 7. C	☐ 7. D	☐ 7. B	☐ 7. D	☐ 7. C	☐ 7. A	☐ 7. D
☐ 8. D	☐ 8. A	☐ 8. A	☐ 8. C	☐ 8. C	☐ 8. E	☐ 8. B	☐ 8. D
☐ 9. E	☐ 9. 7.5	☐ 9. B	☐ 9. A	☐ 9. D	☐ 9. E	☐ 9. B	☐ 9. B
☐ 10. B	☐ 10. 13	☐ 10. A	☐ 10. D	☐ 10. E	☐ 10. C	☐ 10. E	☐ 10. B
☐ 11. A	☐ 11. 100	☐ 11. E	☐ 11. E	☐ 11. B	☐ 11. A	☐ 11. E	☐ 11. B
☐ 12. E	☐ 12. 24	☐ 12. E	☐ 12. B	☐ 12. C	☐ 12. A	☐ 12. D	☐ 12. C
☐ 13. D	☐ 13. 0.2	☐ 13. E	☐ 13. C	☐ 13. A	☐ 13. D	☐ 13. B	☐ 13. D
☐ 14. B	or 1/5	☐ 14. C	☐ 14. A	☐ 14. A	☐ 14. B	☐ 14. D	☐ 14. B
☐ 15. A	☐ 14. 4	☐ 15. C	☐ 15. D	☐ 15. D	☐ 15. A	☐ 15. D	
☐ 16. C	☐ 15. 0.8	☐ 16. A	☐ 16. B	☐ 16. B	☐ 16. A	☐ 16. E	
☐ 17. C	☐ 16. 5		☐ 17. A	☐ 17. C	☐ 17. C	☐ 17. C	
☐ 18. C	☐ 17. 9		☐ 18. A	☐ 18. D	☐ 18. D	☐ 18. B	
☐ 19. E	☐ 18. 10		☐ 19. D	☐ 19. B	☐ 19. C	☐ 19. C	
☐ 20. C			☐ 20. C	☐ 20. A		☐ 20. B	
			☐ 21. B	☐ 21. C		☐ 21. E	
			☐ 22. C	☐ 22. B		☐ 22. C	
			☐ 23. E	☐ 23. C		☐ 23. C	
			☐ 24. D	☐ 24. E		☐ 24. E	
						☐ 25. B	
						☐ 26. C	
						☐ 27. E	
						☐ 28. A	
						☐ 29. C	
						☐ 30. A	
						☐ 31. B	
						☐ 32. B	
						☐ 33. D	
						☐ 34. E	
						☐ 35. A	

# Right (A):	Questions 1–8 # Right (A):	# Right (A):	# Right (A):	# Right (A):	# Right (A):	# Right (A)	# Right (A):
# Wrong (B):	# Wrong (B):	# Wrong (B):	# Wrong (B):	# Wrong (B):	# Wrong (B):	# Wrong (B):	# Wrong (B):
# (A) − 1/4 (B):	# (A) − 1/4 (B):	# (A) − 1/4 (B):	# (A) − 1/4 (B):	# (A) − 1/4 (B):	# (A) − 1/4 (B):	# (A) − 1/4 (B):	# (A) − 1/4 (B):

Questions 9–18
Right (A):

SCORE CONVERSION TABLE

How to score your test

Use the answer key on the previous page to determine your raw score on each section. **Your raw score on each section except Section 5 is simply the number of correct answers minus ¼ of the number of wrong answers. On Section 5, your raw score is the sum of the number of correct answers for questions 1–18 minus ¼ of the number of wrong answers for questions 1–8.** Next, add the raw scores from Sections 3, 4, and 7 to get your Math raw score, and add the raw scores from Sections 6 and 9 to get your Writing raw score. Write the three raw scores here:

Raw Critical Reading score: _____　　Raw Math score: _____　　Raw Writing score: _____

Use the table below to convert these to scaled scores.

Scaled scores:　　Critical Reading: _____　　Math: _____　　Writing: _____

Raw Score	Critical Reading Scaled Score	Math Scaled Score	Writing Scaled Score	Raw Score	Critical Reading Scaled Score	Math Scaled Score	Writing Scaled Score
67	800			32	520	550	610
66	800			31	510	550	600
65	790			30	510	540	580
64	780			29	500	530	570
63	760			28	490	530	560
62	750			27	490	520	550
61	730			26	480	510	540
60	720			25	480	500	530
59	700			24	470	490	520
58	700			23	460	480	510
57	690			22	460	480	500
56	680			21	450	470	490
55	670			20	440	460	480
54	660	800		19	440	450	470
53	650	790		18	430	450	460
52	650	760		17	420	440	450
51	640	740		16	420	430	440
50	630	720		15	410	420	440
49	620	710	800	14	400	410	430
48	620	700	800	13	400	410	420
47	610	680	800	12	390	400	410
46	600	670	790	11	380	390	400
45	600	660	780	10	370	380	390
44	590	650	760	9	360	370	380
43	590	640	740	8	350	360	380
42	580	630	730	7	340	350	370
41	570	630	710	6	330	340	360
40	570	620	700	5	320	330	350
39	560	610	690	4	310	320	340
38	550	600	670	3	300	310	320
37	550	590	660	2	280	290	310
36	540	580	650	1	270	280	300
35	540	580	640	0	250	260	280
34	530	570	630	−1	230	240	270
33	520	560	620	−2 or less	210	220	250

SCORE CONVERSION TABLE FOR WRITING COMPOSITE
[ESSAY + MULTIPLE CHOICE]

Calculate your writing raw score as you did on the previous page and grade your essay from a 1 to a 6 according to the standards that follow in the detailed answer key.

Essay score: _____ Raw Writing score: _____

Use the table below to convert these to scaled scores.

Scaled score: Writing: _____

Raw Score	Essay Score 0	Essay Score 1	Essay Score 2	Essay Score 3	Essay Score 4	Essay Score 5	Essay Score 6
−2 or less	280	230	250	280	310	340	370
−1	210	240	260	290	320	360	380
0	230	260	280	300	340	370	400
1	240	270	290	320	350	380	410
2	250	280	300	330	360	390	420
3	260	290	310	340	370	400	430
4	270	300	320	350	380	410	440
5	280	310	330	360	390	420	450
6	290	320	340	360	400	430	460
7	290	330	340	370	410	440	470
8	300	330	350	380	410	450	470
9	310	340	360	390	420	450	480
10	320	350	370	390	430	460	490
11	320	360	370	400	440	470	500
12	330	360	380	410	440	470	500
13	340	370	390	420	450	480	510
14	350	380	390	420	460	490	520
15	350	380	400	430	460	500	530
16	360	390	410	440	470	500	530
17	370	400	420	440	480	510	540
18	380	410	420	450	490	520	550
19	380	410	430	460	490	530	560
20	390	420	440	470	500	530	560
21	400	430	450	480	510	540	570
22	410	440	460	480	520	550	580
23	420	450	470	490	530	560	590
24	420	460	470	500	540	570	600
25	430	460	480	510	540	580	610
26	440	470	490	520	550	590	610
27	450	480	500	530	560	590	620
28	460	490	510	540	570	600	630
29	470	500	520	550	580	610	640
30	480	510	530	560	590	620	650
31	490	520	540	560	600	630	660
32	500	530	570	570	610	640	670
33	510	540	580	580	620	650	680
34	510	550	560	590	630	660	690
35	520	560	570	600	640	670	700
36	530	560	580	610	650	680	710
37	540	570	590	620	660	690	720
38	550	580	600	630	670	700	730
39	560	600	610	640	680	710	740
40	580	610	620	650	690	720	750
41	590	620	640	660	700	730	760
42	600	630	650	680	710	740	770
43	610	640	660	690	720	750	780
44	620	660	670	700	740	770	800
45	640	670	690	720	750	780	800
46	650	690	700	730	770	800	800
47	670	700	720	750	780	800	800
48	680	720	730	760	800	800	800
49	680	720	730	760	800	800	800

Detailed Answer Key

Section 1

The following essay received 12 points out of a possible 12, meaning that it demonstrates *clear and consistent competence* in that it

- develops an insightful point of view on the topic
- demonstrates exemplary critical thinking
- uses effective examples, reasons, and other evidence to support its thesis
- is consistently focused, coherent, and well-organized
- demonstrates skillful and effective use of language and sentence structure
- is largely (but not necessarily completely) free of grammatical and usage errors

Consider carefully the issue discussed in the following passage, then write an essay that answers the question posed in the assignment.

> An entertainment-driven culture runs the risk of encouraging passivity among its citizens. If they can experience something vicariously through a movie, television show or video game, why should they get involved with the activity itself? It's safer, after all, to watch someone scale a mountain than to do it yourself. The effect of this passivity, of course, is an apathetic frame of mind. We cease to care deeply about so many things because they are experienced, at best, second-hand.

Assignment: **Is apathy a problem in today's society?** Write an essay in which you answer this question and discuss your point of view on this issue. Support your position logically with examples from literature, the arts, history, politics, science and technology, current events, or your experience or observation.

SAMPLE STUDENT ESSAY

Every society seems to have platitudes about laziness, like "idle hands are the devil's workshop." This is because, to a society, the value of an individual is little more than his or her productivity. For many people, the worst kind of laziness is apathy, being too lazy to even care. But the fact is that we couldn't survive if we cared about everything that was worth caring about. We would go insane. Furthermore, those who complain about apathy are usually the great manipulators of the world, trying to blame others for their own failures.

Holden Caulfield seemed to be apathetic to his teachers at Pencey Prep. But he was far from apathetic; indeed, he probably cared too much. His brother's death and the suicide of a classmate affected him deeply, although he had trouble articulating his grief. He saw what the adults in his world seemed unable to see: the hypocrisy and meanness in the world. If he didn't get away from the things that the teachers and other adults wanted him to care about, he probably would have gone crazy. Indeed, those adults thought he was crazy, but to Holden, it was the hypocritical world that was mad. His desperation to protect himself from the unbearable "phoniness" in the world led him, ironically, to often be phony himself. He hated his own hypocrisy, but he had to experience it to understand it. What others saw as apathy and cynicism was just his way of making it in the world.

Holden was quick to see that those who complained about his laziness and apathy were just the ones who wanted to control him because they couldn't control their own lives. Teachers too often assume that, if their students aren't "performing," they must be lazy and apathetic. "You're so smart. You would do well if you would just apply yourself." Teachers see this kind of comment as supporting, but it is supremely degrading, and it covers up the teachers' inability to inspire or even understand their students.

Some people even go so far as to assume that entire societies are lazy or apathetic, simply because they do not share their same sensibilities or "productivity," failing to see that productivity is often the product, not just of hard work, but of material and logistical advantage. I don't have to work as hard, for instance, to be "productive" as a teenager in rural China, because I have free access to a computer, the internet, a local library, and helpful adult professionals. The Chinese teenager might be far more intelligent, diligent and resourceful than I, but far less "productive."

Perhaps a sign of maturity and virtue in a society is the degree to which it values its citizens independently of their "productivity." Every human being desires to build a better world in his or her own way. Sometimes that way does not involve making more money, getting better grades, or doing what society has established as "productive."

The following essay received 8 points out of a possible 12, meaning that it demonstrates *adequate competence* in that it

- develops a point of view on the topic
- demonstrates some critical thinking, but perhaps not consistently
- uses some examples, reasons, and other evidence to support its thesis, but perhaps not adequately
- shows a general organization and focus, but shows occasional lapses in this regard
- demonstrates adequate but occasionally inconsistent facility with language
- contains occasional errors in grammar, usage, and mechanics

---

SAMPLE STUDENT ESSAY

The greatest danger to the modern world is not terrorists who have been indoctrinated into a twisted world view, but the masses of people who are indifferent to them, or even sympathize with them. "Live and let live," so many people say. "They have a right to their point of view that women are animals and that someone who speaks against their religion should have his tongue cut out. That is just their way of thinking." This apathy to the dangers of the world is even more dangerous than the terrorists themselves.

In Madrid, a band of Al Qaeda terrorists decided that it was a good idea, in March of 2004, to blow up 200 innocent commuters on a train so that they could influence the upcoming elections in Spain. They proclaimed that they love death more than westerners love life. They were hoping that the Spanish people would then be so frightened that they would elect a leader who would take Spain's troops out of Iraq, as Al Qaeda wished. And that is exactly what happened.

The people of Spain didn't care enough to realize that they were doing exactly what the terrorists were hoping they would do. The voters of Spain probably believed that they were making it less likely that the terrorists would strike again, but it was probably the exact opposite. The terrorists love to know that their violence scares people, and the Spanish people gave them what they wanted. Contrast this with the American response to terrorism: zero tolerance.

The worst evil occurs when good people do nothing. Millions of supposedly "good" German people sat on their hands as millions of "unwanted" Jews, gays and foreigners were slaughtered. Now, millions of people sit on their hands as religious fanatics look at the slaughter of innocent people as their ticket to paradise. It is unreasonable to believe that those with warped hatred of western cultures will stop their hatred and their evil deeds merely because they are appeased by weak governments.

The following essay received 4 points out of a possible 12, meaning that it demonstrates *some incompetence* in that it

- has a seriously limited point of view
- demonstrates weak critical thinking
- uses inappropriate or insufficient examples, reasons, and other evidence to support its thesis
- is poorly focused and organized, and has serious problems with coherence
- demonstrates frequent problems with language and sentence structure
- contains errors in grammar and usage that obscure the author's meaning seriously

SAMPLE STUDENT ESSAY

When people don't care about something, it's hard to get anything done. If a team has players that don't really want to play, for instance, it's almost impossible to get them to win a game, even if you're a master motivator. That's why it's so important to care about things and not have apathy.

If you don't care about something, also, it's just really difficult to be happy. You don't have anything to look forward to in life. Some people don't really care about school, and they just listen to their iPods and can't wait to hang out with their friends or play their XBoxes when they get home. College doesn't mean anything to them, and you can tell that they are miserable people. It's one thing to question your teachers and wonder whether the things you learn in school are relevant for your life, but it's entirely different to not even care about what you do in school even a little bit.

Research has shown that you can't really get anywhere without an education, so if you don't care about school you might as well not care about having any kind of successful life. If they would just find something important that they could care about, like a sport or a musical instrument or a job or something like that, then they might have something they could focus there life for, and have some positive purpose in life. Criminals probably come about because early on they didn't really learn to care about anything important, and that is the real tragedy and foreigners were slaughtered. Now, millions of people sit on their hands as religious fanatics look at the slaughter of innocent people as their ticket to paradise. It is unreasonable to believe that those with warped hatred of western cultures will stop their hatred and their evil deeds merely because they are appeased by weak governments.

Detailed Answer Key

Section 2

1. **E**   Just substitute 3 for x:

	$5x = 3x + y$
Substitute:	$5(3) = 3(3) + y$
Simplify:	$15 = 9 + y$
Subtract 9:	$6 = y$

2. **B**   To buy 48 batteries in packages of 24, you will need two packages, which will cost $2(\$12) = \$24$. To buy them in packages of 6, you will need 8 packages, which will cost $8(\$4) = \$32$. Buying in packages of 24 will save $\$32 - \$24 = \$8$.

3. **E**   You can probably solve this one best by quickly graphing each point and just inspecting. Clearly, (5, 5) lies outside the region.

4. **D**   Interpret the statement as an equation:

$$(\tfrac{1}{3})(2x) = 5$$

Multiply by 2: $(\tfrac{2}{3})(2x) = 10$

Multiply by 2: $(\tfrac{2}{3})(4x) = 20$

5. **C**   The smallest positive integer that is divisible by 12 and 16 is 48. If n is 48, the only factor among the choices is (C) 48.

6. **D**   The sum of the angles in a triangle is 180°, so

	$a + b + 40 = 180$
Subtract 40:	$a + b = 140$
Add the given equation:	$\underline{\ + (a - b) = 10\ }$
	$2a = 150$
Divide by 2:	$a = 75$

7. **E**   Choose $n = 1$ as an example. Plugging this in to the choices gives answers of (A) $\tfrac{1}{2}$ (B) 3 (C) 3 (D) 1 (E) 2. The only even number here is (E) 2.

8. **D**   Let c be the number of colas that Mike sold and r be the number of root beers. Since the total sold is 48, $c + r = 48$. Since he sold twice as many colas as root beers, $c = 2r$. Substituting this into the first equation gives

	$2r + r = 48$
Simplify:	$3r = 48$
Divide by 3:	$r = 16$

9. **E**   Pick two perfect squares for m and n, like 4 and 9. Plugging these in to the examples gives (A) 36 (B) 36 (C) 16 (D) 324 (E) –45. The only choice that is not a perfect square is (E) –45.

10. **B**   One option is to solve each equation by plugging in 10 for a:

	$a + b = 10 + b = 9$
Subtract 10:	$b = -1$
Second equation:	$10 - c = 14$
Subtract 10:	$-c = 4$
Divide by –1:	$c = -4$

So $c - b = -4 - (-1) = -4 + 1 = -3$.

11. **A**   To maximize $5x - 5y$, maximize the value of x and minimize the value of y. The greatest x can be is $\tfrac{5}{6}$, and the least y can be is $\tfrac{1}{6}$. So $5x - 5y = 5(\tfrac{5}{6}) - 5(\tfrac{1}{6}) = \tfrac{25}{6} - \tfrac{5}{6} = \tfrac{20}{6} = \tfrac{10}{3}$.

12. **E**   Fill in the table above and to the left of the x by following the rule, like this:

0	1	2	3	4	5
1	2	4	7		
2	4	8	15		
3	7	15	x		
4					
5					

This shows that $x = 15 + 15 = 30$.

13. **D**   To maximize c you must minimize the value of $a + b$. Since the numbers must be positive and even, the least values that a and b can have are 2 and 4:

$$a + b + c = 60$$

Plug in: $2 + 4 + c = 60$
Simplify: $6 + c = 60$
Subtract 6: $c = 54$

14. **B**   It is easier to pick a simple value for the "starting" population in 1980, like 100. Since the population increased by 10% from 1980 to 1990, the 1990 population must have been $(100)(1.10) = 110$. Since it decreased by 10% from 1990 to 2000, the 2000 population must have been $(110)(0.90) = 99$. From 1980 to 2000, then, the percent change was $(99 - 100)/100 = -1/100 = -1\%$.

15. **A**   An egg-producing female lays 100 eggs. Only 30% of these eggs become egg-producing females, which is $(30)(100) = 30$ egg-producing females the next year. These 30 lay 100 eggs each, or 3,000 eggs. If 30% of these eggs become egg-producing females the next year, this yields $(0.30)(3,000) = 900$ in 2 years.

16. **C**   Although you may substitute $5y$ for x as a first step, it's probably easier to simplify the expression first:

$$\sqrt{(x^2 - 2xy + y^2)}$$

Factor: $\sqrt{(x - y)^2}$
Simplify: $|x - y|$
Substitute: $|5x - y|$
Simplify: $|4y| = 4y$

17. **C**   Think of numbers that are larger than their squares. This excludes negatives, because the squares of negatives are always positive. It also excludes numbers greater than 1, because the squares of these are bigger than the original numbers. Therefore, $0 < x < 1$. This means I and II are true, but not III.

18. **C**   Believe it or not, you don't need to find the 2 midpoints in order to answer this question. You need to know only that the distance between the 2 midpoints is half of the distance between the 2 endpoints. The distance between the endpoints is $(3x + 2) - (-x - 4) = 3x + 2 + x + 4 = 4x + 6$. Half of this is $2x + 3$.

19. **E**   Since all radii of a triangle are equal, $PQ = PR$. Since $PQ = QR$ too, the triangle must be equilateral. Since its area is $9\sqrt{3}$, the lengths have the measures shown in the diagram. The circle has a radius of 6. The shaded region is equal to the area of the sector minus the area of the triangle. Since the central angle is 60°, the sector has an area that is $^1/_6$ of the whole circle, or $(^1/_6)(\pi(6)^2) = 6\pi$. Subtracting the area of the triangle gives $6\pi - 9\sqrt{3}$.

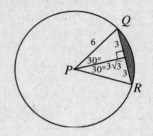

20. **C**   If the ratio of boys to girls in a class is 3 to 5, then $3/(3 + 5) = ^3/_8$ of the class is boys and $5/(3 + 5) = 5/8$ of the class is girls. This means there are $(^3/_8)(160) = 60$ boys and $(^5/_8)(160) = 100$ girls in the senior class. Similarly, the fraction of boys in the junior class is $^3/_5$ and the fraction of girls is $^2/_5$. If there are x students in the junior class, then there are $(^3/_5)x$ boys and $(^2/_5)x$ girls in the junior class. If the ratio of boys to girls is 1:1 when the classes are combined, then

$$60 + (^3/_5)x = 100 + (^2/_5)x$$

Subtract 60 and $(^2/_5)x$: $(^1/_5)x = 40$
Multiply by 5: $x = 200$

Section 3

1. **A** A *six-month hiatus* (break) would cause her skills to *weaken*, something she might fear. *atrophy* = weaken from disuse; *align* = line up; *disseminate* = spread like seed.

2. **C** *Domineering* opinions are overbearing and preachy. *vindictive* = inspired by revenge; *pedantic* = acting like a know-it-all; *conciliatory* = acting to bring people together; *treacherous* = betraying someone's confidence; *didactic* = preachy; *dogmatic* = condescendingly preachy; *prosaic* = ordinary.

3. **A** The missing word must refer to Walter's *inability to make up his mind. vacillation* = inability to make up one's mind; *solicitation* = request for help; *rejuvenation* = restoration of one's youth; *admonishment* = mild reproof.

4. **D** If a writer is *successful . . . even in the face of . . . rejections*, he or she must be very *persistent. affluence* = wealth; *haughty* = arrogant; *pertinacity* = strong persistence; *resilient* = able to endure hardship; *tenacity* = ability to hold fast; *relentless* = unwilling to give up; *stoutness* = courage or sturdiness; *craven* = cowardly.

5. **B** The missing word must be in contrast to *direct, forceful stances. pontification* = haughty, self-important speech; *circumlocution* = indirect, evasive speech; *brevity* = conciseness.

6. **E** The parallelism of the two clauses helps you to complete the sentence. If counselors *believe that criminals can change*, then they must *have faith in their changeability*. If they realize *that they can often return to their old habits*, they must be wary of *recidivism* (tendency to fall into old habits). *mutability* = changeability; *astuteness* = keen ability; *transcendence* = the quality of exceeding; *malleability* = ability to be bent; *relapse* = falling back into old ways.

7. **B** If something is out of place in time, it is an *anachronism. anachronism* = something out of place in time; *idiom* = phrase with a meaning that is different from its literal meaning; *interlocutor* = someone who takes part in a conversation.

8. **C** The sentence indicates that the "h" was evidence of an earlier time. *inference* = conclusion based on evidence; *analogy* = useful comparison; *vestige* = remaining trace; *anomaly* = unusual event; *quandary* = perplexing situation.

9. **A** The passage states that language is used as *impenetrable walls* (line 7) between people, having biased connotations favoring one group over another.

10. **D** By saying that *we infer volumes* (lines 3–4), the author means that *we draw a lot of conclusions*.

11. **E** The passage states that instructing a child to tie shoes *the right way will defeat the child's growing attempt at self-mastery* (lines 12–14).

12. **B** The last sentence states that *nagging* is a *constant reminder of his or her lack of self-control* (lines 21–22).

13. **C** The author states that Modernism is *egotistical* (line 20) and *self-conscious* (line 21) and also that it *begins nowhere and with no one in particular* (line 13), suggesting that it is both *self-centered* and *ill-defined*, but the paragraph does not mention Modernism being *politically oriented*.

14. **A** The passage states that *Critics and academics . . . prefer their artistic movements to be readily comprehensible* (lines 8–10), so they do *not* like those that are hard to understand.

15. **D** The quotation from James Joyce in the next sentence describes these *landmines as enigmas and puzzles that . . . will keep the professors busy for centuries arguing over what I meant* (lines 23–26). In other words, they are literary devices placed in his novels to baffle professors.

16. **B** The passage states that *plots . . . are submerged beneath wave after wave of . . . hyper-literary and meta-literary indulgences* (lines 33–39), so it suggests that plot is not as important as other things.

17. **A** The author states that it is *hard not to love modernism* (line 40) but also uses critical terms like *posturing* (line 20) *aberrations* (line 20) to describe it. In the last two lines, he refers to modernism as *reprehensive but somehow roguishly likeable*. This is a very *ambivalent* characterization of modernism.

18. **A** The comparison is a *metaphor* but not a *simile* because it states that the *modernist novel is a sociopath. Juxtaposition* is the placement of two images one on top of another, as in *a sociopath and a cad. Personification* is giving human qualities to something that is not human.

19. **D**   The purpose of the passage is to introduce the reader to the new science of genomics.

20. **C**   A *pathogen* (line 9) is not part of the *immune system* (line 8) but rather what the immune system responds to.

21. **B**   The *orchestrated response* of *the immune system* (lines 7–8) is mentioned as an example of how *molecules convey information* (lines 9–10).

22. **E**   The fact that *through genomics massive amounts of information can be converted into an electronic format* (lines 39–40) is what *facilitates a dramatically new framework for understanding life* (lines 42–43).

23. **C**   The passage suggests that *information theory ... may seem unfit for... science* (lines 53–54) because *information... implies an underlying intent* (lines 51–52).

24. **D**   The final paragraph indicates that genomic advances *have helped to propel the remarkable development of the computer and telecommunication industries* (lines 60–63) and suggests that they may help to *improve human health* (line 64). This discusses *actual and potential consequences*.

Section 4

1. **A**   The sentence is correct.

2. **E**   The underlined phrase should be a noun phrase that represents *one of the best features of the journalist's lifestyle*. Only (C) and (E) are noun phrases, and (E) is much clearer.

3. **B**   The opening participial phrase modifies *Greg* and not *Greg's search*.

4. **C**   Idiom requires *neither* to be followed by *nor*, and parallelism requires the *nor* to be followed by an adjective.

5. **D**   The past participle of *to take* is *taken*, not *took*.

6. **C**   Although choice (D) is parallel in structure, its phrasing is nonstandard. The phrasing in (C) is both parallel and clear.

7. **A**   The pronoun *he* is the subject of an implied verb: *he (did)*, so it is correctly in the subjective form. Also, the phrase *admire his acting* is correct, because the object of the verb is *acting*, not *him*.

8. **B**   *Neither* is the singular subject of the verb, so the verb should be *was*, not *were*, and the pronoun should be *his* (since rams are male and each ram can only feel his own pain).

9. **B**   The participle *walking* modifies *Liz*, not *Liz's family*. Choice (D) makes this correction, but the modifiers are awkward and unclear.

10. **E**   The phrase *if not better* is an interrupter, so the sentence should read well even if it is omitted. The only phrasing that meets this criterion is (E).

11. **E**   The original is not a sentence but a fragment.

12. **D**   The phrase *much closer* modifies the verb *study* and so should be in adverbial form: *much more closely*.

13. **B**   The two clauses must be parallel: *has been so popular* would make this clause parallel to the first.

14. **D**   This is a diction error. *Respectfully* means full of respect, which makes no sense here. The word should be *respectively*.

15. **D**   The verb *would have considered* is in the wrong tense and mood. It should be *consider*.

16. **E**   The sentence is correct.

17. **C**   The *fund deficit and the disillusionment* are not a single problem, but two *problems*.

18. **B**   The subject of the verb is *either accepting or rejecting*. If the subject of a verb is an *either . . . or* construction, the verb must agree with the noun after the *or*, which in this case is *rejecting*. Since this is a singular noun, the verb should be *was*.

19. **C**   Since *defense attorneys* can be counted, the correct comparative word is *fewer*, not *less*.

20. **B**   It is illogical to compare *service* to *other restaurants*. The phrase should be *the service at the other restaurants*.

21. **E**   The sentence is correct.

22. **C**   This pronoun refers to *a child*, so it must be the singular *his or her*.

23. **C**   The phrase *not only A but also B* indicates a parallel structure. To make the structure parallel, the phrase should be replaced with *by*.

24. **E**   The sentence is correct.

25. **B**   The pronoun *he* is ambiguous. We are not certain which individual it is referring to. To correct the error, *he* should be changed to either Thomas Cowher or the Senator.

26. **C**   The sentence indicates that this occurred in the past by saying those who *were observing*. Therefore *are* should instead be *were*.

27. **E**   The sentence is correct

28. **A**   Between my brother and *I* should instead be between my brother and *me*. Subjective pronouns, such as *I*, should only be used as subjects. Objective pronouns, including *me*, can be used as objects of verbs or as objects of prepositions.

29. **C**   The critic is writing about a *duo*, which is a singular subject. The *their* should therefore be replaced by *its*.

30. **A**   Choice (A) is the most concise and clear, and the phrasing is parallel.

31. **B**   Sentence 3 presents an example of Plato's reasoning as described in sentence 2. Choice (C) may be tempting, but since the sentence does not extend the idea from sentence 2 but only provides an example, the word *furthermore* is inappropriate.

32. **B**   The pronoun *they* and the noun *approximations* should agree in number. Choice (B) provides the most straightforward phrasing.

33. **D**   Sentence 6 does not fit because it shifts the discussion to what students dislike, rather than the nature of mathematical objects.

34. **E**   Choice (E) provides the most logical, concise, and clear phrasing.

35. **A**   Choice (A) provides the most logical, concise, and clear phrasing.

Section 5

1. **E**   If $2x = 10$, then $4x = 20$, and if $3y = 12$, then $6y = 24$, so $4x + 6y = 20 + 24 = 44$.

2. **D**   Set up the equation: $(a + b + 4)/3 = 5$
   Multiply by 3: $a + b + 4 = 15$
   Subtract 4: $a + b = 11$

3. **C**   If $b = 2a$, then $a + 2a = 180$, because the 2 angles form a linear pair. So $3a = 180$ and $a = 60$. Your diagram should now look like this:

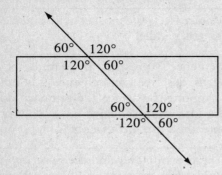

So $d + e + g + h = 60 + 60 + 120 + 60 = 300$.

---

4. **A**   Substitute $x = 100$ into the function:

$$\sqrt{\sqrt{100} - 1} = \sqrt{10 - 1} = \sqrt{9} = 3$$

---

5. **B**   If $2^m = 8$, then $m = 3$. So $3^{k+3} = 243$. Checking the powers of 3 shows that $k + 3 = 5$. Therefore, $k = 2$, so $2^k = 2^2 = 4$.

---

6. **A**   If four numbers have an average of 50, they have a sum of $4 \times 50 = 200$. The numbers are all *different* and all *even*. To minimize 1 of the numbers, you must maximize the other 3. If none is greater than 60, then the greatest the 3 numbers can be is 60, 58, and 56.

So	$60 + 58 + 56 + x = 200$
Simplify:	$174 + x = 200$
Subtract 174:	$x = 26$

---

7. **C**   Each of the 5 teams must play 4 other teams 3 times apiece. In other words, each team must play in $4 \times 3 = 12$ games. Since there are 5 teams, it might seem at first that there are a total of $5 \times 12 = 60$ games, but since each game needs 2 teams, the total number of games is $60/2 = 30$.

---

8. **A**   If pump A can fill the tank in 3 hours, then it will fill $\frac{1}{3}$ of the tank in 1 hour, leaving $\frac{2}{3}$ of the tank to fill. Pump B can fill $\frac{1}{2}$ of the tank in an hour, so working together, the two pumps can fill $\frac{1}{2} + \frac{1}{3} = \frac{5}{6}$ of the tank per hour. To fill $\frac{2}{3}$ of the tank working together, then, takes $(\frac{2}{3}) \div (\frac{5}{6}) = \frac{4}{5}$ hour, which equals $(\frac{4}{5})(60) = 48$ minutes.

---

9. **7.5**   Translate into an equation:

	$4x - 5 = 25$
Add 5:	$4x = 30$
Divide by 4:	$x = 7.5$

---

10. **13** $<<7>> = 7 + 6 + 5 + 4 + 3 + 2 + 1$
$<<5>> = 5 + 4 + 3 + 2 + 1$
So $<<7>> - <<5>> = 7 + 6 = 13$

---

11. **100**   Circumference $= \pi d$, so you can find the diameter:

	$\pi d = 10\pi$
Divide by π:	$d = 10$

This diameter is also the hypotenuse of a right triangle, so by the Pythagorean Theorem, $a^2 + b^2 = d^2 = 10^2 = 100$.

---

12. **24**   This is a "counting" problem, so it helps to know the Fundamental Counting Principle from Chapter 12, Lesson 5. Since you are making a 3-letter arrangement, there are 3 decisions to be made. The number of choices for the first letter is 4; then there are 3 letters left for the second spot, then 2 left for the third spot. This gives a total of $4 \times 3 \times 2 = 24$ possible arrangements.

---

13. **0.2 or 1/5**   This is a simple substitution. You can substitute 10,200 for $96,878 \times x^2$ because they are equal. So $10,200/(5 \times 96,878 \times x^2) = 10,200/(5 \times 10,200) = \frac{1}{5}$. Notice that the 10,200s "cancel."

14. 4 If each term is 1 less than 3 times the *previous* term, then each term is also 1/3 of the number that is 1 greater than the *successive* term. Since the 4th term is 95, the 3rd term must be 1/3 of 96, which is 32. Repeating this shows that the 2nd term is 11 and the 1st term is 4. Check your work by confirming that the sequence satisfies the formula.

---

15. 0.8 If $4 + \sqrt{b} = 7.2$ then $\sqrt{b} = 3.2$

So $4 - \sqrt{b} = 4 - 3.2 = 0.8$.

(Notice that you don't really have to deal with the root!)

---

16. 5 If there are a adults, there must be $30 - a$ children, because the total number of people is 30.

Therefore	$10a + 5(30 - a) = 175$
Distribute:	$10a + 150 - 5a = 175$
Simplify:	$5a + 150 = 175$
Subtract 150:	$5a = 25$
Divide by 5:	$a = 5$

Now check: if there are 5 adults, there must be 25 children, and the tickets would cost $5(10) + 25(5) = 50 + 125 = 175$ (yes!).

---

17. 9 Since $a = (2/3)b$, the perimeter of the triangle is $b + b + (2/3)b = (8/3)b$. The perimeter is 24, so

	$(8/3)b = 24$
Multiply by 3/8:	$b = 9$

---

18. 10

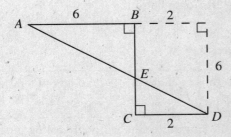

Mark the diagram with the given information. The dotted lines show that AD is the hypotenuse of a right triangle with legs of length 8 and 6. So to find it, just use the Pythagorean Theorem: $6^2 + 8^2 = (AD)^2$

Simplify:	$100 = (AD)^2$
Take the square root:	$10 = AD$

Section 6

1. A Because the signal was *strange*, it was clearly not an expected result, but it was also not from outside of the telescope, so it was a *strange happening* from the telescope itself. *malfunction* = disruption of the normal workings; *bulwark* = defensive fortification; *anthology* = collection of literary works; *mutation* = change in form.

---

2. B The problem is one that may never be solved, so it is *difficult* or *stubborn*. *impotent* = weak and ineffective; *intractable* = hard to manage, stubborn; *evanescent* = likely to vanish; *irate* = angry; *insipid* = dull, tasteless.

---

3. E If the general was *surprised* at the ease with which the defenses were breached, he must have expected the resistance to be much *stronger*. *ephemeral* = short-lived; *compatible* = working well together; *egregious* = blatant or extreme; *imposing* = intimidating.

---

4. B A *dependence on electronic devices* would be expected to *tax* the power grid, although *increased efficiency* of those devices would be expected to ease the burden. *abated* = decreased in intensity; *attenuated* = caused to be less intense; *compromised* = rendered vulnerable; *flourished* = thrived.

---

5. E The word *although* indicates a contrast. Although the persecution *vanquished* (conquered) the will of some, it must have *strengthened* the will of others. *despotic* = tyrannical; *squandered* = wasted; *amenable* = obedient; *celebrated* = eminent; *ruthless* = merciless; *forged* = established.

---

6. C The passage says that *Rousseau's writings* (line 1) were what led *Goethe to say that "feeling is all"* (lines 4–5). Therefore, Goethe was influenced by Rousseau.

---

7. D The passage says that Kant *forgot to take his . . . daily walk* because *he was so absorbed in reading Rousseau's Émile* (lines 15–16).

8. **C** Passage 1 states that *by emphasizing feeling* (line 3) Rousseau inspired the Romantic movement and Goethe in particular, while Passage 2 criticizes Rousseau's *worship of emotion* (line 35) as encouraging poor parenting.

9. **D** Passage 1 states that Rousseau *inspired the French Revolution* (lines 9–10) and Passage 2 give Rousseau credit for laying the *philosophical foundation of American independence* (lines 31–32).

10. **E** By saying *"It would be a good idea,"* Gandhi indicated that civilization in the West had not really been realized.

11. **B** The *voices* are those who are *bankrolled by large corporations* and who are *saying such things* (lines 15–16) as that America is a *model of free-market capitalism* (line 11). This would certainly not include Mahatma Gandhi, but the passage indicates that it would include *politicians* and those in *corporate news and entertainment media* (lines 9–10).

12. **C** The second paragraph explains how *the concept of free trade* (line 21) works, so it is explaining a concept.

13. **A** The statement suggests that the rules of free trade would work differently if the parties involved were different, suggesting that the rules are selectively applied.

14. **A** This paragraph indicates that these words are being used ironically. It states that the Indians *(gave in to Western pressure)* (lines 57–58), so the agreement was not a completely free one. Also, the words "liberalize" and "liberalization" are used ironically because they refer to actions that in fact reduced competition and were *a great blow to free markets* (line 66).

15. **D** The *triumph* was also described as *a great blow to free markets* (line 66).

16. **B** The paragraph indicates that *businesses are ...expected to wager their own capital on success in the marketplace* (lines 68–69) but that some pharmaceutical companies don't need to.

17. **C** The instruction is described as having made his inquiries *clear and facile* (line 15).

18. **D** The phrase *clear and facile to my apprehension* means *easy to understand.*

19. **B** The narrator says that *a mind of moderate capacity which closely pursues one study must infallibly arrive at great proficiency* (line 25), thereby suggesting that only *diligence* is required for proficiency.

20. **A** The narrator was *as well acquainted with the theory and practice of natural philosophy as depended on the lessons of any of the professors at Ingolstadt* (lines 34–37), which means he had learned all he could from them.

21. **C** This *supernatural enthusiasm* describes the narrator's passion for his studies.

22. **B** The human bodies are described as changing from *the seat of beauty and strength* in life to *food for the worm* (line 71) in death.

23. **C** The rest of the sentence describes how the processes of death change a formerly living body. In saying that he *beheld the corruption of death succeed to the blooming cheek of life*, he is saying that death and decay have replaced or defeated life.

24. **E** The narrator reveals his sense of privilege in this discovery by stating that he is *alone* (line 86) among the *many men of genius* (line 84) who had studied this topic before.

Section 7

1. **C** 16 is equal to 2(7) + 2, so it is two more than a multiple of 7.

2. **E** Five oranges can be bought for 5¢ more than the price of 4, which is 4(20¢) + 5¢ = 85¢. $3.40 is equivalent to 4(.85), so it will buy 4(5) = 20 oranges.

3. **A** If r is positive, then $-r$ is negative. If you add another negative, then the result will be even more negative.

4. D 12 less than the product of 3 and $x + 1$ can be represented as

$$3(x + 1) - 12$$

Distribute: $3x + 3 - 12$

Simplify: $3x - 9$

---

5. C The square has an area of $200 \times 200 = 40,000$ square feet. $40,000 \div 5,000 = 8$, so this will require 8 bags of seed at $25 apiece. $8 \times \$25 = \$200$.

---

6. C Analyzing the right angle shows that $x + y = 90$. Since the sum of the angles in a triangle is always 180°,

$$x + y + w = 180$$

Substitute $x + y = 90$: $90 + w = 180$

Subtract 90: $w = 90$

---

7. D If the numbers have a product of 0, then at least one must equal 0. Call the numbers x, y, and 0. The problem also says that $x + y = 7$ and $x - y = 11$.

Add the equations:
$$x + y = 7$$
$$+ (x - y = 11)$$
$$2x = 18$$

Divide by 2: $x = 9$

Plug back in, solve for y: $9 + y = 7$

Subtract 9: $y = -2$

So the least of the numbers is -2.

---

8. A You can draw a diagram and see that there are only 4 possible triangles:

If you prefer to look at it as a "combination" problem, the number of triangles is the number of ways of choosing 3 things from a set of 4, or $_4C_3 = 4$.

---

9. B The only way that abc would not be a multiple of 4 is if none of the 3 numbers is a multiple of 4 *and* no 2 of them are even (because the product of 2 evens is always a multiple of 4). One simple example is $a = 1$, $b = 2$, and $c = 3$. This example rules out choices A, C, D, and E.

---

10. A A large percent change from 2002 to 2003 is represented by a point in which the y-coordinate is much greater than the x-coordinate. Point A represents a change from 30 in 2003 to 70 in 2003, which is a percent change of $(70 - 30)/30 \times 100\% = 133\%$.

---

11. E If both classes have 100 students, then class B had 30 students participate in 2002 and 50 in 2003, for a total of 80. Class E had 80 in 2002 and 60 in 2003, for a total of 140. The difference, then, is $140 - 80 = 60$.

---

12. E Substitute $x = -1$ into the equation to find c.

Simplify: $1 = -4 + c$

Add 4: $5 = c$

So the equation is $x^2 = 4x + 5$

Subtract $(4x + 5)$: $x^2 - 4x - 5 = 0$

Factor the quadratic (remember that since $x = -1$ is a solution, $(x + 1)$ must be a factor): $x^2 - 4x - 5 = (x + 1)(x - 5)$

Therefore $(x + 1)(x - 5) = 0$

So the solutions are $x = 1$ and $x = 5$.

---

13. E If class D has 120 students, then 80% of 120, or 96 students participated in 2002. If the same number participated from class C, then 96 is 60% of the number of students in class C. If the number of students in class C is x, then $.60x = 96$. Divide by .6: $x = 160$.

---

14. C To create a 3-digit number, 3 decisions must be made: you must choose the 1st digit, then choose where to put the 2, then choose the final digit. Since the 1st digit must be odd, there are 3 options for the 1st digit. Since the 2 may be placed in either the 2nd or the 3rd slot, there are 2 options. Then there are 3 digits left to choose for the final slot. This means there are $3 \times 2 \times 3 = 18$ possibilities.

---

15. C Since 1 pound feeds 5 chickens, 4 pounds are needed to feed 20 chickens. This leaves $10 - 4 = 6$ pounds of feed. Since each pound can feed 2 pigs, 6 pounds can feed $2 \times 6 = 12$ pigs.

16. A   Since 120° is 1/3 of 360°, the shaded region has 1/3 the area of the circle. Therefore, the circle has an area of 3(3π) = 9π. Since A = πr², the radius is 3 centimeters. The circumference of the circle, then, is 2πr = 2π(3) = 6π, and the arc of the shaded region has length (1/3)(6π) = 2π. The perimeter of the shaded region, then, is 3 + 3 + 2π = 2π + 6.

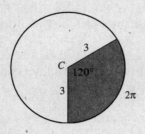

Section 8

1. D   The word *rather* indicates the important contrast between the 2 ideas. The 2nd word indicates something specific to a *single director* rather than *many visions. conglomeration* = collection; *insubordination* = disobedience; *prudence* = careful management; *bastion* = a well-fortified area; *synthesis* = a fusion of different elements; *conspiracy* = secret agreement to commit a crime.

2. B   The fact that modern readers *read a book once and then discard it* suggests that their interest in it is only *temporary*, rather than *timeless. immoral* = unethical; *fleeting* = short-lived.

3. A   *Although* indicates a contrast in ideas, so the missing word must mean *prolonged* rather than *short term. protracted* = prolonged; *contemporaneous* = living or existing at the same time; *transient* = short-lived; *surreptitious* = secretive; *fickle* = tending to change one's mind often.

4. C   Since the sentence says that athletes are treated like successful warriors, you should look for a word like *celebrated. invoked* = called on or cited; *repudiated* = having its validity rejected; *lionized* = treated like a celebrity; *vilified* = defamed; *beguiled* = deceived by charm.

5. E   The word *although* indicates a contrast. Although the persecution *vanquished* (conquered) the will of some, it must have *strengthened* the will of others. *despotic* = tyrannical; *squandered* = wasted; *amenable* = obedient; *celebrated* = eminent; *ruthless* = merciless; *forged* = established.

6. B   If she was an *opponent of the male hegemony* (dominance of one group over another) she must have been an *outspoken* critic of the *male-dominated* society. *matriarchal* = female-dominated; *pugnacious* = belligerent; *patriarchal* = male-dominated; *vociferous* = outspoken; *avuncular* = like a good-natured uncle; *belligerent* = inclined to picking fights; *rudimentary* = basic; *liberal* = free-thinking.

7. C   The author begins by making the point that *the spelling profession* (line 1) kills genius. By saying that Shakespeare was not a good speller but was more of a genius than Noah Webster, he is reinforcing the point, thereby suggesting that Webster is someone in the "spelling profession."

8. E   The previous two sentences discuss the fact that any attempt to make spelling easier would undermine the author's *excuse for bad spelling* (line 19).

9. E   Serena's plan is to have people avoid spelling words with silent letters, but not change the way they pronounce words. This would require a change in writing habits.

10. C   Serena's plan is to *boycott* (line 80) words with superfluous letters. Boycotting is a form of protest. By saying that her plan is more American than his, the author suggests that Americans are inclined to protest things.

11. A   The author says he wants to *set the idle letters to work* (lines 53–54) by pronouncing them, while Serena plans to *ignore all words that contain superfluous letters* (line 79).

12. A   In the final paragraph of Passage 1, the author says that he *replaced* the *Platonic friendship* he had with Serena with *ardent love* (line 89) because he didn't know how to spell the word *friend*.

13. D   The *chaos* is mentioned as the result of failing to impose standards for spelling particular words and instead spelling a word in many different ways according to how it is pronounced in different dialects.

14. **B** Passage 2 says that standardized spelling *obscures those spoken dialects that are so often used to stratify and separate us* (lines 122–123).

15. **A** Passage 2 says that the silent letters in the word "eight" are *a treasure trove* (line 132) to those who study the history of language.

16. **A** Passage 1 is clearly intended to be humorous, while Passage 2 is very systematic in discussing the problems with the spelling reform movement.

17. **D** Passage 1 says that *Americans do not like sudden changes* (line 31) to suggest the difficulty in enacting spelling reform. Similarly, Passage 2 says that *languages are not influenced very much by plan or reason* (lines 135–136).

18. **D** Because the final paragraph of Passage 2 discusses the problem of enacting a *plan* to change the conventions of language, the author of Passage 2 would likely regard such a plan as unworkable.

19. **C** The first passage discusses *although* as a word with too many silent letters, while Passage 2 discusses it because it contains a letter sequence that can be pronounced in many different ways.

Section 9

1. **C** The original sentence is a run-on sentence. Answer choice (C) properly coordinates the two ideas.

2. **B** In the original sentence *a better debator* should instead be *better debaters,* the plural form. Answer choice (B) corrects this error.

3. **B** *Billy the Bobcat* is a singular subject and the verb *have* is plural. It should instead be *has*.

4. **B** The pronoun *when* should be used only to refer to a time. It should be replaced by *who*.

5. **A** This sentence is correct as written.

6. **E** The original sentence is phrased awkwardly. As constructed it suggests that the U.S. enjoyed *peace and economic well being* more than *any time* did, which makes no sense. Answer choice (E) corrects this comparison error.

7. **D** The phrase *because of* is awkward. Answer choice (D) corrects the error in the most concise and logical fashion.

8. **D** The sentence requires parallel structure. Jerry Lewis hosted *a variety show* and *an annual telethon.* Answer choice (D) corrects the error.

9. **B** You should not begin the clause after a semicolon with *and* because it is supposed to be an *independent* clause. Answer choice (B) properly coordinates the two ideas.

10. **B** As originally constructed, the sentence suggests that the children themselves contain violent imagery, rather than the video games contain violent imagery. Answer choice (B) corrects this error.

11. **B** The opening participial phrase, *walking hand-in-hand* improperly modifies the *vendor* rather than *the couple.* Answer choice (B) corrects this error.

12. **C** The original sentence is awkward and wordy. The phrasing in answer choice (C) is the most concise and logical of the choices.

13. **D** This question presents an illogical comparison. As written the parents today spend more time working than 30 years ago did. The sentence is *trying* to say that parents today spend more time working than *parents did* 30 years ago. Answer choice (D) corrects the error.

14. **B** The phrase *if they would have* in (E) is incorrect subjunctive form, and the comparison between the *language* and the *Borneans* is illogical.

PRACTICE TEST 10

ANSWER SHEET

Last Name: _____   First Name: _____

Date: _____   Testing Location: _____

Directions for Test

- Remove these answer sheets from the book and use them to record your answers to this test.
- This test will require 3 hours and 20 minutes to complete. Take this test in one sitting.
- The time allotment for each section is written clearly at the beginning of each section. This test contains six 25-minute sections, two 20-minute sections, and one 10-minute section.
- This test is 25 minutes shorter than the actual SAT, which will include a 25-minute "experimental" section that does not count toward your score. That section has been omitted from this test.
- You may take one short break during the test, of no more than 10 minutes in length.
- You may only work on one section at any given time.
- You must stop ALL work on a section when time is called.
- If you finish a section before the time has elapsed, check your work on that section. You may NOT work on any other section.
- Do not waste time on questions that seem too difficult for you.
- Use the test book for scratchwork, but you will receive credit only for answers that are marked on the answer sheets.
- You will receive one point for every correct answer.
- You will receive no points for an omitted question.
- For each wrong answer on any multiple-choice question, your score will be reduced by ¼ point.
- For each wrong answer on any numerical "grid-in" question, you will receive no deduction.

SECTION 2

1. Ⓐ Ⓑ Ⓒ Ⓓ Ⓔ	11. Ⓐ Ⓑ Ⓒ Ⓓ Ⓔ	21. Ⓐ Ⓑ Ⓒ Ⓓ Ⓔ	31. Ⓐ Ⓑ Ⓒ Ⓓ Ⓔ
2. Ⓐ Ⓑ Ⓒ Ⓓ Ⓔ	12. Ⓐ Ⓑ Ⓒ Ⓓ Ⓔ	22. Ⓐ Ⓑ Ⓒ Ⓓ Ⓔ	32. Ⓐ Ⓑ Ⓒ Ⓓ Ⓔ
3. Ⓐ Ⓑ Ⓒ Ⓓ Ⓔ	13. Ⓐ Ⓑ Ⓒ Ⓓ Ⓔ	23. Ⓐ Ⓑ Ⓒ Ⓓ Ⓔ	33. Ⓐ Ⓑ Ⓒ Ⓓ Ⓔ
4. Ⓐ Ⓑ Ⓒ Ⓓ Ⓔ	14. Ⓐ Ⓑ Ⓒ Ⓓ Ⓔ	24. Ⓐ Ⓑ Ⓒ Ⓓ Ⓔ	34. Ⓐ Ⓑ Ⓒ Ⓓ Ⓔ
5. Ⓐ Ⓑ Ⓒ Ⓓ Ⓔ	15. Ⓐ Ⓑ Ⓒ Ⓓ Ⓔ	25. Ⓐ Ⓑ Ⓒ Ⓓ Ⓔ	35. Ⓐ Ⓑ Ⓒ Ⓓ Ⓔ
6. Ⓐ Ⓑ Ⓒ Ⓓ Ⓔ	16. Ⓐ Ⓑ Ⓒ Ⓓ Ⓔ	26. Ⓐ Ⓑ Ⓒ Ⓓ Ⓔ	36. Ⓐ Ⓑ Ⓒ Ⓓ Ⓔ
7. Ⓐ Ⓑ Ⓒ Ⓓ Ⓔ	17. Ⓐ Ⓑ Ⓒ Ⓓ Ⓔ	27. Ⓐ Ⓑ Ⓒ Ⓓ Ⓔ	37. Ⓐ Ⓑ Ⓒ Ⓓ Ⓔ
8. Ⓐ Ⓑ Ⓒ Ⓓ Ⓔ	18. Ⓐ Ⓑ Ⓒ Ⓓ Ⓔ	28. Ⓐ Ⓑ Ⓒ Ⓓ Ⓔ	38. Ⓐ Ⓑ Ⓒ Ⓓ Ⓔ
9. Ⓐ Ⓑ Ⓒ Ⓓ Ⓔ	19. Ⓐ Ⓑ Ⓒ Ⓓ Ⓔ	29. Ⓐ Ⓑ Ⓒ Ⓓ Ⓔ	39. Ⓐ Ⓑ Ⓒ Ⓓ Ⓔ
10. Ⓐ Ⓑ Ⓒ Ⓓ Ⓔ	20. Ⓐ Ⓑ Ⓒ Ⓓ Ⓔ	30. Ⓐ Ⓑ Ⓒ Ⓓ Ⓔ	40. Ⓐ Ⓑ Ⓒ Ⓓ Ⓔ

SECTION 3

1. Ⓐ Ⓑ Ⓒ Ⓓ Ⓔ	11. Ⓐ Ⓑ Ⓒ Ⓓ Ⓔ	21. Ⓐ Ⓑ Ⓒ Ⓓ Ⓔ	31. Ⓐ Ⓑ Ⓒ Ⓓ Ⓔ
2. Ⓐ Ⓑ Ⓒ Ⓓ Ⓔ	12. Ⓐ Ⓑ Ⓒ Ⓓ Ⓔ	22. Ⓐ Ⓑ Ⓒ Ⓓ Ⓔ	32. Ⓐ Ⓑ Ⓒ Ⓓ Ⓔ
3. Ⓐ Ⓑ Ⓒ Ⓓ Ⓔ	13. Ⓐ Ⓑ Ⓒ Ⓓ Ⓔ	23. Ⓐ Ⓑ Ⓒ Ⓓ Ⓔ	33. Ⓐ Ⓑ Ⓒ Ⓓ Ⓔ
4. Ⓐ Ⓑ Ⓒ Ⓓ Ⓔ	14. Ⓐ Ⓑ Ⓒ Ⓓ Ⓔ	24. Ⓐ Ⓑ Ⓒ Ⓓ Ⓔ	34. Ⓐ Ⓑ Ⓒ Ⓓ Ⓔ
5. Ⓐ Ⓑ Ⓒ Ⓓ Ⓔ	15. Ⓐ Ⓑ Ⓒ Ⓓ Ⓔ	25. Ⓐ Ⓑ Ⓒ Ⓓ Ⓔ	35. Ⓐ Ⓑ Ⓒ Ⓓ Ⓔ
6. Ⓐ Ⓑ Ⓒ Ⓓ Ⓔ	16. Ⓐ Ⓑ Ⓒ Ⓓ Ⓔ	26. Ⓐ Ⓑ Ⓒ Ⓓ Ⓔ	36. Ⓐ Ⓑ Ⓒ Ⓓ Ⓔ
7. Ⓐ Ⓑ Ⓒ Ⓓ Ⓔ	17. Ⓐ Ⓑ Ⓒ Ⓓ Ⓔ	27. Ⓐ Ⓑ Ⓒ Ⓓ Ⓔ	37. Ⓐ Ⓑ Ⓒ Ⓓ Ⓔ
8. Ⓐ Ⓑ Ⓒ Ⓓ Ⓔ	18. Ⓐ Ⓑ Ⓒ Ⓓ Ⓔ	28. Ⓐ Ⓑ Ⓒ Ⓓ Ⓔ	38. Ⓐ Ⓑ Ⓒ Ⓓ Ⓔ
9. Ⓐ Ⓑ Ⓒ Ⓓ Ⓔ	19. Ⓐ Ⓑ Ⓒ Ⓓ Ⓔ	29. Ⓐ Ⓑ Ⓒ Ⓓ Ⓔ	39. Ⓐ Ⓑ Ⓒ Ⓓ Ⓔ
10. Ⓐ Ⓑ Ⓒ Ⓓ Ⓔ	20. Ⓐ Ⓑ Ⓒ Ⓓ Ⓔ	30. Ⓐ Ⓑ Ⓒ Ⓓ Ⓔ	40. Ⓐ Ⓑ Ⓒ Ⓓ Ⓔ

ANSWER SHEET

SECTION 4

1. Ⓐ Ⓑ Ⓒ Ⓓ Ⓔ
2. Ⓐ Ⓑ Ⓒ Ⓓ Ⓔ
3. Ⓐ Ⓑ Ⓒ Ⓓ Ⓔ
4. Ⓐ Ⓑ Ⓒ Ⓓ Ⓔ
5. Ⓐ Ⓑ Ⓒ Ⓓ Ⓔ
6. Ⓐ Ⓑ Ⓒ Ⓓ Ⓔ
7. Ⓐ Ⓑ Ⓒ Ⓓ Ⓔ
8. Ⓐ Ⓑ Ⓒ Ⓓ Ⓔ
9. Ⓐ Ⓑ Ⓒ Ⓓ Ⓔ
10. Ⓐ Ⓑ Ⓒ Ⓓ Ⓔ

11. Ⓐ Ⓑ Ⓒ Ⓓ Ⓔ
12. Ⓐ Ⓑ Ⓒ Ⓓ Ⓔ
13. Ⓐ Ⓑ Ⓒ Ⓓ Ⓔ
14. Ⓐ Ⓑ Ⓒ Ⓓ Ⓔ
15. Ⓐ Ⓑ Ⓒ Ⓓ Ⓔ
16. Ⓐ Ⓑ Ⓒ Ⓓ Ⓔ
17. Ⓐ Ⓑ Ⓒ Ⓓ Ⓔ
18. Ⓐ Ⓑ Ⓒ Ⓓ Ⓔ
19. Ⓐ Ⓑ Ⓒ Ⓓ Ⓔ
20. Ⓐ Ⓑ Ⓒ Ⓓ Ⓔ

21. Ⓐ Ⓑ Ⓒ Ⓓ Ⓔ
22. Ⓐ Ⓑ Ⓒ Ⓓ Ⓔ
23. Ⓐ Ⓑ Ⓒ Ⓓ Ⓔ
24. Ⓐ Ⓑ Ⓒ Ⓓ Ⓔ
25. Ⓐ Ⓑ Ⓒ Ⓓ Ⓔ
26. Ⓐ Ⓑ Ⓒ Ⓓ Ⓔ
27. Ⓐ Ⓑ Ⓒ Ⓓ Ⓔ
28. Ⓐ Ⓑ Ⓒ Ⓓ Ⓔ
29. Ⓐ Ⓑ Ⓒ Ⓓ Ⓔ
30. Ⓐ Ⓑ Ⓒ Ⓓ Ⓔ

31. Ⓐ Ⓑ Ⓒ Ⓓ Ⓔ
32. Ⓐ Ⓑ Ⓒ Ⓓ Ⓔ
33. Ⓐ Ⓑ Ⓒ Ⓓ Ⓔ
34. Ⓐ Ⓑ Ⓒ Ⓓ Ⓔ
35. Ⓐ Ⓑ Ⓒ Ⓓ Ⓔ
36. Ⓐ Ⓑ Ⓒ Ⓓ Ⓔ
37. Ⓐ Ⓑ Ⓒ Ⓓ Ⓔ
38. Ⓐ Ⓑ Ⓒ Ⓓ Ⓔ
39. Ⓐ Ⓑ Ⓒ Ⓓ Ⓔ
40. Ⓐ Ⓑ Ⓒ Ⓓ Ⓔ

SECTION 5

1. Ⓐ Ⓑ Ⓒ Ⓓ Ⓔ
2. Ⓐ Ⓑ Ⓒ Ⓓ Ⓔ
3. Ⓐ Ⓑ Ⓒ Ⓓ Ⓔ
4. Ⓐ Ⓑ Ⓒ Ⓓ Ⓔ

5. Ⓐ Ⓑ Ⓒ Ⓓ Ⓔ
6. Ⓐ Ⓑ Ⓒ Ⓓ Ⓔ
7. Ⓐ Ⓑ Ⓒ Ⓓ Ⓔ
8. Ⓐ Ⓑ Ⓒ Ⓓ Ⓔ

9. 10. 11. 12. 13.

14. 15. 16. 17. 18.

ANSWER SHEET

SECTION 6

1. A B C D E	11. A B C D E	21. A B C D E	31. A B C D E
2. A B C D E	12. A B C D E	22. A B C D E	32. A B C D E
3. A B C D E	13. A B C D E	23. A B C D E	33. A B C D E
4. A B C D E	14. A B C D E	24. A B C D E	34. A B C D E
5. A B C D E	15. A B C D E	25. A B C D E	35. A B C D E
6. A B C D E	16. A B C D E	26. A B C D E	36. A B C D E
7. A B C D E	17. A B C D E	27. A B C D E	37. A B C D E
8. A B C D E	18. A B C D E	28. A B C D E	38. A B C D E
9. A B C D E	19. A B C D E	29. A B C D E	39. A B C D E
10. A B C D E	20. A B C D E	30. A B C D E	40. A B C D E

SECTION 7

1. A B C D E	11. A B C D E	21. A B C D E	31. A B C D E
2. A B C D E	12. A B C D E	22. A B C D E	32. A B C D E
3. A B C D E	13. A B C D E	23. A B C D E	33. A B C D E
4. A B C D E	14. A B C D E	24. A B C D E	34. A B C D E
5. A B C D E	15. A B C D E	25. A B C D E	35. A B C D E
6. A B C D E	16. A B C D E	26. A B C D E	36. A B C D E
7. A B C D E	17. A B C D E	27. A B C D E	37. A B C D E
8. A B C D E	18. A B C D E	28. A B C D E	38. A B C D E
9. A B C D E	19. A B C D E	29. A B C D E	39. A B C D E
10. A B C D E	20. A B C D E	30. A B C D E	40. A B C D E

SECTION 8

1. A B C D E	11. A B C D E	21. A B C D E	31. A B C D E
2. A B C D E	12. A B C D E	22. A B C D E	32. A B C D E
3. A B C D E	13. A B C D E	23. A B C D E	33. A B C D E
4. A B C D E	14. A B C D E	24. A B C D E	34. A B C D E
5. A B C D E	15. A B C D E	25. A B C D E	35. A B C D E
6. A B C D E	16. A B C D E	26. A B C D E	36. A B C D E
7. A B C D E	17. A B C D E	27. A B C D E	37. A B C D E
8. A B C D E	18. A B C D E	28. A B C D E	38. A B C D E
9. A B C D E	19. A B C D E	29. A B C D E	39. A B C D E
10. A B C D E	20. A B C D E	30. A B C D E	40. A B C D E

SECTION 9

1. A B C D E	11. A B C D E	21. A B C D E	31. A B C D E
2. A B C D E	12. A B C D E	22. A B C D E	32. A B C D E
3. A B C D E	13. A B C D E	23. A B C D E	33. A B C D E
4. A B C D E	14. A B C D E	24. A B C D E	34. A B C D E
5. A B C D E	15. A B C D E	25. A B C D E	35. A B C D E
6. A B C D E	16. A B C D E	26. A B C D E	36. A B C D E
7. A B C D E	17. A B C D E	27. A B C D E	37. A B C D E
8. A B C D E	18. A B C D E	28. A B C D E	38. A B C D E
9. A B C D E	19. A B C D E	29. A B C D E	39. A B C D E
10. A B C D E	20. A B C D E	30. A B C D E	40. A B C D E

Section 1

Time—25 minutes

Directions for Writing Essays

Plan and write an essay that answers the question below. Do NOT write on another topic. An essay on another topic will receive a score of 0.

Two readers will grade your essay based on how well you develop your point of view, organize and explain your ideas, use specific and relevant examples to support your thesis, and use clear and effective language. How well you write is much more important than how much you write, but to cover the topic adequately you should plan to write several paragraphs.

Your essay must be written on separate lined sheets of paper. Keep your handwriting to a reasonable size. Your essay will be read by people who are not familiar with your handwriting, so write legibly.

You may use this sheet for notes and outlining, but these will not be graded as part of your essay.

Consider carefully the issue discussed in the following passage, then write an essay that answers the question posed in the assignment.

> The best leaders are not those who seek power, or have great political skill. Great leaders—and these are exceptionally rare, especially today—represent the best selves of the people they represent.

Assignment: **What are the most important qualities of a leader?** Write an essay in which you answer this question and discuss your point of view on this issue. Support your position logically with examples from literature, the arts, history, politics, science and technology, current events, or your experience or observation.

Write your essay on separate sheets of paper.

Section 2

Time — 25 minutes
24 Questions

Each sentence below has one or two blanks, each blank indicating that something has been omitted. Beneath the sentence are five words or sets of words labeled A through E. Choose the word or set of words that, when inserted in the sentence, best fits the meaning of the sentence as a whole.

Example:

Medieval kingdoms did not become constitutional republics overnight; on the contrary, the change was ————.

(A) unpopular   (B) unexpected
(C) advantageous   (D) sufficient
(E) gradual

Correct response: (E)

1 Even though Alisha had every reason to hold a grudge, she felt that _____ was not a healthful emotion.

(A) resentment
(B) fortitude
(C) sarcasm
(D) elation
(E) fondness

2 Those who expected the governor to be inarticulate were surprised by his _____.

(A) intolerance
(B) fatigue
(C) eloquence
(D) endurance
(E) violence

3 Before the Realist movement, novelists rarely utilized the _____ language of commoners, preferring the more _____ parlance of the upper classes.

(A) normal ... ordinary
(B) elite ... fancy
(C) sympathetic ... wasteful
(D) colloquial ... refined
(E) effective ... utilitarian

4 Many college students are attracted to the _____ life of a journalist; the prospect of exploring the world is very appealing, even if the pay is not.

(A) peripatetic
(B) conventional
(C) tolerant
(D) coordinated
(E) remunerative

5 A position that requires public speaking would be very difficult for one as _____ as he.

(A) vivacious
(B) garrulous
(C) amiable
(D) decent
(E) reticent

6 One example of a ____ relationship is provided by the tickbird, which gets protection and a free meal of ticks from the hippopotamus and in turn supplies free pest removal services.

(A) competitive
(B) deteriorating
(C) symbiotic
(D) regressive
(E) vacillating

7 Early philosophers used ____ alone to reach their conclusions; unlike modern scientists, they did not value the ____ information that comes only from close observation and experimentation.

(A) reason ... empirical
(B) coercion ... mathematical
(C) deduction ... clerical
(D) computation ... intuitive
(E) compassion ... numerical

8 The _____ of many media companies under a single owner is troublesome to those who believe that _____ is essential to the fair and balanced presentation of the news.

(A) retraction ... differentiation
(B) consolidation ... independence
(C) collaboration ... sharing
(D) unification ... dissemination
(E) disintegration ... variety

GO ON TO THE NEXT PAGE ▶▶▶

2

The passages below are followed by questions based on their content. Answer each question based on what is stated or implied in the passages or the introductory material that precedes them.

Questions 9–12 are based on the following passages.

Passage 1

Line   Education, then, beyond all other devices of
        human origin, is the great equalizer of the
        conditions of men—the balance-wheel of the
        social machinery. It gives each man the
5   independence and the means by which he
        can resist the selfishness of other men. It
        does better than to disarm the poor of their
        hostility toward the rich; it prevents being
        poor. The spread of education, by enlarging
10   the cultivated class or caste, will open a
        wider area over which the social feelings will
        expand, and, if this education should be
        universal and complete, it would do more
        than all things else to obliterate factitious
15   distinctions in society.

Passage 2

        For most students, the main product of
        schooling is not education but the acceptance
        of one's place in society and of the power of
        that society to mete out the symbols of status.
20   Education is the acquisition of competence,
        power, wisdom and discernment. These come
        only from the unadulterated struggle for
        sense in the world, and it is this struggle
        that is denied by schooling, which dictates
25   experience and then evaluates that experience
        as it chooses. But only the experiencer can
        really evaluate an experience.

9   Unlike Passage 1, Passage 2 focuses on the
        distinction between

(A)   educating the poor and educating
        the wealthy
(B)   power and knowledge
(C)   teachers and students
(D)   educated people and uneducated
        people
(E)   schooling and education

First paragraph: Horace Mann, *The Case for Public Schools*,
  a report to the Massachusetts Board of Education in 1848.
Second paragraph: Printed with the permission of its author,
  Christopher Black and College Hill Coaching. © 2005

10   Passage 1 mentions each of the following as
        benefits of public education to the poor
        EXCEPT

(A)   the diminishment of social distinctions
(B)   the improvement of living standards
(C)   better ability to counteract greed
(D)   increased self-sufficiency
(E)   the reduction of crime

11   Passage 1 suggests that the obliteration of
        "factitious distinctions" (lines 14–15) requires

(A)   unlimited access to education
(B)   a rigorous curriculum in civics
(C)   hostility toward the rich
(D)   dedicated teachers
(E)   aggressive legislation

12   The author of Passage 2 characterizes the
        "struggle" (line 22) as

(A)   regretful
(B)   empowering
(C)   illusionary
(D)   unwinnable
(E)   foreign

GO ON TO THE NEXT PAGE ▸▸▸

The questions below are based on the content of the passage that precedes them. The questions are to be answered on the basis of what is stated or implied in the passage or in the introductory material that precedes it.

Questions 13–18 are based on the following passage.

The following is an essay from a textbook on the history of philosophy published in 1999.

Line The scientists of the Renaissance brought about the most fundamental alterations in the world of thought, and they accomplished this feat by devising a new method for
5 discovering knowledge. Unlike the medieval thinkers, who proceeded for the most part by reading traditional texts, the early modern scientists laid greatest stress upon observation and the formation of temporary hypotheses.
10 The method of observation implied two things: namely, that traditional explanations of the behavior of nature should be empirically demonstrated, the new assumption being that such explanations
15 could very well be wrong, and that new information might be available to scientists if they could penetrate beyond the superficial appearances of things. People now began to look at the heavenly bodies with a new attitude,
20 hoping not solely to find the confirmation of Biblical statements about the firmament but, further, to discover the principles and laws that describe the movements of bodies. Observation was directed not only upon the
25 stars but also in the opposite direction, toward the minutest constituents of physical substance.
    To enhance the exactness of their observations, they invented various scientific
30 instruments. Tippershey, a Dutchman, invented the telescope in 1608, although Galileo was the first to make dramatic use of it. In 1590 the first compound microscope was created. The principle of the barometer
35 was discovered by Galileo's pupil Torricelli. The air pump, which was so important in creating a vacuum for the experiment that proved that all bodies regardless of their weight or size fall at the same rate when

40 there is no air resistance, was invented by Otto von Guericke (1602–1686). With the use of instruments and imaginative hypotheses, fresh knowledge began to unfold. Galileo discovered the moons around Jupiter, and
45 Anton Leeuwenhoek (1632–1723) discovered spermatozoa, protozoa, and bacteria. Whereas Nicolaus Copernicus (1473–1543) formed a new hypothesis of the revolution of the earth around the sun, Harvey (1578–1657)
50 discovered the circulation of the blood. William Gilbert (1540–1603) wrote a major work on the magnet, and Robert Boyle (1627–1691), the father of chemistry, formulated his famous law concerning the
55 relation of temperature, volume, and pressure of gases. Added to these inventions and discoveries was the decisive advance made in mathematics, especially by Sir Isaac Newton and Leibniz, who independently
60 invented differential and integral calculus. The method of observation and mathematical calculation now became the hallmarks of modern science.
    The new scientific mode of thought in
65 time influenced philosophic thought in two important ways. First, the assumption that the basic processes of nature are observable and capable of mathematical calculation and description had the effect of engendering
70 another assumption, namely, that everything consists of bodies in motion, that everything conforms to a mechanical model. The heavens above and the smallest particles below all exhibit the same laws of motion.
75 Even human thought was soon explained in mechanical terms, not to mention the realm of human behavior, which the earlier moralists described as the product of free will.

13 Which of the following is the best title for this passage?

(A) The Beginnings of the Scientific Method
(B) Scientific Instruments of the Renaissance
(C) The Art and Science of the Renaissance
(D) Biblical Influence on the Scientific Mode of Thought
(E) The Importance of Hypotheses in Scientific Thinking

GO ON TO THE NEXT PAGE ▸▸▸

Excerpted from "The Renaissance Interlude," in *Socrates to Sartre*, by Samuel Enoch Stumpf, McGraw-Hill, New York, 1999, pp. 203–204

14 As it is used in line 8, "stress" most nearly means

(A) anxiety   (B) pressure
(C) emphasis   (D) desperation
(E) contortion

2

15 It can be inferred from the passage that if pre-Renaissance scientists observed the motions of heavenly bodies, they did so most likely in order to

(A) confirm the formulas that describe the motions of the planets and stars
(B) distinguish the motions of various planets
(C) validate what the Bible says about those bodies
(D) demonstrate the utility of their newly invented instruments
(E) refute the hypotheses of their rival scientists

16 The passage indicates that Galileo did which of the following?

   I. invented an important optical instrument
   II. instructed another famous scientist
   III. made an important astronomical discovery

(A) II only   (B) III only
(C) I and II only (D) II and III only
(E) I, II, and III

17 The passage indicates that, unlike the "earlier moralists" (lines 77–78), Renaissance scientists began to perceive human behavior as

(A) a matter of free choice
(B) influenced by heavenly bodies
(C) controlled by a metaphysical spirit
(D) affected by animalistic impulses
(E) subject to the laws of physical motion

18 The primary function of the last paragraph is to

(A) propose a solution to a problem
(B) identify those responsible for a discovery
(C) discuss the effects of a change
(D) refute a misconception
(E) address an objection to the author's thesis

Questions 19–24 are based on the following passage.

The following passage is from a recent book on the history of warfare.

Line   One of the high points of any production of Shakespeare's *Henry V* is the Saint Crispin's Day speech at the Battle of Agincourt, in which the English king rhapsodizes over the
5   glorious plight of his vastly outnumbered army with the words "We few, we happy few, we band of brothers." What prompts this outpouring of fraternal emotion is the Earl of Westmoreland's complaint that if only they
10   had "ten thousand of those men in England that do no work today," they would at least have a fighting chance. But Henry will have none of that, and delivers his justly famous rejoinder:

15   *If we are marked to die, we are enow*
        To do our country loss; and if to live,
        The fewer men, the greater share of honor.
        God's will! I pray thee wish not one
        man more.

20   This is usually assumed to be a show of stoic bravado that harks back to the prebattle speeches recorded by ancient historians (notably Thucydides and Xenophon), speeches in which an outnumbered force
25   cement their solidarity by reveling in their numerical disadvantage. "The fewer men, the greater the honor" was by Shakespeare's time a well-known proverb, trotted out in many instances of the glorious, fighting few.
30   In Froissart's account of the Battle of Poitiers in 1356, for example, the Prince of Wales harangues his men prior to the battle in a speech that closely parallels Henry's. Shakespeare was undoubtedly familiar
35   with it.

        Now, my gallant fellows, what though we
        be a small body when compared to the
        army of our enemies; do not let us be cast
        down on that account, for victory does not
40   *always follow numbers, but where the*
        Almighty God wishes to bestow it. If,
        through good fortune, the day shall be ours,
        we shall gain the greatest honor and glory
        in this world; if the contrary should
45   *happen, and we be slain, I have a father*
        and beloved brethren alive, and you all have

some relations, or good friends, who will be
sure to revenge our deaths. I
50 *therefore entreat of you to exert yourselves,*
and combat manfully; for, if it please God
and St. George, you shall see me this day
act like a true knight.

Of course the race does not always go to the
55 swift nor the battle to the stronger in
number. Despite being outmanned, both
King Henry and Prince Edward managed to
prevail quite handily due to the incompetence
of their opponents. In each instance, the
60 French squandered their numerical advantage
by charging before they were ready, by
bunching up, and by underestimating the
range and accuracy of the English longbow.
The numbers not only fail to tell the whole
65 story, but they actually obscure it. Ten
thousand more men might actually have
hindered the English, whereas fewer men
(and less overconfidence) might have saved
the French. It seems that in fact, as these and
70 many other examples show, strength is not
always proportional to size.

19 The passage suggests that Henry V requests
"not one man more" (line 18) because

(A) his strategy can work only with a
small band of fighters.
(B) he considers it more honorable to
fight while outnumbered
(C) the opposing soldiers are unreliable
(D) no other fighters have the skills of the
ones he has assembled
(E) he does not wish to be victorious

20 In line 28, the phrase "trotted out" most
nearly means

(A) abused
(B) removed
(C) employed for rhetorical effect
(D) spared an indignity
(E) used flippantly

Damn the Torpedoes, Brian Burrell, McGraw-Hill, New York,
1999, pp. 109–110

21 In line 36, the word "body" most nearly
means

(A) stature
(B) strength
(C) corpse
(D) group
(E) anthology

22 In line 61, the word "charging" most nearly
means

(A) accusing
(B) inspiring
(C) resting
(D) attacking
(E) prevailing

23 The passage indicates that the Battle of
Agincourt and the Battle of Poitiers were
similar in that in each case

I. the victorious army was the smaller
II. the French army was defeated
III. one side committed tactical errors

(A) I only
(B) I and II only
(C) I and III only
(D) II and III only
(E) I, II, and III

24 The passage suggests that the "whole story"
(line 64) should include the possibility that

(A) numerical supremacy would not have
been an advantage to the British
(B) King Henry had more soldiers available than was previously believed
(C) the English longbow was not as
accurate as the French soldiers
believed it to be
(D) confidence aided the French more
than the British
(E) the French did not really outman the
British

STOP

You may check your work, on this
section only, until time is called.

Section 3

Time—25 miinutes
20 Questions

Directions for Multiple-Choice Questions

In this section, solve each problem, using any available space on the page for scratchwork. Then decide which is the best of the choices given and fill in the corresponding oval on the answer sheet.

- You may use a calculator on any problem. All numbers used are real numbers.
- Figures are drawn as accurately as possible EXCEPT when it is stated that the figure is not drawn to scale.
- All figures lie in a plane unless otherwise indicated.

Reference Information

$A = \pi r^2$ $A = \ell w$
$C = 2\pi r$ $A = \frac{1}{2}bh$ $V = \ell wh$ $V = \pi r^2 h$ $c^2 = a^2 + b^2$ Special Right Triangles

The arc of a circle measures 360°.
Every straight angle measures 180°.
The sum of the measures of the angles in a triangle is 180°.

---

1 If n is 3 times an even number, then which of the following could be n?

(A) 14
(B) 15
(C) 16
(D) 17
(E) 18

2 A machine can produce 50 computer chips in 2 hours. At this rate, how many computer chips can the machine produce in 7 hours?

(A) 175
(B) 200
(C) 225
(D) 250
(E) 275

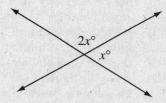

3 In the figure above, what is the value of x?

(A) 40
(B) 45
(C) 60
(D) 75
(E) 90

4 Any positive integer that is divisible by 6 and 15 must also be divisible by

(A) 12
(B) 21
(C) 30
(D) 72
(E) 90

GO ON TO THE NEXT PAGE ▶▶▶

5 If n percent of 20 is 4, what is n?

(A) ⅕
(B) 2
(C) 5
(D) 20
(E) 500

6 If $f(x) = 3x + n$, where n is a constant, and $f(2) = 0$, then $f(0) =$

(A) −6
(B) −2
(C) 0
(D) 2
(E) 6

7 A square has the same area as a right triangle with sides of lengths 6, 8, and 10. What is the length of 1 side of the square?

(A) 4
(B) $2\sqrt{3}$
(C) $\sqrt{15}$
(D) $2\sqrt{6}$
(E) 12

8 If $12v = 3w$ and $v \neq 0$, then which of the following is equivalent to $2w - 8v$?

(A) 0
(B) $4w$
(C) $-6w$
(D) $2v$
(E) $-2v$

9 If x is a negative number and $2|x| + 1 > 5$, then which of the following must be true?

(A) $x < -3$
(B) $x < -2.5$
(C) $x < -2$
(D) $x < -2$
(E) $x < -5$

10 If $x = -2$, then $-x^2 - 8x - 5 =$

(A) 3
(B) 7
(C) 15
(D) 23
(E) 25

11 If $\dfrac{5}{m} \leq \dfrac{2}{3}$ then what is the smallest possible positive value of m?

(A) 6
(B) 6.5
(C) 7
(D) 7.5
(E) 8

12 Theo wants to buy a sweater that is priced at $60.00 before tax. The store charges a 6% sales tax on all purchases. If he gives the cashier $70.00 for the sweater, how much should he receive in change?

(A) $3.60
(B) $6.40
(C) $7.40
(D) $9.40
(E) $66.40

13 When m is subtracted from n, the result is r. Which of the following expresses the result when $2m$ is added to s?

(A) $s + 2n - 2r$ (B) $s + 2n + 2r$
(C) $2s + 2n - 2r$ (D) $2s + 2n + 2r$
(E) $s - 2n + 2r$

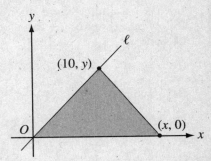

Note: Figure not drawn to scale.

14 In the figure above, the slope of line l is $\dfrac{3}{5}$ and the area of the triangle is 48 square units. What is the value of $x + y$?

(A) 13
(B) 14
(C) 19
(D) 22
(E) 96

GO ON TO THE NEXT PAGE ▸▸▸

15 Ellen takes a trip that is y miles long in total, where $y > 20$. She travels the first 15 miles at an average speed of 30 miles per hour and the rest of the trip at an average speed of 40 miles per hour. Which of the following represents the total time of the trip, in hours?

(A) $\dfrac{1}{2} + \dfrac{y-15}{40}$

(B) $2 + \dfrac{y-15}{40}$

(C) $\dfrac{1}{2} + 40y - 15$

(D) $2 + 40(y-15)$

(E) $\dfrac{1}{2} + 40y - 15$

16 If y varies directly as m and inversely as the square of n, and if $y = 8$ when $m = 16$ and $n = 1$, then what is the value of y when $m = 8$ and $n = 4$?

(A) 0.125
(B) 0.25
(C) 0.5
(D) 1
(E) 2

17 If $a + b = s$ and $a - b = t$, then which of the following expresses the value of ab in terms of s and t?

(A) st

(B) $\dfrac{(s-t)}{2}$

(C) $\dfrac{(s+t)}{2}$

(D) $\dfrac{(s^2 - t^2)}{4}$

(E) $\dfrac{(s^2 - t^2)}{2}$

18 If $y = m^4 = n^3$ and y is greater than 1, then $mn =$

(A) $y^{1/12}$
(B) $y^{1/7}$
(C) $y^{7/12}$
(D) y^7
(E) y^{12}

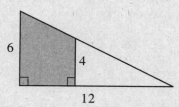

6   4   12

Note: Figure not drawn to scale.

19 In the figure above, what is the area of the shaded region?

(A) 20
(B) 22
(C) 24
(D) 26
(E) 28

20 Every car at a certain dealership is either a convertible, a sedan, or both. If one-fifth of the convertibles are also sedans and one-third of the sedans are also convertibles, which of the following could be the total number of cars at the dealership?

(A) 28
(B) 29
(C) 30
(D) 31
(E) 32

STOP

You may check your work, on this section only, until time is called.

Section 4

Time — 25 miinutes
18 Questions

Directions for Multiple-Choice Questions

In this section, solve each problem, using any available space on the page for scratchwork. Then decide which is the best of the choices given and fill in the corresponding oval on the answer sheet.

- You may use a calculator on any problem. All numbers used are real numbers.
- Figures are drawn as accurately as possible EXCEPT when it is stated that the figure is not drawn to scale.
- All figures lie in a plane unless otherwise indicated.

4

Reference Information

$A = \pi r^2$
$C = 2\pi r$

$A = \ell w$

$A = \frac{1}{2}bh$

$V = \ell w h$

$V = \pi r^2 h$

$c^2 = a^2 + b^2$

Special Right Triangles

The arc of a circle measures 360°.
Every straight angle measures 180°.
The sum of the measures of the angles in a triangle is 180°.

---

1 A square has a perimeter of 36 centimeters. What is its area in square centimeters?

(A) 24
(B) 36
(C) 49
(D) 64
(E) 81

2 If b is a positive integer less than 100, then how many integer pairs (a, b) satisfy the equation $\frac{a}{b} = \frac{1}{10}$?

(A) 7
(B) 8
(C) 9
(D) 10
(E) 11

3

Cleaning Costs in the McKenzie Office Building

Room Type	Number of Rooms in the Building	Cost per Room to Clean
Bathrooms	10	$20
Offices	30	$15

According to the table above, how much will it cost, in dollars, to clean each bathroom twice and each office once in the McKenzie Office Building?

(A) 200
(B) 400
(C) 450
(D) 600
(E) 850

GO ON TO THE NEXT PAGE ▶▶▶

4 If $a^2 - b^2 = 10$ and $a - b = 2$, what is the value of $a + b$?

(A) 5
(B) 6
(C) 7
(D) 8
(E) 9

5 For all integers n greater than 1, let $f(n) = k$, where k is the sum of all the prime factors of n. What is the value of $f(14) - f(6)$?

(A) 4
(B) 5
(C) 6
(D) 9
(E) 14

6 The average (arithmetic mean) of 4 different positive integers is 20. What is the greatest possible value of any of these integers?

(A) 68
(B) 70
(C) 73
(D) 74
(E) 77

7 The radius of circle A is twice the radius of circle B. If the sum of their circumferences is 36π, then what is the radius of circle A?

(A) 9
(B) 12
(C) 14
(D) 16
(E) 18

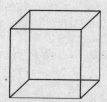

8 The figure above represents a cube. How many different planes can be drawn if each plane must contain *exactly 2* edges of the cube?

(A) 4
(B) 5
(C) 6
(D) 7
(E) 8

Directions for Student-Produced Response Questions

Each of the questions in this section requires you to solve the problem and enter your answer in a grid, as shown below.

- If your answer is ⅔ or .666 ..., you must enter **the most accurate value the grid can accommodate**, but you may do this in one of four ways:

Start in first column

Grid result here

Start in second column

Grid as a truncated decimal

Grid as a rounded decimal

- In the example above, gridding a response of 0.67 or 0.66 is **incorrect** because it is less accurate than those above.

- The scoring machine cannot read what is written in the top row of boxes. You **MUST** fill in the numerical grid accurately to get credit for answering any question correctly. You should write your answer in the top row of boxes only to aid your gridding.

- Do **not** grid in a mixed fraction like $3\frac{1}{2}$ as $\boxed{3\,|\,1\,/\,2}$ because it will be interpreted as $\frac{31}{2}$. Instead, convert it to an improper fraction like $\frac{7}{2}$ or a decimal like 3.5 before gridding.

- None of the answers will be negative, because there is no negative sign in the grid.

- Some of the questions may have more than one correct answer. You must grid only one of the correct answers.

- You may use a calculator on any of these problems.

- All numbers in these problems are real numbers.

- Figures are drawn as accurately as possible EXCEPT when it is stated that the figure is not drawn to scale.

- All figures lie in a plane unless otherwise indicated.

 9 If 10 less than $2x$ is 22, then what is the value of x?

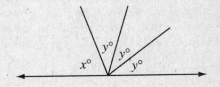

10 In the figure above, if $x = 2y$, then what is the value of y?

GO ON TO THE NEXT PAGE ▸▸▸

11 If $8x + 4y = 20$, then $2x + y =$

12 If the average (arithmetic mean) of x, y, and 20 is 30 and x is 10 greater than y, then what is the value of y?

13 The ratio of men to women in a room is 4:5. If the room contains 3 more women than men, how many women are in the room?

14 If, for some constant value b, the equation $y = |2x - b|$ is satisfied by the point (5, 2), then what is 1 possible value of b?

15 A mixture of water and sucrose is 10% sucrose by weight. How many grams of pure sucrose must be added to a 200-gram sample of this mixture to produce a mixture that is 20% sucrose?

16 A runner runs a 16-mile race at an average speed of 8 miles per hour. By how many <u>minutes</u> can she improve her time in this race if she trains and increases her average speed by 25%?

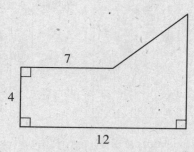

<u>Note:</u> Figure not drawn to scale.

17 The area of the figure above is 78. What is its perimeter?

18 Every sophomore at Hillside High School is required to study at least 1 language among Spanish, French, and Latin, but no one may study more than 2. If 120 sophomores study Spanish, 80 study French, 75 study Latin, and 50 study 2 of the 3 languages, how many sophomores are there at Hillside High School?

STOP

You may check your work, on this section only, until time is called.

Section 5

Time—25 minutes
24 Questions

Each sentence below has one or two blanks, each blank indicating that something has been omitted. Beneath the sentence are five words or sets of words labeled A through E. Choose the word or set of words that, when inserted in the sentence, *best* fits the meaning of the sentence as a whole.

Example:

Medieval kingdoms did not become constitutional republics overnight; on the contrary, the change was ———.

(A) unpopular   (B) unexpected
(C) advantageous   (D) sufficient
(E) gradual

Correct response: (E)

1 The _____ with which the advisor managed the funds forced his clients to seek more reliable advice regarding investment.

(A) skill
(B) caution
(C) ineptitude
(D) recognition
(E) bitterness

2 As an Armenian born in Iran and educated in Lebanon, Vartan Gregorian brought _____ flavor to the presidency of Brown University that was unprecedented in the Ivy League.

(A) a perpetual
(B) an authoritative
(C) a structured
(D) an artificial
(E) a cosmopolitan

3 The lawyers did not have time to consider the contract in great detail; rather, they were able to give it only a ——— reading before they had to make their presentation on its merits.

(A) verbatim
(B) meandering
(C) tormented
(D) cursory
(E) substantial

4 The _____ in many parts of the city has made the _____ of infectious diseases more rapid, because pathogens spread quickly in close quarters.

(A) overcrowding ... propagation
(B) squalor ... circulation
(C) poverty ... deterioration
(D) congestion ... elimination
(E) proximity ... resilience

5 Much research in neuroscience today endeavors to _____ the mechanisms by which our brains turn the _____ data from our sense organs into coherent and understandable information.

(A) enhance ... quality of
(B) restore ... absence of
(C) enlighten ... source of
(D) attenuate ... dearth of
(E) elucidate ... deluge of

The passages below are followed by questions based on their content. Answer each question based on what is stated or implied in the passages.

Questions 6–7 are based on the following passage.

Line   Towards the middle and the end of the
        sixteenth century there were many students
        and scholars possessing a great deal of
        erudition, but very little means of
5   subsistence. Nor were their prospects very
        encouraging. They first went through that
        bitter experience, which, since then, so many
        have made after them—that whoever seeks
        a home in the realm of intellect runs the risk
10   of losing the solid ground on which the fruits
        for maintaining human life grow. The eye
        directed towards the Parnassus is not the
        most apt to spy out the small tortuous paths
        of daily gain. To get quick returns of interest,
15   even though it be small, from the capital of
        knowledge and learning has always been, and
        still is, a question of difficult solution.

6   The "fruits" mentioned in line 10 represent

(A)   spiritual growth
(B)   artistic skill
(C)   technological progress
(D)   the means of acquiring food and
       shelter
(E)   scientific knowledge

7   The "question" in line 17 is whether

(A)   money can buy happiness
(B)   intellectuals can earn a good living
(C)   society can construct effective
       schools
(D)   old ideas are relevant to modern
       society
(E)   scholars are happier than merchants

Questions 8–9 are based on the following passage.

Line   When there exists an inherited or instinctive
        tendency to the performance of an action, or
        an inherited taste for certain kinds of food,
        some degree of habit in the individual is
5   often or generally requisite. We find this in
        the paces of the horse, and to a certain extent
        in the pointing of dogs; although some young
        dogs point excellently the first time they are
        taken out, yet they often associate the proper
10   inherited attitude with a wrong odour, and
        even with eyesight. I have heard it asserted
        that if a calf be allowed to suck its mother
        only once, it is much more difficult afterwards
        to rear it by hand. Caterpillars which have
15   been fed on the leaves of one kind of tree,
        have been known to perish from hunger
        rather than to eat the leaves of another tree,
        although this afforded them their proper
        food, under a state of nature.

8   The "pointing of dogs" (line 8) is mentioned
       primarily as an example of

(A)   an innate habit
(B)   a behavior that humans find useful
(C)   a skill that is hard to learn
(D)   an ability that many other animals
       also have
(E)   a skill that helps animals to find food

9   Which of the following best summarizes the
       main point of the paragraph?

(A)   People will eat only what they are
       genetically determined to eat.
(B)   All animal behavior is instinctive.
(C)   Cows and other animals should not
       be fed by humans.
(D)   Habits in animals are impossible to
       break.
(E)   Inherited tendencies manifest them-
       selves in behavioral habits.

First paragraph: Jacob Feis, *Shakspere and Montaigne*, c. 1890.
    Public domain
Second paragraph: Charles Darwin, *The Expression of the
    Emotions in Man and Animals*, 1872. Public domain

GO ON TO THE NEXT PAGE ▶▶▶

The passages below are followed by questions based on their content. The questions are to be answered on the basis of what is stated or implied in the passage itself or in the introductory material that precedes them.

Questions 10–16 are based on the following passage.

The following is an excerpt from an essay entitled Political Ideals, written in 1917 by Bertrand Russell.

Line   It is not one ideal for all men, but a separate ideal for each separate man, that has to be realized if possible. Every man has it in his being to develop into something good or bad:
5   there is a best possible for him, and a worst possible. His circumstances will determine whether his capacities for good are developed or crushed, and whether his bad impulses are strengthened or gradually diverted into better
10   channels.

But although we cannot set up in any detail an ideal of character which is to be universally applicable—although we cannot say, for instance, that all men ought to be
15   industrious, or self-sacrificing, or fond of music—there are some broad principles which can be used to guide our estimates as to what is possible or desirable.

We may distinguish two sorts of goods,
20   and two corresponding sorts of impulses. There are goods in regard to which individual possession is possible, and there are goods in which all can share alike. The food and clothing of one man is not the food and
25   clothing of another; if the supply is insufficient, what one man has is obtained at the expense of some other man. This applies to material goods generally, and therefore to the greater part of the present economic life
30   of the world. On the other hand, mental and spiritual goods do not belong to one man to the exclusion of another. If one man knows a science, that does not prevent others from knowing it; on the contrary, it helps them to
35   acquire the knowledge. If one man is a great artist or poet, that does not prevent others from painting pictures or writing poems, but helps to create the atmosphere in which such things are possible. If one man is full of
40   good-will toward others, that does not mean

that there is less goodwill to be shared among the rest; the more goodwill one man has, the more he is likely to create among others.

In such matters there is no possession,
45   because there is not a definite amount to be shared; any increase anywhere tends to produce an increase everywhere.

There are two kinds of impulses, corresponding to the two kinds of goods.
50   There are possessive impulses, which aim at acquiring or retaining private goods that cannot be shared; these center in the impulse of property. And there are creative or constructive impulses, which aim at bringing
55   into the world or making available for use the kind of goods in which there is no privacy and no possession.

The best life is the one in which the creative impulses play the largest part and
60   the possessive impulses the smallest. This is no new discovery. The Gospel says: "Take no thought, saying, What shall we eat? or What shall we drink? Or Wherewithal shall we be clothed?" The thought we give to these
65   things is taken away from matters of more importance. And what is worse, the habit of mind engendered by thinking of these things is a bad one; it leads to competition, envy, domination, cruelty, and almost all the moral
70   evils that infest the world. In particular, it leads to the predatory use of force. Material possessions can be taken by force and enjoyed by the robber. Spiritual possessions cannot be taken in this way. You may kill an
75   artist or a thinker, but you cannot acquire his art or his thought. You may put a man to death because he loves his fellow-men, but you will not by so doing acquire the love which made his happiness. Force is impotent
80   in such matters; it is only as regards material goods that it is effective. For this reason the men who believe in force are the men whose thoughts and desires are preoccupied with material goods.

GO ON TO THE NEXT PAGE ▶▶▶

10 Which of the following best summarizes the main point of the passage?

(A) People should strive harder to appreciate the arts.
(B) Nothing can be possessed exclusively by one person.
(C) Societies need strong laws against stealing.
(D) Creativity is of higher value than possessiveness.
(E) Scarce resources should be shared equally in a society.

11 The passage mentions "food and clothing" (lines 23–24) primarily as examples of things that

(A) everyone needs to survive
(B) create a positive atmosphere of sharing
(C) many underdeveloped countries lack
(D) cannot be shared as freely as other things
(E) are hard to find

12 As it is used in line 44, "such matters" can be inferred to refer to situations in which

(A) people must compete for ownership of goods
(B) artists struggle to sell their works
(C) people strive to be industrious
(D) philosophers endeavor to define human ideals
(E) possessing a good does not deny it to someone else

13 In line 52, the phrase "impulse of" most nearly means

(A) reaction against
(B) restriction of
(C) sharing of
(D) fear of
(E) desire for

14 According to the author, "force is impotent in such matters" (line 79–80) because

(A) violence cannot influence another person's thoughts
(B) moral people do not engage in violence
(C) spiritual things cannot be acquired coercively
(D) a good person will always be protected by friends
(E) reason is more powerful than physical force

15 In the last paragraph, the author indicates that his thesis is not

(A) ancient
(B) a matter of logic
(C) relevant to those who are already happy
(D) original
(E) universal

16 Which of the following examples, if it existed, would most directly refute the main point of the author?

(A) a person who finds a large sum of money and gives it to charity
(B) an invention that benefits all of humankind even though it was created only to make money for its inventor
(C) a tyrant who murders intellectuals in order to maintain his authority
(D) a thief who steals in order to feed his starving family
(E) an army that invades another country and plunders its wealth

GO ON TO THE NEXT PAGE ▶▶▶

Questions 17–24 are based on the following passage.

The following passage was written for The Atlantic Monthly *in 1902 by Native American writer Zitkala-Sa, also known as Gertrude Simmons Bonnin.*

Line   The racial lines, which once were bitterly
        real, now serve nothing more than marking
        out a living mosaic of human beings. And
        even here men of the same color are like the
5   ivory keys of one instrument where each
        represents all the rest, yet varies from them
        in pitch and quality of voice. Thus with a
        compassion for all echoes in human guise,
        I greet the solemn-faced "native preacher"
10   whom I find awaiting me. I listen with respect
        for God's creature, though he mouth most
        strangely the jangling phrases of a bigoted
        creed.
            As our tribe is one large family, where
15   every person is related to all the others,
        he addressed me:
            "Cousin, I came from the morning church
        service to talk with you."
            "Yes," I said interrogatively, as he paused
20   for some word from me.
            Shifting uneasily about in the straight-
        backed chair he sat upon, he began: "Every
        holy day (Sunday) I look about our little
        God's house, and not seeing you there, I am
        disappointed.
25   This is why I come today. Cousin, as I watch
        you from afar, I see no unbecoming behavior
        and hear only good reports of you, which all
        the more burns me with the wish that you
        were a church member. Cousin, I was taught
30   long years ago by kind missionaries to read
        the holy book. These godly men taught me
        also the folly of our old beliefs.
            "There is one God who gives reward or
        punishment to the race of dead men. In the
35   upper region the Christian dead are gathered
        in unceasing song and prayer. In the deep pit
        below, the sinful ones dance in torturing
        flames.
            "Think upon these things, my cousin, and
40   choose now to avoid the after-doom of hell
        fire!" Then followed a long silence in which
        he clasped tighter and unclasped again his
        interlocked fingers.

45   Like instantaneous lightning flashes came
        pictures of my own mother's making, for she,
        too, is now a follower of the new superstition.
            "Knocking out the chinking of our log
        cabin, some evil hand thrust in a burning
        taper of braided dry grass, but failed of his
50   intent, for the fire died out and the half burned
        brand fell inward to the floor. Directly above
        it, on a shelf, lay the holy book. This is what
        we found after our return from a several
        days' visit. Surely some great power is hid in
55   the sacred book!"
            Brushing away from my eyes many like
        pictures, I offered midday meal to the
        converted Indian sitting wordless and with
        downcast face. No sooner had he risen from
60   the table with "Cousin, I have relished it,"
        than the church bell rang.
            Thither he hurried forth with his afternoon
        sermon. I watched him as he hastened along,
        his eyes bent fast upon the dusty road till he
65   disappeared at the end of a quarter of a mile.
            The little incident recalled to mind the
        copy of a missionary paper brought to my
        notice a few days ago, in which a "Christian"
        pugilist[1] commented upon a recent article of
70   mine, grossly perverting the spirit of my pen.
        Still I would not forget that the pale-faced
        missionary and the aborigine are both God's
        creatures, though small indeed their own
        conceptions of Infinite Love. A wee child
75   toddling in a wonder world, I prefer to their
        dogma my excursions into the natural
        gardens where the voice of the Great Spirit is
        heard in the twittering of birds, the rippling
        of mighty waters, and the sweet breathing of
80   flowers. If this is Paganism, then at present,
        at least, I am a Pagan.

17   The main purpose of the passage as a whole
        is to

(A)   describe one person's perspective on
       an attempt at religious conversion
(B)   compare Native American religious
       tradition to European religious
       tradition
(C)   analyze the rise of Christianity in
       Native American tribes
(D)   refute a misconception about the
       nature of Paganism
(E)   describe a conflict between the
       author and her mother

[1]One who fights for a cause; also, a prize fighter

GO ON TO THE NEXT PAGE ▶▶▶

18 The reference to "pitch and quality of voice" (line 7) serves to emphasize

(A) the variety in vocal quality of religious singers

(B) the harshness with which many preachers rebuke their congregations

(C) the sounds that the author hears in nature

(D) the author's inability to understand what the native preacher is saying

(E) the differences among members of the same race

5 **19** In the first paragraph, the author characterizes the preacher primarily as

(A) respectful

(B) articulate

(C) uneducated

(D) intolerant

(E) compassionate

20 According to the passage, the preacher addressed the author as "cousin" because

(A) it is customary for preachers to refer to church members with that term

(B) the tribe members are all related

(C) the preacher's mother and the author's mother are sisters

(D) the preacher had forgotten the author's name

(E) the author refused to answer to her given name

21 According to the passage, the native preacher and the author's mother are alike in that they both

(A) have experienced attempted arson

(B) must travel a great deal

(C) have similar religious beliefs

(D) relish the midday meal

(E) enjoy excursions into the natural gardens

22 In line 70, the word "spirit" most nearly means

(A) apparition

(B) lively nature

(C) intent

(D) fear

(E) presence

23 In the final paragraph, the author characterizes herself primarily as

(A) mature

(B) creative

(C) vengeful

(D) repressed

(E) awed

24 The author mentions "conceptions of Infinite Love" (line 74) in order to emphasize which of the following characteristics of the "pale-faced missionary" (lines 71–72)?

(A) small-mindedness

(B) reluctance to persist in the attempt to convert the author to Christianity

(C) generosity toward aborigines

(D) sympathy for animals

(E) high intelligence

STOP

You may check your work, on this section only, until time is called.

Section 6

Time—25 Minutes
35 Questions

Directions for "Improving Sentences" Questions

Each of the sentences below contains one underlined portion. The portion may contain one or more errors in grammar, usage, construction, precision, diction (choice of words), or idiom. Some of the sentences are correct.

Consider the meaning of the original sentence, and choose the answer that best expresses that meaning. If the original sentence is best, choose (A), because it repeats the original phrasing. Choose the phrasing that creates the clearest, most precise and most effective sentence.

EXAMPLE:

The children couldn't hardly believe their eyes.

   (A)   couldn't hardly believe their eyes
   (B)   would not hardly believe their eyes
   (C)   could hardly believe their eyes
   (D)   couldn't nearly believe their eyes
   (E)   could hardly believe his or her eyes

Example answer: (C)

---

1 Claims about harmful effects of the genetic alteration of vegetables <u>is more speculation than documented fact.</u>

   (A)   is more speculation than documented fact
   (B)   are more with speculation than of a documented fact
   (C)   is more of a speculation than a documented fact
   (D)   are more speculation than documented fact
   (E)   are a matter of more speculation than documented fact

2 <u>Having passed</u> the test for certification, Mackenzie was looking forward to finding a challenging teaching position in her home town.

   (A)   having passed
   (B)   passing
   (C)   being that she passed
   (D)   if she had passed
   (E)   for her passing

3 Having once been a provincial schoolmaster, <u>Jean-Paul Sartre's writing was always oriented more toward clear instruction than pontification.</u>

   (A)   Jean-Paul Sartre's writing was always oriented more toward clear instruction than pontification
   (B)   Jean-Paul Sartre always wrote to instruct more than to pontificate
   (C)   the writings of Jean-Paul Sartre were always oriented more toward instruction than pontification
   (D)   Jean-Paul Sartre was oriented in his writing more toward instruction than pontification
   (E)   Jean-Paul Sartre's writing was more to instruct than to pontificate

4 Adam Smith was a professor of philosophy, <u>a commissioner of customs, and founded the field of modern economics.</u>

   (A)   a commissioner of customs, and founded the field of modern economics
   (B)   worked as commissioner of customs, and founded the field of modern economics
   (C)   a commissioner of customs, and the founder of the field of modern economics
   (D)   commissioned customs, and was the founder of the field of modern economics
   (E)   a commissioner of customs, and was the founder of the field of modern economics

6

GO ON TO THE NEXT PAGE ▶▶▶

5 John Locke was one of the first philosophers to attack the principle of <u>primogeniture, the practice of handing the monarchy down</u> to the king's first-born son.

- (A) primogeniture, the practice of handing the monarchy down
- (B) primogeniture; the practice of handing the monarchy down
- (C) primogeniture being the practice of handing the monarchy down
- (D) primogeniture that which handed down the monarchy
- (E) primogeniture this was the practice of handing the monarchy down

6 The nation's fledgling economy struggled <u>because the investment from other countries into its major industries was lacking from most of them</u>.

- (A) because the investment from other countries into its major industries was lacking from most of them
- (B) because few other countries were willing to invest in its major industries
- (C) due to the fact that few other countries would have invested in its major industries
- (D) because of the lack of investment from few other countries in its major industries
- (E) for the lack of investment in its major industries from other countries

7 The corporation began construction on the new building in January, but <u>there is still no completion</u>.

- (A) there is still no completion
- (B) they have yet to complete it
- (C) it has yet to complete the project
- (D) they have not still completed it yet
- (E) it isn't hardly done yet

8 Having spread more quickly than antibiotics could be distributed, <u>doctors were prevented from effectively treating the virulent disease</u>.

- (A) doctors were prevented from effectively treating the virulent disease
- (B) doctors could not effectively treat the virulent disease because it thwarted them
- (C) the doctors who were trying to treat it effectively were prevented by the virulent disease

- (D) the virulent disease prevented itself from its being treated effectively by the doctors
- (E) the virulent disease prevented the doctors from treating it effectively

9 Although psychologist B. F. <u>Skinner, who is best known as the man who popularized behaviorism, he</u> also wrote a utopian novel entitled *Walden Two*.

- (A) Skinner, who is best known as the man who popularized behaviorism, he
- (B) Skinner, who is best known as the man who popularized behaviorism,
- (C) Skinner is best known as the man who popularized behaviorism, he
- (D) Skinner popularized behaviorism, for which he is well known, nevertheless he
- (E) Skinner, who is best known as the man who popularized behaviorism, is the one who

10 <u>Singing for over 2 hours, Anita's hoarseness prevented her hitting the high notes</u>.

- (A) Singing for over 2 hours, Anita's hoarseness prevented her hitting the high notes.
- (B) Singing for over 2 hours, Anita was unable to hit the high notes because of her hoarseness.
- (C) Having sung for over 2 hours, Anita's hoarseness prevented her from hitting the high notes.
- (D) Having sung for over 2 hours, Anita was no longer able to hit the high notes because of her hoarseness.
- (E) Having sung for over 2 hours, Anita's ability to hit the high notes was prevented by her hoarseness.

11 Some philosophers maintain that language is essential to formulating certain <u>thoughts; others, that</u> even the most complex thoughts are independent of words.

- (A) thoughts; others, that
- (B) thoughts, however, that others maintain that
- (C) thoughts others suggest that
- (D) thoughts and that others believe
- (E) thoughts but others, however, that

GO ON TO THE NEXT PAGE ▶▶▶

Directions for Identifying Sentence Error Questions

The following sentences may contain errors in grammar, usage, diction (choice of words), or idiom. Some of the sentences are correct. No sentence contains more than 1 error.

If the sentence contains an error, it is underlined and lettered. The parts that are not underlined are correct.

If there is an error, select the part that must be changed to correct the sentence.

If there is no error, choose (E).

EXAMPLE:

By the time <u>they reached</u> the halfway point
               A
<u>in the race,</u> most of the runners <u>hadn't</u> <u>hardly</u>
    B   C   D
begun to hit their stride. <u>No error</u>
                                    E

Sample answer: (D)

---

12 Ellen turned around <u>quick</u> and noticed
                          A
<u>that the dog</u> that <u>had been following</u> her was
      B   C
now <u>gone</u>. <u>No error</u>
       D   E

13 Marlena was honored not only for her

<u>initiative</u> in establishing the fund for war
    A
refugees but also <u>in devoting</u> so much
                       B
<u>of her own time</u> and money <u>to its success</u>.
        C   D
<u>No error</u>
    E

14 The Medieval era in music <u>is considered</u>
                                    A
<u>by most</u> scholars <u>to begin</u> during the reign
    B   C
of Pope Gregory and to have ended <u>around</u>

<u>the middle of</u> the 15th century. <u>No error</u>
        D   E

15 Neither the artists <u>who were</u> at the vanguard
                            A
of the Expressionist movement <u>or even</u> the
                                   B
critics <u>of the era</u> could have foreseen
            C
<u>the impact</u> of this new mode on the general
    D
public. <u>No error</u>
            E

16 Several members <u>of the safety commission</u>
                            A
<u>suggested</u> that lowering the speed limit
    B
<u>on the road</u> would not necessarily result in
    C
<u>less</u> accidents. <u>No error</u>
    D   E

17 By the time the operation <u>was completed</u>,
                                    A
5 surgeons <u>spent</u> over 20 hours <u>performing</u>
                B   C
more than a dozen <u>procedures</u>. <u>No error</u>
                        D   E

18 Not until the recent scandal <u>has</u> the
                                      A
newspapers published <u>anything</u> even
                          B
vaguely <u>negative</u> about the company or
            C
<u>its executives</u>. <u>No error</u>
        D   E

19 <u>After falling asleep</u> on a horse-drawn bus in
        A
Belgium in 1865, Friedrick Kekule had a

<u>dream, it led</u> to <u>his discovery</u> of the structure
        B   C
<u>of the benzene molecule</u>. <u>No error</u>
            D   E

GO ON TO THE NEXT PAGE ▶▶▶

20 The movement <u>to establish</u> women's issues
        A
as important <u>subjects of study</u> <u>have had</u>
              B   C
a profound impact on the curricula

<u>offered in colleges</u> today. <u>No error</u>
        D   E

21 Legends and folk stories inevitably become

transformed and <u>exaggerated</u> as they are
                  A
<u>passed down</u> through the generations, often
   B
in order <u>to conform</u> to changing political
          C
and <u>social standards</u>. <u>No error</u>
        D   E

6

22 Although the remarks <u>were made</u> to the
                          A
entire group, <u>everyone</u> at the meeting could
               B
tell <u>that they were</u> particularly intended
     C
<u>for Maria and I</u>. <u>No error</u>
      D   E

23 By all accounts, the restructuring of the

federal department was <u>successive</u>,
                         A
<u>eliminating</u> unnecessary layers
  B
<u>of bureaucracy</u> and dozens of
  C
<u>wasteful procedures</u>. <u>No error</u>
     D   E

24 The professor <u>suggested</u> that
                      A
<u>those who wished</u> to attend the lecture next
   B
week <u>be in the classroom</u> 10 minutes
       C
<u>earlier than usual</u>. <u>No error</u>
     D   E

25 While in office a President <u>can usually</u>
                                   A
pass more legislation, <u>and with fewer</u>
                         B
procedural obstacles, when the Congress,

and the administration are <u>underneath</u> the
                             C
<u>control of</u> the same political party.
   D
<u>No error</u>
   E

26 A quick <u>inspection</u> of Kurt's art collection
                A
<u>would show clearly</u> that <u>he has</u> a discerning
   B   C
eye for <u>exemplary works</u> of art. <u>No error</u>
         D   E

27 <u>Surprisingly</u> absent from the debate <u>were</u>
   A   B
the vice president's arrogance <u>that</u> he
                                 C
typically displays <u>in such</u> forums. <u>No error</u>
                    D   E

28 Of the numerous strains of *Streptococcus*

bacteria <u>that are known</u> to cause
              A
infections, type B is the <u>more</u> dangerous
                           B
<u>for pregnant women</u> about <u>to give</u>
   C   D
birth. <u>No error</u>
         E

29 Since 2001, the company <u>has spent</u>
                                A
<u>more time on</u> employee training than
   B
<u>they did</u> in the previous 10 years <u>combined</u>.
   C   D
<u>No error</u>
   E

Questions 30–35 are based on the following passage.

(1) *Most great scientists and artists are familiar with the so-called "eureka phenomenon."* (2) *This is the experience that a thinker has when, after they thought about a problem long and hard, they suddenly come upon a solution in a flash when they are no longer thinking about it.* (3) *The name of the phenomenon comes from the legend of Archimedes.* (4) *He had been thinking for days about a hard problem that had come from the king, King Hieron II.* (5) *The problem was how to determine whether the king's crown was pure gold without destroying it.* (6) *As he was bathing, the solution to the problem came to Archimedes in a flash and he ran naked through the streets of Syracuse shouting "Eureka!" meaning "I have found it!"*

(7) *Students should understand this also.* (8) *You have probably had the experience of thinking about a paper or a math problem for so long that it's like one's brain gets frozen.* (9) *When this happens, it is best to get away from the problem for a while rather than obsess about it.* (10) *Isaac Asimov, one of the most prolific writers of all time, used to go to the movies every time he got writer's block.* (11) *He claimed that he always came out of the movie knowing exactly how to get his story back on track.*

(12) *Unfortunately, many students today don't have time for that.* (13) *They feel so much pressure to get everything done—their homework, their jobs, their sports, their extracurricular activities—that they think that taking "time out" to relax their brains is just a costly waste of time.* (14) *This is really too bad because very often relaxation is more valuable to a student than just more hard work.*

30 Which of the following is the best revision of the underlined portion of sentence 2 (reproduced below)?

This is the experience <u>that a thinker has when, after they thought about a problem long and hard, they suddenly come upon a solution in a flash</u> when they are no longer thinking about it.

(A) that a thinker has when, after they thought long and hard about a problem, their solution suddenly arises like a flash

(B) that thinkers have when a solution suddenly had arisen like a flash after they were thinking long and hard about a problem

(C) that a thinker has when, after having thought long and hard about a problem, they suddenly come upon a solution

(D) that thinkers have when, after having thought long and hard about a problem, they suddenly come upon a solution

(E) that thinkers have when, thinking long and hard about a problem, they suddenly come upon a solution in a flash

31 Which of the following is the best way to combine sentences 3, 4, and 5?

(A)   The name of the phenomenon comes from the legend of Archimedes, who had been thinking for days about how to determine whether King Hieron II's crown was pure gold without destroying it.

(B)   Archimedes had been thinking for days about how to determine whether King Hieron II's crown was pure gold without destroying it, and this is where the name of the phenomenon comes from.

(C)   The legend of Archimedes thinking about how to determine whether King Hieron II's crown was pure gold without destroying it is the origin of the name of the phenomenon.

(D)   The phenomenon is named for Archimedes and his thinking for days about how to determine whether King Hieron II's crown was pure gold without destroying it.

(E)   The name of the phenomenon was from Archimedes, and his thinking for days about how to determine without destroying it whether King Hieron II's crown was pure gold.

32 Which of the following revisions of sentence 7 most clearly and logically introduces the second paragraph?

(A)   This historical episode is something that all students should learn about in school.

(B)   Understanding this phenomenon may help students to improve their studies.

(C)   Nevertheless, this episode is something that all students should know.

(D)   Understanding this episode requires a more thorough understanding of its historical setting.

(E)   Many have tried to understand this phenomenon, but few have succeeded.

33 Which of the following is the best revision of the underlined portion of sentence 8 (reproduced below)?

You have probably had the experience of thinking about a paper or a math problem for so long that it's like one's brain gets frozen.

(A)   it seems that your brain gets frozen
(B)   one's brain gets frozen
(C)   your brain seems to freeze
(D)   your brains seem to freeze
(E)   one's brain seems to freeze

34 Where is the best place to insert the following sentence?

Perhaps if students could work such little excursions into their busy study schedules, they would have similar "eureka" experiences.

(A)   after sentence 7
(B)   after sentence 8
(C)   after sentence 9
(D)   after sentence 10
(E)   after sentence 11 (as the last sentence of the second paragraph)

35 In context, which of the following revisions of the underlined portion of sentence 12 (reproduced below) is most effective at making it clearer and more specific?

Unfortunately, many students today don't have time for that.

(A)   today have hardly even 1 hour for such things

(B)   today, unlike those in Archimedes' time, don't have time to go to the movies

(C)   today don't have time for such excursions

(D)   of modern times lack sufficient time for the kinds of things explained above

(E)   today lack sufficient time for things like this

STOP

You may check your work, on this section only, until time is called.

Section 7

Time — 20 minutes
16 Questions

Directions for Multiple-Choice Questions

In this section, solve each problem, using any available space on the page for scratchwork. Then decide which is the best of the choices given and fill in the corresponding oval on your answer sheet.

- You may use a calculator on any problem. All numbers used are real numbers.
- Figures are drawn as accurately as possible EXCEPT when it is stated that the figure is not drawn to scale.
- All figures lie in a plane unless otherwise indicated.

Reference Information

$A = \pi r^2$　　$A = \ell w$　　　　$A = \frac{1}{2}bh$　　$V = \ell wh$　　$V = \pi r^2 h$　　$c^2 = a^2 + b^2$　　Special Right Triangles
$C = 2\pi r$

The arc of a circle measures 360°.
Every straight angle measures 180°.
The sum of the measures of the angles in a triangle is 180°.

---

1 If four apples cost 20 cents, then, at this rate, how much would 10 apples cost?

(A) $.40
(B) $.50
(C) $.60
(D) $.70
(E) $.80

2 If $2^b = 8$, then $3^b =$

(A) 6
(B) 9
(C) 27
(D) 64
(E) 81

3 How much greater is the average (arithmetic mean) of a, b, and 18 than the average of a, b, and 12?

(A) 2
(B) 3
(C) 4
(D) 5
(E) 6

4 The first day of a particular month is a Tuesday. What day of the week will it be on the 31st day of the month?

(A) Wednesday
(B) Thursday
(C) Friday
(D) Saturday
(E) Sunday

5 How many integer pairs (m, n) satisfy the statements $0 < m + n < 50$ and $\frac{m}{n} = 8$?

(A) 5
(B) 6
(C) 7
(D) 8
(E) more than 8

GO ON TO THE NEXT PAGE ▶▶▶

6 If y% of 50 is 32, then what is 200% of y?

(A) 16
(B) 32
(C) 64
(D) 128
(E) 256

7 For $x > 0$, the function $g(x)$ is defined by the equation $g(x) = x + x^{1/2}$. What is the value of $g(16)$?

(A) 16
(B) 20
(C) 24
(D) 64
(E) 272

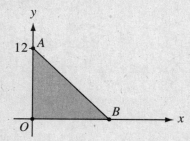

Note: Figure not drawn to scale.

8 In the figure above, if the slope of $\overline{AB}$ is $-\frac{3}{4}$, what is the area of $\triangle ABO$?

(A) 54
(B) 72
(C) 96
(D) 108
(E) 192

9   −1, 1, 2, −1, 1, 2, −1, 1, 2, ...

The sequence above continues according to the pattern shown. What is the sum of the first 25 terms of this sequence?

(A) 15
(B) 16
(C) 18
(D) 19
(E) 21

10 A jar contains only white and blue marbles of identical size and weight. The ratio of the number of white marbles to the number of blue marbles is 4 to b. If the probability of choosing a white marble from the jar at random is $\frac{1}{4}$, then what is the value of b?

(A) 1
(B) 2
(C) 6
(D) 12
(E) 16

11 The area of a right triangle is 10 square centimeters. If the length of each leg, in centimeters, is a positive integer, then what is the *least* possible length, in centimeters, of the hypotenuse?

(A) $\sqrt{29}$
(B) $\sqrt{41}$
(C) $\sqrt{101}$
(D) $\sqrt{104}$
(E) $\sqrt{401}$

12 If y is a number less than 0 but greater than −1, which of the following expressions has the greatest value?

(A) $100y$
(B) y^2
(C) y^3
(D) y^4
(E) y^5

13 If at least one wuzzle is grumpy, then some fuzzles are lumpy. If the statement above is true, then which of the following must also be true?

(A) If all wuzzles are grumpy, then all fuzzles are lumpy.
(B) If no wuzzle is grumpy, then all fuzzles are lumpy.
(C) If all fuzzles are lumpy, then all wuzzles are grumpy.
(D) If no wuzzle is grumpy, then no fuzzle is lumpy.
(E) If no fuzzle is lumpy, then no wuzzle is grumpy.

14 Six buses are to carry 200 students on a field trip. If each bus must have no more than 40 students and no fewer than 30 students, then what is the greatest number of buses that can have 40 students?

(A) 6
(B) 5
(C) 4
(D) 3
(E) 2

16 In a set of 30 different positive integers, every number is even and/or a multiple of 3. If 22 of these numbers are even and 15 are multiples of 3, then how many of these numbers are multiples of 6?

(A) 23
(B) 22
(C) 15
(D) 11
(E) 7

15 The volume of right cylinder A is twice the volume of right cylinder B. If the height of cylinder B is twice the height of cylinder A, then what is the ratio of the radius of cylinder A to the radius of cylinder B?

(A) 1 to 2
(B) 1 to 1
(C) $\sqrt{2}$ to 1
(D) 2 to 1
(E) 4 to 1

You may check your work, on this section only, until time is called.

Section 8

Time — 20 minutes
19 Questions

Each of the sentences below is missing one or two portions. Read each sentence, then select the word or words that most logically completes the sentence, taking into account the meaning of the sentence as a whole.

Example:

Rather than accepting the theory unquestioningly, Deborah regarded it with ———.

(A) mirth   (B) sadness
(C) responsibility (D) ignorance
(E) skepticism

Correct response: (E)

8

1 The evidence for ESP is _____ at best, so very few reputable scientists are willing to even _____ that the phenomenon exists.

(A) meager ... regret
(B) unconvincing ... suggest
(C) plentiful ... admit
(D) paltry ... deny
(E) strong ... assume

2 The concept that the Earth is round was once _____ theory, but is now accepted as an inarguable truth.

(A) an incontrovertible
(B) a mellifluous
(C) an admirable
(D) a dubious
(E) an accurate

3 The controversy within the party produced a _____ that broke it into several factions even before the matter could be fully discussed among the members.

(A) unanimity
(B) schism
(C) caucus
(D) commemoration
(E) prognostication

4 Horace Mann, widely acknowledged as the father of American public schooling, _____ the Massachusetts legislature to institute a system for _____ universal access to education.

(A) petitioned ... restricting
(B) established ... denying
(C) persuaded ... ensuring
(D) tolerated ... requiring
(E) discouraged ... vouchsafing

5 The light from most stars takes millions of years to reach us, so not only is the present existence of these stars _____, but so are the very concepts of "the present" and "existence."

(A) debatable   (B) methodical
(C) indecorous   (D) imperious
(E) profuse

6 Although many parents prefer to be _____ when their children broach sensitive personal subjects, others resort instead to _____ so as to make any potentially offensive matters seem less objectionable.

(A) honest ... anachronism
(B) intolerant ... laudation
(C) clandestine ... obligation
(D) candid ... euphemism
(E) forthright ... coercion

GO ON TO THE NEXT PAGE ▶▶▶

The passages below are followed by questions based on their content and the relationship between the passages. The questions are to be answered on the basis of what is stated or implied in the passages or the introductory material that precedes them.

Questions 7–19 are based on the following passages.

The following 2 passages concern the use of "reinforcers," which are rewards or punishments used to encourage desired behaviors, and "contingencies," which are the arrangements of those reinforcers to shape behavior.

Passage 1

Line   "Avoid compulsion," said Plato in *The Republic*, "and let your children's lessons take the form of play." Horace, among others, recommended rewarding a child with
5   cakes. Erasmus tells of an English gentleman who tried to teach his son Greek and Latin without punishment. He taught the boy to use a bow and arrow and set up targets in the shape of Greek and Latin letters, rewarding
10   each hit with a cherry. He also fed the boy letters cut from delicious biscuits. Privileges and favors are often suggested, and the teacher may be personally reinforcing as friend or entertainer. In industrial education
15   students are paid for learning. Certain explicit contrived reinforcers, such as marks, grades, and diplomas, are characteristic of education as an institution. (These suggest progress, but like progress they must be
20   made reinforcing for other reasons.) Prizes are intrinsically reinforcing. Honors and medals derive their power from prestige or esteem. This varies between cultures and epochs. In 1876 Oscar Wilde, then 22 years
25   old and halfway toward his B.A. at Oxford, got a "first in Mods." He wrote to a friend: "… I did not know what I had got till the next morning at 12 o'clock, breakfasting at the Mitre, I read it in the *Times*. Altogether I
30   swaggered horribly but am really pleased with myself. My poor mother is in great delight, and I was overwhelmed with telegrams on Thursday from everyone I knew." The contemporary student graduating
35   *summa cum laude* is less widely acclaimed.

Although free of some of the by-products of aversive control, positive reinforcers of this sort are not without their problems. Many are effective only in certain states of
40   deprivation which are not always easily arranged. Making a student hungry in order to reinforce him with food would raise personal issues which are not entirely avoided with other kinds of reinforcers.
45   We cannot all get prizes, and if some students get high grades, others must get low.

But the main problem again is the contingencies. Much of what the child is to do in school does not have the form of play,
50   with its naturally reinforcing consequences, nor is there any natural connection with food or a passing grade or a medal. Such contingencies must be arranged by the teacher, and the arrangement is often
55   defective. The boy mentioned by Erasmus may have salivated slightly upon seeing a Greek or Latin text, and he was probably a better archer, but his knowledge of Greek and Latin could not have been appreciably
60   improved. Grades are almost always given long after the student has stopped behaving as a student. We must know that such contingencies are weak because we would never use them to shape skilled behavior.
65   In industrial education pay is usually by the hour—in other words, contingent mainly on being present. Scholarships are contingent on a general level of performance. All these contingencies could no doubt be improved,
70   but there is probably good reason why they remain defective.

Passage 2

Even if they don't study it as a philosophical matter, all teachers must at some point confront the issue of whether, when, and how
75   to punish or reward student behavior. Unless a teacher is blessed with a class full of highly motivated adult-pleasers, it is nearly impossible to avoid the need to nudge students in one direction or another.

First passage: B. F. Skinner, *The Technology of Teaching*, © 1968 Prentice-Hall, pp. 149–150
Second passage: © 2004 Christopher Black. All rights reserved. Reprinted by permission of the author.

GO ON TO THE NEXT PAGE ▶▶▶

80 Simple suggestion works occasionally, but
not frequently enough. Reasoning sometimes
works, too, but explaining the logical
nuances of behavioral standards is often
time-consuming and too often falls on deaf
85 ears. So the practical question becomes: the
carrot or the stick?

Most educators and psychologists agree
that reward is always better than punishment,
but a small yet vocal group of psychologists
have maintained since the 1960s that reward
90 is often just as harmful as punishment, if not
more so. Their arguments are subtle but very
persuasive. Educators like Alfie Kohn and
psychologists like Edward Deci claim that
careful study has shown that the introduction
95 of a reward system, like gold stars on an
attendance sheet or extra recess time for
good behavior, changes the nature of the
desired behavior completely, and not for the
better. For instance, Deci conducted a study
100 in which people were given a puzzle to solve.
Some were given money as a "reward" for
solving the puzzle and others were simply
asked to solve the puzzle. Afterwards, both
groups were left alone but watched carefully.
105 Those who had been paid stopped playing,
but those who had not been paid continued.
Deci concluded that the subjects who were
paid probably construed the task as being
manipulative: the experimenter was trying to
110 get them to do something through bribery.
The unpaid subjects, however, were more
likely to see the task as fun and worth doing
for its own sake.

This study and many like it have profound
115 implications for the classroom. Several
experiments have demonstrated that
"pay-to-read" programs, where students are
given money or certificates to read books,
have surprisingly negative effects on literacy.
120 Such programs usually get kids to "read" a
lot more books, but their reading skills and,
far more importantly, their love of reading
decline. Such programs, research suggests,
turn reading into a performance rather than
125 a fulfilling personal experience. They
encourage students to read books only
superficially and only to get the reward.
What is worse, like Deci's puzzlesolvers, the
students don't want to continue reading after
130 the payments stop. Books have become only
enrichment for the pocket, not enrichment
for the mind.

Of course, the human mind is an enormously
complex machine, and it would be a mistake
135 to use these few experiments to generalize
that all rewards are bad. Certainly, honest
and mindful praise from a respected teacher
can do a great deal to encourage not only
good behavior but rigorous intellectual
140 curiosity. Parents and teachers, however,
need to be very aware of children's need to
feel in control of themselves.

7 It can be inferred that the "English gentleman" (line 5) believed that good teaching
utilized

(A) punishment
(B) well-written books
(C) reward
(D) humor
(E) careful grading

8 The parenthetical remark in lines 18–20 is
intended to caution educators against

(A) failing to make grades and diplomas
meaningful to students
(B) punishing students unnecessarily
(C) employing dull lessons
(D) emphasizing entertainment over rigor
(E) using rewards as reinforcers

9 Passage 1 indicates that "cultures and
epochs" (lines 23–24) vary in the ways that

(A) universities choose from among their
applicants
(B) academic awards are effective as
motivators
(C) universities teach literature
(D) students are paid money for learning
(E) the media portray educational crises

10 The Wilde story in lines 24–33, "In 1876 . . . everyone I knew," is intended to illustrate

(A) how the modern cultural perception of academic honors differs from that of a previous era
(B) a particularly effective teaching strategy
(C) how a famous author used rewards to teach his students
(D) the dangerous effects of using academic rewards
(E) the point that Plato makes in the first sentence

11 Passage 1 mentions which of the following as "problems" (line 38) inherent in the use of positive reinforcers in education?

I. difficulties in scheduling the reinforcers
II. limitations in the supply of reinforcers
III. the fact that rewards encourage only superficial learning

(A) I only
(B) II only
(C) I and II only
(D) I and III only
(E) I, II, and III

12 In the final paragraph of Passage 1, the author suggests that grades are problematic as reinforcers because they

(A) cannot be given to every student
(B) do not provide sensual gratification, as food does
(C) are not publicized enough
(D) are not given immediately after the desired behavior is exhibited
(E) are not as useful to the student as money

13 The sentence that begins on line 81, "Reasoning sometimes works ... on deaf ears" is intended to describe the interaction between

(A) those who promote the use of punishments and those who oppose it
(B) educators and philosophers
(C) parents and teachers
(D) teachers and administrators
(E) teachers and students

14 In Passage 2, Alfie Kohn and Edward Deci (lines 92–93) are mentioned as examples of

(A) teachers who use rewards as reinforcers
(B) experts who question the effectiveness of rewards as reinforcers
(C) scientists on opposite sides of a debate
(D) educators who prefer negative reinforcers to positive reinforcers
(E) educators who advocate a careful schedule of contingencies for students

15 In saying that "the introduction of a reward system ... changes the nature of the desired behavior" (lines 93–95), the author of Passage 2 indicates that

(A) many people object to the use of punishments in school
(B) teachers find it difficult to find the right kinds of rewards for student performance
(C) experts disagree about the effects of rewards on human behavior
(D) such systems tend to decrease student interest in the activity for its own sake
(E) not enough study has been done on the effectiveness of rewards in education

16 Deci's conclusion about the experiment described in Passage 2 (lines 96–109) assumes that the subjects in the study

(A) are well educated
(B) are highly proficient at solving puzzles
(C) have not participated in reward systems before
(D) can make inferences about the motives of the experimenter
(E) have some teaching experience

GO ON TO THE NEXT PAGE ▶▶▶

17 The author of Passage 2 mentions that "the human mind is an enormously complex machine" (lines 134–135) in order to suggest that

(A) a simplistic theory about the effectiveness of rewards is unwise
(B) people cannot be easily fooled
(C) many learning disabilities require special attention
(D) teachers often find it hard to teach certain subjects
(E) Deci's experiment was poorly constructed

18 The description of the "problems" (line 38) with positive reinforcers in Passage 1 would most likely be regarded by Edward Deci as

(A) thorough and fair
(B) presumptuous and incomplete
(C) unfair to educators
(D) erroneous in concluding that the methods of the "gentleman" were ineffective
(E) likely correct, but worthy of further study

19 Which of the following assumptions is shared by the authors of both passages?

(A) Rewards are ineffective as reinforcers of behavior.
(B) Honors and grades are necessary elements of institutional education.
(C) Good teaching is always focused on play.
(D) Negative feedback is not an effective teaching tool.
(E) If prizes are to be used in a classroom, there must be enough for all students.

STOP

You may check your work, on this section only, until time is called.

Section 9

Time—10 Minutes
14 Questions

Directions for "Improving Sentences" Questions

Each of the sentences below contains one underlined portion. The portion may contain one or more errors in grammar, usage, construction, precision, diction (choice of words), or idiom. Some of the sentences are correct.

Consider the meaning of the original sentence, and choose the answer that best expresses that meaning. If the original sentence is best, choose (A), because it repeats the original phrasing. Choose the phrasing that creates the clearest, most precise and most effective sentence.

EXAMPLE:

The children <u>couldn't hardly believe their eyes.</u>

    (A) couldn't hardly believe their eyes
    (B) would not hardly believe their eyes
    (C) could hardly believe their eyes
    (D) couldn't nearly believe their eyes
    (E) could hardly believe his or her eyes

Example answer: (C)

---

1 <u>Choreographer Alvin Ailey's works, whose style is rooted in the techniques of modern dance, jazz dance and ballet, draw upon African American themes.</u>

(A) Choreographer Alvin Ailey's works, whose style is rooted in the techniques of modern dance, jazz dance and ballet, draw upon African American themes.

(B) Alvin Ailey has a style of a choreographer that is rooted in the techniques of modern dance, jazz dance and ballet of which also draws upon African American themes.

(C) The works of choreographer Alvin Ailey, which draw upon African American themes, have a style that is rooted in the techniques of modern dance, jazz dance, and ballet.

(D) Choreographer Alvin Ailey's works, which have a style that is rooted in the techniques of modern dance, jazz dance, and ballet, drawing upon African American themes.

(E) Alvin Ailey's style, a choreographer, is rooted in the techniques of modern dance and jazz dance and ballet which also draws upon African American themes.

2 <u>The mountain climbers getting this far, they</u> did not want to return without having reached the peak.

(A) The mountain climbers getting this far, they

(B) Having gotten this far, the mountain climbers

(C) To have gotten this far, the mountain climbers

(D) The mountain climbers having gotten so far that they

(E) Mountain climbers getting this far

3 Although usually even-tempered, <u>Rachel's irritation with her supervisor caused her to become</u> uncharacteristically cantankerous.

(A) Rachel's irritation with her supervisor caused her to become

(B) Rachel being irritated by her supervisor caused her to become

(C) Rachel was irritated by her supervisor, and so became

(D) her supervisor caused Rachel through irritation to become

(E) Rachel, due to her supervisor's irritation, caused her to become

GO ON TO THE NEXT PAGE ▶▶▶

4 Because Alberta worked harder than her associates, she assumed that her salary <u>would be higher than the</u> other workers in the firm.

(A) would be higher than the
(B) was higher than that of the
(C) had been higher than the
(D) being higher than the salary of
(E) was highest of the

5 The police chief was hoping that by assigning an extra officer to the patrol he <u>would decrease the amount of elicit</u> behavior in the neighborhood.

(A) would decrease the amount of elicit
(B) would be able to decrease the elicit
(C) would decrease the amount of illicit
(D) might be able to lessen that of the illicit
(E) decreases the amount of illicit

6 <u>Watching from the balcony</u>, the paraders marched triumphantly through the streets below us.

(A) Watching from the balcony
(B) While watching from the balcony
(C) As we had been watching from the balcony
(D) As we watched from the balcony
(E) From the balcony, while watching,

7 By the time we arrived at the campsite where the troop would be staying, <u>the counselors set up all the tents.</u>

(A) the counselors set up all the tents
(B) setting up all the tents were the counselors
(C) set up by the counselors are the tents
(D) the tents are set up by the counselors
(E) the counselors had set up all the tents

8 By the time the movie had finished, <u>neither Eric nor his daughters was able to stay awake because of the boredom caused by the film's inferior plot</u>.

(A) neither Eric nor his daughters was able to stay awake because of the boredom caused by the film's inferior plot
(B) staying awake was an impossibility for Eric and his daughters because of the boredom caused by the inferiority of the plot
(C) neither Eric nor his daughters were able to stay awake because of the boredom caused by the film's inferior plot
(D) Eric and his daughters was unable to stay awake because of the boredom caused by the film's inferior plot
(E) the film's inferior plot had made it impossible for neither Eric nor his daughters to stay awake

9 An outstanding tennis player, Erica was concerned not only with working her way to the top of the national rankings, but <u>also wanted to compete with class and dignity</u>.

(A) also wanted to compete with class and dignity
(B) also with competing with class and dignity
(C) also with wanting to have competed with class and dignity
(D) she also wanted to compete with class and dignity
(E) she was also wanting to compete with class and dignity

10 Roberto volunteered to be an usher, not wanting to be the one <u>that had to clean up the petals after the ceremony</u>.

(A) that had to clean up the petals after the ceremony
(B) which had to clean up the petals after the ceremony
(C) who had to clean up the petals after the ceremony
(D) cleaning the petals up after the ceremony
(E) who was to be cleaning the petals after the ceremony

GO ON TO THE NEXT PAGE ▶▶▶

11 Rebecca liked to read <u>books, of which she found autobiographies to be the most interesting</u>.

(A) books, of which she found autobiographies to be the most interesting

(B) books, the most fascinating of which to her she found the autobiographies

(C) books, autobiographies being the most interesting she found

(D) books; she found autobiographies to be the most interesting

(E) books, to which autobiographies were the most interesting

12 Forced to live apart from his family and to move from place to place to avoid detection by the government's ubiquitous informers, <u>St. Pierre adopting a number of disguises</u>.

(A) St. Pierre adopting a number of disguises

(B) St. Pierre having adopted a number of disguises

(C) had adopted for St. Pierre a number of disguises

(D) a number of disguises by St. Pierre had adopted

(E) St. Pierre had to adopt a number of disguises

13 The Santa Catalina <u>Mountains, forming 12 million years ago during a period when the Western North American Continent was stretching</u>, cracking into blocks, bordered by steep faults.

(A) Mountains, forming 12 million years ago during a period when the Western North American Continent was stretching

(B) Mountains were formed 12 million years ago during a period when the Western North American Continent was being stretched

(C) Mountains, having been formed 12 million years ago during a period when the Western North American Continent was stretching

(D) Mountains was formed 12 million years ago during a period when the Western North American Continent was being stretched.

(E) Mountains had been formed during a period 12 million years ago when the Western North American Continent was stretching.

14 The most challenging aspect of the project is <u>we have to coordinate our work carefully</u>.

(A) we have to coordinate our work carefully

(B) we must coordinate our work carefully

(C) our coordination of our work carefully

(D) coordinating our work carefully

(E) in careful coordination of our work

STOP

You may check your work, on this section only, until time is called.

ANSWER KEY

Section 3 Math	Section 4 Math	Section 7 Math	Section 2 Critical Reading	Section 5 Critical Reading	Section 8 Critical Reading	Section 6 Writing	Section 9 Writing
☐ 1. E	☐ 1. E	☐ 1. B	☐ 1. A	☐ 1. C	☐ 1. B	☐ 1. D	☐ 1. C
☐ 2. A	☐ 2. C	☐ 2. C	☐ 2. C	☐ 2. E	☐ 2. D	☐ 2. A	☐ 2. B
☐ 3. C	☐ 3. E	☐ 3. A	☐ 3. D	☐ 3. D	☐ 3. B	☐ 3. B	☐ 3. C
☐ 4. C	☐ 4. A	☐ 4. B	☐ 4. A	☐ 4. A	☐ 4. C	☐ 4. C	☐ 4. B
☐ 5. D	☐ 5. A	☐ 5. A	☐ 5. E	☐ 5. E	☐ 5. A	☐ 5. A	☐ 5. C
☐ 6. A	☐ 6. D	☐ 6. D	☐ 6. C	☐ 6. D	☐ 6. D	☐ 6. B	☐ 6. D
☐ 7. D	☐ 7. B	☐ 7. B	☐ 7. A	☐ 7. B	☐ 7. C	☐ 7. C	☐ 7. E
☐ 8. A	☐ 8. C	☐ 8. C	☐ 8. B	☐ 8. A	☐ 8. A	☐ 8. E	☐ 8. C
☐ 9. C	☐ 9. 16	☐ 9. A	☐ 9. E	☐ 9. E	☐ 9. B	☐ 9. C	☐ 9. B
☐ 10. B	☐ 10. 36	☐ 10. D	☐ 10. B	☐ 10. D	☐ 10. A	☐ 10. D	☐ 10. C
☐ 11. D	☐ 11. 5	☐ 11. B	☐ 11. A	☐ 11. D	☐ 11. C	☐ 11. A	☐ 11. D
☐ 12. B	☐ 12. 30	☐ 12. B	☐ 12. B	☐ 12. E	☐ 12. D	☐ 12. A	☐ 12. E
☐ 13. A	☐ 13. 15	☐ 13. E	☐ 13. A	☐ 13. E	☐ 13. E	☐ 13. B	☐ 13. B
☐ 14. D	☐ 14. 8 or 12	☐ 14. E	☐ 14. C	☐ 14. C	☐ 14. B	☐ 14. C	☐ 14. D
☐ 15. A	☐ 15. 25	☐ 15. D	☐ 15. C	☐ 15. D	☐ 15. D	☐ 15. B	
☐ 16. B	☐ 16. 24	☐ 16. E	☐ 16. D	☐ 16. B	☐ 16. D	☐ 16. D	
☐ 17. D	☐ 17. 52		☐ 17. E	☐ 17. A	☐ 17. A	☐ 17. B	
☐ 18. C	☐ 18. 225		☐ 18. C	☐ 18. E	☐ 18. B	☐ 18. A	
☐ 19. A			☐ 19. B	☐ 19. D	☐ 19. D	☐ 19. B	
☐ 20. A			☐ 20. C	☐ 20. B		☐ 20. C	
			☐ 21. D	☐ 21. C		☐ 21. E	
			☐ 22. D	☐ 22. C		☐ 22. D	
			☐ 23. E	☐ 23. E		☐ 23. A	
			☐ 24. A	☐ 24. A		☐ 24. E	
						☐ 25. C	
						☐ 26. E	
						☐ 27. B	
						☐ 28. B	
						☐ 29. C	
						☐ 30. D	
						☐ 31. A	
						☐ 32. B	
						☐ 33. C	
						☐ 34. E	
						☐ 35. C	

# Right (A):	Questions 1–8 # Right (A):	# Right (A):	# Right (A):	# Right (A):	# Right (A):	# Right (A)	# Right (A):
# Wrong (B):	 # Wrong (B):	# Wrong (B):	# Wrong (B):	# Wrong (B):	# Wrong (B):	# Wrong (B):	# Wrong (B):
# (A) – ¼ (B):	# (A) – ¼ (B):	# (A) – ¼ (B):	# (A) – ¼ (B):	# (A) – ¼ (B):	# (A) – ¼ (B):	# (A) – ¼ (B):	# (A) – ¼ (B):
	Questions 9–18 # Right (A):						

SCORE CONVERSION TABLE

How to score your test

Use the answer key on the previous page to determine your raw score on each section. **Your raw score on each section except Section 4 is simply the number of correct answers minus ¼ of the number of wrong answers. On Section 4, your raw score is the sum of the number of correct answers for questions 1–18 minus ¼ of the number of wrong answers for questions 1–8.** Next, add the raw scores from Sections 3, 4, and 7 to get your Math raw score, add the raw scores from Sections 6 and 9 to get your Writing raw score. Write the three raw scores here:

Raw Critical Reading score: _____ Raw Math score: _____ Raw Writing score: _____

Use the table below to convert these to scaled scores.

Scaled scores: Critical Reading: _____ Math: _____ Writing: _____

Raw Score	Critical Reading Scaled Score	Math Scaled Score	Writing Scaled Score	Raw Score	Critical Reading Scaled Score	Math Scaled Score	Writing Scaled Score
67	800			32	520	550	610
66	800			31	510	550	600
65	790			30	510	540	580
64	780			29	500	530	570
63	760			28	490	520	560
62	750			27	490	530	550
61	730			26	480	510	540
60	720			25	480	500	530
59	700			24	470	490	520
58	700			23	460	480	510
57	690			22	460	480	500
56	680			21	450	470	490
55	670			20	440	460	480
54	660	800		19	440	450	470
53	650	790		18	430	450	460
52	650	760		17	420	440	450
51	640	740		16	420	430	440
50	630	720		15	410	420	440
49	620	710	800	14	400	410	430
48	620	700	800	13	400	410	420
47	610	680	800	12	390	400	410
46	600	670	790	11	380	390	400
45	600	660	780	10	370	380	390
44	590	650	760	9	360	370	380
43	590	640	740	8	350	360	380
42	580	630	730	7	340	350	370
41	570	630	710	6	330	340	360
40	570	620	700	5	320	330	350
39	560	610	690	4	310	320	340
38	550	600	670	3	300	310	320
37	550	590	660	2	280	290	310
36	540	580	650	1	270	280	300
35	540	580	640	0	250	260	280
34	530	570	630	−1	230	240	270
33	520	560	620	−2 or less	210	220	250

SCORE CONVERSION TABLE FOR WRITING COMPOSITE
[ESSAY + MULTIPLE CHOICE]

Calculate your writing raw score as you did on the previous page and grade your essay from a 1 to a 6 according to the standards that follow in the detailed answer key.

Essay score: _____   Raw Writing score: _____

Use the table below to convert these to scaled scores.

Scaled score: Writing: _____

Raw Score	Essay Score 0	Essay Score 1	Essay Score 2	Essay Score 3	Essay Score 4	Essay Score 5	Essay Score 6
−2 or less	200	230	250	280	310	340	370
−1	210	240	260	290	320	360	380
0	230	260	280	300	340	370	400
1	240	270	290	320	350	380	410
2	250	280	300	330	360	390	420
3	260	290	310	340	370	400	430
4	270	300	320	350	380	410	440
5	280	310	330	360	390	420	450
6	290	320	340	360	400	430	460
7	290	330	340	370	410	440	470
8	300	330	350	380	410	450	470
9	310	340	360	390	420	450	480
10	320	350	370	390	430	460	490
11	320	360	370	400	440	470	500
12	330	360	380	410	440	470	500
13	340	370	390	420	450	480	510
14	350	380	390	420	460	490	520
15	350	380	400	430	460	500	530
16	360	390	410	440	470	500	530
17	370	400	420	440	480	510	540
18	380	410	420	450	490	520	550
19	380	410	430	460	490	530	560
20	390	420	440	470	500	530	560
21	400	430	450	480	510	540	570
22	410	440	460	480	520	550	580
23	420	450	470	490	530	560	590
24	420	460	470	500	540	570	600
25	430	460	480	510	540	580	610
26	440	470	490	520	550	590	610
27	450	480	500	530	560	590	620
28	460	490	510	540	570	600	630
29	470	500	520	550	580	610	640
30	480	510	530	560	590	620	650
31	490	520	540	560	600	630	660
32	500	530	550	570	610	640	670
33	510	540	550	580	620	650	680
34	510	550	560	590	630	660	690
35	520	560	570	600	640	670	700
36	530	560	580	610	650	680	710
37	540	570	590	620	660	690	720
38	550	580	600	630	670	700	730
39	560	600	610	640	680	710	740
40	580	610	620	650	690	720	750
41	590	620	640	660	700	730	760
42	600	630	650	680	710	740	770
43	610	640	660	690	720	750	780
44	620	660	670	700	740	770	800
45	640	670	690	720	750	780	800
46	650	690	700	730	770	800	800
47	670	700	720	750	780	800	800
48	680	720	730	760	800	800	800
49	680	720	730	760	800	800	800

Detailed Answer Key

Section 1

The following essay received 12 points out of a possible 12. This means that, according to the graders, it

- develops an insightful point of view on the topic
- demonstrates exemplary critical thinking
- uses effective examples, reasons, and other evidence to support its thesis
- is consistently focused, coherent, and well-organized
- demonstrates skillful and effective use of language and sentence structure
- is largely (but not necessarily completely) free of grammatical and usage errors

Consider carefully the issue discussed in the following passage, then write an essay that answers the question posed in the assignment.

> The best leaders are not those who seek power, or have great political skill. Great leaders—and these are exceptionally rare, especially today—represent the best selves of the people they represent.

Assignment: **What are the most important qualities of a leader?** Write an essay in which you answer this question and discuss your point of view on this issue. Support your position logically with examples from literature, the arts, history, politics, science and technology, current events, or your experience or observation.

SAMPLE STUDENT ESSAY

There is no more important decision that a citizen can make than one's choice of a leader. I am inclined to agree with Thomas Hobbes, who believed that humans are hardly better than other mammals without a social contract that binds us to work together as a society. Artists could not survive in a society that does not provide a means of trading art for food. Great teachers cannot survive in a society without a means of trading wisdom for shelter. This requires a social order, a division of labor, and a group we call leaders. Yet we know that power corrupts, and absolute power corrupts absolutely. So how do we maintain a just society when we must bestow corrupting powers upon members of that society?

Those who seek power are too often not our best leaders, but rather our best politicians. George Bush, John F. Kennedy and Ronald Reagan came to power not so much because of their visionary leadership but because of their appeal to a television-viewing audience. The problems with democracy are well known. In order to become elected, most politicians must appeal to a broad range of citizens. To gain this appeal, they must pander to their constituents, and often take conflicting or equivocal stances on issues. Of course, the politicians claim that they are taking

"forceful stances" to "bring the people together." But it is far more likely that they are simply doing their best to make everyone happy without putting their feet in their mouths.

So why is democracy the best way of electing a leader? Because the alternatives are much worse. To gain power, one must either use force or pander to those who do. Which is a better alternative? A country is weak if its people do not support it, and, at the very least, a democracy can claim a good degree of public support. Even more importantly, only a democracy allows for the possibility of finding a reluctant leader with genuine leadership skills. It doesn't happen often enough, but when it does, it is breathtaking. Witness the phenomenon of Howard Dean's campaign for the 2004 Democratic nomination for president, or Ross Perot's run in 1992. Neither was ultimately successful, but both demonstrated the potential of motivated citizens to change their country.

Without democracy, there is no hope for an ordinary citizen to change his or her country. What makes America great is not that its policies are always correct. Indeed, they are often deeply flawed. What makes America great is that it is run by those who are not even seeking power: the citizens.

The following essay received 8 points out of a possible 12, meaning that it demonstrates *adequate competence* in that it

- develops a point of view on the topic
- demonstrates some critical thinking, but perhaps not consistently
- uses some examples, reasons, and other evidence to support its thesis, but perhaps not adequately
- shows a general organization and focus, but shows occasional lapses in this regard
- demonstrates adequate but occasionally inconsistent facility with language
- contains occasional errors in grammar, usage, and mechanics

SAMPLE STUDENT ESSAY

Someone once said that great men don't seek greatness but have it thrust upon them. I think this is true, because those who have really changed the world were not slick politicians but rather people who had such great leadership skill and charisma that others forced them into leadership roles. Good examples of this are Jesus, Mahatma Gandhi, Mother Theresa and George Washington.

After his great victories in the American Revolutionary War against Great Britain, George Washington wanted to retire to his farm in Virginia and live out the rest of his days as a humble farmer. He did not want to become the political leader of a brand new country. But the Continental Congress looked to him for leadership, and sought him out to be the first President of the United States. Washington saw that his country needed him and answered the call.

Similarly, Mahatma Gandhi did not seek personal power, but only justice for his people. His humility and selflessness are what made him one of the great leaders of the twentieth century, and a model for the cause of nonviolent activism.

It is unfortunate that today only millionaires with big political connections seem to have any chance at being elected to national office. Maybe they have a shot at a local race, but the congress and the presidency seem to be off limits. The answer is to get more involved in politics yourself, as a voter, and avoid voting for candidates just because they are popular but instead because they have good souls.

The following essay received 4 points out of a possible 12, meaning that it demonstrates *some incompetence* in that it

- has a seriously limited point of view
- demonstrates weak critical thinking
- uses inappropriate or insufficient examples, reasons, and other evidence to support its thesis
- is poorly focused and organized, and has serious problems with coherence
- demonstrates frequent problems with language and sentence structure
- contains errors in grammar and usage that obscure the author's meaning seriously

SAMPLE STUDENT ESSAY

I'm not sure how it can be that you can be the best person to be in power if you don't want to be. In this country, at least, running for president or something like that takes a lot of effort, and I think you have to be a really hard worker in order to become president or senator.

An example of somebody who is a hard worker who got into office is former president Bill Clinton. Although many people think he had indiscretions in office, he came from a very poor family where he was only raised by his mother because his father left the family when he was young. He worked really hard and became a Rhodes scholar and was elected as governor at a very young age. He knew even when he was a very young kid that he wanted to become a great leader like John F. Kennedy.

Clinton was a good leader because he understood where a lot of people were coming from. He wasn't just a rich guy who got into office because he had rich relatives who got him there. I don't think you can say that the best leaders are the ones who don't want to be in office. If you didn't want to be in office, then you shouldn't run.

Detailed Answer Key

Section 2

1. A Alisha was holding a *grudge*, which is a feeling of resentment. *resentment* = ill will; *fortitude* = strength of mind to endure; *sarcasm* = wit used to ridicule; *elation* = extreme joy.

2. C There were people who expected the governor to be *inarticulate* (unable to speak clearly), so they would be surprised if he were *articulate*. *intolerance* = inability to put up with something; *fatigue* = tiredness; *eloquence* = persuasiveness in speech; *endurance* = ability to last, often through hard times.

3. D The *language of commoners* would be logically described as *common*. But the novelists preferred another kind of *parlance* (speech): that of the *upper* classes. A word such as *elegant* would work nicely. *elite* = superior; *sympathetic* = compassionate; *colloquial* = characteristic of everyday language; *refined* = precise, elegant; *utilitarian* = practical, stressing utility.

4. A The second half of this sentence presents a definition. The word in the blank should mean *"exploring the world."* *peripatetic* = walking from place to place; *conventional* = customary; *tolerant* = willing to put up with something; *coordinated* = well-matched; *remunerative* = profitable.

5. E A position that requires public speaking would be *difficult* for a person who does not like to speak or is afraid of crowds. *vivacious* = full of life; *garrulous* = talkative; *amiable* = friendly; *reticent* = hesitant to share one's feelings or opinions with others.

6. C The tickbird gets something from the hippopotamus, and the hippopotamus gets something from the tickbird; it's a *give-and-receive* relationship. *deteriorating* = diminishing in quality; *symbiotic* = of mutual benefit; *regressive* = going backwards; *vacillating* = going back and forth.

7. A This sentence establishes a contrast between how *modern scientists* think and how *early philosophers* thought. The contrast shows that the early philosophers were not using experiments as much as their own minds to draw conclusions and that the modern scientists rely more on experimental data to draw their conclusions. *empirical* = relying on the observations made from experiments; *coercion* = pressure on someone to act; *deduction* = reaching a conclusion through the use of logic; *clerical* = relating to office work; *intuitive* = known innately.

8. B The first blank should be a word like *merging* or *unification*, because many companies are under a *single owner*. This would be *troublesome* to those who value *independence*. *retraction* = taking something back; *differentiation* = finding a difference between 2 things; *consolidation* = combining of multiple things into 1 common entity; *collaboration* = working together on something; *dissemination* = the spread of something.

9. E Passage 2 distinguishes between education and schooling. It states that the *main product of schooling is not education* (lines 16–17) and that the struggle that defines education *is denied by schooling* (line 24). Passage 1 makes no such distinction, and speaks of education as if it is inseparable from the idea of schooling.

10. B Farmers raise most food by *a rotation of plants belonging to the most different orders: nature follows what may be called a simultaneous rotation*. They both are using a similar system.

11. A The passage suggests that education *is the great equalizer* and that *the spread of education will open a wider area over which the social feelings will expand*. It concludes by commenting that *if this education should be universal and complete* it would *obliterate factitious distinctions in society*.

12. B Passage 2 states that education, which is *the acquisition of competence, power, wisdom and discernment* (lines 20–21), is achieved only through the *struggle for sense in the world* (lines 22–23). Therefore, this struggle is empowering.

13. A "The Beginnings of the Scientific Method" is the best title, because this passage begins by discussing the scientists of the Renaissance and how they *brought about the most fundamental alterations in the world of thought ... by devising a new method for discovering knowledge* (lines 1–5). This new method was the scientific method.

14. C Saying that *the early modern scientists laid greatest stress upon observation and the formation of temporary hypotheses* (lines 7–9) is like saying they *emphasized* observation and hypotheses.

15. C In lines 19–21 the passage suggests that earlier scientists were simply trying *to find the confirmation of Biblical statements about the firmament*.

16. D Choice II is confirmed in lines 34–35: *The principle of the barometer was discovered by Galileo's **pupil** (student) Torricelli.* Choice III is confirmed in lines 44–45: *Galileo discovered the moons around Jupiter.*

17. E The final paragraph states that Renaissance scientists believed *that everything consists of bodies in motion, that everything conforms to a mechanical model. The heavens above and the smallest particles below all exhibit the same laws of motion*—even, as it says in the next sentence, *human thought* (lines 70–75).

18. C The final paragraph discusses how the scientific method changed the way science was done.

19. B The passage mentions in lines 25–26 that many military leaders *cement their solidarity by reveling* (taking delight) *in their numerical disadvantage.* They considered it more honorable to fight with fewer men and beat a larger opponent.

20. C Stating that *a well-known proverb was **trotted out** in many instances of the glorious, fighting few* (lines 28–29), in this context, is like saying that the proverb was *used for rhetorical effect* because it was used to persuade and inspire the troops.

21. D When the prince says that *we be a small **body** when compared to the army of our enemies,* he is saying that they are a small army or group of men.

22. D This sentence is discussing the tactical errors of the French in two different battles. The phrase *charging before they were ready* simply means *attacking before they were ready.*

23. E All 3 of these facts are true and are mentioned in the passage.

24. A The passage states in the final paragraph that *ten thousand more men might actually have hindered the English* (lines 66–67) and that *it seems that in fact ... strength is not always proportional to size* (lines 70–71).

Section 3

1. E Since *n* is equal to 3 times an even number, you can eliminate any answer choice that is not a multiple of 3 (A, C, and D). Answer choice B: $15 = 3 \times 5$; 5 is an odd number, so this answer choice is out. Answer choice E: $18 = 3 \times 6$; 6 is an even number.

2. A Set up a ratio: $\dfrac{50 \text{ chips}}{2 \text{ hours}} = \dfrac{x \text{ chips}}{7 \text{ hours}}$

Cross-multiply: $350 = 2x$
Divide by 2: $175 = x$

3. C Angles that form a straight angle have a sum of 180°:

$$x + 2x = 180°$$
Combine like terms: $3x = 180°$
Divide by 3: $x = 60°$

4. C Find the smallest number that is divisible by both 15 and 6 and see which answer choice works.
Multiples of 15: 15, **30**, 45, ...
Multiples of 6: 6, 12, 18, 24, **30**, ...

5. D *n*% of 20 is 4

$$\frac{n}{100} \times 20 = 4$$

Simplify: $.20n = 4$
Divide by .20: $n = 20$

6. A $f(x) = 3x + n$
Plug in 2 for *x*: $f(2) = 3(2) + n = 0$
Simplify: $6 + n = 0$
Subtract 6: $n = -6$
Substitute for *n*: $f(x) = 3x - 6$
Plug in 0 for *x*: $f(0) = 3(0) - 6 = -6$

7. D First find the area of the right triangle:

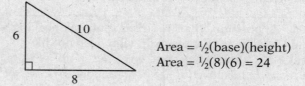

Area = ½(base)(height)
Area = ½(8)(6) = 24

Next, set up an equation for the area of a square.
Area = (side)²

Substitute 24 for area: 24 = (side)²
Take the square root: $\sqrt{24}$ = side
Simplify the radical: $2\sqrt{6}$ = side

8. A   You are told that: $12v = 3w$
           Divide by 3: $4v = w$
           Multiply by 2: $8v = 2w$
The question asks for the value of: $2w - 8v$
           Substitute for $2w$: $8v - 8v = 0$
Alternatively, you can try finding values for v and w that work, like 1 and 4, and plug them in to $2w - 8v$ and into the choices and find the match.

---

9. C $2|x| + 1 > 5$
           Subtract 1: $2|x| > 4$
           Divide by 2: $|x| > 2$
Interpret the absolute value: $x > 2$ OR $x < -2$
You are told that x is negative, so $x < -2$ is the answer.

---

10. B
                              $-x^2 - 8x - 5$
           Substitute -2 for x: $-(-2)^2 - 8(-2) - 5$
           Square -2: $-(4) - 8(-2) - 5$
           Simplify: $-(4) + 16 - 5 = 7$
When evaluating $-x^2$, don't forget to square the value *before* taking its opposite!

---

11. D
                              $\dfrac{5}{m} \le \dfrac{2}{3}$

           Cross-multiply: $15 \le 2m$
           Divide by 2: $7.5 \le m$
Since m is greater than *or equal to* 7.5, D is the answer.

---

12. B   First find the price after the 6% sales tax:
           $\$60.00 \times .06 = \$3.60$ tax
           $\$60.00 + \$3.60 = \$63.60$ price with tax
(A simpler way is just to multiply 60 by 1.06.)
           Now find how much change Theo received:
           $\$70.00 - \$63.00 = \$6.40$ change

---

13. A   Write an equation for the first sentence.
                              $n - m = r$
Because none of the answer choices contain m, solve for m in terms of r and n: $n - m = r$
           Add m: $n = r + m$
           Subtract r: $n - r = m$
Now write an expression for what the question asks for:
                              $s + 2m$
           Substitute for m: $s + 2(n - r)$
           Distribute: $s + 2n - 2r$
Alternatively, you can substitute numbers for n, m, and r, making sure they "work," and get a numerical answer to the question.

---

14. D   Two points on line l are $(0, 0)$ and $(10, y)$.
           Find the slope of the line:

$$m = \frac{y_2 - y_1}{x_2 - x_1} = \frac{y - 0}{10 - 0} = \frac{y}{10} = \frac{3}{5}$$

           Cross-multiply: $5y = 30$
           Divide by 5: $y = 6$
Since $y = 6$, the height of the triangle is 6. Find the area:
                              $A = \frac{1}{2}(\text{base})(\text{height})$
           Substitute 48 for A: $48 = \frac{1}{2}(\text{base})(6)$
           Simplify: $48 = 3(\text{base})$
           Divide by 3: $16 = \text{base} = x$
Now find $x + y = 16 + 6 = 22$.

---

15. A   Ellen travels the first 15 miles at 30 miles per hour. Find out how much time that takes:
                              $d = (rate)(time)$
           Plug in known values: $15 = 30t$
           Divide by 30: $\frac{1}{2}$ hour $= t$
The rest of the trip, which is $(y - 15)$ miles long, she travels at an average speed of 40 miles per hour:
                              $d = (rate)(time)$
           Plug in known values: $(y - 15) = 40t$

           Divide by 40: $\dfrac{y - 15}{40} = t$

Add the 2 times together to find the total time:

$$\frac{1}{2} + \frac{y - 15}{40}$$

16. B   Set up the relationship in equation form:

$$y = \frac{km}{n^2}$$

Plug in what you're given: $8 = \dfrac{k(16)}{(1)^2}$

Simplify: $8 = 16k$

Divide by 16: $\frac{1}{2} = k$

Write the new equation: $y = \dfrac{\frac{1}{2}(m)}{(n^2)}$

Plug in new values: $y = \dfrac{\frac{1}{2}(8)}{(4)^2} = \dfrac{4}{16} = \dfrac{1}{4}$

17. D

$$a + b = s$$
$$\underline{a - b = t}$$

Add straight down: $2a = s + t$

Divide by 2: $a = \dfrac{s+t}{2}$

$$a + b = s$$
$$\underline{a - b = t}$$

Subtract straight down: $2b = s - t$

Divide by 2: $b = \dfrac{s-t}{2}$

Find the product: $(a)(b) = \left(\dfrac{s+t}{2}\right)\left(\dfrac{s-t}{2}\right) = \left(\dfrac{s^2 - t^2}{4}\right)$

18. C $y = m^4 = n^3$

The answer is in terms of y alone, so find m and n in terms of y:
$$y = m^4$$

Take the 4th root: $y^{1/4} = m$
$$y = n^3$$

Take the cube root: $y^{1/3} = n$

Find the product mn: $mn = (y^{1/4})(y^{1/3})$
$$= y^{1/3 + 1/4}$$

Add exponents: $mn = y^{7/12}$

19. A   This question deals with similar triangles:

Set up ratio: $\dfrac{6}{14} = \dfrac{4}{x}$

Cross-multiply: $6x = 48$

Divide by 6: $x = 8$

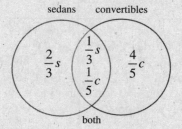

Area of big triangle = ½(base)(height) = ½(12)(6) = 36
Area of small triangle = ½(base)(height) = ½(8)(4) = 16
Shaded area = area of big triangle – area of small triangle = 36 – 16 = 20

20. A   Set up a Venn diagram to visualize the information.

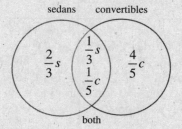

Notice that ⅓ the number of sedans must equal ⅕ the number of convertibles. Say the number of convertible sedans is x. If this is ⅓ the number of sedans, then there must be $3x$ sedans in total, and $3x - x = 2x$ of these are *not* convertibles. Similarly, if x is ⅕ the number of convertibles, then there must be $5x$ convertibles altogether, and $5x - x = 4x$ of these are *not* sedans. So now your diagram can look like this:

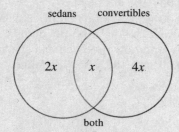

So there must be a total of $2x + x + 4x = 7x$ cars at the dealership. The only choice that is a multiple of 7 is A: 28.

Section 4

1. E

Perimeter of a square = $4s$

$$36 = 4s$$

Divide by 4: $\quad 9 = s$

Area of a square $\quad = (s)^2$

Area = $(9)^2 = 81$

2. C

$$\frac{a}{b} = \frac{1}{10}$$

Cross-multiply: $\quad b = 10a$

Try positive integer values of a to see how many work:

a	1	2	3	4	5	6	7	8	9
b	10	20	30	40	50	60	70	80	90

There are 9 integer pairs that satisfy the equation.

3. E The 10 bathrooms cost $20 each to clean:

Total cost = $20 × 10 = $200

To clean each bathroom twice would cost:

$200 × 2 = $400

There are 30 offices, and they cost $15 each to clean:

Total cost = $15 × 30 = $450

To clean each office once and each bathroom twice will cost: $400 + $450 = $850

4. A Remember the "difference of squares" factoring formula: $\quad a^2 - b^2 = (a - b)(a + b)$

Substitute: $\quad 10 = (2)(a + b)$

Divide by 2: $\quad 5 = a + b$

5. A

To find the value of $f(14)$, find all the factors of 14:

1, 2, 7, 14

There are two prime factors, 2 and 7.

$$2 + 7 = 9$$
$$f(14) = 9$$

To find the value of $f(6)$, find all the factors of 6:

1, 2, 3, 6

There are two prime factors, 2 and 3.

$$2 + 3 = 5$$
$$f(6) = 5$$
$$f(14) - f(6) = 9 - 5 = 4$$

6. D First write an equation to find the average.

$$\frac{a + b + c + d}{4} = 20$$

Multiply by 4: $\quad a + b + c + d = 80$

If you want a to be as large as possible, make b, c, and d as small as possible. You are told that they are all *different* positive integers: $a + b + c + d = 80$

Let $b = 1$, $c = 2$, $d = 3$: $\quad a + 1 + 2 + 3 = 80$

Combine like terms: $\quad a + 6 = 80$

Subtract 6: $\quad a = 74$

7. B Let the radius of circle A = a and the radius of circle B = b. It is given that $a = 2b$. The circumference of a circle can be found with the equation $C = 2\pi r$. The sum of their circumferences is 36π:

$$36\pi = 2\pi a + 2\pi b$$

Divide by π: $\quad 36 = 2a + 2b$

Substitute for a: $\quad 36 = 2(2b) + 2b$

Simplify: $\quad 36 = 4b + 2b$

Combine like terms: $\quad 36 = 6b$

Divide by 6: $\quad 6 = b$

Solve for a: $\quad a = 2(b) = 2(6) = 12$

8. C This is a visualization problem. The 6 possible planes are illustrated below. Notice that the 6 faces of the cube "don't count," because each of those contains 4 edges of the cube.

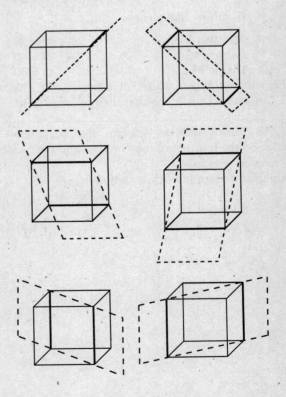

9. **16**   Set up an equation: $2x - 10 = 22$
        Add 10: $2x = 32$
        Divide by 2: $x = 16$

10. **36**

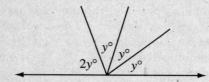

        There are 180° on 1 side of a line:
                     $2y + y + y + y = 180°$
        Combine like terms: $5y = 180°$
        Divide by 5: $y = 36°$

11. **5**   Think simple: What's the simplest way to turn $8x + 4y$ into $2x + y$? Just divide by 4!
                        $8x + 4y = 20$
        Divide by 4: $2x + y = 5$

12. **30**   Set up equations: $\dfrac{x + y + 20}{3} = 30$

                            $x = y + 10$

        Substitute for x: $\dfrac{y + 10 + y + 20}{3} = 30$

        Combine like terms: $\dfrac{2y + 30}{3} = 30$

        Multiply by 3: $2y + 30 = 90$
        Subtract 30 $2y = 60$
        Divide by 2: $y = 30$
Check by noticing that the 3 numbers are 20, 30, and 40. You should easily see that their average is 30.

13. **15**   Ratios such as 4:5 can also be written as $4x{:}5x$. So the number of men m is $4x$ and the number of women w is $5x$.
Plug those values into the equation $w = m + 3$
                   $5x = 4x + 3$
        Subtract $4x$: $x = 3$
        Plug 3 in to $5x$: $w = 5x = 5(3) = 15$

14. **8 or 12** $y = |2x - b|$
        Plug in (5, 2): $2 = |2(5) - b|$
        Simplify: $2 = |10 - b|$
                 $(10 - b) = 2$ or $(10 - b) = -2$
        Subtract 10: $-b = -8$ or $-b = -12$
        Multiply by −1: $b = 8$ or $b = 12$

15. **25**   First calculate how many grams of sucrose there are in 200 grams of a 10% mixture.
        (200 grams)(0.10) = 20 grams of sucrose
Since you will be adding x grams of sucrose, the total weight of sucrose will be $20 + x$ grams, and the total weight of the mixture will be $200 + x$ grams. Since the fraction that will be sucrose is 20%,

$$\frac{20 + x}{200 + x} = \frac{20}{100}$$

Cross-multiply: $(20 + x)(100) = 20(200 + x)$
Distribute: $2,000 + 100x = 4,000 + 20x$
Subtract 2,000: $100x = 2,000 + 20x$
Subtract $20x$: $80x = 2,000$
Divide by 80: $x = 25$

16. **24**   First calculate how long the race took.
                distance = *rate* × *time*
                   $16 = (8)(time)$
     Divide by 8:   2 hours = *time* = 120 minutes
Next, find the new rate that is 25% faster:
           new rate = (8)(1.25) = 10 mph
Calculate how long the new race would take:
                distance = *rate* × *time*
                   $16 = (10)(time)$
     Divide by 10: 1.6 hours = time = 96 minutes
So she can improve her time by (120 − 96) =
24 minutes.

17. 52
Break a shape like this into recogniz- able 4-sided fig- ures and triangles that are easier to deal with. The area of the rectangle on the left is 7 × 4 = 28.

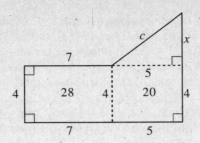

The area of the rectangle on the right is 5 × 4 = 20. The sum of those two areas is 28 + 20 = 48. The area remaining for the triangle is the difference 78 − 48 = 30. Set up an equation for the area of a triangle to solve for *x:*

$$\text{Area} = \tfrac{1}{2}(\text{base})(\text{height})$$
$$30 = \tfrac{1}{2}(5)(\text{height})$$

Divide by ½: 60 = 5(height)
Divide by 5:   12 = height

To find the hypotenuse of the right triangle, set up the Pythagorean Theorem and solve:

$$5^2 + 12^2 = c^2$$
$$25 + 144 = c^2$$
$$169 = c^2$$
$$c = 13$$

(Or just notice that it's a 5-12-13 triangle!)
To find the perimeter of the figure, add up all of the sides:

$$13 + 12 + 4 + 5 + 7 + 4 + 7 = 52$$

18. 225 Set up a 3-circle Venn diagram to visualize this information.

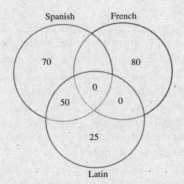

Fifty students study 2 of the 3 languages, so let's say that 50 students study both Spanish and Latin. (It doesn't matter *which* 2 languages those 50 students take; the result turns out the same.) This means that 0 students study both Spanish and French both French and Latin and 0 students study all three languages.
There are 120 Spanish students in all. There are therefore 120 − 150 = 70 students who study Spanish

alone. There are 80 French students in all, all of whom study just French, and there are 75 total Latin students including 75 − 50 = 25 students who study only Latin.
This means that there are 70 + 50 + 80 + 25 = 225 sophomores at Hillside High School.

Section 5

1. C The clients were forced to seek more *reliable* investment advice, so the manager must have man- aged their funds badly. *ineptitude* = lack of skill.

2. E Vartan is Armenian; he was born in Iran and educated in Lebanon and is now president of the American Brown University. He has a lot of *worldly* experience. *perpetual* = lasting forever; *authoritative* = showing authority; *cosmopolitan* = worldly.

3. D They didn't consider it in great detail, so the reading must have been *without great care*. *verbatim* = word for word; *meandering* = wandering; *tormented* = feeling anguish or pain; *cursory* = quick and without care; *substantial* = of substance, quite large.

4. A If the *pathogens* (infectious agents) spread more quickly in close quarters, the *crowding* would be a problem. This would cause the disease to *spread*. *propagation* = reproduction, increase in number; *squalor* = horrible or dirty conditions; *circulation* = moving of something around from place to place; *poverty* = state of being poor; *deterioration* = wearing down; *congestion* = crowdedness; *proximity* = close- ness; *resilience* = ability to recover from a challenge.

5. E The purpose of research is to find answers to questions of interest. Therefore, the research *endeavors* (attempts) to *determine* or *understand* the mechanisms by which our brains do things. If the data must be turned into *coherent and understand- able information*, it must not have been coherent to begin with, but rather just a big rush of information. *enhance* = make better; *attenuate* = reduce in amount; *dearth* = scarcity, lack; *elucidate* = make clear; *deluge* = huge flood.

6. D The *fruits* mentioned in line 10 refer to the means of acquiring food and shelter, because they are described as the *fruits for maintaining human life.*

7. B The question is whether one can *get quick returns of interest* (make money) *from the capital of knowledge and learning* (from one's education) (lines 15–16).

8. **A** The pointing of dogs is mentioned as an *instinctive tendency to the performance of an action* (lines 15–16).

9. **E** Inherited tendencies tend to show themselves in the behavior of an organism. The paragraph mentions the calf and the caterpillar as examples of organisms with instincts that show themselves in later behavior.

10. **D** The final paragraph begins with *The best life is the one in which the creative impulses play the largest part and the possessive impulses the smallest* (lines 57–59).

11. **D** Lines 22–26 say that *the food and clothing of one man is not the food and clothing of another; if the supply is insufficient, what one man has is obtained at the expense of some other man.* Therefore, food and clothing exist in finite amounts and can be used up.

12. **E** This section of the passage discusses matters such as *good will* (line 39), *science* (line 32), and *painting pictures or writing poems* (line 36) as things that are not denied to someone else when 1 person possesses them.

13. **E** This sentence discusses the *possessive impulses* (line 49) as distinct from the *creative impulses* discussed in the next sentence. The *impulse of property* in lines 51–52 is the *desire to possess property*.

14. **C** This statement echoes the point made in lines 72–73 that *spiritual possessions cannot be taken in this way,* that is, by force.

15. **D** Lines 59–60 say *This is no new discovery* and goes on to cite the Gospel as a prior source expressing the same opinions as Russell's.

16. **B** The author's main point is that creativity is of higher value than possessiveness. The invention mentioned in answer choice B was created to make money for its inventor (a possessive and materialistic motive) but has the side effect of benefiting all of humankind.

17. **A** The passage discusses the perspective one Native American has on the appearance of the *new superstition* (line 46). It discusses how some villagers have taken to the new religion and also mentions one fellow tribe member's attempting to convert the main character.

18. **E** In saying that *men of the same color are like the ivory keys of one instrument where each represents all the rest, yet varies from them in pitch and quality of voice* (lines 4–6), the author is saying that people of the same race possess important differences.

19. **D** The author describes the preacher as *mouth[ing] most strangely the jangling phrases of a bigoted creed* (lines 12–13), indicating that she considers him to be an intolerant person. She describes herself as having *compassion* (line 8) and *respect* (line 10), but does not attribute these qualities to the preacher.

20. **B** Lines 14–15 say that *our tribe is one large family, where every person is related to all the others.*

21. **C** Both the preacher and the author's mother have become followers of *the new superstition* (line 46).

22. **C** In saying that a *pugilist commented upon a recent article of mine, grossly perverting the spirit of my pen* (lines 69–70) the author is saying that the pugilist distorted the author's words in a grotesque way.

23. **E** The author characterizes herself as *a wee child toddling in a wonder world* (lines 74–75), indicating that she is in awe of the world around her. Although one might expect her to be vengeful in response to the *pugilist* (line 69) who *grossly pervert[ed] the spirit of [her] pen* (line 70), there is no indication in the paragraph that she is vengeful.

24. **A** The author says in lines 71–74 that *still I would not forget that the pale-faced missionary and the aborigine are both God's creatures, though **small indeed in their own conceptions of Infinite Love***. In other words, the author respects the missionary but believes he is small-minded.

Section 6

1. **D** The verb must agree with the plural subject *claims.* Choice D is most concise and correct.

2. **A** The original sentence is best.

3. **B** The participial phrase opening the sentence modifies Sartre himself, not his *writing*. This being the case, the phrase dangles.

4. **C** Choice C best follows the law of parallelism.

5. **A** The original sentence is best.

6. **B** Choice B is the most concise, logical, and complete.

7. **C** The original phrasing contains an incomplete thought. Choice C is by far the most concise and direct.

8. **E** The participle *having spread* modifies the *disease*, not the *doctors*.

9. **C** The original phrasing contains an incomplete thought. Choice C is by far the most concise and direct.

10. **D** The participle *singing* modifies *Anita*, not her hoarseness. Furthermore, the participle is in the wrong form; it should be in the perfect form *having sung*, because only the *previous* singing could have contributed to her hoarseness.

11. **A** The original sentence is best.

12. **A** The word *quick* is an adjective and can thus modify only a noun. But since it modifies the verb *turned*, the adverb *quickly* is needed here.

13. **B** This sentence violates the law of parallelism. If she is known *for her initiative*, she should also be known *for devoting her own time.*

14. **C** Since the Medieval era is long past, its *beginning* is "completed" or, in grammar terms, "perfect." So this phrase should be the "perfect" form of the infinitive: *to have begun.*

15. **B** The word *neither* is almost always part of the phrase *neither of …* or *neither A nor B*. So choice B should read *nor even.*

16. **D** The word *less* is used to compare only quantities that can't be counted. If the quantities are countable, as accidents are, the word should be *fewer.*

17. **B** To convey the proper sequence of events, the perfect tense is required: *had spent.*

18. **A** The subject of the verb *has* is the plural noun *newspapers*. (The sentence is "inverted," because the subject follows the verb.) The proper form of the verb, then, is *have.*

19. **B** The original sentence has a "comma splice" that incorrectly joins 2 sentences with only a comma. A better phrasing is *dream that led.*

20. **C** The subject of the verb is the singular noun *movement*, so the proper verb form is *has led.*

21. **E** The sentence is correct as written.

22. **D** This is a prepositional phrase, so the pronoun is the object of the preposition and should be in the objective case. The correct phrasing is *for Maria and me.*

23. **A** The word *successive* means *consecutive*, so it does not make sense in this context. The right word is *successful.*

24. **E** The sentence is correct as written.

25. **C** The word *underneath* means that it is physically *below* something else. It should be changed to *under.*

26. **E** The sentence is correct as written.

27. **B** The subject of the verb *were* is *arrogance*, which is singular. It should instead be *was.*

28. **B** The sentence mentions there are *numerous* strains of the bacteria, which means that *more* should instead be *most.*

29. **C** The subject *company* is singular. Therefore, *they* should instead be *it.*

30. **D** Choice D is most consistent, logical, and concise.

31. **A** Choice A is most logical.

32. **B** The first paragraph ends with the description of an idea. The second paragraph begins with an illustration of how students experience this idea in their daily lives and then goes on to explain how it can help them get through their *brain freezes*. Choice B is the best introduction to the paragraph, because it explains that a student using the phenomenon can improve his or her studies.

33. **C** The sentence begins using the pronoun *you*, so that usage should be maintained throughout the sentence. Option D is incorrect because a person has only 1 brain.

34. **E** Sentence 11 concludes a discussion of Isaac Asimov's "eureka" experience. The additional sentence expands upon that idea, relating it back to the lives of students.

35. **C** Choice C is the most concise and logical revision.

Section 7

1. B   Set up a ratio to solve this problem:

$$\frac{4 \text{ apples}}{20 \text{ cents}} = \frac{10 \text{ apples}}{x \text{ cents}}$$

Cross-multiply: $4x = 200$
Divide by 4: $x = 50$ cents

---

2. C   Solve for b: $2^b = 8$
                     $b = 3$
Plug in 3: $3^b = 3^3 = 27$

---

3. A   The sum of a, b, and 18 is 6 greater than the sum of a, b, and 12. Since there are 3 terms in the group, it follows that the average of a, b, and 18 would be $6 \div 3 = 2$ greater than the average of a, b, and 12.

---

4. B   If you have the patience, you can write out a quick calendar for yourself to track the days:

Su	M	T	W	**Th**	F	Sa
		1	2	3	4	5
6	7	8	9	10	11	12
13	14	15	16	17	18	19
20	21	22	23	24	25	26
27	28	29	30	**31**		

Or you can use the simple fact that successive Tuesdays (like any other days) are always 7 days apart. Therefore, if the 1st of the month is a Tuesday, so are the 8th, the 15th, the 22nd, and the 29th. Therefore, the 30th is a Wednesday and the 31st is a Thursday.

---

5. A   From the given information: $m = 8n$
                          $0 < m + n < 50$
Substitute for m: $0 < 8n + n < 50$
Combine like terms: $0 < 9n < 50$
Divide by 9: $0 < n < 5^{5/9}$
Since n must be an integer, n can be 1, 2, 3, 4, or 5.

---

6. D   First find the value of y: $y\%$ of 50 is 32.

Simplify: $\frac{y}{100} \times 50 = 32$

Cross-multiply: $50y = 3{,}200$
Divide by 50: $y = 64$
What is 200% of 64?
Interpret: $2.00 \times 64 = 128$

---

7. B $g(x) = x + x^{1/2}$
Plug in 16 for x $g(16) = 16 + 16^{1/2}$
Take square root of 16: $g(16) = 16 + 4$
Combine like terms: $g(16) = 20$

---

8. C   The slope of the line is $-\frac{3}{4}$, so use the slope equation and the coordinates of point A (0, 12) to find the coordinates of point B (x, 0):

$$m = \frac{y_2 - y_1}{x_2 - x_1} = \frac{0 - 12}{x - 0} = \frac{-12}{x} = -\frac{3}{4}$$

Cross-multiply: $4(-12) = -3(x)$
Simplify: $-48 = -3x$
Divide by -3: $16 = x$
The base of the triangle is 16, and its height is 12.
              Area = ½(base)(height)
Substitute: Area = ½(16)(12)
Simplify: Area = 96

---

9. A   Find the sum of each repetition of the pattern:
$-1 + 1 + 2 = 2$
Next, determine how many times the pattern repeats in the first 25 terms: $25 \div 3 = 8$ with a remainder of 1.
Multiply the sum of the pattern by 8 to obtain the sum of the first 24 terms: $2 \times 8 = 16$
The 25th term is -1, which makes the sum $16 \pm 1 = 15$.

---

10. D   The ratio of white marbles to blue marbles is 4 to b. The probability of randomly selecting a white marble from the jar is ¼. This means that 1 out of every 4 marbles in the jar is white and 3 out of every 4 marbles are blue. If there are 4 white marbles, then there are $4 \times 3 = 12$ blue marbles.

---

11. B   Area = ½(base)(height)
Substitute: $10 = ½(\text{base})(\text{height})$
Divide by ½: $20 = (\text{base})(\text{height})$
The base and the height are both integers. Find all the "factor pairs" of 20: 1, 20; 2, 10; and 4, 5
Plug each pair into the Pythagorean Theorem to find the least possible length of the hypotenuse:
               $a^2 + b^2 = c^2$
               $4^2 + 5^2 = c^2$
Combine like terms: $41 = c^2$
Take square root: $\sqrt{41} = c$
               $a^2 + b^2 = c^2$
               $2^2 + 10^2 = c^2$
Combine like terms: $104 = c^2$
Take square root: $\sqrt{104} = c$
               $a^2 + b^2 = c^2$
               $1^2 + 20^2 = c^2$
Combine like terms: $401 = c^2$
Take square root: $\sqrt{401} = c$
$\sqrt{41}$ is the shortest possible hypotenuse.

---

12. B $-1 < y < 0$
This means that y is a negative decimal fraction. Answer choices A, C, and E will all be negative numbers. Answer choices B and D are positive numbers.

When you raise a simple fraction to a positive number larger than 1, it gets smaller. $y^4 < y^2$, which makes B the greatest value. Pick a value like $y = -\frac{1}{2}$ and see.

13. **E**   Any statement of the form *"If A is true, then B is true"* is logically equivalent to *"If B is not true, then A is not true."* Try this with some common-sense examples of such statements. For instance, saying *"If I am under 16 years old, then I am not allowed to drive"* is the same as saying *"If I am allowed to drive, then I must not be under 16 years old."* The statement in E is logically equivalent to the original.

14. **E**   If each bus contained only the minimum number of students, the buses would accommodate $6 \times 3 = 180$ students. But since you have 200 students to accommodate, you have 20 more students to place. To maximize the number of 40-student buses, place 10 more students in 2 of the buses. Therefore, a maximum of 2 buses can have 40 students.

15. **D**   The volume of a cylinder is equal to $\pi r^2 h$. Let's say that the radius of cylinder A is a and the radius of cylinder B is b. Since the height of cylinder B is twice the height of cylinder A, if the height of cylinder A is h, then the height of cylinder B is $2h$. The volume of A is twice that of B:

$$\pi a^2 h = 2\pi b^2(2h)$$
Simplify: $\pi a^2 h = 4\pi b^2 h$
Divide by π: $a^2 h = 4b^2 h$
Divide by h: $a^2 = 4b^2$
Take the square root of both sides: $a = 2b$
Divide by b: $\dfrac{a}{b} = \dfrac{2}{1}$

16. **E**   First notice that any multiple of 6 is an even number that is divisible by 3, since $2 \times 3 = 6$. Set up a Venn diagram to help visualize the information, letting x represent how many of the numbers are multiples of 6.

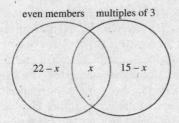

even members   multiples of 3

There are 30 numbers in the set, so set up an equation using the values in the Venn diagram and solve for x:
$$(22 - x) + (x) + (15 - x) = 30$$
Combine like terms: $37 - x = 30$
Add x: $37 = 30 + x$
Subtract 30: $7 = x$
So there are 7 multiples of 6 in this set.

Section 8

1. **B**   A *reputable* scientist is well-known and well-respected. Saying *the evidence is _____ at best* indicates that there is not much evidence at all. It must be *flimsy*. Reputable scientists would not likely *admit* that a phenomenon exists if the evidence is weak. *meager* = scanty, deficient; *regret* = feel bad about an action, wish it hadn't happened; *paltry* = lacking worth.

2. **D**   The concept that the Earth is round is *now accepted as an inarguable truth*. It can be inferred that it was at some point a fact that was thought to be wrong. *incontrovertible* = cannot be questioned; *mellifluous* = smooth flowing; *dubious* = doubtful.

3. **B**   A profound break of a political party or religion into factions is a *schism*. (The Latin word *schisma* = split.) *unanimity* = full agreement; *schism* = division into factions; *caucus* = meeting of party members; *commemoration* = event that honors something or someone; *prognostication* = prediction.

4. **C**   As the father of the American public school system, Horace Mann would *pressure* or *push* the Massachusetts legislature to institute a system for *ensuring* or *guaranteeing* universal access to education. *petitioned* = requested, lobbied for; *vouchsafing* = conceding, granting.

5. **A**   Since the light from most stars takes millions of years to reach us, it is plausible to imagine that by the time we see the light the star might actually no longer be there. This would make the present existence of these stars *questionable*. *debatable* = disputable; *methodical* = systematic; *indecorous* = not proper; *imperious* = acting as if one is superior to another; *profuse* = abundant.

6. **D**   The *although* establishes a contrast. Something that makes *any potentially offensive matters seem less objectionable* is, by definition, a *euphemism*. The 1st blank should therefore be a word that contrasts with euphemism, like *straightforward*. *anachronism* = something out of place in time; *intolerant* = unable to put up with something; *laudation* = extreme praise; *clandestine* = secret, hidden; *candid* = honest, straightforward; *euphemism* = the substitution of an inoffensive term for an offensive one; *forthright* = honest; *coercion* = pressure on someone to act.

7. **C**   The English gentleman *tried to teach his son Greek and Latin without punishment, ... rewarding his son with cherries and biscuits* (lines 5–11).

8. A In saying that *marks, grades, and diplomas … must be made reinforcing for other reasons* (lines 16–20), the author is saying that such things will not reinforce behavior by themselves but must be made to represent something more meaningful.

9. B The passage says that how *honors and medals derive their power from prestige or esteem* is what *varies between cultures and epochs* (lines 21–24). When Oscar Wilde got *a "first in Mods"* in 1876, he was the talk of the town. But the contemporary student graduating *summa cum laude* is *less widely acclaimed* (lines 34–35).

10. A The story follows the statement that how *honors and medals derive their power from prestige or esteem* is what *varies between cultures and epochs*. Therefore, the story is intended to illustrate that fact.

11. C Statement I is supported by lines 40–41, which say that certain kinds of reinforcements (like food) *are not always easily arranged*. Statement II is supported by line 43: *We cannot all get prizes*. The selection does not mention anything about rewards' encouraging only superficial learning.

12. D In lines 60–62, the passage says that *grades are almost always given long after the student has stopped behaving as a student*. It then goes on to discuss how *such contingencies are weak* (lines 60–61).

13. E The paragraph as a whole discusses the need for teachers to address the issues of whether, when, and how to punish or reward student behavior, so it is about teacher-student interactions.

14. B Kohn and Deci are mentioned as examples of experts who believe *that reward is often just as harmful as punishment, if not more so* (lines 89–90).

15. D The second paragraph of Passage 2 goes on to argue that those who are doing a task without a reward continue to perform the task because they see it as being "fun," whereas those who do it for a reward stop playing because they are no longer being paid to continue. The activity's sole value comes from the payment they get for it, not from the enjoyment they get from participating.

16. D We are told that Deci concluded that the *subjects who were paid probably construed* (interpreted) *the task as being manipulative* (lines 108–109). In order to draw such conclusions, the subjects would have to make inferences about the motivations of the experimenter.

17. A The author follows that statement with *it would be a mistake to use these few experiments to generalize that all rewards are bad* (lines 135–136). These statements caution against an overly simplistic theory about the effectiveness of rewards.

18. B Deci's opinion is that the introduction of a reward system changes things for the worse. He would see the description of the *problems* mentioned in line 38 as presumptuous because they presume that the rewards actually have a positive effect and incomplete because they do not mention all of the problems that he sees in reward systems.

19. D Both authors agree that positive feedback is a more effective teaching mechanism than negative feedback. Passage 1 mentions the need of good educators to *teach … without punishment* (lines 6–7) and mentions the negative *by-products of aversive control* (control by punishment) (lines 36–37). Passage 2 mentions that *most educators and psychologists agree that reward is always better than punishment* (lines 87–88), and since the writer goes on to criticize even reward systems, he implies that punishment is most certainly a bad teaching technique.

Section 9

1. C The word *whose* should refer to Alvin Ailey, but the way the sentence is constructed, it is referring to Alvin Ailey's *works*. Answer choice (C) corrects this error in the most concise and logical fashion.

2. B When a participle is used to indicate an action that is completed before another action, it should be *perfect*. *Getting* this far should instead be *Having gotten*.

3. C The sentence is improperly describing Rachel's irritation as being even-tempered. In reality, it should be *Rachel* who is even-tempered. Answer choice (C) corrects this error.

4. B This is a comparisons error. The literal translation of the sentence as written suggests that Alberta's salary is higher in the air than her co-workers are. It needs to be changed so that the sentence is comparing Alberta's salary to the *salary of her coworkers*.

5. C The word *elicit* means to call forth or draw out. The word should be *illicit*, which means unlawful.

6. D The paraders were not watching from the balcony. The sentence needs to be changed so that the subjects represented by the final pronoun *us* are the ones watching from the balcony.

7. **E**   The sentence contains two past tense verbs and one event was completed before the other. The tents were set up before they arrived. So *set up* needs to be in the past perfect tense—*had set up*.

8. **C**   When using neither … nor … phrasing, the verb should match in number the subject that follows the *nor*. Because daughters is plural, *was* should instead be *were*.

9. **B**   When using not only A but also B, the words or phrases that replace A and B must be parallel. It should be replaced by not only *with working* but also *with wanting*.

10. **C**   To correct this sentence, the word *that* should be replaced with *who*, sine Roberto is a *person*.

11. **D**   Answer choice (D) connects the two clauses most effectively.

12. **E**   When reading this sentence you should ask yourself: "who was forced to live apart from his family?" The answer to that question, St. Pierre, is what should immediately follow the comma after *informers*.

13. **B**   The gerund form, *forming*, is not correct and needs to be changed to past tense *formed*. Choice (B) works best.

14. **D**   What follows the linking verb is must be a noun phrase representing *the most challenging aspect*, not an independent clause, as in the original. Choice (D) works best.

PRACTICE TEST 11

ANSWER SHEET

Last Name: _____   First Name: _____

Date: _____   Testing Location: _____

Directions for Test

- Remove these answer sheets from the book and use them to record your answers to this test.
- This test will require 3 hours and 20 minutes to complete. Take this test in one sitting.
- The time allotment for each section is written clearly at the beginning of each section. This test contains six 25-minute sections, two 20-minute sections, and one 10-minute section.
- This test is 25 minutes shorter than the actual SAT, which will include a 25-minute "experimental" section that does not count toward your score. That section has been omitted from this test.
- You may take one short break during the test, of no more than 10 minutes in length.
- You may only work on one section at any given time.
- You must stop ALL work on a section when time is called.
- If you finish a section before the time has elapsed, check your work on that section. You may NOT work on any other section.
- Do not waste time on questions that seem too difficult for you.
- Use the test book for scratchwork, but you will receive credit only for answers that are marked on the answer sheets.
- You will receive one point for every correct answer.
- You will receive no points for an omitted question.
- For each wrong answer on any multiple-choice question, your score will be reduced by ¼ point.
- For each wrong answer on any "numerical grid-in" question, you will receive no deduction.

SECTION 2

1. Ⓐ Ⓑ Ⓒ Ⓓ Ⓔ   11. Ⓐ Ⓑ Ⓒ Ⓓ Ⓔ   21. Ⓐ Ⓑ Ⓒ Ⓓ Ⓔ   31. Ⓐ Ⓑ Ⓒ Ⓓ Ⓔ
2. Ⓐ Ⓑ Ⓒ Ⓓ Ⓔ   12. Ⓐ Ⓑ Ⓒ Ⓓ Ⓔ   22. Ⓐ Ⓑ Ⓒ Ⓓ Ⓔ   32. Ⓐ Ⓑ Ⓒ Ⓓ Ⓔ
3. Ⓐ Ⓑ Ⓒ Ⓓ Ⓔ   13. Ⓐ Ⓑ Ⓒ Ⓓ Ⓔ   23. Ⓐ Ⓑ Ⓒ Ⓓ Ⓔ   33. Ⓐ Ⓑ Ⓒ Ⓓ Ⓔ
4. Ⓐ Ⓑ Ⓒ Ⓓ Ⓔ   14. Ⓐ Ⓑ Ⓒ Ⓓ Ⓔ   24. Ⓐ Ⓑ Ⓒ Ⓓ Ⓔ   34. Ⓐ Ⓑ Ⓒ Ⓓ Ⓔ
5. Ⓐ Ⓑ Ⓒ Ⓓ Ⓔ   15. Ⓐ Ⓑ Ⓒ Ⓓ Ⓔ   25. Ⓐ Ⓑ Ⓒ Ⓓ Ⓔ   35. Ⓐ Ⓑ Ⓒ Ⓓ Ⓔ
6. Ⓐ Ⓑ Ⓒ Ⓓ Ⓔ   16. Ⓐ Ⓑ Ⓒ Ⓓ Ⓔ   26. Ⓐ Ⓑ Ⓒ Ⓓ Ⓔ   36. Ⓐ Ⓑ Ⓒ Ⓓ Ⓔ
7. Ⓐ Ⓑ Ⓒ Ⓓ Ⓔ   17. Ⓐ Ⓑ Ⓒ Ⓓ Ⓔ   27. Ⓐ Ⓑ Ⓒ Ⓓ Ⓔ   37. Ⓐ Ⓑ Ⓒ Ⓓ Ⓔ
8. Ⓐ Ⓑ Ⓒ Ⓓ Ⓔ   18. Ⓐ Ⓑ Ⓒ Ⓓ Ⓔ   28. Ⓐ Ⓑ Ⓒ Ⓓ Ⓔ   38. Ⓐ Ⓑ Ⓒ Ⓓ Ⓔ
9. Ⓐ Ⓑ Ⓒ Ⓓ Ⓔ   19. Ⓐ Ⓑ Ⓒ Ⓓ Ⓔ   29. Ⓐ Ⓑ Ⓒ Ⓓ Ⓔ   39. Ⓐ Ⓑ Ⓒ Ⓓ Ⓔ
10. Ⓐ Ⓑ Ⓒ Ⓓ Ⓔ   20. Ⓐ Ⓑ Ⓒ Ⓓ Ⓔ   30. Ⓐ Ⓑ Ⓒ Ⓓ Ⓔ   40. Ⓐ Ⓑ Ⓒ Ⓓ Ⓔ

SECTION 3

1. Ⓐ Ⓑ Ⓒ Ⓓ Ⓔ   11. Ⓐ Ⓑ Ⓒ Ⓓ Ⓔ   21. Ⓐ Ⓑ Ⓒ Ⓓ Ⓔ   31. Ⓐ Ⓑ Ⓒ Ⓓ Ⓔ
2. Ⓐ Ⓑ Ⓒ Ⓓ Ⓔ   12. Ⓐ Ⓑ Ⓒ Ⓓ Ⓔ   22. Ⓐ Ⓑ Ⓒ Ⓓ Ⓔ   32. Ⓐ Ⓑ Ⓒ Ⓓ Ⓔ
3. Ⓐ Ⓑ Ⓒ Ⓓ Ⓔ   13. Ⓐ Ⓑ Ⓒ Ⓓ Ⓔ   23. Ⓐ Ⓑ Ⓒ Ⓓ Ⓔ   33. Ⓐ Ⓑ Ⓒ Ⓓ Ⓔ
4. Ⓐ Ⓑ Ⓒ Ⓓ Ⓔ   14. Ⓐ Ⓑ Ⓒ Ⓓ Ⓔ   24. Ⓐ Ⓑ Ⓒ Ⓓ Ⓔ   34. Ⓐ Ⓑ Ⓒ Ⓓ Ⓔ
5. Ⓐ Ⓑ Ⓒ Ⓓ Ⓔ   15. Ⓐ Ⓑ Ⓒ Ⓓ Ⓔ   25. Ⓐ Ⓑ Ⓒ Ⓓ Ⓔ   35. Ⓐ Ⓑ Ⓒ Ⓓ Ⓔ
6. Ⓐ Ⓑ Ⓒ Ⓓ Ⓔ   16. Ⓐ Ⓑ Ⓒ Ⓓ Ⓔ   26. Ⓐ Ⓑ Ⓒ Ⓓ Ⓔ   36. Ⓐ Ⓑ Ⓒ Ⓓ Ⓔ
7. Ⓐ Ⓑ Ⓒ Ⓓ Ⓔ   17. Ⓐ Ⓑ Ⓒ Ⓓ Ⓔ   27. Ⓐ Ⓑ Ⓒ Ⓓ Ⓔ   37. Ⓐ Ⓑ Ⓒ Ⓓ Ⓔ
8. Ⓐ Ⓑ Ⓒ Ⓓ Ⓔ   18. Ⓐ Ⓑ Ⓒ Ⓓ Ⓔ   28. Ⓐ Ⓑ Ⓒ Ⓓ Ⓔ   38. Ⓐ Ⓑ Ⓒ Ⓓ Ⓔ
9. Ⓐ Ⓑ Ⓒ Ⓓ Ⓔ   19. Ⓐ Ⓑ Ⓒ Ⓓ Ⓔ   29. Ⓐ Ⓑ Ⓒ Ⓓ Ⓔ   39. Ⓐ Ⓑ Ⓒ Ⓓ Ⓔ
10. Ⓐ Ⓑ Ⓒ Ⓓ Ⓔ   20. Ⓐ Ⓑ Ⓒ Ⓓ Ⓔ   30. Ⓐ Ⓑ Ⓒ Ⓓ Ⓔ   40. Ⓐ Ⓑ Ⓒ Ⓓ Ⓔ

ANSWER SHEET

SECTION 4

1. Ⓐ Ⓑ Ⓒ Ⓓ Ⓔ
2. Ⓐ Ⓑ Ⓒ Ⓓ Ⓔ
3. Ⓐ Ⓑ Ⓒ Ⓓ Ⓔ
4. Ⓐ Ⓑ Ⓒ Ⓓ Ⓔ
5. Ⓐ Ⓑ Ⓒ Ⓓ Ⓔ
6. Ⓐ Ⓑ Ⓒ Ⓓ Ⓔ
7. Ⓐ Ⓑ Ⓒ Ⓓ Ⓔ
8. Ⓐ Ⓑ Ⓒ Ⓓ Ⓔ
9. Ⓐ Ⓑ Ⓒ Ⓓ Ⓔ
10. Ⓐ Ⓑ Ⓒ Ⓓ Ⓔ

11. Ⓐ Ⓑ Ⓒ Ⓓ Ⓔ
12. Ⓐ Ⓑ Ⓒ Ⓓ Ⓔ
13. Ⓐ Ⓑ Ⓒ Ⓓ Ⓔ
14. Ⓐ Ⓑ Ⓒ Ⓓ Ⓔ
15. Ⓐ Ⓑ Ⓒ Ⓓ Ⓔ
16. Ⓐ Ⓑ Ⓒ Ⓓ Ⓔ
17. Ⓐ Ⓑ Ⓒ Ⓓ Ⓔ
18. Ⓐ Ⓑ Ⓒ Ⓓ Ⓔ
19. Ⓐ Ⓑ Ⓒ Ⓓ Ⓔ
20. Ⓐ Ⓑ Ⓒ Ⓓ Ⓔ

21. Ⓐ Ⓑ Ⓒ Ⓓ Ⓔ
22. Ⓐ Ⓑ Ⓒ Ⓓ Ⓔ
23. Ⓐ Ⓑ Ⓒ Ⓓ Ⓔ
24. Ⓐ Ⓑ Ⓒ Ⓓ Ⓔ
25. Ⓐ Ⓑ Ⓒ Ⓓ Ⓔ
26. Ⓐ Ⓑ Ⓒ Ⓓ Ⓔ
27. Ⓐ Ⓑ Ⓒ Ⓓ Ⓔ
28. Ⓐ Ⓑ Ⓒ Ⓓ Ⓔ
29. Ⓐ Ⓑ Ⓒ Ⓓ Ⓔ
30. Ⓐ Ⓑ Ⓒ Ⓓ Ⓔ

31. Ⓐ Ⓑ Ⓒ Ⓓ Ⓔ
32. Ⓐ Ⓑ Ⓒ Ⓓ Ⓔ
33. Ⓐ Ⓑ Ⓒ Ⓓ Ⓔ
34. Ⓐ Ⓑ Ⓒ Ⓓ Ⓔ
35. Ⓐ Ⓑ Ⓒ Ⓓ Ⓔ
36. Ⓐ Ⓑ Ⓒ Ⓓ Ⓔ
37. Ⓐ Ⓑ Ⓒ Ⓓ Ⓔ
38. Ⓐ Ⓑ Ⓒ Ⓓ Ⓔ
39. Ⓐ Ⓑ Ⓒ Ⓓ Ⓔ
40. Ⓐ Ⓑ Ⓒ Ⓓ Ⓔ

SECTION 5

1. Ⓐ Ⓑ Ⓒ Ⓓ Ⓔ
2. Ⓐ Ⓑ Ⓒ Ⓓ Ⓔ
3. Ⓐ Ⓑ Ⓒ Ⓓ Ⓔ
4. Ⓐ Ⓑ Ⓒ Ⓓ Ⓔ

5. Ⓐ Ⓑ Ⓒ Ⓓ Ⓔ
6. Ⓐ Ⓑ Ⓒ Ⓓ Ⓔ
7. Ⓐ Ⓑ Ⓒ Ⓓ Ⓔ
8. Ⓐ Ⓑ Ⓒ Ⓓ Ⓔ

9. 10. 11. 12. 13.

14. 15. 16. 17. 18.

ANSWER SHEET

SECTION 6

1. Ⓐ Ⓑ Ⓒ Ⓓ Ⓔ
2. Ⓐ Ⓑ Ⓒ Ⓓ Ⓔ
3. Ⓐ Ⓑ Ⓒ Ⓓ Ⓔ
4. Ⓐ Ⓑ Ⓒ Ⓓ Ⓔ
5. Ⓐ Ⓑ Ⓒ Ⓓ Ⓔ
6. Ⓐ Ⓑ Ⓒ Ⓓ Ⓔ
7. Ⓐ Ⓑ Ⓒ Ⓓ Ⓔ
8. Ⓐ Ⓑ Ⓒ Ⓓ Ⓔ
9. Ⓐ Ⓑ Ⓒ Ⓓ Ⓔ
10. Ⓐ Ⓑ Ⓒ Ⓓ Ⓔ

11. Ⓐ Ⓑ Ⓒ Ⓓ Ⓔ
12. Ⓐ Ⓑ Ⓒ Ⓓ Ⓔ
13. Ⓐ Ⓑ Ⓒ Ⓓ Ⓔ
14. Ⓐ Ⓑ Ⓒ Ⓓ Ⓔ
15. Ⓐ Ⓑ Ⓒ Ⓓ Ⓔ
16. Ⓐ Ⓑ Ⓒ Ⓓ Ⓔ
17. Ⓐ Ⓑ Ⓒ Ⓓ Ⓔ
18. Ⓐ Ⓑ Ⓒ Ⓓ Ⓔ
19. Ⓐ Ⓑ Ⓒ Ⓓ Ⓔ
20. Ⓐ Ⓑ Ⓒ Ⓓ Ⓔ

21. Ⓐ Ⓑ Ⓒ Ⓓ Ⓔ
22. Ⓐ Ⓑ Ⓒ Ⓓ Ⓔ
23. Ⓐ Ⓑ Ⓒ Ⓓ Ⓔ
24. Ⓐ Ⓑ Ⓒ Ⓓ Ⓔ
25. Ⓐ Ⓑ Ⓒ Ⓓ Ⓔ
26. Ⓐ Ⓑ Ⓒ Ⓓ Ⓔ
27. Ⓐ Ⓑ Ⓒ Ⓓ Ⓔ
28. Ⓐ Ⓑ Ⓒ Ⓓ Ⓔ
29. Ⓐ Ⓑ Ⓒ Ⓓ Ⓔ
30. Ⓐ Ⓑ Ⓒ Ⓓ Ⓔ

31. Ⓐ Ⓑ Ⓒ Ⓓ Ⓔ
32. Ⓐ Ⓑ Ⓒ Ⓓ Ⓔ
33. Ⓐ Ⓑ Ⓒ Ⓓ Ⓔ
34. Ⓐ Ⓑ Ⓒ Ⓓ Ⓔ
35. Ⓐ Ⓑ Ⓒ Ⓓ Ⓔ
36. Ⓐ Ⓑ Ⓒ Ⓓ Ⓔ
37. Ⓐ Ⓑ Ⓒ Ⓓ Ⓔ
38. Ⓐ Ⓑ Ⓒ Ⓓ Ⓔ
39. Ⓐ Ⓑ Ⓒ Ⓓ Ⓔ
40. Ⓐ Ⓑ Ⓒ Ⓓ Ⓔ

SECTION 7

1. Ⓐ Ⓑ Ⓒ Ⓓ Ⓔ
2. Ⓐ Ⓑ Ⓒ Ⓓ Ⓔ
3. Ⓐ Ⓑ Ⓒ Ⓓ Ⓔ
4. Ⓐ Ⓑ Ⓒ Ⓓ Ⓔ
5. Ⓐ Ⓑ Ⓒ Ⓓ Ⓔ
6. Ⓐ Ⓑ Ⓒ Ⓓ Ⓔ
7. Ⓐ Ⓑ Ⓒ Ⓓ Ⓔ
8. Ⓐ Ⓑ Ⓒ Ⓓ Ⓔ
9. Ⓐ Ⓑ Ⓒ Ⓓ Ⓔ
10. Ⓐ Ⓑ Ⓒ Ⓓ Ⓔ

11. Ⓐ Ⓑ Ⓒ Ⓓ Ⓔ
12. Ⓐ Ⓑ Ⓒ Ⓓ Ⓔ
13. Ⓐ Ⓑ Ⓒ Ⓓ Ⓔ
14. Ⓐ Ⓑ Ⓒ Ⓓ Ⓔ
15. Ⓐ Ⓑ Ⓒ Ⓓ Ⓔ
16. Ⓐ Ⓑ Ⓒ Ⓓ Ⓔ
17. Ⓐ Ⓑ Ⓒ Ⓓ Ⓔ
18. Ⓐ Ⓑ Ⓒ Ⓓ Ⓔ
19. Ⓐ Ⓑ Ⓒ Ⓓ Ⓔ
20. Ⓐ Ⓑ Ⓒ Ⓓ Ⓔ

21. Ⓐ Ⓑ Ⓒ Ⓓ Ⓔ
22. Ⓐ Ⓑ Ⓒ Ⓓ Ⓔ
23. Ⓐ Ⓑ Ⓒ Ⓓ Ⓔ
24. Ⓐ Ⓑ Ⓒ Ⓓ Ⓔ
25. Ⓐ Ⓑ Ⓒ Ⓓ Ⓔ
26. Ⓐ Ⓑ Ⓒ Ⓓ Ⓔ
27. Ⓐ Ⓑ Ⓒ Ⓓ Ⓔ
28. Ⓐ Ⓑ Ⓒ Ⓓ Ⓔ
29. Ⓐ Ⓑ Ⓒ Ⓓ Ⓔ
30. Ⓐ Ⓑ Ⓒ Ⓓ Ⓔ

31. Ⓐ Ⓑ Ⓒ Ⓓ Ⓔ
32. Ⓐ Ⓑ Ⓒ Ⓓ Ⓔ
33. Ⓐ Ⓑ Ⓒ Ⓓ Ⓔ
34. Ⓐ Ⓑ Ⓒ Ⓓ Ⓔ
35. Ⓐ Ⓑ Ⓒ Ⓓ Ⓔ
36. Ⓐ Ⓑ Ⓒ Ⓓ Ⓔ
37. Ⓐ Ⓑ Ⓒ Ⓓ Ⓔ
38. Ⓐ Ⓑ Ⓒ Ⓓ Ⓔ
39. Ⓐ Ⓑ Ⓒ Ⓓ Ⓔ
40. Ⓐ Ⓑ Ⓒ Ⓓ Ⓔ

SECTION 8

1. Ⓐ Ⓑ Ⓒ Ⓓ Ⓔ
2. Ⓐ Ⓑ Ⓒ Ⓓ Ⓔ
3. Ⓐ Ⓑ Ⓒ Ⓓ Ⓔ
4. Ⓐ Ⓑ Ⓒ Ⓓ Ⓔ
5. Ⓐ Ⓑ Ⓒ Ⓓ Ⓔ
6. Ⓐ Ⓑ Ⓒ Ⓓ Ⓔ
7. Ⓐ Ⓑ Ⓒ Ⓓ Ⓔ
8. Ⓐ Ⓑ Ⓒ Ⓓ Ⓔ
9. Ⓐ Ⓑ Ⓒ Ⓓ Ⓔ
10. Ⓐ Ⓑ Ⓒ Ⓓ Ⓔ

11. Ⓐ Ⓑ Ⓒ Ⓓ Ⓔ
12. Ⓐ Ⓑ Ⓒ Ⓓ Ⓔ
13. Ⓐ Ⓑ Ⓒ Ⓓ Ⓔ
14. Ⓐ Ⓑ Ⓒ Ⓓ Ⓔ
15. Ⓐ Ⓑ Ⓒ Ⓓ Ⓔ
16. Ⓐ Ⓑ Ⓒ Ⓓ Ⓔ
17. Ⓐ Ⓑ Ⓒ Ⓓ Ⓔ
18. Ⓐ Ⓑ Ⓒ Ⓓ Ⓔ
19. Ⓐ Ⓑ Ⓒ Ⓓ Ⓔ
20. Ⓐ Ⓑ Ⓒ Ⓓ Ⓔ

21. Ⓐ Ⓑ Ⓒ Ⓓ Ⓔ
22. Ⓐ Ⓑ Ⓒ Ⓓ Ⓔ
23. Ⓐ Ⓑ Ⓒ Ⓓ Ⓔ
24. Ⓐ Ⓑ Ⓒ Ⓓ Ⓔ
25. Ⓐ Ⓑ Ⓒ Ⓓ Ⓔ
26. Ⓐ Ⓑ Ⓒ Ⓓ Ⓔ
27. Ⓐ Ⓑ Ⓒ Ⓓ Ⓔ
28. Ⓐ Ⓑ Ⓒ Ⓓ Ⓔ
29. Ⓐ Ⓑ Ⓒ Ⓓ Ⓔ
30. Ⓐ Ⓑ Ⓒ Ⓓ Ⓔ

31. Ⓐ Ⓑ Ⓒ Ⓓ Ⓔ
32. Ⓐ Ⓑ Ⓒ Ⓓ Ⓔ
33. Ⓐ Ⓑ Ⓒ Ⓓ Ⓔ
34. Ⓐ Ⓑ Ⓒ Ⓓ Ⓔ
35. Ⓐ Ⓑ Ⓒ Ⓓ Ⓔ
36. Ⓐ Ⓑ Ⓒ Ⓓ Ⓔ
37. Ⓐ Ⓑ Ⓒ Ⓓ Ⓔ
38. Ⓐ Ⓑ Ⓒ Ⓓ Ⓔ
39. Ⓐ Ⓑ Ⓒ Ⓓ Ⓔ
40. Ⓐ Ⓑ Ⓒ Ⓓ Ⓔ

SECTION 9

1. Ⓐ Ⓑ Ⓒ Ⓓ Ⓔ
2. Ⓐ Ⓑ Ⓒ Ⓓ Ⓔ
3. Ⓐ Ⓑ Ⓒ Ⓓ Ⓔ
4. Ⓐ Ⓑ Ⓒ Ⓓ Ⓔ
5. Ⓐ Ⓑ Ⓒ Ⓓ Ⓔ
6. Ⓐ Ⓑ Ⓒ Ⓓ Ⓔ
7. Ⓐ Ⓑ Ⓒ Ⓓ Ⓔ
8. Ⓐ Ⓑ Ⓒ Ⓓ Ⓔ
9. Ⓐ Ⓑ Ⓒ Ⓓ Ⓔ
10. Ⓐ Ⓑ Ⓒ Ⓓ Ⓔ

11. Ⓐ Ⓑ Ⓒ Ⓓ Ⓔ
12. Ⓐ Ⓑ Ⓒ Ⓓ Ⓔ
13. Ⓐ Ⓑ Ⓒ Ⓓ Ⓔ
14. Ⓐ Ⓑ Ⓒ Ⓓ Ⓔ
15. Ⓐ Ⓑ Ⓒ Ⓓ Ⓔ
16. Ⓐ Ⓑ Ⓒ Ⓓ Ⓔ
17. Ⓐ Ⓑ Ⓒ Ⓓ Ⓔ
18. Ⓐ Ⓑ Ⓒ Ⓓ Ⓔ
19. Ⓐ Ⓑ Ⓒ Ⓓ Ⓔ
20. Ⓐ Ⓑ Ⓒ Ⓓ Ⓔ

21. Ⓐ Ⓑ Ⓒ Ⓓ Ⓔ
22. Ⓐ Ⓑ Ⓒ Ⓓ Ⓔ
23. Ⓐ Ⓑ Ⓒ Ⓓ Ⓔ
24. Ⓐ Ⓑ Ⓒ Ⓓ Ⓔ
25. Ⓐ Ⓑ Ⓒ Ⓓ Ⓔ
26. Ⓐ Ⓑ Ⓒ Ⓓ Ⓔ
27. Ⓐ Ⓑ Ⓒ Ⓓ Ⓔ
28. Ⓐ Ⓑ Ⓒ Ⓓ Ⓔ
29. Ⓐ Ⓑ Ⓒ Ⓓ Ⓔ
30. Ⓐ Ⓑ Ⓒ Ⓓ Ⓔ

31. Ⓐ Ⓑ Ⓒ Ⓓ Ⓔ
32. Ⓐ Ⓑ Ⓒ Ⓓ Ⓔ
33. Ⓐ Ⓑ Ⓒ Ⓓ Ⓔ
34. Ⓐ Ⓑ Ⓒ Ⓓ Ⓔ
35. Ⓐ Ⓑ Ⓒ Ⓓ Ⓔ
36. Ⓐ Ⓑ Ⓒ Ⓓ Ⓔ
37. Ⓐ Ⓑ Ⓒ Ⓓ Ⓔ
38. Ⓐ Ⓑ Ⓒ Ⓓ Ⓔ
39. Ⓐ Ⓑ Ⓒ Ⓓ Ⓔ
40. Ⓐ Ⓑ Ⓒ Ⓓ Ⓔ

Section 1

1➤ **Time—25 minutes**

Directions for Writing the Essay

Plan and write an essay that answers the question below. Do NOT write on another topic. An essay on another topic will receive a score of 0.

Two readers will grade your essay based on how well you develop your point of view, organize and explain your ideas, use specific and relevant examples to support your thesis, and use clear and effective language. How well you write is much more important than how much you write, but to cover the topic adequately you should plan to write several paragraphs.

Your essay must be written on separate lined sheets of paper. Keep your handwriting to a reasonable size. Your essay will be read by people who are not familiar with your handwriting, so write legibly.

You may use this sheet for notes and outlining, but these will not be graded as part of your essay.

Consider carefully the issue discussed in the following passage, then write an essay that answers the question posed in the assignment.

> Many among us like to blame violence and immorality in the media for a "decline in morals" in society. Yet these people seem to have lost touch with logic. Any objective examination shows that our society is far less violent or exploitative than virtually any society in the past. Early humans murdered and enslaved each other with astonishing regularity, without the help of gangsta rap or Jerry Bruckheimer films.

Assignment: **Does violence and immorality in the media make our society more dangerous and immoral?** Write an essay in which you answer this question and discuss your point of view on this issue. Support your position logically with examples from literature, the arts, history, politics, science and technology, current events, or your experience or observation.

Write your essay on separate sheets of paper.

Section 2

Time–25 minutes
20 Questions

Directions for Multiple-Choice Questions

In this section, solve each problem, using any available space on the page for scratchwork. Then decide which is the best of the choices given and fill in the corresponding oval on the answer sheet.

- You may use a calculator on any problem. All numbers used are real numbers.
- Figures are drawn as accurately as possible EXCEPT when it is stated that the figure is not drawn to scale.
- All figures lie in a plane unless otherwise indicated.

Reference Information

$A = \pi r^2$ $A = \ell w$ $A = \frac{1}{2}bh$ $V = \ell wh$ $V = \pi r^2 h$ $c^2 = a^2 + b^2$ Special Right Triangles
$C = 2\pi r$

The arc of a circle measures 360°.
Every straight angle measures 180°.
The sum of the measures of the angles in a triangle is 180°.

---

1 If $(x + 4) + 7 + 14$, what is the value of x?

(A) 3
(B) 7
(C) 11
(D) 17
(E) 25

2 Erica spends $.95 each day for her newspaper subscriptions. She would like to determine the approximate amount she spends during the month of July, which has 31 days. Which of the following would provide her with the best estimate?

(A) $.50 \times 30$
(B) 1.00×30
(C) 1.50×30
(D) $.50 \times 35$
(E) 1.00×35

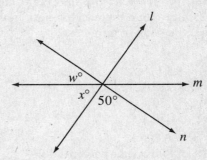

Note: Figure not drawn to scale.

3 In the figure above, lines l, m, and n intersect in a single point. What is the value of $w + x$?

(A) 40
(B) 70
(C) 90
(D) 130
(E) 140

GO ON TO THE NEXT PAGE ▶▶▶

2

4 Let the function g be defined by the equation $g(x) = 3x + 4$. What is the value of $g(5)$?

(A) 8
(B) 11
(C) 15
(D) 19
(E) 23

5 If $x > y$, which of the following equations expresses the fact that when the difference between x and y is multiplied by their sum, the product is 18?

(A) $(x - y)^2 = 18$
(B) $(x + y)^2 = 18$
(C) $(x - y) \div (x + y) = 18$
(D) $x^2 - y^2 = 18$
(E) $x^2 + y^2 = 18$

6 If $3\sqrt{x} - 7 = 20$, what is the value of x?

(A) 3
(B) 9
(C) 27
(D) 36
(E) 81

7 Chris buys a chocolate bar and a pack of gum for \$1.75. If the chocolate bar costs \$.25 more than the pack of gum, how much does the pack of gum cost?

(A) \$.25
(B) \$.50
(C) \$.75
(D) \$1.00
(E) \$1.50

8 40% of 80 is what percent of 96?

(A) 20%
(B) 30%
(C) 33⅓%
(D) 50%
(E) 66⅔%

9 If l, m, and n are positive integers greater than 1; $lm = 21$; and $mn = 39$, then which of the following must be true?

(A) $n > l > m$
(B) $m > n > l$
(C) $m > l > n$
(D) $l > n > m$
(E) $n > m > l$

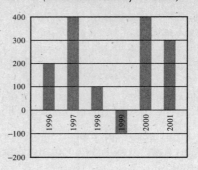

Annual Profits for ABC Company
(in thousands of dollars)

10 According to the graph above, ABC Company showed the greatest change in profits between which 2 years?

(A) 1996 and 1997
(B) 1997 and 1998
(C) 1998 and 1999
(D) 1999 and 2000
(E) 2000 and 2001

11 In a 9th-grade class, 12 students play soccer, 7 students play tennis, and 9 students play lacrosse. If 4 students play exactly 2 of the 3 sports and all other students play only 1, how many students are in the class?

(A) 28
(B) 24
(C) 20
(D) 18
(E) 16

12 The point (14, 14) is the center of a circle, and (2, 9) is a point on the circle. What is the length of a diameter of the circle?

(A) 24
(B) 26
(C) 50
(D) 144π
(E) 169π

13 The population of Boomtown doubles every 18 months. In January of 2000, its population was exactly 12,000. At this rate, approximately when should the population reach 96,000?

(A) January 2003
(B) July 2004
(C) January 2006
(D) July 2007
(E) January 2012

GO ON TO THE NEXT PAGE ▶▶▶

14 In how many different ways can 5 students of different heights be arranged in a line if the tallest student cannot be on either end?

(A)   24
(B)   25
(C)   72
(D)   96
(E)   120

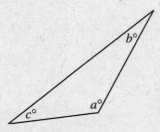

Note: Figure not drawn to scale.

15 In the figure above, $a > 90$ and $b = c + 3$. If a, b, and c are all integers, what is the greatest possible value of b?

(A)   43
(B)   46
(C)   60
(D)   86
(E)   89

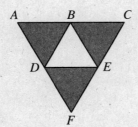

16 In the figure above, $\triangle ACF$ is equilateral, with sides of length 4. If B, D, and E are the mid-points of their respective sides, what is the sum of the areas of the shaded regions?

(A) $3\sqrt{2}$
(B) $3\sqrt{3}$
(C) $4\sqrt{2}$
(D) $4\sqrt{3}$
(E) $6\sqrt{3}$

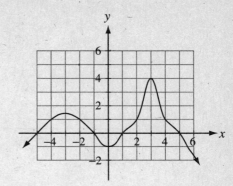

17 Given the graph of $y = f(x)$ above, which of the following sets represents all values of x for which $f(x) \geq 1$?

(A)   all real numbers
(B) $x \geq 1$
(C) $-5 \leq x \leq -1; 1 \leq x \leq 5$
(D) $-4 \leq x \leq -2; 2 \leq x \leq 4$
(E) $x \leq -4; x \geq 4$

X: {2, 4, 6, 8, 10}
Y: {1, 3, 5, 7, 9}

18 If a is a number chosen randomly from set X and b is a number chosen randomly from set Y, what is the probability that ab is greater than 20 but less than 50?

(A)   1/5
(B)   6/5
(C)   7/25
(D)   3/5
(E)   18/25

19 If $w^a \times w^5 = w^{15}$ and $(w^4)^b = w^{12}$, what is the value of $a + b$?

(A)   6
(B)   7
(C)   11
(D)   12
(E)   13

GO ON TO THE NEXT PAGE ▶▶▶

2

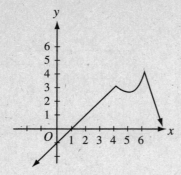

20 Given the graph of $y = f(x)$ above, which of the following represents the graph of $y = f(x - 2)$?

(A)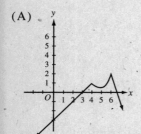

(B)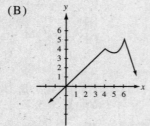

(C)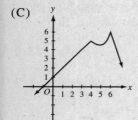

(D)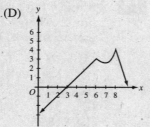

(E)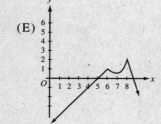

You may check your work, on this section only, until time is called.

Section 3

Time—25 minutes
24 Questions

Each of the sentences below is missing one or two portions. Read each sentence, then select the word or words that most logically completes the sentence, taking into account the meaning of thesentence as a whole.

Example:

Rather than accepting the theory unquestioningly, Deborah regarded it with _____.

(A) mirth   (B) sadness
(C) responsibility   (D) ignorance
(E) skepticism

Correct response: (E)

1 Although he purchased his computer only 10 months ago, rapid improvements in technology have left Raúl with ——— machine.

(A) an obsolete   (B) an adjunct
(C) a novel   (D) an automated
(E) an elusive

2 Only if the number of applicants continues to ——— can the admissions committee justify offering more scholarships in order to increase the number of applications.

(A) mushroom   (B) expand
(C) plummet   (D) satiate
(E) burgeon

3 My father is so ——— that he will never even consider another person's viewpoint to be valid if it is different from his own.

(A) pragmatic   (B) dogmatic
(C) phlegmatic   (D) cordial
(E) curt

4 J. K. Rowling's *Harry Potter* series is a collection of works that are ——— for children but are still ——— to adults.

(A) penned ... prosaic
(B) employed ... morose
(C) censored ... incongruous
(D) designed ... tedious
(E) authored ... engaging

5 Julia approaches her homework assignments in such ——— way that it is very difficult to believe that she is at the top of her class.

(A) an adept   (B) a diligent
(C) a fanatical   (D) an extroverted
(E) a laggardly

6 The President was such a ——— orator that his opponents were always supremely cautious about agreeing to debate him.

(A) redoubtable   (B) staid
(C) magnanimous   (D) weak
(E) stoic

7 The newest clothing line revealed at the show was an eclectic mix that ranged from the modest and unadorned to the ——— and garish.

(A) austere   (B) prophetic
(C) cordial   (D) ostentatious
(E) solitary

8 Neil Campbell's textbook *Biology* is ——— and yet ———; it includes all of the essential information without ever being verbose.

(A) compendious ... circumlocutory
(B) reprehensible ... terse
(C) comprehensive ... concise
(D) praiseworthy ... grandiloquent
(E) painstaking ... redundant

GO ON TO THE NEXT PAGE ▶▶▶

The passages below are followed by questions based on their content. Answer each question based on what is stated or implied in the passages or the introductory material preceding them.

Questions 9–12 are based on the following passages.

Passage 1

The following is from President Bill Clinton's first inaugural address.

Line   Today, a generation raised in the shadows of
the Cold War assumes new responsibilities in
a world warmed by the sunshine of freedom,
but threatened still by ancient hatreds
5   and new plagues. Raised in unrivaled
prosperity, we inherit an economy that is still
the world's strongest, but is weakened by
business failures, stagnant wages, increasing
inequality, and deep divisions among our
10   own people. When George Washington first
took the oath I have just sworn to uphold,
news traveled slowly across the land by
horseback, and across the ocean by boat.
Now the sights and sounds of this ceremony
15   are broadcast instantaneously to billions
around the world. Communications and
commerce are global. Investment is mobile.
Technology is almost magical, and ambition
for a better life is now universal.

Passage 2

The following is a commentary on America written in 2005 by an American writer.

20   The people of the world, save the majority
of our own citizens, are growing to
appreciate the difference between America
and the United States. America is the heart
and mind of the world. It is an ideal to which
25   all free-thinking men and women aspire.
It is the spirit of hope, freedom, vision and
creativity. But the United States, at least since
the turn of the century, has become
something different. It constantly grasps at
30   the cloak of America, but this cloak fits our
current leaders quite poorly. Our leaders have
become dominated by fear and its value as a
political tool. They speak incessantly of
freedom but revel in repression. They speak

35   of a "culture of life" but revel in the culture
of siege and war. The hope, freedom, vision
and creativity of America have slipped
through their fingers, and they have little
hope of recapturing it. In America, that task
40   is left to the people.

9 The word "unrivaled" in line 5 most nearly means

(A) without enemies
(B) supremely abundant
(C) militarily superior
(D) unimaginable
(E) highly intelligent

10 Which of the following best describes the contrast between the "people" (line 10) as characterized in Passage 1 and the "citizens" (line 21) as characterized in Passage 2?

(A) the "people" are ignorant, while the "citizens" are well-educated
(B) the "people" lack fortitude, while the "citizens" are courageous
(C) the "people" are worldly, while the "citizens" are parochial
(D) the "people" are proud of their leaders, while the "citizens" are not
(E) the "people" lack unity, while the "citizens" lack awareness

11 Passage 1 makes all of the following claims about the state of society EXCEPT that

(A) an increasing number of people are happy with their lives
(B) information is disseminated more rapidly than in the past
(C) the current economy is strong
(D) social inequities are deepening
(E) workers' incomes are not increasing

12 Unlike the author of Passage 1, the author of Passage 2 does which of the following?

(A) contrasts an ideal with a reality
(B) explains a study
(C) compares the past with the present
(D) describes an injustice
(E) acknowledges a responsibility

GO ON TO THE NEXT PAGE ▶▶▶

The passages below are followed by questions based on their content. The questions are to be answered on the basis of what is stated or implied in the passage itself or in the introductory material that precedes them.

Questions 13–19 are based on the following passage.

The following passage is adapted from a short story published by a Russian author in the late 1970s.

Line   What is all this? he thought, terrified. And
        yet … do I love her, or don't I? That is the
        question!
            But she, now that the most important and
5   difficult thing had at last been said, breathed
        lightly and freely. She, too, stood up and,
        looking straight into Ognev Alexeyich's face,
        began to talk quickly, irrepressibly and
        ardently.
10   Just as a man who is suddenly
        overwhelmed by terror cannot afterwards
        remember the exact order of sounds
        accompanying the catastrophe which stuns
        him, Ognev could not remember Vera's words
15   and phrases. His memory retained only the
        substance of her speech itself and the
        sensation her speech produced in him.
        He remembered her voice, as though it were
        choked and slightly hoarse from excitement,
20   and the extraordinary music and passion of
        her intonation. Crying, laughing, the tears
        glittering on her eyelashes, she was telling
        him that even from the first days of their
        acquaintance she had been struck by his
25   originality, his intellect, his kind intelligent
        eyes, with the aims and objects of his life;
        that she had fallen passionately, madly and
        deeply in love with him; that whenever she
        had happened to come into the house from
30   the garden that summer and had seen his
        coat in the vestibule or heard his voice in the
        distance, her heart had felt a cold thrill of
        delight, a foretaste of happiness; that even
        the silliest jokes made her laugh helplessly,
35   and in each figure of his copybook she could
        see something extraordinarily clever and
        grandiose; that his knotted walking stick
        seemed to her more beautiful than the trees.
            The forest and the wisps of fog and the
40   black ditches alongside the road seemed to
        fall silent, listening to her, but something bad
        and strange was taking place in Ognev's
        heart … Vera was enchantingly beautiful as
        she told him of her love, she spoke with
45   eloquence and passion, but much as he
        wanted to, he could feel no joy, no
        fundamental happiness, but only compassion
        for Vera, and pain and regret that a good
        human being should be suffering because of
50   him. The Lord only knows whether it was his
        bookish mind that now began to speak, or
        whether he was affected by that irresistible
        habit of objectivity which so often prevents
        people from living, but Vera's raptures and
55   suffering seemed to him only cloying and
        trivial. At the same time he was outraged
        with himself and something whispered to
        him that what he was now seeing and
        hearing was, from the point of view of
60   human nature and his personal happiness,
        more important than any statistics, books or
        philosophical truths … And he was annoyed
        and blamed himself even though he himself
        did not understand why he was to blame.

GO ON TO THE NEXT PAGE ▶▶▶

13 Which of the following best describes the characterization of the man and the woman in the first two paragraphs?

(A)   He is confused, while she is passionate.
(B)   He is angry, while she is jocular.
(C)   He is stoic, while she is serene.
(D)   He is ambivalent, while she is anxious.
(E)   He is disdainful, while she is whimsical.

14 The author suggests that one "who is suddenly overwhelmed by terror" (line 11) is temporarily

(A)   vindictive
(B)   defensive
(C)   cautious
(D)   disoriented
(E)   resentful

15 The description of "the catastrophe" (line 13) serves primarily to suggest that

(A)   the couple has endured a terrible accident
(B)   Ognev is devastated by Vera's harsh words
(C)   Ognev is deeply troubled by Vera's passionate expression of love
(D)   Ognev holds Vera responsible for a crime
(E)   Vera has told Ognev a horrible secret

16 In line 26, "objects" most nearly means

(A)   possessions
(B)   facts
(C)   decorations
(D)   goals
(E)   complaints

17 The passage suggests that the "bad and strange" (lines 41–42) thing that was taking place in Ognev's heart was his

(A)   eagerness
(B)   sadism
(C)   jealousy
(D)   hatred
(E)   disaffection

18 In lines 61–62, "statistics, books or philosophical truths" are mentioned as examples of things that

(A)   Vera does not understand
(B)   Ognev and Vera share reluctantly
(C)   Ognev abandoned long ago
(D)   Vera loves passionately
(E)   Ognev inexplicably values more highly than passion

19 The primary function of the final paragraph is to show Ognev's

(A)   struggle to understand his own feelings
(B)   anger about Vera's misrepresentation of her feelings
(C)   frustration with the voices in his head
(D)   outrage with his inability to understand a philosophical concept
(E)   appreciation of Vera's beauty

GO ON TO THE NEXT PAGE ▶▶▶

Questions 20–24 are based on the following passage.

The following is part of an introduction to the publication of a speech delivered by President Lyndon B. Johnson in the 1960s.

Line "Somehow you never forget what poverty and hatred can do when you see its scars on the hopeful face of a young child." So spoke President Lyndon B. Johnson in the course of

5 one of the most deeply felt, and deeply moving, addresses ever delivered by an American president. The date was March 15th, 1965; the occasion was an extraordinary joint session at night of the Senate and the

10 House of Representatives, televised across the nation. It was the "time of Selma"—only a few days after the historic mass demonstration in support of voter registration in Alabama, in which many of the peaceful marchers were

15 physically at tacked and one of them, a white clergyman from the north, was killed. The nation itself was a shocked witness, via television, of much of that unforgettable scene: the long rows of marchers, a cross

20 section of African Americans and whites, Californians and New Yorkers, resolutely striding, smiling, singing to hide their exhaustion, trying not to see the hatet-wisted faces and shouting menace of the

25 side-walk crowd, trying not to fear the armored troopers and police with their notorious supporting artillery of dogs, clubs, and cattle prods.

This was the moment chosen by the

30 President, himself a Southerner with a reputation for compromise, to bear witness before the nation, and to call upon his former associates of Congress to stand up and be counted with him—more specifically, to take

35 action on a bill which would correct the conspicuous weakness of the 1964 Civil Rights Bill, its failure to protect the right of African Americans to vote "when local officials are determined to deny it."

40 In forthright terms, President Johnson spelled out the full cruelty and ingenuity of that discrimination, and crisply defined the central issue involved: "There is no Constitutional issue here. The command of

45 the Constitution is plain. There is no moral issue. It is wrong—deadly wrong—to deny any of your fellow Americans the right to

vote in this country. There is no issue of state's rights or national rights. There is only

50 the struggle for human rights."

The President spoke slowly, solemnly, with unmistakable determination. His words and his manner were perfectly synchronized; indeed he made the nationwide audience

55 aware of how deeply personal the issue of African American rights was to him. He recalled his own southern origins, and his shattering encounter with Mexican-American children as a young schoolteacher ("They

60 never seemed to know why people disliked them, but they knew it was so because I saw it in their eyes.") He spoke more directly, more explicitly, and more warmly of the human experience of prejudice than any

65 president before him. But he also placed the problem of African American rights in a broader frame of reference—that of poverty and ignorance, bigotry and fear. "Their cause must be our cause too. Because it is not just

70 African Americans, but really it's all of us, who must overcome the crippling legacy of bigotry and injustice. And we shall overcome."

20 In the first paragraph, the marchers are characterized as

(A) ruthless
(B) gleeful
(C) intellectual
(D) stoic
(E) shocked

21 The passage indicates that the 1964 Civil Rights Act was deficient in that it did not

(A) sufficiently pressure local officials to extend voting privileges to all citizens
(B) provide enough funds to promote voter registration drives
(C) punish felons who committed hate crimes
(D) provide military protection for the Selma marchers
(E) invest in minority-owned businesses

GO ON TO THE NEXT PAGE ▶▶▶

22 In line 58, *shattering* most nearly means

(A) exploding
(B) disturbing
(C) fragmenting
(D) violent
(E) loud

3 ➡

23 The quotation in lines 59–62 ("They never seemed ... in their eyes") indicates that Johnson

(A) understood the political process at a young age
(B) was unfamiliar with Mexican-American customs
(C) empathized strongly with his students
(D) was a victim of bigotry
(E) was unaware of the difficulties his students faced

24 The passage indicates that Johnson, unlike previous presidents, handled the issue of civil rights by

(A) successfully integrating the issue into his reelection campaign
(B) approaching the cause with objectivity and impartiality
(C) speaking clearly to reporters using terms they wanted to hear
(D) focusing primarily on the Mexican American population
(E) directly addressing the public on the issue and describing it in personal terms

STOP

You may check your work, on this section only, until time is called.

Section 4

**Time—25 minutes
35 Questions**

Directions for "Improving Sentences" Questions

Each of the sentences below contains one underlined portion. The portion may contain one or more errors in grammar, usage, construction, precision, diction (choice of words), or idiom. Some of the sentences are correct.

Consider the meaning of the original sentence, and choose the answer that best expresses that meaning. If the original sentence is best, choose (A), because it repeats the original phrasing. Choose the phrasing that creates the clearest, most precise, and most effective sentence.

EXAMPLE:

The children <u>couldn't hardly believe their eyes.</u>
- (A) couldn't hardly believe their eyes
- (B) would not hardly believe their eyes
- (C) could hardly believe their eyes
- (D) couldn't nearly believe their eyes
- (E) could hardly believe his or her eyes

Example answer: (C)

---

1 Exhausted from a day of hiking across steep, rain-soaked paths, the <u>group of campers were relieved upon the final reaching of the car.</u>

- (A) group of campers were relieved upon the final reaching of the car
- (B) camping group became relieved after they got to the car
- (C) group of campers was relieved to finally reach the car
- (D) campers were relieved after the car was finally reached
- (E) group was relieved after the campers finally reached the car

2 Theodore Roosevelt's first term as President <u>was marked by a ferocious battle between labor and management</u> in Pennsylvania's anthracite coal mines.

- (A) was marked by a ferocious battle between labor and management
- (B) marked a ferocious battle between labor and management
- (C) battled ferociously with labor and management
- (D) was marked ferociously by labor and management's battle
- (E) was marking a ferocious battle between labor and management

3 Timid and self-conscious, <u>Timothy never managed to give full expression towards his feelings for Jessica</u>.

- (A) Timothy never managed to give full expression towards his feelings for Jessica.
- (B) Timothy never managed full expression of his feelings towards Jessica.
- (C) Jessica never heard Timothy's full expression of his feelings.
- (D) Timothy never managed to fully express his feelings for Jessica.
- (E) Timothy's full expression of his feelings never reached Jessica.

4 Knowing that this was his last chance, Sherman stayed up all night <u>studying in preparation for the exam</u>.

- (A) studying in preparation for the exam.
- (B) studying for the exam.
- (C) studying for preparation for the exam.
- (D) to study in order to get ready for the exam.
- (E) for studying for the exam.

GO ON TO THE NEXT PAGE ▶▶▶

4 ➤

5 Disgruntled with the United States and disillusioned by battle, Hemingway <u>led an exodus of expatriate authors on an overseas journey</u> across the Atlantic Ocean following World War I.

(A) led an exodus of expatriate authors on an overseas journey

(B) leads an exodus of expatriate authors on an overseas journey

(C) led an exodus of expatriate authors

(D) led expatriate authors on an overseas exodus

(E) during an expatriate author exodus, journeyed

6 Renowned for his straightforward, honest presentation of the news, <u>Walter Cronkite, which became a fixture in the homes</u> of an entire American generation.

(A) Walter Cronkite, which became a fixture in the homes

(B) Walter Cronkite, who became a fixture in the homes

(C) Walter Cronkite became a home fixture

(D) Walter Cronkite, who was a fixture, became home

(E) Walter Cronkite became a fixture in the homes

7 <u>Known for his patience, understanding, and how easily he can be approached</u>, Professor Wilson has developed close relationships with many of his colleagues and students.

(A) Known for his patience, understanding, and how easily he can be approached

(B) Known for his patience, understanding, and the ability to be approached

(C) Known for his patience, understanding, and approachability

(D) Knowing his patience, understanding, and ability to be approached

(E) Known for his patience, for his understanding, and his approachability

8 Auto racing, often thought of as a regional phenomenon, <u>therefore is quite popular</u> throughout the nation.

(A) therefore is quite popular

(B) henceforth is quite popular

(C) is thus quite popular

(D) is actually quite popular

(E) in retrospect, is quite popular

9 Unable to wait until her birthday, <u>Julia sneaked downstairs in an effort to open</u> several of her presents.

(A) Julia sneaked downstairs in an effort to open

(B) Julia, sneaking downstairs and opening

(C) Julia sneaked downstairs and opened

(D) Julia sneaked downstairs in opening

(E) Julia, as a result of sneaking downstairs, opened

10 Many parents detest music featuring explicit lyrics, <u>believing that which encourages inappropriate behavior</u>.

(A) believing that which encourages inappropriate behavior

(B) that which they believe encourages inappropriate behavior

(C) believing that it encourages inappropriate behavior

(D) of the belief that it encourages inappropriate behavior

(E) that which encourages inappropriate behavior, they believe

11 Perhaps best known for his untiring defense of the downtrodden, <u>Clarence Darrow's stunning oratory often devastated his opponents</u>.

(A) Clarence Darrow's stunning oratory often devastated his opponents

(B) Clarence Darrow often devastated his opponents with his stunning oratory

(C) the stunning oratory of Clarence Darrow often devastated his opponents

(D) Clarence Darrow devastated his opponents often with the stunning nature of his oratory

(E) Clarence Darrow's devastated opponents were stunned by his oratory

GO ON TO THE NEXT PAGE ▶▶▶

Directions for "Identifying Sentence Error" Questions

The following sentences may contain errors in grammar, usage, diction (choice of words), or idiom. Some of the sentences are correct. No sentence contains more than 1 error.

If the sentence contains an error, it is underlined and lettered. The parts that are not underlined are correct.

If there is an error, select the part that must be changed to correct the sentence.

If there is no error, choose (E).

EXAMPLE:

By the time <u>they reached</u> the halfway point
            A
<u>in the race,</u> <u>most of the runners</u> <u>hadn't hardly</u>
   B   C   D
begun to hit their stride. <u>No error</u>
                       E

Sample answer: D

12 The local dairy company is <u>one of the most</u>
                               A
<u>efficient</u> in the state, <u>so</u> it is surprising that
   B   C
the delivery of our milk products over the

last few days <u>have been</u> late. <u>No error</u>
             D   E

13 <u>Last summer</u> <u>we stayed in</u> a charming
       A   B
cottage <u>whose rooms are</u> spacious and
          C
<u>well decorated.</u> <u>No error</u>
      D   E

14 <u>This holiday season</u>, several members of
         A
the committee <u>are</u> sponsoring a dinner
          B
to raise money for their <u>efforts</u> to
               C
encourage <u>responsible</u> driving. <u>No error</u>
        D   E

15 The lavish photographs and fascinating
diagrams <u>in the biology textbook</u> <u>was</u> so
         A   B
engaging that I seriously <u>considered</u>
                C
becoming a <u>zoologist.</u> <u>No error</u>
      D   E

16 Behavioral scientists <u>believe</u> that the way
              A
chimpanzees <u>form friendships</u> and
          B
alliances is <u>very similar</u> <u>to humans</u>.
         C   D
<u>No error</u>
 E

17 When the window <u>was opened</u>, <u>affects</u>
              A   B
of the cool spring breeze were

<u>felt immediately</u> by the
   C
<u>uncomfortable workers.</u> <u>No error</u>
      D   E

18 The probability <u>of getting hit</u> by lightning
             A
<u>are fewer than</u> the probability of <u>winning</u>
     B   C
the lottery, <u>although both</u> are minuscule.
           D
<u>No error</u>
 E

19 My mother <u>has always believed</u> that
            A
everyone <u>should clean</u> <u>their</u> room
         B   C
<u>thoroughly</u> each morning or risk bad
   D
luck all day. <u>No error</u>
         E

4

20 Eric <u>was so grateful</u> to us for <u>allowing him</u>
    A   B
to spend a weekend <u>on the island</u> that he
                     C
<u>bought</u> us back a lovely fruit basket.
  D
<u>No error</u>
  E

21 <u>Although</u> we had expected poor service
    A
at the resort, <u>we were</u> more than
           B
<u>satisfied at</u> the attention <u>we received</u>
  C   D
throughout our stay. <u>No error</u>
              E

22 After we <u>had ate</u> a leisurely meal,
        A
we walked <u>down the street</u> and
         B
<u>discovered</u> a jazz club where a talented
  C
young trio <u>was playing</u>. <u>No error</u>
        D   E

23 <u>Jules and I</u> have been at the same school
  A
<u>since</u> we <u>were</u> 5 years old and <u>will even go</u>
  B   C   D
to college together next fall. <u>No error</u>
                 E

24 <u>Despite</u> the fact that <u>they had</u> lived in
  A   B
France <u>until they were</u> 8 years old, neither
      C
of the boys <u>are</u> able to speak French
        D
any more. <u>No error</u>
      E

25 Some doctors <u>believe that</u> taking vitamins
        A
<u>on a daily basis</u> <u>help</u> decrease a patient's
  B   C
susceptibility <u>to infection</u>. <u>No error</u>
       D   E

26 When my parents <u>went</u> out to dinner, they
          A
left me <u>underneath</u> the <u>control</u> of our
      B   C
babysitter, <u>who lived</u> next door to us.
        D
<u>No error</u>
  E

27 Since 2001, the company <u>has spent more on</u>
               A B
employee training than <u>they did</u> in the
               C
previous 10 years <u>combined</u>. <u>No error</u>
         D   E

28 <u>When teaching</u> high-school students, <u>one</u>
  A   B
must not only command respect but
<u>one should</u> develop rapport <u>as well</u>.
  C   D
<u>No error</u>
  E

29 Since the experiments began, the scientists
<u>have discovered</u> that <u>they</u> can separate the
  A   B
reagents more effectively <u>by using</u> a
             C
centrifuge machine <u>and not</u> by shaking
         D
the tubes. <u>No error</u>
      E

Questions 30–35 pertain to the following passage.

(1) *While known when he was the President for his abundant energy and muscular build as an adult, Theodore Roosevelt's build as a child was actually quite puny.* (2) *Stricken with asthma, he was taught early that strenuous physical activity might be dangerous to his health and that, in fact, it might even be fatal.* (3) *Determined to overcome this obstacle, Roosevelt trained his body relentlessly and built his impressive girth through sheer grit and determination.* (4) *That these childhood passions stayed with him throughout his adult life should not be surprising.* (5) *Physical activities, though, were not the only childhood fascination to play a prominent role later in his life.*

(6) *A skilled hunter, Roosevelt spent much of his leisure time hunting various forms of game.* (7) *Beginning during his undergraduate days at Harvard, he spent significant time in snow-covered Maine forests as well as the arid deserts of the Dakota territory.* (8) *As a child, Theodore was so enraptured by birds, he would spend hours observing and writing about them, even phonetically spelling out their various calls and songs.* (9) *Upon reaching government office, Roosevelt became the first true conservationist, pushing for laws to protect wildlife and resources.* (10) *He cherished nature in all its forms, seeking to understand its variety through research and experience.*

(11) *By openly maintaining these passions while in political office, Roosevelt redefined the role of the American politician.* (12) *While his predecessors had often been aloof with regard to their own personal feelings, Roosevelt advertised his sense of morality by talking openly about it repeatedly with citizens and reporters in speeches and newspapers.* (13) *In the dawning of a new, industrialized age, Roosevelt chose to take on*

controversial issues, battling through the spoils system, disputes between management and labor, and the question of imperialism.

30 In context, which of the following is the best revision of sentence 1 (reproduced below)?

While known when he was the President for his abundant energy and muscular build as an adult, Theodore Roosevelt's build as a child was actually quite puny.

(A) While Theodore Roosevelt was known for his energy and muscular build, but the President was actually a quite puny child.

(B) Although known for his abundant energy and muscular build as an adult, President Theodore Roosevelt was actually quite puny as a child.

(C) While puny as a child, Theodore Roosevelt was known for his abundant energy and muscular build while being President.

(D) As President, Theodore Roosevelt was known for his abundant energy and muscular build, not for being puny as a child.

(E) Theodore Roosevelt was puny as a child and was known for his abundant energy and muscular build as President.

31 In context, which of the following is the best revision of the underlined portion of sentence 3 (reproduced below)?

Determined <u>to overcome this obstacle</u>, Roosevelt trained his body relentlessly and built his impressive girth through sheer grit and determination.

(A) (no revision needed)
(B) that this obstacle should be overcome
(C) to overcome such ideas that became obstacles
(D) not to allow this to become an obstacle standing in his way
(E) to take obstacles out of his way

GO ON TO THE NEXT PAGE ▸▸▸

32 Where is the most appropriate place to move sentence 4?

(A) before sentence 1
(B) before sentence 2
(C) before sentence 6, to start the 2nd paragraph
(D) after sentence 10, to end the 2nd paragraph
(E) after sentence 13

4 ➤ **33** Which of the following provides the most logical ordering of the sentences in paragraph 2?

(A) 7, 9, 10, 6, 8
(B) 8, 10, 7, 6, 9
(C) 8, 10, 9, 6, 7
(D) 9, 7, 8, 10, 6
(E) 7, 10, 8, 6, 9

34 If the author wanted to make sentence 7 more specific, which of the following details would fit best in the context of the 2nd paragraph?

(A) Roosevelt's age
(B) information about Roosevelt's course of study
(C) details of Roosevelt's activities in the deserts and forests
(D) an explanation of why the climate of Maine is so different from the climate of the Dakota territory
(E) information about Roosevelt's political affiliation prior to these excursions

35 Where is the best place to insert the following sentence?

His brazen moves were often criticized, but Theodore Roosevelt will go down in the annals of history as a man who was always true to himself, whether as a private citizen or as President of the United States.

(A) before sentence 1
(B) after sentence 1
(C) after sentence 5
(D) before sentence 11
(E) after sentence 13

STOP

You may check your work, on this section only, until time is called.

Section 5

Time – 25 Minutes
18 Questions

Directions for Multiple-Choice Questions

In this section, solve each problem, using any available space on the page for scratchwork. Then decide which is the best of the choices given and fill in the corresponding oval on the answer sheet.

- You may use a calculator on any problem. All numbers used are real numbers.
- Figures are drawn as accurately as possible EXCEPT when it is stated that the figure is not drawn to scale.
- All figures lie in a plane unless otherwise indicated.

5

Reference Information

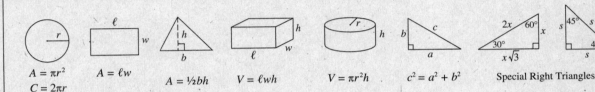

$A = \pi r^2$
$C = 2\pi r$

$A = \ell w$

$A = \frac{1}{2}bh$

$V = \ell wh$

$V = \pi r^2 h$

$c^2 = a^2 + b^2$

Special Right Triangles

The arc of a circle measures 360°.
Every straight angle measures 180°.
The sum of the measures of the angles in a triangle is 180°.

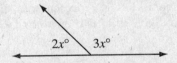

Note: Figure not drawn to scale.

1
In the figure above, what is the value of $2x$?

(A) 36
(B) 72
(C) 90
(D) 108
(E) 132

---

2 While at the laundromat, Erica wrote down the phone number for a nearby pizzeria. Unfortunately, the paper got wet and she could no longer read the last 2 digits. If she dials what she knows of the number and guesses on the missing digits, how many phone numbers does she have to choose from, if she knows only that neither of the last 2 digits is odd?

(A) 5
(B) 25
(C) 36
(D) 50
(E) 100

GO ON TO THE NEXT PAGE ▶▶▶

3

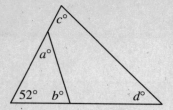

In the figure above, what is the value of $a + b + c + d$?

(A) 56
(B) 128
(C) 256
(D) 264
(E) 322

4

If $f(x) = x^2 - 4$, for what positive value of x does $f(x) = 32$?

(A) 5
(B) 6
(C) 7
(D) 8
(E) 9

5

If the average (arithmetic mean) of x, $x + 1$, $x + 4$, $2x$, and $5x$ is 11, what is the median of these numbers?

(A) 5
(B) 9
(C) 10
(D) 11
(E) 25

6

Twenty students in a chemistry class took a test on which the overall average score was 75. If the average score for 12 of those students was 83, what was the average score for the remaining members of the class?

(A) 60
(B) 61
(C) 62
(D) 63
(E) 64

7

In the figure above, the vertices of square $EFGH$ are on the diagonals of square $ABCD$. If $EF = 8\sqrt{2}$ and $AB = 14\sqrt{2}$, what is the sum of the lengths $AE + BF + CG + DH$ (heavier lines)?

(A) 24
(B) 28
(C) 32
(D) 36
(E) 38

8

$$\begin{array}{r} RS \\ +SR \\ \hline TR4 \end{array}$$

In the correctly worked addition problem above, each letter represents a different nonzero digit. What is the value of $2R + T$?

(A) 4
(B) 5
(C) 10
(D) 11
(E) 13

GO ON TO THE NEXT PAGE ▶▶▶

Directions for Student-Produced Response Questions

Each of the questions in this section requires you to solve the problem and enter your answer in a grid, as shown below.

- If your answer is ⅔ or .666..., you must enter **the most accurate value the grid can accommodate**, but you may do this in one of four ways.

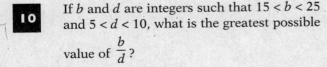

Start in first column

Grid result here

Start in second column

Grid as a truncated decimal

Grid as a rounded decimal

5

- In the example above, gridding a response of 0.67 or 0.66 is **incorrect** because it is less accurate than those above.
- The scoring machine cannot read what is written in the top row of boxes. You **MUST** fill in the numerical grid accurately to get credit for answering any question correctly. You should write your answer in the top row of boxes only to aid your gridding.
- Do **not** grid in a mixed fraction like $3\frac{1}{2}$ as $\boxed{3 \ 1 \ / \ 2}$ because it will be interpreted as $\frac{31}{2}$. Instead, convert it to an improper fraction like ⅞ or a decimal like 3.5 before gridding.
- None of the answers will be negative, because there is no negative sign in the grid.
- Some of the questions may have more than one correct answer. You must grid only one of the correct answers.
- You may use a calculator on any of these problems.
- All numbers in these problems are real numbers.
- Figures are drawn as accurately as possible EXCEPT when it is stated that the figure is not drawn to scale.
- All figures lie in a plane unless otherwise indicated.

9 For all real numbers n, let $\boxed{n}$ be defined by $\boxed{n} = \dfrac{n^2}{16}$ What is the value of $\boxed{4}^2$

11 If the sum of two numbers is 4 and their difference is 2, what is their product?

10 If b and d are integers such that $15 < b < 25$ and $5 < d < 10$, what is the greatest possible value of $\dfrac{b}{d}$?

GO ON TO THE NEXT PAGE ▶▶▶

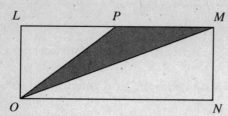

Note: Figure not to scale.

12 In rectangle LMNO above, P is the midpoint of side $\overline{LM}$. If the perimeter of the rectangle is 48 and side $\overline{LM}$ is twice the length of side $\overline{LO}$, what is the area of the shaded region?

13 If $64^3 = 4^x$, what is the value of x?

14 Points P, Q, R, and S lie on a line in that order. If $\overline{PS}$ is twice as long as $\overline{PR}$ and 4 times as long as $\overline{PQ}$, what is the value of $\dfrac{QS}{PQ}$?

15 If $f(x) = \dfrac{(x-1)(2x-1)}{(x-2)(3x-1)}$, what is one possible value of x for which $f(x)$ is not a real number?

16 If the sum of five consecutive even integers is 110, what is the value of the least of these integers?

NUMBER OF APPLICANTS TO COLLINS COLLEGE	
YEAR	APPLICANTS
1980	15,000
1985	18,000
1990	20,000
1995	24,000
2000	25,000

17 According to the data in the table above, by what percent did the number of applicants to Collins College increase from 1990 to 1995? (Disregard the % symbol when entering your answer into the grid. For instance, grid 50% as 50.)

18 A jar contains only black, white, and red marbles. If randomly choosing a black marble is 4 times as likely as randomly choosing a white marble and randomly choosing a red marble is 5 times as likely as randomly choosing a black marble, then what is the smallest possible number of marbles in the jar?

STOP

You may check your work, on this section only, until time is called.

Section 6

Time—25 minutes
24 Questions

Each of the sentences below is missing one or two portions. Read each sentence, then select the word or words that most logically completes the sentence, taking into account the meaning of the sentence as a whole.

Example:

Rather than accepting the theory unquestioningly, Deborah regarded it with ———.

(A) mirth   (B) sadness
(C) responsibility   (D) ignorance
(E) skepticism

Correct response: (E)

1 If John had not been there to ——— when tensions began to rise at the meeting, a fight would surely have ensued.

(A) intervene
(B) coalesce
(C) harass
(D) intermingle
(E) exacerbate

2 The defendant hoped that the testimony of the surprise witness would corroborate his alibi and ——— him of the crime of which he had been accused.

(A) convoke
(B) synthesize
(C) impeach
(D) absolve
(E) magnify

3 Rachel's ——— driving is not surprising, given that she spends ——— hours each day ensnarled in traffic delays.

(A) antipathy for ... delightful
(B) penchant for ... uncountable
(C) predilection for ... dreary
(D) proclivity for ... desperate
(E) aversion to ... insufferable

4 Many medical practices once considered "state of the art" are now thought to be ——— by physicians who are often incredulous that such barbaric acts were once ———.

(A) primitive ... sanctioned
(B) ingenious ... approved
(C) boorish ... censured
(D) innovative ... endorsed
(E) foolhardy ... condemned

5 The Prime Minister had vetoed the proposal several times in the past; thus, it came as a great surprise to the public when he ——— the same law in his most recent speech.

(A) articulated
(B) sanctioned
(C) denounced
(D) initiated
(E) abbreviated

6

GO ON TO THE NEXT PAGE ▶▶▶

The passages below are followed by questions based on their content. Answer each question based on what is stated or implied in the passages or the introductory material preceding them.

Questions 6–7 are based on the following passage.

Line   The reverence for their goddess of protection
       accounts for the respect Navajos show to the
       women of their tribe. The tradition is that a
       man never lifts his hand against a woman,
5   although it is not an unusual thing for a
       squaw to administer a sound thrashing to a
       warrior husband who has offended her. All of
       the sheep, which constitute the great wealth
       of the tribe, are owned by the women, and in
10   the various families the line of descent is
       always on the side of the women. The
       Navajos have little or no idea of a future
       existence but are firm believers in the
       transmigration of souls. For this reason they
15   have great reverence for different animals
       and birds, which are supposed to be the re-
       embodiment of departed spirits of Navajos.

6 Based on the information in the passage,
       with which of the following statements
       would the author most likely agree?

(A)   Navajo warriors obey their wives
       obsequiously.
(B)   Birds are a particularly vital food
       source for the Navajo.
(C)   A Navajo man who disrespects a
       woman would likely face censure.
(D)   The Navajo do not believe in reincar-
       nation.
(E)   In the winter, the Navajo migrate to
       warmer climates.

7 The word "administer" in line 6 most nearly
       means

(A)   manage
(B)   maintain
(C)   govern
(D)   rehearse
(E)   dispense

Questions 8–9 are based on the following passage.

Line   "Dying with dignity" is a topic that has
       inspired deep debate among the members of
       the medical community. Should an individual
       be allowed to determine when he or she
5   wants to die? Should a person who is merely
       receiving palliative care that provides no
       hope of a cure be allowed to tell a doctor to
       stop all treatment so she can die in peace?
       How can a doctor know if a patient has the
10   mental capacity to decide for herself that the
       time has come to stop fighting the disease?
       It is a challenging and persistent debate.

8 As used in line 6, "palliative" most nearly
       means

(A)   punitive
(B)   remedial
(C)   analgesic
(D)   curative
(E)   altruistic

9 The passage suggests that in cases of
       extreme illness, doctors may have difficulty
       in determining their patients'

(A)   state of mind
(B)   prognosis
(C)   quality of life
(D)   tolerance of pain
(E)   ability to remember facts

GO ON TO THE NEXT PAGE ▶▶▶

First paragraph: *The Navajo Indians*, William M. Edwardy; *Harper's Weekly*, July 1890
Second paragraph: Copyright 2004 Mark Anestis. All rights reserved.

The passages below are followed by questions based on their contents. Answer each question based on what is stated or implied in the passages or the introductory material preceding them.

Questions 10–16 pertain to the following passage.

The following passage is excerpted from a recent book about seismology, the study of earthquakes.

Line   In the 1970s, there was great optimism about earthquake prediction. A few so-called earthquake precursors had come to light, and there was even a theory (known as dilatancy)
5   put forth to explain many of the phenomena that come before a large earthquake. A series of foreshocks is an example of a precursor. However, since foreshocks look just like any other earthquakes, they are not in themselves
10   very useful in prediction. From all points around the globe, there are numerous anecdotal reports about other precursors, earthquake folklore, if you will.
    Many widely reported earthquake
15   precursors are related to groundwater. A few hours before a large earthquake, marked changes have been reported in the level or flow of wells and springs. Groundwater has also reportedly changed temperature, become
20   cloudy, or acquired a bad taste. Occasionally, electrostatic phenomena such as earthquake lights (similar to St. Elmo's fire that appears on ships during electrical storms) and changes in the local magnetic field have been
25   reported. Anecdotal reports also persistently include the strange behavior of animals, which might be linked to electrostatic phenomena or foreshocks. Changes in strain and creep (silent tectonic motion, without
30   accompanying earthquake) along a fault normally locked by friction could also be considered precursors.
    In China in the 1970s, it became popular
35   for people to predict earthquakes using "backyard" measurements such as the monitoring of well levels and observation of farm animals. At least one earthquake, the Haicheng quake in 1975, was successfully
40   predicted and a town evacuated, proving that, at least in some cases, earthquake prediction is possible. The Haicheng

earthquake had hundreds of foreshocks, making it an easier-than-average earthquake
45   to predict. Groundwater changes and anomalous animal behavior were also reported (for example, hibernating snakes supposedly awoke and froze to death). In China, "evacuation" meant that compulsory
50   outdoor movies were shown, so that when the quake did happen and the town was severely damaged, no one was killed. But Chinese seismologists missed predicting the catastrophic Tangshan earthquake, in which
55   at least 250,000 reportedly perished.

10   Which of the following is the best title for this passage?

(A)   The Effects of Earthquakes on Groundwater
(B)   The Search for Earthquake Precursors
(C)   A Novel Theory of the Origin of Earthquakes
(D)   A History of Chinese Earthquakes
(E)   How Animals Anticipate Earthquakes

11   The passage indicates that foreshocks are *not ... very useful* (lines 9–10) in predicting earthquakes because they

(A)   are exceptionally difficult to detect
(B)   occur simultaneously with changes in groundwater
(C)   are not part of the theory of dilatancy
(D)   interfere with electrostatic phenomena
(E)   are impossible to distinguish from earthquakes themselves

12   According to the passage, which of the following features of groundwater have been reported to change immediately prior to an earthquake (lines 16–20)?

     I.   density
     II.   clarity
     III.   flow

(A)   II only
(B)   III only
(C)   I and II only
(D)   II and III only
(E)   I, II, and III

GO ON TO THE NEXT PAGE ▸▸▸

Excerpted from *Furious Earth* by Ellen J. Prager, McGraw-Hill, New York, 2000, pp. 80–81

13 Which of the following could be considered a logical inconsistency in the passage?

(A) The passage states that foreshocks are not useful predictors of earthquakes but then cites foreshocks as instrumental to predicting an earthquake.

(B) The passage says that the Chinese are interested in predicting earthquakes but then says that they were devastated by the Tangshan earthquake.

(C) The passage reports that animals behaved strangely before an earthquake but then attributes this behavior to electrostatic phenomena.

(D) The passage states that the town of Haicheng was safely evacuated but then says that its citizens were forced to watch outdoor movies.

(E) The passage suggests that both strain and creep could be considered earthquake precursors.

14 Which of the following best describes the function of the third paragraph?

(A) to describe an application of a theory
(B) to provide an alternative perspective
(C) to recount a scientific experiment
(D) to summarize the ancient origins of a theory
(E) to demonstrate the difficulties of employing a technique

15 The passage suggests that the Tangshan earthquake

(A) was caused by strain and creep
(B) was preceded by changes in the groundwater
(C) caused more damage than the Haicheng earthquake did
(D) was preceded by several foreshocks
(E) was anticipated by the theory of dilatancy

16 In line 49, the word "evacuation" is placed in quotations in order to

(A) imply that an action was ineffective
(B) indicate that it is an archaic term
(C) emphasize the primitiveness of Chinese scientific methods
(D) suggest that a certain practice was unconventional
(E) underscore that an action was intended, but not implemented

Questions 17–24 pertain to the following passage.

The following passage contains an excerpt taken from an anthology of autobiographies of American women.

Line   On landing in America, a grievous
        disappointment awaited us; my father did
        not meet us. He was in New Bedford,
        Massachusetts, nursing his grief and
5   preparing to return to England, for he had
        been told that the *John Jacob Westervelt* had
        been lost at sea with every soul on board.
        One of the missionaries who met the ship
        took us under his wing and conducted us to a
10   little hotel, where we remained until father
        had received his incredible news and rushed
        to New York. He could hardly believe that we
        were really restored to him; and even now,
        through the mists of more than half a
15   century, I can still see the expression in his
        wet eyes as he picked me up and tossed me
        into the air.
            I can see, too, the toys he brought me—a
        little saw and a hatchet, which became the
20   dearest treasures of my childish days. They
        were fatidical[1] gifts, that saw and hatchet; in
        the years ahead of me I was to use tools as
        well as my brothers did, as I proved when
        I helped to build our frontier home.
25   We went to New Bedford with father, who
        had found work there at his old trade; and
        here I laid the foundations of my first
        childhood friendship, not with another child,
        but with my next-door neighbor, a ship-
30   builder. Morning after morning, this man
        swung me on his big shoulder and took me to
        his shipyard, where my hatchet and saw had
        violent exercise as I imitated the workers
        around me. Discovering that my tiny
35   petticoats were in my way, my new friends
        had a little boy's suit made for me; and thus
        emancipated, at this tender age, I worked
        unwearyingly at his side all day long and day
        after day.
40   The move to Michigan meant a complete
        upheaval in our lives. In Lawrence we had
        around us the fine flower of New England
        civilization. We children went to school; our
        parents, though they were in very humble

[1]prophetic

GO ON TO THE NEXT PAGE ▸▸▸

45   circumstances, were associated with the
      leading spirits and the big movements of the
      day. When we went to Michigan, we went to
      the wilderness, to the wild pioneer life of
      those times, and we were all old enough to
50   keenly feel the change.
          Every detail of our journey through the
      wilderness is clear in my mind. My brother
      James met us at Grand Rapids with what, in
      those days, was called a lumber-wagon, but
55   which had a horrible resemblance to a
      vehicle from the health department. My
      sisters and I gave it one cold look and turned
      from it; we were so pained by its appearance
      that we refused to ride in it through the
60   town. Instead, we started off on foot, trying
      to look as if we had no association with it,
      and we climbed into the unwieldy vehicle
      only when the city streets were far behind us.

17   Immediately upon arriving in America, the
        author was cared for by

      (A)   John Jacob Westervelt
      (B)   her father
      (C)   a missionary
      (D)   a childhood friend
      (E)   a shipbuilder neighbor

18   In line 13, the word "restored" most nearly
        means

      (A)   updated
      (B)   refurbished
      (C)   put into storage
      (D)   deposited
      (E)   returned

19   Which of the following best describes the
        relationship between the narrator and the
        men in her life?

      (A)   She gladly provides for their needs.
      (B)   She considers herself their equal.
      (C)   She feels overly dependent on them.
      (D)   She wishes to avoid them.
      (E)   She believes that they suppress her
             wishes.

20   The author was "emancipated" (line 36) so
        that she might more easily

      (A)   spend time with her father
      (B)   play with her young friends
      (C)   travel throughout New Bedford
      (D)   work with tools
      (E)   move to Michigan

21   In line 43, the word "movements" most nearly
        means

      (A)   travels
      (B)   cosmetic alterations
      (C)   cultural changes
      (D)   physical actions
      (E)   mechanical workings

22   The author indicates that she regarded New
        England as superior to Michigan in that
        New England

             I.   had humbler citizens
             II.   was more culturally developed
             III. had finer gardens
      (A)   II only
      (B)   III only
      (C)   I and II only
      (D)   II and III only
      (E)   I, II, and III

23   The author's attitude toward her move to
        Michigan is best described as

      (A)   eager
      (B)   awed
      (C)   fearful
      (D)   resentful
      (E)   bewildered

24   The sisters refused to ride in the lumber
        wagon mainly because

      (A)   they were embarrassed by its appearance
      (B)   they felt it was unsafe
      (C)   they had bad memories of it
      (D)   it was cold
      (E)   it lacked sufficient room for both of
             them

Excerpted from "The Story of a Pioneer" by Anna Howard Shaw, in *Autobiographies of American Women: An Anthology* © 1992 by Jill Ker Conway, ed., pp. 475–477

STOP

You may check your work, on this section only, until time is called.

Section 7

Time—20 Minutes
16 Questions

Directions for Multiple-Choice Questions

In this section, solve each problem, using any available space on the page for scratchwork. Then decide which is the best of the choices given and fill in the corresponding oval on your answer sheet.

- You may use a calculator on any problem. All numbers used are real numbers.
- Figures are drawn as accurately as possible EXCEPT when it is stated that the figure is not drawn to scale.
- All figures lie in a plane unless otherwise indicated.

Reference Information

$A = \pi r^2$ $A = \ell w$ $A = \frac{1}{2}bh$ $V = \ell wh$ $V = \pi r^2 h$ $c^2 = a^2 + b^2$ Special Right Triangles
$C = 2\pi r$

The number of degrees of arc in a circle measures 360.
The measure in degrees of a straight angle is 180.
The sum of the measures in degrees of the angles of a triangle is 180.

---

1 If $4x + 5 = 20$, what is the value of $4x + 8$?

(A) 3
(B) 7
(C) 16
(D) 23
(E) 30

2 If one serving of cereal is $\frac{1}{3}$ cup, how many servings are in 3 pints of cereal? (1 pint = 2 cups)

(A) 3
(B) 9
(C) 18
(D) 27
(E) 36

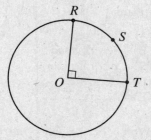

3 If the radius of the circle with center O above is 4, what is the length of arc RST?

(A) 2π
(B) 4π
(C) 8π
(D) 12π
(E) 16π

GO ON TO THE NEXT PAGE ▸▸▸

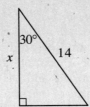

Note: Figure not drawn to scale.

4 In the triangle above, what is the value of x?

(A) 7
(B) $7\sqrt{2}$
(C) $7\sqrt{3}$
(D) $14\sqrt{3}$
(E) $28\sqrt{3}$

5 For $x > 0$, let $= \triangle x$ be defined by the equation $\nabla x = 3x - 3$. Which of the following is equivalent to $\dfrac{\nabla 7}{\nabla 3}$?

(A) $\nabla 2$
(B) $\nabla 3$
(C) $\nabla 6$
(D) $\nabla 8$
(E) $\nabla 9$

6 Stephanie can clean a pool in 1 hour, and Mark can clean the same pool in 1.5 hours. If the rate at which they work together is the sum of their rates working separately, how many minutes should they need to clean the pool if they work together? (1 hour = 60 minutes)

(A) 24 minutes
(B) 36 minutes
(C) 60 minutes
(D) 72 minutes
(E) 100 minutes

7 Which of the following has the greatest value?

(A) $(100^3)^4$
(B) $(100^5)(100^6)$
(C) $(10,000)^4$
(D) $(100^2 \times 100^2)^2$
(E) $(1,000,000)^3$

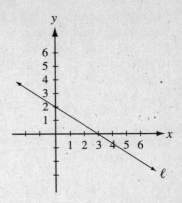

8 Line m (not shown) is the reflection of line l over the x-axis. What is the slope of line m?

(A) 3/2
(B) 2/3
(C) 0
(D) −2/3
(E) −3/2

9 If $a^2 + b^2 = 4$ and $ab = 5$, what is the value of $(a + b)^2$?

(A) 10
(B) 12
(C) 14
(D) 16
(E) 18

10

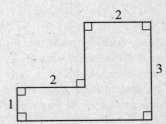

The figure above shows the dimensions, in feet, of a stone slab. How many of these slabs are required to construct a rectangular patio 24 feet long and 12 feet wide?

(A) 18
(B) 20
(C) 24
(D) 36
(E) 48

GO ON TO THE NEXT PAGE ▶▶▶

11 $12,000 in winnings for a golf tournament were distributed in the ratio of 7:2:1 to the 1st-, 2nd-, and 3rd-place finishers, respectively. How much money did the 1st-place finisher receive?

(A) $1,200
(B) $1,700
(C) $2,400
(D) $8,400
(E) $10,000

12 If $2x + 3y = 7$ and $4x - 5y = 12$, what is the value of $6x - 2y$?

(A) 5
(B) 8
(C) 15
(D) 17
(E) 19

13 If r and s are positive integers and $s + 1 = 2r$, which of the following must be true?

   I. s is odd
   II. r is even
   III. $\dfrac{s}{r} + \dfrac{1}{r}$ is an integer

(A) I only
(B) III only
(C) I and II only
(D) I and III only
(E) I, II, and III

14 A bag contains 6 chips, numbered 1 through 6. If 2 chips are chosen at random without replacement and the values on those 2 chips are multiplied, what is the probability that this product will be greater than 20?

(A) 1/30
(B) 1/15
(C) 2/15
(D) 1/5
(E) 13/15

15
$$2, -4, -8, \ldots$$
In the sequence above, each term after the 2nd is equal to the product of the 2 preceding terms. For example, the 3rd term, -8, is the product of 2 and -4. How many of the first 100 terms of this sequence are negative?

(A) 33
(B) 34
(C) 50
(D) 66
(E) 67

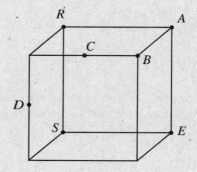

16 In the figure above, points C and D are midpoints of edges of a cube. A triangle is to be drawn with R and S as 2 of the vertices. Which of the following points should be the 3rd vertex of the triangle if it is to have the largest possible perimeter?

(A) A
(B) B
(C) C
(D) D
(E) E

You may check your work, on this section only, until time is called.

Section 8

Time—20 minutes
19 Questions

Each of the sentences below is missing one or two portions. Read each sentence, then select the word or words that most logically completes the sentence, taking into account the meaning of the sentence as a whole.

Example:

Rather than accepting the theory unquestioningly, Deborah regarded it with ———.

(A) mirth   (B) sadness
(C) responsibility   (D) ignorance
(E) skepticism

Correct response: (E)

1 The latest review for the restaurant was ———, suggesting that the ——— cuisine came close to compensating for the insipid decor.

(A) glowing ... indefatigable
(B) banal ... mediocre
(C) ambivalent ... sublime
(D) severe ... piquant
(E) antiquated ... tepid

2 As unexpected as the results of the experiment were, Dr. Thompson refused to characterize them as ———.

(A) meticulous
(B) belligerent
(C) anomalous
(D) convergent
(E) warranted

3 The executives could only hope that the company's poor 1st-quarter performance was not ——— of the year to come.

(A) an amalgam
(B) a harbinger
(C) an arbiter
(D) a deception
(E) a talisman

4 Around 1850, abolitionist and author Frederick Douglass sought to ——— those oppressed by slavery by facilitating the underground railroad, a widespread network of individuals and organizations that worked to transport former slaves out of bondage.

(A) evaluate   (B) encumber
(C) unfetter   (D) disorient
(E) forgo

5 Known for her ——— and decorative poetry, the author demonstrated her ——— by scribing a keenly analytical mystery novel.

(A) flamboyant ... immutability
(B) austere ... elegance
(C) unadorned ... flexibility
(D) florid ... versatility
(E) grandiloquent ... insurgence

6 Because the mechanisms by which cancers attack the body are so ———, scientists have been ——— in their efforts to find a universal cure.

(A) efficacious ... bilked
(B) multifarious ... stymied
(C) conspicuous ... thwarted
(D) consistent ... hampered
(E) lucid ... proscribed

7

GO ON TO THE NEXT PAGE ▶▶▶

Questions 7–19 pertain to the following passages.

The following passages are excerpts from a recent debate between two well-known astronomers. The author of passage 1 is a professor of geological sciences and the author of passage 2 is a principal scientist in the Department of Space Studies in Boulder, Colorado.

Passage 1

Line   There is a cultural assumption that there are many alien civilizations. This stems in no small way from the famous estimate by Frank Drake—known as the "Drake
5   Equation"—that was later amended by Drake and Carl Sagan. They arrived at an estimate that there are perhaps a million intelligent civilizations in the Milky Way Galaxy alone.

The Drake and Sagan estimate was based
10   on their best guess about the number of planets in the galaxy, the percentage of those that might harbor life, and the percentage of planets on which life not only could exist but could have advanced to culture. Since our
15   galaxy is but one of hundreds of billions of galaxies in the universe, the number of intelligent alien species would be numbered in the billions. Surely, if there are so many intelligent aliens out there, then the number
20   of planets with life must be truly astronomical. But what if the Drake and Sagan estimates are way off? If, as could be the reality, our civilization is unique in the galaxy, does that mean that there might be
25   much less life in general as well?

In my view, life in the form of microbes or their equivalents is very common in the universe, perhaps more common than even Drake and Sagan envisioned. However,
30   complex life is likely to be far more rare than commonly assumed. Life on earth evolved from single celled organisms to multi-cellular creatures with tissues and organs, climaxing in animals and higher planets. But is Earth's
35   particular history of life—one of increasing complexity to an animal grade of evolution— an inevitable result of evolution, or even a common one? Perhaps life is common, but complex life— anything that is multicellular—
40   is not. On Earth, evolution has undergone a progressive development of ever more complex and sophisticated forms leading ultimately to human intelligence. Complex life—and even intelligence—could
45   conceivably arise faster than it did on Earth. A planet could go from an abiotic state to a civilization in 100 million years, as compared to the nearly 4 billion years it took on Earth. Evolution on Earth has been affected by
50   chance events, such as the configuration of the continents produced by continental drift. Furthermore, I believe that the way the solar system was produced, with its characteristic number and planetary positions, may have
55   had a great impact on the history of life here.

It has always been assumed that attaining the evolutionary grade we call animals would be the final and decisive step. Once we are at this level of evolution, a long and continuous
60   progression toward intelligence should occur. However, recent research shows that while attaining the stage of animal life is one thing, maintaining that level is quite another. The geologic record has shown that once evolved,
65   complex life is subject to an unending succession of planetary disasters, creating what are known as "mass extinction" events. These rare but devastating events can reset the evolutionary timetable and destroy
70   complex life while sparing simpler life forms. Such discoveries suggest that the conditions allowing the rise and existence of complex life are far more rigorous than are those for life's formation. On some planets, then, life
75   might arise and animals eventually evolve— only to be soon destroyed by a global catastrophe.

GO ON TO THE NEXT PAGE ▶▶▶

First passage: Peter Ward, Great Debates Part I, *Astrobiology Magazine*, 2003
Second passage: David Grinspoon, Great Debates Part III, *Astrobiology Magazine*, 2003

PART 2 / PRACTICE TEST 11

Passage 2

It is always shaky when we generalize from
experiments with a sample size of one. So we
80 have to be a bit cautious when we fill
the cosmos with creatures based on the time
scales of Earth history (it happened so fast
here, therefore it must be easy) and the
resourcefulness of Earth life (they are
85 everywhere where there is water). This is one
history, and one example of life.

I am not convinced that the Earth's
carbon-in-water example is the only way for
the universe to solve the life riddle. I am not
90 talking about silicon, which is a bad idea, but
systems of chemical complexity that we have
not thought of, which may not manifest
themselves at room temperature in our
oxygen atmosphere. The universe is
95 constantly more clever than we are, and we
learn about complex phenomena, like life,
more through exploration than by theorizing
and modeling. I think there are probably
forms of life out there which use different
100 chemical bases than we, and which we will
know about only when we find them, or
when they find us.

An obvious rejoinder to this is, "But no
one has invented another system that works
105 as well as carbon-in-water." That is true. But
to this I would answer, "We did not invent
carbon-in-water!" We discovered it. I don't
believe that we are clever enough to have
thought of life based on nucleic acids and
110 proteins if we hadn't had this example
handed to us. This makes me wonder what
else the universe might be using for its
refined, evolving complexity elsewhere, in
other conditions that seem hostile to life as
115 we know it.

I think it is a mistake to look at the many
specific peculiarities of Earth's biosphere and
how unlikely such a combination of
characteristics seems, and to then conclude
120 that complex life is rare. This argument can
only be used to justify the conclusion that
planets exactly like Earth, with life exactly
like Earth-life, are rare.

My cat, "Wookie" survived life as a near
125 starving alley cat and wound up as a beloved
house cat through an unlikely series of
biographical accidents, which I won't take up
space describing but, trust me, given all of
the incredible things that had to happen in
130 just the right way, it is much more likely that
there would be no Wookie than Wookie.
From this I do not conclude that there are no
other cats (The Rare Cat Hypothesis), only
that there are no other cats exactly like
135 Wookie.

Life has evolved together with the Earth.
Life is opportunistic. The biosphere has
taken advantage of the myriad of strange
idiosyncrasies that our planet has to offer. So
140 it is easy to look at our biosphere and
conclude that this is the best of all possible
worlds; that only on such a world could
complex life evolve. My bet is that many
other worlds, with their own peculiar
145 characteristics and histories, co-evolve their
own biospheres. The complex creatures on
those worlds, upon first developing
intelligence and science, would observe how
incredibly well adapted life is to the many
150 unique features of their home world. They
might naively assume that these qualities,
very different from Earth's, are the only ones
that can breed complexity.

7 The discussion of the Drake equation in the
first paragraph indicates that the author
holds which of the following assumptions?

(A) The Drake equations are too complicated for most people to understand.

(B) Mathematical formulas can influence
public opinion.

(C) Sagan did not substantially alter the
Drake equation.

(D) Mathematics tend to obscure scientific exploration.

(E) Drake was not as reputable a scientist
as Sagan was.

8 Which of the following best describes the function of the third paragraph?

(A) It asks more questions similar to those posed in the second paragraph.

(B) It provides more background information on the debate discussed in the passage.

(C) It explains a comment made in the second paragraph.

(D) It defines an important term mentioned in the second paragraph.

(E) It presents an opinion contrary to one presented in the second paragraph.

9 In line 47, the word "abiotic" most nearly means

(A) resistant to bacteria
(B) devoid of life
(C) highly populated
(D) extremely advanced
(E) quick growing

10 Which of the following best summarizes the main idea of Passage 1?

(A) The conditions that support complex life may be much more difficult to maintain than is widely assumed.

(B) The Drake equation is not a valid predictor of life in the universe.

(C) Evolution on Earth has made it very unlikely that there would be complex life on other planets.

(D) The number of planets in the universe with complex life is astronomical.

(E) Conditions allowing for the existence of microbes are rare.

11 In line 57, "grade" most nearly means

(A) level
(B) slope
(C) evaluation
(D) life
(E) quantity

12 The author of Passage 1 makes all of the following claims in support of his argument EXCEPT

(A) Complex life on Earth was due in part to haphazard events.

(B) Higher life forms sometimes face the likelihood of extinction due to catastrophic events.

(C) The Earth's carbon-in-water example is probably not the only way for life to come into existence.

(D) Simple forms of life are far more common than highly evolved life forms.

(E) The evolution of life can be affected by the positions of planets around a star.

13 The "sample size of one" (line 79) refers to

(A) the Milky Way galaxy
(B) Drake and Sagan's data
(C) the planet Earth
(D) the Sun of our solar system
(E) mass extinction events

14 The quotations in lines 102–107 serve to

(A) show how the author would respond to someone who disagrees with him

(B) illustrate an argument for why there is no life on neighboring planets

(C) explain a theory the author has disagreed with his entire career

(D) describe a conversation the author had with a colleague

(E) illustrate the author's confusion about the origin of alternate life forms

15 The author includes the anecdote in lines 124–134 in order to

(A) compare his cat to the complex life forms in nearby galaxies

(B) give supporting evidence to the claim that life in the universe is unique to the Earth

(C) caution scientists about drawing premature conclusions from one specific occurrence

(D) mock scientists who believe that animals such as cats can live on other planets

(E) show the result of an evolutionary process

16 In saying that "Life is opportunistic" (line 137), the author of Passage 2 suggests that

(A) only the most cunning animals survive

(B) evolution takes advantage of the unique features of many different environments

(C) humans will likely always be the dominant species on Earth

(D) the theory of evolution is probably wrong

(E) all life forms seek to dominate others

17 The author of Passage 2 suggests that the "complex creatures" discussed in lines 146–150 are likely to believe that

(A) technological advancements are critical to their survival

(B) life is unique to planet Earth

(C) there is no life on other planets

(D) life on all planets originates in the same manner

(E) carbon is essential to the creation of life

18 The author of Passage 1 would most likely respond to the statement in Passage 2 that "The biosphere ... offer" (lines 137–139) by saying that

(A) our planet also offers many dangers to the biosphere

(B) the biosphere is filled with far more complex life forms

(C) life on Earth has not evolved to such a high level

(D) our planet does not offer so many idiosyncrasies

(E) carbon is one of the most complex elements in the universe

19 The authors of both passages would most likely agree with which of the following statements?

(A) The estimates made by the Drake Equation are surprisingly accurate.

(B) Mass extinction events are not a factor in predicting the existence of extraterrestrial life.

(C) Mathematical models are the most helpful means of learning about the development of life in the universe.

(D) There is likely an abundance of life in the universe that has yet to be discovered.

(E) Complex life is very common in the universe.

8

STOP

You may check your work, on this section only, until time is called.

Section 9

Time – 10 Minutes
14 Questions

1 His morning routine included eating an English muffin with grape jelly, <u>then to drink coffee from a styrofoam cup</u>, and sitting down to draw his daily comic strip.

(A) then to drink coffee from a styrofoam cup
(B) drinking coffee from a styrofoam cup
(C) then drink coffee from a styrofoam cup
(D) from a styrofoam cup he would drink coffee
(E) he would drink coffee from a styrofoam cup

2 Pretending to be hurt to avoid running sprints at the end of practice, <u>Mark's attempt failed to convince</u> his coach.

(A) Mark's attempt failed to convince
(B) Mark's attempted to fail to convince
(C) Mark attempt to convince failed
(D) Mark failed to convince
(E) Mark failed but attempt to convince

3 The flier describing the details of the blood drive requested that we <u>are in the hospital lobby</u> promptly at 10 A.M.

(A) are in the hospital lobby
(B) should get at the hospital lobby
(C) be in the hospital lobby
(D) would be to the hospital lobby
(E) should have been at the lobby of the hospital

4 <u>Known for his temper, impatience, and how easily he can be irritated</u>, Dr. McGee was not well-liked by his patients.

(A) Known for his temper, impatience, and how easily he can be irritated
(B) Knowing his temper, impatience and irritability
(C) Known for his temper, impatience and irritability
(D) Known for his temper, impatience and irritation
(E) Known for his temper, for his impatience and his irritability

5 <u>Winning</u> the final match, Courtney gave a gracious speech thanking her competitor, the sponsors, and the spectators.

(A) Winning
(B) Having won
(C) Being that she won
(D) If she had won
(E) For her winning

6 Generally regarded as the most influential social science treatise of the 20th century, <u>John Maynard Keynes wrote a book, *The General Theory of Employment Interest and Money* that</u> forever changed the way scientists looked at the economy.

(A) John Maynard Keynes wrote a book, *The General Theory of Employment Interest and Money* that

(B) a book by John Maynard Keynes, *The General Theory of Employment Interest and Money,* that

(C) John Maynard Keynes' book *The General Theory of Employment Interest and Money* had already

(D) John Maynard Keynes wrote a book *The General Theory of Employment Interest and Money* having

(E) John Maynard Keynes' book *The General Theory of Employment Interest and Money*

7 <u>Neither of the warriors were aware of the massive wounds they had suffered</u> because each was so intently focused on vanquishing the other.

(A) Neither of the warriors were aware of the massive wounds they had suffered

(B) Neither of the warriors was aware of the massive wounds they had suffered

(C) The wounds suffered by the warriors who were not aware

(D) Having suffered massive wounds, neither of the warriors was aware

(E) Despite the wounds suffered, neither of the warriors was aware

8 The Chief of Staff stayed up the entire night to <u>prepare</u> the President's speech for the following night.

(A) to prepare
(B) in preparing
(C) for the preparation of
(D) in order for preparation of
(E) for preparing

9 Twenty-foot high waves crashed into the shore, covering the stores along the <u>boardwalk and many cars in the parking lots were swept away.</u>

(A) boardwalk and many cars in the parking lots were swept away

(B) boardwalk with many cars in the parking lot having been swept away

(C) boardwalk and sweeping away many cars in the parking lot

(D) boardwalk, and the sweeping away of many cars in the parking lot

(E) boardwalk; sweeping away many cars having been in the parking lot

10 <u>The life of the ShinZanu tribesmen of the Australian Outback, which are realistically depicted in the books written by Ronald Skinner.</u>

(A) The life of the ShinZanu tribesmen of the Australian Outback, which are realistically depicted in the books written by Ronald Skinner.

(B) The books written by Ronald Skinner realistically depict the life of the ShinZanu tribesmen of the Australian Outback.

(C) The life of the ShinZanu tribesmen of the Australian Outback being realistically depicted in the books written by Ronald Skinner.

(D) Ronald Skinner realistically depicting in his books the life of the ShinZanu tribesmen of the Australian Outback.

(E) Ronald Skinner, whose books realistically depicting the life of the ShinZanu tribesmen of the Australian Outback.

GO ON TO THE NEXT PAGE ▶▶▶

11 <u>At the age of seven, my father took me to a baseball game for the very first time</u>.

(A) At the age of seven, my father took me to a baseball game for the very first time.
(B) At the age of seven, my father took me to my first baseball game.
(C) My father took me at seven years old to a baseball game for the first time.
(D) When I was seven years old, my father took me to my first baseball game.
(E) At the age of seven, I was being taken by my father to my first baseball game.

12 Dealing skillfully with Congress, President Ronald Reagan <u>obtained legislation to stimulate economic growth, curb inflation, increase employment, and strengthen national defense</u>.

(A) obtained legislation to stimulate economic growth, curb inflation, increase employment, and strengthen national defense
(B) obtained legislation to stimulate economic growth, curb inflation, increase employment, and strengthening national defense
(C) obtaining legislation to stimulate economic growth, curbing inflation, increasing employment, and strengthening national defense
(D) obtained legislation to stimulate economic growth, to curb inflation, increasing employment, and strengthen national defense
(E) had obtained legislation to stimulate economic growth, to curb inflation, to increase employment, and to strengthen national defense

13 <u>If anyone asks for a doctor, send them</u> directly to the nurses' station for immediate assistance.

(A) if anyone asks for a doctor, send them
(B) having asked for a doctor, send them
(C) when anyone asks for a doctor, they should be sent
(D) had anyone asked for a doctor, send them
(E) send anyone who asks for a doctor

14 <u>Even if they have been declawed as kittens</u>, adult cats often run their paws along tall objects as if to sharpen their claws.

(A) even if they have been declawed as kittens
(B) even though they should have been declawed when being kittens
(C) even when being declawed as kittens
(D) declawed when kittens nevertheless
(E) declawed as kittens

STOP

You may check your work, on this section only, until time is called.

ANSWER KEY

Section 2 Math	Section 5 Math	Section 7 Math	Section 3 Critical Reading	Section 6 Critical Reading	Section 8 Critical Reading	Section 4 Writing	Section 9 Writing
☐ 1. A	☐ 1. B	☐ 1. D	☐ 1. A	☐ 1. A	☐ 1. C	☐ 1. C	☐ 1. B
☐ 2. B	☐ 2. B	☐ 2. C	☐ 2. C	☐ 2. D	☐ 2. C	☐ 2. A	☐ 2. D
☐ 3. D	☐ 3. C	☐ 3. A	☐ 3. B	☐ 3. E	☐ 3. B	☐ 3. D	☐ 3. C
☐ 4. D	☐ 4. B	☐ 4. C	☐ 4. E	☐ 4. A	☐ 4. C	☐ 4. B	☐ 4. C
☐ 5. D	☐ 5. B	☐ 5. A	☐ 5. E	☐ 5. B	☐ 5. D	☐ 5. C	☐ 5. B
☐ 6. E	☐ 6. D	☐ 6. B	☐ 6. A	☐ 6. C	☐ 6. B	☐ 6. E	☐ 6. C
☐ 7. C	☐ 7. A	☐ 7. A	☐ 7. D	☐ 7. E	☐ 7. B	☐ 7. C	☐ 7. B
☐ 8. C	☐ 8. D	☐ 8. B	☐ 8. C	☐ 8. C	☐ 8. E	☐ 8. D	☐ 8. A
☐ 9. A	☐ 9. 1	☐ 9. C	☐ 9. B	☐ 9. A	☐ 9. B	☐ 9. C	☐ 9. C
☐ 10. D	☐ 10. 4	☐ 10. D	☐ 10. E	☐ 10. B	☐ 10. A	☐ 10. C	☐ 10. B
☐ 11. B	☐ 11. 3	☐ 11. D	☐ 11. A	☐ 11. E	☐ 11. A	☐ 11. B	☐ 11. D
☐ 12. B	☐ 12. 32	☐ 12. E	☐ 12. A	☐ 12. D	☐ 12. C	☐ 12. D	☐ 12. A
☐ 13. B	☐ 13. 9	☐ 13. D	☐ 13. A	☐ 13. A	☐ 13. C	☐ 13. C	☐ 13. E
☐ 14. C	☐ 14. 3	☐ 14. C	☐ 14. D	☐ 14. A	☐ 14. A	☐ 14. E	☐ 14. A
☐ 15. B	☐ 15. 2 or 1/3 or .333	☐ 15. D	☐ 15. C	☐ 15. C	☐ 15. C	☐ 15. B	
☐ 16. B		☐ 16. B	☐ 16. D	☐ 16. D	☐ 16. B	☐ 16. D	
☐ 17. D	☐ 16. 18		☐ 17. E	☐ 17. C	☐ 17. D	☐ 17. B	
☐ 18. C	☐ 17. 20		☐ 18. E	☐ 18. E	☐ 18. A	☐ 18. B	
☐ 19. E	☐ 18. 25		☐ 19. A	☐ 19. B	☐ 19. D	☐ 19. C	
☐ 20. D			☐ 20. D	☐ 20. D		☐ 20. D	
			☐ 21. A	☐ 21. C		☐ 21. C	
			☐ 22. B	☐ 22. A		☐ 22. A	
			☐ 23. C	☐ 23. D		☐ 23. E	
			☐ 24. E	☐ 24. A		☐ 24. D	
						☐ 25. C	
						☐ 26. B	
						☐ 27. C	
						☐ 28. E	
						☐ 29. B	
						☐ 30. B	
						☐ 31. A	
						☐ 32. D	
						☐ 33. B	
						☐ 34. C	
						☐ 35. E	

# Right (A):	Questions 1–8 # Right (A):	# Right (A):	# Right (A):	# Right (A):	# Right (A):	# Right (A)	# Right (A):
# Wrong (B):	# Wrong (B):	# Wrong (B);	# Wrong (B):	# Wrong (B):	# Wrong (B):	# Wrong (B):	# Wrong (B):
# (A) – ¼ (B):	# (A) – ¼ (B):	# (A) – ¼ (B):	# (A) – ¼ (B):	# (A) – ¼ (B):	# (A) – ¼ (B):	# (A) – ¼ (B):	# (A) – ¼ (B):
	Questions 9–18 # Right (A):						

SCORE CONVERSION TABLE

How to score your test

Use the answer key on the previous page to determine your raw score on each section. **Your raw score on each section except Section 5 is simply the number of correct answers minus ¼ of the number of wrong answers. On Section 5, your raw score is the sum of the number of correct answers for questions 1–18 minus ¼ of the number of wrong answers for questions 1–8.** Next, add the raw scores from Sections 3, 4, and 7 to get your Math raw score, and add the raw scores from Sections 6 and 9 to get your Writing raw score. Write the three raw scores here:

Raw Critical Reading score: _____   Raw Math score: _____   Raw Writing score: _____

Use the table below to convert these to scaled scores.

Scaled scores: Critical Reading: _____   Math: _____   Writing: _____

Raw Score	Critical Reading Scaled Score	Math Scaled Score	Writing Scaled Score	Raw Score	Critical Reading Scaled Score	Math Scaled Score	Writing Scaled Score
67	800			32	520	550	610
66	800			31	510	550	600
65	790			30	510	540	580
64	780			29	500	530	570
63	760			28	490	530	560
62	750			27	490	520	550
61	730			26	480	510	540
60	720			25	480	500	530
59	700			24	470	490	520
58	700			23	460	480	510
57	690			22	460	480	500
56	680			21	450	470	490
55	670			20	440	460	480
54	660	800		19	440	450	470
53	650	790		18	430	450	460
52	650	760		17	420	440	450
51	640	740		16	420	430	440
50	630	720		15	410	420	440
49	620	710	800	14	400	410	430
48	620	700	800	13	400	410	420
47	610	680	800	12	390	400	410
46	600	670	790	11	380	390	400
45	600	660	780	10	370	380	390
44	590	650	760	9	360	370	380
43	590	640	740	8	350	360	380
42	580	630	730	7	340	350	370
41	570	630	710	6	330	340	360
40	570	620	700	5	320	330	350
39	560	610	690	4	310	320	340
38	550	600	670	3	300	310	320
37	550	590	660	2	280	290	310
36	540	580	650	1	270	280	300
35	540	580	640	0	250	260	280
34	530	570	630	−1	230	240	270
33	520	560	620	−2 or less	210	220	250

SCORE CONVERSION TABLE FOR WRITING COMPOSITE
[ESSAY + MULTIPLE CHOICE]

Calculate your writing raw score as you did on the previous page and grade your essay from a 1 to a 6 according to the standards that follow in the detailed answer key.

Essay score: _____ Raw Writing score: _____

Use the table below to convert these to scaled scores.

Scaled score: Writing: _____

Raw Score	Essay Score 0	Essay Score 1	Essay Score 2	Essay Score 3	Essay Score 4	Essay Score 5	Essay Score 6
−2 or less	200	230	250	280	310	340	370
−1	210	240	260	290	320	360	380
0	230	260	280	300	340	370	400
1	240	270	290	320	350	380	410
2	250	280	300	330	360	390	420
3	260	290	310	340	370	400	430
4	270	300	320	350	380	410	440
5	280	310	330	360	390	420	450
6	290	320	340	360	400	430	460
7	290	330	340	370	410	440	470
8	300	330	350	380	410	450	470
9	310	340	360	390	420	450	480
10	320	350	370	390	430	460	490
11	320	360	370	400	440	470	500
12	330	360	380	410	440	470	500
13	340	370	390	420	450	480	510
14	350	380	390	420	460	490	520
15	350	380	400	430	460	500	530
16	360	390	410	440	470	500	530
17	370	400	420	440	480	510	540
18	380	410	420	450	490	520	550
19	380	410	430	460	490	530	560
20	390	420	440	470	500	530	560
21	400	430	450	480	510	540	570
22	410	440	460	480	520	550	580
23	420	450	470	490	530	560	590
24	420	460	470	500	540	570	600
25	430	460	480	510	540	580	610
26	440	470	490	520	550	590	610
27	450	480	500	530	560	590	620
28	460	490	510	540	570	600	630
29	470	500	520	550	580	610	640
30	480	510	530	560	590	620	650
31	490	520	540	560	600	630	660
32	500	530	550	570	610	640	670
33	510	540	550	580	620	650	680
34	510	550	560	590	630	660	690
35	520	560	570	600	640	670	700
36	530	560	580	610	650	680	710
37	540	570	590	620	660	690	720
38	550	580	600	630	670	700	730
39	560	600	610	640	680	710	740
40	580	610	620	650	690	720	750
41	590	620	640	660	700	730	760
42	600	630	650	680	710	740	770
43	610	640	660	690	720	750	780
44	620	660	670	700	740	770	800
45	640	670	690	720	750	780	800
46	650	690	700	730	770	800	800
47	670	700	720	750	780	800	800
48	680	720	730	760	800	800	800
49	680	720	730	760	800	800	800

Detailed Answer Key

Section 1

The following essay received 12 points out of a possible 12. This means that, according to the graders, it

- develops an insightful point of view on the topic
- demonstrates exemplary critical thinking
- uses effective examples, reasons, and other evidence to support its thesis
- is consistently focused, coherent, and well-organized
- demonstrates skillful and effective use of language and sentence structure
- is largely (but not necessarily completely) free of grammatical and usage errors

Consider carefully the issue discussed in the following passage, then write an essay that answers the question posed in the assignment.

> Many among us like to blame violence and immorality in the media for a "decline in morals" in society. Yet these people seem to have lost touch with logic. Any objective examination shows that our society is far less violent or exploitative than virtually any society in the past. Early humans murdered and enslaved each other with astonishing regularity, without the help of gangsta rap or Jerry Bruckheimer films.

Assignment: **Does violence and immorality in the media make our society more dangerous and immoral?** Write an essay in which you answer this question and discuss your point of view on this issue. Support your position logically with examples from literature, the arts, history, politics, science and technology, current events, or your experience or observation.

SAMPLE STUDENT ESSAY

One of the most misguided notions of conventional wisdom is that depicting violence in the media makes our society more violent. A close examination shows that this claim is baseless. Societies with severe restrictions on violence in the media tend to be more, not less, violent than those with no such restrictions. Indeed, despite the popular myth of a more peaceful past, societies were far more violent before the advent of movies, television, and video games. Societies that restrict access to "immoral" western movies are the same ones that call their citizens to violent and irrational holy war.

As Michael Moore pointed out poignantly in the movie "Bowling for Columbine," Americans kill each other with firearms at a far greater rate than almost any other first-world nation. But he is quick to point out that our media is not more violent than those in Japan or Germany or even Canada, which have rates of violence that are a full order of magnitude lower

than ours. Indeed, the killers among us are not likely to spend a lot of time listening to Marilyn Manson or playing Mortal Kombat on their Playstations, despite what our more nearsighted and sanctimonious politicians and preachers would like us to believe. Ted Kaczynski, the Unabomber, lived in a one-room shack without electricity or running water, let alone cable. But even if murderers like Kaczynski were video game addicts, attributing their motives to media violence would be missing the point entirely.

People who are habitually violent have adopted a "war mentality." They tend to see the world in black-and-white, us-against-them terms. Tragically, our leaders tend to have this very same mentality, but they couch it in "patriotism." Lobbing cruise missiles and landing marines in another country is not considered a horrible last resort, but a patriotic duty. If we wish to understand why Americans are more violent than the Japanese, violence in the media will hold no answers; Japanese kids watch just as much violence. Foreign policy is far more telling: which country has leaders who engage in violence against other countries at every opportunity, and constantly try to convince us that it's right?

If our pundits and politicians were truly concerned about making a safer world—and there are many reasons to believe they are not, since they profit the most from a fearful citizenry—they would begin by acknowledging that violence is almost a desperate grab for control from a person or people who believe they are being repressed. If we want a more peaceful and noble society, then we will stop coercing other countries with violence and economic oppression. As Franklin Roosevelt said, "We have nothing to fear but fear itself." We are the most fearful nation on the planet, and we are paying for it.

The following essay received 8 points out of a possible 12, meaning that it demonstrates *adequate competence* in that it

- develops a point of view on the topic
- demonstrates some critical thinking, but perhaps not consistently
- uses some examples, reasons, and other evidence to support its thesis, but perhaps not adequately
- shows a general organization and focus, but shows occasional lapses in this regard
- demonstrates adequate but occasionally inconsistent facility with language
- contains occasional errors in grammar, usage, and mechanics

---

SAMPLE STUDENT ESSAY

People say that society today is much more violent due to all of the media portrayal of violence we see on a daily basis. The nightly news is often made up entirely of stories about murders, muggings, arson, and other gruesome crimes. The most successful shows on television are the investigative crime shows in which they solve disturbing murder mysteries. Movies like the Lord of the Rings contain gory fight scenes that show the death of hundreds of characters. It's hard even to find a video game anymore that doesn't somehow relate back to fighting.

Those who don't believe that violence breeds violence would argue that the United States murder rate had declined to its lowest level in 30 years and that this is proof that the violence in the media has not in fact made for a more violent society. But what they conveniently leave out is the fact that at the same time, youth gun killings were on the rise. This is who is being affected by the increased exposure to violence—the children. It is perhaps the video game violence and television/movie violence that can be held responsible.

Kids today are growing up in a society where violence is everywhere. It is difficult for a child to go through the day without witnessing some violent act on TV or hearing about a gruesome murder on the radio. A recent study we learned about in class concluded that because of what they see on television, children become immune to violence, accept it as something that is part of a "normal" life, and they often times will attempt to imitate what they see on television because it "looks fun."

Something needs to be done to reverse this trend of growing violence in our country and tighter regulation of the amount of violence on television, in music, and in the movies would be a great place to start. The youth of this country need to be reminded that violence is not an acceptable part of daily existence and that it should be avoided at all costs.

The following essay received 4 points out of a possible 12, meaning that it demonstrates *some incompetence* in that it

- has a seriously limited point of view
- demonstrates weak critical thinking
- uses inappropriate or insufficient examples, reasons, and other evidence to support its thesis
- is poorly focused and organized and has serious problems with coherence
- demonstrates frequent problems with language and sentence structure
- contains errors in grammar and usage that obscure the author's meaning seriously

SAMPLE STUDENT ESSAY

Believing that the violence in the media has made the members of our society like violent murderers is an absurd notion. Sure, there are lots video games on the market that involve fighting ninjas and battling army troops. Yes, nightly television shows on the public television networks show many a violent episode. Sure, the nightly news is covered with violent crimes and such. For instance, the popular music of this era is full of violent references and foul language. But, no experiment or statistics that I have seen proves the above statement to be true. Just because a teenager kills over 500 fake people on his ninja fighting video game, it does not mean that after he turns off the game console that he will run outside in his ninja costume and start attacking the people in his neighborhood. It is absurd to say that violence is because of all the violence on video games television. Actually I think that video games make you better at eye-hand coordination which is a valuable skill. Hundreds of years before video games and movies and television, there were murder and violence. Human beings are violent people and the exposure to violence does not make us more violent than we already were. If we did not have all of these impressive technological advances such as radio, television and film, we would still be committing acts of violence. There will always be violent humans that are ready to hurt others to get what they want and eliminating violent references from our music and television shows might even make people madder.

Detailed Answer Key

Section 2

---

1. A

$(x + 4) + 7 = 14$

Subtract 7: $\quad x + 4 = 7$

Subtract 4: $\quad\quad x = 3$

---

2. B Write out a mathematical equation for how you would actually find the cost for the month: $.95 × 31. Answer choice B, $1.00 × 30, is closest to that amount.

---

3. D A linear angle measures 180°. Write an equation:

$$w + x + 50 = 180°$$

Subtract 50°: $\quad w + x = 130°$

---

4. D

$g(x) = 3x + 4$

Substitute 5 for x: $\quad g(5) = 3(5) + 4$

Simplify: $\quad g(5) = 15 + 4 = 19$

---

5. D The difference between x and y is $(x - y)$. The sum of x and y is $(x + y)$. The product of those two is equal to 18:

$$(x - y)(x + y) = 18$$

FOIL: $\quad x^2 - xy + xy - y^2 = 18$

Combine like terms: $\quad x^2 - y^2 = 18$

---

6. E

$3\sqrt{x} - 7 = 20$

Add 7: $\quad 3\sqrt{x} = 27$

Divide by 3: $\quad \sqrt{x} = 9$

Square both sides: $\quad x = 81$

---

7. C Let b = cost of chocolate bar and g = cost of gum.

$b + g = \$1.75$

Chocolate bar is $.25 more: $b = \$.25 + g$

Substitute for b: $\$.25 + g + g = \$1.75$

Combine like terms: $\$.25 + 2g = \$1.75$

Subtract $.25: $\quad 2g = \$1.50$

Divide by 2: $\quad g = \$.75$

---

8. C First find 40% of 80: $.40 × 80 = 32$

Now find what percent of 96 is 32.

Translate: $\dfrac{x}{100} × 96 = 32$

Multiply by 100: $\quad 96x = 3,200$

Divide by 96: $\quad x = 33\tfrac{1}{3}$

---

9. A If $lm = 21$ and both l and m are integers, then m must either 1, 3, 7, or 21. If $mn = 39$, however, then m must also be a factor of 39, so it must be 3. Therefore, $l = 21/3 = 7$ and $n = 39/3 = 13$, so $n > l > m$.

---

10. D There's no need to do a lot of calculation here. Look for the 2 adjacent bars with the greatest positive difference between them. Since 1999 shows the least profits of all the years on the graph and 2000 shows the greatest profits of any year on the graph, 1999–2000 must have the greatest change in profit.

---

11. B A Venn diagram can help you with this problem: Imagine that the 4 students who play 2 sports play soccer and tennis. (It doesn't matter which specific pair of sports they play.) This means that $12 - 4 = 8$ students play just soccer, $7 - 4 = 63$ students play just tennis, and 9 students play just lacrosse. This shows that there is a total of $9 + 8 + 4 + 3 = 24$ students.

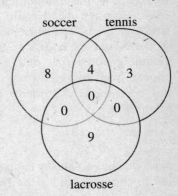

12. **B**   To solve this problem, you need to find the distance between the center of the circle (14, 14) and the point on the circle (2, 9). To do this, you can use the distance formula.

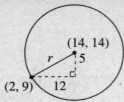

You can also draw a right triangle connecting the two points. It gives you a triangle with one leg of 5 and one leg of 12. Set up the Pythagorean Theorem and solve for r.

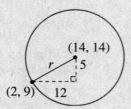

$$5^2 + 12^2 = r^2$$

Simplify: $25 + 144 = r^2$
Combine like terms: $169 = r^2$
Take square root: $13 = r$

The diameter is twice the radius = $2(r) = 2(13) = 26$.

13. **B**   The population doubles every 18 months. Start with January of 2000 and start doubling.

	January 2000	12,000
18 months later:	July 2001	24,000
18 months later:	January 2003	48,000
18 months later:	July 2004	96,000

14. **C**   Use the Fundamental Counting Principle from Chapter 12 Lesson 5. To arrange these students, 5 choices must be made. First select the students for each end. Since one of the 5 (the tallest) cannot go on either end, you have 4 students to choose from for 1 end and then, once that choice has been made, 3 students to choose from for the other end:

$$\underset{*}{\underline{\;4\;}} \;\;\underline{\;\;\;\;}\;\; \underline{\;\;\;\;}\;\; \underline{\;\;\;\;}\;\; \underset{*}{\underline{\;3\;}}$$

Now fill the remaining spots. There are 3 students left to choose from for the 2nd spot:

$$\underset{*}{\underline{\;4\;}} \;\;\underline{\;3\;}\;\; \underline{\;\;\;\;}\;\; \underline{\;\;\;\;}\;\; \underset{*}{\underline{\;3\;}}$$

Then, once that selection has been made, there are 2 for the next spot, then 1 for the remaining spot:

$$\underline{\;4\;} \;\;\underline{\;3\;}\;\; \underline{\;2\;}\;\; \underline{\;1\;}\;\; \underline{\;3\;}$$

To find the total number of possible arrangements, simply multiply: $4 \times 3 \times 2 \times 1 \times 3 = 72$.

15. **B**   From the diagram, we know that $a + b + c = 180$, and we know that $b = c + 3$.
If you want b to be as large as possible, then you need to make the sum of a and c as small as possible. The smallest integer value of a possible is 91. So let's say that $a = 91$.

Substitute 91 for a:	$91 + b + c$	$= 180$
Substitute $c + 3$ for b:	$91 + c + 3 + c$	$= 180$
Combine like terms:	$94 + 2c$	$= 180$
Subtract 94:	$2c$	$= 86$
Divide by 2:	c	$= 43$

So 43 is the largest possible value of c; this means that $43 + 3 = 46$ is the largest possible value of b.

16. **B**   Begin by finding the area of the big equilateral triangle. An equilateral triangle with sides of length 4 has a height of $2\sqrt{3}$, because the height divides the triangle into
2 30° 60° 90° triangles.
Area = ½(base)(height)
       = ½ (4)($2\sqrt{3}$) = $4\sqrt{3}$

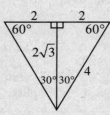

The big triangle is divided into 4 equal parts, 3 of which are shaded, so the shaded area is ¾ of the total area.
Shaded area = ¾($4\sqrt{3}$) = $3\sqrt{3}$

17. **D**   Just look at the graph and draw a line at $y = 1$. The y-values of the graph are at or above that line from $x = -4$ to $x = -2$ and from $x = 2$ to $x = 4$.

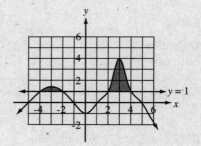

18. C This table shows all of the $5 \times 5 = 25$ possible values of ab:

x	2	4	6	8	10
1	2	4	6	8	10
3	6	12	18	24	30
5	10	20	30	40	50
7	14	28	42	56	70
9	18	36	54	72	90

Of those, only the 7 shaded values are greater than 20 and less than 50, so the probability is 7/25.

19. E

$$(w^a)(w^5) = w^{15}$$

Simplify: $w^{5+a} = w^{15}$

Equate the exponents: $5 + a = 15$

Subtract 5: $a = 10$

$$(w^4)^b = w^{12}$$

Simplify: $w^{4b} = w^{12}$

Equate the exponents: $4b = 12$

Divide by 4: $b = 3$

So $a + b = 10 + 3 = 13$.

20. D The graph of $y = f(x - 2)$ is the graph of $y = f(x)$ shifted to the right 2 units without changing its shape. Therefore, the "peak" at point (6, 4) should shift to (8, 4).

Section 3

1. A The word *although* indicates a contrast. Raúl purchased his computer only 10 months ago, but technology has been improving so fast that it is already *outdated*. *obsolete* = outdated; *adjunct* = auxiliary, or additional; *novel* = new, innovative; *elusive* = hard to catch.

2. C The admissions committee is looking to justify offering more scholarships to increase the number of applications, so the number of applicants must be *decreasing*. *mushroom* = expand rapidly; *plummet* = decrease rapidly; *satiate* = satisfy; *burgeon* = grow.

3. B If the father will not consider another person's viewpoint to be valid if it differs from his own, he must be pretty *stubborn* or *arrogant*. *pragmatic* = practical; *dogmatic* = arrogantly authoritative; *phlegmatic* = sluggish; *cordial* = polite; *curt* = abrupt and rude.

4. E The books are written for children but are still *enjoyable* to adults. *penned* = written; *prosaic* = dull; *morose* = gloomy; *censored* = cleansed of profanity; *incongruous* = not compatible; *tedious* = boring, dull; *authored* = written; *engaging* = captivating, interesting.

5. E Julia is at the top of her class, but if this is hard to believe, she must approach her work in a *lazy* or *irresponsible* way. *adept* = skilled; *diligent* = hardworking; *fanatical* = obsessive and crazy; *extroverted* = outgoing; *laggardly* = slow-moving, lagging behind.

6. A The President's opponents were always cautious about debating him, so the President must be *highly skilled* or *intimidating* or *mean*. *redoubtable* = formidable, imposing; *staid* = calm, not outwardly emotional; *magnanimous* = generous; *stoic* = indifferent to pain or pleasure.

7. D The new clothing line was described as being *eclectic* (containing much variety). It ranged from *modest* (not showy) and *unadorned* (undecorated) to ———— and *garish* (flashy). By parallelism, the missing word should be in opposition to the word *modest*. *austere* = severe, stern; *prophetic* = able to tell the future; *cordial* = polite; *ostentatious* = showy; *solitary* = alone.

8. C The textbook *includes all of the essential information* but it is not *verbose* (wordy); the 2 missing words should be parallel to *containing lots of information* and *not verbose*. *compendious* = succinct; *circumlocutory* = talking around the subject, indirect; *reprehensible* = blameworthy; *terse* = concise; *comprehensive* = including a large amount of information; *concise* = brief and to the point; *grandiloquent* = speaking in a pompous manner; *painstaking* = done with great care; *redundant* = repetitive.

9. B Saying that we were *raised in unrivaled prosperity* is like saying that the economy has been very strong and *abundant*.

10. E The "people" are plagued by *deep divisions* (line 9), and the *citizens* are the only ones who are not *growing to appreciate the difference between America and the United States* (lines 21–23). Therefore, the *people* lack unity, while the *citizens* lack awareness.

11. **A** Don't miss the word *EXCEPT* in the question. Choice B is supported in line 14, choice C in line 7, choice D in line 8, and choice E in line 8. The last lines say that *ambition for a better life is universal*, implying that *not* everyone is happy with the status of their lives.

12. **A** Unlike Passage 1, Passage 2 discusses the difference between the ideal of America and the reality of the United States.

13. **A** The questions in the opening lines show the man's *confusion*, and the woman is said to talk *ardently* (passionately).

14. **D** The author says that one *who is suddenly overwhelmed by terror cannot afterwards remember the exact order of sounds accompanying the castastrophe which stuns him*—that is, he becomes disoriented.

15. **C** Line 13 suggests that Ognev is stunned by a *catastrophe*. The context of the passage makes it clear that this catastrophe is the expression of love from Vera, which Ognev has difficulty understanding.

16. **D** In saying that *she had been struck by ... the aims and objects of his life* (lines 24–26) the author is saying that she was impressed with Ognev's *life goals*.

17. **E** In lines 45–47, the passage states that *much as he wanted to, he could feel no joy; no fundamental happiness*. In other words, the *bad and strange* thing was *disaffection*.

18. **E** In lines 54–56, the passage states that *Vera's raptures and suffering seemed to him* (Ognev) *to be only cloying* (excessively sweet) *and trivial* (of little significance). He felt her passion to be unimportant and was *outraged at himself* for feeling this way. To him, his *statistics, books or philosophical truths* were more important than this passion.

19. **A** The final sentence of the passage states that *he was annoyed and blamed himself even though he himself did not understand why he was to blame*. Ognev is confused and uncertain about how he *should* feel about Vera's passion. He feels indifference but thinks he should feel something different.

20. **D** In lines 22–23 the marchers are described as *singing to hide their exhaustion* and then as *trying not to fear... .* This commitment to hiding emotion is *stoicism*.

21. **A** Lines 36–39 criticize the bill's *failure to protect the right of African Americans to vote "when local officials are determined to deny it."* In other words, it did not sufficiently pressure local officials to extend voting rights to all citizens.

22. **B** In context, saying that *his ... encounter with Mexican-American children* was *shattering* is like saying that the encounter bothered the President and had a major impact on the way he approached civil rights issues later in his career.

23. **C** Johnson indicates that he inferred, by looking into his students' eyes, that they knew that others disliked them. This indicates a strong empathy with his students, because he inferred it not from their words but from their expressions.

24. **E** Lines 54–56 say that Johnson *made the nationwide audience aware of how deeply personal the issue of African American rights was to him* and lines 62–65 that *he spoke more directly, more explicitly, and more warmly of the human experience of prejudice than any president before him*. In other words, he addressed it directly and in personal terms.

Section 4

1. **C** The word *group* is the singular subject, so the verb should be *was*.

2. **A** The original phrasing is best.

3. **D** *Timothy* must follow the opening modifiers, because he is the one who is *timid and self-conscious*. The original phrasing is wrong, however, because *give full expression towards* is awkward and unidiomatic. Choice B is wrong because *managed full expression of* is awkward and unidiomatic.

4. **B** The phrase *studying in preparation for* is awkward, redundant, and unidiomatic.

5. **C**   The phrase *on an overseas journey* is redundant because the next phrase is *across the Atlantic Ocean*.

6. **E**   The original phrasing is a sentence fragment. Choice E is better than choice C because, idiomatically, being a *home fixture* means being an *appliance*, while being a *fixture in the homes* means being a *welcome figure in the homes*.

7. **C**   This phrasing is most parallel and concise.

8. **D**   The use of *therefore* in the original phrasing is illogical, because the ideas in the sentence are related not as a cause and effect but rather as a contrast. The use of *actually* in choice D conveys the appropriate irony.

9. **C**   Because the sneaking is not a part of the *effort to open several of her presents* but rather an action that preceded it, the original phrasing is awkward and illogical.

10. **C**   The definite pronoun *it* is required to relate it to its antecedent *music*.

11. **B**   The opening participial phrase modifies *Clarence Darrow*, not his oratory, so the original phrasing leaves a dangling participle. Choice B is less awkward than D.

12. **D**   The subject of this verb is *delivery*, which is singular, so the verb should be *has been*.

13. **C**   The pronoun *whose* is personal and so should not refer to an inanimate object like a *charming cottage*. A better phrase here is *with rooms that are*.

14. **E**   The sentence is correct.

15. **B**   The subject of this verb is *photographs … and diagrams*, which is plural, so the verb should be *were*.

16. **D**   This is a comparison error. The *way in which chimpanzees form friendships* cannot logically be compared to *humans*. Instead, the phrase should be *to the way humans form friendships*.

17. **B**   As a noun, *affects* means *feelings or emotions*, so its use here is a diction error. The proper word is *effects*.

18. **B**   There are 2 errors in this phrase. First, the subject *probability* is singular, so the verb should be *is*. Second, a probability can be *lower* than another, but not *fewer* than another.

19. **C**   *Everyone* is singular, so the pronoun should be changed to the singular *his or her*.

20. **D**   The word *bought* is the past tense of the verb *to buy*. But Eric clearly did not *buy back* the basket.
The correct word here is *brought*.

21. **C**   People are satisfied *with* things, not *at* them.

22. **A**   The phrase *had ate* is an incorrect past perfect form. The correct form is *had eaten*. In this case, however, the word *after* conveys the time sequence, so the past perfect form isn't strictly necessary: *ate* (but not *had ate*) is an acceptable alternative.

23. **E**   The sentence is correct.

24. **D**   The word *neither* is a singular subject of the verb, so the correct form is *is*.

25. **C**   The subject of the verb *help* is *taking*, which is singular. Think of the subject as *it*. The word *help* should instead be *helps*.

26. **B**   The word *underneath* means physically below something. The word should instead be *under*.

27. **C**   The subject *they* is referring to *the company*, which is singular. *They* should instead be *it*.

28. **E**   The sentence is correct.

29. **B**   The subject *they* is ambiguous. It is not easy to tell if the *they* is referring to the *experiments* or the *scientists*.

30. **B**   This phrasing is the most concise and logical of the choices.

31. **A**   The original phrasing is best.

32. **D**   Because the sentence refers to *these passions*, it is most logically placed after those passions are described. It also provides a logical transition to the third paragraph.

33. **B**   This order places the sentences in proper logical and chronological order: (8) identifies his childhood passion, (10) identifies his goals for this passion, (7) proceeds to his college years, (6) mentions where he pursued his passions, and (9) describes the connection between these passions and his later career.

34. **C**   The paragraph as a whole discusses Roosevelt's passion for nature, so details about his activities in these natural settings would be relevant.

35. **E**   This sentence would be a good conclusion to the passage because it gives historical perspective to the specific ideas in the passage.

Section 5

1. **B**   There are 180°on the side of a line.
$$2x + 3x = 180°$$
Combine like terms: $5x = 180°$
Divide by 5: $x = 36°$
Multiply by 2: $2x = 72°$

2. **B**   Erica knows that *neither* of the last two digits is odd, so each is 0, 2, 4, 6, or 8. Since there are 5 possibilities for each digit, there are $5 \times 5 = 25$ possible arrangements.

3. **C**   There are 180° in a triangle. Set up equations for the two triangles in the figure.
$$a + b + 52 = 180$$
Subtract 52: $a + b = 128$
$$c + d + 52 = 180$$
Subtract 52: $c + d = 128$
$$a + b + c + d =$$
Substitute: $128 + 128 = 256$

4. **B**
$$f(x) = x^2 - 4$$
Set $f(x)$ equal to 32: $x^2 - 4 = 32$
Add 4: $x^2 = 36$
Take positive square root: $x = 6$

5. **B**   Set up an equation to find the average.
$$\frac{x + (x + 1) + (x + 4) + 2x + 5x}{5} = 11$$
Multiply by 5: $x + (x + 1) + (x + 4) + 2x + 5x = 55$
Combine like terms: $10x + 5 = 55$
Subtract 5: $10x = 50$
Divide by 10: $x = 5$
Plug in 5 for x to find the values:
$$x, (x + 1), (x + 4), 2x, 5x$$
$$5, 6, 9, 10, 25$$
The median is the middle number, which is 9.

6. **D**   If 20 students scored an average of 75 points, then the sum of their scores is $20 \times 75 = 1{,}500$ total points.
If 12 of those students scored an average of 83 points, then the sum of their scores is $12 \times 83 = 996$ points. Therefore, the remaining 8 students scored $1{,}500 - 996 = 504$ points altogether, so their average score is $504 \div 8 = 63$ points.

7. **A**   The sides of square *EFGH* all have length $\left(8\sqrt{2}\right)^2$ A diagonal of this square can be found with the

Pythagorean Theorem: $\left(8\sqrt{2}\right)^2 + \left(8\sqrt{2}\right)^2 \overline{EG}^2$.
          Simplify: $128 + 128 = \overline{EG}^2$
                               $256 = \overline{EG}^2$
          Take square root: $16 = \overline{EG}$
(Or, more simply, you can remember that the length of the diagonal of a 45° –45° –90° triangle is the length of the side times $\sqrt{2}$. So the diagonal is $14\sqrt{2} \times \sqrt{2} = 16$.) By the same reasoning, since the sides of square *ABCD* all have length $14\sqrt{2}$: $\overline{AD} = 14\sqrt{2} \times \sqrt{2} = 28$.

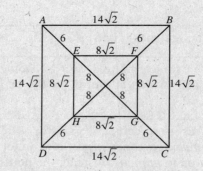

Notice that $\overline{AC} = \overline{AE} + \overline{EG} + \overline{CG}$; therefore, $28 = \overline{AE} + 16 + \overline{CG}$, so $\overline{AE} + \overline{CG} = 12$. By the same reasoning, $\overline{BF} + \overline{DH} = 12$, so $\overline{AE} + \overline{BF} + \overline{CG} + \overline{DH} = 24$.

8. D Although you were probably taught to add the "rightmost" digits first, here the "leftmost" digits provide more information about the number, so it's best to start there.

$$\begin{array}{r} RS \\ +SR \\ \hline TR4 \end{array}$$

The largest possible 3-digit number that can be formed by adding two 2-digit numbers is $99 + 99 = 198$. Therefore, T must be 1.

$$\begin{array}{r} RS \\ +SR \\ \hline 1R4 \end{array}$$

Therefore, there must be a "carry" of 1 from the addition of $R + S$ in the 10s column. Looking at the units column tells us that $S + R$ yields a units digit of 4, so $S + R = 14$. The addition in the 10s column tells us that $R + S + 1 = R + 10$. (The "+10" is needed for the carry into the 100s column.)

$$R + S + 1 = R + 10$$
Substitute $R + S = 14$: $14 + 1 = R + 10$
Subtract 10: $5 = R$
So $2R + T = 2(5) + 1 = 11$.

9. 1

$$\boxed{n} = \frac{n^2}{16}$$

If it helps, you can think of this as $f(n) = \dfrac{n^2}{16}$

Find the value of $(f(4))^2$

Plug in 4 for n: $f(4) = \dfrac{4^2}{16} = \dfrac{16}{16} = 1$

Plug in 1 for $f(4)$: $(f(4))^2 = (1)^2 = 1$

10. 4 To find the greatest possible value of b/d, find the greatest possible value of b and the least possible positive value of d. Since they are both integers, the greatest possible value of b is 24 and the least possible value of d is 6. $24 \div 6 = 4$.

11. 3 Set up equations: $x + y = 4$

$$\begin{array}{r} x + y = 2 \\ \hline \end{array}$$

Add straight down: $2x = 6$
Divide by 2: $x = 3$
Plug in 3 for x: $3 + y = 4$
Subtract 3: $y = 1$
Final product: $(x)(y) = (3)(1) = 3$

12. 32 Let $LM = x$, and let $LO = y$. Since x is twice the length of y, $x = 2y$.

$$x + x + y + y = P$$
Substitute for x: $2y + 2y + y + y = P$
Combine terms: $6y = P$
Plug in 48 for P: $6y = 48$
Divide by 6: $y = 8$
Solve for x: $x = 2y = 2(8) = 16$

To find the area of the shaded region, you might notice that if PM is the base of the shaded triangle, then LO is the height, so area = ½ (base)(height) = ½ (8)(8) = 32. If you don't notice this, you can find the shaded area by finding the area of the rectangle and subtracting the areas of the two unshaded triangles.

Area of rectangle = (length)(width)
Area of rectangle = (x) (y) = (16)(8) = 128
Area of triangle PLO = ½(base)(height)

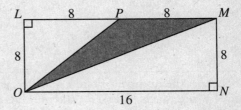

Area of triangle PLO = ½(8)(8) = 32
Area of triangle MNO = ½(base)(height)
Area of triangle MNO = ½(16)(8) = 64
Area of triangle OPM = 128 − 64 − 32 = 32

13. 9 $64^3 = 4^x$
Substitute 4^3 for 64: $(4^3)^3 = 4^x$
Simplify: $4^9 = 4^x$
Equate the exponents: $x = 9$

14. 3 Draw a line with points P, Q, R, and S on the line in that order. You are given that $\overline{PS} = 2\overline{PR}$ and that $\overline{PS} = 4\overline{PQ}$, so choose values for those lengths, like $\overline{PS} = 12$, $\overline{PR} = 6$, and $\overline{PQ} = 3$.

$$\begin{array}{ccccc} & 3 & 3 & 6 & \\ \bullet & \bullet & \bullet & & \bullet \\ P & Q & R & & S \end{array}$$

This means that $\overline{QS} = 9$, so $\overline{QS} / \overline{PQ} = 9/3 = 3$.

15. 2   or ⅓ or .333
If $f(x)$ is not a real number, it must have a denominator of 0. Therefore, either $(x − 2)$ or $(3x − 1)$ is 0.
Set $(x − 2) = 0$ and solve for x: $(x − 2) = 0$
Add 2: $x = 2$
Set $(3x − 1) = 0$ and solve for x: $(3x − 1) = 0$
Add 1: $3x = 1$
Divide by 3: $x = ⅓$

16. **18**   Since these numbers are "evenly spaced," their mean (average) is equal to their median (middle number). The average is easy to calculate: 110/5 =22. Therefore, the middle number is 22, so the numbers are 18, 20, 22, 24, and 26.

Alternatively, you can set up an equation to find the sum of 5 consecutive unknown even integers, where x is the least of these:

$$x + (x + 2) + (x + 4) + (x + 6) + (x + 8) = 110$$

Combine like terms:	$5x + 20 = 110$
Subtract 20:	$5x = 90$
Divide by 5:	$x = 18$

So the 5 integers are 18, 20, 22, 24, and 26.

---

17. **20**   Use the percent change formula:

$$\frac{Final - Original}{Original} \times (100\%)$$

$$\frac{24,000 - 20,000}{20,000} \times (100\%) = 20\%$$

---

18. **25**   Let b = the number of black marbles, w = the number of white marbles, and r = the number of red marbles in the jar. If you are 4 times as likely to choose a black marble as a white one, then $b = 4w$. If you are 5 times as likely to choose a red marble as a black one, then $r = 5b$. To find the least possible number of marbles in the jar, imagine you have only 1 white marble. This would mean you have $4(1) = 4$ black marbles and $5(4) = 20$ red marbles, for a total of $1 + 4 + 20 = 25$ marbles.

In general, you can represent the total number of marbles as

	total $= b + w + r$
Since $r = 5b$:	total $= b + w + 5b$
Since $b = 4w$:	total $= 4w + w + 5(4w)$
Simplify:	total $= 4w + w + 20w$
Simplify:	total $= 25w$

In other words, the number of marbles in the jar must be a multiple of 25. The smallest positive multiple of 25 is, of course, 25.

Section 6

1. **A**   If the fight did not ensue, John must have *intervened* to stop it. *intervene* = get in the way of something; *coalesce* = fuse together; *intermingle* = mix together; *exacerbate* = make worse.

---

2. **D**   The defendant hoped the testimony would *corroborate* (support) his alibi, which would *clear him of blame*. *convoke* = call together; *synthesize* = generate; *absolve* = free of blame; *impeach* = accuse.

3. **E**   Being *ensnarled* (tied up) in traffic is an unpleasant experience that Rachel would have an *aversion to* or *dislike for*. *antipathy* = feeling against; *penchant* = liking; *predilection* = liking; *proclivity* = tendency to do something; *aversion* = feeling of dislike; *insufferable* = intolerable.

---

4. **A**   If the practices are no longer considered *state of the art*, they must now be considered *outdated* or *unsophisticated*. The physicians are *incredulous* (not able to believe) that such barbaric acts were once *supported* or *condoned*. *primitive* = old, unsophisticated; *sanctioned* = approved; *ingenious* = incredible, brilliant; *boorish* = rude; *censured* = publicly condemned; *innovative* = new; *endorsed* = supported; *foolhardy* = recklessly bold; *condemned* = criticized.

---

5. **B**   The Prime Minister had vetoed the law in the past many times, so he didn't want it to pass. What would come *as a great surprise?* The Prime Minister's suddenly *supporting* the law. *articulated* = expressed clearly; *championed* = defended; *denounced* = spoke out against; *initiated* = began; *abbreviated* = shortened.

---

6. **C**   Lines 3–4 state that the *tradition is that a man never lifts his hand against a woman*. Furthermore, if a man offends a woman, she is entitled to give him *a sound thrashing* (line 6). Therefore, a man who disrespected a woman would face *censure*.

---

7. **E**   Saying that *it is not an unusual thing for a squaw to administer a sound thrashing to a warrior husband* (lines 5–7) is like saying that it is not unusual for her to *give* him a beating, or *dispense* it.

---

8. **C**   Lines 5–6 say that *merely receiving palliative care ... provides no hope of a cure*. Therefore, palliative care only reduces the discomfort of the symptoms, without curing the disease, as something *analgesic* does.

---

9. **A**   Lines 9–11 ask, *How can a doctor know if a patient has the mental capacity to decide for herself that the time has come to stop fighting the disease?* This question indicates that there may be some difficulty in determining a patient's *state of mind*.

---

10. **B**   The first sentence of the passage says *there was great optimism about earthquake prediction*. Each paragraph discusses potential *precursors*, or predictors, of earthquakes.

11. E Lines 8–10 say that because *foreshocks look just like any other earthquake, they are not in themselves very useful in prediction.*

12. D Support for choice II can be found in line 19, which says that groundwater has *become cloudy* prior to an earthquake. Choice III is supported in lines 16–18, which say that *before a large earthquake, marked changes have been reported in the level or flow of wells and springs.* Nothing is said about density changes in the groundwater.

13. A The passage says (lines 8–10) that *since foreshocks look just like any other earthquakes, they are not in themselves very useful in prediction* but later (lines 42–45) mentions that because *the Haicheng earthquake had hundreds of foreshocks,* it was *easier than average ... to predict,* thereby suggesting that foreshocks are, in fact, useful in predicting earthquakes.

14. A This paragraph describes a particular application of the theory of earthquake prediction, described in the previous paragraphs, which led to scientists' predicting a large earthquake and saving many lives. Although this is said to have *prov[ed] that ... earthquake prediction is possible* (lines 39–40), it was not a scientific experiment, as there was no control group.

15. C Lines 53–54 mention that *seismologists missed predicting* the Tangshan earthquake and that over 250,000 people died. This was far worse than the Haicheng earthquake, which was *successfully predicted,* so that many lives were saved.

16. D The word "evacuation" in line 49 is placed in quotations to indicate that it is not being used in the traditional sense. The task of evacuating a population from a natural disaster does not typically involve showing movies, so doing so is unconventional.

17. C Lines 8–9 say that *one of the missionaries who met the ship took us under his wing.*

18. E Saying that *he could hardly believe that we were really restored to him* is like saying he couldn't believe that we were returned to him.

19. B The narrator states that she could *use tools as well as [her] brothers did* (lines 22–23), that her first childhood friendship was with a male ship-builder next door, and that she was eager and able to work with the ship-builders around her. Thus, she conveys a clear sense that she considers herself the equal of the males in her life.

20. D The author was emancipated from her confining clothing so that she could work with tools, such as her hatchet, in the shipyard.

21. C The *big movements of the day* refer to the changes in culture and *civilization* (line 43).

22. A Choice II is supported by lines 42–43, which say that *we had around us the fine flower of New England civilization,* as opposed to Michigan, which the author characterizes as *the wilderness* (line 48). The passage does not suggest that New England had finer gardens or humbler citizens than Michigan had.

23. D The author describes the move to Michigan as a *complete upheaval* (lines 40–41), and an unwelcome move from the *fine flower of New England civilization* (lines 42–43), thereby suggesting that she resents the move. She conveys no sign of bewilderment, fear or awe in this passage, since she describes the move with insight and equanimity.

24. A The passage says that the sisters *were so pained by* (the lumber wagon's) *appearance that we refused to ride in it* (lines 58–59) and that they wanted to *look as if we had no association with it* (line 61).

Section 7

1. D

	$4x + 5 = 20$
Add 3:	$4x + 8 = 23$

2. C First find out how many cups are in 3 pints.

Set up a ratio: $\dfrac{1 \text{ pint}}{2 \text{ cups}} = \dfrac{3 \text{ pint}}{x \text{ cups}}$

Cross-multiply: $x = 6$ cups
Set up ratio to solve for servings:

$\dfrac{1 \text{ serving}}{\frac{1}{3} \text{ cups}} = \dfrac{x \text{ servings}}{6 \text{ cups}}$

Cross-multiply: $\frac{1}{3}x = 6$
Divide by ⅓: $x = 18$

3. A Since the angle shown is a right angle, the arc represents ¼ of the circumference.

	length of arc = ¼(2πr)
Substitute 4 for *r*:	length of arc = ¼(2π(4))
Simplify:	length of arc = 2π

4. C This question tests your understanding of 30°–60°–90° triangles. The hypotenuse, which corresponds to $2x$, is 14. This means that the base is $x = 7$. The height is therefore $x\sqrt{3} = \sqrt{3}$.

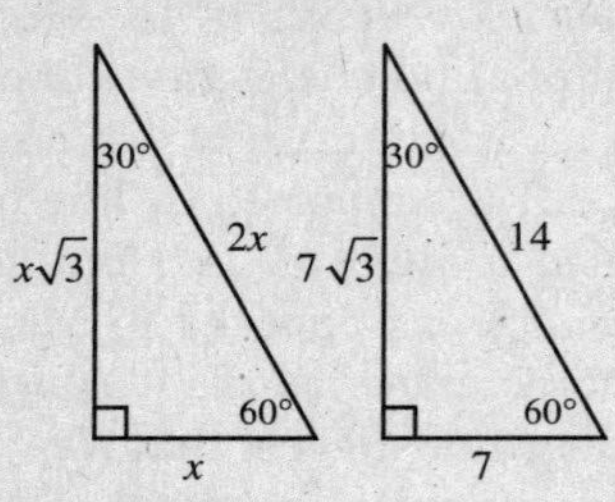

5. A Given that $\nabla x = 3x - 3$, find $\nabla 7$.

$$\nabla 7 = 3x - 3$$

Plug in 7 for x: $3(7) - 3 = 18$

Find $\nabla 3$: $\nabla 3 = 3x - 3$

Plug in 3 for x: $3(3) - 3 = 6$

$$\frac{\nabla 7}{\nabla 3} = \frac{18}{6} = 3$$

Be careful not to pick answer choice (B) $\nabla 3$, because $\nabla 3 = 3(3) - 3 = 6$, not 3. Answer choice (A) $\nabla 2$ is correct, because $\nabla 2 = 3(2) - 3 = 3$.

6. B A little common sense should tell you that they will not need a full hour to clean the pool, because Stephanie can clean it in an hour all by herself, but Mark is helping. Therefore, you should eliminate choices (C), (D), and (E) right away. You might also notice that it can't take less than 30 minutes, because that is how long it would take if they both cleaned 1 pool per hour (so that the 2 working together could clean it in half the time), but Mark is slower, so they can't clean it quite that fast. This eliminates choice (A) and leaves (B) as the only possibility.

But you should know how to solve this problem if it were not a multiple-choice question, as well:

Stephanie's rate for cleaning the pool is 1 pool per hour. Mark's rate for cleaning the pool is 1 pool ÷ 1.5 hours = $\frac{2}{3}$ pools per hour. Combined, they can clean $1 + \frac{2}{3} = \frac{5}{3}$ pools per hour. Set up a rate equation using this rate to determine how much time it would take to clean 1 pool:

1 pool = ($\frac{5}{3}$ pools per hour)(time)

Divide by $\frac{5}{3}$: $\frac{3}{5}$ hours to clean the pool

Multiply by 60: $\frac{3}{5}(60) = 36$ minutes

7. A Change each expression to a base-10 exponential:

(A) $= ((10^2)^3)^4 = 10^{24}$

(B) $= ((10^2)^5)((10^2)^6) = (10^{10})(10^{12}) = 10^{22}$

(C) $= ((10^4)^4) = 10^{16}$

(D) $= (((10^2)^2)((10^2)^2))^2 = ((10^4)(10^4))^2 = (10^8)^2 = 10^{16}$

(E) $= (10^6)^3 = 10^{18}$

8. B Consider the points (0, 2) and (3, 0) on line l. When these points are reflected over the x-axis, (0, 2) transforms to (0, –2) and (3, 0) stays at (3, 0) because it is on the x-axis. You can then use the slope formula to find the slope of line m:

$$\frac{y_2 - y_1}{x_2 - x_1} = \frac{0 - (-2)}{3 - 0} = \frac{2}{3}$$

It's helpful to notice that whenever a line is reflected over the x-axis (or the y-axis, for that matter—try it), its slope becomes the opposite of the original slope.

9. C $(a + b)^2 = (a + b)(a + b)$

FOIL: $a^2 + ab + ab + b^2$

Combine like terms: $a^2 + 2ab + b^2$

Plug in 5 for ab: $a^2 + 2(5) + b^2$

Simplify: $a^2 + b^2 + 10$

Plug in 4 for $a^2 + b^2$: $4 + 10 = 14$

10. D The total area of the patio to be constructed is $24 \times 12 = 288$ ft^2. The slab shown in the figure has an area of 8 ft^2. Therefore, to fill the patio you will need $288 \div 8 = 36$ slabs.

11. D The prize money ratio can also be written as $7x{:}2x{:}1x$. Because the total prize money is $12,000,

$$7x + 2x + 1x = 12{,}000$$

Combine like terms: $10x = 12{,}000$

Divide by 10: $x = 1{,}200$

The first place prize is $7x = 7(1{,}200) = \$8{,}400$.

12. E Always read the problem carefully and notice what it's asking for. Don't assume that you must solve for x and y here. Finding the value of $6x - 2y$ is much simpler than solving the entire system:

$$2x + 3y = 7$$
$$4x - 5y = 12$$

Add straight down: $6x - 2y = 19$

13. D Think carefully about the given information and what it implies, then try to find counterexamples to disprove the given statements. For instance, try to disprove statement I by showing that s can be even. Imagine $s = 2$:

$$s + 1 = 2r$$

Substitute 6 for s: $6 + 1 = 2r$

Combine like terms: $7 = 2r$

Divide by 2: $3.5 = r$ (nope)

This doesn't work because r must be an integer. Why didn't it work? Because $2r$ must be even, but if s is even, then $s + 1$ must be odd and cannot equal an even number, so s must always be odd and statement I is true. (Eliminate choice (B).)

Statement II can be disproven with $r = 1$:

$$s + 1 = 2r$$

Substitute 1 for r: $s + 1 = 2(1)$

Subtract 1: $s = 1$ (okay)

Since 1 is an integer, we've proven that r is not necessarily even, so II is false. (Eliminate choices (C) and (E).)

Since we still have 2 choices remaining, we have to check ugly old statement III. Try the values we used before. If $r = 1$ and $s = 1$, then $\dfrac{s}{r} + \dfrac{1}{r} = \dfrac{1}{1} + \dfrac{1}{1} = 2$,

which is an integer. But is it always an integer? Plugging in more examples can't prove that it will ALWAYS be an integer, because we can never test all possible solutions. We can prove it easily with algebra, though. Since $s + 1 = 2r$:

Divide by r: $\dfrac{s + 1}{r} = 2$

Distribute: $\dfrac{s}{r} + \dfrac{1}{r} = 2$

Since 2 is an integer, statement III is necessarily true.

---

14. C Find all the possible products of the values on two chips: $(1)(2) = 2$; $(1)(3) = 3$; $(1)(4) = 4$; $(1)(5) = 5$; $(1)(6) = 6$; $(2)(3) = 6$; $(2)(4) = 8$; $(2)(5) = 10$; $(2)(6) = 12$; $(3)(4) = 12$; $(3)(5) = 15$; $(3)(6) = 18$; $(4)(5) = 20$; $(4)(6) = 24$; $(5)(6) = 30$. There are 15 different combinations of chips. Of these, only the last 2 yield products that are greater than 20. So the probability is 2/15.

---

15. D In this problem, only the signs of the terms matter. By following the rule of the sequence, you should see that the first 6 terms of the sequence are: $+, -, -, +, -, -, \ldots$ The pattern $\{+, -, -\}$ repeats forever. In the first 100 terms, the pattern repeats $100 \div 3 = 33\frac{1}{3}$ times. Because each repetition contains 2 negative numbers, in 33 full repetitions there are $33 \times 2 = 66$ negative numbers. The 100th term is the 1st term of the next pattern, which is positive, so the total number of negative terms is 66.

---

16. B Draw the 5 triangles. The simplest way to solve this problem is to compare the choices 1 pair at a time. For instance, it should be clear just by inspection that $RB > RA$ and $SB > SA$, so we can eliminate A. Similarly, it should be clear that $RB > RC$ and $SB > SC$, so we can eliminate C. Likewise, since $RB > RD$ and $SB > SD$, we can eliminate D. Finally, we compare B with E. Since RB and RE are each a diagonal of one of the square faces, they must be equal. But SB is clearly longer than SE, because SB is the hypotenuse of triangle SEB, while SE is one of the legs.

Section 8

---

1. C If the review suggested that the décor of the restaurant was insipid (tasteless), but that the cuisine came close to *compensating* for it, the review must have been part positive and part negative, that is, *ambivalent*. *indefatigable* = untiring; *banal* = lacking originality; *ambivalent* = characterized by conflicting feelings; *sublime* = supreme, impressive; *piquant* = spicy; *tepid* = lukewarm.

---

2. C The sentence suggests that Dr. Thompson should have characterized the results as unusual, but didn't. *meticulous* = concerned with detail; *belligerent* = prone to fighting; *anomalous* = deviating from the norm; *convergent* = coming together; *warranted* = appropriate to the situation.

---

3. B They would hope that bad news did not predict further bad news. *amalgam* = a combination of diverse elements; *harbinge* = omen; *arbiter* = judge; *talisman* = an object with magical power.

---

4. C To bring slaves *out of bondage* is to *free* or *unfetter* them. *encumber* = burden; *forgo* = relinquish.

---

5. D A writer who can produce both *decorative poetry* and a *keenly analytical mystery novel* is a *versatile* writer, that is, she is able to write in divergent styles. *flamboyant* = ornate; *immutability* = permanence, unchangeability; *austere* = plain; *florid* = ornate; *grandiloquent* = characterized by pompous language.

---

6. B The word *because* indicates that the sentence shows a cause-and-effect relationship. There are several ways to complete this sentence logically, but the only one among the choices is (B), because *multifarious* (widely varied) mechanisms would logically "stymie" (impede) scientists who are trying to investigate them. *efficacious* = capable of producing a desired effect; *bilked* = cheated; *conspicuous* = obvious; *thwarted* = prevented; *hampered* = hindered; *lucid* = clear; *proscribed* = forbidden.

---

7. B If the *cultural assumption that there are many alien civilizations ... stems in no small way from ... the "Drake Equation,"* then this equation has had quite an influence on public opinion.

---

8. E The first two paragraphs discuss how the Drake Equation has led to the belief that there are many alien civilizations in the universe. The third paragraph discusses the author's contrasting view that there is indeed probably much simple life in the universe but very little if any other complex life.

9. B The sentence states that *a planet could go from an abiotic state to a civilization in 100 million years* thereby implying that a *civilization* must, by definition, not be *abiotic*. B is the only choice that necessarily cannot apply to a civilization.

10. A The author states his thesis in lines 38–39: *perhaps life is common, but complex life is not,* and goes on to explain this thesis, stating in lines 61–67 that *research shows that while attaining the stage of animal life is one thing, maintaining that level is quite another ... Complex life is subject to an unending succession of planetary disasters, creating what are known as mass-extinction events.*

11. A The phrase *the evolutionary grade we call animals* refers to the *level* of life form produced by evolution.

12. C Statement (A) is supported in lines 48–50, statement (B) is supported in lines 74–77, statement (D) is supported in lines 38–40, and statement (E) is supported in lines 52–55.

13. C The *sample size of one* refers to the uniqueness of *Earth history* (line 82).

14. A The first quotation in lines 103–105 is described as a *rejoinder,* or an opposing response, to the author's thoughts. The author then responds with his own quotation.

15. C The author says that he does not *conclude that there are no other cats (Rare Cat Hypothesis), only that there are no other cats exactly like Wookie* in order to convey the idea that one should not draw conclusions based on 1 occurrence.

16. B The author says that *life is opportunistic* to summarize the next statement that *the biosphere has taken advantage of the myriad of strange idiosyncrasies that our planet has to offer.*

17. D The passage says that these creatures *might naively assume that these qualities, very different from Earth's, are the only ones that can breed complexity,* that is, that all life evolved the same way.

18. A The author of Passage 1 believes that complex life, once evolved, faces numerous dangers that push it toward extinction. The author would point this fact out in response to the statement in lines 136–137 of Passage 2.

19. D The author of Passage 1 says in line 26, *In my view, life in the form of microbes or their equivalents is very common in the universe, perhaps more common than even Drake and Sagan envisioned.* The author of Passage 2 says in line 143, *My bet is that many other worlds, with their own peculiar characteristics and histories, co-evolve their own biospheres.* Both authors seem to agree that there is a lot of undiscovered life out there in the universe.

Section 9

1. B When you list items in a sentence, the items should have the same grammatical form. If the first item is in the gerund, they should all be in the gerund. Because the sentence says *Eating* an english muffin and *sitting* down, *drink coffee* should instead be *drinking coffee.*

2. D As written the sentence suggests that Mark's *attempt* was pretending to be hurt rather than Mark himself. Answer choice (D) corrects this error.

3. C The verb *are* is the improper tense. It should be *be* as in answer choice (C).

4. C When you list items in a sentence, the items should have the same grammatical form. If the first term is in the noun form, then they all should be in the noun form. Because the sentence says *his temper, impatience, how easily he can be irritated* should instead be *irritability.*

5. B Before she gave the *gracious speech,* she won the match. The verb *winning* should instead be in the *past perfect form, having won.*

6. C The sentence begins by describing something that was the most influential science treatise of the 20th century. The pronoun to follow the comma should describe this treatise. Choice (C) corrects the error in the most logical and concise fashion.

7. B The subject *neither* is singular and therefore *were* should instead be *was.*

8. A This sentence is correct as written.

9. C Because the waves were described to have been *covering* the stores (gerund form), the verb *swept* should also be in the gerund form—*sweeping.*

10. B The problem with this question is that it is not a complete sentence as written. Answer choice (B) corrects that flaw in the most logical fashion.

11. D The problem with this sentence is that it suggests that the father was 7 years old when he took his son to the game. That is not likely. Answer choice (D) best corrects the problem.

12. A This sentence is correct as written.

13. E The pronoun them refers to a plural subject. However, anyone is singular. Answer choice (E) clears up this pronoun-antecedent disagreement in the most concise and logical way.

14. A Although the original phrasing is not the most concise option, it is the only one that logically coordinates the ideas in the sentence.

PRACTICE TEST 12

ANSWER SHEET

Last Name: _____   First Name: _____

Date: _____   Testing Location: _____

Directions for Test

- Remove these answer sheets from the book and use them to record your answers to this test.
- This test will require 3 hours and 20 minutes to complete. Take this test in one sitting.
- The time allotment for each section is written clearly at the beginning of each section. This test contains six 25-minute sections, two 20-minute sections, and one 10-minute section.
- This test is 25 minutes shorter than the actual SAT, which will include a 25-minute "experimental" section that does not count toward your score. That section has been omitted from this test.
- You may take one short break during the test, of no more than 10 minutes in length. You may only work on one section at any given time.
- You must stop ALL work on a section when time is called.
- If you finish a section before the time has elapsed, check your work on that section. You may NOT work on any other section.
- Do not waste time on questions that seem too difficult for you.
- Use the test book for scratchwork, but you will receive credit only for answers that are marked on the answer sheets.
- You will receive one point for every correct answer.
- You will receive no points for an omitted question.
- For each wrong answer on any multiple-choice question, your score will be reduced by ¼ point.
- For each wrong answer on any "numerical grid-in" question, you will receive no deduction.

SECTION 2

1. Ⓐ Ⓑ Ⓒ Ⓓ Ⓔ   11. Ⓐ Ⓑ Ⓒ Ⓓ Ⓔ   21. Ⓐ Ⓑ Ⓒ Ⓓ Ⓔ   31. Ⓐ Ⓑ Ⓒ Ⓓ Ⓔ
2. Ⓐ Ⓑ Ⓒ Ⓓ Ⓔ   12. Ⓐ Ⓑ Ⓒ Ⓓ Ⓔ   22. Ⓐ Ⓑ Ⓒ Ⓓ Ⓔ   32. Ⓐ Ⓑ Ⓒ Ⓓ Ⓔ
3. Ⓐ Ⓑ Ⓒ Ⓓ Ⓔ   13. Ⓐ Ⓑ Ⓒ Ⓓ Ⓔ   23. Ⓐ Ⓑ Ⓒ Ⓓ Ⓔ   33. Ⓐ Ⓑ Ⓒ Ⓓ Ⓔ
4. Ⓐ Ⓑ Ⓒ Ⓓ Ⓔ   14. Ⓐ Ⓑ Ⓒ Ⓓ Ⓔ   24. Ⓐ Ⓑ Ⓒ Ⓓ Ⓔ   34. Ⓐ Ⓑ Ⓒ Ⓓ Ⓔ
5. Ⓐ Ⓑ Ⓒ Ⓓ Ⓔ   15. Ⓐ Ⓑ Ⓒ Ⓓ Ⓔ   25. Ⓐ Ⓑ Ⓒ Ⓓ Ⓔ   35. Ⓐ Ⓑ Ⓒ Ⓓ Ⓔ
6. Ⓐ Ⓑ Ⓒ Ⓓ Ⓔ   16. Ⓐ Ⓑ Ⓒ Ⓓ Ⓔ   26. Ⓐ Ⓑ Ⓒ Ⓓ Ⓔ   36. Ⓐ Ⓑ Ⓒ Ⓓ Ⓔ
7. Ⓐ Ⓑ Ⓒ Ⓓ Ⓔ   17. Ⓐ Ⓑ Ⓒ Ⓓ Ⓔ   27. Ⓐ Ⓑ Ⓒ Ⓓ Ⓔ   37. Ⓐ Ⓑ Ⓒ Ⓓ Ⓔ
8. Ⓐ Ⓑ Ⓒ Ⓓ Ⓔ   18. Ⓐ Ⓑ Ⓒ Ⓓ Ⓔ   28. Ⓐ Ⓑ Ⓒ Ⓓ Ⓔ   38. Ⓐ Ⓑ Ⓒ Ⓓ Ⓔ
9. Ⓐ Ⓑ Ⓒ Ⓓ Ⓔ   19. Ⓐ Ⓑ Ⓒ Ⓓ Ⓔ   29. Ⓐ Ⓑ Ⓒ Ⓓ Ⓔ   39. Ⓐ Ⓑ Ⓒ Ⓓ Ⓔ
10. Ⓐ Ⓑ Ⓒ Ⓓ Ⓔ   20. Ⓐ Ⓑ Ⓒ Ⓓ Ⓔ   30. Ⓐ Ⓑ Ⓒ Ⓓ Ⓔ   40. Ⓐ Ⓑ Ⓒ Ⓓ Ⓔ

SECTION 3

1. Ⓐ Ⓑ Ⓒ Ⓓ Ⓔ   11. Ⓐ Ⓑ Ⓒ Ⓓ Ⓔ   21. Ⓐ Ⓑ Ⓒ Ⓓ Ⓔ   31. Ⓐ Ⓑ Ⓒ Ⓓ Ⓔ
2. Ⓐ Ⓑ Ⓒ Ⓓ Ⓔ   12. Ⓐ Ⓑ Ⓒ Ⓓ Ⓔ   22. Ⓐ Ⓑ Ⓒ Ⓓ Ⓔ   32. Ⓐ Ⓑ Ⓒ Ⓓ Ⓔ
3. Ⓐ Ⓑ Ⓒ Ⓓ Ⓔ   13. Ⓐ Ⓑ Ⓒ Ⓓ Ⓔ   23. Ⓐ Ⓑ Ⓒ Ⓓ Ⓔ   33. Ⓐ Ⓑ Ⓒ Ⓓ Ⓔ
4. Ⓐ Ⓑ Ⓒ Ⓓ Ⓔ   14. Ⓐ Ⓑ Ⓒ Ⓓ Ⓔ   24. Ⓐ Ⓑ Ⓒ Ⓓ Ⓔ   34. Ⓐ Ⓑ Ⓒ Ⓓ Ⓔ
5. Ⓐ Ⓑ Ⓒ Ⓓ Ⓔ   15. Ⓐ Ⓑ Ⓒ Ⓓ Ⓔ   25. Ⓐ Ⓑ Ⓒ Ⓓ Ⓔ   35. Ⓐ Ⓑ Ⓒ Ⓓ Ⓔ
6. Ⓐ Ⓑ Ⓒ Ⓓ Ⓔ   16. Ⓐ Ⓑ Ⓒ Ⓓ Ⓔ   26. Ⓐ Ⓑ Ⓒ Ⓓ Ⓔ   36. Ⓐ Ⓑ Ⓒ Ⓓ Ⓔ
7. Ⓐ Ⓑ Ⓒ Ⓓ Ⓔ   17. Ⓐ Ⓑ Ⓒ Ⓓ Ⓔ   27. Ⓐ Ⓑ Ⓒ Ⓓ Ⓔ   37. Ⓐ Ⓑ Ⓒ Ⓓ Ⓔ
8. Ⓐ Ⓑ Ⓒ Ⓓ Ⓔ   18. Ⓐ Ⓑ Ⓒ Ⓓ Ⓔ   28. Ⓐ Ⓑ Ⓒ Ⓓ Ⓔ   38. Ⓐ Ⓑ Ⓒ Ⓓ Ⓔ
9. Ⓐ Ⓑ Ⓒ Ⓓ Ⓔ   19. Ⓐ Ⓑ Ⓒ Ⓓ Ⓔ   29. Ⓐ Ⓑ Ⓒ Ⓓ Ⓔ   39. Ⓐ Ⓑ Ⓒ Ⓓ Ⓔ
10. Ⓐ Ⓑ Ⓒ Ⓓ Ⓔ   20. Ⓐ Ⓑ Ⓒ Ⓓ Ⓔ   30. Ⓐ Ⓑ Ⓒ Ⓓ Ⓔ   40. Ⓐ Ⓑ Ⓒ Ⓓ Ⓔ

ANSWER SHEET

SECTION 4

1. Ⓐ Ⓑ Ⓒ Ⓓ Ⓔ
2. Ⓐ Ⓑ Ⓒ Ⓓ Ⓔ
3. Ⓐ Ⓑ Ⓒ Ⓓ Ⓔ
4. Ⓐ Ⓑ Ⓒ Ⓓ Ⓔ
5. Ⓐ Ⓑ Ⓒ Ⓓ Ⓔ
6. Ⓐ Ⓑ Ⓒ Ⓓ Ⓔ
7. Ⓐ Ⓑ Ⓒ Ⓓ Ⓔ
8. Ⓐ Ⓑ Ⓒ Ⓓ Ⓔ
9. Ⓐ Ⓑ Ⓒ Ⓓ Ⓔ
10. Ⓐ Ⓑ Ⓒ Ⓓ Ⓔ

11. Ⓐ Ⓑ Ⓒ Ⓓ Ⓔ
12. Ⓐ Ⓑ Ⓒ Ⓓ Ⓔ
13. Ⓐ Ⓑ Ⓒ Ⓓ Ⓔ
14. Ⓐ Ⓑ Ⓒ Ⓓ Ⓔ
15. Ⓐ Ⓑ Ⓒ Ⓓ Ⓔ
16. Ⓐ Ⓑ Ⓒ Ⓓ Ⓔ
17. Ⓐ Ⓑ Ⓒ Ⓓ Ⓔ
18. Ⓐ Ⓑ Ⓒ Ⓓ Ⓔ
19. Ⓐ Ⓑ Ⓒ Ⓓ Ⓔ
20. Ⓐ Ⓑ Ⓒ Ⓓ Ⓔ

21. Ⓐ Ⓑ Ⓒ Ⓓ Ⓔ
22. Ⓐ Ⓑ Ⓒ Ⓓ Ⓔ
23. Ⓐ Ⓑ Ⓒ Ⓓ Ⓔ
24. Ⓐ Ⓑ Ⓒ Ⓓ Ⓔ
25. Ⓐ Ⓑ Ⓒ Ⓓ Ⓔ
26. Ⓐ Ⓑ Ⓒ Ⓓ Ⓔ
27. Ⓐ Ⓑ Ⓒ Ⓓ Ⓔ
28. Ⓐ Ⓑ Ⓒ Ⓓ Ⓔ
29. Ⓐ Ⓑ Ⓒ Ⓓ Ⓔ
30. Ⓐ Ⓑ Ⓒ Ⓓ Ⓔ

31. Ⓐ Ⓑ Ⓒ Ⓓ Ⓔ
32. Ⓐ Ⓑ Ⓒ Ⓓ Ⓔ
33. Ⓐ Ⓑ Ⓒ Ⓓ Ⓔ
34. Ⓐ Ⓑ Ⓒ Ⓓ Ⓔ
35. Ⓐ Ⓑ Ⓒ Ⓓ Ⓔ
36. Ⓐ Ⓑ Ⓒ Ⓓ Ⓔ
37. Ⓐ Ⓑ Ⓒ Ⓓ Ⓔ
38. Ⓐ Ⓑ Ⓒ Ⓓ Ⓔ
39. Ⓐ Ⓑ Ⓒ Ⓓ Ⓔ
40. Ⓐ Ⓑ Ⓒ Ⓓ Ⓔ

SECTION 5

1. Ⓐ Ⓑ Ⓒ Ⓓ Ⓔ
2. Ⓐ Ⓑ Ⓒ Ⓓ Ⓔ
3. Ⓐ Ⓑ Ⓒ Ⓓ Ⓔ
4. Ⓐ Ⓑ Ⓒ Ⓓ Ⓔ

5. Ⓐ Ⓑ Ⓒ Ⓓ Ⓔ
6. Ⓐ Ⓑ Ⓒ Ⓓ Ⓔ
7. Ⓐ Ⓑ Ⓒ Ⓓ Ⓔ
8. Ⓐ Ⓑ Ⓒ Ⓓ Ⓔ

9. 10. 11. 12. 13.

14. 15. 16. 17. 18.

ANSWER SHEET

SECTION 6

1. Ⓐ Ⓑ Ⓒ Ⓓ Ⓔ   11. Ⓐ Ⓑ Ⓒ Ⓓ Ⓔ   21. Ⓐ Ⓑ Ⓒ Ⓓ Ⓔ   31. Ⓐ Ⓑ Ⓒ Ⓓ Ⓔ
2. Ⓐ Ⓑ Ⓒ Ⓓ Ⓔ   12. Ⓐ Ⓑ Ⓒ Ⓓ Ⓔ   22. Ⓐ Ⓑ Ⓒ Ⓓ Ⓔ   32. Ⓐ Ⓑ Ⓒ Ⓓ Ⓔ
3. Ⓐ Ⓑ Ⓒ Ⓓ Ⓔ   13. Ⓐ Ⓑ Ⓒ Ⓓ Ⓔ   23. Ⓐ Ⓑ Ⓒ Ⓓ Ⓔ   33. Ⓐ Ⓑ Ⓒ Ⓓ Ⓔ
4. Ⓐ Ⓑ Ⓒ Ⓓ Ⓔ   14. Ⓐ Ⓑ Ⓒ Ⓓ Ⓔ   24. Ⓐ Ⓑ Ⓒ Ⓓ Ⓔ   34. Ⓐ Ⓑ Ⓒ Ⓓ Ⓔ
5. Ⓐ Ⓑ Ⓒ Ⓓ Ⓔ   15. Ⓐ Ⓑ Ⓒ Ⓓ Ⓔ   25. Ⓐ Ⓑ Ⓒ Ⓓ Ⓔ   35. Ⓐ Ⓑ Ⓒ Ⓓ Ⓔ
6. Ⓐ Ⓑ Ⓒ Ⓓ Ⓔ   16. Ⓐ Ⓑ Ⓒ Ⓓ Ⓔ   26. Ⓐ Ⓑ Ⓒ Ⓓ Ⓔ   36. Ⓐ Ⓑ Ⓒ Ⓓ Ⓔ
7. Ⓐ Ⓑ Ⓒ Ⓓ Ⓔ   17. Ⓐ Ⓑ Ⓒ Ⓓ Ⓔ   27. Ⓐ Ⓑ Ⓒ Ⓓ Ⓔ   37. Ⓐ Ⓑ Ⓒ Ⓓ Ⓔ
8. Ⓐ Ⓑ Ⓒ Ⓓ Ⓔ   18. Ⓐ Ⓑ Ⓒ Ⓓ Ⓔ   28. Ⓐ Ⓑ Ⓒ Ⓓ Ⓔ   38. Ⓐ Ⓑ Ⓒ Ⓓ Ⓔ
9. Ⓐ Ⓑ Ⓒ Ⓓ Ⓔ   19. Ⓐ Ⓑ Ⓒ Ⓓ Ⓔ   29. Ⓐ Ⓑ Ⓒ Ⓓ Ⓔ   39. Ⓐ Ⓑ Ⓒ Ⓓ Ⓔ
10. Ⓐ Ⓑ Ⓒ Ⓓ Ⓔ 20. Ⓐ Ⓑ Ⓒ Ⓓ Ⓔ   30. Ⓐ Ⓑ Ⓒ Ⓓ Ⓔ   40. Ⓐ Ⓑ Ⓒ Ⓓ Ⓔ

SECTION 7

1. Ⓐ Ⓑ Ⓒ Ⓓ Ⓔ   11. Ⓐ Ⓑ Ⓒ Ⓓ Ⓔ   21. Ⓐ Ⓑ Ⓒ Ⓓ Ⓔ   31. Ⓐ Ⓑ Ⓒ Ⓓ Ⓔ
2. Ⓐ Ⓑ Ⓒ Ⓓ Ⓔ   12. Ⓐ Ⓑ Ⓒ Ⓓ Ⓔ   22. Ⓐ Ⓑ Ⓒ Ⓓ Ⓔ   32. Ⓐ Ⓑ Ⓒ Ⓓ Ⓔ
3. Ⓐ Ⓑ Ⓒ Ⓓ Ⓔ   13. Ⓐ Ⓑ Ⓒ Ⓓ Ⓔ   23. Ⓐ Ⓑ Ⓒ Ⓓ Ⓔ   33. Ⓐ Ⓑ Ⓒ Ⓓ Ⓔ
4. Ⓐ Ⓑ Ⓒ Ⓓ Ⓔ   14. Ⓐ Ⓑ Ⓒ Ⓓ Ⓔ   24. Ⓐ Ⓑ Ⓒ Ⓓ Ⓔ   34. Ⓐ Ⓑ Ⓒ Ⓓ Ⓔ
5. Ⓐ Ⓑ Ⓒ Ⓓ Ⓔ   15. Ⓐ Ⓑ Ⓒ Ⓓ Ⓔ   25. Ⓐ Ⓑ Ⓒ Ⓓ Ⓔ   35. Ⓐ Ⓑ Ⓒ Ⓓ Ⓔ
6. Ⓐ Ⓑ Ⓒ Ⓓ Ⓔ   16. Ⓐ Ⓑ Ⓒ Ⓓ Ⓔ   26. Ⓐ Ⓑ Ⓒ Ⓓ Ⓔ   36. Ⓐ Ⓑ Ⓒ Ⓓ Ⓔ
7. Ⓐ Ⓑ Ⓒ Ⓓ Ⓔ   17. Ⓐ Ⓑ Ⓒ Ⓓ Ⓔ   27. Ⓐ Ⓑ Ⓒ Ⓓ Ⓔ   37. Ⓐ Ⓑ Ⓒ Ⓓ Ⓔ
8. Ⓐ Ⓑ Ⓒ Ⓓ Ⓔ   18. Ⓐ Ⓑ Ⓒ Ⓓ Ⓔ   28. Ⓐ Ⓑ Ⓒ Ⓓ Ⓔ   38. Ⓐ Ⓑ Ⓒ Ⓓ Ⓔ
9. Ⓐ Ⓑ Ⓒ Ⓓ Ⓔ   19. Ⓐ Ⓑ Ⓒ Ⓓ Ⓔ   29. Ⓐ Ⓑ Ⓒ Ⓓ Ⓔ   39. Ⓐ Ⓑ Ⓒ Ⓓ Ⓔ
10. Ⓐ Ⓑ Ⓒ Ⓓ Ⓔ 20. Ⓐ Ⓑ Ⓒ Ⓓ Ⓔ   30. Ⓐ Ⓑ Ⓒ Ⓓ Ⓔ   40. Ⓐ Ⓑ Ⓒ Ⓓ Ⓔ

SECTION 8

1. Ⓐ Ⓑ Ⓒ Ⓓ Ⓔ   11. Ⓐ Ⓑ Ⓒ Ⓓ Ⓔ   21. Ⓐ Ⓑ Ⓒ Ⓓ Ⓔ   31. Ⓐ Ⓑ Ⓒ Ⓓ Ⓔ
2. Ⓐ Ⓑ Ⓒ Ⓓ Ⓔ   12. Ⓐ Ⓑ Ⓒ Ⓓ Ⓔ   22. Ⓐ Ⓑ Ⓒ Ⓓ Ⓔ   32. Ⓐ Ⓑ Ⓒ Ⓓ Ⓔ
3. Ⓐ Ⓑ Ⓒ Ⓓ Ⓔ   13. Ⓐ Ⓑ Ⓒ Ⓓ Ⓔ   23. Ⓐ Ⓑ Ⓒ Ⓓ Ⓔ   33. Ⓐ Ⓑ Ⓒ Ⓓ Ⓔ
4. Ⓐ Ⓑ Ⓒ Ⓓ Ⓔ   14. Ⓐ Ⓑ Ⓒ Ⓓ Ⓔ   24. Ⓐ Ⓑ Ⓒ Ⓓ Ⓔ   34. Ⓐ Ⓑ Ⓒ Ⓓ Ⓔ
5. Ⓐ Ⓑ Ⓒ Ⓓ Ⓔ   15. Ⓐ Ⓑ Ⓒ Ⓓ Ⓔ   25. Ⓐ Ⓑ Ⓒ Ⓓ Ⓔ   35. Ⓐ Ⓑ Ⓒ Ⓓ Ⓔ
6. Ⓐ Ⓑ Ⓒ Ⓓ Ⓔ   16. Ⓐ Ⓑ Ⓒ Ⓓ Ⓔ   26. Ⓐ Ⓑ Ⓒ Ⓓ Ⓔ   36. Ⓐ Ⓑ Ⓒ Ⓓ Ⓔ
7. Ⓐ Ⓑ Ⓒ Ⓓ Ⓔ   17. Ⓐ Ⓑ Ⓒ Ⓓ Ⓔ   27. Ⓐ Ⓑ Ⓒ Ⓓ Ⓔ   37. Ⓐ Ⓑ Ⓒ Ⓓ Ⓔ
8. Ⓐ Ⓑ Ⓒ Ⓓ Ⓔ   18. Ⓐ Ⓑ Ⓒ Ⓓ Ⓔ   28. Ⓐ Ⓑ Ⓒ Ⓓ Ⓔ   38. Ⓐ Ⓑ Ⓒ Ⓓ Ⓔ
9. Ⓐ Ⓑ Ⓒ Ⓓ Ⓔ   19. Ⓐ Ⓑ Ⓒ Ⓓ Ⓔ   29. Ⓐ Ⓑ Ⓒ Ⓓ Ⓔ   39. Ⓐ Ⓑ Ⓒ Ⓓ Ⓔ
10. Ⓐ Ⓑ Ⓒ Ⓓ Ⓔ 20. Ⓐ Ⓑ Ⓒ Ⓓ Ⓔ   30. Ⓐ Ⓑ Ⓒ Ⓓ Ⓔ   40. Ⓐ Ⓑ Ⓒ Ⓓ Ⓔ

SECTION 9

1. Ⓐ Ⓑ Ⓒ Ⓓ Ⓔ   11. Ⓐ Ⓑ Ⓒ Ⓓ Ⓔ   21. Ⓐ Ⓑ Ⓒ Ⓓ Ⓔ   31. Ⓐ Ⓑ Ⓒ Ⓓ Ⓔ
2. Ⓐ Ⓑ Ⓒ Ⓓ Ⓔ   12. Ⓐ Ⓑ Ⓒ Ⓓ Ⓔ   22. Ⓐ Ⓑ Ⓒ Ⓓ Ⓔ   32. Ⓐ Ⓑ Ⓒ Ⓓ Ⓔ
3. Ⓐ Ⓑ Ⓒ Ⓓ Ⓔ   13. Ⓐ Ⓑ Ⓒ Ⓓ Ⓔ   23. Ⓐ Ⓑ Ⓒ Ⓓ Ⓔ   33. Ⓐ Ⓑ Ⓒ Ⓓ Ⓔ
4. Ⓐ Ⓑ Ⓒ Ⓓ Ⓔ   14. Ⓐ Ⓑ Ⓒ Ⓓ Ⓔ   24. Ⓐ Ⓑ Ⓒ Ⓓ Ⓔ   34. Ⓐ Ⓑ Ⓒ Ⓓ Ⓔ
5. Ⓐ Ⓑ Ⓒ Ⓓ Ⓔ   15. Ⓐ Ⓑ Ⓒ Ⓓ Ⓔ   25. Ⓐ Ⓑ Ⓒ Ⓓ Ⓔ   35. Ⓐ Ⓑ Ⓒ Ⓓ Ⓔ
6. Ⓐ Ⓑ Ⓒ Ⓓ Ⓔ   16. Ⓐ Ⓑ Ⓒ Ⓓ Ⓔ   26. Ⓐ Ⓑ Ⓒ Ⓓ Ⓔ   36. Ⓐ Ⓑ Ⓒ Ⓓ Ⓔ
7. Ⓐ Ⓑ Ⓒ Ⓓ Ⓔ   17. Ⓐ Ⓑ Ⓒ Ⓓ Ⓔ   27. Ⓐ Ⓑ Ⓒ Ⓓ Ⓔ   37. Ⓐ Ⓑ Ⓒ Ⓓ Ⓔ
8. Ⓐ Ⓑ Ⓒ Ⓓ Ⓔ   18. Ⓐ Ⓑ Ⓒ Ⓓ Ⓔ   28. Ⓐ Ⓑ Ⓒ Ⓓ Ⓔ   38. Ⓐ Ⓑ Ⓒ Ⓓ Ⓔ
9. Ⓐ Ⓑ Ⓒ Ⓓ Ⓔ   19. Ⓐ Ⓑ Ⓒ Ⓓ Ⓔ   29. Ⓐ Ⓑ Ⓒ Ⓓ Ⓔ   39. Ⓐ Ⓑ Ⓒ Ⓓ Ⓔ
10. Ⓐ Ⓑ Ⓒ Ⓓ Ⓔ 20. Ⓐ Ⓑ Ⓒ Ⓓ Ⓔ   30. Ⓐ Ⓑ Ⓒ Ⓓ Ⓔ   40. Ⓐ Ⓑ Ⓒ Ⓓ Ⓔ

Section 1

Time—25 minutes

Directions for Writing the Essay

Plan and write an essay that answers the question below. Do NOT write on another topic. An essay on another topic will receive a score of 0.

Two readers will grade your essay based on how well you develop your point of view, organize and explain your ideas, use specific and relevant examples to support your thesis, and use clear and effective language. How well you write is much more important than how much you write, but to cover the topic adequately you should plan to write several paragraphs.

Your essay must be written on separate lined sheets of paper. Keep your handwriting to a reasonable size. Your essay will be read by people who are not familiar with your handwriting, so write legibly.

You may use this sheet for notes and outlining, but these will not be graded as part of your essay.

Consider carefully the issue discussed in the following passage, then write an essay that answers the question posed in the assignment.

> We like to believe that physical phenomena, animals, people and societies obey predictable rules, but such rules, even when carefully ascertained, have their limits. Every rule has its exceptions.

Assignment: **What is one particularly interesting "exception" to a rule?** Write an essay in which you answer this question and discuss your point of view on this issue. Support your position logically with examples from literature, the arts, history, politics, science and technology, current events, or your experience or observation.

Write your essay on separate sheets of paper.

GO ON TO THE NEXT PAGE ▶▶▶

Section 2

Time — 25 minutes
20 Questions

Directions for Multiple-Choice Questions

In this section, solve each problem, using any available space on the page for scratchwork. Then decide which is the best of the choices given and fill in the corresponding oval on the answer sheet.

- You may use a calculator on any problem. All numbers used are real numbers.
- Figures are drawn as accurately as possible EXCEPT when it is stated that the figure is not drawn to scale.
- All figures lie in a plane unless otherwise indicated.

Reference Information

$A = \pi r^2$
$C = 2\pi r$

$A = \ell w$

$A = \frac{1}{2}bh$

$V = \ell wh$

$V = \pi r^2 h$

$c^2 = a^2 + b^2$

Special Right Triangles

The arc of a circle measures 360°.
Every straight angle measures 180°.
The sum of the measures of the angles in a triangle is 180°.

---

1 A playground with an area of 3,600 square feet is to be divided into 6 different play stations. What is the average (arithmetic mean) area, in square feet, of the 6 stations?

(A) 400
(B) 500
(C) 600
(D) 700
(E) 800

2 If $3a = 15$ and $4b = 10$, what is the value of $\frac{a}{b}$?

(A) $\frac{1}{2}$

(B) $\frac{2}{3}$

(C) $\frac{3}{2}$

(D) 2

(E) $\frac{5}{2}$

3

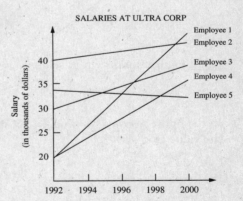

SALARIES AT ULTRA CORP

The graph above shows the salaries of 5 employees at UltraCorp over an 8-year period. Which employee's salary has risen at the fastest rate over this period?

(A) Employee 1
(B) Employee 2
(C) Employee 3
(D) Employee 4
(E) Employee 5

GO ON TO THE NEXT PAGE ▶▶▶

4 One bucket of fried chicken serves either 3 adults or 5 children. If the Memorial Day fair committee wants to have enough chicken to serve 100 children and 60 adults, how many buckets of chicken are needed?

2 ▶

(A)   29
(B)   32
(C)   35
(D)   40
(E)   45

5 $(5x - 3x + 4)(3x + 6x - 2) =$

(A) $9x^2 + 16x - 4$
(B) $18x^2 + 32x - 8$
(C) $18x^2 - 40x + 8$
(D) $72x^2 + 20x - 8$
(E) $72x^2 - 20x + 8$

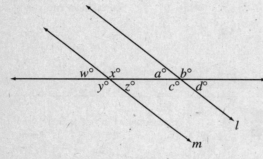

Note: Figure not drawn to scale.

6 In the figure above, $l \parallel m$ and $z = 55$. What is the value of $a + b + c$?

(A)   235
(B)   265
(C)   275
(D)   305
(E)   315

7 If $7\sqrt{x} + 16 = 79$, what is the value of x?

(A)   3
(B)   6
(C)   9
(D)   27
(E)   81

8 Each term in a sequence of numbers, except for the 1st term, is 2 less than the square root of the previous term. If the 3rd term of this sequence is 1, what is the 1st term?

(A)   1
(B)   9
(C)   11
(D)   121
(E)   123

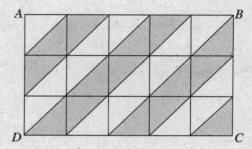

9 In the figure above, rectangle $ABCD$ has an area of 90 and is divided into 15 smaller squares. What is the sum of the areas of the shaded regions?

(A)   39
(B)   42
(C)   45
(D)   48
(E)   51

10 For all x greater than ☆2☆, let ☆x☆ be defined as the sum of the positive integers less than x.

What is the value of ☆16☆ − ☆13☆ ?

(A)   27
(B)   29
(C)   42
(D)   45
(E)   54

11

$$X3Y$$
$$\underline{+5YX}$$
$$1,33X$$

In the correctly worked addition problem above, X and Y represent 2 different digits. What digit does X represent?

(A)   0
(B)   1
(C)   4
(D)   8
(E)   9

12

$$x, y, 3y$$

If the average (arithmetic mean) of the 3 numbers above is $3x$ and $x \neq 0$, what is y in terms of x?

(A) $\dfrac{x}{2}$

(B) $2x$
(C) $3x$
(D) $x+7$
(E) $3x-3$

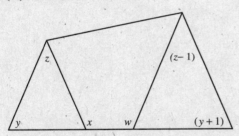

Note: Figure not drawn to scale.

13   In the figure above, what is the value of x in terms of w?

(A) $w-2$
(B) $w-1$
(C) w
(D) $w+1$
(E) $w+2$

14   When r is divided by 10, the remainder is 9. What is the remainder when $r + 2$ is divided by 5?

(A)   0
(B)   1
(C)   3
(D)   4
(E)   14

15   If five distinct lines lie in a plane, then at most how many distinct points can lie on two or more of these lines?

(A)   6
(B)   7
(C)   8
(D)   9
(E)   10

16   A pile of playing cards consists of only kings, jacks, and queens. If the probability of randomly choosing a king is ¼ and the probability of randomly choosing a queen is ²⁄₇, what is the probability of randomly choosing a jack?

(A) $\dfrac{3}{7}$

(B) $\dfrac{13}{28}$

(C) $\dfrac{15}{28}$

(D) $\dfrac{4}{7}$

(E) $\dfrac{9}{14}$

17

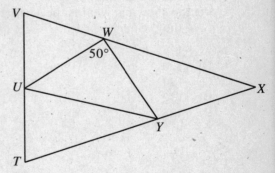

Note: Figure not drawn to scale.

In the figure above, ΔVXT is equilateral and $WU = WY$. If the measure of $\angle VWU$ is twice the measure of $\angle VUW$, what is the measure of $\angle TUY$?

(A)   55°
(B)   60°
(C)   65°
(D)   70°
(E)   75°

GO ON TO THE NEXT PAGE ▶▶▶

18 If m and n are positive numbers, what percent of $m - 4$ is $n + 2$?

(A) $\dfrac{100(n + 2)}{(m - 4)}\%$

(B) $\dfrac{m - 4}{n + 2}(100)\%$

(C) $\dfrac{100n + 2}{(m - 4)}\%$

(D) $\dfrac{m - 4}{100n}\%$

(E) $\dfrac{n + 2}{m - 4}\%$

19 The Greenwich Cinema charges the same price for every ticket it sells. At a matinee showing, the theater sold tickets for all but 6 seats. At the evening showing, the theater sold tickets for every seat, as well as 5 additional standing-room-only tickets at full price. If the theater collected $912 in ticket revenue for the matinee and $1,000 for the evening showing, what is the seating capacity of the theater?

(A) 116
(B) 120
(C) 124
(D) 130
(E) 135

20 The price of a certain stock was d dollars on January 1, 2003. The price decreased by 20% in January, increased by 40% in February, decreased by 25% in March, and increased by 25% in April. In terms of d, what was the price of the stock at the end of April?

(A) $0.80d$
(B) $0.84d$
(C) $1.05d$
(D) $1.12d$
(E) $1.20d$

STOP

You may check your work, on this section only, until time is called.

Section 3

Time—25 minutes
24 Questions

Each of the sentences below is missing one or two portions. Read each sentence, then select the word or words that most logically completes the sentence, taking into account the meaning of the sentence as a whole.

Example:

Rather than accepting the theory unquestioningly, Deborah regarded it with ———.

(A) mirth   (B) sadness   (C) responsibility
(D) ignorance   (E) skepticism

Correct response: (E)

---

1 Jacques Lugard's world-renowned 34th-Street bistro is known best for its ——— main courses, but many go there simply to enjoy the restaurant's ——— desserts.

(A) delectable ... scrumptious
(B) unpalatable ... tantalizing
(C) divine ... bland
(D) debilitating ... uninspired
(E) savory ... mediocre

2 Decades of political ——— have left the region on the brink of war; the slightest —— could cause it to explode into destructive conflict.

(A) dissension ... construct
(B) tension ... communication
(C) harmony ... instigation
(D) strife ... provocation
(E) unanimity ... agitation

3 For over 500 years, the *Mona Lisa*'s smile has been the source of much ——— among art historians, who continue to interpret her enigmatic smile in many different ways.

(A) assent   (B) deliberation
(C) concurrence   (D) remuneration
(E) reconciliation

4 Even after his death, Elvis Presley continues to be one of the most ——— singers of all time; every year hundreds of thousands of fans travel to his hometown to pay tribute to his memory.

(A) satirized   (B) unexalted
(C) revered   (D) despised
(E) shunned

5 Professional poker player Howard Lederer is known as "the professor" because of the —— tactics he uses to outthink his opponents.

(A) entertaining (B) obscure
(C) cerebral   (D) transparent
(E) outlandish

6 Detractors of the new building say that it is ——— aesthetically and furthermore that, far from being the financial ——— that its developers claimed it would be, the project has cost the city dearly in lost revenue.

(A) an eyesore ... adversary
(B) an enhancement ... gratuity
(C) an embellishment ... windfall
(D) a defacement ... calamity
(E) an atrocity ... boon

7 Nineteenth-century author Edgar Allen Poe was acclaimed for his ——— inventiveness; he had an unmatched ability to write ——— tales of cruelty and torture that mesmerized his readers.

(A) tenuous ... spellbinding
(B) grotesque ... enthralling
(C) interminable ... sacrilegious
(D) eclectic ... sadistic
(E) chimerical ... mundane

8 DNA evidence taken from the scene of the crime was used to ——— the defendant; the genomic "fingerprint" taken from the blood sample was not a match for the accused, thus proving his innocence.

(A) perambulate   (B) expedite
(C) incriminate   (D) exculpate
(E) equivocate

GO ON TO THE NEXT PAGE ▶▶▶

The passages below are followed by questions based on their content. Answer each question based on what is stated or implied in the passages or the introductory material preceding them.

3

Questions 9–10 are based on the following passage.

Line Debussy, though less radical harmonically
than Schoenberg, preceded him in starting
the breakdown of the old system. Debussy,
one of the most instinctive musicians who
5   ever lived, was the first composer of our time
who dared to make his ear the sole judge of
what was good harmonically. With Debussy,
analysts found chords that could no longer
be explained according to the old harmony.
10   If one had asked Debussy why he used such
chords, I am sure he would have given the
only possible answer: "I like it that way!" It
was as if one composer finally had
confidence in his ear. I exaggerate a little, for,
15   after all, composers have never had to wait
for theoreticians to tell them what or what
not to do. On the contrary, it has always been
the other way about—theoreticians have
explained the logic of the composer's thought
20   after he has instinctively put it down.

9 It can be inferred from the passage that the "old system" (line 3) most likely involved

(A) a way of developing musical intuition
(B) a rigid method for writing musical harmonies
(C) a means by which musicians could incorporate the ideas of theoreticians into their music
(D) a method of transcribing music that arose spontaneously from a musician's imagination
(E) methods that theoreticians used for distinguishing the harmonies of different composers

10 The passage characterizes Debussy primarily as being

(A) less self-assured than other composers of his time
(B) reverential of traditional musical forms
(C) preoccupied more with musical theory than with practice
(D) harmonically inventive
(E) derisive of musical theoreticians

Questions 11–12 are based on the following passage.

Imagine flying in a hot-air balloon over the
lush, green canopy of a rainforest.
Line Through the clouds and mist you can barely
make out the treetops and a few of the birds
5   flying among them. What lies hidden in the
undergrowth? How many organisms are
there, what do they look like, and how do
they behave? Using a rope and bucket you
blindly drag the rainforest from above hoping
10   to ensnare some of its inhabitants or the
materials that make up its infrastructure. But
alas, with such feeble and limited means you
can learn little about the environment and
life below. For years this is essentially how
15   we have studied the ocean—blindly sampling
the sea with limited and relatively ineffective
methods. Even today, with technology as

GO ON TO THE NEXT PAGE ▶▶▶

First paragraph: *What to Listen for in Music*, Aaron Copland, McGraw-Hill, 1957, pp. 73–74
Second paragraph: *The Oceans*, Ellen J. Prager; McGraw-Hill, 2000, pp. xii–xiii

advanced as it is, study of the ocean remains a difficult and expensive task. Whether
20 through large-scale satellite imagery, small-scale chemical and biological measures, or even the collecting of fossil impressions of ancient sea creatures, all aspects of oceanographic study require some type of
25 observation or sample collection, and herein lies the problem.

11 The passage describes a trip in a hot-air balloon primarily in order to

(A) describe the variety of life forms in the rainforest
(B) make an analogy to ocean exploration
(C) exemplify the advanced equipment that land-based biologists have at their disposal
(D) show the difficulties that most biologists encounter in extracting samples from the rainforest
(E) demonstrate how methods of biological exploration have evolved over time

12 The "small-scale chemical and biological measures" (lines 20–21) are mentioned primarily as examples of

(A) methods that are not as cost-effective or simple as the author would like
(B) challenges for the explorer of the rainforest
(C) technologies that hold great promise for revealing the nature of oceanic life
(D) techniques that require little or no training to employ
(E) inexpensive means of exploring the deepest parts of the ocean

The passages below are followed by questions based on their content. Answer each question based on what is stated or implied in the passages or the introductory material preceding them.

Questions 13–17 are based on the following passage.

The following is an excerpt from a book about the history of primitive art.

Pictures from the earliest artistic periods are the traces of a primal concept of the
Line world. In spite of the thematic treatment of real creatures we can still recognize,
5 paintings of animals or men from the early Stone Age are charged with magical strength, exaggerated and concentrated as they are into forms of existential experience. They fulfilled still other functions beyond the mere
10 representation of the visible.

The degree of naïveté in archaic primitive art varies. A certain naïveté is always present when observation of nature is not overlaid with rational thought. Art first had to
15 discover the world and to invent ways of making it perceivable. Along with visible things, invisible forces too were given form and substance and began to make their appearance. And as they achieved form they
20 took on permanence.

The early hunters attempted to influence the chance fortunes of the hunt through magical practices. The power of magic was as real to them as the power of the stone ax they
25 had invented. Art ensnared the form of the animal. Whenever the figure of woman appears it is a sign of fertility; representations of men are rarer, and when they occur they show him in his role as
30 hunter. Man does not yet look beyond the borders of existence that mark his practical life. Magic precedes the fall of man into knowledge.

It must have meant a considerable
35 revolution in prehistoric times when man discovered that he did not have to live solely from hunting, that not only the animals but indeed all of nature round about him was full of life. Stars and seasons take their rhythms

40   from unknown forces; a mysterious power
      functioning beyond human understanding,
      propitious or forbidding, helpful or
      threatening; forces of ancestors, spirits, and
      demons, and forces of the departed and the
45   coming gods.
          With the transition from the early to the
      late Stone Age there appears the first stylistic
      change in art. The original naturalism based
      on observation and experience gives way to a
50   geometrically stylized world of forms
      discoverable only through thought and
      speculation.
          Prehistoric man, leaving behind him the
      life of the hunter and gatherer, invents
55   abbreviations and pictographic signs which
      are no longer pictures proper but rather
      thought models, reflections of his more
      settled existence as a beginning herdsman
      and farmer.
60   Following the late Stone Age, the art of
      the Bronze Age—which in Asia dates from
      the middle of the third millennium B.C. and
      which began in Europe around 2100 B.C.—
      contains, as does the art of the Iron Age as
65   well, elements of naïveté and inventive
      immediacy side by side with highly
      developed, formalized compositions. The
      bronze sculptures of the Celts and the
      Illyrians are ample witnesses to them. With
70   the substitution of conceptual rationalization
      for more primitive, mythical explanations of
      the world, a kind of art arises in which
      objective criteria of reality and the natural
      laws of optics come into play. The simplicity
75   and vividness of the naïve become more rare.
          The art of the period of the catacombs was
      informed with the naturalistic naïveté of late
      antiquity. In medieval Christian art, which
      was averse to any spatial illusions, a "moral"
80   perspective dominated; all action was pressed
      onto the holy, two-dimensional surface.
          While the primitive and instinctual
      accompanies the course of art until
      the Renaissance, it recedes in the face of the
85   humanistic concept of the world and the
      discovery of linear and aerial perspective.
      High art forsakes the realm of instinct in
      exchange for the province of reason.
          But parallel with it, in folk art and among
90   so-called primitive peoples, naïve
      representation lives on.

13 The first paragraph suggests that the "primal
concept of the world" (lines 2–3) involved

(A)   a belief that art was more important
      even than hunting
(B)   a need to preserve a record of events
      for the future
(C)   a focus on the realistic depiction of
      animals
(D)   a sense that paintings can have
      powers beyond what can be seen
(E)   a desire to communicate with animals

14 In line 6, the word "charged" most nearly
means

(A)   exchanged   (B)   approached violently
(C)   accused   (D)   trampled
(E)   filled

15 The "stylistic change" (lines 47–48) is a transition from

(A)   representations of real things to rep-
      resentations of ideas
(B)   magical applications of art to repre-
      sentations of hunting scenes
(C)   depictions of gods to depictions of
      herdsmen
(D)   art used to depict the natural environ-
      ment to art used for magical rituals
(E)   a focus on the theme of hunting to a
      focus on the theme of fertility

16 The "bronze sculptures of the Celts and the
Illyrians" (lines 67–68) are mentioned primarily as examples of

(A)   a new appreciation of three-dimen-
      sional art
(B)   art with both primitive and formal
      characteristics
(C)   a revival of the art of the Stone Age
(D)   illustrations of the herding life
(E)   art with moralistic themes

17 The passage indicates that, unlike the "art of
the period of the catacombs" (line 76),
Renaissance art is characterized by

(A)   an appreciation of three-dimensional
      forms
(B)   an emphasis on religious themes
(C)   representations of magical creatures
(D)   a primitive view of the world
(E)   a focus on the realm of instinct

Questions 18–24 are based on the following passage.

The following passage, from a modern textbook on anthropology, discusses a debate among biologists and anthropologists about how humans evolved.

Line   Does evolution occur gradually or in
"punctuated equilibria"? Charles Darwin, a
gradualist, maintained that life forms arise
from others in a gradual and orderly fashion.
5 Small modifications that accumulate over the
generations add up to major changes after
millions of years. Gradualists cite
intermediate fossils as evidence for their
position, contending that there would be
10 even more transitional forms if it weren't for
gaps in the fossil record.

    The advocates of the punctuated
equilibrium model believe that long periods
of equilibrium, during which species change
15 little, are interrupted (punctuated) by sudden
changes—evolutionary leaps. One reason for
such jumps in the fossil record may be
extinction followed by invasion by a closely
related species. For example, a sea species
20 may die out when a shallow body of water
dries up, while a closely related species will
survive in deeper waters. Then, later, when
the sea reinvades the first locale, the
protected species will extend its range to the
25 first area. Another possibility is that when
barriers are removed, a group may replace,
rather than succeed, a related one because it
has a trait that makes it adaptively superior
in the environment they now share.
30   When a major environmental change occurs
suddenly, one possibility is for the pace of
evolution to increase. Another possibility is
extinction. The earth has witnessed several
mass extinctions—worldwide ecosystem
35 catastrophes that affect multiple species. The
biggest one divided the era of "ancient life"
(the Paleozoic) from the era of "middle life"
(the Mesozoic). This mass extinction
occurred 245 million years ago, when
40 4.5 million of the earth's estimated 5 million
species (mostly invertebrates) were wiped
out. The second biggest extinction, which
occurred 65 million years ago, destroyed the
dinosaurs and many other Mesozoic species.
45 One explanation for the extinction of the
dinosaurs is that a massive, long-lasting
cloud of gas and dust arose from the impact
of a huge meteorite. The cloud blocked solar
radiation and therefore photosynthesis,
50 ultimately destroying most plants and the
chain of animals that fed on them.

    The hominid fossil record exemplifies
both gradual and rapid change, confirming
that evolution can be faster or slower
55 depending on the rate of environmental
change, the speed with which geographic
barriers rise or fall, and the value of the
group's adaptive response. Australopithecine
teeth and skulls show some gradual
60 transitions. For example, some of the fossils
that are intermediate between
Australopithecus and early *Homo* combine a
larger brain (characteristic of *Homo*) with
huge back teeth and supportive structures
65 (characteristic of the australopithecines).
However, there is no doubt that the pace of
hominid evolution sped up around 18 million
years ago. This spurt resulted in the
emergence (in just 200,000 years) of *Homo*
70 *erectus*. This was followed by a long period of
relative stability. The probable key to the
rapid emergence of *Homo erectus* was a
dramatic change in adaptive strategy: greater
reliance on hunting through improved tools
75 and other cultural means of adaptation. The
new economy, tools, and phenotype arose
and spread rapidly, then remained fairly
stable for about 1 million years.

18   The passage suggests that the existence
of "transitional forms" (line 10) would
demonstrate

(A)   how some species have come to dominate others
(B)   how life first arose on earth
(C)   the gradual nature of evolution
(D)   the divisions in the scientific community over the manner in which evolution occurs
(E)   how barriers arise between species

GO ON TO THE NEXT PAGE ▶▶▶

Anthropology: *The Exploration of Human Diversity*, Conrad Phillip Kottak, McGraw-Hill, 1997, p. 161

19 The example of the two "sea species" (line 19) described in the second paragraph is intended to demonstrate

(A) the differences between the demands of an aquatic environment and the demands of a terrestrial environment
(B) how the fossil record can misrepresent the history of a species
(C) the manner in which one species gradually evolves into a more advanced one
(D) a current theory of how mass extinctions occur
(E) how punctuated evolution can occur

20 According to the passage, the dinosaurs most likely became extinct because

(A) they were struck by a large meteorite
(B) their food supply was eliminated
(C) a more dominant species invaded their environment and destroyed them
(D) the earth's temperature increased dramatically after the impact of a meteorite
(E) a sudden ice age destroyed their environment

21 In line 64, the word "supportive" most nearly means

(A) providing evidence
(B) secondary
(C) emotionally sustaining
(D) weight-bearing
(E) scientific

22 According to the passage, the early Mesozoic era differed from the late Paleozoic era chiefly in that the early Mesozoic era

(A) was no longer dominated by the dinosaurs
(B) was characterized by the rise of *Homo erectus*
(C) was characterized by a greater diversity of life than that in the late Paleozoic era
(D) was far colder than the late Paleozoic era
(E) contained far fewer species than the late Paleozoic era did

23 According to the passage, "the pace of hominid evolution sped up around 18 million years ago" (lines 66–68) most likely because

(A) *Australopithecus* developed a larger brain
(B) *Homo erectus* developed better means of hunting and social interaction
(C) *Homo erectus* invaded and took over the environment of *Australopithecus*
(D) *Australopithecus* developed large teeth, which enabled it to eat a wider variety of foods
(E) a natural catastrophe, perhaps a meteor, destroyed many species that were competing with the hominids

24 Given the information in the passage as a whole, how would the author most likely answer the opening question of the passage?

(A) The gaps in the fossil record indicate clearly that all organisms evolve in punctuated equilibrium.
(B) The example of *Homo erectus* demonstrates that no species can remain stable for very long.
(C) The rapidity with which species evolve depends on many factors, so evolution can occur gradually or in a punctuated manner.
(D) Only occasional mass extinctions interrupt the gradual evolution of species.
(E) The father of evolution, Charles Darwin, was correct in believing that all species evolve gradually over long periods of time.

STOP

You may check your work, on this section only, until time is called.

Section 4

Time — 25 Minutes
35 Questions

Directions for "Improving Sentences" Questions

Each of the sentences below contains one underlined portion. The portion may contain one or more errors in grammar, usage, construction, precision, diction (choice of words), or idiom. Some of the sentences are correct.

Consider the meaning of the original sentence, and choose the answer that best expresses that meaning. If the original sentence is best, choose (A), because it repeats the original phrasing. Choose the phrasing that creates the clearest, most precise, and most effective sentence.

EXAMPLE:

The children <u>couldn't hardly believe their eyes.</u>
(A) couldn't hardly believe their eyes
(B) would not hardly believe their eyes
(C) could hardly believe their eyes
(D) couldn't nearly believe their eyes
(E) could hardly believe his or her eyes

Example answer: (C)

---

1 Renowned for his skills on the trumpet, Louis Armstrong also <u>thrilling listeners with his remarkable and unique singing voice</u>.

(A) thrilling listeners with his remarkable and unique singing voice
(B) thrilled listeners with his remarkable and unique singing voice
(C) with his remarkable and unique singing voice thrilled listeners
(D) thrilled listeners remarkably with his singing voice that was unique
(E) thrilling listeners, his remarkable and unique singing voice

2 Like children, cats often develop a love for certain <u>toys, creating games and diversions</u> that can occupy them for hours.

(A) toys, creating games and diversions
(B) toys and creating games and diverting
(C) toys and in creating games and diversions
(D) toys; and these create games and diversions
(E) toys, the creation of games and diversions

3 Marcus Garvey argued that assimilation into mainstream culture, far from being a panacea for African Americans, <u>would be a distracting factor from their ultimate goals</u>.

(A) would be a distracting factor from their ultimate goals
(B) would factor to distract them from their ultimate goals
(C) would, for their ultimate goals, be a distraction
(D) distracting them from their ultimate goals
(E) would distract them from their ultimate goals

4 Pretending to be sick to avoid taking her chemistry test, <u>Chandra's attempt failed to convince</u> her parents.

(A) Chandra's attempt failed to convince
(B) Chandra's attempt to convince failed
(C) Chandra attempted to fail to convince
(D) Chandra failed to convince
(E) Chandra failed but attempted to convince

5 <u>Believing his speech to be superior to the other candidates</u>, Walter walked confidently into the assembly hall.

(A) Believing his speech to be superior to the other candidates

(B) Believing his speech superior to the other candidates

(C) Of the belief that his speech was superior to the other candidates

(D) Believing his speech to be superior to those of the other candidates

(E) Of the belief that his speech was superior over the other candidates

6 <u>Undeterred by her parents' opposition</u>, Rachel changed majors during her junior year, convinced that she had found her calling in the study of romantic poetry.

(A) Undeterred by her parents' opposition

(B) Undeterred and opposed by her parents

(C) Undeterred by her parents whose opposition

(D) Her parents' opposition undeterring her

(E) Undeterred to her parents opposition

7 The field commanders quickly realized that they had lost command of their troops, who had become scattered, <u>undisciplined, and most were becoming demoralized</u>.

(A) undisciplined, and most were becoming demoralized

(B) were losing discipline and morale

(C) undisciplined, and demoralized

(D) were undisciplined, and they were demoralized

(E) and had become undisciplined and demoralized

8 Standardized tests, some argue, do not indicate a student's academic skill but <u>rather their ability to memorize and use a set of test-taking tricks</u>.

(A) rather their ability to memorize and use a set of test-taking tricks

(B) instead it tests your ability to memorize and use test-taking tricks

(C) also the ability to memorize and use a set of test-taking tricks

(D) rather the ability to memorize and use a set of test-taking tricks

(E) instead the ability of memorizing and using a set of test-taking tricks

9 Muhammad Ali, known almost as much for his controversies outside the ring as for his glory within <u>it, becoming a great American icon.</u>

(A) it, becoming a great American icon

(B) it, has become a great American icon

(C) it; has thereby become a great American icon

(D) it; he has become a great American icon

(E) it, and so has become a great American icon

10 The brochure describing the camp requested that we <u>are at the registration center</u> promptly at noon.

(A) are at the registration center

(B) should be getting to the registration center

(C) should get at the registration center

(D) would be to the registration center

(E) be at the registration center

11 Without such detailed information about the disaster, the agency could not <u>have allocated the proper resources to distribute</u> the necessary food, medicine, and clothing.

(A) have allocated the proper resources to distribute

(B) allocate the proper resources in order for the distribution of

(C) be allocating the proper resources to distribute

(D) have been allocating the proper resources for the distribution of

(E) allocated the proper resources to distribute

GO ON TO THE NEXT PAGE ▶▶▶

12 After all the children's names were wrote
                        A   B
down, they were allowed to proceed to
                     C
recess, joining the rest of their classmates
               D
outside. No error
          E

13 Because each of the candidates had a very

different position on the matter, the voters
     A   B
were able to select from a very diverse set of
        C
options from which to choose. No error
            D   E

14 The film was a watershed in art history: its
                     A   B
stylistic innovations catalyzed a revolution
                          C
in American movies. No error
     D   E

15 An astute tactician, an experienced player,
        A
and charismatic as a leader, Terrence was
        B
an obvious choice to be the next captain
     C
of the soccer team. No error
     D   E

16 His chronic back pain and strong dislike for
                              A
manual labor were a reason why Thomas
                    B
refused to help the others shovel snow from
     C   D
the driveway. No error
              E

17 Tabitha had a maddening habit of extending
                     A
trips unnecessarily, leading friends on
          B   C
roundabout, circuitous routes. No error
          D   E

18 The subtle oration left Perry confused; he
        A   B
was not confident that he truly understood
                              C
the message eluded to by the speaker.
                 D
No error
  E

19 Still nervous hours after watching the
                     A
horror movie, Annie clutching her sheets
                        B
tighter every time a noise from the street
     C
reached her ear. No error
     D   E

20 Throwing her shoe, stomping on the floor,
                        A
and screaming at the top of her lungs, the

demonstrative girl persisted in arguing her
     B   C
point, leaving her parents at a loss as to how
           D
to subdue her. No error
                E

21 Ariel was <u>dumbfounded</u> when she did not
                    A
get into <u>her favorite college</u>, because her
              B
grade point average was higher than

<u>the rest of her classmates</u> and her
              C
after-school activities were <u>so impressive</u>.
                                          D

<u>No error</u>
    E

22 The <u>emissary for</u> the committee stated that
              A
<u>their</u> position <u>on the matter</u> remained
    B   C
neutral and that no amount of <u>cajolery</u>
                                          D
would cause a shift in either direction.

<u>No error</u>
    E

23 Brian hopes that his training program

<u>will help</u> him <u>to become faster</u> and stronger
    A   B
than <u>both</u> of his chief rivals for the position
        C
of quarterback, each of whom <u>receive</u> more
                                          D
practice time with the varsity team.

<u>No error</u>
    E

24 The magician's skill <u>left</u> the children
                              A
both <u>awestruck and inspired</u>; they all
              B
left the party <u>convinced that</u>, if they
                      C
<u>tried hard enough</u>, they could pull a rabbit
        D
out of any hat. <u>No error</u>
                    E

25 The genre of romance literature, now

<u>primarily associated</u> with love stories,
        A
actually <u>encompass</u> a much broader range
              B
of themes <u>including</u> chivalry, heroism
                  C
<u>and travel</u> to foreign lands. <u>No error</u>
    D   E

26 The settlers <u>experimented</u> for months
                        A
<u>to find</u> the best method <u>to channel</u> water
    B   C
from the river to <u>their</u> fields and homes.
                          D
<u>No error</u>
    E

27 Ms. Parker <u>read</u> the account with <u>so much</u>
                    A   B
emotion and urgency <u>as</u> we could clearly
                              C
envision ourselves <u>embroiled</u> in the battle
                              D
ourselves. <u>No error</u>
                    E

28 Several college coaches came to the

tournament hoping to find <u>perspective</u>
                                      A
players <u>who</u> demonstrated <u>not only</u>
              B   C
strong basketball skills but also the ability

<u>to work</u> as members of a team. <u>No error</u>
    D   E

29 In the school's new camp <u>for the performing</u>
                                          A
<u>arts</u> students choreograph <u>their own</u> dances,
                                        B
develop <u>their acting skills</u>, and <u>will write</u>
                  C   D
and perform their own plays. <u>No error</u>
                                          E

Directions for "Improving Paragraphs" Questions

Below is an early draft of an essay. It requires revision in many areas.

The questions that follow ask you to make improvements in sentence structure, diction, organization, and development. Answering the questions may require you to understand the context of the passage as well as the rules of standard written English.

Questions 30–35 refer to the following passage.

(1) *Few people have had as strong an impact on an industry as the impact that Charlie Chaplin had on the world of film.* (2) *Born into an impoverished London family, Chaplin crossed the Atlantic and became a pioneer in silent comedic movies.* (3) *Charlie's mother suffered from severe mental illness, which forced her to spend time institutionalized.* (4) *Early in his film career, Chaplin developed his signature character, the "Little Tramp," who amused audiences repeatedly with his clever physical comedy and endearing sensitivity.* (5) *Modest yet clearly intelligent, shy yet always at the center of action, the Tramp's embodiment was of the genius of Chaplin's artistry.*

(6) *Being writer, director, and editing his own work, Chaplin faced a daunting challenge with the rise of "talkie" films, which dried up the market for the Tramp.* (7) *His response was to take on the additional role of composer, writing beautiful scores to accompany his work and thus allowing the Tramp to remain speechless.* (8) *Whether it was the mastery of his work or the audience's tendency, during the Great Depression, to identify with his character, Chaplin managed to defy the odds and maintain a tremendous level of popularity and success in the face of technological advancement.*

(9) *A vocal liberal in a time of conservative rule, he became a target for men like Senator Joseph McCarthy and his House Un-American Activities Committee.* (10) *While he managed to avoid being named to McCarthy's Hollywood Ten, a list of blacklisted entertainment industry figures suspected of Communist connections, he drew the ire of J. Edgar Hoover with the messages imbedded within his films.* (11) *The fascination with Chaplin went beyond his artistic genius, however.*

(12) *Chaplin saw the dangers in Hitler's rise to power before most of the world had heard of the dictator.* (13) *He saw industry becoming mechanized and impersonal and believed in a connection between the atomic bomb and murder.* (14) *Outraged at what they viewed as subversive propaganda created by an immoral man, the United States government revoked Chaplin's re-entry visa during a trip to London in 1952.* (15) *Sixty-three years old and tired of fighting against a force unwilling to hear his message, Chaplin agreed to exile rather than to going back to America and facing interrogation and lived the rest of his years in Europe.* (16) *He returned twenty years later to receive an Academy Award for lifetime achievement.*

30 Which of the following is the best revision of the underlined portion of sentence 1 (reproduced below)?

Few people have had as strong an impact on an industry as <u>the impact that Charlie Chaplin had on the world of film</u>.

(A) the impact that Charlie Chaplin had on the world of film

(B) Charlie Chaplin had on the world of film

(C) the impact upon the world of film by Charlie Chaplin

(D) Charlie Chaplin's impact on the world of film

(E) Charlie Chaplin and his impact on the world of film

31 Which sentence contributes least to the unity of the first paragraph?

(A) sentence 1   (B) sentence 2
(C) sentence 3   (D) sentence 4
(E) sentence 5

GO ON TO THE NEXT PAGE ▶▶▶

32 Which of the following is the best version of the underlined portion of sentence 5 (reproduced below)?

Modest yet clearly intelligent, shy yet always at the center of action, the <u>Tramp's embodiment was of the genius of Chaplin's artistry.</u>

(A) (no revision needed)
(B) Tramp was embodied for the genius of Chaplin's artistry
(C) Tramp and his embodiment of the genius of Chaplin's artistry
(D) Tramp embodied the genius of Chaplin's artistry
(E) Tramp's embodiment and the genius of Chaplin's artistry

33 Which of the following is the best version of the underlined portion of sentence 6 (reproduced below)?

<u>Being writer, director, and editing his own work,</u> Chaplin faced a daunting challenge with the rise of "talkie" films, which dried up the market for the Tramp.

(A) (no revision needed)
(B) Writing, directing, and being editor of his own work
(C) Being writer of his own work, directing and editing too
(D) Writing his own work, directing, and editing also
(E) As the writer, director, and editor of his own work

34 What is the most logical way to rearrange the sentences in paragraph 3?

(A) 11, 9, 10   (B) 10, 11, 9
(C) 11, 10, 9   (D) 9, 11, 10
(E) 10, 9, 11

35 In context, which of the following sentences best precedes sentence 12 as an introduction to the 4th paragraph?

(A) But Chaplin did not let his politics overwhelm his art.
(B) Chaplin's films allowed audiences to escape from hard political and economic times.
(C) Chaplin's fame and power came to dominate Hollywood.
(D) These messages addressed political and moral issues both inside and outside of the United States.
(E) Chaplin would never again be the same actor he once was.

You may check your work, on this section only, until time is called.

Section 5

Time—20 minutes
18 Questions

Directions for Multiple-Choice Questions

In this section, solve each problem, using any available space on the page for scratchwork. Then decide which is the best of the choices given and fill in the corresponding oval on your answer sheet.

- You may use a calculator on any problem. All numbers used are real numbers.
- Figures are drawn as accurately as possible EXCEPT when it is stated that the figure is not drawn to scale.
- All figures lie in a plane unless otherwise indicated.

5

Reference Information

$A = \pi r^2$
$C = 2\pi r$

$A = \ell w$

$A = \frac{1}{2}bh$

$V = \ell wh$

$V = \pi r^2 h$

$c^2 = a^2 + b^2$

Special Right Triangles

The arc of a circle measures 360°.
Every straight angle measures 180°.
The sum of the measures of the angles in a triangle is 180°.

---

1 Eric earns a 5% commission on each $200 stereo that he sells. How many stereos must he sells to earn $100?

(A) 5
(B) 10
(C) 15
(D) 20
(E) 25

2

Jane's Discount Music Superstore
Holiday Sales

	CDs	DVDs	Total
New		4,500	7,500
Used			
Total	7,000		14,000

Jane's Discount Music Superstore sells both new and used CDs and DVDs. On the basis of the information listed above, how many used DVDs were sold during the holiday season?

(A) 2,500
(B) 3,000
(C) 4,000
(D) 6,500
(E) 7,000

GO ON TO THE NEXT PAGE ▶▶▶

3 One bag of potatoes of a certain brand weighs 40 ounces. Five pounds of these potatoes cost $4.00. If Larry has exactly $20.00 to spend on potatoes, what is the maximum number of bags he can buy? (1 pound = 16 ounces)

(A) 7
(B) 8
(C) 9
(D) 10
(E) 11

4

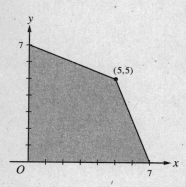

What is the area of the shaded region in the figure above?

(A) 15
(B) 20
(C) 25
(D) 30
(E) 35

5 The rectangular solid above is constructed of 12 cubes that each have a volume of 8 cubic inches. What is the surface area of the solid?

(A) 32
(B) 48
(C) 96
(D) 128
(E) 144

6 Set M consists of the consecutive integers from −15 to y, inclusive. If the sum of all of the integers in set M is 70, how many numbers are in the set?

(A) 33
(B) 34
(C) 35
(D) 36
(E) 37

7 In a round robin tennis tournament involving 7 players, each player will play every other player twice. How many total matches will be played in the tournament?

(A) 21
(B) 28
(C) 42
(D) 48
(E) 56

8

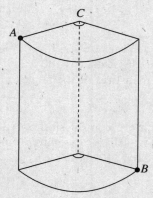

The figure above shows a right prism, the base of which is a quarter of a circle with center C. If the area of each base of the prism is 12.5π and the volume of the solid is 300π, what is the distance from point A to point B?

(A) 24
(B) 26
(C) 28
(D) 30
(E) 32

Directions for Student-Produced Response Questions

Each of the questions in this section requires you to solve the problem and enter your answer in a grid, as shown below.

- If your answer is ⅔ or .666..., you must enter **the most accurate value the grid can accommodate**, but you may do this in one of four ways.

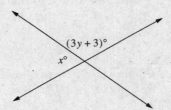

- In the example above, gridding a response of 0.67 or 0.66 is **incorrect** because it is less accurate than those above.
- The scoring machine cannot read what is written in the top row of boxes. You **MUST** fill in the numerical grid accurately to get credit for answering any question correctly. You should write your answer in the top row of boxes only to aid your gridding.
- Do **not** grid in a mixed fraction like $3\frac{1}{2}$ as $\boxed{3\ \ 1\ /\ 2}$ because it will be interpreted as $\frac{31}{2}$. Instead, convert it to an improper fraction like ½ or a decimal like 3.5 before gridding.
- None of the answers will be negative, because there is no negative sign in the grid.
- Some of the questions may have more than one correct answer. You must grid only one of the correct answers.
- You may use a calculator on any of these problems.
- All numbers in these problems are real numbers.
- Figures are drawn as accurately as possible EXCEPT when it is stated that the figure is not drawn to scale.
- All figures lie in a plane unless otherwise indicated.

9

In the figure above, if $x = y + 1$, what is the value of $3y + 3$?

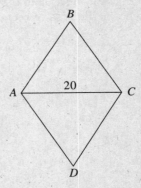

Note: Figure not drawn to scale.

10 In the figure above, $AB = BC = CD = AD$ and quadrilateral $ABCD$ has an area of 480 square inches. What is the perimeter, in inches, of quadrilateral $ABCD$?

GO ON TO THE NEXT PAGE ▶▶▶

11

$$f(x) = 7x + 2$$

$$g(x) = x^2 - 5$$

Given the functions above, what is the value of $f(g(3))$?

12 How much less than x is $\dfrac{6x - 9}{5} - \dfrac{x + 6}{5}$?

13 If a and b are positive integers, $a + b < 20$, and the product ab is an even number, what is the largest possible value of a?

U	V
W	X
Y	Z

Note: Figure not drawn to scale.

14 In the figure above, a large rectangle is divided into 6 smaller rectangles that each have integer lengths and widths. The areas of rectangles U, V, and W are 18, 21, and 12, respectively. If the area of the entire figure is 117, what is the area of rectangle Z?

15 An elementary school class of 55 students is planning a field trip to a nearby aquarium. The price of admission is $15 per person. However, for groups of 60 or more people, the price is reduced to $13 per person. How much money would the class save by buying 60 tickets at the discounted price and using only 55 of them, instead of buying 55 individual tickets?

16 Points W, X, Y, and Z lie on a line in that order. If $WY = 15$, X is the midpoint of $\overline{WY}$ and $YZ = 2WX$, what is the length of $\overline{XZ}$?

17 For all numbers r and s, let $r \square s$ be defined by $r \square s = \dfrac{rs^2}{r - s}$. If $3 \square 2 = x$, what is the value of $x \square 3$?

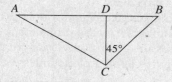

Note: Figure not drawn to scale.

18 In $\triangle ABC$ above, $\overline{DC}$ is perpendicular to $\overline{AB}$, $BC = 5\sqrt{2}$, and $AD = 2DB$. What is the area of $\triangle ABC$?

STOP

You may check your work, on this section only, until time is called.

Section 6

Time—25 minutes
24 Questions

Each of the sentences below is missing one or two portions. Read each sentence, then select the word or words that most logically complete the sentence, taking into account the meaning of the sentence as a whole.

Example:

Rather than accepting the theory unquestioningly, Deborah regarded it with ———.

(A) mirth   (B) sadness   (C) responsibility
(D) ignorance   (E) skepticism

Correct response: (E)

---

1 The knee-jerk reflex is nearly ——— because it produces an immediate muscular response without sending information to the brain.

(A) transient   (B) instantaneous
(C) stagnant   (D) revitalized
(E) consecutive

2 Although starved and emaciated, the 2 stray cats nevertheless summoned the energy to fight ——— for the scraps of food.

(A) humanely   (B) vigilantly
(C) fluently   (D) ferociously
(E) dispassionately

3 Jennifer's ——— demeanor irritated her peers, who hated listening to her supercilious and pretentious remarks.

(A) reticent   (B) belligerent
(C) lofty   (D) self-effacing
(E) discomfited

4 The art of the sushi master takes years to grasp; only after years of ——— will a chef in training have the ——— to create his or her own work.

(A) apprenticeship ... autonomy
(B) tutelage ... ineptitude
(C) dormancy ... sovereignty
(D) cultivation ... boorishness
(E) quiescence ... authority

5 The journalist had been called ——— by her editors because of her ability to get news stories before anyone else, but she later admitted that she had received early information from privileged sources, rather than through ———, as many thought.

(A) prophetic ... prescience
(B) premeditated ... predilection
(C) dismissive ... omniscience
(D) preeminent ... reluctance
(E) insolvent ... foresight

6

GO ON TO THE NEXT PAGE ▶▶▶

The passages below are followed by questions based on their content. Answer each question based on what is stated or implied in the passages or the introductory material preceding them.

Questions 6–9 are based on the following passages.

Passage 1

Line   The very differentness of the medieval
        universe from our own invites our study of it,
        for we cannot fully appreciate the world we
        live in until we contrast it with a different
        weltanschauung, or "world picture," and the
5   older cosmology is indeed very unlike our
        own. For example, C. S. Lewis has pointed
        out that where our universe is thought to be
        dark, the other one was presumed to be
        illuminated; and while Pascal could be
10   disturbed by the silence of the vast spaces
        between the stars, the universe was formerly
        thought to produce the "music of the
        spheres" that only the wise man could hear.
        Furthermore, the often-heard charge that the
15   earth-centered universe of former times was
        the product of man's sense of self-importance
        is questionable, for we may observe in a
        medieval poet and philosopher like Dante
        that although the spheres are first described
20   as surrounding the earth, they are then more
        properly seen in an inverted order surrounding
        God, so that God, not man, is at the center.

Passage 2

        The mystical works of Hildegard of Bingen, a
25   12th century German nun and daughter of a
        knight, reveal a great deal about the medieval
        mind. One of the earliest known composers
        of hymns, she also wrote plays and other
        works based on her migraine-inspired
30   visions. She also composed treatises, like
        Physica, that analyzed the physical world
        from a religious perspective. Hildegard's
        science was based on the Aristotelian
        categories of earth, water, air and fire, and on
35   the then-common view of the relationship
        between mankind and nature: "All the

elements served mankind and, sensing that man was alive, they busied themselves in aiding his life in every way."

6 Both passages are primarily concerned with

(A)   describing the discoveries of great medieval scientists
(B)   providing examples of how medieval thinkers perceived the world
(C)   disproving modern assumptions about medieval history
(D)   questioning medieval scientific theories
(E)   showing the influence of religion on everyday life in medieval Europe

7 In Passage 1, the "other one" (line 9) refers to

(A)   the far side of the galaxy
(B)   the earth in contrast with outer space
(C)   the sun
(D)   the medieval universe
(E)   an alternative cosmological theory

8 Pascal is mentioned in the passage primarily as an example of someone

(A)   who could hear the "music of the spheres"
(B)   who was among the first scientists to explore the medieval universe
(C)   whose "world picture" was different from that of medieval times
(D)   whose cosmology is very similar to that of poets like Dante
(E)   who assumed that the universe was illuminated

9 Hildegard's view of the world as described in Passage 2 differs from Dante's view of the world as described in Passage 1 primarily in terms of its

(A)   focus on religion
(B)   assumption that the universe is ordered
(C)   application of scientific methods
(D)   public acceptance
(E)   anthropocentrism

GO ON TO THE NEXT PAGE ▸▸▸

First paragraph: *The Literature of Medieval England,* D. W. Robertson, Jr., McGraw-Hill, 1970, p. 10
Second paragraph: Christopher Black 2005. All Rights reserved.

The passages below are followed by questions based on their content. Answer each question based on what is stated or implied in the passages or the introductory material preceding them.

Questions 10–16 pertain to the following passage.

The following passage was written by a naturalist about his studies of the wildlife in the African plains, particularly Serengeti National Park in Tanzania.

Line   How can so many wild animals manage to
       survive in the Serengeti? Their migrations of
       course tell part of the story. By moving from
       place to place with the changing seasons,
5   they do not overuse and damage the grass in
       any one area. But other, less obvious factors
       also are involved.
              Here on the eastern plains in January, it is
       clear that most of the animals are eating the
10   abundant grass that springs up like a well-
       mown lawn between low clumps of Sodom
       apple and indigo plants. Nearly all of them,
       from 1,500-pound eland bulls to tiny 10-
       pound Thomson's gazelle calves, are grazers,
15   rather than browsers, which feed on shrubs
       or the leaves of trees. Singly or in pairs, long
       lines, or little groups, they move over the
       green pastures, never remaining long in one
       place. Where the grass is all short, as it will
20   be when it has been heavily grazed, all the
       animals apparently eat much the same sort of
       grass. But where the grass is of varied lengths
       and toughness, we can see that each animal
       copes differently with the available fodder.
25   The herds of zebras tend to roam in areas
       separate from the rest of the grazing
       multitude. Unlike all the other grazers on the
       plain, they have teeth in both jaws. This
       enables them to deal with taller, coarser grass
30   than can the other herbivores. All the rest are
       various species of antelope, which nip off the
       grass between their lower incisors and
       toothless upper palates. Thus, the zebras eat
       down the longer grasses to a certain level

35   and then move on.
              Following the zebras come the wildebeests
       and, in better-wooded areas, hartebeests.
       These animals eat the grass down a stage
       further, until it is really short. (They also eat
40   new growth before it has had a chance to
       grow tall.) Then the Thomson's gazelles take
       over. With their tails flicking constantly, they
       nibble at the individual leaves of the tussocks
       and on the tiny plants that grow between
45   them. By the time all of them have finished,
       the plain resembles a closely but rather
       unevenly mown lawn.
              Thus, one species or another of animal
       often predominates over a great expanse of
50   the plain, depending on the height to which
       the grass has grown or has been grazed.
       Finally, when all has been eaten down rather
       short, most of the grazers leave the area
       altogether.
55   Two or three weeks later, when more rain
       has brought on fresh growth, the herds may
       return to feed over the area again. Perhaps
       they move about in response to the intensity
       of local showers, which can vary a good deal
60   over a distance of only a mile or two. In any
       case, the result of their returning again and
       again to the same areas is to keep the grass
       green and short, just as the repeated mowing
       of a lawn in summer does.
65   If, as a result of badly drawn park
       boundaries or some other cause, the migrant
       herds of Serengeti were confined to either the
       western woodlands or the eastern short-grass
       plains, they would be forced to return to the
70   same areas too often and would eventually so
       weaken the grass that it would die out. But as
       they eat it down, they move away and the
       grass recovers.

6

GO ON TO THE NEXT PAGE ▶▶▶

Excerpted from *The Life of the African Plains*, Leslie Brown, McGraw-Hill, 1972, pp. 69–71.

10   As a whole, this passage is primarily concerned with

(A) criticizing human intervention in a natural habitat
(B) describing the life cycle of particular plants
(C) suggesting a way to avert a natural disaster
(D) showing how to distinguish grazers from browsers
(E) describing how a particular ecosystem works

11   Lines 22–24 ("Where the grass ... the available fodder") discuss the relationship between

(A) what they eat
(B) the seasons and relative animal populations
(C) plant size and dietary variety
(D) zebras and antelopes
(E) climate and plant health

12   According to the passage, browsers differ from grazers primarily in terms of

(A) what they eat
(B) how quickly they eat
(C) their weight
(D) how they digest their food
(E) the season in which they migrate

13   The passage indicates that the various species of antelope that graze on the Serengeti

(A) feed on shrubs and leaves of trees
(B) lack upper teeth
(C) can easily eat tall and coarse grass
(D) usually graze with zebras
(E) tend to consume all of the vegetation in an area before moving on

14   The passage suggests that the sequence of grazers described in the 3rd and 4th paragraphs—zebras followed by wildebeests followed by Thomson's gazelles—is generally maintained UNLESS

(A) the grazers arrive at a new pasture
(B) the grass is of various lengths and textures
(C) there are browsers among them
(D) fresh rains have fallen
(E) all of the available grass is short

15   According to the passage, rain affects the feeding habits of Serengeti grazers primarily by

(A) flooding and destroying some of the pastures
(B) forcing the browsers to take shelter under trees
(C) rendering the plants edible again
(D) weakening the grass
(E) confining the herds to high plateaus

16   The final paragraph suggests that maintaining the grasslands of the Serengeti requires

(A) freedom of the grazers to move as they wish
(B) frequent rainless periods
(C) frequent removal of dead plants
(D) the restriction of grazers to the woodlands
(E) a separation of grazers and browsers

Questions 17–24 are based on the following passage.

The following is an excerpt from an essay by George Bernard Shaw, written in 1889, on the economic basis of socialism.

Line   All economic analyses begin with the cultivation of the earth. To the mind's eye of the astronomer the earth is a ball spinning in space without ulterior motives. To the bodily
5   eye of the primitive cultivator it is a vast green plain, from which, by sticking a spade into it, wheat and other edible matters can be made to spring. To the eye of the sophisticated city man this vast green plain
10   appears rather as a great gaming table, your chances in the game depending chiefly on the place where you deposit your stakes. To the economist, again, the green plain is a sort of burial place of hidden treasure, where all the
15   forethought and industry of man are set at naught by the caprice of the power which hid the treasure. The wise and patient workman strikes his spade in here, and with heavy toil can discover nothing but a poor quality of

20 barley, some potatoes, and plentiful nettles,
with a few dock leaves to cure his stings. The
foolish spendthrift on the other side of the
hedge, gazing idly at the sand glittering in the
sun, suddenly realizes that the earth is
25 offering him gold—is dancing it before his
listless eyes lest it should escape him.
Another man, searching for some more of
this tempting gold, comes upon a great hoard
of coal, or taps a jet of petroleum. Thus is
30 Man mocked by Earth his stepmother, and
never knows as he tugs at her closed hand
whether it contains diamonds or flints, good
red wheat or a few clayey and blighted
cabbages. Thus too he becomes a gambler,
35 and scoffs at the theorists who prate of
industry and honesty and equality. Yet
against this fate he eternally rebels. For since
in gambling the many must lose in order that
the few may win; since dishonesty is mere
40 shadow-grasping where everyone is
dishonest; and since inequality is bitter to all
except the highest, and miserably lonely for
him, men come greatly to desire that these
capricious gifts of Nature might be
45 intercepted by some agency having the power
and the goodwill to distribute them justly
according to the labor done by each in the
collective search for them. This desire is
Socialism; and, as a means to its fulfillment,
50 Socialists have devised communes,
kingdoms, principalities, churches, manors,
and finally, when all these had succumbed to
the old gambling spirit, the Social
Democratic State, which yet remains to be
55 tried. As against Socialism, the gambling
spirit urges man to allow no rival to come
between his private individual powers and
Stepmother Earth, but rather to secure some
acres of her and take his chance of getting
60 diamonds instead of cabbages. This is private
property or Unsocialism. Our own choice is
shown by our continual aspiration to possess
property, our common hailing of it as sacred,
our setting apart of the word Respectable for
65 those who have attained it, our ascription of
pre-eminent religiousness to commandments
forbidding its violation, and our identification
of law and order among men with its
protection. Therefore is it vital to a living

70 knowledge of our society that Private
Property should be known in every step of its
progress from its source in cupidity to its end
in confusion.

17 Which of the following best summarizes the
main idea of this passage?

(A) Socialism provides the best means
for humanity to manage the capriciousness of nature.
(B) Astronomers, farmers, and economists
have much to learn from each other.
(C) Patient and diligent farmers will
always be rewarded.
(D) Foolish people are often just as lucky
as industrious workers.
(E) All people properly aspire to own
property and earn respectability.

18 The "primitive cultivator" (line 5) is

(A) a supernatural creator
(B) an astronomer
(C) a farmer
(D) a machine
(E) a philosopher

19 According to the passage, the perspective of
the "astronomer" (line 3) differs primarily
from the perspective of the "foolish spendthrift" (line 22) in that the astronomer views
the earth as

(A) generous, while the spendthrift views
the earth as stingy
(B) a beautiful gem, while the spendthrift
views the earth as a dull, sandy expanse
(C) dangerously capricious, while the
spendthrift views the earth as a
source of unlimited riches
(D) lacking regard for humankind, while
the spendthrift views the earth as
generous
(E) moving in an orderly fashion, while
the spendthrift views the earth's
movements as dangerously random

6

GO ON TO THE NEXT PAGE ▶▶▶

Shaw, George Bernard and H. G. Wilshire. Various authors. See Contents. *Fabian Essays in Socialism*. New York: Humboldt Publishing
Co., ed. George Bernard Shaw, H. G. Wilshire, and W. D. P. Bliss, 1891. [Online] available from http://www.econlib.org/library/

20 The "closed hand" in line 31 refers to

(A) the strength of the farmer
(B) the tendency of the earth to hide its treasures
(C) the abundance of resources that spring from the earth
(D) the laziness of the foolish spendthrift
(E) the fact that the earth is inanimate and lacking will

21 The author mentions "industry and honesty and equality" (line 36) in order to make the point that

(A) some moral habits are not as valuable as many claim
(B) fate tends to favor those who are virtuous
(C) too many people disdain ethical behavior
(D) the natural order reflects a moral order
(E) hard work and morality are their own reward

22 The "fate" mentioned in line 37 is the fate of

(A) the hard-working farmer
(B) the theorist who preaches honesty and equality
(C) the gambler
(D) the owner of private property
(E) the socialist

23 The author qualifies his view of the "Social Democratic State" by indicating that it

(A) appeals to the gambling instinct
(B) will discourage workers from being industrious
(C) places a high value on selfishness
(D) encourages people to be wasteful
(E) has not yet been attempted

24 The sentence "Our own choice ... its protection" (lines 61–69) suggests that most people of the author's era

(A) are deeply religious
(B) are becoming skeptical of the concept of respectability
(C) place a high value on the concept of private property
(D) desire a socialist democratic state
(E) are not as industrious as they believe themselves to be

STOP

You may check your work, on this section only, until time is called.

Section 7

Time — 20 minutes
16 Questions

Directions for Multiple-Choice Questions

In this section, solve each problem, using any available space on the page for scratchwork. Then decide which is the best of the choices given and fill in the corresponding oval on the answer sheet.

- You may use a calculator on any problem. All numbers used are real numbers.
- Figures are drawn as accurately as possible EXCEPT when it is stated that the figure is not drawn to scale.
- All figures lie in a plane unless otherwise indicated.

Reference Information

$A = \pi r^2$ $A = \ell w$
$C = 2\pi r$ $A = \frac{1}{2}bh$ $V = \ell wh$ $V = \pi r^2 h$ $c^2 = a^2 + b^2$ Special Right Triangles

The number of degrees of arc in a circle is 360°.
The measure in degress of a straight angle is 180°.
The sum of the measures of the angles in a triangle is 180°.

---

1 If $3x + 5x + 8x = 32$, what is the value of x?

(A) 1
(B) 2
(C) 3
(D) 4
(E) 5

2 If $\left(\dfrac{1}{x}\right)\left(\dfrac{x}{3}\right)(6x) = 8$, then $x =$

(A) 1
(B) 2
(C) 3
(D) 4
(E) 5

3 If $5b - 10 \geq 15$, which of the following expresses all of the possible values of b?

(A) $b \geq 5$
(B) $b \geq 1$
(C) $b \geq 9$
(D) $b \leq 1$
(E) $b \leq 5$

4 If $t\%$ of 60 is 30% of 50, what is the value of t?

(A) 12
(B) 15
(C) 25
(D) 30
(E) 35

5 If it takes 40 minutes to write h holiday cards, then in terms of h, how many holiday cards can be written at that rate in 8 hours?

(A) $\dfrac{5}{h}$

(B) $8h$

(C) $12h$

(D) $\dfrac{5}{h}$

(E) $\dfrac{12}{h}$

GO ON TO THE NEXT PAGE ▸▸▸

6

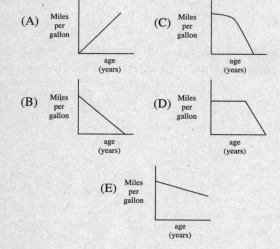

A number line with points labeled A, B, C at approximately −2, −1.5, −0.75, D at 0.5, E at 2, with markings at −2, −1, 0, 1, 2.

Which of the labeled points on the number line above could represent the product −1.5 ×1.25?

(A) A
(B) B
(C) C
(D) D
(E) E

7

If 4 people share 100 baseball cards and each person must receive a different positive whole number of cards, what is the <u>greatest</u> possible number of cards any one person may have?

(A) 28
(B) 29
(C) 94
(D) 95
(E) 97

Fuel Efficiency over Time

Age of car (in years)	1	2	3	4	5
Miles per gallon	36	35	31	26	20

8

Which of the following graphs best represents the data presented in the table above?

(A) Miles per gallon vs age (years) — increasing line

(C) Miles per gallon vs age (years) — flat then decreasing

(B) Miles per gallon vs age (years) — decreasing line

(D) Miles per gallon vs age (years) — flat then decreasing

(E) Miles per gallon vs age (years) — gently decreasing line

9

If the sum of 7 integers is even, at most how many of these integers could be odd?

(A) 3
(B) 4
(C) 5
(D) 6
(E) 7

10

In a particular year, if January 22 is the 4th Wednesday of the month, what is the date of the 4th Monday in January?

(A) January 20
(B) January 21
(C) January 26
(D) January 27
(E) January 28

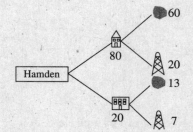

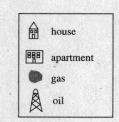

11

The graph above shows the number of teachers in Hamden who live in a house, the number of teachers who live in an apartment and the number of each who use gas or oil heat. Of the teachers who use gas heat, what fraction live in a house?

(A) $\dfrac{60}{100}$

(B) $\dfrac{73}{100}$

(C) $\dfrac{60}{80}$

(D) $\dfrac{60}{73}$

(E) $\dfrac{73}{80}$

GO ON TO THE NEXT PAGE ▶▶▶

12 If $5x + 7y = 18$ and $2x - 4y = 6$, what is the value of $7x + 3y$?

(A) 7
(B) 12
(C) 19
(D) 24
(E) 31

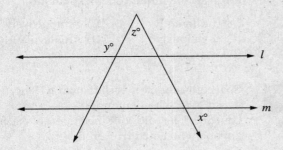

13 In the figure above, if $l \parallel m$, what is the value of x in terms of y and z?

(A) $y - z$
(B) $z - y$
(C) $z + y$
(D) $180 - y - z$
(E) $90 - z - y$

14 Julie Ann commutes to work one morning at an average speed of 40 mph. She returns home along the same route at an average speed of 24 mph. If she spends a total of 2 hours traveling to and from work that day, how many miles is her commute to work?

(A) 24
(B) 30
(C) 32
(D) 34
(E) 40

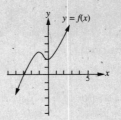

<u>Note:</u> Figure not drawn to scale.

15 Given the graph of $y = f(x)$ above, which of the following represents the graph of $y = f(x - 2) + 4$?

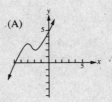

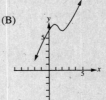

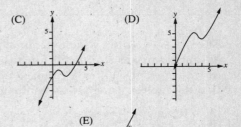

(E)

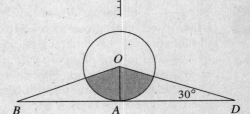

16 Line segment $\overline{BD}$ is tangent to the circle with center O at point A. If $DO = BO = 12$, what is the area of the *unshaded* region of $\triangle BOD$?

(A) $36\sqrt{3} - 12\pi$

(B) $36\sqrt{2} - 12\pi$

(C) $36 - 12\pi$

(D) $72\sqrt{2} - 36\pi$

(E) $72\sqrt{3} - 36\pi$

STOP

You may check your work, on this section only, until time is called.

Section 8

Time—20 minutes
19 Questions

Each of the sentences below is missing one or two portions. Read each sentence, then select the word or words that most logically complete the sentence, taking into account the meaning of the sentence as a whole.

Example:

Rather than accepting the theory unquestioningly, Deborah regarded it with ———.

(A) mirth   (B) sadness
(C) responsibility (D) ignorance
(E) skepticism

Correct response: (E)

8 ➡

1 The ——— with which technology is advancing makes it difficult for businesses to stay current, and as a result, they often find themselves using ——— equipment.

(A) urgency ... progressive
(B) swiftness ... conventional
(C) torpidity ... antiquated
(D) lassitude ... innovative
(E) rapidity ... outdated

2 The ——— of James Joyce's early works, which used clear prose to reveal the inner dimensions of his characters, gave way to ——— and arcane style of writing in such books as *Ulysses* and *Finnegans Wake*, which explored character through neologisms and obscure literary tricks.

(A) inspiration ... an emotional
(B) lucidity ... an opaque
(C) vagueness ... a simple
(D) popularity ... a concise
(E) anachronism ... a derivative

3 Critics of former British Prime Minister Winston Churchill complained that he too often acted ———, choosing his strategies arbitrarily without much explanation.

(A) diligently   (B) impulsively
(C) viciously   (D) malevolently
(E) savagely

4 Sixteenth-century British monarch Henry VIII was a king who demanded ——— from his courtiers; he did not hesitate to execute anyone who acted irreverently.

(A) insolence   (B) impudence
(C) truculence   (D) deference
(E) ignominy

5 In the 1600s, Italian scientist Galileo Galilei was ——— and sentenced to life in prison for being a ——— when, contrary to church teachings, he proposed that the sun, rather than the earth, was the center of the universe.

(A) ostracized ... hermit
(B) venerated ... demagogue
(C) hallowed ... revisionist
(D) denounced ... heretic
(E) reviled ... luminary

6 Known for her ——— and iconoclastic stance on most political matters, the Senator had a hard time securing the votes of the more ——— party members during her presidential campaign.

(A) contentious ... orthodox
(B) controversial ... litigious
(C) disingenuous ... vituperative
(D) dissident ... idolatrous
(E) heretical ... polemical

GO ON TO THE NEXT PAGE ➤➤➤

The passages below are followed by questions based on their content and the relationship between them. Answer the questions on the basis of what is stated or implied in the passages or the introductory material that precedes them.

Questions 7–19 are based on the following passages.

The following passages present 2 viewpoints on the assimilation of ex-slaves into American culture in the late 19th century. Passage 1 is from a speech given by Booker T. Washington, an African American ex-slave and prominent educator, at the Atlanta Exposition in 1895. Passage 2 is an excerpt from a paper entitled The Conservation of Races *written by W. E. B. Du Bois in 1897.*

Passage I

Line A ship lost at sea for many days suddenly
sighted a friendly vessel. From the mast of the
unfortunate vessel was seen a signal, "Water,
water; we die of thirst!" The answer from the
5 friendly vessel at once came back, "Cast
down your bucket where you are." And a
second, third and fourth signal for water
were answered, "Cast down your bucket
where you are." The captain of the distressed
10 vessel, at last heeding the injunction, cast
down his bucket, and it came up full of fresh,
sparkling water from the mouth of the
Amazon River. To those of my race who
depend upon bettering their condition in a
15 foreign land or who underestimate the
importance of cultivating friendly relations
with the Southern white man, who is their
next-door neighbor, I would say: "Cast down
your bucket where you are"— cast it down in
20 making friends in every manly way of the
people of all races by whom we are
surrounded.
        Cast it down in agriculture, in mechanics,
in commerce, in domestic service, and in the
25 professions. And in this connection it is well
to bear, when it comes to business, pure and
simple, it is in the South that the Negro[1] is
given a man's chance in the commercial
world, and in nothing is this Exposition more

30 eloquent than in emphasizing this chance.
Our greatest danger is that in the great leap
from slavery to freedom we may overlook the
fact that the masses of us are to live by the
production of our hands, and fail to keep in
35 mind that we shall prosper in proportion as
we learn to dignify and glorify common labor
and put brains and skill into the common
occupations of life; shall prosper in
proportion as we learn to draw the line
40 between the superficial and the substantial,
the ornamental gew-gaws of life and the
useful. No race can prosper till it learns that
there is as much dignity in tilling a field as in
writing a poem. It is at the bottom of life we
45 must begin, and not at the top. Nor should
we permit our grievances to overshadow our
opportunities.
        To those of the white race who look to the
incoming of those of foreign birth and
50 strange tongue and habits for the prosperity
of the South, were I permitted I would repeat
what I say to my own race, "Cast down your
bucket where you are." Cast it down among
the eight millions of Negroes whose habits
55 you know, whose fidelity and love you have
tested in days when to have proved
treacherous meant the ruin of your firesides.
Cast down your bucket among these people
who have, without strikes and labor wars,
60 tilled your fields, cleared your forests, built
your railroads and cities, and brought forth
treasures from the bowels of the earth, and
helped make possible this magnificent
representation of the progress of the South.
65 Casting down your bucket among my people,
helping and encouraging them as you are
doing on these grounds, and to education of
head, hand and heart, you will find that they
will buy your surplus land, make blossom the
70 waste places in your fields, and run your
factories.

Passage 2

Here, then, is the dilemma, and it is a
puzzling one, I admit. No Negro who has
given earnest thought to the situation of his
75 people in America has failed, at some time in
life, to find himself at these cross-roads; has
failed to ask himself at some time: What,

8

GO ON TO THE NEXT PAGE ▸▸▸

1 African American

after all, am I? Am I an American or am I a Negro? Can I be both? Or is it my duty to
80 cease to be a Negro as soon as possible and be an American? If I strive as a Negro, am I not perpetuating the very cleft that threatens and separates Black and White America? Is not my only possible practical aim the
85 subduction of all that is Negro in me to the American? Does my black blood place upon me any more obligation to assert my nationality than German, or Irish or Italian blood would?
90   It is such incessant self-questioning and the hesitation that arises from it, that is making the present period a time of vacillation and contradiction for the American Negro; combined race action is stifled, race
95 responsibility is shirked, race enterprises languish, and the best blood, the best talent, the best energy of the Negro people cannot be marshalled to do the bidding of the race. They stand back to make room for every
100 rascal and demagogue who chooses to cloak his selfish deviltry under the veil of race pride.
        Is this right? Is it rational? Is it good policy? Have we in America a distinct
105 mission as a race—a distinct sphere of action and an opportunity for race development, or is selfobliteration the highest end to which Negro blood dare aspire?
        If we carefully consider what race
110 prejudice really is, we find it, historically, to be nothing but the friction between different groups of people; it is the difference in aim, in feeling, in ideals of two different races; if, now, this difference exists touching territory,
115 laws, language, or even religion, it is manifest that these people cannot live in the same territory without fatal collision; but if, on the other hand, there is substantial agreement in laws, language and religion; if there is a
120 satisfactory adjustment of economic life, then there is no reason why, in the same country and on the same street, two or three great national ideals might not thrive and develop, that men of different races might not strive
125 together for their race ideals as well, perhaps even better, than in isolation. Here, it seems to me, is the reading of the riddle that puzzles so many of us. We are Americans, not only by birth and by citizenship, but by
130 our political ideals, our language, our religion. Farther than that, our Americanism

does not go. At that point, we are Negroes, members of a vast historic race that from the very dawn of creation has slept, but half
135 awakening in the dark forests of its African fatherland. We are the first fruits of this new nation, the harbinger of that black tomorrow which is yet destined to soften the whiteness of the Teutonic today. We are that people
140 whose subtle sense of song has given America its only American music, its only American fairy tales, its only touch of pathos and humor amid its mad money-getting plutocracy. As such, it is our duty to conserve
145 our physical powers, our intellectual endowments, our spiritual ideals; as a race we must strive by race organization, by race solidarity, by race unity to the realization of that broader humanity which freely
150 recognizes differences in men, but sternly deprecates inequality in their opportunities of development.

7 Passage 1 is primarily concerned with

(A) educating former slave owners about the social plight of African Americans
(B) describing the many cultural contributions of African Americans
(C) presenting an argument for creating schools to educate former slaves
(D) convincing African Americans and white Americans to work together to build a vibrant Southern economy
(E) preventing future labor strikes

8 The author of Passage 1 specifically addresses each of the following audiences EXCEPT

(A) Southern whites who were active in the movement to end slavery
(B) Southern whites who are considering hiring foreign laborers
(C) African Americans who seek to improve their social conditions
(D) Southern whites who have employed African Americans in the past
(E) African Americans who do not consider it necessary to build friendly relationships with Southern whites

9 Passage 1 suggests that, upon hearing the first response from the friendly vessel, the captain of the distressed vessel was

(A) elated
(B) arrogant
(C) incredulous
(D) indifferent
(E) angry

10 In the sentence beginning on line 25, "And in this connection ... emphasizing this chance," the author of Passage 1 suggests that the Exposition at which he is speaking

(A) is overly concerned with superficial things
(B) does not represent the full spectrum of the American population
(C) provides excellent economic opportunities for African Americans
(D) is in distress, much like the ship in his story
(E) will encourage African Americans to seek employment in the North

11 The author of Passage 1 mentions "writing a poem" in line 44 in order to suggest that

(A) manual labor is a worthy activity
(B) poetry can convey emotions more effectively than prose
(C) expanding literacy should be a major focus of the Exposition
(D) African Americans should consider careers in writing
(E) political leaders should be more articulate

12 The questions in lines 77–89 are intended to represent the thoughts of

(A) a former slave owner
(B) one who is doubtful about the morality of slavery
(C) an African American who is seeking a new life in a foreign country
(D) an African American who is concerned with the issue of race identity
(E) any political leader who represents a substantial population of African Americans

13 In line 98, the word "marshalled" most nearly means

(A) arrested
(B) discovered
(C) organized for a purpose
(D) interrogated
(E) determined

14 The sentence that begins on line 98, "They stand back ... the veil of race pride," suggests that those who incessantly question themselves run the risk of

(A) violating the law
(B) alienating friends
(C) losing gainful employment
(D) falling under the influence of disreputable people
(E) squandering their education

15 The phrase "that point" in line 132 refers to the boundary between

(A) the needs of the dominant class of society and the needs of the minority classes
(B) the past and the future
(C) white Americans and African Americans
(D) the qualities that bind all Americans and the qualities that make one race unique
(E) those who support racial discrimination and those who oppose it

16 The term "broader humanity" (line 149) refers to people who

(A) hinder the progress of African Americans
(B) acknowledge the substantial cultural contributions African Americans have made to American culture
(C) believe that all races deserve equal opportunity in society
(D) seek a better life outside of their home countries
(E) have little understanding of cultures beyond their own

GO ON TO THE NEXT PAGE ▶▶▶

17 The 2 passages differ in their characterizations of the contributions of African Americans to American culture in that the 1st passage emphasizes

(A) agricultural contributions, while the 2nd emphasizes scientific innovations

(B) religious heritage, while the 2nd emphasizes political contributions

(C) musical innovations, while the 2nd emphasizes social contributions

(D) contributions of the past, while the 2nd focuses only on potential contributions in the future

(E) economic contributions, while the 2nd emphasizes artistic contributions

18 Unlike the "black tomorrow" (line 137) described in Passage 2, the vision of the future of African Americans described in Passage 1 involves

8

(A) the incorporation of African Americans into the dominant system rather than a change in dominant American cultural values

(B) the restructuring of political institutions rather than maintenance of the status quo

(C) the reeducation of all Americans rather than the submission of one race to another

(D) a strong reliance on the lessons of the past rather than a complete rejection of the past

(E) travel to foreign lands rather than the commitment to stay in America

19 Which of the following best characterizes the tone each author takes toward the dominant American culture of his time?

(A) The author of Passage 1 is sarcastic, while the author of Passage 2 is respectful.

(B) The author of Passage 1 is tongue-in-cheek, while the author of Passage 2 is didactic.

(C) The author of Passage 1 is aggressive, while the author of Passage 2 is nonchalant.

(D) The author of Passage 1 is pontifical, while the author of Passage 2 is colloquial.

(E) The author of Passage 1 is deferential, while the author of Passage 2 is assertive.

STOP

You may check your work, on this section only, until time is called.

Section 9

Time—10 Minutes
14 Questions

Directions for "Improving Sentences" Questions

Each of the sentences below contains one underlined portion. The portion may contain one or more errors in grammar, usage, construction, precision, diction (choice of words), or idiom. Some of the sentences are correct.

Consider the meaning of the original sentence, and choose the answer that best expresses that meaning. If the original sentence is best, choose (A), because it repeats the original phrasing. Choose the phrasing that creates the clearest, most precise and most effective sentence.

EXAMPLE:

The children <u>couldn't hardly believe their eyes</u>.

   (A)   couldn't hardly believe their eyes
   (B)   would not hardly believe their eyes
   (C)   could hardly believe their eyes
   (D)   couldn't nearly believe their eyes
   (E)   could hardly believe his or her eyes

Example answer: (C)

---

1 Neither the strength of the army <u>nor how agile they were</u> was able to compensate for the superior strategy of its enemy.

   (A)   nor how agile they were
   (B)   nor their agility
   (C)   nor its agility
   (D)   or how agile it was
   (E)   or its agility

2 Although Georgia preferred to perform with her fellow band members, <u>they were not used by her</u> when she sang at the opening ceremony.

   (A)   they were not used by her
   (B)   they were not used by she
   (C)   it was her who did not use them
   (D)   she had not used them
   (E)   she did not use them

3 <u>Without rehearsing</u> at all the previous week, the troupe performed the first act of the play in full costume.

   (A)   Without rehearsing
   (B)   Being that they didn't rehearse
   (C)   They didn't rehearse
   (D)   Without having rehearsed
   (E)   They hadn't even rehearsed

4 Not since the beginning of the resistance movement <u>has the major media outlets acknowledged the scope of the opposition</u>.

   (A)   has the major media outlets acknowledged the scope of the opposition
   (B)   have the major media outlets acknowledged the scope of the opposition
   (C)   have the scope of the opposition been acknowledged by the major media outlets
   (D)   has it been acknowledged by the major media outlets what the scope is of the opposition
   (E)   have the major media outlets been acknowledging the scope of the opposition

5 We would be healthier today if <u>we have had to hunt and scavenge</u> for our food as our ancestors did.

   (A)   if we have had to hunt and scavenge
   (B)   having hunted and scavenged
   (C)   if we would have hunted and scavenged
   (D)   for hunting and scavenging
   (E)   if we had to hunt and scavenge

9

GO ON TO THE NEXT PAGE ▶▶▶

6 <u>Against popular opinion</u>, college students with strong reasoning skills are more successful than students with strong memorization skills.

(A) Against popular opinion
(B) Not what popular opinion says
(C) Contrary to popular opinion
(D) Opposite to what popular opinion says
(E) Contrary to what popular opinion says

7 The school renovations should be planned <u>so as to minimize disruption and inconvenience to teachers and students</u>.

(A) so as to minimize disruption and inconvenience to teachers and students
(B) for the minimizing of disruptions and inconvenience to teachers and students
(C) so that teachers and students have minimum disruptions and inconvenience
(D) to minimize disruption and inconvenience on the part of teachers and students
(E) in order for the minimization of disruption and inconvenience to teachers and students

8 Dina, having struggled for months <u>to find a job as a writer</u>; she finally took a position at a local advertising agency.

(A) to find a job as a writer; she finally
(B) to find a job as a writer, finally
(C) for finding a job as a writer, finally
(D) finding a job as a writer, finally
(E) to find a job as a writer, so she finally

9 The fall of the Roman Empire was precipitated not so much by foreign invaders as <u>by the delusions and indulgences of its ruling class</u>.

(A) by the delusions and indulgences of its ruling class
(B) because of the delusions and indulgences of their ruling class
(C) the delusions and indulgences of its ruling class did
(D) it was by the delusions and indulgences of its ruling class
(E) the delusions and indulgences of its ruling class

10 If the preliminary sales numbers are reliable, then Hannigan's first book appears <u>like it is a success</u>.

(A) like it is a success
(B) like a success
(C) a success
(D) to be a success
(E) as a success

11 The response to the revised proposal has been much more favorable than <u>the original one</u>.

(A) the original one
(B) the original one was
(C) the response to the original one
(D) to the one that was originally given
(E) to the original one

12 The discovery was made by a team of <u>scientists trying to locate a gene responsible for producing a particular enzyme, but they found instead</u> a set of genetic triggers for a predisposition to heart disease.

(A) scientists trying to locate a gene responsible for producing a particular enzyme, but they found instead
(B) scientists; trying to locate a gene responsible for producing a particular enzyme, but they found instead
(C) scientists who, trying to locate a gene responsible for producing a particular enzyme, instead found
(D) scientists that tried to locate a gene responsible for producing a particular enzyme, instead finding
(E) scientists who instead, in trying to find a gene responsible for producing a particular enzyme, found

13 The strongest opposition to the sale of alcohol in the United States came in the late nineteenth century, <u>and this is the time when religious movements</u> preaching temperance were sweeping the nation.

(A) and this is the time when religious movements
(B) when religious movements were
(C) and this is when religious movements
(D) at the time in which religious movements were
(E) when religious movements

14 Professor Angleton valued conciseness highly, telling his students to edit their papers thoroughly <u>for eliminating any extra superfluous</u> information in the text.

(A) for eliminating any extra superfluous
(B) to eliminate any extra superfluous
(C) and eliminate any superfluous
(D) having eliminated any superfluous
(E) in eliminating any superfluous

STOP *You may check your work, on this section only, until time is called.*

9

ANSWER KEY

Section 2 Math	Section 5 Math	Section 7 Math	Section 3 Critical Reading	Section 6 Critical Reading	Section 8 Critical Reading	Section 4 Writing	Section 9 Writing
☐ 1. C	☐ 1. B	☐ 1. B	☐ 1. A	☐ 1. B	☐ 1. E	☐ 1. B	☐ 1. C
☐ 2. D	☐ 2. A	☐ 2. D	☐ 2. D	☐ 2. D	☐ 2. B	☐ 2. A	☐ 2. E
☐ 3. A	☐ 3. D	☐ 3. A	☐ 3. B	☐ 3. C	☐ 3. B	☐ 3. E	☐ 3. D
☐ 4. D	☐ 4. E	☐ 4. C	☐ 4. C	☐ 4. A	☐ 4. D	☐ 4. D	☐ 4. B
☐ 5. B	☐ 5. D	☐ 5. C	☐ 5. C	☐ 5. A	☐ 5. D	☐ 5. D	☐ 5. E
☐ 6. D	☐ 6. C	☐ 6. A	☐ 6. E	☐ 6. B	☐ 6. A	☐ 6. A	☐ 6. C
☐ 7. E	☐ 7. C	☐ 7. C	☐ 7. B	☐ 7. D	☐ 7. D	☐ 7. C	☐ 7. A
☐ 8. D	☐ 8. B	☐ 8. C	☐ 8. D	☐ 8. C	☐ 8. A	☐ 8. D	☐ 8. B
☐ 9. C	☐ 9. 135	☐ 9. D	☐ 9. B	☐ 9. E	☐ 9. C	☐ 9. B	☐ 9. A
☐ 10. C	☐ 10. 104	☐ 10. D	☐ 10. D	☐ 10. E	☐ 10. C	☐ 10. E	☐ 10. D
☐ 11. D	☐ 11. 30	☐ 11. D	☐ 11. B	☐ 11. C	☐ 11. A	☐ 11. A	☐ 11. C
☐ 12. B	☐ 12. 3	☐ 12. D	☐ 12. A	☐ 12. A	☐ 12. D	☐ 12. B	☐ 12. C
☐ 13. C	☐ 13. 18	☐ 13. A	☐ 13. D	☐ 13. B	☐ 13. C	☐ 13. D	☐ 13. E
☐ 14. B	☐ 14. 28	☐ 14. B	☐ 14. E	☐ 14. E	☐ 14. D	☐ 14. E	☐ 14. C
☐ 15. E	☐ 15. 45	☐ 15. B	☐ 15. A	☐ 15. C	☐ 15. D	☐ 15. B	
☐ 16. B	☐ 16. 22.5	☐ 16. A	☐ 16. B	☐ 16. A	☐ 16. C	☐ 16. B	
☐ 17. E	☐ 17. 12		☐ 17. A	☐ 17. A	☐ 17. E	☐ 17. D	
☐ 18. A	☐ 18. 37.5		☐ 18. C	☐ 18. C	☐ 18. A	☐ 18. D	
☐ 19. B			☐ 19. E	☐ 19. D	☐ 19. E	☐ 19. B	
☐ 20. C			☐ 20. B	☐ 20. B		☐ 20. E	
			☐ 21. D	☐ 21. A		☐ 21. C	
			☐ 22. E	☐ 22. C		☐ 22. B	
			☐ 23. B	☐ 23. E		☐ 23. D	
			☐ 24. C	☐ 24. C		☐ 24. E	
						☐ 25. B	
						☐ 26. C	
						☐ 27. C	
						☐ 28. A	
						☐ 29. D	
						☐ 30. B	
						☐ 31. C	
						☐ 32. D	
						☐ 33. E	
						☐ 34. A	
						☐ 35. D	

# Right (A):	Questions 1–8 # Right (A):	# Right (A):	# Right (A):	# Right (A):	# Right (A):	# Right (A)	# Right (A):
# Wrong (B):	# Wrong (B):	# Wrong (B):	# Wrong (B):	# Wrong (B):	# Wrong (B):	# Wrong (B):	# Wrong (B):
# (A) – $\frac{1}{4}$ (B):	# (A) – $\frac{1}{4}$ (B):	# (A) – $\frac{1}{4}$ (B):	# (A) – $\frac{1}{4}$ (B):	# (A) – $\frac{1}{4}$ (B):	# (A) – $\frac{1}{4}$ (B):	# (A) – $\frac{1}{4}$ (B):	# (A) – $\frac{1}{4}$ (B):
	Questions 9–18 # Right (A):						

SCORE CONVERSION TABLE

How to score your test

Use the answer key on the previous page to determine your raw score on each section. **Your raw score on each section except Section 4 is simply the number of correct answers minus ¼ of the number of wrong answers. On Section 4, your raw score is the sum of the number of correct answers for questions 1–8 minus ¼ of the number of wrong answers for questions 1–8 plus the total number of correct answers for questions 9–18.** Next, add the raw scores from Sections 3, 4, and 7 to get your Math raw score, and add the raw scores from Sections 6 and 9 to get your Writing raw score. Write the three raw scores here:

Raw Critical Reading score: _____ Raw Math score: _____ Raw Writing score: _____

Use the table below to convert these to scaled scores.

Scaled scores: Critical Reading: _____ Math: _____ Writing: _____

Raw Score	Critical Reading Scaled Score	Math Scaled Score	Writing Scaled Score	Raw Score	Critical Reading Scaled Score	Math Scaled Score	Writing Scaled Score
67	800			32	520	550	610
66	800			31	510	550	600
65	790			30	510	540	580
64	780			29	500	530	570
63	760			28	490	520	560
62	750			27	490	530	550
61	730			26	480	510	540
60	720			25	480	500	530
59	700			24	470	490	520
58	700			23	460	480	510
57	690			22	460	480	500
56	680			21	450	470	490
55	670			20	440	460	480
54	660	800		19	440	450	470
53	650	790		18	430	450	460
52	650	760		17	420	440	450
51	640	740		16	420	430	440
50	630	720		15	410	420	440
49	620	710	800	14	400	410	430
48	620	700	800	13	400	410	420
47	610	680	800	12	390	400	410
46	600	670	790	11	380	390	400
45	600	660	780	10	370	380	390
44	590	650	760	9	360	370	380
43	590	640	740	8	350	360	380
42	580	630	730	7	340	350	370
41	570	630	710	6	330	340	360
40	570	620	700	5	320	330	350
39	560	610	690	4	310	320	340
38	550	600	670	3	300	310	320
37	550	590	660	2	280	290	310
36	540	580	650	1	270	280	300
35	540	580	640	0	250	260	280
34	530	570	630	−1	230	240	270
33	520	560	620	−2 or less	210	220	250

SCORE CONVERSION TABLE FOR WRITING COMPOSITE
[ESSAY + MULTIPLE CHOICE]

Calculate your writing raw score as you did on the previous page and grade your essay from a 1 to a 6 according to the standards that follow in the detailed answer key.

Essay score: _____ Raw Writing score: _____

Use the table below to convert these to scaled scores.

Scaled score: Writing: _____

Raw Score	Essay Score 0	Essay Score 1	Essay Score 2	Essay Score 3	Essay Score 4	Essay Score 5	Essay Score 6
−2 or less	200	230	250	280	310	340	370
−1	210	240	260	290	320	360	380
0	230	260	280	300	340	370	400
1	240	270	290	320	350	380	410
2	250	280	300	330	360	390	420
3	260	290	310	340	370	400	430
4	270	300	320	350	380	410	440
5	280	310	330	360	390	420	450
6	290	320	340	360	400	430	460
7	290	330	340	370	410	440	470
8	300	330	350	380	410	450	470
9	310	340	360	390	420	450	480
10	320	350	370	390	430	460	490
11	320	360	370	400	440	470	500
12	330	360	380	410	440	470	500
13	340	370	390	420	450	480	510
14	350	380	390	420	460	490	520
15	350	380	400	430	460	500	530
16	360	390	410	440	470	500	530
17	370	400	420	440	480	510	540
18	380	410	420	450	490	520	550
19	380	410	430	460	490	530	560
20	390	420	440	470	500	530	560
21	400	430	450	480	510	540	570
22	410	440	460	480	520	550	580
23	420	450	470	490	530	570	590
24	420	460	470	500	540	570	600
25	430	460	480	510	540	580	610
26	440	470	490	520	550	590	610
27	450	480	500	530	560	590	620
28	460	490	510	540	570	600	630
29	470	500	520	550	580	610	640
30	480	510	530	560	590	620	650
31	490	520	540	560	600	630	660
32	500	530	550	570	610	640	670
33	510	540	550	580	620	650	680
34	510	550	560	590	630	660	690
35	520	560	570	600	640	670	700
36	530	560	580	610	650	680	710
37	540	570	590	620	660	690	720
38	550	580	600	630	670	700	730
39	560	600	610	640	680	710	740
40	580	610	620	650	690	720	750
41	590	620	640	660	700	730	760
42	600	630	650	680	710	740	770
43	610	640	660	690	720	750	780
44	620	660	670	700	740	770	800
45	640	670	690	720	750	780	800
46	650	690	700	730	770	800	800
47	670	700	720	750	780	800	800
48	680	720	730	760	800	800	800
49	680	720	730	760	800	800	800

Detailed Answer Key

Section 1

The following essay received 12 points out of a possible 12 meaning that it demonstrates *clear and consistent mastery* in that it

- develops an insightful point of view on the topic
- demonstrates exemplary critical thinking
- uses effective examples, reasons, and other evidence to support its thesis
- is consistently focused, coherent, and well-organized
- demonstrates skillful and effective use of language and sentence structure
- is largely (but not necessarily completely) free of grammatical and usage errors

Consider carefully the issue discussed in the following passage, then write an essay that answers the question posed in the assignment.

> We like to believe that physical phenomena, animals, people and societies obey predictable rules, but such rules, even when carefully ascertained, have their limits. Every rule has its exceptions.

Assignment: **What is one particularly interesting "exception" to a rule?** Write an essay in which you answer this question and discuss your point of view on this issue. Support your position logically with examples from literature, the arts, history, politics, science and technology, current events, or your experience or observation.

SAMPLE STUDENT ESSAY

One particularly interesting exception to a rule is the orbit of Mercury. For hundreds of years, Sir Isaac Newton's laws of motion and gravity stood as a testament to the power of mathematics to describe the universe. Newton's equations showed that the moon did not revolve around the earth because the gods willed it to, or because of the abstract perfection of a circular orbit. Rather, it circled the earth because doing so obeyed a simple mathematical formula: Newton's Universal Law of Gravitation. It was a singular achievement in the history of science.

The equation was not only elegant, but enormously powerful. It was used to predict the existence of two new planets before they were even seen: Neptune and Pluto. Astronomers actually began to doubt the power of the Universal Law of Gravitation when they noticed that Uranus was not behaving the way the equation said it should. Its orbit was wobblier than Newton's law predicted. Could the law be incorrect? A few careful scientists noticed that the law could still be correct if another planet, further from the sun, were tugging at Uranus. Indeed, astronomers looked carefully and found a planet

they called Neptune. As even further confirmation of Newton's law, irregularities in Neptune's orbit led astronomers to find Pluto exerting yet another tiny gravitational tug at the edge of the solar system. It seemed that Newton's equation could do no wrong.

But it was wrong. When astronomers began to notice irregularities in Mercury's orbit, they surmised, naturally, that another planet must be near the sun tugging at Mercury. They even went so far as to call the undiscovered planet Vulcan. But even the most careful observations revealed no such planet. How could this equation, so powerful and elegant, be wrong? It turned out that Newton's equation broke down a bit as gravitational force became great, as it did near the sun. It wasn't until the 20th century that Einstein's theory of General Relativity tweaked Newton's equation to make it explain the precession of Mercury's orbit.

The value of Mercury's orbit, in fact, lies not so much in its ability to "prove" Einstein's theory as in its ability to disprove Newton's. It was the exception to a very powerful rule. It seems to suggest that, in science, nothing is truly sacred; everything must be examined. If one of the most powerful and elegant equations in all of science—one that had been "proven" time and again by rigorous experiment—could turn out to be wrong (albeit only by a tiny bit, in most ordinary circumstances), how much can we trust our own beloved "truths" about our universe? So many of us believe we know at least a few things that are "absolutely true." But can we say that we are more insightful, intelligent, or rigorous than Isaac Newton? Perhaps we should be more like the scientists, and look for the holes in our theories.

The following essay received 8 points out of a possible 12, meaning that it demonstrates *adequate competence* in that it

- develops a point of view on the topic
- demonstrates some critical thinking, but perhaps not consistently
- uses some examples, reasons, and other evidence to support its thesis, but perhaps not adequately
- shows a general organization and focus, but shows occasional lapses in this regard
- demonstrates adequate but occasionally inconsistent facility with language
- contains occasional errors in grammar, usage, and mechanics

---

SAMPLE STUDENT ESSAY

When we are children, everyone—parents, teachers and friends—tells us that we should never lie. It's even one of the ten commandments in the Bible. This is a rule that many believe should have no exceptions. It is just something you should not do. Lying is bad, and being truthful is good. End of story.

But I believe that this rule has its exceptions, as many rules do. Sometimes lying can even be considered the right thing to do. It's obviously not good to lie just because you don't feel like telling the truth or just because you might look better if you lie. There has to be a good reason to deceive someone in order for it to be a valid action.

For instance, sometimes telling the truth can really hurt a situation more than it helps. For example, my friend is in a dance company, and I went to see her in the Nutcracker dance performance this past weekend. Even though she was pretty good, the whole thing was long, boring, and a lot of the dancers were not very good. I know that she would not want to hear that. So instead of telling her the truth, I lied and told her how great it was. This is what is called a "white lie." Yes, I was deceiving her, but there was really very little to come from telling her the truth that the show was a disaster. What is the point of telling the truth there if it is only going to hurt everyone involved?

Recently, I watched a documentary about the Vietnam War. The documentary focused on a troop of 25 soldiers and their experience in the war and how they grew closer together as a group as the time went by. One of the soldiers, a 16-year-old boy who had lied about his age so that he could fight, died because he made a bad decision and chased after a Vietnamese soldier into the woods without anyone else to back him up. Part of the reasoning behind this action, they explained, was because he spent his entire life trying to prove to his parents that he was not a failure at everything and that he could be a hero. A fellow troop mate knew what he had done, knew the struggle for respect he was going through at home, and wrote the formal letter home to the family telling them how their son had died in an honorable fashion saving several members of the troop with his heroism. Some might argue that it was bad to lie about his death, but I would argue that this was a valiant thing done by the soldier who wrote the letter because it allowed the family to feel better about the death of their young son in a war so many miles away.

To summarize, in general, it is best not to lie. But there are in fact situations where it is better to tell partial truths than the whole truth. It is important to avoid lying whenever possible, but it is also important to know when it is OK to tell a slight variation to the truth.

The following essay received 4 points out of a possible 12, meaning that it demonstrates *some incompetence* in that it

- has a seriously limited point of view
- demonstrates weak critical thinking
- uses inappropriate or insufficient examples, reasons, and other evidence to support its thesis
- is poorly focused and organized, and has serious problems with coherence
- demonstrates frequent problems with language and sentence structure
- contains errors in grammar and usage that obscure the author's meaning seriously

SAMPLE STUDENT ESSAY

A lot of rules have exceptions because there are different circumstances for everybody and also people grow up and the old rules don't apply anymore. One afternoon back in elementary school, I got in trouble when I took my friend's Capri-Sun drink out of his lunchbox and took a sip without asking his permission. My teacher caught me in the act and yelled at me reciting the "Golden Rule." She said: How would you feel if he took your drink and had some without asking you? I guess I would have been pretty annoyed. I hate it when people drink from the same glass as me. It seemed like a pretty fair rule that I should only do things to other people that I would be OK with them doing to me.

This interaction with my 3rd grade teacher stuck with me throughout my education experience and I heard her voice in my head many times as I was about to perform questionable acts upon others around me. It kept me from doing a lot of pranks like I used to do like tie Eric's shoelaces together and putting hot pepper flakes in Steve's sandwich one afternoon while he went off to get himself another cup of water.

But this rule seemed to get a bit more difficult to follow as I got older and found myself in more complex relationships. Sometimes I wanted to be treated in ways that my friends did not want to be treated. I wanted my friends to call me each night so that we could talk and catch up on the day's events so I would call each of them every night to chat. This annoyed my friends though who did not like talking on the phone. Or, I would always point out to my friends when something they were wearing did not look good because I wanted to be told such things so that I did not embarrass myself. This made a LOT of my friends very angry at me and cost me a few good friendships.

"Do unto others" is a rule that requires a bit of thought and a lot of good judgment. Doing unto others things that I was hoping they would do to me sometimes cost myself friendships. I think it is better to reserve that rule for things that I might consider negative rather than positive.

Detailed Answer Key

Section 2

---

1. C It does not matter how big each station is. All that matters is the total area and *how many* stations there are.

$$\text{average} = \frac{\text{total}}{\text{pieces}} = \frac{3{,}600 \text{ ft}^2}{6 \text{ stations}} = 600 \text{ ft}^2$$

---

2. D Solve for a and b: $3a = 15$
Divide by 3: $a = 5$
                                        $4b = 10$
Divide by 4: $b = 2.5$

Plug in a and b: $\dfrac{a}{b} = \dfrac{5}{2.5} = 2$

---

3. A Pick the employee whose line has the largest positive slope. This is Employee 1. Her line has the largest "rise over run." Her salary increases approximately $20,000 in 8 years, or roughly $2,500 per year.

---

4. D Use unit analysis and solve:

$$100 \text{ children} \times \frac{1 \text{ bucket}}{5 \text{ children}} = 20 \text{ buckets}$$

$$60 \text{ adults} \times \frac{1 \text{ bucket}}{3 \text{ adults}} = 20 \text{ buckets}$$

Total number of buckets = 20 + 20 = 40

---

5. B $(5x - 3x + 4)(3x + 6x - 2)$
Combine like terms: $(2x + 4)(9x - 2)$
FOIL: $(18x^2 - 4x + 36x - 8)$
Combine like terms: $18x^2 + 32x - 8$

---

6. D

Linear pair: $z + x = 180$
Substitute: $55 + x = 180$
Subtract 55: $x = 125$
Since lines l and m are parallel:
    Corresponding: $z = d = 55$
                                        $x = c = 125$
    Alternate interior: $z = a = 55$
                                        $x = c = 125$

$a + b + c = 55 + 125 + 125 = 305$

---

7. E $7\sqrt{x} + 16 = 79$

Subtract 16: $7\sqrt{x} = 63$

Divide by 7: $\sqrt{x} = 9$
Square both sides: $x = 81$

---

8. D Work backwards with this problem. Each term, starting with the second, is 2 less than the square root of the previous term. So to work backwards and find the previous term, add 2 and then square the sum: 2nd term $= (1 + 2)^2 = 3^2 = 9$
                        1st term $= (9 + 2)^2 = 11^2 = 121$

---

9. C Before trying to solve this with geometrical formulas, analyze the figure. The rectangle is divided into 15 squares. Each of the 15 squares is split into 2 identical triangles, which means there are 30 triangles total. Of those 30 triangles, 15 of them are shaded in, or *half* of the figure. This means that half of the area, or 45, is shaded.

---

10. C The long way:

⭐16 = 15 + 14 + 13 + 12 + 11 + 10 + 9 + 8 + 7 + 6 + 5 + 4 + 3 + 2 + 1 = 120

⭐13 = 12 + 11 + 10 + 9 + 8 + 7 + 6 + 5 + 4 + 3 + 2 + 1 = 78

⭐16 − ⭐13 = 120 − 78 = 42

More simply, this can be solved without actually calculating the sums. Just focus on the terms in the sum of

⭐16 that are not "cancelled" by the terms in ⭐13:

⭐16 − ⭐13 = 15 + 14 + 13 = 42

11. D   Look at the right (units) column first.

$$Y + X = X$$

Subtract X: $Y = 0$

Look at the 10s column: $3 + Y = 3$

Because $Y = 0$, we know there is no carried digit. Look at the left (1,000s) column:

$$X + 5 = 13$$

Subtract 5: $X = 8$

---

12. B   Write out an equation given the average:

$$\frac{x + y + 3y}{3} = 3x$$

Multiply by 3: $x + y + 3y = 9x$
Combine like terms: $x + 4y = 9x$
Subtract x: $4y = 8x$
Divide by 4: $y = 2x$

---

13. C

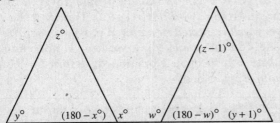

The simplest method is to use the Triangle External Angle Theorem, which says that the measure of an "exterior angle" of a triangle equals the sum of the measures of the two "remote interior angles," so $x = y + z$ and $w = (z-1) + (y + 1) = y + z$. Therefore, $w = x$.

Another, more involved method is to write an equation for each triangle:

Triangle on left: $y + z + (180 - x) = 180$
Subtract 180: $y + z - x = 0$
Add x: $y + z = x$
Triangle on right: $(y + 1) + (z - 1) + (180 - w) = 180$
Subtract 180 and simplify: $y + z - w = 0$
Add w: $y + z = 0$
Substitute w for $y + z$: $w = x$

---

14. B   Pick a value for r, like 19, that makes this statement true. (r must be 9 more than some multiple of 10.) If r is 19, then $r + 2$ is 21. When 21 is divided by 5, it leaves a remainder of 1.

15. E

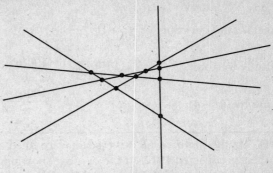

The best way to solve this problem is to draw the lines. With each line you draw, attempt to create as many intersection points as possible. The maximum number of intersection points possible with 5 lines is 10, as shown above.

---

16. B   The probability of selecting a king is ¼, and the probability of selecting a queen is ²∕₇. To find the probability of randomly choosing a jack, add up the probabilities of choosing a king and a queen and subtract that sum from 1. $\frac{1}{4} + \frac{2}{7}$

Find a common denominator: $\frac{7}{28} + \frac{8}{28} = \frac{15}{28}$
Subtract from 1: $1 - \frac{15}{28} = \frac{13}{28}$

---

17. E

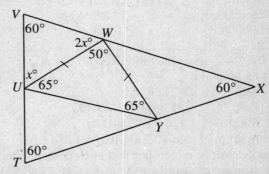

Since $\triangle VXT$ is equilateral, its angles all measure 60°. Mark the diagram as shown.
If $WU = WY$, then $\angle WUY = \angle WYU = 65°$.
$\angle VWU$ ($2x°$) is twice as large as $\angle VUW$ ($x°$).
There are 180 degrees in a triangle: $x + 2x + 60° = 180°$

Combine like terms: $3x + 60° = 180°$
Subtract 60°: $3x = 120°$
Divide by 3: $x = 40°$

The angles on one side of a line add up to 180°:

$$40° + 65° + \angle TUY = 180°$$

Combine like terms: $105° + \angle TUY = 180°$
Subtract 105°: $\angle TUY = 75°$

18. A The question asks: what percent of $m - 4$ is $n + 2$?

Translate the question: $\dfrac{x}{100} \times (m - 4) = n + 2$

Multiply by 100: $\qquad\qquad x(m - 4) = 100(n + 2)$

Divide by $(m - 4)$: $\qquad\qquad x = \dfrac{100(n + 2)}{m - 4}$

---

19. B At the matinee, all but 6 seats were filled and the theater collected $912. At the evening showing, all the seats were sold plus 5 extra tickets and they collected $1,000. Let x = the number of seats in the theater. Let y = the price per ticket in the theater. Set up equations to represent the amount of money collected:

Matinee showing: $\qquad\qquad (x - 6)y = \$912$

Divide by $(x - 6)$: $\qquad\qquad y = \dfrac{912}{(x - 6)}$

Evening showing: $\qquad\qquad (x + 5)y = \$1{,}000$

Divide by $(x - 5)$: $\qquad\qquad y = \dfrac{1000}{(x + 5)}$

Set up equation: $\qquad\qquad \dfrac{912}{(x - 6)} = \dfrac{1000}{(x + 5)}$

Cross-multiply: $\qquad (912)(x + 5) = (1{,}000)(x - 6)$
Distribute: $\qquad\quad 912x + 4{,}560 = 1{,}000x - 6{,}000$
Add 6,000: $\qquad\quad 912x + 10{,}560 = 1{,}000x$
Subtract 912x: $\qquad\quad 10{,}560 = 88x$
Divide by 88: $\qquad\qquad 120 = x$

---

20. C Work month by month with the price:
Start of Jan: $\quad d$
After Jan: $\quad d - .2d = .8d$
After Feb: $\quad .8d + (.4)(.8d) = 1.12d$
After Mar: $\quad 1.12d - (.25)(1.12d) = .84d$
After Apr: $\quad .84d + (.25)(.84d) = 1.05d$
Or, more simply, remember that each percent change is a simple multiplication: $d(.8)(1.4)(.75)(1.25) = 1.05d$.

Section 3

1. A The bistro is world-renowned, so it is *famous* and *successful*. Both words should be positive. *delectable* = pleasing to the taste; *scrumptious* = delicious; *unpalatable* = bad tasting; *tantalizing* = exciting because kept out of reach; *debilitating* = sapping energy; *savory* = pleasing to the taste.

2. D The 1st word represents something that could put a country on the *brink of war*. The 2nd word represents something that could cause it to *explode into destructive conflict*. *dissension* = disagreement; *harmony* = concord; *instigation* = provocation; *strife* = violent disagreement; *provocation* = rousing of anger; *unanimity* = complete agreement; *agitation* = disturbance.

3. B For over 500 years, art historians have argued about the emotion behind the *Mona Lisa's* *enigmatic* (mysterious) smile. This would make the painting the source of much *debate* or *discussion*. *assent* = agreement; *deliberation* = discussion of all sides of an issue; *concurrence* = agreement; *remuneration* = payment for goods or services; *reconciliation* = the act of resolving an issue.

4. C Every year, crowds of people travel to Elvis's hometown to pay *tribute* (respect). Therefore, he was a very *well-respected* or *admired* musician. *satirized* = made fun of, mocked; *unexalted* = not praised; *revered* = respected, worshipped; *despised* = hated; *shunned* = avoided.

5. C The poker player uses *tactics* (strategies) to *out-think* his opponents, so his tactics must be intellectual. This is why he is called "the professor." *obscure* = not well understood; *cerebral* = using intellect; *transparent* = easily understood; *outlandish* = bizarre, unusual.

6. E Detractors are critics who would likely say something negative about the aesthetics of the building, whereas its developers would likely claim that the project would be a *great success*. *adversary* = opponent; *enhancement* = something that improves the appearance or function of something else; *gratuity* = tip; *embellishment* = decoration or exaggeration; *windfall* = unexpected benefit; *defacement* = act of vandalism; *calamity* = disaster; *atrocity* = horrific crime; *boon* = benefit.

7. B Poe wrote tales of cruelty and torture, so they must have been *horrific*. His tales mesmerized his readers, so they must have been *hypnotizing*. *tenuous* = flimsy; *spellbinding* = mesmerizing; *grotesque* = distorted, horrifying, outlandish; *enthralling* = captivating; *interminable* = never-ending; *sacrilegious* = grossly disrespectful; *eclectic* = deriving from a variety of sources; *sadistic* = taking pleasure in others' pain; *chimerical* = unrealistically fanciful, illusory; *mundane* = everyday, common.

8. D The DNA evidence was vital to proving the defendant's innocence. The missing word should mean to *prove innocent* or *free from blame. perambulate* = walk through; *expedite* = speed up; *incriminate* = accuse of a crime; *exculpate* = free from blame; *equivocate* = avoid telling the whole truth.

9. B Debussy is said to have started the *breakdown of the old system* (line 3) and then to have been the *first ... who dared to make his ear the sole judge of what was good harmonically* (lines 6–7). Therefore, the old system did not allow this and was a rigid method for writing harmonies.

10. D The passage as a whole describes Debussy's inventiveness as a composer of musical harmony.

11. B The hot-air balloon trip is an analogy for the difficulties involved in exploring the ocean.

12. A These are examples of the *limited and relatively ineffective methods* (lines 16–17) that make ocean exploration *a difficult and expensive task* (line 19).

13. D This *primal concept* is revealed by the fact that the paintings of Stone Age artists are charged with *magical strength* and *fulfilled ... other functions beyond the mere representation of the visible* (lines 9–10).

14. E To be *charged with magical strength* is to be *filled with magical strength*.

15. A The *stylistic change* was from the *naturalism based on observation and experience* to a *geometrically stylized world of forms discoverable ... through thought and speculation* (lines 49–52). In other words, artists were depicting ideas rather than just objects and animals.

16. B The sculptures are said to be *ample witnesses* (line 69) to the fact that art of this period contained *elements of naïveté ... side by side with ... formalized compositions* (lines 65–67).

17. A The passage states that Renaissance art is characterized by the *discovery of linear and aerial perspective* (line 86), that is, the ability to imply depth in painting, while the earlier *art of the period of the catacombs* (line 76) *was averse to any spatial illusions* and contained action *pressed onto the holy, two-dimensional surface* (lines 80–81).

18. C *Transitional forms* (line 10) are described as fossils that gradualists would cite as *evidence for their position* (line 8), which is that evolution proceeds gradually.

19. E This case is mentioned as an illustration of the theory of *punctuated equilibrium* (lines 12–13).

20. B The passage says that one *explanation for the extinction of the dinosaurs* is that a meteorite created a *cloud of gas and dust* that destroyed *most plants and the chain of animals that fed on them* (lines 45–51).

21. D This sentence is discussing fossil evidence. The supportive structures are those bones that support the weight of the body.

22. E The passage states in lines 35–38 that the biggest mass extinction in history happened between the Paleozoic era and the Mesozoic era, thereby implying that there were far fewer species in the early Mesozoic era than there were in the late Paleozoic era.

23. B In lines 71–75, the passage states that *the probable key to the rapid emergence* of Homo erectus *was a dramatic change in adaptive strategy: greater reliance on hunting through improved tools and other cultural means of adaptation.*

24. C The author presents several examples of mass extinctions and environmental changes that would likely lead to punctuated evolution but also describes species like *Homo erectus,* which *remained fairly stable for about 1 million years* (lines 77–78).

Section 4

1. **B** The original phrasing is a fragment. Choice B completes the thought clearly and concisely.

2. **A** The original phrasing is best.

3. **E** This phrasing is concise, complete, and in the active voice.

4. **D** The participle *pretending* modifies *Chandra* and not *Chandra's attempt*, so the participle dangles. Choice D corrects the problem most concisely.

5. **D** The original phrasing contains a comparison error, comparing *his speech* to the *candidates*. Choice D best corrects the mistake.

6. **A** The original phrasing is best.

7. **C** The original phrasing is not parallel. Choice C maintains parallelism by listing 3 consecutive adjectives.

8. **D** The pronoun *their* does not agree with its antecedent, *student*. Choice (C) is close, but including the word *also* implies that the tests do indicate academic skill.

9. **B** The original phrasing is a sentence fragment. Choices (C) and (D) are incorrect because semicolons must separate independent clauses.

10. **E** The phrase *requested that* indicates that the idea to follow is **subjunctive**. The correct subjunctive form here is *be*.

11. **A** The original phrasing is best.

12. **B** The past participle form of *to write* is *written*.

13. **D** This phrase is redundant and should be omitted.

14. **E** The sentence is correct.

15. **B** This phrase lacks parallel structure. A good revision is *a charismatic leader*.

16. **B** The sentence indicates two reasons, not one.

17. **D** This phrase is redundant. *Circuitous* means *roundabout*.

18. **D** *Eluded* means *evaded*, so this is a diction error. The correct word here is *alluded*, meaning *hinted at*.

19. **B** As it is written, the sentence is a fragment. Change *clutching* to *clutched* to complete the thought.

20. **E** The sentence is correct.

21. **C** This is a comparison error. A *grade point average* cannot be higher than *her classmates*, but rather higher than *those of the rest of her classmates*.

22. **B** Both the *emissary* and the *committee* are singular, so the pronoun *their* should be changed to *its* (if it refers to the committee) or *his* or *her* (if it refers to the emissary).

23. **D** The verb *receive* does not agree with the singular subject *each* and so should be changed to *receives*.

24. **E** The sentence is correct.

25. **B** The subject of this sentence is *genre*, so the correct conjugation of the verb is *encompasses*.

26. **C** The proper idiom is *method of channeling* or *method for channeling*.

27. **C** The sentence does not make a comparison, but rather indicates a result, so the word *as* should be replaced with *that*.

28. **A** The word *perspective* is a noun meaning point of view. In this context, the proper word is *prospective*, which is an adjective meaning *having the potential to be*.

29. **D** The list of camp activities should be parallel. The verbs should consistently be in the present tense, so *will write* should be changed to *write*.

30. B This phrasing is concise and parallel and makes a logical comparison.

31. C Chaplin's mother's mental illness is not pertinent to the main ideas of paragraph 1.

32. D In the original phrasing, the opening modifiers are left dangling. Choice D corrects this problem most concisely.

33. E This choice is most parallel.

34. A Sentence 11 introduces the idea that some were interested in more than Chaplin's art. Sentence 9 expands on this fact with the specific example of Senator McCarthy's interest in Chaplin's political beliefs. Sentence 10 extends the ideas in sentence 9.

35. D This sentence provides the best transition from the idea that Chaplin's films contained political messages to a discussion of their specific messages about domestic and international issues.

Section 5

1. B Eric earns a 5% commission on each $200 stereo, so he makes ($200)(.05) = $10 per stereo. So if he makes $100 on x stereos,

$$10x = 100$$

Divide by 10: $\quad x = 10$

2. A Fill in the table:

Jane's Discount Music Superstore
Holiday Sales

	CDs	DVDs	Total
New	*3,000*	4,500	7,500
Used	*4,000*	**2,500**	6,500
Total	7,000	*7,000*	14,000

Since 7,000 out of the total of 14,000 items sold were CDs, 14,000 − 7,000 = 7,000 were DVDs. Since 4,500 of these DVDs were new, 7,000 − 4,500 = 2,500 were used.

3. D Set up a ratio: $\dfrac{5\ \text{pounds}}{\$4.00} = \dfrac{x\ \text{pounds}}{\$20.00}$

Cross-multiply: $\quad 4x = 100$
Divide by 4: $\quad x = 25$

$$25\ \text{pounds} \times \frac{16\ \text{ounces}}{1\ \text{pound}} = 400\ \text{ounces}$$

Set up a proportion: $\dfrac{1\ \text{bag}}{40\ \text{ounces}} = \dfrac{x\ \text{bags}}{400\ \text{ounces}}$

Cross-multiply: $\quad 40x = 400$
Divide by 40: $\quad x = 10\ \text{bags}$

4. E
Divide this complex-looking shape into a square and 2 right triangles.

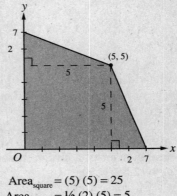

$$\text{Area}_{\text{square}} = (5)(5) = 25$$
$$\text{Area}_{\text{triangle}} = \tfrac{1}{2}(2)(5) = 5$$

Total shaded area = $\text{Area}_{\text{square}} + \text{Area}_{\text{triangle}} + \text{Area}_{\text{triangle}} = 2 + 5 + 5 = 35$.

5. D If each of the small cubes has a volume of 8 cubic inches, then each side of the smaller cubes must be 2 inches long. So the dimensions of the box are 6, 4, and 4. To find the surface area, use the formula:

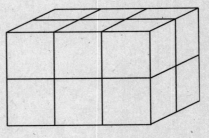

$$SA = 2lw + 2lh + 2wh$$
Plug in values: $\quad SA = 2(6)(4) + 2(6)(4) + 2(4)(4)$
Simplify: $\quad SA = 48 + 48 + 32 = 128$

6. C   Don't waste time doing the calculation: $-15 + -14 + -13 + -12 + -11 + -10 + -9 + -8 + -7 + -6 + -5 + -4 + -3 + -2 + -1 + 0 + 1 + 2 + 3 + 4 + 5 + 6 + 7 + 8 + 9 + 10 + 11 + 12 + 13 + 14 + 15 + 16 + 17 + 18 + 19$. Instead, think logically. The sum of the numbers from -15 to $+15$ is 0. They cancel out completely $-15: +15 = 0$, $-14 + 14 = 0$, $-13 + 13 = 0$, etc. Therefore, y must be greater than 15. With a little checking, it's easy to see that $16 + 17 + 18 + 19 = 70$, so $y = 19$. The total number of integers from -15 to 19, inclusive, is $19 - (-15) + 1 = 35$

---

7. C   The general strategy is to find out how many matches there are if each plays every other player once and multiply that by 2.

Opponents:

Player 1: 2, 3, 4, 5, 6, 7	6
Player 2: 3, 4, 5, 6, 7	5
Player 3: 4, 5, 6, 7	4
Player 4: 5, 6, 7	3
Player 5: 6, 7	2
Player 6: 7	1
Total head to-head-matchups:	21

Since they play each opponent twice, there is a total of $21 \times 2 = 42$ matches.

---

8. B   The area of the base of the prism is 12.5π. Since this is one-quarter of a circle, the entire circle has an area of $4(12.5\pi) = 50\pi$.

$$\pi r^2 = \text{area}$$

Substitute: $\pi r^2 = 50\pi$

Divide by π: $r^2 = 50$

Take square root: $r = \sqrt{50}$

You are told that the volume of the prism is 300π. Since this is ¼ of a cylinder, the entire cylinder would have a volume of $4(300\pi) = 1,200\pi$.

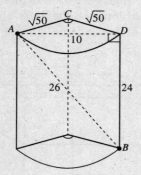

$\pi r^2 h = \text{volume of a cylinder}$

Substitute: $r^2 h = 1,200\pi$

Divide by π: $r^2 h = 1,200$

Substitute: $r = \sqrt{50}: (\sqrt{50})^2 h = 1,200$

Simplify: $50h = 1,200$

Divide by 50: $h = 24$

Finally, to find the distance from point A to point B, notice that AB is the hypotenuse of a right triangle with legs AD and DB. First you must find the value of AD:

$$\left(\sqrt{50}\right)^2 + \left(\sqrt{50}\right)^2 = \left(AD\right)^2$$

Simplify: $50 + 50 = 100 = (AD)^2$

Take square root: $10 = AD$

Solve for AB: $(AD)^2 + (DB)^2 = (AB)^2$

Substitute: $(10)^2 + (24)^2 = (AB)^2$

Simplify: $100 + 576 = (AB)^2$

Combine like terms: $676 = (AB)^2$

Take square root: $26 = AB$

---

9. 135

Set up an equation:	$x + (3y + 3) = 180°$
Substitute $y + 1$ for x:	$y + 1 + 3y + 3 = 180°$
Combine like terms:	$4y + 4 = 180°$
Subtract 4:	$4y = 176°$
Divide by 4:	$y = 44°$
Solve for $3y + 3$:	$3(44) + 3 = 135°$

---

10. 104

Quadrilateral $ABCD$ is composed of 2 identical triangles, each with an area of 240 square inches.

Area of $\triangle ABC = \frac{1}{2}bh$

$240 = \frac{1}{2}(20)(h)$

$h = 24$ inches

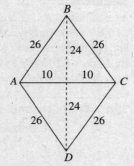

To solve for side BC, set up the Pythagorean Theorem:

$$10^2 + 24^2 = (BC)^2$$

Simplify: $100 + 576 = (BC)^2$

Combine like terms: $676 = (BC)^2$

Take the square root: $26 = BC$

(Or simply notice that each right triangle is a classic 5-12-13 triangle times 2: 10-24-26.)

The perimeter of quadrilateral $ABCD = 26 + 26 + 26 + 26 = 104$

11. 30 If 2 things are equal, you can substitute either one for the other. Since $g(x) = x^2 - 5$,

$$f(g(x)) = f(x^2 - 5)$$

Plug $x^2 - 5$ into $f(x)$ and simplify:

$$f(x) = 7(x^2 - 5) + 2$$

Distribute: $\qquad\qquad 7x^2 - 35 + 2$

Plug in 3 for x: $\qquad\quad 7(3)^2 - 35 + 2$

Simplify: $\qquad\qquad 63 - 35 + 2 = 30$

---

12. 3 Start by simplifying the expression:

$$\frac{6x - 9}{5} - \frac{x + 6}{5} = \frac{6x - 9 - x - 6}{5}$$

Combine like terms: $\qquad \dfrac{5x - 15}{5}$

Simplify: $\qquad\qquad\qquad x - 3$

This expression is 3 less than x.

---

13. 18 Approach this problem logically, but keep the restrictions in mind. If we want the *largest* possible value of a and $a + b < 20$, try $a = 19$. But that is not a possibility, because b is a positive integer and so can be no less than 1, and $19 + 1$ is equal to, not less than 20. Therefore, the largest value of a that fits the restriction is 18. If $a = 18$ and $b = 1$, then $ab = (18)(1) = 18$, an even number.

---

14. 28 Since rectangle U and rectangle V share a side with integer length, this length must be a common factor of 18 and 21. Similarly, the side that rectangle U and rectangle W share must be a common factor of 18 and 12. Therefore, the common side between U and V is 3, and the common side between U and W is 6. So U is a 6-by-3 rectangle, V is a 7-by-3 rectangle, and W is a 6-by-2 rectangle, which means rectangle X must have an area of 14. The sum of the areas of those 4

	6	7
U	3	V
W	6 / 2	7 / X
Y	6 / x	7 / Z

rectangles is $18 + 21 + 12 + 14 = 65$. The area of the entire rectangle is given as 117. Thus, the area of rectangles Y and Z together must be $117 - 65 = 52$. Set up an equation:

$$6x + 7x = 52$$

Combine like terms: $\qquad 13x = 52$

Divide by 13: $\qquad\qquad x = 4$

If $x = 4$, then the area of rectangle Z is $4 \times 7 = 28$.

---

15. 45 Begin by finding the amount the class would spend on 55 regular-price tickets: $55 \times \$15 = \$825$. Then calculate how much 60 discounted tickets cost: $60 \times \$13 = \$780$. Then subtract to find the amount saved: $\$825 - \$780 = \$45$.

---

16. 22.5

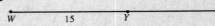

The length of $\overline{WY}$, as shown above, is 15.

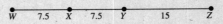

Point X is the midpoint of $\overline{WY}$, so $WX = XY = 7.5$. $YZ = 2WX = 2(7.5) = 15$. So $XZ = 22.5$.

---

17. 12

$$r \,\square\, s = \frac{rs^2}{r - s}$$

Solve for x: $\qquad 3 \,\square\, 2 = \dfrac{(3)(2^2)}{3 - 2} = \dfrac{12}{1} = 12 = x$

$$x \,\square\, 3 = 12 \,\square\, 3 = \frac{(12)(3^2)}{12 - 3} = \frac{108}{9} = 12$$

---

18. 37.5

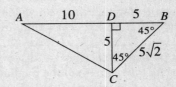

Since $\overline{DC} \perp \overline{AB}$, angle CDB is a right angle, so $\triangle CDB$ is a 45°-45°-90° right triangle. Therefore, $DB = DC = 5$. Since $AD = 2DB$, $AD = (5)(2) = 10$. The area of $\triangle ABC = \frac{1}{2}(b)(h) = \frac{1}{2}(15)(5) = 37.5$.

Section 6

1. B The reflex produces an *immediate* (or *instantaneous*) response. *transient* = short-lived; *stagnant* = not moving; *revitalized* = filled with new life and energy.

---

2. D Although the cats are *emaciated* (excessively thin) and *starved for food*, summoning energy would help them to fight *hard* or *aggressively* for the scraps. *humanely* = with mercy; *vigilantly* = in a watchful way; *fluently* = smoothly; *ferociously* = fiercely.

GO ON TO THE NEXT PAGE ▶▶▶

3. C Jennifer *irritated* her peers with her *supercilious* (overly proud) and *pretentious* (haughty) remarks. These are characteristic of an arrogant or showy demeanor. *reticent* = reserved, unwilling to speak; *belligerent* = warlike; *lofty* = pompous; *self effacing* = modest; *discomfited* = uneasy, uncomfortable.

4. A The first part of the sentence indicates that a sushi master's work is not easily learned. Therefore, much *training* and *studying* are required to become a master chef. *Apprenticeship, tutelage,* and *cultivation* are all good choices for the 1st word. This training will give someone the *autonomy* to create his or her own work. *apprenticeship* = working as a beginner under the assistance of an instructor; *autonomy* = independence; *tutelage* = instruction; *ineptitude* = lack of skill; *dormancy* = lack of activity; *sovereignty* = supreme authority; *cultivation* = the act of improving; *boorish* = rude, lacking manners; *quiescent* = not active.

5. A The journalist had a reputation for breaking news early, almost as if she were *able to see the future*. Later she admitted that she had privileged sources and did not use *prophecy* at all. *prophetic* = able to tell the future; *prescience* = knowledge of future events; *premeditated* = planned ahead of time; *predilection* = preference; *dismissive* = indifferent; *omniscience* = total knowledge; *preeminent* = superior; *reluctance* = resistance; *insolvent* = bankrupt; *foresight* = thinking ahead.

6. B Neither passage describes a discovery, but rather the world picture (line 5) of the medieval mind (lines 26–27), that is, medieval theories about the nature of the universe. Although Passage 1 provides a counter-example to an often-heard charge (lines 15–16), Passage 2 does not attempt to disprove any assumptions. Neither passage questions the medieval theories presented. Instead, the passages merely describe those theories. Lastly, neither passage discusses the everyday life in medieval Europe.

7. D The passage states that where our universe is thought to be dark, the other one was presumed to be illuminated, which means that the medieval universe was perceived to be full of light, unlike our modern universe.

8. C Pascal is said to be *disturbed by the silence of the vast spaces between the stars* (lines 10–11), in contrast to the medieval thinkers who *formerly thought* that the universe produced *the "music of the spheres"* (lines 13–14).

9. E Dante's theory is described in Passage 1 to counter the charge that medieval thinkers were focused on man's sense of self-importance (lines 21–23), but Hildegard's theory presented in the final sentence of Passage 2 is clearly anthropocentric, or human-centered. The world views of both Dante and Hildegard are focused on religion and an ordered hierarchy, but neither addresses scientific methods. Lastly, Passage 1 does not discuss the public acceptance of Dante's theory.

10. E This passage is concerned primarily with describing the relationships among the plants, animals and climate of the Serengeti. Therefore, it is describing how a particular ecosystem works. Although the passage mentions human intervention tangentially in the last paragraph, where it refers to badly drawn park boundaries, it is not a central focus of the passage. Although it does mention individual plants, the passage as a whole does not focus on them, but instead shows how they play a role in a larger ecosystem. It does not mention natural disasters, and only mentions the distinction between grazers and browsers as a minor point.

11. C These sentences suggest that the variety in the diet of grazers increases with the length of the grass. When the grass is short, all the animals apparently eat much the same sort of grass, but when it is long, they diversify their diets.

12. A Browsers are said to *feed on shrubs or the leaves of trees* (lines 15–16), as opposed to the grazers, which eat *the abundant grass that springs up like a well-mown lawn* (lines 10–11).

13. B The passage states that *unlike all the other grazers on the plain*, (zebras) *have teeth in both jaws* (lines 27–28). *All the rest* (besides the zebras) *are various species of antelope* (lines 30–31), which have *toothless upper palates* (lines 32–33).

14. E The second paragraph states that *where the grass is all short ... all the animals apparently eat the same sort of grass ... but where the grass is of varied lengths ... each animal copes differently with the available fodder* (lines 19–24). This difference is then described in the third paragraph, where the grazing sequence is specified.

15. C The rains are said to bring on *fresh growth* (line 56), encouraging the grazers to return to old grazing lands.

16. **A** This paragraph states that if the *migrant herds ... were confined* (lines 65–67), they would *so weaken the grass that it would die out* (lines 67–68). So maintaining the grasslands requires that the animals not be confined.

17. **A** The thesis of the passage is that *men come greatly to desire that these capricious gifts of Nature* (that is, the natural resources that are hard for some and easy for others to find, by luck alone) *might be intercepted by some agency having the power and the goodwill to distribute them justly .... This desire is Socialism* (lines 44–49).

18. **C** This primitive cultivator is a person who tries to stick a spade into the earth and make wheat and other edible matters spring from it. This is a farmer. Although the author uses figurative and metaphorical language throughout the passage, this particular phrase is being used literally.

19. **D** The *astronomer* is said to regard the earth as simply *a ball ... without ulterior motives* (lines 3–4), while the *foolish spendthrift ... suddenly realizes that the earth is offering him gold* (lines 22–24). Therefore, the astronomer regards the earth as impersonal, while the spendthrift regards it as generous.

20. **B** The *closed hand* represents the tendency of the *Earth* to hide its *diamonds* and *good red wheat* (lines 32–33).

21. **A** The author is discussing how capricious nature is in revealing its resources, and suggests that anyone trying to harvest the earth's resources must become a gambler (line 34), and scoff at theorists who prate (speak inconsequentially) of moral virtues such as industry and honesty and equality. Therefore, the author is suggesting that these virtues are not as valuable as many people claim they are.

22. **C** This fate is the fate of the *gambler* (line 34), who is at the whim of mother earth.

23. **E** The author states that the *Social Democratic State ... remains to be tried* (lines 54–55).

24. **C** The author states that *our own choice* (that is, the choice of his society) *is shown by our continual aspiration to possess property* (lines 62–63).

Section 7

1. **B**

	$3x + 5x + 8x = 32$
Combine like terms:	$16x = 32$
Divide by 16:	$x = 2$

2. **D**

$$\left(\frac{1}{x}\right)\left(\frac{x}{3}\right)(6x) = 8$$

Simplify: $2x = 8$
Divide by 2: $x = 4$

3. **A**

	$5b - 10 \geq 15$
Add 10:	$5b \geq 25$
Divide by 5:	$b \geq 5$

4. **C** First find 30% of 50: $(.3)(50) = 15$
t% of 60 is 15
Set up equation: $\dfrac{t}{100} = \dfrac{15}{100}$

Cross-multiply: $60t = 1{,}500$
Divide by 60: $t = 25$

5. **C** First convert 8 hours into minutes:

$$\frac{8 \text{ hours}}{x \text{ minutes}} = \frac{1 \text{ hour}}{60 \text{ minutes}}$$

Cross-multiply: $x = 480$ minutes
Then set up a ratio to answer the question:

$$\frac{480 \text{ minutes}}{y \text{ cards}} = \frac{40 \text{ minutes}}{h \text{ cards}}$$

Cross-multiply: $40y = 480h$
Divide by 40: $y = 12h$

6. **A** First find the product of -1.5×1.25: -1.875. Point A is closest to -1.875 on the number line presented.

7. **C** If the 4 people must each have a different positive number of cards, then the least that 3 may have is 1, 2, and 3 cards. This leaves a maximum of $100 - 6 = 94$ for the remaining person.

8. C A quick plot of the data listed in the table will point you to answer choice C. Since the miles per gallon are decreasing as the age increases, you can eliminate choice A. There is no point where the data levels out, which eliminates answer choice D. Finally, because it is not decreasing at a constant rate, you can eliminate choices B and E.

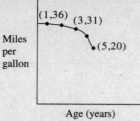

9. D If the question is *at most* how many of these integers *could* be odd, begin by imagining that ALL of them are odd. The integers may be the same, so imagine that they are all 1: $1 + 1 + 1 + 1 + 1 + 1 + 1 = 7$. But 7 is odd, so try 6 odds and 1 even: $1 + 1 + 1 + 1 + 1 + 1 + 2 = 8$. Therefore, the most that could be odd is 6.

10. D You can write out a quick calendar for yourself to track the days:

Su	M	T	W	**Th**	F	Sa
		1	2	3	4	5
6	7	8	9	10	11	12
13	14	15	16	17	18	19
20	21	22	23	24	25	26
27	28	29	30	**31**		

If you do this problem too quickly, you might assume that since the 4th Wednesday is the 22nd, the 4th Monday would be the 20th. But the 1st Monday comes after the 1st Wednesday, which makes the 4th Monday the 27th.

11. D Be careful with this question. Make sure you understand the chart before choosing an answer. The question asks about teachers who use gas heat. There are $60 + 13 = 73$ teachers who use gas heat, and 60 of these live in a house.

12. D "Stack" the equations:

$$5x + 7y = 18$$
$$\underline{2x - 4y = 6}$$

Add straight down: $7x + 3y = 24$

13. A

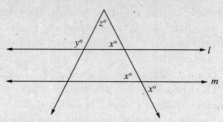

Starting with the angle marked $x°$ in the original figure, you can mark its vertical angle $x°$ as well. Since line l is parallel to line m, the corresponding angle in the top triangle is also $x°$. Set up an equation for the triangle:

$$x + z + (180 - y) = 180$$

Subtract 180: $x + z - y = 0$

Add y: $x + z = y$

(You might also simply notice that the angle marked $y°$ is an "exterior" angle to the triangle, so its measure is equal to the sum of the 2 "remote interior" angles: $y = x + z$.)

Subtract z: $x = y - z$

14. B This problem involves rates, so it helps to recall the rate equation: $d = rt$.

Because she travels home *along the same route*, you can use d for the distance both to and from work. Because she spends a total of 2 hours in the car, if she spends t hours on the way to work, she will spend $2 - t$ hours on the way home from work. Set up rate equations for both legs of the trip:

To work: $d = 40(t)$

From work: $d = 24(2 - t)$

Set the expressions equal: $40t = 24(2 - t)$

Distribute: $40t = 48 - 24t$

Add 24: $64t = 48$

Divide by 64: $t = .75$

Plug 0.75 in for t and solve for d: $d = 40(.75) = 30$

Check by confirming that plugging $t = .75$ into the other rate equation gives the same distance from home to work.

15. B The graph of the original function will be shifted up 4 and right 2. Answer choice B shows the proper representation of the new graph.

16. A

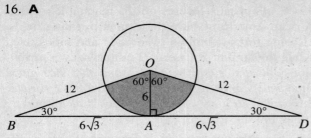

Line segment $\overline{BD}$ is tangent to the circle at point *A*, so angles *BAO* and *DAO* are right angles. This means that both ΔDAO and ΔBAO are 30°-60°-90° triangles.

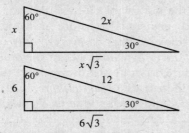

Using the 30°-60°-90° reference information at the beginning of this section, you can find the values of the remaining sides of the triangles.

Find the area of ΔBOD: Area $= \dfrac{1}{2}$(base)(height)

Plug in values: Area $= \dfrac{1}{2}(12\sqrt{3})(6) = 36\sqrt{3}$

The radius of the circle is 6, so the area of the entire circle can be found using the equation Area $= \pi r^2 = \pi(6)^2 = 36\pi$.

The shaded region of the circle makes up 120°, or ⅓ of the circle. Therefore, the area of the shaded region is equal to ⅓$(\pi r^2) = $ ⅓$(36\pi) = 12\pi$.

The area of the unshaded region of the triangle can be found by subtracting the area of the shaded region from the total area of the triangle: $36\sqrt{3} - 12\pi$.

Section 8

1. E If businesses are having a hard time staying current, their equipment must be *old* or *outdated* because technology is advancing at a *fast rate. urgency* = pressing importance; *progressive* = advancing forward; *conventional* = standard; *torpidity* = lethargy; *antiquated* = outdated; *lassitude* = lack of energy; *innovative* = inventive, novel.

2. B The sentence states that one feature of Joyce's work *gave way* to another, suggesting that first missing word is a noun that directly contrasts the adjective in the second blank. The second word is paired with *arcane,* which means *secret* or *little-understood.* This word must also describe works that feature *neologisms* (invented words) and *obscure literary tricks.* Therefore the first word should mean something like *clarity* and the second phrase should include an adjective like *hard to understand. lucidity* = clarity; *opaque* = very difficult to understand or translate; *concise* = brief and to the point; *anachronism* = quality of being out of place in time; *derivative* = copied from others.

3. B Churchill was known to *choose his strategies arbitrarily* (without logical reason), so he was *whimsical* or *impulsive. diligent* = working with great effort; *impulsive* = acting without thought; *vicious* = evil, harsh; *malevolent* = wishing harm, malicious.

4. D If the king executed those who acted irreverently (without respect), he must have demanded *utmost respect. insolence* = brazen rudeness; *impudence* = disrespect; *truculence* = inclination to pick fights; *deference* = respect; *ignominy* = humiliation.

5. D Since Galileo contradicted church teachings, he was a *heretic. ostracized* = cut off from society; *hermit* = one who seeks solitude; *venerated* = worshipped; *demagogue* = powerful leader; *hallowed* = respected as holy; *revisionist* = one who rethinks or reshapes a commonly accepted view; *denounced* = accused or condemned for being a villain; *heretic* = one who holds controversial opinions; *reviled* = attacked with harsh language; *luminary* = one who inspires others.

6. A The Senator is known for her *iconoclastic* views, which means that she goes against the party line. Because of this, she would have a tough time getting *traditional* party members to support her. *Contentious* = quarrelsome; *orthodox* = traditional; *litigious* = prone to bringing lawsuits; *disingenuous* = insincere; *vituperative* = using harsh censure or condemnation; *dissident* = disagreeing; *heretical* = going against standard beliefs; *polemical* = pertaining to a highly controversial political or intellectual position.

7. D This is an address to the Atlanta Exposition (as the introduction indicates), and the author is clearly addressing those in *the commercial world* (lines 28–29) and entreating ex-slaves and Southern whites to work together for their mutual benefit.

8. **A**   The author does not directly address those in the antislavery movement but does address (B) *those of the white race who look to the incoming of those of foreign birth ... for the prosperity of the South* (lines 49–51), (C) *those of my race who depend upon bettering their condition* (lines 13–14), (D) those for whom African Americans have *tilled your fields, cleared your forests ...* (line 60), and (E) those African Americans who *underestimate the importance of cultivating friendly relations with the Southern white man* (lines 15–17).

9. **C**   The captain did not heed the 1st, 2nd, or 3rd call but heeded the 4th call *at last* (line 10), suggesting that he did not believe the responses were helpful at first.

10. **C**   The phrase *this chance* refers to the *man's chance* (that African Americans can have) *in the commercial world* (lines 28–29).

11. **A**   In saying that *there is as much dignity in tilling a field as in writing a poem* (lines 43–44), the author is saying that such manual labor is valuable work.

12. **D**   These indicate the thoughts of a *Negro who has given earnest thought to the situation of his people in America* (lines 74–75).

13. **C**   In saying that because of *incessant self-questioning* (line 90) ... *the best energy of the Negro people cannot be marshalled to do the bidding of the race* (lines 97–98), the author means that introspection keeps African Americans from organizing themselves to meet the needs of their race.

14. **D**   Such people are said to *make room for every rascal and demagogue who chooses to cloak his selfish deviltry under the veil of race pride* (lines 99–101); that is, they allow themselves to be influenced by selfish and evil people.

15. **D**   *That point* refers to the point *farther than* (which) *our Americanism does not go* (lines 131–132). In other words, this is the point up to which African Americans share much in common with all Americans but beyond which they are a unique people.

16. **C**   This *broader humanity* is that which *freely recognizes differences in men, but sternly deprecates* (disapproves of) *inequality in their opportunities of development* (lines 149–153). In other words, its members value equal opportunity for all races.

17. **E**   Passage 1 focuses on the manual labor that African Americans have performed in tilling fields, clearing forests, building railroads and cities, etc., while the author of Passage 2 emphasizes contributions like *the subtle sense of song that has given America its only American music, its only American fairy tales, its only touch of pathos and humor ....* (lines 140–143).

18. **A**   The *black tomorrow* in Passage 2 is the influence of African Americans in softening *the whiteness of the Teutonic today* (line 139), which suggests a change in the dominant culture. Passage 1, on the other hand, envisions a future in which African Americans make *friends in every manly way of the people of all races by whom we are surrounded* (lines 20–23) and incorporate themselves into the existing dominant industries of *agriculture, mechanics, ... commerce, ... (and) domestic service* (lines 23–24).

19. **E**   Passage 1 indicates that the dominant culture can give the African American *a man's chance in the commercial world* (lines 28–29) and contains many *opportunities* (line 47). Passage 2 is more assertive in suggesting that African Americans have changed and will continue to change the dominant culture: *We are the first fruits of this new nation, the harbinger of that black tomorrow which is yet destined to soften the whiteness of the Teutonic today* (lines 138–139).

Section 9

1. **C**   The parallel idiom *neither ... nor* requires that the phrase following *neither* and the phrase following *nor* have the same grammatical form. The only choice that maintains proper idiom and parallelism is C.

2. **E**   This sentence contains three clauses, each of which has the same subject, *Georgia*. The underlined clause, however, is in the passive voice, unlike the other two. It should be changed to the active voice like the others.

3. **D**   Since any rehearsal would have been completed before the performance, the participle in the underlined phrase should be in the perfect form *having rehearsed*. Choice B also uses the nonstandard phrase *being that*, and choices C and E create run-on sentences.

4. B In the original sentence, the subject *outlets* does not agree with the verb *has acknowledged*. In choice C, the subject *scope* disagrees with the verb *have been acknowledged*. Choice D is awkward and choice E uses an illogical verb tense. Choice B conveys the idea clearly and grammatically.

5. E The original verb *have had* is in the imperative mood, but should be in the subjunctive mood because it conveys a hypothetical condition. Choice E conveys the mood correctly.

6. C The statement made in the main clause is not *against* popular opinion, but rather is *contrary* to it. Although choice E uses the proper modifier, it illogically suggests that an opinion can *say* something.

7. A The original sentence is the most logical and effective option.

8. B The original phrase misuses the semicolon, because the phrase preceding it is not an independent clause. Similarly, choice E uses the conjunction *so* to join two clauses, but the first is not independent, so the sentence is ungrammatical. Choices C and D use the unidiomatic phrases *struggled for finding* and *struggled finding*. Choice B avoids these problems, and is clear and effective.

9. A The original phrasing is best. It provides the parallel form required by the comparative idiom *not so much by ... as by ...*, whereas the others violate parallel form.

10. D The original phrasing is unidiomatic. The correct idiom is *A appears to be B*.

11. C The comparison is logically between the *response* to the revised proposal and the *response* to the original proposal. Choice C is the only one that makes the correct logical and parallel comparison.

12. C The original phrasing breaks the idea into two independent clauses. But since it conveys one central idea, it is more effectively phrased with a single independent clause and a modifying phrase. Choice C does this effectively, idiomatically and concisely.

13. E The original phrasing is unnecessarily wordy and does not effectively coordinate the ideas in the sentence. Choice C has the same problem. Choices B and D create clauses with uncoordinated verbs. Only choice E conveys the idea concisely and effectively.

14. C The phrase *extra superfluous* is redundant, and the phrase *to edit for eliminating* is unidiomatic. Choice C is clear and concise.

PSAT/NMSQT PRACTICE TEST

ANSWER SHEET

Last Name: _____   First Name: _____

Date: _____   Testing Location: _____

Administering the Test

- Remove these answer sheets from the book and use them to record your answers to this test.
- This test will require 2 hours and 30 minutes to complete. Take this test in one sitting.
- Use a stopwatch to time yourself on each other section. The time limit for each section is written clearly at the beginning of each section. The first four sections are 25 minutes long, and last section is 30 minutes long.
- Each response must completely fill the oval. Erase all stray marks completely, or they may be interpreted as responses.
- You must stop ALL work on a section when time is called.
- If you finish a section before the time has elapsed, check your work on that section. You may NOT move on to the next section until time is called.
- Do not waste time on questions that seem too difficult for you.
- Use the test book for scratchwork, but you will only receive credit for answers that are marked on the answer sheets.

Scoring the Test

- Your scaled score, which will be determined from a conversion table, is based on your raw score for each section.
- You will receive one point toward your raw score for every correct answer.
- You will receive no points toward your raw score for an omitted question.
- For each wrong answer on any multiple-choice question, your raw score will be reduced by ¼ point. For each wrong answer on any numerical "grid-in" question (Section 4, questions 29–38), your raw score will receive no deduction.

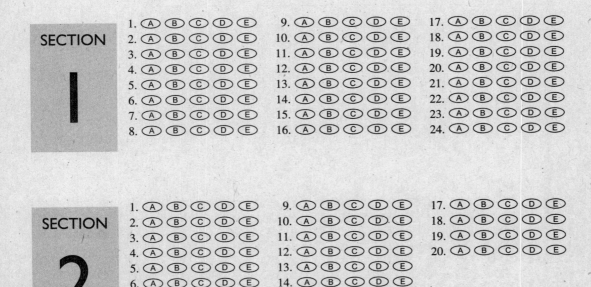

ANSWER SHEET

SECTION 3

25. Ⓐ Ⓑ Ⓒ Ⓓ Ⓔ 33. Ⓐ Ⓑ Ⓒ Ⓓ Ⓔ 41. Ⓐ Ⓑ Ⓒ Ⓓ Ⓔ
26. Ⓐ Ⓑ Ⓒ Ⓓ Ⓔ 34. Ⓐ Ⓑ Ⓒ Ⓓ Ⓔ 42. Ⓐ Ⓑ Ⓒ Ⓓ Ⓔ
27. Ⓐ Ⓑ Ⓒ Ⓓ Ⓔ 35. Ⓐ Ⓑ Ⓒ Ⓓ Ⓔ 43. Ⓐ Ⓑ Ⓒ Ⓓ Ⓔ
28. Ⓐ Ⓑ Ⓒ Ⓓ Ⓔ 36. Ⓐ Ⓑ Ⓒ Ⓓ Ⓔ 44. Ⓐ Ⓑ Ⓒ Ⓓ Ⓔ
29. Ⓐ Ⓑ Ⓒ Ⓓ Ⓔ 37. Ⓐ Ⓑ Ⓒ Ⓓ Ⓔ 45. Ⓐ Ⓑ Ⓒ Ⓓ Ⓔ
30. Ⓐ Ⓑ Ⓒ Ⓓ Ⓔ 38. Ⓐ Ⓑ Ⓒ Ⓓ Ⓔ 46. Ⓐ Ⓑ Ⓒ Ⓓ Ⓔ
31. Ⓐ Ⓑ Ⓒ Ⓓ Ⓔ 39. Ⓐ Ⓑ Ⓒ Ⓓ Ⓔ 47. Ⓐ Ⓑ Ⓒ Ⓓ Ⓔ
32. Ⓐ Ⓑ Ⓒ Ⓓ Ⓔ 40. Ⓐ Ⓑ Ⓒ Ⓓ Ⓔ 48. Ⓐ Ⓑ Ⓒ Ⓓ Ⓔ

SECTION 4

21. Ⓐ Ⓑ Ⓒ Ⓓ Ⓔ 25. Ⓐ Ⓑ Ⓒ Ⓓ Ⓔ
22. Ⓐ Ⓑ Ⓒ Ⓓ Ⓔ 26. Ⓐ Ⓑ Ⓒ Ⓓ Ⓔ
23. Ⓐ Ⓑ Ⓒ Ⓓ Ⓔ 27. Ⓐ Ⓑ Ⓒ Ⓓ Ⓔ
24. Ⓐ Ⓑ Ⓒ Ⓓ Ⓔ 28. Ⓐ Ⓑ Ⓒ Ⓓ Ⓔ

[Grid-in response boxes for questions 29–38]

SECTION 5

1. Ⓐ Ⓑ Ⓒ Ⓓ Ⓔ   11. Ⓐ Ⓑ Ⓒ Ⓓ Ⓔ   21. Ⓐ Ⓑ Ⓒ Ⓓ Ⓔ   31. Ⓐ Ⓑ Ⓒ Ⓓ Ⓔ
2. Ⓐ Ⓑ Ⓒ Ⓓ Ⓔ   12. Ⓐ Ⓑ Ⓒ Ⓓ Ⓔ   22. Ⓐ Ⓑ Ⓒ Ⓓ Ⓔ   32. Ⓐ Ⓑ Ⓒ Ⓓ Ⓔ
3. Ⓐ Ⓑ Ⓒ Ⓓ Ⓔ   13. Ⓐ Ⓑ Ⓒ Ⓓ Ⓔ   23. Ⓐ Ⓑ Ⓒ Ⓓ Ⓔ   33. Ⓐ Ⓑ Ⓒ Ⓓ Ⓔ
4. Ⓐ Ⓑ Ⓒ Ⓓ Ⓔ   14. Ⓐ Ⓑ Ⓒ Ⓓ Ⓔ   24. Ⓐ Ⓑ Ⓒ Ⓓ Ⓔ   34. Ⓐ Ⓑ Ⓒ Ⓓ Ⓔ
5. Ⓐ Ⓑ Ⓒ Ⓓ Ⓔ   15. Ⓐ Ⓑ Ⓒ Ⓓ Ⓔ   25. Ⓐ Ⓑ Ⓒ Ⓓ Ⓔ   35. Ⓐ Ⓑ Ⓒ Ⓓ Ⓔ
6. Ⓐ Ⓑ Ⓒ Ⓓ Ⓔ   16. Ⓐ Ⓑ Ⓒ Ⓓ Ⓔ   26. Ⓐ Ⓑ Ⓒ Ⓓ Ⓔ   36. Ⓐ Ⓑ Ⓒ Ⓓ Ⓔ
7. Ⓐ Ⓑ Ⓒ Ⓓ Ⓔ   17. Ⓐ Ⓑ Ⓒ Ⓓ Ⓔ   27. Ⓐ Ⓑ Ⓒ Ⓓ Ⓔ   37. Ⓐ Ⓑ Ⓒ Ⓓ Ⓔ
8. Ⓐ Ⓑ Ⓒ Ⓓ Ⓔ   18. Ⓐ Ⓑ Ⓒ Ⓓ Ⓔ   28. Ⓐ Ⓑ Ⓒ Ⓓ Ⓔ   38. Ⓐ Ⓑ Ⓒ Ⓓ Ⓔ
9. Ⓐ Ⓑ Ⓒ Ⓓ Ⓔ   19. Ⓐ Ⓑ Ⓒ Ⓓ Ⓔ   29. Ⓐ Ⓑ Ⓒ Ⓓ Ⓔ   39. Ⓐ Ⓑ Ⓒ Ⓓ Ⓔ
10. Ⓐ Ⓑ Ⓒ Ⓓ Ⓔ 20. Ⓐ Ⓑ Ⓒ Ⓓ Ⓔ   30. Ⓐ Ⓑ Ⓒ Ⓓ Ⓔ

Section 1

**Time—25 minutes
24 Questions**

Each of the sentences below is missing one or two portions. Read each sentence. Then select the choice that most logically completes the sentence, taking into account the meaning of the sentence as a whole.

Example:

Rather than accepting the theory unquestioningly, Deborah regarded it with ———.

(A) mirth   (B) sadness
(C) responsibility   (D) ignorance
(E) skepticism

Correct response: (E)

1 Hillary opened the door quietly and sneaked into her seat in order to remain as ——— as possible.

(A) inconspicuous
(B) coincidental
(C) tolerant
(D) inspired
(E) offensive

2 The speech began with focused and riveting vignettes about the life of a diplomat, but then deteriorated into a ——— list of unrelated facts.

(A) reflexive
(B) declining
(C) spellbinding
(D) superb
(E) rambling

3 The clothing stores in the new mall cater to the ——— and ever-changing tastes of their clientele, and so have a much more ——— inventory than typical boutiques.

(A) modest .. expensive
(B) diverse .. eclectic
(C) subtle .. permanent
(D) conservative .. extravagant
(E) redundant .. corporate

4 Some languages have very rigid rules of ———, while others allow many different possible arrangements of words to convey the same idea.

(A) pronunciation
(B) emphasis
(C) syntax
(D) acceptance
(E) symbolism

5 The ex-mayor's reputation has become so tainted that even members of his own party ——— at the mere mention of his name.

(A) recoil
(B) applaud
(C) defer
(D) pontificate
(E) calculate

6 Although few voters pay close attention to a presidential candidate's ——— policies, it is such ——— the economy that often affect citizens' lives most dramatically.

(A) foreign .. differences about
(B) political .. deliberations on
(C) domestic .. retreats on
(D) corporate .. indifference to
(E) fiscal .. stances on

7 When the editor learned that much of the information in the news article was ———, she quickly ——— the story and reprimanded the journalist who wrote it.

(A) verifiable .. published
(B) improbable .. marketed
(C) refutable .. compensated
(D) spurious .. retracted
(E) polished .. disowned

GO ON TO THE NEXT PAGE ▶▶▶

8

Many developing nations face the choice of, on the one hand, cultivating ——— and self-sufficient economy or, on the other hand, creating an international system of trade that renders them ——— the industries of many other nations.

(A) a free .. tolerant of
(B) an impoverished .. ignorant of
(C) an unregulated .. pursued by
(D) an isolated .. dependent on
(E) a robust .. superior to

The passages below are followed by questions based on their content and the relationship between the passages. Answer each question based on what is stated or implied in the passages.

Questions 9–12 are based on the following passages.

Passage 1

Line The currently fashionable criticism of the media as "liberal" is an interesting one. The term derives from the Latin *liber*, meaning free. A free-thinking press, independent
5 of a self-serving government, is central to American values as embodied in the Constitution. So why do right-wing pundits use it so derisively? The answer to this question goes to the heart of what it means
10 to be a conservative as well as what it means to be a good journalist. Conservatism depends, in large measure, on verifying that the status quo is working, so that the current power structure can remain in place. It is
15 founded on a need for comfort and a disdain for change. Good journalism, on the other hand, requires a divestment from governmental and corporate ideologies. Conservatives are wary of those who would
20 look closely at things with a mind open to changing them if necessary. Good journalists, however, examine worldly issues with a free and open mind. All good journalists are proud to be called liberals.

Passage 2

25 Those who debate whether the media are too "liberal" or too "conservative" fundamentally misconstrue the problem with the way news is presented to the American public. The very fabric of the media is corporate. The object
30 of the major news enterprises is not impartial analysis. Even if they employ the most capable and scrupulous journalists, the corporate goal is to make a profit. This inescapable fact molds the "news" in myriad
35 important ways. The issues, be they liberal or conservative, must be packaged for the least common consumer. Deep analysis or, God forbid, instruction, only causes consumers to tune out. The media have mastered the

GO ON TO THE NEXT PAGE ▶▶▶

40 formula of "scare, titillate, and reassure" in twenty words or less. Television and newspaper editors are essentially marketing executives, responsible not to the tenets of journalism but to what sells.

9 The primary purpose of Passage 1 is to

(A) examine the history of a term
(B) criticize a social policy
(C) propose a means of educating journalists
(D) recast a criticism into a compliment
(E) analyze a phenomenon objectively

10 Unlike Passage 1, Passage 2 focuses on

(A) conservatism
(B) the profit motive
(C) the rights of journalists
(D) the liberal nature of the media
(E) the need for social change

11 In line 29, the word "object" most nearly means

(A) criticism
(B) instrument
(C) goal
(D) insight
(E) obstacle

12 The authors of the two passages differ in their analysis of journalists in that the author of Passage 1 focuses on their

(A) freedom, while the author of Passage 2 focuses on their constraints
(B) incompetence, while the author of Passage 2 focuses on their skills
(C) political affiliations, while the author of Passage 2 focuses on their education
(D) appeal to consumers, while the author of Passage 2 focuses on their professionalism
(E) cynicism, while the author of Passage 2 focuses on their optimism

The questions that follow are to be answered on the basis of what is stated or implied in the passage below or the introductory material that precedes the passage.

Questions 13–18 are based on the following passage.

The following is an excerpt from a biography of Paul Erdös, an eccentric and prolific mathematician of the late 20th century.

Line   It was dinnertime in Greenbrook, New Jersey, on a cold spring day in 1987, and Paul Erdös, then seventy-four, had lost four mathematical colleagues, who were sitting
5 fifty feet in front of him, sipping green tea. Squinting, Erdös scanned the tables of the small Japanese restaurant, one arm held out to the side like a scarecrow's. He was angry with himself for letting his friends slip out of
10 sight. His mistake was to pause at the coat check while they charged ahead. His arm was flapping wildly now, and he was coughing. "I don't understand why the SF has seen fit to give me a cold," he wheezed. (The SF is the
15 Supreme Fascist, the Number-One Guy Up There, God, who was always tormenting Erdös by hiding his glasses, stealing his Hungarian passport, or, worse yet, keeping to Himself the elegant solutions to all sorts of
20 intriguing mathematical problems.) "The SF created us to enjoy our suffering," Erdös said. "The sooner we die, the sooner we defy his plans."

Erdös still didn't see his friends, but his
25 anger dissipated—his arm dropped to his side—as he heard the high-pitched squeal of a small boy, who was dining with his parents. "An epsilon!" Erdös said. (*Epsilon* was Erdös's word for a small child; in
30 mathematics that Greek letter is used to represent small quantities.) Erdös moved slowly toward the child, navigating not so much by sight as by the sound of the boy's voice. "Hello," he said, as he reached into his
35 ratty gray overcoat and extracted a bottle of Benzedrine. He dropped the bottle from shoulder height and with the same hand caught it a split second later. The epsilon was

not at all amused, but perhaps to be polite,
40 his parents made a big production of
applauding. Erdös repeated the trick a few
more times, and then he was rescued by one
of his confederates, Ronald Graham, a
mathematician at AT & T, who called him
45 over to the table where he and Erdös's other
friends were waiting.

The waitress arrived, and Erdös, after
inquiring about each item on the long menu,
ordered fried squid balls. While the waitress
50 took the rest of the orders, Erdös turned over
his placemat and drew a tiny sketch vaguely
resembling a rocket passing through a
hulahoop. His four dining companions
leaned forward to get a better view of the
55 world's most prolific mathematician plying
his craft. "There are still many edges that will
destroy chromatic number three," Erdös said.
"This edge destroys bipartiteness." With that
pronouncement Erdös closed his eyes and
60 seemed to fall asleep.

Mathematicians, unlike other scientists,
require no laboratory equipment—a practice
that reportedly began with Archimedes, who,
after emerging from his bath and rubbing
65 himself with olive oil, discovered the
principles of geometry by using his fingernails
to trace figures on his oily skin. A Japanese
restaurant, apparently, is as good a place as
any to do mathematics. Mathematicians need
70 only peace of mind and, occasionally, paper
and pencil. "That's the beauty of it," Graham
said. "You can lie back, close your eyes, and
work. Who knows what problem Paul's
thinking about now?"
75 "There was a time at Trinity College, in
the 1930s I believe, when Erdös and my
husband, Harold, sat thinking in a public
place for more than an hour without uttering
a single word," recalled Anne Davenport, the
80 widow of one of Erdös's English collaborators.
"Then Harold broke the long silence, by
saying, 'It is not nought. It is one.' Then all
was relief and joy. Everyone around
them thought they were mad. Of course,
85 they were."

13 In the first paragraph, Erdös is characterized primarily as

(A) domineering
(B) playful
(C) disoriented
(D) charismatic
(E) stoic

14 The passage suggests that Erdös's extended
arm indicates his

(A) desire for silence
(B) illustration of a mathematical
concept
(C) attempt to entertain children
(D) anger
(E) efforts to signal a waitress

15 The quotations from Erdös in the passage
demonstrate that he feels most keenly
oppressed by

(A) his fellow mathematicians
(B) his waitress
(C) God
(D) small children
(E) scientists

16 In line 52, the word "craft" most nearly
means

(A) skill
(B) creation
(C) means of transportation
(D) deception
(E) artwork

17 The reference to Archimedes in lines 65–67
serves primarily to emphasize Erdös's

(A) use of tricks to entertain small
children
(B) prolific mathematical output
(C) ability to do mathematical work
almost anywhere
(D) disregard for his surroundings
(E) lack of self-consciousness

18 The story in the final paragraph (lines 75–85)
characterizes Erdös as

(A) impatient
(B) reclusive
(C) jocular
(D) distractible
(E) focused

GO ON TO THE NEXT PAGE ▶▶▶

Questions 19–24 are based on the following passage.

The following passage discusses the principles of aesthetics, the study of the nature and meaning of art.

Line   Since it is our purpose to develop an
        adequate idea of art, it might seem as if a
        definition were rather our goal than our
        starting point; yet we must identify the field
5   of our investigations and mark it off from
        other regions; and this we can do only by
        means of a preliminary definition, which the
        rest of our study may then enrich and
        complete.
10   We shall find it fruitful to begin with the
        definition recently revived by Crocc: art is
        expression, and expression we may describe,
        for our own ends, as the putting forth of
        purpose, feeling, or thought into a sensuous
15   medium, where they can be experienced
        again by the one who expresses himself and
        communicated to others. Thus, in this sense,
        a lyric poem is an expression—a bit of a
        poet's intimate experience put into words;
20   epic and dramatic poetry are expressions—
        visions of a larger life made manifest in the
        same medium. Pictures and statues are also
        expressions, for they are embodiments in
        color and space-forms of the artists' ideas of
25   visible nature and man. Works of architecture
        and the other industrial arts are embodiments
        of purpose and the well-being that comes
        from purpose fulfilled.
            This definition, good so far as it goes, is,
30   however, too inclusive, for plainly, although
        every work of art is an expression, not every
        expression is a work of art. Automatic
        expressions, instinctive overflowings of
        emotion into motor channels, like the cry
35   of pain or the shout of joy, are not aesthetic.
        Practical expressions also, all such as are
        only means or instruments for the realization
        of ulterior purposes—the command of the
        officer, the conversation of the market
40   place, a saw—are not aesthetic. Works of
        art—the *Ninth Symphony*, the *Ode to the West
        Wind*—are not of this character.

No matter what further purposes artistic
expressions may serve, they are produced
45 and valued for themselves; we linger in them;
we neither merely execute them mechanically,
as we do automatic expressions, nor hasten
through them, our minds fixed upon some
future end to be gained by them, as is the
50 case with practical expressions. Both for the
artist and the appreciator, they are ends in
themselves. Compare, for example, a love
poem with a declaration of love. The poem is
esteemed for the rhythmic emotional
55 experience it gives the writer or reader; the
declaration, even when enjoyed by the suitor,
has its prime value in its consequences, and
the quicker it is over and done with and its
end attained the better. The one, since it has
60 its purpose within itself, is returned to and
repeated; the other, being chiefly a means to
an end, would be senseless if repeated, once
the end that called it forth is accomplished.
The value of the love poem, although
65 written to persuade a lady, cannot be
measured in terms of its mere success; for if
beautiful, it remains of worth after the lady
has yielded, nay, even if it fails to win her.
Any sort of practical purpose may be one
70 motive in the creation of
a work of art, but its significance is broader
than the success or failure of that motive.
The Russian novel is still significant, even
now, after the revolution. As beautiful, it is of
75 perennial worth and stands out by itself.
But practical expressions are only transient
links in the endless chain of means,
disappearing as the wheel of effort revolves.
Art is indeed expression, but free or
80 autonomous expression.

19 The purpose of the passage as a whole is to

(A) contrast several different modes of artistic expression

(B) discuss the effects of art on modern society

(C) establish the importance of defining terms as a prelude to philosophical discourse

(D) distinguish between artistic expression and nonartistic expression

(E) compare modern definitions of art with definitions from the past

GO ON TO THE NEXT PAGE ▶▶▶

20 As it is used in line 15, "medium" most nearly means

(A) moderate position
(B) environment
(C) prediction
(D) artist
(E) mode of creation

21 According to the passage, "the cry of pain or the shout of joy" (lines 34–35) is

(A) a potential reaction to a moving work of art
(B) something that could hinder creativity
(C) an expression of emotion that can inspire a great work of art
(D) an action that in itself lacks meaning as art
(E) an outburst that could interfere with the appreciation of a work of art

22 The author mentions the *Ninth Symphony* in line 41 primarily as an example of

(A) an underappreciated masterpiece
(B) a work that was inspired by an instinctive expression of emotion
(C) an expression that has a purpose in itself, rather than as a means to something else
(D) a piece of art that was intended as a declaration of love
(E) a musical piece that is not held in high regard by critics

23 The "success" mentioned in line 67 refers to the ability of

(A) a sentimental expression to influence a particular person
(B) an artist to sell a work of art at a high price
(C) an artwork to remain popular after many years
(D) an artist to maintain high aesthetic standards
(E) a society to appreciate the meaning of art

24 The sentence beginning on line 69 ("Any sort of … of that motive") conveys the author's opinion that

(A) every work of art must have an ulterior motive
(B) few works of art have any significant effect on historical events
(C) a work of art has meaning beyond its intended purpose
(D) art does not need a wide audience in order to be successful
(E) a musical piece that is not held in high regard by critics

STOP   *You may check your work, on this section only, until time is called.*

Section 2

Time—25 minutes
20 Questions

Directions for Multiple-Choice Questions

In this section, solve each problem, using any available space on the page for scratchwork. Then decide which is the best of the choices given and fill in the corresponding oval on the answer sheet.

- You may use a calculator on any problem. All numbers used are real numbers.
- Figures are drawn as accurately as possible EXCEPT when it is stated that the figure is not drawn to scale.
- All figures lie in a plane unless otherwise indicated.

Reference Information

$A = \pi r^2$ $A = \ell w$ $A = \frac{1}{2}bh$ $V = \ell wh$ $V = \pi r^2 h$ $c^2 = a^2 + b^2$ Special Right Triangles
$C = 2\pi r$

The arc of a circle measures 360°.
Every straight angle measures 180°.
The sum of the measures of the angles in a triangle is 180°.

---

1 If $x = 5$ and $y + 2 = 10$, what is the value of xy?

(A) 13
(B) 17
(C) 40
(D) 50
(E) 60

2 The average (arithmetic mean) of four numbers is 10. If three of the numbers are 8, 9, and 10, what is the fourth number?

(A) 10
(B) 11
(C) 12
(D) 13
(E) 17

3 Two of the angles in a triangle measure 70° and 60°. What is the measure of the third angle?

(A) 40°
(B) 50°
(C) 60°
(D) 80°
(E) 230°

4 The ratio of 5 to 6 is equal to the ratio of 30 to what number?

(A) 25
(B) 31
(C) 36
(D) 38
(E) 40

5 If $k = 2m \neq 0$, what is the value of $\frac{m}{k} \times 16$?

(A) 4
(B) 8
(C) 16
(D) 32
(E) 64

GO ON TO THE NEXT PAGE ▶▶▶

VOTING RESULTS FOR CLASS ELECTION

	Student A	Student B	Total
Boys	19		
Girls			40
Total	35		67

6 The table above represents the results of a vote for a class election between Student A and Student B. How many girls voted for Student B?

(A) 8
(B) 16
(C) 24
(D) 27
(E) 32

7 Caroline and Mark together own 36 DVDs, but Caroline owns 6 more than Mark does. How many DVDs does Caroline own?

(A) 12
(B) 15
(C) 18
(D) 21
(E) 24

8 How many ounces of nuts must be added to 12 ounces of raisins if the resulting mixture is to be 25% nuts, by weight?

(A) 3
(B) 4
(C) 8
(D) 36
(E) 48

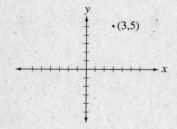

9 The point (3, 5) undergoes three consecutive transformations: first, a reflection over the x-axis, then a reflection over the y-axis, and then a reflection over the x-axis. What are the coordinates of the resulting point?

(A) (3, −5)
(B) (−3, −5)
(C) (−3, 5)
(D) (−5, 3)
(E) (−5, −3)

10 If $m + 6n = 40$ and m and n are positive integers, then what is the least possible value of m?

(A) 1
(B) 4
(C) 6
(D) 8
(E) 10

11 If k is divisible by both 27 and 36, it must also be divisible by which of the following?

(A) 8
(B) 10
(C) 16
(D) 54
(E) 72

$$1, 1, 2, 3, 5, 8, \ldots$$

12 Each term in the sequence above, except the first, is the sum of the previous two terms. How many of the first 60 of these terms are even?

(A) 18
(B) 20
(C) 30
(D) 40
(E) 42

13 At a certain store, the price of a sweater is discounted by 10% after each week that it is on the shelf. What is the price of a sweater after 4 weeks on the shelf if its original price was $100?

(A) $59.05
(B) $60.00
(C) $65.61
(D) $72.90
(E) $93.44

14 If $9x^2 - 9y^2 = 36$ and $x + y = 2$, then how much greater is x than y?

(A) 2
(B) 4
(C) 6
(D) 8
(E) 10

GO ON TO THE NEXT PAGE ▶▶▶

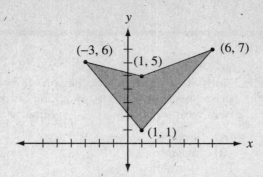

15 What is the area, in square units, of the shaded region above?

(A) 22
(B) 21
(C) 20
(D) 19
(E) 18

16 Points A, B, C, and D lie on a line, in that order. If $AC = 6BC$ and $BD = 5AB$, then $\dfrac{CD}{AC} =$

(A) $\dfrac{1}{4}$

(B) $\dfrac{1}{3}$

(C) $\dfrac{3}{4}$

(D) 3

(E) 4

17 If some aggles are iggles and all aggles are uggles, then which of the following statements must be true?

   I. All iggles are uggles.
  II. Some uggles are iggles.
 III. There are no uggles that are not aggles.

(A) I only
(B) II only
(C) III only
(D) I and II only
(E) II and III only

18 If x gallons of paint cost d dollars, and each gallon of paint covers 500 square feet, how much would it cost, in dollars, to purchase enough paint to cover m square feet?

(A) $\dfrac{md}{500x}$

(B) $\dfrac{500md}{x}$

(C) $\dfrac{500x}{md}$

(D) $\dfrac{500m}{dx}$

(E) $\dfrac{m}{500dx}$

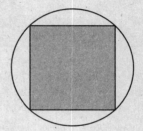

19 In the figure above, a square is inscribed in a circle. If the circle has an area of 16π, what is the area of the square?

(A) 12
(B) 16
(C) 32
(D) 36
(E) 38

20 Let $r \diamond t \diamond s$ be defined by the equation $r \diamond t \diamond s = r^s + t^s$. If m and n are postive integers and $m \diamond n \diamond 2 = 100$, what is the value of $m + n$?

(A) 10
(B) 11
(C) 12
(D) 13
(E) 14

You may check your work, on this section only, until time is called.

Section 3

Time—25 minutes
24 Questions

Each of the sentences below is missing one or two portions. Read each sentence. Then select the word or words that most logically completes the sentence, taking into account the meaning of the sentence as a whole.

Example:

Rather than accepting the theory unquestioningly, Deborah regarded it with ———.

(A) mirth   (B) sadness
(C) responsibility   (D) ignorance
(E) skepticism

Correct response: (E)

25 As activists, they knew that they could not remain _____ while their most precious values were being attacked.

(A) repetitive
(B) passive
(C) memorable
(D) confrontational
(E) generalized

26 Although he was _____ by a strained tendon, Schilling did not allow this_____ to keep him from pitching a masterful game.

(A) hobbled .. impediment
(B) weakened .. inspiration
(C) disabled .. aid
(D) deterred .. promotion
(E) consoled .. hurdle

27 Martin Gardner is considered one of the most _____ writers in science and mathematics, having authored over 65 books and countless magazine articles.

(A) conservative
(B) ingenuous
(C) obscure
(D) prolific
(E) desperate

28 Normally a sympathetic person, Jerry surprised his supporters by attacking his opponent with seemingly _____ remarks.

(A) stoic
(B) delicate
(C) synthetic
(D) venerable
(E) callous

29 The _____ display advertising the new video game, which included a garish neon sign, was a marked departure from the more _____ promotions that the company had used in the past.

(A) listless .. lethargic
(B) dynamic .. insightful
(C) ostentatious .. subdued
(D) beguiling .. volatile
(E) nondescript .. mutable

GO ON TO THE NEXT PAGE ▶▶▶

Each passage below is followed by questions based on its content. Answer each question based on what is stated or implied in the passage or the introductory material that precedes it.

Questions 30–31 are based on the following passage.

Line   The American Revolution overspread
       Nantucket like a pall. Trade and
       communication with the outside world were
       reduced to a trickle. Vessels arriving home
5   were necessarily laid up, as there was too
       much risk of life and property to venture out
       again. Moreover, the Provincial Congress of
       Massachusetts and later the Continental
       Congress restricted such voyages. Some
10   people resorted to surreptitious trade in
       swift, light vessels designed to outrun a
       pursuer, but this often proved disastrous
       since they carried such a press of sail that
       they were frequently swamped and their
15   crews drowned. Because the majority of the
       islanders were members of the Society of
       Friends, they were opposed to war and thus
       took no active part in the conflict; but this
       did not keep its consequences from their
20   shores.

30 The passage characterizes the effects of the American Revolution primarily as

(A) political
(B) restrictive
(C) triumphant
(D) bloody
(E) hopeful

31 The passage suggests that, during the American Revolution, members of the Society of Friends were

(A) patriots
(B) pacifists
(C) adventurers
(D) entrepreneurs
(E) conservatives

Questions 32–33 are based on the following passage.

Line   About 500 years ago, a new dimension was
       added to man's age-old attempt to satisfy his
       insatiable curiosity about the nature of the
       universe—people began to verify their
5   scientific hypotheses by stringent tests. It was
       Galileo Galilei who ushered in the era of
       modern science 400 years ago when he
       conducted the first verifiable experiments
       during his investigation of freely falling
10   bodies. Compared to Galileo's throwing rocks
       off the leaning tower of Pisa, our using
       gigantic particle detectors to penetrate to the
       heart of matter seems to represent something
       of an entirely different order. Yet the
15   principle behind both kinds of experiments,
       and the excitement of discovery they engender,
       remains the same: when we conduct an
       experiment we put a question to nature, and
       nature is forced to yield an answer.
20   Frequently the answer is rather complicated
       and we have enormous difficulty understanding
       it. Sometimes, however, the answer is simpler
       than anticipated. When insights suddenly
       appear and new ideas are born—these are the
25   great moments of science, when it becomes
       as sublime as a great work of art.

32 The author compares one of Galileo's experiments with a modern one primarily to make the point that

(A) Galileo's experiments did not yield accurate results
(B) modern equipment is often inordinately expensive
(C) stringent scientific tests are a recent development
(D) the scientific method has endured many centuries
(E) modern physicists are much more knowledgeable than the scientists of centuries ago

33 The passage suggests that "insights" (line 23) are produced primarily through

(A) imagination
(B) experimentation
(C) re-examination of traditional texts
(D) the use of systematic logic
(E) synthesizing divergent viewpoints

GO ON TO THE NEXT PAGE ▶▶▶

Questions 34–48 are based on the following passages.

The following passages examine the issue of global warming. The first was written in 1997, the second in 2004.

Passage 1

Line   A small, vocal minority of skeptics claims
there is no scientific evidence to support the
theory that man-made emissions of greenhouse
gases will alter the Earth's climate. They
5   claim that global warming is liberal, left-
wing, claptrap science and a ploy by the
scientific community to ensure funding for
yet another "Chicken Little" scare. Others
suggest that attempts to reduce greenhouse-
10   gas emissions by changing energy or land use
policies would needlessly cost the American
taxpayer tens to hundreds of billions of
dollars annually and that it is really part of
an international conspiracy to undermine
15   America's competitiveness in the global
marketplace.
    The truth, however, is quite different. The
overwhelming majority of scientific experts
believes human-induced climate change is
20   inevitable. The question is not *whether*
climate will change in response to human
activities, but rather *where, when* and by *how
much*.
    We must keep in mind the following
25   points about current scientific understanding
of the climate system:
    First, human activities undoubtedly are
increasing atmospheric concentrations of
greenhouse gases, which tend to warm the
30   atmosphere. The most important greenhouse
gas directly affected by human activities is
carbon dioxide, which has increased by
nearly 30 percent since 1700, primarily
because of changes in land use and the
35   burning of coal, oil and gas.
    Second, there is no doubt that the Earth's
climate has changed during the last 100
years. The global mean air-surface
temperature over the land and ocean has
40   warmed between 0.6 and 1.1 degrees
Fahrenheit, glaciers have retreated globally,
and sea level has risen by 10 to 25
centimeters.
    Third, comparing the observed changes in
45   global mean temperature with model
simulations that incorporate the effect of
increases in greenhouse gases in aerosols
suggests that the observed changes during
the last century are unlikely to be due
50   entirely to natural causes. In addition, the
increase in the frequency of heavy rains in
the United States is yet another signal
consistent with human-induced global
warming.
55   Many people, especially those in colder
climes, question whether we should care if
the climate becomes warmer. The answer is
quite simple: a warmer climate will be
accompanied by changes in precipitation,
60   floods, droughts, heat waves and rises in
sea level.
    Policymakers are faced with responding to
the risks posed by human-induced emissions
of greenhouse gases. Decisions made during
65   the next few years are particularly important
because climate-induced environmental
changes cannot be reversed for decades, if
not millennia.

Passage 2

    We live in an age in which facts and logic
70   have a hard time competing with rhetoric—
especially when the rhetoric is political
alarmism over global warming. We continue
to hear that "the science is settled" in the
global warming debate, that we know enough
75   to take significant action to counter it. Those
who hold this view believe emissions of
carbon dioxide are the primary cause of any
change in global temperature and inevitably
will lead to serious environmental harm in
80   the decades ahead.
    In 1997, for instance, Vice President Al
Gore played a leading role in the negotiation
of the Kyoto Protocol, the international
agreement to deal with the fears about global
85   warming. He was willing to embrace severe
reductions in U.S. emissions, even though the
Clinton administration's own Department of
Energy estimated that Kyoto-like restrictions
could cost $300 billion annually. Then, when
90   it became clear that the Senate would not
agree to a treaty that would harm the
economy and exempt developing countries
like China and India, the Clinton
administration did not forward it for
95   ratification. Since then, the treaty's flaws
have become more evident, and too few
countries have ratified it to allow it to "enter
into force."

GO ON TO THE NEXT PAGE ▶▶▶

The Bush administration, as an alternative
100 to such energy-suppressing measures, has
focused on filling gaps in our state of
knowledge, promoting the development of
new technology, encouraging voluntary
programs and working with other nations on
105 controlling the growth of greenhouse gas
emissions. Collectively, these actions involve
spending more than $4 billion annually, and
the U.S. is doing more than any other nation
to address the climate-change issue.
110 Of these efforts, filling the gaps in our
knowledge may be the most important. What
we know for sure is quite limited. For
example, we know that since the early 1900s,
the Earth's surface temperature has risen
115 about 1 degree Fahrenheit. We also know
that carbon dioxide, a greenhouse gas, has
been increasing in the atmosphere. And we
know that the theory that increasing
concentrations of greenhouse gases like
120 carbon dioxide will lead to further warming
is at least an oversimplification. It is
inconsistent with the fact that satellite
measurements over 35 years show no
significant warming in the lower atmosphere,
125 which is an essential part of the global-
warming theory.
Much of the warming in the 20th century
happened from 1900 to 1940. That warming
was followed by atmospheric cooling from
130 1940 to around 1975. During that period,
frost damaged crops in the Midwest during
summer months, and glaciers in Europe
advanced. This happened despite the rise in
greenhouse gases. These facts, too, are not in
135 dispute.
And that's just our recent past. Taking a
longer view of climate history deepens our
perspective. For example, during what's
known as the Climatic Optimum of the early
140 Middle Ages, the Earth's temperatures were
1 to 2 degrees warmer than they are today.
That period was succeeded by the Little Ice
Age, which lasted until the early 19th century.
Neither of these climate periods had anything
145 to do with man-made greenhouse gases.
The lessons of our recent history and of
this longer history are clear: It is not possible
to know now how much of the warming over
the last 100 or so years was caused by human
150 activities and how much was because of
natural forces. Acknowledging that we know
too little about a system as complicated as
the planet's climate is not a sign of neglect by
policymakers or the scientific community.

155 Indeed, admitting that there is much we do
not know is the first step to greater
understanding.
Meanwhile, it is important that we not be
unduly influenced by political rhetoric and
160 scare tactics. Wise policy involves a continued
emphasis on science, technology, engagement
of the business community on voluntary
programs and balancing actions with
knowledge and economic priorities. As a
165 nation, by focusing on these priorities, we
show leadership and concern about the well-
being of this generation and the ones to follow.

34 The main purpose of the first paragraph of
Passage 1 is to

(A) describe the author's perspective on
global warming
(B) present an objective viewpoint
(C) rally support for a little-known cause
(D) outline a scientific theory
(E) present positions to be refuted

35 The argument described in lines 8–16
appeals to the reader's

(A) love of nature
(B) fear of rising sea levels
(C) fiscal responsibility
(D) sense of humor
(E) political loyalties

36 The "minority" mentioned in line 1 and the
"others" mentioned in line 8 agree that

(A) global warming is a serious concern
(B) greenhouse gas emissions have not
been increasing
(C) efforts to counteract global warming
are ill-conceived
(D) the costs of curbing gas emissions are
much less than most people think
(E) scientists should do more to study
global warming

First passage: *Global Warming Opposing Viewpoints*, Watson,
Robert, Greenhaven Press. ©1997 p. 18–22.
Second passage: "*Cold Facts on Global Warming*" by James
Schlesinger. *The Los Angeles Times*, January 22, 2004.

GO ON TO THE NEXT PAGE ▶▶▶

37 Which of the following, if true, would most directly weaken a claim made in the sixth paragraph of Passage 1 (lines 44–54)?

(A) The activities of many factories and power plants are regulated by the government.

(B) The emission of greenhouse gases has greatly accelerated in the last 50 years.

(C) The effects of global warming are more pronounced near the Earth's poles.

(D) The computer models used to simulate climate changes do not account for significant environmental variables.

(E) Scientists have been analyzing climate changes for over one hundred years.

38 The author discusses "changes in precipitation" in line 59 primarily in order to

(A) persuade those who doubt that global warming is a serious concern

(B) demonstrate the effectiveness of a particular scientific model

(C) show that a prediction is incorrect

(D) explain a potential benefit

(E) describe a way to slow global warming

39 Which of the following does the author of Passage 1 specifically cite as a potential result of global warming?

    I.   widespread extinctions
   II.   rising sea levels
  III.   longer growing seasons

(A) II only

(B) I and II only

(C) I and III only

(D) II and III only

(E) I, II, and III

40 With which of the following statements would the author of Passage 2 most likely agree?

(A) The belief that global surface temperatures have risen in the last 100 years is false.

(B) The U.S. Senate should ratify the Kyoto Protocol.

(C) Research indicates that Americans should immediately reduce greenhouse emissions.

(D) We do not yet know enough about the science of climate change to base environmental policy on it.

(E) The United States is not addressing the issue of climate change to the degree that other nations are.

41 The author of Passage 2 regards the statement that "the science is settled" (line 73) with

(A) reluctant acceptance

(B) skepticism

(C) urgent agreement

(D) indifference

(E) surprise

42 The author of Passage 2 objects to the Kyoto Protocol chiefly because it

(A) does not cut carbon dioxide emissions sufficiently

(B) does not incorporate current climatological research

(C) is too costly and unfairly applied

(D) does not promote new technology

(E) has not been ratified by the U.S. Senate

43 In line 132, the author of Passage 2 mentions damage done to crops primarily to make the point that

(A) global warming has hurt American agriculture

(B) the effects of global warming seem to be localized, rather than global

(C) more must be done to protect American farmlands

(D) increased carbon dioxide emissions can have a positive effect

(E) the climate has not been consistently warming over the last 50 years

GO ON TO THE NEXT PAGE ▶▶▶

44 The author of Passage 2 discusses the "Climatic Optimum" (line 140) because it

(A) illustrates the effects of unbridled carbon dioxide emissions
(B) shows a general cooling trend over the centuries
(C) is an example of political alarmism
(D) demonstrates a defect in the Kyoto Protocol
(E) seems to contradict a widely held theory

45 In line 153, the term "system" refers to a

(A) complex scientific phenomenon
(B) way of making environmental policy decisions
(C) means by which scientists can work together
(D) method of communication
(E) governmental bureaucracy

46 The author of Passage 2 suggests that the "scientific community" (line 155) should

(A) be active in publicizing its findings
(B) become more involved in policymaking
(C) be more cautious in making claims
(D) work more closely with industry
(E) change the focus of its study

47 With which of the following statements would the authors of BOTH passages likely agree?

   I. Global surface temperatures have increased over the last 100 years.
  II. The atmospheric concentration of greenhouse gases has been increasing.
 III. The extent to which human activities have contributed to global warming is well known.

(A) I only
(B) I and II only
(C) I and III only
(D) II and III only
(E) I, II, and III only

48 The author of Passage 2 would most likely respond to the observation noted in Passage 1 that "global mean air-surface temperature . . . has warmed" (lines 38–40) by noting that this observation is

(A) false
(B) inconsistent with other measured trends in atmospheric temperature
(C) based on political dogma rather than scientific study
(D) not addressed in the Kyoto Protocol
(E) the result of increased carbon dioxide emissions

STOP

You may check your work, on this section only, until time is called.

Section 4

Time—25 minutes
18 Questions

Directions for Multiple-Choice Questions

In this section, solve each problem, using any available space on the page for scratchwork. Then decide which is the best of the choices given and fill in the corresponding oval on the answer sheet.

- You may use a calculator on any problem. All numbers used are real numbers.
- Figures are drawn as accurately as possible EXCEPT when it is stated that the figure is not drawn to scale.
- All figures lie in a plane unless otherwise indicated.

Reference Information

$A = \pi r^2$ $A = \ell w$
$C = 2\pi r$ $A = \frac{1}{2}bh$ $V = \ell wh$ $V = \pi r^2 h$ $c^2 = a^2 + b^2$ Special Right Triangles

The arc of a circle measures 360°.
Every straight angle measures 180°.
The sum of the measures of the angles in a triangle is 180°.

21

$$2a + 3b + c = 20$$
$$3b + c = 24$$

If a, b, and c satisfy the equations above, what is the value of a?

(A) −8
(B) −4
(C) −2
(D) 2
(E) 4

22 If $0.00035 = 3.5 \times 10^n$, then $n =$

(A) −5
(B) −4
(C) −3
(D) 3
(E) 4

23 What is 25 percent of $\left(12x + \dfrac{1}{2}\right)$?

(A) $3x + \dfrac{1}{8}$

(B) $3x + \dfrac{1}{2}$

(C) $3x + \dfrac{1}{6}$

(D) $4x + \dfrac{1}{2}$

(E) $6x + \dfrac{1}{8}$

GO ON TO THE NEXT PAGE ▶▶▶

9 in

9 in

9 in

24 If a and b are the coordinates of the points on the number line above, then which of the following best describes the location of ab on the number line?

(A) between −1.5 and −1.0
(B) between −1.0 and −0.5
(C) between −0.5 and 0
(D) between 0 and 0.5
(E) between 0.5 and 1.0

27 The solid cube of wood shown above is to be cut into two congruent pieces with a cut that is parallel to two of the faces. What is the surface area (in square inches) of <u>one</u> of these two pieces?

(A) 243
(B) 283.5
(C) 324
(D) 364.5
(E) 445.5

25 The greatest of 4 consecutive positive even integers is k. If the average (arithmetic mean) of these integers is m and the median of these integers is n, which of the following must be true?

    I. m is odd
    II. $k - m = 3$
    III. $m = n$

(A) I only
(B) II only
(C) I and II only
(D) II and III only
(E) I, II, and III

28 For all positive integers n, let $\{n\}$ be defined as follows:

$\{n\} = \dfrac{n}{2}$ if n is a multiple of 4

$\{n\} = 4n$ if n is <u>not</u> a multiple of 4

Which of the following is equivalent to $[[6]]$?
(A) $\{3\}$
(B) $\{6\}$
(C) $\{12\}$
(D) $\{20\}$
(E) $\{22\}$

26 $2^{2x} \cdot 4^{3x} =$

(A) 2^{8x}
(B) 2^{12x^2}
(C) 4^{3x^2}
(D) 8^{5x}
(E) 8^{6x^2}

Directions for Student-Produced Response Questions

Each of the questions in this section requires you to solve the problem and enter your answer in a grid, as shown below.

- If your answer is ⅔ or .666 ..., you must enter **the most accurate value the grid can accommodate**, but you may do this in one of four ways:

| Start in first column | Start in second column | Grid as a truncated decimal | Grid as a rounded decimal |

Grid result here

- In the example above, gridding a response of 0.67 or 0.66 is **incorrect** because it is less accurate than those above.
- The scoring machine cannot read what is written in the top row of boxes. You **MUST** fill in the numerical grid accurately to get credit for answering any question correctly. You should write your answer in the top row of boxes only to aid your gridding.
- Do **not** grid in a mixed fraction like $3\frac{1}{2}$ as $\boxed{3\,1\,/\,2}$ because it will be interpreted as $\frac{31}{2}$. Instead, convert it to an improper fraction like ⅞ or a decimal like 3.5 before gridding.
- None of the answers will be negative, because there is no negative sign in the grid.
- Some of the questions may have more than one correct answer. You must grid only one of the correct answers.
- You may use a calculator on any of these problems.
- All numbers in these problems are real numbers.
- Figures are drawn as accurately as possible EXCEPT when it is stated that the figure is not drawn to scale.
- All figures lie in a plane unless otherwise indicated.

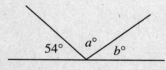

Note: Figure not drawn to scale.

29 In the figure above, if $a = 2b$, what is the value of a?

$$m, 12, m + 10$$

30 If the numbers above are the first three terms of an arithmetic sequence written in increasing order, what is the value of m?

31 If $p + r = 5$, what is the average (arithmetic mean) of 5, $3p$, 12, and $3r$?

32 How many integers between 10 and 99 contain either a 3 or a 5, but not both?

GO ON TO THE NEXT PAGE ▶▶▶

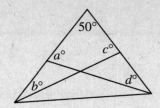

Note: Figure not drawn to scale.

33 In the figure above, what is the value of $a + b + c + d$?

34 Each of four cards contains a different positive integer less than 10. The following three conditions are met.

(1) Exactly three of the four numbers are prime.
(2) Two of the numbers are multiples of 3.
(3) None of the numbers is even.

What is the sum of the four numbers on these cards?

35 At a certain store, employees may buy clothing at a 20% discount from the original price, but must pay a 6% sales tax. If the final cost of a sweater purchased by an employee is $55.12, what is the original price of the sweater, before the discount and tax? (Disregard the $ symbol when gridding.)

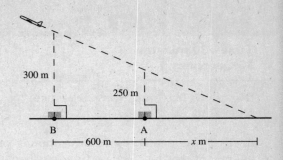

Note: Figure not drawn to scale.

36 Two detectors, located 600 meters apart on a flat airport runway, measure the altitude of airplanes as they pass overhead. Detector A determines that, when a certain plane passes directly above it, the plane has an altitude of 250 meters. A short time later, detector B determines that, when the same plane passes over it, the plane has an altitude of 300 meters, as shown in the diagram above. If the plane follows a straight path once it leaves the ground, how many meters from detector A did the plane first leave the ground?

37 If pump A, working at a constant rate, can fill a tank in 6 hours, and pump B, working at a constant rate, can fill the same tank in 2 hours, how many hours should it take them to fill the tank if they work together?

38 In a group of 500 students, 150 are studying physics, 220 are studying biology, and 100 are studying chemistry. At least 25 students are studying more than one of these sciences. What is the greatest possible number of these students that might NOT be studying any of these sciences?

STOP

You may check your work, on this section only, until time is called.

Section 5

Time—30 minutes
39 Questions

Directions for "Improving Sentences" Questions

Each of the sentences below contains one underlined portion. The portion may contain one or more errors in grammar, usage, construction, precision, diction (choice of words), or idiom. Some of the sentences are correct.

Consider the meaning of the original sentence, and choose the answer that best expresses that meaning. If the original sentence is best, choose (A), because it repeats the original phrasing. Choose the phrasing that creates the clearest, most precise, and most effective sentence.

EXAMPLE:

The children <u>couldn't hardly believe their eyes,</u>

(A) couldn't hardly believe their eyes
(B) would not hardly believe their eyes
(C) could hardly believe their eyes
(D) couldn't nearly believe their eyes
(E) could hardly believe his or her eyes

Example answer: (C)

---

1 <u>Despite having received</u> a majority of the votes, few people regarded Mark Lemann's election as a qualified representative.

(A) Despite having received
(B) Although having received
(C) Although he had received
(D) While receiving
(E) In his receiving

2 The radiation from naturally occurring carbon-14 atoms <u>are used to determine</u> the age of many ancient artifacts.

(A) are used to determine
(B) determining
(C) are what are used to determine
(D) is used to determine
(E) are determining

3 Nelson has written and directed many acclaimed films, <u>but he is</u> best known as a character actor.

(A) but he is
(B) is
(C) but being
(D) so is
(E) although

4 Although Magnus was clearly inspired by the romance novelists of the early nineteenth century, <u>they were deliberately not imitated by him</u>.

(A) they were deliberately not imitated by him
(B) he deliberately avoided imitating them
(C) the imitation was deliberately avoided by him
(D) he was avoiding the imitation of them by deliberation
(E) his avoidance to imitate them was deliberate

5 Many economists believe that, when used judiciously, <u>you can stimulate a stagnant economy with deficit spending</u>.

(A) you can stimulate a stagnant economy with deficit spending
(B) one can stimulate, with deficit spending, a stagnant economy
(C) deficit spending can, for a stagnant economy, stimulate it
(D) a stagnant economy can be stimulated by deficit spending
(E) deficit spending can stimulate a stagnant economy

GO ON TO THE NEXT PAGE ▶▶▶

6 When a nation is at war, the military conflict tends to override <u>what controversies, if any, that may exist</u> within the government.

(A) what controversies, if any, that may exist
(B) the controversies, if there are any, that are
(C) any controversies
(D) the controversies, if any exist
(E) what the controversies are that are

7 The vast landscape of the Bonneville Salt Flats in Utah is utterly devoid of plant life and geographical irregularities <u>and hence is an ideal location for racing</u> high-speed vehicles.

(A) and hence is an ideal location for racing
(B) which are ideal for racing
(C) providing the ideal location for racing
(D) that are ideal to race
(E) making these ideal for racing

8 Weighed down by an overloaded backpack, <u>David's search for a place to rest was urgent</u>.

(A) David's search for a place to rest was urgent
(B) David's urgent search was for a place to rest
(C) a place to rest was what David urgently needed
(D) a place to rest for which David urgently searched
(E) David searched urgently for a place to rest

9 The small breach in the hull of the ship soon became a gaping hole, quickly flooding the hold and <u>it made the possibility of repairing the damage almost impossible</u>.

(A) it made the possibility of repairing the damage almost impossible
(B) it made repairing the damage almost impossible
(C) making it almost impossible to repair the damage
(D) this fact made it almost impossible to repair the damage
(E) rendering the possibility of repairing the damage almost impossible

10 Yearning for a new challenge in college, <u>the forensics team provided me with a strong sense of camaraderie and teamwork</u>.

(A) the forensics team provided me with a strong sense of camaraderie and teamwork
(B) I found a strong sense of camaraderie and teamwork in the forensics team
(C) a strong sense of camaraderie and teamwork was what I found in the forensics team
(D) providing me with a strong sense of camaraderie and teamwork was the forensics team
(E) I was by the forensics team provided with a strong sense of camaraderie and teamwork

5

11 <u>The base camp had an insufficient supply of oxygen tanks, which were not enough for those climbers who required them as a necessity</u>.

(A) The base camp had an insufficient supply of oxygen tanks, which were not enough for those climbers who required them as a necessity.
(B) The insufficient supply of oxygen tanks at the base camp was not enough for those climbers who needed them.
(C) Lacking a sufficient supply of oxygen tanks, the base camp did not have enough for the climbers who needed them.
(D) The base camp did not have enough oxygen tanks for the climbers who needed them.
(E) The climbers' need for oxygen tanks was not met by the insufficient supply of them at the base camp.

12 Today's political campaigns rely so much on scare tactics and superficial sound bites <u>that voters rarely get any substantial perspective</u> on policy issues.

(A) that voters rarely get any substantial perspective

(B) so voters get rarely any substantial perspective

(C) and the substantial perspective is hardly gotten by voters

(D) and they don't give voters any substantial perspective

(E) that the substantial perspective is not really received by voters

13 In medieval times, many doctors believed that <u>if you had a disease it was because of an imbalance in your bodily "humours."</u>

(A) if you had a disease it was because of an imbalance in your bodily "humours"

(B) diseases were caused because you had an imbalance in your bodily "humours"

(C) diseases were caused by the fact of your bodily "humours" not being in balance

(D) diseases were being caused by imbalances in the "humours" in your body

(E) diseases were caused by imbalances in the bodily "humours"

14 <u>The charity finally reaching its goal through a pledge drive,</u> it did not want to neglect to thank its many benefactors.

(A) The charity finally reaching its goal through a pledge drive, it

(B) It reached its goal through a pledge drive, the charity

(C) To reach its goal through a pledge drive, the charity

(D) The charity reaching its goal through a pledge drive

(E) Having finally reached its goal through a pledge drive, the charity

15 In some ostensibly democratic countries, elections rarely take place, <u>unlike every year in the United States</u>.

(A) unlike every year in the United States

(B) where in the United States they take place every year

(C) unlike in the United States, where they take place every year

(D) unlike the United States' having them every year

(E) unlike the elections that take place every year in the United States

16 To become a *Jeopardy!* champion requires not only a broad knowledge base, but also <u>you must have quick reflexes and be able</u> to decipher hidden clues.

(A) you must have quick reflexes and be able

(B) your reflexes must be quick and the ability

(C) quick reflexes and the ability

(D) to have quick reflexes and the ability

(E) to have quick reflexes and to be able

17 A longstanding national tradition permits the monarch, regardless of his or her tribe of origin, <u>to be proclaimed as an honorary elder of every clan</u>.

(A) to be proclaimed as an honorary elder of every clan

(B) to have been proclaimed in every clan as an honorary member of it

(C) being proclaimed as an honorary elder of every clan

(D) as an honorary elder of every clan

(E) for being proclaimed an honorary elder of every clan

18 The tests performed to assess the age of the painting have produced inconclusive <u>results, and</u> many historians continue to insist that it predated the Renaissance.

(A) results, and

(B) results because

(C) results; thus

(D) results for

(E) results, but

19 Confident in its ability to hold on to its sizable lead, <u>the second half saw the team lose focus and allow its opponent to seize the momentum</u>.

(A) the second half saw the team lose focus and allow its opponent to seize the momentum

(B) the team allowed its opponent to seize the momentum in the second half because it lost its focus

(C) the momentum was seized by the opponent when the team lost its focus in the second half

(D) the team lost its focus in the second half and allowed its opponent to seize the momentum

(E) its opponents seized the momentum in the second half because the team lost its focus

20 An increasing number of feature films are starting to be regarded not so much as works of art or even as commercial products, <u>but rather as</u> advertisements for embedded products.

(A) but rather as

(B) or even as

(C) but not as

(D) but also as

(E) but are instead

5

> ## Directions for Identifying Sentence Error Questions
>
> The following sentences may contain errors in grammar, usage, diction (choice of words), or idiom. Some of the sentences are correct. No sentence contains more than one error.
>
> If the sentence contains an error, it is in one of the parts that are underlined and lettered. The parts that are not underlined are correct.
>
> If there is an error, select the part that must be changed to correct the sentence.
>
> If there is no error, choose (E).
>
> EXAMPLE:
>
> By the time <u>they reached</u> the halfway point
>   A
> <u>in the race,</u> most <u>of the runners</u> <u>hadn't hardly</u>
>   B   C   D
> begun to hit their stride. <u>No error</u>
>   E
>
> ***Example answer: (C)***

5 ➤

21 The twelve <u>choral pieces</u> that the choir <u>sung</u>
               A   B
in the spring concert were <u>chosen</u> for their
               C
vibrant melodies and <u>intricate</u> harmonies.
               D
<u>No error</u>
  E

22 The effects <u>of the decision</u> to invade Iraq
             A
<u>has been felt</u> not only in the Middle East
  B
but <u>throughout</u> the world <u>as well</u> <u>No error</u>
     C   D   E

23 Partisanship <u>still divides</u> the state legislature,
             A
<u>with</u> some representatives <u>tenaciously</u>
  B   C
demanding tax relief and others <u>insist on</u>
                    D
balancing the budget. <u>No error</u>
             E

24 Ever since the university vowed <u>to dedicate</u>
                       A
more of its resources to professional
studies, <u>there have been</u> <u>less</u> courses available
       B   C
<u>in the arts and humanities</u>. <u>No error</u>
        D   E

25 Although over 80 percent of citizens <u>profess</u>
                        A
a strong opinion <u>on the issue</u>, a much lower
             B
<u>percentage</u> actually intend <u>on voting</u> on the
  C   D
referendum. <u>No error</u>
         E

26 This year's geography bee, which was the
first to be held <u>on a college campus</u>, <u>drew</u>
            A   B
nearly three hundred <u>more</u> participants
               C
than <u>last year</u>. <u>No error</u>
    D   E

27 One of the <u>first challenges</u> that most first-year
             A
college students must address <u>is</u> coordinating
                    B
<u>his or her</u> academic schedules <u>with</u>
  C   D
many new social opportunities. <u>No error</u>
                    E

28 Our opponents in the debate <u>had prepared</u>
                      A
very well for their opening presentation,
<u>but they did not fare</u> well with the challenging
  B
questions <u>posed</u> by <u>Denitra and myself</u>.
        C   D
<u>No error</u>
  E

29 Although <u>they</u> deliberated for
                     A
<u>over four full days</u>, the jury members
                B
could not <u>agree for</u> the verdict, because
                     C
several key pieces of evidence had been

<u>called into</u> question. <u>No error</u>
        D   E

30 By virtue of <u>its ability</u> to use echolocation,
                          A
dolphins can, <u>even</u> while blindfolded,
                      B
<u>retrieve</u> small objects that are
    C
<u>dozens of meters</u> away. <u>No error</u>
           D   E

31 <u>If expecting</u> a clever and comic masterpiece
        A
<u>like</u> Bryant's debut novel, the second install-
 B
ment <u>of this trilogy</u> is <u>likely</u> to disappoint
              C   D
you. <u>No error</u>
        E

32 Many in the embassy <u>believe</u> that, if nego-
                                A
tiations <u>between</u> the two disputing factions
                 B
<u>had been given</u> more of a chance, civil war
           C
might have been <u>averted</u>. <u>No error</u>
                          D   E

33 The board soon <u>realized that</u>, in order to
                             A
avoid the need <u>to declare</u> bankruptcy, the
                        B
company would have to eliminate not only

<u>millions of dollars</u> in annual costs, but also
           C
<u>get rid of</u> hundreds of jobs. <u>No error</u>
        D   E

34 Many students who are <u>critics about</u> the
                                  A
current administration <u>remarked</u> that <u>their</u>
                              B   C
greatest fear is that the president will mis-

interpret his election <u>as a mandate</u> for his
                                D
economic policies. <u>No error</u>
                              E

5

GO ON TO THE NEXT PAGE ▸▸▸

Directions for Improving Paragraphs Questions

Below is an early draft of an essay. It requires revision in many areas.

The questions that follow ask you to make improvements in sentence structure, diction, organization, and development. Answering the questions may require that you understand the context of the passage as well as the rules of standard written English.

5

Questions 35–39 pertain to the following passage.

(1) *In the Copper Canyons of northwestern Mexico lives a remarkable people called the Tarahumara.* (2) *They are know by many as the Running Indians.* (3) *Running being such an integral part of their lifestyle, and so they are ready to take off on a long run at almost any time.*

(4) *You may never have heard of them because they rarely run in the big marathons around the world.* (5) *Believe it or not, this is because many of their runners think that such races are too short.* (6) *Where they excel is at the super-long races, many of which are well over 100 miles long.* (7) *Their economy is based on the trade of corn beer, which they make themselves.* (8) *Even over rocky and treacherous terrain, they often run barefoot, or with sandals handmade of old tires.* (9) *They do not use rigorous training methods, nor do they stretch or warm up before races.*

(10) *The Tarahumara may be among the best ultra marathoners in the world.* (11) *Although most runners consider their nontraditional running methods dangerous and unwise, it is because they have a very different perspective on the meaning of running.* (12) *One common ritual is the rarajipari, an all-out running race that pits one village against another.* (13) *After a night of drinking corn beer and betting, the two teams will run for 24 to 40 straight hours kicking a wooden ball over a predetermined course.* (14) *Often, the ball careens into a crevice and must be retrieved by one of the runners.* (15) *The race can easily cover over 100 miles.* (16) *Most runners would consider this an ordeal only to be endured for some personal victory, but to the Tarahumara it's just a heck of a lot of fun.*

35 Which of the following changes should be made to sentence 1?

(A)   Change *of* to *to*.
(B)   Insert a semicolon after *people*.
(C)   Omit the phrase *called the*.
(D)   Insert the phrase *which are* after *people*.
(E)   Change *lives* to *live*.

36 Which of the following is the best revision of sentence 3 (reproduced below)?

Running being such an integral part of their lifestyle, and so they are ready to take off on a long run at almost any time.

(A)   Because they are ready to take off on a long run at almost any time, and so running is an integral part of their lifestyle.
(B)   Running is such an integral part of their lifestyle that they are ready to take off on a long run at almost any time.
(C)   Being able to take off on a long run at almost any time, running is an integral part of their lifestyle.
(D)   Running being such an integral part of their lifestyle, and being ready to take off on a long run at almost any time.
(E)   Running being such an integral part of their lifestyle that they are ready to take off on a long run at almost any time.

37 The unity of the second paragraph can best be improved by deleting which of the following sentences?

(A)   sentence 4
(B)   sentence 5
(C)   sentence 7
(D)   sentence 8
(E)   sentence 9

GO ON TO THE NEXT PAGE ▶▶▶

38 In context, which of the following best replaces *"The Tarahumara"* in sentence 10?

(A) secondly, the Tarahumara
(B) cultures like that of the Tarahumara
(C) nevertheless, the Tarahumara
(D) while the Tarahumara
(E) in this sense, the Tarahumara

39 In context, which of the following is the best revision of the underlined portion of sentence 11 (reproduced below)?

Although most runners consider their nontraditional running methods dangerous and unwise, it is because they have a very different perspective on the meaning of running.

(A) most runners consider the nontraditional running methods of the Tarahumara to be dangerous and unwise, but the Tarahumara
(B) because most runners consider their nontraditional running methods to be dangerous and unwise, the Tarahumara
(C) considering the nontraditional running methods of the Tarahumara to be dangerous and unwise, the Tarahumara, to most runners
(D) considered by most runners, the nontraditional running methods of the Tarahumara are dangerous and unwise, but they
(E) although most runners would consider the running methods of the Tarahumara to be nontraditional, dangerous and unwise, they therefore

5

STOP

You may check your work, on this section only, until time is called.

ANSWER KEY

Section 1 Critical Reading	Section 3 Critical Reading	Section 2 Math	Section 4 Math	Section 5 Writing
☐ 1. A	☐ 25. B	☐ 1. C	☐ 21. C	☐ 1. C
☐ 2. E	☐ 26. A	☐ 2. D	☐ 22. B	☐ 2. D
☐ 3. B	☐ 27. D	☐ 3. B	☐ 23. A	☐ 3. A
☐ 4. C	☐ 28. E	☐ 4. C	☐ 24. B	☐ 4. B
☐ 5. A	☐ 29. C	☐ 5. B	☐ 25. E	☐ 5. E
☐ 6. E	☐ 30. B	☐ 6. C	☐ 26. A	☐ 6. C
☐ 7. D	☐ 31. B	☐ 7. D	☐ 27. C	☐ 7. A
☐ 8. D	☐ 32. D	☐ 8. B	☐ 28. A	☐ 8. E
☐ 9. D	☐ 33. B	☐ 9. C	# Right (A):	☐ 9. C
☐ 10. B	☐ 34. E	☐ 10. B	# Wrong (B):	☐ 10. B
☐ 11. C	☐ 35. C	☐ 11. D	# (A) $\frac{1}{4}$ (B):	☐ 11. D
☐ 12. A	☐ 36. C	☐ 12. B	☐ 29. 84	☐ 12. A
☐ 13. C	☐ 37. D	☐ 13. C	☐ 30. 7	☐ 13. E
☐ 14. D	☐ 38. A	☐ 14. A	☐ 31. 28	☐ 14. E
☐ 15. C	☐ 39. A	☐ 15. E	☐ 32. 32	☐ 15. C
☐ 16. A	☐ 40. D	☐ 16. E	☐ 33. 260	☐ 16. C
☐ 17. C	☐ 41. B	☐ 17. B	☐ 34. 24	☐ 17. A
☐ 18. E	☐ 42. C	☐ 18. A	☐ 35. 65	☐ 18. E
☐ 19. D	☐ 43. E	☐ 19. C	☐ 36. 3000	☐ 19. D
☐ 20. E	☐ 44. E	☐ 20. E	☐ 37. 3/2 or 1.5	☐ 20. A
☐ 21. D	☐ 45. A			☐ 21. B
☐ 22. C	☐ 46. C			☐ 22. B
☐ 23. A	☐ 47. B			☐ 23. D
☐ 24. C	☐ 48. B			☐ 24. C
				☐ 25. D
				☐ 26. D
				☐ 27. C
				☐ 28. D
				☐ 29. C
				☐ 30. A
				☐ 31. A
				☐ 32. E
				☐ 33. D
				☐ 34. A
				☐ 35. E
				☐ 36. B
				☐ 37. C
				☐ 38. C
				☐ 39. A

# Right (A):	# Right (A):	# Right (A):	# Right (A):	# Right (A):
# Wrong (B):	# Wrong (B):	# Wrong (B):		# Wrong (B):
# (A) $- \frac{1}{4}$(B):	# (A) $- \frac{1}{4}$ (B):	# (A) $- \frac{1}{4}$ (B):		# (A) $- \frac{1}{4}$ (B):

SCORE CONVERSION TABLE

How to score your test

Use the answer key on the previous page to determine your raw score on each section. Remember to add the raw scores from Sections 1 and 3 to get your Critical Reading raw score, and to add the raw scores from Sections 2 and 4 to get your Math raw score. Write the three raw scores here:

Raw Critical Reading score (Section 1 + Section 3): _____

Raw Math score (Section 2 + Section 4): _____

Raw Writing score (Section 5): _____

Use the table below to convert these to scaled scores.

Scaled scores: Critical Reading: _____ Math: _____ Writing: _____

Raw Score	Critical Reading Scaled Score	Math Scaled Score	Writing Scaled Score	Raw Score	Critical Reading Scaled Score	Math Scaled Score	Writing Scaled Score
48	80			20	49	52	54
47	80			19	48	51	52
46	78			18	47	50	51
45	76			17	46	48	50
44	74			16	45	47	49
43	72			15	44	46	48
42	71			14	43	45	46
41	69			13	42	44	45
40	68			12	41	43	44
39	67		80	11	40	42	43
38	66	80	80	10	39	41	41
37	64	77	78	9	38	40	40
36	63	74	77	8	37	39	39
35	62	72	76	7	36	38	37
34	62	70	74	6	34	36	36
33	61	68	73	5	33	35	35
32	60	66	71	4	32	34	33
31	59	65	69	3	30	32	32
30	58	64	68	2	29	30	31
29	57	62	66	1	27	29	30
28	56	61	65	0	25	26	29
27	55	60	63	−1	22	23	28
26	54	59	62	−2	20	20	27
25	54	58	60	−3	20	20	25
24	54	57	59	−4	20	20	24
23	52	55	57	−5	20	20	22
22	51	54	56	−6	20	20	21
21	50	53	55	−7 or less	20	20	20

Detailed Answer Key

Section I

1. A The fact that Hillary opened the door *quietly* and *sneaked* into the room suggests that she was trying not to be noticed. *inconspicuous* = not readily noticed; *coincidental* = occurring together by chance.

2. E The word *but* indicates a contrast in tone from the description of the speech as *focused and riveting*. The missing word should mean something opposite to focused. *reflexive* = referring to an action that is automatic and unintentional; *spellbinding* = riveting; *rambling* = unfocused.

3. B If the stores *cater* to a clientele with *everchanging tastes*, they must carry a wide variety of clothing. Both missing words should mean something like *varied*. *modest* = humble; *diverse* = varied; *eclectic* = deriving from a wide variety of sources; *subtle* = not obvious; *conservative* = traditional; *extravagant* = extremely abundant; *redundant* = characterized by needless repetition; *corporate* = appropriate to the business world.

4. C This sentence indicates a contrast between *rigid rules* on the one hand and more flexible rules on the other. The missing word must mean *rules for arranging words to convey an idea*. *emphasis* = the placement of stress or significance; *syntax* = the rules that govern word-order in a language; *symbolism* = the use of symbols to represent concepts.

5. A A *tainted* reputation is one that is damaged, usually by a scandal. If one's reputation is particularly tainted, the mention of one's name might cause even one's friends to *cringe*. *recoil* = cringe or shrink from; *applaud* = praise highly; *defer* = to submit to the wishes of another; *pontificate* = to speak haughtily; *calculate* = plan deliberately.

6. E Reading the whole sentence makes it clear that the subject of the sentence is a candidate's *economic policies*. Policies are positions on how an organization like the government should be run. *deliberations* = careful discussions to reach a decision; *domestic* = pertaining to one's own country rather than foreign ones; *retreats* = withdrawals from previous positions; *indifference* = apathy; *fiscal* = pertaining to financial matters; *stances* = official positions.

7. D If the editor *reprimanded* (scolded) the journalist, the journalist must have done something wrong. One common mistake in journalism is publishing incorrect information, which must later be withdrawn. *verifiable* = capable of being proved true; *marketed* = advertised for sale; *refutable* = capable of being proven incorrect; *compensated* = provided payment for a good or service; *spurious* = invalid, false; *retracted* = withdrew published material, usually because it contained erroneous information; *polished* = perfected; *disowned* = refused to claim as one's own.

8. D The sentence describes a contrast between two kinds of economy. The first is *self-sufficient*, so the second must *rely* on other nations. Such an economy is necessarily not *disconnected* with the outside world. *impoverished* = poor; *unregulated* = without rules designed to govern behavior; *pursued* = chased; *isolated* = set apart from the outside world; *robust* = vigorous and strong.

9. D The passage begins by describing a *currently fashionable criticism* (line 1), namely, that the press is *liberal*. It ends with the conclusion that *all good journalists are proud to be called liberals* (lines 24–25), so the overall purpose of the passage is to recast a criticism into a compliment. Although the origin of the term "liberty" is briefly discussed, it is not the main idea of the passage. It also does not discuss social policy or education. Lastly, it is not an *objective* analysis because it contains subjective evaluations of *good* journalism.

10. B The main point of the second passage is that *the very fabric of the media is corporate* (lines 28–29) and that *the corporate goal* [of journalism] *is to make a profit* (lines 32–33).

11. C In saying that *the object of the major news enterprises is not impartial analysis*, the author means that the *goal* of the media is not to give objective information.

12. A The first passage focuses on the fact that journalists should be independent of *governmental and corporate ideologies* (line 18), while the second suggests that they cannot be independent of corporate ideologies and are constrained by the need *to make a profit*. Neither passage discusses the skill level, education, or optimism of journalists.

13. C The first paragraph says that Erdös *had lost four mathematical colleagues* (lines 3–4), although they were sitting in front of him, so he was somewhat disoriented. There is nothing in the paragraph to suggest that he is *domineering* (overbearing and controlling), *playful* (although he certainly becomes more playful in the *second* paragraph), *charismatic* (showing natural leadership qualities), or *stoic* (deliberately unemotional).

14. D At two points in the passage, the author suggests that Erdös's extended arm indicates his anger. In lines 8–9, the author states that Erdös *was angry with himself* immediately after stating that he had *one arm held out to the side like a scarecrow's* (lines 7–8). Later the author states that *his anger dissipated—his arm dropped to his side* (lines 25–26).

15. C The passage states that *God . . . was always tormenting Erdös by hiding his glasses . . . or, worse yet, keeping to Himself the elegant solutions to all sorts of intriguing mathematical problems* (lines 18–20).

16. A In this context, the phrase *plying his craft* means exercising his skill, since it is referring to Erdös's explanation of an obscure mathematical proof.

17. C Archimedes is mentioned as an example of a mathematician who required *no laboratory equipment* and who could solve problems on his oil-drenched skin, much as Erdös was able to do complicated mathematics on a restaurant napkin.

18. E The last paragraph is a short vignette about Erdös and a colleague *thinking . . . for more than an hour without uttering a single word* (lines 78–79). Clearly, this requires a good deal of focus, and so Erdös is clearly not portrayed as *impatient* or *distractible*. And although there was *joy* at the resolution of the problem, the joy was not the result of a joke, and so Erdös is not portrayed as *jocular*.

19. D The first paragraph indicates that the author's purpose is to *develop an adequate idea of art* (lines 1–2) and to *identify the field of our investigation and mark it off from other regions* (lines 4–5). The essay then goes on to define art as a type of *expression* (line 12) that is distinct from nonartistic expression such as *automatic expressions* (lines 32–33) and *practical expressions* (line 36). Therefore, the main purpose of the essay is to distinguish artistic expression from nonartistic expression.

20. E In saying that *expression [is] the putting forth of purpose, feeling, or thought into a sensuous medium* (lines 12–15), the author is saying that artistic expressions must be made through some means that is detectable by the senses. Such a means is a *mode of creation*.

21. D The author refers to *the cry of pain or the shout of joy* (line 35) as an example of *automatic expression*, which are *instinctive overflowings of emotion* (lines 33–34). These, the author claims, are *not aesthetic* (line 35); that is, they are not expressions of true art.

22. C When the author states that a *work of art* such as the *Ninth Symphony [is] not of this character*, he indicates that it is not *only* [a means or instrument] *for the realization of ulterior purposes* (lines 37–38). That is, the *Ninth Symphony* has its purpose in itself.

23. A The word *success* in this sentence refers to the ability of a *love poem . . . to persuade a lady* (lines 64–65). Therefore, it refers to the ability of a sentimental expression to influence a particular person.

24. C This sentence states that a *work of art* has significance [that] *is broader than the success or failure of* [its] *motive*. That is, even if a piece of art was created for a specific purpose, such as to *persuade a lady* or to inspire a revolution, the work must still have meaning beyond the original purpose in order to be considered true art. This idea is summarized in choice (C). The sentence indicates that a work of art has meaning *despite* its ulterior motive, not *because* of it; therefore choice (A) is incorrect. The sentence does not refer to *historical events*, an *audience*, or *critics*; therefore choices (B), (D), and (E) are incorrect.

Section 2

1. C
$$y + 2 = 10$$
Subtract 2: $y = 8$
Therefore $xy = (5)(8) = 40$

2. D If the average of 4 numbers is 10, then the sum of the four numbers must be $4 \times 10 = 40$. Since the other three numbers have a sum of $8 + 9 + 10 = 27$, the fourth number must be $40 - 27 = 13$.

3. B The measure of the angles in a triangle adds up to 180°, so

$$70 + 60 + x = 180$$
Simplify: $\quad 130 + x = 180$
Subtract 130: $\quad x = 50$

4. C Set up the proportion: $\dfrac{5}{6} = \dfrac{30}{x}$

Cross-multiply: $\quad 5x = 180$
Divide by 5: $\quad x = 36$

5. B Simply substitute $2m$ for k (because they are equal) and simplify: $\dfrac{m}{k} \times 16 = \dfrac{m}{2m} \times 16 = \dfrac{1}{2} \times 16 = 8.$

6. C Notice first that the column showing the votes for Student A contains two numbers, so you can easily find the missing number. Since a total of 35 students voted for Student A and 19 of these were boys, 35 – 19 = 16 of them must have been girls. (Write this number into the table.) Since the "girls" row indicates that a total of 40 girls voted and since you just determined that 16 of them voted for Student A, then 40 – 16 = 24 girls must have voted for Student B.

7. D Start by saying that Caroline owns c DVDs. Since she owns 6 more than Mark does, Mark must own $c - 6$ DVDs. Since they own 36 altogether,

$$c + c - 6 = 36$$
Simplify: $\quad 2c - 6 = 36$
Add 6: $\quad 2c = 42$
Divide by 2: $\quad c = 21$

8. B Start by saying that you will add x ounces of nuts. If the resulting mixture is to be 25% nuts, then

$$\frac{\text{ounces of nuts}}{\text{ounces of mixture}} = \frac{x}{x+12} = \frac{25}{100}$$

Simplify: $\quad \dfrac{x}{x+12} = \dfrac{1}{4}$

Cross-multiply: $\quad 4x = x + 12$
Subtract x: $\quad 3x = 12$
Divide by 3: $\quad x = 4$

9. C The figure below shows the three consecutive transformations. The resulting point is at (–3, 5).

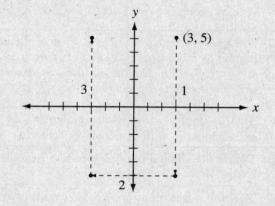

10. B Since the sum $m + 6n$ is fixed at 40, minimizing the value of m means <u>maximizing</u> the value of $6n$. Since both m and n are positive integers, $6n$ must be a multiple of 6. The greatest multiple of 6 less than 40 is 36, so the maximum possible value of n is 6. If n were 7 or greater, then m would have to be negative for the sum to equal 40, which would contradict the given information. Therefore, for the minimum value of m,

$$m + 36 = 40$$
Subtract 36: $\quad m = 4$

11. D The prime factorization of 27 is $3 \times 3 \times 3$, and the prime factorization of 36 is $2 \times 2 \times 3 \times 3$. The least common multiple of 27 and 36 is therefore $2 \times 2 \times 3 \times 3 \times 3 = 108$. Therefore, if an integer is divisible by both 27 and 36, it must also be divisible by 108. Any number that is divisible by 108 must also be divisible by 54, since 54 is a factor of 108 ($54 \times 2 = 108$).

12. B Looking at the 6 given terms, notice that the sequence is:

odd, odd, even, odd, odd, even . . .

In other words, one out of every three consecutive terms is even. Since 60 is divisible by 3, the total number of even numbers in the first 60 is $60 \div 3 = 20$.

---

13. C Reducing a number by 10% is equivalent to multiplying that number by 0.9. After 4 weeks, the sweater would have been discounted 4 times, so the final price would be $\$100(0.9)(0.9)(0.9)(0.9) = \$65.61$.

---

14. A

$$9x^2 - 9y^2 = 36$$

$$\text{Divide by 9:} \quad x^2 - y^2 = 4$$

$$\text{Factor:} \quad (x - y)(x + y) = 4$$

$$\text{Substitute 2 for } x + y: \quad (x - y)(2) = 4$$

$$\text{Divide by 2:} \quad x - y = 2$$

This means that x is 2 greater than y.

---

15. E Divide the shaded regions into two triangles with a vertical line as shown here:

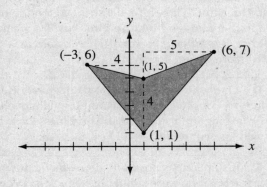

One triangle has a base of 4 and a height of 4, and the other has a base of 4 and a height of 5. The first triangle, then, has an area of $(4)(4)/2 = 8$, and the second has an area of $(4)(5)/2 = 10$. Altogether, then, the shaded region has an area of $8 + 10 = 18$.

---

16. E Start by drawing a line segment with points labeled A, B, C, and D, in that order. You don't have to worry about drawing it perfectly to scale.

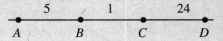

Assume, for simplicity's sake, that $BC = 1$. If $AC = 6BC$, then $AC = 6(1) = 6$. This means that $AB = 6 - 1 = 5$. If $BD = 5AB$, then $BD = 5(5) = 25$, and so $CD = 25 - 1 = 24$. Therefore, $CD/AC = 24/6 = 4$.

---

17. B A Venn diagram is very handy in a problem like this. If some aggles are iggles, then the circle representing the set of aggles must intersect the circle representing the set of iggles. If all aggles are uggles, then the circle representing the set of aggles must be *completely contained* in the circle representing the set of all uggles. Your diagram, then, should look something like this:

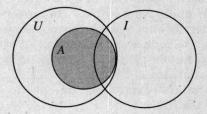

Now look at statement I: are all iggles also uggles? The diagram shows a lot of space inside the "iggles" circle that is not inside the "uggles" circle. Therefore, it is possible that there are iggles that are not uggles. So statement I is not necessarily true. [This lets you eliminate choices (A) and (D).] Now look at statement II: are some uggles also iggles? The diagram suggests yes, because part of the "uggles" circle must overlap the "iggles" circle in order to completely contain the "aggles" circle. This means at least some uggles are necessarily iggles. Therefore, statement II is necessarily true. [And you can eliminate choice (C).] Now look at statement III: are all uggles also aggles? Not necessarily, because there is a lot of space within the "uggles" circle that is not inside the "aggles" circle, so there could be some uggles that are not aggles, and therefore statement III is not necessarily true, and the correct answer is (B).

18. A You can solve this problem numerically, by "plugging in" values for the unknowns, or algebraically, by "converting" *m* square feet to the corresponding number of dollars. To use the "plugging-in" method, just pick simple values for the unknowns, like $x = 2$, $d = 20$, and $m = 1000$. (Think about the problem situation and notice why these are particularly convenient choices for the unknown values.) This suggests that 2 gallons of paint cost $20, so 1 gallon must cost $10. This one gallon covers 500 square feet, so it costs $10 to buy enough paint to cover 500 square feet. Since 1,000 square feet is twice as much as 500 square feet, it must cost twice as much, or $20. Therefore, when you plug in $x = 2$, $d = 20$, and $m = 1,000$ to the answer choices, the correct answer must equal 20. Notice that only choice (A) has a value of 20 in this case.

Alternatively, you can solve this with simple algebra:

$$m \text{ square feet} \times \frac{1 \text{ gallon}}{500 \text{ square feet}} \times \frac{d \text{ dollars}}{x \text{ gallons}} = \frac{md}{500x} \text{ dollars}$$

Notice that here you convert *m* square feet into dollars by multiplying by two "conversion factors." Notice that the numerator and denominator in each conversion factor are equal, and that all of the units "cancel" except for the one you're looking for: dollars.

19. C Use the circle area formula to find the radius of the circle:

$$16\pi = \pi r^2$$

Divide by π: $16 = r^2$
Take the square root: $4 = r$

Now write this information into the diagram. You might notice that the square can be divided up and reassembled as shown to form two squares that have an area of $4^2 = 16$. Therefore the entire shaded region has an area of $2(16) = 32$.

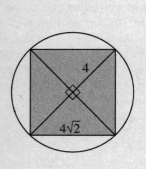
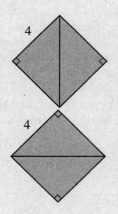

Alternatively, you might notice that each radius of the circle sketched in the diagram above is also a leg of a 45°–45°–90° triangle. Using the relationships among sides in this "special" triangle shows that each side of the inscribed square is $4\sqrt{2}$. Therefore the area of this square is $(4\sqrt{2})^2 = 32$.

20. E

$$m \diamond n \diamond 2 = 100$$
Translate using definition: $m^2 + n^2 = 100$

The fact that *m* and *n* must be positive integers and that $10^2 = 100$ suggests that *m* and *n* must each be an integer from 1 to 9. A small amount of trial and error should quickly show that the only possible solution is $6^2 + 8^2 = 100$. Therefore $m + n = 6 + 8 = 14$.

Section 3

25. B *Activists* are people who take political action for causes that are important to them. As an activist, one could not remain *idle* while one's values were being attacked. *passive* = inactive; *confrontational* = inclined to starting fights.

26. A The word *although* indicates that it is surprising that Schilling was not kept from pitching a masterful game. Therefore, his strained tendon must have been a real *hindrance* to him. *hobbled* = caused to limp; *impediment* = hindrance; *deterred* = prevented from taking action.

27. D One who has *authored over 65 books* is very *productive*. *conservative* = resistant to change; *ingenuous* = lacking sophistication or worldliness; *obscure* = not well known; *prolific* = very productive.

28. E If someone is normally *sympathetic*, it would be surprising if he were suddenly *mean*. *stoic* = deliberately unemotional; *synthetic* = artificial or = man-made; *venerable* = honorable; *callous* = emotionally hardened, insensitive.

29. C *Garish* means gaudy or excessively flashy. If such a display was a *departure*, their promotions must have previously been more *tame*. *listless* = lacking energy; *lethargic* = sluggish; *dynamic* = energetic; *ostentatious* = showy; *subdued* = modest; *beguiling* = charming in a deceitful way; *volatile* = explosive; *nondescript* = lacking in distinctive qualities; *mutable* = changeable.

30. **B** The passage states that, as a result of the Revolution, *trade and communication with the outside world were reduced to a trickle* (lines 2–4), and *the Continental Congress restricted* (line 8–9) voyages. This indicates that the revolution had a very restrictive effect on the people of Nantucket.

31. **B** The passage states that, as members of the Society of Friends, islanders were *opposed to war.* This means that they were *pacifists*.

32. **D** The overall purpose of the passage is to discuss briefly the effectiveness of experimentation and the scientific method over the last 500 years. The author compares one of Galileo's ancient experiments with a modern one primarily to make the point that *the principle behind both kinds of experiments, and the excitement of discovery they engender, remains the same* (lines 14–17). In other words, the scientific method has endured many centuries. Although the passage does suggest subtly that Galileo's experiments were cruder than modern ones, it does not state or even suggest that Galileo's experiments were inaccurate, that Galileo was less knowledgeable than modern scientists, or that modern scientific equipment is too expensive.

33. **B** The *insights* mentioned in line 23 are part of the discussion of the results of well-conducted *experimentation*.

34. **E** The viewpoints presented in the first paragraph are later refuted by the author, so they cannot represent the *author's perspective*. The fact that the author argues against these viewpoints indicates that they are not *objective*, nor are they part of a *scientific theory*. This paragraph is clearly presenting *positions to be refuted*.

35. **C** The argument described in lines 10–13 suggests that *changing energy or land use policies would needlessly cost the American taxpayer tens to hundreds of billions of dollars annually*. Although the author clearly disagrees with this argument, it is also clear that this argument is appealing to the reader's concerns about money, or *fiscal responsibility*.

36. **C** The two perspectives described in the first paragraph emphasize different points, but agree that *efforts to counteract global warming are ill-conceived*, either because there is no such thing as global warming or because the remedies would undermine America's competitiveness.

37. **D** The claim in the sixth paragraph that *the observed changes during the last century are unlikely to be due entirely to natural causes* (lines 44–50) is based on *model simulations* (lines 45–46) of the environment. If these simulations are innacurate, or do not consider important variables, then this conclusion would be called into question.

38. **A** The *changes in precipitation* and other effects of global warming are mentioned in order to convince those who *question whether we should care if the climate becomes warmer* (lines 56–57).

39. **A** On lines 60–61, the author mentions *rises in sea level* as one effect of global warming, but does not mention widespread extinctions or longer growing seasons anywhere in the passage.

40. **D** The thesis of Passage 2 is that the belief that *we know enough to take significant action to counter* [global warming] (lines 74–75) is incorrect. Therefore, he would clearly agree with the statement that *we do not yet know enough about the science of climate change to base environmental policy on it.*

41. **B** The overall purpose of the passage is to question some common conceptions about global warming and environmental policy. The claim that *the science* [about climate change] *is settled* is refuted throughout the passage by pointing out the *gaps in our state of knowledge* (lines 101–102). Thus, the author has clearly adopted a *skeptical* view of this statement.

42. **C** The author of Passage 2 states that *Kyoto-like restrictions could cost $300 billion annually* (lines 88–89) and that the Kyoto Protocol *would harm the economy and exempt developing countries like China and India* (lines 91–93). This means that the author believes that the treaty is too expensive and unfair.

43. **E** The author states that *frost damaged crops* (line 132) during a period of *atmospheric cooling from 1940 to around 1975* (lines 130–131), which occurred *despite the rise in greenhouse gases* (lines 134–135). This refutes the idea that greenhouse gases have produced a steady atmospheric warming effect over the last 50 years.

44. **E** The author discusses the warming during the Climatic Optimum, in which *the Earth's temperatures were 1 to 2 degrees warmer than they are today* (lines 141–142), even though this warming had nothing *to do with man-made greenhouse gases* (line 146) in order to discredit the widely held assumption that there is a strong connection between greenhouse gases and atmospheric warming.

45. **A** The *system* in line 153 is that of *the planet's climate*, which is a complex scientific phenomenon.

46. **C** The overall thesis of Passage 2 is that we do not know enough about the science of global warming to base environmental policy on it. According to the author, the common claims about the science of global warming are suspect. The author states that the *scientific community* (line 155) should acknowledge that *we know too little about a system as complicated as the planet's climate* (lines 152–154) and therefore should be cautious in making claims about it.

47. **B** Both authors acknowledge that the Earth's surface temperature has increased over the last 100 years: the author of Passage 1 in lines 38–41 and the author of Passage 2 in lines 115–116. They also both acknowledge that the atmospheric concentration of greenhouse gases has been increasing: the author of Passage 1 in lines 28–29 and the author of Passage 2 in lines 117–118. The author of Passage 2, however, clearly disagrees with statement III.

48. **B** The author of Passage 2 acknowedges (in lines 115–116) that the global surface temperature has warmed, but says that this fact is *inconsistent with the fact that satellite measurements over 35 years show no significant warming in the lower atmosphere, which is an essential part of the global-warming theory* (lines 123–127). Although the author of Passage 2 does criticize *political alarmism* (lines 71–72) surrounding global warming, he does not suggest that this statement is an example of it.

Section 4

21. **C**

Subtract the equations:
$$2a + 3b + c = 20$$
$$-(3b + c) = -24$$
$$2a = -4$$

Divide by 2: $a = -2$

22. **B** Remember that multiplying a number by 10^{-n} is the same as dividing that number by 10^n, which is the same as moving the decimal point of the number n places to the left. Therefore $0.00035 = 3.5 \times 10^{-4}$.

23. **A** 25% is the same as 1/4.

Distribute: $\frac{1}{4}\left(12x + \frac{1}{2}\right) = 3x + \frac{1}{8}$

24. **B** One simple approach to this problem is to estimate the values of a and b and then multiply them. a is approximately –1.1 and b is approximately 0.6, so ab is approximately $(-1.1)(0.6) = -0.66$, which is between –1.0 and –0.5.

25. **E** Consider any 4 consecutive positive even integers, like 2, 4, 6, and 8. Notice that, in this case, the largest number, k, is 8. The average, m, is $(2+4+6+8)/4 = 20/4 = 5$. The median of the set, n, is the average of the two middle numbers, which is $(4+6)/2 = 5$ also. Is this just a coincidence? No: you should know that the median of any set of "evenly spaced" numbers is always equal to the average. In this example, and with any other example you choose, all three statements are true.

26. **A** There are two basic approaches to this problem: plugging in for x and simplification. To plug in, choose a simple value for x, like 1. Thus $2^{2x} \cdot 4^{3x} = 2^2 \cdot 4^3 = 4 \cdot 64 = 256$. Next, plug in $x = 1$ to the choices and eliminate all that are not equal to 256:

(A) $2^8 = 256$ Yes
(B) $2^{12} = 4096$ No
(C) $4^3 = 64$ No
(D) $8^5 = 32768$ No
(E) $8^6 = 262144$ No

So the correct answer is clearly (A).
Alternatively, if you are confident with using the rules of exponents, simplifying this expression is fairly simple. The key is to notice that 4 is a power of 2:
$$2^{2x} \cdot 4^{3x}$$
Write 4 as 2^2: $2^{2x} \cdot (2^2)^{3x}$
Simplify the second exponential: $2^{2x} \cdot 2^{6x}$
Simplify the product of the exponentials: 2^{8x}

27. C The resulting box will have 6 faces: two 9 × 9 faces and four 9 × 4.5 faces. The total surface area, then, is 2(9 × 9) + 4(9 × 4.5) = 162 + 162 = 324.

28. A Since 6 is <u>not</u> a multiple of 4, [6] = 4(6) = 24. Therefore, [[6]] = [24]. Since 24 <u>is</u> a multiple of 4, [24] = 24 ≠ 2 = 12. If you've gotten this far, be careful not to jump to choice (C) [12], because [12] does not equal 12, but rather 12/2 = 6. The only choice that is equal to 12 is (A) [3] = 4(3) = 12.

29. 84 First remember that a straight angle measures 180°, so 54 + a + b = 180. Since a = 2b,

$$54 + 2b + b = 180$$
Simplify: $\quad 54 + 3b = 180$
Subtract 54: $\quad 3b = 126$
Divide by 3: $\quad b = 42$
Substitute to find a: $\quad a = 2b = 2(42) = 84$

30. 7 Recall that an arithmetic sequence is one in which the difference between consecutive terms is always the same. Since the third term, m + 10, is 10 greater than the first term, m, the difference beween consecutive terms must be 5. Since the middle term is 12, the terms must be 7, 12, 17. Notice that each term is 5 more than the previous one.

31. 8 Recall that the average (arithmetic mean) of a set of numbers is its sum divided by the number of numbers. So the average of this set is

$$\frac{5 + 3p + 12 + 3r}{4}$$

Recall given equation: $\quad p + r = 5$
Subtract r: $\quad p = 5 - r$

Substitute 5 − r for p: $\quad \dfrac{5 + 3(5 - r) + 12 + 3r}{4}$

Distribute multiplication: $\quad \dfrac{5 + 15 - 3r + 12 + 3r}{4}$

Simplify numerator: $\quad \dfrac{32}{4} = 8$

32. 32 Notice first that any integer between 10 and 99 is a two-digit number. Next, find the number of integers containing a 3. These are 13, 23, 30–39, 43, 53, 63, 73, 83, and 93: a total of 18 numbers. Next find the integers containing a 5. These are 15, 25, 35,

45, 50–59, 65, 75, 85, and 95: a total of 18 more numbers. To count all the numbers that contain either a 3 or a 5, we combine these two sets, subtracting the number of "overlapping" terms, which are 35 and 53. Therefore, the number of 2-digit integers containing a 3 or a 5 is 18 + 18 − 2 = 34. But now we must remove 35 and 53 from this set (that's right—they're still counted in the set even though we're no longer "double-counting" them), so the number of 2-digit integers with a 3 or a 5 but not both is 34 − 2 = 32.

33. 260 Notice that this figure contains two triangles with angles that add up to 180°.

First triangle: $\quad 50 + a + d = 180$
Second triangle: $\quad 50 + b + c = 180$
Add two equations: $\quad 100 + a + b + c + d = 360$
Subtract 100: $\quad a + b + c + d = 360$

34. 24 You must find the four positive integers from 1 to 9 that satisfy the given conditions. The only primes in this set are 2, 3, 5, and 7. Since none of the numbers is even, 2 cannot be in the set, so three of the numbers are 3, 5, and 7. Since two of the numbers must be multiples of 3, and only one of the numbers we already have is a multiple of 3, the fourth number must be 6 or 9. It cannot be 6 since none of the numbers can be even, so the four numbers must be 3, 5, 7, and 9. These numbers have a sum of 24.

35. 65 Call the original price (in dollars) x. With a discount of 20% and a tax of 6%, the final price will be (.80)(1.06)x. Set up an equation:

$$(.80)(1.06)x = 55.12$$
Simplify: $\quad .848x = 55.12$
Divide by .848: $\quad x = 65$

36. 3000 The key is seeing that the two triangles in the diagram are similar. This means that the corresponding sides are proportional.

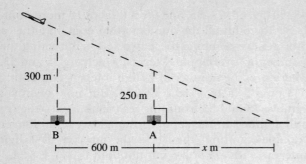

Set up the proportion: $\dfrac{x}{250} = \dfrac{x+600}{300}$

Cross-multiply: $300x = 250x + 150,000$
Subtract $250x$: $50x = 150,000$
Divide by 50: $x = 3,000$

---

37. 3/2 or 1.5   Pump A works at a rate of 1/6 of a tank per hour, and pump B works at a rate of 1/2 of a tank per hour. Together, then, they work at a rate of 1/6 + 1/2 = 2/3 of a tank per hour. This is equivalent to 3/2 of an *hour* per *tank*.

---

38. 280   To maximize the number of students who do NOT take any of these sciences, you must minimize the number of students who DO take those sciences. The minimum possible number of students taking any of those sciences is 220, as this Venn diagram shows:

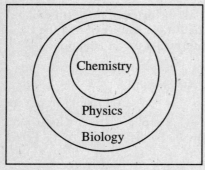

Entire Class

To minimize the number of science students, the sets of science students must be "nested" so that all the chemistry students also take physics, and all the physics students also take biology. This means that only 220 students in all take any kind of science, so there can be at most 500 – 220 = 280 students who don't take any science class at all.

Section 5

1. C   In the original sentence, the participle *having received* is dangling because the noun that it modifies—*Mark Lemann* or *he*—does not immediately follow the comma. Since you cannot change the portion of the sentence that is not underlined, the only way to fix the problem is to incorporate the subject *he* into the opening phrase.

---

2. D   The subject of the verb is *radiation*, which is singular, so the verb should be *is used*.

---

3. A   The original sentence is correct, because it concisely shows the contrast between the two clauses.

---

4. B   The original sentence lacks parallel form and therefore reads very awkwardly. The two clauses have the same subject and so should both be in the active voice. Choice (B) accomplishes this most concisely.

---

5. E   In the original sentence, the participle *used* dangles, and the usage of the pronoun *you* is unnecessary. Since *deficit spending* is what is *used*, it is what should follow the comma.

---

6. C   The original phrasing is redundant and hence needlessly wordy. Choice (C) provides the most concise phrasing without any loss of meaning.

---

7. A   The original phrasing is the most concise and logical. Choices (B), (C), (D), and (E) suggest that the *irregularities* are ideal, rather than the *Salt Flats*.

---

8. E   The participle *weighed down* modifies *David*, which must follow the comma.

---

9. C   The underlined phrase must be parallel to the phrase *flooding the hold*. Choice (C) provides that parallelism by beginning with a gerund. Choice (E) provides this as well, but includes the absurdity of an *impossible possibility*.

---

10. B   The participle *yearning* modifies *I*, which must follow the comma. Choice (E) does this, but contains a misplaced modifier, *by the forensics team*.

---

11. D   The original phrase contains redundancies like *insufficient* and *not enough* as well as *required them as a necessity*. Choice (D) is the most concise of all the choices.

12. **A** The original sentence is correct.

13. **E** Since this sentence is about an ancient theory about diseases, it should not address the reader directly. The use of *you* and *your* is improper in the other choices.

14. **E** Since the goal was reached before the benefactors could be thanked, the past perfect tense should be used with the past tense to show the proper sequence. Choice (E) is the only one that provides the proper sequencing.

15. **C** The contrast in this sentence is between what it is like *in some ostensibly democratic countries* and what it is like *in the United States*. Choice (C) is the only one that provides a logical and parallel contrast.

16. **C** The sentence indicates two things that *Jeopardy!* champions need, the first being *a broad knowledge base*. The second item must be parallel in phrasing to the first, and so should be an impersonal common noun, as in (C).

17. **A** The original sentence is correct.

18. **E** The original sentence does not connect the clauses logically since there is a clear contrast between the ideas. Choice (E) provides the logical contrast.

19. **D** The adjective *confident* modifies *the team*, so *the team* must follow the comma so that the modifier does not dangle. With choice (B), the adjective no longer dangles, but the pronouns *it* and *its* at the end have unclear antecedents.

20. **A** This sentence is correct. It completes the parallel structure *not so much as A but rather as B*.

21. **B** The past tense of *sing is sang*.

22. **B** The subject of the verb *has been felt* is *effects*, which is plural. Therefore, the correct verb conjugation is *have been felt*.

23. **D** The phrasing in choice (D) is not parallel with the previous phrasing. Since some are *demanding*, others are *insisting*.

24. **C** The word *less* should only be used in a comparison of a quantity that is uncountable. Since *courses* are countable things, the word should be *fewer*.

25. **D** The correct idiom is *intend to vote*, not *intend on voting*.

26. **D** This comparison is illogical. The comparison is to *this year's geography bee*, so the phrase should be *last year's bee*.

27. **C** The antecedent is *students*, so the pronoun should be *they*.

28. **D** This phrase is the indirect object of the verb *posed* and therefore should be in the objective case, *Denitra and me*.

29. **C** The correct idiom is *agree on* (or *upon*) *the verdict*.

30. **A** The antecedent of the pronoun is *dolphins*, so it should be the plural pronoun *their*.

31. **A** As it is worded, the participle *expecting* dangles, because the noun it modifies does not follow the participial phrase. To correct this, the subject should be incorporated into the phrase: *If you are expecting*.

32. **E** The sentence is correct.

33. **D** In the phrase *not only A but also B*, the phrases *A* and *B* must be parallel. In order for this phrase to be completed in a parallel way, the phrase in (D) must be eliminated.

34. **A** The correct idiom is *critics of*.

35. **E** The subject of the verb is the plural noun *people*, so the verb form is *live*.

36. **B** Choice (B) is the only one that coordinates the two clauses logically.

37. **C** In a paragraph about the running habits of the Tarahumara, sentence 7, about its beer-based economy, is out of place.

38. **C** Since the previous sentences described the primitive nature of the Tarahumara's training and equipment, the statement that they are *among the best ultramarathoners in the world* is surprising. Therefore, this sentence should begin with a contrasting transition, as in choice (C).

39. **A** The two clauses should be coordinated to contrast each other, as in choice (A). Choice (B) indicates an illogical cause and effect. Choice (C) contains a dangling participle. Choices (D) and (E) are awkward, and in both cases, the pronoun *they* has an ambiguous antecedent.